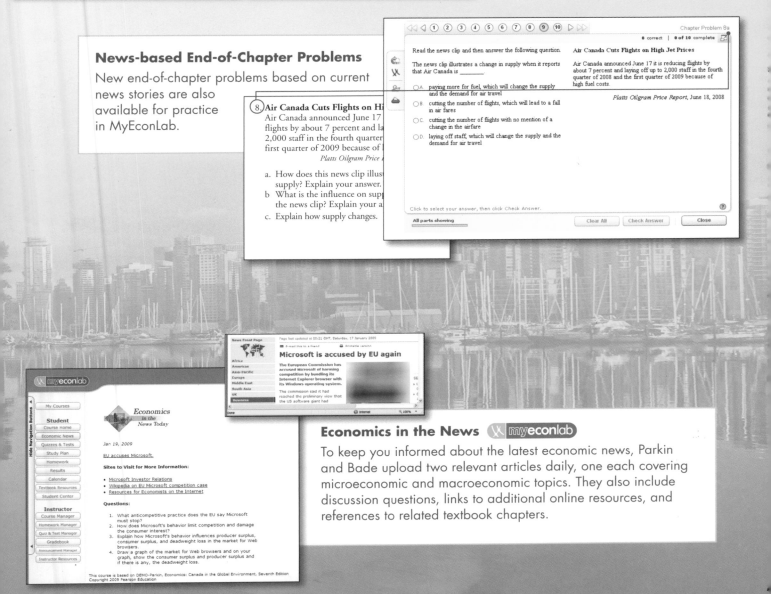

Reading Between the Lines

At the end of each chapter, *Reading Between the Lines* uses economic tools to critically evaluate a news article about the chapter-opening issue.

News-based End-of-Chapter Problems

New end-of-chapter problems based on current news stories are also available for practice in MyEconLab.

Economics in the News

To keep you informed about the latest economic news, Parkin and Bade upload two relevant articles daily, one each covering microeconomic and macroeconomic topics. They also include discussion questions, links to additional online resources, and references to related textbook chapters.

Get Ahead of the Curve

Save Time. Improve Results!

Use *MyEconLab* to prepare for tests and exams and to go to class ready to learn.

When you use *MyEconLab* you don't just learn more about economics—you learn how to learn.

Since 2002, more than 70 000 students have used *MyEconLab* at more than 600 institutions around the world.

We asked some of these students what they thought about *MyEconLab*. Here are some of the things they had to say:

"*MyEconLab allowed me to see where I stood on all the topics so I knew what to study more.*"

"*MyEconLab was a good asset to the course. It almost serves as an online tutor when you don't have an answer.*"

"*I was able to study better and teach myself without costly errors. I could see where I went wrong and go back and understand the concept.*"

"*MyEconLab helped me master economic concepts. Using it put the textbook to work before test day.*"

90% of students surveyed who used the Study Plan practice questions and feedback felt it helped them to prepare for tests.

87% of students who regularly used *MyEconLab* felt it improved their grades.

84% said they would recommend *MyEconLab* to a friend.

Save Time. Improve Results. www.myeconlab.com

Personalized Learning!

The *MyEconLab* Study Plan is based on your specific learning needs.

Auto-Graded Tests and Assignments

MyEconLab comes with two pre-loaded Sample Tests for each chapter so you can self-assess your understanding of the material.

Personalized Study Plan

A Study Plan is generated based on your results on Sample Tests and instructor assignments. You can clearly see which topics you have mastered and, more importantly, which topics you need to work on!

"I just wanted to let you know how helpful the Study Plan in MyEconLab is. Everything's clicking... so two thumbs up!"
—Student, Ryerson University

Practice Problems

Use the Study Plan exercises to get practice where you need it. To check how you're doing, click Results to get an overview of all your scores.

Save Time. Improve Results. www.myeconlab.com

Unlimited Practice!

MyEconLab offers a wide variety of problems that let you practise the theories and models being learned.

Graphing Tools and Questions

MyEconLab offers questions that allow you to draw graphs and plot data, as well as manipulate interactive model-based graphs.

Practice Problems

Many Study Plan and instructor-assigned problems contain algorithmically generated values, ensuring you get as much practice as you need.

Learning Resources

Each problem links to the eText page discussing the very concept being applied. You also have access to guided solutions and a suite of other practice tools.

MICHAEL PARKIN ◆ ROBIN BADE

University of Western Ontario

ECONOMICS

CANADA IN THE GLOBAL ENVIRONMENT

SEVENTH EDITION

Pearson Canada
Toronto

Library and Archives Canada Cataloguing in Publication

Parkin, Michael, 1939–
    Economics : Canada in the global environment / Michael Parkin, Robin
Bade. — 7th ed.

Includes index.
ISBN 978-0-321-56389-7

1. Economics—Textbooks.   2. Canada—Economic conditions—1991- —Textbooks.
I. Bade, Robin   II. Title.

HB171.5.P26 2009   330   C2009-900064-4

ISBN-13: 978-0-321-56389-7

ISBN-10: 0-321-56389-1

Vice President, Editorial Director: Gary Bennett
Acquisitions Editor: Gary Bennett
Marketing Manager: Leigh-Anne Graham
Associate Editor: Catherine Belshaw
Production Editor: Leanne Rancourt/Cheryl Jackson
Copy Editor: Sally Glover
Proofreader: Lu Cormier
Production Coordinator: Deborah Starks
Compositor: Christine Velakis
Photo/Permissions Researcher: Lisa Brant
Art Director: Julia Hall
Technical Illustrator: Richard Parkin
Cover and Interior Designer: Anthony Leung
Cover Image: Getty Images

2 3 4 5   13 12 11 10

Printed and bound in the United States.

TO

OUR STUDENTS

ABOUT
THE AUTHORS

Michael Parkin received his training as an economist at the Universities of Leicester and Essex in England. Currently in the Department of Economics at the University of Western Ontario, Canada, Professor Parkin has held faculty appointments at Brown University, the University of Manchester, the University of Essex, and Bond University. He is a past president of the Canadian Economics Association and has served on the editorial boards of the *American Economic Review* and the *Journal of Monetary Economics* and as managing editor of the *Canadian Journal of Economics*. Professor Parkin's research on macroeconomics, monetary economics, and international economics has resulted in over 160 publications in journals and edited volumes, including the *American Economic Review*, the *Journal of Political Economy*, the *Review of Economic Studies*, the *Journal of Monetary Economics*, and the *Journal of Money, Credit and Banking*. He became most visible to the public with his work on inflation that discredited the use of wage and price controls. Michael Parkin also spearheaded the movement towards European monetary union.

Robin Bade earned degrees in mathematics and economics at the University of Queensland and her Ph.D. at the Australian National University. She has held faculty appointments at the University of Edinburgh in Scotland, at Bond University in Australia, and at the Universities of Manitoba, Toronto, and Western Ontario in Canada. Her research on international capital flows appears in the *International Economic Review* and the *Economic Record*.

Professor Parkin and Dr. Bade are the joint authors of *Foundations of Economics* (Addison Wesley), *Modern Macroeconomics* (Pearson Education Canada), an intermediate text, and have collabrated on many research and textbook writing projects. They are both experienced and dedicated teachers of introductory economics.

BRIEF
CONTENTS

PART 1
INTRODUCTION 1
CHAPTER 1   What Is Economics? 1
CHAPTER 2   The Economic Problem 31

PART 2
HOW MARKETS WORK 57
CHAPTER 3   Demand and Supply 57
CHAPTER 4   Elasticity 85
CHAPTER 5   Efficiency and Equity 107
CHAPTER 6   Government Actions in Markets 129
CHAPTER 7   Global Markets in Action 153

PART 3
HOUSEHOLDS' CHOICE 181
CHAPTER 8   Utility and Demand 181
CHAPTER 9   Possibilities, Preferences, and Choices 203

PART 4
FIRMS AND MARKETS 227
CHAPTER 10   Organizing Production 227
CHAPTER 11   Output and Costs 251
CHAPTER 12   Perfect Competition 273
CHAPTER 13   Monopoly 299
CHAPTER 14   Monopolistic Competition 323
CHAPTER 15   Oligopoly 341

PART 5
MARKET FAILURE AND GOVERNMENT 373
CHAPTER 16   Externalities 373
CHAPTER 17   Public Goods and Common Resources 393

PART 6
FACTOR MARKETS AND INEQUALITY 417
CHAPTER 18   Markets for Factors of Production 417
CHAPTER 19   Economic Inequality 441

PART 7
MONITORING MACROECONOMIC TRENDS AND FLUCTUATIONS 467
CHAPTER 20   Measuring GDP and Economic Growth 467
CHAPTER 21   Monitoring Jobs and Inflation 489

PART 8
MACROECONOMIC TRENDS 515
CHAPTER 22   Economic Growth 515
CHAPTER 23   Finance, Saving, and Investment 543
CHAPTER 24   Money, the Price Level, and Inflation 567
CHAPTER 25   The Exchange Rate and the Balance of Payments 593

PART 9
MACROECONOMIC FLUCTUATIONS 625
CHAPTER 26   Aggregate Supply and Aggregate Demand 625
CHAPTER 27   Expenditure Multipliers: The Keynesian Model 649
CHAPTER 28   Canadian Inflation, Unemployment, and Business Cycle 679

PART 10
MACROECONOMIC POLICY 707
CHAPTER 29   Fiscal Policy 707
CHAPTER 30   Monetary Policy 731

PREFACE

Historic is a big word. Yet it accurately describes the economic events and policy responses that followed the sub-prime mortgage crisis of August 2007. Economics moved from the business pages to the front page as fear gripped producers, consumers, financial institutions, and governments. The unimaginable repeat of a Great Depression gradually became imaginable as U.S. house prices plunged, credit markets froze, financial institutions failed, governments in Canada, the United States, and around the world mounted massive bailouts and rescues, central banks made loans and bought debts of a quality that they don't normally touch, and the prices of items from gasoline and food to stocks and currencies fluctuated wildly.

Even the *idea* that the market is an efficient mechanism for allocating scarce resources came into question as some political leaders trumpeted the end of capitalism and the dawn of a new economic order in which tighter regulation reigned in unfettered greed.

Rarely do teachers of economics have such a rich feast on which to draw. And rarely are the principles of economics more surely needed to provide the solid foundation on which to think about economic events and navigate the turbulence of economic life.

Although thinking like an economist can bring a clearer perspective to and deeper understanding of today's events, students don't find the economic way of thinking easy or natural. *Economics* seeks to put clarity and understanding in the grasp of the student through its careful and vivid exploration of the tension between self-interest and the social interest, the role and power of incentives—of opportunity cost and marginal benefit—and demonstrating the possibility that markets, supplemented by other mechanisms, might allocate resources efficiently.

Parkin and Bade students begin to think about issues the way real economists do and learn how to explore difficult policy problems and make more informed decisions in their own economic lives.

The Seventh Edition Revision

The seventh edition of *Economics* retains all of the improvements achieved in its predecessors: a thorough and detailed presentation of the principles of economics, an emphasis on real-world examples and applications, the development of critical thinking skills, diagrams renowned for pedagogy and precision, and path-breaking technology.

This comprehensive revision also incorporates and responds to the suggestions for improvements made by reviewers and users, in both the broad architecture of the text and chapter-by-chapter.

Current issues organize each chapter. News stories about today's major economic events tie each chapter together, from new chapter-opening vignettes to end-of-chapter problems and online practice. Students learn to use economic tools to analyze their own daily decisions and recent real-world events and issues.

Each chapter includes a discussion of a critical issue of our time to demonstrate how economic theory can be applied to explore a particular debate or question. Issues of central importance include

- Gains and tensions from globalization, the rise of Asia, and the changing structure of the global economy in Chapters 2, 7, and 22
- High and rising cost of food in Chapters 2 and 3
- Fluctuations in gas and oil prices and the effects of high gas prices on auto sales in Chapters 3, 4, and 18
- Changing patterns of consumption in the information age in Chapter 8
- Climate change in Chapter 16
- Efficient use of natural resources and today's tragedies of the commons in Chapter 17
- Bank of Canada and government rescues and bailouts in Chapters 23 and 30
- Financial instability of 2008 in Chapters 23, 26, and 30
- Currency fluctuations in Chapter 25
- Recession of 2008–2009 in Chapters 26, 27, 28, and 29
- Real-world examples and applications appear in the body of each chapter and in the end-of-chapter problems and applications. Each chapter has approximately 10 additional problems tied to current news and events. All of these problems have parallel questions in MyEconLab.

Questions that appear weekly in *Economics in the News* in MyEconLab are also available for assignment in MyEconLab as homework, quizzes, or tests.

Highlights of the Micro Revision

In addition to being thoroughly updated and revised to include the topics and features just described, the microeconomics chapters feature the following six major changes:

1. ***Global Markets in Action*** (Chapter 7): This new chapter explains the sources and effects of international trade, its winners and losers, and the effects of trade protection (tariffs and import quotas) on economic welfare. The chapter applies the tools of demand and supply, consumer and producer surplus, and deadweight loss explained in two earlier chapters. Offshore outsourcing and the ongoing failure of the Doha negotiations feature in this chapter.

2. ***Utility and Demand*** (Chapter 8): Extensively revised and reorganized, this chapter provides a more intuitive and less graphical analysis of utility maximization. Changes in consumer choices for recorded music, in which digital downloads have almost driven CDs out of the market, illustrate the predictions of marginal utility theory. The chapter includes an explanation of behavioural economics and neuroeconomics. (Material on the budget line found in the previous edition is omitted from this chapter but can be found in the first part of Chapter 9, an alternative chapter on indifference curves.)

3. ***Monopoly*** (Chapter 13): The final section of this chapter now covers the regulation of natural monopoly, which was previously found in a separate chapter. This change enables monopoly regulation to be explained when the material on unregulated monopoly and its inefficiency is fresh in the student's mind.

4. ***Monopolistic Competition*** (Chapter 14): In the seventh edition, this market type has its own full-chapter treatment. High selling costs are illustrated with the breakdown of the price of a pair of running shoes between manufacturing and selling. An example focused on cell phones illustrates product differentiation.

5. ***Oligopoly*** (Chapter 15): This market type also has its own chapter and is expanded to include a section on anti-combine law. As with the change

in the monopoly chapter, this change enables anti-combine law to be studied when the coverage of cartels and the temptation to fix prices is still in the student's mind.

6. ***Externalities*** (Chapter 16): This chapter in the seventh edition focuses on climate change and the economic debate it engenders, as we feature these topics at several points as the major example of a negative externality and the alternative ways of dealing with it.

Highlights of the Macro Revision

The thoroughly updated coverage of macroeconomics is now organized in four parts: *monitoring the trends and fluctuations*, *understanding the trends*, *understanding the fluctuations*, and *macroeconomic policy*.

The introductory chapter of previous editions is redistributed across the other chapters as needed. Economic growth and the long-term trends in output growth have been brought forward and the content of the previous edition's chapter on the classical model of potential GDP is incorporated into the economic growth chapter.

Following economic growth is a new chapter on financial markets. This chapter enables students to understand the financial crisis of 2007–2008. Then follows two chapters on money and the exchange rate in which the emphasis is on understanding inflation and exchange rate trends.

The aggregate supply–aggregate demand model, the Keynesian model of aggregate expenditure, and the short-run tradeoff between real variables and inflation come next. This group of chapters can be covered right after Chapter 21 if desired.

The treatment of fiscal policy and monetary policy is radically revised to pay attention to the roles of policy in influencing both trends and fluctuations. The chapter in previous editions on fiscal and monetary interaction has been dropped from this edition.

In addition to these organizational changes, the chapters feature the following eight major revisions:

1. ***Measuring GDP and Economic Growth*** (Chapter 20): This chapter now includes a description and discussion of the recent history of real GDP growth and fluctuations found in the previous edition's introductory macro chapter. The explanation of the real GDP calculation has been simplified, and the current chain-dollar method of real GDP calculation is presented in a new Mathematical Note at the end of the chapter.

2. ***Monitoring Jobs and Inflation*** (Chapter 21):
This substantially revised chapter has a simplified
coverage of the anatomy and types of unemployment, but a more comprehensive explanation of
the sources of unemployment. As today's unemployment is compared with that of the Great
Depression, the empirical relationship between
cyclical unemployment and the output gap is
more clearly illustrated. The measurement of the
price level and inflation is motivated with a discussion of inflation and why it is a problem. The
chapter also includes new material on alternative
price indexes, including the personal consumption expenditure deflator as well as the concept of
core inflation. The chapter now concludes with a
brief section on the general use of real variables in
macroeconomics.

3. ***Economic Growth*** (Chapter 22): The process of
economic growth now begins with an explanation
of what determines potential GDP (adapted from
the previous edition's classical model chapter),
which is followed by an explanation of what
makes potential GDP grow. The sources of labour
productivity growth are thoroughly explored.

4. ***Finance, Saving, and Investment*** (Chapter 23):
New to the seventh edition, this chapter provides
a thorough and extensive explanation of financial
markets and institutions and their role in providing the funds for investment, an engine of economic growth. The circular flow model of
Chapter 20 is extended to include the flows in the
market for loanable funds that finance investment. The chapter explains the role of government in the market for loanable funds and
explains crowding out and the role of debt and
the government budget deficit. The chapter also
includes a discussion of borrowing and lending in
the global loanable funds market. The credit crisis
of 2008 is a central example used to illustrate the
working of this vital macroeconomic market.

5. ***Money, the Price Level, and Inflation*** (Chapter
24): This chapter is heavily revised to simplify the
explanation of the money creation process. A
Mathematical Note at the end of the chapter provides a more comprehensive analysis of this
process. The chapter includes an explanation of
the role and functions of the Bank of Canada. It
also includes coverage of the U.S. Federal
Reserve's role in the 2008 credit crisis.

6. ***The Exchange Rate and the Balance of
Payments*** (Chapter 25): This chapter is heavily
revised to incorporate an explanation of the determination of the balance of payments found in the
international trade chapter of the previous edition. The chapter also looks at the recent dramatic
fluctuations in the Canadian dollar in 2007 and
2008.

7. ***Aggregate Supply and Aggregate Demand***
(Chapter 26): This chapter is a streamlined version of the previous edition's content, but with a
new and more detailed explanation and illustration of Canada's business cycle. The added clarity
and focus of this chapter reflects the tone and
goals of the seventh edition.

8. ***Fiscal Policy*** (Chapter 29) and ***Monetary Policy***
(Chapter 30): These chapters are revised to incorporate the dramatic policy responses to the ongoing slowdown and increasingly likely recession of
2008–2009.

Features to Enhance Teaching and Learning

Chapter Objectives

Each chapter opens with a list of learning objectives,
which enables students to see exactly where the chapter
is going and to set their goals before they begin.

Chapter Openers

Each chapter opens with a student-friendly vignette that
raises questions to motivate the student and focus the
chapter. This chapter-opening story is woven into the
main body of the chapter and is explored in the *Reading
Between the Lines* feature that ends each chapter.

Key Terms

Highlighted terms simplify the student's task of learning the vocabulary of economics. Each highlighted
term appears in an end-of-chapter list with page numbers, in an end-of-book glossary with page numbers,
boldfaced in the index, in the Web glossary, and in the
Web Flash Cards.

Diagrams that Show the Action

Through the past six editions, this book has set new standards of clarity in its diagrams; the seventh edition continues to uphold this tradition. Our goal has always been to show "where the economic action is." The diagrams in this book continue to generate an enormously positive response, which confirms our view that graphical analysis is the most powerful tool available for teaching and learning economics.

Because many students find graphs hard to work with, we have developed the entire art program with the study and review needs of the student in mind.

The diagrams feature

- Original curves consistently shown in blue
- Shifted curves, equilibrium points, and other important features highlighted in red
- Colour-blended arrows to suggest movement
- Graphs paired with data tables
- Diagrams labelled with boxed notes
- Extended captions that make each diagram and its caption a self-contained object for study and review.

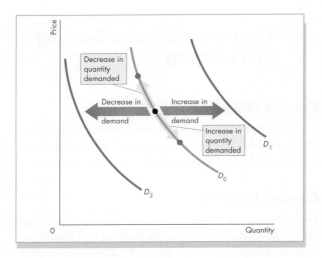

Reading Between the Lines

In *Reading Between the Lines*, which appears at the end of each chapter, students apply the tools they have just learned by analyzing an article from a newspaper or news Web site. Each article sheds additional light on the questions first raised in the Chapter Opener.

Questions about the article also appear with the end-of-chapter problems and applications.

In-Text Review Quizzes

A review quiz at the end of each major section enables students to determine whether a topic needs further study before moving on. This feature includes a reference to the appropriate MyEconLab Study Plan to help students further test their understanding.

End-of-Chapter Study Material

Each chapter closes with a concise summary organized by major topics, lists of key terms, figures and tables (all with page references), and problems and applications. These learning tools provide students with a summary for review and exam preparation.

News-Based End-of-Chapter Problems and Applications

Each chapter's problems and applications section now includes an additional set of news-based real-world problems that are new to the seventh edition. All of the problems and applications are also available for self-assessment or assignment as homework, a quiz, or a test in MyEconLab.

Interviews with Economists

Each major part of the text closes with a summary feature that includes an interview with a leading economist whose research and expertise correlates to what the student has just learned. These interviews explore the background, education, and research these prominent economists have conducted, as well as advice for those who want to continue the study of economics. New interviewees in this seventh edition are David Card of University of California at Berkeley, Susan Athey and Drew Fudenberg of Harvard University, Jadgish Baghwati, Xavier Sala-i-Martin, and Stephanie Schmitt-Grohé of Columbia University, and Ricardo Cabellaro of MIT. The interview with Peter Howitt of Brown University has been updated.

◆ For the Instructor

This book enables you to achieve three objectives in your principles course:

- Focus on the economic way of thinking
- Explain the issues and problems of our time
- Choose your own course structure

Focus on the Economic Way of Thinking

As an instructor, you know how hard it is to encourage a student to think like an economist. But that is your goal. Consistent with this goal, the text focuses on and repeatedly uses the central ideas: choice; tradeoff; opportunity cost; the margin; incentives; the gains from voluntary exchange; the forces of demand, supply, and equilibrium; the pursuit of economic rent; the tension between self-interest and the social interest; and the scope and limitations of government actions.

Explain the Issues of Our Global Economy

Students must *use* the central ideas and tools if they are to begin to *understand* them. There is no better way to motivate students than by using the tools of economics to explain the issues that confront today's world. Issues such as globalization and the emergence of China and India as major economic forces; the credit crisis, the recent bankruptcy, absorption, or government-funded bailout of U.S. banks, stock market fluctuations, the new economy with new near-monopolies such as eBay and Google; the widening income gap between rich and poor; the reallocation of resources towards counterterrorism; disappearing tropical rainforests and the challenge that this tragedy of the commons creates; the challenge of managing the world's water resources; rising international deficits and debt; and the fluctuating value of currencies on the foreign exchange market.

Flexible Structure

You have preferences for how you want to teach your course. We have organized this book to enable you to do so. The flexibility chart and alternative sequences tables that appear on pages xvii–xix demonstrate this book's flexibility. Whether you want to teach a traditional course that blends theory and policy or focuses on current policy issues, *Economics: Canada in the Global Environment* gives you the choice.

Supplemental Resources

Instructor's Manual We have streamlined and reorganized the Instructor's Manual to reflect the focus and intuition of the seventh edition. The Instructor's Manual integrates the teaching and learning package and serves as a guide to all the supplements.

Each chapter contains

- A chapter overview
- A list of what's new in the seventh edition
- *Lecture Notes* Ready-to-use lecture notes from each chapter enable a new user of Parkin and Bade to walk into a classroom ready to deliver a polished lecture. The lecture notes provide an outline of the chapter; concise statements of key material; alternate tables and figures, key terms, definitions, and boxes that highlight key concepts, provide an interesting anecdote, or suggest how to handle a difficult idea; additional discussion questions; and additional problems with solutions. The chapter outline and teaching suggestions sections are keyed to the PowerPoint® lecture notes.

Solutions Manual For ease of use and instructor reference, a comprehensive Solutions Manual provides instructors with solutions to the Review Quizzes and the end-of-chapter problems. The Solutions Manual is available in hard copy and electronically on the Instructor's Resource Centre CD-ROM, and in the instructor's resources section of MyEconLab and on the Instructor's Resource Centre.

Test Bank The seventh edition Test Bank, with more than 3,000 multiple-choice questions, has been prepared by Jeannie Gillmore of the University of Western Ontario. Jeannie has reviewed and edited all questions in the sixth edition Test Bank to ensure their clarity and consistency with the seventh edition and has incorporated new questions. These new questions follow the style and format of the end-of chapter text problems and provide the instructor with a whole new set of testing opportunities and/or homework assignments. Additionally, end-of-part tests contain questions that cover all the chapters in the part and feature integrative questions that span more than one chapter.

Computerized Test Bank in TestGen Pearson TestGen enables instructors to view and edit test bank questions, generate tests, and print tests in a variety of formats. Powerful search and sort functions make it easy to locate questions and arrange them in any order desired. TestGen also enables instructors to administer tests on a local area network, have tests graded electronically, and have the results prepared in electronic or printed reports. Pearson TestGen is compatible with Windows® or Macintosh® systems. This test bank is also available as a Test Item File in Microsoft Word® and Adobe Acrobat® formats

PowerPoint® Resources We have developed a full-colour Microsoft PowerPoint® Lecture Presentation for each chapter that includes all the figures and tables from the text, animated graphs, and speaking notes. The lecture notes in the Instructor's Manual and the slide outlines are correlated, and the speaking notes are based on the Instructor's Manual teaching suggestions.

A separate set of PowerPoint® files containing large-scale versions of all the text's figures (most of them animated) and tables are also available. The presentations can be used electronically in the classroom or can be printed to create hard copy transparency masters. This item is available for Macintosh® and Windows®.

Clicker-Ready PowerPoint® Resources This edition features the addition of clicker-ready PowerPoint® slides for the Personal Response System you use. Each chapter of the text includes 10 multiple-choice questions that test important concepts. Instructors can assign these as in-class assignments or review quizzes.

Instructor's Resource Centre CD-ROM The Instructor's Resource CD includes all of the instructor supplements for the seventh edition: the Instructor's Manual in Microsoft Word® and Adobe Acrobat® formats, Solutions Manual, Test Bank, PowerPoint® Resources, and Clicker Questions. The Instructor's Resource CD is compatible with both Windows® and Macintosh® systems.

Most of these instructor supplements are also available for download from a password-protected section of Pearson Education Canada's online catalogue (vig.pearsoned.ca). Navigate to this book's catalogue page to view a list of the supplements that are available. See your local sales representative for details and access.

Technology Specialists Pearson's technology specialists work with faculty and campus course designers to ensure that Pearson technology products, assessment tools, and online course materials are tailored to meet your specific needs. This highly qualified team is dedicated to helping schools take full advantage of a wide range of educational resources by assisting in the integration of a variety of instructional materials and media formats. Your local Pearson Education sales representative can provide you with more details on this service program.

Study Guide The seventh edition Study Guide by Avi Cohen of York University and Harvey King of the University of Regina is carefully coordinated with the text, MyEconLab, and the Test Bank. Each chapter of the Study Guide contains

- Key concepts
- Helpful hints
- True/false/uncertain questions that ask students to explain their answers
- Multiple-choice questions
- Short-answer questions
- Each Part Wrapup allows students to test their cumulative understanding with questions that go across chapters and to work a sample midterm examination.

MyEconLab Pearson Canada's online resource, MyEconLab, offers instructors and students all of their resources in one place, written and designed to accompany this text. MyEconLab creates a perfect pedagogical loop that provides not only text-specific assessment and practice problems, but also tutorial support to make sure students learn from their mistakes.

MyEconLab is available to instructors by going to www.myeconlab.com and following the instructions. Students access MyEconLab with an access code that is available with the purchase of a new text.

At the core of MyEconLab are the following features:

Auto-Graded Tests and Assignments MyEconLab comes with two preloaded Sample Tests for each chapter. Students can use these tests for self-assessment and obtain immediate feedback. Instructors can assign the

Sample Tests or use them along with Test Bank questions or their own exercises to create tests or quizzes.

Study Plan A Study Plan is generated from each student's results on Sample Tests and instructor assignments. Students can clearly see which topics they have mastered—and, more importantly, which they need to work on. The Study Plan consists of material from the in-text Review Quizzes and end-of-chapter Problems and Applications. The Study Plan links to additional practice problems and tutorial help on those topics.

Unlimited Practice Many Study Plan and instructor-assigned exercises contain algorithmically generated values to ensure that students get as much practice as they need. Every problem links students to learning resources that further reinforce concepts they need to master.

Learning Resources Each practice problem contains a link to the eText page that discusses the concept being applied. Students also have access to guided solutions, animated graphs with audio narrative, flashcards, and live tutoring.

Economics in the News Weekly news updates during the school year are available in MyEconLab. Each week, the authors post links to two news articles from the week's headlines. One links students to a microeconomics article, and the other to a macroeconomics article. Each article is accompanied by additional links, discussion questions, and a reference to relevant textbook chapters. An archive of *Economics in the News* articles and questions is also available.

New to the seventh edition are instructor-assignable *Economics in the News* questions. These news analysis questions are updated routinely to ensure that the latest news and news analysis problems are available for assignment.

Economics Videos and Assignable Questions Featuring abcNEWS Economics videos featuring ABC news enliven your course with short news clips featuring real-world issues. These 10 videos, available in MyEconLab, feature news footage and commentary by economists. Questions and problems for each video clip are available for assignment in MyEconLab.

Pearson Tutoring Services powered by SMARTHINKING A subscription to MyEconLab includes complimentary access to Pearson Tutor Services, powered by SMARTHINKING Inc. Highly qualified tutors use whiteboard technology and feedback tools to help students understand and master the major concepts of economics. Students can receive real-time, one-on-one instruction, submit questions for a response within 24 hours, and view archives of past sessions.

Access to MyEconLab and the Complete eText A student access code card for MyEconLab is packaged with every new copy of this book. Students may purchase access to MyEconLab online at www.myeconlab.com or through their campus bookstore.

CourseSmart eTextbook CourseSmart is a new way for instructors and students to access this textbook online anytime from anywhere. With thousands of titles across hundreds of courses, CourseSmart helps instructors chose the best textbook for their class and give their students a new option for buying the assigned textbook as a lower cost eTextbook. For more information visit www.coursesmart.com.

◆ Acknowledgments

We thank our current and former colleagues and friends at the University of Western Ontario who have taught us so much. They are Jim Davies, Jeremy Greenwood, Ig Horstmann, Peter Howitt, Greg Huffman, David Laidler, Phil Reny, Chris Robinson, John Whalley, and Ron Wonnacott. We also thank Doug McTaggart and Christopher Findlay, co-authors of the Australian edition, and Melanie Powell and Kent Matthews, co-authors of the European edition. Suggestions arising from their adaptations of earlier editions have been helpful to us in preparing this edition.

We thank the several thousand students whom we have been privileged to teach. The instant response that comes from the look of puzzlement or enlightenment has taught us how to teach economics.

It is a special joy to thank the many outstanding editors, media specialists, and others at Pearson Education Canada who contributed to the concerted publishing effort that brought this edition to completion. Allan Reynolds, President and CEO, and Steve O'Hern, President of Higher Education, have once again provided outstanding corporate direction. They have worked hard to build a culture that brings out the best in its editors and authors. Gary Bennett, Vice-President and Editorial Director for Higher Education, played a major role in bringing this new edition to completion. Gary, ably assisted by Catherine Belshaw, found and managed a team of outstanding supplements authors and editorial resources.

Leanne Rancourt brought a fresh eye to the development and production process. Anthony Leung designed the cover and text. Jennifer Parks directed the development and production of MyEconLab and ensured that all our media assets were correctly assembled. Leigh-Anne Graham provided inspired marketing strategy and direction. Sally Glover provided a careful, consistent, and intelligent copy edit, Lu Cormier, our proofreader, caught many slips, and Kit Pasula, our accuracy checker, found some errors of substance, which we are relieved to have had the opportunity to correct. We thank Lisa Brant, our photo researcher and permissions editor, for her thorough work.

We thank Luke Armstrong of Lee College for providing the news-based applications that appear at the end of each chapter. Luke has been using this type of material with his students and has now shared his talent with a wider audience.

We thank our talented seventh edition supplements authors—Avi Cohen and Harvey King wrote the Study Guide, Jeannie Gillmore updated and revised the Test Bank.

We thank the many exceptional reviewers who have shared their insights through the various editions of this book. Their contributions have been invaluable.

We thank the people who work directly with us. Jeannie Gillmore provided outstanding research assistance on many topics, including the *Reading Between the Lines* news articles. Richard Parkin created the electronic art files and offered many ideas that improved the figures in this book. He also created all the animated figures for the ebook and the PowerPoint® slides. And Laurel Davies managed an ever-growing and ever more complex MyEconLab database.

Classroom experience will test the value of this book. We would appreciate hearing from instructors and students about how we can continue to improve it in future editions.

Michael Parkin
Robin Bade
London, Ontario, Canada
michael.parkin@uwo.ca
robin@econ100.com

◆ Reviewers

Syed Ahmed, Red Deer Community College
Ather H. Akbari, Saint Mary's University
Benjamin Amoah, University of Guelph
Terri Anderson, Fanshawe College
Torben Andersen, Red Deer College
Syed Ashan, Concordia University
Fred Aswani, McMaster University
Iris Au, University of Toronto, Scarborough
Keith Baxter, Bishop's University
Andy Baziliauskas, University of Winnipeg
Dick Beason, University of Alberta
Karl Bennett, University of Waterloo
Ronald Bodkin, University of Ottawa
Caroline Boivin, Concordia University
Paul Booth, University of Alberta
John Boyd, University of British Columbia
John Brander, University of New Brunswick
Larry Brown, Selkirk College
Bogdan Buduru, Concordia University
Lutz-Alexander Busch, University of Waterloo
Alan Tak Yan Chan, Atlantic Baptist University
Beverly J. Cameron, University of Manitoba
Norman Cameron, University of Manitoba
Emanuel Carvalho, University of Waterloo
Francois Casas, University of Toronto
Robert Cherneff, University of Victoria
Jason Childs, University of New Brunswick, Saint John
Saud Choudhry, Trent University
Louis Christofides, University of Guelph
Kam Hon Chu, Memorial University of Newfoundland
George Churchman, University of Manitoba
Avi J. Cohen, York University
Marilyn Cottrell, Brock University
Rosilyn Coulson, Douglas College
Brian Coulter, University College of the Fraser Valley
Stanya Cunningham, Concordia Universiry College of Alberta
Douglas Curtis, Trent University
Garth Davies, OIds College
Vaughan Dickson, University of New Brunswick (Fredericton)
Mohammed Dore, Brock University
Torben Drewes, Trent University
Byron Eastman, Laurentian Universty
Fahira Eston, Humber College
Brian Ferguson, University of Guelph
Len Fitzpatrick, Carleton University
Peter Fortura, Algonquin College
Oliver Franke, Athabasca University

Bruno Fullone, George Brown College
Donald Garrie, Georgian College
Philippe Ghayad, Dawson College and Concordia University
David Gray, University of Ottawa
Rod Hill, University of New Brunswick
Eric Kam, Ryerson University
Susan Kamp, University of Alberta
Cevat Burc Kayahan, University of Guelph
Peter Kennedy, Simon Fraser University
Harvey King, University of Regina
Patricia Koss, Concordia University
Robert Kunimoto, Mt. Royal College
David Johnson, Wilfrid Laurier University
Eva Lau, University of Waterloo
Gordon Lee, University of Alberta
Anastasia M. Lintner, University of Guelph
Scott Lynch, Memorial University
Dan MacKay, SIAST
Keith MacKinnon, York University
Mohammad Mahbobi, Thompson Rivers University
S. Manchouri, University of Alberta
Christian Marfels, Dalhousie University
Raimo Martalla, Malaspina University College
Perry Martens, University of Regina
Roberto Martínez-Espíneira, St. Francis Xavier University
Livio Di Matteo, Lakehead University
Dennis McGuire, Okanagan University College
Rob Moir, University of New Brunswick Saint John
Saeed Moshiri, University of Manitoba
Joseph Muldoon, Trent University
David Murrell, University of New Brunswick (Fredericton)
Robin Neill, Carleton University
A. Gyasi Nimarko, Vanier College
Sonia Novkovic, Saint Mary's University
John O'Brien, Concordia University
Arne Paus-Jenssen, University of Saskatchewan
Derek Pyne, Memorial University of Newfoundland.
Stephen Rakoczy, Humber College
Don Reddick, Kwantlen University College
E. Riser, Memorial University
Roberta Robb, Brock University
Nick Rowe, Carleton University
Michael Rushton, University of Regina
Balbir Sahni, Concordia University
Brian Scarfe, University of Regina
Marlyce Searcy, SIAST Palliser
Jim Sentance, University of Prince Edward Island
Lance Shandler, Kwantlen University College
Stan Shedd, University of Calgary

Peter Sinclair, Wilfrid Laurier University
Ian Skaith, Fanshawe College
Judith Skuce, Georgian College
George Slasor, University of Toronto
Norman Smith, Georgian College
Bert Somers, John Abbott College
Lewis Soroka, Brock University
Glen Stirling, University of Western Ontario
Irene Trela, University of Western Ontario
Russell Uhler, University of British Columbia
Jane Waples, Memorial University of Newfoundland
Tony Ward, Brock University
Bruce Wilkinson, University of Alberta
Christopher Willmore, University of Victoria
Arthur Younger, Humber College Institute of Technology and
    Advanced Learning
Andrew Wong, Grant MacEwan College
Peter Wylie, University of British Colombia, Okanagan
Ayoub Yousefi, University of Western Ontario
Weiqiu Yu, University of New Brunswick (Fredericton)

FLEXIBILITY
BY CHAPTER

Core

1 What Is Economics?

2 The Economic Problem

3 Demand and Supply

4 Elasticity

5 Efficiency and Equity

11 Output and Costs

12 Perfect Competition

13 Monopoly

14 Monopolistic Competition

15 Oligopoly

18 Markets for Factors of Production

20 Measuring GDP and Economic Growth

21 Monitoring Jobs and Inflation

22 Economic Growth

23 Finance, Saving, and Investment

24 Money, the Price Level, and Inflation

26 Aggregate Supply and Aggregate Demand

Policy

6 Government Actions in Markets

7 Global Markets in Action

16 Externalities

17 Public Goods and Common Resources

19 Economic Inequality

29 Fiscal Policy

30 Monetary Policy

Optional

1 Appendix: Graphs in Economics

8 Utility and Demand

9 Possibilities, Preferences, and Choices

10 Organizing Production

25 The Exchange Rate and the Balance of Payments

27 Expenditure Multipliers: The Keynesian Model

28 Canadian Inflation, Unemployment, and Business Cycle

FOUR ALTERNATIVE
MICRO SEQUENCES

Traditional Theory and Policy

1 What Is Economics?
2 The Economic Problem
3 Demand and Supply
4 Elasticity
5 Efficiency and Equity
6 Government Actions in Markets
7 Global Markets in Action
8 Utility and Demand
10 Organizing Production
11 Output and Costs
12 Perfect Competition
13 Monopoly
14 Monopolistic Competition
15 Oligopoly
18 Markets for Factors of Production
19 Economic Inequality

Challenging Theory Emphasis

1 What Is Economics?
2 The Economic Problem
3 Demand and Supply
4 Elasticity
5 Efficiency and Equity
6 Government Actions in Markets
7 Global Markets in Action
9 Possibilities, Preferences, and Choices
10 Organizing Production
11 Output and Costs
12 Perfect Competition
13 Monopoly
14 Monopolistic Competition
15 Oligopoly
18 Markets for Factors of Production

Public Choice Emphasis

1 What Is Economics?
2 The Economic Problem
3 Demand and Supply
4 Elasticity
5 Efficiency and Equity
6 Government Actions in Markets
7 Global Markets in Action
8 Utility and Demand
10 Organizing Production
11 Output and Costs
12 Perfect Competition
13 Monopoly
14 Monopolistic Competition
15 Oligopoly
16 Externalities
17 Public Goods and Common Resources

Policy Emphasis (Shorter)

1 What Is Economics?
2 The Economic Problem
3 Demand and Supply
4 Elasticity
5 Efficiency and Equity
6 Government Actions in Markets
7 Global Markets in Action
16 Externalities
17 Public Goods and Common Resources
18 Markets for Factors of Production
19 Economic Inequality

THREE ALTERNATIVE
MACRO SEQUENCES

Classical Perspective

1 What Is Economics?

2 The Economic Problem

3 Demand and Supply

20 Measuring GDP and Economic Growth

21 Monitoring Jobs and Inflation

22 Economic Growth

23 Finance, Saving, and Investment

24 Money, the Price Level, and Inflation

25 The Exchange Rate and the Balance of Payments

26 Aggregate Supply and Aggregate Demand

28 Canadian Inflation, Unemployment, and Business Cycle

29 Fiscal Policy

30 Monetary Policy

Keynesian Perspective

1 What Is Economics?

2 The Economic Problem

3 Demand and Supply

20 Measuring GDP and Economic Growth

21 Monitoring Jobs and Inflation

27 Expenditure Multipliers: The Keynesian Model

26 Aggregate Supply and Aggregate Demand

28 Canadian Inflation, Unemployment, and Business Cycle (omit real business cycles)

29 Fiscal Policy (omit supply-side sections)

24 Money, the Price Level, and Inflation

30 Monetary Policy

22 Economic Growth

23 Finance, Saving, and Investment

25 The Exchange Rate and the Balance of Payments

Monetarist Perspective

1 What Is Economics?

2 The Economic Problem

3 Demand and Supply

20 Measuring GDP and Economic Growth

21 Monitoring Jobs and Inflation

24 Money, the Price Level, and Inflation

25 The Exchange Rate and the Balance of Payments

26 Aggregate Supply and Aggregate Demand

28 Canadian Inflation, Unemployment, and Business Cycle (omit real business cycles)

30 Monetary Policy

29 Fiscal Policy

22 Economic Growth

23 Finance, Saving, and Investment

TABLE OF

CONTENTS

PART 1
INTRODUCTION   1

CHAPTER 1 ◆ **What Is Economics?**   1

Definition of Economics   2
  Microeconomics   2
  Macroeconomics   2

Two Big Economic Questions   3
  What, How, and For Whom?   3
  How Can the Pursuit of Self-Interest Promote the
    Social Interest?   5
  Self-Interest and the Social Interest   5

The Economic Way of Thinking   8
  Choices and Tradeoffs   8
  What, How, and For Whom Tradeoffs   8
  Choices Bring Change   9
  Opportunity Cost   9
  Choosing at the Margin   10
  Responding to Incentives   10
  Human Nature, Incentives, and Institutions   10

Economics as Social Science and Policy Tool   11
  Economics as Social Science   11
  Economics as Policy Tool   12

*Summary (Key Points, Key Figures and Tables, and
Key Terms), and Problems and Applications appear
at the end of each chapter.*

Appendix Graphs in Economics   15

Graphing Data   15
  Time-Series Graphs   16
  Cross-Section Graphs   16
  Scatter Diagrams   17

Graphs Used in Economic Models   18
  Variables That Move in the Same Direction   18
  Variables That Move in Opposite Directions   19
  Variables That Have a Maximum or a
    Minimum   20
  Variables That Are Unrelated   21

The Slope of a Relationship   22
  The Slope of a Straight Line   22
  The Slope of a Curved Line   23

**Graphing Relationships Among More Than
Two Variables**   24

MATHEMATICAL NOTE
Equations of Straight Lines   26

CHAPTER 2 ◆ The Economic Problem 31

Production Possibilities and Opportunity Cost 32

Production Possibilities Frontier 32
Production Efficiency 33
Tradeoff Along the *PPF* 33
Opportunity Cost 33

Using Resources Efficiently 35

The *PPF* and Marginal Cost 35
Preferences and Marginal Benefit 36
Allocative Efficiency 37

Economic Growth 38

The Cost of Economic Growth 38
A Nation's Economic Growth 39

Gains from Trade 40

Comparative Advantage and Absolute
Advantage 40
Achieving the Gains from Trade 41
Dynamic Comparative Advantage 43

Economic Coordination 43

Firms 43
Markets 44
Property Rights 44
Money 44
Circular Flows Through Markets 44
Coordinating Decisions 44

READING BETWEEN THE LINES
The Rising Opportunity Cost of Food 46

PART ONE **WRAP-UP**

Understanding the Scope of Economics
Your Economic Revolution 53

Talking with
Jagdish Bhagwati 54

PART 2
HOW MARKETS WORK 57

CHAPTER 3 ◆ Demand and Supply 57

Markets and Prices 58

Demand 59

The Law of Demand 59
Demand Curve and Demand Schedule 59
A Change in Demand 60
A Change in the Quantity Demanded Versus a
Change in Demand 62

Supply 64

The Law of Supply 64
Supply Curve and Supply Schedule 64
A Change in Supply 65
A Change in the Quantity Supplied Versus a
Change in Supply 66

Market Equilibrium 68

Price as a Regulator 68
Price Adjustments 69

Predicting Changes in Price and Quantity 70

An Increase in Demand 70
A Decrease in Demand 70
An Increase in Supply 71
A Decrease in Supply 71
All the Possible Changes in Demand and
Supply 75

READING BETWEEN THE LINES
Demand and Supply: The Price of Gasoline 76

MATHEMATICAL NOTE
Demand, Supply, and Equilibrium 78

CHAPTER 4 ◆ Elasticity 85

Price Elasticity of Demand 86
Calculating Price Elasticity of Demand 87
Inelastic and Elastic Demand 88
Elasticity Along a Straight-Line Demand
  Curve 89
Total Revenue and Elasticity 90
Your Expenditure and Your Elasticity 91
The Factors That Influence the Elasticity of
  Demand 91

More Elasticities of Demand 93
Cross Elasticity of Demand 93
Income Elasticity of Demand 94

Elasticity of Supply 96
Calculating the Elasticity of Supply 96
The Factors That Influence the Elasticity of
  Supply 97

READING BETWEEN THE LINES
The Elasticities of Demand for Gasoline, Trucks,
  and Cars 100

CHAPTER 5 ◆ Efficiency and Equity 107

Resource Allocation Methods 108
Market Price 108
Command 108
Majority Rule 108
Contest 108
First-Come, First-Served 108
Lottery 109
Personal Characteristics 109
Force 109

Demand and Marginal Benefit 110
Demand, Willingness to Pay, and Value 110
Individual Demand and Market Demand 110
Consumer Surplus 111

Supply and Marginal Cost 112
Supply, Cost, and Minimum Supply-Price 112
Individual Supply and Market Supply 112
Producer Surplus 113

Is the Competitive Market Efficient? 114
Efficiency of Competitive Equilibrium 114
Underproduction and Overproduction 115
Obstacles to Efficiency 116
Alternatives to the Market 117

Is the Competitive Market Fair? 118
It's Not Fair If the *Result* Isn't Fair 118
It's Not Fair If the *Rules* Aren't Fair 120
Case Study: A Water Shortage in a Natural
  Disaster 120

READING BETWEEN THE LINES
Is Water Use Efficient? 122

CHAPTER 6 ◆ **Government Actions in Markets** 129

A Housing Market with a Rent Ceiling 130
A Housing Shortage 130
Increased Search Activity 130
A Black Market 130
Inefficiency of a Rent Ceiling 131
Are Rent Ceilings Fair? 132

A Labour Market with a Minimum Wage 133
Minimum Wage Brings Unemployment 133
Inefficiency of a Minimum Wage 133
Is the Minimum Wage Fair? 134

Taxes 135
Tax Incidence 135
A Tax on Sellers 135
A Tax on Buyers 136
Equivalence of Tax on Buyers and Sellers 136
Tax Incidence and Elasticity of Demand 137
Tax Incidence and Elasticity of Supply 138
Taxes and Efficiency 139
Taxes and Fairness 140

Production Quotas and Subsidies 141
Production Quotas 141
Subsidies 142

Markets for Illegal Goods 144
A Free Market for a Drug 144
A Market for an Illegal Drug 144
Legalizing and Taxing Drugs 145

READING BETWEEN THE LINES
The Minimum Wage in Action 146

CHAPTER 7 ◆ **Global Markets in Action** 153

How Global Markets Work 154
International Trade Today 154
What Drives International Trade? 154
Why Canada Imports T-Shirts 155
Why Canada Exports Regional Jets 156

Winners, Losers, and the Net Gain from Trade 157
Gains and Losses from Imports 157
Gains and Losses from Exports 158

International Trade Restrictions 159
Tariffs 159
Import Quotas 162
Other Import Barriers 164
Export Subsidies 164

The Case Against Protection 165
The Infant-Industry Argument 165
The Dumping Argument 165
Saves Jobs 166
Allows Us to Compete with Cheap Foreign Labour 166
Penalizes Lax Environmental Standards 166
Prevents Rich Countries from Exploiting Developing Countries 167
Offshore Outsourcing 167
Avoiding Trade Wars 168
Why Is International Trade Restricted? 168
Compensating Losers 169

READING BETWEEN THE LINES
The United States Protects Its Lumber Producers 170

PART TWO **WRAP-UP** ◆

Understanding How Markets Work
The Amazing Market 177

Talking with
Susan Athey 178

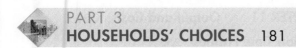

PART 3
HOUSEHOLDS' CHOICES 181

CHAPTER 8 ◆ Utility and Demand 181

Maximizing Utility 182
Total Utility 182
Marginal Utility 182
Graphing Lisa's Utility Schedules 183
The Utility-Maximizing Choice 184
Choosing at the Margin 184
The Power of Marginal Analysis 186

Predictions of Marginal Utility Theory 187
A Fall in the Price of a Movie 187
A Rise in the Price of Pop 189
A Rise in Income 190
The Paradox of Value 191
Temperature: An Analogy 192

New Ways of Explaining Consumer Choices 194
Behavioural Economics 194
Neuroeconomics 195
Controversy 195

READING BETWEEN THE LINES
The Marginal Utility of Food 196

CHAPTER 9 ◆ Possibilities, Preferences, and Choices 203

Consumption Possibilities 204
Budget Equation 205

Preferences and Indifference Curves 207
Marginal Rate of Substitution 208
Degree of Substitutability 209

Predicting Consumer Choices 210
Best Affordable Choice 210
A Change in Price 211
A Change in Income 212
Substitution Effect and Income Effect 213
Back to the Facts 214

Work-Leisure Choices 214
Labour Supply 214
The Labour Supply Curve 215

READING BETWEEN THE LINES
Paper Books Versus e-Books 216

PART **THREE WRAP-UP**

Understanding Households' Choices
Making the Most of Life 223

Talking with
Steven D. Levitt 224

PART 4
FIRMS AND MARKETS 227

CHAPTER 10 ◆ Organizing Production 227

The Firm and Its Economic Problem 228
  The Firm's Goal 228
  Accounting Profit 228
  Economic Accounting 228
  A Firm's Opportunity Cost of Production 228
  Economic Accounting: A Summary 229
  Decisions 229
  The Firm's Constraints 230

Technological and Economic Efficiency 231
  Technological Efficiency 231
  Economic Efficiency 231

Information and Organization 233
  Command Systems 233
  Incentive Systems 233
  Mixing the Systems 233
  The Principal–Agent Problem 234
  Coping with the Principal–Agent Problem 234
  Types of Business Organization 234
  Pros and Cons of Different Types of Firms 235

Markets and the Competitive Environment 237
  Measures of Concentration 238
  Limitations of Concentration Measures 240

Market and Firms 242
  Market Coordination 242
  Why Firms? 242

READING BETWEEN THE LINES
  Battling for Markets in Internet Search 244

CHAPTER 11 ◆ Output and Costs 251

Decision Time Frames 252
  The Short Run 252
  The Long Run 252

Short-Run Technology Constraint 253
  Product Schedules 253
  Product Curves 253
  Total Product Curve 254
  Marginal Product Curve 254
  Average Product Curve 256

Short-Run Cost 257
  Total Cost 257
  Marginal Cost 258
  Average Cost 258
  Marginal Cost and Average Cost 258
  Why the Average Total Cost Curve Is
    U-Shaped 258
  Cost Curves and Product Curves 260
  Shifts in the Cost Curves 260

Long-Run Cost 262
  The Production Function 262
  Short-Run Cost and Long-Run Cost 262
  The Long-Run Average Cost Curve 264
  Economies and Diseconomies of Scale 264

READING BETWEEN THE LINES
  Cutting the Cost of Clean Electricity 266

CHAPTER 12 ◆ Perfect Competition 273

What Is Perfect Competition? 274
How Perfect Competition Arises 274
Price Takers 274
Economic Profit and Revenue 274
The Firm's Decisions 275

The Firm's Output Decision 276
Marginal Analysis and the Supply Decision 277
Temporary Shutdown Decision 278
The Firm's Supply Curve 279

Output, Price, and Profit in the Short Run 280
Market Supply in the Short Run 280
Short-Run Equilibrium 281
A Change in Demand 281
Profits and Losses in the Short Run 281
Three Possible Short-Run Outcomes 282

Output, Price, and Profit in the Long Run 283
Entry and Exit 283
A Closer Look at Entry 284
A Closer Look at Exit 284
Long-Run Equilibrium 285

Changing Tastes and Advancing Technology 286
A Permanent Change in Demand 286
External Economies and Diseconomies 287
Technological Change 289

Competition and Efficiency 290
Efficient Use of Resources 290
Choices, Equilibrium, and Efficiency 290

READING BETWEEN THE LINES
Temporary Shutdown or Exit 292

CHAPTER 13 ◆ Monopoly 299

Monopoly and How It Arises 300
How Monopoly Arises 300
Monopoly Price-Setting Strategies 301

A Single-Price Monopoly's Output and Price Decision 302
Price and Marginal Revenue 302
Marginal Revenue and Elasticity 303
Price and Output Decision 304

Single-Price Monopoly and Competition Compared 306
Comparing Price and Output 306
Efficiency Comparison 307
Redistribution of Surpluses 308
Rent Seeking 308
Rent-Seeking Equilibrium 308

Price Discrimination 309
Capturing Consumer Surplus 309
Profiting by Price Discriminating 310
Perfect Price Discrimination 311
Efficiency and Rent Seeking with Price Discrimination 312

Monopoly Regulation 313
Efficient Regulation of a Natural Monopoly 313
Second-Best Regulation of a Natural Monopoly 314

READING BETWEEN THE LINES
European View of Microsoft 316

CHAPTER 14 ◆ Monopolistic Competition 323

What Is Monopolistic Competition? 324
    Large Number of Firms 324
    Product Differentiation 324
    Competing on Quality, Price, and Marketing 324
    Entry and Exit 325
    Examples of Monopolistic Competition 325

Price and Output in Monopolistic Competition 326
    The Firm's Short-Run Output and Price
       Decision 326
    Profit Maximizing Might Be Loss
       Minimizing 326
    Long-Run: Zero Economic Profit 327
    Monopolistic Competition and Perfect
       Competition 328
    Is Monopolistic Competition Efficient? 329

Product Development and Marketing 330
    Innovation and Product Development 330
    Advertising 330
    Using Advertising to Signal Quality 332
    Brand Names 333
    Efficiency of Advertising and Brand Names 333

READING BETWEEN THE LINES
    Product Differentiation in the 3G Cell Phone
       Market 334

CHAPTER 15 ◆ Oligopoly 341

What Is Oligopoly? 342
    Barriers to Entry 342
    Small Number of Firms 343
    Examples of Oligopoly 343

Two Traditional Oligopoly Models 344
    The Kinked Demand Curve Model 344
    Dominant Firm Oligopoly 344

Oligopoly Games 346
    What Is a Game? 346
    The Prisoners' Dilemma 346
    An Oligopoly Price-Fixing Game 348
    Other Oligopoly Games 352
    The Disappearing Invisible Hand 353
    A Game of Chicken 354

Repeated Games and Sequential Games 355
    A Repeated Duopoly Game 355
    A Sequential Entry Game in a Contestable
       Market 356

Anti-Combine Law 358
    Canada's Anti-Combine Law 358
    Some Major Anti-Combine Cases 358

READING BETWEEN THE LINES
    Dell and HP in a Market Share Game 362

PART FOUR **WRAP-UP** ◆

    Understanding Firms and Markets
    Managing Change and Limiting Market
       Power 369

    Talking with
    Drew Fudenberg 370

PART 5
MARKET FAILURE AND GOVERNMENT 373

CHAPTER 16 ◆ Externalities 373

Externalities in Our Lives 374
Negative Production Externalities 374
Negative Consumption Externalities 376
Positive Production Externalities 376
Positive Consumption Externalities 376

Negative Externalities: Pollution 377
Private Costs and Social Costs 377
Production and Pollution: How Much? 377
Property Rights 377
The Coase Theorem 379
Government Actions in the Face of External Costs 380

Positive Externalities: Knowledge 381
Private Benefits and Social Benefits 381
Government Actions in the Face of External Benefits 383

READING BETWEEN THE LINES
Fighting Carbon Emissions with a Carbon Tax and Solar Subsidy 386

CHAPTER 17 ◆ Public Goods and Common Resources 393

Classifying Goods and Resources 394
Excludable 394
Rival 394
A Fourfold Classification 394

Public Goods 395
The Free-Rider Problem 395
Marginal Social Benefit of a Public Good 395
Marginal Social Cost of a Public Good 396
Efficient Quantity of a Public Good 396
Inefficient Private Provision 396
Efficient Public Provision 396
Inefficient Public Overprovision 397
Two Types of Political Equilibrium 399
Why Government Is Large and Growing 399
Voters Strike Back 399

Common Resources 400
The Tragedy of the Commons 400
Sustainable Production 400
An Overfishing Equilibrium 401
The Efficient Use of the Commons 402
Achieving an Efficient Outcome 403
Public Choice and the Political Equilibrium 405

READING BETWEEN THE LINES
Rainforests: A Tragedy of the Commons 406

PART FIVE **WRAP-UP** ◆

Understanding Market Failure and Government
Making the Rules 413

Talking with
Caroline M. Hoxby 414

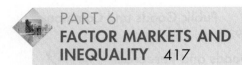

PART 6
FACTOR MARKETS AND INEQUALITY   417

CHAPTER 18 ◆ Markets for Factors of Production   417

The Anatomy of Factor Markets   418
Markets for Labour Services   418
Markets for Capital Services   418
Markets for Land Services and Natural Resources   418
Entrepreneurship   418

The Demand for a Factor of Production   419
Value of Marginal Product   419
A Firm's Demand for Labour   419
A Firm's Demand for Labour Curve   420
Changes in a Firm's Demand for Labour   421

Labour Markets   422
A Competitive Labour Market   422
A Labour Market with a Union   424
Scale of the Union–Nonunion Wage Gap   426
Trends and Differences in Wage Rates   427

Capital and Natural Resource Markets   428
Capital Rental Markets   428
Land Rental Markets   428
Nonrenewable Natural Resource Markets   429

READING BETWEEN THE LINES
Canada's Oilsands   432

MATHEMATICAL NOTE
Present Value and Discounting   434

CHAPTER 19 ◆ Economic Inequality   441

Measuring Economic Inequality   442
The Distribution of Income   442
The Income Lorenz Curve   443
The Distribution of Wealth   444
Wealth or Income?   444
Annual or Lifetime Income and Wealth?   445
Trends in Inequality   445
Poverty   447

The Sources of Economic Inequality   448
Human Capital   448
Discrimination   451
Unequal Wealth   452

Income Redistribution   453
Income Taxes   453
Income Maintenance Programs   453
Subsidized Services   453
The Big Tradeoff   454
A Major Welfare Challenge   455

READING BETWEEN THE LINES
Trends in Poverty   456

PART SIX WRAP-UP ◆
Understanding Factor Markets and Inequality
For Whom?   463
Talking with
David Card   464

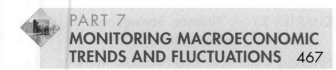

PART 7
MONITORING MACROECONOMIC TRENDS AND FLUCTUATIONS 467

CHAPTER 20 ◆ Measuring GDP and Economic Growth 467

Gross Domestic Product 468
GDP Defined 468
GDP and the Circular Flow of Expenditure and Income 469
Why Is Domestic Product "Gross"? 470

Measuring Canada's GDP 471
The Expenditure Approach 471
The Income Approach 471
Nominal GDP and Real GDP 473
Calculating Real GDP 473

The Uses and Limitations of Real GDP 474
The Standard of Living Over Time 474
The Standard of Living Across Countries 476
Limitations of Real GDP 477

READING BETWEEN THE LINES
Real GDP in the Slowing Economy of 2008 480

MATHEMATICAL NOTE
Chained-Dollar Real GDP 482

CHAPTER 21 ◆ Monitoring Jobs and Inflation 489

Employment and Unemployment 490
Why Unemployment Is a Problem 490
The Labour Force Survey 491
Four Labour Market Indicators 491

Unemployment and Full Employment 494
Underutilized Labour Excluded 494
"Natural" Unemployment 494
Real GDP and Unemployment Over the Cycle 496

The Price Level and Inflation 498
Why Inflation Is a Problem 498
The Consumer Price Index 498
Reading the CPI Numbers 498
Constructing the CPI 499
Measuring the Inflation Rate 500
Distinguishing High Inflation from a High Price Level 501
The Biased CPI 501
The Magnitude of the Bias 502
Some Consequences of the Bias 502
Alternative Price Indexes 502
Core Inflation 502
The Real Variables in Macroeconomics 503

READING BETWEEN THE LINES
Jobs in the Slowdown of 2008 504

PART SEVEN **WRAP-UP** ◆

Understanding Macroeconomic Trends and Fluctuations
The Big Picture 511

Talking with
Peter Howitt 512

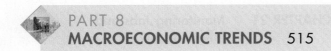

PART 8
MACROECONOMIC TRENDS 515

CHAPTER 22 ◆ Economic Growth 515

The Basics of Economic Growth 516
Calculating Growth Rates 516
The Magic of Sustained Growth 516
Applying the Rule of 70 517

Economic Growth Trends 518
Growth in the Canadian Economy 518
Real GDP Growth in the World Economy 519
How Potential GDP Grows 521
How Potential GDP is Determined 521
What Makes Potential GDP Grow? 523

Why Labour Productivity Grows 526
Preconditions for Labour Productivity
   Growth 526
Physical Capital Growth 526
Human Capital Growth 527
Technological Advances 527
Growth Accounting 528

Growth Theories and Policies 531
Classical Growth Theory 531
Neoclassical Growth Theory 531
New Growth Theory 533
New Growth Theory Versus Malthusian
   Theory 534
Sorting Out the Theories 535
Achieving Faster Growth 535

READING BETWEEN THE LINES
Economic Growth in China 536

CHAPTER 23 ◆ Finance, Saving, and
                          Investment 543

Financial Institutions and Financial Markets 544
Finance and Money 544
Physical Capital and Financial Capital 544
Capital and Investment 544
Wealth and Saving 544
Markets for Financial Capital 545
Financial Institutions 546
Solvency and Liquidity 547
Interest Rates and Asset Prices 548

The Market for Loanable Funds 548
Funds that Finance Investment 548
The Real Interest Rate 549
The Demand for Loanable Funds 550
The Supply of Loanable Funds 551
Equilibrium in the Market for Loanable
   Funds 552
Changes in Demand and Supply 552

Government in the Market for Loanable
Funds 555
A Government Budget Surplus 555
A Government Budget Deficit 555

The Global Loanable Funds Market 557
International Capital Mobility 557
International Borrowing and Lending 557
Demand and Supply in the Global and National
   Markets 557

READING BETWEEN THE LINES
Bailing Out Troubled U.S. Financial Markets 560

CHAPTER 24 ◆ Money, the Price Level, and Inflation 567

What Is Money? 568
Medium of Exchange 568
Unit of Account 568
Store of Value 569
Money in Canada Today 569

The Banking System 571
Depository Institutions 571
The Bank of Canada 572
The Payments System 573

How Banks Create Money 575
Creating Deposits by Making Loans 575
The Money Creation Process 576
The Money Multiplier 577

The Market for Money 578
The Influences on Money Holding 578
The Demand for Money 579
Shifts in the Demand for Money Curve 579
Money Market Equilibrium 581

The Quantity Theory of Money 582

READING BETWEEN THE LINES
The Quantity Theory of Money in Zimbabwe 584

MATHEMATICAL NOTE
The Money Multiplier 586

CHAPTER 25 ◆ The Exchange Rate and the Balance of Payments 593

Currencies and Exchange Rates 594
The Foreign Exchange Market 594
Exchange Rates 594
Nominal and Real Exchange Rates 594
Canadian-Dollar Effective Exchange Rate Index 596
Questions About the Exchange Rate 596

The Foreign Exchange Market 597
The Demand for One Money Is the Supply of Another Money 597
Demand in the Foreign Exchange Market 597
The Law of Demand for Foreign Exchange 597
Demand Curve for Canadian Dollars 598
Supply in the Foreign Exchange Market 599
The Law of Supply of Foreign Exchange 599
Supply Curve for Canadian Dollars 599
Market Equilibrium 600

Changes in Demand and Supply: Exchange Rate Fluctuations 601
A Change in the Demand for Canadian Dollars 601
Changes in the Supply of Canadian Dollars 602
Changes in the Exchange Rate 602
Exchange Rate Expectations 604
Instant Exchange Rate Response 604
The Nominal and Real Exchange Rates in the Short Run and in the Long Run 605

Financing International Trade 606
Balance of Payments Accounts 606
Borrowers and Lenders 608
Debtors and Creditors 608
Is the United States Borrowing for Consumption? 608
Current Account Balance 609
Net Exports 609
Where Is the Exchange Rate? 610

Exchange Rate Policy 611
   Flexible Exchange Rate   611
   Fixed Exchange Rate   611
   Crawling Peg   612

READING BETWEEN THE LINES
   The Rising Chinese Yuan   614

PART EIGHT **WRAP-UP**

Understanding Macroeconomic Trends
Expanding the Frontier   621
Talking with
Xavier Sala-i-Martin   622

PART 9
**MACROECONOMIC
FLUCTUATIONS** 625

CHAPTER 26 ◆ **Aggregate Supply and
                Aggregate Demand** 625

Aggregate Supply 626
   Quantity Supplied and Supply   626
   Long-Run Aggregate Supply   626
   Short-Run Aggregate Supply   627
   Changes in Aggregate Supply   628

Aggregate Demand 630
   The Aggregate Demand Curve   630
   Changes in Aggregate Demand   631

Explaining Macroeconomic Fluctuations 634
   Short-Run Macroeconomic Equilibrium   634
   Long-Run Macroeconomic Equilibrium   635
   Economic Growth in the *AS–AD* Model   635
   Inflation in the *AS–AD* Model   636
   The Business Cycle in the *AS–AD* Model   636
   Fluctuations in Aggregate Demand   638
   Fluctuations in Aggregate Supply   639

Macroeconomic Schools of Thought 640
   The Classical View   640
   The Keynesian View   640
   The Monetarist View   641
   The Way Ahead   641

READING BETWEEN THE LINES
   Aggregate Supply and Aggregate Demand in
      Action   642

CHAPTER 27 ◆ Expenditure Multipliers: The Keynesian Model 649

Fixed Prices and Expenditure Plans 650

Expenditure Plans 650
Consumption and Saving Plans 650
Marginal Propensities to Consume and Save 652
Slopes and Marginal Propensities 652
Consumption as a Function of Real GDP 653
Import Function 653

Real GDP with a Fixed Price Level 654

Aggregate Planned Expenditure 654
Actual Expenditure, Planned Expenditure, and Real GDP 655
Equilibrium Expenditure 656
Convergence to Equilibrium 657

The Multiplier 658

The Basic Idea of the Multiplier 658
The Multiplier Effect 658
Why Is the Multiplier Greater than 1? 659
The Size of the Multiplier 659
The Multiplier and the Slope of the *AE* Curve 660
Imports and Income Taxes 661
The Multiplier Process 661
Business Cycle Turning Points 662

The Multiplier and the Price Level 663

Adjusting Quantities and Prices 663
Aggregate Expenditure and Aggregate Demand 663
Deriving the Aggregate Demand Curve 663
Changes in Aggregate Expenditure and Aggregate Demand 664
Equilibrium Real GDP and the Price Level 665

READING BETWEEN THE LINES
Recession Coming 668

MATHEMATICAL NOTE
The Algebra of the Keynesian Model 670

CHAPTER 28 ◆ Canadian Inflation, Unemployment, and Business Cycle 679

Inflation Cycles 680

Demand-Pull Inflation 680
Cost-Push Inflation 682
Expected Inflation 684
Forecasting Inflation 685
Inflation and the Business Cycle 685

Inflation and Unemployment: The Phillips Curve 686

The Short-Run Phillips Curve 686
The Long-Run Phillips Curve 687
Changes in the Natural Unemployment Rate 687

The Business Cycle 689

Mainstream Business Cycle Theory 689
Real Business Cycle Theory 690

READING BETWEEN THE LINES
Onset of Recession in Canada and the United States 696

PART NINE **WRAP-UP** ◆

Understanding Macroeconomic Fluctuations
Boom and Bust 703

Talking with
Ricardo J. Cabellero 704

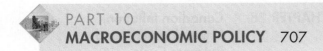

PART 10
MACROECONOMIC POLICY 707

CHAPTER 29 ◆ Fiscal Policy 707

Government Budgets 708
Budget Making 708
Highlights of the 2008 Budget 708
The Budget in Historical Perspective 709

Supply-Side Effects of Fiscal Policy 714
Full Employment and Potential GDP 714
The Effects of the Income Tax 714
Taxes on Expenditure and the Tax Wedge 715
Taxes and the Incentive to Save 716
Tax Revenues and the Laffer Curve 717
The Supply-Side Debate 717

Stabilizing the Business Cycle 718
Government Expenditure Multiplier 718
The Autonomous Tax Multiplier 718
The Balanced Budget Multiplier 718
Discretionary Fiscal Stabilization 718
Limitations of Discretionary Fiscal Policy 720
Automatic Stabilizers 720

READING BETWEEN THE LINES
Global Coordinated Fiscal Policy 724

CHAPTER 30 ◆ Monetary Policy 731

Monetary Policy Objective and Framework 732
Monetary Policy Objective 732
Responsibility for Monetary Policy 733

The Conduct of Monetary Policy 734
Choosing a Policy Instrument 734
The Overnight Rate 734
The Bank's Decision-Making Process 735
Hitting the Overnight Rate Target 736
How an Open Market Operation Works 736
Equilibrium in the Market for Reserves 738

Monetary Policy Transmission 739
Quick Overview 739
Interest Rate Changes 739
Exchange Rate Fluctuations 740
Money and Bank Loans 741
The Long-Term Real Interest Rate 741
Expenditure Plans 741
The Change in Aggregate Demand, Real GDP, and
     the Price Level 742
The Bank of Canada Fights Recession 742
The Bank of Canada Fights High Inflation 744
Loose Links and Long and Variable Lags 745

Alternative Monetary Policy Strategies 747
Overnight Rate Instrument Rule 747
Monetary Base Instrument Rule 747
Exchange Rate Targeting Rule 747
Money Targeting Rule 748
Why Rules? 749

READING BETWEEN THE LINES
Monetary Policy in Action 750

PART TEN WRAP-UP

Understanding Macroeconomic Policy
Tradeoffs and Free Lunches 757

Talking with
Stephanie Schmitt Grohé 758

Glossary **G-1**
Index **I-1**
Credits **C-1**

1 What Is Economics?

After studying this chapter,
you will be able to

- Define economics and distinguish between microeconomics and macroeconomics
- Explain the two big questions of economics
- Explain the key ideas that define the economic way of thinking
- Explain how economists go about their work as social scientists

You are studying economics at a time of extraordinary change. Canada is one of the world's richest nations, but China, India, Brazil, and Russia, nations with a combined population that dwarfs our own, are emerging to play ever greater roles in an expanding global economy. The technological change that is driving this expansion has brought us the laptops, wireless broadband, iPods, DVDs, cell phones, and video games that have transformed the way Canadians work and play. But this expanding global economy has also brought us sky-rocketing food and fuel prices and is contributing to global warming and climate change.

Your life will be shaped by the challenges you face and the opportunities you create. But to face those challenges and seize the opportunities they present, you must understand the powerful forces at play. The economics that you're about to learn will become your most reliable guide. This chapter gets you started. It describes the questions that economists try to answer and the ways in which they search for the answers.

◆ Definition of Economics

All economic questions arise because we want more than we can get. We want a peaceful and secure world. We want clean air, lakes, and rivers. We want long and healthy lives. We want good schools, colleges, and universities. We want spacious and comfortable homes. We want an enormous range of sports and recreational gear, from running shoes to jet skis. We want the time to enjoy sports, games, novels, movies, music, travel, and hanging out with our friends.

What each one of us can get is limited by time, by the incomes we earn, and by the prices we must pay. Everyone ends up with some unsatisfied wants. What we can get as a society is limited by our productive resources. These resources include the gifts of nature, human labour and ingenuity, and tools and equipment that we have produced.

Our inability to satisfy all our wants is called **scarcity**. The poor and the rich alike face scarcity. A child wants a $1.00 can of pop and two 50¢ packs of gum but has only $1.00 in his pocket. He faces scarcity. A millionaire wants to spend the weekend playing golf *and* spend the same weekend attending a business strategy meeting. She faces scarcity. A society wants to provide improved health care, install a computer in every classroom, upgrade the public transit system, clean polluted lakes and rivers, and so on. Society faces scarcity. Even parrots face scarcity!

Faced with scarcity, we must *choose* among the available alternatives. The child must *choose* the pop *or* the gum. The millionaire must *choose* the golf game *or* the meeting. As a society, we must *choose* among health care, national defence, and education.

Not only do I want a cracker—we all want a cracker!

© The New Yorker Collection 1985, Frank Modell from
cartoonbank.com. All Rights Reserved.

The choices that we make depend on the incentives that we face. An **incentive** is a reward that encourages an action or a penalty that discourages one. If the price of pop falls, the child has an *incentive* to choose more pop. If a profit of $10 million is at stake, the millionaire has an *incentive* to skip the golf game. As computer prices tumble, school boards have an *incentive* to connect more classrooms to the Internet.

Economics is the social science that studies the *choices* that individuals, businesses, governments, and entire societies make as they cope with *scarcity* and the *incentives* that influence and reconcile those choices. The subject divides into two main parts:

- Microeconomics
- Macroeconomics

Microeconomics

Microeconomics is the study of the choices that individuals and businesses make, the way these choices interact in markets, and the influence of governments. Some examples of microeconomic questions are: Why are people buying more DVDs and fewer movie tickets? How would a tax on e-commerce affect eBay?

Macroeconomics

Macroeconomics is the study of the performance of the national economy and the global economy. Some examples of macroeconomic questions are: Why did inflation in Canada start to increase in 2008? Can the Bank of Canada keep our inflation rate under control by raising interest rates?

Review Quiz ◆

1 List some examples of scarcity in Canada today.
2 Use the headlines in today's news to provide some examples of scarcity around the world.
3 Use today's news to illustrate the distinction between microeconomics and macroeconomics.

 Work Study Plan 1.1
and get instant feedback.

◆ Two Big Economic Questions

Two big questions summarize the scope of economics:

- How do choices end up determining *what*, *how*, and *for whom* goods and services are produced?
- How can choices made in the pursuit of *self-interest* also promote the *social interest*?

What, How, and For Whom?

Goods and services are the objects that people value and produce to satisfy human wants. *Goods* are physical objects, such as cell phones and automobiles. *Services* are tasks performed for people, such as cell phone service and auto-repair service.

What? What we produce changes over time. Sixty-five years ago, almost 20 percent of Canadians worked on farms. That number has shrunk to less than 3 percent today. Over the same period, the number of people who produce goods—in mining, construction, and manufacturing—has shrunk from 60 percent to less than 25 percent. The decrease in farming and manufacturing is reflected in an increase in services. Sixty-five years ago, 20 percent of the population produced services. Today, more than 75 percent of working Canadians have service jobs. Figure 1.1 shows these trends.

What determines these patterns of production? How do choices end up determining the quantities of cell phones, automobiles, cell phone service, auto-repair service, and the millions of other items that are produced in Canada and around the world?

How? Goods and services are produced by using productive resources that economists call **factors of production**. Factors of production are grouped into four categories:

- Land
- Labour
- Capital
- Entrepreneurship

Land The "gifts of nature" that we use to produce goods and services are called **land**. In economics, land is what in everyday language we call *natural resources*. It includes land in the everyday sense together with minerals, oil, gas, coal, water, air, forests, and fish.

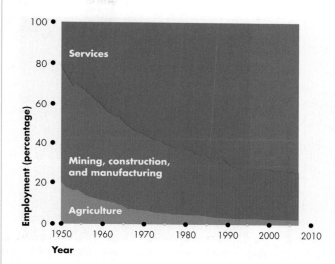

FIGURE 1.1 Trends in What We Produce

Services have expanded and agriculture, mining, construction, and manufacturing have shrunk.

Source of data: Statistics Canada.

myeconlab animation

Our land surface and water resources are renewable and some of our mineral resources can be recycled. But the resources that we use to create energy are nonrenewable—they can be used only once.

Labour The work time and work effort that people devote to producing goods and services is called **labour**. Labour includes the physical and mental efforts of all the people who work on farms and construction sites and in factories, shops, and offices.

The *quality* of labour depends on **human capital**, which is the knowledge and skill that people obtain from education, on-the-job training, and work experience. You are building your own human capital right now as you work on your economics course, and your human capital will continue to grow as you gain work experience.

Human capital expands over time. Today, 92 percent of the adult population of Canada have completed high school and more than 62 percent have a college or university degree. Figure 1.2 shows these measures of the growth of human capital in Canada over the past few decades.

FIGURE 1.2   A Measure of Human Capital

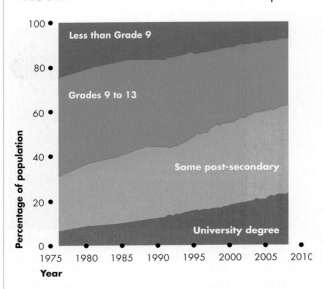

Today, 23 percent of the adult population have university degrees and another 40 percent have post-secondary certificates. A further 30 percent have completed high school.

Source of data: Statistics Canada.

myeconlab animation

Capital   The tools, instruments, machines, buildings, and other constructions that businesses use to produce goods and services are called **capital**.

In everyday language, we talk about money, stocks, and bonds as being "capital." These items are *financial* capital. Financial capital plays an important role in enabling businesses to borrow the funds that they use to buy physical capital. But because financial capital is not used to produce goods and services, it is not a productive resource.

Entrepreneurship   The human resource that organizes labour, land, and capital is called **entrepreneurship**. Entrepreneurs come up with new ideas about what and how to produce, make business decisions, and bear the risks that arise from these decisions.

What determines the quantities of factors of production that are used to produce goods and services?

For Whom?   Who consumes the goods and services that are produced depends on the incomes that people earn. A large income enables a person to buy large

quantities of goods and services. A small income leaves a person with few options and small quantities of goods and services.

People earn their incomes by selling the services of the factors of production they own:

- Land earns **rent**.
- Labour earns **wages**.
- Capital earns **interest**.
- Entrepreneurship earns **profit**.

Which factor of production earns the most income? The answer is labour. Wages and fringe benefits are around 70 percent of total income. Land, capital, and entrepreneurship share the rest. These percentages have been remarkably constant over time.

Knowing how income is shared among the factors of production doesn't tell us how it is shared among individuals. And the distribution of income among individuals is extremely unequal. You know of some people who earn very large incomes: Mike Lazaridis of Research in Motion earned more than $2.66 billion in 2007 and Frank Stronach, chairman of Canada's largest auto parts company, was paid more than $27 million.

You know of even more people who earn very small incomes. Servers at Tim Hortons average about $8.75 an hour; checkout clerks, cleaners, and textile workers all earn less than $10 an hour.

You probably know about other persistent differences in incomes. Men, on the average, earn more than women; whites earn more than minorities; college graduates earn more than high-school graduates.

We can get a good sense of who consumes the goods and services produced by looking at the percentages of total income earned by different groups of people. The poorest 20 percent of the population earn about 5 percent of total income; the richest 20 percent earn close to 50 percent of total income. So the richest 20 percent, on average, earn more than 10 times what the poorest 20 percent earn.

Why is the distribution of income so unequal? Why do women and minorities earn less than men?

Economics provides some answers to all these questions about what, how, and for whom goods and services are produced and much of the rest of this book will help you to understand those answers.

We're now going to look at the second big question of economics: When does the pursuit of self-interest promote the social interest? This question is a difficult one both to appreciate and to answer.

How Can the Pursuit of Self-Interest Promote the Social Interest?

Every day, you and 32 million other Canadians, along with 6.7 billion people in the rest of the world, make economic choices that result in *what*, *how*, and *for whom* goods and services are produced.

Self-Interest A choice is in your **self-interest** if you think that choice is the best one available for you. You make most of your choices in your self-interest. You use your time and other resources in the ways that make most sense to you, and you don't think too much about how your choices affect other people. You order a home delivery pizza because you're hungry and want to eat. You don't order it thinking that the delivery person needs an income.

When you act on your self-interested economic choices, you come into contact with thousands of other people who produce and deliver the goods and services that you decide to buy or who buy the things that you sell. These people have made their own choices—what to produce and how to produce it, who to hire or whom to work for, and so on—in their self-interest. When the pizza delivery person shows up at your door, he's not doing you a favour. He's earning his income and hoping for a good tip.

Social Interest Self-interested choices promote the **social interest** if they lead to an outcome that is the best for society as a whole—an outcome that uses resources efficiently and distributes goods and services equitably (or fairly) among individuals.

Resources are used efficiently when goods and services are produced

1. At the lowest possible cost, and
2. In the quantities that give the greatest possible benefit.

The Big Question How can we organize our economic lives so that when each one of us makes choices that are in our self-interest, it turns out that these choices also promote the social interest? Does voluntary trading in free markets achieve the social interest? Do we need government action to guide our choices to achieve the social interest? Do we need international cooperation and treaties to achieve the global social interest?

Let's put some flesh on these broad questions with some examples.

Self-Interest and the Social Interest

To get started thinking about the tension between self-interest and the social interest, we'll consider five topics that generate discussion in today's world. Here, we will briefly introduce the topics and identify some of the economic questions that they pose. We'll return to each one of them as you learn more of the economic ideas and tools that can be used to understand these issues. The topics are

- Globalization
- The information-age economy
- Global warming
- Natural resource depletion
- Economic instability

Globalization The term *globalization* means the expansion of international trade, borrowing and lending, and investment.

Whose self-interest does globalization serve? Is it only in the self-interest of the multinational firms that produce in low-cost regions and sell in high-price regions? Is globalization in the interest of consumers who buy lower-cost goods? Is globalization in the interest of the worker in Malaysia who sews your new running shoes? Is globalization in your self-interest and in the social interest? Or should we limit globalization and restrict imports of cheap foreign-produced goods and services?

Globalization Today
Life in a Small and Ever-Shrinking World

Every day, 40,000 people travel by air between North America and Asia and Europe. A phone call or a video conference with people who live 15,000 kilometres away is a common and easily affordable event.

When Roots produces yoga pants, people in Taiwan get work. When Apple designs a new generation iPod, electronics factories in China, Japan, Korea, and Taiwan produce and assemble the parts. When Nintendo creates a new game for the Wii, programmers in India write the code. And when China Airlines buys new regional jets, Canadians who work at Bombardier build them.

While globalization brings expanded production and job opportunities for Asian workers, it destroys many North American jobs. Workers across the manufacturing industries must learn new skills, or take lower-paid service jobs, or retire earlier than planned.

The Information-Age Economy The technological change of the 1990s and 2000s has been called the *Information Revolution.*

During the Information Revolution were scarce resources used in the best possible way? Who benefitted from Bill Gates' decision to quit Harvard and create Microsoft? Did Microsoft produce operating systems for the personal computer that served the social interest? Did it sell its programs for prices that served the social interest? Did Bill Gates have to be paid what has now grown to $55 billion to produce successive generations of Windows, Microsoft Office, and other programs? Did Intel make the right quality of chips and sell them in the right quantities for the right prices? Or was the quality too low and the price too high? Would the social interest have been better served if Microsoft and Intel had faced competition from other firms?

The Source of the Information Age

So Much from One Tiny Chip

The microprocessor or computer chip created the information age. Gordon Moore of Intel predicted in 1965 that the number of transistors that could be placed on one chip would double every 18 months (Moore's law). This prediction turned out to be remarkably accurate. In 1980, an Intel chip had 60,000 transistors. In 2008, Intel's Core 2 Duo processor—that you might be using on your personal computer—has 291 million transistors.

The spinoffs from faster and cheaper computing were widespread. Telecommunications became clearer and faster; music and movie recording became more realistic; routine tasks that previously required human decision and action were automated.

All the new products and processes, and the low-cost computing power that made them possible, were produced by people who made choices in their own self-interest. They did not result from any grand design or government economic plan.

When Gordon Moore set up Intel and started making chips, no one had told him to do so, and he wasn't thinking how much easier it would be for you to turn in your essay on time if you had a faster laptop. When Bill Gates quit Harvard to set up Microsoft, he wasn't thinking about making it easier to use a computer. Moore, Gates, and thousands of other entrepreneurs were in hot pursuit of the big prizes that many of them succeeded in winning.

Global Warming Global warming and its effect on climate change is a huge political issue today. Every serious political leader is acutely aware of the problem and of the popularity of having proposals that might lower carbon emissions.

Every day, when you make self-interested choices to use electricity and gasoline, you contribute to carbon emissions; you leave your carbon footprint. You can lessen your carbon footprint by walking, riding a bike, taking a cold shower, or planting a tree.

But can each one of us be relied upon to make decisions that affect the Earth's carbon-dioxide concentration in the social interest? Must governments change the incentives we face so that our self-interested choices advance the social interest? How can governments change incentives? How can we encourage the use of wind and solar power to replace the burning of fossil fuels that bring climate change?

A Hotter Planet

Melting Ice and the Changing Climate

Retreating polar icecaps are a vivid illustration of a warming planet. Over the past 100 years, Earth's surface air temperature is estimated to have risen by about three-quarters of a degree Celsius. Uncertainty surrounds the causes, likely future amount, and effects of this temperature increase.

The consensus is that the temperature is rising because the amount of carbon dioxide in the Earth's atmosphere is increasing, and that human economic activity is a source of the increased carbon concentration.

Forests convert carbon dioxide to oxygen and so act as carbon sinks, but they are shrinking.

Two-thirds of the world's carbon emissions come from the United States, China, the European Union, Russia, and India. The fastest growing emissions are coming from India and China.

Burning fossil fuels—coal and oil—to generate electricity and to power airplanes, automobiles, and trucks pours a staggering 28 billion tonnes, or 4 tonnes per person, of carbon dioxide into the atmosphere each year.

The amount of future global warming and its effects are uncertain. If the temperature rise continues, the Earth's climate will change, ocean levels will rise, and low-lying coastal areas will need to be protected against the rising tides by expensive barriers.

Natural Resource Depletion Tropical rainforests and ocean fish stocks are disappearing quickly. No one owns these resources and everyone is free to take what they want. When Japanese, Spanish, and Russian trawlers scoop up fish in international waters, no one keeps track of the quantities of fish they catch and no one makes them pay. The fish are free.

Each one of us makes self-interested economic choices to buy products that destroy natural resources and kill wild fish stocks. When you buy soap or shampoo or eat fish and contribute to the depletion of natural resources, are your self-interested choices damaging the social interest? If they are, what can be done to change your choices so that they serve the social interest?

Economic Instability The past 20 years have been ones of remarkable economic stability, so much so that they've been called the *Great Moderation*. Even the economic shockwaves after 9/11 brought only a small dip in the strong pace of Canadian and global economic expansion. But in August 2007, a period of financial stress began.

Running Out of Natural Resources

Disappearing Forests and Fish

Tropical rainforests in South America, Africa, and Asia support the lives of 30 million species of plants, animals, and insects—approaching 50 percent of all the species on the planet. These rainforests provide us with the ingredients for many goods, including soaps, mouthwashes, shampoos, food preservatives, rubber, nuts, and fruits. The Amazon rainforest alone converts about 1 trillion pounds of carbon dioxide into oxygen each year.

Yet tropical rainforests cover less than 2 percent of the earth's surface and are heading for extinction. Logging, cattle ranching, mining, oil extraction, hydroelectric dams, and subsistence farming destroy an area the size of two football fields every second, or an area larger than New York City every day. At the current rate of destruction, almost all the tropical rainforest ecosystems will be gone by 2030.

What is happening to the tropical rainforests is also happening to ocean fish stocks. Overfishing has almost eliminated cod from the Atlantic Ocean and the southern bluefin tuna from the South Pacific Ocean. Many other species of fish are on the edge of extinction in the wild and are now available only from fish farms.

Banks' choices to lend and people's choices to borrow were made in self-interest. But did this lending and borrowing serve the social interest? Did the Federal Reserve's bailout of troubled U.S. banks serve the global social interest? Or might the Federal Reserve's rescue action encourage U.S. banks around the world to repeat their dangerous lending in the future?

The End of the Great Moderation

A Credit Crunch

Flush with funds, and offering record low interest rates, U.S. banks went on a lending spree to home buyers. Rapidly rising U.S. home prices made home owners feel well off and they were happy to borrow and spend. Home loans were bundled into securities that were sold and resold to banks around the world.

In 2006, U.S. interest rates began to rise, the rate of rise in home prices slowed, and borrowers defaulted on their loans. What started as a trickle became a flood. By mid-2007, banks took losses that totalled billions of dollars as more people defaulted.

Global credit markets stopped working, and people began to fear a prolonged slowdown in economic activity. Some even feared the return of the economic trauma of the *Great Depression* of the 1930s. The Federal Reserve, determined to avoid a catastrophe, started lending on a very large scale to the troubled U.S. banks.

Review Quiz

1 Describe the broad facts about *what*, *how*, and *for whom* goods and services are produced.
2 Use headlines from the recent news to illustrate the potential for conflict between self-interest and the social interest.

myeconlab Work Study Plan 1.2 and get instant feedback.

We've looked at five topics that illustrate the big question: How can choices made in the pursuit of self-interest also promote the social interest? While working through this book, you will encounter the principles that help economists figure out when the social interest is being served, when it is not, and what might be done when the social interest is not being served.

◆ The Economic Way of Thinking

The questions that economics tries to answer tell us about the *scope of economics*. But they don't tell us how economists *think* about these questions and go about seeking answers to them.

You're now going to begin to see how economists approach economic questions. We'll look at the ideas that define the *economic way of thinking*. This way of thinking needs practice, but it is powerful, and as you become more familiar with it, you'll begin to see the world around you with a new and sharper focus.

Choices and Tradeoffs

Because we face scarcity, we must make choices. And when we make a choice, we select from the available alternatives. For example, you can spend Saturday night studying for your next economics test or having fun with your friends, but you can't do both of these activities at the same time. You must choose how much time to devote to each. Whatever choice you make, you could have chosen something else.

You can think about your choice as a tradeoff. A **tradeoff** is an exchange—giving up one thing to get something else. When you choose how to spend your Saturday night, you face a tradeoff between studying and hanging out with your friends.

Guns Versus Butter The classic tradeoff is between guns and butter. "Guns" and "butter" stand for any pair of goods. They might actually be guns and butter. Or they might be broader categories, such as national defence and food. Or they might be any pair of specific goods or services, such as cola and pizza, baseball bats and tennis rackets, colleges and hospitals, realtor services and career counseling.

Regardless of the specific objects that guns and butter represent, the guns-versus-butter tradeoff captures a hard fact of life: If we want more of one thing, we must give up something else to get it: to get more "guns" we must give up some "butter."

The idea of a tradeoff is central to economics. We'll look at some examples, beginning with the big questions: What, How, and For Whom goods and services are produced? We can view each of these questions in terms of tradeoffs.

What, How, and For Whom Tradeoffs

The questions what, how, and for whom goods and services are produced all involve tradeoffs that are similar to that between guns and butter.

What Tradeoffs What goods and services are produced depends on choices made by each one of us, by our government, and by the businesses that produce the things we buy. Each of these choices involves a tradeoff.

Each of us faces a tradeoff when we choose how to spend our income. You go to the movies this week, but you forgo a few cups of coffee to buy the movie ticket. You trade off coffee for a movie.

The federal government faces a tradeoff when it chooses how to spend our tax dollars. It votes for more national defence but cuts back on educational programs. The government trades off education for national defence.

Businesses face a tradeoff when they decide what to produce. Nike hires Tiger Woods and allocates resources to designing and marketing a new golf ball but cuts back on its development of a new running shoe. Nike trades off running shoes for golf balls.

How Tradeoffs How businesses produce the goods and services we buy depends on their choices. These choices involve tradeoffs. For example, when Tim Hortons opens a new store with an automated production line and closes one with a traditional kitchen, it trades off labour for capital. When Air Canada replaces check-in agents with self check-in kiosks, it also trades off labour for capital.

For Whom Tradeoffs For whom goods and services are produced depends on the distribution of buying power. Buying power can be redistributed—transferred from one person to another—in three ways: by voluntary payments, by theft, or through taxes and benefits organized by the government. Redistribution brings tradeoffs.

Each of us faces a tradeoff when we choose how much to contribute to the United Nations' famine relief fund. You donate $50 and cut your spending. You trade off your own spending for a small increase in economic equality. We also face a tradeoff when we vote to increase the resources for catching thieves and enforcing the law. We trade off goods and services for an increase in the security of our property.

We also face a *for whom* tradeoff when we vote for taxes and social programs that redistribute buying power from the rich to the poor. These redistribution programs confront society with what has been called the **big tradeoff**—the tradeoff between equality and efficiency. Taxing the rich and making transfers to the poor brings greater economic equality. But taxing productive activities such as running a business, working hard, and developing a more productive technology discourages these activities. So taxing productive activities means producing less. A more equal distribution means there is less to share.

Think of the problem of how to share a pie that everyone contributes to baking. If each person receives a share of the pie that is proportional to her or his effort, everyone will work hard and the pie will be as large as possible. But if the pie is shared equally, regardless of contribution, some talented bakers will slack off and the pie will shrink. The big tradeoff is one between the size of the pie and how equally it is shared. We trade off some pie for increased equality.

Choices Bring Change

What, how, and for whom goods and services are produced changes over time. The quantity and range of goods and services available today is much greater than it was a generation ago. But the quality of economic life (and its rate of improvement) does not depend purely on nature and on luck. It depends on many of the choices made by each one of us, by governments, and by businesses. These choices also involve tradeoffs.

One choice is how much of our income to consume and how much to save. Our saving can be channelled through the financial system to finance businesses and pay for new capital that increases production. The more we save, the more financial capital is available for businesses to use to buy physcial capital, so the more goods and services we can produce in the future. When you decide to save an extra $1,000 and forgo a vacation, you trade off the vacation for a higher future income. If everyone saves an extra $1,000 and businesses buy more equipment that increases production, future consumption per person rises. As a society, we trade off current consumption for economic growth and higher future consumption.

A second choice is how much effort to devote to education and training. By becoming better educated and more highly skilled, we become more productive

and are able to produce more goods and services. When you decide to remain in school for another two years to complete a professional degree and forgo a huge chunk of leisure time, you trade off leisure today for a higher future income. If everyone becomes better educated, production increases and income per person rises. As a society, we trade off current consumption and leisure time for economic growth and higher future consumption.

A third choice is how much effort to devote to research and the development of new products and production methods. Ford Motor Company can hire people either to design a new robotic assembly line or to operate the existing plant and produce cars. The robotic plant brings greater productivity in the future but means less current production—a tradeoff of current production for greater future production.

Seeing choices as tradeoffs emphasizes the idea that to get something, we must give up something. What we give up is the cost of what we get. Economists call this cost the *opportunity cost*.

Opportunity Cost

"There's no such thing as a free lunch" expresses the central idea of economics: Every choice has a cost. The **opportunity cost** of something is the highest-valued alternative that we must give up to get it.

For example, you face an opportunity cost of being in school. That opportunity cost is the highest-valued alternative that you would do if you were not in school. If you quit school and take a job at Tim Hortons, you will earn enough to go to hockey games and movies and will have lots of free time to spend with your friends. If you remain in school, you can't afford these things. You will be able to buy them when you graduate and get a job, and that is one of the payoffs from being in school. But for now, when you've bought your books, you have nothing left for games and movies. Working on assignments leaves even less time for hanging out with your friends. Giving up hockey games, movies, and free time is part of the opportunity cost of being in school.

All the *what, how,* and *for whom* tradeoffs involve opportunity costs. The opportunity cost of a gun is the butter forgone; the opportunity cost of a movie ticket is the number of cups of coffee forgone.

The choices that bring change also involve opportunity costs. The opportunity cost of more goods and services in the future is less consumption today.

Choosing at the Margin

You can allocate the next hour between studying and instant messaging your friends. But the choice is not all or nothing. You must decide how many minutes to allocate to each activity. To make this decision, you compare the benefit of a little bit more study time with its cost—you make your choice at the **margin**.

The benefit that arises from an increase in an activity is called **marginal benefit**. For example, suppose that you're spending four nights a week studying and your grade point average (GPA) is 3.0. You decide that you want a higher GPA, so you study an extra night each week. Your GPA rises to 3.5. The marginal benefit from studying for one extra night a week is the 0.5 increase in your GPA. It is *not* the 3.5. You already have a 3.0 from studying for four nights a week, so we don't count this benefit as resulting from the decision you are now making.

The cost of an increase in an activity is called **marginal cost**. For you, the marginal cost of increasing your study time by one night a week is the cost of the additional night not spent with your friends (if that is your best alternative use of the time). It does not include the cost of the four nights you are already studying.

To make your decision, you compare the marginal benefit from an extra night of studying with its marginal cost. If the marginal benefit exceeds the marginal cost, you study the extra night. If the marginal cost exceeds the marginal benefit, you do not study the extra night.

By evaluating marginal benefits and marginal costs and choosing only those actions that bring greater benefit than cost, we use our scarce resources in the way that makes us as well off as possible.

Responding to Incentives

When we make choices we respond to incentives. A change in marginal cost or a change in marginal benefit changes the incentives that we face and leads us to change our choice.

For example, suppose your economics instructor gives you a set of problems and tells you that all the problems will be on the next test. The marginal benefit from working these problems is large, so you diligently work them all. In contrast, if your math instructor gives you a set of problems and tells you that none of the problems will be on the next test, the marginal benefit from working these problems is lower, so you skip most of them.

The central idea of economics is that we can predict how choices will change by looking at changes in incentives. More of an activity is undertaken when its marginal cost falls or its marginal benefit rises; less of an activity is undertaken when its marginal cost rises or its marginal benefit falls.

Incentives are also the key to reconciling self-interest and social interest. When our choices are *not* in the social interest, it is because of the incentives we face. One of the challenges for economists is to figure out the incentive systems that result in self-interested choices also being in the social interest.

Human Nature, Incentives, and Institutions

Economists take human nature as given and view people as acting in their self-interest. All people—consumers, producers, politicians, and public servants—pursue their self-interest.

Self-interested actions are not necessarily *selfish* actions. You might decide to use your resources in ways that bring pleasure to others as well as to yourself. But a self-interested act gets the most value for *you* based on *your* view about value.

If human nature is given and if people act in their self-interest, how can we take care of the social interest? Economists answer this question by emphasizing the crucial role that institutions play in influencing the incentives that people face as they pursue their self-interest.

A system of laws that protects private property and markets that enable voluntary exchange are the fundamental institutions. You will learn as you progress with your study of economics that where these institutions exist, self-interest can indeed promote the social interest.

Review Quiz

1   Provide three everyday examples of tradeoffs and describe the opportunity cost involved in each.
2   Provide three everyday examples to illustrate what we mean by choosing at the margin.
3   How do economists predict changes in choices?
4   What do economists say about the role of institutions in promoting the social interest?

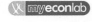 Work Study Plan 1.3 and get instant feedback.

Economics as Social Science and Policy Tool

Economics is both a science and a set of tools that can be used to make policy decisions.

Economics as Social Science

As social scientists, economists seek to discover how the economic world works. In pursuit of this goal, like all scientists, they distinguish between two types of statements: positive and normative.

Positive Statements *Positive* statements are about what is. They say what is currently believed about the way the world operates. A positive statement might be right or wrong, but we can test a positive statement by checking it against the facts. "Our planet is warming because of the amount of coal that we're burning" is a positive statement. "A rise in the minimum wage will bring more teenage unemployment" is another positive statement. Each statement might be right or wrong, and it can be tested.

A central task of economists is to test positive statements about how the economic world works and to weed out those that are wrong. Economics first got off the ground in the late 1700s, so economics is a young subject compared with, for example, math and physics, and much remains to be discovered.

Normative Statements *Normative* statements are statements about what ought to be. These statements depend on values and cannot be tested. The statement "We ought to cut back on our use of coal" is a normative statement. "The minimum wage should not be increased" is another normative statement. You may agree or disagree with either of these statements, but you can't test them. They express an opinion, but they don't assert a fact that can be checked. They are not economics.

Unscrambling Cause and Effect Economists are especially interested in positive statements about cause and effect. Are computers getting cheaper because people are buying them in greater quantities? Or are people buying computers in greater quantities because they are getting cheaper? Or is some third factor causing both the price of a computer to fall and the quantity of computers bought to increase?

To answer questions such as these, economists create and test economic models. An **economic model** is a description of some aspect of the economic world that includes only those features that are needed for the purpose at hand. For example, an economic model of a cell phone network might include features such as the prices of calls, the number of users, and the volume of calls. But the model would ignore details such as cell phone colours and ringtones.

A model is tested by comparing its predictions with the facts. But testing an economic model is difficult because we observe the outcomes of the simultaneous operation of many factors. To cope with this problem, economists use natural experiments, statistical investigations, and economic experiments.

Natural Experiment A natural experiment is a situation that arises in the ordinary course of economic life in which the one factor of interest is different and other things are equal (or similar). For example, Canada has higher unemployment benefits than the United States, but the people in the two nations are similar. So to study the effect of unemployment benefits on the unemployment rate, economists might compare Canada with the United States.

Statistical Investigation A statistical investigation looks for correlation—a tendency for the values of two variables to move together (either in the same direction or in opposite directions) in a predictable and related way. For example, cigarette smoking and lung cancer are correlated. Sometimes a correlation shows a causal influence of one variable on the other. For example, smoking causes lung cancer. But sometimes the direction of causation is hard to determine.

Steven Levitt, the author of *Freakonomics* and whom you can meet on pp. 224–226, is a master in the use of a combination of the natural experiment and statistical investigation to unscramble cause and effect. He has used the tools of economics to investigate the effects of good parenting on education (not very strong), to explain why drug dealers live with their mothers (because they don't earn enough to live independently), and (controversially) the effects of abortion law on crime.

Economic Experiment An economic experiment puts people in a decision-making situation and varies the influence of one factor at a time to discover how they respond.

Economics as Policy Tool

Economics is useful. It is a toolkit for making decisions. And you don't need to be a fully fledged economist to think like one and to use the insights of economics as a policy tool.

Economics provides a way of approaching problems in all aspects of our lives. Here, we'll focus on the three broad areas of:

- Personal economic policy
- Business economic policy
- Government economic policy

Personal Economic Policy Should you take out a student loan? Should you get a weekend job? Should you buy a used car or a new one? Should you rent an apartment or take out a loan and buy a condominium? Should you pay off your credit card balance or make just the minimum payment? How should you allocate your time between study, working for a wage, caring for family members, and having fun? How should you allocate your time between studying economics and your other subjects? Should you quit school after getting a bachelor's degree or should you go for a master's or a professional qualification?

All these questions involve a marginal benefit and a marginal cost. And although some of the numbers might be hard to pin down, you will make more solid decisions if you approach these questions with the tools of economics.

Business Economic Policy Should Sony make only flat panel televisions and stop making conventional ones? Should Bell Canada outsource its online customer services to India or run the operation from Quebec? Should Encana explore the Deep Panuke natural gas field off the coast of Nova Scotia or expand its oil sands project in North Alberta? Can Microsoft compete with Google in the search engine business? Can eBay compete with the surge of new Internet auction services? Is Allan Burnett really worth $13,200,000 to the Blue Jays?

Like personal economic questions, these business questions involve the evaluation of a marginal benefit and a marginal cost. Some of the questions require a broader investigation of the interactions of individuals and firms. But again, by approaching these questions with the tools of economics and by hiring economists as advisors, businesses can make better decisions.

Government Economic Policy How can provincial and federal governments balance their budgets? Should the federal governments cut taxes? Should provincial governments raise taxes? How can the Canadian tax system be simplified? Should people be permitted to buy private health insurance just as they already buy private travel insurance? Should there be a special tax to penalize corporations that send jobs overseas? Should cheap foreign imports of furniture and textiles be limited? Should egg, dairy, and milk farmers receive subsidies? Should wheat and barley growers be able to sell their output on the world market and not be restricted to sell to the Canadian Wheat Board?

These government policy questions call for decisions that involve the evaluation of a marginal benefit and a marginal cost and an investigation of the interactions of individuals and businesses. Yet again, by approaching these questions with the tools of economics, governments make better decisions.

Notice that all the policy questions we've just posed involve a blend of the positive and the normative. Economics can't help with the normative part—the objective. But for a given objective, economics provides a method of evaluating alternative solutions. That method is to evaluate the marginal benefits and marginal costs and to find the solution that brings the greatest available gain.

Review Quiz

1 What is the distinction between a positive statement and a normative statement? Provide an example (different from those in the chapter) of each type of statement.
2 What is a model? Can you think of a model that you might use (probably without thinking of it as a model) in your everyday life?
3 What are the three ways in which economists try to disentangle cause and effect?
4 How is economics used as a policy tool?
5 What is the role of marginal benefit and marginal cost in the use of economics as a policy tool?

 Work Study Plan 1.4 and get instant feedback.

SUMMARY

Key Points

Definition of Economics (p. 2)

- All economic questions arise from scarcity—from the fact that wants exceed the resources available to satisfy them.
- Economics is the social science that studies the choices that people make as they cope with scarcity.
- The subject divides into microeconomics and macroeconomics.

Two Big Economic Questions (pp. 3–7)

- Two big questions summarize the scope of economics:

  1. How do choices end up determining *what*, *how*, and *for whom* goods and services are produced?
  2. When do choices made in the pursuit of *self-interest* also promote the *social interest*?

The Economic Way of Thinking (pp. 8–10)

- Every choice is a tradeoff—exchanging more of something for less of something else.

- The classic guns-versus-butter tradeoff represents all tradeoffs.
- All economic questions involve tradeoffs.
- The big social tradeoff is that between equality and efficiency.
- The highest-valued alternative forgone is the opportunity cost of what is chosen.
- Choices are made at the margin and respond to incentives.

Economics as Social Science and Policy Tool (pp. 11–12)

- Economists distinguish between positive statements—what is—and normative statements—what ought to be.
- To explain the economic world, economists create and test economic models.
- Economics is used in personal, business, and government economic policy decisions.
- The main policy tool is the evaluation and comparison of marginal cost and marginal benefit.

Key Terms

Big tradeoff, 9
Capital, 4
Economic model, 11
Economics, 2
Entrepreneurship, 4
Factors of production, 3
Goods and services, 3
Human capital, 3
Incentive, 2

Interest, 4
Labour, 3
Land, 3
Macroeconomics, 2
Margin, 10
Marginal benefit, 10
Marginal cost, 10
Microeconomics, 2
Opportunity cost, 9

Profit, 4
Rent, 4
Scarcity, 2
Self-interest, 5
Social interest, 5
Tradeoff, 8
Wages, 4

PROBLEMS and APPLICATIONS

 Work problems 1–6 in Chapter 1 Study Plan and get instant feedback.
Work problems 7–11 as Homework, a Quiz, or a Test if assigned by your instructor.

1. Apple Computer Inc. decides to make songs freely available in unlimited quantities at the iTunes Store.
   a. How does Apple's decision change the opportunity cost of downloading a song?
   b. Does Apple's decision change the incentives that people face?
   c. Is Apple's decision an example of a microeconomic or a macroeconomic issue?

2. Which of the following pairs does not match?
   a. Labour and wages
   b. Land and rent
   c. Entrepreneurship and profit
   d. Capital and profit

3. Explain how the following news headlines concern self-interest and the social interest:
   a. Roots Expands in China
   b. McDonald's Moves into Salads
   c. Food Must Be Labelled with Nutrition Information

4. The night before a test, you decide to go to the movies instead of working your MyEconLab Study Plan. You get 50 percent on your test, not the 70 percent that you normally score.
   a. Did you face a tradeoff?
   b. What was the opportunity cost of your evening at the movies?

5. Which of the following statements is positive, which is normative, and which can be tested?
   a. The federal government should increase production of biofuels.
   b. China is Canada's largest trading partner.
   c. If the price of antiretroviral drugs increases, HIV/AIDS sufferers will decrease their consumption of the drugs.

6. As London prepares to host the 2012 Olympic Games, concern about the cost of the event is increasing. An example:

   Costs Soar for London Olympics

   The regeneration of East London is set to add extra £1.5 billion to taxpayers' bill.
   The Times, London, July 6, 2006

   Is the cost of regenerating East London an opportunity cost of hosting the 2012 Olympic Games? Explain why or why not.

7. Before starring as Tony Stark in *Iron Man*, Robert Downey Jr. had acted in 45 movies that had average first-weekend box office revenues of a bit less than $5 million. *Iron Man* grossed $102 million on its opening weekend.
   a. How do you expect the success of *Iron Man* to influence the opportunity cost of hiring Robert Downey Jr.?
   b. How have the incentives for a movie producer to hire Robert Downey Jr. changed?

8. How would you classify a movie star as a factor of production?

9. How does the creation of a successful movie influence what, how, and for whom goods and services are produced?

10. How does the creation of a successful movie illustrate self-interested choices that are also in the social interest?

11. Look at today's *National Post*.
    a. What is the top economic news story? With which of the big questions does it deal? (It must deal with at least one of them and might deal with more than one.)
    b. What tradeoffs does the news item discuss or imply?
    c. Write a brief summary of the news item using the economic vocabulary that you have learned in this chapter and as many as possible of the key terms listed on p. 13.

12. Use the link in MyEconLab (Textbook Resources, Chapter 1) to visit *Resources for Economists on the Internet*. This Web site is a good place from which to search for economic information on the Internet. Click on "Blogs, Commentaries, and Podcasts" and then click on the Becker-Posner Blog.

    a. Read the latest blog by these two outstanding economists.
    b. As you read this blog, think about what it is saying about the "what," "how," and "for whom" questions.
    c. As you read the blog, also think about what it is saying about self-interest and the social interest.

APPENDIX

Graphs in Economics

After studying this appendix, you will be able to

- Make and interpret a time-series graph, a cross-section graph, and a scatter diagram

- Distinguish between linear and nonlinear relationships and between relationships that have a maximum and a minimum

- Define and calculate the slope of a line

- Graph relationships among more than two variables

Graphing Data

A graph represents a quantity as a distance on a line. In Fig. A1.1, a distance on the horizontal line represents temperature, measured in degrees Celsius. A movement from left to right shows an increase in temperature. The point 0 represents zero degrees Celsius. To the right of 0, the temperature is positive. To the left of 0 (as indicated by the minus sign), the temperature is negative. A distance on the vertical line represents height, measured in thousands of feet. The point 0 represents sea level. Points above 0 represent feet above sea level. Points below 0 (indicated by a minus sign) represent feet below sea level.

By setting two scales perpendicular to each other, as in Fig. A1.1, we can visualize the relationship between two variables. The scale lines are called *axes*. The vertical line is the *y-axis*, and the horizontal line is the *x-axis*. Each axis has a zero point, which is shared by the two axes and called the *origin*.

We need two bits of information to make a two-variable graph: the value of the *x* variable and the value of the *y* variable. For example, off the coast of British Columbia, the temperature is 10 degrees—the value of *x*. A fishing boat is located at 0 feet above sea level—the value of *y*. These two bits of information appear as point *A* in Fig. A1.1. A climber at the top of Mount McKinley on a cold day is 6,194 metres

FIGURE A1.1 Making a Graph

Graphs have axes that measure quantities as distances. Here, the horizontal axis (*x*-axis) measures temperature, and the vertical axis (*y*-axis) measures height. Point *A* represents a fishing boat at sea level (0 on the *y*-axis) on a day when the temperature is 10°C. Point *B* represents a climber at the top of Mt. McKinley, 6,194 metres above sea level in a zero-degree gale. Point *C* represents a climber at the top of Mt. McKinley, 6,194 metres above sea level, at a temperature of 10°C.

myeconlab   animation

above sea level in a zero-degree gale. These two pieces of information appear as point *B*. On a warmer day, a climber might be at the peak of Mt. McKinley when the temperature is 10 degrees, at point *C*.

We can draw two lines, called *coordinates*, from point *C*. One, called the *y-coordinate*, runs from *C* to the horizontal axis. Its length is the same as the value marked off on the *y*-axis. The other, called the *x-coordinate*, runs from *C* to the vertical axis. Its length is the same as the value marked off on the *x*-axis. We describe a point on a graph by the values of its *x*-coordinate and its *y*-coordinate.

Graphs like that in Fig. A1.1 can show any type of quantitative data on two variables. Economists use three types of graphs based on the principles in Fig. A1.1 to reveal and describe the relationships among variables. They are

- Time-series graphs
- Cross-section graphs
- Scatter diagrams

Time-Series Graphs

A **time-series graph** measures time (for example, months or years) on the *x*-axis and the variable or variables in which we are interested on the *y*-axis. Figure A1.2 is an example of a time-series graph. It provides information about the price of gasoline (the variable we're interested in). In this figure, we measure time in months starting in January 2006. We measure the price of gasoline on the *y*-axis.

The point of a time-series graph is to enable us to visualize how a variable has changed over time and how its value in one period relates to its value in another period.

A time-series graph conveys an enormous amount of information quickly and easily, as this example illustrates. It shows

- The *level* of the price of gasoline—when it is *high* and *low*. When the line is a long way from the *x*-axis, the price is high, as it was, for example, in May 2008. When the line is close to the *x*-axis, the price is low, as it was, for example, in October 2006.

- How the price *changes*—whether it *rises* or *falls*. When the line slopes upward, as in January 2008, the price is rising. When the line slopes downward, as in July 2007, the price is falling.

- The *speed* with which the price changes—whether it rises or falls *quickly* or *slowly*. If the line is very steep, then the price rises or falls quickly. If the line is not steep, the price rises or falls slowly. For example, the price rose quickly between March 2008 and May 2008 and slowly between December 2007 and February 2008. The price fell quickly between August 2006 and September 2006 and slowly between July 2007 and August 2007.

A time-series graph also reveals whether there is a **trend**—a general tendency for a variable to move in one direction. A trend might be upward or downward. In Fig. A1.2, the price of gasoline had a general tendency to rise from January 2006 to May 2008. Although the price rose and fell, the general tendency was for it to rise—the price had an upward trend. A time-series graph also helps us to detect fluctuations in a variable around its trend. You can see some peaks and troughs in the price of gasoline in Fig. A1.2.

Finally, a time-series graph also lets us quickly compare the variable in different periods. Figure A1.2 shows that the price of gasoline fluctuated more

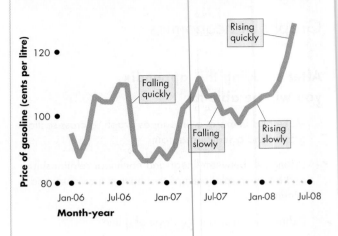

FIGURE A1.2 A Time-Series Graph

A time-series graph plots the level of a variable on the *y*-axis against time (day, week, month, or year) on the *x*-axis. This graph shows the price of gasoline (in 2006 dollars per litre) each month from January 2006 to July 2008. It shows us when the price of gasoline was *high* and when it was *low*, when the price *increased* and when it *decreased*, and when the price changed *quickly* and when it changed *slowly*.

myeconlab animation

during 2006 and 2007 than it did in the first six months of 2008.

You can see that a time-series graph conveys a wealth of information, and it does so in much less space than we have used to describe only some of its features. But you do have to "read" the graph to obtain all this information.

Cross-Section Graphs

A **cross-section graph** shows the values of an economic variable for different groups or categories at a point in time. Figure A1.3, called a *bar chart*, is an example of a cross-section graph.

The bar chart in Fig. A1.3 shows the number of visitors to each province in 2004. The length of each bar indicates the number of visitors. This figure enables you to compare the number of visitors across the provinces. And you can do so much more quickly and clearly than you could by looking at a list of numbers.

FIGURE A1.3 A Cross-Section Graph

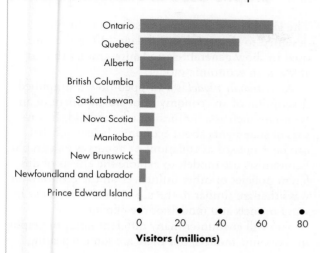

A cross-section graph shows the level of a variable across categories or groups. This bar chart shows the number of visitors to each province in 2004.

myeconlab animation

Scatter Diagrams

A **scatter diagram** plots the value of one variable against the value of another variable. Such a graph reveals whether a relationship exists between two variables and describes their relationship. Figure A1.4(a) shows the relationship between expenditure and income. Each point shows expenditure per person and income per person in a given year from 1997 to 2007. The points are "scattered" within the graph. The point labelled *A* tells us that in 2000, income per person was $20,840 and expenditure per person was $19,421. The dots in this graph form a pattern, which reveals that as income increases, expenditure increases.

Figure A1.4(b) shows the relationship between the number of computers sold and the price of a computer. This graph shows that as the price of a computer falls, number of computers sold increases.

Figure A1.4(c) shows a scatter diagram of the inflation rate and the unemployment rate in Canada. Here, the dots show no clear relationship between these two variables.

FIGURE A1.4 Scatter Diagrams

(a) **Expenditure and income**   (b) **Computer sales and prices**   (c) **Unemployment and inflation**

A scatter diagram reveals the relationship between two variables. Part (a) shows the relationship between expenditure and income. Each point shows the values of the two variables in a specific year. For example, point *A* shows that in 2000, average income was $20,840 and average expenditure was $19,421. The pattern formed by the points shows that as income increases, expenditure increases.

Part (b) shows the relationship between the price of a computer and the number of computers sold from 1990 to 2006. This graph shows that as the price of a computer falls, the number of computers sold increases.

Part (c) shows a scatter diagram of the inflation rate and the unemployment rate from 1997 to 2007. This graph shows that inflation and unemployment are not closely related.

myeconlab animation

Breaks in the Axes Two of the graphs you've just looked at, Fig. A1.4(a) and Fig. A1.4(c), have breaks in their axes, as shown by the small gaps. The breaks indicate that there are jumps from the origin, 0, to the first values recorded.

In Fig. A1.4(a), the breaks are used because the lowest value of expenditure exceeds $15,000 and the lowest value of income exceeds $15,000. With no breaks in the axes, there would be a lot of empty space, all the points would be crowded into the top right corner, and we would not be able to see whether a relationship exists between these two variables. By breaking the axes, we are able to bring the relationship into view.

Putting a break in one or both axes is like using a zoom lens to bring the relationship into the centre of the graph and magnify it so that the relationship fills the graph.

Misleading Graphs Breaks can be used to highlight a relationship, but they can also be used to mislead—to make a graph that lies. The most common way of making a graph lie is to use axis breaks and either to stretch or to compress a scale. For example, suppose that in Fig. A1.4(a), the *y*-axis that measures expenditure ran from zero to $30,000 while the *x*-axis was the same as the one shown. The graph would now create the impression that despite a huge increase in income, expenditure had barely changed.

To avoid being misled, it is a good idea to get into the habit of always looking closely at the values and the labels on the axes of a graph before you start to interpret it.

Correlation and Causation A scatter diagram that shows a clear relationship between two variables, such as Fig. A1.4(a) or Fig. A1.4(b), tells us that the two variables have a high correlation. When a high correlation is present, we can predict the value of one variable from the value of the other variable. But correlation does not imply causation.

Sometimes a high correlation is a coincidence, but sometimes it does arise from a causal relationship. It is likely, for example, that rising income causes rising expenditure, in Fig. A1.4(a), and that the falling price of a computer causes more computers to be sold, in Fig. A1.4(b).

You've now seen how we can use graphs in economics to show economic data and to reveal relationships. Next, we'll learn how economists use graphs to construct and display economic models.

◆ Graphs Used in Economic Models

The graphs used in economics are not always designed to show real-world data. Often they are used to show general relationships among the variables in an economic model.

An *economic model* is a stripped-down, simplified description of an economy or of a component of an economy such as a business or a household. It consists of statements about economic behaviour that can be expressed as equations or as curves in a graph. Economists use models to explore the effects of different policies or other influences on the economy in ways that are similar to the use of model airplanes in wind tunnels and models of the climate.

You will encounter many different kinds of graphs in economic models, but there are some repeating patterns. Once you've learned to recognize these patterns, you will instantly understand the meaning of a graph. Here, we'll look at the different types of curves that are used in economic models, and we'll see some everyday examples of each type of curve. The patterns to look for in graphs are the four cases in which

- Variables move in the same direction.
- Variables move in opposite directions.
- Variables have a maximum or a minimum.
- Variables are unrelated.

Let's look at these four cases.

Variables That Move in the Same Direction

Figure A1.5 shows graphs of the relationships between two variables that move up and down together. A relationship between two variables that move in the same direction is called a **positive relationship** or a **direct relationship**. A line that slopes upward shows such a relationship.

Figure A1.5 shows three types of relationships: one that has a straight line and two that have curved lines. But all the lines in these three graphs are called curves. Any line on a graph—no matter whether it is straight or curved—is called a *curve*.

A relationship shown by a straight line is called a linear relationship. Figure A1.5(a) shows a **linear relationship** between the number of kilometres travelled in 5 hours and speed. For example, point *A* shows that we will travel 200 kilometres in 5 hours if our

FIGURE A1.5 Positive (Direct) Relationships

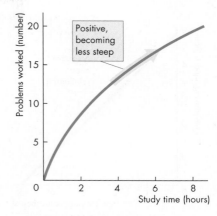

(a) Positive, linear relationship   **(b) Positive, becoming steeper**   **(c) Positive, becoming less steep**

Each part of this figure shows a positive (direct) relationship between two variables. That is, as the value of the variable measured on the x-axis increases, so does the value of the variable measured on the y-axis. Part (a) shows a linear relationship—as the two variables increase together, we move along a straight line. Part (b) shows a positive relationship such that as the two variables increase together, we move along a curve that becomes steeper. Part (c) shows a positive relationship such that as the two variables increase together, we move along a curve that becomes flatter.

myeconlab animation

speed is 40 kilometres an hour. If we double our speed to 80 kilometres an hour, we will travel 400 kilometres in 5 hours.

Figure A1.5(b) shows the relationship between distance sprinted and recovery time (the time it takes the heart rate to return to its normal resting rate). This relationship is an upward-sloping one that starts out quite flat but then becomes steeper as we move along the curve away from the origin. The reason this curve slopes upward and becomes steeper is because the additional recovery time needed from sprinting an additional 100 metres increases. It takes less than 5 minutes to recover from sprinting 100 metres but more than 10 minutes to recover from sprinting 200 metres.

Figure A1.5(c) shows the relationship between the number of problems worked by a student and the amount of study time. This relationship is an upward-sloping one that starts out quite steep and becomes flatter as we move along the curve away from the origin. Study time becomes less productive as the student spends more hours studying and becomes more tired.

Variables That Move in Opposite Directions

Figure A1.6 shows relationships between things that move in opposite directions. A relationship between variables that move in opposite directions is called a **negative relationship** or an **inverse relationship**.

Figure A1.6(a) shows the relationship between the hours spent playing squash and the hours spent playing tennis when the total number of hours available is 5. One extra hour spent playing tennis means one hour less playing squash and vice versa. This relationship is negative and linear.

Figure A1.6(b) shows the relationship between the cost per kilometre travelled and the length of a journey. The longer the journey, the lower is the cost per kilometre. But as the journey length increases, even though the cost per kilometre decreases, the fall in the cost is smaller. This feature of the relationship is shown by the fact that the curve slopes downward, starting out steep at a short journey length and then becoming flatter as the journey length increases. This relationship arises because some of the costs don't depend on the journey length, such as auto insurance, and these costs are spread over a longer journey.

FIGURE A1.6 Negative (Inverse) Relationships

(a) Negative, linear relationship

(b) Negative, becoming less steep

(c) Negative, becoming steeper

Each part of this figure shows a negative (inverse) relationship between two variables. That is, as the value of the variable measured on the *x*-axis increases, the value of the variable measured on the *y*-axis decreases. Part (a) shows a linear relationship. The total time spent playing tennis and squash is 5 hours. As the time spent playing tennis increases, the time spent playing squash decreases, and we move along a straight line.

Part (b) shows a negative relationship such that as the journey length increases, the travel cost decreases as we move along a curve that becomes less steep.

Part (c) shows a negative relationship such that as leisure time increases, the number of problems worked decreases as we move along a curve that becomes steeper.

myeconlab animation

Figure A1.6(c) shows the relationship between the amount of leisure time and the number of problems worked by a student. Increasing leisure time produces an increasingly large reduction in the number of problems worked. This relationship is a negative one that starts out with a gentle slope at a small number of leisure hours and becomes steeper as the number of leisure hours increases. This relationship is a different view of the idea shown in Fig. A1.5(c).

Variables That Have a Maximum or a Minimum

Many relationships in economic models have a maximum or a minimum. For example, firms try to make the maximum possible profit and to produce at the lowest possible cost. Figure A1.7 shows relationships that have a maximum or a minimum.

Figure A1.7(a) shows the relationship between rainfall and wheat yield. When there is no rainfall, wheat will not grow, so the yield is zero. As the rainfall increases up to 10 days a month, the wheat yield increases. With 10 rainy days each month, the wheat yield reaches its maximum at 2 tonnes per hectare (point *A*). Rain in excess of 10 days a month starts to lower the yield of wheat. If every day is rainy, the wheat suffers from a lack of sunshine and the yield decreases to zero. This relationship is one that starts out sloping upward, reaches a maximum, and then slopes downward.

Figure A1.7(b) shows the reverse case—a relationship that begins sloping downward, falls to a minimum, and then slopes upward. Most economic costs are like this relationship. An example is the relationship between the cost per kilometre and speed for a car trip. At low speeds, the car is creeping in a traffic jam. The number of kilometres per litre is low, so the cost per kilometre is high. At high speeds, the car is travelling faster than its efficient speed, using a large quantity of gasoline, and again the number of kilometres per litre is low and the cost per kilometre is high. At a speed of 100 kilometres an hour, the cost per kilometre is at its minimum (point *B*). This relationship is one that starts out sloping downward, reaches a minimum, and then slopes upward.

FIGURE A1.7 Maximum and Minimum Points

(a) Relationship with a maximum

(b) Relationship with a minimum

Part (a) shows a relationship that has a maximum point, A. The curve slopes upward as it rises to its maximum point, is flat at its maximum, and then slopes downward.

Part (b) shows a relationship with a minimum point, B. The curve slopes downward as it falls to its minimum, is flat at its minimum, and then slopes upward.

myeconlab animation

Variables That Are Unrelated

There are many situations in which no matter what happens to the value of one variable, the other variable remains constant. Sometimes we want to show the independence between two variables in a graph, and Fig. A1.8 illustrates two ways of achieving this.

In describing the graphs in Fig. A1.5 through A1.7, we have talked about curves that slope upward or slope downward, and curves that become less steep or steeper. Let's spend a little time discussing exactly what we mean by slope and how we measure the slope of a curve.

FIGURE A1.8 Variables That Are Unrelated

(a) Unrelated: *y* constant

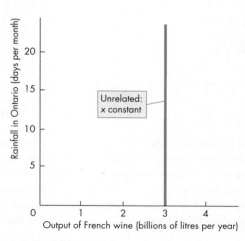

(b) Unrelated: *x* constant

This figure shows how we can graph two variables that are unrelated. In part (a), a student's grade in economics is plotted at 75 percent on the *y*-axis regardless of the price of bananas on the *x*-axis. The curve is horizontal.

In part (b), the output of the vineyards of France on the *x*-axis does not vary with the rainfall in Ontario on the *y*-axis. The curve is vertical.

myeconlab animation

◆ The Slope of a Relationship

We can measure the influence of one variable on another by the slope of the relationship. The **slope** of a relationship is the change in the value of the variable measured on the y-axis divided by the change in the value of the variable measured on the x-axis. We use the Greek letter Δ (*delta*) to represent "change in." Thus Δy means the change in the value of the variable measured on the y-axis, and Δx means the change in the value of the variable measured on the x-axis. Therefore the slope of the relationship is

$$\Delta y / \Delta x.$$

If a large change in the variable measured on the y-axis (Δy) is associated with a small change in the variable measured on the x-axis (Δx), the slope is large and the curve is steep. If a small change in the variable measured on the y-axis (Δy) is associated with a large change in the variable measured on the x-axis (Δx), the slope is small and the curve is flat.

We can make the idea of slope clearer by doing some calculations.

The Slope of a Straight Line

The slope of a straight line is the same regardless of where on the line you calculate it. The slope of a

FIGURE A1.9 The Slope of a Straight Line

(a) Positive slope

(b) Negative slope

To calculate the slope of a straight line, we divide the change in the value of the variable measured on the y-axis (Δy) by the change in the value of the variable measured on the x-axis (Δx) as we move along the curve.

Part (a) shows the calculation of a positive slope. When x increases from 2 to 6, Δx equals 4. That change in x

brings about an increase in y from 3 to 6, so Δy equals 3. The slope ($\Delta y/\Delta x$) equals 3/4.

Part (b) shows the calculation of a negative slope. When x increases from 2 to 6, Δx equals 4. That increase in x brings about a decrease in y from 6 to 3, so Δy equals –3. The slope ($\Delta y/\Delta x$) equals –3/4.

straight line is constant. Let's calculate the slopes of the lines in Fig. A1.9. In part (a), when x increases from 2 to 6, y increases from 3 to 6. The change in x is $+4$—that is, Δx is 4. The change in y is $+3$—that is, Δy is 3. The slope of that line is

$$\frac{\Delta y}{\Delta x} = \frac{3}{4}.$$

In part (b), when x increases from 2 to 6, y decreases from 6 to 3. The change in y is *minus* 3—that is, Δy is –3. The change in x is *plus* 4—that is, Δx is 4. The slope of the curve is

$$\frac{\Delta y}{\Delta x} = \frac{-3}{4}.$$

Notice that the two slopes have the same magnitude (3/4), but the slope of the line in part (a) is positive ($+3/+4 = 3/4$) while the slope in part (b) is negative ($-3/+4 = -3/4$). The slope of a positive relationship is positive; the slope of a negative relationship is negative.

The Slope of a Curved Line

The slope of a curved line is trickier. The slope of a curved line is not constant, so the slope depends on where on the curved line we calculate it. There are two ways to calculate the slope of a curved line: You can calculate the slope at a point, or you can calculate the slope across an arc of the curve. Let's look at the two alternatives.

Slope at a Point To calculate the slope at a point on a curve, you need to construct a straight line that has the same slope as the curve at the point in question. Figure A1.10 shows how this is done. Suppose you want to calculate the slope of the curve at point A. Place a ruler on the graph so that it touches point A and no other point on the curve, then draw a straight line along the edge of the ruler. The straight red line is this line, and it is the tangent to the curve at point A. If the ruler touches the curve only at point A, then the slope of the curve at point A must be the same as the slope of the edge of the ruler. If the curve and the ruler do not have the same slope, the line along the edge of the ruler will cut the curve instead of just touching it.

Now that you have found a straight line with the same slope as the curve at point A, you can calculate

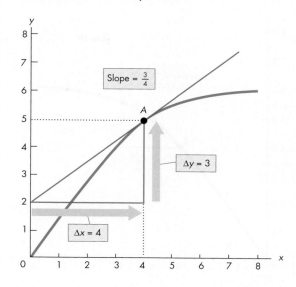

FIGURE A1.10 Slope at a Point

To calculate the slope of the curve at point A, draw the red line that just touches the curve at A—the tangent. The slope of this straight line is calculated by dividing the change in y by the change in x along the line. When x increases from 0 to 4, Δx equals 4. That change in x is associated with an increase in y from 2 to 5, so Δy equals 3. The slope of the red line is 3/4. So the slope of the curve at point A is 3/4.

myeconlab animation

the slope of the curve at point A by calculating the slope of the straight line. Along the straight line, as x increases from 0 to 4 ($\Delta x = 4$) y increases from 2 to 5 ($\Delta y = 3$). Therefore the slope of the straight line is

$$\frac{\Delta y}{\Delta x} = \frac{3}{4}.$$

So the slope of the curve at point A is 3/4.

Slope Across an Arc An arc of a curve is a piece of a curve. In Fig. A1.11, you are looking at the same curve as in Fig. A1.10. But instead of calculating the slope at point A, we are going to calculate the slope across the arc from B to C. You can see that the slope at B is greater than at C. When we calculate the slope across an arc, we are calculating the average slope between two points. As we move along the arc from B to C, x increases from 3 to 5 and y increases from 4 to

FIGURE A1.11 Slope Across an Arc

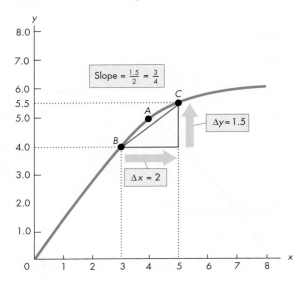

$$\text{Slope} = \frac{1.5}{2} = \frac{3}{4}$$

$\Delta y = 1.5$

$\Delta x = 2$

To calculate the average slope of the curve along the arc *BC*, draw a straight line from *B* to *C*. The slope of the line *BC* is calculated by dividing the change in *y* by the change in *x*. In moving from *B* to *C*, Δx equals 2 and Δy equals 1.5. The slope of the line *BC* is 1.5 divided by 2, or 3/4. So the slope of the curve across the arc *BC* is 3/4.

myeconlab animation

5.5. The change in *x* is 2 ($\Delta x = 2$), and the change in *y* is 1.5 ($\Delta y = 1.5$). Therefore the slope is

$$\frac{\Delta y}{\Delta x} = \frac{1.5}{2} = \frac{3}{4}.$$

So the slope of the curve across the arc *BC* is 3/4.

This calculation gives us the slope of the curve between points *B* and *C*. The actual slope calculated is the slope of the straight line from *B* to *C*. This slope approximates the average slope of the curve along the arc *BC*. In this particular example, the slope across the arc *BC* is identical to the slope of the curve at point *A*. But the calculation of the slope of a curve does not always work out so neatly. You might have fun constructing some more examples and a few counterexamples.

You now know how to make and interpret a graph. But so far, we've limited our attention to graphs of two variables. We're now going to learn how to graph more than two variables.

Graphing Relationships Among More Than Two Variables

We have seen that we can graph the relationship between two variables as a point formed by the *x*- and *y*-coordinates in a two-dimensional graph. You might be thinking that although a two-dimensional graph is informative, most of the things in which you are likely to be interested involve relationships among many variables, not just two. For example, the amount of ice cream consumed depends on the price of ice cream and the temperature. If ice cream is expensive and the temperature is low, people eat much less ice cream than when ice cream is inexpensive and the temperature is high. For any given price of ice cream, the quantity consumed varies with the temperature; and for any given temperature, the quantity of ice cream consumed varies with its price.

Figure A1.12 shows a relationship among three variables. The table shows the number of litres of ice cream consumed each day at various temperatures and ice cream prices. How can we graph these numbers?

To graph a relationship that involves more than two variables, we use the *ceteris paribus* assumption.

Ceteris Paribus ***Ceteris paribus*** means "if all other relevant things remain the same." To isolate the relationship of interest in a laboratory experiment, we hold other things constant. We use the same method to graph a relationship with more than two variables.

Figure A1.12(a) shows an example. There, you can see what happens to the quantity of ice cream consumed when the price of ice cream varies when the temperature is held constant. The line labelled 21°C shows the relationship between ice cream consumption and the price of ice cream if the temperature remains at 21°C. The numbers used to plot that line are those in the third column of the table in Fig. A1.12. For example, if the temperature is 21°C, 10 litres are consumed when the price is 60¢ a scoop, and 18 litres are consumed when the price is 30¢ a scoop. The curve labelled 32°C shows consumption as the price varies if the temperature remains at 32°C.

We can also show the relationship between ice cream consumption and temperature when the price of ice cream remains constant, as shown in Fig. A1.12(b). The curve labelled 60¢ shows how the consumption of ice cream varies with the

FIGURE A1.12   Graphing a Relationship Among Three Variables

(a) Price and consumption at a given temperature

(b) Temperature and consumption at a given price

(c) Temperature and price at a given consumption

Price (cents per scoop)	Ice cream consumption (litres per day)			
	−10°C	10°C	21°C	32°C
15	12	18	25	50
30	10	12	18	37
45	7	10	13	27
60	5	7	10	20
75	3	5	7	14
90	2	3	5	10
105	1	2	3	6

Ice cream consumption depends on its price and the temperature. The table tells us how many litres of ice cream are consumed each day at different prices and different temperatures. For example, if the price is 60¢ a scoop and the temperature is 21°C, 10 litres of ice cream are consumed. This set of values is highlighted in the table and each part of the figure.

To graph a relationship among three variables, the value of one variable is held constant. Part (a) shows the relationship between price and consumption when temperature is held constant. One curve holds temperature at 32°C and the other holds it at 21°C. Part (b) shows the relationship between temperature and consumption when price is held constant. One curve holds the price at 60¢ a scoop and the other holds it at 15¢ a scoop. Part (c) shows the relationship between temperature and price when consumption is held constant. One curve holds consumption at 10 litres and the other holds it at 7 litres.

temperature when the price of ice cream is 60¢ a scoop, and a second curve shows the relationship when the price is 15¢ a scoop. For example, at 60¢ a scoop, 10 litres are consumed when the temperature is 21°C and 20 litres are consumed when the temperature is 32°C.

Figure A1.12(c) shows the combinations of temperature and price that result in a constant consumption of ice cream. One curve shows the combinations that result in 10 litres a day being consumed, and the other shows the combinations that result in 7 litres a

day being consumed. A high price and a high temperature lead to the same consumption as a lower price and a lower temperature. For example, 10 litres of ice cream are consumed at 21°C and 60¢ a scoop, at 32°C and 90¢ a scoop, and at 10°C and 45¢ a scoop.

◆ With what you have learned about graphs, you can move forward with your study of economics. There are no graphs in this book that are more complicated than those that have been explained in this appendix.

MATHEMATICAL NOTE

Equations of Straight Lines

If a straight line in a graph describes the relationship between two variables, we call it a linear relationship. Figure 1 shows the *linear relationship* between a person's expenditure and income. This person spends $100 a week (by borrowing or spending previous savings) when income is zero. And out of each dollar earned, this person spends 50 cents (and saves 50 cents).

All linear relationships are described by the same general equation. We call the quantity that is measured on the horizontal axis (or *x*-axis) *x*, and we call the quantity that is measured on the vertical axis (or *y*-axis) *y*. In the case of Fig. 1, *x* is income and *y* is expenditure.

A Linear Equation

The equation that describes a straight-line relationship between *x* and *y* is

$$y = a + bx.$$

In this equation, *a* and *b* are fixed numbers and they are called constants. The values of *x* and *y* vary, so these numbers are called variables. Because the equation describes a straight line, the equation is called a *linear equation*.

The equation tells us that when the value of *x* is zero, the value of *y* is *a*. We call the constant *a* the *y*-axis intercept. The reason is that on the graph the straight line hits the *y*-axis at a value equal to *a*. Figure 1 illustrates the *y*-axis intercept.

For positive values of *x*, the value of *y* exceeds *a*. The constant *b* tells us by how much *y* increases above *a* as *x* increases. The constant *b* is the slope of the line.

Slope of Line

As we defined in the chapter, the *slope* of a relationship is the change in the value of *y* divided by the change in the value of *x*. We use the Greek letter Δ (*delta*) to represent "change in." So Δy means the change in the value of the variable measured on the *y*-axis, and Δx means the change in the value of the variable measured on the *x*-axis. Therefore the slope of the relationship is

$$\Delta y / \Delta x.$$

To see why the slope is *b*, suppose that initially the value of *x* is x_1, or $200 in Fig. 2. The corresponding value of *y* is y_1, also $200 in Fig. 2. The equation of the line tells us that

$$y_1 = a + bx_1. \tag{1}$$

Now the value of *x* increases by Δx to $x_1 + \Delta x$ (or $400 in Fig. 2). And the value of *y* increases by Δy to $y_1 + \Delta y$ (or $300 in Fig. 2).

The equation of the line now tells us that

$$y_1 + \Delta y = a + b(x_1 + \Delta x). \tag{2}$$

Figure 1 Linear relationship

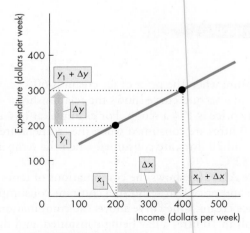

Figure 2 Calculating slope

To calculate the slope of the line, subtract equation (1) from equation (2) to obtain

$$\Delta y = b \Delta x \qquad (3)$$

and now divide equation (3) by Δx to obtain

$$\Delta y / \Delta x = b.$$

So the slope of the line is b.

Position of Line

The y-axis intercept determines the position of the line on the graph. Figure 3 illustrates the relationship between the y-axis intercept and the position of the line. In this graph, the y-axis measures saving and the x-axis measures income.

When the y-axis intercept, a, is positive, the line hits the y-axis at a positive value of y—as the blue line does. Its y-axis intercept is 100. When the y-axis intercept, a, is zero, the line hits the y-axis at the origin—as the purple line does. Its y-axis intercept is 0. When the y-axis intercept, a, is negative, the line hits the y-axis at a negative value of y—as the red line does. Its y-axis intercept is –100.

As the equations of the three lines show, the value of the y-axis intercept does not influence the slope. All three lines have a slope equal to 0.5.

Positive Relationships

Figure 1 shows a positive relationship—the two variables x and y move in the same direction. All positive relationships have a slope that is positive. In the equation of the line, the constant b is positive. In this example, the y-axis intercept, a, is 100. The slope b equals $\Delta y / \Delta x$, which in Fig. 2 is 100/200 or 0.5. The equation of the line is

$$y = 100 + 0.5x.$$

Negative Relationships

Figure 4 shows a negative relationship—the two variables x and y move in the opposite direction. All negative relationships have a slope that is negative. In the equation of the line, the constant b is negative. In the example in Fig. 4, the y-axis intercept, a, is 30. The slope, b, equals $\Delta y / \Delta x$, which is –20/2 or –10. The equation of the line is

$$y = 30 + (-10)x$$

or

$$y = 30 - 10x.$$

Example

A straight line has a y-axis intercept of 50 and a slope of 2. What is the equation of this line? The equation of a straight line is

$$y = a + bx$$

where a is the y-axis intercept and b is the slope. The equation is

$$y = 50 + 2x.$$

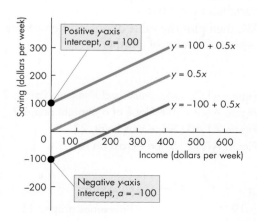

Figure 3 The y-axis intercept

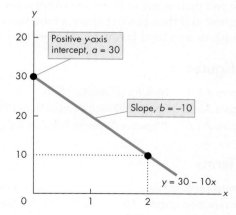

Figure 4 Negative relationship

Review Quiz

1 What are the three types of graphs used to show economic data?
2 Give an example of a time-series graph.
3 List three things that a time-series graph shows quickly and easily.
4 Give three examples, different from those in the chapter, of scatter diagrams that show a positive relationship, a negative relationship, and no relationship.
5 Draw some graphs to show the relationships between two variables that
   a. Move in the same direction.
   b. Move in opposite directions.
   c. Have a maximum and have a minimum.
6 Which of the relationships in question 5 is a positive relationship and which is a negative relationship?
7 What are the two ways of calculating the slope of a curved line?
8 How do we graph a relationship among more than two variables?

 Work Study Plan 1.A and get instant feedback.

SUMMARY

Key Points

Graphing Data (pp. 15–18)

■ A time-series graph shows the trend and fluctuations in a variable over time.
■ A cross-section graph shows how the value of a variable changes across the members of a population.
■ A scatter diagram shows the relationship between two variables. It shows whether two variables are positively related, negatively related, or unrelated.

Graphs Used in Economic Models (pp. 18–21)

■ Graphs are used to show relationships among variables in economic models.
■ Relationships can be positive (an upward-sloping curve), negative (a downward-sloping curve), positive and then negative (have a maximum point), negative and then positive (have a minimum point), or unrelated (a horizontal or vertical curve).

The Slope of a Relationship (pp. 22–24)

■ The slope of a relationship is calculated as the change in the value of the variable measured on the y-axis divided by the change in the value of the variable measured on the x-axis—that is, $\Delta y/\Delta x$.
■ A straight line has a constant slope.
■ A curved line has a varying slope. To calculate the slope of a curved line, we calculate the slope at a point or across an arc.

Graphing Relationships Among More Than Two Variables (pp. 24–25)

■ To graph a relationship among more than two variables, we hold constant the values of all the variables except two.
■ We then plot the value of one of the variables against the value of another.

Key Figures

Figure A1.1   Making a Graph, 15
Figure A1.5   Positive (Direct) Relationships, 19
Figure A1.6   Negative (Inverse) Relationships, 20

Figure A1.7   Maximum and Minimum Points, 21
Figure A1.9   The Slope of a Straight Line, 22
Figure A1.10 Slope at a Point, 23
Figure A1.11 Slope Across an Arc, 24

Key Terms

Ceteris paribus, 24
Cross-section graph, 16
Direct relationship, 18
Inverse relationship, 19

Linear relationship, 18
Negative relationship, 19
Positive relationship, 18
Scatter diagram, 17

Slope, 22
Time-series graph, 16
Trend, 16

PROBLEMS and APPLICATIONS ◆

myeconlab Work problems 1–5 in Chapter 1A Study Plan and get instant feedback.
Work problems 6–10 as Homework, a Quiz, or a Test if assigned by your instructor.

1. The spreadsheet provides data on the Canadian economy: Column A is the year, column B is the inflation rate, column C is the interest rate, column D is the growth rate, and column E is the unemployment rate.

	A	B	C	D	E
1	1997	1.6	3.6	4.2	9.2
2	1998	0.9	5.0	4.1	8.4
3	1999	1.7	4.9	5.6	7.6
4	2000	3.1	5.7	5.2	6.8
5	2001	2.1	3.9	1.8	7.2
6	2002	2.2	2.9	2.9	7.7
7	2003	2.8	2.3	1.9	7.6
8	2004	1.8	2.8	3.1	7.2
9	2005	2.2	4.2	2.9	6.8
10	2006	2.0	4.6	3.1	6.3
11	2007	2.2	3.5	2.7	6.0

a. Draw a time-series graph of the inflation rate.
b. In which year(s) (i) was inflation highest, (ii) was inflation lowest, (iii) did it increase, (iv) did it decrease, (v) did it increase most, and (vi) did it decrease most?
c. What was the main trend in inflation?
d. Draw a scatter diagram of the inflation rate and the interest rate. Describe the relationship.
e. Draw a scatter diagram of the growth rate and the unemployment rate. Describe the relationship.

2. **"Hulk" Tops Box Office with Sales of $54.5 Million**

Movie	Theatres (number)	Revenue (dollars per theatre)
Hulk	3,505	15,560
The Happening	2,986	10,214
Zohan	3,462	4,737
Crystal Skull	3,804	3,561

Bloomberg.com, June 15, 2008

a. Draw a graph to show the relationship between the revenue per theatre on the *y*-axis and the number of theatres on the *x*-axis. Describe the relationship.
b. Calculate the slope of the relationship between 3,462 and 3,804 theatres.

3. Calculate the slope of the following relationship.

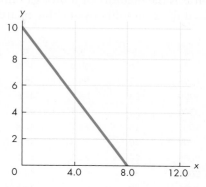

4. Calculate the slope of the following relationship:

a. At point *A* and at point *B*.
b. Across the arc *AB*.

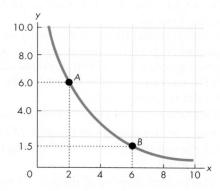

5. The table gives the price of a balloon ride, the temperature, and the number of rides a day.

Price (dollars per ride)	Balloon rides (number per day)		
	10°C	20°C	30°C
5	32	40	50
10	27	32	40
15	18	27	32

Draw graphs to show the relationship between
a. The price and the number of rides, holding the temperature constant. Describe this relationship.
b. The number of rides and temperature, holding the price constant.

6. The spreadsheet provides data on oil and gasoline: Column A is the year, column B is the price of crude oil (dollars per barrel), column C is the price of motor gasoline (cents per litre), column D is the quantity of crude oil produced, and column E is the quantity of motor gasoline produced (both in millions of cubic metres).

	A	B	C	D	E
1	1997	16	60.6	38.6	112.7
2	1998	9	56.2	38.7	117.1
3	1999	24	58.3	41.0	111.0
4	2000	22	70.9	42.2	116.4
5	2001	18	78.7	43.8	118.2
6	2002	30	72.5	45.9	126.9
7	2003	28	72.2	45.8	134.7
8	2004	36	91.8	44.9	139.3
9	2005	52	92.2	43.9	136.2
10	2006	57	97.0	42.0	143.8
11	2007	90	101.4	43.8	150.3

a. Draw a time-series graph of the quantity of motor gasoline.
b. In which year(s) (i) was the quantity of motor gasoline highest, (ii) was the quantity of motor gasoline lowest, (iii) did it increase, (iv) did it decrease, (v) did it increase most, and (vi) did it decrease most?
c. What was the main trend in this quantity?
d. Draw a scatter diagram of the price of crude oil and the quantity of crude oil. Describe the relationship.
e. Draw a scatter diagram of the price of motor gasoline and the quantity of motor gasoline. Describe the relationship.

7. Draw a graph that shows the relationship between the two variables x and y:

x	0	1	2	3	4	5
y	25	24	22	18	12	0

a. Is the relationship positive or negative?
b. Does the slope of the relationship increase or decrease as the value of x increases?
c. Think of some economic relationships that might be similar to this one.
d. Calculate the slope of the relationship between x and y when x equals 3.
e. Calculate the slope of the relationship across the arc as x increases from 4 to 5.

8. Calculate the slope of the relationship at point A.

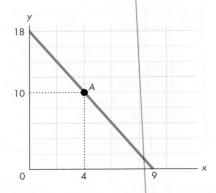

9. Calculate the slope of the relationship:

a. At point A and at point B.
b. Across the arc AB.

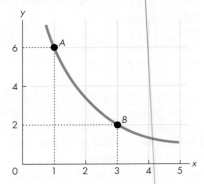

10. The table gives information about umbrellas: price, the number purchased, and rainfall.

Price (dollars per umbrella)	Umbrellas (number per day)		
	0	1	2
	(mms of rainfall)		
20	4	7	8
30	2	4	7
40	1	2	4

Draw graphs to show the relationship between

a. Price and the number of umbrellas purchased, holding the amount of rainfall constant. Describe this relationship.
b. The number of umbrellas purchased and the amount of rainfall, holding the price constant. Describe this relationship.

2

The Economic Problem

After studying this chapter, you will be able to

- Define the production possibilities frontier and calculate opportunity cost

- Distinguish between production possibilities and preferences and describe an efficient allocation of resources

- Explain how current production choices expand future production possibilities

- Explain how specialization and trade expand our production possibilities

- Describe the economic institutions that coordinate decisions

Why does food cost much more today

than it did a few years ago? One reason is that many countries now use part of their corn crops to produce ethanol, a clean biofuel substitute for gasoline. Another reason is that drought in some parts of the world has decreased global grain production. In this chapter, you will study an economic model—the production possibilities frontier—and you will learn why ethanol production and drought have increased the cost of producing food. You will also learn how to assess whether it is a good idea to increase corn production to produce fuel; how we can expand our production possibilities; how we gain by trading with others; and why the social institutions of firms, markets, property rights, and money that make trade possible have evolved. At the end of the chapter, in *Reading Between the Lines*, we'll apply what you've learned to understanding why ethanol production is raising the cost of food.

Production Possibilities and Opportunity Cost

Every working day, in mines, factories, shops, and offices and on farms and construction sites across Canada, 18 million people produce a vast variety of goods and services valued at $5 billion. But the quantities of goods and services that we can produce are limited both by our available resources and by technology. And if we want to increase our production of one good, we must decrease our production of something else—we face a tradeoff. You are going to learn about the production possibilities frontier, which describes the limit to what we can produce and provides a neat way of thinking about and illustrating the idea of a tradeoff.

The **production possibilities frontier** (*PPF*) is the boundary between those combinations of goods and services that can be produced and those that cannot. To illustrate the *PPF*, we focus on two goods at a time and hold the quantities produced of all the other goods and services constant. That is, we look at a *model* economy in which everything remains the same except for the production of the two goods we are considering.

Let's look at the production possibilities frontier for cola and pizza, which stand for *any* pair of goods or services.

Production Possibilities Frontier

The *production possibilities frontier* for cola and pizza shows the limits to the production of these two goods, given the total resources and technology available to produce them. Figure 2.1 shows this production possibilities frontier. The table lists some combinations of the quantities of pizza and cola that can be produced in a month given the resources available. The figure graphs these combinations. The *x*-axis shows the quantity of pizzas produced, and the *y*-axis shows the quantity of cola produced.

The *PPF* illustrates *scarcity* because we cannot attain the points outside the frontier. These points describe wants that can't be satisfied. We can produce at any point *inside* the *PPF* or *on* the *PPF*. These points are attainable. Suppose that in a typical month, we produce 4 million pizzas and 5 million cans of cola. Figure 2.1 shows this combination as point *E* and as possibility *E* in the table. The figure

FIGURE 2.1   Production Possibilities Frontier

Possibility	Pizzas (millions)		Cola (millions of cans)
A	0	and	15
B	1	and	14
C	2	and	12
D	3	and	9
E	4	and	5
F	5	and	0

The table lists six production possibilities for cola and pizzas. Row *A* tells us that if we produce no pizza, the maximum quantity of cola we can produce is 15 million cans. Points *A*, *B*, *C*, *D*, *E*, and *F* in the figure represent the rows of the table. The curve passing through these points is the production possibilities frontier (*PPF*).

The *PPF* separates the attainable from the unattainable. Production is possible at any point *inside* the orange area or *on* the frontier. Points outside the frontier are unattainable. Points inside the frontier, such as point *Z*, are inefficient because resources are wasted or misallocated. At such points, it is possible to use the available resources to produce more of either or both goods.

also shows other production possibilities. For example, we might stop producing pizza and move all the people who produce it into producing cola. Point *A* in the figure and possibility *A* in the table show this case. The quantity of cola produced increases to 15 million cans, and pizza production dries up. Alternatively, we might close the cola factories and switch all the resources into producing pizza. In this situation, we produce 5 million pizzas. Point *F* in the figure and possibility *F* in the table show this case.

Production Efficiency

We achieve **production efficiency** if we produce goods and services at the lowest possible cost. This outcome occurs at all the points *on* the *PPF.* At points *inside* the *PPF,* production is inefficient because we are giving up more than necessary of one good to produce a given quantity of the other good.

For example, at point *Z* in Fig. 2.1, we produce 3 million pizzas and 5 million cans of cola. But we could produce 3 million pizzas and 9 million cans of cola. Our pizzas cost more cola than necessary. We can get them for a lower cost. Only when we produce *on* the *PPF* do we incur the lowest possible cost of production.

Production is *inefficient* inside the *PPF* because resources are either *unused* or *misallocated* or both.

Resources are *unused* when they are idle but could be working. For example, we might leave some of the factories idle or some workers unemployed.

Resources are *misallocated* when they are assigned to tasks for which they are not the best match. For example, we might assign skilled pizza chefs to work in a cola factory and skilled cola producers to work in a pizza shop. We could get more pizzas *and* more cola from these same workers if we reassigned them to the tasks that more closely match their skills.

Tradeoff Along the *PPF*

Every choice *along* the *PPF* involves a *tradeoff.* On the *PPF* in Fig. 2.1, we trade off cola for pizzas.

Tradeoffs arise in every imaginable real-world situation, and you reviewed several of them in Chapter 1. At any given point in time, we have a fixed amount of labour, land, capital, and entrepreneurship. By using our available technologies, we can employ these resources to produce goods and services, but we are limited in what we can produce. This limit defines a boundary between what we can attain and what we cannot attain. This boundary is the real world's production possibilities frontier, and it defines the tradeoffs that we must make. On our real-world *PPF,* we can produce more of any one good or service only if we produce less of some other goods or services.

When doctors want to spend more on AIDS and cancer research, they face a tradeoff: more medical research for less of some other things. When the prime minister wants to spend more on education and health care, he faces a tradeoff: more education and health care for less national defence or less private spending (because of higher taxes). When an environmental group argues for less logging, it is suggesting a tradeoff: greater conservation of endangered wildlife for less paper. When you want to study more, you face a tradeoff: more study time for less leisure or sleep.

All tradeoffs involve a cost—an opportunity cost.

Opportunity Cost

The **opportunity cost** of an action is the highest-valued alternative forgone. The *PPF* makes this idea precise and enables us to calculate opportunity cost. Along the *PPF,* there are only two goods, so there is only one alternative forgone: some quantity of the other good. Given our current resources and technology, we can produce more pizzas only if we produce less cola. The opportunity cost of producing an additional pizza is the cola we *must* forgo. Similarly, the opportunity cost of producing an additional can of cola is the quantity of pizza we must forgo.

In Fig. 2.1, if we move from point *C* to point *D,* we get 1 million more pizzas but 3 million fewer cans of cola. The additional 1 million pizzas *cost* 3 million cans of cola. One pizza costs 3 cans of cola.

We can also work out the opportunity cost of moving in the opposite direction. In Fig. 2.1, if we move from point *D* to point *C,* the quantity of cola produced increases by 3 million cans and the quantity of pizzas produced decreases by 1 million. So if we choose point *C* over point *D,* the additional 3 million cans of cola *cost* 1 million pizzas. One can of cola costs 1/3 of a pizza.

Opportunity Cost Is a Ratio   Opportunity cost is a ratio. It is the decrease in the quantity produced of one good divided by the increase in the quantity produced of another good as we move along the production possibilities frontier.

Because opportunity cost is a ratio, the opportunity cost of producing an additional can of cola is equal to the *inverse* of the opportunity cost of producing an additional pizza. Check this proposition by returning to the calculations we've just worked through. When we move along the *PPF* from *C* to *D*, the opportunity cost of a pizza is 3 cans of cola. The inverse of 3 is 1/3. If we decrease the production of pizza and increase the production of cola by moving from *D* to *C*, the opportunity cost of a can of cola must be 1/3 of a pizza. That is exactly the number that we calculated for the move from *D* to *C*.

Increasing Opportunity Cost   The opportunity cost of a pizza increases as the quantity of pizzas produced increases. The outward-bowed shape of the *PPF* reflects increasing opportunity cost. When we produce a large quantity of cola and a small quantity of pizzas—between points *A* and *B* in Fig. 2.1—the frontier has a gentle slope. An increase in the quantity of pizzas costs a small decrease in the quantity of cola—the opportunity cost of a pizza is a small quantity of cola.

Increasing Opportunity Cost

Opportunity Cost on the Oil Patch

It costs about $30 a barrel to get crude oil out of the ground and into a tanker or pipeline to deliver it to a refinery. So for every barrel of oil produced, we forgo $30-worth of other goods and services.

Between 2003 and 2006, the price of crude oil on the global oil market doubled; and between 2006 and 2008, it doubled again. With the price of oil at such levels, it becomes worthwhile for owners of oil resources to pump them at a faster rate and to extract from higher-cost sources.

Such changes have taken place on the Alberta and Newfoundland oil patches. The opportunity cost of extracting oil in these regions is probably around $30-worth of other goods and services. But as production increases, the opportunity cost rises.

In Alberta, production increased by 12 percent from 2003 to 2006 and by 3 percent in 2007. The marginal oil in Alberta is in tar sands, and the opportunity cost of extracting this oil is around $50 a barrel.

As Canada produces more crude oil, we slide around our *PPF* and the opportunity cost of producing oil rises.

When we produce a large quantity of pizzas and a small quantity of cola—between points *E* and *F* in Fig. 2.1—the frontier is steep. A given increase in the quantity of pizzas *costs* a large decrease in the quantity of cola, so the opportunity cost of a pizza is a large quantity of cola.

The *PPF* is bowed outward because resources are not all equally productive in all activities. People with many years of experience working for PepsiCo are good at producing cola but not very good at making pizzas. So if we move some of these people from PepsiCo to Domino's, we get a small increase in the quantity of pizzas but a large decrease in the quantity of cola.

Similarly, people who have spent years working at Domino's are good at producing pizzas, but they have no idea how to produce cola. So if we move some of these people from Domino's to PepsiCo, we get a small increase in the quantity of cola but a large decrease in the quantity of pizzas. The more of either good we try to produce, the less productive are the additional resources we use to produce that good and the larger is the opportunity cost of a unit of that good.

Review Quiz

1 How does the production possibilities frontier illustrate scarcity?
2 How does the production possibilities frontier illustrate production efficiency?
3 How does the production possibilities frontier show that every choice involves a tradeoff?
4 How does the production possibilities frontier illustrate opportunity cost?
5 Why is opportunity cost a ratio?
6 Why does the *PPF* for most goods bow outward so that opportunity cost increases as the quantity of the good produced increases?

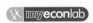 Work Study Plan 2.1 and get instant feedback.

We've seen that what we can produce is limited by the production possibilities frontier. We've also seen that production on the *PPF* is efficient. But we can produce many different quantities on the *PPF*. How do we choose among them? How do we know which point on the *PPF* is the best one?

Using Resources Efficiently

We achieve *production efficiency* at every point on the *PPF*. But which point is best? The answer is the point on the *PPF* at which goods and services are produced in the quantities that provide the greatest possible benefit. When goods and services are produced at the lowest possible cost and in the quantities that provide the greatest possible benefit, we have achieved **allocative efficiency**.

The questions that we raised when we reviewed the five big issues in Chapter 1 are questions about allocative efficiency. To answer such questions, we must measure and compare costs and benefits.

The *PPF* and Marginal Cost

The **marginal cost** of a good is the opportunity cost of producing one more unit of it. We calculate marginal cost from the slope of the *PPF*. As the quantity of pizzas produced increases, the *PPF* gets steeper and the marginal cost of a pizza increases. Figure 2.2 illustrates the calculation of the marginal cost of a pizza.

Begin by finding the opportunity cost of pizza in blocks of 1 million pizzas. The cost of the first million pizzas is 1 million cans of cola; the cost of the second million pizzas is 2 million cans of cola; the cost of the third million pizzas is 3 million cans of cola, and so on. The bars in part (a) illustrate these calculations.

The bars in part (b) show the cost of an average pizza in each of the 1 million pizza blocks. Focus on the third million pizzas—the move from *C* to *D* in part (a). Over this range, because 1 million pizzas cost 3 million cans of cola, one of these pizzas, on average, costs 3 cans of cola—the height of the bar in part (b).

Next, find the opportunity cost of each additional pizza—the marginal cost of a pizza. The marginal cost of a pizza increases as the quantity of pizzas produced increases. The marginal cost at point *C* is less than it is at point *D*. On the average over the range from *C* to *D*, the marginal cost of a pizza is 3 cans of cola. But it exactly equals 3 cans of cola only in the middle of the range between *C* and *D*.

The red dot in part (b) indicates that the marginal cost of a pizza is 3 cans of cola when 2.5 million pizzas are produced. Each black dot in part (b) is interpreted in the same way. The red curve that passes through these dots, labelled *MC*, is the marginal cost curve. It shows the marginal cost of a pizza at each quantity of pizzas as we move along the *PPF*.

FIGURE 2.2 The *PPF* and Marginal Cost

(a) *PPF* **and opportunity cost**

(b) Marginal cost

Marginal cost is calculated from the slope of the *PPF*. As the quantity of pizzas produced increases, the *PPF* gets steeper and the marginal cost of a pizza increases. The bars in part (a) show the opportunity cost of pizza in blocks of 1 million pizzas. The bars in part (b) show the cost of an average pizza in each of these 1 million blocks. The red curve, *MC*, shows the marginal cost of a pizza at each point along the *PPF*. This curve passes through the centre of each of the bars in part (b).

 animation

Preferences and Marginal Benefit

Look around your classroom and notice the wide variety of shirts, pants, and shoes that you and your fellow students are wearing today. Why is there such a huge variety? Why don't you all wear the same styles and colours? The answer lies in what economists call preferences. **Preferences** are a description of a person's likes and dislikes.

You've seen that we have a concrete way of describing the limits to production: the *PPF*. We need a similarly concrete way of describing preferences. To describe preferences, economists use the concept of marginal benefit. The **marginal benefit** from a good or service is the benefit received from consuming one more unit of it.

We measure the marginal benefit from a good or service by the most that people are *willing to pay* for an additional unit of it. The idea is that you are willing to pay less for a good than it is worth to you but you are not willing to pay more than it is worth. So the most you are willing to pay for something measures its marginal benefit.

Economists illustrate preferences using the **marginal benefit curve**, which is a curve that shows the relationship between the marginal benefit from a good and the quantity consumed of that good. It is a general principle that the more we have of any good or service, the smaller is its marginal benefit and the less we are willing to pay for an additional unit of it. This tendency is so widespread and strong that we call it a principle—the *principle of decreasing marginal benefit*.

The basic reason why marginal benefit from a good or service decreases as we consume more of it is that we like variety. The more we consume of any one good or service, the more we tire of it and would prefer to switch to something else.

Think about your willingness to pay for a pizza. If pizza is hard to come by and you can buy only a few slices a year, you might be willing to pay a high price to get an additional slice. But if pizza is all you've eaten for the past few days, you are willing to pay almost nothing for another slice.

You've learned to think about cost as opportunity cost, not as a dollar cost. You can think about marginal benefit and willingness to pay in the same way. The marginal benefit, measured by what you are willing to pay for something, is the quantity of other goods and services that you are willing to forgo. Let's continue with the example of cola and pizza and illustrate preferences this way.

FIGURE 2.3 Preferences and the Marginal Benefit Curve

Possibility	Pizzas (millions)	Willingness to pay (cans of cola per pizza)
A	0.5	5
B	1.5	4
C	2.5	3
D	3.5	2
E	4.5	1

The smaller the quantity of pizzas produced, the more cola people are willing to give up for an additional pizza. If pizza production is 0.5 million, people are willing to pay 5 cans of cola per pizza. But if pizza production is 4.5 million, people are willing to pay only 1 can of cola per pizza. Willingness to pay measures marginal benefit. A universal feature of people's preferences is that marginal benefit decreases.

 myeconlab animation

Figure 2.3 illustrates preferences as the willingness to pay for pizza in terms of cola. In row *A*, pizza production is 0.5 million, and at that quantity, people are willing to pay 5 cans of cola per pizza. As the quantity of pizzas produced increases, the amount that people are willing to pay for a pizza falls. When pizza production is 4.5 million, people are willing to pay only 1 can of cola per pizza.

Let's now use the concepts of marginal cost and marginal benefit to describe allocative efficiency.

FIGURE 2.4   Efficient Use of Resources

(a) On the PPF

(b) Marginal benefit equals marginal cost

The greater the quantity of pizzas produced, the smaller is the marginal benefit (*MB*) from pizza—the less cola people are willing to give up to get an additional pizza. But the greater the quantity of pizzas produced, the greater is the marginal cost (*MC*) of a pizza—the more cola people must give up to get an additional pizza. When marginal benefit equals marginal cost, resources are being used efficiently.

 animation

Allocative Efficiency

At *any* point on the *PPF*, we cannot produce more of one good without giving up some other good. At the *best* point on the *PPF*, we cannot produce more of one good without giving up some other good that provides greater benefit. We are producing at the point of allocative efficiency—the point on the *PPF* that we prefer above all other points.

Suppose that in Fig. 2.4, we produce 1.5 million pizzas. The marginal cost of a pizza is 2 cans of cola, and the marginal benefit from a pizza is 4 cans of cola. Because someone values an additional pizza more highly than it costs to produce, we can get more value from our resources by moving some of them out of producing cola and into producing pizza.

Now suppose we produce 3.5 million pizzas. The marginal cost of a pizza is now 4 cans of cola, but the marginal benefit from a pizza is only 2 cans of cola. Because the additional pizza costs more to produce than anyone thinks it is worth, we can get more value from our resources by moving some of them away from producing pizza and into producing cola.

Suppose we produce 2.5 million pizzas. Marginal cost and marginal benefit are now equal at 3 cans of cola. This allocation of resources between pizza and cola is efficient. If more pizzas are produced, the forgone cola is worth more than the additional pizzas. If fewer pizzas are produced, the forgone pizzas are worth more than the additional cola.

Review Quiz

1 What is marginal cost? How is it measured?
2 What is marginal benefit? How is it measured?
3 How does the marginal benefit from a good change as the quantity produced of that good increases?
4 What is allocative efficiency and how does it relate to the production possibilities frontier?
5 What conditions must be satisfied if resources are used efficiently?

myeconlab Work Study Plan 2.2 and get instant feedback.

You now understand the limits to production and the conditions under which resources are used efficiently. Your next task is to study the expansion of production possibilities.

◆ Economic Growth

During the past 30 years, production per person in Canada has doubled. Such an expansion of production is called **economic growth**. Economic growth increases our *standard of living,* but it doesn't overcome scarcity and avoid opportunity cost. To make our economy grow, we face a tradeoff—the faster we make production grow, the greater is the opportunity cost of economic growth.

The Cost of Economic Growth

Economic growth comes from technological change and capital accumulation. **Technological change** is the development of new goods and of better ways of producing goods and services. **Capital accumulation** is the growth of capital resources, including *human capital.*

Because of technological change and capital accumulation, we have an enormous quantity of cars that provide us with more transportation than was available when we had only horses and carriages; we have satellites that provide global communications on a much larger scale than that available with the earlier cable technology. But if we use our resources to develop new technologies and produce capital, we must decrease our production of consumption goods and services. New technologies and new capital have an opportunity cost. Let's look at this opportunity cost.

Instead of studying the *PPF* of pizza and cola, we'll hold the quantity of cola produced constant and examine the *PPF* for pizzas and pizza ovens. Figure 2.5 shows this *PPF* as the blue curve *ABC*. If we devote no resources to producing pizza ovens, we produce at point *A.* If we produce 3 million pizzas, we can produce 6 pizza ovens at point *B.* If we produce no pizza, we can produce 10 ovens at point *C.*

The amount by which our production possibilities expand depends on the resources we devote to technological change and capital accumulation. If we devote no resources to this activity (point *A*), our *PPF* remains at *ABC*—the blue curve in Fig. 2.5. If we cut the current production of pizza and produce 6 ovens (point *B*), then in the future, we'll have more capital and our *PPF* will rotate outward to the position shown by the red curve. The fewer resources we use for producing pizza and the more resources we use for producing ovens, the greater is the future expansion of our production possibilities.

FIGURE 2.5 Economic Growth

PPF_0 shows the limits to the production of pizza and pizza ovens, with the production of all other goods and services remaining the same. If we devote no resources to producing pizza ovens and produce 5 million pizzas, our production possibilities will remain the same PPF_0. But if we decrease pizza production to 3 million and produce 6 ovens, at point *B,* our production possibilities expand. After one period, the *PPF* rotates outward to PPF_1 and we can produce at point *B',* a point outside the original PPF_0. We can rotate the *PPF* outward, but we cannot avoid opportunity cost. The opportunity cost of producing more pizzas in the future is fewer pizzas today.

Economic growth is not free. To make it happen, we use more resources to produce new ovens and fewer resources to produce pizzas. In Fig. 2.5, we move from *A* to *B.* There is no free lunch. The opportunity cost of more pizzas in the future is fewer pizzas today. Also, economic growth is no magic formula for abolishing scarcity. On the new production possibilities frontier, we continue to face a tradeoff and opportunity cost.

The ideas about economic growth that we have explored in the setting of the pizza industry also apply to nations. Hong Kong and Canada provide an interesting case study.

Economic Growth

Hong Kong Overtakes Canada

In 1968, the production possibilities per person in Canada were much larger than those in Hong Kong (see the figure). Canada devotes one-fifth of its resources to accumulating capital and in 1968 was at point *A* on its *PPF*. Hong Kong devotes one-third of its resources to accumulating capital and in 1968, Hong Kong was at point *A* on its *PPF*.

Since 1968, both countries have experienced economic growth, but because Hong Kong devotes a bigger fraction of its resources to accumulating capital, its production possibilities have expanded more quickly.

By 2008, production possibilities per person in Hong Kong had exceeded those in Canada. If Hong Kong continues to devote more resources to accumulating capital than Canada does (at point *B* on its 2008 *PPF*), Hong Kong will continue to grow more rapidly. But if Hong Kong decreases capital accumulation (moving to point *D* on its 2008 *PPF*), then its rate of economic growth will slow.

Hong Kong is typical of the fast-growing Asian economies, which include Taiwan, Thailand, South Korea, and China. Production possibilities expand in these countries by between 5 and 10 percent a year. If such high economic growth rates are maintained, these other Asian countries will continue to close the gap between themselves and Canada.

Economic Growth in Canada and Hong Kong

To catch up with Hong Kong, Canada must devote more than one-third of its resources to accumulating capital.

A Nation's Economic Growth

The experiences of Canada and Hong Kong make a striking example of the effects of our choices about what to produce and how to produce it on the rate of economic growth.

If a nation devotes all its factors of production to producing consumption goods and services and none to advancing technology and accumulating capital, its production possibilities in the future will be the same as they are today.

To expand production possibilities in the future, a nation must devote fewer resources to producing consumption goods and services and some resources to accumulating capital and developing new technologies. As production possibilities expand, consumption in the future can increase. The decrease in today's consumption is the opportunity cost of tomorrow's increase in consumption.

Review Quiz

1 What generates economic growth?
2 How does economic growth influence the production possibilities frontier?
3 What is the opportunity cost of economic growth?
4 Why has Hong Kong experienced faster economic growth than Canada?
5 Does economic growth overcome scarcity?

 Work Study Plan 2.3 and get instant feedback.

Next, we're going to study another way in which we expand our production possibilities—the amazing fact that *both* buyers and sellers gain from specialization and trade.

◢ Gains from Trade

People can produce for themselves all the goods and services that they consume, or they can produce one good or a few goods and trade with others. Producing only one good or a few goods is called *specialization*. We are going to learn how people gain by specializing in the production of the good in which they have a *comparative advantage* and trading with others.

Comparative Advantage and Absolute Advantage

A person has a **comparative advantage** in an activity if that person can perform the activity at a lower opportunity cost than anyone else. Differences in opportunity costs arise from differences in individual abilities and from differences in the characteristics of other resources.

No one excels at everything. One person is an outstanding pitcher but a poor catcher; another person is a brilliant lawyer but a poor teacher. In almost all human endeavours, what one person does easily, someone else finds difficult. The same applies to land and capital. One plot of land is fertile but has no mineral deposits; another plot of land has outstanding views but is infertile. One machine has great precision but is difficult to operate; another is fast but often breaks down.

Although no one excels at everything, some people excel and can outperform others in a large number of activities—perhaps even in all activities. A person who is more productive than others has an **absolute advantage**.

Absolute advantage involves comparing productivities—production per hour—whereas comparative advantage involves comparing opportunity costs.

Notice that a person who has an absolute advantage does not have a *comparative* advantage in every activity. Joni Mitchell is a better folk singer and a better painter than most people. She has an absolute advantage in these two activities. But compared to others, she is a better folk singer than a painter, so her *comparative* advantage is in folk singing.

Because ability and resources vary from one person to another, people have different opportunity costs of producing various goods. These differences in opportunity cost are the source of comparative advantage.

Let's explore the idea of comparative advantage by looking at two smoothie bars: one operated by Liz and the other operated by Joe.

Liz's Smoothie Bar Liz produces smoothies and salads. In Liz's high-tech bar, she can turn out either a smoothie or a salad every 2 minutes—see Table 2.1. If Liz spends all her time making smoothies, she can produce 30 an hour. And if she spends all her time making salads, she can also produce 30 an hour. If she splits her time equally between the two, she can produce 15 smoothies and 15 salads an hour. For each additional smoothie Liz produces, she must decrease her production of salads by one, and for each additional salad she produces, she must decrease her production of smoothies by one. So

> Liz's opportunity cost of producing 1 smoothie is 1 salad,

and

> Liz's opportunity cost of producing 1 salad is 1 smoothie.

Liz's customers buy smoothies and salads in equal quantities, so she splits her time equally between the two items and produces 15 smoothies and 15 salads an hour.

Joe's Smoothie Bar Joe also produces smoothies and salads, but his bar is smaller than Liz's. Also, Joe has only one blender, and it's a slow, old machine. Even if Joe uses all his resources to produce smoothies, he can produce only 6 an hour—see Table 2.2. But Joe is good at making salads, so if he uses all his resources to make salads, he can produce 30 an hour.

Joe's ability to make smoothies and salads is the same regardless of how he splits an hour between the two tasks. He can make a salad in 2 minutes or a smoothie in 10 minutes. For each additional

TABLE 2.1   Liz's Production Possibilities

Item	Minutes to produce 1	Quantity per hour
Smoothies	2	30
Salads	2	30

TABLE 2.2   Joe's Production Possibilities

Item	Minutes to produce 1	Quantity per hour
Smoothies	10	6
Salads	2	30

smoothie Joe produces, he must decrease his production of salads by 5. And for each additional salad he produces, he must decrease his production of smoothies by 1/5 of a smoothie. So

Joe's opportunity cost of producing 1 smoothie is 5 salads,

and

Joe's opportunity cost of producing 1 salad is 1/5 of a smoothie.

Joe's customers, like Liz's, buy smoothies and salads in equal quantities. So Joe spends 50 minutes of each hour making smoothies and 10 minutes of each hour making salads. With this division of his time, Joe produces 5 smoothies and 5 salads an hour.

Liz's Absolute Advantage   Table 2.3(a) summarizes the production of Liz and Joe. You can see that Liz is three times as productive as Joe—her 15 smoothies and salads an hour are three times Joe's 5. Liz has an absolute advantage over Joe in producing both smoothies and salads. But Liz has a comparative advantage in only one of the activities.

Liz's Comparative Advantage   In which of the two activities does Liz have a comparative advantage? Recall that comparative advantage is a situation in which one person's opportunity cost of producing a good is lower than another person's opportunity cost of producing that same good. Liz has a comparative advantage in producing smoothies. Her opportunity cost of a smoothie is 1 salad, whereas Joe's opportunity cost of a smoothie is 5 salads.

Joe's Comparative Advantage   If Liz has a comparative advantage in producing smoothies, Joe must have a comparative advantage in producing salads. Joe's opportunity cost of a salad is 1/5 of a smoothie, whereas Liz's opportunity cost of a salad is 1 smoothie.

Achieving the Gains from Trade

Liz and Joe run into each other one evening in a singles bar. After a few minutes of getting acquainted, Liz tells Joe about her amazing smoothie business. Her only problem, she tells Joe, is that she would like to produce more because potential customers leave when her lines get too long.

Joe isn't sure whether to risk spoiling his chances by telling Liz about his own struggling business. But he takes the risk. When he explains to Liz that he spends 50 minutes of every hour making 5 smoothies and 10 minutes making 5 salads, Liz's eyes pop. "Have I got a deal for you!" she exclaims.

Here's the deal that Liz sketches on a table napkin. Joe stops making smoothies and allocates all his time to producing salads. And Liz stops making salads and allocates all her time to producing smoothies. That is, they both specialize in producing the good in which they have a comparative advantage. Together they produce 30 smoothies and 30 salads—see Table 2.3(b).

TABLE 2.3   Liz and Joe Gain from Trade

(a) Before trade	Liz	Joe
Smoothies	15	5
Salads	15	5
(b) Specialization	**Liz**	**Joe**
Smoothies	30	0
Salads	0	30
(c) Trade	**Liz**	**Joe**
Smoothies	sell 10	buy 10
Salads	buy 20	sell 20
(d) After trade	**Liz**	**Joe**
Smoothies	20	10
Salads	20	10
(e) Gains from trade	**Liz**	**Joe**
Smoothies	+5	+5
Salads	+5	+5

They then trade. Liz sells Joe 10 smoothies and Joe sells Liz 20 salads—the price of a smoothie is 2 salads—see Table 2.3(c).

After the trade, Joe has 10 salads—the 30 he produces minus the 20 he sells to Liz. He also has the 10 smoothies that he buys from Liz. So Joe now has increased the quantities of smoothies and salads that he can sell—see Table 2.3(d).

Liz has 20 smoothies—the 30 she produces minus the 10 she sells to Joe. She also has the 20 salads that she buys from Joe. Liz has increased the quantities of smoothies and salads that she can sell—see Table 2.3(d). Liz and Joe both gain 5 smoothies and 5 salads an hour—see Table 2.3(e).

To illustrate her idea, Liz grabs a fresh napkin and draws the graphs in Fig. 2.6. The blue *PPF* in part (a) shows Joe's production possibilities. Before trade, he is producing 5 smoothies and 5 salads an hour at point *A*.

The blue *PPF* in part (b) shows Liz's production possibilities. Before trade, she is producing 15 smoothies and 15 salads an hour at point *A*.

Liz's proposal is that they each specialize in producing the good in which they have a comparative advantage. Joe produces 30 salads and no smoothies at point *B* on his *PPF*. Liz produces 30 smoothies and no salads at point *B* on her *PPF*.

Liz and Joe then trade smoothies and salads at a price of 2 salads per smoothie or 1/2 a smoothie per salad. Joe gets smoothies from Liz for 2 salads each, which is less than the 5 salads it costs him to produce a smoothie. Liz gets salads from Joe for 1/2 a smoothie each, which is less than the 1 smoothie that it costs her to produce a salad.

With trade, Joe has 10 smoothies and 10 salads at point *C*—a gain of 5 smoothies and 5 salads. Joe moves to a point *outside* his *PPF*.

FIGURE 2.6   The Gains from Trade

(a) Joe

(b) Liz

Joe initially produces at point *A* on his *PPF* in part (a), and Liz initially produces at point *A* on her *PPF* in part (b). Joe's opportunity cost of producing a salad is less than Liz's, so Joe has a comparative advantage in producing salads. Liz's opportunity cost of producing a smoothie is less than Joe's, so Liz has a comparative advantage in producing smoothies. If Joe specializes in making salads, he produces 30 salads and no smoothies at point *B* on his *PPF*. If Liz specializes in

making smoothies, she produces 30 smoothies and no salads at point *B* on her *PPF*. They exchange salads for smoothies along the red "Trade line." Liz buys salads from Joe for less than her opportunity cost of producing them. Joe buys smoothies from Liz for less than his opportunity cost of producing them. Each goes to point *C*—a point outside his or her *PPF*. Both Joe and Liz increase production by 5 smoothies and 5 salads with no change in resources.

With trade, Liz has 20 smoothies and 20 salads at point *C*—a gain of 5 smoothies and 5 salads. Liz moves to a point *outside* her *PPF.*

Despite Liz's absolute advantage in producing smoothies and salads, both Liz and Joe gain from specializing—producing the good in which they have a comparative advantage—and trading.

The gains that we achieve from international trade are similar to those achieved by Joe and Liz in this example. When Canadians buy T-shirts from China and when China buys regional jets from Canada, both countries gain. We get our shirts at a lower cost than that at which we can produce them, and China gets its regional jets at a lower cost than that at which it can produce them.

Dynamic Comparative Advantage

At any given point in time, the resources and technologies available determine the comparative advantages that individuals and nations have. But just by repeatedly producing a particular good or service, people become more productive in that activity, a phenomenon called **learning-by-doing.** Learning-by-doing is the basis of *dynamic* comparative advantage. **Dynamic comparative advantage** is a comparative advantage that a person (or country) has acquired by specializing in an activity and becoming the lowest-cost producer as a result of learning-by-doing.

Singapore, for example, pursued dynamic comparative advantage when it decided to begin a biotechnology industry in which it initially didn't have a comparative advantage.

Review Quiz

1 What gives a person a comparative advantage?
2 Distinguish between comparative advantage and absolute advantage.
3 Why do people specialize and trade?
4 What are the gains from specialization and trade?
5 What is the source of the gains from trade?
6 How does dynamic comparative advantage arise?

 Work Study Plan 2.4 and get instant feedback.

Economic Coordination

People gain by specializing in the production of those goods and services in which they have a comparative advantage and then trading with each other. Liz and Joe, whose production of salads and smoothies we studied earlier in this chapter, can get together and make a deal that enables them to enjoy the gains from specialization and trade. But for billions of individuals to specialize and produce millions of different goods and services, their choices must somehow be coordinated.

Two competing economic coordination systems have been used: central economic planning and decentralized markets.

Central economic planning might appear to be the best system because it can express national priorities. But when this system was tried in Russia for 60 years and in China for 30 years, it was a miserable failure. Today, most previously planned economies are adopting a decentralized market system.

To make decentralized coordination work, four complementary social institutions that have evolved over many centuries are needed. They are

- Firms
- Markets
- Property rights
- Money

Firms

A **firm** is an economic unit that hires factors of production and organizes those factors to produce and sell goods and services. Examples of firms are your local gas station, Canadian Tire, and Roots.

Firms coordinate a huge amount of economic activity. For example, Canadian Tire buys or rents large buildings, equips them with storage shelves and checkout lanes, and hires labour. Canadian Tire directs the labour and decides what goods to buy and sell.

But Canadian Tire doesn't produce the goods that it sells. It could do so. It could own and coordinate the production of all the things that it sells in all its stores. It could also produce all the raw materials that are used to produce the things that it sells. But John W. and Alfred J. Billes would not have created one of Canada's great retailers if they had followed that path.

The reason is that if a firm gets too big, it can't keep track of all the information needed to coordinate its activities. It is more efficient for firms to specialize (just as Liz and Joe did) and trade with each other. This trade between firms takes place in markets.

Markets

In ordinary speech, the word *market* means a place where people buy and sell goods such as fish, meat, fruits, and vegetables. In economics, a *market* has a more general meaning. A **market** is any arrangement that enables buyers and sellers to get information and to do business with each other. An example is the market in which oil is bought and sold—the world oil market. The world oil market is not a place. It is the network of oil producers, oil users, wholesalers, and brokers who buy and sell oil. These decision makers do not meet physically. They make deals by telephone, fax, and direct computer link.

Markets have evolved because they facilitate trade. Without organized markets, we would miss out on a substantial part of the potential gains from trade. Enterprising individuals and firms, each pursuing their own self-interest, have profited from making markets—standing ready to buy or sell the items in which they specialize. But markets can work only when property rights exist.

Property Rights

The social arrangements that govern the ownership, use, and disposal of anything that people value are called **property rights**. *Real property* includes land and buildings—the things we call property in ordinary speech—and durable goods such as plant and equipment. *Financial property* includes stocks and bonds and money in the bank. *Intellectual property* is the intangible product of creative effort. This type of property includes books, music, computer programs, and inventions of all kinds and is protected by copyrights and patents.

Where property rights are enforced, people have the incentive to specialize and produce the goods in which they have a comparative advantage. Where people can steal the production of others, resources are devoted not to production but to protecting possessions. Without property rights, we would still be hunting and gathering as our Stone Age ancestors did.

Money

Money is any commodity or token that is generally acceptable as a means of payment. Liz and Joe didn't use money in the example above. They exchanged salads and smoothies. In principle, trade in markets can exchange any item for any other item. But you can perhaps imagine how complicated life would be if we exchanged goods for other goods. The "invention" of money makes trading in markets much more efficient.

Circular Flows Through Markets

Figure 2.7 shows the flows that result from the choices that households and firms make. Households specialize and choose the quantities of labour, land, capital, and entrepreneurial services to sell or rent to firms. Firms choose the quantities of factors of production to hire. These (red) flows go through the *factor markets*. Households choose the quantities of goods and services to buy, and firms choose the quantities to produce. These (red) flows go through the *goods markets*. Households receive incomes and make expenditures on goods and services (the green flows).

How do markets coordinate all these decisions?

Coordinating Decisions

Markets coordinate decisions through price adjustments. To see how, think about your local market for hamburgers. Suppose that too few hamburgers are available and some people who want to buy hamburgers are not able to do so. To make buying and selling plans the same, either more hamburgers must be offered for sale or buyers must scale down their appetites (or both). A rise in the price of a hamburger produces this outcome. A higher price encourages producers to offer more hamburgers for sale. It also encourages some people to change their lunch plans. Fewer people buy hamburgers, and more buy hot dogs. More hamburgers (and more hot dogs) are offered for sale.

Alternatively, suppose that more hamburgers are available than people want to buy. In this case, to make the choices of buyers and sellers compatible, more hamburgers must be bought or fewer hamburgers must be offered for sale (or both). A fall in the price of a hamburger achieves this outcome. A lower price encourages firms to produce a smaller quantity of hamburgers. It also encourages people to buy more hamburgers.

FIGURE 2.7 Circular Flows in the Market Economy

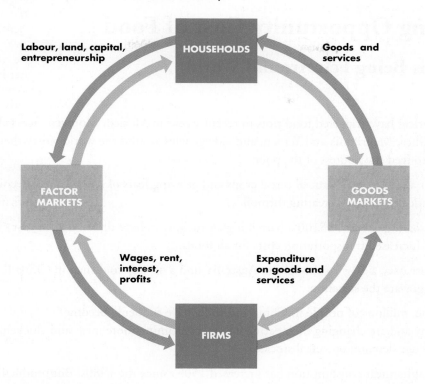

Households and firms make economic choices and markets coordinate these choices.

Households choose the quantities of labour, land, capital, and entrepreneurial services to sell or rent to firms in exchange for wages, rent, interest, and profit. Households also choose how to spend their incomes on the various types of goods and services available.

Firms choose the quantities of factors of production to hire and the quantities of goods and services to produce.

Goods markets and factor markets coordinate these choices of households and firms.

The counterclockwise red flows are real flows—the flow of factors of production from households to firms and the flow of goods and services from firms to households. The clockwise green flows are the payments for the red flows. They are the flow of incomes from firms to households and the flow of expenditure on goods and services from households to firms.

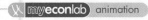 animation

Review Quiz

1 Why are social institutions such as firms, markets, property rights, and money necessary?

2 What are the main functions of markets?

3 What are the flows in the market economy that go from firms to households and the flows from households to firms?

 Work Study Plan 2.5
and get instant feedback.

◆ You have now begun to see how economists approach economic questions. Scarcity, choice, and divergent opportunity costs explain why we specialize and trade and why firms, markets, property rights, and money have developed. You can see all around you the lessons you've learned in this chapter. *Reading Between the Lines* on pp. 46–47 provides an opportunity to apply the *PPF* model to deepen your understanding of the reasons for the increase in the cost of food associated with the increase in corn production.

The Rising Opportunity Cost of Food

Food Crisis Being Felt Around World

April 1, 2008

Sharply rising prices have triggered food riots in recent weeks in Mexico, Morocco, Senegal, Uzbekistan, Guinea, Mauritania and Yemen, and aid agencies around the world worry they may be unable to feed the poorest of the poor. …

Rising prices for all the world's crucial cereal crops and growing fears of scarcity are careening through international markets, creating turmoil. …

With crude oil soaring above US$100 a barrel, higher fuel prices have driven up the cost of production and increased transportation costs for all foods.

Pests in Southeast Asia, a 10-year drought in Australia, and a 45-day cold snap in China have combined to aggravate the situation.

At the same time, millions of people in China and India have suddenly become relatively wealthy and are changing their eating habits, consuming more meat and chicken, which places a huge demand on cereal stocks.

In China, per-capita meat consumption has increased 150% since the 1980s. But producing more meat requires more feed to raise more animals. …

Also influencing the food crisis is the move in North America and Europe to biofuel in an effort to ease global warming and reduce reliance on imported energy.

A surge in demand for biofuel has resulted in a sharp decline in agricultural land planted for food crops. About 16% of U.S. agricultural land formerly planted with soybeans and wheat is now growing corn for biofuel.

Material reprinted with the express permission of "The National Post Company," a Canwest Partnership.

Essence of the Story

- A swelling global population explains only part of the problem of food shortages.

- The dramatic price rises have been driven by factors such as turning food into fuel, high crude oil prices (which boost trucking costs), and greater consumption of meat products as incomes rise (which raises the demand for animal feedstuffs).

- Pests in Southeast Asia, a long drought in Australia, and a 45-day cold snap in China have limited grain production and also raised the cost of food.

- Driven by fears of global warming, biofuel has become big business, especially in the United States and the European Union.

Economic Analysis

- Ethanol is made from corn, so biofuel and food compete to use the same resources.

- To produce more ethanol, farmers increased the number of hectares devoted to corn production.

- In 2008, the amount of land devoted to corn production increased by 20 percent in the United States and by 2 percent in the rest of the world.

- Figure 1 shows the U.S. production possibilities frontier, PPF, for corn and other goods and services.

- The increase in the production of corn is illustrated by a movement along the PPF in Fig. 1 from point A in 2007 to point B in 2008.

- In moving from point A to point B, the United States incurs a higher opportunity cost of producing corn, indicated by the greater slope of the PPF at point B.

- In other regions of the world, despite the fact that more land was devoted to corn production, the amount of corn produced didn't change.

- The reason is that drought in Australia, pests in Southeast Asia, and a cold snap in China lowered the crop yield per hectare.

- Figure 2 shows the rest of the world's PPF for corn and other goods and services in 2007 and 2008.

- The increase in the amount of land devoted to producing corn is illustrated by a movement along PPF_{07}.

- With a decrease in the crop yield, production possibilities decreased and the PPF rotated inward.

- The rotation from PPF_{07} to PPF_{08} illustrates this decrease in production possibilities.

- The opportunity cost of producing corn in the rest of the world increased for two reasons: the movement along its PPF and the inward rotation of the PPF.

- With a higher opportunity cost of producing corn, the cost of both biofuel and food increases.

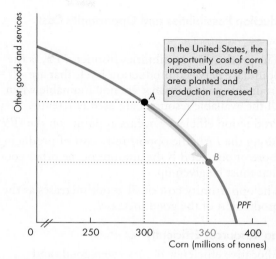

In the United States, the opportunity cost of corn increased because the area planted and production increased

Figure 1 U.S. PPF

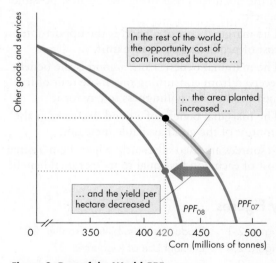

In the rest of the world, the opportunity cost of corn increased because ...

... the area planted increased ...

... and the yield per hectare decreased

Figure 2 Rest of the World PPF

47

SUMMARY ◆

Key Points

Production Possibilities and Opportunity Cost (pp. 32–34)

- The production possibilities frontier, *PPF*, is the boundary between production levels that are attainable and those that are not attainable when all the available resources are used efficiently.
- Production efficiency occurs at points on the *PPF*.
- Along the *PPF*, the opportunity cost of producing more of one good is the amount of the other good that must be given up.
- The opportunity cost of all goods increases as the production of the good increases.

Using Resources Efficiently (pp. 35–37)

- Allocative efficiency occurs when goods and services are produced at the least possible cost and in the quantities that bring the greatest possible benefit.
- The marginal cost of a good is the opportunity cost of producing one more unit.
- The marginal benefit from a good is the benefit received from consuming one more unit of it, measured by the willingness to pay for it.
- The marginal benefit of a good decreases as the amount of the good available increases.
- Resources are used efficiently when the marginal cost of each good is equal to its marginal benefit.

Economic Growth (pp. 38–39)

- Economic growth, which is the expansion of production possibilities, results from capital accumulation and technological change.
- The opportunity cost of economic growth is forgone current consumption.

Gains from Trade (pp. 40–43)

- A person has a comparative advantage in producing a good if that person can produce the good at a lower opportunity cost than everyone else.
- People gain by specializing in the activity in which they have a comparative advantage and trading with others.
- Dynamic comparative advantage arises from learning-by-doing.

Economic Coordination (pp. 43–45)

- Firms coordinate a large amount of economic activity, but there is a limit to the efficient size of a firm.
- Markets coordinate the economic choices of people and firms.
- Markets can work efficiently only when property rights exist.
- Money makes trading in markets more efficient.

Key Figures

Figure 2.1   Production Possibilities Frontier, 32
Figure 2.4   Efficient Use of Resources, 37
Figure 2.5   Economic Growth, 38
Figure 2.6   The Gains from Trade, 42
Figure 2.7   Circular Flows in the Market Economy, 45

Key Terms

Absolute advantage, 40
Allocative efficiency, 35
Capital accumulation, 38
Comparative advantage, 40
Dynamic comparative advantage, 43
Economic growth, 38
Firm, 43
Learning-by-doing, 43
Marginal benefit, 36
Marginal benefit curve, 36
Marginal cost, 35
Market, 44
Money, 44
Opportunity cost, 33
Preferences, 36
Production efficiency, 33
Production possibilities frontier, 32
Property rights, 44
Technological change, 38

PROBLEMS and APPLICATIONS

 Work problems 1–11 in Chapter 2 Study Plan and get instant feedback.
Work problems 12–21 as Homework, a Quiz, or a Test if assigned by your instructor.

1. Brazil produces ethanol from sugar, and the land used to grow sugar can be used to grow food crops. Suppose that Brazil's production possibilities for ethanol and food crops are as follows:

Ethanol (barrels per day)		Food crops (tonnes per day)
70	and	0
64	and	1
54	and	2
40	and	3
22	and	4
0	and	5

   a. Draw a graph of Brazil's *PPF* and explain how your graph illustrates scarcity.
   b. If Brazil produces 40 barrels of ethanol a day, how much food must it produce if it achieves production efficiency?
   c. Why does Brazil face a tradeoff on its *PPF*?
   d. If Brazil increases its production of ethanol from 40 barrels per day to 54 barrels per day, what is the opportunity cost of the additional ethanol?
   e. If Brazil increases its production of food crops from 2 tonnes per day to 3 tonnes per day, what is the opportunity cost of the additional food?
   f. What is the relationship between your answers to d and e?
   g. Does Brazil face an increasing opportunity cost of ethanol? What feature of the *PPF* that you've drawn illustrates increasing opportunity cost?

2. Define marginal cost and use the information provided in problem 1 to calculate the marginal cost of producing a tonne of food when the quantity produced is 2.5 tonnes per day.

3. Define marginal benefit, explain how it is measured, and explain why the information provided in the table in problem 1 does not enable you to calculate the marginal benefit of food.

4. Distinguish between *production efficiency* and *allocative efficiency*. Explain why many production possibilities achieve production efficiency but only one achieves allocative efficiency.

5. Harry enjoys tennis but wants a high grade in his economics course. The figure shows the limits to what he can achieve: his *PPF*.

   The following figure shows Harry's *MB* curve for tennis.

   a. What is Harry's marginal cost of tennis if he plays for (i) 3 hours a week; (ii) 5 hours a week; and (iii) 7 hours a week?
   b. If Harry uses his time to achieve allocative efficiency, what is his economics grade and how many hours of tennis does he play?
   c. Explain why Harry would be worse off getting a grade higher than your answer to b.
   d. If Harry becomes a tennis superstar with big earnings from tennis, what happens to his *PPF*, *MB* curve, and efficient time allocation?

e. If Harry suddenly finds high grades in economics easier to attain, what happens to his *PPF*, *MB* curve, and efficient time allocation?

6. A farm grows wheat and produces pork. The marginal cost of producing each of these products increases as more of it is produced.

   a. Make a graph that illustrates the farm's *PPF*.
   b. The farm adopts a new technology that allows it to use fewer resources to fatten pigs. Use your graph to illustrate the impact of the new technology on the farm's *PPF*.
   c. With the farm using the new technology described in b, has the opportunity cost of producing a tonne of wheat increased, decreased, or remained the same? Explain and illustrate your answer.
   d. Is the farm more efficient with the new technology than it was with the old one? Why?

7. In an hour, Sue can produce 40 caps or 4 jackets and Tessa can produce 80 caps or 4 jackets.

   a. Calculate Sue's opportunity cost of producing a cap.
   b. Calculate Tessa's opportunity cost of producing a cap.
   c. Who has a comparative advantage in producing caps?
   d. If Sue and Tessa specialize in producing the good in which each of them has a comparative advantage, and they trade 1 jacket for 15 caps, who gains from the specialization and trade?

8. Suppose that Tessa buys a new machine for making jackets that enables her to make 20 jackets an hour. (She can still make only 80 caps per hour.)

   a. Who now has a comparative advantage in producing jackets?
   b. Can Sue and Tessa still gain from trade?
   c. Would Sue and Tessa still be willing to trade 1 jacket for 15 caps? Explain your answer.

9. "America's baby-boomers are embracing tea for its health benefits," said the *Economist* (July 8, 2005, p. 65). The article went on to say, "Even though the climate is suitable, tea-growing [in the United States] is simply too costly, since the process is labour-intensive and resists automation."

   Using this information:

   a. Sketch a *PPF* for the production of tea and other goods and services in India.
   b. Sketch a *PPF* for the production of tea and other goods and services in the United States.
   c. Sketch a marginal cost curve for the production of tea in India.
   d. Sketch a marginal cost curve for the production of tea in the United States.
   e. Sketch the marginal benefit curve for tea in the United States before and after the baby-boomers began to appreciate the health benefits of tea.
   f. Explain why the United States does not produce tea and instead imports it from India.
   g. Explain how the quantity of tea that achieves allocative efficiency has changed.
   h. Does the change in preferences towards tea affect the opportunity cost of producing tea?

10. Brazil produces ethanol from sugar at a cost of 22 cents per litre. The United States produces ethanol from corn at a cost of 30 cents per litre. Sugar grown on one hectare of land produces twice the quantity of ethanol as the corn grown on a hectare. The United States imports 5 percent of its ethanol consumption and produces the rest itself. Since 2003, U.S. ethanol production has more than doubled and U.S. corn production has increased by 45 percent.

    a. Does Brazil or the United States have a comparative advantage in producing ethanol?
    b. Do you expect the opportunity cost of producing ethanol in the United States to have increased since 2003? Explain why.
    c. Sketch the *PPF* for ethanol and other goods and services for the United States.
    d. Sketch the *PPF* for ethanol and other goods and services for Brazil.
    e. Sketch a figure similar to Fig. 2.6 on p. 42 to show how both the United States and Brazil can gain from specialization and trade.
    f. Do you think the United States has achieved production efficiency in its manufacture of ethanol? Explain why or why not.
    g. Do you think the United States has achieved allocative efficiency in its manufacture of ethanol? Explain why or why not.

11. For 50 years, Cuba has had a centrally planned economy in which the government decides the allocation of resources. Why would you expect Cuba's production possibilities (per person) to be smaller than those of Canada? What social institutions that help the Canadian economy achieve allocative efficiency are missing in Cuba?

12. Suppose that a country's production possibilities are

Food (kilograms per month)		Sunscreen (litres per month)
300	and	0
200	and	50
100	and	100
0	and	150

a. Draw a graph of the country's *PPF* and explain how your graph illustrates a tradeoff.
b. If the country produces 150 kilograms of food per month, how much sunscreen must it produce to achieve production efficiency?
c. What is the opportunity cost of producing 1 kilogram of food?
d. What is the opportunity cost of producing 1 litre of sunscreen?
e. What is the relationship between your answers to c and d?
f. Does the country face an increasing opportunity cost of food? What feature of a *PPF* illustrates increasing opportunity cost and why does your *PPF* not have this feature?

13. What is the marginal cost of a kilogram of food in the country in problem 12 when the quantity produced is 150 kilograms a month? What is special about the marginal cost of food in this country?

14. The table describes the preferences in the country in problem 12.

Sunscreen (litres per month)	Willingness to pay (kilograms of food per litre)
25	3
75	2
125	1

a. What is the marginal benefit from sunscreen and how is it measured?
b. What information provided in the table above and the table in problem 12 do we need to be able to calculate the marginal benefit from sunscreen?
c. Draw a graph of the marginal benefit from sunscreen.

15. "Dr. Arata Kochi, the World Health Organization malaria chief, ... [says that] eradication is counterproductive. With enough money, he said, current tools like nets, medicines, and DDT could drive down malaria cases 90 percent. 'But eliminating the last 10 percent is a tremendous task and very expensive,' Dr. Kochi said. 'Even places like South Africa should think twice before taking this path.'"

New York Times, March 4, 2008

a. Is Dr. Kochi talking about *production efficiency* or *allocative efficiency* or both?
b. Make a graph with the percentage of malaria cases eliminated on the *x*-axis and the marginal cost and marginal benefit of driving down malaria cases on the *y*-axis. On your graph,
   (i) Draw a marginal cost curve that is consistent with Dr. Kochi's opinion reported in the news article.
   (ii) Draw a marginal benefit curve that is consistent with Dr. Kochi's opinion reported in the news article.
   (iii) Identify the quantity of malaria eradicated that achieves allocative efficiency.

16. Capital accumulation and technological change bring economic growth, which means that the *PPF* keeps shifting outward: Production that was unattainable yesterday becomes attainable today; and production that is unattainable today will become attainable tomorrow. Why doesn't this process of economic growth mean that scarcity is being defeated and will one day be gone?

17. "Inexpensive broadband access has done far more for online video than enable the success of services like YouTube and iTunes. By unchaining video watchers from their TV sets, it has opened the floodgates to a generation of TV producers for whom the Internet is their native medium."

New York Times, December 2, 2007

a. How has inexpensive broadband changed the production possibilities of video entertainment and other goods and services?
b. Sketch a *PPF* for video entertainment and other goods and services before broadband.
c. Show how the arrival of inexpensive broadband has changed the *PPF*.
d. Sketch a marginal benefit curve for video entertainment. Show how opening the "floodgates to a generation of TV producers for whom the Internet is their native medium" might have changed the marginal benefit from video entertainment.
e. Explain how the quantity of video entertainment that achieves allocative efficiency has changed.

18. Kim can produce 40 pies an hour or 400 cookies an hour. Liam can produce 100 pies an hour or 200 cookies an hour.

    a. Calculate Kim's opportunity cost of producing a pie and Liam's opportunity cost of producing a pie. Who has a comparative advantage in producing pies?
    b. If Kim and Liam spend 30 minutes of each hour producing pies and 30 minutes producing cookies, how many pies and cookies does each of them produce?
    c. Suppose that Kim and Liam increase the time they spend producing the good in which they have a comparative advantage by 15 minutes. What will be the increase in the total number of pies and cookies they produce?
    d. What is the highest price of a pie at which Kim and Liam would agree to trade pies and cookies?
    e. If Kim and Liam specialize and trade, what are the gains from trade?

19. Tony and Patty produce skis and snowboards. The tables show their production possibilities. Each week, Tony produces 5 snowboards and 40 skis and Patty produces 10 snowboards and 5 skis.

Tony's Production Possibilities

Snowboards (per week)		Skis (per week)
25	and	0
20	and	10
15	and	20
10	and	30
5	and	40
0	and	50

Patty's Production Possibilities

Snowboards (per week)		Skis (per week)
20	and	0
10	and	5
0	and	10

    a. Who has a comparative advantage in producing snowboards? And who has a comparative advantage in producing skis?
    b. If Tony and Patty specialize and trade 1 snowboard for 1 ski, what are the gains from trade?

20. "A two-time N.B.A. All-Star, Barron Davis has quietly been moonlighting as a [movie] producer since 2005, when he and a high school buddy, Cash Warren, formed a production company called Verso Entertainment.

    In January, Verso's first feature-length effort, "Made in America," had its premiere to good reviews at Sundance Film Festival and is being courted by distributors."

    New York Times, February 24, 2008

    a. Does Barron Davis have an absolute advantage in basketball and movie directing and is this the reason for his success in both activities?
    b. Does Barron Davis have a comparative advantage in basketball or movie directing or both and is this the reason for his success in both activities?
    c. Sketch a *PPF* between playing basketball and producing other goods and services for Barron Davis and for yourself.
    d. How do you (and people like you) and Barron Davis (and people like him) gain from specialization and trade?

21. After you have studied *Reading Between the Lines* on pp. 46–47, answer the following questions:

    a. Why has corn production in the United States increased?
    b. Why would you expect an increase in the quantity of corn produced to raise the opportunity cost of producing corn?
    c. Why did the cost of producing corn increase in the rest of the world?
    d. Is it possible that the increased quantity of corn produced, despite the higher cost of production, moves the United States closer to allocative efficiency?

22. Use the links on MyEconLab (Textbook Resources, Chapter 2, Weblinks) to obtain data on the tuition and other costs of enrolling in the MBA program at a school that interests you.

    a. Draw a *PPF* that shows the tradeoff that you would face if you decided to enroll in the MBA program.
    b. Do you think your marginal benefit of an MBA exceeds your marginal cost?
    c. Based on your answer to b, do you plan to enroll in an MBA program? Is your answer to this question consistent with using your time to achieve your self-interest?

UNDERSTANDING THE SCOPE OF ECONOMICS

Your Economic Revolution

Three periods in human history stand out as ones of economic revolution. The first, the *Agricultural Revolution*, occurred 10,000 years ago. In what is today Iraq, people learned to domesticate animals and plant crops. People stopped roaming in search of food and settled in villages, towns, and cities, where they specialized in the activities in which they had a comparative advantage and developed markets in which to exchange their products. Wealth increased enormously.

You are studying economics at a time that future historians will call the *Information Revolution*. Over the entire world, people are embracing new information technologies and prospering on an unprecedented scale.

Economics was born during the *Industrial Revolution*, which began in England during the 1760s. For the first time, people began to apply science and create new technologies for the manufacture of textiles and iron, to create steam engines, and to boost the output of farms.

During all three economic revolutions, many have prospered but many have been left behind. It is the range of human progress that poses the greatest question for economics and the one that Adam Smith addressed in the first work of economic science: What causes the differences in wealth among nations?

Many people had written about economics before **Adam Smith**, *but he made economics a science. Born in 1723 in Kirkcaldy, a small fishing town near Edinburgh, Scotland, Smith was the only child of the town's customs officer. Lured from his professorship (he was a full professor at 28) by a wealthy Scottish duke who gave him a pension of £300 a year—ten times the average income at that time—Smith devoted ten years to writing his masterpiece:* An Inquiry into the Nature and Causes of the **Wealth of Nations**, *published in 1776.*

Why, Adam Smith asked, are some nations wealthy while others are poor? He was pondering these questions at the height of the Industrial Revolution, and he answered by emphasizing the role of the division of labour and free markets.

To illustrate his argument, Adam Smith described two pin factories. In the first, one person, using the hand tools available in the 1770s, could make 20 pins a day. In the other, by using those same hand tools but breaking the process into a number of individually small operations in which people specialize—by the division of labour—ten people could make a staggering 48,000 pins a day. One

"It is not from the benevolence of the butcher, the brewer, or the baker that we expect our dinner, but from their regard to their own interest."

ADAM SMITH
The Wealth of Nations

draws out the wire, another straightens it, a third cuts it, a fourth points it, a fifth grinds it. Three specialists make the head, and a fourth attaches it. Finally, the pin is polished and packaged.

But a large market is needed to support the division of labour: One factory employing ten workers would need to sell more than 15 million pins a year to stay in business!

TALKING
WITH

Jagdish Bhagwati

Jagdish Bhagwati is University Professor at Columbia University. Born in India in 1934, he studied at Cambridge University in England, MIT, and Oxford University before returning to India. He returned to teach at MIT in 1968 and moved to Columbia in 1980. A prolific scholar, Professor Bhagwati also writes in leading newspapers and magazines throughout the world. He has been much honoured for both his scientific work and his impact on public policy. His greatest contributions are in international trade but extend also to developmental problems and the study of political economy.

Michael Parkin and Robin Bade talked with Jagdish Bhagwati about his work and the progress that economists have made in understanding the benefits of economic growth and international trade since the pioneering work of Adam Smith.

Professor Bhagwati, what attracted you to economics?

When you come from India, where poverty hits the eye, it is easy to be attracted to economics, which can be used to bring prosperity and create jobs to pull up the poor into gainful employment.

I learned later that there are two broad types of economist: those who treat the subject as an arid mathematical toy and those who see it as a serious social science.

If Cambridge, where I went as an undergraduate, had been interested in esoteric mathematical economics, I would have opted for something else. But the Cambridge economists from whom I learned—many among the greatest figures in the discipline—saw economics as a social science. I therefore saw the power of economics as a tool to address India's poverty and was immediately hooked.

Who had the greatest impact on you at Cambridge?

Most of all, it was Harry Johnson, a young Canadian of immense energy and profound analytical gifts. Quite unlike the shy and reserved British dons, Johnson was friendly, effusive, and supportive of students who flocked around him. He would later move to Chicago, where he became one of the most influential members of the market-oriented Chicago school. Another was Joan Robinson, arguably the world's most impressive female economist.

When I left Cambridge for MIT, going from one Cambridge to the other, I was lucky to transition from one phenomenal set of economists to another. At MIT, I learned much from future Nobel laureates Paul Samuelson and Robert Solow. Both would later become great friends and colleagues when I joined the MIT faculty in 1968.

After Cambridge and MIT, you went to Oxford and then back to India. What did you do in India?

I joined the Planning Commission in New Delhi, where my first big job was to find ways of raising the bottom 30 percent of India's population out of poverty to a "minimum income" level.

And what did you prescribe?

My main prescription was to "grow the pie." My research suggested that the share of the bottom 30 percent of the pie did not seem to vary dramatically with differences in economic and political systems. So growth in the pie seemed to be the principal (but not the only) component of an anti-poverty strategy. To supplement growth's good effects on the poor, the Indian planners were also dedicated to education, health, social reforms, and land reforms. Also, the access of the lowest-income and socially disadvantaged groups to the growth process and its benefits was to be improved in many ways, such as extension of credit without collateral.

Today, this strategy has no rivals. Much empirical work shows that where growth has occurred, poverty has lessened. It is nice to know that one's basic take on an issue of such central importance to humanity's well-being has been borne out by experience!

You left India in 1968 to come to the United States and an academic job at MIT. Why?

While the decision to emigrate often reflects personal factors—and they were present in my case—the offer of a professorship from MIT certainly helped me make up my mind. At the time, it was easily the world's most celebrated department. Serendipitously, the highest-ranked departments at MIT were not in engineering and the sciences but in linguistics (which had Noam Chomsky) and economics (which had Paul Samuelson). Joining the MIT faculty was a dramatic breakthrough: I felt stimulated each year by several fantastic students and by several of the world's most creative economists.

We hear a lot in the popular press about fair trade and level playing fields. What's the distinction between free trade and fair trade? How can the playing field be unlevel?

Free trade simply means allowing no trade barriers such as tariffs, subsidies, and quotas. Trade barriers

> My main prescription was to "grow the pie" ... Today, this strategy has no rivals. Much empirical work shows that where growth has occurred, poverty has lessened.

> Fair trade ... is almost always a sneaky way of objecting to free trade.

make domestic prices different from world prices for traded goods. When this happens, resources are not being used efficiently. Basic economics from the time of Adam Smith tells us why free trade is good for us and why barriers to trade harm us, though our understanding of this doctrine today is far more nuanced and profound than it was at its creation.

Fair trade, on the other hand, is almost always a sneaky way of objecting to free trade. If your rivals are hard to compete with, you are not likely to get protection simply by saying that you cannot hack it. But if you say that your rival is an "unfair" trader, that is an easier sell! As international competition has grown fiercer, cries of "unfair trade" have therefore multiplied. The lesser rogues among the protectionists ask for "free and fair trade," whereas the worst ones ask for "fair, not free, trade."

At the end of World War II, the General Agreement of Tariffs and Trade (GATT) was established and there followed several rounds of multilateral trade negotiations and reductions in barriers to trade. How do you assess the contribution of GATT and its successor, the World Trade Organization (WTO)?

The GATT has made a huge contribution by overseeing massive trade liberalization in industrial goods among the developed countries. GATT rules, which "bind" tariffs to negotiated ceilings, prevent the raising of tariffs and have prevented tariff wars like those of the 1930s in which mutual and retaliatory tariff barriers were raised, to the detriment of everyone.

The GATT was folded into the WTO at the end of the Uruguay Round of trade negotiations, and the WTO is institutionally stronger. For instance, it has a binding dispute settlement mechanism, whereas the GATT had no such teeth. It is also more ambitious in its scope, extending to new areas such as the environment, intellectual property protection, and investment rules.

Running alongside the pursuit of multilateral free trade has been the emergence of bilateral trade agreements such as NAFTA and the European Union (EU). How do you view the bilateral free trade areas in today's world?

We now have a world of uncoordinated and inefficient trade policies.

Unfortunately, there has been an explosion of bilateral free trade areas today. By some estimates, the ones in place and others being plotted approach 400! Each bilateral agreement gives preferential treatment to its trading partner over others. Because there are now so many bilateral agreements, such as those between the United States and Israel and between the United States and Jordan, the result is a chaotic pattern of different tariffs depending on where a product comes from. Also, "rules of origin" must be agreed upon to determine whether a product is, say, Jordanian or Taiwanese if Jordan qualifies for a preferential tariff but Taiwan does not and Taiwanese inputs enter the Jordanian manufacture of the product.

I have called the resulting crisscrossing of preferences and rules of origin the "spaghetti bowl" problem. The world trading system is choking under these proliferating bilateral deals. Contrast this complexity with the simplicity of a multilateral system with common tariffs for all WTO members.

We now have a world of uncoordinated and inefficient trade policies. The EU makes bilateral free trade agreements with different non-EU countries, so the United States follows with its own bilateral agreements; and with Europe and the United States doing it, the Asian countries, long wedded to multilateralism, have now succumbed to the mania.

Instead, if the United States had provided leadership by rewriting rules to make the signing of such bilateral agreements extremely difficult, this plague on the trading system today might well have been averted.

Despite the benefits that economics points to from multilateral free trade, the main organization that pursues this goal, the WTO, is having a very hard time with the anti-globalization movement. What can we say about globalization that puts the WTO and its work in proper perspective?

The anti-globalization movement contains a diverse set of activists. Essentially, they all claim to be stakeholders in the globalization phenomenon. But there are those who want to drive a stake through the system, as in Dracula films, and there are those who want to exercise their stake in the system. The former want to be heard; the latter, to be listened to. For a while, the two disparate sets of critics were milling around together, seeking targets of opportunity at international conferences such as WTO's November 2000 meeting in Seattle, where the riots broke out. Now things have settled down, and the groups that want to work systematically and seriously at improving the global economy's functioning are much more in play.

But the WTO is also seen, inaccurately for the most part, as imposing trade sanctions that override concerns such as environmental protection. For example, U.S. legislation bans the importing of shrimp that is harvested without the use of turtle-excluding devices. India and others complained, but the WTO upheld the U.S. legislation. Ignorant of the facts, demonstrators took to the streets dressed as turtles protesting the WTO decision!

What advice do you have for a student who is just starting to study economics? Is economics a good subject in which to major?

I would say: enormously so. In particular, we economists bring three unique insights to good policy making.

First, economists look for second- and subsequent-round effects of actions.

Second, we correctly emphasize that a policy cannot be judged without using a counterfactual. It is a witticism that an economist, when asked how her husband was, said, "compared to what?"

Third, we uniquely and systematically bring the principle of social cost and social benefit to our policy analysis.

3 Demand and Supply

After studying this chapter,
you will be able to

■ Describe a competitive market and think about price as an opportunity cost

■ Explain the influences on demand

■ Explain the influences on supply

■ Explain how demand and supply determine prices and quantities bought and sold

■ Use the demand and supply model to make predictions about changes in prices and quantities

What makes the prices of oil and gasoline
double in just one year? Will these prices keep on rising? Are the oil companies taking advantage of people? This chapter enables you to answer these and similar questions about prices—prices that rise, prices that fall, and prices that fluctuate.

You already know that economics is about the choices people make to cope with scarcity and how those choices respond to incentives. Prices act as incentives. You're going to see how people respond to prices and how prices get determined by demand and supply. The demand and supply model that you study in this chapter is the main tool of economics. It helps us to answer the big economic question: What, how,

and for whom are goods and services produced? It also helps us to say more about what it takes for the pursuit of self-interest to promote the social interest.

At the end of the chapter, in *Reading Between the Lines*, we'll apply the model to the market for gasoline and explain why the price is expected to rise again by 2010.

◆ Markets and Prices

When you need a new pair of running shoes, want a bagel and a latte, plan to upgrade your cell phone, or need to fly home for Thanksgiving, you must find a place where people sell those items or offer those services. The place in which you find them is a *market*. You learned in Chapter 2 (p. 44) that a market is any arrangement that enables buyers and sellers to get information and to do business with each other.

A market has two sides: buyers and sellers. There are markets for *goods* such as apples and hiking boots, for *services* such as haircuts and tennis lessons, for *resources* such as computer programmers and earth-movers, and for other manufactured *inputs* such as memory chips and auto parts. There are also markets for money such as Japanese yen and for financial securities such as Yahoo! stock. Only our imagination limits what can be traded in markets.

Some markets are physical places where buyers and sellers meet and where an auctioneer or a broker helps to determine the prices. Examples of this type of market are live car auction markets and wholesale fish, meat, and produce markets.

Some markets are groups of people spread around the world who never meet and know little about each other but are connected through the Internet or by telephone and fax. Examples are the e-commerce markets and the markets for foreign currency.

But most markets are unorganized collections of buyers and sellers. You do most of your trading in this type of market. An example is the market for basketball shoes. The buyers in this $3 billion-a-year market are the 45 million North Americans who play basketball (or who want to make a fashion statement). The sellers are the tens of thousands of retail sports equipment and footwear stores. Each buyer can visit several different stores, and each seller knows that the buyer has a choice of stores.

Markets vary in the intensity of competition that buyers and sellers face. In this chapter, we're going to study a **competitive market**—a market that has many buyers and many sellers, so no single buyer or seller can influence the price.

Producers offer items for sale only if the price is high enough to cover their opportunity cost. And consumers respond to changing opportunity cost by seeking cheaper alternatives to expensive items.

We are going to study how people respond to *prices* and the forces that determine prices. But to pursue these tasks, we need to understand the relationship between a price and an opportunity cost.

In everyday life, the *price* of an object is the number of dollars that must be given up in exchange for it. Economists refer to this price as the **money price**.

The *opportunity cost* of an action is the highest-valued alternative forgone. If, when you buy a cup of coffee, the highest-valued thing you forgo is some gum, then the opportunity cost of the coffee is the *quantity* of gum forgone. We can calculate the quantity of gum forgone from the money prices of the coffee and the gum.

If the money price of coffee is $2 a cup and the money price of gum is $1 a pack, then the opportunity cost of one cup of coffee is two packs of gum. To calculate this opportunity cost, we divide the price of a cup of coffee by the price of a pack of gum and find the *ratio* of one price to the other. The ratio of one price to another is called a **relative price**, and a *relative price is an opportunity cost.*

We can express the relative price of coffee in terms of gum or any other good. The normal way of expressing a relative price is in terms of a "basket" of all goods and services. To calculate this relative price, we divide the money price of a good by the money price of a "basket" of all goods (called a *price index*). The resulting relative price tells us the opportunity cost of the good in terms of how much of the "basket" we must give up to buy it.

The demand and supply model that we are about to study determines *relative prices*, and the word "price" means *relative* price. When we predict that a price will fall, we do not mean that its *money* price will fall—although it might. We mean that its *relative* price will fall. That is, its price will fall *relative* to the average price of other goods and services.

Review Quiz ◆

1 What is the distinction between a money price and a relative price?
2 Explain why a relative price is an opportunity cost.
3 Think of examples of goods whose relative price has risen or fallen by a large amount.

 Work Study Plan 3.1 and get instant feedback.

Let's begin our study of demand and supply, starting with demand.

◆ Demand

If you demand something, then you

1. Want it,
2. Can afford it, and
3. Plan to buy it.

Wants are the unlimited desires or wishes that people have for goods and services. How many times have you thought that you would like something "if only you could afford it" or "if it weren't so expensive"? Scarcity guarantees that many—perhaps most—of our wants will never be satisfied. Demand reflects a decision about which wants to satisfy.

The **quantity demanded** of a good or service is the amount that consumers plan to buy during a given time period at a particular price. The quantity demanded is not necessarily the same as the quantity actually bought. Sometimes the quantity demanded exceeds the amount of goods available, so the quantity bought is less than the quantity demanded.

The quantity demanded is measured as an amount per unit of time. For example, suppose that you buy one cup of coffee a day. The quantity of coffee that you demand can be expressed as 1 cup per day, 7 cups per week, or 365 cups per year.

Many factors influence buying plans, and one of them is the price. We look first at the relationship between the quantity demanded of a good and its price. To study this relationship, we keep all other influences on buying plans the same and we ask: How, other things remaining the same, does the quantity demanded of a good change as its price changes?

The law of demand provides the answer.

The Law of Demand

The **law of demand** states

> Other things remaining the same, the higher the price of a good, the smaller is the quantity demanded; and the lower the price of a good, the greater is the quantity demanded.

Why does a higher price reduce the quantity demanded? For two reasons:

- Substitution effect
- Income effect

Substitution Effect When the price of a good rises, other things remaining the same, its *relative* price—its opportunity cost—rises. Although each good is unique, it has *substitutes*—other goods that can be used in its place. As the opportunity cost of a good rises, the incentive to economize on its use and switch to a substitute becomes stronger.

Income Effect When a price rises, other things remaining the same, the price rises *relative* to income. Faced with a higher price and an unchanged income, people cannot afford to buy all the things they previously bought. They must decrease the quantities demanded of at least some goods and services. Normally, the good whose price has increased will be one of the goods that people buy less of.

To see the substitution effect and the income effect at work, think about the effects of a change in the price of an energy bar. Several different goods are substitutes for an energy bar. For example, an energy drink could be consumed instead of an energy bar.

Suppose that an energy bar initially sells for $3 and then its price falls to $1.50. People now substitute energy bars for energy drinks—the substitution effect. And with a budget that now has some slack from the lower price of an energy bar, people buy even more energy bars—the income effect. The quantity of energy bars demanded increases for these two reasons.

Now suppose that an energy bar initially sells for $3 and then the price doubles to $6. People now buy fewer energy bars and more energy drinks—the substitution effect. And faced with a tighter budget, people buy even fewer energy bars—the income effect. The quantity of energy bars demanded decreases for these two reasons.

Demand Curve and Demand Schedule

You are now about to study one of the two most used curves in economics: the demand curve. And you are going to encounter one of the most critical distinctions: the distinction between *demand* and *quantity demanded*.

The term **demand** refers to the entire relationship between the price of a good and the quantity demanded of that good. Demand is illustrated by the demand curve and the demand schedule. The term *quantity demanded* refers to a point on a demand curve—the quantity demanded at a particular price.

Figure 3.1 shows the demand curve for energy bars. A **demand curve** shows the relationship between the quantity demanded of a good and its price when all other influences on consumers' planned purchases remain the same.

The table in Fig. 3.1 is the demand schedule for energy bars. A *demand schedule* lists the quantities demanded at each price when all the other influences on consumers' planned purchases remain the same. For example, if the price of a bar is 50¢, the quantity demanded is 22 million a week. If the price is $2.50, the quantity demanded is 5 million a week. The other rows of the table show the quantities demanded at prices of $1.00, $1.50, and $2.00.

We graph the demand schedule as a demand curve with the quantity demanded on the x-axis and the price on the y-axis. The points on the demand curve labelled A through E correspond to the rows of the demand schedule. For example, point A on the graph shows a quantity demanded of 22 million energy bars a week at a price of 50¢ a bar.

Willingness and Ability to Pay   Another way of looking at the demand curve is as a willingness-and-ability-to-pay curve. The willingness and ability to pay is a measure of *marginal benefit.*

If a small quantity is available, the highest price that someone is willing and able to pay for one more unit is high. But as the quantity available increases, the marginal benefit of each additional unit falls and the highest price that someone is willing and able to pay also falls along the demand curve.

In Fig. 3.1, if only 5 million energy bars are available each week, the highest price that someone is willing to pay for the 5 millionth bar is $2.50. But if 22 million energy bars are available each week, someone is willing to pay 50¢ for the last bar bought.

A Change in Demand

When any factor that influences buying plans other than the price of the good changes, there is a **change in demand**. Figure 3.2 illustrates an increase in demand. When demand increases, the demand curve shifts rightward and the quantity demanded at each price is greater. For example, at $2.50 a bar, the quantity demanded on the original (blue) demand curve is 5 million energy bars a week. On the new (red) demand curve, at $2.50 a bar, the quantity demanded is 15 million bars a week. Look closely at the numbers in the table and check that the quantity demanded at each price is greater.

FIGURE 3.1   The Demand Curve

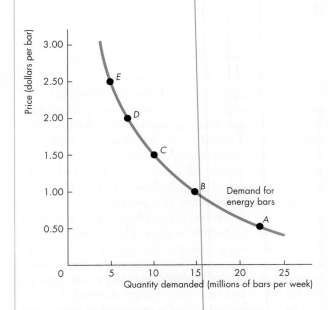

	Price (dollars per bar)	Quantity demanded (millions of bars per week)
A	0.50	22
B	1.00	15
C	1.50	10
D	2.00	7
E	2.50	5

The table shows a demand schedule for energy bars. At a price of 50¢ a bar, 22 million bars a week are demanded; at a price of $1.50 a bar, 10 million bars a week are demanded. The demand curve shows the relationship between quantity demanded and price, other things remaining the same. The demand curve slopes downward: As the price decreases, the quantity demanded increases.

The demand curve can be read in two ways. For a given price, the demand curve tells us the quantity that people plan to buy. For example, at a price of $1.50 a bar, people plan to buy 10 million bars a week. For a given quantity, the demand curve tells us the maximum price that consumers are willing and able to pay for the last bar available. For example, the maximum price that consumers will pay for the 15 millionth bar is $1.00.

FIGURE 3.2   An Increase in Demand

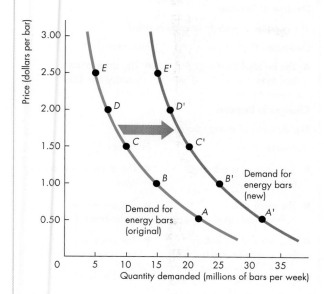

A change in any influence on buyers' plans other than the price of the good itself results in a new demand schedule and a shift of the demand curve. A change in income changes the demand for energy bars. At a price of $1.50 a bar, 10 million bars a week are demanded at the original income (row C of the table) and 20 million bars a week are demanded at the new higher income (row C'). A rise in income increases the demand for energy bars. The demand curve shifts rightward, as shown by the shift arrow and the resulting red curve.

Original demand schedule Original income		New demand schedule New higher income	
Price (dollars per bar)	**Quantity demanded** (millions of bars per week)	**Price** (dollars per bar)	**Quantity demanded** (millions of bars per week)
A 0.50	22	A' 0.50	32
B 1.00	15	B' 1.00	25
C 1.50	10	C' 1.50	20
D 2.00	7	D' 2.00	17
E 2.50	5	E' 2.50	15

Six main factors bring changes in demand. They are changes in

- The prices of related goods
- Expected future prices
- Income
- Expected future income and credit
- Population
- Preferences

Prices of Related Goods The quantity of energy bars that consumers plan to buy depends in part on the prices of substitutes for energy bars. A **substitute** is a good that can be used in place of another good. For example, a bus ride is a substitute for a train ride; a hamburger is a substitute for a hot dog; and an energy drink is a substitute for an energy bar. If the price of a substitute for an energy bar rises, people buy less of the substitute and more energy bars. For example, if the price of an energy drink rises, people buy fewer energy drinks and more energy bars. The demand for energy bars increases.

The quantity of energy bars that people plan to buy also depends on the prices of complements with energy bars. A **complement** is a good that is used in conjunction with another good. Hamburgers and fries are complements, and so are energy bars and exercise. If the price of an hour at the gym falls, people buy more gym time *and more* energy bars.

Expected Future Prices If the price of a good is expected to rise in the future and if the good can be stored, the opportunity cost of obtaining the good for future use is lower today than it will be when the price has increased. So people retime their purchases—they substitute over time. They buy more of the good now before its price is expected to rise (and less afterward), so the demand for the good today increases.

For example, suppose that a Florida frost damages the season's orange crop. You expect the price of orange juice to rise, so you fill your freezer with enough frozen juice to get you through the next six months. Your current demand for frozen orange juice has increased, and your future demand has decreased.

Similarly, if the price of a good is expected to fall in the future, the opportunity cost of buying the good today is high relative to what it is expected to be in the future. So again, people retime their purchases. They buy less of the good now before its price falls, so the demand for the good decreases today and increases in the future.

Computer prices are constantly falling, and this fact poses a dilemma. Will you buy a new computer now, in time for the start of the school year, or will you wait until the price has fallen some more? Because people expect computer prices to fall, the current demand for computers is less (and the future demand is greater) than it otherwise would be.

Income Consumers' income influences demand. When income increases, consumers buy more of most goods; and when income decreases, consumers buy less of most goods. Although an increase in income leads to an increase in the demand for *most* goods, it does not lead to an increase in the demand for *all* goods. A **normal good** is one for which demand increases as income increases. An **inferior good** is one for which demand decreases as income increases. As incomes increase, the demand for air travel (a normal good) increases and the demand for long-distance bus trips (an inferior good) decreases.

Expected Future Income and Credit When income is expected to increase in the future, or when credit is easy to obtain, demand might increase now. For example, a salesperson gets the news that she will receive a big bonus at the end of the year, so she goes into debt and buys a new car right now.

Population Demand also depends on the size and the age structure of the population. The larger the population, the greater is the demand for all goods and services; the smaller the population, the smaller is the demand for all goods and services.

For example, the demand for parking spaces or movies or just about anything that you can imagine is much greater in the Greater Toronto Area (population 5.6 million) than it is in Thunder Bay (population 124,000).

Also, the larger the proportion of the population in a given age group, the greater is the demand for the goods and services used by that age group.

For example, in 2007, there were 2.3 million 20- to 24-year-olds in Canada compared with 2.4 million in 1987. As a result, the demand for university places in 2007 was similar to what it was in 1987. Over this same period, the number of Canadians age 85 years and over increased by 313,000. As a result, the demand for nursing home services increased.

TABLE 3.1 The Demand for Energy Bars

The Law of Demand

The quantity of energy bars demanded

Decreases if:	Increases if:
■ The price of an energy bar rises	■ The price of an energy bar falls

Changes in Demand

The demand of energy bars

Decreases if:	Increases if:
■ The price of a substitute falls	■ The price of a substitute rises
■ The price of a complement rises	■ The price of a complement falls
■ The price of an energy bar is expected to fall	■ The price of an energy bar is expected to rise
■ Income falls*	■ Income rises*
■ Expected future income falls or credit becomes harder to get	■ Expected future income rises or credit becomes easier to get
■ The population decreases	■ The population increases

*An energy bar is a normal good.

Preferences Demand depends on preferences. *Preferences* determine the value that people place on each good and service. Preferences depend on such things as the weather, information, and fashion. For example, greater health and fitness awareness has shifted preferences in favour of energy bars, so the demand for energy bars has increased.

Table 3.1 summarizes the influences on demand and the direction of those influences.

A Change in the Quantity Demanded Versus a Change in Demand

Changes in the influences on buyers' plans bring either a change in the quantity demanded or a change in demand. Equivalently, they bring either a movement along the demand curve or a shift of the demand curve. The distinction between a change in the quantity demanded and a change in demand is the same as that between a movement along the demand curve and a shift of the demand curve.

A point on the demand curve shows the quantity demanded at a given price. So a movement along the demand curve shows a **change in the quantity demanded**. The entire demand curve shows demand. So a shift of the demand curve shows a *change in demand*. Figure 3.3 illustrates these distinctions.

Movement Along the Demand Curve   If the price of the good changes but no other influence on buying plans changes, we illustrate the effect as a movement along the demand curve.

A fall in the price of a good increases the quantity demanded of it. In Fig. 3.3, we illustrate the effect of a fall in price of the good as a movement down along the demand curve D_0.

A rise in the price of a good decreases the quantity demanded of it. In Fig. 3.3, we illustrate the effect of a rise in price of the good as a movement up along the demand curve D_0.

A Shift of the Demand Curve   If the price of a good remains constant but some other influence on buyers' plans changes, there is a change in demand for that good. We illustrate a change in demand as a shift of the demand curve. For example, if more people work out at the gym, consumers buy more energy bars regardless of the price of a bar. That is what a rightward shift of the demand curve shows—more energy bars are demanded at each price.

In Fig. 3.3, there is a *change in demand* and the demand curve shifts when any influence on buyers' plans change, other than the price of the good. Demand *increases* and the demand curve *shifts rightward* (to the red demand curve D_1) if the price of a substitute rises, the price of a complement falls, the expected future price of the good rises, income increases (for a normal good), expected future income or credit increases, or the population increases. Demand *decreases* and the demand curve *shifts leftward* (to the red demand curve D_2) if the price of a substitute falls, the price of a complement rises, the expected future price of the good falls, income decreases (for a normal good), expected future income or credit decreases, or the population decreases. (For an inferior good, the effects of changes in income are in the opposite direction to those described above.)

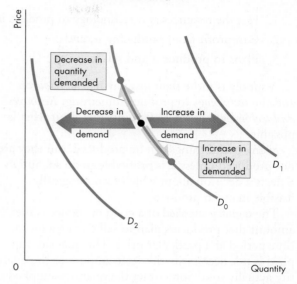

FIGURE 3.3   A Change in the Quantity Demanded Versus a Change in Demand

When the price of the good changes, there is a movement along the demand curve and *a change in the quantity demanded,* shown by the blue arrows on demand curve D_0. When any other influence on buyers' plans changes, there is a shift of the demand curve and a *change in demand.* An increase in demand shifts the demand curve rightward (from D_0 to D_1). A decrease in demand shifts the demand curve leftward (from D_0 to D_2).

 animation

Review Quiz

1   Define the quantity demanded of a good or service.
2   What is the law of demand and how do we illustrate it?
3   What does the demand curve tell us about the price that consumers are willing to pay?
4   List all the influences on buying plans that change demand, and for each influence, say whether it increases or decreases demand.
5   Why does demand not change when the price of a good changes with no change in the other influences on buying plans?

myeconlab   Work Study Plan 3.2 and get instant feedback.

Supply

If a firm supplies a good or service, the firm

1. Has the resources and technology to produce it,
2. Can profit from producing it, and
3. Plans to produce it and sell it.

A supply is more than just having the *resources* and the *technology* to produce something. *Resources and technology* are the constraints that limit what is possible.

Many useful things can be produced, but they are not produced unless it is profitable to do so. Supply reflects a decision about which technologically feasible items to produce.

The **quantity supplied** of a good or service is the amount that producers plan to sell during a given time period at a particular price. The quantity supplied is not necessarily the same amount as the quantity actually sold. Sometimes the quantity supplied is greater than the quantity demanded, so the quantity sold is less than the quantity supplied.

Like the quantity demanded, the quantity supplied is measured as an amount per unit of time. For example, suppose that GM produces 1,000 cars a day. The quantity of cars supplied by GM can be expressed as 1,000 a day, 7,000 a week, or 365,000 a year. Without the time dimension, we cannot tell whether a particular quantity is large or small.

Many factors influence selling plans, and again one of them is the price of the good. We look first at the relationship between the quantity supplied of a good and its price. Just as we did when we studied demand, to isolate the relationship between the quantity supplied of a good and its price, we keep all other influences on selling plans the same and ask: How does the quantity supplied of a good change as its price changes when other things remain the same?

The law of supply provides the answer.

The Law of Supply

The **law of supply** states:

> Other things remaining the same, the higher the price of a good, the greater is the quantity supplied; and the lower the price of a good, the smaller is the quantity supplied.

Why does a higher price increase the quantity supplied? It is because *marginal cost increases.* As the quantity produced of any good increases, the marginal cost of producing the good increases. (You can refresh your memory of increasing marginal cost in Chapter 2, p. 35.)

It is never worth producing a good if the price received for the good does not at least cover the marginal cost of producing it. When the price of a good rises, other things remaining the same, producers are willing to incur a higher marginal cost, so they increase production. The higher price brings forth an increase in the quantity supplied.

Let's now illustrate the law of supply with a supply curve and a supply schedule.

Supply Curve and Supply Schedule

You are now going to study the second of the two most used curves in economics: the supply curve. And you're going to learn about the critical distinction between *supply* and *quantity supplied.*

The term **supply** refers to the entire relationship between the price of a good and the quantity supplied of it. Supply is illustrated by the supply curve and the supply schedule. The term *quantity supplied* refers to a point on a supply curve—the quantity supplied at a particular price.

Figure 3.4 shows the supply curve of energy bars. A **supply curve** shows the relationship between the quantity supplied of a good and its price when all other influences on producers' planned sales remain the same. The supply curve is a graph of a supply schedule.

The table in Fig. 3.4 sets out the supply schedule for energy bars. A *supply schedule* lists the quantities supplied at each price when all the other influences on producers' planned sales remain the same. For example, if the price of a bar is 50¢, the quantity supplied is zero—in row *A* of the table. If the price of a bar is $1.00, the quantity supplied is 6 million energy bars a week—in row *B*. The other rows of the table show the quantities supplied at prices of $1.50, $2.00, and $2.50.

To make a supply curve, we graph the quantity supplied on the *x*-axis and the price on the *y*-axis, just as in the case of the demand curve. The points on the supply curve labelled *A* through *E* correspond to the rows of the supply schedule. For example, point *A* on the graph shows a quantity supplied of zero at a price of 50¢ an energy bar.

FIGURE 3.4   The Supply Curve

	Price (dollars per bar)	Quantity supplied (millions of bars per week)
A	0.50	0
B	1.00	6
C	1.50	10
D	2.00	13
E	2.50	15

The table shows the supply schedule of energy bars. For example, at a price of $1.00, 6 million bars a week are supplied; at a price of $2.50, 15 million bars a week are supplied. The supply curve shows the relationship between the quantity supplied and the price, other things remaining the same. The supply curve slopes upward: As the price of a good increases, the quantity supplied increases.

A supply curve can be read in two ways. For a given price, the supply curve tells us the quantity that producers plan to sell at that price. For example, at a price of $1.50 a bar, producers are willing to sell 10 million bars a week. For a given quantity, the supply curve tells us the minimum price at which producers are willing to sell one more bar. For example, if 15 million bars are produced each week, the lowest price at which a producer is willing to sell the 15 millionth bar is $2.50.

myeconlab animation

Minimum Supply Price   The supply curve can be interpreted as a minimum-supply-price curve—a curve that shows the lowest price at which someone is willing to sell. This lowest price is the *marginal cost.*

If a small quantity is produced, the lowest price at which someone is willing to sell one more unit is low. But as the quantity produced increases, the marginal cost of each additional unit rises, so the lowest price at which someone is willing to sell one more unit rises along the supply curve.

In Fig. 3.4, if 15 million bars are produced each week, the lowest price at which someone is willing to sell the 15 millionth bar is $2.50. But if 10 million bars are produced each week, someone is willing to accept $1.50 for the last bar produced.

A Change in Supply

When any factor that influences selling plans other than the price of the good changes, there is a **change in supply**. Six main factors bring changes in supply. They are changes in

- The prices of factors of production
- The prices of related goods produced
- Expected future prices
- The number of suppliers
- Technology
- The state of nature

Prices of Factors of Production   The prices of the factors of production used to produce a good influence its supply. To see this influence, think about the supply curve as a minimum-supply-price curve. If the price of a factor of production rises, the lowest price that a producer is willing to accept for that good rises, so supply of the good decreases. For example, during 2008, as the price of jet fuel increased, the supply of air service decreased. Similarly, a rise in the minimum wage decreases the supply of hamburgers.

Prices of Related Goods Produced   The prices of related goods that firms produce influence supply. For example, if the price of energy gel rises, firms switch production from bar to gel. The supply of energy bars decreases. Energy bars and energy gel are *substitutes in production*—goods that can be produced by using the same resources. If the price of beef rises, the supply of cowhide increases. Beef and cowhide are *complements in production*—goods that must be produced together.

Expected Future Prices If the price of a good is expected to rise, the return from selling the good in the future is higher than it is today. So supply decreases today and increases in the future.

The Number of Suppliers The larger the number of firms that produce a good, the greater is the supply of the good. And as firms enter an industry, the supply in that industry increases. As firms leave an industry, the supply in that industry decreases.

Technology The term "technology" is used broadly to mean the way that factors of production are used to produce a good. A technology change occurs when a new method is discovered that lowers the cost of producing a good. For example, new methods used in the factories that produce computer chips have lowered the cost and increased the supply of chips.

The State of Nature The state of nature includes all the natural forces that influence production. It includes the state of the weather and, more broadly, the natural environment. Good weather can increase the supply of many agricultural products and bad weather can decrease their supply. Extreme natural events such as earthquakes, tornadoes, and hurricanes can also influence supply.

Figure 3.5 illustrates an increase in supply. When supply increases, the supply curve shifts rightward and the quantity supplied at each price is larger. For example, at $1.00 per bar, on the original (blue) supply curve, the quantity supplied is 6 million bars a week. On the new (red) supply curve, the quantity supplied is 15 million bars a week. Look closely at the numbers in the table in Fig. 3.5 and check that the quantity supplied is larger at each price.

Table 3.2 summarizes the influences on supply and the directions of those influences.

A Change in the Quantity Supplied Versus a Change in Supply

Changes in the influences on producers' planned sales bring either a change in the quantity supplied or a change in supply. Equivalently, they bring either a movement along the supply curve or a shift of the supply curve.

A point on the supply curve shows the quantity supplied of a good at a given price. A movement along the supply curve shows a **change in the quantity supplied**. The entire supply curve shows supply. A shift of the supply curve shows a *change in supply*.

FIGURE 3.5   An Increase in Supply

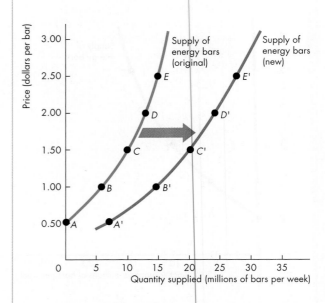

Original supply schedule Old technology			New supply schedule New technology		
	Price (dollars per bar)	Quantity supplied (millions of bars per week)		Price (dollars per bar)	Quantity supplied (millions of bars per week)
A	0.50	0	A'	0.50	7
B	1.00	6	B'	1.00	15
C	1.50	10	C'	1.50	20
D	2.00	13	D'	2.00	25
E	2.50	15	E'	2.50	27

A change in any influence on sellers' plans other than the price of the good itself results in a new supply schedule and a shift of the supply curve. For example, a new, cost-saving technology for producing energy bars changes the supply of energy bars. At a price of $1.50 a bar, 10 million bars a week are supplied when producers use the old technology (row C of the table) and 20 million energy bars a week are supplied when producers use the new technology (row C'). An advance in technology *increases* the supply of energy bars. The supply curve shifts *rightward*, as shown by the shift arrow and the resulting red curve.

Figure 3.6 illustrates and summarizes these distinctions. If the price of the good falls and other things remain the same, the quantity supplied of that good decreases and there is a movement down along the supply curve S_0. If the price of the good rises and other things remain the same, the quantity supplied of that good increases and there is a movement up along the supply curve S_0. When any other influence on selling plans changes, the supply curve shifts and there is a *change in supply*. If supply increases, the supply curve shifts rightward to S_1. If supply decreases, the supply curve shifts leftward to S_2.

TABLE 3.2   The Supply of Energy Bars

The Law of Supply

The quantity of energy bars supplied

Decreases if:	*Increases if:*
■ The price of an energy bar falls	■ The price of an energy bar rises

Changes in Supply

The supply of energy bars

Decreases if:	*Increases if:*
■ The price of a factor of production used to produce energy bars rises	■ The price of a factor of production used to produce energy bars falls
■ The price of a substitute in production rises	■ The price of a substitute in production falls
■ The price of a complement in production falls	■ The price of a complement in production rises
■ The price of an energy bar is expected to rise	■ The price of an energy bar is expected to fall
■ The number of suppliers of bars decreases	■ The number of suppliers of bars increases
■ A technology change decreases energy bar production	■ A technology change increases energy bar production
■ A natural event decreases energy bar production	■ A natural event increases energy bar production

FIGURE 3.6   A Change in the Quantity Supplied Versus a Change in Supply

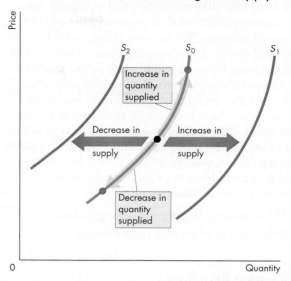

When the price of the good changes, there is a movement along the supply curve and *a change in the quantity supplied*, shown by the blue arrows on supply curve S_0. When any other influence on selling plans changes, there is a shift of the supply curve and a *change in supply*. An increase in supply shifts the supply curve rightward (from S_0 to S_1), and a decrease in supply shifts the supply curve leftward (from S_0 to S_2).

 animation

Review Quiz

1   Define the quantity supplied of a good or service.
2   What is the law of supply and how do we illustrate it?
3   What does the supply curve tell us about the producer's minimum supply price?
4   List all the influences on selling plans, and for each influence, say whether it changes supply.
5   What happens to the quantity of cell phones supplied and the supply of cell phones if the price of a cell phone falls?

myeconlab Work Study Plan 3.3 and get instant feedback.

Now we're going to combine demand and supply and see how prices and quantities are determined.

Market Equilibrium

We have seen that when the price of a good rises, the quantity demanded *decreases* and the quantity supplied *increases*. We are now going to see how the price adjusts to coordinate the plans of buyers and sellers and achieve an equilibrium in the market.

An *equilibrium* is a situation in which opposing forces balance each other. Equilibrium in a market occurs when the price balances the plans of buyers and sellers. The **equilibrium price** is the price at which the quantity demanded equals the quantity supplied. The **equilibrium quantity** is the quantity bought and sold at the equilibrium price. A market moves towards its equilibrium because

- Price regulates buying and selling plans.
- Price adjusts when plans don't match.

Price as a Regulator

The price of a good regulates the quantities demanded and supplied. If the price is too high, the quantity supplied exceeds the quantity demanded. If the price is too low, the quantity demanded exceeds the quantity supplied. There is one price at which the quantity demanded equals the quantity supplied. Let's work out what that price is.

Figure 3.7 shows the market for energy bars. The table shows the demand schedule (from Fig. 3.1) and the supply schedule (from Fig. 3.4). If the price of a bar is 50¢, the quantity demanded is 22 million bars a week but no bars are supplied. There is a shortage of 22 million bars a week. This shortage is shown in the final column of the table. At a price of $1.00 a bar, there is still a shortage, but only of 9 million bars a week. If the price of a bar is $2.50, the quantity supplied is 15 million bars a week but the quantity demanded is only 5 million. There is a surplus of 10 million bars a week. The one price at which there is neither a shortage nor a surplus is $1.50 a bar. At that price, the quantity demanded is equal to the quantity supplied: 10 million bars a week. The equilibrium price is $1.50 a bar, and the equilibrium quantity is 10 million bars a week.

Figure 3.7 shows that the demand curve and the supply curve intersect at the equilibrium price of $1.50 a bar. At each price *above* $1.50 a bar, there is a surplus of bars. For example, at $2.00 a bar, the surplus is 6 million bars a week, as shown by the blue arrow.

FIGURE 3.7   Equilibrium

Price (dollars per bar)	Quantity demanded	Quantity supplied	Shortage (−) or surplus (+)
	(millions of bars per week)		
0.50	22	0	−22
1.00	15	6	−9
1.50	10	10	0
2.00	7	13	+6
2.50	5	15	+10

The table lists the quantity demanded and the quantity supplied as well as the shortage or surplus of bars at each price. If the price is $1.00 a bar, 15 million bars a week are demanded and 6 million are supplied. There is a shortage of 9 million bars a week, and the price rises.

If the price is $2.00 a bar, 7 million bars a week are demanded and 13 million are supplied. There is a surplus of 6 million bars a week, and the price falls.

If the price is $1.50 a bar, 10 million bars a week are demanded and 10 million bars are supplied. There is neither a shortage nor a surplus. Neither buyers nor sellers have an incentive to change the price. The price at which the quantity demanded equals the quantity supplied is the equilibrium price. The quantity, 10 million bars a week, is the equilibrium quantity.

myeconlab   animation

At each price *below* $1.50 a bar, there is a shortage of bars. For example, at $1.00 a bar, the shortage is 9 million bars a week, as shown by the red arrow.

Price Adjustments

You've seen that if the price is below equilibrium, there is a shortage and that if the price is above equilibrium, there is a surplus. But can we count on the price to change and eliminate a shortage or a surplus? We can, because such price changes are beneficial to both buyers and sellers. Let's see why the price changes when there is a shortage or a surplus.

A Shortage Forces the Price Up   Suppose the price of an energy bar is $1. Consumers plan to buy 15 million bars a week, and producers plan to sell 6 million bars a week. Consumers can't force producers to sell more than they plan, so the quantity that is actually offered for sale is 6 million bars a week. In this situation, powerful forces operate to increase the price and move it towards the equilibrium price. Some producers, noticing lines of unsatisfied consumers, raise the price. Some producers increase their output. As producers push the price up, the price rises towards its equilibrium. The rising price reduces the shortage because it decreases the quantity demanded and increases the quantity supplied. When the price has increased to the point at which there is no longer a shortage, the forces moving the price stop operating and the price comes to rest at its equilibrium.

A Surplus Forces the Price Down   Suppose the price of a bar is $2. Producers plan to sell 13 million bars a week, and consumers plan to buy 7 million bars a week. Producers cannot force consumers to buy more than they plan, so the quantity that is actually bought is 7 million bars a week. In this situation, powerful forces operate to lower the price and move it towards the equilibrium price. Some producers, unable to sell the quantities of bars they planned to sell, cut their prices. In addition, some producers scale back production. As producers cut the price, the price falls towards its equilibrium. The falling price decreases the surplus because the quantity demanded increases and the quantity supplied decreases. When the price has fallen to the point at which there is no longer a surplus, the forces moving the price stop operating and the price comes to rest at its equilibrium.

The Best Deal Available for Buyers and Sellers   When the price is below equilibrium, it is forced upward. Why don't buyers resist the increase and refuse to buy at the higher price? Because they value the good more highly than the current price and they can't satisfy their demand at the current price. In some markets—for example, the markets that operate on eBay—the buyers might even be the ones who force the price up by offering to pay more.

When the price is above equilibrium, it is bid downward. Why don't sellers resist this decrease and refuse to sell at the lower price? Because their minimum supply price is below the current price and they cannot sell all they would like to at the current price. Normally, it is the sellers who force the price down by offering lower prices to gain market share.

At the price at which the quantity demanded and the quantity supplied are equal, neither buyers nor sellers can do business at a better price. Buyers pay the highest price they are willing to pay for the last unit bought, and sellers receive the lowest price at which they are willing to supply the last unit sold.

When people freely make offers to buy and sell and when demanders try to buy at the lowest possible price and suppliers try to sell at the highest possible price, the price at which trade takes place is the equilibrium price—the price at which the quantity demanded equals the quantity supplied. The price coordinates the plans of buyers and sellers, and no one has an incentive to change it.

Review Quiz

1   What is the equilibrium price of a good or service?
2   Over what range of prices does a shortage arise? What happens to the price when there is a shortage?
3   Over what range of prices does a surplus arise? What happens to the price when there is a surplus?
4   Why is the price at which the quantity demanded equals the quantity supplied the equilibrium price?
5   Why is the equilibrium price the best deal available for both buyers and sellers?

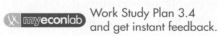 Work Study Plan 3.4 and get instant feedback.

Predicting Changes in Price and Quantity

The demand and supply model that we have just studied provides us with a powerful way of analyzing influences on prices and the quantities bought and sold. According to the model, a change in price stems from a change in demand, a change in supply, or a change in both demand and supply. Let's look first at the effects of a change in demand.

An Increase in Demand

When more and more people join health clubs, the demand for energy bars increases. The table in Fig. 3.8 shows the original and new demand schedules for energy bars (the same as those in Fig. 3.2) as well as the supply schedule of energy bars.

When demand increases, there is a shortage at the original equilibrium price of $1.50 a bar. To eliminate the shortage, the price must rise. The price that makes the quantity demanded and quantity supplied equal again is $2.50 a bar. At this price, 15 million bars are bought and sold each week. When demand increases, both the price and the quantity increase.

Figure 3.8 shows these changes. The figure shows the original demand for and supply of energy bars. The original equilibrium price is $1.50 an energy bar, and the quantity is 10 million energy bars a week. When demand increases, the demand curve shifts rightward. The equilibrium price rises to $2.50 an energy bar, and the quantity supplied increases to 15 million energy bars a week, as highlighted in the figure. There is an *increase in the quantity supplied* but *no change in supply*—a movement along, but no shift of, the supply curve.

A Decrease in Demand

We can reverse this change in demand. Start at a price of $2.50 a bar with 15 million energy bars a week being bought and sold, and then work out what happens if demand decreases to its original level. Such a decrease in demand might arise if people switch to energy gel (a substitute for energy bars). The decrease in demand shifts the demand curve leftward. The equilibrium price falls to $1.50 a bar, and the equilibrium quantity decreases to 10 million bars a week.

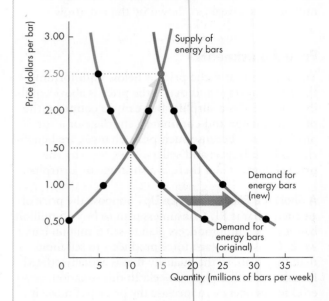

FIGURE 3.8 The Effects of a Change in Demand

Price (dollars per bar)	Quantity demanded (millions of bars per week)		Quantity supplied (millions of bars per week)
	Original	New	
0.50	22	32	0
1.00	15	25	6
1.50	**10**	**20**	**10**
2.00	7	17	13
2.50	5	15	15

Initially, the demand for energy bars is the blue demand curve. The equilibrium price is $1.50 a bar, and the equilibrium quantity is 10 million bars a week. When more health-conscious people do more exercise, the demand for energy bars increases and the demand curve shifts rightward to become the red curve.

At $1.50 a bar, there is now a shortage of 10 million bars a week. The price of a bar rises to a new equilibrium of $2.50. As the price rises to $2.50, the quantity supplied increases—shown by the blue arrow on the supply curve—to the new equilibrium quantity of 15 million bars a week. Following an increase in demand, the quantity supplied increases but supply does not change—the supply curve does not shift.

 animation

We can now make our first two predictions:

1. When demand increases, both the price and the quantity increase.
2. When demand decreases, both the price and the quantity decrease.

An Increase in Supply

When Nestlé (the producer of PowerBar) and other energy bar producers switch to a new cost-saving technology, the supply of energy bars increases. The table in Fig. 3.9 shows the new supply schedule (the same one that was shown in Fig. 3.5). What are the new equilibrium price and quantity? The price falls to $1.00 a bar, and the quantity increases to 15 million bars a week. You can see why by looking at the quantities demanded and supplied at the old price of $1.50 a bar. The quantity supplied at that price is now 20 million bars a week, and there is a surplus of bars. The price falls. Only when the price is $1.00 a bar does the quantity supplied equal the quantity demanded.

Figure 3.9 illustrates the effect of an increase in supply. It shows the demand curve for energy bars and the original and new supply curves. The initial equilibrium price is $1.50 a bar, and the quantity is 10 million bars a week. When supply increases, the supply curve shifts rightward. The equilibrium price falls to $1.00 a bar, and the quantity demanded increases to 15 million bars a week, highlighted in the figure. There is an *increase in the quantity demanded* but *no change in demand*—a movement along, but no shift of, the demand curve.

A Decrease in Supply

Start out at a price of $1.00 a bar with 15 million bars a week being bought and sold. Then suppose that the cost of labour or raw materials rises and the supply of energy bars decreases. The decrease in supply shifts the supply curve leftward. The equilibrium price rises to $1.50 a bar, and the equilibrium quantity decreases to 10 million bars a week.

We can now make two more predictions:

1. When supply increases, the quantity increases and the price falls.
2. When supply decreases, the quantity decreases and the price rises.

FIGURE 3.9 The Effects of a Change in Supply

Price (dollars per bar)	Quantity demanded (millions of bars per week)	Quantity supplied (millions of bars per week)	
		Original	New
0.50	22	0	7
1.00	15	6	15
1.50	**10**	**10**	20
2.00	7	13	25
2.50	5	15	27

Initially, the supply of energy bars is shown by the blue supply curve. The equilibrium price is $1.50 a bar, and the equilibrium quantity is 10 million bars a week. When the new cost-saving technology is adopted, the supply of energy bars increases and the supply curve shifts rightward to become the red curve.

At $1.50 a bar, there is now a surplus of 10 million bars a week. The price of an energy bar falls to a new equilibrium of $1.00 a bar. As the price falls to $1.00, the quantity demanded increases—shown by the blue arrow on the demand curve—to the new equilibrium quantity of 15 million bars a week. Following an increase in supply, the quantity demanded increases but demand does not change—the demand curve does not shift.

How Markets Interact to Reallocate Resources

Fuel, Food, and Fertilizer

The demand and supply model provides insights into all competitive markets. Here, we'll apply what you've learned to the markets for

- Crude oil
- Corn
- Fertilizers

Crude Oil

Crude oil is like the life-blood of the global economy. It is used to fuel our cars, airplanes, trains, and buses, to generate electricity, and to produce a wide range of plastics. When the price of crude oil rises, the cost of transportation, power, and materials all increase.

In 2006, the price of a barrel of oil was $50. In 2008, the price reached $135. While the price of oil has been rising, the quantity of oil produced and consumed has barely changed. Since 2006, the world has produced a steady 85 million barrels of oil a day. Who or what has been raising the price of oil? Is it the fault of greedy oil producers?

Oil producers might be greedy, and some of them might be big enough to withhold supply and raise the price, but it wouldn't be in their self-interest to do so. The higher price would bring forth a greater quantity supplied from other producers and the profit of the one limiting supply would fall.

Producers could try to cooperate and jointly withhold supply. The Organization of Petroleum Exporting Countries, OPEC, is such a group of suppliers. But OPEC doesn't control the world supply and the self-interest of each of its members is to produce the quantity that gives it the maximum attainable profit.

So even though the global oil market has some big players, they don't fix the price. Instead, the actions of thousands of buyers and sellers and the forces of demand and supply determine the price of oil. So how have demand and supply changed?

Because the price has increased with an unchanged quantity, demand must have increased and supply must have decreased.

Demand has increased for two reasons. First, world production, particularly in China and India, is expanding at a rapid rate. The increased production of electricity, gasoline, plastics, and other oil-using goods has increased the demand for oil.

Second, the rapid expansion of production in China, India, and other developing economies is expected to continue. So the demand for oil is expected to keep increasing at a rapid rate. As the demand for oil keeps increasing, the price of oil will keep rising *and be expected* to keep rising.

A higher expected future price increases demand today yet further. It also decreases supply today because producers know they can get a greater return from their oil by leaving it in the ground and selling it in a later year. So an *expected* rise in price brings both an increase in demand and a decrease in supply, which in turn brings an *actual* rise in price.

Because an expected price rise brings an actual price rise, it is possible for expectations to create a process called a **speculative bubble**. In a speculative bubble, the price rises purely because it is expected to rise and events reinforce the expectation. No one knows yet whether the world oil market was in a bubble in 2008, but bubbles always burst, so eventually we will know.

Figure 1 illustrates the events that we've just described and summarizes the forces at work on demand and supply in the world market for oil.

Figure 1 The Market for Crude Oil

Corn

Corn is used as food, animal feed, and a source of ethanol. Global corn production increased during the past few years, but the price also increased.

The story of the production and price of corn, like the story of the price of oil, begins in China and India. Greater production and higher incomes in these countries have increased the demand for corn.

Some of the increase in demand is for corn as food. But more of the increase is for corn as cattle feed, driven by an increased demand for beef—it takes 7 kilograms of corn to produce 1 kilogram of beef.

In addition, mandated targets for ethanol production in the United States have increased the demand for corn as a source of biofuel.

While the demand for corn has increased, the supply has decreased. Drought in several parts of the world cut production and decreased supply. Higher fertilizer prices increased the cost of growing corn, which also decreased supply.

So the demand for corn increased and the supply of corn decreased. This combination of changes in demand and supply raised the price of corn. Also, the increase in demand was greater than the decrease in supply, so the quantity of corn increased.

Figure 2 provides a summary of the events that we've just described in the market for corn.

Fertilizers

Nitrogen, potassium, and potash are not on your daily shopping list, but you consume them many times each day. They are the reason why our farms are so productive. And like the prices of oil and corn, the prices of fertilizers have gone skyward.

The increase in the global production of corn and other grains as food and sources of biofuels has increased the demand for fertilizers.

All fertilizers are costly to produce and use energy-intensive processes. Nitrogen is particularly energy intensive and uses natural gas. Potash is made from deposits of chloride and sodium chloride that are found 900 metres or deeper underground, and energy is required to bring the material to the surface and more energy is used to separate the chemicals and turn them into fertilizer.

All energy sources are substitutes, so the rise in the price of oil has increased the prices of all other energy sources. Consequently, the energy cost of producing fertilizers has risen. This higher cost of production has decreased the supply of fertilizers.

The increase in demand and the decrease in supply combine to raise the price. The increase in demand has been greater than the decrease in supply, so the quantity of fertilizer has increased. Figure 3 illustrates the market for fertilizers.

Figure 2 The Market for Corn

Figure 3 The Market for Fertilizer

FIGURE 3.10 The Effects of All the Possible Changes in Demand and Supply

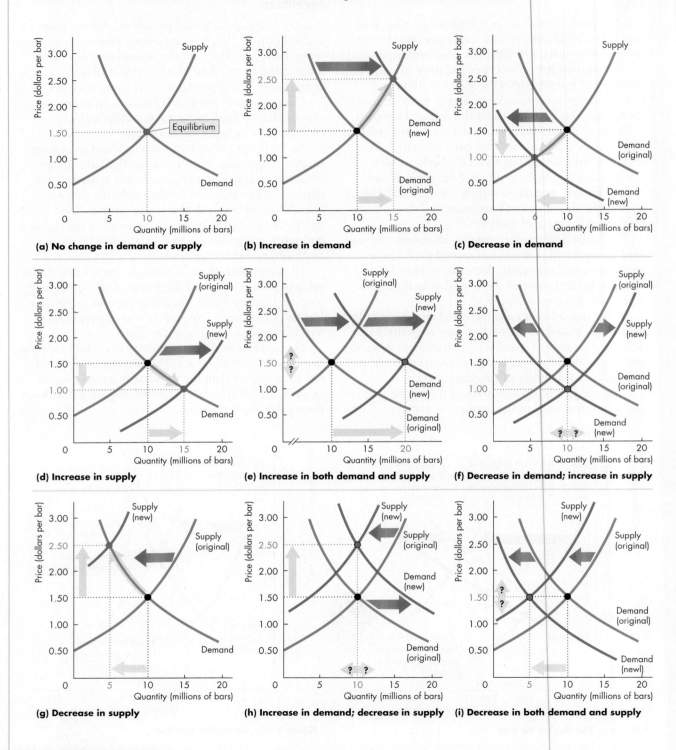

(a) No change in demand or supply

(b) Increase in demand

(c) Decrease in demand

(d) Increase in supply

(e) Increase in both demand and supply

(f) Decrease in demand; increase in supply

(g) Decrease in supply

(h) Increase in demand; decrease in supply

(i) Decrease in both demand and supply

myeconlab animation

All the Possible Changes in Demand and Supply

Figure 3.10 brings together and summarizes the effects of all the possible changes in demand and supply. With what you've learned about the effects of a change in *either* demand or supply, you can predict what happens if *both* demand and supply change together. Let's begin by reviewing what you already know.

Change in Demand with No Change in Supply The first row of Fig. 3.10, parts (a), (b), and (c), summarizes the effects of a change in demand with no change in supply. In part (a), with no change in either demand or supply, neither the price nor the quantity changes. With an *increase* in demand and no change in supply in part (b), both the price and quantity increase. And with a *decrease* in demand and no change in supply in part (c), both the price and the quantity decrease.

Change in Supply with No Change in Demand The first column of Fig. 3.10, parts (a), (d), and (g), summarizes the effects of a change in supply with no change in demand. With an *increase* in supply and no change in demand in part (d), the price falls and quantity increases. And with a *decrease* in supply and no change in demand in part (g), the price rises and the quantity decreases.

Increase in Both Demand and Supply You've seen that an increase in demand raises the price and increases the quantity. And you've seen that an increase in supply lowers the price and increases the quantity. Fig. 3.10(e) combines these two changes. Because either an increase in demand or an increase in supply increases the quantity, the quantity also increases when both demand and supply increase. But the effect on the price is uncertain. An increase in demand raises the price and an increase in supply lowers the price, so we can't say whether the price will rise or fall when both demand and supply increase. We need to know the magnitudes of the changes in demand and supply to predict the effects on price. In the example in Fig. 3.10(e), the price does not change. But notice that if demand increases by slightly more than the amount shown in the figure, the price will rise. And if supply increases by slightly more than the amount shown in the figure, the price will fall.

Decrease in Both Demand and Supply Figure 3.10(i) shows the case in which demand and supply *both decrease*. For the same reasons as those we've just reviewed, when both demand and supply decrease, the quantity decreases, and again the direction of the price change is uncertain.

Decrease in Demand and Increase in Supply You've seen that a decrease in demand lowers the price and decreases the quantity. You've also seen that an increase in supply lowers the price and increases the quantity. Figure 3.10(f) combines these two changes. Both a decrease in demand and an increase in supply lower the price, so the price falls. But a decrease in demand decreases the quantity and an increase in supply increases the quantity, so we can't predict the direction in which the quantity will change unless we know the magnitudes of the changes in demand and supply. In Fig. 3.10(f), the quantity does not change. But notice that if demand decreases by slightly more than the amount shown in the figure, the quantity will decrease; if supply increases by slightly more than the amount shown in the figure, the quantity will increase.

Increase in Demand and Decrease in Supply Figure 3.10(h) shows the case in which demand increases and supply decreases. Now, the price rises, but the direction of the quantity change is uncertain.

Review Quiz

What is the effect on the price of an MP3 player (such as an iPod) and the quantity of MP3 players if

1 The price of a PC falls or the price of an MP3 download rises? (Draw the diagrams!)
2 More firms produce MP3 players or electronics workers' wages rise? (Draw the diagrams!)
3 Any two of the events in questions 1 and 2 occur together? (Draw the diagrams!)

myeconlab Work Study Plan 3.5 and get instant feedback.

Now that you understand the demand and supply model and the predictions that it makes, try to get into the habit of using it in your everyday life. To see how you might use the model, take a look at *Reading Between the Lines* on pp. 76–77, which uses the tools of demand and supply to explain the rising price of gasoline in 2008.

Demand and Supply: The Price of Gasoline

"Mass Exodus" from Roads: Surging Gas Prices May Park Millions of Cars

June 27, 2008

Gasoline prices are becoming so high that one of Canada's top banks is predicting a "mass exodus" of vehicles from U.S. highways within four years, with a slightly less dramatic drop in Canada. …

CIBC World Markets said in a report yesterday that gas prices in the U.S. will hit $7 US a gallon—the equivalent of $1.86 Canadian a litre—two summers from now. That marks a 70 percent increase over today's record levels. …

The meteoric rise in crude oil prices has been a major factor in soaring pump prices. CIBC predicts crude will hit $200 a barrel by 2010.

The average pump price in Canada yesterday was $1.38 a litre, nearly 30 cents higher than it was a year ago, according to the price-tracking website Gasbuddy.com. …

CIBC senior economist Benjamin Tal said: there will be about 700,000 fewer cars on Canadian roads by 2012 and a 10 percent decrease in average kilometres driven.

"Canada will feel the pain, but it's not going to be the same as in the U.S.," Tal said in an interview. …

"In Canada, more low-income Canadians have access to public transportation, therefore the adjustment will not come from them," he said. "The adjustment will come from middle-class families that will start giving up the second or third cars."

"With Americans abandoning their gas-guzzling SUVs and pickup trucks for small, more fuel-efficient vehicles, we estimate that the average fuel-efficiency of this year's fleet has climbed by nearly 20 percent from the previous model year," said auto industry specialist Carlos Gomes. …

The trend is less pronounced in Canada, where there has traditionally been a greater appetite for fuel-efficient vehicles, Gomes said in an interview

Reprinted courtesy of *The Hamilton Spectator*.

Essence of the Story

- The average price of gasoline in Canada on June 27, 2008 was $1.38 a litre, up 30 cents from June, 2007.

- A CIBC economist made four predictions for Canada in 2010.

- First, the price of gasoline will rise to $1.86 a litre.

- Second, the price of crude oil to rise to $200 a barrel.

- Third, there will be 700,000 fewer cars on the road and average kilometres driven will be down 10 percent.

- Fourth, low-income people will use more public transportation and middle-class families will give up the second and third cars.

Economic Analysis

- Figure 1 shows the market for gasoline in Canada in June 2008. The demand curve is D, the supply curve is S_{08}, and the market equilibrium is at 110 million litres a day and $1.38 a litre, the price reported in the news article.

- Gasoline is made from crude oil and when the price of crude oil rises, the cost of producing gasoline also rises, and the supply of gasoline decreases.

- The news article predicts that the price of crude oil will rise to $200 a barrel by 2010. This rise in price will decrease the supply of gasoline.

- We have no information about the likely change in the demand for gasoline. It is likely to change but by much less than the change in supply and we will assume no change in the demand for gasoline.

- The forecast in the news article is that the price of gasoline will rise to $1.86 a litre in 2010 and that the number of kilometres driven will decrease by 10 percent. We will assume that the quantity of gasoline used will also fall by 10 percent.

- Figure 2 shows the market for gasoline in 2010 that is consistent with these forecasts. Supply decreases and the supply curve shifts leftward from S_{08} to S_{10}.

- With no change in demand, the demand curve remains the same as in Fig. 1. The decrease in supply raises the price of gasoline to $1.86 a litre and the quantity decreases to 99 million litres a day—a decrease of 10 percent.

- The quantity of gasoline demanded decreases—shown as a movement up along the demand curve—by 10 percent.

- This decrease in the quantity demanded occurs as the higher price of gasoline induces low-income drivers to use public transport and middle-income families to operate fewer cars.

- This analysis of the market for gasoline emphasizes the distinction between a change in demand and a *change in the quantity demanded* and the distinction between a change in supply and a *change in the quantity supplied.*

- In this example, supply changes, demand remains constant, and the quantity demanded changes.

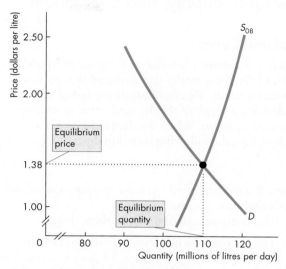

Figure 1 The gasoline market in 2008

Figure 2 Forecast of the gasoline market in 2010

MATHEMATICAL NOTE

Demand, Supply, and Equilibrium

Demand Curve

The law of demand says that as the price of a good or service falls, the quantity demanded of that good or service increases. We can illustrate the law of demand by drawing a graph of the demand curve or writing down an equation. When the demand curve is a straight line, the following equation describes it:

$$P = a - bQ_D$$

where P is the price and Q_D is the quantity demanded. The a and b are positive constants.

The demand equation tells us three things:

1. The price at which no one is willing to buy the good (Q_D is zero). That is, if the price is a, then the quantity demanded is zero. You can see the price a in Fig. 1. It is the price at which the demand curve hits the y-axis—what we call the demand curve's "intercept on the y-axis."

2. As the price falls, the quantity demanded increases. If Q_D is a positive number, then the price P must be less than a. And as Q_D gets larger, the price P becomes smaller. That is, as the quantity increases, the maximum price that buyers are willing to pay for the last unit of the good falls.

3. The constant b tells us how fast the maximum price that someone is willing to pay for the good falls as the quantity increases. That is, the constant b tells us about the steepness of the demand curve. The equation tells us that the slope of the demand curve is $-b$.

Supply Curve

The law of supply says that as the price of a good or service rises, the quantity supplied of that good or service increases. We can illustrate the law of supply by drawing a graph of the supply curve or writing down an equation. When the supply curve is a straight line, the following equation describes it:

$$P = c + dQ_S$$

where P is the price and Q_S is the quantity supplied. The c and d are positive constants.

The supply equation tells us three things:

1. The price at which sellers are not willing to supply the good (Q_S is zero). That is, if the price is c, then no one is willing to sell the good. You can see the price c in Fig. 2. It is the price at which the supply curve hits the y-axis—what we call the supply curve's "intercept on the y-axis."

2. As the price rises, the quantity supplied increases. If Q_S is a positive number, then the price P must be greater than c. And as Q_S increases, the price P becomes larger. That is, as the quantity increases, the minimum price that sellers are willing to accept for the last unit rises.

3. The constant d tells us how fast the minimum price at which someone is willing to sell the good rises as the quantity increases. That is, the constant d tells us about the steepness of the supply curve. The equation tells us that the slope of the supply curve is d.

Figure 1 Demand curve

Figure 2 Supply curve

Market Equilibrium

Demand and supply determine market equilibrium. Figure 3 shows the equilibrium price (P^*) and equilibrium quantity (Q^*) at the intersection of the demand curve and the supply curve.

We can use the equations to find the equilibrium price and equilibrium quantity. The price of a good adjusts until the quantity demanded Q_D equals the quantity supplied Q_S. So at the equilibrium price (P^*) and equilibrium quantity (Q^*),

$$Q_D = Q_S = Q^*.$$

To find the equilibrium price and equilibrium quantity, substitute Q^* for Q_D in the demand equation and Q^* for Q_S in the supply equation. Then the price is the equilibrium price (P^*), which gives

$$P^* = a - bQ^*$$
$$P^* = c + dQ^*.$$

Notice that

$$a - bQ^* = c + dQ^*.$$

Now solve for Q^*:

$$a - c = bQ^* + dQ^*$$
$$a - c = (b + d)Q^*$$
$$Q^* = \frac{a - c}{b + d}.$$

To find the equilibrium price, (P^*), substitute for Q^* in either the demand equation or the supply equation.

Using the demand equation, we have

$$P^* = a - b\left(\frac{a - c}{b + d}\right)$$
$$P^* = \frac{a(b + d) - b(a - c)}{b + d}$$
$$P^* = \frac{ad + bc}{b + d}.$$

Alternatively, using the supply equation, we have

$$P^* = c + d\left(\frac{a - c}{b + d}\right)$$
$$P^* = \frac{c(b + d) - d(a - c)}{b + d}$$
$$P^* = \frac{ad + bc}{b + d}.$$

An Example

The demand for ice cream cones is

$$P = 800 - 2Q_D.$$

The supply of ice cream cones is

$$P = 200 + 1Q_S.$$

The price of a cone is expressed in cents, and the quantities are expressed in cones per day.

To find the equilibrium price (P^*) and equilibrium quantity (Q^*), substitute Q^* for Q_D and Q_S and P^* for P. That is,

$$P^* = 800 - 2Q^*$$
$$P^* = 200 + 1Q^*.$$

Now solve for Q^*:

$$800 - 2Q^* = 200 + 1Q^*$$
$$600 = 3Q^*$$
$$Q^* = 200.$$

And

$$P^* = 800 - 2(200)$$
$$= 400.$$

The equilibrium price is \$4 a cone, and the equilibrium quantity is 200 cones per day.

Figure 3 Market equilibrium

SUMMARY ◆

Key Points

Markets and Prices (p. 58)

- A competitive market is one that has so many buyers and sellers that no single buyer or seller can influence the price.
- Opportunity cost is a relative price.
- Demand and supply determine relative prices.

Demand (pp. 59–63)

- Demand is the relationship between the quantity demanded of a good and its price when all other influences on buying plans remain the same.
- The higher the price of a good, other things remaining the same, the smaller is the quantity demanded—the law of demand.
- Demand depends on the prices of related goods (substitutes and complements), expected future prices, income, expected future income and credit, population, and preferences.

Supply (pp. 64–67)

- Supply is the relationship between the quantity supplied of a good and its price when all other influences on selling plans remain the same.
- The higher the price of a good, other things remaining the same, the greater is the quantity supplied—the law of supply.

- Supply depends on the prices of factors of production used to produce a good, the prices of related goods produced, expected future prices, the number of suppliers, technology, and the state of nature.

Market Equilibrium (pp. 68–69)

- At the equilibrium price, the quantity demanded equals the quantity supplied.
- At any price above equilibrium, there is a surplus and the price falls.
- At any price below equilibrium, there is a shortage and the price rises.

Predicting Changes in Price and Quantity (pp. 70–75)

- An increase in demand brings a rise in the price and an increase in the quantity supplied. A decrease in demand brings a fall in the price and a decrease in the quantity supplied.
- An increase in supply brings a fall in the price and an increase in the quantity demanded. A decrease in supply brings a rise in the price and a decrease in the quantity demanded.
- An increase in demand and an increase in supply bring an increased quantity but an uncertain price change. An increase in demand and a decrease in supply bring a higher price but an uncertain change in quantity.

Key Figures

Figure 3.1   The Demand Curve, 60
Figure 3.3   A Change in the Quantity Demanded Versus a Change in Demand, 63
Figure 3.4   The Supply Curve, 65

Figure 3.6   A Change in the Quantity Supplied Versus a Change in Supply, 67
Figure 3.7   Equilibrium, 68
Figure 3.10   The Effects of All the Possible Changes in Demand and Supply, 74

Key Terms

Change in demand, 60
Change in supply, 65
Change in the quantity demanded, 63
Change in the quantity supplied, 66
Competitive market, 58
Complement, 61

Demand, 59
Demand curve, 60
Equilibrium price, 68
Equilibrium quantity, 68
Inferior good, 62
Law of demand, 59
Law of supply, 64
Money price, 58

Normal good, 62
Quantity demanded, 59
Quantity supplied, 64
Relative price, 58
Speculative bubble, 72
Substitute, 61
Supply, 64
Supply curve, 64

PROBLEMS and APPLICATIONS

 Work problems 1–13 in Chapter 3 Study Plan and get instant feedback.
Work problems 15–27 as Homework, a Quiz, or a Test if assigned by your instructor.

1. In December 1862, William Gregg, a mill owner, placed a notice in the *Edgehill Advertiser* announcing his willingness to exchange cloth for food and other items. Here is an extract:

   1 yard of cloth for 1 pound of bacon

   2 yards of cloth for 1 pound of butter

   4 yards of cloth for 1 pound of wool

   8 yards of cloth for 1 bushel of salt

   a. What is the relative price of butter in terms of wool?
   b. If the money price of bacon was 20¢ a pound, what do you predict was the money price of butter?
   c. If the money price of bacon was 20¢ a pound and the money price of salt was $2.00 a bushel, do you think anyone would accept Mr. Gregg's offer of cloth for salt?

2. The price of food increased during the past year.

   a. Explain why the law of demand applies to food just as it does to all other goods and services.
   b. Explain how the substitution effect influences food purchases and provide some examples of substitutions that people might make when the price of food rises and other things remain the same.
   c. Explain how the income effect influences food purchases and provide examples of the income effect that might occur when the price of food rises and other things remain the same.

3. Place the following goods and services into pairs of likely substitutes and pairs of likely complements. (You may use an item in more than one pair.) The goods and services are coal, oil, natural gas, wheat, corn, rye, pasta, pizza, sausage, skateboard, roller blades, video game, laptop, iPod, cell phone, text message, e-mail, phone call, and voice mail.

4. During 2008, the average income in China increased by 10 percent. Compared to 2007, how do you expect the following would change:

   a. The demand for beef? Explain your answer.
   b. The demand for rice? Explain your answer.

5. The following events occur one at a time in the market for cell phones:

   - The price of a cell phone falls.
   - Everyone believes that the price of a cell phone will fall next month.
   - The price of a call made from a cell phone falls.
   - The price of a call made from a land-line phone increases.
   - The introduction of camera phones makes cell phones more popular.

   a. Explain the effect of each event on the demand for cell phones.
   b. Use a graph to illustrate the effect of each event.
   c. Does any event (or events) illustrate the law of demand?

6. On July 22, 2008, the *Montreal Gazette* reported: "Pump prices have fluctuated over the past few months from the $1.20 range upwards to nearly $1.50 a litre, driving down consumption." Assume that there were no changes in average income, population, or any other influence on buying plans. How would you expect the rise in the price of gasoline to affect

   a. The demand for gasoline? Explain your answer.
   b. The quantity of gasoline demanded? Explain your answer.

7. Timber beams are made from logs and in the process of making beams the mill produces sawdust, which is made into pressed wood. In the market for timber beams, the following events occur one at a time:

   - The wage rate of sawmill workers rises.
   - The price of sawdust rises.
   - The price of a timber beam rises.
   - The price of a timber beam is expected to rise next year.
   - Environmentalists convince Parliament to introduce a new law that reduces the amount of forest that can be cut for timber products.
   - A new technology lowers the cost of producing timber beams.

a. Explain the effect of each event on the supply of timber beams.

b. Use a graph to show the effect of each event.

c. Does any event (or events) illustrate the law of supply?

8. **Air Canada Cuts Flights on High Jet Prices**
Air Canada announced June 17 it is reducing flights by about 7 percent and laying off up to 2,000 staff in the fourth quarter of 2008 and the first quarter of 2009 because of high fuel costs.
Platts Oilgram Price Report, June 18, 2008

a. How does this news clip illustrate a change in supply? Explain your answer.

b What is the influence on supply identified in the news clip? Explain your answer.

c. Explain how supply changes.

9. **Oil Soars to New Record Over $135**
The price of oil hit a record high above $135 a barrel on Thursday—more than twice what it cost a year ago ... OPEC has so far blamed price rises on speculators and says there is no shortage of oil.
BBC News, May 22, 2008

a. Explain how the price of oil can rise even though there is no shortage of oil.

b. If a shortage of oil does occur, what does that imply about price adjustments and the role of price as a regulator in the market for oil?

c. If OPEC is correct, what factors might have changed demand and/or supply and shifted the demand curve and/or the supply curve to cause the price to rise?

10. "As more people buy computers, the demand for Internet service increases and the price of Internet service decreases. The fall in the price of Internet service decreases the supply of Internet service." Is this statement true or false? Explain.

11. The following events occur one at a time:
    (i)   The price of crude oil rises.
    (ii) The price of a car rises.
    (iii) All speed limits on highways are abolished.
    (iv) Robots cut car production costs.

Which of these events will increase or decrease (state which occurs)

a. The demand for gasoline?
b. The supply of gasoline?
c. The quantity of gasoline demanded?
d. The quantity of gasoline supplied?

12. The demand and supply schedules for gum are

Price (cents per pack)	Quantity demanded	Quantity supplied
	(millions of packs a week)	
20	180	60
40	140	100
60	100	140
80	60	180
100	20	220

a. Draw a graph of the gum market, label the axes and the curves, and mark in the equilibrium price and quantity.

b. Suppose that the price of gum is 70¢ a pack. Describe the situation in the gum market and explain how the price adjusts.

c. Suppose that the price of gum is 30¢ a pack. Describe the situation in the gum market and explain how the price adjusts.

d. A fire destroys some factories that produce gum and the quantity of gum supplied decreases by 40 million packs a week at each price. Explain what happens in the market for gum and illustrate the changes on your graph.

e. If at the same time as the fire occurs in d, there is an increase in the teenage population, which increases the quantity of gum demanded by 40 million packs a week at each price, what are the new equilibrium price and quantity of gum? Illustrate these changes in your graph.

13. **Eurostar Boosted by *Da Vinci Code***
Eurostar, the train service linking London to Paris, ... said on Wednesday first-half sales rose 6 per cent, boosted by devotees of the blockbuster Da Vinci movie.
CNN, July 26, 2006

a. Explain how *Da Vinci Code* fans helped to raise Eurostar's sales.

b. What markets in Paris did these fans influence? Explain the influence on three markets.

14. Use the link on MyEconLab (Textbook Resources, Chapter 3, Web Links) to obtain data on the prices and quantities of bananas in 1985 and 2002.

a. Make a graph to illustrate the market for bananas in 1985 and 2002.

b. On the graph, show the changes in demand, supply, the quantity demanded, and the quantity supplied that are consistent with the data.

c. Why did the demand and supply change?

15. What features of the world market for crude oil make it a competitive market?

16. The money price of a textbook is $90 and the money price of the Wii game *Super Mario Galaxy* is $45.

    a. What is the opportunity cost of a textbook in terms of the Wii game?

    b. What is the relative price of the Wii game in terms of textbooks?

17. The price of gasoline increased during the past year.

    a. Explain why the law of demand applies to gasoline just as it does to all other goods and services.

    b. Explain how the substitution effect influences gasoline purchases and provide some examples of substitutions that people might make when the price of gasoline rises and other things remain the same.

    c. Explain how the income effect influences gasoline purchases and provide some examples of the income effects that might occur when the price of gasoline rises and other things remain the same.

18. Classify the following pairs of goods and services as substitutes, complements, substitutes in production, or complements in production.

    a. Bottled water and health club memberships

    b. French fries and baked potatoes

    c. Leather purses and leather shoes

    d. SUVs and compact cars

    e. Diet coke and regular coke

    f. Low-fat milk and cream

19. Think about the demand for the three popular game consoles: XBox, PS3, and Wii. Explain the effect of the following events on the demand for XBox games and the quantity of XBox games demanded, other things remaining the same.

    a. The price of an XBox falls.

    b. The prices of a PS3 and a Wii fall.

    c. The number of people writing and producing XBox games increases.

    d. Consumers' incomes increase.

    e. Programmers who write code for XBox games become more costly to hire.

    f. The price of an XBox game is expected to fall.

    g. A new game console comes onto the market, which is a close substitute for XBox.

20. **Rising Corn Prices Hit Grocery Shoppers' Pocketbooks**

    The rising demand for corn as a source of ethanol-blended fuel is largely to blame for increasing food costs. ... Food prices rose 10 per cent in 2006, "driven mainly by surging prices of corn, wheat and soybean oil in the second part of the year," the International Monetary Fund said in a report. "Looking ahead, rising demand for biofuels will likely cause the prices of corn and soybean oil to rise further," ...

    Statistics Canada says consumers in the country paid 3.8 per cent more for food in April 2007, compared to the same month last year.

    CBC News Online, May 22, 2008

    a. Explain why the demand for ethanol has influenced the price of corn.

    b. Use graphs to show why the higher price of corn affects the price of food.

21. **G.M. Cuts Production for Quarter**

    General Motors cut its fourth-quarter production schedule by 10 percent on Tuesday as a tightening credit market caused sales at the Ford Motor Company, Chrysler, and even Toyota to decline in August. ... Bob Carter, group vice president for Toyota Motor Sales USA, said ... dealerships were still seeing fewer potential customers browsing the lots.

    New York Times, September 5, 2007

    Explain whether this news clip illustrates

    a. A change in supply.

    b. A change in the quantity supplied.

    c. A change in demand.

    d. A change in the quantity demanded.

22. **"Popcorn Movie" Experience Gets Pricier**

    ... cinemas are raising ... prices. ... Demand for field corn, used for animal feed, ... corn syrup and ... ethanol, has caused its price to explode. That's caused some farmers to shift from popcorn to easier-to-grow field corn, cutting supply and pushing its price higher, too. ...

    USA Today, May 24, 2008

    Explain and illustrate graphically the events described in the news clip in the markets for

    a. Popcorn.

    b. Cinema tickets.

    c. Field corn.

23. The figure illustrates the market for pizza.

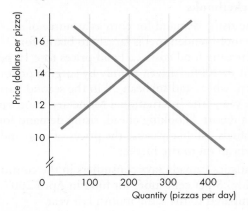

a. Label the curves. Which curve shows the willingness to pay for a pizza?
b. If the price of a pizza is $16, is there a shortage or a surplus and does the price rise or fall?
c. Sellers want to receive the highest possible price, so why would they be willing to accept less than $16 a pizza?
d. If the price of a pizza is $12, is there a shortage or a surplus and does the price rise or fall?
e. Buyers want to pay the lowest possible price, so why would they be willing to pay more than $12 for a pizza?

24. What is the effect on the equilibrium price and equilibrium quantity of orange juice if the price of apple juice decreases and the wage rate paid to orange grove workers increases?

25. The table sets out the demand and supply schedules for potato chips.

Price (cents per bag)	Quantity demanded	Quantity supplied
	(millions of bags per week)	
50	160	130
60	150	140
70	140	150
80	130	160
90	120	170
100	110	180

a. Draw a graph of the potato chip market and mark in the equilibrium price and quantity.
b. If the price is 60¢ a bag, is there a shortage or a surplus, and how does the price adjust?
c. If a new dip increases the quantity of potato chips that people want to buy by 30 million bags per week at each price, how does the demand and/or supply of chips change?
d. If a new dip has the effect described in c, how does the price and quantity of chips change?
e. If a virus destroys potato crops and the quantity of potato chips produced decreases by 40 million bags a week at each price, how does the supply of chips change?
f. If the virus described in e hits just as the new dip in c comes onto the market, how do the price of chips and the quantity bought change?

26. **Consumer Tech: Blu-Ray Wins, but Does Anyone Care?**
Toshiba Corp. yesterday raised the white flag in the war over the next-generation home movie format, announcing the end of its HD DVD business in a victory for Sony Corp.'s Blu-ray technology.
Canadian Business Online, July 9, 2008
How would you expect the end of Toshiba's HD DVD format to influence

a. The price of a used Toshiba player on eBay? Would the outcome that you predict result from a change in demand or a change in supply or both, and in which directions?
b. The price of a Blu-ray player?
c. The demand for Blu-ray format movies?
d. The supply of Blu-ray format movies?
e. The price of Blu-ray format movies?
f. The quantity of Blu-ray format movies?

27. After you have studied *Reading Between the Lines* on pp. 76–77, answer the following questions:

a. What substitutions did drivers make to decrease the quantity of gasoline demanded?
b. What were the two main factors that influenced the demand for gasoline in 2008 and how did they change demand?
c. What was the main influence on the supply of gasoline during early 2008 and how did supply change?
d. How did the combination of the factors you have noted in c and d influence the price and quantity of gasoline?
e. Did the quantity demanded or the quantity supplied change?

4 Elasticity

After studying this chapter, you will be able to

- Define, calculate, and explain the factors that influence the price elasticity of demand

- Define, calculate, and explain the factors that influence the cross elasticity of demand and the income elasticity of demand

- Define, calculate, and explain the factors that influence the elasticity of supply

What are the effects of a high gasoline price on buying plans? You can see some of the biggest effects at car dealers' lots, where SUVs and other gas guzzlers remain unsold while sub-compacts and hybrids sell in greater quantities. But how big are these effects? When the price of gasoline doubles, as it has done over the past few years, by how much does the quantity of SUVs sold decrease, and by how much does the quantity of sub-compacts sold increase?

And what about gasoline purchases? Do we keep filling our tanks and spending more on gas? Or do we find substitutes on such a large scale that we end up cutting our expenditure on gas?

This chapter introduces you to elasticity: a tool that addresses these quantitative questions. At the end of the chapter, in *Reading Between the Lines*, we'll use the concept of elasticity to explain what was happening in the markets for gasoline and automobiles in 2008. But we'll explain and illustrate elasticity by studying another familiar market: the market for pizza.

85

◆ Price Elasticity of Demand

You know that when supply increases, the equilibrium price falls and the equilibrium quantity increases. But does the price fall by a large amount and the quantity increase by a little? Or does the price barely fall and the quantity increase by a large amount?

The answer depends on the responsiveness of the quantity demanded to a change in price. You can see why by studying Fig. 4.1, which shows two possible scenarios in a local pizza market. Figure 4.1(a) shows one scenario, and Fig. 4.1(b) shows the other.

In both cases, supply is initially S_0. In part (a), the demand for pizza is shown by the demand curve D_A. In part (b), the demand for pizza is shown by the demand curve D_B. Initially, in both cases, the price is $20 a pizza and the equilibrium quantity is 10 pizzas an hour.

Now a large pizza franchise opens up, and the supply of pizza increases. The supply curve shifts rightward to S_1. In case (a), the price falls by an enormous $15 to $5 a pizza, and the quantity increases by only 3 to 13 pizzas an hour. In contrast, in case (b), the price falls by only $5 to $15 a pizza and the quantity increases by 7 to 17 pizzas an hour.

The different outcomes arise from differing degrees of responsiveness of the quantity demanded to a change in price. But what do we mean by responsiveness? One possible answer is slope. The slope of demand curve D_A is steeper than the slope of demand curve D_B.

In this example, we can compare the slopes of the two demand curves, but we can't always make such a comparison. The reason is that the slope of a demand curve depends on the units in which we measure the price and quantity. And we often must compare the demand for different goods and services that are measured in unrelated units. For example, a pizza producer might want to compare the demand for pizza with the demand for soft drinks. Which quantity demanded is more responsive to a price change? This question can't be answered by comparing the slopes of two demand curves. The units of measurement of pizza and soft drinks are unrelated. The question can be answered with a measure of responsiveness that is independent of units of measurement. Elasticity is such a measure.

The **price elasticity of demand** is a units-free measure of the responsiveness of the quantity demanded of a good to a change in its price when all other influences on buying plans remain the same.

FIGURE 4.1 How a Change in Supply Changes Price and Quantity

(a) Large price change and small quantity change

(b) Small price change and large quantity change

Initially, the price is $20 a pizza and the quantity sold is 10 pizzas an hour. Then supply increases from S_0 to S_1. In part (a), the price falls by $15 to $5 a pizza, and the quantity increases by 3 to 13 pizzas an hour. In part (b), the price falls by only $5 to $15 a pizza, and the quantity increases by 7 to 17 pizzas an hour. The price change is smaller and the quantity change is larger in case (b) than in case (a). The quantity demanded is more responsive to the change in the price in case (b) than in case (a).

Calculating Price Elasticity of Demand

We calculate the *price elasticity of demand* by using the formula:

$$\text{Price elasticity of demand} = \frac{\text{Percentage change in quantity demanded}}{\text{Percentage change in price}}.$$

To use this formula, we need to know the quantities demanded at different prices when all other influences on buying plans remain the same. Suppose we have the data on prices and quantities demanded of pizza and we calculate the price elasticity of demand for pizza.

Figure 4.2 zooms in on the demand curve for pizza and shows how the quantity demanded responds to a small change in price. Initially, the price is $20.50 a pizza and 9 pizzas an hour are sold—the original point in the figure. The price then falls to $19.50 a pizza, and the quantity demanded increases to 11 pizzas an hour—the new point in the figure. When the price falls by $1 a pizza, the quantity demanded increases by 2 pizzas an hour.

To calculate the price elasticity of demand, we express the changes in price and quantity demanded as percentages of the *average price* and the *average quantity*. By using the average price and average quantity, we calculate the elasticity at a point on the demand curve midway between the original point and the new point. The original price is $20.50 and the new price is $19.50, so the average price is $20. The $1 price decrease is 5 percent of the average price. That is,

$$\Delta P/P_{ave} = (\$1/\$20) \times 100 = 5\%.$$

The original quantity demanded is 9 pizzas and the new quantity demanded is 11 pizzas, so the average quantity demanded is 10 pizzas. The 2 pizza increase in the quantity demanded is 20 percent of the average quantity. That is,

$$\Delta Q/Q_{ave} = (2/10) \times 100 = 20\%.$$

So the price elasticity of demand, which is the percentage change in the quantity demanded (20 percent) divided by the percentage change in price (5 percent) is 4. That is,

$$\text{Price elasticity of demand} = \frac{\%\Delta Q}{\%\Delta P}$$

$$= \frac{20\%}{5\%} = 4.$$

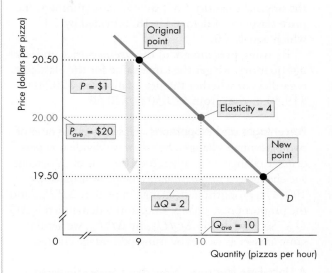

FIGURE 4.2   Calculating the Elasticity of Demand

The elasticity of demand is calculated by using the formula:*

$$\text{Price elasticity of demand} = \frac{\text{Percentage change in quantity demanded}}{\text{Percentage change in price}}$$

$$= \frac{\%\Delta Q}{\%\Delta P}$$

$$= \frac{\Delta Q/Q_{ave}}{\Delta P/P_{ave}}$$

$$= \frac{2/10}{1/20}$$

$$= 4.$$

This calculation measures the elasticity at an average price of $20 a pizza and an average quantity of 10 pizzas an hour.

*In the formula, the Greek letter delta Δ stands for "change in" and %Δ stands for "percentage change in."

 ⊗ myeconlab animation

Average Price and Quantity Notice that we use the *average* price and *average* quantity. We do this because it gives the most precise measurement of elasticity—at the midpoint between the original price and the new price. If the price falls from $20.50 to $19.50, the $1 price change is 4.9 percent of $20.50. The 2 pizza change in quantity is 22.2 percent of 9 pizzas, the original quantity. So if we use these numbers, the price elasticity of demand is 22.2 divided by 4.9, which equals 4.5. If the price rises from $19.50 to $20.50, the $1 price change is 5.1 percent of $19.50. The 2 pizza change in quantity is 18.2 percent of 11 pizzas, the original quantity. So if we use these numbers, the price elasticity of demand is 18.2 divided by 5.1, which equals 3.6.

By using percentages of the *average* price and *average* quantity, we get the same value for the elasticity regardless of whether the price falls from $20.50 to $19.50 or rises from $19.50 to $20.50.

Percentages and Proportions   Elasticity is the ratio of two percentage changes. So when we divide one percentage change by another, the 100s cancel. A percentage change is a *proportionate* change multiplied by 100. The proportionate change in price is $\Delta P / P_{ave}$, and the proportionate change in quantity demanded is $\Delta Q / Q_{ave}$. So if we divide $\Delta Q / Q_{ave}$ by $\Delta P / P_{ave}$ we get the same answer as we get by using percentage changes.

A Units-Free Measure   Now that you've calculated a price elasticity of demand, you can see why it is a *units-free measure*. Elasticity is a units-free measure because the percentage change in each variable is independent of the units in which the variable is measured. And the ratio of the two percentages is a number without units.

Minus Sign and Elasticity   When the price of a good *rises*, the quantity demanded *decreases*. Because a *positive* change in price brings a *negative* change in the quantity demanded, the price elasticity of

demand is a negative number. But it is the magnitude, or *absolute value*, of the price elasticity of demand that tells us how responsive the quantity demanded is. So to compare price elasticities of demand, we use the *magnitude* of the elasticity and ignore the minus sign.

Inelastic and Elastic Demand

Figure 4.3 shows three demand curves that cover the entire range of possible elasticities of demand. In Fig. 4.3(a), the quantity demanded is constant regardless of the price. If the quantity demanded remains constant when the price changes, then the price elasticity of demand is zero and the good is said to have a **perfectly inelastic demand**. One good that has a very low price elasticity of demand (perhaps zero over some price range) is insulin. Insulin is of such importance to some diabetics that if the price rises or falls, they do not change the quantity they buy.

If the percentage change in the quantity demanded equals the percentage change in the price, then the price elasticity equals 1 and the good is said to have a **unit elastic demand**. The demand in Fig. 4.3(b) is an example of unit elastic demand.

Between the cases shown in Fig. 4.3(a) and Fig. 4.3(b) is the general case in which the percentage change in the quantity demanded is more than the percentage change in the price. In this case, the price elasticity of demand is between 1 and infinity and the good is said to have an **inelastic demand**. Food and shelter are examples of goods with inelastic demand.

FIGURE 4.3   Inelastic and Elastic Demand

(a) Perfectly inelastic demand   **(b) Unit elastic demand**   **(c) Perfectly elastic demand**

Each demand illustrated here has a constant elasticity. The demand curve in part (a) illustrates the demand for a good that has a zero elasticity of demand. The demand curve in part (b) illustrates the demand for a good with a unit elasticity of demand. And the demand curve in part (c) illustrates the demand for a good with an infinite elasticity of demand.

myeconlab animation

If the quantity demanded changes by an infinitely large percentage in response to a tiny price change, then the price elasticity of demand is infinity and the good is said to have a **perfectly elastic demand**. Figure 4.3(c) shows a perfectly elastic demand. An example of a good that has a very high elasticity of demand (almost infinite) is a soft drink from two campus machines located side by side. If the two machines offer the same soft drinks for the same price, some people buy from one machine and some from the other. But if one machine's price is higher than the other's, by even a small amount, no one will buy from the machine with the higher price. Soft drinks from the two machines are perfect substitutes. The demand for a good that has a perfect substitute is perfectly elastic.

Between the cases shown in Fig. 4.3(a) and Fig. 4.3(b) is the general case in which the percentage change in the quantity demanded is less than the percentage change in the price. In this case, the price elasticity of demand is between zero and 1 and the good is said to have an **elastic demand**. Automobiles and furniture are examples of goods that have elastic demand.

Elasticity Along a Straight-Line Demand Curve

Elasticity and slope are not the same, but they are related. To understand how they are related, let's look at elasticity along a straight-line demand curve—a demand curve that has a constant slope.

Figure 4.4 illustrates the calculation of elasticity along a straight-line demand curve. First, suppose the price falls from $25 to $15 a pizza. The quantity demanded increases from zero to 20 pizzas an hour. The average price is $20 a pizza, and the average quantity is 10 pizzas. So

$$\text{Price elasticity of demand} = \frac{\Delta Q/Q_{ave}}{\Delta P/P_{ave}}$$
$$= \frac{20/10}{10/20}$$
$$= 4.$$

That is, the price elasticity of demand at an average price of $20 a pizza is 4.

Next, suppose that the price falls from $15 to $10 a pizza. The quantity demanded increases from 20 to 30 pizzas an hour. The average price is now $12.50 a pizza, and the average quantity is 25 pizzas an hour. So

$$\text{Price elasticity of demand} = \frac{10/25}{5/12.50}$$
$$= 1.$$

That is, the price elasticity of demand at an average price of $12.50 a pizza is 1.

Finally, suppose that the price falls from $10 to zero. The quantity demanded increases from 30 to 50 pizzas an hour. The average price is now $5 a pizza and the average quantity is 40 pizzas an hour. So

$$\text{Price elasticity of demand} = \frac{20/40}{10/5}$$
$$= 1/4.$$

That is, the price elasticity of demand at an average price of $5 a pizza is 1/4.

You've now seen how elasticity changes along a straight-line demand curve. At the midpoint of the curve, demand is unit elastic. Above the midpoint, demand is elastic. Below the midpoint, demand is inelastic.

FIGURE 4.4 Elasticity Along a Straight-Line Demand Curve

On a straight-line demand curve, elasticity decreases as the price falls and the quantity demanded increases. Demand is unit elastic at the midpoint of the demand curve (elasticity is 1). Above the midpoint, demand is elastic; below the midpoint, demand is inelastic.

Total Revenue and Elasticity

The **total revenue** from the sale of a good equals the price of the good multiplied by the quantity sold. When a price changes, total revenue also changes. But a rise in price does not always increase total revenue. The change in total revenue depends on the elasticity of demand in the following way:

- If demand is elastic, a 1 percent price cut increases the quantity sold by more than 1 percent and total revenue increases.
- If demand is inelastic, a 1 percent price cut increases the quantity sold by less than 1 percent and total revenue decreases.
- If demand is unit elastic, a 1 percent price cut increases the quantity sold by 1 percent and total revenue does not change.

Figure 4.5 shows how we can use this relationship between elasticity and total revenue to estimate elasticity using the total revenue test. The **total revenue test** is a method of estimating the price elasticity of demand by observing the change in total revenue that results from a change in the price, when all other influences on the quantity sold remain the same.

- If a price cut increases total revenue, demand is elastic.
- If a price cut decreases total revenue, demand is inelastic.
- If a price cut leaves total revenue unchanged, demand is unit elastic.

In Fig. 4.5(a), over the price range from $25 to $12.50, demand is elastic. Over the price range from $12.50 to zero, demand is inelastic. At a price of $12.50, demand is unit elastic.

Figure 4.5(b) shows total revenue. At a price of $25, the quantity sold is zero, so total revenue is zero. At a price of zero, the quantity demanded is 50 pizzas an hour and total revenue is again zero. A price cut in the elastic range brings an increase in total revenue—the percentage increase in the quantity demanded is greater than the percentage decrease in price. A price cut in the inelastic range brings a decrease in total revenue—the percentage increase in the quantity demanded is less than the percentage decrease in price. At unit elasticity, total revenue is at a maximum.

FIGURE 4.5   Elasticity and Total Revenue

(a) Demand

(b) Total revenue

When demand is elastic, in the price range from $25 to $12.50, a decrease in price (part a) brings an increase in total revenue (part b). When demand is inelastic, in the price range from $12.50 to zero, a decrease in price (part a) brings a decrease in total revenue (part b). When demand is unit elastic, at a price of $12.50 (part a), total revenue is at a maximum (part b).

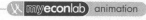 animation

Your Expenditure and Your Elasticity

When a price changes, the change in your expenditure on the good depends on *your* elasticity of demand.

- If your demand is elastic, a 1 percent price cut increases the quantity you buy by more than 1 percent and your expenditure on the item increases.
- If your demand is inelastic, a 1 percent price cut increases the quantity you buy by less than 1 percent and your expenditure on the item decreases.
- If your demand is unit elastic, a 1 percent price cut increases the quantity you buy by 1 percent and your expenditure on the item does not change.

So if you spend more on an item when its price falls, your demand for that item is elastic; if you spend the same amount, your demand is unit elastic; and if you spend less, your demand is inelastic.

The Factors That Influence the Elasticity of Demand

What makes the demand for some goods elastic and the demand for others inelastic? The elasticity of demand for a good depends on

- The closeness of substitutes
- The proportion of income spent on the good
- The time elapsed since a price change

Closeness of Substitutes   The closer the substitutes for a good or service, the more elastic is the demand for it. For example, oil from which we make gasoline has substitutes but none that are currently very close (imagine a steam-driven, coal-fuelled car). So the demand for oil is inelastic. Plastics are close substitutes for metals, so the demand for metals is elastic.

The degree of substitutability between two goods also depends on how narrowly (or broadly) we define them. For example, a personal computer has no really close substitutes, but a Dell PC is a close substitute for a Hewlett-Packard PC. So the elasticity of demand for personal computers is lower than the elasticity of demand for a Dell or a Hewlett-Packard.

In everyday language we call goods such as food and shelter *necessities* and goods such as exotic vacations *luxuries*. A necessity is a good that has poor substitutes and that is crucial for our well-being. So generally, a necessity has an inelastic demand.

A luxury is a good that usually has many substitutes, one of which is not buying it. So a luxury generally has an elastic demand.

Some Real-World Elasticities of Demand

Elastic and Inelastic Demand

The real-world elasticities of demand in the table range from 1.52 for metals, the item with the most elastic demand in the table, to 0.05 for oil, the item with the most inelastic demand in the table.

Oil and food, which have poor substitutes and inelastic demands, might be classified as necessities. Furniture and motor vehicles, which have good substitutes and elastic demands, might be classified as luxuries.

Price Elasticities of Demand

Good or Service	Elasticity
Elastic Demand	
Metals	1.52
Electrical engineering products	1.39
Mechanical engineering products	1.30
Furniture	1.26
Motor vehicles	1.14
Instrument engineering products	1.10
Professional services	1.09
Transportation services	1.03
Inelastic Demand	
Gas, electricity, and water	0.92
Chemicals	0.89
Drinks (all types)	0.78
Clothing	0.64
Tobacco	0.61
Banking and insurance services	0.56
Housing services	0.55
Agricultural and fish products	0.42
Books, magazines, and newspapers	0.34
Food	0.12
Oil	0.05

Sources of data: Ahsan Mansur and John Whalley, "Numerical Specification of Applied General Equilibrium Models: Estimation, Calibration, and Data," in *Applied General Equilibrium Analysis*, eds. Herbert E. Scarf and John B. Shoven (New York: Cambridge University Press, 1984), 109, and Henri Theil, Ching-Fan Chung, and James L. Seale, Jr., *Advances in Econometrics, Supplement 1, 1989, International Evidence on Consumption Patterns* (Greenwich, Conn.: JAI Press Inc., 1989), and Geoffrey Heal, Columbia University, Web site.

Proportion of Income Spent on the Good   Other things remaining the same, the greater the proportion of income spent on the good, the more elastic is the demand for it.

Think about your own elasticity of demand for chewing gum and housing. If the price of chewing gum doubles, you consume almost as much gum as before. Your demand for gum is inelastic. If apartment rents double, you shriek and look for more students to share your apartment. Your demand for

Price Elasticities of Demand for Food

How Inelastic?

As the average income in a country increases and the proportion of income spent on food decreases, the demand for food becomes more inelastic.

The figure shows that the price elasticity of demand for food (green bars) is greatest in the poorest countries. The larger the proportion of income spent on food, the larger is the price elasticity of demand for food. In Tanzania, a nation where 62 percent of income is spent on food, the price elasticity of demand for food is 0.77. In contrast, in Canada, where 14 percent of income is spent on food, the price elasticity of demand for food is 0.13.

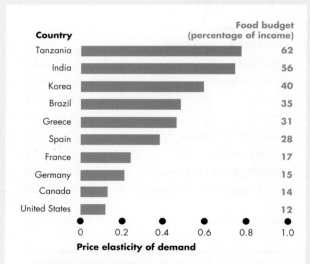

Price Elasticities in 10 Countries

Source of data: Henri Theil, Ching-Fan Chung, and James L. Seale, Jr., *Advances in Econometrics, Supplement 1, 1989, International Evidence on Consumption Patterns* (Greenwich, Conn.: JAI Press, Inc., 1989).

housing is not as inelastic as your demand for gum. Why the difference? Housing takes a large proportion of your budget, and gum takes only a tiny proportion. You don't like either price increase, but you hardly notice the higher price of gum, while the higher rent puts your budget under severe strain.

Time Elapsed Since Price Change   The longer the time that has elapsed since a price change, the more elastic is demand. When the price of oil increased by 400 percent during the 1970s, people barely changed the quantity of oil and gasoline they bought. But gradually, as more efficient auto and airplane engines were developed, the quantity bought decreased. The demand for oil has become more elastic as more time has elapsed since the huge price hike. Similarly, when the price of a PC fell, the quantity of PCs demanded increased only slightly at first. But as more people have become better informed about the variety of ways of using a PC, the quantity of PCs bought has increased sharply. The demand for PCs has become more elastic.

Review Quiz

1   Why do we need a units-free measure of the responsiveness of the quantity demanded of a good or service to a change in its price?
2   Define the price elasticity of demand and show how it is calculated.
3   Why, when we calculate the price elasticity of demand, do we express the change in price as a percentage of the *average* price and the change in quantity as a percentage of the *average* quantity?
4   What is the total revenue test? Explain how it works.
5   What are the main influences on the elasticity of demand that make the demand for some goods elastic and the demand for other goods inelastic?
6   Why is the demand for a luxury generally more elastic than the demand for a necessity?

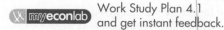 Work Study Plan 4.1 and get instant feedback.

You've now completed your study of the *price* elasticity of demand. Two other elasticity concepts tell us about the effects of other influences on demand. Let's look at these other elasticities of demand.

More Elasticities of Demand

Back at the pizzeria, you are trying to work out how a price rise by the burger shop next door will affect the demand for your pizza. You know that pizzas and burgers are substitutes. And you know that when the price of a substitute for pizza rises, the demand for pizza increases. But by how much?

You also know that pizza and soft drinks are complements. And you know that if the price of a complement of pizza rises, the demand for pizza decreases. So you wonder: By how much will the demand for your pizza decrease if the price of a soft drink rises?

To answer these questions, you need to calculate the cross elasticity of demand. Let's examine this elasticity measure.

Cross Elasticity of Demand

We measure the influence of a change in the price of a substitute or complement by using the concept of the cross elasticity of demand. The **cross elasticity of demand** is a measure of the responsiveness of the demand for a good to a change in the price of a substitute or complement, other things remaining the same. We calculate the *cross elasticity of demand* by using the formula:

$$\text{Cross elasticity} \atop \text{of demand} = \frac{\text{Percentage change} \atop \text{in quantity demanded}}{\text{Percentage change in price} \atop \text{of a substitute or complement}}.$$

The cross elasticity of demand can be positive or negative. It is *positive* for a *substitute* and *negative* for a *complement*.

Substitutes Suppose that the price of pizza is constant and people buy 9 pizzas an hour. Then the price of a burger rises from $1.50 to $2.50. No other influence on buying plans changes and the quantity of pizzas bought increases to 11 an hour.

The change in the quantity demanded is +2 pizzas—the new quantity, 11 pizzas, minus the original quantity, 9 pizzas. The average quantity is 10 pizzas. So the quantity of pizzas demanded increases by 20 percent. That is,

$$\Delta Q / Q_{ave} = (+2/10) \times 100 = +20\%.$$

The change in the price of a burger, a substitute for pizza, is +$1—the new price, $2.50, minus the original price, $1.50. The average price is $2 a burger. So the price of a burger rises by 50 percent. That is,

$$\Delta P / P_{ave} = (+\$1/\$2) \times 100 = +50\%.$$

The cross elasticity of demand for pizza with respect to the price of a burger is

$$\frac{+20\%}{+50\%} = 0.4.$$

Figure 4.6 illustrates the cross elasticity of demand. Pizzas and burgers are substitutes. Because they are substitutes, when the price of a burger rises, the demand for pizza increases. The demand curve for pizza shifts rightward from D_0 to D_1. Because a *rise* in the price of a burger brings an *increase* in the demand for pizza, the cross elasticity of demand for pizza with respect to the price of a burger is *positive*. Both the price and the quantity change in the same direction.

FIGURE 4.6 Cross Elasticity of Demand

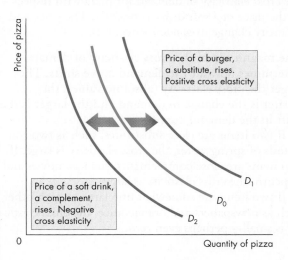

A burger is a *substitute* for pizza. When the price of a burger rises, the demand for pizza increases and the demand curve for pizza shifts rightward from D_0 to D_1. The cross elasticity of demand is *positive*.

A soft drink is a *complement* of pizza. When the price of a soft drink rises, the demand for pizza decreases and the demand curve for pizza shifts leftward from D_0 to D_2. The cross elasticity of demand is *negative*.

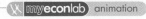 myeconlab animation

Complements Now suppose that the price of pizza is constant and 11 pizzas an hour are bought. Then the price of a soft drink rises from $1.50 to $2.50. No other influence on buying plans changes and the quantity of pizzas bought falls to 9 an hour.

The change in the quantity demanded is the opposite of what we've just calculated: The quantity of pizzas demanded decreases by 20 percent (–20%).

The change in the price of a soft drink, a complement of pizza, is the same as the percentage change in the price of a burger that we've just calculated. The price rises by 50 percent (+50%). So the cross elasticity of demand for pizza with respect to the price of a soft drink is

$$\frac{-20\%}{+50\%} = -0.4.$$

Because pizza and soft drinks are complements, when the price of a soft drink rises, the demand for pizza decreases. The demand curve for pizza shifts leftward from D_0 to D_2. Because a *rise* in the price of a soft drink brings a *decrease* in the demand for pizza, the cross elasticity of demand for pizza with respect to the price of a soft drink is *negative*. The price and quantity change in *opposite* directions.

The magnitude of the cross elasticity of demand determines how far the demand curve shifts. The larger the cross elasticity (absolute value), the greater is the change in demand and the larger is the shift in the demand curve.

If two items are close substitutes, such as two brands of spring water, the cross elasticity is large. If two items are close complements, such as movies and popcorn, the cross elasticity is large.

If two items are somewhat unrelated to each other, such as newspapers and orange juice, the cross elasticity is small—perhaps even zero.

Income Elasticity of Demand

Suppose the economy is expanding and people are enjoying rising incomes. This prosperity brings an increase in the demand for most types of goods and services. But by how much will the demand for pizza increase? The answer depends on the **income elasticity of demand**, which is a measure of the responsiveness of the demand for a good or service to a change in income, other things remaining the same.

The income elasticity of demand is calculated by using the formula:

$$\text{Income elasticity of demand} = \frac{\text{Percentage change in quantity demanded}}{\text{Percentage change in income}}.$$

Income elasticities of demand can be positive or negative and they fall into three interesting ranges:

- Greater than 1 (*normal* good, income elastic)
- Positive and less than 1 (*normal* good, income inelastic)
- Negative (*inferior* good)

Income Elastic Demand Suppose that the price of pizza is constant and 9 pizzas an hour are bought. Then incomes rise from $975 to $1,025 a week. No other influence on buying plans changes and the quantity of pizzas sold increases to 11 an hour.

The change in the quantity demanded is +2 pizzas. The average quantity is 10 pizzas, so the quantity demanded increases by 20 percent. The change in income is +$50 and the average income is $1,000, so incomes increase by 5 percent. The income elasticity of demand for pizza is

$$\frac{20\%}{5\%} = 4.$$

The demand for pizza is income elastic. The percentage increase in the quantity of pizza demanded exceeds the percentage increase in income. *When the demand for a good is income elastic, the percentage of income spent on that good increases as income increases.*

Income Inelastic Demand If the income elasticity of demand is positive but less than 1, demand is income inelastic. The percentage increase in the quantity demanded is positive but less than the percentage increase in income. *When the demand for a good is income inelastic, the percentage of income spent on that good decreases as income increases.*

Inferior Goods If the income elasticity of demand is negative, the good is an *inferior* good. The quantity demanded of an inferior good and the amount spent on it *decrease* when income increases. Goods in this category include small motorcycles, potatoes, and rice. Low-income consumers buy most of these goods.

Income Elasticities of Demand

Necessities and Luxuries

The table shows estimates of some real-world income elasticities of demand. The demand for a necessity such as food or clothing is income inelastic, while the demand for a luxury such as transportation, which includes airline and foreign travel, is income elastic.

But what is a necessity and what is a luxury depends on the level of income. For people with a low income, food and clothing can be luxuries. So the *level* of income has a big effect on income elasticities of demand.

The figure shows this effect on the income elasticity of demand for food in 10 countries. In countries with low incomes, such as Tanzania and India, the income elasticity of demand for food is high. In countries with high incomes, such as Canada, the income

elasticity of demand for food is low. That is, as income increases, the income elasticity of demand for food decreases. Low-income consumers spend a larger percentage of any increase in income on food than do high-income consumers.

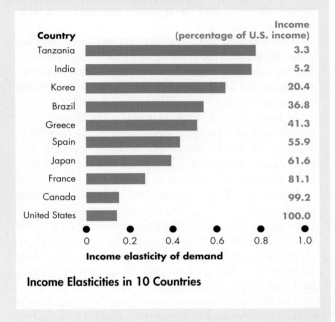

Income Elasticities in 10 Countries

Real-World Income Elasticities of Demand

Income Elastic Demand

Airline travel	5.82
Movies	3.41
Foreign travel	3.08
Electricity	1.94
Restaurant meals	1.61
Local buses and trains	1.38
Haircuts	1.36
Automobiles	1.07

Income Inelastic Demand

Tobacco	0.86
Alcoholic drinks	0.62
Furniture	0.53
Clothing	0.51
Newspapers and magazines	0.38
Telephone	0.32
Food	0.14

Sources of data: H.S. Houthakker and Lester D. Taylor, *Consumer Demand in the United States* (Cambridge, Mass.: Harvard University Press, 1970), and Henri Theil, Ching-Fan Chung, and James L. Seale, Jr., *Advances in Econometrics, Supplement 1, 1989, International Evidence on Consumption Patterns* (Greenwich, Conn.: JAI Press, Inc., 1989).

Review Quiz

1 What does the cross elasticity of demand measure?
2 What does the sign (positive versus negative) of the cross elasticity of demand tell us about the relationship between two goods?
3 What does the income elasticity of demand measure?
4 What does the sign (positive versus negative) of the income elasticity of demand tell us about a good?
5 Why does the level of income influence the magnitude of the income elasticity of demand?

 Work Study Plan 4.2 and get instant feedback.

You've now completed your study of the cross *elasticity* of demand and the *income elasticity* of demand. Let's look at the other side of the market and examine the elasticity of supply.

Elasticity of Supply

You know that when demand increases, the equilibrium price rises and the equilibrium quantity increases. But does the price rise by a large amount and the quantity increase by a little? Or does the price barely rise and the quantity increase by a large amount?

The answer depends on the responsiveness of the quantity supplied to a change in price. You can see why by studying Fig. 4.7, which shows two possible scenarios in a local pizza market. Figure 4.7(a) shows one scenario, and Fig. 4.7(b) shows the other.

In both cases, demand is initially D_0. In part (a), supply is shown by the supply curve S_A. In part (b), supply is shown by the supply curve S_B. Initially, in both cases, the price is $20 a pizza and the equilibrium quantity is 10 pizzas an hour.

Now increases in incomes and population increase the demand for pizza. The demand curve shifts rightward to D_1. In case (a), the price rises by $10 to $30 a pizza, and the quantity increases by only 3 to 13 pizzas an hour. In contrast, in case (b), the price rises by only $1 to $21 a pizza, and the quantity increases by 10 to 20 pizzas an hour.

The different outcomes arise from differing degrees of responsiveness of the quantity supplied to a change in price. We measure the degree of responsiveness by using the concept of the elasticity of supply.

Calculating the Elasticity of Supply

The **elasticity of supply** measures the responsiveness of the quantity supplied to a change in the price of a good when all other influences on selling plans remain the same. It is calculated by using the formula:

$$\text{Elasticity of supply} = \frac{\text{Percentage change in quantity supplied}}{\text{Percentage change in price}}.$$

We use the same method that you learned when you studied the elasticity of demand. (Refer back to p. 87 to check this method.) Let's calculate the elasticity of supply along the supply curves in Fig. 4.7.

In Fig. 4.7(a), when the price rises from $20 to $30, the price rise is $10 and the average price is $25, so the price rises by 40 percent of the average price. The quantity increases from 10 to 13 pizzas an hour,

FIGURE 4.7   How a Change in Demand Changes Price and Quantity

(a) Large price change and small quantity change

(b) Small price change and large quantity change

Initially, the price is $20 a pizza, and the quantity sold is 10 pizzas an hour. Then the demand for pizza increases. The demand curve shifts rightward to D_1. In part (a), the price rises by $10 to $30 a pizza, and the quantity increases by 3 to 13 pizzas an hour. In part (b), the price rises by only $1 to $21 a pizza, and the quantity increases by 10 to 20 pizzas an hour. The price change is smaller and the quantity change is larger in case (b) than in case (a). The quantity supplied is more responsive to a change in the price in case (b) than in case (a).

 animation

so the increase is 3 pizzas, the average quantity is 11.5 pizzas an hour, and the quantity increases by 26 percent. The elasticity of supply is equal to 26 percent divided by 40 percent, which equals 0.65.

In Fig. 4.7(b), when the price rises from $20 to $21, the price rise is $1 and the average price is $20.50, so the price rises by 4.9 percent of the average price. The quantity increases from 10 to 20 pizzas an hour, so the increase is 10 pizzas, the average quantity is 15 pizzas, and the quantity increases by 67 percent. The elasticity of supply is equal to 67 percent divided by 4.9 percent, which equals 13.67.

Figure 4.8 shows the range of elasticities of supply. If the quantity supplied is fixed regardless of the price, the supply curve is vertical and the elasticity of supply is zero. Supply is perfectly inelastic. This case is shown in Fig. 4.8(a). A special intermediate case occurs when the percentage change in price equals the percentage change in quantity. Supply is then unit elastic. This case is shown in Fig. 4.8(b). No matter how steep the supply curve is, if it is linear and passes through the origin, supply is unit elastic. If there is a price at which sellers are willing to offer any quantity for sale, the supply curve is horizontal and the elasticity of supply is infinite. Supply is perfectly elastic. This case is shown in Fig. 4.8(c).

The Factors That Influence the Elasticity of Supply

The elasticity of supply of a good depends on

- Resource substitution possibilities
- Time frame for the supply decision

Resource Substitution Possibilities   Some goods and services can be produced only by using unique or rare productive resources. These items have a low, perhaps even a zero, elasticity of supply. Other goods and services can be produced by using commonly available resources that could be allocated to a wide variety of alternative tasks. Such items have a high elasticity of supply.

A Van Gogh painting is an example of a good with a vertical supply curve and a zero elasticity of supply. At the other extreme, wheat can be grown on land that is almost equally good for growing corn, so it is just as easy to grow wheat as corn. The opportunity cost of wheat in terms of forgone corn is almost constant. As a result, the supply curve of wheat is almost horizontal and its elasticity of supply is very large. Similarly, when a good is produced in many different countries (for example, sugar and beef), the supply of the good is highly elastic.

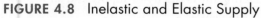

FIGURE 4.8   Inelastic and Elastic Supply

(a) Perfectly inelastic supply

(b) Unit elastic supply

(c) Perfectly elastic supply

Each supply illustrated here has a constant elasticity. The supply curve in part (a) illustrates the supply of a good that has a zero elasticity of supply. The supply curve in part (b) illustrates the supply of a good with a unit elasticity of supply. All linear supply curves that pass through the origin illustrate supplies that are unit elastic. The supply curve in part (c) illustrates the supply of a good with an infinite elasticity of supply.

The supply of most goods and services lies between these two extremes. The quantity produced can be increased but only by incurring a higher cost. If a higher price is offered, the quantity supplied increases. Such goods and services have an elasticity of supply between zero and infinity.

Time Frame for the Supply Decision To study the influence of the amount of time elapsed since a price change, we distinguish three time frames of supply:

1.   Momentary supply
2.   Long-run supply
3.   Short-run supply

When the price of a good rises or falls, the *momentary supply curve* shows the response of the quantity supplied immediately following the price change.

Some goods, such as fruits and vegetables, have a perfectly inelastic momentary supply—a vertical supply curve. The quantities supplied depend on crop-planting decisions made earlier. In the case of oranges, for example, planting decisions have to be made many years in advance of the crop being available. The momentary supply curve is vertical because, on a given day, no matter what the price of oranges, producers cannot change their output. They have picked, packed, and shipped their crop to market, and the quantity available for that day is fixed.

In contrast, some goods have a perfectly elastic momentary supply. Long-distance phone calls are an example. When many people simultaneously make a call, there is a big surge in the demand for telephone cables, computer switching, and satellite time, and the quantity supplied increases. But the price remains constant. Long-distance carriers monitor fluctuations in demand and reroute calls to ensure that the quantity supplied equals the quantity demanded without changing the price.

The *long-run supply curve* shows the response of the quantity supplied to a price change after all the technologically possible ways of adjusting supply have been exploited. In the case of oranges, the long run is the time it takes new plantings to grow to full maturity—about 15 years. In some cases, the long-run adjustment occurs only after a completely new production plant has been built and workers have been trained to operate it—typically a process that might take several years.

The *short-run supply curve* shows how the quantity supplied responds to a price change when only *some*

of the technologically possible adjustments to production have been made. The short-run response to a price change is a sequence of adjustments. The first adjustment that is usually made is in the amount of labour employed. To increase output in the short run, firms work their labour force overtime and perhaps hire additional workers. To decrease their output in the short run, firms either lay off workers or reduce their hours of work. With the passage of time, firms can make additional adjustments, perhaps training additional workers or buying additional equipment.

The short-run supply curve slopes upward because producers can take actions quite quickly to change the quantity supplied in response to a price change. For example, if the price of oranges falls, growers can stop picking and leave oranges to rot on the trees. Or if the price rises, they can use more fertilizer and improved irrigation to increase the yields of their existing trees. In the long run, they can plant more trees and increase the quantity supplied even more in response to a given price rise.

Review Quiz

1   Why do we need a units-free measure of the responsiveness of the quantity supplied of a good or service to a change in its price?
2   Define the elasticity of supply and show how it is calculated.
3   What are the main influences on the elasticity of supply that make the supply of some goods elastic and the supply of other goods inelastic?
4   Provide examples of goods or services whose elasticities of supply are (a) zero, (b) greater than zero but less than infinity, and (c) infinity.
5   How does the time frame over which a supply decision is made influence the elasticity of supply? Explain your answer.

myeconlab   Work Study Plan 4.3 and get instant feedback.

You have now learned about the elasticities of demand and supply. Table 4.1 summarizes all the elasticities that you've met in this chapter. *Reading Between the Lines* on pp. 100–101 puts the elasticity of demand to work and looks at the markets for gasoline and automobiles. In the next chapter, we study the efficiency of competitive markets.

TABLE 4.1   A Compact Glossary of Elasticities

Price Elasticities of Demand

A relationship is described as	When its magnitude is	Which means that
Perfectly elastic	Infinity	The smallest possible increase in price causes an infinitely large decrease in the quantity demanded*
Elastic	Less than infinity but greater than 1	The percentage decrease in the quantity demanded exceeds the percentage increase in price
Unit elastic	1	The percentage decrease in the quantity demanded equals the percentage increase in price
Inelastic	Greater than zero but less than 1	The percentage decrease in the quantity demanded is less than the percentage increase in price
Perfectly inelastic	Zero	The quantity demanded is the same at all prices

Cross Elasticities of Demand

A relationship is described as	When its value is	Which means that
Close substitutes	Large	The smallest possible increase in the price of one good causes an infinitely large increase in the quantity demanded of the other good
Substitutes	Positive	If the price of one good increases, the quantity demanded of the other good also increases
Unrelated goods	Zero	If the price of one good increases, the quantity demanded of the other good remains the same
Complements	Negative	If the price of one good increases, the quantity demanded of the other good decreases

Income Elasticities of Demand

A relationship is described as	When its value is	Which means that
Income elastic (normal good)	Greater than 1	The percentage increase in the quantity demanded is greater than the percentage increase in income
Income inelastic (normal good)	Less than 1 but greater than zero	The percentage increase in the quantity demanded is less than the percentage increase in income
Negative (inferior good)	Less than zero	When income increases, quantity demanded decreases

Elasticities of Supply

A relationship is described as	When its magnitude is	Which means that
Perfectly elastic	Infinity	The smallest possible increase in price causes an infinitely large increase in the quantity supplied
Elastic	Less than infinity but greater than 1	The percentage increase in the quantity supplied exceeds the percentage increase in the price
Inelastic	Greater than zero but less than 1	The percentage increase in the quantity supplied is less than the percentage increase in the price
Perfectly inelastic	Zero	The quantity supplied is the same at all prices

*In each description, the directions of change may be reversed. For example, in this case, the smallest possible decrease in price causes an infinitely large increase in the quantity demanded.

The Elasticities of Demand for Gasoline, Trucks, and Cars

GM Canada Truck Sales Fall 35%

July 2, 2008

Canadian sales of cars and light trucks, which had been holding up remarkably well for the most part in the first five months of 2008, took a sharp turn for the worse last month as the high price of gasoline cut demand for pickups, SUVs and gas guzzlers.

General Motors of Canada, the country's biggest auto maker, reported a 23.8 per cent skid in overall June sales as the company sold a total of 32,365 cars and light trucks last month, down from 42,466 in June 2007.

GM's truck sales were especially hard-hit, plunging more than 35 per cent compared with a year ago. ...

"GM Canada's June sales reflected the significant ongoing market impact of rising gas prices and the resulting further consumer shift toward cars and smaller crossovers," stated Marc Comeau, the automaker's vice-president of sales.

But GM wasn't alone in suffering a weak June.

Overall Canadian sales of light trucks last month fell by 17.6 per cent to 63,540, compared with June last year, while car sales actually increased to 95,989, up 4.3 per cent from 92,052 a year ago.

Subaru Canada also announced that it set a new record for June. Its sales volume rose by 34.9 per cent to 1,822 from 1,351.

The Canadian Press

Essence of the Story

- Faced with high gas prices, Canadians cut their demand for pickups, SUVs, and gas guzzlers.

- GM sales of cars and light trucks fell 23.8 percent in June 2008.

- GM truck sales plunged 35 percent from June 2007 to June 2008.

- Canadian sales of light trucks fell 17.6 percent to 63,540 in June, while car sales increased by 4.3 percent to 95,989 from 92,052 a year ago.

Economic Analysis

- Statistics Canada provides data on the price of gasoline. Table 1 summarizes the information on the quantity and price, and assuming that no other influences on buying plans changed, we can estimate the price elasticity of demand, using the midpoint method.

Table 1 Price Elasticity of Demand for Gasoline

	Quantity (millions of litres)	Price (dollars per litre)
June-07	110	1.07
June-08	108	1.20
Change	–2	0.13
Average	109	1.14
% change	–1.8	11.4
Elasticity	**0.16**	

- Figure 1 illustrates the calculation of the price elasticity of demand for gasoline.

- The price elasticity of demand for gasoline in Canada is 0.16, and the demand for gasoline is inelastic. A large percentage change in price brings a small percentage change in the quantity of gasoline demanded.

- Information in the news article allows us to estimate the cross elasticities of demand for GM trucks, light trucks, and cars with respect to the price of gasoline.

- Table 2 provides additional data on the quantities sold and the price of gasoline in June 2007 and June 2008.

Table 2 Cross Elasticities of Demand

	June 07	June 08	% change	Cross elasticity
	Number of vehicles			
GM trucks	22,014	14,243	–42.9	–3.76
Light trucks	77,112	63,540	–19.3	–1.69
Cars	92,052	95,898	4.1	0.36
Price of gasoline	1.07	1.20	11.4	

(dollars per litre)

- The cross elasticities of demand are calculated using the formula on p. 93.

- The cross elasticity of demand for cars is positive. A rise in the price of gasoline increases the demand for these types of automobiles. A car and gasoline are *substitutes*—a car is used in place of a large gas bill.

- Figure 2 illustrates the cross elasticity of demand for cars with respect to the price of gasoline.

Figure 1 Price elasticity of demand for gasoline

Figure 2 Cross elasticity: cars and price of gasoline

Figure 3 Cross elasticity: GM trucks and price of gasoline

- The cross elasticities of demand for the GM trucks and light trucks are negative and large. A rise in the price of gasoline decreases the demand for trucks. A truck and gasoline are *complements*.

- Figure 3 illustrates the cross elasticity of demand for trucks with respect to the price of gasoline.

SUMMARY ◆

Key Points

Price Elasticity of Demand (pp. 86–92)

- Elasticity is a measure of the responsiveness of the quantity demanded of a good to a change in its price, other things remaining the same.
- Price elasticity of demand equals the percentage change in the quantity demanded divided by the percentage change in the price.
- The larger the magnitude of the price elasticity of demand, the greater is the responsiveness of the quantity demanded to a given price change.
- If demand is elastic, a cut in price leads to an increase in total revenue. If demand is unit elastic, a cut in price leaves total revenue unchanged. And if demand is inelastic, a cut in price leads to a decrease in total revenue.
- Price elasticity of demand depends on how easily one good serves as a substitute for another, the proportion of income spent on the good, and the length of time elapsed since the price change.

More Elasticities of Demand (pp. 93–95)

- Cross elasticity of demand measures the responsiveness of the demand for one good to a change in the price of a substitute or a complement, other things remaining the same.
- The cross elasticity of demand with respect to the price of a substitute is positive. The cross elasticity of demand with respect to the price of a complement is negative.
- Income elasticity of demand measures the responsiveness of demand to a change in income, other things remaining the same. For a normal good, the income elasticity of demand is positive. For an inferior good, the income elasticity of demand is negative.
- When the income elasticity of demand is greater than 1 (income elastic), the percentage of income spent on the good increases as income increases.
- When the income elasticity of demand is less than 1 (income inelastic and inferior), the percentage of income spent on the good decreases as income increases.

Elasticity of Supply (pp. 96–98)

- Elasticity of supply measures the responsiveness of the quantity supplied of a good to a change in its price, other things remaining the same.
- The elasticity of supply is usually positive and ranges between zero (vertical supply curve) and infinity (horizontal supply curve).
- The elasticity of supply depends on resource substitution possibilities and the time frame for the supply decision.
- Momentary supply refers to the response of the quantity supplied to a price change at the instant that the price changes.
- Long-run supply refers to the response of the quantity supplied to a price change when all the technologically feasible adjustments in production have been made.
- Short-run supply refers to the response of the quantity supplied to a price change after some of the technologically feasible adjustments in production have been made.

Key Figures and Table

Figure 4.2   Calculating the Elasticity of Demand, 87
Figure 4.3   Inelastic and Elastic Demand, 88
Figure 4.4   Elasticity Along a Straight-Line Demand Curve, 89
Figure 4.5   Elasticity and Total Revenue, 90
Figure 4.6   Cross Elasticity of Demand, 93
Table 4.1   A Compact Glossary of Elasticities, 99

Key Terms

Cross elasticity of demand, 93
Elastic demand, 89
Elasticity of supply, 96
Income elasticity of demand, 94
Inelastic demand, 88
Perfectly elastic demand, 89
Perfectly inelastic demand, 88
Price elasticity of demand, 86
Total revenue, 90
Total revenue test, 90
Unit elastic demand, 88

PROBLEMS and APPLICATIONS ◆

myeconlab Work problems 1–12 in Chapter 4 Study Plan and get instant feedback.
Work problems 14–28 as Homework, a Quiz, or a Test if assigned by your instructor.

1. Rain spoils the strawberry crop. As a result, the price rises from $4 to $6 a box and the quantity demanded decreases from 1,000 to 600 boxes a week. Over this price range,
   a. What is the price elasticity of demand?
   b. Describe the demand for strawberries.

2. When the price of a good increased by 10 percent, the quantity demanded of it decreased by 2 percent.
   a. Is the demand for this good elastic, unit elastic, or inelastic?
   b. Are substitutes for this good easy to find or does it have poor substitutes? Is this good more likely to be a necessity or a luxury? Is the good more likely to be narrowly or broadly defined? Why?
   c. Calculate the price elasticity of demand for this good and explain how the total revenue from the sale of this good has changed.
   d. Explain which of the goods in the following list this good is most likely to be: orange juice, bread, toothpaste, theatre tickets, clothing, blue jeans, Stanley Cup tickets.

3. The demand schedule for hotel rooms is

Price (dollars per night)	Quantity demanded (rooms per night)
200	10,000
250	8,000
400	5,000
500	4,000
800	2,500

   a. What happens to total revenue if the price falls from $400 to $250 a night?
   b. What happens to total revenue if the price falls from $250 to $200 a night?
   c. At what price is total revenue at a maximum? Explain and interpret your answer.
   d. Is the demand for hotel rooms elastic, unit elastic, or inelastic?

4. In 2003, when music downloading first took off, Universal Music slashed the price of a CD from an average of $21 to an average of $15. The company said that it expected the price cut to boost the quantity of CDs sold by 30 percent, other things remaining the same.
   a. What was Universal Music's estimate of the price elasticity of demand for CDs?
   b. Given your answer in a, if you were making the pricing decision at Universal Music, would you cut the price, raise the price, or not change the price? Explain your decision.

5. **Why the Tepid Response to Rising Gasoline Prices?**
   Estimates of the long-run response to past movements in [gasoline] prices imply that a 10 percent price rise causes 5 to 10 percent less consumption, other things being equal. ... The nationwide average price of gasoline surged 53 percent from 1998 to 2004, after adjusting for inflation. Yet consumption was up 10 percent in this period.
   Of course, many other things changed in this period. Perhaps most important, [incomes] grew by 19 percent. ... This would ordinarily be expected to push gasoline sales up about 20 percent. ...
   New York Times, October 13, 2005
   a. What does the above information tell us about the responsiveness of the quantity of gasoline demanded to a change in the price a long time after the price change occurs?
   b. Calculate the income elasticity of demand for gasoline implied by the above information.
   c. If other things remained the same except for the increase in income and the rise in price, what would the data for 1998 to 2004 imply about the price elasticity of demand for gasoline?
   d. List all the factors you can think of that might bias the estimate of the price elasticity of demand for gasoline, using just the data for 1998 to 2004.

6. If a 12 percent rise in the price of orange juice decreases the quantity of orange juice demanded by 22 percent and increases the quantity of apple juice demanded by 14 percent, calculate the
   a. Price elasticity of demand for orange juice.
   b. Cross elasticity of demand for apple juice with respect to the price of orange juice.

7. **Swelling Textbook Costs Have College Students Saying "Pass"**

   Textbook prices have been rising at double the rate of inflation. ... [and] nearly 60 percent of students nationwide choose not to buy all the course materials. ... For students working to pay for school or for those whose parents sweat every increase in tuition, book prices can be a nasty surprise. ... And plenty of students come up with their own strategies: Hunting down used copies and selling books back at the end of the semester; buying online, which is sometimes cheaper than the campus store; asking professors to put a copy in the library and waiting around till it's free. Or borrowing, copying, taking careful notes in class—and gambling that the exam questions don't come from the text.

   Washington Post, January 23, 2006

   Explain what this news clip implies about

   a. The price elasticity of demand for college text-books.
   b. The income elasticity of demand for college textbooks.
   c. The cross elasticity of demand for college text-books from the campus bookstore with respect to the online price of a textbook.

8. **Home Depot Earnings Hammered**

   As home prices slump across the country, fewer people are spending money to renovate their homes, and the improvements that they are mak-ing are not as expensive. ... People are spending on small ticket types of repairs, ... not big ticket renovations ... With gas and food prices increas-ing ... people have less extra income to spend on major home improvements.

   CNN, May 20, 2008

   What does this news clip imply about the income elasticity of demand for big-ticket home-improvement items? Would the income elasticity of demand be greater or less than 1? Explain.

9. **Spam Sales Rise as Food Costs Soar**

   Sales of Spam—that much maligned meat—are rising as consumers are turning more to lunch meats and other lower-cost foods to extend their already stretched food budgets. ... Consumers are quick to realize that meats like Spam and other processed foods can be substituted for costlier cuts as a way of controlling costs.

   AOL Money & Finance, May 28, 2008

   a. Is Spam a normal good or inferior good? Explain.
   b. Would the income elasticity of demand for Spam be negative or positive? Explain.

10. When the price of a pizza falls from $9 to $7 and other things remain the same, the quantity of pizza demanded increases from 100 to 200 an hour, the quantity of burgers demanded decreases from 200 to 100 an hour, and the quantity of cola demanded increases from 150 to 250 cans an hour.

    a. Calculate the cross elasticity of demand for cola with respect to pizza.
    b. Calculate the cross elasticity of demand for burgers with respect to pizza.
    c. Of what use are these two cross elasticities of demand to the owner of a business that sells burgers and cola?

11. You are told that a 10 percent increase in the price of a good increases the quantity supplied of it after a month by 1 percent and after a year by 25 percent.

    a. Is the supply of this good elastic, unit elastic, or inelastic? Is this good likely to be produced using productive resources that are easily obtained?
    b. What is the elasticity of supply of this good after one year? Has the supply of this good become more elastic or less elastic? Why?

12. The quantity demanded of good *A* increases by 5 percent when the price of good *B* rises by 10 percent and other things remain the same. Are goods *A* and *B* complements or substitutes? Describe how the demand for good *A* changes and calculate the cross elasticity of demand.

13. Use the links on MyEconLab (Textbook Resources, Chapter 4, Web links) to find the number of litres in a barrel of oil and the prices of crude oil and gasoline in the summer of 2007 and 2008.

    a. What are the other costs that make up the total cost of a litre of gasoline?
    b. If the price of crude oil falls by 10 percent, by what percentage will the price of gasoline change, other things remaining the same?
    c. Which demand do you think is more elastic: that for crude oil or gasoline? Why?
    d. Use the concepts of demand, supply, and elasticity to explain recent changes in the prices of crude oil and gasoline.

14. With higher fuel costs, airlines raise their fares. The average fare rises from 75¢ per passenger mile to $1.25 per passenger mile and the number of passenger miles decreases from 2.5 million a day to 1.5 million a day. Over this price range,

    a. What is the price elasticity of demand for air travel?
    b. Describe the demand for air travel.

15. The figure shows the demand for DVD rentals.

    a. Calculate the elasticity of demand when the price rises from $3 to $5 a DVD.
    b. At what price is the elasticity of demand for DVDs equal to 1?

16. Use the data in the *Reading Between the Lines* on p. 77 to calculate the price elasticity of demand for gasoline in Canada.

17. If the quantity of dental services demanded increases by 10 percent when the price of dental services falls by 10 percent, is the demand for dental services inelastic, elastic, or unit elastic?

18. The demand schedule for computer chips is

Price (dollars per chip)	Quantity demanded (millions of chips per year)
200	50
250	45
300	40
350	35
400	30

    a. What happens to total revenue if the price falls from $400 to $350 a chip?
    b. What happens to total revenue if the price falls from $350 to $300 a chip?
    c. At what price is total revenue at a maximum?

    d. At an average price of $350, is the demand for chips elastic, inelastic, or unit elastic? Use the total revenue test to answer this question.
    e. At $250 a chip, is the demand for chips elastic or inelastic? Use the total revenue test to answer this question.

19. Your price elasticity of demand for bananas is 4. If the price of bananas rises by 5 percent, what is

    a. The percentage change in the quantity of bananas you buy?
    b. The change in your expenditure on bananas?

20. You are told that a 5 percent increase in the price of a good has led to an 8 percent increase in the quantity supplied of the good after one month and a 10 percent increase in the quantity supplied after one year.

    a. Is the supply of this good elastic, unit elastic, or inelastic in the short run?
    b. Is this good likely to be produced using productive resources that are easily obtained?
    c. Has the supply of this good become more elastic or less elastic in the long run? Why?

21. **Why Gasoline Follows Oil Up but Not Down**
    If it seems like gasoline prices are quick to skyrocket when the price of oil goes up, but then take their sweet ol' time coming back down when crude prices sink, the answer is simple: They do. "There is a rocket and feather aspect." ... The service stations are still selling the same amount of gasoline when wholesale prices fall ... "so there's no reason to drop. ...[Service stations] typically react [to a spike in oil prices] by pushing prices higher, even before they replace their inventories ..." Eventually, the free market steps in and prices begin going down when other nearby stations reduce their price.
    CNN, January 12, 2007

    a. Explain the link between the elasticity of supply of gasoline and gas price fluctuations.
    b. Explain the connection between the elasticity of demand for gasoline and the "rocket and feather" tendency of price fluctuations.

22. **As Gasoline Prices Soar, Americans Slowly Adapt**
    ... in March, Americans drove 11 billion fewer miles than in March 2007 ... "People have recognized that prices are not going down and are

adapting to higher energy cost." ... Americans spend 3.7 percent of their disposable income on transportation fuels. At its lowest point, that share was 1.9 percent in 1998, and at its highest it reached 4.5 percent in 1981 ... "We actually have a lot of choices, based on what car we drive, where we live, how much time we choose to drive, and where we choose to go." For many people, higher energy costs mean fewer restaurant meals, deferred weekend outings, ... less air travel and more time closer to home. ...

International Herald Tribune, May 23, 2008

a. List and explain the elasticities of demand that are implicitly referred to in the news clip.

b. Explain the factors identified in the news clip that may make the demand for gasoline inelastic.

23. When Alex's income increased from $3,000 to $5,000, he increased his consumption of bagels from 4 to 8 a month and decreased his consumption of doughnuts from 12 to 6 a month. Calculate Alex's income elasticity of demand for

a. Bagels.

b. Doughnuts.

24. **Wal-Mart's Recession-Time Pet Project**

Wal-Mart ... is "redefining" the pets business in its stores, including repositioning pet food and supplies right in front of its other fast-growing business, baby products. There lies the connection, according to retail industry experts, ... even in a recession, dogs will be fed and kids will get their toys. ...

CNN, May 13, 2008

a. What does this news clip imply about the income elasticity of demand for pet food and baby products?

b. Would the income elasticity of demand be greater or less than 1? Explain.

25. **Netflix to Offer Online Movie Viewing**

Online movie rental service Netflix introduced a new feature Tuesday to allow customers to watch movies and television series on their personal computers. ... Netflix has been competing with video rental retailer Blockbuster, which has added an online rental service to the in-store rental service.

CNN, January 16, 2007

a. How will the offering of online movie viewing influence the price elasticity of demand for in-store movie rentals?

b. Would the cross elasticity of demand for online movies and in-store movie rentals be negative or positive? Explain.

c. Would the cross elasticity of demand for online movies with respect to high-speed Internet service be negative or positive? Explain.

26. **To Love, Honor, and Save Money**

Nearly half of caterers and event planners surveyed ... said they were seeing declines in wedding spending in response to the economic slowdown; 12% even reported wedding cancellations because of financial concerns.

Time, June 2, 2008

a. Based upon this news clip, are wedding events a normal good or inferior good? Explain.

b. Are wedding events more of a necessity or luxury? Explain.

c. Given your answer to b, would that make the income elasticity of demand greater than 1, less than 1, or equal to 1?

27. The table gives the supply schedule of long-distance phone calls.

Price (cents per minute)	Quantity supplied (millions of minutes per day)
10	200
20	400
30	600
40	800

Calculate the elasticity of supply when

a. The price falls from 40¢ to 30¢ a minute.

b. The average price is 20¢ a minute.

28. Study *Reading Between the Lines* on pp. 100–101. Then answer the following questions.

a. What factors other than the price of gasoline would you expect to influence motorists' planned purchases of gasoline?

b. Explain how the factors you identified in a would change the demand for gasoline.

c. How would the changes in the demand for gasoline in b have biased our estimate of the price elasticity of demand for gasoline?

d. Given the influence of the price of gasoline on the demand for cars and light trucks, how would you expect the prices of cars and light trucks (pickups) to have changed in 2008?

e. What elasticities do you need to know to predict the magnitude of the changes in the prices of cars and pickups?

5

Efficiency and Equity

After studying this chapter, you will be able to

- Describe the alternative methods of allocating scarce resources
- Explain the connection between demand and marginal benefit and define consumer surplus
- Explain the connection between supply and marginal cost and define producer surplus
- Explain the conditions under which markets are efficient and inefficient
- Explain the main ideas about fairness and evaluate claims that markets result in unfair outcomes

Every time you pour a glass of water or order a pizza, you express your view about how scarce resources should be used and you make choices in your *self-interest*. Markets coordinate your choices along with those of everyone else. But do markets do a good job? Do they allocate resources between water, pizza, and everything else efficiently?

The market economy generates huge income inequality. You can afford to buy a bottle of fresh spring water, while a student in India must make the best of dirty well water or expensive water from a tanker. Is this situation fair?

The *social interest* has the two dimensions that we've just discussed: efficiency and fairness (or equity). So our central question in this chapter is: Do markets operate in the social interest? At the end of the chapter, in *Reading Between the Lines*, we return to the issue of the use of the water resources. Do we use markets and other arrangements that allocate scarce water efficiently and fairly?

Resource Allocation Methods

The goal of this chapter is to evaluate the ability of markets to allocate resources efficiently and fairly. But to see whether the market does a good job, we must compare it with its alternatives. Resources are scarce, so they must be allocated somehow. And trading in markets is just one of several alternative methods.

Resources might be allocated by

- Market price
- Command
- Majority rule
- Contest
- First-come, first-served
- Lottery
- Personal characteristics
- Force

Let's briefly examine each method.

Market Price

When a market price allocates a scarce resource, the people who are willing and able to pay that price get the resource. Two kinds of people decide not to pay the market price: those who can afford to pay but choose not to buy and those who are too poor and simply can't afford to buy.

For many goods and services, distinguishing between those who choose not to buy and those who can't afford to buy doesn't matter. But for a few items, it does matter. For example, poor people can't afford to pay school fees and doctors' fees. Because poor people can't afford items that most people consider to be essential, these items are usually allocated by one of the other methods.

Command

A **command system** allocates resources by the order (command) of someone in authority. In the Canadian economy, the command system is used extensively inside firms and government departments. For example, if you have a job, most likely someone tells you what to do. Your labour is allocated to specific tasks by a command.

A command system works well in organizations in which the lines of authority and responsibility are clear and it is easy to monitor the activities being performed. But a command system works badly when the range of activities to be monitored is large and when it is easy for people to fool those in authority. The system works so badly in North Korea, where it is used extensively in place of markets, that it fails even to deliver an adequate supply of food.

Majority Rule

Majority rule allocates resources in the way that a majority of voters choose. Societies use majority rule to elect representative governments that make some of the biggest decisions. For example, majority rule decides the tax rates that end up allocating scarce resources between private use and public use. And majority rule decides how tax dollars are allocated among competing uses such as education and health care.

Majority rule works well when the decisions being made affect large numbers of people and self-interest must be suppressed to use resources most effectively.

Contest

A contest allocates resources to a winner (or a group of winners). Sporting events use this method. Tiger Woods competes with other golfers, and the winner gets the biggest payoff. But contests are more general than those in a sports arena, though we don't normally call them contests. For example, Bill Gates won a contest to provide the world's personal computer operating system.

Contests do a good job when the efforts of the "players" are hard to monitor and reward directly. When a manager offers everyone in the company the opportunity to win a big prize, people are motivated to work hard and try to become the winner. Only a few people end up with a big prize, but many people work harder in the process of trying to win. The total output produced by the workers is much greater than it would be without the contest.

First-Come, First-Served

A first-come, first-served method allocates resources to those who are first in line. Many casual restaurants won't accept reservations. They use first-come, first-served to allocate their scarce tables. Highway space is allocated in this way too: The first to arrive at the on-ramp gets the road space. If too many vehicles enter the highway, the speed slows and people wait in line for some space to become available.

First-come, first-served works best when, as in the above examples, a scarce resource can serve just one user at a time in a sequence. By serving the user who arrives first, this method minimizes the time spent waiting for the resource to become free.

Lottery

Lotteries allocate resources to those who pick the winning number, draw the lucky cards, or come up lucky in some other gaming system. State lotteries and casinos reallocate millions of dollars worth of goods and services every year.

But lotteries are more widespread than jackpots and roulette wheels in casinos. They are used to allocate landing slots to airlines at some airports and have been used to allocate fishing rights and the electromagnetic spectrum used by cell phones.

Lotteries work best when there is no effective way to distinguish among potential users of a scarce resource.

Personal Characteristics

When resources are allocated on the basis of personal characteristics, people with the "right" characteristics get the resources. Some of the resources that matter most to you are allocated in this way. For example, you will choose a marriage partner on the basis of personal characteristics. But this method is also used in unacceptable ways. Allocating the best jobs to white males and discriminating against visible minorities and women is an example.

Force

Force plays a crucial role, for both good and ill, in allocating scarce resources. Let's start with the ill.

War, the use of military force by one nation against another, has played an enormous role historically in allocating resources. The economic supremacy of European settlers in the Americas and Australia owes much to the use of this method.

Theft, the taking of the property of others without their consent, also plays a large role. Both large-scale organized crime and small-scale petty crime collectively allocate billions of dollars worth of resources annually.

But force plays a crucial positive role in allocating resources. It provides the state with an effective method of transferring wealth from the rich to the poor, and it provides the legal framework in which voluntary exchange in markets takes place.

A legal system is the foundation on which our market economy functions. Without courts to enforce contracts, it would not be possible to do business. But the courts could not enforce contracts without the ability to apply force if necessary. The state provides the ultimate force that enables the courts to do their work.

More broadly, the force of the state is essential to uphold the principle of the rule of law. This principle is the bedrock of civilized economic (and social and political) life. With the rule of law upheld, people can go about their daily economic lives with the assurance that their property will be protected—that they can sue for violations against their property (and be sued if they violate the property of others).

Free from the burden of protecting their property and confident in the knowledge that those with whom they trade will honour their agreements, people can get on with focusing on the activity at which they have a comparative advantage and trading for mutual gain.

Review Quiz

1 Why do we need methods of allocating scarce resources?
2 Describe the alternative methods of allocating scarce resources.
3 Provide an example of each allocation method that illustrates when it works well.
4 Provide an example of each allocation method that illustrates when it works badly.

 Work Study Plan 5.1 and get instant feedback.

In the next sections, we're going to see how a market can achieve an efficient use of resources, examine the obstacles to efficiency, and see how sometimes an alternative method might improve on the market. After looking at efficiency, we'll turn our attention to the more difficult issue of fairness.

Demand and Marginal Benefit

Resources are allocated efficiently when they are used in the ways that people value most highly. This outcome occurs when marginal benefit equals marginal cost (Chapter 2, pp. 35–37). So to determine whether a competitive market is efficient, we need to see whether, at the market equilibrium quantity, marginal benefit equals marginal cost. We begin by seeing how market demand reflects marginal benefit.

Demand, Willingness to Pay, and Value

In everyday life, we talk about "getting value for money." When we use this expression, we are distinguishing between *value* and *price*. Value is what we get, and price is what we pay.

The value of one more unit of a good or service is its marginal benefit. And we measure marginal benefit by the maximum price that is willingly paid for another unit of the good or service. But willingness to pay determines demand. *A demand curve is a marginal benefit curve.*

In Fig. 5.1(a), Lisa is willing to pay $1 for the 30th slice of pizza and $1 is her marginal benefit from that slice. In Fig. 5.1(b), Nick is willing to pay $1 for the 10th slice of pizza and $1 is his marginal benefit from that slice. But at what quantity is the market willing to pay $1 for the marginal slice? The answer is provided by the market demand curve.

Individual Demand and Market Demand

The relationship between the price of a good and the quantity demanded by one person is called *individual demand*. And the relationship between the price of a good and the quantity demanded by all buyers is called *market demand*.

> The market demand curve is the horizontal sum of the individual demand curves and is formed by adding the quantities demanded by all the individuals at each price.

Figure 5.1(c) illustrates the market demand for pizza if Lisa and Nick are the only people in the market. Lisa's demand curve in part (a) and Nick's demand curve in part (b) sum horizontally to the market demand curve in part (c).

FIGURE 5.1   Individual Demand, Market Demand, and Marginal Social Benefit

(a) Lisa's demand   **(b) Nick's demand**   **(c) Market demand**

At a price of $1 a slice, the quantity demanded by Lisa is 30 slices and the quantity demanded by Nick is 10 slices, so the quantity demanded by the market is 40 slices. Lisa's demand curve in part (a) and Nick's demand curve in part (b) sum horizontally to the market demand curve in part (c). The market demand curve is the marginal social benefit (MSB) curve.

myeconlab animation

At a price of $1 a slice, Lisa demands 30 slices and Nick demands 10 slices, so the market quantity demanded at $1 a slice is 40 slices. From the market demand curve, we see that the economy is willing to pay $1 for 40 slices a day. *The market demand curve is the marginal social benefit (MSB) curve.*

Although here the price is in dollars, think of the price as the number of *dollars' worth of other goods willingly forgone* to obtain one more slice of pizza.

Consumer Surplus

We don't always have to pay what we are willing to pay—we get a bargain. When people buy something for less than it is worth to them, they receive a consumer surplus. A **consumer surplus** is the value (or marginal benefit) of a good minus the price paid for it, summed over the quantity bought.

Figure 5.2(a) shows Lisa's consumer surplus from pizza when the price is $1 a slice. At this price, she buys 30 slices a month because the 30th slice is worth exactly $1 to her. But Lisa is willing to pay $2 for the 10th slice, so her marginal benefit from this slice is $1 more than she pays for it—she receives a surplus of $1 on the 10th slice.

Lisa's consumer surplus is the sum of the surpluses on *all of the slices she buys*. This sum is the area of the green triangle—the area below the demand curve and above the market price line. The area of this triangle is equal to its base (30 slices) multiplied by its height ($1.50) divided by 2, which is $22.50. The area of the blue rectangle in Fig. 5.2(a) shows what Lisa pays for 30 slices of pizza.

Figure 5.2(b) shows Nick's consumer surplus, and part (c) shows the consumer surplus for the market. The consumer surplus for the market is the sum of the consumer surpluses of Lisa and Nick.

All goods and services, like pizza, have decreasing marginal benefit, so people receive more benefit from their consumption than the amount they pay.

Review Quiz

1 How do we measure the value or marginal benefit of a good or service?
2 What is consumer surplus? How is it measured?

 Work Study Plan 5.2 and get instant feedback.

FIGURE 5.2 Demand and Consumer Surplus

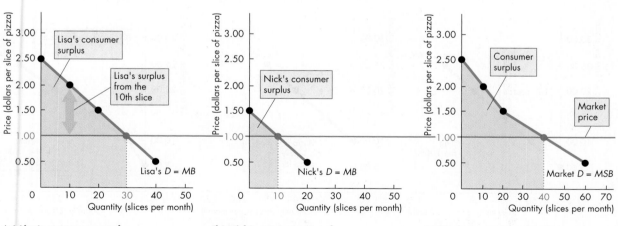

(a) Lisa's consumer surplus   **(b) Nick's consumer surplus**   **(c) Market consumer surplus**

Lisa is willing to pay $2 for her 10th slice of pizza in part (a). At a market price of $1 a slice, Lisa receives a surplus of $1 on the 10th slice. The green triangle shows her consumer surplus on the 30 slices she buys at $1 a slice.

The green triangle in part (b) shows Nick's consumer surplus on the 10 slices that he buys at $1 a slice. The green area in part (c) shows the consumer surplus for the market. The blue rectangles show the amounts spent on pizza.

Supply and Marginal Cost

We are now going to see how market supply reflects marginal cost. This section closely parallels the related ideas about market demand and marginal benefit that you've just studied. Firms are in business to make a profit. To do so, they must sell their output for a price that exceeds the cost of production. Let's investigate the relationship between cost and price.

Supply, Cost, and Minimum Supply-Price

Firms make a profit when they receive more from the sale of a good or service than the cost of producing it. Just as consumers distinguish between value and price, so producers distinguish between cost and price. Cost is what a producer gives up, and price is what a producer receives.

The cost of producing one more unit of a good or service is its marginal cost. Marginal cost is the minimum price that producers must receive to induce them to offer one more unit of a good or service for sale. But the minimum supply-price determines supply. *A supply curve is a marginal cost curve.*

In Fig. 5.3(a), Max is willing to produce the 100th pizza for $15, his marginal cost of that pizza. In Fig. 5.3(b), Mario is willing to produce the 50th pizza for $15, his marginal cost of that pizza. But what quantity is this market willing to produce for $15 a pizza? The answer is provided by the *market supply curve.*

Individual Supply and Market Supply

The relationship between the price of a good and the quantity supplied by one producer is called *individual supply*. And the relationship between the price of a good and the quantity supplied by all producers is called *market supply*.

> The market supply curve is the horizontal sum of the individual supply curves and is formed by adding the quantities supplied by all the producers at each price.

Figure 5.3(c) illustrates the market supply if Max and Mario are the only producers of pizzas. Max's supply curve in part (a) and Mario's supply curve in part (b) sum horizontally to the market supply curve in part (c).

FIGURE 5.3 Individual Supply, Market Supply, and Marginal Social Cost

(a) Max's supply

(b) Mario's supply

(c) Market supply

At a price of $15 a pizza, the quantity supplied by Max is 100 pizzas and the quantity supplied by Mario is 50 pizzas, so the quantity supplied by the market is 150 pizzas. Max's supply curve in part (a) and Mario's supply curve in part (b) sum horizontally to the market supply curve in part (c). The market supply curve is the marginal social cost (MSC) curve.

myeconlab animation

At a price of $15 a pizza, Max supplies 100 pizzas and Mario supplies 50 pizzas, so the quantity supplied by the market at $15 a pizza is 150 pizzas.

From the market supply curve, we see that the market is willing to supply 150 pizzas a month for $15 each. *The market supply curve is the marginal social cost (MSC) curve.*

Again, although we're measuring price in dollars, think of the price as telling us the number of *dollars' worth of other goods and services that must be forgone* to produce one more pizza.

Producer Surplus

When price exceeds marginal cost, the firm receives a producer surplus. A **producer surplus** is the price received for a good minus its minimum supply-price (or marginal cost), summed over the quantity sold.

Figure 5.4(a) shows Max's producer surplus from pizza when the price is $15 a pizza. At this price, he sells 100 pizzas a month because the 100th pizza costs him $15 to produce. But Max is willing to produce the 50th pizza for his marginal cost, which is $10, so he receives a surplus of $5 on this pizza.

Max's producer surplus is the sum of the surpluses on the pizzas he sells. This sum is the area of the blue triangle—the area below the market price and above the supply curve. The area of this triangle is equal to its base (100) multiplied by its height ($10) divided by 2, which is $500.

The red area in Fig. 5.4(a) is what it costs Max to produce 100 pizzas.

The area of the blue triangle in Fig. 5.4(b) shows Mario's producer surplus and the blue area in Fig. 5.4(c) shows the producer surplus for the market. The producer surplus for the market is the sum of the producer surpluses of Max and Mario.

Review Quiz

1 What is the relationship between the marginal cost, minimum supply-price, and supply?
2 What is producer surplus? How is it measured?

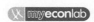 Work Study Plan 5.3 and get instant feedback.

Consumer surplus and producer surplus can be used to measure the efficiency of a market. Let's see how we can use these concepts to study the efficiency of a competitive market.

FIGURE 5.4   Supply and Producer Surplus

(a) Max's producer surplus

(b) Mario's producer surplus

(c) Market producer surplus

Max is willing to produce the 50th pizza for $10 in part (a). At a market price of $15 a pizza, Max gets a surplus of $5 on the 50th pizza. The blue triangle shows his producer surplus on the 100 pizzas he sells at $15 each. The blue triangle in part (b) shows Mario's producer surplus on the 50 pizzas that he sells at $15 each. The blue area in part (c) shows producer surplus for the market. The red areas show the cost of producing the pizzas sold.

myeconlab animation

Is the Competitive Market Efficient?

Figure 5.5(a) shows the market for pizza. The market forces that you studied in Chapter 3 (pp. 68–69) pull the pizza market to its equilibrium price of $15 a pizza and equilibrium quantity of 10,000 pizzas a day. Buyers enjoy a consumer surplus (green area) and sellers enjoy a producer surplus (blue area), but is this competitive equilibrium efficient?

Efficiency of Competitive Equilibrium

You've seen that the demand curve tells us the marginal benefit from a pizza. If the only people who benefit from pizza are the people who buy it, then the demand curve for pizzas measures the marginal benefit to the entire society from pizza. We call the marginal benefit to the entire society, marginal *social* benefit, *MSB*. In this case, the demand curve is also the *MSB* curve.

You've also seen that the supply curve tells us the marginal cost of a pizza. If the only people who bear the cost of pizza are the people who produce it, then the supply curve of pizzas measures the marginal cost of a pizza to the entire society. We call the marginal cost to the entire society, marginal *social* cost, *MSC*. In this case, the supply curve is also the *MSC* curve.

So where the demand curve and the supply curve intersect in part (a), marginal social benefit equals marginal social cost in part (b). This condition delivers an efficient use of resources for the entire society.

If production is less than 10,000 pizzas a day, the marginal pizza is valued more highly than it costs to produce. If production exceeds 10,000 pizzas a day, the marginal pizza costs more to produce than the value that consumers place on it. Only when 10,000 pizzas a day are produced is the marginal pizza worth exactly what it costs.

The competitive market pushes the quantity of pizzas produced to its efficient level of 10,000 a day. If production is less than 10,000 pizzas a day, a shortage raises the price, which increases production. If production exceeds 10,000 pizzas a day, a surplus of pizzas lowers the price, which decreases production. So a competitive pizza market is efficient.

When the efficient quantity is produced, the *total surplus* (the sum of consumer surplus and producer surplus) is maximized. Buyers and sellers acting in their self-interest end up promoting the social interest.

FIGURE 5.5 An Efficient Market for Pizza

(a) Equilibrium and surpluses

(b) Efficiency

Competitive equilibrium in part (a) occurs when the quantity demanded equals the quantity supplied. Consumer surplus is the area under the demand curve and above the market price (the green triangle). Producer surplus is the area above the supply curve and below the market price (the blue triangle). Resources are used efficiently in part (b) when marginal social benefit, *MSB*, equals marginal social cost, *MSC*.

The efficient quantity in part (b) is the same as the equilibrium quantity in part (a). The competitive pizza market produces the efficient quantity of pizzas.

 myeconlab animation

Markets at Work

The Invisible Hand

Writing in his *Wealth of Nations* in 1776, Adam Smith was the first to suggest that competitive markets send resources to the uses in which they have the highest value (see p. 53). Smith believed that each participant in a competitive market is "led by an invisible hand to promote an end [the efficient use of resources] which was no part of his intention."

You can see the invisible hand at work in the cartoon and in the world today.

Umbrella for Sale The cold drinks vendor has cold drinks and shade and he has a marginal cost and a minimum supply-price of each. The reader on the park bench has a marginal benefit and willingness to pay for each. The reader's marginal benefit from shade exceeds the vendor's marginal cost; but the vendor's marginal cost of a cold drink exceeds the reader's marginal benefit. They trade the umbrella. The vendor gets a producer surplus from selling the shade for more than its marginal cost, and the reader gets a consumer surplus from buying the shade for less than its marginal benefit. Both are better off and the umbrella has moved to its highest-valued use.

The Invisible Hand at Work Today The market economy relentlessly performs the activity illustrated in the cartoon to achieve an efficient allocation of resources.

A Florida frost cuts the supply of oranges. With fewer oranges available in Canada, the marginal social benefit from oranges increases. A shortage of oranges raises their price, so the market allocates the smaller quantity available to the people who value them most highly.

A new technology cuts the cost of producing a computer. With a lower production cost, the supply of computers increases and the price of a computer falls. The lower price encourages an increase in the quantity demanded of this now less-costly tool. The

© The New Yorker Collection 1985 Mike Twohy from cartoonbank.com. All Rights Reserved.

marginal social benefit from a computer is brought to equality with its marginal social cost.

In both the oranges and computer examples, market forces persistently bring marginal social cost and marginal social benefit to equality, allocate scarce resources efficiently, and maximize total surplus (consumer surplus plus producer surplus).

Underproduction and Overproduction

Inefficiency can occur because either too little of an item is produced (underproduction) or too much is produced (overproduction).

Underproduction In Fig. 5.6(a), the quantity of pizzas produced is 5,000 a day. At this quantity, consumers are willing to pay $20 for a pizza that costs only $10 to produce. By producing only 5,000 pizzas a day, total surplus is smaller than its maximum possible level. The quantity produced is inefficient—there is underproduction.

We measure the scale of inefficiency by **deadweight loss**, which is the decrease in total surplus that results

FIGURE 5.6 Underproduction and Overproduction

(a) Underproduction

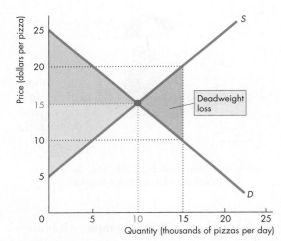

(b) Overproduction

If pizza production is 5,000 a day in part (a), total surplus (shown by the green and blue areas) is smaller than its maximum level by the amount of the deadweight loss (shown by the grey triangle). At all production levels below 10,000 pizzas a day, the benefit from one more pizza exceeds its cost.

If pizza production is 15,000 a day in part (b), total surplus is also smaller than its maximum level by the amount of the deadweight loss. At all production levels in excess of 10,000 pizzas a day, the cost of one more pizza exceeds its benefit.

myeconlab animation

from an inefficient level of production. The grey triangle in Fig. 5.6(a) shows the deadweight loss.

Overproduction In Fig. 5.6(b), the quantity of pizzas produced is 15,000 a day. At this quantity, consumers are willing to pay only $10 for a pizza that costs $20 to produce. By producing the 15,000th pizza, $10 of resources are wasted. Again, the grey triangle shows the deadweight loss, which reduces the total surplus to less than its maximum.

The deadweight loss is borne by the entire society: It is a *social* loss.

Obstacles to Efficiency

The obstacles to efficiency that bring underproduction or overproduction are

- Price and quantity regulations
- Taxes and subsidies
- Externalities
- Public goods and common resources
- Monopoly
- High transactions costs

Price and Quantity Regulations *Price regulations* that put a cap on the rent a landlord is permitted to charge and laws that require employers to pay a minimum wage sometimes block the price adjustments that balance the quantity demanded and the quantity supplied and lead to underproduction. *Quantity regulations* that limit the amount that a farm is permitted to produce also lead to underproduction.

Taxes and Subsidies *Taxes* increase the prices paid by buyers and lower the prices received by sellers. So taxes decrease the quantity produced and lead to underproduction. *Subsidies*, which are payments by the government to producers, decrease the prices paid by buyers and increase the prices received by sellers. So subsidies increase the quantity produced and lead to overproduction.

Externalities An *externality* is a cost or a benefit that affects someone other than the seller or the buyer. An *external cost* arises when an electric utility burns coal and emits carbon dioxide. The utility doesn't consider the cost of climate change when it decides how much power to produce. The result is overproduction. An *external benefit* arises when an apartment owner installs a smoke detector and decreases her neighbour's fire risk. She doesn't consider the benefit to her neighbour when she decides how many detectors to install. The result is underproduction.

Public Goods and Common Resources A *public good* is a good or service that is consumed simultaneously by everyone even if they don't pay for it. National defence is an example. Competitive markets would underproduce national defence because it is in each person's interest to free ride on everyone else and avoid paying for her or his share of such a good.

A *common resource* is owned by no one but available to be used by everyone. Atlantic cod is an example. It is in everyone's self-interest to ignore the costs they impose on others when they decide how much of a common resource to use. The result is that the resource is overused.

Monopoly A *monopoly* is a firm that is the sole provider of a good or service. Local water supply and cable television are supplied by firms that are monopolies. The monopoly's self-interest is to maximize its profit. Because the monopoly has no competitors, it can set the price to achieve its self-interested goal. To achieve its goal, a monopoly produces too little and charges too high a price. It leads to underproduction.

High Transactions Costs Stroll around a shopping mall and observe the retail markets in which you participate. You'll see that these markets employ enormous quantities of scarce labour and capital resources. It is costly to operate any market. Econom-ists call the opportunity costs of making trades in a market **transactions costs**.

To use market price as the allocator of scarce resources, it must be worth bearing the opportunity cost of establishing a market. Some markets are just too costly to operate. For example, when you want to play tennis on your local "free" court, you don't pay a market price for your slot on the court. You hang around until the court becomes vacant, and you "pay" with your waiting time. When transactions costs are high, the market might underproduce.

You now know the conditions under which resource allocation is efficient. You've seen how a competitive market can be efficient, and you've seen some obstacles to efficiency. Can alternative allocation methods improve on the market?

Alternatives to the Market

When a market is inefficient, can one of the alternative nonmarket methods that we described at the beginning of this chapter do a better job? Sometimes it can.

Often, majority rule might be used in an attempt to improve the allocation of resources. But majority rule has its own shortcomings. A group that pursues the self-interest of its members can become the majority. For example, a price or quantity regulation that creates inefficiency is almost always the result of a self-interested group becoming the majority and imposing costs on the minority. Also, with majority rule, votes must be translated into actions by bureaucrats who have their own agendas based on their self-interest.

Managers in firms issue commands and avoid the transactions costs that they would incur if they went to a market every time they needed a job done.

First-come, first-served works best in some situations. Think about the scene at a busy ATM. Instead of waiting in line, people might trade places at a "market" price. But someone would need to ensure that trades were honoured. At a busy ATM, first-come, first-served is the most efficient arrangement.

There is no one efficient mechanism that allocates all resources efficiently. But markets, when supplemented by other mechanisms such as majority rule, command systems, and first-come, first-served, do an amazingly good job.

Review Quiz

1 Do competitive markets use resources efficiently? Explain why or why not.
2 What is deadweight loss and under what conditions does it occur?
3 What are the obstacles to achieving an efficient allocation of resources in the market economy?

 Work Study Plan 5.4 and get instant feedback.

Is an efficient allocation of resources also a fair allocation? Does the competitive market provide people with fair incomes for their work? Do people always pay a fair price for the things they buy? Don't we need the government to step into some competitive markets to prevent the price from rising too high or falling too low? Let's now study these questions.

Is the Competitive Market Fair?

When a natural disaster strikes, such as a severe winter storm or a hurricane, the prices of many essential items jump. The reason prices jump is that the demand and willingness to pay for these items has increased, but the supply has not changed. So the higher prices achieve an efficient allocation of scarce resources. News reports of these price hikes almost never talk about efficiency. Instead, they talk about equity or fairness. The claim that is often made is that it is unfair for profit-seeking dealers to cheat the victims of natural disaster.

Similarly, when low-skilled people work for a wage that is below what most would regard as a "living wage," the media and politicians talk of employers taking unfair advantage of their workers.

How do we decide whether something is fair or unfair? You know when you *think* something is unfair. But how do you *know?* What are the *principles* of fairness?

Philosophers have tried for centuries to answer this question. Economists have offered their answers too. But before we look at the proposed answers, you should know that there is no universally agreed upon answer.

Economists agree about efficiency. That is, they agree that it makes sense to make the economic pie as large as possible and to produce it at the lowest possible cost. But they do not agree about equity. That is, they do not agree about what are fair shares of the economic pie for all the people who make it. The reason is that ideas about fairness are not exclusively economic ideas. They touch on politics, ethics, and religion. Nevertheless, economists have thought about these issues and have a contribution to make. Let's examine the views of economists on this topic.

To think about fairness, think of economic life as a game—a serious game. All ideas about fairness can be divided into two broad groups. They are

- It's not fair if the *result* isn't fair.
- It's not fair if the *rules* aren't fair.

It's Not Fair If the *Result* Isn't Fair

The earliest efforts to establish a principle of fairness were based on the view that the result is what matters. The general idea was that it is unfair if people's incomes are too unequal. For example, it is

unfair that a bank president earns millions of dollars a year while a bank teller earns only thousands of dollars. It is unfair that a store owner makes a larger profit and her customers pay higher prices in the aftermath of a winter storm.

During the nineteenth century, economists thought they had made the incredible discovery: Efficiency requires equality of incomes. To make the economic pie as large as possible, it must be cut into equal pieces, one for each person. This idea turns out to be wrong. But there is a lesson in the reason that it is wrong, so this idea is worth a closer look.

Utilitarianism The nineteenth century idea that only equality brings efficiency is called *utilitarianism*. **Utilitarianism** is a principle that states that we should strive to achieve "the greatest happiness for the greatest number." The people who developed this idea were known as utilitarians. They included the most eminent thinkers, such as Jeremy Bentham and John Stuart Mill.

Utilitarians argued that to achieve "the greatest happiness for the greatest number," income must be transferred from the rich to the poor up to the point of complete equality—to the point at which there are no rich and no poor.

They reasoned in the following way: First, everyone has the same basic wants and a similar capacity to enjoy life. Second, the greater a person's income, the smaller is the marginal benefit of a dollar. The millionth dollar spent by a rich person brings a smaller marginal benefit to that person than the marginal benefit that the thousandth dollar spent brings to a poorer person. So by transferring a dollar from the millionaire to the poorer person, more is gained than is lost. The two people added together are better off.

Figure 5.7 illustrates this utilitarian idea. Tom and Jerry have the same marginal benefit curve, *MB*. (Marginal benefit is measured on the same scale of 1 to 3 for both Tom and Jerry.) Tom is at point *A*. He earns $5,000 a year, and his marginal benefit from a dollar is 3 units. Jerry is at point *B*. He earns $45,000 a year, and his marginal benefit from a dollar is 1 unit. If a dollar is transferred from Jerry to Tom, Jerry loses 1 unit of marginal benefit and Tom gains 3 units. So together, Tom and Jerry are better off—they are sharing the economic pie more efficiently. If a second dollar is transferred, the same thing happens: Tom gains more than Jerry loses. And the same is true for every dollar transferred until they both reach

FIGURE 5.7   Utilitarian Fairness

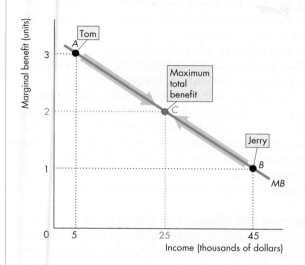

Tom earns $5,000 and has 3 units of marginal benefit at point A. Jerry earns $45,000 and has 1 unit of marginal benefit at point B. If income is transferred from Jerry to Tom, Jerry's loss is less than Tom's gain. Only when each of them has $25,000 and 2 units of marginal benefit (at point C) can the sum of their total benefit increase no further.

myeconlab animation

point *C*. At point *C*, Tom and Jerry have $25,000 each and a marginal benefit of 2 units. Now they are sharing the economic pie in the most efficient way. It brings the greatest happiness to Tom and Jerry.

The Big Tradeoff One big problem with the utilitarian ideal of complete equality is that it ignores the costs of making income transfers. Recognizing the costs of making income transfers leads to what is called the **big tradeoff**, which is a tradeoff between efficiency and fairness.

The big tradeoff is based on the following facts. Income can be transferred from people with high incomes to people with low incomes only by taxing the high incomes. Taxing people's income from employment makes them work less. It results in the quantity of labour being less than the efficient quantity. Taxing people's income from capital makes them save less. It results in the quantity of capital being less than the efficient quantity. With smaller quantities of both labour and capital, the quantity of goods and services produced is less than the efficient quantity. The economic pie shrinks.

The tradeoff is between the size of the economic pie and the degree of equality with which it is shared. The greater the amount of income redistribution through income taxes, the greater is the inefficiency—the smaller is the economic pie.

There is a second source of inefficiency. A dollar taken from a rich person does not end up as a dollar in the hands of a poorer person. Some of the dollar is spent on administration of the tax and transfer system. The cost of tax-collecting agencies, such as Canada Revenue Agency, and welfare-administering agencies, such as Human Resources and Social Development Canada, must be paid with some of the taxes collected. Also, taxpayers hire accountants, auditors, and lawyers to help them ensure that they pay the correct amount of taxes. These activities use skilled labour and capital resources that could otherwise be used to produce goods and services that people value.

When all these costs are taken into account, taking a dollar from a rich person does not give a dollar to a poor person. It is possible that with high taxes, people with low incomes might end up being worse off. Suppose, for example, that highly taxed entrepreneurs decide to work less hard and shut down some of their businesses. Low-income workers get fired and must seek other, perhaps even lower-paid, work.

Today, because of the big tradeoff, no one says that fairness requires equality of incomes.

Make the Poorest as Well Off as Possible A new solution to the big tradeoff problem was proposed by philosopher John Rawls in a classic book entitled *A Theory of Justice*, published in 1971. Rawls says that, taking all the costs of income transfers into account, the fair distribution of the economic pie is the one that makes the poorest person as well off as possible. The incomes of rich people should be taxed, and after paying the costs of administering the tax and transfer system, what is left should be transferred to the poor. But the taxes must not be so high that they make the economic pie shrink to the point at which the poorest person ends up with a smaller piece. A bigger share of a smaller pie can be less than a smaller share of a bigger pie. The goal is to make the piece enjoyed by the poorest person as big as possible. Most likely, this piece will not be an equal share.

The "fair results" idea requires a change in the results after the game is over. Some economists say that these changes are themselves unfair and propose a different way of thinking about fairness.

It's Not Fair If the *Rules* Aren't Fair

The idea that it's not fair if the rules aren't fair is based on a fundamental principle that seems to be hardwired into the human brain: the symmetry principle. The **symmetry principle** is the requirement that people in similar situations be treated similarly. It is the moral principle that lies at the centre of all the big religions and that says, in some form or other, "Behave towards other people in the way you expect them to behave towards you."

In economic life, this principle translates into *equality of opportunity*. But equality of opportunity to do what? This question is answered by the philosopher Robert Nozick in a book entitled *Anarchy, State, and Utopia*, published in 1974.

Nozick argues that the idea of fairness as an outcome or result cannot work and that fairness must be based on the fairness of the rules. He suggests that fairness obeys two rules:

1. The state must enforce laws that establish and protect private property.
2. Private property may be transferred from one person to another only by voluntary exchange.

The first rule says that everything that is valuable must be owned by individuals and that the state must ensure that theft is prevented. The second rule says that the only legitimate way a person can acquire property is to buy it in exchange for something else that the person owns. If these rules, which are the only fair rules, are followed, then the result is fair. It doesn't matter how unequally the economic pie is shared, provided that the pie is made by people, each one of whom voluntarily provides services in exchange for the share of the pie offered in compensation.

These rules satisfy the symmetry principle. If these rules are not followed, the symmetry principle is broken. You can see these facts by imagining a world in which the laws are not followed.

First, suppose that some resources or goods are not owned. They are common property. Then everyone is free to participate in a grab to use them. The strongest will prevail. But when the strongest prevails, the strongest effectively *owns* the resources or goods in question and prevents others from enjoying them.

Second, suppose that we do not insist on voluntary exchange for transferring ownership of resources from one person to another. The alternative is *involuntary* transfer. In simple language, the alternative is theft.

Both of these situations violate the symmetry principle. Only the strong acquire what they want. The weak end up with only the resources and goods that the strong don't want.

In a majority rule political system, the strong are those in the majority or those with enough resources to influence opinion and achieve a majority.

In contrast, if the two rules of fairness are followed, everyone, strong and weak, is treated in a similar way. Everyone is free to use their resources and human skills to create things that are valued by themselves and others and to exchange the fruits of their efforts with each other. This set of arrangements is the only one that obeys the symmetry principle.

Fairness and Efficiency   If private property rights are enforced and if voluntary exchange takes place in a competitive market, resources will be allocated efficiently if there are no

1. Price and quantity regulations
2. Taxes and subsidies
3. Externalities
4. Public goods and common resources
5. Monopolies
6. High transactions costs

And according to the Nozick rules, the resulting distribution of income and wealth will be fair. Let's study an example to check the claim that if resources are allocated efficiently, they are also allocated fairly.

Case Study: A Water Shortage in a Natural Disaster

An earthquake has broken the pipes that deliver drinking water to a city. Bottled water is available, but there is no tap water. What is the fair way to allocate the bottled water?

Market Price   Suppose that if the water is allocated by market price, the price jumps to $8 a bottle—five times its normal price. At this price, the people who own water can make a large profit by selling it. People who are willing and able to pay $8 a bottle get the water. And because most people can't afford the $8 price, they end up either without water or consuming just a few drops a day.

You can see that the water is being used efficiently. There is a fixed amount available, some people are willing to pay $8 to get a bottle, and the water goes to those people. The people who own and sell water receive a large producer surplus and total surplus is maximized.

In the rules view, the outcome is fair. No one is denied the water they are willing to pay for. In the results view, the outcome would most likely be regarded as unfair. The lucky owners of water make a killing, and the poorest end up the thirstiest.

Nonmarket Methods Suppose that by a majority vote, the citizens decide that the government will buy all the water, pay for it with a tax, and use one of the nonmarket methods to allocate the water to the citizens. The possibilities now are

Command Someone decides who is the most deserving and needy. Perhaps everyone is given an equal share. Or perhaps government officials and their families end up with most of the water.

Contest Bottles of water are prizes that go to those who are best at a particular contest.

First-come, first-served Water goes to the first off the mark or to those who place the lowest value on their time and can afford to wait in line.

Lottery Water goes to those in luck.

Personal characteristics Water goes to those with the "right" characteristics. Perhaps the old, the young, or pregnant women get the water.

Except by chance, none of these methods delivers an allocation of water that is either fair or efficient. It is unfair in the rules view because the tax involves involuntary transfers of resources among citizens. And it is unfair in the results view because the poorest don't end up being made as well off as possible.

The allocation is inefficient for two reasons. First, resources have been used to operate the allocation scheme. Second, some people are willing to pay for more water than the quantity they have been allocated and others have been allocated more water than they are willing to pay for.

The second source of inefficiency can be overcome if, after the nonmarket allocation, people are permitted to trade water at its market price. Those who value the water they have at less than the market price sell, and people who are willing to pay the market price to obtain more water buy. Those who value the water most highly are the ones who consume it.

Market Price with Taxes Another approach is to allocate the scarce water using the market price but then to alter the redistribution of buying power by taxing the sellers and providing benefits to the poor.

Suppose water owners are taxed on each bottle sold and the revenue from these taxes is given to the poorest people. People are then free, starting from this new distribution of buying power, to trade water at the market price.

Because the owners of water are taxed on what they sell, they have a weaker incentive to offer water for sale and the supply decreases. The equilibrium price rises to more than $8 a bottle. There is now a deadweight loss in the market for water—similar to the loss that arises from underproduction on pp. 115–116. (We study the effects of a tax and show its inefficiency in Chapter 6 on pp. 135–140.)

So the tax is inefficient. In the rules view, the tax is also unfair because it forces the owners of water to make a transfer to others. In the results view, the outcome might be regarded as being fair.

This brief case study illustrates the complexity of ideas about fairness. Economists have a clear criterion of efficiency but no comparably clear criterion of fairness. Most economists regard Nozick as being too extreme and want a fair tax system. But there is no consensus about what a fair tax system looks like.

Review Quiz

1 What are the two big approaches to thinking about fairness?
2 What is the utilitarian idea of fairness and what is wrong with it?
3 Explain the big tradeoff. What idea of fairness has been developed to deal with it?
4 What is the idea of fairness based on fair rules?

 Work Study Plan 5.5 and get instant feedback.

You've now studied the two biggest issues that run through the whole of economics: efficiency and equity, or fairness. In the next chapter, we study some sources of inefficiency and unfairness. At many points in this book—and in your life—you will return to and use the ideas about efficiency and fairness that you've learned here. *Reading Between the Lines* on pp. 122–123 looks at an example of an inefficiency in our economy today.

Is Water Use Efficient?

India Digs Deeper, but Wells Are Drying Up, and a Farming Crisis Looms

September 30, 2006

... Across India, where most people still live off the land, the chief source of irrigation is groundwater, at least for those who can afford to pump it.

Indian law has virtually no restrictions on who can pump groundwater, how much and for what purpose. Anyone, it seems, can—and does—extract water as long as it is under his or her patch of land. That could apply to homeowner, farmer or industry. ...

"We forgot that water is a costly item," lamented K. P. Singh, regional director of the Central Groundwater Board, in his office in the city of Jaipur. "Our feeling about proper, judicious use of water vanished."

... On a parched, hot morning ... a train pulled into the railway station at a village called Peeplee Ka Bas. Here, the wells have run dry and the water table fallen so low that it is too salty even to irrigate the fields.

The train came bearing precious cargo: 15 tankers loaded with nearly 120,000 gallons of clean, sweet drinking water.

The water regularly travels more than 150 miles, taking nearly two days, by pipeline and then by rail, so that the residents of a small neighbouring town can fill their buckets with water for 15 minutes every 48 hours.

It is a logistically complicated, absurdly expensive proposition. Bringing the water here costs the state about a penny a gallon; the state charges the consumer a monthly flat rate of 58 cents for about 5,300 gallons, absorbing the loss. ...

Essence of the Story

- In India, groundwater is the chief source of irrigation.
- Indian law has few restrictions on who can pump groundwater.
- A regional director of the Central Groundwater Board laments that Indians are behaving as if water were a free resource.
- Where the wells have run dry, water is delivered by pipeline and then by train.
- Water is rationed by permitting residents to fill their buckets with water for 15 minutes every 48 hours.
- Transporting water costs 1 cent per gallon, but consumers pay about 11 cents per 1,000 gallons.

Economic Analysis

- Water is one of the world's most vital resources, and it is used inefficiently.

- Markets in water are not competitive. They are controlled by governments or private producers, and they do not work like the competitive markets that deliver an efficient use of resources.

- The major problem in achieving an efficient use of water is to get it from the places where it is most abundant to the places in which it has the most valuable uses.

- Some places have too little water, and some have too much.

- The news article tells us that the owners of land that has groundwater under it pump the water and sell it and pay little attention to the fact that they will pump the well dry.

- Figure 1 illustrates this situation. The curve D shows the demand for water and its marginal social benefit, MSB. The curve S shows the supply of water and its marginal social cost, MSC.

- Ignoring the high marginal social cost, land owners produce W_A litres a day, which is greater than the efficient quantity. Farmers are willing to pay B, which is less than the marginal social cost C but enough to earn the land owner a profit.

- A deadweight loss arises from overproduction.

- Figure 2 shows the situation in places where the wells have run dry.

- A limited quantity of water, W_B, is transported in, and each consumer is restricted to the quantity that can be put into a bucket in 15 minutes every 48 hours.

- Consumers are willing to pay B per litre, which is much more than the marginal social cost C.

- The green area shows the consumer surplus, and the red rectangle shows the cost of the water, which is paid by the government and borne by the taxpayers.

- A deadweight loss arises from underproduction.

- The situation in India is replicated in thousands of places around the world.

Figure 1 Overproduction where wells are not dry

Figure 2 Underproduction where wells run dry

SUMMARY

Key Points

Resource Allocation Methods (pp. 108–109)

- Because resources are scarce, some mechanism must allocate them.
- The alternative allocation methods are market price; command; majority rule; contest; first-come, first-served; lottery; personal characteristics; and force.

Demand and Marginal Benefit (pp. 110–111)

- The maximum price willingly paid is marginal benefit, so a demand curve is also a marginal benefit curve.
- The market demand curve is the horizontal sum of the individual demand curves and is the marginal social benefit curve.
- Value is what people are *willing to* pay; price is what people *must* pay.
- Consumer surplus equals value minus price, summed over the quantity bought.

Supply and Marginal Cost (pp. 112–113)

- The minimum supply-price is marginal cost, so a supply curve is also a marginal cost curve.
- The market supply curve is the horizontal sum of the individual supply curves and is the marginal social cost curve.

- Cost is what producers pay; price is what producers receive.
- Producer surplus equals price minus marginal cost, summed over the quantity sold.

Is the Competitive Market Efficient? (pp. 114–117)

- In a competitive equilibrium, marginal social benefit equals marginal social cost and resource allocation is efficient.
- Buyers and sellers acting in their self-interest end up promoting the social interest.
- The sum of consumer surplus and producer surplus is maximized.
- Producing less than or more than the efficient quantity creates deadweight loss.
- Price and quantity regulations; taxes and subsidies; externalities; public goods and common resources; monopoly; and high transactions costs can lead to underproduction or overproduction and create inefficiency.

Is the Competitive Market Fair? (pp. 118–121)

- Ideas about fairness can be divided into two groups: fair *results* and fair *rules*.
- Fair-results ideas require income transfers from the rich to the poor.
- Fair-rules ideas require property rights and voluntary exchange.

Key Figures

Figure 5.1   Individual Demand, Market Demand, and Marginal Social Benefit, 110
Figure 5.2   Demand and Consumer Surplus, 111
Figure 5.3   Individual Supply, Market Supply, and Marginal Social Cost, 112
Figure 5.4   Supply and Producer Surplus, 113
Figure 5.5   An Efficient Market for Pizza, 114
Figure 5.6   Underproduction and Overproduction, 116

Key Terms

Big tradeoff, 119
Command system, 108
Consumer surplus, 111
Deadweight loss, 115
Producer surplus, 113
Symmetry principle, 120
Transactions costs, 117
Utilitarianism, 118

PROBLEMS and APPLICATIONS ◆

myeconlab Work problems 1–9 in Chapter 5 Study Plan and get instant feedback.
Work problems 10–16 as Homework, a Quiz, or a Test if assigned by your instructor.

1. At West, recognized as the "jewel in Vancouver's culinary crown," reservations are essential. At Le Bistro Chez Michel, a restaurant in North Vancouver, reservations are recommended. At Vij's, a restaurant not too far from the University of British Columbia, reservations are not accepted.

   a. Describe the method of allocating scarce table resources at these three restaurants.
   b. Why do you think restaurants have different reservations policies?
   c. Why might each restaurant be using an efficient allocation method?
   d. Why do you think restaurants don't use the market price to allocate their tables?

2. The table provides information on the demand schedules for train travel for Ann, Beth, and Cy, who are the only buyers in the market.

Price	Quantity demanded (kilometres)		
(dollars per kilometre)	Ann	Beth	Cy
3	30	25	20
4	25	20	15
5	20	15	10
6	15	10	5
7	10	5	0
8	5	0	0
9	0	0	0

   a. Construct the market demand schedule.
   b. What are the maximum prices that Ann, Beth, and Cy are willing to pay to travel 20 kilometres? Why?
   c. What is the marginal social benefit when the total distance travelled is 60 kilometres?
   d. What is the marginal private benefit for each person when they travel a total distance of 60 kilometres and how many kilometres does each of the people travel?
   e. What is each traveller's consumer surplus when the price is $4 a kilometre?
   f. What is the market consumer surplus when the price is $4 a kilometre?

3. **eBay Saves Billions for Bidders**
   If you think you would save money by bidding

on eBay auctions, you would likely be right. ... Two associate professors ... calculate the difference between the actual purchase price paid for auction items and the top price bidders stated they were willing to pay ... and the Maryland researchers found it averaged at least $4 per auction.

Information Week, January 28, 2008

   a. What method is used to allocate goods on eBay?
   b. How do eBay auctions influence consumer surplus?

4. The table provides information on the supply schedules of hot air balloon rides by Xavier, Yasmin, and Zack, who are the only sellers in the market.

Price	Quantity supplied (rides per week)		
(dollars per ride)	Xavier	Yasmin	Zack
100	30	25	20
90	25	20	15
80	20	15	10
70	15	10	5
60	10	5	0
50	5	0	0
40	0	0	0

   a. Construct the market supply schedule.
   b. What are the minimum prices that Xavier, Yasmin, and Zack are willing to accept to supply 20 rides? Why?
   c. What is the marginal social cost when the total number of rides is 30?
   d. What is the marginal cost for each supplier when the total number of rides is 30 and how many rides does each of the firms supply?
   e. What is each firm's producer surplus when the price is $70 a ride?
   f. What is the market producer surplus when the price is $70 a ride?

5. Based on the information provided in the news clip in problem 3,

   a. Can an eBay auction give the seller a surplus?

b. Draw a graph to illustrate an eBay auction and show the consumer surplus and producer surplus that it generates.

6. The figure illustrates the market for cell phones.

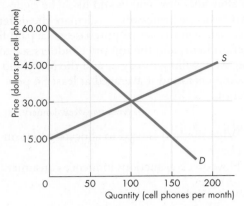

a. What are the equilibrium price and equilibrium quantity of cell phones?
b. Shade in and label the consumer surplus and the producer surplus.
c. Shade in and label the cost of producing the cell phones sold.
d. Calculate total surplus.
e. What is the efficient quantity of cell phones?

7. The table gives the demand and supply schedules for sunscreen.

Price	Quantity demanded	Quantity supplied
(dollars per bottle)	(bottles per day)	
0	400	0
5	300	100
10	200	200
15	100	300
20	0	400

Sunscreen factories are required to limit production to 100 bottles a day.

a. What is the maximum price that consumers are willing to pay for the 100th bottle?
b. What is the minimum price that producers are willing to accept for the 100th bottle?
c. Describe the situation in this market.
d. How can the 100 bottles be allocated to beachgoers? Which possible methods would be fair and which would be unfair?

8. **Wii Sells Out Across Japan**

... Japan finally came in for its share of Wii

madness this weekend. ... However, given the large amount of interest in the console—which Nintendo has flogged with a TV-ad blitz for the past two months—demand is expected to be much higher than supply. ... Yodobashi Camera was selling Wii games on a first-come, first-served basis, so eager customers showed up early so as not to miss out on their favorite titles. [But] customers who tried to get in the ... line after 6 or 7 a.m. were turned away. ... [and] many could be spotted rushing off to the smaller Akihabara stores that were holding raffles to decide who got a Wii.

Gamespot News, December 1, 2006

a. Why was the quantity demanded of Wii expected to exceed the quantity supplied?
b. Did Nintendo produce the efficient quantity of Wii? Explain.
c. Can you think of reasons why Nintendo might want to underproduce and leave the market with fewer Wii than people want to buy?
d. What are the two methods of resource allocation described in the news clip?
e. Is either method of allocating Wii efficient?
f. What do you think some of the people who managed to buy a Wii did with it?
g. Explain which is the fairer method of allocating the Wii: the market price or the two methods described in the news clip.

9. **New Zealand's Private Forests**

In the late 1980s, New Zealand decided it was time to quit cold turkey. Its addiction was government. ... By the early 1990s, New Zealand had [sold] half of the country's total plantation forests to the highest bidder, introducing an era of privately-owned forests. "We want [timber companies] to behave like farmers. Farmers make sure they don't destroy the soil or run down its fertility. Farmers look after their farms to make them continuously productive."

Reuters, September 7, 2007

a. In the late 1980s, did logging companies operate in the social interest or self-interest?
b. Since the early 1990s, has the New Zealand timber industry been efficient? Have logging companies operated in the social interest?
c. What incentive do private timber companies have to ensure that they "behave like farmers"?

10. The table gives the supply schedules for jet-ski rides by three owners: Rick, Sam, and Tom, the only suppliers of jet-ski rides.

Price	Quantity supplied (rides per day)		
(dollars per ride)	Rick	Sam	Tom
10.00	0	0	0
12.50	5	0	0
15.00	10	5	0
17.50	15	10	5
20.00	20	15	10

a. What is each owner's minimum supply-price of 10 rides a day?

b. Which owner has the largest producer surplus when the price of a ride is $17.50? Explain.

c. What is the marginal social cost of producing 45 rides a day?

d. Construct the market supply schedule of jet-ski rides.

11. The table gives the demand and supply schedules for sandwiches.

Price	Quantity demanded	Quantity supplied
(dollars per sandwich)	(sandwiches per hour)	
0	300	0
1	250	50
2	200	100
3	150	150
4	100	200
5	50	250
6	0	300

a. What is the maximum price that consumers are willing to pay for the 200th sandwich?

b. What is the minimum price that producers are willing to accept for the 200th sandwich?

c. Are 200 sandwiches an hour less than or greater than the efficient quantity?

d. If sandwich makers produce 200 sandwiches an hour, what is the deadweight loss?

e. If the sandwich market is efficient, what is the consumer surplus, what is the producer surplus, and what is the total surplus?

f. If the demand for sandwiches increases and sandwich makers produce the efficient quantity, what happens to consumer surplus and producer surplus?

12. **The Right Price for Digital Music: Why 99 Cents per Song is Too Much, and Too Little**

Apple's 99-cents-for-everything model isn't perfect. Isn't 99 cents too much to pay for music that appeals to just a few people? What we need is a system that will continue to pack the corporate coffers yet be fair to music lovers. The solution: a real-time commodities market that combines aspects of Apple's iTunes, Nasdaq, the Chicago Mercantile Exchange, Priceline, and eBay. ... Songs would be priced strictly on demand. The more people who download [a particular song] ... the higher the price [of that song] will go. ... The fewer people who buy a [particular] song, the lower the price [of that song] goes. ... In essence, this is a pure free-market solution—the market alone would determine price.

Slate, December 5, 2005

Assume that the marginal social cost of downloading a song from the iTunes Store is zero. (This assumption means that the cost of operating the iTunes Store doesn't change if people download more songs.)

a. Draw a graph of the market for downloadable music with a price of 99 cents for everything. On your graph, show consumer surplus and producer surplus.

b. With a price of 99 cents for everything, is the market efficient or inefficient? If it is inefficient, show the deadweight loss on your graph.

c. If the pricing scheme described in the news clip were adopted, how would consumer surplus, producer surplus, and the deadweight loss change?

d. If the pricing scheme described in the news clip were adopted, would the market be efficient or inefficient? Explain.

e. Is the pricing scheme described in the news clip a "pure free-market solution"? Explain.

13. A winter storm cuts the power supply and isolates a small town in the mountains. The people rush to buy candles from the town store, which is the only source of candles. The store owner decides to ration the candles to one per family but to keep the price of a candle unchanged.

a. Who gets to use the candles? Who receives the consumer surplus and who receives the producer surplus on candles?

b. Is the allocation efficient? Is the allocation fair?

14. **Ticketmaster Accused of "Price Gouging" in Canada**

    As if the imminent Live Nation ticketing venture wasn't enough for Ticketmaster, the company now has to deal with accusations of "price gouging" by angry Elton John fans in Saskatchewan. When tickets for Elton John's performance in the capital city of Saskatoon went on sale, fans discovered that Ticketmaster had already sold out of their allotment, and instead recommended fans try to buy tickets at Tickets Now, a secondary ticketing site owned by Ticketmaster. Not only did Tickets Now already have tickets for sale, but they were also demanding much higher prices than originally posted on Ticketmaster, leading fans to accuse the company of scalping. ...

    Ticketmaster said they were not aware they were shuffling fans to Tickets Now and has since removed the link. The company's head of ticketing in Saskatchewan said, "The inventory belongs to the promoter and artist, and the artist determines who has what privileges in advance of the public on sale or not, like fan clubs for instance."

    Rolling Stone, July 14, 2008

    a. What is "price gouging"? Is price gouging in the social interest or self-interest?
    b. Explain the effect of the company's "scalping" on consumer surplus and producer surplus.
    c. Evaluate the "fairness" of Ticketmaster "shuffling fans to Tickets Now" when the concert tickets went on sale to the public.
    d. Describe the allocation method used when "the artist determines who has what privileges in advance of the public on sale or not, like fan clubs for instance."

15. **Fight over Water Rates; Escondido Farmers Say Increase would Put Them out of Business**

    The city is considering significant increases in water rates for agriculture, which historically has paid less than residential and business users. ... [S]ince 1993, water rates have gone up more than 90 percent for residential customers while agricultural users ... have seen increases of only about 50 percent, ...

    San Diego Union-Tribune, June 14, 2006

    a. Do you think that the allocation of water among San Diego agricultural and residential users is likely to be efficient? Explain your answer.
    b. If agricultural users pay a higher price for water, will the allocation of resources become more efficient?
    c. If agricultural users pay a higher price for water, what will happen to consumer surplus and producer surplus from water?
    d. Is the difference in price paid by agricultural and residential users fair?

16. After you have studied *Reading Between the Lines* on pp. 122–123, answer the following questions:

    a. What is the major problem in achieving an efficient use of the world's water?
    b. If there were a global market in water, like there is in oil, how do you think the market would work?
    c. Would a free world market in water achieve an efficient use of the world's water resources? Explain why or why not.
    d. Would a free world market in water achieve a fair use of the world's water resources? Explain why or why not and be clear about the concept of fairness that you are using.

17. Use the link on MyEconLab (Chapter Resources, Chapter 5, Web links) to visit the Web site of Health Action International and read the article by Catrin Schulte-Hillen entitled "Study concerning the availability and price of AZT." Then answer the following questions and explain your answers using the concepts of marginal benefit, marginal cost, price, consumer surplus, and producer surplus.

    a. What is the range of retail prices of AZT across the countries covered by the study?
    b. What, if anything, do you think could be done to increase the quantity of AZT and decrease its price?
    c. Canadian online pharmacies sell AZT to Americans for a price below the U.S. price. Does this practice increase or decrease consumer surplus, producer surplus, and deadweight loss from AZT in the United States?

6 Government Actions in Markets

After studying this chapter, you will be able to

- Explain how rent ceilings create housing shortages and inefficiency
- Explain how minimum wage laws create unemployment and inefficiency
- Explain the effects of a tax
- Explain the effects of production quotas and subsidies on production, costs, and prices
- Explain how markets for illegal goods work

Even though house prices are falling, home renters across Canada saw their rents rise by an average of 2.6 percent in 2007. Can governments cap rents to help renters live in affordable housing? Or instead, can governments make housing more affordable by raising incomes with minimum wage laws?

Taxes put the hand of government in almost every pocket and market. We pay income taxes and Employment Insurance taxes in the labour market and sales taxes in the markets for almost everything we buy. You probably think that you pay more than your fair share of taxes. But who actually pays and who benefits when a tax is cut: buyers or sellers?

In some markets, governments intervene with the opposite of a tax: a subsidy. For example, in the market for farm products, governments often subsidize producers to lower the price faced

by consumers. Sometimes, governments limit the quantities that farms may produce. Do subsidies and production limits help to make markets efficient?

Price caps, tax cuts, and subsidies, three of the major topics that you study in this chapter, have been proposed as ways of dealing with the high price of gasoline. In *Reading Between the Lines* at the end of the chapter, we apply what you've learned to the labour market for young workers and explore the effects of a proposed increase in the provincial minimum wage in British Columbia.

A Housing Market with a Rent Ceiling

We spend more of our income on housing than on any other good or service, so it isn't surprising that rents can be a political issue. When rents are high, or when they jump by a large amount, renters might lobby the government for limits on rents.

A government regulation that makes it illegal to charge a price higher than a specified level is called a **price ceiling** or **price cap**.

The effects of a price ceiling on a market depend crucially on whether the ceiling is imposed at a level that is above or below the equilibrium price.

A price ceiling set *above the equilibrium price* has no effect. The reason is that the price ceiling does not constrain the market forces. The force of the law and the market forces are not in conflict. But a price ceiling *below the equilibrium price* has powerful effects on a market. The reason is that the price ceiling attempts to prevent the price from regulating the quantities demanded and supplied. The force of the law and the market forces are in conflict.

When a price ceiling is applied to a housing market, it is called a **rent ceiling**. A rent ceiling set below the equilibrium rent creates

- A housing shortage
- Increased search activity
- A black market

A Housing Shortage

At the equilibrium price, the quantity demanded equals the quantity supplied. In a housing market, when the rent is at the equilibrium level, the quantity of housing supplied equals the quantity of housing demanded and there is neither a shortage nor a surplus of housing.

But at a rent set below the equilibrium rent, the quantity of housing demanded exceeds the quantity of housing supplied—there is a shortage. So if a rent ceiling is set below the equilibrium rent, there will be a shortage of housing.

When there is a shortage, the quantity available is the quantity supplied and, somehow, this quantity must be allocated among the frustrated demanders. One way in which this allocation occurs is through increased search activity.

Increased Search Activity

The time spent looking for someone with whom to do business is called **search activity**. We spend some time in search activity almost every time we make a purchase. When you're shopping for the latest hot new cell phone, and you know four stores that stock it, how do you find which store has the best deal? You spend a few minutes on the Internet, checking out the various prices. In some markets, such as the housing market, people spend a lot of time checking the alternatives available before making a choice.

When a price is regulated and there is a shortage, search activity increases. In the case of a rent-controlled housing market, frustrated would-be renters scan the newspapers, not only for housing ads but also for death notices! Any information about newly available housing is useful, and apartment seekers race to be first on the scene when news of a possible supplier breaks.

The *opportunity cost* of a good is equal not only to its price but also to the value of the search time spent finding the good. So the opportunity cost of housing is equal to the rent (a regulated price) plus the time and other resources spent searching for the restricted quantity available. Search activity is costly. It uses time and other resources, such as phone calls, automobiles, and gasoline that could have been used in other productive ways.

A rent ceiling controls only the rent portion of the cost of housing. The cost of increased search activity might end up making the full cost of housing *higher* than it would be without a rent ceiling.

A Black Market

A rent ceiling also encourages illegal trading in a **black market**, an illegal market in which the equilibrium price exceeds the price ceiling. Black markets occur in rent-controlled housing and many other markets. For example, scalpers run black markets in tickets for big sporting events and rock concerts.

When a rent ceiling is in force, frustrated renters and landlords constantly seek ways of increasing rents. One common way is for a new tenant to pay a high price for worthless fittings, such as charging $2,000 for threadbare drapes. Another is for the tenant to pay an exorbitant price for new locks and keys—called "key money."

The level of a black market rent depends on how tightly the rent ceiling is enforced. With loose enforcement, the black market rent is close to the unregulated rent. But with strict enforcement, the black market rent is equal to the maximum price that a renter is willing to pay.

Figure 6.1 illustrates the effects of a rent ceiling. The demand for housing is *D* and the supply is *S*. A rent ceiling is imposed at $800 a month. Rents that exceed $800 a month are in the grey-shaded illegal region in the figure. You can see that the equilibrium rent, where the demand and supply curves intersect, is in the illegal region.

At a rent of $800 a month, the quantity of housing supplied is 60,000 units and the quantity demanded is 100,000 units. So with a rent of $800 a month, there is a shortage of 40,000 units of housing.

To rent the 60,000th unit, someone is willing to pay $1,200 a month. They might pay this amount by incurring search costs that bring the total cost of housing to $1,200 a month, or they might pay a black market price of $1,200 a month. Either way, they end up incurring a cost that exceeds what the equilibrium rent would be in an unregulated market.

Inefficiency of a Rent Ceiling

A rent ceiling set below the equilibrium rent results in an inefficient underproduction of housing services. The *marginal social benefit* from housing exceeds its *marginal social cost* and a deadweight loss shrinks the producer surplus and consumer surplus (Chapter 5, pp. 115–116).

Figure 6.2 shows this inefficiency. The rent ceiling ($800 per month) is below the equilibrium rent ($1,000 per month) and the quantity of housing supplied (60,000 units) is less than the efficient quantity (80,000 units).

Because the quantity of housing supplied (available) is less than the efficient quantity, a deadweight loss arises, as shown by the grey triangle. Producer surplus shrinks to the blue triangle and consumer surplus shrinks to the green triangle. The red rectangle represents the potential loss from increased search activity. This loss is borne by consumers and the full loss from the rent ceiling is the sum of the deadweight loss and the increased cost of search activity.

FIGURE 6.1 A Rent Ceiling

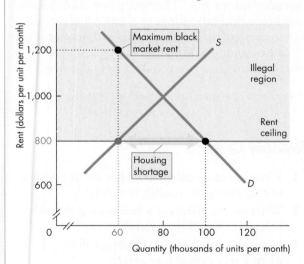

A rent above the rent ceiling of $800 a month is illegal (in the grey-shaded illegal region). At a rent of $800 a month, the quantity of housing supplied is 60,000 units. Frustrated renters spend time searching for housing and they make deals with landlords in a black market. Someone is willing to pay $1,200 a month for the 60,000th unit.

FIGURE 6.2 The Inefficiency of a Rent Ceiling

Without a rent ceiling, the market produces an efficient 80,000 units of housing at a rent of $1,000 a month. A rent ceiling of $800 a month decreases the quantity of housing supplied to 60,000 units. Producer surplus and consumer surplus shrink and a deadweight loss arises. The red rectangle represents the cost of resources used in increased search activity. The full loss from the rent ceiling equals the sum of the red rectangle and grey triangle.

Are Rent Ceilings Fair?

Rent ceilings might be inefficient, but don't they achieve a fairer allocation of scarce housing? Let's explore this question.

Chapter 5 (pp. 118–121) reviews two key ideas about fairness. According to the *fair rules* view, anything that blocks voluntary exchange is unfair, so rent ceilings are unfair. But according to the *fair result* view, a fair outcome is one that benefits the less well off. So according to this view, the fairest outcome is the one that allocates scarce housing to the poorest people. To see whether rent ceilings help to achieve a fairer outcome in this sense, we need to consider how the market allocates scarce housing resources in the face of a rent ceiling.

Blocking rent adjustments doesn't eliminate scarcity. Rather, because a rent ceiling decreases the quantity of housing available, it creates an even bigger challenge for the housing market. Somehow, the market must ration a smaller quantity of housing and allocate that housing among the people who are willing to rent housing at the rent ceiling.

When the rent is not permitted to allocate scarce housing, what other mechanisms are available, and are *they* fair? Some possible mechanisms are

- A lottery
- First-come, first-served
- Discrimination

A lottery allocates housing to those who are lucky, not to those who are poor. First-come, first-served (a method used to allocate housing in England after World War II) allocates housing to those who have the greatest foresight and who get their names on a list first, not to the poorest. Discrimination allocates scarce housing based on the views and self-interest of the owner of the housing. In the case of public housing, it is the self-interest of the bureaucracy that administers the allocation that counts.

In principle, self-interested owners and bureaucrats could allocate housing to satisfy some criterion of fairness, but they are not likely to do so. Discrimination based on friendship, family ties, and criteria such as race, ethnicity, or sex is more likely to enter the equation. We might make such discrimination illegal, but we cannot prevent it from occurring.

It is hard, then, to make a case for rent ceilings on the basis of fairness. When rent adjustments are blocked, other methods of allocating scarce housing resources operate that do not produce a fair outcome.

Rent Ceilings in Practice
The Rich and the Famous Win

New York, San Francisco, London, and Paris, four of the world's great cities, have rent ceilings in some parts of their housing markets. Winnipeg has rent ceilings and Toronto had them from 1975 to the late 1990s. Other Canadian cities, including Calgary, Edmonton, and Vancouver, do not have rent ceilings.

To see the effects of rent ceilings in practice we can compare the housing markets in cities with ceilings with those without ceilings. We learn two main lessons from such a comparison.

First, rent ceilings definitely create a housing shortage. Second, they do lower the rents for some but raise them for others.

A survey[*] conducted in the United States in 1997 showed that the rents of housing units *actually available for rent* were 2.5 times the average of all rents in New York City, but equal to the average rent in Philadelphia where there is no rent ceiling. The winners from rent ceilings in New York City are families that have lived there for a long time, including some rich and famous ones. The voting power of the winners keeps the rent ceilings in place, while mobile newcomers are the losers in a city with rent ceilings.

The bottom line is that, in principle and in practice, rent ceilings are inefficient and unfair.

[*]William Tucker, "How Rent Control Drives Out Affordable Housing."

Review Quiz

1 What is a rent ceiling and what are its effects if it is set above the equilibrium rent?
2 What are the effects of a rent ceiling that is set below the equilibrium rent?
3 How are scarce housing resources allocated when a rent ceiling is in place?
4 Why does a rent ceiling create an inefficient and unfair outcome in the housing market?

myeconlab   Work Study Plan 6.1 and get instant feedback.

You now know how a price ceiling (rent ceiling) works. Next, we'll learn about the effects of a price floor by studying a minimum wage in a labour market.

A Labour Market with a Minimum Wage

For each one of us, the labour market is the market that influences the jobs we get and the wages we earn. Firms decide how much labour to demand, and the lower the wage rate, the greater is the quantity of labour demanded. Households decide how much labour to supply, and the higher the wage rate, the greater is the quantity of labour supplied. The wage rate adjusts to make the quantity of labour demanded equal to the quantity supplied.

When wage rates are low, or when they fail to keep up with rising prices, labour unions might turn to governments and lobby for a higher wage rate.

A government-imposed regulation that makes it illegal to charge a price lower than a specified level is called a **price floor**.

The effects of a price floor on a market depend crucially on whether the floor is imposed at a level that is above or below the equilibrium price.

A price floor set *below the equilibrium price* has no effect. The reason is that the price floor does not constrain the market forces. The force of the law and the market forces are not in conflict. But a price floor *above the equilibrium price* has powerful effects on a market. The reason is that the price floor attempts to prevent the price from regulating the quantities demanded and supplied. The force of the law and the market forces are in conflict.

When a price floor is applied to a labour market, it is called a **minimum wage**. A minimum wage imposed at a level that is above the equilibrium wage creates unemployment. Let's look at the effects of a minimum wage.

Minimum Wage Brings Unemployment

At the equilibrium price, the quantity demanded equals the quantity supplied. In a labour market, when the wage rate is at the equilibrium level, the quantity of labour supplied equals the quantity of labour demanded: There is neither a shortage of labour nor a surplus of labour.

But at a wage rate above the equilibrium wage, the quantity of labour supplied exceeds the quantity of labour demanded—there is a surplus of labour. So when a minimum wage is set above the equilibrium wage, there is a surplus of labour. The demand for labour determines the level of employment, and the surplus of labour is unemployed.

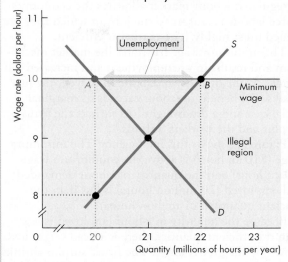

FIGURE 6.3 Minimum Wage and Unemployment

The minimum wage rate is set at $10 an hour. Any wage rate below $10 an hour is illegal (in the grey-shaded illegal region). At the minimum wage of $10 an hour, 20 million hours are hired but 22 million hours are available. Unemployment—AB—of 2 million hours a year is created. With only 20 million hours demanded, someone is willing to supply the 20 millionth hour for $8.

myeconlab animation

Figure 6.3 illustrates the effect of the minimum wage on unemployment. The demand for labour curve is *D* and the supply of labour curve is *S*. The horizontal red line shows the minimum wage set at $10 an hour. A wage rate below this level is illegal, in the grey-shaded illegal region of the figure. At the minimum wage rate, 20 million hours of labour are demanded (point *A*) and 22 million hours of labour are supplied (point *B*), so 2 million hours of available labour are unemployed.

With only 20 million hours demanded, someone is willing to supply that 20 millionth hour for $8. Frustrated unemployed workers spend time and other resources searching for hard-to-find jobs.

Inefficiency of a Minimum Wage

In the labour market, the supply curve measures the marginal social cost of labour to workers. This cost is leisure forgone. The demand curve measures the marginal social benefit from labour. This benefit is the value of the goods and services produced. An unregulated labour market allocates the economy's scarce labour resources to the jobs in which they are valued most highly. The market is efficient.

The minimum wage frustrates the market mechanism and results in unemployment and increased job search. At the quantity of labour employed, the marginal social benefit of labour exceeds its marginal social cost and a deadweight loss shrinks the firms' surplus and the workers' surplus.

Figure 6.4 shows this inefficiency. The minimum wage ($10 an hour) is above the equilibrium wage ($9 an hour) and the quantity of labour demanded and employed (20 million hours) is less than the efficient quantity (21 million hours).

Because the quantity of labour employed is less than the efficient quantity, there is a deadweight loss, shown by the grey triangle. The firms' surplus shrinks to the blue triangle and the workers' surplus shrinks to the green triangle. The red rectangle shows the potential loss from increased job search, which is borne by workers. The full loss from the minimum wage is the sum of the deadweight loss and the increased cost of job search.

FIGURE 6.4   The Inefficiency of a Minimum Wage

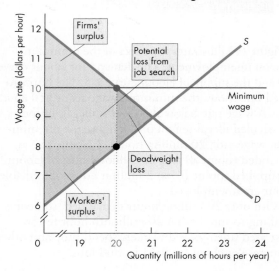

A minimum wage decreases employment. Firms' surplus (blue area) and workers' surplus (green area) shrink and a deadweight loss (grey area) arises. Job search increases and the red area shows the loss from this activity.

myeconlab animation

The Minimum Wage in Practice

Unscrambling Cause and Effect

Provincial governments in Canada set minimum wage rates. In 2008, minimum wage rates ranged from a low of $7.50 an hour in New Brunswick and Prince Edward Island to a high of $10.00 an hour in Nunavut.

Does the minimum wage result in unemployment, and if so, how much unemployment does it create? The consensus answer is that a 10 percent rise in the minimum wage decreases teenage employment by between 1 and 3 percent.

This consensus answer has been challenged by David Card of the University of California at Berkeley (see pp. 464–466) and Alan Krueger of Princeton University.

Card and Krueger say that increases in the minimum wage have *increased* teenage employment and *decreased* unemployment.

Card and Krueger studied minimum wages in California, New Jersey, and Texas, and they say that the employment rate of low-income workers increased following a rise in the minimum wage. They argue that a higher wage *increases* employment by making workers become more conscientious and productive and less likely to quit, which lowers

Is the Minimum Wage Fair?

The minimum wage is unfair on both views of fairness: It delivers an unfair *result* and imposes an unfair *rule*.

The *result* is unfair because only those people who have jobs and keep them benefit from the minimum wage. The unemployed end up worse off than they would be with no minimum wage. Some of those who search for jobs and find them end up worse off because of the increased cost of job search they incur. Also those who find jobs aren't always the least well off. When the wage rate doesn't allocate labour, other mechanisms determine who finds a job. One such mechanism is discrimination, which is yet another source of unfairness.

The minimum wage imposes an unfair *rule* because it blocks voluntary exchange. Firms are willing to hire more labour and people are willing to work more, but they are not permitted by the minimum wage law to do so.

unproductive labour turnover. Card and Krueger also argue that a higher wage rate makes managers seek ways to increase labour productivity.

Most economists are skeptical about Card and Krueger's argument. Why, economists ask, don't firms freely pay wage rates above the equilibrium wage to encourage more productive work habits? Also, they point to other explanations for the employment responses that Card and Krueger found.

According to Daniel Hamermesh of the University of Texas at Austin, Card and Krueger got the timing wrong. Hamermesh says that firms cut employment *before* the minimum wage is increased in anticipation of the increase. If he is correct, looking for the effects of an increase *after* it has occurred misses its main effects.

Finis Welch of Texas A&M University and Kevin Murphy of the University of Chicago say the employment effects that Card and Krueger found are caused by regional differences in economic growth, not by changes in the minimum wage.

One effect of the minimum wage is an increase in the quantity of labour supplied. If this effect occurs, it might show up as an increase in the number of people who quit school to look for work before completing high school. Some economists say that this response does occur.

Review Quiz

1 What is a minimum wage and what are its effects if it is set above the equilibrium wage?

2 What are the effects of a minimum wage set below the equilibrium wage?

3 Explain how scarce jobs are allocated when a minimum wage is in place.

4 Explain why a minimum wage creates an inefficient allocation of labour resources.

5 Explain why a minimum wage is unfair.

 Work Study Plan 6.2 and get instant feedback.

Next we're going to study a more widespread government action in markets: taxes. We'll see how taxes change prices and quantities. You will discover the surprising fact that while the government can impose a tax, it can't decide who will pay the tax! And you will see that a tax creates a deadweight loss.

Taxes

Everything you earn and almost everything you buy is taxed. Income taxes and Social Security taxes are deducted from your earnings, and provincial sales tax and GST are added to the bill when you buy something. Employers also pay an Employment Insurance tax for their workers, and producers of tobacco products, alcoholic drinks, and gasoline pay a tax every time they sell something.

Who *really* pays these taxes? Because the income tax and the Employment Insurance tax are deducted from your pay, and the sales taxes are added to the prices that you pay, isn't it obvious that *you* pay these taxes? Isn't it equally obvious that your employer pays the Employment Insurance tax and that tobacco producers pay the tax on cigarettes?

You're going to discover that it isn't obvious who *really* pays a tax and that lawmakers don't make that decision. We begin with a definition of tax incidence.

Tax Incidence

Tax incidence is the division of the burden of a tax between buyers and sellers. When the government imposes a tax on the sale of a good*, the price paid by buyers might rise by the full amount of the tax, by a lesser amount, or not at all. If the price paid by buyers rises by the full amount of the tax, then the burden of the tax falls entirely on buyers—the buyers pay the tax. If the price paid by buyers rises by a lesser amount than the tax, then the burden of the tax falls partly on buyers and partly on sellers. And if the price paid by buyers doesn't change at all, then the burden of the tax falls entirely on sellers.

Tax incidence does not depend on the tax law. The law might impose a tax on sellers or on buyers, but the outcome is the same in either case. To see why, let's look at the tax on cigarettes in Ontario.

A Tax on Sellers

On February 1, 2006, Ontario upped the tax on the sale of cigarettes to $3.09 a pack of 25 cigarettes. To work out the effects of this tax (rounded to $3) on the sellers of cigarettes, we begin by examining the effects on demand and supply in the market for cigarettes.

---

* These propositions also apply to services and factors of production (land, labour, capital).

In Fig. 6.5, the demand curve is D, and the supply curve is S. With no tax, the equilibrium price is $6 per pack and 350 million packs a year are bought and sold.

A tax on sellers is like an increase in cost, so it decreases supply. To determine the position of the new supply curve, we add the tax to the minimum price that sellers are willing to accept for each quantity sold. You can see that without the tax, sellers are willing to offer 350 million packs a year for $6 a pack. So with a $3 tax, they will offer 350 million packs a year only if the price is $9 a pack. The supply curve shifts to the red curve labelled *S + tax on sellers*.

Equilibrium occurs where the new supply curve intersects the demand curve at 325 million packs a year. The price paid by buyers rises by $2 to $8 a pack. And the price received by sellers falls by $1 to $5 a pack. So buyers pay $2 of the tax and sellers pay the other $1.

A Tax on Buyers

Suppose that instead of taxing sellers, Ontario taxes cigarette buyers $3 a pack.

A tax on buyers lowers the amount they are willing to pay sellers, so it decreases demand and shifts the demand curve leftward. To determine the position of this new demand curve, we subtract the tax from the maximum price that buyers are willing to pay for each quantity bought. You can see in Fig. 6.6 that without the tax, buyers are willing to buy 350 million packs a year for $6 a pack. So with a $3 tax, they are willing to buy 350 million packs a year only if the price including the tax is $6 a pack, which means that buyers are willing to pay sellers only $3 a pack. The demand curve shifts downward to become the red curve labelled *D – tax on buyers*.

Equilibrium occurs where the new demand curve intersects the supply curve at a quantity of 325 million packs a year. The price received by sellers is $5 a pack, and the price paid by buyers is $8.

Equivalence of Tax on Buyers and Sellers

You can see that the tax on buyers in Fig. 6.6 has the same effects as the tax on sellers in Fig. 6.5. In both cases, the equilibrium quantity decreases to 325 million packs a year, the price paid by buyers rises to $8 a pack, and the price received by sellers falls to $5 a pack. Buyers pay $2 of the $3 tax, and sellers pay the other $1 of the tax.

FIGURE 6.5   A Tax on Sellers

With no tax, 350 million packs a year are bought and sold at $6 a pack. A tax on sellers of $3 a pack shifts the supply curve leftward to *S + tax on sellers*. The equilibrium quantity decreases to 325 million packs a year, the price paid by buyers rises to $8 a pack, and the price received by sellers falls to $5 a pack. The tax raises the price paid by buyers by less than the tax and lowers the price received by sellers, so buyers and sellers share the burden of the tax.

myeconlab   animation

Can We Share the Burden Equally?   Suppose that the government of Ontario wants the burden of the cigarette tax to fall equally on buyers and sellers and declares that a $1.50 tax be imposed on each. Is the burden of the tax then shared equally?

You can see that it is not. The tax is still $3 a pack. And you've seen that the tax has the same effect regardless of whether it is imposed on sellers or buyers. So imposing half the tax on one and half on the other is like an average of the two cases you've examined. (Draw the demand–supply graph and work out what happens in this case. The demand curve shifts downward by $1.50 and the supply curve shifts upward by $1.50. The new equilibrium quantity is still 325 million packs a year. Buyers pay $8 a pack, of which $1.50 is tax. Sellers receive $6.50 from buyers but must pay a $1.50 tax, so sellers net $5 a pack.)

When a transaction is taxed, there are two prices: the price paid by buyers, which includes the tax; and the price received by sellers, which excludes the tax.

FIGURE 6.6   A Tax on Buyers

With no tax, 350 million packs a year are bought and sold at $6 a pack. A tax on buyers of $3 a pack shifts the demand curve leftward to *D – tax on buyers*. The equilibrium quantity decreases to 325 million packs a year, the price paid by buyers rises to $8 a pack, and the price received by sellers falls to $5 a pack. The tax raises the price paid by buyers by less than the tax and lowers the price received by sellers, so buyers and sellers share the burden of the tax.

myeconlab animation ▶   ◆

Buyers respond to the price that *includes* the tax and sellers respond to the price that *excludes* the tax.

A tax is like a wedge between the price buyers pay and the price sellers receive. The size of the wedge determines the effects of the tax, not the side of the market on which the government imposes the tax.

The Employment Insurance Tax The Employment Insurance tax is an example of a tax that the federal government imposes on *both* buyers of labour (employers) and sellers of labour (employees). But the principles you've just learned apply to this tax too. The market for labour, not the federal government, decides how the burden of the Employment Insurance tax is divided between firms and workers.

In the Ontario cigarette tax example, buyers bear twice the burden of the tax borne by sellers. In special cases, either buyers or sellers bear the entire burden. The division of the burden of a tax between buyers and sellers depends on the elasticities of demand and supply, as you will now see.

Tax Incidence and Elasticity of Demand

The division of the tax between buyers and sellers depends in part on the elasticity of demand. There are two extreme cases:

- Perfectly inelastic demand—buyers pay.
- Perfectly elastic demand—sellers pay.

Perfectly Inelastic Demand Figure 6.7 shows the market for insulin, a vital daily medication for people with diabetes. Demand is perfectly inelastic at 100,000 doses a day, regardless of the price, as shown by the vertical demand curve *D*. That is, a diabetic would sacrifice all other goods and services rather than not consume the insulin dose that provides good health. The supply curve of insulin is S. With no tax, the price is $2 a dose and the quantity is 100,000 doses a day.

If insulin is taxed at 20¢ a dose, we must add the tax to the minimum price at which drug companies are willing to sell insulin. The result is the new supply curve *S + tax*. The price rises to $2.20 a dose, but the quantity does not change. Buyers pay the entire tax of 20¢ a dose.

FIGURE 6.7   Tax with Perfectly Inelastic Demand

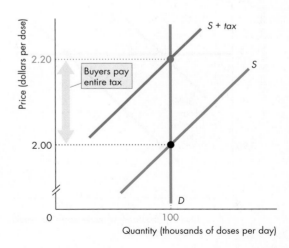

In this market for insulin, demand is perfectly inelastic. With no tax, the price is $2 a dose and the quantity is 100,000 doses a day. A tax of 20¢ a dose shifts the supply curve to *S + tax*. The price rises to $2.20 a dose, but the quantity bought does not change. Buyers pay the entire tax.

myeconlab animation ▶   ◆

Perfectly Elastic Demand Figure 6.8 shows the market for pink marker pens. Demand is perfectly elastic at $1 a pen, as shown by the horizontal demand curve *D*. If pink pens are less expensive than the other colours, everyone uses pink. If pink pens are more expensive than other colours, no one uses pink. The supply curve is *S*. With no tax, the price of a pink pen is $1 and the quantity is 4,000 pens a week.

Suppose that the government imposes a tax of 10¢ a pen on pink marker pens but not on other colours. The new supply curve is *S* + *tax*. The price remains at $1 a pen, and the quantity decreases to 1,000 pink pens a week. The 10¢ tax leaves the price paid by buyers unchanged but lowers the amount received by sellers by the full amount of the tax. Sellers pay the entire tax of 10¢ a pink pen.

We've seen that when demand is perfectly inelastic, buyers pay the entire tax and when demand is perfectly elastic, sellers pay the entire tax. In the usual case, demand is neither perfectly inelastic nor perfectly elastic and the tax is split between buyers and sellers. But the division depends on the elasticity of demand: The more inelastic the demand, the larger is the amount of the tax paid by buyers.

FIGURE 6.8 Tax with Perfectly Elastic Demand

In this market for pink pens, demand is perfectly elastic. With no tax, the price of a pen is $1 and the quantity is 4,000 pens a week. A tax of 10¢ per pink pen shifts the supply curve to *S* + *tax*. The price remains at $1 a pen, and the quantity of pink pens sold decreases to 1,000 a week. Sellers pay the entire tax.

Tax Incidence and Elasticity of Supply

The division of the tax between buyers and sellers also depends, in part, on the elasticity of supply. Again, there are two extreme cases:

- Perfectly inelastic supply—sellers pay.
- Perfectly elastic supply—buyers pay.

Perfectly Inelastic Supply Figure 6.9(a) shows the market for water from a mineral spring that flows at a constant rate that can't be controlled. Supply is perfectly inelastic at 100,000 bottles a week, as shown by the supply curve *S*. The demand curve for the water from this spring is *D*. With no tax, the price is 50¢ and the quantity is 100,000 bottles.

Suppose this spring water is taxed at 5¢ a bottle. The supply curve does not change because the spring owners still produce 100,000 bottles a week, even though the price they receive falls. But buyers are willing to buy the 100,000 bottles only if the price is 50¢ a bottle, so the price remains at 50¢ a bottle. The tax reduces the price received by sellers to 45¢ a bottle, and sellers pay the entire tax.

Perfectly Elastic Supply Figure 6.9(b) shows the market for sand from which computer-chip makers extract silicon. Supply of this sand is perfectly elastic at a price of 10¢ a kilogram, as shown by the supply curve *S*. The demand curve for sand is *D*. With no tax, the price is 10¢ a kilogram and 5,000 pounds a week are bought.

If this sand is taxed at 1¢ a kilogram, we must add the tax to the minimum supply-price. Sellers are now willing to offer any quantity at 11¢ a kilogram along the curve *S* + *tax*. A new equilibrium is determined where the new supply curve intersects the demand curve: at a price of 11¢ a kilogram and a quantity of 3,000 pounds a week. The tax has increased the price buyers pay by the full amount of the tax—1¢ a kilogram—and has decreased the quantity sold. Buyers pay the entire tax.

We've seen that when supply is perfectly inelastic, sellers pay the entire tax; and when supply is perfectly elastic, buyers pay the entire tax. In the usual case, supply is neither perfectly inelastic nor perfectly elastic and the tax is split between buyers and sellers. But how the tax is split depends on the elasticity of supply: The more elastic the supply, the larger is the amount of the tax paid by buyers.

FIGURE 6.9   Tax and the Elasticity of Supply

(a) Perfectly inelastic supply

(b) Perfectly elastic supply

Part (a) shows the market for water from a mineral spring. Supply is perfectly inelastic. With no tax, the price is 50¢ a bottle. With a tax of 5¢ a bottle, the price remains at 50¢ a bottle. The number of bottles bought remains the same, but the price received by sellers decreases to 45¢ a bottle. Sellers pay the entire tax.

Part (b) shows the market for sand. Supply is perfectly elastic. With no tax, the price is 10¢ a kilogram. A tax of 1¢ a kilogram increases the minimum supply-price to 11¢ a kilogram. The supply curve shifts to S + tax. The price increases to 11¢ a kilogram. Buyers pay the entire tax.

Taxes and Efficiency

A tax drives a wedge between the buying price and the selling price and results in inefficient underproduction. The price buyers pay is also the buyers' willingness to pay, which measures *marginal social benefit*. The price sellers receive is also the sellers' minimum supply-price, which equals *marginal social cost*.

A tax makes marginal social benefit exceed marginal social cost, shrinks the producer surplus and consumer surplus, and creates a deadweight loss.

Figure 6.10 shows the inefficiency of a tax on MP3 players. The demand curve, *D*, shows marginal social benefit, and the supply curve, *S*, shows marginal social cost. Without a tax, the market produces the efficient quantity (5,000 players a week).

With a tax, the sellers' minimum supply-price rises by the amount of the tax and the supply curve shifts to *S + tax*. This supply curve does *not* show marginal social cost. The tax component isn't a *social* cost of

FIGURE 6.10   Taxes and Efficiency

With no tax, 5,000 players a week are produced. With a $20 tax, the buyers' price rises to $210, the sellers' price falls to $190, and the quantity decreases to 4,000 players a week. Consumer surplus shrinks to the green area, and the producer surplus shrinks to the blue area. Part of the loss of consumer surplus and producer surplus goes to the government as tax revenue (the purple area) and part becomes a deadweight loss (the grey area).

production. It is a transfer of resources to the government. At the new equilibrium quantity (4,000 players a week), both consumer surplus and producer surplus shrink. Part of each surplus goes to the government in tax revenue—the purple area. And part becomes a deadweight loss—the grey area.

Only in the extreme cases of perfectly inelastic demand and perfectly inelastic supply does a tax not change the quantity bought and sold so that no deadweight loss arises.

Taxes and Fairness

We've examined the incidence and the efficiency of taxes. But when political leaders debate tax issues, it is fairness, not incidence and efficiency, that gets the most attention. The NDP complains that tax cuts are unfair because they give the benefits of lower taxes to the rich. Conservatives counter that it is fair that the rich get most of the tax cuts because they pay most of the taxes. No easy answers are available to the questions about the fairness of taxes.

Economists have proposed two conflicting principles of fairness to apply to a tax system:

- The benefits principle
- The ability-to-pay principle

The Benefits Principle The *benefits principle* is the proposition that people should pay taxes equal to the benefits they receive from the services provided by government. This arrangement is fair because it means that those who benefit most pay the most taxes. It makes tax payments and the consumption of government-provided services similar to private consumption expenditures.

The benefits principle can justify high fuel taxes to pay for highways, high taxes on alcoholic beverages and tobacco products to pay for public health-care services, and high rates of income tax on high incomes to pay for the benefits from law and order and from living in a secure environment, from which the rich might benefit more than the poor.

The Ability-to-Pay Principle The *ability-to-pay principle* is the proposition that people should pay taxes according to how easily they can bear the burden of the tax. A rich person can more easily bear the burden than a poor person can, so the ability-to-pay principle can reinforce the benefits principle to justify high rates of income tax on high incomes.

Taxes in Practice
Workers and Consumers Pay the Most

Personal income taxes and provincial sales taxes plus GST generate most of the tax revenues in Canada. Because the elasticity of supply of labour is low and the elasticity of demand for labour is high, workers pay most of the income taxes. Because the elasticities of demand for alcohol, tobacco, and gasoline are low and the elasticities of supply are high, the burden of these taxes (excise taxes) falls more heavily on buyers than on sellers.

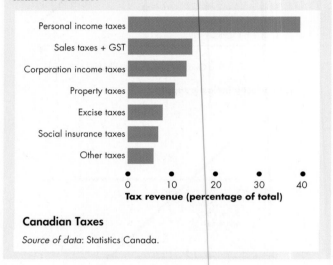

Canadian Taxes

Source of data: Statistics Canada.

Review Quiz

1 How does the elasticity of demand influence the effect of a tax on the price buyers pay, the price sellers receive, the quantity bought, the tax revenue, and the deadweight loss?
2 How does the elasticity of supply influence the effect of a tax on the price buyers pay, the price sellers receive, the quantity bought, the tax revenue, and the deadweight loss?
3 Why is a tax inefficient?
4 When would a tax be efficient?
5 What are the two principles of fairness that are applied to tax systems?

 Work Study Plan 6.3 and get instant feedback.

Your next task is to study two other types of government actions in markets: production quotas and subsidies. These tools are often used to influence the markets for farm products.

Production Quotas and Subsidies

An early or late frost, a hot, dry summer, or a wet spring present just a few of the challenges that fill the lives of farmers with uncertainty and sometimes with economic hardship. Fluctuations in the weather bring fluctuations in farm output and prices and sometimes leave farmers with low incomes. To help farmers avoid low prices and low incomes, governments intervene in the markets for farm products.

Price floors that work a bit like the minimum wage that you've already studied might be used. But as you've seen, this type of government action creates a surplus and is inefficient. These same conclusions apply to the effects of a price floor for farm products.

Governments often use two other methods of intervention in the markets for farm products:

- Production quotas
- Subsidies

Production Quotas

In the markets for milk, eggs, and poultry (among others), governments have, from time to time, imposed production quotas. A **production quota** is an upper limit to the quantity of a good that may be produced in a specified period. To discover the effects of a production quota, let's look at what a quota does to the market for milk.

Suppose that dairy farmers want to limit total production of milk to get a higher price. They persuade the government to introduce a production quota on milk.

The effect of the production quota depends on whether it is set below or above the equilibrium quantity. If the government introduced a production quota above the equilibrium quantity, nothing would change because milk growers would already be producing less than the quota. But a production quota set *below the equilibrium quantity* has big effects, which are

- A decrease in supply
- A rise in price
- A decrease in marginal cost
- Inefficient underproduction
- An incentive to cheat and overproduce

Figure 6.11 illustrates these effects.

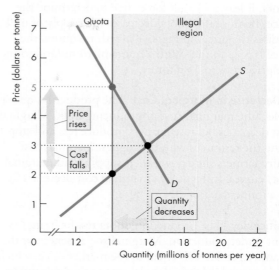

FIGURE 6.11 The Effects of a Production Quota

With no quota, farmers produce 16 million tonnes of milk a year and the price is $3 a tonne. A production quota of 14 million tonnes a year restricts total production to that amount. The quantity produced decreases to 14 million tonnes a year, the price rises to $5 a tonne, and the farmers' marginal cost falls to $2 a tonne. Because marginal social cost (on the supply curve) is less than marginal social benefit (on the demand curve), a deadweight loss arises from the underproduction.

myeconlab animation

A Decrease in Supply A production quota on milk decreases the supply of milk. Each farmer is assigned a production limit that is less than the amount that would be produced—and supplied—without the quota. The total of the farmers' limits equals the quota, and any production in excess of the quota is illegal.

The quantity supplied becomes the amount permitted by the production quota, and this quantity is fixed. The supply of milk becomes perfectly inelastic at the quantity permitted under the quota.

In Fig. 6.11, with no quota, farmers would produce 16 million tonnes of milk a year—the market equilibrium quantity. With a production quota set at 14 million tonnes a year, the grey-shaded area shows the illegal region. As in the case of price ceilings and price floors, market forces and political forces are in conflict in this illegal region.

The vertical red line labelled "Quota" becomes the supply curve of milk at prices above $2 a tonne.

A Rise in Price The production quota raises the price of milk. When the government sets a production quota, it leaves market forces free to determine the price. Because the quota decreases the supply of milk, it raises the price. In Fig. 6.11, with no quota, the price is $3 a tonne. With a quota of 14 million tonnes, the price rises to $5 a tonne.

A Decrease in Marginal Cost The production quota lowers the marginal cost of producing milk. Marginal cost decreases because farmers produce less and stop using the resources with the highest marginal cost. Dairy farmers slide down their supply (and marginal cost) curves. In Fig. 6.11, marginal cost decreases to $2 a tonne.

Inefficiency The production quota results in inefficient underproduction. Marginal social benefit at the quantity produced is equal to the market price, which has increased. Marginal social cost at the quantity produced has decreased and is less than the market price. So marginal social benefit exceeds marginal social cost and a deadweight loss arises.

An Incentive to Cheat and Overproduce The production quota creates an incentive for farmers to cheat and produce more than their individual production limit. With the quota, the price exceeds marginal cost, so the farmer can get a larger profit by producing one more unit. Of course, if all farmers produce more than their assigned limit, the production quota becomes ineffective, and the price falls to the equilibrium (no quota) price.

To make the production quota effective, farmers must set up a monitoring system to ensure that no one cheats and overproduces. But it is costly to set up and operate a monitoring system and difficult to detect and punish producers who violate their quotas.

Because of the difficulty of operating a quota, producers often lobby governments to establish a quota and provide the monitoring and punishment systems that make it work.

Subsidies

In Canada, the European Union, and the United States, the producers of grain, meat, milk, eggs, and many other farm products receive subsidies. A **subsidy** is a payment made by the government to a producer.

The effects of a subsidy are similar to the effects of a tax but they go in the opposite directions. These effects are

- An increase in supply
- A fall in price and increase in quantity produced
- An increase in marginal cost
- Payments by government to farmers
- Inefficient overproduction

To see the effects of a subsidy, we'll look at a market for grain. Figure 6.12 illustrates these effects.

An Increase in Supply In Fig. 6.12, with no subsidy, the demand curve D and the supply curve S determine the price of grain at $40 a tonne and the quantity of grain at 40 million tonnes a year.

Suppose that the government introduces a subsidy of $20 a tonne to grain farmers. A subsidy is like a negative tax. A tax is equivalent to an increase in cost, so a subsidy is equivalent to a decrease in cost. The subsidy brings an increase in supply.

To determine the position of the new supply curve, we subtract the subsidy from the farmers' minimum supply-price. In Fig. 6.12, with no subsidy, farmers are willing to offer 40 million tonnes a year at a price of $40 a tonne. With a subsidy of $20 a tonne, they will offer 40 million tonnes a year if the price is as low as $20 a tonne. The supply curve shifts to the red curve labelled *S – subsidy*.

A Fall in Price and Increase in Quantity Produced The subsidy lowers the price of grain and increases the quantity produced. In Fig. 6.12, equilibrium occurs where the new supply curve intersects the demand curve at a price of $30 a tonne and a quantity of 60 million tonnes a year.

An Increase in Marginal Cost The subsidy lowers the price paid by consumers but increases the marginal cost of producing grain. Marginal cost increases because farmers grow more grain, which means that they must begin to use some resources that are less ideal for growing grain. Farmers slide up along their supply (and marginal cost) curves. In Fig. 6.12, marginal cost increases to $50 a tonne.

Payments by Government to Farmers The government pays a subsidy to farmers on each tonne of grain produced. In this example, farmers increase production to 60 million tonnes a year and receive a subsidy

FIGURE 6.12 The Effects of a Subsidy

With no subsidy, farmers produce 40 million tonnes a year at $40 a tonne. A subsidy of $20 a tonne shifts the supply curve rightward to *S – subsidy*. The equilibrium quantity increases to 60 million tonnes a year, the price falls to $30 a tonne, and the price plus the subsidy received by farmers rises to $50 a tonne. In the new equilibrium, marginal social cost (on the supply curve) exceeds marginal social benefit (on the demand curve) and the subsidy results in inefficient overproduction.

 animation

of $20 a tonne. So grain farmers receive payments from the government that total $1,200 million a year.

Inefficient Overproduction The subsidy results in inefficient overproduction. At the quantity produced with the subsidy, marginal social benefit is equal to the market price, which has fallen. Marginal social cost has increased and it exceeds the market price. Because marginal social cost exceeds marginal social benefit, the increased production brings inefficiency.

Subsidies spill over to the rest of the world. Because a subsidy lowers the domestic market price, subsidized farmers will offer some of their output for sale on the world market. The increase in supply on the world market lowers the price in the rest of the world. Faced with lower prices, farmers in other countries decrease production and receive smaller revenues.

Farm Subsidies Today
Producing Food in the Wrong Places

Farm subsidies are a major obstacle to achieving an efficient use of resources in the global markets for farm products and are a source of tension between rich and developing nations.

Canada, the European Union, and the United States pay their farmers subsidies that create inefficient overproduction of food in these rich economies.

One international study concluded that Canadians would be better off if they imported *all* their food rather than producing any themselves!

At the same time, rich country's subsidies make it difficult for farmers in the poorer developing nations of Africa, Asia, and Central and South America to compete in global food markets. Farmers in these countries can often produce at a lower opportunity cost than Canadian, European, and U.S. farmers.

Two rich countries, Australia and New Zealand, have stopped subsidizing farmers. The result has been an improvement in the efficiency of farming in these countries. New Zealand is so efficient at producing lamb and dairy products that it has been called the Saudi Arabia of milk (an analogy with Saudi Arabia's huge oil reserve and production.)

International opposition to farm subsidies is strong. Opposition to farm subsidies inside Canada, the European Union, and the United States is growing, but it isn't as strong as the pro-farm lobby, so don't expect an early end to these subsidies.

Review Quiz

1 Summarize the effects of a production quota on the market price and the quantity produced.
2 Explain why a production quota is inefficient.
3 Explain why a voluntary production quota is difficult to operate.
4 Summarize the effects of a subsidy on the market price and the quantity produced.
5 Explain why a subsidy is inefficient.

myeconlab   Work Study Plan 6.4 and get instant feedback.

Governments intervene in some markets by making it illegal to trade in a good. Let's now see how these markets work.

Markets for Illegal Goods

The markets for many goods and services are regulated, and buying and selling some goods is illegal. The best-known examples of such goods are drugs, such as marijuana, cocaine, ecstasy, and heroin.

Despite the fact that these drugs are illegal, trade in them is a multibillion-dollar business. This trade can be understood by using the same economic model and principles that explain trade in legal goods. To study the market for illegal goods, we're first going to examine the prices and quantities that would prevail if these goods were not illegal. Next, we'll see how prohibition works. Then we'll see how a tax might be used to limit the consumption of these goods.

A Free Market for a Drug

Figure 6.13 shows the market for a drug. The demand curve, D, shows that, other things remaining the same, the lower the price of the drug, the larger is the quantity of the drug demanded. The supply curve, S, shows that, other things remaining the same, the lower the price of the drug, the smaller is the quantity supplied. If the drug were not illegal, the quantity bought and sold would be Q_C and the price would be P_C.

A Market for an Illegal Drug

When a good is illegal, the cost of trading in the good increases. By how much the cost increases and who bears the cost depend on the penalties for violating the law and the degree to which the law is enforced. The larger the penalties and the better the policing, the higher are the costs. Penalties might be imposed on sellers, buyers, or both.

Penalties on Sellers Drug dealers in Canada face large penalties if their activities are detected. For example, a marijuana dealer caught with less than 3 kilograms could serve a 5-year-less-one-day prison term. A heroin dealer or a marijuana dealer caught with 3 or more kilograms could be imprisoned for life. These penalties are part of the cost of supplying illegal drugs, and they bring a decrease in supply. To determine the new supply curve, we add the cost of breaking the law to the minimum price that drug dealers are willing to accept. In Fig. 6.13, the cost of breaking the law by selling drugs (*CBL*) is added to the minimum price that dealers will accept and the

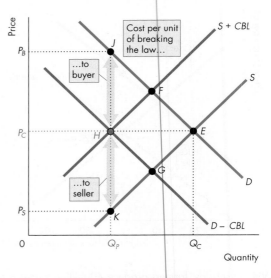

FIGURE 6.13   A Market for an Illegal Good

The demand curve for drugs is D, and the supply curve is S. If drugs are not illegal, the quantity bought and sold is Q_C at a price of P_C—point E. If selling drugs is illegal, the cost of breaking the law by selling drugs (*CBL*) is added to the minimum supply-price and supply decreases to $S + CBL$. The market moves to point F. If buying drugs is illegal, the cost of breaking the law is subtracted from the maximum price that buyers are willing to pay, and demand decreases to $D - CBL$. The market moves to point G. With both buying and selling illegal, the supply curve and the demand curve shift and the market moves to point H. The market price remains at P_C, but the market price plus the penalty for buying rises—point J—and the market price minus the penalty for selling falls—point K.

X myeconlab animation

supply curve shifts leftward to $S + CBL$. If penalties were imposed only on sellers, the market equilibrium would move from point E to point F.

Penalties on Buyers In Canada, it is illegal to *possess* drugs such as marijuana, cocaine, ecstasy, and heroin. Possession of marijuana can bring a prison term of 6 months and a fine of $1,000. Possession of heroin can bring a prison term of 7 years. Penalties fall on buyers, and the cost of breaking the law must be subtracted from the value of the good to determine the maximum price buyers are willing to pay for drugs. Demand decreases, and the demand curve shifts leftward. In Fig. 6.13, the demand curve shifts to $D - CBL$. If penalties were imposed only on buyers, the market equilibrium would move from point E to point G.

Penalties on Both Sellers and Buyers

If penalties are imposed on both sellers *and* buyers, both supply and demand decrease and both the supply curve and the demand curve shift. In Fig. 6.13, the costs of breaking the law are the same for both buyers and sellers, so both curves shift leftward by the same amount. The market equilibrium moves to point H. The market price remains at the competitive market price P_C, but the quantity bought decreases to Q_P. Buyers pay P_C plus the cost of breaking the law, which equals P_B. Sellers receive P_C minus the cost of breaking the law, which equals P_S.

The larger the penalties and the greater the degree of law enforcement, the larger is the decrease in demand and/or supply. If the penalties are heavier on sellers, the supply curve shifts farther than the demand curve and the market price rises above P_C. If the penalties are heavier on buyers, the demand curve shifts farther than the supply curve and the market price falls below P_C. In Canada, the penalties on sellers are larger than those on buyers, so the quantity of drugs traded decreases and the market price increases compared with a free market.

With high enough penalties and effective law enforcement, it is possible to decrease demand and/or supply to the point at which the quantity bought is zero. But in reality, such an outcome is unusual. It does not happen in Canada in the case of illegal drugs. The key reason is the high cost of law enforcement and insufficient resources for the police to achieve effective enforcement. Because of this situation, some people suggest that drugs (and other illegal goods) should be legalized and sold openly but also taxed at a high rate in the same way that legal drugs such as alcohol are taxed. How would such an arrangement work?

Legalizing and Taxing Drugs

From your study of the effects of taxes, it is easy to see that the quantity bought of a drug could be decreased if the drug was legalized and taxed. Imposing a sufficiently high tax could decrease the supply, raise the price, and achieve the same decrease in the quantity bought as does a prohibition on drugs. The government would collect a large tax revenue.

Illegal Trading to Evade the Tax It is likely that an extremely high tax rate would be needed to cut the quantity of drugs bought to the level prevailing with a prohibition. It is also likely that many drug dealers and buyers would try to cover up their activities to evade the tax on drugs. If they did act in this way, they would face the cost of breaking the law—the tax law. If the penalty for tax law violation is as severe and as effectively policed as drug-dealing laws, the analysis we've already conducted also applies to this case. The quantity of drugs bought would depend on the penalties for law breaking and on the way in which the penalties are assigned to buyers and sellers.

Taxes Versus Prohibition: Some Pros and Cons Which is more effective: prohibition or a tax? In favour of a tax and against prohibition is the fact that the tax revenue can be used to make law enforcement more effective. It can also be used to run a more effective education campaign against illegal drug use. In favour of prohibition and against a tax is the fact that prohibition sends a signal that might influence preferences, decreasing the demand for illegal drugs. Also, some people intensely dislike the idea of the government profiting from trade in harmful substances.

Review Quiz

1   How does the imposition of a penalty for selling an illegal drug influence demand, supply, price, and the quantity of the drug consumed?
2   How does the imposition of a penalty for possessing an illegal drug influence demand, supply, price, and the quantity of the drug bought?
3   How do penalties for selling and possessing an illegal drug influence demand, supply, price, and the quantity of the drug bought?
4   Is there any case for legalizing drugs?

 Work Study Plan 6.5 and get instant feedback.

You now know how to use the demand and supply model to predict prices, to study government actions in markets, and to study the sources and costs of inefficiency. *Reading Between the Lines* on pp. 146–147 applies what you've learned and shows why a rise in the minimum wage rate in British Columbia will not alleviate poverty.

The Minimum Wage in Action

Increasing Minimum Wage Good Intention, Lousy Policy

January 8, 2009

... [T]he B.C. Federation of Labour, among others, wants a $10 per hour minimum wage, up from $8, a 25-percent hike. Minimum wage advocates argue that increases are needed to reduce poverty among the "working poor" and that it can miraculously be done without negatively affecting employment. ...

The most damaging impact of minimum wage increases is that ... [it] results in higher unemployment for low-skilled workers and young people.

This unpleasant reality is well-documented. ... The Canadian research indicates that a 10-percent increase in the minimum wage is likely to decrease employment by three to six percent among all young workers (aged 15 to 24). For those young workers most directly affected—earning between the current $8 per hour and the proposed $10—the impact is more acute, experiencing employment losses of 4.5 to 20 percent. ... [I]ncreasing B.C.'s minimum wage by 25 percent to $10 per hour will lead to a loss of between 11,000 to 52,000 jobs for workers aged 15 to 24.

... [H]igher minimum wages have also been associated with increased school dropout rates. When minimum wages increase, more young people leave school in search of employment. Less education, fewer employment opportunities and less training is a deadly cocktail of results, given that experience, education, and skills development are critical drivers of higher wages.

The latest available data from Statistics Canada reveals that only 3.4 percent of workers in B.C. earned the minimum wage. Of these, 56 percent were between 15 and 24 years old, most of whom (87 percent) were living at home with family. Many of the remaining individuals earning minimum wages were adults supplementing their family income with part-time work.

Of course some minimum wage earners will benefit, but the typical minimum wage earner is not the person depicted by the advocates of higher minimum wages. ... [M]inimum wage work is largely a temporary experience. Research shows that after one year, more than 60 percent of minimum wage workers earn more than the minimum wage, with a typical wage gain of about 20 percent.

Essence of the Story

- In 2008, 56 percent of minimum wage earners in British Columbia were young people and 87 percent of these lived with their families.

- A high and rising minimum wage does not help the working poor, increases the unemployment rate, decreases the amount of on-the-job training, and increases the number of school dropouts.

- Earning the minimum wage is temporary: More than 60 percent of minimum wage earners move above the minimum after one year with a typical wage gain of 20 percent.

Economic Analysis

- In 2008, the minimum wage in Canada ranged from $7.75 an hour in New Brunswick and Prince Edward Island to $10.00 an hour in Nunavut. Figure 1 shows the data.

- The minimum wage affects younger low-skilled workers more than older and more skilled workers.

- A rise in the minimum wage rate in British Columbia will decrease employment and increase the unemployment rate of young workers.

- Figure 2 shows the British Columbia's labour market for young workers. The demand curve is LD and the supply curve is LS. (The assumed elasticity of the demand for labour is 0.5 and the assumed elasticity of the supply of labour is 0.25.)

- In July 2008, when the minimum wage rate was $8.00 an hour, 370,000 young people were employed and approximately 40,000 were unemployed.

- The rise in the minimum wage rate decreases the quantity of labour demanded, increases the quantity of labour supplied, and increases the unemployment of young workers.

- Some of the increase in the quantity of labour supplied is labour services supplied by school dropouts.

- With the assumed elasticities of demand and supply of labour, a rise in the minimum wage rate to $10 an hour will increase unemployment to more than 100,000 young workers.

- If the elasticities are smaller than those assumed, unemployment will increase by a smaller number.

- Figure 3 is a scatter diagram of the relationship between the minimum wage rate (x-axis) and the unemployment rate of young workers measured as a ratio of the unemployment rate of older workers (y-axis).

- Figure 3 shows a positive relationship between the minimum wage rate and the unemployment rate of young workers relative to that of older workers.

- But the correlation between these two variables is not perfect. The reason is that other things are not the same across the provinces and factors other than the minimum wage influence the unemployment rate of young workers.

Figure 1 Minimum wage rates across Canada

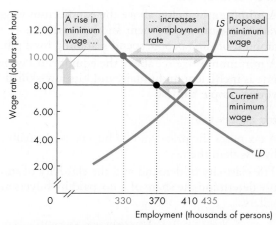

Figure 2 British Columbia's labour market for young workers

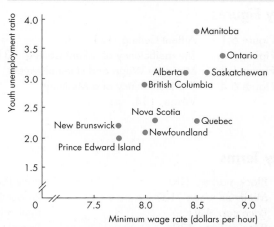

Figure 3 Minimum wage and youth unemployment rates

147

SUMMARY ◆

Key Points

A Housing Market with a Rent Ceiling (pp. 130–132)
- A rent ceiling that is set above the equilibrium rent has no effect.
- A rent ceiling that is set below the equilibrium rent creates a housing shortage, increased search activity, and a black market.
- A rent ceiling that is set below the equilibrium rent is inefficient and unfair.

A Labour Market with a Minimum Wage (pp. 133–135)
- A minimum wage set below the equilibrium wage rate has no effect.
- A minimum wage set above the equilibrium wage rate creates unemployment and increases the amount of time people spend searching for a job.
- A minimum wage set above the equilibrium wage rate is inefficient and unfair, and hits low-skilled young people hardest.

Taxes (pp. 135–140)
- A tax raises the price paid by buyers, but usually by less than the tax.
- The elasticity of demand and the elasticity of supply determine the share of a tax paid by buyers and sellers.

- The less elastic the demand or the more elastic the supply, the larger is the share of the tax paid by buyers.
- If demand is perfectly elastic or supply is perfectly inelastic, sellers pay the entire tax. And if demand is perfectly inelastic or supply is perfectly elastic, buyers pay the entire tax.

Production Quotas and Subsidies (pp. 141–143)
- A production quota leads to inefficient under-production, which raises the price.
- A subsidy is like a negative tax. It lowers the price, increases the cost of production, and leads to inefficient overproduction.

Markets for Illegal Goods (pp. 144–145)
- Penalties on sellers increase the cost of selling the good and decrease the supply of the good.
- Penalties on buyers decrease their willingness to pay and decrease the demand for the good.
- Penalties on buyers and sellers decrease the quantity of the good, raise the price buyers pay, and lower the price sellers receive.
- Legalizing and taxing can achieve the same outcome as penalties on buyers and sellers.

Key Figures

Figure 6.1   A Rent Ceiling, 131
Figure 6.2   The Inefficiency of a Rent Ceiling, 131
Figure 6.3   Minimum Wage and Unemployment, 133
Figure 6.4   The Inefficiency of a Minimum Wage, 134
Figure 6.5   A Tax on Sellers, 136
Figure 6.6   A Tax on Buyers, 137
Figure 6.10   Taxes and Efficiency, 139
Figure 6.11   The Effects of a Production Quota, 141
Figure 6.12   The Effects of a Subsidy, 143
Figure 6.13   A Market for an Illegal Good, 144

Key Terms

Black market, 130
Minimum wage, 133
Price cap, 130
Price ceiling, 130
Price floor, 133
Production quota, 141
Rent ceiling, 130
Search activity, 130
Subsidy, 142
Tax incidence, 135

PROBLEMS and APPLICATIONS

myeconlab   Work problems 1–9 in Chapter 6 Study Plan and get instant feedback.
Work problems 10–17 as Homework, a Quiz, or a Test if assigned by your instructor.

1. The graph illustrates the market for rental housing.

a. What are the equilibrium rent and equilibrium quantity of rental housing?
b. If a rent ceiling is set at $600 a month, what is the quantity of housing rented and the shortage of housing?

   If a rent ceiling is set at $300 a month, what is
c. The quantity of housing rented?
d. The shortage of housing?
e. The maximum price that someone is willing to pay for the last unit of housing available?

2. **Rent Control Regime Stifles Manitoba Market**

   Manitoba may soon be the only western "have not" province in terms of supply, availability, and quality of rental accommodation, a commodity which is paramount to the attraction and retention of the talented young people who drive the economy. ... Alberta and Saskatchewan have abolished rent controls. British Columbia reinstituted rent controls in 2004 but with a guideline based on CPI plus two percent. ... In essence, B.C.'s rent control system is almost a market economy system.

   As a consequence of using market systems, all three of our western neighbours have enjoyed growth in available units over the past few years. In contrast, Manitoba has seen a net loss of more than 1,000 units between 1998 and 2004 and our vacancy rates have decreased from 5.5 percent to 1.1 percent over the past decade, well below the 2.7 percent national average.

   Winnipeg Free Press, September 25, 2005

a. Explain the effect of the rent control in Manitoba on the quantity of rental units supplied and the quantity demanded.
b. Draw a demand and supply graph to illustrate the effects of a rent control in the market for rental units in Winnipeg.
c. Explain why the vacancy rate over the past few years has fallen in Manitoba and increased in the three other western provinces.
d. The *Winnipeg Free Press* also reported that "Every year, Manitobans see more rental units converted to condominiums." Do rent controls protect any segment of the population?
e. Explain what changes would occur in the rental housing market if rent controls in Winnipeg were abolished. What would happen to total surplus and deadweight loss?

3. The table shows the demand and supply schedules for on-campus housing.

Rent (dollars per room)	Quantity demanded	Quantity supplied
	(rooms)	
500	2,500	2,000
550	2,250	2,000
600	2,000	2,000
650	1,750	2,000
700	1,500	2,000

a. If the college puts a rent ceiling of $650 a month on rooms, what is the rent paid, how many rooms are rented, and is the on-campus housing market efficient?
b. If the college strictly enforced a rent ceiling of $550 a month, what is the rent paid, how many rooms are rented, and is the on-campus housing market efficient?
c. Suppose that with a strictly enforced rent ceiling of $550 a month, a black market develops. How high might the black market rent be? Would the on-campus housing market be fair? Explain your answer.

4. Suppose the government introduced a ceiling on lawyers' fees. How would the amount of work done by lawyers, the consumer surplus of people who hire lawyers, and the producer surplus of

law firms change? Would this fee ceiling result in an efficient use of resources? Why or why not?

5. The table gives the demand and supply schedules of teenage labour.

Wage rate (dollars per hour)	Quantity demanded	Quantity supplied
	(hours per month)	
4	3,000	1,000
5	2,500	1,500
6	2,000	2,000
7	1,500	2,500
8	1,000	3,000

a. What are the equilibrium wage rate and number of hours worked?
b. What is the quantity of unemployment?

If a minimum wage for teenagers is $5 an hour,

c. How many hours do they work?
d. How many hours of teenage labour are unemployed?

If a minimum wage for teenagers is $7 an hour,

e. How many hours do teenagers work and how many hours are unemployed?
f. Demand for teenage labour increases by 500 hours a month. What is the wage rate paid to teenagers and how many hours of teenage labour are unemployed?

6. The table gives the demand and supply schedules for chocolate brownies.

Price (cents per brownie)	Quantity demanded	Quantity supplied
	(millions per day)	
50	5	3
60	4	4
70	3	5
80	2	6
90	1	7

a. If brownies are not taxed, what is the price of a brownie and how many are bought?
b. If sellers are taxed 20¢ a brownie, what are the price and quantity bought? Who pays the tax?
c. If buyers are taxed 20¢ a brownie, what are the price and quantity bought? Who pays the tax?
d. If a tax of 20¢ is imposed on brownies, what is the government's tax revenue and what is the deadweight loss?

7. The demand and supply schedules for rice are

Price (dollars per box)	Quantity demanded	Quantity supplied
	(boxes per week)	
1.00	3,500	500
1.10	3,250	1,000
1.20	3,000	1,500
1.30	2,750	2,000
1.40	2,500	2,500
1.50	2,250	3,000
1.60	2,000	3,500

What are the price, the marginal cost of producing rice, and the quantity produced if the government

a. Sets a production quota for rice of 2,000 boxes a week?
b. Introduces a subsidy to rice growers of 30¢ a box?

8. The figure shows the market for a banned substance.

What are the market price and the quantity bought if a penalty of $20 a unit is imposed on

a. Sellers only?
b. Buyers only?
c. Both sellers and buyers?

9. **Battling Foreign Farm Subsidies**
... On the farm subsidy front, farmers in Europe received subsidies of about $6 a bushel, U.S. farmers got $2.50 a bushel, Canadian farmers received subsidies of only 40 cents a bushel.
CBC News Online, August 6, 2004

In which market do you think the surplus (as a percentage of equilibrium output) is largest and which market is the most inefficient?

10. Coal Shortage at China Plants

Chinese power plants have run short of coal, an unintended effect of government-mandated price controls—a throwback to communist central planning—to shield the public from rising global energy costs. ... Beijing has also frozen retail prices of gasoline and diesel. That helped farmers and the urban poor, but it has spurred sales of gas-guzzling luxury cars and propelled double-digit annual growth in fuel consumption.

Oil refiners say they are suffering heavy losses and some began cutting production last year, causing fuel shortages in parts of China's south.

CNN, May 20, 2008

a. Are China's price controls described in the news clip price floors or price ceilings?

b. Explain how China's price controls have created shortages or surpluses in the markets for coal, gasoline, and diesel.

c. Illustrate your answer to b graphically by using the supply and demand model.

d. Explain how China's price controls have changed consumer surplus, producer surplus, total surplus, and the deadweight loss in the markets for coal, gasoline, and diesel.

e. Illustrate your answer to d graphically by using the supply and demand model.

11. The figure shows the rental housing market.

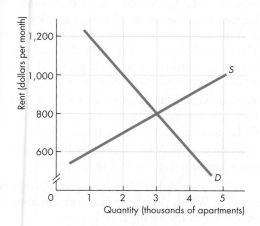

a. What is the rent and how many apartments are rented? If a rent ceiling is set at $900 a month, what is the rent and how many apartments are rented?

b. If a rent ceiling is set at $600 a month, what is the rent and how many apartments are rented? If a black market develops, how high could the black market rent be? Explain.

c. With a strictly enforced rent ceiling of $600 a month, is the housing market efficient? What is the deadweight loss? Is the housing market fair? Explain why or why not.

12. India Steps Up Pressure for Minimum Wage for Its Workers in the Gulf

Oil-rich countries in the [Persian] Gulf, already confronted by strong labour protests, are facing renewed pressure from India to pay minimum wages for unskilled workers. The effort by India—the largest source of migrant workers in the region, with five million—is the strongest push yet by home countries to win better conditions for their citizens. ...

International Herald Tribune, March 27, 2008

If the Persian Gulf countries paid a minimum wage above the equilibrium wage to Indian workers,

a. How would the market for labour be affected in the Gulf countries? Draw a supply and demand graph to illustrate your answer.

b. How would the market for labour be affected in India? Draw a supply and demand graph to illustrate your answer. [Be careful: the minimum wage is in the Gulf countries, not in India.]

c. Would migrant Indian workers be better off, worse off, or unaffected by the minimum wage?

13. The figure shows the market for tomatoes. The government now introduces a subsidy for tomatoes at $4 per kilogram.

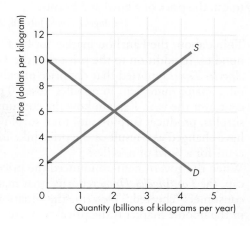

a. Before the subsidy is introduced, what are the equilibrium price and quantity of tomatoes? Is the market for tomatoes efficient?

b. After the government introduces the subsidy what is the quantity of tomatoes produced, the quantity demanded, and the subsidy received by tomato farmers?

c. With the subsidy, is the market for tomatoes efficient? Who gains and who loses from the subsidy and what is the deadweight loss? Could the subsidy be regarded as being fair?

14. The demand and supply schedules for tulips are

Price (dollars per bunch)	Quantity demanded	Quantity supplied
	(bunches per week)	
10	100	40
12	90	60
14	80	80
16	70	100
18	60	120

a. If tulips are not taxed, what is the price and how many bunches are bought?

b. If tulips are taxed $6 a bunch, what are the price and quantity bought? Who pays the tax?

15. **Chinese City Stews over Rising Cost of Beef Noodles**

Lanzhou, China—Mention this city's name in China and people think beef noodles. Today, more than 1,000 beef noodle shops cater to this western industrial city of 3 million. ...So when one shop after another bumped up the price of a bowl from 33 cents to 40 cents last month, it came as something of a jolt. ...The outcry over the beef noodle price hike prompted the local government on June 26 to cap the price of a bowl at 33 cents.

Los Angeles Times, July 28, 2007

a. Think about the Lanzhou market for beef noodles. In addition to the price rise, the *Los Angeles Times* reported that the price of palm oil, a major ingredient in noodles, rose 20 percent over the year. Explain how the consumer surplus, producer surplus, and total surplus have changed as a result of the price hike to 40 cents for a bowl of noodles?

b. When the government announced the price cap, the *Los Angeles Times* reported that many consumers "cheered." Describe the situation in the noodle market if the price cap were

enforced. Is the consumer surplus larger or smaller than before the price was capped?

c. The *Los Angeles Times* reported that with no penalty for violating the cap, shops "are defying the directive." Is this black market efficient or inefficient? And is it fair or unfair?

16. The table gives the demand and supply schedules for an illegal drug.

Price (dollars per unit)	Quantity demanded	Quantity supplied
	(units per day)	
50	500	300
60	400	400
70	300	500
80	200	600
90	100	700

a. If there are no penalties on buying or selling the drug, what is the price and how many units are consumed?

b. If the penalty on sellers is $20 a unit, what are the price and quantity consumed?

c. If the penalty on buyers is $20 a unit, what are the price and quantity consumed?

17. Study *Reading Between the Lines* (pp. 146–147) about the market for young workers in British Columbia.

a. If the minimum wage in British Columbia were abolished, what do you predict would happen to the quantity of labour employed and the average wage rate?

b. With the abolition of the minimum wage in British Columbia, who would gain and who would lose? Would society gain or lose?

c. Why do you think a large number of British Columbians and the government of British Columbia support the minimum wage?

d. Why do you think Ms. Ivanova wants to raise the minimum wage to $10 an hour?

18. Use the links in MyEconLab (Chapter Resources, Chapter 6, Web links) to get information about production quotas on sugar in Europe.

a. Why do you think the European nations assign production quotas for sugar?

b. If the European sugar quotas are less than the equilibrium quantities, who benefits from the quotas? Who loses from the production quotas?

7 ◆ Global Markets in Action

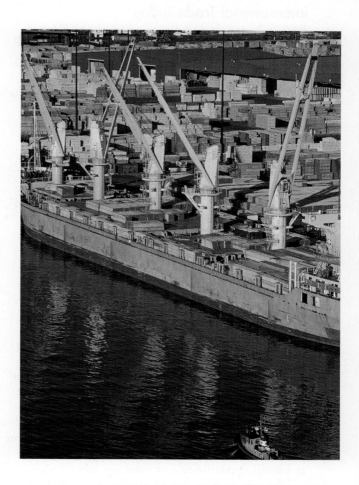

After studying this chapter, you will be able to

- Explain how markets work with international trade

- Identify the gains from international trade and its winners and losers

- Explain the effects of international trade barriers

- Explain and evaluate arguments used to justify restricting international trade

iPods, Wii games, and Roots sweaters are just three of the items you might buy that are not produced in Canada. In fact, most of the goods that you buy are produced abroad, often in Asia, and transported here in container ships or cargo jets. And it's not only goods produced abroad that you buy—it is services too. When you make a technical support call, most likely you'll be talking with someone in India, or to a voice recognition system that was programmed in India. Satellites or fibre cables will carry your conversation along with huge amounts of other voice messages, video images, and data.

All these activities are part of the globalization process that is having a profound effect on our lives. Globalization is controversial and generates heated debate. Many Canadians want to know how we can compete with people whose wages are a fraction of our own.

Why do we go to such lengths to trade and communicate with others in faraway places? You will find some answers in this chapter. And in *Reading Between the Lines* at the end of the chapter, you can apply what you've learned and examine the effects of the softwood lumber deal between Canada and the United States.

How Global Markets Work

Because we trade with people in other countries, the goods and services that we can buy and consume are not limited by what we can produce. The goods and services we buy from other countries are our **imports**. The goods and services we sell to people in other countries are our **exports**.

International Trade Today

Global trade today is enormous. In 2008, global exports and imports were $35 trillion, which is more than half the value of global production. The United States is the world's largest international trader and accounts for 10 percent of world exports and 15 percent of world imports. Germany and China, which rank second and third behind the United States, lag by a large margin.

In 2008, total Canadian exports were $535 billion, which is about 34 percent of the value of Canadian production. Total Canadian imports were $503 billion, which is about 32 percent of the value of total expenditure in Canada.

Canada trades both goods and services. In 2008, exports of services were about 13 percent of total exports, and imports of services were about 18 percent of total imports.

What Drives International Trade?

Comparative advantage is the fundamental force that drives international trade. Comparative advantage (see Chapter 2, p. 40) is a situation in which a person can perform an activity or produce a good or service at a lower opportunity cost than anyone else. This same idea applies to nations. We can define *national comparative advantage* as a situation in which a nation can perform an activity or produce a good or service at a lower opportunity cost than any other nation.

The opportunity cost of producing a T-shirt is lower in China than in Canada, so China has a comparative advantage in producing T-shirts. The opportunity cost of producing a regional jet is lower in Canada than in China, so Canada has a comparative advantage in producing regional jets.

You saw in Chapter 2 how Liz and Joe reap gains from trade by specializing in the production of the good at which they have a comparative advantage and trading. Both are better off.

Canada's Most Traded Items
Trading Energy for Automobiles

The figure shows Canada's four largest exports and imports by value. Motor vehicles and parts and crude petroleum are large exports *and* imports. But Canada is a *net importer* of motor vehicles and parts and a *net exporter* of crude oil. Natural gas is another big export. So Canadians trade energy products in exchange for motor vehicles and parts.

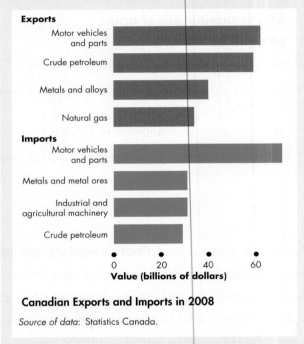

Canadian Exports and Imports in 2008

Source of data: Statistics Canada.

This same principle applies to trade among nations. Because China has a comparative advantage at producing T-shirts and Canada has a comparative advantage at producing regional jets, the people of both countries can gain from specialization and trade. China can buy regional jets from Canada at a lower opportunity cost than that at which Chinese firms can produce them. And Canadians can buy T-shirts from China for a lower opportunity cost than that at which firms in Canada can produce them. Also, through international trade, Chinese producers can get higher prices for their T-shirts and Bombardier can sell regional jets for a higher price. Both countries gain from international trade.

Let's now illustrate the gains from trade that we've just described by studying demand and supply in the global markets for T-shirts and regional jets.

Why Canada Imports T-Shirts

Canada imports T-shirts because the rest of the world has a comparative advantage in producing T-shirts. Figure 7.1 illustrates how this comparative advantage generates international trade and how trade affects the price of a T-shirt and the quantities produced and bought.

The demand curve D_{Can} and the supply curve S_{Can} show the demand and supply in Canada's domestic market only. The demand curve tells us the quantity of T-shirts that Canadians are willing to buy at various prices. The supply curve tells us the quantity of T-shirts that Canadian garment makers are willing to sell at various prices—that is, the quantity supplied at each price when all T-shirts sold in Canada are produced in Canada.

Figure 7.1(a) shows what the Canadian T-shirt market would be like with no international trade.

The price of a shirt would be $8 and 4 million shirts a year would be produced by Canadian garment makers and bought by Canadian consumers.

Figure 7.1(b) shows the market for T-shirts with international trade. Now the price of a T-shirt is determined in the world market, not Canada's domestic market. The world price is less than $8 a T-shirt, which means that the rest of the world has a comparative advantage in producing T-shirts. The world price line shows the world price at $5 a shirt.

The Canadian demand curve D_{Can} tells us that at $5 a shirt, Canadians buy 6 million shirts a year. The Canadian supply curve S_{Can} tells us that at $5 a shirt, Canadian garment makers produce 2 million T-shirts a year. To buy 6 million T-shirts when only 2 million are produced in Canada, we must import T-shirts from the rest of the world. The quantity of T-shirts imported is 4 million a year.

FIGURE 7.1 A Market with Imports

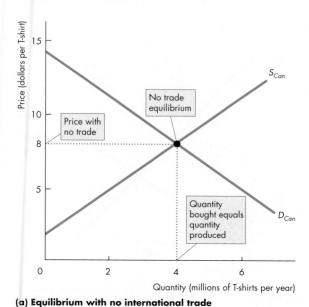

(a) Equilibrium with no international trade

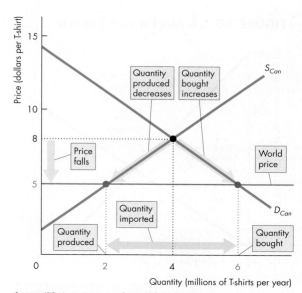

(b) Equilibrium in a market with imports

Part (a) shows the Canadian market for T-shirts with no international trade. The domestic demand curve D_{Can} and domestic supply curve S_{Can} determine the price of a T-shirt at $8 and the quantity produced and bought in Canada at 4 million T- shirts a year.

Part (b) shows the Canadian market for T-shirts with international trade. World demand and world supply determine the world price of a T-shirt, which is $5. The price in the Canadian market falls to $5 a shirt. Canadian purchases of T-shirts increase to 6 million a year, and Canadian production of T-shirts decreases to 2 million a year. Canada imports 4 million T-shirts a year.

Why Canada Exports Regional Jets

Figure 7.2 illustrates international trade in regional jets. The demand curve D_{Can} and the supply curve S_{Can} show the demand and supply in Canada's domestic market only. The demand curve tells us the quantity of regional jet that airlines in Canada are willing to buy at various prices. The supply curve tells us the quantity of regional jets that Bombardier is willing to sell at various prices.

Figure 7.2(a) shows what the Canadian market for regional jets would be like with no international trade. The price of a regional jet would be $100 million and 40 a year would be produced by Bombardier and bought by Canadian airlines.

Figure 7.2(b) shows the Canadian market for regional jets with international trade. Now the price of a regional jet is determined in the world market and the world price is higher than $100 million, which means that Canada has a comparative

advantage in producing regional jets. The world price line shows the world price at $150 million.

The Canadian demand curve D_{Can} tells us that at a price of $150 million, Canadian airlines buy 20 regional jets a year. The Canadian supply curve S_{Can} tells us that at a price of $150 million, Bombardier produces 70 regional jets a year. The quantity produced in Canada (70 a year) minus the quantity purchased by Canadian airlines (20 a year) is the quantity exported, which is 50 regional jets a year.

Review Quiz

1   Describe the situation in the market for a good or service that Canada imports.
2   Describe the situation in the market for a good or service that Canada exports.

myeconlab Work Study Plan 7.1 and get instant feedback.

FIGURE 7.2   A Market with Exports

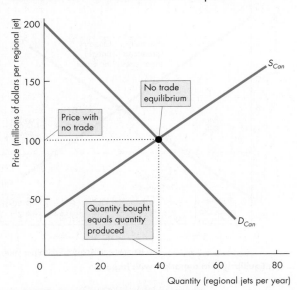

(a) Equilibrium without international trade

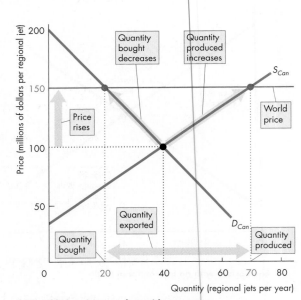

(b) Equilibrium in a market with exports

In part (a), the Canadian market with no international trade, the domestic demand curve D_{Can} and the domestic supply curve S_{Can} determine the price of a regional jet at $100 million and 40 jets are produced and bought each year.

In part (b), the Canadian market with international

trade, world demand and world supply determine the world price of a regional jet at $150 million. The price in Canada rises. Bombardier increases production to 70 a year, and Canadian airlines decrease their purchases to 20 a year. Canada exports 50 regional jets a year.

myeconlab animation

Winners, Losers, and the Net Gain from Trade

International trade has winners but it also has losers. That's why you often hear people complaining about international competition. We're now going to see who wins and who loses from international trade. You will then be able to understand who complains about international competition and why. You will learn why we hear producers complaining about cheap foreign imports. You will also see why we never hear consumers of imported goods and services complaining and why we never hear exporters complaining except when they want greater access to foreign markets.

Gains and Losses from Imports

We measure the gains and losses from imports by examining their effect on consumer surplus, producer surplus, and total surplus. The winners are those whose surplus increases and the losers are those whose surplus decreases.

Figure 7.3(a) shows what consumer surplus and producer surplus would be with no international trade in T-shirts. Canadian domestic demand D_{Can} and domestic supply S_{Can} determine the price and quantity. The green area shows consumer surplus and the blue area shows producer surplus. Total surplus is the sum of consumer surplus and producer surplus.

Figure 7.3(b) shows how these surpluses change when the Canadian market opens to imports. The price in Canada falls to the world price. The quantity bought increases to the quantity demanded at the world price and consumer surplus expands from A to the larger green area $A + B + D$. The quantity produced in Canada decreases to the quantity supplied at the world price and producer surplus shrinks to the smaller blue area C.

Part of the gain in consumer surplus, the area B, is a loss of producer surplus—a redistribution of total surplus. But the other part of the increase in

FIGURE 7.3 Gains and Losses in a Market with Imports

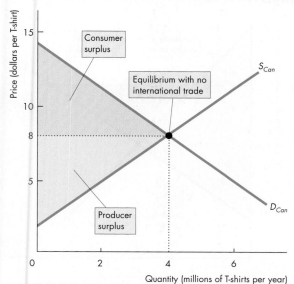

(a) Consumer surplus and producer surplus with no international trade

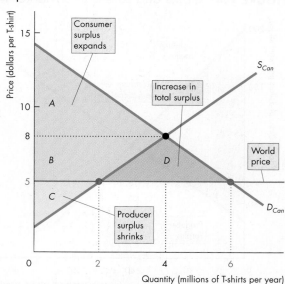

(b) Gains and losses from imports

In part (a), with no international trade, the green area shows the consumer surplus and the blue area shows the producer surplus.

In part (b), with international trade, the price falls to the world price of $5 a shirt. Consumer surplus expands to area $A + B + D$. Producer surplus shrinks to area C. Area B is a transfer of surplus from producers to consumers. Area D is an increase in total surplus—the gain from imports.

myeconlab animation

consumer surplus, the area D, is a net gain. This increase in total surplus results from the lower price and increased purchases and is the gain from imports.

Gains and Losses from Exports

We measure the gains and losses from exports just as we measured those from imports, by their effect on consumer surplus, producer surplus, and total surplus.

Figure 7.4(a) shows what the consumer surplus and producer surplus would be with no international trade. Domestic demand D_{Can} and domestic supply S_{Can} determine the price and quantity. The green area shows consumer surplus and the blue area shows producer surplus. The two surpluses sum to total surplus.

Figure 7.4(b) shows how the consumer surplus and producer surplus change when the good is exported. The price rises to the world price. The quantity bought decreases to the quantity demanded at the world price and the consumer surplus shrinks

to the green area A. The quantity produced increases to the quantity supplied at the world price and the producer surplus expands from the blue area C to the larger blue area $B + C + D$.

Part of the gain of producer surplus, the area B, is a loss in consumer surplus—a redistribution of the total surplus. But the other part of the increase in producer surplus, the area D, is a net gain. This increase in total surplus results from the higher price and increased production and is the gain from exports.

Review Quiz

1 How is the gain from imports distributed between consumers and domestic producers?
2 How is the gain from exports distributed between consumers and domestic producers?
3 Why is the net gain from international trade positive?

myeconlab   Work Study Plan 7.2 and get instant feedback.

FIGURE 7.4 Gains and Losses in a Market with Exports

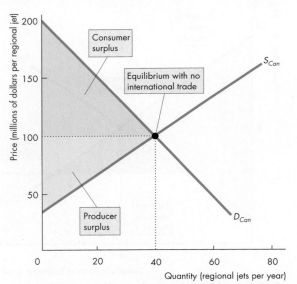

(a) Consumer surplus and producer surplus with no international trade

(b) Gains and losses from exports

In part (a), the Canadian market with no international trade, the green area shows the consumer surplus and the blue area shows the producer surplus. In part (b), the Canadian market with international trade, the price rises

to the world price. Consumer surplus shrinks to area A. Producer surplus expands to area $B + C + D$. Area B is a transfer of consumer surplus to producers. Area D is an increase in total surplus—the gain from exports.

myeconlab animation

International Trade Restrictions

Governments use four sets of tools to influence international trade and protect domestic industries from foreign competition. They are

- Tariffs
- Import quotas
- Other import barriers
- Export subsidies

Tariffs

A **tariff** is a tax on a good that is imposed by the importing country when an imported good crosses its international boundary. For example, the government of India imposes a 100 percent tariff on wine imported from Ontario. So when an Indian imports a $10 bottle of Ontario wine, he pays the Indian government a $10 import duty.

The temptation for governments to impose tariffs is a strong one. First, they provide revenue to the government. Second, they enable the government to satisfy the self-interest of the people who earn their incomes in the import-competing industries. But as you will see, tariffs and other restrictions on free international trade decrease the gains from trade and are not in the social interest. Let's see why.

The Effects of a Tariff To see the effects of a tariff, let's return to the example in which Canada imports T-shirts. With free trade, the T-shirts are imported and sold at the world price. Then, under pressure from Canadian garment makers, the government of Canada imposes a tariff on imported T-shirts. Buyers of T-shirts must now pay the world price plus the tariff. Several consequences follow, as Fig. 7.5 illustrates.

Figure 7.5(a) shows the situation with free international trade. Canada produces 2 million T-shirts a year and imports 4 million a year at the world price of $5 a shirt. Figure 7.5(b) shows what happens with

FIGURE 7.5   The Effects of a Tariff

(a) Free trade

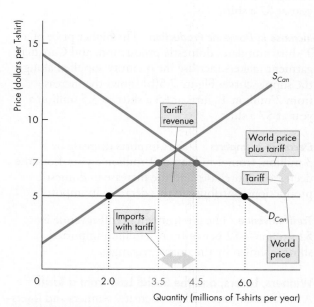

(b) Market with tariff

The world price of a T-shirt is $5. With free trade in part (a), Canadians buy 6 million T-shirts a year. Canadian garment makers produce 2 million T-shirts a year and Canada imports 4 million a year.

With a tariff of $2 per T-shirt in part (b), the price in

Canada rises to $7 a T-shirt. Canadian production increases, Canadian purchases decrease, and the quantity imported decreases. The government collects a tariff revenue of $2 on each T-shirt imported, which is shown by the purple rectangle.

a tariff set at $2 per T-shirt. The following changes occur in the market for T-shirts:

- The price of a T-shirt in Canada rises by $2.
- The quantity of T-shirts bought in Canada decreases.
- The quantity of T-shirts produced in Canada increases.
- The quantity of T-shirts imported into Canada decreases.
- The Canadian government collects a tariff revenue.

Rise in Price of a T-Shirt   To buy a T-shirt, Canadians must pay the world price plus the tariff, so the price of a T-shirt rises by $2 to $7. Figure 7.5(b) shows the new domestic price line, which lies $2 above the world price line.

Decrease in Purchases   The higher price of a T-shirt brings a decrease in the quantity demanded along the demand curve. Figure 7.5(b) shows the decrease from 6 million T-shirts a year at $5 a shirt to 4.5 million a year at $7 a shirt.

Increase in Domestic Production   The higher price of a T-shirt stimulates domestic production, and Canadian garment makers increase the quantity supplied along the supply curve. Figure 7.5(b) shows the increase from 2 million T-shirts at $5 a shirt to 3.5 million a year at $7 a shirt.

Decrease in Imports   T-shirt imports decrease by 3 million, from 4 million to 1 million a year. Both the decrease in purchases and the increase in domestic production contribute to this decrease in imports.

Tariff Revenue   The government's tariff revenue is $2 million—$2 per shirt on 1 million imported shirts—shown by the purple rectangle.

Winners, Losers, and the Social Loss from a Tariff

A tariff on an imported good creates winners and losers and a social loss. When the government of Canada imposes a tariff on an imported good,

- Canadian consumers of the good lose.
- Canadian producers of the good gain.
- Canadian consumers lose more than Canadian producers gain.
- Society loses: a deadweight loss arises.

Canadian Consumers of the Good Lose   Because the price of a T-shirt in Canada rises, the quantity of T-shirts demanded decreases. The combination of a higher price and smaller quantity bought decreases consumer surplus—the loss to Canadian consumers that arises from a tariff.

Canadian Producers of the Good Gain   Because the price of an imported T-shirt rises by the amount of the tariff, Canadian T-shirt producers are now able to sell their T-shirts for the world price plus the tariff. At the higher price, the quantity of T-shirts supplied by Canadian producers increases. The combination of a higher price and larger quantity produced increases producer surplus—the gain to Canadian producers from the tariff.

Canadian Consumers Lose More Than Canadian Producers Gain   Consumer surplus decreases for four reasons: Some becomes producer surplus, some is lost in a higher cost of production (domestic producers have higher costs than foreign producers), some is lost because imports decrease, and some goes to the government as tariff revenue. Figure 7.6 shows these sources of lost consumer surplus.

Figure 7.6(a) shows the consumer surplus and producer surplus with free international trade in T-shirts. Figure 7.6(b) shows the consumer surplus and producer surplus with a $2 tariff on imported T-shirts. By comparing Fig. 7.6(b) with Fig. 7.6(a), you can see how a tariff changes these surpluses.

Consumer surplus—the green area—shrinks. The decrease in consumer surplus is made up of four parts. First, some of the consumer surplus is transferred to producers. The blue area B represents this loss (and gain of producer surplus). Second, part of the consumer surplus is lost in the higher cost of domestic production. The grey area C shows this loss. Third, some of the consumer surplus is transferred to the government. The purple area D shows this loss (and gain of government revenue). Fourth, some of the consumer surplus is lost because imports decrease. The grey area E shows this loss.

Society Loses: A Deadweight Loss Arises   Some of the loss of consumer surplus is transferred to producers and some is transferred to the government and spent on government programs that people value. But the increase in production cost and the loss from decreased imports is transferred to no one: It is a social loss—a deadweight loss. The grey areas labelled C and E represent this deadweight loss.

FIGURE 7.6   The Winners and Losers from a Tariff

(a) Free trade

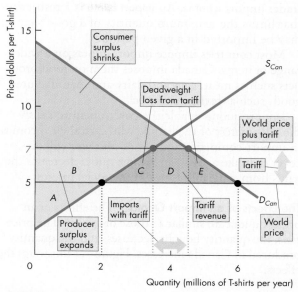

(b) Market with tariff

The world price of a T-shirt is $5. In part (a), with free trade, Canada imports 4 million T-shirts. Consumer surplus, producer surplus, and the gains from free trade are as large as possible.

In part (b), a tariff of $2 per T-shirt raises the Canadian price of a T-shirt to $7. The quantity imported decreases. Consumer surplus shrinks by the areas B, C, D, and E. Producer surplus expands by area B. The government's tariff revenue is area D, and the tariff creates a deadweight loss equal to the area $C + E$.

myeconlab   animation

Canadian Tariffs

Almost Gone

Canadian tariffs were in place before Confederation. They increased sharply in the 1870s and remained high until the 1930s. Since the establishment of the **General Agreement on Tariffs and Trade (GATT)**, in 1947, tariffs have steadily declined in a series of negotiating rounds, the most significant of which are identified in the figure. Tariffs have almost gone, but other trade barriers persist.

Sources of data: Adapted from the Statistics Canada publication "Historical Statistics of Canada." Catalogue 11-516. Released July 29, 1999, and from the Statistics Canada CANSIM database Tables 380-0002 and 380-0034.

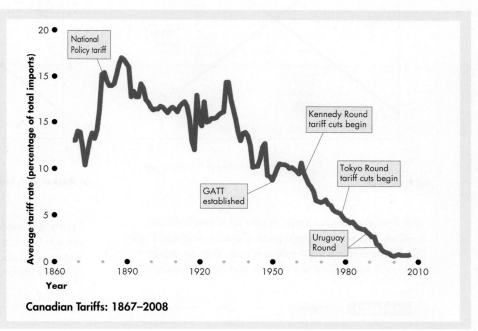

Canadian Tariffs: 1867–2008

Import Quotas

We now look at the second tool for restricting trade: import quotas. An **import quota** is a restriction that limits the maximum quantity of a good that may be imported in a given period.

Most countries impose import quotas on a wide range of items. Canada imposes them on food products such as meat, eggs and dairy and manufactured goods such as textiles and steel.

Import quotas enable the government to satisfy the self-interest of the people who earn their incomes in import-competing industries. But you will discover that like a tariff, an import quota decreases the gains from trade and is not in the social interest.

The Effects of an Import Quota   The effects of an import quota are similar to those of a tariff. The price rises, the quantity bought decreases, and the quantity produced in Canada increases. Figure 7.7 illustrates the effects.

Figure 7.7(a) shows the situation with free international trade. Figure 7.7(b) shows what happens with an import quota of 1 million T-shirts a year. The Canadian supply curve of T-shirts becomes the domestic supply curve S_{Can} plus the quantity that the import quota permits. So the supply curve becomes $S_{Can} + quota$. The price of a T-shirt rises to $7, the quantity of T-shirts bought in Canada decreases to 4.5 million a year, the quantity of T-shirts produced in Canada increases to 3.5 million a year, and the quantity of T-shirts imported into Canada decreases to the quota quantity of 1 million a year. All the effects of this quota are identical to the effects of a tariff of $2 per T-shirt, as you can check in Fig. 7.6(b).

Winners, Losers, and the Social Loss from an Import Quota   An import quota creates winners and losers that are similar to those of a tariff but with an interesting difference.

FIGURE 7.7   The Effects of an Import Quota

(a) Free trade

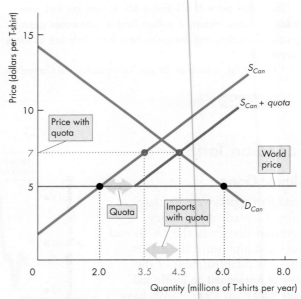

(b) Market with import quota

With free international trade, in part (a), Canadians buy 6 million T-shirts at the world price. Canada produces 2 million T-shirts and imports 4 million a year. With an import quota of 1 million T-shirts a year, in part (b), the supply of

T-shirts in Canada is shown by the curve $S_{Can} + quota$. The price in Canada rises to $7 a T-shirt. Canadian production increases, Canadian purchases decrease, and the quantity of T-shirts imported decreases.

When the government imposes an import quota,

- Canadian consumers of the good lose.
- Canadian producers of the good gain.
- Importers of the good gain.
- Society loses: a deadweight loss arises.

Figure 7.8 shows these gains and losses. By comparing Fig. 7.8(b) with a quota and Fig. 7.8(a) with free trade, you can see how an import quota of 1 million T-shirts a year changes the consumer and producer surpluses.

Consumer surplus—the green area—shrinks. This decrease is the loss to consumers from the import quota. The decrease in consumer surplus is made up of four parts. First, some of the consumer surplus is transferred to producers. The blue area B represents this loss of consumer surplus (and gain of producer surplus). Second, part of the consumer surplus is lost because the domestic cost of production is higher

than the world price. The grey area C represents this loss. Third, part of the consumer surplus is transferred to importers who buy T-shirts for $5 (the world price) and sell them for $7 (the Canadian domestic price). The two blue areas D represent this loss of consumer surplus and profit for importers. Fourth, part of the consumer surplus is lost because imports decrease. The grey area E represents this loss.

The losses of consumer surplus from the higher cost of production and the decrease in imports is a social loss—a deadweight loss. The grey areas labelled C and E represent this deadweight loss. Total surplus decreases by the area C + E.

You can now see the one difference between a quota and a tariff. A tariff brings in revenue for the government while a quota brings profit for the importers. All the other effects are the same, provided the quota is set at the same quantity of imports that results from the tariff.

FIGURE 7.8 The Winners and Losers from an Import Quota

(a) Free trade

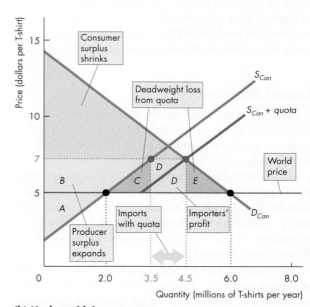

(b) Market with import quota

The world price of a T-shirt is $5. In part (a), with free trade, Canada produces 2 million T-shirts a year and imports 4 million. Consumer surplus, producer surplus, and the gain from free trade (the darker green area) are as large as possible.

In part (b), the import quota raises the price of a T-shirt to $7. The quantity imported decreases. Consumer surplus shrinks by the areas B, C, D, and E. Producer surplus expands by area B. Importers' profit is the two areas D, and the quota creates a deadweight loss equal to C + E.

Other Import Barriers

Two sets of policies that influence imports are

- Health, safety, and regulation barriers
- Voluntary export restraints

Health, Safety, and Regulation Barriers   Thousands of detailed health, safety, and other regulations restrict international trade. For example, Canadian food imports are examined by the Canadian Food Inspection Agency, which "is mandated to safeguard Canada's food supply and the plants and animals upon which safe and high-quality food depends." The discovery of BSE (mad cow disease) in just one cow on May 20, 2003, led to an immediate worldwide ban on Canadian beef exports. The European Union bans imports of most genetically modified foods, such as Canadian canola. Although regulations of this type are not designed to limit international trade, they have that effect.

Voluntary Export Restraints   A *voluntary export restraint* is like a quota allocated to a foreign exporter of a good. This type of trade barrier isn't common. It was initially used during the 1980s when Japan voluntarily limited its exports of car parts to North America.

Export Subsidies

A *subsidy* is a payment by the government to a producer. You studied the effects of a subsidy on the quantity produced and the price of a subsidized farm product in Chapter 6, pp. 142–143.

An *export subsidy* is a payment by the government to the producer of an exported good. Export subsidies are illegal under a number of international agreements, including the North American Free Trade Agreement (NAFTA), and the rules of the World Trade Organization (WTO).

Although export subsidies are illegal, the subsidies that the Canadian, U.S., and European Union governments pay to farmers end up increasing domestic production, some of which gets exported. These exports of subsidized farm products make it harder for producers in other countries, notably in Africa and Central and South America, to compete in global markets. Export subsidies bring gains to domestic producers, but they result in inefficient underproduction in the rest of the world and create a deadweight loss.

Failure in Doha
Self-Interest Beats the Social Interest

The **World Trade Organization (WTO)** is an international body established by the world's major trading nations for the purpose of supervising international trade and lowering the barriers to trade.

In 2001, at a meeting of trade ministers from all the WTO member-countries held in Doha, Qatar, an agreement was made to begin negotiations to lower tariff barriers and quotas that restrict international trade in farm products and services. These negotiations are called the **Doha Development Agenda** or the **Doha Round**.

In the period since 2001, thousands of hours of conferences in Cancún in 2003, Geneva in 2004, and Hong Kong in 2005, and ongoing meetings at WTO headquarters in Geneva, costing millions of taxpayers' dollars, have made disappointing progress.

Rich nations, led by the United States, the European Union, and Japan, want greater access to the markets of developing nations in exchange for allowing those nations greater access to the rich world's markets, especially for farm products.

Developing nations, led by Brazil, China, India, and South Africa, want access to the farm product markets of the rich world, but they also want to protect their infant industries.

With two incompatible positions, these negotiations are stalled and show no signs of a breakthrough. The self-interest of rich and developing nations is preventing the achievement of the social interest.

Review Quiz

1 What tools can a country use to restrict international trade?
2 Explain the effects of a tariff on domestic production, the quantity bought, and the price.
3 Explain who gains and who loses from a tariff and why the losses exceed the gains.
4 Explain the effects of an import quota on domestic production, consumption, and price.
5 Explain who gains and who loses from an import quota and why the losses exceed the gains.

 Work Study Plan 7.3 and get instant feedback.

The Case Against Protection

For as long as nations and international trade have existed, people have debated whether a country is better off with free international trade or with protection from foreign competition. The debate continues, but for most economists, a verdict has been delivered and is the one you have just seen. Free trade promotes prosperity for all countries; protection is inefficient. We've studied the most powerful case for free trade—it brings gains for consumers that exceed any losses incurred by producers, so there is a net gain for society.

But there is a broader range of issues in the free trade versus protection debate. Let's review these issues.

Two classical arguments for restricting international trade are

- The infant-industry argument
- The dumping argument

The Infant-Industry Argument

The **infant-industry argument** for protection is that it is necessary to protect a new industry to enable it to grow into a mature industry that can compete in world markets. The argument is based on the idea of *dynamic comparative advantage*, which can arise from *learning-by-doing* (see Chapter 2, p. 43).

Learning-by-doing, a powerful engine of productivity growth, and on-the-job experience can change comparative advantage. But these facts do not justify protection.

First, the infant-industry argument is valid only if the benefits of learning-by-doing *not only* accrue to the owners and workers of the firms in the infant industry but also *spill over* to other industries and parts of the economy. For example, there are huge productivity gains from learning-by-doing in the manufacture of aircraft.

But almost all of these gains benefit the stockholders and workers of Bombardier and other aircraft producers. Because the people making the decisions, bearing the risk, and doing the work are the ones who benefit, they take the dynamic gains into account when they decide on the scale of their activities. In this case, almost no benefits spill over to other parts of the economy, so there is no need for government assistance to achieve an efficient outcome.

Second, even if the case is made for protecting an infant industry, it is more efficient to do so by giving the firms in the industry a subsidy, which is financed out of taxes. Such a subsidy would encourage the industry to mature and to compete with efficient world producers and keep the price faced by consumers at the world price.

The Dumping Argument

Dumping occurs when a foreign firm sells its exports at a lower price than its cost of production. Dumping might be used by a firm that wants to gain a global monopoly. In this case, the foreign firm sells its output at a price below its cost to drive domestic firms out of business. When the domestic firms have gone, the foreign firm takes advantage of its monopoly position and charges a higher price for its product. Dumping is illegal under the rules of the WTO and is usually regarded as a justification for temporary tariffs, which are called *antidumping duties*.

But there are powerful reasons to resist the dumping argument for protection. First, it is virtually impossible to detect dumping because it is hard to determine a firm's costs. As a result, the test for dumping is whether a firm's export price is below its domestic price. But this test is a weak one because it can be rational for a firm to charge a low price in a market in which the quantity demanded is highly sensitive to price and a higher price in a market in which demand is less price-sensitive.

Second, it is hard to think of a good that is produced by a *global* monopoly. So even if all the domestic firms in some industry were driven out of business, it would always be possible to find alternative foreign sources of supply and to buy the good at a price determined in a competitive market.

Third, if a good or service were a truly global monopoly, the best way of dealing with it would be by regulation—just as in the case of domestic monopolies (see Chapter 13, pp. 313–315). Such regulation would require international cooperation.

The two arguments for protection that we've just examined have an element of credibility. The counterarguments are in general stronger, however, so these arguments do not make the case for protection. But they are not the only arguments that you might encounter. There are many other new arguments against globalization and for protection. The most common ones are that protection

- Saves jobs
- Allows us to compete with cheap foreign labour
- Penalizes lax environmental standards
- Prevents rich countries from exploiting developing countries

Saves Jobs

First, free trade does cost some jobs, but it also creates other jobs. It brings about a global rationalization of labour and allocates labour resources to their highest-valued activities. International trade in textiles has cost thousands of jobs in Canada as textile mills and other factories have closed. But thousands of jobs have been created in other countries as textile mills have opened. And thousands of Canadian workers got better-paying jobs than as textile workers because Canadian export industries expanded and created new jobs. More jobs have been created than destroyed.

Although protection saves particular jobs, it does so at a high cost. A striking example of the cost of quotas is that of the quotas on the import of textiles. Quotas imposed under the international agreement called the Multifiber Arrangement (which ended in 2005) protected textile jobs, especially in the United States. The U.S. International Trade Commission (ITC) has estimated that because of import quotas, 72,000 jobs existed in the textile industry that would otherwise have disappeared and that the annual clothing expenditure in the United States was $15.9 billion ($160 per family) higher than it would have been with free trade. Equivalently, the ITC estimated that each textile job saved cost $221,000 a year.

Imports don't only destroy jobs. They create jobs for retailers that sell imported goods and for firms that service those goods. Imports also create jobs by creating incomes in the rest of the world, some of which are spent on domestic-made goods and services.

Allows Us to Compete with Cheap Foreign Labour

With the removal of tariffs on trade between Canada, the United States, and Mexico, people said we would hear a "giant sucking sound" as jobs rushed to Mexico. Let's see what's wrong with this view.

The labour cost of a unit of output equals the wage rate divided by labour productivity. For example, if a Canadian autoworker earns $30 an hour and produces 15 units of output an hour, the average labour cost of a unit of output is $2. If a Mexican auto assembly worker earns $3 an hour and produces 1 unit of output an hour, the average labour cost of a unit of output is $3. Other things remaining the same, the higher a worker's productivity, the higher is the worker's wage rate. High-wage workers have high productivity; low-wage workers have low productivity.

Although high-wage Canadian workers are more productive, on average, than low-wage Mexican workers, there are differences across industries. Canadian labour is relatively more productive in some activities than in others. For example, the productivity of Canadian workers in producing financial services and telephone systems is relatively higher than their productivity in the production of metals and some standardized machine parts. The activities in which Canadian workers are relatively more productive than their Mexican counterparts are those in which Canada has a *comparative advantage*.

By engaging in free trade, increasing our production and exports of the goods and services in which we have a comparative advantage and decreasing our production and increasing our imports of the goods and services in which our trading partners have a comparative advantage, we can make ourselves and the citizens of other countries better off.

Penalizes Lax Environmental Standards

Another argument for protection is that many poorer countries, such as China and Mexico, do not have the same environmental policies that we have and, because they are willing to pollute and we are not, we cannot compete with them without tariffs. So if poorer countries want free trade with the richer and "greener" countries, they must raise their environmental standards.

This argument for trade restrictions is weak. First, a poor country cannot afford to be as concerned about its environmental standard as a rich country can. Today, some of the worst pollution of air and water is found in China, Mexico, and the former communist countries of Eastern Europe. But only a few decades ago, London and Los Angeles led the pollution league table. The best hope for cleaner air in Beijing and Mexico City is rapid income growth. Free trade contributes to that growth. As incomes in developing countries grow, they will have the *means* to match their desires to improve their environmental standard. Second, a poor country might have a comparative advantage at doing "dirty" work, which helps it to raise its income and at the same time enables the global economy to achieve a higher environmental standard than would otherwise be possible.

Prevents Rich Countries from Exploiting Developing Countries

Another argument for protection is that international trade must be restricted to prevent the people of the rich industrial world from exploiting the poorer people of the developing countries and forcing them to work for slave wages.

Child labour and near-slave labour are serious problems that are rightly condemned. But by trading with poor countries, we increase the demand for the goods that these countries produce and, more significantly, we increase the demand for their labour. When the demand for labour in developing countries increases, the wage rate also increases. So, rather than exploiting people in developing countries, trade can expand their opportunities and increase their incomes.

The arguments for protection that we've reviewed leave free-trade unscathed. But a new phenomenon is at work in our economy: *offshore outsourcing*. Surely we need protection from this new source of foreign competition. Let's investigate.

Offshore Outsourcing

Roots, Canadian Tire, and BlackBerry: What do these Canadian icons have in common? They all send jobs that could be done in Canada to China, India, Thailand, or even the United States—they are offshoring. What exactly is offshoring?

What Is Offshoring?   A firm in Canada can obtain the things that it sells in any of four ways:

1. Hire Canadian labour and produce in Canada.
2. Hire foreign labour and produce in other countries.
3. Buy finished goods, components, or services from other firms in Canada.
4. Buy finished goods, components, or services from other firms in other countries.

Activities 3 and 4 are **outsourcing**, and activities 2 and 4 are **offshoring**. Activity 4 is **offshore outsourcing**.

Notice that offshoring includes activities that take place inside Canadian firms. If a Canadian firm opens its own facilities in another country, then it is offshoring.

Offshoring has been going on for hundreds of years, but it expanded rapidly and became a source of concern during the 1990s as many Canadian firms moved information technology services and general office services such as finance, accounting, and human resources management overseas.

Why Did Offshoring of Services Boom During the 1990s?   The gains from specialization and trade that you saw in the previous section must be large enough to make it worth incurring the costs of communication and transportation. If the cost of producing a T-shirt in China isn't lower than the cost of producing the T-shirt in Canada by more than the cost of transporting the shirt from China to Canada, then it is more efficient to produce T-shirts in Canada and avoid the transport costs.

The same considerations apply to trade in services. If services are to be produced offshore, then the cost of delivering those services must be low enough to leave the buyer with an overall lower cost. Before the 1990s, the cost of communicating across large distances was too high to make the offshoring of business services efficient. But during the 1990s, when satellites, fibre-optic cables, and computers cut the cost of a phone call between Canada and India to less than a dollar an hour, a huge base of offshore resources became competitive with similar resources in Canada.

What Are the Benefits of Offshoring?   Offshoring brings gains from trade identical to those of any other type of trade. We could easily change the names of the items traded from T-shirts and regional jets (the examples in the previous sections of this chapter) to banking services and call centre services (or any other pair of services). A Canadian bank might export banking services to Indian firms, and Indians might provide call centre services to Canadian firms. This type of trade would benefit both Canadians and Indians provided that Canada has a comparative advantage in banking services and India has a comparative advantage in call centre services.

Comparative advantages like these emerged during the 1990s. India has the world's largest educated English-speaking population and is located in a time zone half a day ahead of North America's east coast and midway between Asia and Europe, which facilitates 24/7 operations. When the cost of communicating with a worker in India was several dollars a minute, as it was before the 1990s, tapping these vast resources was just too costly. But at today's cost of a long-distance telephone call or Internet connection, resources in India can be used to produce services in Canada at a lower cost than those services can be produced by using resources located in Canada. Some of the goods and services that Indians buy with the incomes they earn from exporting services, are produced in Canada.

Why Is Offshoring a Concern? Despite the gain from specialization and trade that offshoring brings, many people believe that it also brings costs that eat up the gains. Why?

A major reason is that offshoring is taking jobs in services. The loss of manufacturing jobs to other countries has been going on for decades, but the service sector in Canada has always expanded by enough to create new jobs to replace the lost manufacturing jobs. Now that service jobs are also going overseas, the fear is that there will not be enough jobs for Canadians. This fear is misplaced.

Some service jobs are going overseas, while others are expanding at home. Canada imports call centre services, but it exports education, health care, legal, financial, and a host of other types of services. Jobs in these sectors are expanding and will continue to expand.

The exact number of jobs that have moved to lower-cost offshore locations is not known, and estimates vary. But even the highest estimate is a tiny number compared to the normal rate of job creation.

Winners and Losers Gains from trade do not bring gains for every single person. Canadians, on average, gain from offshore outsourcing. But some people lose. The losers are those who have invested in the human capital to do a specific job that has now gone offshore.

Unemployment benefits provide short-term temporary relief for these displaced workers. But the long-term solution requires retraining and the acquisition of new skills.

Beyond providing short-term relief through unemployment benefits, there is a large role for government in the provision of education and training to enable the labour force of the twenty-first century to be capable of ongoing learning and rapid retooling to take on new jobs that today we can't foresee.

Schools, colleges, and universities will expand and get better at doing their jobs of producing a highly educated and flexible labour force.

Avoiding Trade Wars

We have reviewed the arguments commonly heard in favour of protection and the counterarguments against them. There is one counterargument to protection that is general and quite overwhelming: Protection invites retaliation and can trigger a trade war.

The best example of a trade war occurred during the Great Depression of the 1930s, when the United States introduced the Smoot-Hawley tariff. Country after country retaliated with its own tariff, and in a short period, world trade had almost disappeared. The costs to all countries were large and led to a renewed international resolve to avoid such self-defeating moves in the future. The costs also led to the creation of GATT and are the impetus behind current attempts to liberalize trade.

Why Is International Trade Restricted?

Why, despite all the arguments against protection, is trade restricted? There are two key reasons:

- Tariff revenue
- Rent seeking

Tariff Revenue Government revenue is costly to collect. In the developed countries such as Canada, a well-organized tax collection system is in place that can generate billions of dollars of income tax and sales tax revenues. This tax collection system is made possible by the fact that most economic transactions are done by firms that must keep properly audited financial records. Without such records, the revenue collection agencies (such as the Canada Revenue Agency) would be severely hampered in their work. Even with audited financial accounts, some potential tax revenue is lost. Nonetheless, for industrialized countries, income taxes and sales taxes are the major sources of revenue and tariffs play a very small role.

But governments in developing countries have a difficult time collecting taxes from their citizens. Much economic activity takes place in an informal economy with few financial records, so only a small amount of revenue is collected from income taxes and sales taxes. The one area in which economic transactions are well recorded and audited is international trade. So this activity is an attractive base for tax collection in these countries and is used much more extensively than it is in developed countries.

Rent Seeking   Rent seeking is the major reason why international trade is restricted. **Rent seeking** is lobbying for special treatment by the government to create economic profit or to divert consumer surplus or producer surplus away from others. Free trade increases consumption possibilities *on average*, but not everyone shares in the gain and some people even lose. Free trade brings benefits to some and imposes costs on others, with total benefits exceeding total costs. The uneven distribution of costs and benefits is the principal obstacle to achieving more liberal international trade.

Returning to the example of trade in T-shirts and regional jets, the benefits from free trade accrue to all the people involved in the production of regional jets and to those producers of T-shirts that do not bear the costs of adjusting to a smaller garment industry. These costs are transition costs, not permanent costs. The costs of moving to free trade are borne by the garment producers and their employees who must become producers of other goods and services in which Canada has a comparative advantage.

The number of winners from free trade is large. But because the gains are spread thinly over a large number of people, the gain per person is small. The winners could organize and become a political force lobbying for free trade. But political activity is costly. It uses time and other scarce resources and the gains per person are too small to make the cost of political activity worth bearing.

In contrast, the number of losers from free trade is small, but the loss per person is large. Because the loss per person is large, the people who lose *are* willing to incur considerable expense to lobby against free trade.

Both the winners and losers weigh their benefits and costs and pursue their self-interest. Those who gain from free trade weigh the benefits it brings against the cost of achieving it. Those who lose from free trade and gain from protection weigh the benefit of protection against the cost of maintaining it. Because the protectionists have more at stake, they undertake a larger quantity of political lobbying than do the free traders.

Compensating Losers

If, in total, the gains from free international trade exceed the losses, why don't those who gain compensate those who lose so that everyone is in favour of free trade?

The main answer is that there are serious obstacles to providing direct and correctly calculated compensation. First, the cost of identifying all the losers from free trade and estimating the value of their losses would be enormous. Second, it would never be clear whether a person who has fallen on hard times is suffering because of free trade or for other reasons that might be largely under her or his control. Third, some people who look like losers at one point in time might, in fact, end up gaining. The young autoworker who loses her job in Windsor and becomes a worker in Alberta's oil patch resents the loss of work and the need to move. But a year later, looking back on events, she counts herself fortunate. She has made a move that has increased her income and given her greater job security.

Because we do not, in general, compensate the losers from free international trade, protectionism is a popular and permanent feature of our national economic and political life.

Review Quiz

1 What are the infant industry and dumping arguments for protection? Are they correct?
2 Can protection save jobs and the environment and prevent workers in developing countries from being exploited?
3 What is offshore outsourcing? Who benefits from it and who loses?
4 What are the main reasons for imposing a tariff?
5 Why don't the winners from free trade win the political argument?

    Work Study Plan 7.4 and get instant feedback.

We end this chapter on global markets in action with *Reading Between the Lines* on pp. 170–171. It applies what you've learned by looking at the U.S. countervailing tariffs on Canadian softwood lumber.

The United States Protects its Lumber Producers

Softwood Lumber Dispute

August 23, 2006

Disputes on softwood lumber have simmered for more than 20 years, but the most recent conflict boiled over in May 2002, when the United States imposed duties of 27 percent on Canadian softwood lumber, arguing that Canada unfairly subsidized producers of spruce, pine, and fir lumber. ...

The dispute centred on stumpage fees—set amounts charged to companies that harvest timber on public land. Many in the United States see Canadian stumpage fees as being too low, making them de facto subsidies. A U.S. coalition of lumber producers wants the provincial governments to follow the American system and auction off timber rights at market prices.

The bickering between Canada and the United States over softwood lumber is like a case of sibling rivalry. It dates back several decades. Even within Canada there were divisions. The B.C. Lumber Trade Council argued a trade war with the Americans ... would be costly and should be avoided by accommodating U.S. demands. The Free Trade Lumber Council, which includes lumber producers in Quebec and Ontario, wanted to fight it out. What most Canadian foresters and governments do agree on is their goal: free trade in softwood lumber.

Then, on April 26, 2006, came word that Canada and the United Sates had reached a framework agreement that could form the basis for an end to the dispute. The framework agreement called for the United States to return about 80 per cent of the $5 billion in duties that U.S. Customs has collected in the previous four years. Canadian-sourced lumber would also be kept to no more than its current 34 per cent share of the U.S. softwood market. ... Canada will also collect an export tax on softwood lumber exported to the United States if the price drops below $355 a thousand board feet.

Essence of the Story

- The dispute over trade in softwood lumber has simmered for more than 20 years. U.S. lumber producers argued that Canada was unfairly subsidizng producers because stumpage fees are not determined by auction.

- In May 2002, the United States imposed a 27 percent tariff and collected $5 billion in tariff revenue.

- The deal returns 80 percent of the U.S. tariff revenue collected to Canada and maintains Canada's share at 34 percent of the U.S. market.

- If the price drops below $355 a thousand board feet an export tax kicks in.

Economic Analysis

- Before the 2006 agreement, U.S. imports of Canadian lumber had a 27 percent tariff. The tariff damaged the social interest in Canada and the United States.

- Figure 1 shows the U.S. market for lumber. The demand curve D shows the U.S. demand for lumber.

- There are two supply curves: the supply curve of the Canadian producers, S_C, and the supply curve of U.S. producers, S_{US}. We're assuming that Canada can supply any quantity at a price of $100 a load.

- With a 27 percent tariff on the imports, Canadian lumber is supplied to the U.S. market at $100 plus the tariff, $27, so the supply curve of Canadian lumber becomes S_C + tariff.

- At $127 a load, the quantity of lumber bought in the United States is QC_1. Of this amount, QP_1 is produced in the United States and $QC_1 - QP_1$ is imported from Canada.

- The gain to U.S. producers is area A. The tariff revenue collected by the U.S. government is area C. The deadweight loss created by the tariff is area $B + E$.

- The 2006 trade deal removed the tariff but imposed a quota on Canada's imports at its 2006 level—34 percent of the U.S. market.

- Figure 2 shows the U.S. market after the deal. The supply of lumber in the U.S. market is now the U.S. supply plus the quota on Canadian lumber. The supply curve becomes S_{US} + quota.

- The U.S. price remains at $127 a load, the quantity of lumber bought in the United States remains QC_1, the quantity produced in the United States remains QP_1, and imports from Canada remain $QC_1 - QP_1$.

- The only difference that the quota makes is that the tariff revenue becomes a gain to the U.S. importer who buys for $100 a load in Canada and sells for $127 a load in the United States.

- The differences between the tariff and the quota become more interesting and important when the U.S. demand for lumber increases.

- With a quota, an increase in U.S. demand raises the U.S. price and increases both U.S. producer surplus and the deadweight loss. Imports remain constant.

- With a tariff, an increase in U.S. demand leaves the U.S. price, U.S. producer surplus, and the deadweight loss unchanged and imports increase.

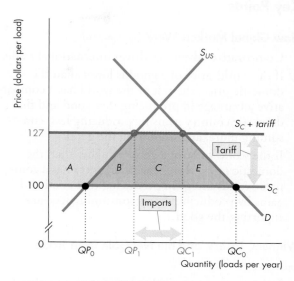

Figure 1 U.S. market with tariff

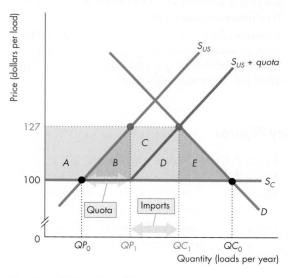

Figure 2 U.S. market with quota

SUMMARY

Key Points

How Global Markets Work (pp. 154–156)

- Comparative advantage drives international trade.
- If the world price of a good is lower than the domestic price, the rest of the world has a comparative advantage in producing that good and the domestic country gains by producing less, consuming more, and importing the good.
- If the world price of a good is higher than the domestic price, the domestic country has a comparative advantage in producing that good and gains by producing more, consuming less, and exporting the good.

Winners, Losers, and the Net Gain from Trade (pp. 157–158)

- Compared to a no-trade situation, in a market with imports, consumer surplus is larger, producer surplus is smaller, and total surplus is larger with free international trade.
- Compared to a no-trade situation, in a market with exports, consumer surplus is smaller, producer surplus is larger, and total surplus is larger with free international trade.

International Trade Restrictions (pp. 159–164)

- Countries restrict international trade by imposing tariffs, import quotas, and other import barriers.
- Trade restrictions raise the domestic price of imported goods, lower the quantity imported, decrease consumer surplus, increase producer surplus, and create a deadweight loss.

The Case Against Protection (pp. 165–169)

- Arguments that protection is necessary for infant industries and to prevent dumping are weak.
- Arguments that protection saves jobs, allows us to compete with cheap foreign labour, is needed to penalize lax environmental standards, and prevents exploitation of developing countries are flawed.
- Offshore outsourcing is just a new way of reaping gains from trade and does not justify protection.
- Trade restrictions are popular because protection brings a small loss per person to a large number of people and a large gain per person to a small number of people. Those who gain have a stronger political voice than those who lose and it is too costly to identify and compensate losers.

Key Figures

Figure 7.1   A Market with Imports, 155
Figure 7.2   A Market with Exports, 156
Figure 7.3   Gains and Losses in a Market with Imports, 157
Figure 7.4   Gains and Losses in a Market with Exports, 158
Figure 7.5   The Effects of a Tariff, 159
Figure 7.6   The Winners and Losers from a Tariff, 161
Figure 7.7   The Effects of an Import Quota, 162
Figure 7.8   The Winners and Losers from an Import Quota, 163

Key Terms

Doha Development Agenda (Doha Round), 164
Dumping, 165
Exports, 154
General Agreement on Tariffs and Trade (GATT), 161
Import quota, 162
Imports, 154
Infant-industry argument, 165
Offshore outsourcing, 167
Offshoring, 167
Outsourcing, 167
Rent seeking, 169
Tariff, 159
World Trade Organization (WTO), 164

PROBLEMS and APPLICATIONS

 Work problems 1–10 in Chapter 7 Study Plan and get instant feedback.
Work problems 11–21 as Homework, a Quiz, or a Test if assigned by your instructor.

1. Canada produces both lumber and wine. Canada exports lumber and imports wine. The rest of the world imports Canadian lumber and exports wine to Canada.

   a. If Canada did not trade with the rest of the world, compare the equilibrium prices of lumber and wine in Canada with the world prices of lumber and wine.
   b. Does Canada or the rest of the world have a comparative advantage in producing lumber? Does Canada or the rest of the world have a comparative advantage in producing wine?
   c. Compare the quantities of wine that Canadian wineries produce and that Canadians buy with and without trade with the rest of the world.
   d. Compare the quantities of lumber that the rest of the world produces and that it buys with and without trade with Canada.
   e. What are the gains from the trade in lumber and wine between Canada and the rest of the world?

2. Wholesalers of roses (the firms that supply local flower shops with roses for Valentine's Day) buy and sell roses in containers that hold 120 stems. The table provides information about the wholesale market for roses. The demand schedule is the wholesalers' demand and the supply schedule is the North American rose growers' supply.

Price (dollars per container)	Quantity demanded	Quantity supplied
	(millions of containers per year)	
100	15	0
125	12	2
150	9	4
175	6	6
200	3	8
225	0	10

North American wholesalers can buy roses at auction in Aalsmeer, Holland, for $125 per container.

   a. Without international trade, what would be the price of a container of roses and how many containers of roses a year would be bought and sold in North America?
   b. At the price in your answer to a, does North America or the rest of the world have a comparative advantage in producing roses?
   c. If North American wholesalers buy roses at the lowest possible price, how many do they buy from local growers and how many do they import?
   d. Draw a graph to illustrate the North American wholesale market for roses. Show the equilibrium in that market with no international trade and the equilibrium with free trade. Mark the quantity of roses produced locally, the quantity imported, and the total quantity bought by North Americans.

3. **Underwater Oil Discovery to Transform Brazil into a Major Exporter**
   A huge underwater oil field discovered late last year has the potential to transform South America's largest country into a sizable exporter.
   ... Just a decade ago the notion that Brazil would become self-sufficient in energy, let alone emerge as an exporter, seemed far-fetched. ... Petrobras was formed five decades ago largely as a trading company to import oil to support Brazil's growing economy. ... Yet two years ago ... Brazil reached its long-sought goal of energy self-sufficiency. ...
   International Herald Tribune, January 11, 2008

   a. Describe Brazil's comparative advantage in producing oil and explain why its comparative advantage has changed.
   b. Draw a graph to illustrate the Brazilian market for oil until a few years ago and explain why it was an importer of oil.
   c. Draw a graph to illustrate the Brazilian market for oil in the near future and explain why Brazil might become an exporter of oil.

4. Use the information on the North American wholesale market for roses in problem 2 to

   a. Explain who gains and who loses from free international trade in roses compared to a situation in which North Americans buy only roses grown locally.
   b. Draw a graph to illustrate the gains and losses from free trade.
   c. Calculate the gain from international trade.

5. **Postcard: Bangalore. Hearts Set on Joining the Global Economy, Indian IT Workers are Brushing up on their Interpersonal Skills**

The huge number of Indian workers staffing the world's tech firms and call centres ... possess cutting-edge technical knowledge, [but] their interpersonal and communication skills lag far behind. ... Enter Bangalore's finishing schools.

Time, May 5, 2008

a. What comparative advantages does this news clip identify?

b. Using the information in this news clip, what services do you predict Bangalore (India) exports and imports?

c. Who will gain and who will lose from the international trade that you described in your answer to b?

6. Use the information on the North American wholesale market for roses in problem 2.

a. If a tariff of $25 per container is imposed on imports of roses, what happens to the North American price of roses, the quantity of roses bought, the quantity produced in North America, and the quantity imported by North American wholesalers?

b. Who gains and who loses from this tariff?

c. Draw a graph to illustrate the gains and losses from the tariff and show the gains and losses, the tariff revenue, and the deadweight loss.

7. Use the information on the North American wholesale market for roses in problem 2.

a. If an import quota of 5 million containers is imposed on roses, what happens to the North American price of roses, the quantity of roses bought, the quantity produced in North America, and the quantity imported by North Americans?

b. Who gains and who loses from this quota?

c. Draw a graph to illustrate the gains and losses from the import quota, the importers' profit, and the deadweight loss created by the import quota.

8. **Car Sales Go Up as Prices Tumble**

Car affordability [in Australia] is now at its best in 20 years, fueling a surge in sales as prices tumble. ... [In 2000, Australia cut the tariff to 15 percent and] on January 1, 2005, the tariff on imported vehicles fell from 15 percent to 10 percent.

Courier Mail, February 26, 2005

a. Explain who gains and who loses from the lower tariff on imported cars.

b. Draw a graph to show how the price of a car, the quantity bought, the quantity produced in Australia, and imports of cars changed.

9. **Chinese Tire Maker Rejects U.S. Charge of Defects**

... regulators in the United States ordered the recall of more than 450,000 faulty tires. ... The Chinese company that produced the tires ... disputed the allegations Tuesday and hinted that the recall might be an effort by foreign competitors to hamper the company's exports to the United States. ... Mounting scrutiny of Chinese-made goods has become a source of new trade frictions between the United States and China and fueled worries among regulators, corporations and consumers about the risks associated with many products imported from China. ...

International Herald Tribune, June 26, 2007

a. What does the information in the news clip imply about the comparative advantage of producing tires in the United States and China?

b. Could product quality be a valid argument against free trade?

c. How would the product-quality argument against free trade be open to abuse by domestic producers of the imported good?

10. **Why the World Can't Afford Food**

As [food] stocks dwindled, some countries placed export restrictions on food to protect their own supplies. This in turn drove up prices, punishing countries—especially poor ones—that depend on imports for much of their food.

Time, May 19, 2008

a. What are the benefits to a country from importing food?

b. What costs might arise from relying on imported food?

c. If a country restricts food exports, what effect does this restriction have in that country on the price of food and the quantities of food produced, consumed, and exported?

d. Draw a graph of the market for food in a country that exports food. Show how the price of food, the quantities of food consumed, produced, and exported change when food exports are restricted.

11. Suppose that the world price of eggs is $1 a dozen, Canada does not trade internationally, and the equilibrium price of eggs in Canada is $3 a dozen. Canada then begins to trade internationally.
   a. How does the price of eggs in Canada change?
   b. Do Canadians buy more or fewer eggs?
   c. Do Canadian egg farmers produce more or fewer eggs?
   d. Does Canada export or import eggs and why?
   e. Would employment in the Canadian egg industry change? If so, how?

12. Suppose that the world price of steel is $100 a tonne, India does not trade internationally, and the equilibrium price of steel in India is $60 a tonne. India then begins to trade internationally.
   a. How does the price of steel in India change?
   b. How does the quantity of steel produced in India change?
   c. How does the quantity of steel bought by India change?
   d. Does India export or import steel and why?

13. A semiconductor is a key component in laptops, cell phones, and iPods. The table provides information about the market for semiconductors in Canada.

Price (dollars per unit)	Quantity demanded	Quantity supplied
	(millions of units per year)	
10	25	0
12	20	20
14	15	40
16	10	60
18	5	80
20	0	100

Producers of semiconductors can get $18 a unit on the world market.
   a. With no international trade, what would be the price of a semiconductor and how many semiconductors a year would be bought and sold in Canada?
   b. At the price in your answer to a, does Canada have a comparative advantage in producing semiconductors?
   c. If Canadian producers of semiconductors sell at the highest possible price, how many do they sell in Canada and how many do they export?

14. **South Korea to Resume U.S. Beef Imports**
South Korea will open its market to most U.S. beef. ... South Korea banned imports of U.S. beef in 2003 amid concerns over a case of mad cow disease in the United States. The ban closed what was then the third-largest market for U.S. beef exporters. ...

CNN, May 29, 2008

   a. Which country, South Korea or the United States, has a comparative advantage in producing beef? What fact in the news clip did you use to answer this question?
   b. Explain how South Korea's import ban on U.S. beef affected beef producers and consumers in South Korea.
   c. Draw a graph of the market for beef in South Korea to illustrate your answer to b. Identify the changes in consumer surplus, producer surplus, and deadweight loss.
   d. Assuming that South Korea is the only importer of U.S. beef, explain how South Korea's import ban on U.S. beef affected beef producers and consumers in the United States.
   e. Draw a graph of the market for beef in the United States to illustrate your answer to d. Identify the changes in consumer surplus, producer surplus, and deadweight loss.

15. **Act Now, Eat Later**
... looming hunger crisis in poor countries ... has its roots in ... misguided policy in the U.S. and Europe of subsidizing the diversion of food crops to produce biofuels like corn-based ethanol ... [That is,] doling out subsidies to put the world's dinner into the gas tank.

Time, May 5, 2008

   a. What is the effect on the world price of corn of the increased use of corn to produce ethanol in the United States and Europe?
   b. How does the change in the world price of corn affect the quantity of corn produced in a poor developing country with a comparative advantage in producing corn, the quantity it consumes, and the quantity that it either exports or imports?
   c. Draw a graph of the market for corn in a poor developing country to illustrate your answer to b. Identify the changes in consumer surplus, producer surplus, and deadweight loss.

16. Before 1995, trade between Canada and Mexico was subject to tariffs. In 1995, Mexico joined NAFTA, and all Canadian and Mexican tariffs are gradually being removed.

a. Explain how the price that Canadian consumers pay for goods from Mexico and the quantity of Canadian imports from Mexico have changed. Who are the winners from free trade? Who are the losers?

b. Explain how the quantity of Canadian exports to Mexico and the Canadian government's tariff revenue from trade with Mexico have changed.

c. Suppose that in 2008, tomato growers in Ontario lobby the Canadian government to impose an import quota on Mexican tomatoes. Explain who in Canada would gain and who would lose from such a quota.

17. Suppose that in response to huge job losses in the Canadian textile industry, the government of Canada imposes a 100 percent tariff on imports of textiles from China.

   a. Explain how the tariff on textiles will change the price that Canadians pay for textiles, the quantity of textiles imported, and the quantity of textiles produced in Canada.

   b. Explain how the Canadian and Chinese gains from trade will change. Who in Canada will lose and who will gain?

18. With free trade between Australia and Canada, Australia would export beef, but Canada imposes an import quota on Australian beef.

   a. Explain how this quota influences the price that Canadians pay for beef, the quantity of beef produced in Canada, and the Canadian and the Australian gains from trade.

   b. Explain who in Canada gains from the quota on beef imports and who loses.

19. **WTO: Farming Exporters Tell Rich Nations to Open Agriculture Markets**

Developing countries and food exporters from rich and poor nations on Sunday demanded that the United States and European Union open their farm markets and eliminate trade-distorting subsidies. ... "Those members responsible for the most significant distortions in global agricultural trade—the EU, U.S. and Japan—bear a heavy responsibility," the Cairns Group of agricultural exporters, which includes Canada, New Zealand, Argentina, South Africa and Thailand, said in a statement. "We can and must now seize this opportunity to secure the main parameters of the

Doha round. The costs of failure are too high."... Zoellick, as former U.S. trade representative, ... said an open and fair trading system would give farmers in developing countries a reason to expand production. Consumers would benefit from lower prices and governments could save on the costs of subsidies and improve their budgets.

Reuters, July 20, 2008

   a. Explain why farmers in developing countries would expand production if EU, U.S., and Japanese subsidies were eliminated.

   b. Explain why EU, U.S., and Japanese consumers would benefit from lower prices that the removal of subsidies would bring.

   c. What are the costs of failure of the Doha Round? Who loses and who gains?

20. Study *Reading Between the Lines* on pp. 170–171 and answer the following questions.

   a. Why, until 2006, did the United States impose a tariff on softwood lumber imports from Canada?

   b. What were the effects of the U.S. tariff on Canadian softwood lumber on Canadian and U.S. production and on Canadian exports?

   c. Who were the winners and who were the losers from the U.S. tariff on Canadian softwood lumber?

   d. When the tariff was replaced by an import quota, how did production and Canadian exports change and who were the winners and losers from the quota?

21. **Vows of New Aid to the Poor Leave the Poor Unimpressed**

... the United States, the European Union, and Japan [plan] to eliminate duties and [import] quotas on almost all goods from up to 50 of the world's poor nations, ... The proposal for duty-free, quota-free treatment is so divisive among developing countries that even some negotiators ... are saying that the plan must be broadened.

New York Times, December 15, 2005

   a. Why do these countries want to eliminate trade barriers for only the poorest countries?

   b. Who will win from the elimination of these trade barriers? Who will lose?

   c. Why is the plan divisive among developing countries?

PART 2

UNDERSTANDING HOW MARKETS WORK

The Amazing Market

The five chapters that you've just studied explain how markets work. The market is an amazing instrument. It enables people who have never met and who know nothing about each other to interact and do business. It also enables us to allocate our scarce resources to the uses that we value most highly. Markets can be very simple or highly organized. Markets are ancient and they are modern.

A simple and ancient market is one that the American historian Daniel J. Boorstin describes in *The Discoverers* (p. 161). In the late fourteenth century,

> *The Muslim caravans that went southward from Morocco across the Atlas Mountains arrived after twenty days at the shores of the Senegal River. There the Moroccan traders laid out separate piles of salt, of beads from Ceutan coral, and cheap manufactured goods. Then they retreated out of sight. The local tribesmen, who lived in the strip mines where they dug their gold, came to the shore and put a heap of gold beside each pile of Moroccan goods. Then they, in turn, went out of view, leaving the Moroccan traders either to take the gold offered for a particular pile or to reduce the pile of their merchandise to suit the offered price in gold. Once again the Moroccan traders withdrew, and the process went on. By this system of commercial etiquette, the Moroccans collected their gold.*

An organized and modern market is an auction at which the Canadian government sells rights to broadcasters and cellular telephone companies for the use of the airwaves.

Everything and anything that can be exchanged is traded in markets—goods, services, and resources; dollars, euros, and yen; goods to be delivered now and for goods to be delivered in the future. Only the imagination places limits on what can be traded in markets.

Alfred Marshall *(1842–1924) grew up in an England that was being transformed by the railroad and by the expansion of manufacturing. Mary Paley was one of Marshall's students at Cambridge, and when Alfred and Mary married, in 1877, celibacy rules barred Alfred from continuing to teach at Cambridge. By 1884, with more liberal rules, the Marshalls returned to Cambridge, where Alfred became Professor of Political Economy.*

Many economists had a hand in refining the demand and supply model, but the first thorough and complete statement of the model as we know it today was set out by Alfred Marshall, with the help of Mary Paley Marshall. Published in 1890, this monumental treatise, The Principles of Economics, became the textbook on economics on both sides of the Atlantic for almost half a century.

"The forces to be dealt with are ... so numerous, that it is best to take a few at a time. ... Thus we begin by isolating the primary relations of supply, demand, and price."

ALFRED MARSHALL
The Principles of Economics

TALKING
WITH

Susan Athey

Susan Athey is Professor of Economics at Harvard University. Born in 1970 in Boston and growing up in Rockville, Maryland, she completed high school in three years, wrapped up three majors—in economics, mathematics, and computer science—at Duke University at 20, completed her Ph.D. at Stanford University at 24, and was voted tenure at MIT and Stanford at 29. After teaching at MIT for six years and Stanford for five, she moved to Harvard in 2006. Among her many honours and awards, the most prestigious is the John Bates Clark Medal given to the best economist under 40. She is the first woman to receive this award.

Professor Athey's research is broad in both scope and style. A government that wants to auction natural resources will turn to her fundamental discoveries (and possibly consult with her) before deciding how to organize the auction. An economist who wants to test a theory using a large data set will use her work on statistics and econometrics.

Michael Parkin and Robin Bade talked with Susan Athey about her research, the progress that economists have made in understanding and designing markets, and her advice to students.

What sparked your interest in economics?

I was studying mathematics and computer science, but I felt that the subjects were not as relevant as I would like.

I discovered economics through a research assistantship with a professor who was working on auctions. I had a summer job working for a firm that sold computers to the government through auctions. Eventually my professor, Bob Marshall, wrote two articles on the topic and testified before Congress to help reform the system for government procurement of computers. That really inspired me and showed me the power of economic ideas to change the world and to make things work more efficiently.

This original inspiration has remained and continues to drive much of your research. Can you explain how economists study auctions?

The study of the design of markets and auction-based marketplaces requires you to use all of the different tools that economics offers.

An auction is a well-defined game. You can write down the rules of the game and a formal theoretical model does a great job capturing the real problem that the players face. And theories do an excellent job predicting behaviour.

Buyers have a valuation for an object that is private information. They do not know the valuations of other bidders, and sometimes they don't even know their own valuation. For example, if they're buying oil rights, there may be uncertainty about how much oil there is in the ground. In that case, information about the amount of oil available is dispersed among the bidders, because each bidder has done their own survey. The bidders face a strategic problem of bidding, and they face an informational problem of trying to draw inferences about how valuable the object will be if they win.

Bidders need to recognize that their bid only matters when they win the auction, and they only win when they bid the most. The knowledge that they were the most optimistic of all the competitors should cause them to revise their beliefs.

From the seller's perspective, there are choices about how an auction is designed—auctions can use sealed bidding, where the seller receives bids and then opens them at a pre-determined time, or alternatively bidding may be interactive, where each bidder has an opportunity to outbid the previous high bidder. There are also different ways to use bids received by the auctioneer to determine the price. The seller may consider revenue, though governments are often most concerned about efficient allocation.

Both revenue and efficiency are affected by auction design. One key question the seller must consider is how the design will affect the participation of bidders, as this will determine how competitive bidding will be as well as whether the object gets to the potential bidder who values the item the most.

What must the designer of an auction-based marketplace take into account?

An example of an auction-based marketplace is eBay, where the market designer sets the rules for buyers and sellers to interact.

When you design an auction-based marketplace, you have a whole new set of concerns. The buyers and sellers themselves are independent agents, each acting in their own interest. The design is a two-step process: You need to design an auction that is going to achieve an efficient allocation; and you need design both the auction and the overall structure of the marketplace to attract participation.

In the case of eBay, the platform itself chooses the possible auction formats: auctions take place over time and bidders have the opportunity to outbid the standing high bidder during that time. The platform also allows sellers to use the "buy it now" option. The platform also makes certain tools and services available, such as the ability to search for items in various ways, track auctions, provide feedback, and monitor reputation. The sellers can select the level of the reserve price, whether they want to have a secret reserve price, how long the auction will last, whether to use "buy it now," what time of day the auction closes, how much information to provide, how many pictures they post.

These are all factors that impact participation of bidders and the revenue the seller will receive. The success of the platform hinges on both buyers and sellers choosing to participate.

Does auction theory enable us to predict the differences in the outcomes of an open ascending-bid English auction and a sealed-bid auction?

Sure. In some of my research, I compared open ascending auctions and pay-your-bid, sealed-bid auctions. I showed how the choice of auction format can make a big difference when you have small bidders bidding against larger, stronger bidders who usually (but not always) have higher valuations.

In an open ascending auction, it is hard for a small weaker bidder to ever win, because a stronger bidder can see their bids, respond to them, and outbid them

But in a pay-your-bid, sealed-bid auction, bidders shade their bids—they bid less than their value, assuring themselves of some profit if they win—and a large bidder doesn't have the opportunity to see and respond to an unusually high bid from a weak bidder. Strong bidders realize that their competition is weak, and they shade their bids a lot—they bid a lot less than their value. That gives a small bidder the opportunity to be aggressive and outbid a larger bidder, even if it has a lower value. So what that does is encourage entry of small bidders. I found empirically that this entry effect was important and it helps sealed-bid auctions generate larger revenue than open ascending-bid auctions.

> Sealed-bid auctions can do a better job of deterring collusion ... and raise more revenue

Does a sealed-bid auction always generate more revenue, other things equal, than an open ascending-bid auction?

Only if you have asymmetric bidders—strong large bidders and weaker small bidders—and even then the effect is ambiguous. It's an empirical question, but it tends to be true. We also showed that sealed-bid auctions can do a better job of deterring collusion. There are theoretical reasons to suggest that sealed-bid auctions are more difficult to collude at than open ascending actions, since at open ascending auctions, bidders can detect an opponent who is bidding higher than an agreement specifies and then respond to that. We found empirically in U.S. Forest Service timber auctions that the gap between sealed-bid auctions and ascending auctions was even greater than what a competitive model would predict, suggesting that some collusion may be at work.

What is the connection between auctions and the supply and demand model?

The basic laws of supply and demand can be seen in evidence in a market like eBay. The more sellers that are selling similar products, the lower the prices they can expect to achieve. Similarly the more buyers there are demanding those objects, the higher the prices the sellers can achieve.

> The basic laws of supply and demand can be seen in evidence in a market like eBay.

An important thing for an auction marketplace is to attract a good balance of buyers and sellers so that both the buyers and the sellers find it more profitable to transact on that marketplace rather than using some other mechanism. From a seller's perspective, the more bidders there are on the platform, the greater the demand and the higher the prices. And from the buyer's perspective, the more sellers there are on the platform, the greater the supply and the lower the prices.

Can we think of this thought experiment you just described as discovering demand and supply curves?

Exactly. When you study supply and demand curves, you wave your hands about how the prices actually get set. In different kinds of market settings, the actual mechanisms for setting prices are different. One way of setting prices is through auctions. But we tend to use auctions in settings where there are unique objects, so there isn't just one market price for the thing you are selling. If you were selling something that had lots of market substitutes, you can think of there being a market price in which this object can transact. An auction is a way to find a market price for something where there might not be a fixed market.

Can we think of an auction as a mechanism for finding the equilibrium price and quantity?

Exactly. We can think of the whole collection of auctions on eBay as being a mechanism to discover a market-clearing price, and individual items might sell a little higher or a little lower but overall we believe that the prices on eBay auctions will represent market-clearing (equilibrium) prices.

Is economics a good subject in which to major? What subjects work well as complements with economics?

Of course I think economics is a fabulous major and I am passionate about it. I think it's a discipline that trains you to think rigorously. And if you apply yourself you'll finish an economics major with a more disciplined mind than when you started. Whether you go into the business world or academics, you'll be able to confront and think in a logical and structured way about whether a policy makes sense, a business model makes sense, or an industry structure is likely to be sustainable. You should look for that in an undergraduate major. You should not be looking to just absorb facts, but you should be looking to train your mind and to think in a way that you will be able to apply to the rest of your career. I think that economics combines well with statistics and mathematics or with more policy-oriented disciplines.

Do you have anything special to say to women who might be making a career choice? Why is economics a good field for a woman?

On the academic side, economics is a fairly objective field, where the best ideas win, so it's a level playing field. Academics is not very family friendly before you get tenured and extremely family friendly after. Within academics or outside of it, there are a wide range of fairly high-paying jobs that still allow some autonomy over your schedule and that have a deeper and more compelling meaning. For both men and women, if you choose to have a family, you reevaluate your career choices and the tradeoff between time and money changes. And you're more likely to stick with and excel in a career if you find some meaning in it. So economics combines some of the advantages of having a strong job market and opportunities to have a large enough salary to pay for child care, and makes it economically worthwhile to stay in the workforce, without sacrificing the sense of the greater good.

8 Utility and Demand

After studying this chapter, you will be able to

- Describe preferences using the concept of utility, distinguish between total utility and marginal utility, and explain the marginal utility theory of consumer choice

- Use marginal utility theory to predict the effects of changes in prices and incomes and to explain the paradox of value

- Describe some new ways of explaining consumer choices

You want Coldplay's latest hit album, *Viva la Vida,* and you want the Justin Timberlake and Madonna single, *Four Minutes.* Will you download the album and the single? Or will you buy two CDs? Or will you buy the album on a CD and download the single? What determines our choices as buyers of recorded music? And how much better off are we because we can download a song for 99 cents?

You know that diamonds are expensive and water is cheap. Doesn't that seem odd? Why do we place a higher value on useless diamonds than on essential-to-life water? You can think of many other examples of this paradox. For example, paramedics who save people's lives get paid a tiny fraction of what a National Hockey League player earns. Do we really place less value on the people who take care of the injured and the sick than we place on those who provide us with entertaining hockey games?

The theory of consumer choice that you're going to study in this chapter answers questions like the ones we've just posed. The main purpose of this theory is to explain the law of demand and the influences on buying plans. To explain the theory, we will study the choices of Lisa, a student who loves movies and has a thirst for pop. But the theory explains all choices including your choices in the market for recorded music as well as the paradox that the prices of water and diamonds are so out of proportion with their benefits. In *Reading Between the Lines* at the end of the chapter, we apply marginal utility theory to yet another choice that you make every day at the grocery store.

Maximizing Utility

Your income and the prices that you face limit your consumption choices. You can buy only the things that you can afford. But you still have lots of choices. Of all the alternative combinations of goods and services that you can afford, what will you buy?

The economist's answer to this question is that you will buy the goods and services that maximize your utility. **Utility** is the benefit or satisfaction that a person gets from the consumption of goods and services. To understand how people's choices maximize utility, we distinguish between two concepts:

- Total utility
- Marginal utility

Total Utility

Total utility is the total benefit that a person gets from the consumption of all the different goods and services. Total utility depends on the level of consumption—more consumption generally gives more total utility.

To make the concept of total utility more concrete, think about the choices of Lisa, a student who spends all her income on two goods: movies and pop. We tell Lisa that we want to measure her utility from these two goods. We can use any scale that we wish to measure utility and give her two starting points:

1. We will call the total utility from no movies and no pop zero utility; and

2. We will call the total utility she gets from seeing 1 movie a month 50 units.

We then ask Lisa to tell us, using the same scale, how much she would like 2 movies, and more, up to 10 a month. We also ask her to tell us, on the same scale, how much she would like 1 case of pop a month, 2 cases, and more, up to 10 cases a month.

In Table 8.1, the columns headed "Total utility" show Lisa's answers. Looking at those numbers, you can say quite a lot about how much Lisa likes pop and movies. She says that 1 case of pop gives her 75 units of utility—50 percent more than the utility that she gets from seeing 1 movie.

But you can also see that her total utility from pop climbs more slowly than her total utility from movies. By the time she is buying 9 cases of pop and seeing 9 movies a month, she gets almost the same

TABLE 8.1   Lisa's Utility from Movies and Pop

Movies			Pop		
Quantity (per month)	Total utility	Marginal utility	Cases (per month)	Total utility	Marginal utility
0	0		0	0	
		50			75
1	50		1	75	
		40			48
2	90		2	123	
		32			36
3	122		3	159	
		28			24
4	150		4	183	
		26			22
5	176		5	205	
		24			20
6	200		6	225	
		22			13
7	222		7	238	
		20			10
8	242		8	248	
		17			7
9	259		9	255	
		16			5
10	275		10	260	

utility from each good. And at 10 of each, she gets more total utility from movies (275 units) than she gets from pop (260 units).

Marginal Utility

Marginal utility is the change in total utility that results from a one-unit increase in the quantity of a good consumed.

In Table 8.1, the columns headed "Marginal utility" show Lisa's marginal utility from movies and pop. You can see that if Lisa increases the pop she buys from 1 to 2 cases a month, her total utility from pop increases from 75 units to 123 units. For Lisa, the marginal utility from the second case each month is 48 units (123 – 75).

The marginal utility numbers appear midway between the quantities of pop because it is the *change* in the quantity she buys from 1 to 2 cases that produces the marginal utility of 48 units.

Marginal utility is *positive,* but it *diminishes* as the quantity consumed of a good increases.

Positive Marginal Utility   All the things that people enjoy and want more of have a positive marginal utility. Some objects and activities can generate negative marginal utility—and lower total utility. Two examples are hard labour and polluted air. But the goods and services that people value and that we are thinking about here all have positive marginal utility: total utility increases as the quantity consumed increases.

Diminishing Marginal Utility As Lisa sees more movies, her total utility from movies increases but her marginal utility from movies decreases. Similarly, as she consumes more pop, her total utility from pop increases but her marginal utility from pop decreases.

The tendency for marginal utility to decrease as the consumption of a good increases is so general and universal that we give it the status of a *principle*—the principle of **diminishing marginal utility**.

You can see Lisa's diminishing marginal utility by calculating a few numbers. Her marginal utility from pop decreases from 75 units from the first case to 48 units from the second case and to 36 units from the third. Her marginal utility from movies decreases from 50 units for the first movie to 40 units for the second and 32 units for the third. Lisa's marginal utility diminishes as she buys more of each good.

You can confirm that the principle of diminishing marginal utility applies to your own utility by thinking about the following two situations: In one, you've been studying all through the day and evening, and you've been too busy finishing an assignment to go shopping. A friend drops by with a can of pop. The utility you get from that pop is the marginal utility from one can. In the second situation, you've been on a pop binge. You've been working on an assignment all day but you've guzzled ten cans of pop while doing so, and are now totally wired. You are happy enough to have one more can, but the thrill that you get from it is not very large. It is the marginal utility from the eleventh can in a day.

Graphing Lisa's Utility Schedules

Figure 8.1(a) illustrates Lisa's total utility from pop. The more pop Lisa consumes in a month, the more total utility she gets. Her total utility curve slopes upward.

Figure 8.1(b) illustrates Lisa's marginal utility from pop. It is a graph of the marginal utility numbers in Table 8.1. This graph shows Lisa's diminishing marginal utility from pop. Her marginal utility curve slopes downward as she consumes more pop.

We've now described Lisa's preferences. Our next task is to see how she chooses what to consume to maximize her utility.

FIGURE 8.1 Total Utility and Marginal Utility

(a) Total utility

(b) Marginal utility

The figure graphs Lisa's total utility and marginal utility from pop based on the numbers for the first 5 cases of pop a month in Table 8.1. Part (a) shows that her total utility increases as her consumption of pop increases—increasing total utility. The bars along the total utility curve show the extra total utility from each additional case of pop—marginal utility. Part (b) shows that Lisa's marginal utility from pop diminishes as her consumption of pop increases—diminishing marginal utility. The bars that measure marginal utility get shorter as pop consumption increases.

The Utility-Maximizing Choice

Suppose that Lisa earns $40 a month and she spends it all on movies and pop. The prices that she faces are $8 for a movie and $4 for a case of pop.

Lisa's most direct way of finding the quantities of movies and pop that maximize her utility is to make a spreadsheet like Table 8.2.

The rows of the table show the combinations of movies and pop that Lisa can afford and that exhaust her $40 income. She can afford smaller quantities of movies and pop than those in the table, but smaller quantities don't maximize her utility. Why? Because her marginal utilities of movies and pop are positive, so the more of each that she buys, the more total utility she gets.

The columns of Table 8.2 show the total utility that Lisa gets from the just-affordable quantities of movies and pop. The middle column adds the total utility from movies to the total utility from pop. This number, the total utility from movies *and* pop, is what Lisa wants to maximize.

In row *A*, Lisa watches no movies and buys 10 cases of pop. She gets no utility from movies and 260 units of utility from pop. Her total utility from movies and pop (the centre column) is 260 units.

In row *C*, highlighted in the table, Lisa sees 2 movies and buys 6 cases of pop. She gets 90 units of utility from movies and 225 units of utility from pop. Her total utility from movies and pop is 315 units. This combination of movies and pop maximizes Lisa's total utility. This is the best Lisa can do, when she has only $40 to spend and given the prices of movies and cases. If Lisa buys 8 cases of pop, she can see only 1 movie. She gets 298 units of total utility, 17 less than the maximum attainable. If she sees 3 movies, she can buy only 4 cases of pop. She gets 305 units of total utility, 10 less than the maximum attainable.

We've just described Lisa's consumer equilibrium. A **consumer equilibrium** is a situation in which a consumer has allocated all of his or her available income in the way that maximizes his or her total utility, given the prices of goods and services. Lisa's consumer equilibrium is 2 movies and 6 cases of pop.

To find Lisa's consumer equilibrium, we measured her *total* utility from all the affordable combinations of movies and pop. But a simpler way of finding a consumer equilibrium uses the idea that choices are made at the margin—an idea that you first met in Chapter 1. Let's look at this approach.

TABLE 8.2   Lisa's Utility-Maximizing Combinations

	Movies $8		Total utility from movies and pop	Pop $4	
	Quantity (per month)	Total utility		Total utility	Cases (per month)
A	0	0	260	260	10
B	1	50	298	248	8
C	2	90	315	225	6
D	3	122	305	183	4
E	4	150	273	123	2
F	5	176	176	0	0

Choosing at the Margin

A consumer's total utility is maximized by following the rule:

- Spend all the available income.
- Equalize the marginal utility per dollar for all goods

Spend All the Available Income   Because more consumption brings more utility, only those choices that exhaust income can maximize utility. For Lisa, combinations of movies and pop that leave her with money to spend don't give her as much total utility as those that spend her entire income of $40 a month.

Equalize Marginal Utility per Dollar   We've defined marginal utility as the increase in total utility from consuming *one more unit* of a good. **Marginal utility per dollar** is the marginal utility from a good obtained by spending *one more dollar* on that good.

The distinction between these two marginal concepts is clearest for a good that is infinitely divisible, such as gasoline. You can buy gasoline by the smallest fraction of a gallon and literally choose to spend one more or one less dollar at the pump. When you buy a movie ticket or a case of pop, you must spend your dollars in bigger lumps. But the principles that apply at the gas pump also apply at the movie house and the convenience store.

Let's see how this marginal approach works.

The Basic Idea The basic idea behind the utility maximizing rule is to move dollars from good *A* to good *B* if doing so increases the utility from good *A* by more than it decreases the utility from good *B*. Such a utility-increasing move is possible if the marginal utility per dollar from good *A* exceeds the marginal utility per dollar from good *B*.

But buying more of good *A* decreases its marginal utility. And buying less of good *B* increases its marginal utility. So by moving dollars from good *A* to good *B*, total utility rises, but the gap between the marginal utilities per dollar gets smaller.

So long as a gap exists—so long as the marginal utility per dollar from good *A* exceeds that from good *B*, total utility can be increased by spending more on *A* and less on *B*. But when enough dollars have been moved from *B* to *A* to make the two marginal utilities per dollar equal, total utility cannot be increased further. Utility is maximized.

Lisa's Marginal Calculation Let's apply the basic idea to Lisa. To calculate Lisa's marginal utility per dollar, we divide her marginal utility numbers for each quantity of each good by the price of the good. Table 8.3 shows these calculations for Lisa. The rows of the table are affordable combinations of movies and pop.

Too Few Movies and Too Much Pop In row *B*, Lisa sees 1 movie and consumes 8 cases of pop a month. Her marginal utility from seeing 1 movie a month is 50 units. Because the price of a movie is $8, Lisa's marginal utility per dollar from movies is 50 units divided by $8, or 6.25 units of utility per dollar.

Lisa's marginal utility from pop when she consumes 8 cases of pop a month is 10 units. Because the price of pop is $4 a case, Lisa's marginal utility per dollar from pop is 10 units divided by $4, or 2.50 units of utility per dollar.

When Lisa sees 1 movie and consumes 8 cases of pop a month, her marginal utility per dollar from movies *exceeds* her marginal utility per dollar from pop. If Lisa spent an extra dollar on movies and a dollar less on pop, her total utility would increase. She would get 6.25 units from the extra dollar spent on movies and lose 2.50 units from the dollar less spent on pop. Her total utility would increase by 3.75 units (6.25 − 2.50).

But if Lisa sees more movies and consumes less pop a month, her marginal utility from movies falls and her marginal utility from pop rises.

TABLE 8.3   Equalizing Marginal Utilities per Dollar

		Movies ($8 each)			Pop ($4 per case)	
	Quantity	Marginal utility	Marginal utility per dollar	Cases	Marginal utility	Marginal utility per dollar
A	0	0		10	5	1.25
B	1	50	6.25	8	10	2.50
C	2	40	5.00	6	20	5.00
D	3	32	4.00	4	24	6.00
E	4	28	3.50	2	48	12.00
F	5	26	3.25	0	0	

Too Many Movies and Too Little Pop In row *D*, Lisa sees 3 movies a month and consumes 4 cases of pop. Her marginal utility from seeing the third movie a month is 32 units. At a price of $8 a movie, Lisa's marginal utility per dollar from movies is 32 units divided by $8, or 4 units of utility per dollar.

Lisa's marginal utility from pop when she buys 4 cases a month is 24 units. At a price of $4 a case, Lisa's marginal utility per dollar from pop is 24 units divided by $4, or 6 units of utility per dollar.

When Lisa sees 3 movies and consumes 4 cases of pop a month, her marginal utility from pop *exceeds* her marginal utility from movies. If Lisa spent an extra dollar on pop and a dollar less on movies, her total utility would increase. She would get 6 units from the extra dollar spent on pop and she would lose 4 units from the dollar less spent on movies. Her total utility would increase by 2 units (6 − 4).

But if Lisa sees fewer movies and consumes more pop, her marginal utility from movies rises and her marginal utility from pop falls.

Utility-Maximizing Movies and Pop In Table 8.3, if Lisa moves from row *B* to row *C*, she increases the movies she sees from 1 to 2 a month and she decreases the pop she consumes from 8 to 6 cases a month. Her marginal utility per dollar from movies falls to 5 and her marginal utility per dollar from pop rises to 5.

Similarly, if Lisa moves from row *D* to row *C*, she decreases the movies she sees from 3 to 2 a month and she increases the pop she consumes from 4 to 6 cases a month. Her marginal utility per dollar from movies rises to 5 and her marginal utility per dollar from pop falls to 5.

At this combination of movies and pop, Lisa is maximizing her utility. If she spent an extra dollar on movies and a dollar less on pop, or an extra dollar on pop and a dollar less on movies, her total utility would not change.

The Power of Marginal Analysis

The method we've just used to find Lisa's utility-maximizing choice of movies and pop is an example of the power of marginal analysis. Lisa doesn't need a computer and a spreadsheet program to maximize utility. She can achieve this goal by comparing the marginal gain from having more of one good with the marginal loss from having less of another good.

The rule that she follows is simple: If the marginal utility per dollar from movies exceeds the marginal utility per dollar from pop, see more movies and buy less pop; if the marginal utility per dollar from pop exceeds the marginal utility per dollar from movies, buy more pop and see fewer movies.

More generally, if the marginal gain from an action exceeds the marginal loss, take the action. You will meet this principle time and again in your study of economics, and you will find yourself using it when you make your own economic choices, especially when you must make big decisions.

Units of Utility In maximizing total utility by making the marginal utility per dollar equal for all goods, the units in which utility is measured do not matter. Any arbitrary units will work. In this respect, utility is like temperature. Predictions about the freezing point of water don't depend on the temperature scale; and predictions about a household's consumption choice don't depend on the units of utility.

When we introduced the idea of utility, we arbitrarily chose 50 units as Lisa's total utility from 1 movie. But we could have given her any number. And as you're now about to discover, we didn't even need to ask Lisa to tell us her preferences. We can figure out Lisa's preferences for ourselves by observing what she buys at various prices. To see how, we need to use a bit of math.

Call the marginal utility from movies MU_M and the price of a movie P_M. Then the marginal utility per dollar from movies is

$$MU_M/P_M.$$

Call the marginal utility from pop MU_P and the price of a case of pop P_P. Then the marginal utility per dollar from pop is

$$MU_P/P_P.$$

When Lisa maximizes utility,

$$MU_P/P_P = MU_M/P_M.$$

Multiply both sides of this equation by P_P to obtain

$$MU_P = MU_M \times P_P/P_M.$$

This equation says that the marginal utility from pop, MU_P, is equal to the marginal utility from movies, MU_M, multiplied by the ratio of the price of pop, P_P, to the price of a movie, P_M.

For Lisa, when P_M = $8 and P_P = $4, we observe that in a month she goes to the movies twice and buys 6 cases of pop. So we know that her MU_P from 6 cases of pop equals her MU_M from 2 movies multiplied by $4/$8 or 0.5. If we call MU_M from the second movie 40, then MU_P from the sixth case of pop is 20. If we observe enough prices and quantities, we can construct an entire utility schedule for an arbitrary starting value.

Review Quiz

1 What is utility and how do we use the concept of utility to describe a consumer's preferences?
2 What is the distinction between total utility and marginal utility?
3 What is the key assumption about marginal utility?
4 What two conditions are met when a consumer is maximizing utility?
5 Explain why equalizing the marginal utility per dollar from each good maximizes utility.

myeconlab   Work Study Plan 8.1
and get instant feedback.

Predictions of Marginal Utility Theory

We're now going to use marginal utility theory to make some predictions. You will see that marginal utility theory predicts the law of demand. The theory also predicts that a fall in the price of a substitute of a good decreases the demand for the good and that for a normal good, a rise in income increases demand. All these effects, which in Chapter 3 we simply assumed, are predictions of marginal utility theory.

To derive these predictions, we will study the effects of three events:

- A fall in the price of a movie
- A rise in the price of pop
- A rise in income

A Fall in the Price of a Movie

With the price of a movie at $8 and the price of pop at $4, Lisa is maximizing utility by seeing 2 movies and buying 6 cases of pop each month. Then, with no change in her $40 income and no change in the price of pop, the price of a movie falls from $8 to $4. How does Lisa change her buying plans?

Finding the New Quantities of Movies and Pop You can find the effect of a fall in the price of a movie on the quantities of movies and pop that Lisa buys in a three-step calculation.

1. Determine the just-affordable combinations of movies and pop at the new prices.
2. Calculate the new marginal utilities per dollar from the good whose price has changed.
3. Determine the quantities of movies and pop that make their marginal utilities per dollar equal.

Affordable Combinations The lower price of a movie means that Lisa can afford more movies or more pop. Table 8.4 shows her new affordable combinations. In row *A*, if she continues to see 2 movies a month, she can now afford 8 cases of pop; and in row *B*, if she continues to buy 6 cases of pop, she can now afford 4 movies. Lisa can afford any of the combinations shown in the rows of Table 8.4.

The next step is to find her new marginal utilities per dollar from movies.

New Marginal Utilities per Dollar from Movies A person's preferences don't change just because a price has changed. With no change in her preferences, Lisa's marginal utilities in Table 8.4 are the same as those in Table 8.1. But because the price of a movie has changed, the marginal utility *per dollar* from movies changes. In fact, with a halving of the price from $8 to $4, the marginal utility per dollar from movies has doubled.

The numbers in Table 8.4 show Lisa's marginal utility per dollar from movies for each quantity of movies. The table also shows Lisa's marginal utility from pop for each quantity.

Equalizing the Marginal Utilities per Dollar You can see that if Lisa continues to see 2 movies a month (row *A*), her marginal utility per dollar from movies is 10 units and if she continues to buy 6 cases of pop a month (row *B*), her marginal utility per dollar from pop is only 5 units. Lisa is buying too much pop and too few movies. If she spends a dollar more on movies and a dollar less on pop, her total utility increases by 5 units (10 − 5).

You can also see that if Lisa continues to buy 6 cases of pop and sees 4 movies (row *B*), her marginal

TABLE 8.4 How a Change in the Price of Movies Affects Lisa's Choices

		Movies ($4 each)			Pop ($4 per case)		
	Quantity	Marginal utility	Marginal utility per dollar	Cases	Marginal utility	Marginal utility per dollar
	0	0		10	5	1.25
	1	50	12.50	9	7	1.75
A	2	40	**10.00**	8	10	2.50
	3	32	8.00	7	13	3.25
B	4	28	7.00	**6**	**20**	**5.00**
	5	26	6.50	5	22	5.50
C	6	24	6.00	4	24	6.00
	7	22	5.50	3	36	9.00
	8	20	5.00	2	48	12.00
	9	17	4.25	1	75	18.75
	10	16	4.00	0	0	

utility per dollar from movies is 7 units and her marginal utility per dollar from pop is only 5 units. Lisa is still buying too much pop and seeing too few movies. If she spends a dollar more on movies and a dollar less on pop, her total utility increases by 2 units (7 − 5).

But if Lisa sees 6 movies and buys 4 cases of pop a month (row C), her marginal utility per dollar from movies (6 units) equals her marginal utility per dollar from pop. Now if she spends a dollar less on pop and a dollar more on movies, her utility doesn't change (6 − 6). She is maximizing utility.

Lisa's increased purchases of movies results from a substitution effect—she substitutes the now lower-priced movies for pop—and an income effect—she can afford more movies.

A Change in the Quantity Demanded Lisa's increase in the quantity of movies that she sees is a change in the quantity demanded. It is the change in the quantity of movies that she plans to see each month when the price of a movie changes and all other influences on buying plans remain the same. We illustrate a change in the quantity demanded by a movement along a demand curve.

Figure 8.2(a) shows Lisa's demand curve for movies. When the price of a movie is $8, Lisa sees 2 movies a month. And when the price of a movie falls to $4, she sees 6 movies a month. Lisa moves downward along her demand curve for movies.

The demand curve traces the quantities that maximize utility at each price, with all other influences remaining the same. You can also see that utility-maximizing choices generate a downward-sloping demand curve. Utility maximization with diminishing marginal utility implies the law of demand.

A Change in Demand Lisa's decrease in the quantity of pop that she buys is the change in the quantity of pop that she plans to buy each month at a given price of pop when the price of a movie changes. It is a change in her demand for pop. We illustrate a change in demand by a shift of a demand curve.

Figure 8.2(b) shows Lisa's demand for pop. The price of pop is fixed at $4 a case. When the price of a movie is $8, Lisa buys 6 cases of pop on demand curve D_0. When the price of a movie falls to $4, Lisa buys 4 cases of pop on demand curve D_1. The fall in the price of a movie decreases Lisa's demand for pop. Her demand curve for pop shifts leftward. For Lisa, pop and movies are substitutes.

FIGURE 8.2 A Fall in the Price of a Movie

(a) Demand for movies

(b) Demand for pop

When the price of a movie falls and the price of pop remains the same, the quantity of movies demanded by Lisa increases, and in part (a), Lisa moves along her demand curve for movies. Also, when the price of a movie falls, Lisa's demand for pop decreases, and in part (b), her demand curve for pop shifts leftward. For Lisa, pop and movies are substitutes.

 animation

A Rise in the Price of Pop

Now suppose that with the price of a movie at $4, the price of pop rises from $4 to $8 a case. How does this price change influence Lisa's buying plans? We find the answer by repeating the three-step calculation with the new price of pop.

Table 8.5 shows Lisa's new affordable combinations. In row *A*, if she continues to buy 4 cases of pop a month she can afford to see only 2 movies; and in row *B*, if she continues to see 6 movies a month, she can afford only 2 cases of pop.

Table 8.5 show Lisa's marginal utility per dollar from pop for each quantity of pop when the price is $8 a case. The table also shows Lisa's marginal utility per dollar from movies for each quantity.

If Lisa continues to buy 4 cases of pop a month (row *A*), her marginal utility per dollar from pop is 3. But she must cut her movies to 2 a month, which gives her 12 units of utility per dollar from movies. Lisa is buying too much pop and too few movies. If she spends a dollar less on pop and a dollar more on movies, her utility increases by 9 units (12 − 3).

But if Lisa sees 6 movies a month and cuts her pop back to 2 cases (row *B*), her marginal utility per dollar from movies (6 units) equals her marginal utility per dollar from pop. She is maximizing utility.

Lisa's decreased purchases of pop results from an income effect—she can afford fewer cases and she buys fewer cases. But she continues to buy the same quantity of movies.

Lisa's Demand for Pop

Now that we've calculated the effect of a change in the price of pop on Lisa's buying plans, we have found two points on her demand curve for pop: When the price of pop is $4 a case, Lisa buys 4 cases a month; and when the price rises to $8 a case, she buys 2 cases a month.

Figure 8.3 shows these points on Lisa's demand curve for pop. It also shows the change in the quantity of pop demanded when the price of pop rises and all other influences on Lisa's buying plans remain the same.

In this particular case, Lisa continues to buy the same quantity of movies. This outcome does not always occur. It is a consequence of Lisa's utility schedule. With different marginal utilities, she might have decreased or increased the quantity of movies that she sees when the price of pop changes.

You've seen that marginal utility theory predicts the law of demand—the way in which the quantity demanded of a good changes when its price changes. Next we'll see how marginal utility theory predicts the effect of a change in income on demand.

TABLE 8.5   How a Change in the Price of Pop Affects Lisa's Choices

	Movies ($4 each)			Pop ($8 per case)		
	Quantity	Marginal utility	Marginal utility per dollar	Cases	Marginal utility	Marginal utility per dollar
	0	0		5	22	2.75
A	2	40	12.00	**4**	24	**3.00**
	4	28	7.00	3	36	4.50
B	6	24	6.00	2	48	6.00
	8	20	5.00	1	75	9.38
	10	16	4.00	0	0	

FIGURE 8.3   A Rise in the Price of Pop

When the price of pop rises and the price of a movie and Lisa's income remain the same, the quantity of pop demanded by Lisa decreases. Lisa moves along her demand curve for pop.

myeconlab animation

A Rise in Income

Suppose that Lisa's income increases from $40 to $56 a month and that the price of a movie is $4 and the price of a case of pop is $4. With these prices and with an income of $40 a month, Lisa sees 6 movies and buys 4 cases of pop a month (Table 8.4). How does the increase in Lisa's income from $40 to $56 change her buying plans?

Table 8.6 shows the calculations needed to answer this question. If Lisa continues to see 6 movies a month, she can now afford to buy 8 cases of pop (row *A*); and if she continues to buy 4 cases of pop, she can now afford to see 10 movies (row *C*).

In row *A*, Lisa's marginal utility per dollar from movies is greater than her marginal utility per dollar from pop. She is buying too much pop and too few movies. In row *C*, Lisa's marginal utility per dollar from movies is less than her marginal utility per dollar from pop. She is buying too little pop and too many movies. But in row *B*, when Lisa sees 8 movies a month and buys 6 cases of pop, her marginal utility per dollar from movies equals that from pop. She is maximizing utility.

Figure 8.4 shows the effects of the rise in Lisa's income on her demand curves for movies and pop. The price of each good is $4. When Lisa's income

TABLE 8.6 Lisa's Choices with an Income of $56 a Month

	Movies ($4 each)			Pop ($4 per case)		
	Quantity	Marginal utility	Marginal utility per dollar	Cases	Marginal utility	Marginal utility per dollar
	4	28	7.00	10	5	1.25
	5	26	6.50	9	7	1.75
A	6	24	**6.00**	8	10	2.50
	7	22	5.50	7	13	3.25
B	8	20	5.00	6	20	5.00
	9	17	4.25	5	22	5.50
C	10	16	4.00	**4**	24	**6.00**

rises to $56 a month, she sees 2 more movies and buys 2 more cases of pop. Her demand curves for both movies and pop shift rightward—her demand for both movies and pop increases. With a larger income, the consumer always buys more of a *normal* good. For Lisa, movies and pop are normal goods.

FIGURE 8.4 The Effects of a Rise in Income

(a) Demand for movies

(b) Demand for pop

When Lisa's income increases, her demand for movies and her demand for pop increase. Lisa's demand curves for

movies, in part (a), and for pop, in part (b), shift rightward. For Lisa, movies and pop are normal goods.

The Paradox of Value

The price of water is low and the price of a diamond is high, but water is essential to life while diamonds are used mostly just for decoration. How can valuable water be so cheap while a relatively useless diamond is so expensive? This so-called *paradox of value* has puzzled philosophers for centuries. Not until the theory of marginal utility had been developed could anyone give a satisfactory answer.

The Paradox Resolved The paradox is resolved by distinguishing between *total* utility and *marginal* utility. The total utility that we get from water is enormous. But remember, the more we consume of something, the smaller is its marginal utility.

We use so much water that its marginal utility—the benefit we get from one more glass of water or another 30 seconds in the shower—diminishes to a small value.

Diamonds, on the other hand, have a small total utility relative to water, but because we buy few diamonds, they have a high marginal utility.

When a household has maximized its total utility, it has allocated its income in the way that makes the marginal utility per dollar equal for all goods. That is, the marginal utility from a good divided by the price of the good is equal for all goods.

This equality of marginal utilities per dollar holds true for diamonds and water: Diamonds have a high price and a high marginal utility. Water has a low price and a low marginal utility. When the high marginal utility from diamonds is divided by the high price of a diamond, the result is a number that equals the low marginal utility from water divided by the low price of water. The marginal utility per dollar is the same for diamonds and water.

Value and Consumer Surplus Another way to think about the paradox of value and illustrate how it is resolved uses *consumer surplus*. Figure 8.5 explains the paradox of value by using this idea. The supply of water in part (a) is perfectly elastic at price P_W, so the quantity of water consumed is Q_W and the consumer surplus from water is the large green area. The supply of diamonds in part (b) is perfectly inelastic at the quantity Q_D, so the price of a diamond is P_D and the consumer surplus from diamonds is the small green area. Water is cheap but brings a large consumer surplus, while diamonds are expensive but bring a small consumer surplus.

FIGURE 8.5 The Paradox of Value

(a) Water

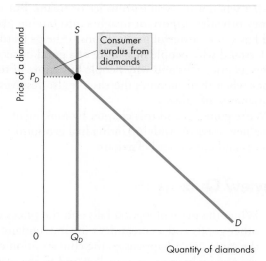

(b) Diamonds

Part (a) shows the demand for and supply of water. Supply is perfectly elastic at the price P_W. At this price, the quantity of water consumed is Q_W and consumer surplus is the large green triangle. Part (b) shows the demand for and supply of diamonds. Supply is perfectly inelastic at the quantity Q_D. At this quantity, the price of a diamond is P_D and consumer surplus is the small green triangle. Water is valuable—has a large consumer surplus—but cheap. Diamonds are less valuable than water—have a smaller consumer surplus—but are expensive.

 animation

Temperature: An Analogy

Utility is similar to temperature. Both are abstract concepts, and both have units of measurement that are arbitrary. You can't *observe* temperature. You can observe water turning to steam if it is hot enough or turning to ice if it is cold enough. And you can construct an instrument—a thermometer—that can help you to predict when such changes will occur. We call the scale on the thermometer *temperature* and we call the units of temperature *degrees*. But these degree units are arbitrary. We can use Celsius units or Fahrenheit units or some other units.

The concept of utility helps us to make predictions about consumption choices in much the same way that the concept of temperature helps us to make predictions about physical phenomena.

Admittedly, marginal utility theory does not enable us to predict how buying plans change with the same precision that a thermometer enables us to predict when water will turn to ice or steam. But the theory provides important insights into buying plans and has some powerful implications. It helps us to understand why people buy more of a good or service when its price falls and why people buy more of most goods when their incomes increase. It also resolves the paradox of value.

We're going to end this chapter by looking at some new ways of studying individual economic choices and consumer behaviour.

Review Quiz

1. When the price of a good falls and the prices of other goods and a consumer's income remain the same, what happens to the consumption of the good whose price has fallen and to the consumption of other goods?
2. Elaborate on your answer to the previous question by using demand curves. For which good does demand change and for which good does the quantity demanded change?
3. If a consumer's income increases and if all goods are normal goods, how does the quantity bought of each good change?
4. What is the paradox of value and how is the paradox resolved?
5. Why are utility and temperature similar?

myeconlab Work Study Plan 8.2 and get instant feedback.

Maximizing Utility in Markets for Recorded Music

Downloads Versus Discs

In 2007, total expenditure on recorded music was $10 billion, down from $14 billion in 2000. But the combined quantity of discs and downloads bought increased from 1 billion in 2000 to 1.8 billion in 2007 and the average price of a unit of recorded music fell from $14 to $5.50.

The average price fell because the mix of formats bought changed dramatically. In 2000, 1 billion CDs were bought; in 2007, only 0.5 billion CDs were bought and 1.3 billion music files were downloaded.

Figure 1 shows the longer history of the changing formats of recorded music.

The music that we buy isn't just one good—it is several goods. Singles and albums are different goods; downloads and discs are different goods; and downloads to a computer and downloads to a cell phone are different goods. There are five major categories (excluding DVDs and cassettes) and the table shows the quantities of each that we bought in 2007.

Format	Singles	Albums
	(millions in 2007)	
Disc	3	500
Download	800	40
Mobile	400	—

Source of data: Recording Industry Association of America.

Most people buy all their music in digital form, but many still buy physical CDs and some people buy both downloads and CDs.

We get utility from the singles and albums that we buy, and the more songs and albums we have, the more utility we get. But our marginal utility from songs and albums decreases as the quantity that we own increases.

We also get utility from convenience. A song that we can buy with a mouse click and play with the spin of a wheel is more convenient both to buy and to use than a song on a CD. The convenience of songs downloaded over the Internet means that, song for song, we get more utility from songs in this format than we get from physical CDs.

But most albums are still played at home on a CD player. So for most people, a physical CD is a more convenient medium for delivering an album. Album for album, people on average get more utility from a CD than from a download.

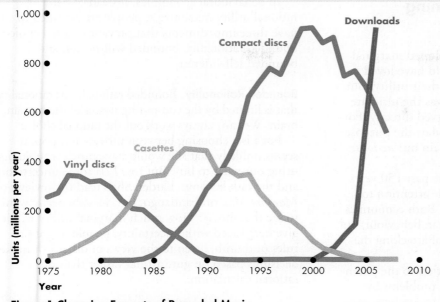

Figure 1 Changing Formats of Recorded Music

Source of data: www.swivel.com.

In the 1970s, recorded music came on vinyl discs. Cassette tapes gradually replaced vinyl, then compact discs gradually replaced cassette tapes, and today, digital files downloaded to computers and mobile devices are replacing physical CDs.

When we decide how many singles and albums to download and how many to buy on CD, we compare the marginal utility per dollar from each type of music in each format. We make the marginal utility per dollar from each type of music in each format equal, as the equations below show.

The market for single downloads has created an enormous consumer surplus. The table shows that the quantity of single downloads demanded at $0.99 each was 800 million in 2007, and the quantity of singles on a disc demanded at $4.75 a disc was 3 million in 2007. If we assume that $4.75 is the most that anyone would pay for a single download (probably an underestimate), the demand curve for single downloads is that shown in Fig. 2.

With the price of a single download at $0.99, consumer surplus (the area of the green triangle) is $1.5 billion.

Figure 2 The Demand for Single Downloads

$$\frac{MU_{single\ downloads}}{P_{single\ downloads}} = \frac{MU_{album\ downloads}}{P_{album\ downloads}} = \frac{MU_{physical\ singles}}{P_{physical\ singles}} = \frac{MU_{physical\ albums}}{P_{physical\ albums}} = \frac{MU_{mobile}}{P_{mobile}}$$

$$\frac{MU_{single\ downloads}}{\$0.99} = \frac{MU_{album\ downloads}}{\$10} = \frac{MU_{physical\ singles}}{\$4.75} = \frac{MU_{physical\ albums}}{\$15} = \frac{MU_{mobile}}{\$2.50}$$

New Ways of Explaining Consumer Choices

When William Stanley Jevons developed marginal utility theory in the 1860s, he would have loved to look inside people's brains to "see" their utility. But he believed that the human brain was the ultimate black box that could never be observed directly. For Jevons, and for most economists today, the purpose of marginal utility theory is to explain our *actions*, not what goes on inside our brains.

Economics has developed over the past 150 years with little help from and paying little attention to advances being made in psychology. Both economics and psychology seek to explain human behaviour, but they have developed different ways of attacking the challenge.

A few researchers *have* paid attention to the potential payoff from exploring economic problems by using the tools of psychology. These researchers, some economists and some psychologists, think that marginal utility theory is based on a view of how people make choices that attributes too much to reason and rationality. They propose an alternative approach based on the methods of psychology.

Other researchers, some economists and some neuroscientists, are using new tools to look inside the human brain and open up Jevons' "black box."

This section provides a very brief introduction to these new and exciting areas of economics. We'll explore the two related research agendas:

- Behavioural economics
- Neuroeconomics

Behavioural Economics

Behavioural economics studies the ways in which limits on the human brain's ability to compute and implement rational decisions influences economic behaviour—both the decisions that people make and the consequences of those decisions for the way markets work.

Behavioural economics starts with observed behaviour. It looks for anomalies—choices that do not seem to be rational. It then tries to account for the anomalies by using ideas developed by psychologists that emphasize features of the human brain that limit rational choice.

In behavioural economics, instead of being rational utility maximizers, people are assumed to have three impediments that prevent rational choice: bounded rationality, bounded will-power, and bounded self-interest.

Bounded Rationality Bounded rationality is rationality that is limited by the computing power of the human brain. We can't always work out the rational choice.

For Lisa, choosing between movies and pop, it seems unlikely that she would have much trouble figuring out what to buy. But toss Lisa some uncertainty and the task becomes harder. She's read the reviews of *Mamma Mia!* on Fandango, but does she really want to see that movie? How much marginal utility will it give her? Faced with uncertainty, people might use rules of thumb, listen to the views of others, or make decisions based on gut instinct rather than on rational calculation.

Bounded Will-Power Bounded will-power is the less-than-perfect will-power that prevents us from making a decision that we know, at the time of implementing the decision, we will later regret.

Lisa might be feeling particularly thirsty when she passes a pop vending machine. Under Lisa's rational utility-maximizing plan, she buys her pop at the discount store, where she gets it for the lowest possible price. Lisa has already bought her pop for this month, but it is at home. Spending $1 on a can now means giving up a movie later this month.

Lisa's rational choice is to ignore the temporary thirst and stick to her plan. But she might not possess the will-power to do so—sometimes she will and sometimes she won't.

Bounded Self-Interest Bounded self-interest is the limited self-interest that results in sometimes suppressing our own interests to help others.

A winter storm hits Newfoundland and Lisa, feeling sorry for the victims, donates $10 to a fundraiser. She now has only $30 to spend on movies and pop this month. The quantities that she buys are not, according to her utility schedule, the ones that maximize her utility.

The main applications of behavioural economics are in two areas: finance, where uncertainty is a key factor in decision making, and savings, where the future is a key factor.

But one behaviour observed by behavioural economists is more general and might affect your choices. It is called the endowment effect.

The Endowment Effect The endowment effect is the tendency for people to value something more highly simply because they own it. If you have allocated your income to maximize utility, the price you are willing to pay for a coffee mug should be the same as the price you would be willing to accept to give up an identical coffee mug that you own.

In experiments, students seem to display the endowment effect: The price they are willing to pay for a coffee mug is less than the price they would be willing to accept to give up an identical coffee mug that they own. Behavioural economists say that this behaviour contradicts marginal utility theory.

Neuroeconomics

Neuroeconomics is the study of the activity of the human brain when a person makes an economic decision. The discipline uses the observational tools and ideas of neuroscience to better understand economic decisions.

Neuroeconomics is an experimental discipline. In an experiment, a person makes an economic decision and the electrical or chemical activity of the person's brain is observed and recorded using the same type of equipment that neurosurgeons use to diagnose brain disorders.

The observations provide information about which regions of the brain are active at different points in the process of making an economic decision.

It has been observed that some economic decisions generate activity in the area of the brain (called the prefrontal cortex) where we store memories, analyze data, and anticipate the consequences of our actions. If people make rational utility-maximizing decisions, it is in this region of the brain that the decision occurs.

But some economic decisions generate activity in the region of the brain (called the hippocampus) where we store memories of anxiety and fear. Decisions that are influenced by activity in this part of the brain might be non-rational and driven by fear or panic.

Neuroeconomists are also able to observe the amount of a brain hormone (called dopamine), the quantity of which increases in response to pleasurable events and decreases in response to disappointing events. These observations might one day enable neuroeconomists to actually measure utility and shine a bright light inside what was once believed to be the ultimate black box.

Controversy

The new ways of studying consumer choice that we've briefly described here are being used more widely to study business decisions and decisions in financial markets, and this type of research is surely going to become more popular.

But behavioural economics and neuroeconomics generate controversy. Most economists hold the view of Jevons that the goal of economics is to explain the decisions that we observe people make, and not to explain what goes on inside people's heads.

Also, most economists would prefer to probe apparent anomalies more deeply and figure out why they are not anomalies after all.

Finally, economists point to the power of marginal utility theory and its ability to explain consumer choice and demand as well as resolve the paradox of value.

Review Quiz

1 Define behavioural economics.
2 What are the three limitations on human rationality that behavioural economics emphasizes?
3 Define neuroeconomics.
4 What do behavioural economics and neuro-economics seek to achieve?

 Work Study Plan 8.3 and get instant feedback.

You have now completed your study of the marginal utility theory and some new ideas about how people make economic choices. You can see marginal utility theory in action once again in *Reading Between the Lines* on pp. 196–197, where it is used to explain how changes in the prices of bread and vegetables have changed the quantities that we buy.

The Marginal Utility of Food

Brace Yourself, Canada, for Higher Grocery Bills

June 12, 2008

Any outsider looking at Canada's most recent consumer price index would be forgiven for concluding that we have somehow managed to dodge the food inflation bullet currently ricocheting around the world.

People in most countries are struggling with unprecedented price hikes in the most widely used foods. But a recent look at the cost of living in this country finds that the typical Canadian food basket in April 2008 was just 1.2 percent more expensive than it was a year earlier.

A little more than 1 percent in a whole year! Well done, Canada. ...

Well, it's time to put away the streamers, the experts say. The warning bells are already sounding. Analysts, farmers and grocery chains all agree that those checkout bills are about to get noticeably bigger.

A look inside the monthly price data from Statistics Canada quickly reveals some ... important anomalies.

Your daily bread

Let's start with our daily bread. As any regular food shopper knows, bread prices have been rising faster than, well, loaves of bread. StatsCan says a typical loaf costs 14 percent more than it did a year earlier. Macaroni is up 25 percent in the same period; the cost of flour grew by 18 percent.

Vegetarians rejoice

... Well, it turns out that the rising cost of pasta, bread and flour have largely been offset by big drops in the price of fresh produce. ... Oranges, grapefruits, apples, carrots, celery, mushrooms, onions, potatoes. You name the product and chances are Canadians have been paying less for it than they did a year ago. Fresh vegetable prices plunged 13 percent in one year, StatsCan said, while fresh fruit prices fell 4 percent. ...

How high will food prices rise?

Statistics Canada notes that this country overall is well positioned to weather the agricultural price jumps hitting the rest of the world. ... We spend an average of just 10 to 15 percent of our disposable income on food, depending on who does the analysis. In some developing countries, people spend upwards of 80 percent of their meagre income on food.

Essence of the Story

- The cost of the typical food basket in April 2008 was only 1 percent higher than in April 2007.

- In other countries, the prices of the most widely consumed foods have risen.

- In Canada, the prices of bread, macaroni, and flour have risen by 14 percent, 25 percent, and 18 percent respectively.

- The prices of fresh vegetables have fallen 13 percent in the last year.

- Canadians spend 10 to 15 percent of income on food.

Economic Analysis

- Consumers allocate their food budgets to maximize utility.

- Utility is maximized when the entire food budget is spent and the marginal utility per dollar from bread equals the marginal utility per dollar from vegetables.

- Call the price of bread P_B, the price of vegetables P_V, the quantity of bread Q_B, and the quantity of vegetables Q_V. The food budget is spent when

$$P_B Q_B + P_V Q_V = \text{Budget.}$$

- Call the marginal utility from bread MU_B and the marginal utility from vegetables MU_V. Utility is maximized when all the food budget is spent and when

$$\frac{MU_B}{P_B} = \frac{MU_V}{P_V}.$$

- From April 2007 to April 2008, the price of bread, P_B, rose by 14 percent while the price of vegetables, P_V, fell by 13 percent.

- The rise in P_B decreased the marginal utility per dollar from bread—MU_B/P_B fell. The fall in P_V increased the marginal utility per dollar from vegetables—MU_V/P_V rose.

- So, with no change in the quantities of bread and vegetables,

$$\frac{MU_B}{P_B} < \frac{MU_V}{P_V}.$$

- To maximize utility, consumers must buy less bread and more vegetables.

- Because marginal utility diminishes as more bread is consumed, the decrease in Q_B increases the marginal utility from bread and increases MU_B/P_B.

- Because marginal utility diminishes as more vgetables are consumed, the increase in Q_V decreases the marginal utility from vegetables and decreases MU_V/P_V.

- We can rearrange the above equation as

$$\frac{MU_B}{MU_V} < \frac{P_B}{P_V}.$$

- The rise in the price of bread and the fall in the price of vegetables means that P_B/P_V increased.

- To maximize utility, consumers adjust the quantities of bread and vegetables to make MU_B/MU_V increase. To do so, they substitute vegetables for bread.

- Despite the price changes, consumers spent the same amount on food in April 2008 as they spent in April 2007.

- As the price of bread rose, the quantity of bread bought decreased. But whether expenditure on bread increased or decreased depends on the price elasticity of demand for bread. The total revenue test tells us that if the demand for bread is price inelastic—which it most likely is—expenditure on bread increased.

- Similarly, as the price of vegetables fell, the quantity of vegetables bought increased. But again, whether expenditure on vegetables increased or decreased depends on the price elasticity of demand for vegetables.

- Again, we can use the total revenue test. Because expenditure on bread increased, expenditure on vegetables must have decreased. If a fall in price brings a decrease in expenditure, then demand is inelastic. We infer that the demand for vegetables, like the demand for bread, is price inelastic.

197

SUMMARY ◈

Key Points

Maximizing Utility (pp. 182–186)

- A household's preferences can be described by a utility schedule that lists the total utility and marginal utility derived from various quantities of goods and services consumed.
- The principle of diminishing marginal utility is that the marginal utility from a good or service decreases as consumption of the good or service increases.
- Total utility is maximized when all the available income is spent and when the marginal utility per dollar from all goods is equal.
- If the marginal utility per dollar for good A exceeds that for good B, total utility increases if the quantity purchased of good A increases and the quantity purchased of good B decreases.

Predictions of Marginal Utility Theory (pp. 187–193)

- Marginal utility theory predicts the law of demand. That is, other things remaining the same, the higher the price of a good, the smaller is the quantity demanded of that good.
- Marginal utility theory also predicts that, other things remaining the same, the larger the consumer's income, the larger is the quantity demanded of a normal good.
- Marginal utility theory resolves the paradox of value.
- Total value is *total* utility or consumer surplus. But price is related to *marginal* utility.
- Water, which we consume in large amounts, has a high total utility and a large consumer surplus, but the price of water is low and the marginal utility from water is low.
- Diamonds, which we buy in small quantities, have a low total utility and a small consumer surplus, but the price of a diamond is high and the marginal utility from diamonds is high.

New Ways of Explaining Consumer Choices
(pp. 194–195)

- Behavioural economics studies limits on the ability of the human brain to compute and implement rational decisions.
- Bounded rationality, bounded will-power, and bounded self-interest are believed to explain some choices.
- Neuroeconomics uses the ideas and tools of neuroscience to study the effects of economic events and choices inside the human brain.

Key Figures

Figure 8.1   Total Utility and Marginal Utility, 183
Figure 8.2   A Fall in the Price of a Movie, 188
Figure 8.3   A Rise in the Price of Pop, 189
Figure 8.4   The Effects of a Rise in Income, 190
Figure 8.5   The Paradox of Value, 191

Key Terms

Behavioural economics, 194
Consumer equilibrium, 184
Diminishing marginal utility, 183
Marginal utility, 182
Marginal utility per dollar, 184
Neuroeconomics, 195
Total utility, 182
Utility, 182

PROBLEMS and APPLICATIONS

myeconlab Work problems 1–9 in Chapter 8 Study Plan and get instant feedback.
Work problems 10–20 as Homework, a Quiz, or a Test if assigned by your instructor.

1. Max enjoys windsurfing and snorkeling. The table shows the total utility he gets from each activity.

Hours per day	Total utility from windsurfing	Total utility from snorkeling
1	120	40
2	220	76
3	300	106
4	360	128
5	396	140
6	412	150
7	422	158

   a. Find Max's marginal utility from windsurfing at each number of hours per day.
   b. Find Max's marginal utility from snorkeling at each number of hours per day.
   c. Do Max's marginal utility from windsurfing and from snorkeling obey the principle of diminishing marginal utility?
   d. Which does Max enjoy more: his 6th hour of windsurfing or his 6th hour of snorkeling?

2. Max in problem 1 has $35 a day to spend, and he can spend as much time as he likes on his leisure pursuits. Windsurfing equipment rents for $10 an hour, and snorkeling equipment rents for $5 an hour.

   a. Make a table that shows the various combinations of hours spent windsurfing and snorkeling that Max can afford.
   b. In your table, add two columns and list Max's marginal utility per dollar from windsurfing and from snorkeling.
   c. How long does Max spend windsurfing and how long does he spend snorkeling to maximize his total utility?
   d. If compared to c, Max spent a dollar more on windsurfing and a dollar less on snorkeling, by how much would his total utility change?
   e. If compared to c, Max spent a dollar less on windsurfing and a dollar more on snorkeling, by how much would his total utility change?
   f. Explain why, if Max equalized the marginal utility per hour from windsurfing and from snorkeling, he would *not* maximize his utility.

3. Max in problems 1 and 2 is offered a special deal on windsurfing equipment: a rental rate of $5 an hour. His income remains at $35 a day and the rental price of snorkeling equipment remains at $5 an hour.

   a. Make a table that shows the new combinations of hours spent windsurfing and snorkeling that Max can afford.
   b. In your table, list Max's marginal utility per dollar from windsurfing and snorkeling.
   c. How many hours does Max now spend windsurfing and how many hours does he spend snorkeling?

4. Given the information about Max in problems 1, 2, and 3,

   a. Find two points on Max's demand curve for rented windsurfing equipment.
   b. Draw Max's demand curve for rented windsurfing equipment.
   c. Is Max's demand for rented windsurfing equipment elastic or inelastic?

5. Max, with the utility schedules in problem 1, gets an increase in income from $35 to $55 a day. Windsurfing equipment rents for $10 an hour, and snorkeling equipment rents for $5 an hour. Show the effect of the increase in Max's income on Max's demand curve for

   a. Rented windsurfing equipment, and explain whether, for Max, windsurfing equipment is a normal good or an inferior good.
   b. Rented snorkeling equipment, and explain whether, for Max, snorkeling equipment is a normal good or an inferior good.

6. **Rising Food Costs Make Prices Hard to Swallow, BMO Says**
Consumers hit as Kraft and others pass on costs.

Rising grain and dairy prices are taking a growing slice out of household incomes as food giants such as Kraft Foods Inc. hike their prices to cover higher input costs. That slice is expected to continue to grow, according to Donald Coxe, global portfolio strategist at BMO Capital Markets.

"I just don't believe that we're going to, three years from now, have the share of people's spending budgets on foods consumed at home anywhere near as low as it is now," Mr. Coxe, who is based in Chicago, said yesterday. "There is nowhere to go but up for food prices, ... "

Mr. Coxe said it was not surprising food costs would once again account for an increasing share of household spending. ... Canadian households spent just over 10% of their total expenditures on food in 2006—the lowest proportion ever, Statistics Canada figures released in February showed. In the 1960s, food represented the largest proportion of household expenditure, at almost 19%.

Financial Post, July 29, 2008

a. Consumers spend part of their food budgets at the grocery stores and part at fast-food restaurants. What is the ratio of the marginal utility per dollar from food eaten at home to the marginal utility per dollar from food eaten at fast-food restaurants?

b. As "food giants such as Kraft Foods Inc. hike their prices," explain the initial effect on the ratio of the marginal utility per dollar from food eaten at home to the marginal utility per dollar from food eaten at fast-food restaurants.

c. As "food giants such as Kraft Foods Inc. hike their prices" and consumers do not change their food budgets, explain how consumers will change the quantity of food bought in grocery stores and the quantity bought in fast-food restaurants.

d. If Canadian households increase the proportion of their total expenditure on food as the price of food rises, does it mean that households do not maximize utility? Explain your answer.

e. If the price of food rises by 10 percent in three years and households increase the proportion of their total expenditure on food to 19 percent, calculate the price elasticity of demand for food and the cross elasticity of other goods with respect to food.

7. **Can Money Buy Happiness?**

"Whoever said money can't buy happiness isn't spending it right."... You know that there must be some connection between money and happiness. If there weren't, you'd be less likely to stay late at work (or even come in at all). ... "Once you get basic human needs met, a lot more money doesn't make a lot more happiness."...

Going from earning less than $20,000 a year to

making more than $50,000 makes you twice as likely to be happy, yet the payoff for then surpassing $90,000 is slight.

CNN, July 18, 2006

a. What does the fundamental assumption of marginal utility theory suggest about the connection between money and happiness?

b. Explain why this news clip is consistent with marginal utility theory.

8. Statistics Canada figures showed on Wednesday, July 30, 2008: The price of homogenized milk was 6.1 percent higher over the year, while the price of bread was up 18.4 percent, flour was up 40.9 percent and macaroni was up 45 percent. Chicken prices rose 4.6 percent over the year ended June, but the prices of most other meats were down, with producers finding it hard to pass on costs.

a. In terms of homogenized milk, what was the change in the relative prices of bread, macaroni, and chicken?

b. What do the prices per unit reported by Statistics Canada tell you about the marginal utility from a carton of milk, a loaf of bread, a serving of macaroni, and chicken?

9. **Exclusive Status: It's in the Bag; $52,500 Purses. 24 Worldwide. 1 in Washington.**

Forget your Coach purse. Put away your Kate Spade. Even Hermes's famous Birkin bag seems positively discount.

The Louis Vuitton Tribute Patchwork is this summer's ultimate status bag, ringing in at $52,500. And it is arriving in Washington. ...

The company ... [is] offering only five for sale in North America and 24 worldwide. ...

The Washington Post, August 21, 2007

a. Use marginal utility theory to explain the facts reported in the news clip.

b. If Louis Vuitton offered 500 Tribute Patchwork bags in North America and 2,400 worldwide, what do you predict would happen to the price that buyers would be willing to pay and what would happen to the consumer surplus?

c. If the Tribute Patchwork bag is copied and thousands are sold illegally, what do you predict would happen to the price that buyers would be willing to pay for a genuine bag and what would happen to the consumer surplus?

10. Cindy enjoys golf and tennis. The table shows the marginal utility she gets from each activity.

Hours per month	Marginal utility from golf	Marginal utility from tennis
1	80	40
2	60	36
3	40	30
4	30	10
5	20	5
6	10	2
7	6	1

Cindy has $70 a month to spend, and she can spend as much time as she likes on her leisure pursuits. The price of an hour of golf is $10, and the price of an hour of tennis is $5.

a. Make a table that shows the various combinations of hours spent playing golf and tennis that Cindy can afford.

b. In your table, add two columns and list Cindy's marginal utility per dollar from golf and from tennis.

c. How long does Cindy spend playing golf and how long does she spend playing tennis to maximize her utility?

d. Compared to c, if Cindy spent a dollar more on golf and a dollar less on tennis, by how much would her total utility change?

e. Compared to c, if Cindy spent a dollar less on golf and a dollar more on tennis, by how much would her total utility change?

f. Explain why, if Cindy equalized the marginal utility per hour of golf and tennis, she would *not* maximize her utility.

11. Cindy's tennis club raises its price of an hour of tennis to $10. The price of golf and Cindy's income remain the same.

a. Make a table that shows the combinations of hours spent playing golf and tennis that Cindy can now afford.

b. In your table, list Cindy's marginal utility per dollar from golf and from tennis.

c. How many hours does Cindy now spend playing golf and how many hours does she spend playing tennis?

12. Given the information in problems 10 and 11,

a. Find two points on Cindy's demand curve for tennis.

b. Draw Cindy's demand curve for tennis.

c. Is Cindy's demand for tennis elastic or inelastic?

d. Explain how Cindy's demand for golf changed when the price of tennis increased.

e. What is Cindy's cross elasticity of demand for golf with respect to the price of tennis?

f. Are tennis and golf substitutes or complements for Cindy?

13. Cindy, with the utility schedules in problem 10, loses her math tutoring job and her income falls to $35 a month. With golf at $10 an hour and tennis at $5 an hour, how does the decrease in Cindy's income change her demand for

a. Golf, and explain whether, for Cindy, golf is a normal good or an inferior good.

b. Tennis, and explain whether, for Cindy, tennis is a normal good or an inferior good.

14. Cindy in problem 10 takes a Club Med vacation, the cost of which includes unlimited activities. With no extra charge for golf and tennis, Cindy allocates a total of 4 hours a day playing them.

a. How many hours does Cindy play golf and how many hours does she play tennis?

b. What is Cindy's marginal utility from golf and from tennis?

c. Why does Cindy equalize the marginal utilities rather than the marginal utility per dollar from golf and from tennis?

15. Ben spends $50 a year on 2 bunches of flowers and $50 a year on 10,000 litres of tap water. Ben is maximizing utility and his marginal utility from water is 0.5 units per litre.

a. Are flowers or water more valuable to Ben?

b. Explain how Ben's expenditure on flowers and water illustrates the paradox of value.

16. **Blu-Ray Format Expected to Dominate, but When?**

Blu-ray stomped HD DVD to become the standard format for high-definition movie discs, but years may pass before it can claim victory over the good old DVD. ... "The group that bought $2,000, 40-inch TVs are the ones that will lead the charge. ... Everyone else will come along when the price comes down." ... Blu-ray machine prices are starting to drop. Wal-Mart Stores Inc. began stocking a $298 Magnavox model. ...

That's cheaper than most alternatives but a hefty price hike from a typical $50 DVD player.

CNN, June 2, 2008

a. What does marginal utility theory predict about the marginal utility from a Magnavox Blu-ray machine compared to the marginal utility from a typical DVD player?

b. What will have to happen to the marginal utility from a Blu-ray machine before it is able to "claim victory over the good old DVD"?

17. **Bling H₂O; Say What?**

Sold as a high-end, über-fashionable bottled water, Bling H₂O is the brainchild of Hollywood writer-producer Kevin G. Boyd. After spending time on studio lots observing celebrities treat their bottled water as a fashion accessory, Boyd decided to create the Cristal of bottled water. The brand features hand-crafted bottles decorated with Swarovski crystals and commands $35 each. At that price, the water is definitely going to be kept in the hands of those who are screaming to be noticed.

So if you're looking to impress folks with your ability to spend way too much on water, just pick up a bottle of Bling H₂O and watch them stifle their laughter as they buy themselves dinner instead.

TMZ, October 18, 2006

a. Assuming that the price of a bottle of Bling H₂0 is $35 in all the major cities, what might its popularity in Hollywood reveal about L.A. consumers' incomes or preferences relative to those in other cities?

b. Why might the marginal utility from a bottle of Bling H₂O decrease more rapidly than the marginal utility from ordinary bottled water?

18. **How to Buy Happiness. Cheap**

Sure, in any given country at any given point in time, the rich tend to be a bit happier than the poor. But across-the-board increases in living standards don't seem to make people any happier. Disposable income for the average American has grown about 80% since 1972, but the percentage describing themselves as "very happy" (roughly a third) has barely budged over the years. ... As living standards increase, most of us respond by raising our own standards. Things that once seemed luxuries now seem necessities. ... As a result, we're working harder than ever to buy stuff that satisfies us less and less.

CNN, October 1, 2004

a. According to this news clip, how do widespread increases in living standards influence total utility?

b. What does the news clip imply about how the total utility from consumption changes over time?

c. What does the news clip imply about how the marginal utility from consumption changes over time?

19. **Putting a Price on Human Life**

What's a healthy human life worth? According to Stanford and University of Pennsylvania Researchers, about $129,000. Using Medicare records on treatment costs for kidney dialysis as a benchmark, the authors tried to pinpoint the threshold beyond which ensuring another "quality" year of life was no longer financially worthwhile. The study comes amid debate over whether Medicare should start rationing health care on a cost-effectiveness basis. ...

Time, June 9, 2008

a. Why might it be necessary for Medicare to ration health care according to treatment that is "financially worthwhile" as opposed to providing as much treatment as is needed by a patient, regardless of costs?

b. What conflict might exist between a person's valuation of his or her own life and the rest of society's valuation of that person's life?

c. How does the potential conflict between self-interest and the social interest complicate setting a financial threshold for Medicare treatments?

20. Study *Reading Between the Lines* (pp. 196–197) about the marginal utility of food. Suppose that over the next year, the price of produce rises by an average of 5 percent while the price of bread continues to rise at 14 percent a year,

a. What happens to the ratio of the marginal utility from bread to the marginal utility of vegetables if consumers do not change the quantity of bread and vegetables that they consume?

b. How do consumers change the quantities of bread and vegetables that they consume to maximize utility?

c. Would you expect that the demand for food in Canada is more price elastic than the demand for food in an undeveloped country? Why?

9 Possibilities, Preferences, and Choices

After studying this chapter, you will be able to

- Describe a household's budget line and show how it changes when prices or income change
- Use indifference curves to map preferences and explain the principle of diminishing marginal rate of substitution
- Predict the effects of changes in prices and income on consumption choices
- Predict the effects of changes in wage rates on work–leisure choices

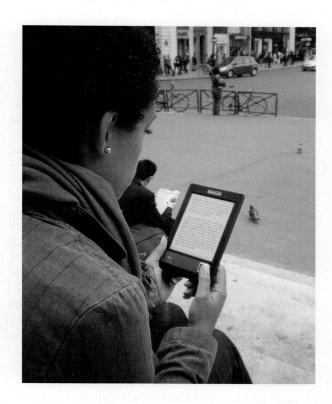

You buy your music online and play it on an iPod. And as the prices of a music download and an iPod have tumbled, the volume of downloads and sales of iPods have skyrocketed. But a similar change hasn't occurred in the way we buy and read our books. Sure, electronic textbooks—e-books—are widely available, and their prices have fallen. At the same time, the prices of old-tech, printed paper books have risen. Yet most students continue to buy printed textbooks. Why, when e-books are cheaper than printed books, have e-books not caught on and replaced printed books in the same way that the new music technologies have replaced physical discs?

Dramatic changes have occurred in the way we spend our time. The average workweek has fallen steadily from 70 hours a week in the nineteenth century to 33 hours a week today. While the average workweek is now much shorter than

it once was, far more people now have jobs. Why has the average workweek declined?

In this chapter, we're going to study a model of choice that predicts the effects of changes in prices and incomes on what people buy and the effects of changes in wage rates on how people allocate their time between leisure and work. At the end of the chapter, in *Reading Between the Lines*, we use the model to explain why e-books are having a hard time replacing printed books.

Consumption Possibilities

Consumption choices are limited by income and by prices. A household has a given amount of income to spend and cannot influence the prices of the goods and services it buys. A household's **budget line** describes the limits to its consumption choices.

Let's look at Lisa's budget line.[*] Lisa has an income of $40 a month to spend. She buys two goods: movies and pop. The price of a movie is $8, and the price of pop is $4 a case.

Figure 9.1 shows alternative combinations of movies and pop that Lisa can afford. In row *A*, she sees no movies and buys 10 cases of pop. In row *F*, she sees 5 movies and buys no pop. Both of these combinations of movies and pop exhaust the $40 available. Check that the combination of movies and pop in each of the other rows also exhausts Lisa's $40 of income. The numbers in the table and the points *A* through *F* in the graph describe Lisa's consumption possibilities.

Divisible and Indivisible Goods Some goods—called divisible goods—can be bought in any quantity desired. Examples are gasoline and electricity. We can best understand household choice if we suppose that all goods and services are divisible. For example, Lisa can see a half a movie a month on the average by seeing one movie every two months. When we think of goods as being divisible, the consumption possibilities are not only the points *A* through *F* shown in Fig. 9.1, but also all the intermediate points that form the line running from *A* to *F*. This line is Lisa's budget line.

Affordable and Unaffordable Quantities Lisa's budget line is a constraint on her choices. It marks the boundary between what is affordable and what is unaffordable. She can afford any point on the line and inside it. She cannot afford any point outside the line. The constraint on her consumption depends on the prices and her income, and the constraint changes when the price of a good or her income changes. To see how, we use a budget equation.

---

[*] If you have studied Chapter 8 on marginal utility theory, you have already met Lisa. This tale of her thirst for pop and zeal for movies will sound familiar to you—up to a point. But in this chapter, we're going to use a different method for representing preferences—one that does not require the idea of utility.

FIGURE 9.1 The Budget Line

Income	$40
Movies	$8 each
Pop	$4 a case

Consumption possibility	Movies (per month)	Pop (cases per month)
A	0	10
B	1	8
C	2	6
D	3	4
E	4	2
F	5	0

Lisa's budget line shows the boundary between what she can and cannot afford. The rows of the table list Lisa's affordable combinations of movies and pop when her income is $40, the price of pop is $4 a case, and the price of a movie is $8. For example, row *A* tells us that Lisa spends all of her $40 income when she buys 10 cases of pop and sees no movies. The figure graphs Lisa's budget line. Points *A* through *F* in the graph represent the rows of the table. For divisible goods, the budget line is the continuous line *AF*. To calculate the equation for Lisa's budget line, start with expenditure equal to income:

$$\$4Q_P + \$8Q_M = \$40.$$

Divide by $4 to obtain

$$Q_P + 2Q_M = 10.$$

Subtract $2Q_M$ from both sides to obtain

$$Q_P = 10 - 2Q_M.$$

myeconlab animation

Budget Equation

We can describe the budget line by using a *budget equation*. The budget equation starts with the fact that

$$\text{Expenditure} = \text{Income}.$$

Expenditure is equal to the sum of the price of each good multiplied by the quantity bought. For Lisa,

$$\text{Expenditure} = (\text{Price of pop} \times \text{Quantity of pop})$$
$$+ (\text{Price of a movie} \times \text{Quantity of movies}).$$

Call the price of pop P_P, the quantity of pop Q_P, the price of a movie P_M, the quantity of movies Q_M, and income Y. We can now write Lisa's budget equation as

$$P_P Q_P + P_M Q_M = Y.$$

Or, using the prices Lisa faces, $4 a case of pop and $8 a movie, and Lisa's income, $40, we get

$$\$4Q_P + \$8Q_M = \$40.$$

Lisa can choose any quantities of pop (Q_P) and movies (Q_M) that satisfy this equation. To find the relationship between these quantities, divide both sides of the equation by the price of pop (P_P) to get

$$Q_P + \frac{P_M}{P_P} \times Q_M = \frac{Y}{P_P}.$$

Now subtract the term $P_M/P_P \times Q_M$ from both sides of this equation to get

$$Q_P = \frac{Y}{P_P} - \frac{P_M}{P_P} \times Q_M.$$

For Lisa, income (Y) is $40, the price of a movie (P_M) is $8, and the price of pop (P_P) is $4 a case. So Lisa must choose the quantities of movies and pop to satisfy the equation

$$Q_P = \frac{\$40}{\$4} - \frac{\$8}{\$4} \times Q_M,$$

or

$$Q_P = 10 - 2Q_M.$$

To interpret the equation, look at the budget line in Fig. 9.1 and check that the equation delivers that budget line. First, set Q_M equal to zero. The budget equation tells us that Q_P, the quantity of pop, is Y/P_P, which is 10 cases. This combination of Q_M and Q_P is the one shown in row A of the table in Fig. 9.1. Next set Q_M equal to 5. Q_P now equals zero (row F of the table). Check that you can derive the other rows.

The budget equation contains two variables chosen by the household (Q_M and Q_P) and two variables that the household takes as given (Y/P_P and P_M/P_P). Let's look more closely at these variables.

Real Income A household's **real income** is its income expressed as a quantity of goods that the household can afford to buy. Expressed in terms of pop, Lisa's real income is Y/P_P. This quantity is the maximum quantity of pop that she can buy. It is equal to her money income divided by the price of pop. Lisa's money income is $40 and the price of pop is $4 a case, so her real income in terms of pop is 10 cases, which is shown in Fig. 9.1 as the point at which the budget line intersects the y-axis.

Relative Price A **relative price** is the price of one good divided by the price of another good. In Lisa's budget equation, the variable P_M/P_P is the relative price of a movie in terms of pop. For Lisa, P_M is $8 a movie and P_P is $4 a case, so P_M/P_P is equal to 2 cases of pop per movie. That is, to see 1 movie, Lisa must give up 2 cases of pop.

You've just calculated Lisa's opportunity cost of seeing a movie. Recall that the opportunity cost of an action is the best alternative forgone. For Lisa to see 1 more movie a month, she must forgo 2 cases of pop. You've also calculated Lisa's opportunity cost of pop. For Lisa to buy 2 more cases of pop a month, she must forgo seeing 1 movie. So her opportunity cost of 2 cases of pop is 1 movie.

The relative price of a movie in terms of pop is the magnitude of the slope of Lisa's budget line. To calculate the slope of the budget line, recall the formula for slope (see the Chapter 1 Appendix): Slope equals the change in the variable measured on the y-axis divided by the change in the variable measured on the x-axis as we move along the line. In Lisa's case (Fig. 9.1), the variable measured on the y-axis is the quantity of pop and the variable measured on the x-axis is the quantity of movies. Along Lisa's budget line, as pop decreases from 10 to 0 cases, movies increase from 0 to 5. So the magnitude of the slope of the budget line is 10 cases divided by 5 movies, or 2 cases of pop per movie. The magnitude of this slope is exactly the same as the relative price we've just calculated. It is also the opportunity cost of a movie.

A Change in Prices When prices change, so does the budget line. The lower the price of the good measured on the x-axis, other things remaining the same, the flatter is the budget line. For example, if the price

FIGURE 9.2 Changes in Prices and Income

(a) A change in price

(b) A change in income

In part (a), the price of a movie changes. A fall in the price from $8 to $4 rotates the budget line outward and makes it flatter. A rise in the price from $8 to $16 rotates the budget line inward and makes it steeper.

In part (b), income falls from $40 to $20 while the prices of movies and pop remain the same. The budget line shifts leftward, but its slope does not change.

 animation

of a movie falls from $8 to $4, real income in terms of pop does not change but the relative price of a movie falls. The budget line rotates outward and becomes flatter, as Fig. 9.2(a) illustrates. The higher the price of the good measured on the x-axis, other things remaining the same, the steeper is the budget line. For example, if the price of a movie rises from $8 to $16, the relative price of a movie increases. The budget line rotates inward and becomes steeper, as Fig. 9.2(a) illustrates.

A Change in Income A change in money income changes real income but does not change the relative price. The budget line shifts, but its slope does not change. An increase in money income increases real income and shifts the budget line rightward. A decrease in money income decreases real income and shifts the budget line leftward.

Figure 9.2(b) shows the effect of a change in money income on Lisa's budget line. The initial budget line when Lisa's income is $40 is the same as in Fig. 9.1. The new budget line shows how much Lisa can buy if her income falls to $20 a month. The two budget lines have the same slope because the relative price is the same. The new budget line is closer to the origin because Lisa's real income has decreased.

Review Quiz

1 What does a household's budget line show?
2 How does the relative price and a household's real income influence its budget line?
3 If a household has an income of $40 and buys only bus rides at $2 each and magazines at $4 each, what is the equation of the household's budget line?
4 If the price of one good changes, what happens to the relative price and the slope of the household's budget line?
5 If a household's money income changes and prices do not change, what happens to the household's real income and budget line?

myeconlab   Work Study Plan 9.1 and get instant feedback.

We've studied the limits to what a household can consume. Let's now learn how we can describe preferences and make a map that contains a lot of information about a household's preferences.

Preferences and Indifference Curves

You are going to discover a very neat idea: that of drawing a map of a person's preferences. A preference map is based on the intuitively appealing idea that people can sort all the possible combinations of goods into three groups: preferred, not preferred, and indifferent. To make this idea more concrete, let's ask Lisa to tell us how she ranks various combinations of movies and pop.

Figure 9.3 shows part of Lisa's answer. She tells us that she currently sees 2 movies and buys 6 cases of pop a month at point C. She then lists all the combinations of movies and pop that she says are just as acceptable to her as her current situation. When we plot these combinations of movies and pop, we get the green curve in Fig. 9.3(a). This curve is the key element in a preference map and is called an indifference curve.

An **indifference curve** is a line that shows combinations of goods among which a consumer is *indifferent*. The indifference curve in Fig. 9.3(a) tells us that Lisa is just as happy to see 2 movies and buy 6 cases of pop a month at point C as she is to have the combination of movies and pop at point G or at any other point along the curve.

Lisa also says that she prefers all the combinations of movies and pop above the indifference curve in Fig. 9.3(a)—the yellow area—to those on the indifference curve. And she prefers any combination on the indifference curve to any combination in the grey area below the indifference curve.

The indifference curve in Fig. 9.3(a) is just one of a whole family of such curves. This indifference curve appears again in Fig. 9.3(b), labelled I_1. The curves labelled I_0 and I_2 are two other indifference curves. Lisa prefers any point on indifference curve I_2 to any point on indifference curve I_1, and she prefers any point on I_1 to any point on I_0. We refer to I_2 as being a higher indifference curve than I_1 and I_1 as being higher than I_0.

A preference map is a series of indifference curves that resemble the contour lines on a map. By looking at the shape of the contour lines on a map, we can draw conclusions about the terrain. Similarly, by looking at the shape of the indifference curves, we can draw conclusions about a person's preferences.

Let's learn how to "read" a preference map.

FIGURE 9.3   A Preference Map

(a) An indifference curve

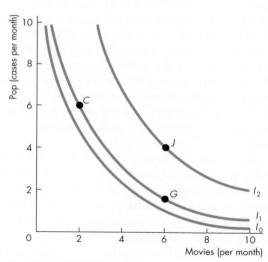

(b) Lisa's preference map

Part (a) shows one of Lisa's indifference curves. She is indifferent between point C (with 2 movies and 6 cases of pop) and all other points on the green indifference curve, such as G. She prefers points above the indifference curve (in the yellow area) to points on it, and she prefers points on the indifference curve to points below it (in the grey area).

Part (b) shows three of the indifference curves—I_0, I_1, and I_2—in Lisa's preference map. She prefers point J to point C or G, and she prefers all the points on I_2 to those on I_1.

 animation

Marginal Rate of Substitution

The **marginal rate of substitution** (*MRS*) is the rate at which a person will give up good *y* (the good measured on the *y*-axis) to get an additional unit of good *x* (the good measured on the *x*-axis) while remaining indifferent (remaining on the same indifference curve). The magnitude of the slope of an indifference curve measures the marginal rate of substitution.

- If the indifference curve is *steep*, the marginal rate of substitution is *high*. The person is willing to give up a large quantity of good *y* to get an additional unit of good *x* while remaining indifferent.
- If the indifference curve is *flat*, the marginal rate of substitution is *low*. The person is willing to give up a small amount of good *y* to get an additional unit of good *x* while remaining indifferent.

Figure 9.4 shows you how to calculate the marginal rate of substitution. At point *C* on indifference curve I_1, Lisa buys 6 cases of pop and sees 2 movies. Her marginal rate of substitution is the magnitude of the slope of the indifference curve at point *C*. To measure this magnitude, place a straight line against, or tangent to, the indifference curve at point *C*. Along that line, as the quantity of pop decreases by 10 cases, the number of movies increases by 5—or 2 cases per movie. At point *C*, Lisa is willing to give up pop for movies at the rate of 2 cases per movie—a marginal rate of substitution of 2.

At point *G* on indifference curve I_1, Lisa buys 1.5 cases of pop and sees 6 movies. Her marginal rate of substitution is measured by the slope of the indifference curve at point *G*. That slope is the same as the slope of the tangent to the indifference curve at point *G*. Now, as the quantity of pop decreases by 4.5 cases, the number of movies increases by 9—or 1/2 case per movie. At point *G*, Lisa is willing to give up pop for movies at the rate of 1/2 case per movie—a marginal rate of substitution of 1/2.

As Lisa sees more movies and buys less pop, her marginal rate of substitution diminishes. Diminishing marginal rate of substitution is the key assumption about preferences. A **diminishing marginal rate of substitution** is a general tendency for a person to be willing to give up less of good *y* to get one more unit of good *x*, while at the same time remaining indifferent as the quantity of *x* increases. In Lisa's case, she is less willing to give up pop to see one more movie as the number of movies she sees increases.

FIGURE 9.4 The Marginal Rate of Substitution

The magnitude of the slope of an indifference curve is called the marginal rate of substitution (*MRS*). The red line at point *C* tells us that Lisa is willing to give up 10 cases of pop to see 5 movies. Her marginal rate of substitution at point *C* is 10 divided by 5, which equals 2. The red line at point *G* tells us that Lisa is willing to give up 4.5 cases of pop to see 9 movies. Her marginal rate of substitution at point *G* is 4.5 divided by 9, which equals 1/2.

myeconlab animation

Your Own Diminishing Marginal Rate of Substitution

Think about your own diminishing marginal rate of substitution. Imagine that in a week, you drink 10 cases of pop and see no movies. Most likely, you are willing to give up a lot of pop so that you can see just 1 movie. But now imagine that in a week, you buy 1 case of pop and see 6 movies. Most likely, you will now not be willing to give up much pop to see a seventh movie. As a general rule, the greater the number of movies you see, the smaller is the quantity of pop you are willing to give up to see one additional movie.

The shape of a person's indifference curves incorporates the principle of the diminishing marginal rate of substitution because the curves are bowed towards the origin. The tightness of the bend of an indifference curve tells us how willing a person is to substitute one good for another while remaining indifferent. Let's look at some examples that make this point clear.

Degree of Substitutability

Most of us would not regard movies and pop as being *close* substitutes, but they are substitutes. No matter how much you love pop, some increase in the number of movies you see will compensate you for being deprived of a can of pop. Similarly, no matter how much you love going to the movies, some number of cans of pop will compensate you for being deprived of seeing one movie.

A person's indifference curves for movies and pop might look something like those for most ordinary goods and services, shown in Fig. 9.5(a).

Close Substitutes
Some goods substitute so easily for each other that most of us do not even notice which we are consuming. The different brands of marker pens and pencils are examples. Most people don't care which brand of these items they use or where they buy them. A marker pen from the campus bookstore is just as good as one from the local grocery store. You would be willing to forgo a pen from the campus store if you could get one more pen from the local grocery

store. When two goods are perfect substitutes, their indifference curves are straight lines that slope downward, as Fig. 9.5(b) illustrates. The marginal rate of substitution is constant.

Complements
Some goods do not substitute for each other at all. Instead, they are complements. The complements in Fig. 9.5(c) are left and right running shoes. Indifference curves of perfect complements are L-shaped. One left running shoe and one right running shoe are as good as one left shoe and two right shoes. Having two of each is preferred to having one of each, but having two of one and one of the other is no better than having one of each.

The extreme cases of perfect substitutes and perfect complements shown here don't often happen in reality, but they do illustrate that the shape of the indifference curve shows the degree of substitutability between two goods. The closer the two goods are to perfect substitutes, the closer the marginal rate of substitution is to being constant (a straight line), rather than diminishing (a curved line). Indifference

FIGURE 9.5   The Degree of Substitutability

(a) Ordinary goods

(b) Perfect substitutes

(c) Perfect complements

The shape of the indifference curves reveals the degree of substitutability between two goods. Part (a) shows the indifference curves for two ordinary goods: movies and pop. To drink less pop and remain indifferent, one must see more movies. The number of movies that compensates for a reduction in pop increases as less pop is consumed. Part (b) shows the indifference curves for two perfect substitutes. For

the consumer to remain indifferent, one fewer marker pen from the local grocery store must be replaced by one extra marker pen from the campus bookstore. Part (c) shows two perfect complements—goods that cannot be substituted for each other at all. Having two left running shoes with one right running shoe is no better than having one of each. But having two of each is preferred to having one of each.

"With the pork I'd recommend an Alsatian white or a Coke."

© The New Yorker Collection 1988, Robert Weber from cartoonbank.com. All Rights Reserved.

curves for poor substitutes are tightly curved and lie between the shapes of those shown in Figs. 9.5(a) and 9.5(c).

As you can see in the cartoon, according to the waiter's preferences, Coke and Alsatian white wine are perfect substitutes and each is a complement of pork. We hope the customers agree with him.

Review Quiz

1 What is an indifference curve and how does a preference map show preferences?
2 Why does an indifference curve slope downward and why is it bowed towards the origin?
3 What do we call the magnitude of the slope of an indifference curve?
4 What is the key assumption about a consumer's marginal rate of substitution?

 Work Study Plan 9.2 and get instant feedback.

The two components of the model of household choice are now in place: the budget line and the preference map. We will now use these components to work out a household's choice and to predict how choices change when prices and income change.

Predicting Consumer Choices

We are now going to predict the quantities of movies and pop that Lisa chooses to buy. We're also going to see how these quantities change when a price changes or when Lisa's income changes. Finally, we're going to see how the *substitution effect* and the *income effect*, two ideas that you met in Chapter 3 (see p. 59), guarantee that for a normal good, the demand curve slopes downward.

Best Affordable Choice

When Lisa makes her best affordable choice of movies and pop, she spends all her income and is on her highest attainable indifference curve. Figure 9.6 illustrates this choice: The budget line is from Fig. 9.1 and the indifference curves are from Fig. 9.3(b). Lisa's best affordable choice is 2 movies and 6 cases of pop at point C—the *best affordable point.*

FIGURE 9.6 The Best Affordable Choice

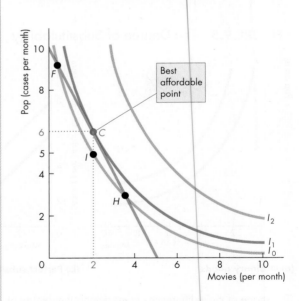

Lisa's best affordable choice is at point C, the point on her budget line and on her highest attainable indifference curve. At point C, Lisa's marginal rate of substitution between movies and pop (the magnitude of the slope of the indifference curve I_1) equals the relative price of movies and pop (the slope of the budget line).

myeconlab animation

On the Budget Line The best affordable point is on the budget line. For every point inside the budget line, such as point *I*, there are points on the budget line that Lisa prefers. For example, she prefers all the points on the budget line between *F* and *H* to point *I*, so she chooses a point on the budget line.

On the Highest Attainable Indifference Curve Every point on the budget line lies on an indifference curve. For example, points *F* and *H* lie on the indifference curve I_0. By moving along her budget line from either *F* or *H* towards *C*, Lisa reaches points on ever higher indifference curves that she prefers to points *F* or *H*. When Lisa gets to point *C*, she is on the highest attainable indifference curve.

Marginal Rate of Substitution Equals Relative Price At point *C*, Lisa's marginal rate of substitution between movies and pop (the magnitude of the slope of the indifference curve) is equal to the relative price of movies and pop (the magnitude of the slope of the budget line). Lisa's willingness to pay for a movie equals her opportunity cost of a movie.

Let's now see how Lisa's choices change when a price changes.

A Change in Price

The effect of a change in the price on the quantity of a good consumed is called the **price effect**. We will use Fig. 9.7(a) to work out the price effect of a fall in the price of a movie. We start with the price of a movie at $8, the price of pop at $4 a case, and Lisa's income at $40 a month. In this situation, she buys 6 cases of pop and sees 2 movies a month at point *C*.

Now suppose that the price of a movie falls to $4. With a lower price of a movie, the budget line rotates outward and becomes flatter. The new budget line is the darker orange one in Fig. 9.7(a). For a refresher on how a price change affects the budget line, check back to Fig. 9.2(a).

Lisa's best affordable point is now point *J*, where she sees 6 movies and drinks 4 cases of pop. Lisa drinks less pop and watches more movies now that movies are cheaper. She cuts her pop purchases from 6 to 4 cases and increases the number of movies she sees from 2 to 6 a month. When the price of a movie falls and the price of pop and her income remain constant, Lisa substitutes movies for pop.

FIGURE 9.7 Price Effect and Demand Curve

(a) Price effect

(b) Demand curve

Initially, Lisa's best affordable point is *C* in part (a). If the price of a movie falls from $8 to $4, Lisa's best affordable point is *J*. The move from *C* to *J* is the price effect.

At a price of $8 a movie, Lisa sees 2 movies a month, at point *A* in part (b). At a price of $4 a movie, she sees 6 movies a month, at point *B*. Lisa's demand curve for movies traces out her best affordable quantity of movies as the price of a movie varies.

The Demand Curve In Chapter 3, we asserted that the demand curve slopes downward. We can now derive a demand curve from a consumer's budget line and indifference curves. By doing so, we can see that the law of demand and the downward-sloping demand curve are consequences of a consumer's choosing her or his best affordable combination of goods.

To derive Lisa's demand curve for movies, lower the price of a movie and find her best affordable point at different prices. We've just done this for two movie prices in Fig. 9.7(a). Figure 9.7(b) highlights these two prices and two points that lie on Lisa's demand curve for movies. When the price of a movie is $8, Lisa sees 2 movies a month at point A. When the price falls to $4, she increases the number of movies she sees to 6 a month at point B. The demand curve is made up of these two points plus all the other points that tell us Lisa's best affordable quantity of movies at each movie price, with the price of pop and Lisa's income remaining the same. As you can see, Lisa's demand curve for movies slopes downward—the lower the price of a movie, the more movies she sees. This is the law of demand.

Next, let's see how Lisa changes her purchases of movies and pop when her income changes.

A Change in Income

The effect of a change in income on buying plans is called the **income effect**. Let's work out the income effect by examining how buying plans change when income changes and prices remain constant. Figure 9.8 shows the income effect when Lisa's income falls. With an income of $40, the price of a movie at $4, and the price of pop at $4 a case, Lisa's best affordable point is J—she buys 6 movies and 4 cases of pop. If her income falls to $28, her best affordable point is K—she sees 4 movies and buys 3 cases of pop. When Lisa's income falls, she buys less of both goods. Movies and pop are normal goods.

The Demand Curve and the Income Effect A change in income leads to a shift in the demand curve, as shown in Fig. 9.8(b). With an income of $40, Lisa's demand curve for movies is D_0, the same as in Fig. 9.7(b). But when her income falls to $28, she plans to see fewer movies at each price, so her demand curve shifts leftward to D_1.

FIGURE 9.8 Income Effect and Change in Demand

(a) Income effect

(b) Demand curve for movies

A change in income shifts the budget line, changes the best affordable point, and changes demand.

In part (a), when Lisa's income decreases from $40 to $28, she sees fewer movies and buys less pop.

In part (b), when Lisa's income is $40, her demand curve for movies is D_0. When Lisa's income falls to $28, her demand curve for movies shifts leftward to D_1. For Lisa, going to the movies is a normal good. Her demand for movies decreases because she now sees fewer movies at each price.

myeconlab animation

Substitution Effect and Income Effect

For a normal good, a fall in its price *always* increases the quantity bought. We can prove this assertion by dividing the price effect into two parts:

- Substitution effect
- Income effect

Figure 9.9(a) shows the price effect, and in Fig. 9.9(b) we separate the price effect into its two parts.

Substitution Effect The **substitution effect** is the effect of a change in price on the quantity bought when the consumer (hypothetically) remains indifferent between the original situation and the new one. To work out Lisa's substitution effect when the price of a movie falls, we cut her income by enough to keep her on the same indifference curve as before.

When the price of a movie falls from $8 to $4, suppose (hypothetically) that we cut Lisa's income to $28. What's special about $28? It is the income that is just enough, at the new price of a movie, to keep Lisa's best affordable point on the same indifference curve as her original point *C*. Lisa's budget line is now the light orange line in Fig. 9.9(b). With the lower price of a movie and a smaller income, Lisa's best affordable point is *K* on indifference curve I_1. The move from *C* to *K* along indifference curve I_1 is the substitution effect of the price change. The substitution effect of the fall in the price of a movie is an increase in the quantity of movies from 2 to 4. The direction of the substitution effect never varies: When the relative price of a good falls, the consumer substitutes more of that good for the other good.

Income Effect To calculate the substitution effect, we gave Lisa a $12 pay cut. To calculate the income effect, we give Lisa back her $12. The $12 increase in income shifts Lisa's budget line outward, as shown in Fig. 9.9(b). The slope of the budget line does not change because both prices remain the same. This change in Lisa's budget line is similar to the one illustrated in Fig. 9.8. As Lisa's budget line shifts outward, her consumption possibilities expand and her best affordable point becomes *J* on indifference curve I_2. The move from *K* to *J* is the income effect of the price change. In this example, as Lisa's income increases, she sees more movies. For Lisa, a movie is a normal good. For a normal good, the income effect reinforces the substitution effect.

FIGURE 9.9 Substitution Effect and Income Effect

(a) Price effect

(b) Substitution effect and income effect

The price effect in part (a) is separated into a substitution effect and an income effect in part (b).

To isolate the substitution effect, we confront Lisa with the new price but keep her on her original indifference curve, I_1. The substitution effect is the move from *C* to *K*.

To isolate the income effect, we confront Lisa with the new price of movies but increase her income so that she can move from the original indifference curve, I_1, to the new one, I_2. The income effect is the move from *K* to *J*.

Inferior Goods The example that we have just studied is that of a change in the price of a normal good. The effect of a change in the price of an inferior good is different. Recall that an inferior good is one whose consumption decreases as income increases. For an inferior good, the income effect is negative and a lower price does not always lead to an increase in the quantity demanded. The lower price has a substitution effect that increases the quantity demanded, but a negative income effect that reduces the demand for the inferior good. The income effect works in the opposite direction to and offsets the substitution effect to some degree. If the negative income effect exceeded the positive substitution effect, the demand curve would slope upward. This case does not appear to occur in the real world.

Back to the Facts

We started this chapter by observing how the way we buy music has changed in recent years. The indifference curve model explains those changes. The best affordable choices determine spending patterns. Changes in prices and incomes change the best affordable choices and change consumption patterns.

Review Quiz

1 When a consumer chooses the combination of goods and services to buy, what is she or he trying to achieve?
2 Explain the conditions that are met when a consumer has found the best affordable combination of goods to buy. (Use the terms budget line, marginal rate of substitution, and relative price in your explanation.)
3 If the price of a normal good falls, what happens to the quantity demanded of that good?
4 Into what two effects can we divide the effect of a price change?
5 For a normal good, does the income effect reinforce the substitution effect or does it partly offset the substitution effect?

 Work Study Plan 9.3 and get instant feedback.

The model of household choice can explain many other household choices. Let's look at one of them.

◆ Work–Leisure Choices

People make many choices other than those about how to spend their income on the various goods and services available. Economists use the indifference curve model to understand many other choices, one of which is how to allocate time between working and leisure activities. This choice determines a person's supply of labour. Let's study this choice.

Labour Supply

Every week, we allocate our 168 hours between working—called *labour*—and all other activities—called *leisure*. How do we decide how to allocate our time between labour and leisure? We can answer this question by using the theory of household choice.

The more hours we spend on *leisure,* the smaller is our income. The relationship between leisure and income is described by an *income-time budget line.* Figure 9.10(a) shows Lisa's income-time budget line. If Lisa devotes the entire week to leisure—168 hours—she has no income and is at point Z. By supplying labour in exchange for a wage, she can convert hours into income along the income-time budget line. The slope of that line is determined by the hourly wage rate. If the wage rate is $5 an hour, Lisa faces the flattest budget line. If the wage rate is $10 an hour, she faces the middle budget line. And if the wage rate is $15 an hour, she faces the steepest budget line.

Lisa "buys" leisure by not supplying labour and by forgoing income. The opportunity cost of an hour of leisure is the hourly wage rate forgone.

Figure 9.10(a) also shows Lisa's indifference curves for income and leisure. Lisa chooses her best attainable point. This choice of income and time allocation is just like her choice of movies and pop. She gets onto the highest possible indifference curve by making her marginal rate of substitution between income and leisure equal to her wage rate.

Lisa's choice depends on the wage rate she can earn. At a wage rate of $5 an hour, Lisa chooses point A and works 20 hours a week (168 minus 148) for an income of $100 a week. At a wage rate of $10 an hour, she chooses point B and works 35 hours a week (168 minus 133) for an income of $350 a week. And at a wage rate of $15 an hour, she chooses point C and works 30 hours a week (168 minus 138) for an income of $450 a week.

FIGURE 9.10 The Supply of Labour

(a) Time allocation decision

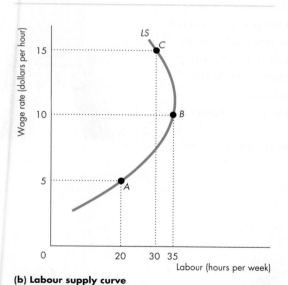

(b) Labour supply curve

In part (a), at a wage rate of $5 an hour, Lisa takes 148 hours of leisure and works 20 hours a week at point A. If the wage rate increases from $5 to $10 an hour, she decreases her leisure to 133 hours and increases her work to 35 hours a week at point B. But if the wage rate increases from $10 to $15 an hour, Lisa *increases* her leisure to 138 hours and *decreases* her work to 30 hours a week at point C.

Part (b) shows Lisa's labour supply curve. Points A, B, and C on the supply curve correspond to Lisa's choices in part (a).

 animation

The Labour Supply Curve

Figure 9.10(b) shows Lisa's labour supply curve. This curve shows that as the wage rate increases from $5 an hour to $10 an hour, Lisa increases the quantity of labour supplied from 20 hours a week to 35 hours a week. But when the wage rate increases to $15 an hour, she decreases her quantity of labour supplied to 30 hours a week.

Lisa's supply of labour is similar to that described for the economy as a whole at the beginning of this chapter. As wage rates have increased, the workweek has shortened. At first, this pattern seems puzzling. We've seen that the wage rate is the opportunity cost of leisure, so a higher wage rate means a higher opportunity cost of leisure. This fact on its own leads to a decrease in leisure and an increase in work hours. But instead, we've cut our work hours. Why? Because our incomes have increased. As the wage rate increases, incomes increase, so people demand more of all normal goods. Leisure is a normal good, so as incomes increase, people demand more leisure.

The higher wage rate has both a *substitution effect* and an *income effect*. The higher wage rate increases the opportunity cost of leisure and so leads to a substitution effect away from leisure. The higher wage rate increases income and so leads to an income effect towards more leisure. This outcome of rational household choice explains why the average workweek has fallen steadily as wage rates have increased. With higher wage rates, people have decided to use their higher incomes in part to "buy" more leisure.

Review Quiz

1 What is the opportunity cost of leisure?
2 Why might a rise in the wage rate lead to an increase in leisure and a decrease in work hours?

myeconlab Work Study Plan 9.4 and get instant feedback.

◆ *Reading Between the Lines* on pp. 216–217 shows you how the theory of household choice explains why e-books have not taken off, and why most people continue to buy their books in traditional paper format.

In the chapters that follow, we study the choices that firms make in their pursuit of profit and how those choices determine the supply of goods and services and the demand for productive resources.

Paper Books Versus e-Books

Are Books Passé?

September 6, 2007

Technology evangelists have predicted the emergence of electronic books for as long as they have envisioned flying cars and video phones. It is an idea that has never caught on with mainstream book buyers. ...

In October, the online retailer Amazon.com will unveil the Kindle, an electronic book reader that has been the subject of industry speculation for a year, according to several people who have tried the device and are familiar with Amazon's plans. The Kindle will be priced at $400 to $500 and will wirelessly connect to an e-book store on Amazon's site. ...

Hopes for e-books began to revive last year with the introduction of the widely marketed Sony Reader. Sony's $300 gadget, the size of a trade paperback, has a six-inch screen, enough memory to hold 80 books and a battery that lasts for 7,500 page turns, according to the company. It uses screen display technology from E Ink, a company based in Cambridge, Mass., that emerged from the Media Lab at the Massachusetts Institute of Technology and creates power-efficient digital screens that uncannily mimic the appearance of paper. ...

Essence of the Story

- Electronic books have not displaced paper books with mainstream book buyers.

- Amazon.com sells an electronic book reader called Kindle that wirelessly connects to Amazon's e-book store.

- Sony sells the Sony Reader, an electronic book reader the size of a paperback that mimics the appearance of paper, priced at $300

Economic Analysis

- Print books and e-books are substitutes although for most people, they are extremely poor substitutes.

- For a committed print-book lover, no quantity of e-books can compensate for a print book—the marginal rate of substitution between print books and e-books is zero.

- Beth is a print-book lover and Fig. 1 shows her indifference curves for print books and e-books.

- With print books on the x-axis, Beth's indifference curves are vertical. They tell us that Beth prefers more print books but gets no benefit from e-books.

- Beth's annual book budget is $500. The price of an e-book reader is $360 (the current price of the Kindle reader). The price of an e-book is $10 and the price of a print book is $20.

- We'll assume that an e-book reader has only a one-year life. (Buyers know they'll want the next generation improved reader next year).

- The orange line is Beth's budget line if she buys a reader. She can afford 14 e-books if she buys no print books ($360 + (14 × $10) = $500) and along this line, by forgoing 2 e-books she can buy 1 print book.

- If Beth doesn't buy an e-book reader, she buys no e-books and can afford 25 print books ($500 ÷ $20 = 25). The red dot shows this affordable point.

- The red dot is also Beth's best affordable choice because this choice gets her on to her highest attainable indifference curve I2.

- Andy differs from Beth: He thinks that print books and e-books are perfect substitutes. But he also likes music and buys albums. Figure 2 shows Andy's indifference curves for books (all types) and albums.

- Andy's annual budget for albums and books is $720. The price of an album is $10 and the prices of an e-book reader, an e-book, and a print book are the same as those that Beth faces.

- Figure 2 shows Andy's two budget lines: one if he buys only e-books and albums and another if he buys only print books and albums.

- If Andy buys e-books, he must spend $360 on a reader, which leaves him with $360 for albums and e-books. If he buys 20 e-books, he can afford 16 albums. [(20 × $10) + (16 × $10) = $360].

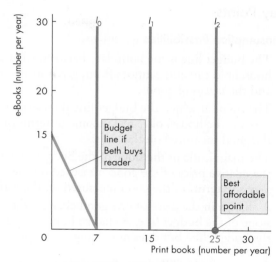

Figure 1 Print books versus e-books for a print-book lover

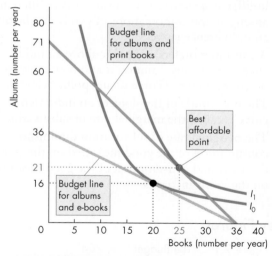

Figure 2 Books versus albums

- If Andy buys print books and albums, he can afford 25 print books and 22 albums [(25 × $20) + (22 × $10) = $720].

- Andy's best affordable choice is 25 print books and 22 albums.

- So even Andy who thinks that e-books and print books are perfect substitutes doesn't buy e-books. But he probably would if he had a larger budget.

SUMMARY ◆

Key Points

Consumption Possibilities (pp. 204–206)

- The budget line is the boundary between what a household can and cannot afford, given its income and the prices of goods.
- The point at which the budget line intersects the y-axis is the household's real income in terms of the good measured on that axis.
- The magnitude of the slope of the budget line is the relative price of the good measured on the x-axis in terms of the good measured on the y-axis.
- A change in the price of one good changes the slope of the budget line. A change in income shifts the budget line but does not change its slope.

Preferences and Indifference Curves (pp. 207–210)

- A consumer's preferences can be represented by indifference curves. The consumer is indifferent among all the combinations of goods that lie on an indifference curve.
- A consumer prefers any point above an indifference curve to any point on it and prefers any point on an indifference curve to any point below it.
- The magnitude of the slope of an indifference curve is called the marginal rate of substitution.
- The marginal rate of substitution diminishes as consumption of the good measured on the y-axis decreases and consumption of the good measured on the x-axis increases.

Predicting Consumer Choices (pp. 210–214)

- A household consumes at its best affordable point. This point is on the budget line and on the highest attainable indifference curve and has a marginal rate of substitution equal to relative price.
- The effect of a price change (the price effect) can be divided into a substitution effect and an income effect.
- The substitution effect is the effect of a change in price on the quantity bought when the consumer (hypothetically) remains indifferent between the original choice and the new choice.
- The substitution effect always results in an increase in consumption of the good whose relative price has fallen.
- The income effect is the effect of a change in income on consumption.
- For a normal good, the income effect reinforces the substitution effect. For an inferior good, the income effect works in the opposite direction to the substitution effect.

Work–Leisure Choices (pp. 214–215)

- The indifference curve model of household choice enables us to understand how a household allocates its time between work and leisure.
- Work hours have decreased and leisure hours have increased because the income effect on the demand for leisure has been greater than the substitution effect.

Key Figures

Figure 9.1   The Budget Line, 204
Figure 9.2   Changes in Prices and Income, 206
Figure 9.3   A Preference Map, 207
Figure 9.4   The Marginal Rate of Substitution, 208
Figure 9.6   The Best Affordable Choice, 210

Figure 9.7   Price Effect and Demand Curve, 211
Figure 9.8   Income Effect and Change in Demand, 212
Figure 9.9   Substitution Effect and Income Effect, 213

Key Terms

Budget line, 204
Diminishing marginal rate of substitution, 208
Income effect, 212

Indifference curve, 207
Marginal rate of substitution, 208
Price effect, 211
Real income, 205

Relative price, 205
Substitution effect, 213

PROBLEMS and APPLICATIONS

myeconlab   Work problems 1–10 in Chapter 9 Study Plan and get instant feedback.
Work problems 11–20 as Homework, a Quiz, or a Test if assigned by your instructor.

1. Sara's income is $12 a week. The price of popcorn is $3 a bag, and the price of a smoothie is $3.
   a. What is Sara's real income in terms of smoothies?
   b. What is her real income in terms of popcorn?
   c. What is the relative price of smoothies in terms of popcorn?
   d. What is the opportunity cost of a smoothie?
   e. Calculate the equation for Sara's budget line (with bags of popcorn on the left side).
   f. Draw a graph of Sara's budget line with the quantity of smoothies on the x-axis.
   g. In f, what is the slope of Sara's budget line? What determines its value?

2. Sara's income falls from $12 to $9 a week, while the price of popcorn remains at $3 a bag and the price of a smoothie remains at $3.
   a. What is the effect of the fall in Sara's income on her real income in terms of smoothies?
   b. What is the effect of the fall in Sara's income on her real income in terms of popcorn?
   c. What is the effect of the fall in Sara's income on the relative price of a smoothie in terms of popcorn?
   d. What is the slope of Sara's new budget line if it is drawn with smoothies on the x-axis?

3. Sara's income is $12 a week. The price of popcorn rises from $3 to $6 a bag, and the price of a smoothie remains at $3.
   a. What is the effect of the rise in the price of popcorn on Sara's real income in terms of smoothies?
   b. What is the effect of the rise in the price of popcorn on Sara's real income in terms of popcorn?
   c. What is the effect of the rise in the price of popcorn on the relative price of a smoothie in terms of popcorn?
   d. What is the slope of Sara's new budget line if it is drawn with smoothies on the x-axis?

4. **The Year in Medicine**

   Sudafed, used to clear up those autumn sniffles, ... contains as one of its active ingredients pseudoephedrine, widely used in backyard labs to make methamphetamine. ... Now, allergy sufferers looking for relief have to ask a pharmacist or salesclerk for their Sudafed, show photo ID, and sign a logbook. Unfortunately, the most common alternative, phenylephrine, isn't as effective.

   Time, December 4, 2006
   a. Draw an indifference curve for Sudafed and phenylephrine that is consistent with this news clip.
   b. On your graph in a, identify combinations that allergy sufferers prefer, do not prefer, and are indifferent among.
   c. Explain how the marginal rate of substitution changes along this indifference curve.

5. Draw figures that show your indifference curves for the following pairs of goods:
   - Right gloves and left gloves
   - Coca-Cola and Pepsi
   - Baseballs and baseball bats
   - Tylenol and acetaminophen (the generic form of Tylenol)
   - Eye glasses and contact lenses
   - Desktop computers and laptop computers
   - Skis and ski poles
   a. For each pair, state whether the goods are perfect substitutes, perfect complements, or neither.
   b. Discuss the shape of your indifference curve for each pair and explain the relationship between its shape and the marginal rate of substitution as the quantities of the two goods change.

6. Pam has chosen her best affordable combination of cookies and comic books. She has spent all of her income on 30 cookies at $1 each and 5 comic books at $2 each. Next month, the price of a cookie falls to 50¢ and the price of a comic book rises to $5.
   a. Will Pam be able to buy, and want to buy, 30 cookies and 5 comic books next month?
   b. Which situation does Pam prefer: cookies at $1 and comic books at $2 or cookies at 50¢ and comic books at $5?
   c. If Pam changes the quantities that she buys, will she buy more or fewer cookies and more or fewer comic books?

d. When the prices change next month, will there be an income effect and a substitution effect at work or just one of them?

7. **Boom Time for "Gently Used" Clothes**

Unlike most retailers who are blaming the economy for their poor sales, one store chain is boldly declaring that an economic downturn can actually be a boon for its business. ... [It] sells used name-brand children's clothes, toys, and furniture. ... Last year, the company took in $20 million in sales, up 5% from the previous year. "Our sales are already up 5% so far this year."

CNN, April 17, 2008

a. According to this article, is used clothing a normal good or an inferior good?
b. If the price of used clothing falls and income remains the same, explain how the quantity of used clothing bought changes.
c. If the price of used clothing falls and income remains the same, describe the substitution effect and the income effect that occur.
d. Draw a graph to illustrate a family's indifference curves for used clothing and other goods and services.
e. On your graph in d, draw two budget lines to show the effect of a fall in income on the quantity of used clothing purchased.

8 **Canada Sees Fewer U.S. Visitors on High Dollar, Gas**

... Trips to Canada by U.S. residents fell 16% in June from a year earlier to 2.56 million, ... Statistics Canada said today. ... "U.S. visitors traditionally have spent a lot of money here, even more than Canadians do, so it's definitely a hit to our ticket sales," Ann Swerdfager, media manager for the Stratford Shakespeare Festival in Stratford, Ontario, said before Monday's report. ... The biggest decline was U.S. tourists taking day trips by car, down 22% from last year, according to the data, which isn't seasonally adjusted. ...

Bloomberg News, August 18, 2008

a. Describe the degree of substitutability between gasoline and festival tickets and draw a preference map that illustrates your description.
b. Draw a budget line for gasoline and festival tickets and identify the best affordable point.
c. Show on your graph how the best affordable point changes when the price of gasoline rises.

9. **Does a Second Income Pay?**

When considering whether two paychecks are worth it, figure out how much of the lower earner's salary will be eaten [up] by expenses incurred if both parents work. Child care is likely to be the biggest cost. ... Also, take into account the costs of going to work. The commute, the clothes, the dry cleaning, the lunches. ... And you may not have as much time or energy to do the housework or make dinner. So you may end up ... doing take-out more often. ...

CNN, March 15, 2006

a. What is the opportunity cost of a parent staying home with her or his children?
b. What is the opportunity cost of a parent working instead of staying home?
c. Why does the opportunity cost of working increase as the number of children in a family increases?
d. How does the number of children in a family influence the marginal rate of substitution between leisure and goods and services?

10. **Floyd Mayweather Jr. Announces Retirement**

Unbeaten world champion boxer Floyd Mayweather Jr. backed out of negotiations for a September rematch against Oscar De La Hoya ... announcing his retirement. ...

In May 2007, Mayweather Jr. won a split-decision over De La Hoya in a bout that established new records for pay-per-view and total revenue. ... [De La Hoya's business partner] didn't believe Mayweather is employing a tactic to earn more money in a De La Hoya fight. ... "He has made enough money to live comfortably for the rest of his life, and if he wants to spend time with his babies, that's a good thing. ..."

Los Angeles Times, June 6, 2008

a. Use the concepts of the substitution effect and the income effect to explain Mayweather's decision.
b. At the income he earns per fight, is Mayweather's labour supply curve upward-sloping or backward-bending?
c. Draw a graph of Mayweather's indifference curves and budget line between leisure time and income and illustrate his decision to fight or not to fight. Show how an increase in the income per fight changes his decision.

11. **Gas Prices Straining Budgets**

... Many say they are staying in and scaling back spending to try to keep up, ... driving as little as possible, cutting back on shopping and eating out, and other discretionary spending.

CNN, February 29, 2008

a. Draw a budget line for a household that consumes only two goods: gasoline and eating out. Identify the combinations of gasoline and eating out that are affordable and those that are unaffordable.

b. Draw a second budget line to show how a rise in the price of gasoline changes the affordable and unaffordable combinations of gasoline and eating out. Describe how the household's consumption possibilities change.

c. How does a rise in the price of gasoline change the relative price of eating out?

d. How does a rise in the price of gasoline change real income in terms of eating out?

12. Rashid buys only books and albums and the figure shows his preferences.

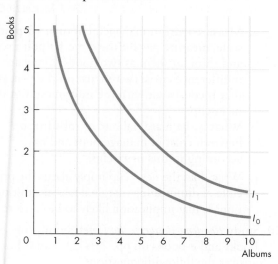

a. If Rashid chooses 3 books and 2 albums, what is his marginal rate of substitution?

b. If Rashid chooses 2 books and 6 albums, what is his marginal rate of substitution?

c. Do Rashid's indifference curves display diminishing marginal rate of substitution? Explain why or why not.

13. Sara's income is $12 a week. The price of popcorn is $3 a bag, and the price of cola is $1.50 a can.

The figure shows Sara's preference map for popcorn and cola.

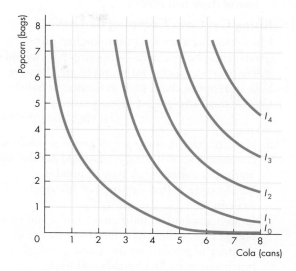

a. What quantities of popcorn and cola does Sara buy?

b. What is Sara's marginal rate of substitution at the point at which she consumes?

14. Now suppose that in problem 13, the price of cola rises to $3 a can and the price of popcorn and Sara's income remain the same.

a. What quantities of cola and popcorn does Sara now buy?

b. What are two points on Sara's demand curve for cola? Draw Sara's demand curve.

c. What is the substitution effect of this price change?

d. What is the income effect of the price change?

e. Is cola a normal good or an inferior good?

15. Jim has made his best affordable choice of muffins and coffee. He spends all of his income on 10 muffins at $1 each and 20 cups of coffee at $2 each. Now the price of a muffin rises to $1.50 and the price of coffee falls to $1.75 a cup.

a. Will Jim now be able and want to buy 10 muffins and 20 coffees?

b. Which situation does Jim prefer: muffins at $1 and coffee at $2 a cup or muffins at $1.50 and coffee at $1.75 a cup?

c. If Jim changes the quantities that he buys, will he buy more or fewer muffins and more or less coffee?

d. When the prices change, is there an income effect and a substitution effect at work or just one of these two effects?

16 **Rising Gas Costs Crimping Budgets**

More [people] are substituting higher-priced goods with cheaper ones—choosing McDonald's coffee over Starbucks, for example, or hitting a bulk warehouse chain such as Costco or Sam's Club instead of a pricier grocery store.

MSNBC, March 20, 2008

a. If an increase in the price of gasoline results in consumers substituting McDonald's coffee for Starbucks coffee, what type of good is McDonald's coffee—normal or inferior? Explain.
b. Draw a graph of an indifference curve and two budget lines to illustrate the effect of a rise in the price of gasoline on the quantity of coffee purchased from McDonald's and from Starbucks.

17. **U-Picks Have More than Fruit**

With their proximity to local markets and the increasing consumer interest in locally grown produce, a growing number of Laval farms have stopped selling to wholesalers and have started selling directly to consumers through roadside kiosks and U-pick operations.

Here's how it works: You visit a farm, pick up some containers at the front entrance, drive out into the farm, stop here and there, pick whatever you want, and pay by the bushel on your way out.

The Sauriol family farm was at the forefront of the U-pick trend 20 years ago. At the time, it sold exclusively to wholesalers. Then it started its own strawberry U-pick, and soon expanded into a wide range of vegetables. ...

The Montreal Gazette, August 30, 2008

a. What is the relationship between gasoline and U-pick vegetables?
b. Draw a Quebecer's preference map and budget line to illustrate the best affordable combination of gasoline and U-pick vegetables.
c. On your graph in b, show the effect of a rise in the price of gasoline on the quantities of gasoline and vegetables picked.

18. The provincial sales tax is a tax on goods. Some people say that the GST, a tax on both goods and services, is a better tax. Explain and illustrate with a graph what would happen, if all provincial sales taxes were replaced with a provincial GST, to

a. The relative price of books and haircuts.
b. The budget line showing the quantities of books and haircuts you can afford to buy.
c. Your purchases of books and haircuts.

19. **You May Be Paid More (or Less) Than You Think**

... If you've ever had to choose between a job you like and a better-paying one that you like less, you probably wished some economist would ... tell you how much job satisfaction is worth. ... Trust in management is by far the biggest component to consider. Say you get a new boss and your trust in management goes up a bit ... (say, up one point on a 10-point scale). That's like getting a 36 percent pay raise. In other words, that increased level of trust will boost your level of overall satisfaction in life by about the same amount as a 36 percent raise would.

CNN, March 29, 2006

a. Measure trust in management on a 10-point scale, measure pay on the same 10-point scale, and think of them as two goods. Draw an indifference curve (with trust on the *x*-axis) that is consistent with the information in the news clip.
b. What is the marginal rate of substitution between trust in management and pay, according to this news clip?
c. What does the news clip imply about the principle of diminishing marginal rate of substitution? Is that implication likely to be correct?

20. Study *Reading Between the Lines* about print books and e-books on pp. 216–217, and then answer the following questions.

a. How do you buy books?
b. Sketch your budget line for books and other goods.
c. Sketch your indifference curves for books and other goods.
d. What would happen to the way you buy books if Amazon gave you its reader free for buying just one e-book?

UNDERSTANDING HOUSEHOLDS' CHOICES

Making the Most of Life

The powerful forces of demand and supply shape the fortunes of families, businesses, nations, and empires in the same unrelenting way that the tides and winds shape rocks and coastlines. You saw in Chapters 3 through 7 how these forces raise and lower prices, increase and decrease quantities bought and sold, cause revenues to fluctuate, and send resources to their most valuable uses.

These powerful forces begin quietly and privately with the choices that each one of us makes. Chapters 8 and 9 probe these individual choices, offering two alternative approaches to explaining both consumption plans and the allocation of time. These explanations of consumption plans can also explain "non-economic" choices, such as whether to marry and how many children to have. In a sense, there are no non-economic choices. If there is scarcity, there must be choice, and economics studies all choices.

The earliest economists (Adam Smith and his contemporaries) did not have a very deep understanding of households' choices. It was not until the nineteenth century that progress was made in this area when Jeremy Bentham (below) introduced the concept of utility and applied it to the study of human choices. Today, Steven Levitt of the University of Chicago, whom you will meet on the following pages, is one of the most influential students of human behaviour.

Jeremy Bentham *(1748–1832), who lived in London, was the son and grandson of lawyers and was himself trained as a barrister. But Bentham rejected the opportunity to maintain the family tradition and, instead, spent his life as a writer, activist, and Member of Parliament in the pursuit of rational laws that would bring the greatest happiness to the greatest number of people.*

Bentham, whose embalmed body is preserved to this day in a glass cabinet in the University of London, was the first person to use the concept of utility to explain human choices. But in Bentham's day, the distinction between explaining and prescribing was not a sharp one, and Bentham was ready to use his ideas to tell people how they ought to behave. He was one of the first to propose pensions for the retired, guaranteed employment, minimum wages, and social benefits such as free education and free medical care.

"... It is the greatest happiness of the greatest number that is the measure of right and wrong."

JEREMY BENTHAM
Fragment on Government

TALKING
WITH

Steven D. Levitt

Steven D. Levitt is Alvin H. Baum Professor of Economics at the University of Chicago. Born in Minneapolis, he was an undergraduate at Harvard and a graduate student at MIT. Among his many honours, he was recently awarded the John Bates Clark Medal, given to the best economist under 40.

Professor Levitt has studied an astonishingly wide range of human choices and their outcomes. He has examined the effects of policing on crime, shown that realtors get a higher price when they sell their own homes than when they sell other people's, devised a test to detect cheating teachers, and studied the choices of drug dealers and gang members. Much of this research has been popularized in *Freakonomics* (Steven D. Levitt and Stephen J. Dubner, HarperCollins, 2005). What unifies this apparently diverse body of research is the use of natural experiments. Professor Levitt has an incredible ability to find just the right set of events and the data the events have generated to enable him to isolate the effect he's looking for.

Michael Parkin and Robin Bade talked with Steven Levitt about his career and the progress that economists have made in understanding how people respond to incentives in all aspects of life.

Why did you become an economist?

As a freshman in college, I took introductory economics. All the ideas made perfect sense to me—it was the way I naturally thought. My friends were befuddled. I thought, "This is the field for me!"

The idea of rational choice made at the margin lies at the heart of economics. Would you say that your work generally supports that idea or challenges it? Can you provide some examples?

I don't like the word "rational" in this context. I think economists model agents as being rational just for convenience. What really matters is whether people respond to incentives. My work very much supports the idea that humans in all types of circumstances respond strongly to incentives. I've seen it with drug dealers, auto thieves, sumo wrestlers, real estate agents, and elementary school teachers, just to name a few examples.

Can you elaborate? What are the incentives to which drug dealers respond? And does an understanding of these responses tell us anything about how public policy might influence drug use?

The incentives people face differ depending on their particular circumstances. Drug dealers, for instance, want to make money, but they also want to avoid being arrested or even killed. In the data we have on drug sellers, we see that when the drug trade is more lucrative, dealers are willing to take greater risks of arrest to carve out a share of the market. On the other hand, they also do their best to minimize their risks. For example, crack sellers used to carry the crack with them. When laws were passed imposing stiff penalties on anyone caught with anything more than a minimal amount of crack, drug dealers responded by storing the crack somewhere else, and retrieving only the amount being sold to the current client. Sumo wrestlers, on the other hand, care mostly about their official ranking. Sometimes matches occur where one wrestler has more to lose or gain than the other wrestler. We find that sumo wrestlers make corrupt deals to make sure the wrestler who needs the win is the one who actually wins.

Why is an economist interested in crime and cheating?

I think of economics as being primarily about a way of looking at the world and a set of tools for thinking clearly. The topics you apply these tools to are unlimited. That is why I think economics has been so powerful. If you understand economics and use the tools wisely, you will be a better business person, doctor, public servant, parent.

> I think of economics as being primarily about a way of looking at the world and a set of tools for thinking clearly.

What is the economic model of crime, and how does it help to design better ways of dealing with criminal activity? Can you illustrate by talking a bit about your work on the behaviour of auto thieves?

The economic model of crime argues that people have a choice of either working for a wage in the legal sector or earning money from illegal activity. The model carefully lays out the set of costs associated with being a criminal (e.g., forgone wages and being punished) and benefits (e.g., the loot) associated with crime and analyzes how a maximizing individual will choose whether to commit crimes and how much crime to commit. One reason the model is useful is because it lays out the various ways in which public policy might influence crime rates. For instance, we can increase the probability of a criminal getting caught or make the prison sentence longer for those who are caught. The government might also try to intervene in the labour market to make legal work more attractive—for instance, with a minimum wage.

What is the problem in figuring out whether more police leads to less crime? How did you find the answer?

We think that when you add more police, crime will fall because the cost of being a criminal goes up because of increased detection. From a public policy perspective, understanding how much crime falls in response to police is an important question. In practice, it is hard to answer this question because we don't randomly hire police. Rather, where crime is bad, there is greater demand for police and thus there are more police. If you just look at different cities, the places with the most police also have the most crime, but it is not because police cause crime, it is because crime causes police to be hired.

To figure out a causal impact of police on crime, you would like to do a randomized experiment where you added a lot of police at random to some cities and took them away in other cities. That is something you cannot really do in real life. So instead, the economist has to look for "natural experiments" to answer the question.

I used the timing of mayoral elections. It turns out that mayors hire a lot of police before elections to "look tough on crime." If elections do not otherwise affect crime, then the election is kind of like a randomizing device that puts more police in some cities every once in a while. Indeed, I found that crime goes down in the year following elections once the police hired are up and running. It is indirect evidence, but it is an example of how economists use their toolbox to handle difficult questions.

Your work shows that legalized abortion leads to less crime. Can you explain how you reach that conclusion? Can you also explain its implications for the pro-life, pro-choice debate?

> If you just look at different cities, the places with the most police also have the most crime, but it is not because police cause crime, it is because crime causes police to be hired.

The theory is simple: Unwanted children have hard lives (including being much more likely to be criminals); after legalized abortion, there are fewer unwanted children. Therefore, there should be less crime (with a 15–20 year lag while the babies grow up and reach high-crime ages).

We looked at what happened to crime 15–20 years after *Roe* v. *Wade*, in states with high and low abortion rates and in states that legalized abortion a few years earlier than the rest of the country. We could even look at people born immediately before or after abortion became legal.

All the evidence pointed the same way: Crime fell a lot because abortion was legalized.

Our results, however, don't have large implications for the abortion debate. If abortion is murder, as pro-life advocates argue, then the changes in crime we see are trivial in comparison. If a woman simply has the right to control her body, as pro-choice advocates argue, then our estimates about crime are likewise irrelevant.

Our results have more to say about unwantedness: There are big benefits to making sure that children who are brought into the world are wanted and well cared for, through either birth control, adoption, abortion, or parental education.

Terrorism is on everyone's minds these days. And presumably, terrorists respond to incentives. Have you thought about how we might be able to use the insights of economics to better understand and perhaps even combat terrorism?

Terrorism is an unusually difficult question to tackle through incentives. The religious terrorists we are most worried about are willing to give up their lives to carry out terrorist acts. So the only punishment we can really offer is preventing them from committing the act by catching them beforehand or maybe minimizing the damage they can do. Unlike typical criminals, the threat of punishing them after the fact will not help deter the crime. Luckily, even among extremists, there are not many people willing to give their lives for a cause.

> ... every time I observed anything in the world I asked myself, "Is that a natural experiment?"

Can a student learn how to use natural experiments or do you have a gift that is hard to teach?

I don't think I have such a gift. Most people who are good at something are good because they have worked hard and practised. That is certainly true with me.

For a while, I just walked around and every time I observed anything in the world I asked myself, "Is that a natural experiment?" Every once in a while I stumbled onto one because I was on the lookout.

What else can a student who wants to become a natural experimenting economist or broader social scientist do to better prepare for that career?

I would say that the best thing students can do is to try to really apply what they are learning to their lives, rather than just memorizing for an exam and quickly forgetting. If you are passionate about economics (or anything else for that matter), you are way ahead of others who are just trying to get by.

10 Organizing Production

After studying this chapter, you will be able to

- Explain what a firm is and describe the economic problem that all firms face

- Distinguish between technological efficiency and economic efficiency

- Define and explain the principal–agent problem and describe how different types of business organizations cope with this problem

- Describe and distinguish between different types of markets in which firms operate

- Explain why markets coordinate some economic activities and why firms coordinate others

In the fall of 1990, a British scientist named Timm Berners-Lee invented the World Wide Web. This remarkable idea paved the way for the creation of thousands of profitable businesses. One of these businesses is Research In Motion (RIM), a Canadian wireless device company that developed the BlackBerry. Mike Lazaridis founded RIM in 1984 in Waterloo, Ontario. How do RIM and the other million or so firms that operate in Canada make their business decisions? How do they operate efficiently?

Most of the firms that you can name don't *make* things; they *buy* and *sell* things. For example, Apple doesn't make the iPod. Toshiba makes the iPod's hard drive, Toshiba and Matsushita make the display module, many other firms make the remaining parts, and a firm in Taiwan called Inventec assembles the components. Why doesn't Apple make its iPod? How do firms decide what to make themselves and what to buy from other firms?

In this chapter, you are going to learn about firms and the choices they make. In *Reading Between the Lines* at the end of the chapter, we'll apply some of what you've learned and look at some of the choices made by Google and Yahoo! in the search engine business.

The Firm and Its Economic Problem

The 2 million firms in Canada differ in size and in the scope of what they do, but they all perform the same basic economic functions. Each **firm** is an institution that hires factors of production and organizes those factors to produce and sell goods and services. Our goal is to predict firms' behaviour. To do so, we need to know a firm's goal and the constraints it faces. We start with the goal.

The Firm's Goal

When economists ask entrepreneurs what they are trying to achieve, they get many different answers. Some talk about making a high-quality product, others about business growth, others about market share, others about the job satisfaction of their workforce, and an increasing number today talk about social and environmental responsibility. All of these goals are pursued by firms, but they are not the fundamental goal: They are the means to that goal.

A firm's goal is to maximize profit. A firm that does not seek to maximize profit is either eliminated or taken over by a firm that does seek that goal.

What is the profit that a firm seeks to maximize? To answer this question, we'll look at Campus Sweaters, Inc., a small producer of knitted sweaters owned and operated by Cindy.

Accounting Profit

In 2008, Campus Sweaters received $400,000 for the sweaters it sold and paid out $80,000 for wool, $20,000 for utilities, $120,000 for wages, $5,000 for the lease of a computer, and $5,000 in interest on a bank loan. These expenses total $230,000, so Campus Sweaters had a cash surplus of $170,000.

To measure the profit of Campus Sweaters, its accountant subtracted a $20,000 depreciation charge from the $170,000 cash surplus. *Depreciation* is the fall in the value of a firm's capital (Campus Sweaters' buildings and knitting machines). To calculate depreciation, accountants use Revenue Canada rules based on standards established by the accounting profession. Using these rules, the accountant calculated that Campus Sweaters made a profit of $150,000 in 2008.

Economic Accounting

Accountants measure a firm's profit to ensure that the firm pays the correct amount of income tax and to show its investors how their funds are being used.

Economists measure a firm's profit to enable them to predict the firm's decisions, and the goal of these decisions is to maximize *economic profit*. **Economic profit** is equal to total revenue minus total cost, with total cost measured as the *opportunity cost of production*.

A Firm's Opportunity Cost of Production

The *opportunity cost* of any action is the highest-valued alternative forgone. The *opportunity cost of production* is the value of the best alternative use of the resources that a firm uses in production.

A firm's opportunity cost of production is the value of real alternatives forgone. We express opportunity cost in money units so that we can compare and add up the value of the alternatives forgone.

A firm's opportunity cost of production is the sum of the cost of using resources

- Bought in the market
- Owned by the firm
- Supplied by the firm's owner

Resources Bought in the Market A firm incurs an opportunity cost when it buys resources in the market. The amount spent on these resources is an opportunity cost of production because the firm could have bought different resources to produce some other good or service. For Campus Sweaters, the resources bought in the market are wool, utilities, labour, a leased computer, and a bank loan. The $230,000 that Campus Sweaters spent on these items in 2008 could have been spent on something else, so it is an opportunity cost of producing sweaters.

Resources Owned by the Firm A firm incurs an opportunity cost when it uses its own capital. The cost of using capital owned by the firm is an opportunity cost of production because the firm could sell the capital that it owns and rent capital from another firm. When a firm uses its own capital, it implicitly rents the capital from itself. In this case, the firm's opportunity cost of using the capital it owns is called the **implicit rental rate** of capital. The implicit rental rate of capital has two components: economic depreciation and forgone interest.

Economic Depreciation Accountants measure *depreciation*, the fall in the value of a firm's capital, using formulas that are unrelated to the change in the market value of capital. **Economic depreciation** is the fall in the *market value* of a firm's capital over a given period. It equals the market price of the capital at the beginning of the period minus the market price of the capital at the end of the period.

Suppose that Campus Sweaters could have sold its buildings and knitting machines on January 1, 2008, for $400,000 and that it can sell the same capital on December 31, 2008, for $375,000. The firm's economic depreciation during 2008 is $25,000 ($400,000 – $375,000). This forgone $25,000 is an opportunity cost of production.

Forgone Interest The funds used to buy capital could have been used for some other purpose, and in their next best use, they would have earned interest. This forgone interest is an opportunity cost of production.

Suppose that Campus Sweaters used $300,000 of its own funds to buy capital. If the firm invested its $300,000 in bonds instead of a knitting factory (and rented the capital it needs to produce sweaters), it would have earned $15,000 a year in interest. This forgone interest is an opportunity cost of production.

Resources Supplied by the Firm's Owner A firm's owner might supply *both* entrepreneurship and labour.

Entrepreneurship The factor of production that organizes a firm and makes its decisions, entrepreneurship, might be supplied by the firm's owner or by a hired entrepreneur. The return to entrepreneurship is profit, and the profit that an entrepreneur earns *on average* is called **normal profit**. Normal profit is the cost of entrepreneurship and is a cost of production.

If Cindy supplies entrepreneurial services herself, and if the normal profit she can earn on these services is $45,000 a year, this amount is an opportunity cost of production at Campus Sweaters.

Owner's Labour Services *In addition* to supplying entrepreneurship, the owner of a firm might supply labour but not take a wage. The opportunity cost of the owner's labour is the wage income forgone by not taking the best alternative job.

If Cindy supplies labour to Campus Sweaters, and if the wage she can earn on this labour at another firm is $55,000 a year, this amount of wages forgone is an opportunity cost of production at Campus Sweaters.

Economic Accounting: A Summary

Table 10.1 summarizes the economic accounting. Campus Sweaters' total revenue is $400,000; its opportunity cost of production is $370,000; and its economic profit is $30,000.

Cindy's personal income is the $30,000 of economic profit plus the $100,000 that she earns by supplying resources to Campus Sweaters.

Decisions

To achieve the objective of maximum economic profit, a firm must make five decisions:

1. What to produce and in what quantities
2. How to produce
3. How to organize and compensate its managers and workers
4. How to market and price its products
5. What to produce itself and buy from others

In all these decisions, a firm's actions are limited by the constraints that it faces. Your next task is to learn about these constraints.

TABLE 10.1   Economic Accounting

Item		Amount
Total Revenue		**$400,000**
Cost of Resources Bought in Market		
Wool	$80,000	
Utilities	20,000	
Wages	120,000	
Computer lease	5,000	
Bank interest	5,000	$230,000
Cost of Resources Owned by Firm		
Economic depreciation	$25,000	
Forgone interest	15,000	$40,000
Cost of Resources Supplied by Owner		
Cindy's normal profit	$45,000	
Cindy's forgone wages	55,000	$100,000
Opportunity Cost of Production		**$370,000**
Economic Profit		**$30,000**

The Firm's Constraints

Three features of a firm's environment limit the maximum economic profit it can make. They are

- Technology constraints
- Information constraints
- Market constraints

Technology Constraints Economists define technology broadly. A **technology** is any method of producing a good or service. Technology includes the detailed designs of machines and the layout of the workplace. It includes the organization of the firm. For example, the shopping mall is one technology for producing retail services. It is a different technology from the catalogue store, which in turn is different from the downtown store.

It might seem surprising that a firm's profits are limited by technology because it seems that technological advances are constantly increasing profit opportunities. Almost every day, we learn about some new technological advance that amazes us. With computers that speak and recognize our own speech and cars that can find the address we need in a city we've never visited, we can accomplish more than ever.

Technology advances over time. But at each point in time, to produce more output and gain more revenue, a firm must hire more resources and incur greater costs. The increase in profit that a firm can achieve is limited by the technology available. For example, by using its current plant and workforce, Ford can produce some maximum number of cars per day. To produce more cars per day, Ford must hire more resources, which increases its costs and limits the increase in profit that it can make by selling the additional cars.

Information Constraints We never possess all the information we would like to have to make decisions. We lack information about both the future and the present. For example, suppose you plan to buy a new computer. When should you buy it? The answer depends on how the price is going to change in the future. Where should you buy it? The answer depends on the prices at hundreds of different computer shops. To get the best deal, you must compare the quality and prices in every shop. But the opportunity cost of this comparison exceeds the cost of the computer!

A firm is constrained by limited information about the quality and efforts of its workforce, the current and future buying plans of its customers, and the plans of its competitors. Workers might make too little effort, customers might switch to competing suppliers, and a competitor might enter the market and take some of the firm's business.

To address these problems, firms create incentives to boost workers' efforts even when no one is monitoring them, conduct market research to lower uncertainty about customers' buying plans, and "spy" on each other to anticipate competitive challenges. But these efforts don't eliminate incomplete information and uncertainty, which limit the economic profit that a firm can make.

Market Constraints The quantity each firm can sell and the price it can obtain are constrained by its customers' willingness to pay and by the prices and marketing efforts of other firms. Similarly, the resources that a firm can buy and the prices it must pay for them are limited by the willingness of people to work for and invest in the firm. Firms spend billions of dollars a year marketing and selling their products. Some of the most creative minds strive to find the right message that will produce a knockout television advertisement. Market constraints and the expenditures firms make to overcome them limit the profit a firm can make.

Review Quiz

1 What is a firm's fundamental goal and what happens if the firm doesn't pursue this goal?
2 Why do accountants and economists calculate a firm's cost and profit in different ways?
3 What are the items that make opportunity cost differ from the accountant's measure of cost?
4 Why is normal profit an opportunity cost?
5 What are the constraints that a firm faces? How does each constraint limit the firm's profit?

 Work Study Plan 10.1 and get instant feedback.

In the rest of this chapter and in Chapters 11 through 14, we study the choices that firms make. We're going to learn how we can predict a firm's decisions as the response to both the constraints it faces and the changes in those constraints. We begin by taking a closer look at the technology constraints that firms face.

Technological and Economic Efficiency

RIM employs a large workforce, and most RIM workers possess a large amount of human capital. But the firm uses a small amount of physical capital. In contrast, a coal-mining company employs a huge amount of mining equipment (physical capital) and almost no labour. Why? The answer lies in the concept of efficiency. There are two concepts of production efficiency: technological efficiency and economic efficiency. **Technological efficiency** occurs when the firm produces a given output by using the least amount of inputs. **Economic efficiency** occurs when the firm produces a given output at the least cost. Let's explore the two concepts of efficiency by studying an example.

Suppose that there are four alternative techniques for making TVs:

A. *Robot production.* One person monitors the entire computer-driven process.
B. *Production line.* Workers specialize in a small part of the job as the emerging TV passes them on a production line.
C. *Hand-tool production.* A single worker uses a few hand tools to make a TV.
D. *Bench production.* Workers specialize in a small part of the job but walk from bench to bench to perform their tasks.

Table 10.2 sets out the amounts of labour and capital required by each of these four methods to make 10 TVs a day.

Which of these alternative methods are technologically efficient?

Technological Efficiency

Recall that *technological efficiency* occurs when the firm produces a given output by using the least amount of inputs. Look at the numbers in the table and notice that method *A* uses the most capital and the least labour. Method *C* uses the most labour and the least capital. Method *B* and method *D* lie between the two extremes. They use less capital and more labour than method *A* and less labour but more capital than method *C*.

Compare methods *B* and *D*. Method *D* requires 100 workers and 10 units of capital to produce 10

TABLE 10.2   Four Ways of Making 10 TVs a Day

	Method	Quantities of inputs	
		Labour	Capital
A	Robot production	1	1,000
B	Production line	10	10
C	Hand-tool production	1,000	1
D	Bench production	100	10

TVs. Those same 10 TVs can be produced by method *B* with 10 workers and the same 10 units of capital. Because method *D* uses the same amount of capital and more labour than method *B*, method *D* is not technologically efficient.

Are any of the other methods not technologically efficient? The answer is no. Each of the other methods is technologically efficient. Method *A* uses more capital but less labour than method *B*, and method *C* uses more labour but less capital than method *B*.

Which of the methods are economically efficient?

Economic Efficiency

Recall that *economic efficiency* occurs when the firm produces a given output at the least cost.

Method *D*, which is technologically inefficient, is also economically inefficient. It uses the same amount of capital as method *B* but 10 times as much labour, so it costs more. A technologically inefficient method is never economically efficient.

One of three technologically efficient methods is economically efficient. The other two are economically inefficient. But which method is economically efficient depends on factor prices.

In Table 10.3(a), the wage rate is $75 per day and the rental rate of capital is $250 per day. By studying Table 10.3(a), you can see that method *B* has the lowest cost and is the economically efficient method.

In Table 10.3(b), the wage rate is $150 a day and the rental rate of capital is $1 a day. Looking at Table 10.3(b), you can see that method *A* has the lowest cost and is the economically efficient method. In this case, capital is so cheap relative to labour that the

TABLE 10.3 The Costs of Different Ways of Making 10 TVs a Day

(a) Wage rate $75 a day; Capital rental rate $250 a day

Method	Inputs Labour	Capital	Labour cost ($75 per day)		Capital cost ($250 per day)		Total cost
A	1	1,000	$75	+	$250,000	=	$250,075
B	10	10	750	+	2,500	=	3,250
C	1,000	1	75,000	+	250	=	75,250

(b) Wage rate $150 a day; Capital rental rate $1 a day

Method	Inputs Labour	Capital	Labour cost ($150 per day)		Capital cost ($1 per day)		Total cost
A	1	1,000	$150	+	$1,000	=	$1,150
B	10	10	1,500	+	10	=	1,510
C	1,000	1	150,000	+	1	=	150,001

(c) Wage rate $1 a day; Capital rental rate $1,000 a day

Method	Inputs Labour	Capital	Labour cost ($1 per day)		Capital cost ($1,000 per day)		Total cost
A	1	1,000	$1	+	$1,000,000	=	$1,000,001
B	10	10	10	+	10,000	=	10,010
C	1,000	1	1,000	+	1,000	=	2,000

method that uses the most capital is the economically efficient method.

In Table 10.3(c), the wage rate is $1 a day and the rental rate of capital is $1,000 a day. You can see that method *C* has the lowest cost and is the economically efficient method. In this case, labour is so cheap relative to capital that the method that uses the most labour is the economically efficient method.

Economic efficiency depends on the relative costs of resources. The economically efficient method is the one that uses a smaller amount of the more expensive resource and a larger amount of the less expensive resource.

A firm that is not economically efficient does not maximize profit. Natural selection favours efficient firms and inefficient firms disappear. Inefficient firms go out of business or are taken over by firms that produce at lower costs.

Review Quiz

1 Is a firm technologically efficient if it uses the latest technology? Why or why not?

2 Is a firm economically inefficient if it can cut its costs by producing less? Why or why not?

3 Explain the key distinction between technological efficiency and economic efficiency.

4 Why do some firms use large amounts of capital and small amounts of labour while others use small amounts of capital and large amounts of labour?

 Work Study Plan 10.2 and get instant feedback.

Next we study the information constraints that firms face and the wide array of organization structures these constraints generate.

Information and Organization

Each firm organizes the production of goods and services by combining and coordinating the factors of production it hires. But the way firms organize production varies and they use a mixture of two systems:

- Command systems
- Incentive systems

Command Systems

A **command system** is a method of organizing production that uses a managerial hierarchy. Commands pass downward through the hierarchy, and information passes upward. Managers spend most of their time collecting and processing information about the performance of the people under their control and making decisions about what commands to issue and how best to get those commands implemented.

The military uses the purest form of command system. A commander-in-chief (in Canada, the Prime Minister) makes the big decisions about strategic goals. Beneath this highest level, generals organize their military resources. Beneath the generals, successively lower ranks organize smaller and smaller units but pay attention to ever-increasing degrees of detail. At the bottom of the managerial hierarchy are the people who operate weapons systems.

Command systems in firms are not as rigid as those in the military, but they share some similar features. A chief executive officer (CEO) sits at the top of a firm's command system. Senior executives who report to and receive commands from the CEO specialize in managing production, marketing, finance, personnel, and perhaps other aspects of the firm's operations. Beneath these senior managers might be several tiers of middle management ranks that stretch downward to the managers who supervise the day-to-day operations of the business. Beneath these managers are the people who operate the firm's machines and who make and sell the firm's goods and services.

Small firms have one or two layers of managers, while large firms have several layers. As production processes have become ever more complex, management ranks have swollen. Today, more people have management jobs than ever before, even though the information revolution of the 1990s slowed the growth of management. In some industries, the information

revolution reduced the number of layers of managers and brought a shakeout of middle managers.

Managers make enormous efforts to be well informed. They try hard to make good decisions and issue commands that end up using resources efficiently. But managers always have incomplete information about what is happening in the divisions of the firm for which they are responsible. For this reason, firms use incentive systems as well as command systems to organize production.

Incentive Systems

An **incentive system** is a method of organizing production that uses a market-like mechanism inside the firm. Instead of issuing commands, senior managers create compensation schemes to induce workers to perform in ways that maximize the firm's profit.

Selling organizations use incentive systems most extensively. Sales representatives who spend most of their working time alone and unsupervised are induced to work hard by being paid a small salary and a large performance-related bonus.

But incentive systems operate at all levels in a firm. The compensation plan of a CEO includes a share in the firm's profit, and factory floor workers sometimes receive compensation based on the quantity they produce.

Mixing the Systems

Firms use a mixture of commands and incentives, and they choose the mixture that maximizes profit. Firms use commands when it is easy to monitor performance or when a small deviation from an ideal performance is very costly. They use incentives when monitoring performance is either not possible or too costly to be worth doing.

For example, Bombardier can easily monitor the performance of workers on a production line. If one person works too slowly, the entire line slows, so a production line is organized with a command system.

In contrast, it is costly to monitor a CEO. For example, what did John Roth (former CEO of Nortel) contribute to the initial success and subsequent problems of Nortel? This question can't be answered with certainty, yet Nortel's stockholders had to put someone in charge of the business and provide that person with an incentive to maximize stockholders' returns. The performance of Nortel illustrates a general problem, known as the principal–agent problem.

The Principal–Agent Problem

The **principal–agent problem** is the problem of devising compensation rules that induce an *agent* to act in the best interest of a *principal*. For example, the stockholders of RIM are *principals,* and the firm's managers are *agents*. The stockholders (the principals) must induce the managers (agents) to act in the stockholders' best interest. Similarly, Steve Jobs (a principal) must induce the designers who are working on the next generation iPhone (agents) to work efficiently.

Agents, whether they are managers or workers, pursue their own goals and often impose costs on a principal. For example, the goal of stockholders of CIBC (principals) is to maximize the firm's profit—its true profit, not some fictitious paper profit. But the firm's profit depends on the actions of its managers (agents), and they have their own goals. Perhaps a manager takes a customer to a hockey game on the pretense that she is building customer loyalty, when in fact she is simply enjoying on-the-job leisure. This same manager is also a principal, and her tellers are agents. The manager wants the tellers to work hard and attract new customers so that she can meet her operating targets. But the workers enjoy conversations with each other and take on-the-job leisure. Nonetheless, the firm constantly strives to find ways of improving performance and increasing profits.

Coping with the Principal–Agent Problem

Issuing commands does not address the principal–agent problem. In most firms, the shareholders can't monitor the managers and often the managers can't monitor the workers. Each principal must create incentives that induce each agent to work in the interests of the principal. Three ways of attempting to cope with the principal–agent problem are

- Ownership
- Incentive pay
- Long-term contracts

Ownership By assigning ownership (or part-ownership) of a business to managers or workers, it is sometimes possible to induce a job performance that increases a firm's profits. Part-ownership is quite common for senior managers but less common for workers. For example, Cando, a Canadian employee-owned company, supplies specialized services, quality materials, and innovative solutions to customers in the rail sector and to industries that depend on the bulk movement of materials. Another is the Edmonton-based construction company PLC.

Incentive Pay Incentive pay—pay related to performance—is very common. Incentives are based on a variety of performance criteria such as profits, production, or sales targets. Promoting an employee for good performance is another example of the use of incentive pay.

Long-Term Contracts Long-term contracts tie the long-term fortunes of managers and workers (agents) to the success of the principal(s)—the owner(s) of the firm. For example, a multiyear employment contract for a CEO encourages that person to take a long-term view and devise strategies that achieve maximum profit over a sustained period.

These three ways of coping with the principal–agent problem give rise to different types of business organization. Each type of business organization is a different response to the principal–agent problem. Each type uses a different combination of ownership, incentives, and long-term contracts. Let's look at the main types of business organization.

Types of Business Organization

The three main types of business organization are

- Sole proprietorship
- Partnership
- Corporation

Sole proprietorship A *sole proprietorship* is a firm with a single owner—a proprietor—who has unlimited liability. *Unlimited liability* is the legal responsibility for all the debts of a firm up to an amount equal to the entire wealth of the owner. If a sole proprietorship cannot pay its debts, those to whom the firm owes money can claim the personal property of the owner. The businesses of some farmers, computer programmers, and artists are examples of sole proprietorships.

The proprietor makes management decisions, receives the firm's profits, and is responsible for its losses. Profits from a sole proprietorship are taxed at the same rate as other sources of the proprietor's personal income.

Partnership A *partnership* is a firm with two or more owners who have unlimited liability. Partners must agree on an appropriate management structure and on how to divide the firm's profits among themselves. The profits of a partnership are taxed as the personal income of the owners, but each partner is legally liable for all the debts of the partnership (limited only by the wealth of that individual partner). Liability for the full debts of the partnership is called *joint unlimited liability*. Most law firms are partnerships.

Corporation A *corporation* is a firm owned by one or more limited liability stockholders. *Limited liability* means that the owners have legal liability only for the value of their initial investment. This limitation of liability means that if the corporation becomes bankrupt, its owners are not required to use their personal wealth to pay the corporation's debts.

Corporations' profits are taxed independently of stockholders' incomes. Stockholders pay tax on dividends and a capital gains tax on the profit they earn when they sell a stock for a higher price than they paid for it. Corporate stocks generate capital gains when a corporation retains some of its profit and reinvests it in profitable activities. So retained earnings are taxed twice because the capital gains they generate are taxed.

Pros and Cons of Different Types of Firms

The different types of business organization arise from firms trying to cope with the principal–agent problem. Each type has advantages in particular situations and because of its special advantages, each type continues to exist. Each type of business organization also has disadvantages.

Table 10.4 summarizes these and other pros and cons of the different types of firms.

TABLE 10.4   The Pros and Cons of Different Types of Firms

Type of Firm	Pros	Cons
Sole proprietorship	■ Easy to set up ■ Simple decision making ■ Profits taxed only once as owner's income	■ Bad decisions not checked; no need for consensus ■ Owner's entire wealth at risk ■ Firm dies with owner ■ Cost of capital and labour is high relative to that of a corporation
Partnership	■ Easy to set up ■ Diversified decision making ■ Can survive withdrawal of partner ■ Profits taxed only once as owners' incomes	■ Achieving consensus may be slow and expensive ■ Owners' entire wealth at risk ■ Withdrawal of partner may create capital shortage ■ Cost of capital and labour is high relative to that of a corporation
Corporation	■ Owners have limited liability ■ Large-scale, low-cost capital available ■ Professional management not restricted by ability of owners ■ Perpetual life ■ Long-term labour contracts cut labour costs	■ Complex management structure can make decisions slow and expensive ■ Profits are taxed twice: as company profit and as stockholders' income

The Size Distribution of Firms in Canada

Many More Small than Large

Industry Canada counts the number of establishments in the Canadian economy and classifies them by size measured by the number of employees. An establishment is not the same as a firm. Some firms operate several, or even many, establishments. For example, Loblaw Companies Limited operates 1,690 grocery stores across Canada. So one large firm operates many small establishments. Keep this fact in mind as you review the data in the figure.

Most establishments in Canada (58 percent of the total) are very small and employ fewer than 5 people. Most of the rest (38 percent of the total) employ between 5 and 99 people. Only 4 percent of establishments employ more than 100 people and only 2,700 establishments (0.3 percent of the total) employ more than 500 people.

The figure shows the distribution of the size of establishments across major industry classes. Most of the largest establishments (shown by the red bars) are found in public administration (government), utilities, and education. Manufacturing, information and culture, and mining, oil, and gas exploration also have some large establishments.

Micro establishments, shown by the blue bars, dominate in agriculture (a group that includes forestry, fishing, and hunting) and professional services, which includes lawyers, accountants, and other types of professional and scientific services.

Most firms in Canada today, regardless of size, are corporations. Many of the very small firms that employ fewer than 5 people find it advantageous to incorporate.

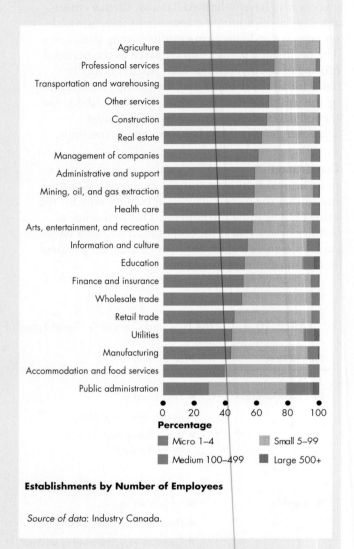

Establishments by Number of Employees

Source of data: Industry Canada.

Review Quiz

1 Explain the distinction between a command system and an incentive system.
2 What is the principal–agent problem? What are three ways in which firms try to cope with it?
3 What are the three types of firms? Explain the major advantages and disadvantages of each.
4 Why do all three types of firms survive and in which sectors is each type most prominent?

myeconlab   Work Study Plan 10.3 and get instant feedback.

You've now seen how technology constraints and information constraints influence firms. You've seen why some firms operate with a large amount of labour and human capital and a small amount of physical capital. You've also seen how firms use a mixture of command and incentive systems and employ different types of business organization to cope with the principal–agent problem.

Your next task is to look at the variety of market situations in which firms operate and classify the different market environments in which firms do business.

Markets and the Competitive Environment

The markets in which firms operate vary a great deal. Some are highly competitive, and profits in these markets are hard to come by. Some appear to be almost free from competition, and firms in these markets earn large profits. Some markets are dominated by fierce advertising campaigns in which each firm seeks to persuade buyers that it has the best products. And some markets display the character of a strategic game.

Economists identify four market types:

1. Perfect competition
2. Monopolistic competition
3. Oligopoly
4. Monopoly

Perfect competition arises when there are many firms, each selling an identical product, many buyers, and no restrictions on the entry of new firms into the industry. The many firms and buyers are all well informed about the prices of the products of each firm in the industry. The worldwide markets for corn, rice, and other grain crops are examples of perfect competition.

Monopolistic competition is a market structure in which a large number of firms compete by making similar but slightly different products. Making a product slightly different from the product of a competing firm is called **product differentiation**. Product differentiation gives a firm in monopolistic competition an element of market power. The firm is the sole producer of a particular version of the good in question. For example, in the market for pizzas, hundreds of firms make their own version of the perfect pizza. Each of these firms is the sole producer of a particular brand. Differentiated products are not necessarily different products. What matters is that consumers perceive them to be different. For example, different brands of potato chips and ketchup might be almost identical but be perceived by consumers to be different.

Oligopoly is a market structure in which a small number of firms compete. Computer software, airplane manufacture, and international air transportation are examples of oligopolistic industries. Oligopolies might produce almost identical products, such as the colas produced by Coke and Pepsi. Or they might produce differentiated products such as Boeing and Airbus aircraft.

Monopoly is a market structure in which there is only one firm and it produces a good or service that has no close substitutes and the firm is protected by a barrier preventing the entry of new firms. In some places, the phone, gas, electricity, cable television, and water suppliers are local monopolies—monopolies restricted to a given location. Microsoft Corporation, the software developer that created Windows and Vista, is an example of a global monopoly.

Perfect competition is the most extreme form of competition. Monopoly is the most extreme absence of competition. The other two market types fall between these extremes.

Many factors must be taken into account to determine which market structure describes a particular real-world market. One of these factors is the extent to which a small number of firms dominates the market. To measure this feature of markets, economists use indexes called measures of concentration. Let's look at these measures.

Measures of Concentration

Economists use two measures of concentration:

- The four-firm concentration ratio
- The Herfindahl-Hirschman Index

The Four-Firm Concentration Ratio The **four-firm concentration ratio** is the percentage of the value of sales accounted for by the four largest firms in an industry. The range of the concentration ratio is from almost zero for perfect competition to 100 percent for monopoly. This ratio is the main measure used to assess market structure.

Table 10.5 shows two calculations of the four-firm concentration ratio: one for tire makers and one for printers. In this example, 14 firms produce tires. The largest four have 80 percent of the sales, so the four-firm concentration ratio is 80 percent. In the printing industry, with 1,004 firms, the largest four firms have only 0.5 percent of the sales, so the four-firm concentration ratio is 0.5 percent.

A low concentration ratio indicates a high degree of competition, and a high concentration ratio indicates an absence of competition. A monopoly has a concentration ratio of 100 percent—the largest (and only) firm has 100 percent of the sales. A four-firm concentration ratio that exceeds 60 percent is regarded as an indication of a market that is highly concentrated and dominated by a few firms in an oligopoly. A ratio of less than 60 percent is regarded as an indication of a competitive market.

The Herfindahl-Hirschman Index The **Herfindahl-Hirschman Index**—also called the HHI—is the square of the percentage market share of each firm summed over the largest 50 firms (or summed over all the firms if there are fewer than 50) in a market. For example, if there are four firms in a market and the market shares of the firms are 50 percent, 25 percent, 15 percent, and 10 percent, the Herfindahl-Hirschman Index is

$$\text{HHI} = 50^2 + 25^2 + 15^2 + 10^2 = 3{,}450.$$

TABLE 10.5   Calculating the Four-Firm Concentration Ratio

Tire makers		Printers	
Firm	Sales (millions of dollars)	Firm	Sales (millions of dollars)
Top, Inc.	200	Fran's	2.5
ABC, Inc.	250	Ned's	2.0
Big, Inc.	150	Tom's	1.8
XYZ, Inc.	100	Jill's	1.7
Largest 4 firms	700	Largest 4 firms	8.0
Other 10 firms	175	Other 1,000 firms	1,592.0
Industry	875	Industry	1,600.0

Four-firm concentration ratios:

Tire makers: $\dfrac{700}{875} \times 100 = 80\%$

Printers: $\dfrac{8}{1{,}600} \times 100 = 0.5\%$

Concentration Measures in the Canadian Economy

A Sweet Monopoly

Statistics Canada calculates and publishes data showing the four-firm concentration ratio for each industry in Canada. The bars in the figure show the four-firm concentration ratio.

Sugar production is highly concentrated and almost a monopoly. Other industries that have a high degree of concentration produce tobacco, beer, tires, soft drinks, and ice. These industries are oligopolies.

Industries that produce clothing, bakery items, textiles, and fabrics have low concentration measures and are highly competitive.

Industries that produce women's and girls' shirts, pharmaceutical products, and wooden windows and doors are moderately concentrated. These industries are examples of monopolistic competition.

Concentration measures are useful indicators of the degree of competition in a market, but they must be supplemented by other information to determine the structure of the market.

Newspapers and automobiles are examples of how the concentration measures give a misleading reading of the degree of competition.

Most newspapers are local. They serve a single city or even smaller area. So despite the low concentration measure, newspapers are concentrated in their own local areas.

Automobiles are traded internationally and foreign cars are freely imported into Canada. Despite the high concentration measure, the automobile industry is competitive.

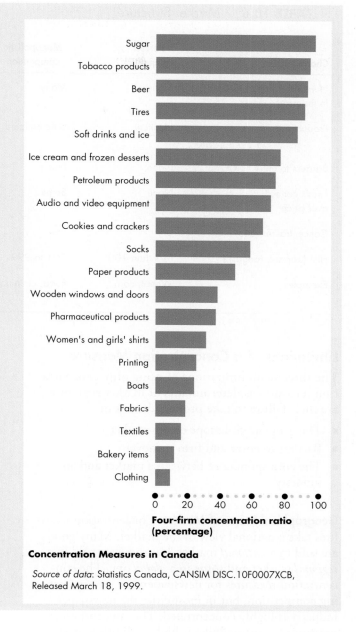

Concentration Measures in Canada

Source of data: Statistics Canada, CANSIM DISC.10F0007XCB, Released March 18, 1999.

In perfect competition, the HHI is small. For example, if each of the largest 50 firms in an industry has a market share of 0.1 percent, then the HHI is $0.1^2 \times 50 = 0.5$. In a monopoly, the HHI is 10,000. The firm has 100 percent of the market: $100^2 = 10,000$.

The HHI can be used to classify markets across a spectrum of types. A market in which the HHI is less than 1,000 is regarded as being competitive—the smaller the number, the greater the degree of competition. A market in which the HHI lies between 1,000 and 1,800 is regarded as being moderately competitive—a form of monopolistic competition. But a market in which the HHI exceeds 1,800 is regarded as being uncompetitive and a potential matter of concern for regulators.

TABLE 10.6   Market Structure

Characteristics	Perfect competition	Monopolistic competition	Oligopoly	Monopoly
Number of firms in industry	Many	Many	Few	One
Product	Identical	Differentiated	Either identical or differentiated	No close substitutes
Barriers to entry	None	None	Moderate	High
Firm's control over price	None	Some	Considerable	Considerable or regulated
Concentration ratio	0	Low	High	100
HHI (approx. ranges)	Less than 100	101 to 999	More than 1,000	10,000
Examples	Wheat, corn	Food, clothing	Automobiles, cereals	Local water supply

Limitations of a Concentration Measure

The three main limitations of using only concentration measures as determinants of market structure are their failure to take proper account of

- The geographical scope of the market
- Barriers to entry and firm turnover
- The correspondence between a market and an industry

Geographical Scope of Market Concentration measures take a national view of the market. Many goods are sold in a *national* market, but some are sold in a *regional* market and some in a *global* one. The concentration measures for newspapers are low, indicating competition, but in most cities the newspaper industry is highly concentrated. The concentration measures for automobiles is high, indicating little competition, but the biggest three North American car makers compete with foreign car makers in a highly competitive global market.

Barriers to Entry and Firm Turnover Some markets are highly concentrated but entry is easy and the turnover of firms is large. For example, small towns have few restaurants, but no restrictions hinder a new restaurant from opening and many attempt to do so.

Also, a market with only a few firms might be competitive because of *potential entry*. The few firms in a market face competition from the many potential firms that will enter the market if economic profit opportunities arise.

Market and Industry Correspondence To calculate concentration ratios, Statistics Canada classifies each firm as being in a particular industry. But markets do not always correspond closely to industries for three reasons.

First, markets are often narrower than industries. For example, the pharmaceutical industry, which has a low concentration ratio, operates in many separate markets for individual products—for example, measles vaccine and cancer drugs. These drugs do not compete with each other, so this industry, which looks competitive, includes firms that are monopolies (or near monopolies) in markets for individual drugs.

Second, most firms make several products. For example, Nortel produces telecommunication equipment and Internet database services, among other things. So this one firm operates in several separate markets. But Statistics Canada classifies Nortel as being in the telecommunication equipment industry. The fact that Nortel competes with other providers of e-commerce database services does not show up in the concentration data for that market.

Market Structures in North America

A Highly Competitive Environment

How competitive are markets in North America? Do most firms operate in competitive markets, in monopolistic competition, in oligopoly, or in monopoly markets?

The data needed to answer these questions are hard to get. The last attempt to answer the questions, in a study by William G. Shepherd, an economics professor at the University of Massachusetts at Amherst, covered the years from 1939 to 1980. The figure shows what he discovered.

In 1980, three-quarters of the value of goods and services bought and sold in North America were traded in markets that are essentially competitive—markets that have almost perfect competition or monopolistic competition. Monopoly and the dominance of a single firm accounted for about 5 percent of sales. Oligopoly, which is found mainly in manufacturing, accounted for about 18 percent of sales.

Over the period studied, the economy became increasingly competitive. The percentage of output sold by firms operating in competitive markets (blue bars) expanded most, and the percentage of output sold by firms operating in oligopoly markets (red bars) shrunk most.

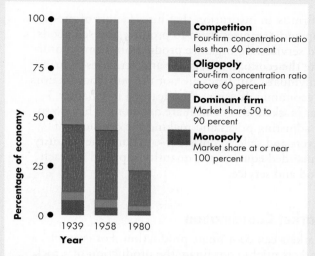

The Market Structure of the Economy

Source of data: William G. Shepherd, "Causes of Increased Competition in the U.S. Economy, 1939–1980," *Review of Economics and Statistics*, November 1982, pp. 613–626. © MIT Press Journals. Reprinted by permission.

But also during the past decades, the economy has become much more exposed to competition from the rest of the world. The data used by William G. Shepherd don't capture this international competition, so the data probably understate the degree of true competition in the North American economy.

Third, firms switch from one market to another depending on profit opportunities. For example, Canadian Pacific Ltd., which today produces hotel services, forest products, coal and petroleum products, as well as rail services, has diversified from being just a railroad company. Bombardier started producing snowmobiles in 1937. Today, it produces aircraft and rail equipment. Publishers of newspapers, magazines, and textbooks are today rapidly diversifying into Internet and multimedia products. These switches among markets show that there is much scope for entering and exiting a market, and so measures of concentration have limited usefulness.

Despite their limitations, concentration measures do provide a basis for determining the degree of competition in a market when they are combined with information about the geographical scope of the market, barriers to entry, and the extent to which large, multiproduct firms straddle a variety of markets.

Review Quiz

1 What are the four market types? Explain the distinguishing characteristics of each.

2 What are the two measures of concentration? Explain how each measure is calculated.

3 Under what conditions do the measures of concentration give a good indication of the degree of competition in a market?

4 Is our economy competitive? Is it becoming more competitive or less competitive?

 Work Study Plan 10.4 and get instant feedback.

You now know the variety of market types and how we identify them. Our final question in this chapter is: What determines the things that firms decide to buy from other firms rather than produce for themselves?

◆ Markets and Firms

A firm is an institution that hires factors of production and organizes them to produce and sell goods and services. To organize production, firms coordinate the economic decisions and activities of many individuals. But firms are not the only coordinators of economic decisions. You learned in Chapter 3 that markets also coordinate decisions. They do so by adjusting prices and making the decisions of buyers and sellers consistent—making the quantity demanded equal to the quantity supplied for each good and service.

Market Coordination

Markets can coordinate production. For example, markets might coordinate the production of a rock concert. A promoter books a stadium, some stage equipment, audio and video recording engineers and technicians, some rock groups, a superstar, a publicity agent, and a ticket agent—all market transactions. The promoter sells tickets to thousands of rock fans, audio rights to a recording company, and video and broadcasting rights to a television network—another set of market transactions. Alternatively, if rock concerts were produced like cornflakes, the firm producing them would own all the capital used (stadiums, stage, sound and video equipment) and would employ all the labour needed (singers, engineers, and salespeople).

Outsourcing, buying parts or products from other firms, is another example of market coordination. Dell uses outsourcing for all the components of the computers it produces. The major automakers use outsourcing for windshields and windows, gearboxes, tires, and many other car parts.

What determines whether a firm or markets coordinate a particular set of activities? How do firms decide whether to buy from another firm or manufacture an item themselves? The answer is cost. Taking account of the opportunity cost of time as well as the costs of the other inputs, firms use the method that costs least. In other words, they use the economically efficient method.

Firms coordinate economic activity when they can perform a task more efficiently than markets can. In such a situation, it is profitable to set up a firm. If markets can perform a task more efficiently than a firm can, firms will use markets, and any attempt to set up a firm to replace such market coordination will be doomed to failure.

Why Firms?

Firms are often more efficient than markets as coordinators of economic activity because they can achieve

- Lower transactions costs
- Economies of scale
- Economies of scope
- Economies of team production

Transactions Costs   The idea that firms exist because there are activities in which firms are more efficient than markets was first suggested by University of Chicago economist and Nobel Laureate Ronald Coase. Coase focused on the firm's ability to reduce or eliminate transactions costs. **Transactions costs** are the costs that arise from finding someone with whom to do business, of reaching an agreement about the price and other aspects of the exchange, and of ensuring that the terms of the agreement are fulfilled. Market transactions require buyers and sellers to get together and to negotiate the terms and conditions of their trading. Sometimes, lawyers have to be hired to draw up contracts. A broken contract leads to still more expense. A firm can lower such transactions costs by reducing the number of individual transactions undertaken.

Consider, for example, two ways of getting your rattling car fixed.

Firm coordination: You take the car to the garage. The garage owner coordinates parts and tools as well as the mechanic's time, and your car gets fixed. You pay one bill for the entire job.

Market coordination: You hire a mechanic, who diagnoses the problems and makes a list of the parts and tools needed to fix them. You buy the parts from the local wrecker's yard and rent the tools from ABC Rentals. You hire the mechanic again to fix the problems. You return the tools and pay your bills—wages to the mechanic, rental to ABC, and the cost of the parts used to the wrecker.

What determines the method you use? The answer is cost. Taking account of the opportunity cost of your own time as well as the costs of the other inputs that you would have to buy, you will use the method that costs least. In other words, you will use the economically efficient method.

The first method requires that you undertake only one transaction with one firm. It's true that the firm has to undertake several transactions—hiring the labour and buying the parts and tools required to do the job. But the firm doesn't have to undertake those transactions simply to fix your car. One set of such transactions enables the firm to fix hundreds of cars. There is an enormous reduction in the number of individual transactions that take place if people get their cars fixed at the garage rather than going through an elaborate sequence of market transactions.

Economies of Scale When the cost of producing a unit of a good falls as its output rate increases, **economies of scale** exist. Automakers, for example, experience economies of scale because as the scale of production increases, the firm can use cost-saving equipment and highly specialized labour. An automaker that produces only a few cars a year must use hand-tool methods that are costly. Economies of scale arise from specialization and the division of labour that can be reaped more effectively by firm coordination rather than market coordination.

Economies of Scope A firm experiences **economies of scope** when it uses specialized (and often expensive) resources to produce a *range of goods and services*. For example, Toshiba uses its designers and specialized equipment to make the hard drive for the iPod. But it makes many different types of hard drives and other related products. As a result, Toshiba produces the iPod hard drive at a lower cost than a firm making only the iPod hard drive could achieve.

Economies of Team Production A production process in which the individuals in a group specialize in mutually supportive tasks is *team production*. Sports provide the best examples of team activity. In baseball, some team members specialize in pitching and others in fielding. In basketball, some team members specialize in defence and some in offence. The production of goods and services offers many examples of team activity. For example, production lines in automobile and TV manufacturing plants work most efficiently when individual activity is organized into teams, each specializing in a small task. You can also think of an entire firm as being a team. The team has buyers of raw material and other inputs, production workers, and salespeople. Each individual member of the team specializes, but the value of the output of the team and the profit that it earns depend on the coordinated activities of all the team's members. The idea that firms arise as a consequence of the economies of team production was first suggested by Armen Alchian and Harold Demsetz of the University of California at Los Angeles.

Because firms can economize on transactions costs, reap economies of scale and economies of scope, and organize efficient team production, it is firms rather than markets that coordinate most of our economic activity. But there are limits to the economic efficiency of firms. If a firm becomes too big or too diversified, the cost of managing its activities, per unit of output, rises. When a firm is too big, it can become more efficient by trimming down and buying more inputs in the market from other firms.

IBM is an example of a firm that became too big to be efficient. In an attempt to restore efficient operations, IBM split up its large organization into a number of "Baby Blues," each of which specializes in a segment of the computer market.

Sometimes firms enter into long-term relationships that make it difficult to see where one firm ends and another begins. For example, GM has long-term relationships with suppliers of windows, tires, and other parts. Wal-Mart has long-term relationships with suppliers of the goods it sells. Such relationships make transactions costs lower than they would be if GM or Wal-Mart went shopping on the world market each time it wanted new supplies.

Review Quiz

1 What are the two ways in which economic activity can be coordinated?

2 What determines whether a firm or markets coordinate production?

3 What are the main reasons why firms can often coordinate production at a lower cost than markets can?

 Work Study Plan 10.5 and get instant feedback.

◆ *Reading Between the Lines* on pp. 244–245 explores the Internet search business. We continue to study firms and their decisions in the next four chapters. In Chapter 11, we learn about the relationships between cost and output at different output levels. These relationships are common to all types of firms in all types of markets. We then turn to problems that are specific to firms in different types of markets.

Battling for Markets in Internet Search

Yawns for Yahoo, Ga-Ga for Google

Earnings from the two search leaders are coming and guess what? Google's eating Yahoo's lunch.

October 13, 2006

... Yahoo stunned Wall Street last month when chief financial officer Sue Decker somewhat casually said at a Goldman Sachs conference in New York that sales for the quarter would be at the low end of the company's forecast due to softness in auto and financial services advertising. ...

Google, on the other hand, keeps wowing the Street. It bested sales and profit forecasts for the second quarter back in July.

And on Monday, Google unveiled a deal to buy YouTube, the popular online video sharing site, for $1.6 billion, a marriage uniting the top search engine and No. 1 video site. Analysts were raving about Google's chances to get a big piece of the potentially lucrative online video advertising market. ...

Yahoo is playing catch-up with Google in the hot market for paid search, ads tied to specific keyword queries. According to the most recent numbers from Web tracking firm comScore Networks, Google widened its lead in search over Yahoo in August. ...

And looking ahead to next year, Yahoo could face a much tougher challenge from Google in so-called display advertising, sales of video ads, banners and other ads not tied to search results, thanks to Google's pending deal for YouTube.

Yahoo has so far maintained an edge over Google in display advertising, which tends to be more attractive to big brand-name companies than search ads. But it is a big market opportunity for Google.

Essence of the Story

- Yahoo! lags behind Google in the market for advertising tied to keyword queries—known as paid search.

- Yahoo! leads Google in sales of video ads, banners, and other ads not tied to search results—known as display advertising.

- By buying YouTube (for $1.6 billion), Google has created a marriage of the top search engine and the top video sharing site.

- Google is expected to gain a large share of the profitable online video advertising market, which big brand-name companies use.

Economic Analysis

- Like all firms, Yahoo! and Google aim to maximize profit.

- Also, like all firms, Yahoo! and Google face constraints imposed by technology and the market.

- Both firms provide search engines to access information on the Internet.

- People who use a search engine demand information, and Yahoo! and Google (and other firms) supply information.

- The equilibrium price of search engine services to users is zero!

- To generate revenue and profit, search engine providers offer advertising services.

- Two types of advertising are offered: paid search and display.

- Google's focus is on paid search—see Figs. 1 and 2. Yahoo!'s focus is on display—see Fig. 3.

- To attract either type of advertising, a firm must be able to offer the advertiser access to a large potential customer base.

- To maximize the use of their search engines, Google and Yahoo! offer a variety of enticements to users.

- One enticement is the quality of the search engine itself. Most people think that Google has the better search technology, but Yahoo! is working on improved search.

- Another enticement is a variety of related attractions. Yahoo!'s photo-sharing service is an example.

- Search engines can also generate more revenue by enabling advertisers to more precisely target their potential customers. Again, the quality of the search technology is the key ingredient. And again, Google is seen by many to have the edge.

- Google hopes to attract even more users and to increase its ability to use video and other display technologies through its acquisition of YouTube.

Figure 1   Paid search advertising

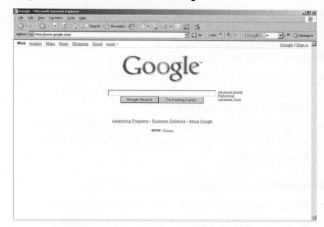

Figure 2   Google's focus is search

Figure 3   Yahoo! features display advertising

SUMMARY ◆

Key Points

The Firm and Its Economic Problem (pp. 228–230)

- Firms hire and organize factors of production to produce and sell goods and services.
- A firm's goal is to maximize economic profit, which is total revenue minus total cost measured as the opportunity cost of production.
- A firm's opportunity cost of production is the sum of the cost of resources bought in the market, using the firm's own resources, and resources supplied by the firm's owner.
- Normal profit is the opportunity cost of entrepreneurship and is part of a firm's opportunity cost.
- Technology, information, and markets limit the economic profit that a firm can make.

Technological and Economic Efficiency (pp. 231–232)

- A method of production is technologically efficient when a firm uses the least amount of inputs to produce a given output.
- A method of production is economically efficient when the cost of producing a given output is as low as possible.

Information and Organization (pp. 233–236)

- Firms use a combination of command systems and incentive systems to organize production.
- Faced with incomplete information and uncertainty, firms induce managers and workers to perform in ways that are consistent with the firms' goals.
- Sole proprietorships, partnerships, and corporations use ownership, incentive pay, and long-term contracts to cope with the principal–agent problem.

Markets and the Competitive Environment (pp. 237–241)

- In perfect competition, many sellers offer an identical product to many buyers and entry is free.
- In monopolistic competition, many sellers offer slightly different products to many buyers and entry is free.
- In oligopoly, a small number of sellers compete and barriers to entry limit the number of firms.
- In monopoly, one firm produces an item that has no close substitutes and the firm is protected by a barrier that prevents the entry of competitors.

Markets and Firms (pp. 242–243)

- Firms coordinate economic activities when they can perform a task more efficiently—at lower cost—than markets can.
- Firms economize on transactions costs and achieve the benefits of economies of scale, economies of scope, and economies of team production.

Key Tables

Table 10.4   The Pros and Cons of Different Types of Firms, 235

Table 10.5   Calculating the Four-Firm Concentration Ratio, 238

Table 10.6   Market Structure, 240

Key Terms

Command system, 233
Economic depreciation, 229
Economic efficiency, 231
Economic profit, 228
Economies of scale, 243
Economies of scope, 243
Firm, 228

Four-firm concentration ratio, 238
Herfindahl-Hirschman Index, 238
Implicit rental rate,   228
Incentive system, 233
Monopolistic competition, 237
Monopoly, 237
Normal profit, 229

Oligopoly, 237
Perfect competition, 237
Principal–agent problem, 234
Product differentiation, 237
Technological efficiency, 231
Technology, 230
Transactions costs, 242

PROBLEMS and APPLICATIONS

myeconlab   Work problems 1–11 in Chapter 10 Study Plan and get instant feedback.
Work problems 12–22 as Homework, a Quiz, or a Test if assigned by your instructor.

1. One year ago, Jack and Jill set up a vinegar-bottling firm (called JJVB). Use the following information to calculate JJVB's opportunity cost of production during its first year of operation:
   - Jack and Jill put $50,000 of their own money into the firm.
   - They bought equipment for $30,000.
   - They hired one employee to help them for an annual wage of $20,000.
   - Jack gave up his previous job, at which he earned $30,000, and spent all his time working for JJVB.
   - Jill kept her old job, which paid $30 an hour, but gave up 10 hours of leisure each week (for 50 weeks) to work for JJVB.
   - JJVB bought $10,000 of goods and services from other firms.
   - The market value of the equipment at the end of the year was $28,000.
   - Jack and Jill have a $100,000 home loan on which they pay an interest rate of 6 percent a year.

2. Joe runs a shoeshine stand at the airport. With no skills and no job experience, Joe has no alternative employment. Other shoeshine stand operators that Joe knows earn $10,000 a year. Joe pays the airport $2,000 a year for the space he uses, and his total revenue from shining shoes is $15,000 a year. He spent $1,000 on a chair, polish, and brushes and paid for these items using his credit card. The interest on his credit card balance is 20 percent a year. At the end of the year, Joe was offered $500 for his business and all its equipment. Calculate Joe's opportunity cost of production and his economic profit.

3. Alternative ways of laundering 100 shirts are

Method	Labour (hours)	Capital (machines)
A	1	10
B	5	8
C	20	4
D	50	1

   a. Which methods are technologically efficient?
   b. Which method is economically efficient if the hourly wage rate and implicit rental rate of capital are

   (i)   Wage rate $1, rental rate $100?
   (ii) Wage rate $5, rental rate $50?
   (iii) Wage rate $50, rental rate $5?

4. Firms in the tattoo industry have the following sales:

Firm	Sales (dollars per year)
Bright Spots	450
Freckles	325
Love Galore	250
Native Birds	200
Other 15 firms	800

   a. Calculate the four-firm concentration ratio.
   b. What is the structure of the tattoo industry?

5. In 2003 and 2004, Lego, the Danish toymaker that produces coloured plastic bricks, incurred economic losses. The firm faced competition from low-cost copiers of its products and a fall in the number of 5- to 9-year-old boys (its main customers) in many rich countries. In 2004, Lego launched a plan to restore profits. It fired 3,500 of its 8,000 workers, closed factories in Switzerland and the United States, opened factories in Eastern Europe and Mexico, and introduced performance-based pay for its managers. Lego reported a return to profit in 2005.

   Based on "Picking up The Pieces," *Economist*, October 28, 2006.

   a. Describe the problems that Lego faced in 2003 and 2004, using the concepts of the three types of constraints that all firms face.
   b. Which of the actions that Lego took to restore profits addressed an inefficiency? How did Lego seek to achieve economic efficiency?
   c. Which of the actions that Lego took to restore profits addressed an information and organization problem? How did Lego change the way in which it coped with the principal–agent problem?
   d. In what type of market does Lego operate?

6. **John Deere's Farm Team**
   Deere ... opened up the Pune [India] centre in 2001 as a way of entering the Indian market. The move was unexpected: Deere is known for its

heavy-duty farm equipment and big construction gear. Many of India's 300 million-plus farmers still use oxen-pulled plows. ...

Fortune, April 14, 2008

a. Why do many Indian farmers still use oxen-pulled plows? Are they efficient or inefficient? Explain.
b. How might making John Deere farm equipment available to Indian farmers change the technology constraint they face?
c. How do you expect John Deere's move into the Indian farm equipment market to influence the firm's profit opportunities?

7. **Here It Is. Now, You Design It!**

The idea is that the most successful companies no longer invent new products and services on their own. They create them along with their customers, and they do it in a way that produces a unique experience for each customer. The important corollary is that no company owns enough resources—or can possibly own enough—to furnish unique experiences for each customer, so companies must organize a constantly shifting global web of suppliers and partners to do the job.

Fortune, May 26, 2008

a. Describe this method of organizing and coordinating production: Does it use a command system or incentive system?
b. How does this method of organizing and coordinating production help firms achieve lower costs?

8. **Rewarding Failure**

Over the past 25 years CEO pay has risen ... faster than corporate profits, economic growth, or average workforce compensation. ... A more sensible alternative to the current compensation system would require CEOs to own a lot of company stock. If the stock is given to the boss, his salary and bonus should be docked to reflect its value. As for bonuses, they should be based on improving a company's cash earnings relative to its cost of capital, not to more easily manipulated measures like earnings per share. ... [Bonuses] should not be capped, but they should be unavailable to the CEO for some period of years.

Fortune, April 28, 2008

a. What is the economic problem that CEO compensation schemes are designed to solve?

b. How do the proposed changes to CEO compensation outlined in the news clip address the problem you described in a?

9. **GameStop Racks Up the Points**

No retailer has more cachet among gamers than GameStop, and only Wal-Mart has a larger share of the market—for now. ... Wal-Mart had a 21.3% market share last year. GameStop's share was 21.1%, and may well overtake Wal-Mart this year ... but [new women gamers] may prefer shopping at Target to GameStop. ... A chance for Wal-Mart and Target to erode GameStop's market share. ...

Fortune, June 9, 2008

a. According to the news clip, what is the structure of the retail video-game market?
b. Estimate a range for the four-firm concentration ratio and the HHI for the market based on the information provided in the news clip.

10. **6 Steps to Creating a Super Startup**

But starting a business is a complicated, risky, all-consuming effort. Indeed, just two-thirds of new small businesses survive at least two years, and only 44 percent survive at least four years. ... You have to be willing to take calculated risks. ... Most entrepreneurs start their businesses by dipping into their savings, and hitting up friends and family. Perhaps half of all startups, in fact, are funded initially by the founder's credit cards. ... Getting a bank loan is tough unless you have assets—and that often means using your home as collateral.

CNN, October 18, 2007

a. When starting a business, what are the risks and potential rewards associated with a proprietorship identified in the news clip?
b. How might a partnership help to overcome the risks identified in the news clip?
c. How might a corporation help to overcome the risks identified in the news clip?

11. Federal Express enters into contracts with independent truck operators who offer FedEx service and who are rewarded by the volume (cubic feet) of packages they carry.

a. Why doesn't FedEx buy more trucks and hire more drivers?
b. What incentive problems might arise from the arrangement that FedEx uses?

12. Lee is a computer programmer who earned $35,000 in 2007. But on January 1, 2008, Lee opened a body board manufacturing business. At the end of the first year of operation, he submitted the following information to his accountant:

- He stopped renting out his cottage for $3,500 a year and used it as his factory. The market value of the cottage increased from $70,000 to $71,000.
- He spent $50,000 on materials, phone, utilities, etc.
- He leased machines for $10,000 a year.
- He paid $15,000 in wages.
- He used $10,000 from his savings account, which earns 5 percent a year interest.
- He borrowed $40,000 at 10 percent a year from the bank.
- He sold $160,000 worth of body boards.
- Normal profit is $25,000 a year.

  a. Calculate Lee's opportunity cost of production and his economic profit.
  b. Lee's accountant recorded the depreciation on his cottage during 2008 as $7,000. According to the accountant, what profit did Lee make?

13. In 2007, Toni taught music and earned $20,000. She also earned $4,000 by renting out her basement. On January 1, 2008, she quit teaching, stopped renting out her basement, and began to use the space as an office for her new Web site design business. She took $2,000 from her savings account to buy a computer. During 2008, she paid $1,500 for the lease of a Web server and $1,750 for high-speed Internet service. She received a total revenue from Web site designing of $45,000 and earned interest at 5 percent a year on her savings account balance. Normal profit is $55,000 a year. At the end of 2008, Toni could have sold her computer for $500. Calculate Toni's opportunity cost of production and her economic profit in 2008.

14. Four methods of completing a tax return and the time taken by each method are: with a PC, 1 hour; with a pocket calculator, 12 hours; with a pocket calculator and paper and pencil, 12 hours; and with a pencil and paper, 16 hours. The PC and its software cost $1,000, the pocket calculator costs $10, and the pencil and paper cost $1.

  a. Which, if any, of the methods is technologically efficient?
  b. Which method is economically efficient if the wage rate is
   (i) $5 an hour?
   (ii) $50 an hour?
   (iii) $500 an hour?

15. Loblaws has more than 1,000 stores from coast to coast, more than 140,000 employees, and total revenues of close to $30 billion. Penny and David Chapman run the family-owned Chapman's Ice Cream in Markdale, Ontario, which employs local people and supplies Loblaws with ice cream.

  a. How do you think Loblaws coordinates its activities? Is it likely to use mainly a command system or also to use incentive systems? Why or why not?
  b. How do you think Penny and David Chapman coordinate the activities of Chapman's Ice Cream? Are they likely to use mainly a command system or also to use incentive systems? Why?
  c. Describe, compare, and contrast the principal–agent problems faced by Loblaws and Chapman's Ice Cream. How might these firms cope with their principal–agent problems?

16. Market shares of chocolate makers are

Firm	Market share (percent)
Mayfair, Inc.	15
Bond, Inc.	10
Magic, Inc.	20
All Natural, Inc.	15
Truffles, Inc.	25
Gold, Inc.	15

  a. Calculate the Herfindahl-Hirschman Index.
  b. What is the structure of the chocolate industry?

17. Two leading design firms, Astro Studios of San Francisco and Hers Experimental Design Laboratory, Inc. of Osaka, Japan, worked with Microsoft to design the Xbox 360 video game console. IBM, ATI, and SiS designed the Xbox 360's hardware. Three firms, Flextronics, Wistron, and Celestica, manufacture the Xbox 360 at their plants in China and Taiwan.

a. Describe the roles of market coordination and coordination by firms in the design, manufacture, and marketing of the Xbox 360.

b. Why do you think Microsoft works with a large number of other firms to bring the Xbox to market, rather than performing all the required tasks at its headquarters in Seattle?

c. What are the roles of transactions costs, economies of scale, economies of scope, and economies of team production in the design, manufacture, and marketing of the Xbox?

d. Why do you think the Xbox is designed in the United States and Japan but built in China and Taiwan?

18. **The Colvin Interview: Chrysler**

The key driver of profitability will be that the focus of the company isn't on profitability. Our focus is on the customer. If we can find a way to give customers what they want better than anybody else, then what can stop us?

Fortune, April 14, 2008

a. In spite of what Chrysler's vice chairman and co-president claims, why is Chrysler's focus actually on profitability?

b. What would happen to Chrysler if they didn't focus on maximizing profits, but instead only focused their production and pricing decisions to "give customers what they want?"

19. **Must Watches**

Stocks too volatile? Bonds too boring? Then try an alternative investment—one you can wear on your wrist. ... [The] typical return on a watch over five to ten years is roughly 10%. [One could] do better in an index fund, but ... what other investment is so wearable?

Fortune, April 14, 2008

a. What is the cost of buying a watch?

b. What is the opportunity cost of owning a watch?

c. Does owning a watch create an economic profit opportunity?

20. **Where Does Google Go Next?**

He made full use of his "20% time," that famous one day a week that Google gives its engineers to work on whatever project they want. ... He and a couple of colleagues did what many of the young geniuses do at Google: They came up with a cool idea. ... At Google, what you often end up

with instead of resource allocation is a laissez-faire mess. ...

Fortune, May 26, 2008

a. Describe Google's method of organizing production with their software engineers.

b. What are the potential gains and opportunity costs associated with this method?

21. **"Bittersweet" Day as Feds Give Farmers $300 million to Exit Dying Tobacco Industry**

The heart of Canada's century-old tobacco-growing industry took another step toward its inexorable demise Friday as ... Ottawa announced $300 million to help them leave their once proud and lucrative business. ...

About 1,000 farm families still produce tobacco on the sandy soil. ... Most growers are now expected to take the money and give up farming altogether or find other cash crops to grow. ...

John Schwager, who owns about $100,000 worth of tobacco-related equipment, said ... "If tobacco goes out, that equipment is worthless, plus we're out of a job."

Canadian Press, August 1, 2008

a. How does offering a payment to exit tobacco growing influence the opportunity cost of growing tobacco?

b. What is the opportunity cost of using the equipment owned by John Schwager?

c. What is the opportunity cost of using the sandy soil on which tobacco grows so well?

d. How would a tobacco farmer decide whether to give up farming rather than find another cash crop to grow?

22. Study *Reading Between the Lines* about Google and Yahoo! on pp. 244–245, and then answer the following questions:

a. What are the products that Google and Yahoo! sell?

b. How do Internet search engine providers generate revenue and earn a profit?

c. What is the distinction between paid search advertising and display advertising? What types of firms use the latter?

d. Why do you think Google bought YouTube? How will this purchase enable Google to increase its revenue and profit?

e. What technological changes might increase the profitability of Internet search engines?

Output and Costs

After studying this chapter, you will be able to

- Distinguish between the short run and the long run
- Explain the relationship between a firm's output and labour employed in the short run
- Explain the relationship between a firm's output and costs in the short run and derive a firm's short-run cost curves
- Explain the relationship between a firm's output and costs in the long run and derive a firm's long-run average cost curve

What do the nation's largest automaker, General Motors, a big electricity supplier in North America, Ontario Power Generation, and a small (fictional) producer of knitwear, Campus Sweaters, have in common? Like every firm, they must decide how much to produce, how many people to employ, and how much and what type of capital equipment to use. How do firms make these decisions?

GM and the other automakers in North America could produce more cars than they can sell. Why do automakers have expensive equipment lying around that isn't fully used?

Ontario Power Generation and the other electricity suppliers in North America use technologies that contribute to climate change and global warming. Why don't they make more use of clean solar and wind technologies?

We are going to answer these questions in this chapter.

To explain the basic ideas as clearly as possible, we are going to focus on the economic decisions of Campus Sweaters Inc. Studying the way Cindy copes with her firm's economic problems will give us a clear view of the problems faced by all firms. We'll then apply what we learn to the real-world costs of producing cars and electricity. In *Reading Between the Lines* at the end of the chapter, we'll look at the effects of changing technologies that aim to lower the cost of clean electricity.

Decision Time Frames

People who operate firms make many decisions, and all of their decisions are aimed at achieving one overriding goal: maximum attainable profit. But not all decisions are equally critical. Some decisions are big ones. Once made, they are costly (or impossible) to reverse. If such a decision turns out to be incorrect, it might lead to the failure of the firm. Other decisions are small. They are easily changed. If one of these decisions turns out to be incorrect, the firm can change its actions and survive.

The biggest decision that an entrepreneur makes is in what industry to establish a firm. For most entrepreneurs, their background knowledge and interests drive this decision. But the decision also depends on profit prospects—on the expectation that total revenue will exceed total cost.

Cindy has already decided to set up Campus Sweaters. She has also decided the most effective method of organizing the firm. But she has not decided the quantity to produce, the factors of production to hire, or the price to charge for sweaters.

Decisions about the quantity to produce and the price to charge depend on the type of market in which the firm operates. Perfect competition, monopolistic competition, oligopoly, and monopoly all confront the firm with their own special problems. But decisions about *how* to produce a given output do not depend on the type of market in which the firm operates. *All* types of firms in *all* types of markets make similar decisions about how to produce.

The actions that a firm can take to influence the relationship between output and cost depend on how soon the firm wants to act. A firm that plans to change its output rate tomorrow has fewer options than one that plans to change its output rate six months or six years from now.

To study the relationship between a firm's output decision and its costs, we distinguish between two decision time frames:

- The short run
- The long run

The Short Run

The **short run** is a time frame in which the quantity of at least one factor of production is fixed. For most firms, capital, land, and entrepreneurship are fixed factors of production and labour is the variable factor of production. We call the fixed factors of production the firm's *plant*: In the short run, a firm's plant is fixed.

For Campus Sweaters, the fixed plant is its factory building and its knitting machines. For an electric power utility, the fixed plant is its buildings, generators, computers, and control systems.

To increase output in the short run, a firm must increase the quantity of a variable factor of production, which is usually labour. So to produce more output, Campus Sweaters must hire more labour and operate its knitting machines for more hours a day. Similarly, an electric power utility must hire more labour and operate its generators for more hours a day.

Short-run decisions are easily reversed. The firm can change its production in the short run by increasing or decreasing the amount of labour it hires.

The Long Run

The **long run** is a time frame in which the quantities of *all* factors of production can be varied. That is, the long run is a period in which the firm can change its *plant*.

To increase output in the long run, a firm can change its plant as well as the quantity of labour it hires. Campus Sweaters can decide whether to install more knitting machines, use a new type of machine, reorganize its management, or hire more labour. Long-run decisions are *not* easily reversed. Once a plant decision is made, the firm usually must live with it for some time. To emphasize this fact, we call the past expenditure on a plant that has no resale value a **sunk cost**. A sunk cost is irrelevant to the firm's current decisions. The only costs that influence its current decisions are the short-run cost of changing its labour inputs and the long-run cost of changing its plant.

Review Quiz

1 Distinguish between the short run and the long run.
2 Why is a sunk cost irrelevant to a firm's current decisions?

[X] **myeconlab** Work Study Plan 11.1 and get instant feedback.

We're going to study costs in the short run and the long run. We begin with the short run and describe a firm's technology constraint.

Short-Run Technology Constraint

To increase output in the short run, a firm must increase the quantity of labour employed. We describe the relationship between output and the quantity of labour employed by using three related concepts:

1. Total product
2. Marginal product
3. Average product

These product concepts can be illustrated either by product schedules or by product curves. Let's look first at product schedules.

Product Schedules

Table 11.1 shows some data that describe the total product, marginal product, and average product of Campus Sweaters. The numbers tell us how the quantity of sweaters increases as Campus Sweaters employs more workers. The numbers also tell us about the productivity of the labour that Campus Sweaters employs.

Focus first on the columns headed "Labour" and "Total product." **Total product** is the maximum output that a given quantity of labour can produce. You can see from the numbers in these columns that as Campus Sweaters employs more labour, total product increases. For example, when 1 worker is employed, total product is 4 sweaters a day, and when 2 workers are employed, total product is 10 sweaters a day. Each increase in employment increases total product.

The **marginal product** of labour is the increase in total product that results from a one-unit increase in the quantity of labour employed, other inputs remaining the same. For example, in Table 11.1, when Campus Sweaters increases employment from 2 to 3 workers and does not change its capital, the marginal product of the third worker is 3 sweaters—total product increases from 10 to 13 sweaters.

Average product tells how productive workers are on average. The **average product** of labour is equal to the total product divided by the quantity of labour employed. For example, in Table 11.1, the average product of 3 workers is 4.33 sweaters per worker—13 sweaters a day divided by 3 workers.

If you look closely at the numbers in Table 11.1, you can see some patterns. As Campus Sweaters hires more labour, marginal product increases initially, and

TABLE 11.1 Total Product, Marginal Product, and Average Product

	Labour (workers per day)	Total product (sweaters per day)	Marginal product (sweaters per additional worker)	Average product (sweaters per worker)
A	0	0		
			4	
B	1	4		4.00
			6	
C	2	10		5.00
			3	
D	3	13		4.33
			2	
E	4	15		3.75
			1	
F	5	16		3.20

Total product is the total amount produced. Marginal product is the change in total product that results from a one-unit increase in labour. For example, when labour increases from 2 to 3 workers a day (row C to row D), total product increases from 10 to 13 sweaters a day. The marginal product of going from 2 to 3 workers is 3 sweaters. Average product is total product divided by the quantity of labour employed. For example, the average product of 3 workers is 4.33 sweaters per worker (13 sweaters a day divided by 3 workers).

then begins to decrease. For example, marginal product increases from 4 sweaters a day for the first worker to 6 sweaters a day for the second worker and then decreases to 3 sweaters a day for the third worker. Average product also increases at first and then decreases. You can see the relationships between the quantity of labour hired and the three product concepts more clearly by looking at the product curves.

Product Curves

Product curves are graphs of the relationships between employment and the three product concepts you've just studied. They show how total product, marginal product, and average product change as employment changes. They also show the relationships among the three concepts. Let's look at the product curves.

Total Product Curve

Figure 11.1 shows the total product curve, *TP*, which is a graph of the total product schedule of Campus Sweaters. Points *A* through *F* correspond to rows *A* through *F* in Table 11.1. To graph the entire total product curve, we vary labour by hours rather than whole days.

Notice the shape of the total product curve. As employment increases from zero to 1 worker a day, the curve becomes steeper. Then, as employment increases to 3, 4, and 5 workers a day, the curve becomes less steep.

The total product curve is similar to the *production possibilities frontier* (explained in Chapter 2). It separates the attainable output levels from those that are unattainable. All the points that lie above the curve are unattainable. Points that lie below the curve, in the orange area, are attainable, but they are inefficient—they use more labour than is necessary to produce a given output. Only the points *on* the total product curve are technologically efficient.

FIGURE 11.1 Total Product Curve

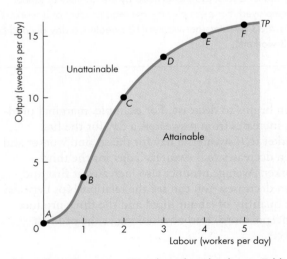

The total product curve, *TP*, is based on the data in Table 11.1. The total product curve shows how the quantity of sweaters produced changes as the quantity of labour employed changes. For example, 2 workers can produce 10 sweaters a day (point *C*). Points *A* through *F* on the curve correspond to the rows of Table 11.1. The total product curve separates attainable outputs from unattainable outputs. Points below the *TP* curve are inefficient.

myeconlab animation

Marginal Product Curve

Figure 11.2 shows the marginal product of labour at Campus Sweaters. Part (a) reproduces the total product curve from Fig. 11.1 and part (b) shows the marginal product curve, *MP*.

In part (a), the orange bars illustrate the marginal product of labour. The height of a bar measures marginal product. Marginal product is also measured by the slope of the total product curve. Recall that the slope of a curve is the change in the value of the variable measured on the *y*-axis—output—divided by the change in the variable measured on the *x*-axis—labour—as we move along the curve. A one-unit increase in labour, from 2 to 3 workers, increases output from 10 to 13 sweaters, so the slope from point *C* to point *D* is 3 sweaters per additional worker, the same as the marginal product we've just calculated.

Again varying the amount of labour in the smallest units possible, we can draw the marginal product curve shown in Fig. 11.2(b). The *height* of this curve measures the *slope* of the total product curve at a point. Part (a) shows that an increase in employment from 2 to 3 workers increases output from 10 to 13 sweaters (an increase of 3). The increase in output of 3 sweaters appears on the *y*-axis of part (b) as the marginal product of going from 2 to 3 workers. We plot that marginal product at the midpoint between 2 and 3 workers. Notice that the marginal product shown in Fig. 11.2(b) reaches a peak at 1.5 workers, and at that point, marginal product is 6 sweaters per additional worker. The peak occurs at 1.5 workers because the total product curve is steepest when employment increases from 1 worker to 2 workers.

The total product and marginal product curves differ across firms and types of goods. GM's product curves are different from those of Ontario Power Generation, whose curves in turn are different from those of Campus Sweaters. But the shapes of the product curves are similar because almost every production process has two features:

- Increasing marginal returns initially
- Diminishing marginal returns eventually

Increasing Marginal Returns Increasing marginal returns occur when the marginal product of an additional worker exceeds the marginal product of the previous worker. Increasing marginal returns arise from increased specialization and division of labour in the production process.

FIGURE 11.2 Total Product and Marginal Product

(a) Total product

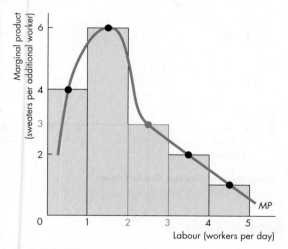

(b) Marginal product

Marginal product is illustrated by the orange bars. For example, when labour increases from 2 to 3 workers a day, marginal product is the orange bar with a height of 3 sweaters. (Marginal product is shown midway between the quantities of labour to emphasize that marginal product results from *changing* the quantity of labour.) The steeper the slope of the total product curve (*TP*) in part (a), the larger is marginal product (*MP*) in part (b). Marginal product increases to a maximum (in this example, when 1.5 workers a day are employed) and then declines—diminishing marginal product.

For example, if Campus Sweaters employs one worker, that person must learn all the aspects of sweater production: running the knitting machines, fixing breakdowns, packaging and mailing sweaters, buying and checking the type and colour of the wool. All these tasks must be performed by that one person.

If Campus Sweaters hires a second person, the two workers can specialize in different parts of the production process and can produce more than twice as much as one worker. The marginal product of the second worker is greater than the marginal product of the first worker. Marginal returns are increasing.

Diminishing Marginal Returns Most production processes experience increasing marginal returns initially, but all production processes eventually reach a point of *diminishing* marginal returns. **Diminishing marginal returns** occur when the marginal product of an additional worker is less than the marginal product of the previous worker.

Diminishing marginal returns arise from the fact that more and more workers are using the same capital and working in the same space. As more workers are added, there is less and less for the additional workers to do that is productive. For example, if Campus Sweaters hires a third worker, output increases but not by as much as it did when it hired the second worker. In this case, after two workers are hired, all the gains from specialization and the division of labour have been exhausted. By hiring a third worker, the factory produces more sweaters, but the equipment is being operated closer to its limits. There are even times when the third worker has nothing to do because the machines are running without the need for further attention. Hiring more and more workers continues to increase output but by successively smaller amounts. Marginal returns are diminishing. This phenomenon is such a pervasive one that it is called a "law"—the law of diminishing returns. The **law of diminishing returns** states that

As a firm uses more of a variable factor of production, with a given quantity of the fixed factor of production, the marginal product of the variable factor eventually diminishes.

You are going to return to the law of diminishing returns when we study a firm's costs. But before we do that, let's look at the average product of labour and the average product curve.

Average Product Curve

Figure 11.3 illustrates the average product of labour at Campus Sweaters and shows the relationship between average product and marginal product. Points *B* through *F* on the average product curve *AP* correspond to those same rows in Table 11.1. Average product increases from 1 to 2 workers (its maximum value at point *C*) but then decreases as yet more workers are employed. Notice also that average product is largest when average product and marginal product are equal. That is, the marginal product curve cuts the average product curve at the point of maximum average product. For the number of workers at which marginal product exceeds average product, average product is *increasing*. For the number of workers at which marginal product is less than average product, average product is *decreasing*.

The relationship between average product and marginal product is a general feature of the relationship between the average and marginal values of any variable—even your grades.

FIGURE 11.3 Average Product

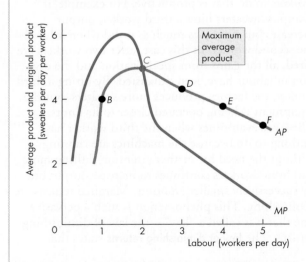

The figure shows the average product of labour and the connection between average product and marginal product. With 1 worker, marginal product exceeds average product, so average product is increasing. With 2 workers, marginal product equals average product, so average product is at its maximum. With more than 2 workers, marginal product is less than average product, so average product is decreasing.

 animation

Marginal Grades and Average Grades

How to Pull Up Your Average

Do you want to pull up your average grade? Then make sure that your next test is better than your current average! Your next test is your marginal test. If your marginal grade exceeds your average grade (like Economics in the figure), your average will rise. If your marginal grade equals your average grade (like English in the figure), your average won't change. If your marginal grade is below your average (like History in the figure), your average will fall.

The relationship between your marginal and average grades is exactly the same as that between marginal product and average product.

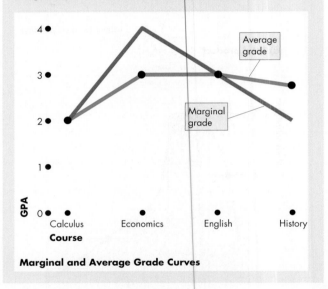

Marginal and Average Grade Curves

Review Quiz

1 Explain how the marginal product of labour and the average product of labour change as the quantity of labour employed increases (a) initially and (b) eventually.
2 What is the law of diminishing returns? Why does marginal product eventually diminish?
3 Explain the relationship between marginal product and average product.

myeconlab   Work Study Plan 11.2 and get instant feedback.

The firm's product curves influence its costs, as you are now going to see.

Short-Run Cost

To produce more output in the short run, a firm must employ more labour, which means that it must increase its costs. We describe the relationship between output and cost by using three cost concepts:

- Total cost
- Marginal cost
- Average cost

Total Cost

A firm's **total cost** (TC) is the cost of *all* the factors of production it uses. We separate total cost into total *fixed* cost and total *variable* cost.

Total fixed cost (TFC) is the cost of the firm's fixed factors. For Campus Sweaters, total fixed cost includes the cost of renting knitting machines and *normal profit*, which is the opportunity cost of Cindy's entrepreneurship (see Chapter 10, p. 229). The quantities of fixed factors don't change as output changes, so total fixed cost is the same at all outputs.

Total variable cost (TVC) is the cost of the firm's variable factors. For Campus Sweaters, labour is the variable factor, so this component of cost is its wage bill. Total variable cost changes as output changes.

Total cost is the sum of total fixed cost and total variable cost. That is,

$$TC = TFC + TVC.$$

The table in Fig. 11.4 shows total costs. Campus Sweaters rents one knitting machine for $25 a day, so its TFC is $25. To produce sweaters, the firm hires labour, which costs $25 a day. TVC is the number of workers multiplied by $25. For example, to produce 13 sweaters a day, in row D, the firm hires 3 workers and TVC is $75. TC is the sum of TFC and TVC, so to produce 13 sweaters a day, TC is $100. Check the calculations in the other rows of the table.

Figure 11.4 shows the total cost curves. The total cost curves graph total cost against output. The green TFC curves is horizontal because total fixed cost ($25 a day) does not change when output changes. The purple TVC curve and the blue TC curve both slope upward because to increase output, more labour must be employed, which increases total variable cost. Total fixed cost equals the vertical distance between the TVC and TC curves.

Let's now look at a firm's marginal cost.

FIGURE 11.4 Total Cost Curves

Labour (workers per day)	Output (sweaters per day)	Total fixed cost (TFC)	Total variable cost (TVC)	Total cost (TC)
		(dollars per day)		
A 0	0	25	0	25
B 1	4	25	25	50
C 2	10	25	50	75
D 3	**13**	**25**	**75**	**100**
E 4	15	25	100	125
F 5	16	25	125	150

Campus Sweaters rents a knitting machine for $25 a day, so this cost is the firm's total fixed cost. The firm hires workers at a wage rate of $25 a day, and this cost is its total variable cost. For example, in row D, Campus Sweaters employs 3 workers and its total variable cost is 3 × $25, which equals $75. Total cost is the sum of total fixed cost and total variable cost. For example, when Campus Sweaters employs 3 workers, total cost is $100—total fixed cost of $25 plus total variable cost of $75.

The graph shows the total cost curves. Total fixed cost is constant—the TFC curve is a horizontal line. Total variable cost increases as output increases, so the TVC curve and the TC curve increase as output increases. The vertical distance between the TC curve and the TVC curve equals total fixed cost, as illustrated by the two arrows.

Marginal Cost

Figure 11.4 shows that total variable cost and total cost increase at a decreasing rate at small outputs, but eventually, as output increases, total variable cost and total cost increase at an increasing rate. To understand this pattern in the change in total cost as output increases, we need to use the concept of *marginal cost*.

A firm's **marginal cost** is the increase in total cost that results from a one-unit increase in output. We calculate marginal cost as the increase in total cost divided by the increase in output. The table in Fig. 11.5 shows this calculation. When, for example, output increases from 10 sweaters to 13 sweaters, total cost increases from $75 to $100. The change in output is 3 sweaters, and the change in total cost is $25. The marginal cost of one of those 3 sweaters is ($25 ÷ 3), which equals $8.33.

Figure 11.5 graphs the marginal cost data in the table as the red marginal cost curve, *MC*. This curve is U-shaped because when Campus Sweaters hires a second worker, marginal cost decreases, but when it hires a third, a fourth, and a fifth worker, marginal cost successively increases.

At small outputs, marginal cost decreases as output increases because of greater specialization and the division of labour, but as output increases further, marginal cost eventually increases because of the *law of diminishing returns*. The law of diminishing returns means that the output produced by each additional worker is successively smaller. To produce an additional unit of output, ever more workers are required, and the cost of producing the additional unit of output—marginal cost—must eventually increase.

Marginal cost tells us how total cost changes as output increases. The final cost concept tells us what it costs, on average, to produce a unit of output. Let's now look at the average costs of Campus Sweaters.

Average Cost

Three average costs of production are

1. Average fixed cost
2. Average variable cost
3. Average total cost

Average fixed cost (*AFC*) is total fixed cost per unit of output. **Average variable cost** (*AVC*) is total variable cost per unit of output. **Average total cost** (*ATC*) is total cost per unit of output. The average cost concepts are calculated from the total cost concepts as follows:

$$TC = TFC + TVC.$$

Divide each total cost term by the quantity produced, *Q*, to get

$$\frac{TC}{Q} = \frac{TFC}{Q} + \frac{TVC}{Q}$$

or

$$ATC = AFC + AVC.$$

The table in Fig. 11.5 shows the calculation of average total cost. For example, in row *C*, output is 10 sweaters. Average fixed cost is ($25 ÷ 10), which equals $2.50, average variable cost is ($50 ÷ 10), which equals $5.00, and average total cost is ($75 ÷ 10), which equals $7.50. Note that average total cost is equal to average fixed cost ($2.50) plus average variable cost ($5.00).

Figure 11.5 shows the average cost curves. The green average fixed cost curve (*AFC*) slopes downward. As output increases, the same constant total fixed cost is spread over a larger output. The blue average total cost curve (*ATC*) and the purple average variable cost curve (*AVC*) are U-shaped. The vertical distance between the average total cost and average variable cost curves is equal to average fixed cost—as indicated by the two arrows. That distance shrinks as output increases because average fixed cost declines with increasing output.

Marginal Cost and Average Cost

The marginal cost curve (*MC*) intersects the average variable cost curve and the average total cost curve *at their minimum points*. When marginal cost is less than average cost, average cost is decreasing, and when marginal cost exceeds average cost, average cost is increasing. This relationship holds for both the *ATC* curve and the *AVC* curve. It is another example of the relationship you saw in Fig. 11.3 for average product and marginal product and in your average and marginal grades.

Why the Average Total Cost Curve Is U-Shaped

Average total cost is the sum of average fixed cost and average variable cost, so the shape of the *ATC* curve combines the shapes of the *AFC* and *AVC* curves. The

FIGURE 11.5 Marginal Cost and Average Costs

Marginal cost is calculated as the change in total cost divided by the change in output. When output increases from 4 to 10 sweaters, an increase of 6 sweaters, total cost increases by $25. Marginal cost is $25 ÷ 6, which is $4.17.

Each average cost concept is calculated by dividing the related total cost by output. When 10 sweaters are produced, AFC is $2.50 ($25 ÷ 10), AVC is $5 ($50 ÷ 10), and ATC is $7.50 ($75 ÷ 10).

The graph shows that the MC curve is U-shaped and intersects the AVC curve and the ATC curve at their minimum points. Average fixed cost curve (AFC) is downward sloping. The ATC curve and AVC curve are U-shaped. The vertical distance between the ATC curve and the AVC curve is equal to average fixed cost, as illustrated by the two arrows.

	Labour (workers per day)	Output (sweaters per day)	Total fixed cost (TFC)	Total variable cost (TVC)	Total cost (TC)	Marginal cost (MC) (dollars per additional sweater)	Average fixed cost (AFC)	Average variable cost (AVC)	Average total cost (ATC)
			(dollars per day)				(dollars per sweater)		
A	0	0	25	0	25		—	—	—
						. . . . 6.25			
B	1	4	25	25	50		6.25	6.25	12.50
						. . . . 4.17			
C	2	10	25	50	75		2.50	5.00	7.50
						. . . . 8.33			
D	3	**13**	25	75	100		**1.92**	**5.77**	**7.69**
						. . . . . . .12.50			
E	4	15	25	100	125		1.67	6.67	8.33
						. . . . . . .25.00			
F	5	16	25	125	150		1.56	7.81	9.38

myeconlab animation

U shape of the *ATC* curve arises from the influence of two opposing forces:

1. Spreading total fixed cost over a larger output
2. Eventually diminishing returns

When output increases, the firm spreads its total fixed cost over a larger output, so its average fixed cost decreases—its *AFC* curve slopes downward.

Diminishing returns means that as output increases, ever-larger amounts of labour are needed to produce an additional unit of output. So as output increases, average variable cost decreases initially but eventually increases, and the *AVC* curve slopes upward. The *AVC* curve is U-shaped.

The shape of the *ATC* curve combines these two effects. Initially, as output increases, both average fixed cost and average variable cost decrease, so average total cost decreases. The *ATC* curve slopes downward.

But as output increases further and diminishing returns set in, average variable cost starts to increase. With average fixed cost decreasing more quickly than average variable cost is increasing, the *ATC* curve continues to slope downward. Eventually, average variable cost starts to increase more quickly than average fixed cost decreases, so average total cost starts to increase. The *ATC* curve slopes upward.

Cost Curves and Product Curves

The technology that a firm uses determines its costs. Figure 11.6 shows the links between the firm's product curves and its cost curves. The upper graph shows the average product curve, *AP*, and the marginal product curve, *MP*—like those in Fig. 11.3. The lower graph shows the average variable cost curve, *AVC*, and the marginal cost curve, *MC*—like those in Fig. 11.5.

As labour increases from 0 to 1.5 workers a day (upper graph), output increases to 6.5 sweaters a day (lower graph). Marginal product and average product rise and marginal cost and average variable cost fall. At the point of maximum marginal product, marginal cost is at a minimum.

As labour increases from 1.5 to 2 workers a day (upper graph), output increases to 10 sweaters a day (lower graph). Marginal product falls and marginal cost rises, but average product continues to rise and average variable cost continues to fall. At the point of maximum average product, average variable cost is at a minimum. As labour increases further, output increases. Average product diminishes and average variable cost increases.

Shifts in the Cost Curves

The position of a firm's short-run cost curves depends on two factors:

- Technology
- Prices of factors of production

Technology A technological change that increases productivity increases the marginal product and average product of labour. With better technology, the same factors of production can produce more output, so the technological advance lowers the costs of production and shifts the cost curves downward.

For example, advances in robot production techniques have increased productivity in the automobile industry. As a result, the product curves of Chrysler, Ford, and GM have shifted upward and their cost curves have shifted downward. But the relationships between their product curves and cost curves have not changed. The curves are still linked in the way shown in Fig. 11.6.

Often, as in the case of robots producing cars, a technological advance results in a firm using more capital, a fixed factor, and less labour, a variable

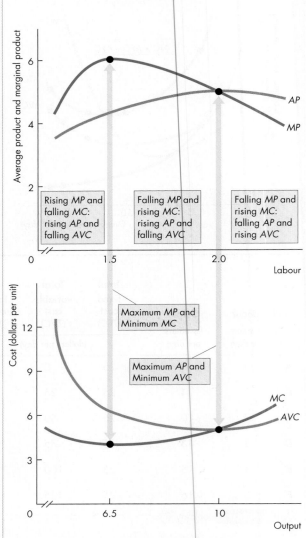

FIGURE 11.6 Product Curves and Cost Curves

A firm's *MP* curve is linked to its *MC* curve. If, as the firm increases its labour from 0 to 1.5 workers a day, its marginal product rises, its marginal cost falls. If marginal product is at a maximum, marginal cost is at a minimum. If, as the firm hires more than 1.5 workers a day, its marginal product diminishes, its marginal cost rises.

A firm's *AP* curve is linked to its *AVC* curve. If, as the firm increases its labour from 0 to 2 workers a day, its average product rises, its average variable cost falls. If average product is at a maximum, average variable cost is at a minimum. If, as the firm hires more than 2 workers a day, its average product diminishes, its average variable cost rises.

TABLE 11.2   A Compact Glossary of Costs

Term	Symbol	Definition	Equation
Fixed cost		Cost that is independent of the output level; cost of a fixed factor of production	
Variable cost		Cost that varies with the output level; cost of a variable factor of production	
Total fixed cost	TFC	Cost of the fixed factors of production	
Total variable cost	TVC	Cost of the variable factors of production	
Total cost	TC	Cost of all factors of production	$TC = TFC + TVC$
Output (total product)	TP	Total quantity produced (output Q)	
Marginal cost	MC	Change in total cost resulting from a one-unit increase in total product	$MC = \Delta TC \div \Delta Q$
Average fixed cost	AFC	Total fixed cost per unit of output	$AFC = TFC \div Q$
Average variable cost	AVC	Total variable cost per unit of output	$AVC = TVC \div Q$
Average total cost	ATC	Total cost per unit of output	$ATC = AFC + AVC$

factor. Another example is the use of ATMs by banks to dispense cash. ATMs, which are fixed capital, have replaced tellers, which are variable labour. Such a technological change decreases total cost but increases fixed costs and decreases variable cost. This change in the mix of fixed cost and variable cost means that at small outputs, average total cost might increase, while at large outputs, average total cost decreases.

Prices of Factors of Production An increase in the price of a factor of production increases the firm's costs and shifts its cost curves. But how the curves shift depends on which factor price changes.

An increase in rent or some other component of *fixed* cost shifts the *TFC* and *AFC* curves upward and shifts the *TC* curve upward but leaves the *AVC* and *TVC* curves and the *MC* curve unchanged. For example, if the interest expense paid by a trucking company increases, the fixed cost of transportation services increases.

An increase in wages, gasoline, or another component of *variable* cost shifts the *TVC* and *AVC* curves upward and shifts the *MC* curve upward but leaves the *AFC* and *TFC* curves unchanged. For example, if

truck drivers' wages or the price of gasoline increases, the variable cost and marginal cost of transportation services increase.

You've now completed your study of short-run costs. All the concepts that you've met are summarized in a compact glossary in Table 11.2.

Review Quiz

1 What relationships do a firm's short-run cost curves show?
2 How does marginal cost change as output increases (a) initially and (b) eventually?
3 What does the law of diminishing returns imply for the shape of the marginal cost curve?
4 What is the shape of the *AFC* curve and why does it have this shape?
5 What are the shapes of the *AVC* curve and the *ATC* curve and why do they have these shapes?

 Work Study Plan 11.3 and get instant feedback.

Long-Run Cost

We are now going to study the firm's long-run costs. In the long run, a firm can vary both the quantity of labour and the quantity of capital, so in the long run, all the firm's costs are variable.

The behaviour of long-run cost depends on the firm's *production function*, which is the relationship between the maximum output attainable and the quantities of both labour and capital.

The Production Function

Table 11.3 shows the production function of Campus Sweaters. The table lists total product schedules for four different quantities of capital. The quantity of capital identifies the plant size. The numbers for plant 1 are for a factory with 1 knitting machine—the case we've just studied. The other three plants have 2, 3, and 4 machines. If Campus Sweaters uses plant 2 with 2 knitting machines, the various amounts of labour can produce the outputs shown in the second column of the table. The other two columns show the outputs of yet larger quantities of capital. Each column of the table could be graphed as a total product curve for each plant.

Diminishing Returns Diminishing returns occur with each of the four plant sizes as the quantity of labour increases. You can check that fact by calculating the marginal product of labour in each of the plants with 2, 3, and 4 machines. With each plant size, as the firm increases the quantity of labour employed, the marginal product of labour (eventually) diminishes.

Diminishing Marginal Product of Capital

Diminishing returns also occur with each quantity of labour as the quantity of capital increases. You can check that fact by calculating the marginal product of capital at a given quantity of labour. The *marginal product of capital* is the change in total product divided by the change in capital when the quantity of labour is constant—equivalently, the change in output resulting from a one-unit increase in the quantity of capital. For example, if Campus Sweaters has 3 workers and increases its capital from 1 machine to 2 machines, output increases from 13 to 18 sweaters a day. The marginal product of the second machine is

TABLE 11.3 The Production Function

Labour (workers per day)	Output (sweaters per day)			
	Plant 1	Plant 2	Plant 3	Plant 4
1	4	10	13	15
2	10	15	18	20
3	13	18	22	24
4	15	20	24	26
5	16	21	25	27
Knitting machines (number)	1	2	3	4

The table shows the total product data for four quantities of capital (plant sizes). The greater the plant size, the larger is the output produced by any given quantity of labour. But for a given plant size, the marginal product of labour diminishes as more labour is employed. For a given quantity of labour, the marginal product of capital diminishes as the quantity of capital used increases.

5 sweaters a day. If the firm increases the number of machines from 2 to 3, output increases from 18 to 22 sweaters a day. The marginal product of the third machine is 4 sweaters a day, down from 5 sweaters a day for the second machine.

Let's now see what the production function implies for long-run costs.

Short-Run Cost and Long-Run Cost

As before, Campus Sweaters can hire workers for $25 a day and rent knitting machines for $25 a day. Using these factor prices and the data in Table 11.3, we can calculate the average total cost and graph the *ATC* curves for factories with 1, 2, 3, and 4 knitting machines. We've already studied the costs of a factory with 1 machine in Figs. 11.4 and 11.5. In Fig. 11.7, the average total cost curve for that case is ATC_1. Figure 11.7 also shows the average total cost curve for a factory with 2 machines, ATC_2, with 3 machines, ATC_3, and with 4 machines, ATC_4.

You can see, in Fig. 11.7, that the plant size has a big effect on the firm's average total cost. Two things stand out:

FIGURE 11.7 Short-Run Costs of Four Different Plants

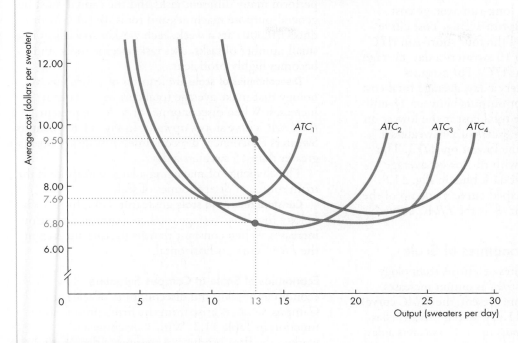

The figure shows short-run average total cost curves for four different quantities of capital at Campus Sweaters. The firm can produce 13 sweaters a day with 1 knitting machine on ATC_1 or with 3 knitting machines on ATC_3 for an average cost of $7.69 a sweater. The firm can produce 13 sweaters a day by using 2 machines on ATC_2 for $6.80 a sweater or by using 4 machines on ATC_4 for $9.50 a sweater.

If the firm produces 13 sweaters a day, the least-cost method of production, *the long-run method*, is with 2 machines on ATC_2.

myeconlab animation

1. Each short-run *ATC* curve is U-shaped.
2. For each short-run *ATC* curve, the larger the plant, the greater is the output at which average total cost is at a minimum.

Each short-run *ATC* curve is U-shaped because as the quantity of labour increases, its marginal product initially increases and then diminishes. This pattern in the marginal product of labour, which we examined in some detail for the plant with 1 knitting machine on pp. 254–255, occurs at all plant sizes.

The minimum average total cost for a larger plant occurs at a greater output than it does for a smaller plant because the larger plant has a higher total fixed cost and therefore, for any given output, a higher average fixed cost.

Which short-run *ATC* curve a firm operates on depends on the plant it has. But in the long run, the firm can choose its plant and the plant it chooses is the one that enables it to produce its planned output at the lowest average total cost.

To see why, suppose that Campus Sweaters plans to produce 13 sweaters a day. In Fig. 11.7, with 1 machine, the average total cost curve is ATC_1 and the

average total cost of 13 sweaters a day is $7.69 a sweater. With 2 machines, on ATC_2, average total cost is $6.80 a sweater. With 3 machines, on ATC_3, average total cost is $7.69 a sweater, the same as with 1 machine. Finally, with 4 machines, on ATC_4, average total cost is $9.50 a sweater.

The economically efficient plant for producing a given output is the one that has the lowest average total cost. For Campus Sweaters, the economically efficient plant to use to produce 13 sweaters a day is the one with 2 machines.

In the long run, Cindy chooses the plant that minimizes average total cost. When a firm is producing a given output at the least possible cost, it is operating on its *long-run average cost curve*.

The **long-run average cost curve** is the relationship between the lowest attainable average total cost and output when the firm can change both the plant it uses and the quantity of labour it employs.

The long-run average cost curve is a planning curve. It tells the firm the plant and the quantity of labour to use at each output to minimize average cost. Once the firm chooses a plant, the firm operates on the short-run cost curves that apply to that plant.

The Long-Run Average Cost Curve

Figure 11.8 shows how a long-run average cost curve is derived. The long-run average cost curve *LRAC* consists of pieces of the four short-run *ATC* curves. For outputs up to 10 sweaters a day, average total cost is the lowest on ATC_1. For outputs between 10 and 18 sweaters a day, average total cost is the lowest on ATC_2. For outputs between 18 and 24 sweaters a day, average total cost is the lowest on ATC_3. And for outputs in excess of 24 sweaters a day, average total cost is the lowest on ATC_4. The piece of each *ATC* curve with the lowest average total cost is highlighted in dark blue in Fig. 11.8. This dark-blue scallop-shaped curve made up of the pieces of the four *ATC* curves is the *LRAC* curve.

Economies and Diseconomies of Scale

Economies of scale are features of a firm's technology that make average total cost *fall* as output increases. When economies of scale are present, the *LRAC* curve slopes downward. In Fig. 11.8, Campus Sweaters has economies of scale for outputs up to 15 sweaters a day.

Greater specialization of both labour and capital is the main source of economies of scale. For example,

if GM produces 100 cars a week, each worker must perform many different tasks and the capital must be general-purpose machines and tools. But if GM produces 10,000 cars a week, each worker specializes in a small number of tasks, uses task-specific tools, and becomes highly proficient.

Diseconomies of scale are features of a firm's technology that make average total cost *rise* as output increases. When diseconomies of scale are present, the *LRAC* curve slopes upward. In Fig. 11.8, Campus Sweaters experiences diseconomies of scale at outputs greater than 15 sweaters a day.

The challenge of managing a large enterprise is the main source of diseconomies of scale.

Constant returns to scale are features of a firm's technology that keep average total cost constant as output increases. When constant returns to scale are present, the *LRAC* curve is horizontal.

Economies of Scale at Campus Sweaters   The economies of scale and diseconomies of scale at Campus Sweaters arise from the firm's production function in Table 11.3. With 1 machine and 1 worker, the firm produces 4 sweaters a day. With 2 machines and 2 workers, total cost doubles but

FIGURE 11.8   Long-Run Average Cost Curve

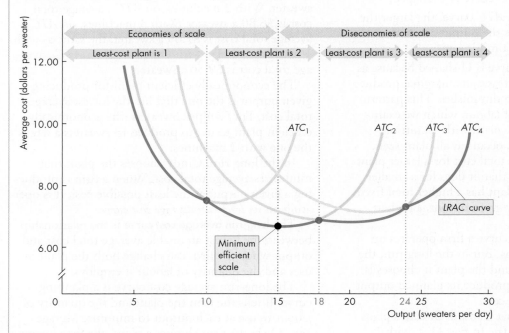

The long-run average cost curve traces the lowest attainable *ATC* when both labour and capital change. The green arrows highlight the output range over which each plant achieves the lowest *ATC*. Within each range, to change the quantity produced, the firm changes the quantity of labour it employs.

Along the *LRAC* curve, economies of scale occur if average cost falls as output increases; diseconomies of scale occur if average cost rises as output increases. Minimum efficient scale is the output at which average cost is lowest, which is 15 sweaters a day.

myeconlab   animation

Economies of Scale at an Auto Plant

Produce More to Cut Cost

Why do GM, Ford, and the other automakers have expensive equipment lying around that isn't fully used? You can answer this question with what you've learned in this chapter.

The basic answer is that auto production enjoys economies of scale. A larger output rate brings a lower long-run average cost—the firm's *LRAC* curve slopes downward.

An auto producer's average total cost curves look like those in the figure. To produce 20 vehicles an hour, the firm installs the plant with the short-run average total cost curve ATC_1. The average cost of producing a vehicle is $20,000.

Producing 20 vehicles an hour doesn't use the plant at its lowest possible average total cost. If the firm could sell enough cars for it to produce 40 vehicles an hour, the firm could use its current plant and produce at an average cost of $15,000 a vehicle.

But if the firm planned to produce 40 vehicles an hour, it would not stick with its current plant. The firm would install a bigger plant with the short-run average total cost curve ATC_2, and produce 40 vehicles an hour for $10,000 a car.

Automobile Plant Average Cost Curves

output more than doubles to 15 sweaters a day, so average cost decreases and Campus Sweaters experiences economies of scale. With 4 machines and 4 workers, total cost doubles again but output less than doubles to 26 sweaters a day, so average cost increases and the firm experiences diseconomies of scale.

Minimum Efficient Scale A firm's **minimum efficient scale** is the smallest output at which long-run average cost reaches its lowest level. At Campus Sweaters, the minimum efficient scale is 15 sweaters a day.

The minimum efficient scale plays a role in determining market structure. In a market in which the minimum efficient scale is small relative to market demand, the market has room for many firms, and the market is competitive. In a market in which the minimum efficient scale is large relative to market demand, only a small number of firms, and possibly only one firm, can make a profit and the market is either an oligopoly or monopoly. We will return to this idea in the next three chapters.

Review Quiz

1 What does a firm's production function show and how is it related to a total product curve?
2 Explain why the law of diminishing returns applies to capital as well as to labour.
3 What does a firm's long-run average cost curve show? How is it related to the firm's short-run average cost curves?
4 What are economies of scale and diseconomies of scale? How do they arise? What do they imply for the shape of the long-run average cost curve?
5 What is a firm's minimum efficient scale?

myeconlab   Work Study Plan 11.4 and get instant feedback.

◆ *Reading Between the Lines* on pp. 266–267 applies what you've learned about a firm's cost curves. It looks at the cost curves for generating electricity using a variety of technologies and compares the total cost and marginal cost of traditional and new technologies.

Cutting the Cost of Clean Electricity

Start-Up: Affordable Solar Power Possible in a Year

April 29, 2008

A Silicon Valley start-up says it has developed technology that can deliver solar power in about a year at prices competitive with coal-fired electricity. ...

SUNRGI's "concentrated photovoltaic" system relies on lenses to magnify sunlight 2,000 times, letting it produce as much electricity as standard panels with a far smaller system. Craig Goodman, head of the National Energy Marketers Association, is expected to announce the breakthrough today. ...

Executives of the year-old company say they'll start producing solar panels by mid-2009 that will generate electricity for about 7 cents a kilowatt hour, including installation. That's roughly the price of cheap coal-fired electricity. ...

Solar power is acclaimed as free of greenhouse gas emissions and able to supply electricity midday when demand is highest. But its cost—20 cents to 30 cents a kilowatt hour—has inhibited broad adoption. Solar makes up less than 1% of U.S. power generation.

An armada of solar technology makers aim to drive solar's price to 10 to 18 cents a kilowatt hour by 2010, and 5 to 10 cents by 2015, at or below utility costs. ...

Essence of the Story

- A new Silicon Valley firm, SUNRGI, says it has developed technology that can deliver solar power for 7 cents per kilowatt hour.

- 7 cents a kilowatt hour is roughly the price of electricity produced by coal.

- Solar power on current technology costs 20 cents to 30 cents per kilowatt hour.

- A large number of solar technology makers aim to bring costs down to 10 to 18 cents per kilowatt hour by 2010 and to 5 to 10 cents by 2015.

Economic Analysis

- Figure 1 shows the average total cost (*ATC*) of producing electricity using seven alternative technologies.

- The cost differences come from differences in fuel and capital costs. Hydro, wind, and solar have zero fuel costs.

- Today's solar technology has the highest average total cost at 15 cents per kilowatt hour.

- The new SUNRGI technology slashes the average total cost of solar power, but the cost doesn't get it down to a level that competes with the other technologies.

- The news article says that SUNRGI's average total cost of 7 cents a kilowatt hour is "roughly the price of cheap coal-fired electricity."

- Figure 1 shows the average total cost of coal-generated electricity at 4 cents per kilowatt hour. Based on this (correct) cost, it appears that SUNRGI cannot compete with coal (if we ignore the emission costs of coal).

- Remember, though, that average total cost varies with the output rate. The costs in Fig. 1 are those for operating plants at their most efficient level—80 percent of maximum capacity. (The closer a plant operates to its theoretical maximum output, the higher are the maintenance costs and so the higher is the average total cost.)

- Figures 2 and 3 compare the *ATC* curves and *MC* curves for producing electricity by using coal and solar technologies.

Figure 1 Average total costs compared

- In Fig. 2, the average total cost of electricity generated by coal has a minimum at 4 cents per kilowatt hour at 80 percent plant capacity.

- In Fig. 3, the average total cost of electricity generated by solar technology decreases as the plant is operated closer to capacity.

- The marginal cost of producing electricity by using coal eventually rises (Fig. 2), but the marginal cost of solar electricity is zero (Fig.3). All the costs for solar power are fixed costs.

Figure 2 Cost curves for coal-generated electricity

Figure 3 Cost curves for solar power

SUMMARY

Key Points

Decision Time Frames (p. 252)

- In the short run, the quantity of at least one factor of production is fixed and the quantities of the other factors of production can be varied.
- In the long run, the quantities of all factors of production can be varied.

Short-Run Technology Constraint (pp. 253–256)

- A total product curve shows the quantity a firm can produce with a given quantity of capital and different quantities of labour.
- Initially, the marginal product of labour increases as the quantity of labour increases, because of increased specialization and the division of labour.
- Eventually, marginal product diminishes because an increasing quantity of labour must share a fixed quantity of capital—the law of diminishing returns.
- Initially, average product increases as the quantity of labour increases, but eventually average product diminishes.

Short-Run Cost (pp. 257–261)

- As output increases, total fixed cost is constant, and total variable cost and total cost increase.
- As output increases, average fixed cost decreases and average variable cost, average total cost, and marginal cost decrease at low outputs and increase at high outputs. These cost curves are U-shaped.

Long-Run Cost (pp. 262–265)

- A firm has a set of short-run cost curves for each plant. For each output, the firm has one least-cost plant. The larger the output, the larger is the plant that will minimize average total cost.
- The long-run average cost curve traces out the lowest attainable average total cost at each output when both capital and labour inputs can be varied.
- With economies of scale, the long-run average cost curve slopes downward. With diseconomies of scale, the long-run average cost curve slopes upward.

Key Figures and Table

Figure 11.2   Total Product and Marginal Product, 255
Figure 11.3   Average Product, 256
Figure 11.5   Marginal Cost and Average Costs, 259
Figure 11.6   Product Curves and Cost Curves, 260
Figure 11.7   Short-Run Costs of Four Different Plants, 263
Figure 11.8   Long-Run Average Cost Curve, 264
Table 11.2   A Compact Glossary of Costs, 261

Key Terms

Average fixed cost, 258
Average product, 253
Average total cost, 258
Average variable cost, 258
Constant returns to scale, 264
Diminishing marginal returns, 255
Diseconomies of scale, 264
Economies of scale, 264
Law of diminishing returns, 255
Long run, 252
Long-run average cost curve, 263
Marginal cost, 258
Marginal product, 253
Minimum efficient scale, 265
Short run, 252
Sunk cost, 252
Total cost, 257
Total fixed cost, 257
Total product, 253
Total variable cost, 257

PROBLEMS and APPLICATIONS ◆

myeconlab Work problems 1–11 in Chapter 11 Study Plan and get instant feedback.
Work problems 12–22 as Homework, a Quiz, or a Test if assigned by your instructor.

1. Which of the following news items involves a short-run decision and which involves a long-run decision? Explain.

   January 31, 2008: Starbucks will open 75 more stores abroad than originally predicted, for a total of 975.

   February 25, 2008: For three hours on Tuesday, Starbucks will shut down every single one of its 7,100 stores so that baristas can receive a refresher course.

   June 2, 2008: Starbucks replaces baristas with vending machines.

   July 18, 2008: Starbucks is closing 616 stores by the end of March.

2. The total product schedule of Sue's Surfboards is

Labour (workers per week)	Output (surfboards per week)
1	30
2	70
3	120
4	160
5	190
6	210
7	220

   a. Draw the total product curve.
   b. Calculate the average product of labour and draw the average product curve.
   c. Calculate the marginal product of labour and draw the marginal product curve.
   d. Over what output range does the firm enjoy the benefits of increased specialization and division of labour?
   e. Over what output range does the firm experience diminishing marginal product of labour?
   f. Over what output range does the firm experience increasing average product of labour but diminishing marginal product of labour?
   g. Explain how it is possible for a firm to experience simultaneously an increasing *average* product but a diminishing *marginal* product.

3. Sue's Surfboards, in problem 2, hires workers at $500 a week and its total fixed cost is $1,000 a week.

   a. Calculate total cost, total variable cost, and total fixed cost of each output in the table. Plot these points and sketch the short-run total cost curves passing through them.
   b. Calculate average total cost, average fixed cost, average variable cost, and marginal cost of each output in the table. Plot these points and sketch the short-run average and marginal cost curves passing through them.
   c. Illustrate the connection between Sue's *AP*, *MP*, *AVC*, and *MC* curves in graphs like those in Fig. 11.6.

4. Sue's Surfboards, in problems 2 and 3, rents a factory building and the rent is increased by $200 a week. If other things remain the same, how do Sue's Surfboards' short-run average cost curves and marginal cost curve change?

5. Workers at Sue's Surfboards, in problems 2 and 3, negotiate an increase in the wage rate to $600 a week. If other things remain the same, explain how Sue's Surfboards' short-run average cost curves and marginal cost curve change.

6. Sue's Surfboards, in problem 2, buys a second plant and the output produced by each worker increases by 50 percent. The total fixed cost of operating each plant is $1,000 a week. Each worker is paid $500 a week.

   a. Calculate the average total cost of producing 180 and 240 surfboards a week when Sue's Surfboards operates two plants. Graph these points and sketch the *ATC* curve.
   b. To produce 180 surfboards a week, is it efficient to operate one or two plants?
   c. To produce 210 surfboards a week, is it efficient for Sue's to operate one or two plants?

7. **Airlines Seek Out New Ways to Save on Fuel as Costs Soar**

   The financial pain of higher fuel prices is particularly acute for airlines because it is their single biggest expense. ... [Airlines] pump about 7,000 gallons into a Boeing 737 and as much as 60,000 gallons into the bigger 747 jet. ... Each generation of aircraft is more efficient. At Northwest, the Airbus A330 long-range jets use 38 percent less fuel than the DC-10s they replaced, while the Airbus A319 medium-range planes are 27 percent more efficient than DC-9s. ...

New York Times, June 11, 2008

a. Is the price of fuel a fixed cost or a variable cost for an airline?
b. Explain how a rise in the price of fuel changes an airline's total average and marginal costs.
c. Draw a graph to show the effects of a rise in the price of fuel on an airline's *TFC, TVC, AFC, AVC,* and *MC* curves.
d. Explain how a technological advance that makes an airplane engine more fuel efficient changes an airline's total product, marginal product, and average product.
e. Draw a graph to illustrate the effects of a more fuel-efficient aircraft on an airline's *TP, MP,* and *AP* curves.
f. Explain how a technological advance that makes an airplane engine more fuel efficient changes an airline's average variable cost, marginal cost, and average total cost.
g. Draw a graph to illustrate the effect of more fuel-efficient airplane engines on an airline's *AVC, MC,* and *ATC* curves.

8. The table shows the production function of Jackie's Canoe Rides.

Labour	Output (rides per day)			
(workers per day)	Plant 1	Plant 2	Plant 3	Plant 4
10	20	40	55	65
20	40	60	75	85
30	65	75	90	100
40	75	85	100	110
Canoes	10	20	30	40

Jackie's pays $100 a day to rent a canoe and $50 a day to hire a canoe operator.

a. Graph the *ATC* curves for Plant 1 and Plant 2.
b. On your graph in a, plot the *ATC* curves for Plant 3 and Plant 4.
c. On the *LRAC* curve, what is the average cost of producing 40, 75, and 85 rides a week?
d. What is Jackie's minimum efficient scale?
e. Explain how Jackie's uses its *LRAC* curve to decide how many canoes to rent.
f. Does Jackie's production function feature economies of scale or diseconomies of scale?

9. **Business Boot Camp**
At a footwear company called Caboots, sales rose from $160,000 in 2000 to $2.3 million in 2006. But in 2007 sales dipped to $1.5 million. Joey and Priscilla Sanchez, who run Caboots, blame the decline partly on a flood that damaged the firm's office and sapped morale.

Based on a *Fortune* article, *CNN*, April 23, 2008

If the Sanchezes are correct in their assumptions and the prices of footwear didn't change, explain the effect of the flood on the total product and marginal product curves of Caboots.

10. **Passengers of Collapsed Discount Airline Zoom Seek New Flights**
Thousands of travellers were trying to book other flights Friday after the sudden collapse of Ottawa-based Zoom Airlines. ...

The airline owes more than $400,000 to the authority that runs the Calgary airport, along with money to the airplanes' owner, ground support and refuellers. The Halifax airport authority is owed nearly $200,000 ... for unpaid landing fees, gate fees and other expenses. ... Ian Lee, ... at Carleton University, said Zoom's demise isn't surprising. ... "They just don't have the economies of scale. They don't have the capital, the deep pockets, to sustain these brutal fuel prices," he said.

CBC News, August 29, 2008

a. Of the costs noted in the news clip, which are fixed costs and which are variable costs?
b. Draw a graph to show your predicted effects of "brutal fuel prices" on the airline's short-run total cost curves.
c. Draw a graph to show your predicted effects of "brutal fuel prices" on Zoom's short-run average cost and marginal cost curves.
d. Explain why small airlines such as Zoom "don't have economies of scale."

11. **Grain Prices Go the Way of the Oil Price**
Every morning millions of [people] confront the latest trend in commodities markets at their kitchen table. ... Rising prices for crops ... have begun to drive up the cost of breakfast.

Economist, July 21, 2007

Explain how the rising price of crops affects the average total cost and marginal cost of producing breakfast cereals.

12. **Coffee King Starbucks Raises Its Prices**

Blame the sour news at Starbucks this week on soaring milk costs. ... The wholesale price [of] milk is up nearly 70% in the 12 months. ... "There's a lot of milk in those [Starbucks] lattes," notes John Glass, CIBC World Markets restaurant analyst.

USA Today, July 24, 2007

a. Is milk a fixed factor of production or a variable factor of production?

b. Describe how the increase in the price of milk changes the short-run cost curves.

13. Bill's Bakery has a fire and Bill loses some of his cost data. The bits of paper that he recovers after the fire provide the information in the following table (all the cost numbers are dollars).

TP	AFC	AVC	ATC	MC
10	120	100	220	
				80
20	*A*	*B*	150	
				90
30	40	90	130	
				130
40	30	*C*	*D*	
				E
50	24	108	132	

Bill asks you to come to his rescue and provide the missing data in the five spaces identified as *A*, *B*, *C*, *D*, and *E*.

14. ProPainters hires students at $250 a week to paint houses. It leases equipment at $500 a week. The table sets out its total product schedule.

Labour (students)	Output (houses painted per week)
1	2
2	5
3	9
4	12
5	14
6	15

a. If ProPainters paints 12 houses a week, calculate its total cost, average total cost, and marginal cost.

b. At what output is average total cost a minimum?

c. Explain why the gap between total cost and total variable cost is the same at all outputs.

15. ProPainters hires students at $250 a week to paint houses. It leases equipment at $500 a week. Suppose that ProPainters doubles the number of students it hires and doubles the amount of equipment it leases. ProPainters experiences diseconomies of scale.

a. Explain how the *ATC* curve with one unit of equipment differs from that when ProPainters uses twice as much equipment.

b. Explain what might be the source of the diseconomies of scale experienced.

16. The table shows the production function of Bonnie's Balloon Rides.

Bonnie's pays $500 a day to rent a balloon and $25 a day to hire a balloon operator.

Labour (workers per day)	Output (rides per day)			
	Plant 1	Plant 2	Plant 3	Plant 4
10	4	10	13	15
20	10	15	18	20
30	13	18	22	24
40	15	20	24	26
50	16	21	25	27
Balloons (number)	1	2	3	4

a. Graph the *ATC* curves for Plant 1 and Plant 2.

b. On your graph in a, plot the *ATC* curves for Plant 3 and Plant 4.

c. On Bonnie's *LRAC* curve, what is the average cost of producing 18 rides and 15 rides a day?

d. Explain how Bonnie's uses its *LRAC* curve to decide how many balloons to rent.

17. A firm is producing at minimum average total cost with its current plant. Sketch the firm's short-run *ATC* curve and its *LRAC* curve for each of the following situations and explain, using the concepts of economies of scale and diseconomies of scale, the circumstances in which

a. The firm can lower its average total cost by increasing its plant.

b. The firm can lower its average total cost by decreasing its plant.

c. The firm cannot lower its average total cost.

18. **Starbucks Unit Brews Up Self-Serve Espresso Bars**

    ... automated, self-serve espresso kiosks are in grocery stores. ... The machines, which grind their own beans, crank out lattes, ... and drip coffees ... take credit and debit cards, [and] cash. ... Concordia Coffee, a small Bellevue coffee equipment maker, builds the self-serve kiosks and sells them to Coinstar for just under $40,000 per unit. Coinstar installs them ... and provides maintenance. The kiosks use Seattle's Best Coffee [from Starbucks]. ... The self-serve kiosks remove the labour costs of having a barista. ... Store personnel handle refills of coffee beans and milk. ...

    MSNBC, June 1, 2008

    a. What is Coinstar's total fixed cost of operating one self-serve kiosk?
    b. What are Coinstar's variable costs of providing coffee at a self-serve kiosk?
    c. Assume that a coffee machine operated by a barista costs less than $40,000. Explain how the fixed costs, variable costs, and total costs of barista-served and self-served coffee differ.
    d. Sketch the marginal cost and average cost curves implied by your answer to c.

19. **A Bakery on the Rise**

    Some 500 customers a day line up to buy Avalon's breads, scones, muffins, and coffee. ... Staffing and management are worries. Avalon now employs 35 ... [and] it will hire 15 more. ... Payroll will climb by 30% to 40%. ... As new CEO, Victor has quickly executed an ambitious agenda that includes the move to a larger space. ... Avalon's costs will soar. ... Its monthly rent, for example, will leap to $10,000, from $3,500.

    CNN, March 24, 2008

    a. Which of Avalon's decisions described in the news clip is a short-run decision and which is a long-run decision?
    b. Why is Avalon's long-run decision riskier than its short-run decision?
    c. By how much will Avalon's short-run decision increase its total variable cost?
    d. By how much will Avalon's long-run decision increase its monthly total fixed cost?
    e. Draw a graph to illustrate Avalon's short-run cost curves before and after the events described in the news clip.

20. **Gap Will Focus on Smaller Scale Stores**

    Gap has too many stores that are 12,500 square feet ... deemed too large. ... "Stores are larger than we need." ... The target size of stores should be 6,000 square feet to 10,000 square feet. In addition, the company plans to combine previously separate concept stores. Some Gap body, adult, maternity, baby and kids stores will be combined in one, rather than in separate spaces as they have been previously.

    CNN, June 10, 2008

    a. Thinking of a Gap store as a production plant, explain why Gap is making a decision to reduce the size of its stores.
    b. Is Gap's decision a long-run decision or a short-run decision? Explain.
    c. How might combining Gap's concept stores into one store help to better take advantage of economies of scale?

21. **The Sunk-Cost Fallacy**

    You have good tickets to a basketball game an hour's drive away. There's a blizzard raging outside, and the game is being televised. You can sit warm and safe at home by a roaring fire and watch it on TV, or you can bundle up, dig out your car, and go to the game. What do you do?

    Slate, September 9, 2005

    a. What type of cost is your expenditure on tickets?
    b. Why is the cost of the ticket irrelevant to your current decision about whether to stay at home or go to the game?

22. Study *Reading Between the Lines* on pp. 266–267 and then answer the following questions.

    a. Sketch the *AFC*, *AVC*, and *ATC* curves for electricity production using seven technologies: (i) nuclear, (ii) coal, (iii) gas, (iv) hydro, (v) wind, (vi) SUNRGI's new solar system, and (vii) today's solar technology.
    b. Sketch the marginal cost curves for electricity production using seven technologies: (i) nuclear, (ii) coal, (iii) gas, (iv) hydro, (v) wind, (vi) SUNRGI's new solar system, and (vii) today's solar technology.
    c. Given the cost differences among the different methods of generating electricity, why do you think we use more than one method? If we could use only one method, which would it be?

12 Perfect Competition

After studying this chapter, you will be able to

- Define perfect competition
- Explain how a firm makes its output decision and why it sometimes shuts down temporarily and lays off its workers
- Explain how price and output are determined in a perfectly competitive market
- Explain why firms enter and leave a competitive market and the consequences of entry and exit
- Predict the effects of a change in demand and of a technological advance
- Explain why perfect competition is efficient

Airlines and producers of trucks, cars, and coaches are facing tough times: Prices are being slashed to drive sales and profits are turning into losses. Airlines are cutting back on flights, charging to check bags and for refreshments, or to use a blanket, and some are even going out of business. Vehicle production has been scaled back and workers have been either laid off temporarily or let go permanently.

Taking a longer view, astonishing transformations have occurred over the past decade. Today, at $600 for a powerful laptop, almost every student owns one. Fifteen years ago, at $6,000 for a heavy, slow portable computer, these machines were a rare sight on campus.

What forces are responsible for this diversity of performance of production, prices, and profits? What are the causes and consequences of firms entering or leaving a market? Why do firms sometimes stop producing and temporarily lay off workers?

To study competitive markets, we are going to build a model of a market in which competition is as fierce and extreme as possible—more extreme than in the examples we've just considered. We call this situation "perfect competition." In *Reading Between the Lines* at the end of the chapter, we'll apply the model to the market for long-distance air travel and see how the effects of high fuel prices are playing out in that market.

◆ What Is Perfect Competition?

The firms that you study in this chapter face the force of raw competition. We call this extreme form of competition perfect competition. **Perfect competition** is a market in which

- Many firms sell identical products to many buyers.
- There are no restrictions on entry into the market.
- Established firms have no advantage over new ones.
- Sellers and buyers are well informed about prices.

Farming, fishing, wood pulping and paper milling, the manufacture of paper cups and shopping bags, grocery retailing, photo finishing, lawn services, plumbing, painting, dry cleaning, and laundry services are all examples of highly competitive industries.

How Perfect Competition Arises

Perfect competition arises if the minimum efficient scale of a single producer is small relative to the market demand for the good or service. In this situation, there is room in the market for many firms. A firm's *minimum efficient scale* is the smallest output at which long-run average cost reaches its lowest level. (See Chapter 11, p. 265.)

In perfect competition, each firm produces a good that has no unique characteristics, so consumers don't care which firm's good they buy.

Price Takers

Firms in perfect competition are price takers. A **price taker** is a firm that cannot influence the market price because its production is an insignificant part of the total market.

Imagine that you are a wheat farmer in Saskatchewan. You have 500 hectares planted—which sounds like a lot. But compared to the millions of hectares across the Canadian prairies and the U. S. mid-west as well as the millions more in Argentina, Australia, and Ukraine, your 500 hectares are a drop in the ocean. Nothing makes your wheat any better than any other farmer's, and all the buyers of wheat know the price at which they can do business.

If the market price of wheat is $300 a tonne, then that is the highest price you can get for your wheat. Ask for $310 and no one will buy from you. Offer it for $290 and you'll be sold out in a flash and have given away $10 a tonne. You take the market price.

Economic Profit and Revenue

A firm's goal is to maximize *economic profit*, which is equal to total revenue minus total cost. Total cost is the *opportunity cost* of production, which includes *normal profit*. (See Chapter 10, p. 228.)

A firm's **total revenue** equals the price of its output multiplied by the number of units of output sold (price × quantity). **Marginal revenue** is the change in total revenue that results from a one-unit increase in the quantity sold. Marginal revenue is calculated by dividing the change in total revenue by the change in the quantity sold.

Figure 12.1 illustrates these revenue concepts. In part (a), the market demand curve, *D*, and market supply curve, *S*, determine the market price. The market price is $25 a sweater. Campus Sweaters is one of many producers of sweaters, so the best it can do is to sell its sweaters for $25 each.

Total Revenue   Total revenue is equal to the price multiplied by the quantity sold. In the table in Fig. 12.1, if Campus Sweaters sells 9 sweaters, its total revenue is $225 (9 × $25).

Figure 12.1(b) shows the firm's total revenue curve (*TR*), which graphs the relationship between total revenue and the quantity sold. At point *A* on the *TR* curve, the firm sells 9 sweaters and has a total revenue of $225. Because each additional sweater sold brings in a constant amount—$25—the total revenue curve is an upward-sloping straight line.

Marginal Revenue   Marginal revenue is the change in total revenue that results from a one-unit increase in quantity sold. In the table in Fig. 12.1, when the quantity sold increases from 8 to 9 sweaters, total revenue increases from $200 to $225, so marginal revenue is $25 a sweater.

Because the firm in perfect competition is a price taker, the change in total revenue that results from a one-unit increase in the quantity sold equals the market price. *In perfect competition, the firm's marginal revenue equals the market price.* Figure 12.1(c) shows the firm's marginal revenue curve (*MR*) as the horizontal line at the market price.

Demand for the Firm's Product   The firm can sell any quantity it chooses at the market price. So the demand curve for the firm's product is a horizontal line at the market price, the same as the firm's marginal revenue curve.

FIGURE 12.1   Demand, Price, and Revenue in Perfect Competition

(a) Sweater market

(b) Campus Sweaters' total revenue

(c) Campus Sweaters' marginal revenue

Quantity sold (Q) (sweaters per day)	Price (P) (dollars per sweater)	Total revenue (TR = P × Q) (dollars)	Marginal revenue (MR = ΔTR/ΔQ) (dollars per additional sweater)
8	25	200	
			 25
9	25	225	
			 25
10	25	250	

In part (a), market demand and market supply determine the market price (and quantity). Part (b) shows the firm's total revenue curve (TR). Point A corresponds to the second row of the table—Campus Sweaters sells 9 sweaters at $25 a sweater, so total revenue is $225. Part (c) shows the firm's marginal revenue curve (MR). This curve is also the demand curve for the firm's sweaters. The demand for sweaters from Campus Sweaters is perfectly elastic at the market price of $25 a sweater.

myeconlab animation

A horizontal demand curve illustrates a perfectly elastic demand, so the demand for the firm's product is perfectly elastic. A sweater from Campus Sweaters is a *perfect substitute* for a sweater from any other factory. But the *market* demand for sweaters is *not* perfectly elastic: Its elasticity depends on the substitutability of sweaters for other goods and services.

The Firm's Decisions

The goal of the competitive firm is to maximize economic profit, given the constraints it faces. To achieve its goal, a firm must decide

1. How to produce at minimum cost
2. What quantity to produce
3. Whether to enter or exit a market

You've already seen how a firm makes the first decision. It does so by operating with the plant that minimizes long-run average cost—by being on its long-run average cost curve. We'll now see how the firm makes the other two decisions. We start by looking at the firm's output decision.

Review Quiz

1 Why is a firm in perfect competition a price taker?

2 In perfect competition, what is the relationship between the demand for the firm's output and the market demand?

3 In perfect competition, why is a firm's marginal revenue curve also the demand curve for the firm's output?

4 What decisions must a firm make to maximize profit?

myeconlab Work Study Plan 12.1 and get instant feedback.

The Firm's Output Decision

A firm's cost curves (total cost, average cost, and marginal cost) describe the relationship between its output and costs (see pp. 257–261). A firm's revenue curves (total revenue and marginal revenue) describe the relationship between its output and revenue (p. 275). From the firm's cost curves and revenue curves, we can find the output that maximizes the firm's economic profit.

Figure 12.2 shows how to do this for Campus Sweaters. The table lists the firm's total revenue and total cost at different outputs, and part (a) of the figure shows the firm's total revenue curve, *TR*, and

total cost curve, *TC*. These curves are graphs of the numbers in the first three columns of the table.

Economic profit equals total revenue minus total cost. The fourth column of the table in Fig. 12.2 shows the economic profit made by Campus Sweaters, and part (b) of the figure graphs these numbers as its economic profit curve, *EP*.

Economic profit is maximized at an output of 9 sweaters a day. At this output, total revenue is $225 a day, total cost is $183 a day, and economic profit is $42 a day. No other output rate achieves a larger profit. At outputs of less than 4 sweaters and more than 12 sweaters a day, the firm incurs an economic loss. At either 4 or 12 sweaters a day, the firm makes zero economic profit, called a *break-even* point.

FIGURE 12.2   Total Revenue, Total Cost, and Economic Profit

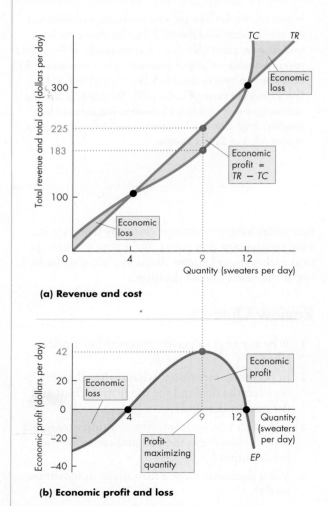

(a) **Revenue and cost**

(b) **Economic profit and loss**

Quantity (Q) (sweaters per day)	Total revenue (TR) (dollars)	Total cost (TC) (dollars)	Economic profit (TR – TC) (dollars)
0	0	22	–22
1	25	45	–20
2	50	66	–16
3	75	85	–10
4	100	100	0
5	125	114	11
6	150	126	24
7	175	141	34
8	200	160	40
9	225	183	42
10	250	210	40
11	275	245	30
12	300	300	0
13	325	360	–35

The table lists the total revenue, total cost, and economic profit of Campus Sweaters. Part (a) graphs the total revenue and total cost curves and part (b) graphs economic profit.

Campus Sweaters makes maximum economic profit, $42 a day ($225 – $183), when it produces 9 sweaters a day. At outputs of 4 sweaters and 12 sweaters a day, Campus Sweaters makes zero economic profit—these are break-even points. At outputs less than 4 sweaters and greater than 12 sweaters a day, Campus Sweaters incurs an economic loss.

Marginal Analysis and the Supply Decision

Another way to find the profit-maximizing output is to use *marginal analysis*, which compares marginal revenue, *MR*, with marginal cost, *MC*. As output increases, marginal revenue is constant but marginal cost eventually increases.

If marginal revenue exceeds the firm's marginal cost (*MR > MC*), then the revenue from selling one more unit exceeds the cost of producing that unit and an increase in output will increase economic profit. If marginal revenue is less than marginal cost (*MR < MC*), then the revenue from selling one more unit is less than the cost of producing that unit and a decrease in output will increase economic profit. If marginal revenue equals marginal cost (*MR = MC*), then the revenue from selling one more unit equals the cost incurred to produce that unit. Economic profit is maximized and either an increase or a decrease in output decreases economic profit.

Figure 12.3 illustrates these propositions. If Campus Sweaters increases its output from 8 sweaters to 9 sweaters a day, marginal revenue ($25) exceeds marginal cost ($23), so by producing the 9th sweater economic profit increases by $2 from $40 to $42 a day. The blue area in the figure shows the increase in economic profit when the firm increases production from 8 to 9 sweaters per day.

If Campus Sweaters increases its output from 9 sweaters to 10 sweaters a day, marginal revenue ($25) is less than marginal cost ($27), so by producing the 10th sweater, economic profit decreases. The last column of the table shows that economic profit decreases from $42 to $40 a day. The red area in the figure shows the economic loss that arises from increasing production from 9 to 10 sweaters a day.

Campus Sweaters maximizes economic profit by producing 9 sweaters a day, the quantity at which marginal revenue equals marginal cost.

A firm's profit-maximizing output is its quantity supplied at the market price. The quantity supplied at a price of $25 a sweater is 9 sweaters a day. If the price were higher than $25 a sweater, the firm would increase production. If the price were lower than $25 a sweater, the firm would decrease production. These profit-maximizing responses to different market prices are the foundation of the law of supply:

Other things remaining the same, the higher the market price of a good, the greater is the quantity supplied of that good.

FIGURE 12.3   Profit-Maximizing Output

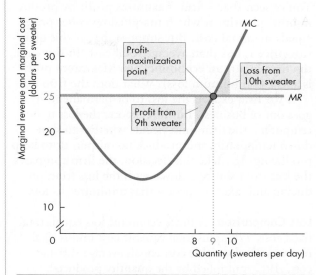

The firm maximizes profit by producing the output at which marginal revenue equals marginal cost and marginal cost is increasing. The table and figure show that marginal cost equals marginal revenue and economic profit is maximized when Campus Sweaters produces 9 sweaters a day.

The table shows that if Campus Sweaters increases output from 8 to 9 sweaters, marginal cost is $23, which is less than the marginal revenue of $25. If output increases from 9 to 10 sweaters, marginal cost is $27, which exceeds the marginal revenue of $25. If marginal revenue exceeds marginal cost, an increase in output increases economic profit. If marginal revenue is less than marginal cost, an increase in output decreases economic profit. If marginal revenue equals marginal cost, economic profit is maximized.

Quantity (Q) (sweaters per day)	Total revenue (TR) (dollars)	Marginal revenue (MR) (dollars per additional sweater)	Total cost (TC) (dollars)	Marginal cost (MC) (dollars per additional sweater)	Economic profit (TR − TC) (dollars)
7	175		141		34
		25		19	
8	200		160		40
		25		23	
9	225		183		42
		25		27	
10	250		210		40
		25		35	
11	275		245		30

Temporary Shutdown Decision

You've seen that a firm maximizes profit by producing the quantity at which marginal revenue (price) equals marginal cost. But suppose that at this quantity, price is less than average total cost. In this case, the firm incurs an economic loss. Maximum profit is a loss (a minimum loss). What does the firm do?

If the firm expects the loss to be permanent, it goes out of business. But if it expects the loss to be temporary, the firm must decide whether to shut down temporarily and produce no output, or to keep producing. To make this decision, the firm compares the loss from shutting down with the loss from producing and takes the action that minimizes its loss.

Loss Comparisons A firm's economic loss equals total fixed cost, *TFC*, plus total variable cost minus total revenue. Total variable cost equals average variable cost, *AVC*, multiplied by the quantity produced, *Q*, and total revenue equals price, *P*, multiplied by the quantity *Q*. So

$$\text{Economic loss} = TFC + (AVC - P) \times Q.$$

If the firm shuts down, it produces no output ($Q = 0$). The firm has no variable costs and no revenue but it must pay its fixed costs, so its economic loss equals total fixed cost.

If the firm produces, then in addition to its fixed costs, it incurs variable costs. But it also receives revenue. Its economic loss equals total fixed cost—the loss when shut down—plus total variable cost minus total revenue. If total variable cost exceeds total revenue, this loss exceeds total fixed cost and the firm shuts down. Equivalently, if average variable cost exceeds price, this loss exceeds total fixed cost and the firm shuts down.

The Shutdown Point A firm's **shutdown point** is the price and quantity at which it is indifferent between producing and shutting down. The shutdown point occurs at the price and the quantity at which average variable cost is a minimum. At the shutdown point, the firm is minimizing its loss and its loss equals total fixed cost. If the price falls below minimum average variable cost, the firm shuts down temporarily and continues to incur a loss equal to total fixed cost. At prices above minimum average variable cost but below average total cost, the firm produces the loss minimizing output and incurs a loss, but a loss that is less than total fixed cost.

Figure 12.4 illustrates the firm's shutdown decision and the shutdown point that we've just described for Campus Sweaters.

The firm's average variable cost curve is *AVC* and the marginal cost curve is *MC*. Average variable cost has a minimum of $17 a sweater when output is 7 sweaters a day. The *MC* curve intersects the *AVC* curve at its minimum. (We explained this relationship between a marginal and average cost in Chapter 11; see pp. 258–259.)

The figure shows the marginal revenue curve *MR* when the price is $17 a sweater, a price equal to minimum average variable cost.

Marginal revenue equals marginal cost at 7 sweaters a day, so this quantity maximizes economic profit (minimizes economic loss). The *ATC* curve shows that the firm's average total cost of producing 7 sweaters a day is $20.14 a sweater. The firm incurs a loss equal to $3.14 a sweater on 7 sweaters a day, so its loss is $22 a day, which equals total fixed cost.

FIGURE 12.4   The Shutdown Decision

The shutdown point is at minimum average variable cost. At a price below minimum average variable cost, the firm shuts down and produces no output. At a price equal to minimum average variable cost, the firm is indifferent between shutting down and producing no output or producing the output at minimum average variable cost. Either way, the firm minimizes its economic loss and incurs a loss equal to total fixed cost.

myeconlab   animation

The Firm's Supply Curve

A perfectly competitive firm's supply curve shows how its profit-maximizing output varies as the market price varies, other things remaining the same. The supply curve is derived from the firm's marginal cost curve and average variable cost curves. Figure 12.5 illustrates the derivation of the supply curve.

When the price *exceeds* minimum average variable cost (more than $17), the firm maximizes profit by producing the output at which marginal cost equals price. If the price rises, the firm increases its output—it moves up along its marginal cost curve.

When the price is *less than* minimum average variable cost (less than $17 a sweater), the firm maximizes profit by temporarily shutting down and producing no output. The firm produces zero output at all prices below minimum average variable cost.

When the price *equals* minimum average variable cost, the firm maximizes profit *either* by temporarily shutting down and producing no output *or* by producing the output at which average variable cost is a minimum—the shutdown point, *T*. The firm never produces a quantity between zero and the quantity at the shutdown point *T* (a quantity greater than zero and less than 7 sweaters a day).

The firm's supply curve in Fig. 12.5(b) runs along the *y*-axis from a price of zero to a price equal to minimum average variable cost, jumps to point *T,* and then, as the price rises above minimum average variable cost, follows the marginal cost curve.

Review Quiz

1 Why does a firm in perfect competition produce the quantity at which marginal cost equals price?
2 What is the lowest price at which a firm produces an output? Explain why.
3 What is the relationship between a firm's supply curve, its marginal cost curve, and its average variable cost curve?

 Work Study Plan 12.2 and get instant feedback.

So far, we have studied a single firm in isolation. We have seen that the firm's profit-maximizing decisions depend on the market price, which the firm takes as given. But how is the market price determined? Let's find out.

FIGURE 12.5   A Firm's Supply Curve

(a) Marginal cost and average variable cost

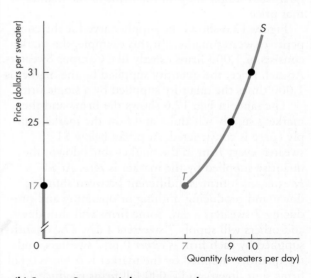

(b) Campus Sweaters' short-run supply curve

Part (a) shows the firm's profit-maximizing output at various market prices. At $25 a sweater, it produces 9 sweaters, and at $17 a sweater, it produces 7 sweaters. At all prices below $17 a sweater, Campus Sweaters produces nothing. Its shutdown point is *T*. Part (b) shows the firm's supply curve—the quantity of sweaters it produces at each price. Its supply curve is made up of the marginal cost curve at all prices above minimum average variable cost and the vertical axis at all prices below minimum average variable cost.

myeconlab animation

Output, Price, and Profit in the Short Run

To determine the price and quantity in a perfectly competitive market, we need to know how market demand and market supply interact. We start by studying a perfectly competitive market in the short run. The short run is a situation in which the number of firms is fixed.

Market Supply in the Short Run

The **short-run market supply curve** shows the quantity supplied by all the firms in the market at each price when each firm's plant and the number of firms remain the same.

You've seen how an individual firm's supply curve is determined. The market supply curve is derived from the individual supply curves. The quantity supplied by the market at a given price is the sum of the quantities supplied by all the firms in the market at that price.

Figure 12.6 shows the supply curve for the competitive sweater market. In this example, the market consists of 1,000 firms exactly like Campus Sweaters. At each price, the quantity supplied by the market is 1,000 times the quantity supplied by a single firm.

The table in Fig. 12.6 shows the firm's and the market's supply schedules and how the market supply curve is constructed. At prices below $17 a sweater, every firm in the market shuts down; the quantity supplied by the market is zero. At $17 a sweater, each firm is indifferent between shutting down and producing nothing or operating and producing 7 sweaters a day. Some firms will shut down, and others will supply 7 sweaters a day. The quantity supplied by each firm is *either* 0 or 7 sweaters, and the quantity supplied by the market is *between* 0 (all firms shut down) and 7,000 (all firms produce 7 sweaters a day each).

The market supply curve is a graph of the market supply schedule, and the points on the supply curve *A* through *D* represent the rows of the table.

To construct the market supply curve, we sum the quantities supplied by all the firms at each price. Each of the 1,000 firms in the market has a supply schedule like Campus Sweaters. At prices below $17 a sweater, the market supply curve runs along the *y*-axis. At $17 a sweater, the market supply curve is horizontal—supply is perfectly elastic. As the price

FIGURE 12.6   Short-Run Market Supply Curve

	Price (dollars per sweater)	Quantity supplied by Campus Sweaters (sweaters per day)	Quantity supplied by market (sweaters per day)
A	17	0 or 7	0 to 7,000
B	20	8	8,000
C	25	9	9,000
D	31	10	10,000

The market supply schedule is the sum of the supply schedules of all the individual firms. A market that consists of 1,000 identical firms has a supply schedule similar to that of one firm, but the quantity supplied by the market is 1,000 times as large as that of the one firm (see the table). The market supply curve is S_M. Points A, B, C, and D correspond to the rows of the table. At the shutdown price of $17 a sweater, each firm produces either 0 or 7 sweaters a day and the quantity supplied by the market is between 0 and 7,000 sweaters a day. The market supply is perfectly elastic at the shutdown price.

myeconlab   animation

rises above $17 a sweater, each firm increases its quantity supplied and the quantity supplied by the market increases by 1,000 times that of one firm.

Short-Run Equilibrium

Market demand and short-run market supply determine the market price and market output. Figure 12.7(a) shows a short-run equilibrium. The short-run supply curve, S, is the same as S_M in Fig. 12.6. If the market demand curve is D_1, the market price is $20 a sweater. Each firm takes this price as given and produces its profit-maximizing output, which is 8 sweaters a day. Because the market has 1,000 identical firms, the market output is 8,000 sweaters a day.

A Change in Demand

Changes in demand bring changes to short-run market equilibrium. Figure 12.7(b) shows these changes.

If demand increases and the demand curve shifts rightward to D_2, the market price rises to $25 a sweater. At this price, each firm maximizes profit by increasing its output to 9 sweaters a day. The market output increases to 9,000 sweaters a day.

If demand decreases and the demand curve shifts leftward to D_3, the market price falls to $17. At this price, each firm maximizes profit by decreasing its output. If each firm produces 7 sweaters a day, the market output decreases to 7,000 sweaters a day.

If the demand curve shifts farther leftward than D_3, the market price remains at $17 a sweater because the market supply curve is horizontal at that price. Some firms continue to produce 7 sweaters a day, and others temporarily shut down. Firms are indifferent between these two activities, and whichever they choose, they incur an economic loss equal to total fixed cost. The number of firms continuing to produce is just enough to satisfy the market demand at a price of $17 a sweater.

Profits and Losses in the Short Run

In short-run equilibrium, although the firm produces the profit-maximizing output, it does not necessarily end up making an economic profit. It might

FIGURE 12.7   Short-Run Equilibrium

(a) Equilibrium

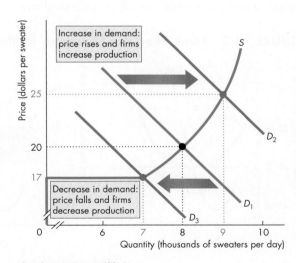

(b) Change in equilibrium

In part (a), the market supply curve is S and the market demand curve is D_1. The market price is $20 a sweater. At this price, each firm produces 8 sweaters a day and the market produces 8,000 sweaters a day.

In part (b), if the market demand increases to D_2, the price rises to $25 a sweater. Each firm produces

9 sweaters a day and market output is 9,000 sweaters a day. If market demand decreases to D_3, the price falls to $17 a sweater and each firm decreases its output. If each firm produces 7 sweaters a day, the market output is 7,000 sweaters a day.

myeconlab   animation

do so, but it might alternatively break even or incur an economic loss. Economic profit (or loss) per sweater is price, P, minus average total cost, ATC. So economic profit (or loss) is $(P - ATC) \times Q$. If price equals average total cost, a firm breaks even—the entrepreneur makes normal profit. If price exceeds average total cost, the firm makes an economic profit. If price is less than average total cost, the firm incurs an economic loss. Figure 12.8 shows these three possible short-run profit outcomes for Campus Sweaters that correspond to the three different levels of market demand that we've just examined.

Three Possible Short-Run Outcomes

Figure 12.8(a) corresponds to the situation in Fig. 12.7(a) where the market demand is D_1. The equilibrium price of a sweater is $20 and the firm produces 8 sweaters a day. Average total cost is $20 a sweater. Price equals average total cost (ATC), so the firm breaks even (makes zero economic profit).

Figure 12.8(b) corresponds to the situation in Fig. 12.7(b) where the market demand is D_2. The equilibrium price of a sweater is $25 and the firm produces 9 sweaters a day. Here, price exceeds average total cost,

so the firm makes an economic profit. Its economic profit is $42 a day, which equals $4.67 per sweater ($25.00 − $20.33) multiplied by 9, the profit-maximizing number of sweaters produced. The blue rectangle shows this economic profit. The height of this rectangle is profit per sweater, $4.67, and the length is the quantity of sweaters produced, 9 a day. So the area of the rectangle is economic profit of $42 a day.

Figure 12.8(c) corresponds to the situation in Fig. 12.7(b) where the market demand is D_3. The equilibrium price of a sweater is $17. Here, the price is less than average total cost, so the firm incurs an economic loss. Price and marginal revenue are $17 a sweater, and the profit-maximizing (in this case, loss-minimizing) output is 7 sweaters a day. Total revenue is $119 a day (7 × $17). Average total cost is $20.14 a sweater, so the economic loss is $3.14 per sweater ($20.14 − $17.00). This loss per sweater multiplied by the number of sweaters is $22. The red rectangle shows this economic loss. The height of this rectangle is economic loss per sweater, $3.14, and the length is the quantity of sweaters produced, 7 a day. So the area of the rectangle is the firm's economic loss of $22 a day. If the price dips below $17 a sweater, the firm temporarily shuts down and incurs an economic loss equal to total fixed cost.

FIGURE 12.8   Three Short-Run Outcomes for the Firm

(a) Break even

(b) Economic profit

(c) Economic loss

In the short run, the firm might break even (make zero economic profit), make an economic profit, or incur an economic loss. In part (a), the price equals minimum average total cost. At the profit-maximizing output, the firm breaks even and makes zero economic profit. In part (b), the market price is $25 a sweater. At the profit-maximizing

output, the price exceeds average total cost and the firm makes an economic profit equal to the area of the blue rectangle. In part (c), the market price is $17 a sweater. At the profit-maximizing output, the price is below minimum average total cost and the firm incurs an economic loss equal to the area of the red rectangle.

myeconlab animation

Production Cutback and Temporary Shutdown

Drop in Demand for Coaches at MCI Winnipeg

Motor Coach Industries (MCI) employs about 1,000 workers at its Winnipeg plant, where it has been building coaches for more than 70 years. In February 2008, the firm delivered some bad news to labour union head, Glen Tomchak: The plant would shut down for a week in April and some workers would be permanently laid off.

MCI officials said that in the current state of the U.S. economy, the demand for coaches was down and prices were depressed.

We can explain this temporary shutdown using the analysis you've learned in this chapter. The shutdown occurred because total revenue was insufficient to cover total *variable* cost.

The firm's permanent cut in its workforce can also be explained by the same analysis. The fall in the price of a coach decreased the profit-maximizing quantity of coaches and MCI cut the quantity of labour employed.

Review Quiz

1 How do we derive the short-run market supply curve in perfect competition?

2 In perfect competition, when market demand increases, explain how the price of the good and the output and profit of each firm changes in the short run.

3 In perfect competition, when market demand decreases, explain how the price of the good and the output and profit of each firm changes in the short run.

 Work Study Plan 12.3 and get instant feedback.

◆ Output, Price, and Profit in the Long Run

In short-run equilibrium, a firm might make an economic profit, incur an economic loss, or break even. Although each of these three situations is a short-run equilibrium, only one of them is a long-run equilibrium. The reason is that in the long run, firms can enter or exit the market.

Entry and Exit

Entry occurs in a market when new firms come into the market and the number of firms increases. Exit occurs when existing firms leave a market and the number of firms decreases.

Firms respond to economic profit and economic loss by either entering or exiting a market. New firms enter a market in which existing firms are making an economic profit. Firms exit a market in which they are incurring an economic loss. Temporary economic profit and temporary economic loss don't trigger entry and exit. It's the prospect of persistent economic profit or loss that triggers entry and exit.

Entry and exit change the market supply, which influences the market price, the quantity produced by each firm, and the firm's economic profit (or loss). If firms enter a market, supply increases and the market supply curve shifts rightward. The increase in supply lowers the market price and eventually eliminates economic profit. When economic profit reaches zero, entry stops.

If firms exit a market, supply decreases and the market supply curve shifts leftward. The market price rises and economic loss decreases. Eventually, economic loss is eliminated and exit stops.

To summarize,

- New firms enter a market in which existing firms are making an economic profit.
- As new firms enter a market, the market price falls and the economic profit of each firm decreases.
- Firms exit a market in which they are incurring an economic loss.
- As firms leave a market, the market price rises and the economic loss incurred by the remaining firms decreases.
- Entry and exit stop when firms make zero economic profit.

A Closer Look at Entry

The sweater market has 800 firms with cost curves like those in Fig. 12.9(a). The market demand curve is D, the market supply curve is S_1, and the price is $25 a sweater in Fig. 12.9(b). Each firm produces 9 sweaters a day and makes an economic profit.

This economic profit is a signal for new firms to enter the market. As entry takes place, supply increases and the market supply curve shifts rightward towards S^*. As supply increases with no change in demand, the market price gradually falls from $25 to $20 a sweater. At this lower price, each firm makes zero economic profit and entry stops.

Entry results in an increase in market output, but each firm's output *decreases*. Because the price falls, each firm moves down its supply curve and produces less. Because the number of firms increases, the market produces more.

A Closer Look at Exit

Now the sweater market has 1,200 firms with cost curves like those in Fig. 12.9(a). The market demand curve is D, the market supply curve is S_2, and the price is $17 a sweater in Fig. 12.9(b). Each firm produces 7 sweaters a day and incurs an economic loss.

This economic loss is a signal for firms to exit the market. As exit takes place, supply decreases and the market supply curve shifts leftward towards S^*. As supply decreases with no change in demand, the market price gradually rises from $17 to $20 a sweater. At this higher price, losses are eliminated, each firm makes zero economic profit, and exit stops.

Exit results in a decrease in market output, but each firm's output *increases*. Because the price rises, each firm moves up its supply curve and produces more. Because the number of firms decreases, the market produces less.

FIGURE 12.9   Entry, Exit, and Long-Run Equilibrium

(a) Campus Sweaters

(b) The sweater market

Each firm has cost curves like those of Campus Sweaters in part (a). The market demand curve is D in part (b). When the market supply in part (b) is S_1, the price is $25 a sweater. In part (a), each firm produces 9 sweaters a day and makes an economic profit. Profit triggers the entry of new firms and as new firms enter, the market supply curve shifts rightward, from S_1 towards S^*. The price falls from $25 to $20 a sweater, and the quantity produced increases from 7,200 to 8,000 sweaters. Each firm's output

decreases to 8 sweaters a day and economic profit is zero.

When the market supply is S_2, the price is $17 a sweater. In part (a), each firm produces 7 sweaters a day and incurs an economic loss. Loss triggers exit and as firms exit, the market supply curve shifts leftward, from S_2 towards S^*. The price rises from $17 to $20 a sweater, and the quantity produced decreases from 8,400 to 8,000 sweaters. Each firm's output increases from 7 to 8 sweaters a day and economic profit is zero.

Entry and Exit in Action

Personal Computers and Farm Machines

An example of entry and falling prices occurred during the 1980s and 1990s in the personal computer market. When IBM introduced its first PC in 1981, IBM had little competition. The price was $7,000 (about $16,850 in today's money) and IBM made a large economic profit selling the new machine.

Observing IBM's huge success, new firms such as Gateway, NEC, Dell, and a host of others entered the market with machines that were technologically identical to IBM's. In fact, they were so similar that they came to be called "clones." The massive wave of entry into the personal computer market increased the market supply and lowered the price. The economic profit for all firms decreased.

Today, a $400 computer is vastly more powerful than its 1981 ancestor that cost 42 times as much.

The same PC market that saw entry during the 1980s and 1990s has seen some exit more recently. In 2001, IBM, the firm that first launched the PC, announced that it was exiting the market. The intense competition from Gateway, NEC, Dell, and others that entered the market following IBM's lead has lowered the price and eliminated the economic profit. So IBM now concentrates on servers and other parts of the computer market.

IBM exited the PC market because it was incurring economic losses. Its exit decreased market supply and made it possible for the remaining firms in the market to make zero economic profit.

International Harvester, a manufacturer of farm equipment, provides another example of exit. For decades, people associated the name "International Harvester" with tractors, combines, and other farm machines. But International Harvester wasn't the only maker of farm equipment. The market became intensely competitive, and the firm began to incur economic losses. Now the firm has a new name, Navistar International, and it doesn't make tractors anymore. After years of economic losses and shrinking revenues, it got out of the farm-machine business in 1985 and started to make trucks.

International Harvester exited because it was incurring an economic loss. Its exit decreased supply and made it possible for the remaining firms in the market to break even.

Long-Run Equilibrium

You've now seen how economic profit induces entry, which in turn eliminates the profit. You've also seen how economic loss induces exit, which in turn eliminates the loss.

When economic profit and economic loss have been eliminated and entry and exit have stopped, a competitive market is in *long-run equilibrium.*

You've seen how a competitive market adjusts towards its long-run equilibrium. But a competitive market is rarely *in* a state of long-run equilibrium. Instead, it is constantly and restlessly evolving towards long-run equilibrium. The reason is that the market is continually bombarded with events that change the constraints that firms face.

Markets are constantly adjusting to keep up with changes in tastes, which change demand, and changes in technology, which change costs.

In the next sections, we're going to see how a competitive market reacts to changing tastes and technology and how it guides resources to their highest-valued use.

Review Quiz

1 What triggers entry in a competitive market? Describe the process that ends further entry.
2 What triggers exit in a competitive market? Describe the process that ends further exit.

myeconlab Work Study Plan 12.4 and get instant feedback.

Changing Tastes and Advancing Technology

Increased awareness of the health hazards of smoking has decreased the demand for tobacco products. The development of inexpensive automobile and air transportation during the 1990s decreased the demand for long-distance trains and buses. Solid-state electronics has decreased the demand for TV and radio repair. The development of good-quality inexpensive clothing has decreased the demand for sewing machines. What happens in a competitive market when there is a permanent decrease in the demand for its product?

Microwave food preparation has increased the demand for paper, glass, and plastic cooking utensils and plastic wrap. The Internet has increased the demand for a personal computer and the widespread use of the computer has increased the demand for high-speed connections and music downloads. What happens in a competitive market when the demand for its output increases?

Advances in technology are constantly lowering the costs of production. New biotechnologies have dramatically lowered the costs of producing many food and pharmaceutical products. New electronic technologies have lowered the cost of producing just about every good and service. What happens in a competitive market for a good when technological change lowers its production costs?

Let's use the theory of perfect competition to answer these questions.

A Permanent Change in Demand

Figure 12.10(a) shows a competitive market that initially is in long-run equilibrium. The demand curve is D_0, the supply curve is S_0, the market price is P_0, and market output is Q_0. Figure 12.10(b) shows a single firm in this initial long-run equilibrium. The firm produces q_0 and makes zero economic profit.

Suppose that demand decreases and the demand curve shifts leftward to D_1, as shown in Fig. 12.10(a). The market price falls to P_1, and the quantity supplied by the market decreases from Q_0 to Q_1 as the market moves down along its short-run supply curve S_0. Figure 12.10(b) shows the situation facing a firm. The market price is now below the firm's minimum average total cost, so the firm incurs an economic

loss. But to minimize its loss, the firm adjusts its output to keep marginal cost equal to price. At a price of P_1, each firm produces an output of q_1.

The market is now in short-run equilibrium but not long-run equilibrium. It is in short-run equilibrium because each firm is maximizing profit; it is not in long-run equilibrium because each firm is incurring an economic loss—its average total cost exceeds the price.

The economic loss is a signal for some firms to exit the market. As they do so, short-run market supply decreases and the market supply curve gradually shifts leftward. As market supply decreases, the price rises. At each higher price, a firm's profit-maximizing output is greater, so the firms remaining in the market increase their output as the price rises. Each firm moves up along its marginal cost or supply curve in Fig. 12.10(b). That is, as some firms exit the market, market output decreases but the output of the firms that remain in the market increases.

Eventually, enough firms have exited the market for the market supply curve to have shifted to S_1 in Fig. 12.10(a). The market price has returned to its original level, P_0. At this price, the firms remaining in the market produce q_0, the same quantity that they produced before the decrease in demand. Because firms are now making zero economic profit, no firm has an incentive to enter or exit the market. The market supply curve remains at S_1, and market output is Q_2. The market is again in long-run equilibrium.

The difference between the initial long-run equilibrium and the final long-run equilibrium is the number of firms in the market. A permanent decrease in demand has decreased the number of firms. Each firm remaining in the market produces the same output in the new long-run equilibrium as it did initially and makes zero economic profit. In the process of moving from the initial equilibrium to the new one, firms incur economic losses.

We've just worked out how a competitive market responds to a permanent *decrease* in demand. A permanent increase in demand triggers a similar response, except in the opposite direction. The increase in demand brings a higher price, economic profit, and entry. Entry increases market supply and eventually lowers the price to its original level and economic profit to zero.

The demand for Internet service increased permanently during the 1990s and huge profit opportunities arose in this market. The result was a massive rate of entry of Internet service providers. The process of

FIGURE 12.10   A Decrease in Demand

(a) Industry

(b) Firm

A market starts out in long-run competitive equilibrium. Part (a) shows the market demand curve D_0, the market supply curve S_0, the market price P_0, and the equilibrium quantity Q_0. Each firm sells its output at the price P_0, so its marginal revenue curve is MR_0 in part (b). Each firm produces q_0 and makes zero economic profit.

Market demand decreases permanently from D_0 to D_1 in part (a) and the market price falls to P_1. Each firm decreases its output to q_1 in part (b), and the market out-

put decreases to Q_1 in part (a).

Firms now incur economic losses and some firms exit the market. As they do so, the market supply curve gradually shifts leftward, from S_0 towards S_1. This shift gradually raises the market price from P_1 back to P_0. While the price is below P_0, firms incur economic losses and some firms exit the market. Once the price has returned to P_0, each firm makes zero economic profit and has no incentive to exit. Each firm produces q_0, and the market output is Q_2.

myeconlab animation

competition and change in the Internet service market is similar to what we have just studied, but with an increase in demand rather than a decrease in demand.

We've now studied the effects of a permanent change in demand for a good. In doing so, we began and ended in a long-run equilibrium and examined the process that takes a market from one equilibrium to another. It is this process, not the equilibrium points, that describes the real world.

One feature of the predictions that we have just generated seems odd: In the long run, regardless of whether demand increases or decreases, the market price returns to its original level. Is this outcome inevitable? In fact, it is not. It is possible for the equilibrium market price in the long run to remain the same, rise, or fall.

External Economies and Diseconomies

The change in the long-run equilibrium price depends on external economies and external diseconomies. **External economies** are factors beyond the control of an individual firm that lower the firm's costs as the *market* output increases. **External diseconomies** are factors outside the control of a firm that raise the firm's costs as the *market* output increases. With no external economies or external diseconomies, a firm's costs remain constant as the market output changes.

Figure 12.11 illustrates these three cases and introduces a new supply concept: the long-run market supply curve.

A **long-run market supply curve** shows how the quantity supplied in a market varies as the market price varies after all the possible adjustments have been made, including changes in each firm's plant and the number of firms in the market.

Figure 12.11(a) shows the case we have just studied—no external economies or diseconomies. The long-run market supply curve (LS_A) is perfectly elastic. In this case, a permanent increase in demand from D_0 to D_1 has no effect on the price in the long run. The increase in demand brings a temporary rise in the price to P_S and in the short run the quantity increases from Q_0 to Q_S. Entry increases short-run supply from S_0 to S_1, which lowers the price from P_S back to P_0 and increases the quantity to Q_1.

Figure 12.11(b) shows the case of external diseconomies. The long-run market supply curve (LS_B) slopes upward. A permanent increase in demand from D_0 to D_1 raises the price in both the short run and the long run. The increase in demand brings a temporary rise in the price to P_S and in the short run the quantity increases from Q_0 to Q_S. Entry increases short-run supply from S_0 to S_2, which lowers the price from P_S to P_2 and increases the quantity to Q_2.

One source of external diseconomies is congestion. The airline market provides a good example. With bigger airline market output, congestion at both airports and in the air increases, resulting in longer delays and extra waiting time for passengers and airplanes. These external diseconomies mean that as the output of air transportation services increases (in the absence of technological advances), average cost increases. As a result, the long-run market supply curve is upward-sloping. A permanent increase in demand brings an increase in quantity and a rise in the price. (Markets with external diseconomies might nonetheless have a falling price because technological advances shift the long-run supply curve downward.)

Figure 12.11(c) shows the case of external economies. The long-run market supply curve (LS_C) slopes downward. A permanent increase in demand from D_0 to D_1 raises the price in the short run and lowers it in the long run. Again, the increase in demand brings a temporary rise in the price to P_S and in the short run the quantity increases from Q_0 to Q_S. Entry increases short-run supply from S_0 to S_3, which lowers the price to P_3 and increases the quantity to Q_3.

An example of external economies is the growth of specialist support services for a market as it expands.

FIGURE 12.11   Long-Run Changes in Price and Quantity

(a) Constant-cost industry   **(b) Increasing-cost industry**   **(c) Decreasing-cost industry**

Three possible changes in price and quantity occur in the long run. When demand increases from D_0 to D_1, entry occurs and the market supply curve shifts rightward from S_0 to S_1. In part (a), the long-run market supply curve, LS_A, is horizontal. The quantity increases from Q_0 to Q_1, and the price remains constant at P_0.

In part (b), the long-run market supply curve is LS_B; the price rises to P_2, and the quantity increases to Q_2. This case occurs in industries with external diseconomies. In part (c), the long-run market supply curve is LS_C; the price falls to P_3, and the quantity increases to Q_3. This case occurs in a market with external economies.

As farm output increased in the nineteenth and early twentieth centuries, the services available to farmers expanded. New firms specialized in the development and marketing of farm machinery and fertilizers. As a result, average farm costs decreased. Farms enjoyed the benefits of external economies. As a consequence, as the demand for farm products increased, the output increased but the price fell.

Over the long term, the prices of many goods and services have fallen, not because of external economies but because of technological change. Let's now study this influence on a competitive market.

Technological Change

Industries are constantly discovering lower-cost techniques of production. Most cost-saving production techniques cannot be implemented, however, without investing in new plant and equipment. As a consequence, it takes time for a technological advance to spread through a market. Some firms whose plants are on the verge of being replaced will be quick to adopt the new technology, while other firms whose plants have recently been replaced will continue to operate with an old technology until they can no longer cover their average variable cost. Once average variable cost cannot be covered, a firm will scrap even a relatively new plant (embodying an old technology) in favour of a plant with a new technology.

New technology allows firms to produce at a lower cost. As a result, as firms adopt a new technology, their cost curves shift downward. With lower costs, firms are willing to supply a given quantity at a lower price or, equivalently, they are willing to supply a larger quantity at a given price. In other words, market supply increases, and the market supply curve shifts rightward. With a given demand, the quantity produced increases and the price falls.

Two forces are at work in a market undergoing technological change. Firms that adopt the new technology make an economic profit, so there is entry by new-technology firms. Firms that stick with the old technology incur economic losses. They either exit the market or switch to the new technology.

As old-technology firms disappear and new-technology firms enter, the price falls and the quantity produced increases. Eventually, the market arrives at a long-run equilibrium in which all the firms use the new technology and make zero economic profit. Because in the long run competition eliminates economic profit, technological change brings only temporary gains to producers. But the lower prices and better products that technological advances bring are permanent gains for consumers.

The process that we've just described is one in which some firms experience economic profits and others experience economic losses. It is a period of dynamic change in a market. Some firms do well, and others do badly. Often, the process has a geographical dimension—the expanding new-technology firms bring prosperity to what was once the boondocks, and traditional industrial regions decline. Sometimes, the new-technology firms are in a foreign country, while the old-technology firms are in the domestic economy. The information revolution of the 1990s produced many examples of changes like these. The computer programming industry, traditionally concentrated in the United States, now flourishes in Canada, the United Kingdom, and India. Television shows and movies, traditionally made in Los Angeles and New York, are now made in large numbers in Toronto and Vancouver.

Technological advances are not confined to the information and entertainment industries. Even food production is undergoing a major technological change because of genetic engineering.

Review Quiz

1 Describe the course of events in a competitive market following a permanent decrease in demand. What happens to output, price, and economic profit in the short run and in the long run?

2 Describe the course of events in a competitive market following a permanent increase in demand. What happens to output, price, and economic profit in the short run and in the long run?

3 Describe the course of events in a competitive market following the adoption of a new technology. What happens to output, price, and economic profit in the short run and in the long run?

 Work Study Plan 12.5 and get instant feedback.

We've seen how a competitive market operates in the short run and the long run, but is a competitive market efficient?

Competition and Efficiency

A competitive market can achieve an efficient use of resources. You first studied efficiency in Chapter 2. Then in Chapter 5, using only the concepts of demand, supply, consumer surplus, and producer surplus, you saw how a competitive market achieves efficiency. Now that you have learned what lies behind the demand and supply curves of a competitive market, you can gain a deeper understanding of the efficiency of a competitive market.

Efficient Use of Resources

Recall that resource use is efficient when we produce the goods and services that people value most highly (see Chapter 2, p. 37 and Chapter 5, p. 110). If someone can become better off without anyone else becoming worse off, resources are *not* being used efficiently. For example, suppose we produce a computer that no one wants and no one will ever use, and, at the same time, some people are clamouring for more video games. If we produce fewer computers and reallocate the unused resources to produce more video games, some people will become better off and no one will be worse off.
So the initial resource allocation was inefficient.

In the more technical language that you have learned, resource use is efficient when marginal social benefit equals marginal social cost. In the computer and video games example, the marginal social benefit of a video game exceeds its marginal social cost; the marginal social cost of a computer exceeds its marginal social benefit. So by producing fewer computers and more video games, we move resources towards a higher-valued use.

Choices, Equilibrium, and Efficiency

We can use what you have learned about the decisions made by consumers and competitive firms and market equilibrium to describe an efficient use of resources.

Choices   Consumers allocate their budgets to get the most value possible out of them. We derive a consumer's demand curve by finding how the best budget allocation changes as the price of a good changes. So consumers get the most value out of their resources at all points along their demand curves. If the people who consume a good or service are the only ones who benefit from it, then the market demand curve measures the benefit to the entire society and is the marginal social benefit curve.

Competitive firms produce the quantity that maximizes profit. We derive the firm's supply curve by finding the profit-maximizing quantity at each price. So firms get the most value out of their resources at all points along their supply curves. If the firms that produce a good or service bear all the costs of producing it, then the market supply curve measures the marginal cost to the entire society and the market supply curve is the marginal social cost curve.

Equilibrium and Efficiency   Resources are used efficiently when marginal social benefit equals marginal social cost. Competitive equilibrium achieves this efficient outcome because for consumers, price equals marginal social benefit, and for producers, price equals marginal social cost.

The gains from trade are the sum of consumer surplus and producer surplus. The gains from trade for consumers are measured by *consumer surplus*, which is the area below the demand curve and above the price paid. (See Chapter 5, p. 111.) The gains from trade for producers are measured by *producer surplus*, which is the area above the supply curve and below the price received. (See Chapter 5, p. 113.) The total gains from trade are the sum of consumer surplus and producer surplus. When the market for a good or service is in equilibrium, the gains from trade are maximized.

Illustrating an Efficient Allocation   Figure 12.12 illustrates the efficiency of perfect competition in long-run equilibrium. Part (a) shows the individual firm, and part (b) shows the market. The equilibrium market price is P^*. At that price, each firm makes zero economic profit and each firm has the plant that enables it to produce at the lowest possible average total cost. Consumers are as well off as possible because the good cannot be produced at a lower cost and the price equals that least possible cost.

In part (b), consumers get the most out of their resources at all points on the market demand curve, $D = MSB$. Consumer surplus is the green area. Producers get the most out of their resources at all points on the market supply curve, $S = MSC$. Producer surplus is the blue area. Resources are used efficiently at the quantity Q^* and price P^*. At this point, marginal social benefit equals marginal social cost, and total surplus (the sum of producer surplus and consumer surplus) is maximized.

FIGURE 12.12   Efficiency of Perfect Competition

(a) A single firm

(b) A market

In part (a), a firm in perfect competition produces at the lowest possible long-run average total cost at q*. In part (b), consumers have made the best available choices and are on the market demand curve and firms are producing at

least cost and are on the market supply curve. With no external benefits or external costs, resources are used efficiently at the quantity Q* and the price P*. Perfect competition achieves an efficient use of resources.

 myeconlab animation

When firms in perfect competition are away from long-run equilibrium, either entry or exit is taking place and the market is moving towards the situation depicted in Fig. 12.12. But the market is still efficient. As long as marginal social benefit (on the market demand curve) equals marginal social cost (on the market supply curve), the market is efficient. But it is only in long-run equilibrium that consumers pay the lowest possible price.

◆ You've now completed your study of perfect competition. *Reading Between the Lines* on pp. 292–293 gives you an opportunity to use what you have learned to understand the recent rise in the price of jet-fuel on the profit of long-distance discount airlines, such as Zoom Airlines.

Although many markets approximate the model of perfect competition, many do not. In Chapter 13 we study markets at the opposite extreme of market power: monopoly. Then we'll study markets that lie between perfect competition and monopoly. In Chapter 14 we study monopolistic competition, and in Chapter 15 we study oligopoly. When you have completed this study, you'll have a tool kit that will enable you to understand the variety of real-world markets.

Review Quiz ◆

1 State the conditions that must be met for resources to be allocated efficiently.

2 Describe the choices that consumers make and explain why consumers are efficient on the market demand curve.

3 Describe the choices that producers make and explain why producers are efficient on the market supply curve.

4 Explain why resources are used efficiently in a competitive market.

 myeconlab   Work Study Plan 12.6 and get instant feedback.

Temporary Shutdown or Exit

Hundreds Stranded, Thousands More Out of Pocket as Airline Fails

August 30, 2008

Hundreds of passengers stranded in airports from Gatwick to San Diego were trying to find a way home yesterday after the collapse of the transatlantic budget airline Zoom.

As many as 40,000 more … were counting the cost of worthless tickets, after high oil costs and pressure from creditors forced the firm into administration. …

Record fuel prices had added £25m to Zoom's operating costs. Efforts to secure an eleventh-hour rescue package failed. …

The news spread rapidly after the company's failure to pay the lease on a plane prevented a Zoom flight, bound for Calgary, taking off from Paris on Wednesday. Its 70 passengers were eventually taken to Vancouver by another airline.

Another Zoom plane due to leave Glasgow airport for Halifax, Canada, was then prevented from taking off on Thursday. The Civil Aviation Authority (CAA) had ordered the grounding because airport charges had not been paid. A third plane full of passengers was held at Cardiff airport. Zoom then halted all its activities at 7 pm on Thursday, cancelling outstanding flights.

The owners of the airline, Scottish brothers John and Hugh Boyle, apologized to the 65,000 passengers affected and their 600 staff. They said they had "left no stone unturned" in their efforts to save the firm.

There was still hope on Thursday afternoon that a refinancing package could be found, but creditors lost confidence in the airline.…

Zoom's demise follows the collapse of two other transatlantic operators. MAXjet folded at the end of 2007, with Eos closing in April. A third luxury airline, Silverjet, closed in May. …

Essence of the Story

- The high price of jet-fuel has put Zoom Airlines into administration.

- Record fuel bills had added £25million to Zoom's operating costs.

- Zoom was not able to pay the lease on an aircraft.

- Zoom had failed to pay Halifax airport its airport charges.

- A number of budget long-distance carriers have gone into administration.

Economic Analysis

- The market for long-distance air travel is not *perfectly* competitive but it is highly competitive and the perfect competition model provides insights into that market.

- In 2008, airlines were being squeezed by the rising cost of jet fuel.

- The quantity of jet fuel bought by an airline varies with the number of trips made, so the cost of jet fuel is part of the airline's *variable* costs.

- Figure 1 shows the cost and revenue curves of an airline such as Zoom Airlines.

- Initially, Zoom's average variable cost curve is AVC_0, its average total cost curve is ATC_0 and its marginal cost curve is MC_0.

- With jet fuel at $70 a barrel, the equilibrium price of a trip is $400 and Zoom breaks even—makes zero economic profit.

- When the price of jet fuel rockets to $147 a barrel, Zoom's average variable cost and marginal cost increase and the firm's AVC and ATC curves shift upward.

- With no change in *fixed* cost, the gap between the AVC curve and the ATC curve doesn't change.

- Figure 2 shows Zoom's higher average cost and marginal cost curves. The average variable cost curve shifts upward to AVC_1, the average total cost curve shifts to ATC_1, and the marginal cost curve shifts to MC_1.

- Zoom maximizes profit by cutting the number of trips to the quantity at which marginal cost equals marginal revenue. It now incurs an economic loss.

- Figure 2 shows Zoom's shutdown point.

- If Zoom believes that the rise in the jet-fuel price is temporary, it will shut down and wait until the price returns to $70 a barrel—temporary shutdown.

- If Zoom believes that the price of jet fuel will be permanently above $70 a barrel, it will exit the market.

- As of November 2008, Zoom was in temporary shutdown and searching for a financial arrangement to help cover its expected temporary losses.

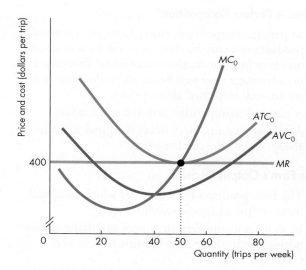

Figure 1 Zoom makes zero profit

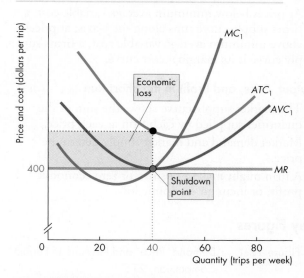

Figure 2 Zoom incurs economic loss

SUMMARY ◆

Key Points

What Is Perfect Competition? (pp. 274–275)

- In perfect competition, many firms sell identical products to many buyers; there are no restrictions on entry into the market; established firms have no advantage over new ones; and sellers and buyers are well informed about prices.
- A perfectly competitive firm is a price taker.
- A perfectly competitive firm's marginal revenue always equals the market price.

The Firm's Output Decision (pp. 276–279)

- The firm produces the output at which marginal revenue (price) equals marginal cost.
- In short-run equilibrium, a firm can make an economic profit, incur an economic loss, or break even.
- If price is less than minimum average variable cost, the firm temporarily shuts down.
- At prices below minimum average variable cost, a firm's supply curve runs along the y-axis; at prices above minimum average variable cost, a firm's supply curve is its marginal cost curve.

Output, Price, and Profit in the Short Run (pp. 280–283)

- The market supply curve shows the sum of the quantities supplied by each firm at each price.
- Market demand and market supply determine price.
- A firm might make a positive or zero economic profit, or incur an economic loss.

Output, Price, and Profit in the Long Run (pp. 283–285)

- Economic profit induces entry and economic loss induces exit.
- Entry increases supply and lowers price and profit. Exit decreases supply and raises price and profit.
- In long-run equilibrium, economic profit is zero. There is no entry or exit.

Changing Tastes and Advancing Technology (pp. 286–289)

- A permanent decrease in demand leads to a smaller market output and a smaller number of firms. A permanent increase in demand leads to a larger market output and a larger number of firms.
- The long-run effect of a change in demand on price depends on whether there are external economies (the price falls) or external diseconomies (the price rises) or neither (the price remains constant).
- New technologies increase supply and in the long run lower the price and increase the quantity.

Competition and Efficiency (pp. 290–291)

- Resources are used efficiently when we produce goods and services in the quantities that people value most highly.
- When there are no external benefits and external costs, perfect competition achieves an efficient allocation. In long-run equilibrium, consumers pay the lowest possible price and marginal social benefit equals marginal social cost.

Key Figures

Figure 12.1   Demand, Price, and Revenue in Perfect Competition, 275
Figure 12.3   Profit-Maximizing Output, 277
Figure 12.4   The Shutdown Decision, 278
Figure 12.5   A Firm's Supply Curve, 279

Figure 12.7   Short-Run Equilibrium, 281
Figure 12.8   Three Short-Run Outcomes for the Firm, 282
Figure 12.9   Entry, Exit, and Long-Run Equilibrium, 284
Figure 12.12   Efficiency of Perfect Competition, 291

Key Terms

External diseconomies, 287
External economies, 287
Long-run market supply curve, 287

Marginal revenue, 274
Perfect competition, 274
Price taker, 274

Short-run market supply curve, 280
Shutdown point, 278
Total revenue, 274

PROBLEMS and APPLICATIONS

myeconlab Work problems 1–9 in Chapter 12 Study Plan and get instant feedback.
Work problems 10–17 as Homework, a Quiz, or a Test if assigned by your instructor.

1. Lin's fortune cookies are identical to the fortune cookies made by dozens of other firms, and there is free entry in the fortune cookie market. Buyers and sellers are well informed about prices.

   a. In what type of market does Lin's operate?
   b. What determines the price of fortune cookies?
   c. What determines Lin's marginal revenue of fortune cookies?
   d. If fortune cookies sell for $10 a box and Lin offers his cookies for sale at $10.50 a box, how many boxes does he sell?
   e. If fortune cookies sell for $10 a box and Lin offers his cookies for sale at $9.50 a box, how many boxes does he sell?
   f. What is the elasticity of demand for Lin's fortune cookies and how does it differ from the elasticity of the market demand for fortune cookies?

2. Pat's Pizza Kitchen is a price taker. Its costs are

Output (pizzas per hour)	Total cost (dollars per hour)
0	10
1	21
2	30
3	41
4	54
5	69

   a. Calculate Pat's profit-maximizing output and economic profit if the market price is
      (i) $14 a pizza.
      (ii) $12 a pizza.
      (iii) $10 a pizza.
   b. What is Pat's shutdown point and what is Pat's economic profit if it shuts down temporarily?
   c. Derive Pat's supply curve.
   d. At what price will firms with costs identical to Pat's exit the pizza market in the long run?
   e. At what price will firms with costs identical to Pat's enter the pizza market in the long run?

3. The market is perfectly competitive and there are 1,000 firms that produce paper. The table sets out the market demand schedule for paper.

Price (dollars per box)	Quantity demanded (thousands of boxes per week)
3.65	500
5.20	450
6.80	400
8.40	350
10.00	300
11.60	250
13.20	200

   Each producer of paper has the following costs when it uses its least-cost plant:

Output (boxes per week)	Marginal cost (dollars per additional box)	Average variable cost	Average total cost
		(dollars per box)	
200	6.40	7.80	12.80
250	7.00	7.00	11.00
300	7.65	7.10	10.43
350	8.40	7.20	10.06
400	10.00	7.50	10.00
450	12.40	8.00	10.22
500	20.70	9.00	11.00

   a. What is the market price of paper?
   b. What is the market's output?
   c. What is the output produced by each firm?
   d. What is the economic profit made or economic loss incurred by each firm?
   e. Do firms have an incentive to enter or exit the paper market in the long run?
   f. What is the number of firms in the long run?
   g. What is the market price in the long run?
   h. What is the equilibrium quantity of paper produced in the long run?

4. **Never Pay Retail Again**

   Not only has scouring the Web for the best possible price become standard protocol before buying a big-ticket item, but more consumers are employing creative strategies for scoring hot deal. … Comparison shopping, haggling and swapping discount codes are all becoming mainstream marks of savvy shoppers … online shoppers can check a comparison service like Price Grabber before making a purchase. …

   CNN, May 30, 2008

a. Explain the effect of the Internet on the degree of competition in the market.
b. Explain how the Internet influences market efficiency.

5. As the quality of computer monitors improves, more people are reading documents online rather than printing them. The demand for paper permanently decreases, and the demand schedule becomes

Price (dollars per box)	Quantity demanded (thousands of boxes per week)
2.95	500
4.13	450
5.30	400
6.48	350
7.65	300
8.83	250
10.00	200
11.18	150

If each producer of paper has the costs set out in problem 3,
a. What is the market price, market output, and economic profit or loss of each firm?
b. What is the long-run equilibrium price, market output, and economic profit or loss of each firm?
c. Does this market experience external economies, external diseconomies, or constant cost? Illustrate by drawing the long-run supply curve.

6. **St. Thomas Plant Cuts Shift and 720 Jobs**
Sterling Trucks is eliminating one of its two remaining shifts and laying off another 720 workers as ... [it] joins the growing ranks of companies being squeezed by an economic slowdown in the United States.

A year ago, Sterling laid off an additional 600 people in St. Thomas when another shift was cut, ... Back when there were three shifts, "We built trucks pretty much 24 hours a day, five days a week," Elliott [CAW president] said.

But with the economy in a slump, "freight's not moving, construction is down—nobody is buying trucks. We really need the economy to turn around ... and hopefully the price of fuel can drop and people will start buying again."

The president of the St. Thomas Chamber of Commerce called the layoffs "devastating" news for the town ... "no way to understate how much

impact 720 relatively high-paying positions have in a community." Each one of those jobs, he said, "can spin to touch at least seven others that sell vehicles, that sell groceries right down to the neighbourhood gas station."

Canadian Press, July 18, 2008
a. Explain how economic slowdown in the United States might cause a producer of trucks to change its output in the short run.
b. On a graph, show the effects of the economic slowdown on Sterling's output in the short run.
c. Explain how the rise in the price of fuel might cause a producer of trucks to change its output in the short run.
d. On a graph, show the effects of the rise in fuel prices on Sterling's output in the short run.
e. Explain why a producer of trucks might incur an economic loss in the short run as the price of fuel rises.
f. If some truck producers decide to exit the market while the price of fuel remains high, explain how the economic profit or loss of the remaining truck producers will change.
g. Explain how the loss of high-paying jobs will affect the economic profit of grocery stores in St. Thomas in the short run.
h. Draw a graph to show the effects of the loss of high-paying jobs on the economic profit of local grocery stores in the short run.

7. In a perfectly competitive market in long-run equilibrium, can
a. Consumer surplus be increased?
b. Producer surplus be increased?
c. A consumer become better off by making a substitution away from this market?
d. The average total cost be reduced?

8. Draw a graph to show how the growing world population is influencing the world market for wheat and a representative wheat farmer.

9. **Airlines in Trouble: A Timeline**
Vancouver-based Harmony Airways announces it will suspend all scheduled service by April 9 [2007].

CBC News, March 27, 2007
Harmony Airways exited the air-travel market before the jet-fuel price rocketed. Illustrate the market and Harmony's situation in April 2007.

10. The market demand schedule for smoothies is

Price (dollars per smoothie)	Quantity demanded (smoothies per hour)
1.90	1,000
2.00	950
2.20	800
2.91	700
4.25	550
5.25	400
5.50	300

The market is perfectly competitive, and each of the 100 firms in the market has the following costs when it uses its least-cost plant:

Output (smoothies per hour)	Marginal cost (dollars per additional smoothie)	Average variable cost (dollars per smoothie)	Average total cost (dollars per smoothie)
3	2.50	4.00	7.33
4	2.20	3.53	6.03
5	1.90	3.24	5.24
6	2.00	3.00	4.67
7	2.91	2.91	4.34
8	4.25	3.00	4.25
9	8.00	3.33	4.44

a. What is the market price of a smoothie?

b. What is the market quantity of smoothies?

c. How many smoothies does each firm sell?

d. What is the economic profit made or economic loss incurred by each firm?

e. Do firms enter or exit the market in the long run?

f. What is the market price and the equilibrium quantity in the long run?

11. **Money in the Tank**

In Marietta, where the road hugs the Susquehanna River, a Rutter's Farm Store gas station stands on one side, a Sheetz gas station on the other. Kelly Bosley, who manages Rutter's, doesn't even have to look across the highway to know when Sheetz changes its price for a gallon of gas. When Sheetz raises prices, her own pumps are busy. When Sheetz lowers prices, she has not a car in sight ... You think you feel helpless at the pump? Bosley makes a living selling gas — and even she has little control over what it costs.

Mining Journal, May 24, 2008

a. Describe the elasticity of demand that each of these gas stations faces.

b. Why does each of these gas stations have so little control over the price of the gasoline they sell?

c. How do these gas stations decide how much gasoline to make available for sale?

12. Quick Copy is one of many copy shops near campus. The figure shows Quick Copy's costs.

If the market price of copying a page is 10 cents, calculate Quick Copy's

a. Marginal revenue.

b. Profit-maximizing output.

c. Economic profit.

13. **Cadillac Plant Shuts Down Temporarily, Future Uncertain**

Delta Truss in Cadillac [Michigan] is shutting down in what [its] parent company, Pro-Build, calls "temporarily discontinuing truss production." Workers fear this temporary shut down will become permanent. About 60 people work at Delta Truss when it's in peak season. Right now, about 20 people work there ... A corporate letter ... says "we are anticipating resuming production at these plants when the spring business begins."

9&10 News, February 18, 2008

a. Explain how the shutdown decision will affect Delta Truss' *TFC, TVC,* and *TC.*

b. Under what conditions would this shutdown decision maximize Delta Truss' economic profit (or minimize its loss)?

c. Under what conditions will Delta Truss start producing again?

d. Under what conditions will Delta Truss make the shutdown permanent and exit the market?

14. **Exxon Mobil Selling All Its Gas Stations to Distributors**

Exxon Mobil Corp. said Thursday it's getting out of the retail gasoline business, following other major oil companies ... "As the highly competitive fuels marketing business ... continues to evolve, we believe this transition is the best way for Exxon Mobil to compete and grow in the future," said Ben Soraci, the director of Exxon Mobil's U.S. retail sales. Exxon Mobil is not alone among Big Oil exiting the retail gas business, a market where profits have gotten tougher as crude oil prices have risen ... Station owners say they're struggling to turn a profit on gas because while wholesale gasoline prices have risen sharply, ... they've been unable to raise pump prices fast enough to keep pace.

Houston Chronicle, June 12, 2008

a. Is Exxon Mobil making a shutdown or exit decision in the retail gasoline market?
b. Under what conditions will this decision maximize Exxon Mobil's economic profit?
c. How might this decision by Exxon Mobil affect the economic profit made by other firms that sell retail gasoline?

15. **Another DVD Format, but This One Says It's Cheaper**

No sooner has the battle for the next-generation high-definition DVD format ended, with Blu-ray triumphing over HD DVD, than a new contender has emerged. A new system ... called HD VMD ... is trying to find a niche. New Medium Enterprises, the London company behind HD VMD, says its system's quality is equal to Blu-ray's but it costs less ... While Blu-ray players typically cost more than $300, an HD VMD unit is priced at $199 ... New Medium's price strategy will fail, said Andy Parsons, chairman of the Blu-ray Disc Association, ... because it relies on a false assumption: Blu-ray technology will always be more expensive. "When you mass produce blue lasers in large quantities, hardware costs will absolutely come down," Mr. Parsons said. "I'm sure we'll eventually be able to charge $90 for a Blu-ray player."

New York Times, March 10, 2008

a. Explain how technological change in Blu-ray production might support Mr. Parsons' prediction of lower prices in the long run and illustrate your explanation with a graph.

b. Even if Blu-ray prices do drop to $90 in the long run, why might the red-laser HD VMD still end up being less expensive at that time?

16. **Cell Phone Sales Hit 1 Billion Mark**

More than 1.15 billion mobile phones were sold worldwide in 2007, a 16 percent increase from the 990.9 million phones sold in 2006 ... "Emerging markets, especially China and India, provided much of the growth as many people bought their first phone," Carolina Milanesi, research director for mobile devices at Gartner, said in a statement. "In mature markets, such as Japan and Western Europe, consumers' appetite for feature-laden phones was met with new models packed with TV tuners, global positioning satellite (GPS) functions, touch screens and high-resolution cameras."

CNET News, February 27, 2008

a. Explain the effects of the global increase in demand for cell phones on the market for cell phones and individual cell phone producers in the short run.
b. Draw a graph to illustrate your explanation in a.
c. Explain the effects of the global increase in demand for cell phones on the market for cell phones in the long run.
d. What factors will determine whether the price of cell phones will rise, fall, or stay the same in the new long-run equilibrium?

17. Study *Reading Between the Lines* about the market for long-distance air travel on pp. 292–293, and then answer the following questions.

a. What are the features of the market for air travel that make it highly competitive?
b. Explain how the market for long-distance discount air travel will get back to a long-run equilibrium if the price of jet fuel falls to $70 a barrel.
c. Draw a graph of the cost and revenue curves of an airline to illustrate the situation in the new long-run equilibrium in b.
d. Explain how the market for long-distance discount air travel will get back to a long-run equilibrium if the jet-fuel price remains above $70 a barrel.
e. Draw a graph of the cost and revenue curves of an airline to illustrate the situation in the new long-run equilibrium in d.

13 ◆ Monopoly

After studying this chapter, you will be able to

- Explain how monopoly arises and distinguish between single-price monopoly and price-discriminating monopoly

- Explain how a single-price monopoly determines its output and price

- Compare the performance and efficiency of single-price monopoly and competition

- Explain how price discrimination increases profit

- Explain how monopoly regulation influences output, price, economic profit, and efficiency

eBay, Google, and Microsoft are dominant players in the markets they serve. Because most Web searchers use Google, most advertisers use it too, which attracts more searchers. Because most online auction buyers use eBay, most online sellers do too, which attracts more buyers. Because most PCs use Windows, programmers write most applications for this operating system, which attracts more users. Each of these firms benefits from a phenomenon called a network externality, which makes it hard for other firms to break into their markets.

eBay, Google, and Microsoft are obviously not like firms in perfect competition. How does their behaviour compare with perfectly competitive firms? Do they charge prices that are too high and that damage the interests of consumers? What benefits do they bring?

In this chapter, we study markets in which the firm can influence the price. We also compare the performance of the firm in such a market with that in a competitive market and examine whether monopoly is as efficient as competition. In *Reading Between the Lines* at the end of the chapter, we'll take a look at what a European court thinks about some of Microsoft's profit-seeking practices.

Monopoly and How It Arises

A **monopoly** is a market with a single firm that produces a good or service for which no close substitute exists and that is protected by a barrier that prevents other firms from selling that good or service.

How Monopoly Arises

Monopoly arises for two key reasons:

- No close substitute
- Barrier to entry

No Close Substitute If a good has a close substitute, even though only one firm produces it, that firm effectively faces competition from the producers of the substitute. A monopoly sells a good or service that has no good substitute. Tap water and bottled water are close substitutes for drinking, but tap water has no effective substitute for showering or washing a car and a local public utility that supplies tap water is a monopoly.

Barrier to Entry A constraint that protects a firm from potential competitors is called a **barrier to entry**. The three types of barrier to entry are

- Natural
- Ownership
- Legal

Natural Barrier to Entry A natural barrier to entry creates a **natural monopoly**: an industry in which economies of scale enable one firm to supply the entire market at the lowest possible cost. The firms that deliver gas, water, and electricity to our homes are examples of natural monopoly.

In Fig. 13.1 the market demand curve for electric power is *D*, and the long-run average cost curve is *LRAC*. Economies of scale prevail over the entire length of the *LRAC* curve.

One firm can produce 4 million kilowatt-hours at 5 cents a kilowatt-hour. At this price, the quantity demanded is 4 million kilowatt-hours. So if the price was 5 cents, one firm could supply the entire market. If two firms shared the market equally, it would cost each of them 10 cents a kilowatt-hour to produce a total of 4 million kilowatt-hours.

In conditions like those shown in Fig. 13.1, one firm can supply the entire market at a lower cost than

FIGURE 13.1   Natural Monopoly

The market demand curve for electric power is *D*, and the long-run average cost curve is *LRAC*. Economies of scale exist over the entire *LRAC* curve. One firm can distribute 4 million kilowatt-hours at a cost of 5 cents a kilowatt-hour. This same total output costs 10 cents a kilowatt-hour with two firms. One firm can meet the market demand at a lower cost than two or more firms can. The market is a natural monopoly.

myeconlab animation

two or more firms can. The market is a natural monopoly.

Ownership Barrier to Entry An ownership barrier to entry occurs if one firm owns a significant portion of a key resource. An example of this type of monopoly occurred during the last century when De Beers controlled up to 90 percent of the world's supply of diamonds. (Today, its share is only 65 percent.)

Legal Barrier to Entry A legal barrier to entry creates a **legal monopoly**: a market in which competition and entry are restricted by the granting of a public franchise, government licence, patent, or copyright.

A *public franchise* is an exclusive right granted to a firm to supply a good or service. An example is Canada Post, which has the exclusive right to deliver first-class mail. A *government licence* controls entry into particular occupations, professions, and industries. Examples of this type of barrier to entry occur in medicine, law, dentistry, school teaching, architecture, and many other professional services. Licensing does not always create a monopoly, but it does restrict competition.

A *patent* is an exclusive right granted to the inventor of a product or service. A *copyright* is an exclusive right granted to the author or composer of a literary, musical, dramatic, or artistic work. Patents and copyrights are valid for a limited time period that varies from country to country. In Canada, a patent is valid for 20 years. Patents encourage the *invention* of new products and production methods. They also stimulate *innovation*—the use of new inventions—by encouraging inventors to publicize their discoveries and offer them for use under licence. Patents have stimulated innovations in areas as diverse as soybean seeds, pharmaceuticals, memory chips, and video games.

Natural Monopoly Today

Information-Age Monopolies

Information-age technologies have created four big natural monopolies. These firms have large plant costs but almost zero marginal cost, so they experience economies of scale.

Microsoft has captured 90 percent of the personal computer operating system market with Windows and 73 percent of the Web browser market with Internet Explorer. eBay has captured 85 percent of the consumer-to-consumer Internet auction market and Google has 78 percent of the search engine market.

New technologies also destroy monopoly. FedEx, Purolator, the fax machine, and e-mail have weakened Canada Post's monopoly, and the satellite dish has weakened the cable TV monopolies.

Market Shares

Monopoly Price-Setting Strategies

A major difference between monopoly and competition is that a monopoly sets its own price. In doing so, the monopoly faces a market constraint: To sell a larger quantity, the monopoly must set a lower price. There are two monopoly situations that create two pricing strategies:

- Single price
- Price discrimination

Single Price   A **single-price monopoly** is a firm that must sell each unit of its output for the same price to all its customers. De Beers sells diamonds (of a given size and quality) for the same price to all its customers. If it tried to sell at a low price to some customers and at a higher price to others, only the low-price customers would buy from De Beers. Others would buy from De Beers' low-price customers. De Beers is a *single-price* monopoly.

Price Discrimination   When a firm practises **price discrimination**, it sells different units of a good or service for different prices. Many firms price discriminate. Microsoft sells its Windows and Office software at different prices to different buyers. Computer manufacturers who install the software on new machines, students and teachers, governments, and businesses all pay different prices. Pizza producers offer a second pizza for a lower price than the first one. These are examples of *price discrimination*.

When a firm price discriminates, it looks as though it is doing its customers a favour. In fact, it is charging the highest possible price for each unit sold and making the largest possible profit.

Review Quiz

1 How does monopoly arise?
2 How does a natural monopoly differ from a legal monopoly?
3 Distinguish between a price-discriminating monopoly and a single-price monopoly.

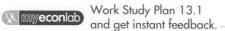 Work Study Plan 13.1 and get instant feedback.

We start with a single-price monopoly and see how it makes its decisions about the quantity to produce and the price to charge to maximize its profit.

A Single-Price Monopoly's Output and Price Decision

To understand how a single-price monopoly makes its output and price decision, we must first study the link between price and marginal revenue.

Price and Marginal Revenue

In a monopoly there is only one firm, so the demand curve facing the firm is the market demand curve. Let's look at Bobbie's Barbershop, the sole supplier of haircuts in Trout River, Newfoundland. The table in Fig. 13.2 shows the market demand schedule. At a price of $20, Bobbie sells no haircuts. The lower the price, the more haircuts she can sell. For example, at $14, consumers demand 3 haircuts an hour (row D).

Total revenue (TR) is the price (P) multiplied by the quantity sold (Q). For example, in row D, Bobbie sells 3 haircuts at $14 each, so total revenue is $42. *Marginal revenue* (MR) is the change in total revenue (TR) resulting from a one-unit increase in the quantity sold. For example, if the price falls from $16 (row C) to $14 (row D), the quantity sold increases from 2 to 3 haircuts. Total revenue increases from $32 to $42, so the change in total revenue is $10. Because the quantity sold increases by 1 haircut, marginal revenue equals the change in total revenue and is $10. Marginal revenue is placed between the two rows to emphasize that marginal revenue relates to the *change* in the quantity sold.

Figure 13.2 shows the market demand curve and marginal revenue curve (MR) and also illustrates the calculation we've just made. Notice that at each level of output, marginal revenue is less than price—the marginal revenue curve lies below the demand curve. Why is marginal revenue *less* than price? It is because when the price is lowered to sell one more unit, two opposing forces affect total revenue. The lower price results in a revenue loss, and the increased quantity sold results in a revenue gain. For example, at a price of $16, Bobbie sells 2 haircuts (point C). If she lowers the price to $14, she sells 3 haircuts and has a revenue gain of $14 on the third haircut. But she now receives only $14 on the first two—$2 less than before. As a result, she loses $4 of revenue on the first 2 haircuts. To calculate marginal revenue, she must deduct this amount from the revenue gain of $14. So her marginal revenue is $10, which is less than the price.

FIGURE 13.2   Demand and Marginal Revenue

	Price (P) (dollars per haircut)	Quantity demanded (Q) (haircuts per hour)	Total revenue (TR = P × Q) (dollars)	Marginal revenue (MR = ΔTR/ΔQ) (dollars per haircut)
A	20	0	0	
				18
B	18	1	18	
				14
C	16	2	32	
				10
D	14	3	42	
				6
E	12	4	48	
				2
F	10	5	50	

The table shows the demand schedule. Total revenue (TR) is price multiplied by quantity sold. For example, in row C, the price is $16 a haircut, Bobbie sells 2 haircuts, and total revenue is $32. Marginal revenue (MR) is the change in total revenue that results from a one-unit increase in the quantity sold. For example, when the price falls from $16 to $14 a haircut, the quantity sold increases by 1 haircut and total revenue increases by $10. Marginal revenue is $10. The demand curve and the marginal revenue curve, MR, are based on the numbers in the table and illustrate the calculation of marginal revenue when the price falls from $16 to $14 a haircut.

myeconlab animation

Marginal Revenue and Elasticity

A single-price monopoly's marginal revenue is related to the *elasticity of demand* for its good. The demand for a good can be *elastic* (the elasticity is greater than 1), *inelastic* (the elasticity is less than 1), or *unit elastic* (the elasticity is equal to 1). Demand is *elastic* if a 1 percent fall in price brings a greater than 1 percent increase in the quantity demanded. Demand is *inelastic* if a 1 percent fall in price brings a less than 1 percent increase in the quantity demanded. Demand is *unit elastic* if a 1 percent fall in price brings a 1 percent increase in the quantity demanded. (See Chapter 4, pp. 86–87.)

If demand is elastic, a fall in price brings an increase in total revenue—the revenue gain from the increase in quantity sold outweighs the revenue loss from the lower price—and marginal revenue is *positive*. If demand is inelastic, a fall in price brings a decrease in total revenue—the revenue gain from the increase in quantity sold is outweighed by the revenue loss from the lower price—and marginal revenue is *negative*. If demand is unit elastic, total revenue does not change—the revenue gain from the increase in the quantity sold offsets the revenue loss from the lower price—and marginal revenue is *zero*. (See Chapter 4, p. 90.)

Figure 13.3 illustrates the relationship between marginal revenue, total revenue, and elasticity. As the price gradually falls from $20 to $10 a haircut, the quantity demanded increases from 0 to 5 haircuts an hour. Over this output range, marginal revenue is positive in part (a), total revenue increases in part (b), and the demand for haircuts is elastic. As the price falls from $10 to $0 a haircut, the quantity of haircuts demanded increases from 5 to 10 an hour. Over this output range, marginal revenue is negative in part (a), total revenue decreases in part (b), and the demand for haircuts is inelastic. When the price is $10 a haircut, marginal revenue is zero in part (a), total revenue is at a maximum in part (b), and the demand for haircuts is unit elastic.

In Monopoly, Demand Is Always Elastic
The relationship between marginal revenue and elasticity of demand that you've just discovered implies that a profit-maximizing monopoly never produces an output in the inelastic range of the market demand curve. If it did so, it could charge a higher price, produce a smaller quantity, and increase its profit. Let's now look at a monopoly's price and output decision.

FIGURE 13.3 Marginal Revenue and Elasticity

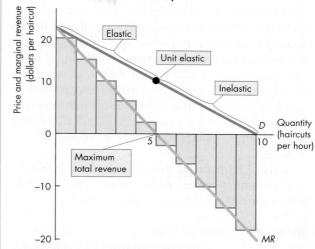

(a) Demand and marginal revenue curves

(b) Total revenue curve

In part (a), the demand curve is *D* and the marginal revenue curve is *MR*. In part (b), the total revenue curve is *TR*. Over the range 0 to 5 haircuts an hour, a price cut increases total revenue, so marginal revenue is positive—as shown by the blue bars. Demand is elastic. Over the range 5 to 10 haircuts an hour, a price cut decreases total revenue, so marginal revenue is negative—as shown by the red bars. Demand is inelastic. At 5 haircuts an hour, total revenue is maximized and marginal revenue is zero. Demand is unit elastic.

myeconlab animation

Price and Output Decision

A monopoly sets its price and output at the levels that maximize economic profit. To determine this price and output level, we need to study the behaviour of both cost and revenue as output varies. A monopoly faces the same types of technology and cost constraints as a competitive firm, so its costs (total cost, average cost, and marginal cost) behave just like those of a firm in perfect competition. A monopoly's revenues (total revenue, price, and marginal revenue) behave in the way we've just described.

Table 13.1 provides information about Bobbie's costs, revenues, and economic profit, and Fig. 13.4 shows the same information graphically.

Maximizing Economic Profit You can see in Table 13.1 and Fig. 13.4(a) that total cost (TC) and total revenue (TR) both rise as output increases, but TC rises at an increasing rate and TR rises at a decreasing rate. Economic profit, which equals TR minus TC, increases at small output levels, reaches a maximum, and then decreases. The maximum profit ($12) occurs when Bobbie sells 3 haircuts for $14 each. If she sells 2 haircuts for $16 each or 4 haircuts for $12 each, her economic profit will be only $8.

Marginal Revenue Equals Marginal Cost You can see Bobbie's marginal revenue (MR) and marginal cost (MC) in Table 13.1 and Fig. 13.4(b).

When Bobbie increases output from 2 to 3 haircuts, MR is $10 and MC is $6. MR exceeds MC by $4 and Bobbie's profit increases by that amount. If Bobbie increases output yet further, from 3 to 4 haircuts, MR is $6 and MC is $10. In this case, MC exceeds MR by $4, so profit decreases by that amount. When MR exceeds MC, profit increases if output increases. When MC exceeds MR, profit increases if output *decreases*. When MC equals MR, profit is maximized.

Figure 13.4(b) shows the maximum profit as price (on the demand curve D) minus average total cost (on the ATC curve) multiplied by the quantity produced—the blue rectangle.

Maximum Price the Market Will Bear Unlike a firm in perfect competition, a monopoly influences the price of what it sells. But a monopoly doesn't set the price at the maximum *possible* price. At the maximum possible price, the firm would be able to sell only one unit of output, which in general is less than the profit-maximizing quantity. Rather, a monopoly produces the profit-maximizing quantity and sells that quantity for the highest price it can get.

TABLE 13.1   A Monopoly's Output and Price Decision

Price (P) (dollars per haircut)	Quantity demanded (Q) (haircuts per hour)	Total revenue (TR = P × Q) (dollars)	Marginal revenue (MR = ΔTR/ΔQ) (dollars per haircut)	Total cost (TC) (dollars)	Marginal cost (MC = ΔTC/ΔQ) (dollars per haircut)	Profit (TR − TC) (dollars)
20	0	0		20		−20
			18		1	
18	1	18		21		−3
			14		3	
16	2	32		24		+8
			10		6	
14	3	42		30		+12
			6		10	
12	4	48		40		+8
			2		15	
10	5	50		55		−5

This table gives the information needed to find the profit-maximizing output and price. Total revenue (*TR*) equals price multiplied by the quantity sold. Profit equals total revenue minus total cost (*TC*). Profit is maximized when 3 haircuts are sold at a price of $14 each. Total revenue is $42, total cost is $30, and economic profit is $12 ($42 − $30).

FIGURE 13.4   A Monopoly's Output and Price

(a) Total revenue and total cost curves

(b) Demand and marginal revenue and cost curves

In part (a), economic profit is the vertical distance equal to total revenue (*TR*) minus total cost (*TC*) and it is maximized at 3 haircuts an hour. In part (b), economic profit is maximized when marginal cost (*MC*) equals marginal revenue (*MR*). The profit-maximizing output is 3 haircuts an hour. The price is determined by the demand curve (*D*) and is $14 a haircut. The average total cost of a haircut is $10, so economic profit, the blue rectangle, is $12—the profit per haircut ($4) multiplied by 3 haircuts.

All firms maximize profit by producing the output at which marginal revenue equals marginal cost. For a competitive firm, price equals marginal revenue, so price also equals marginal cost. For a monopoly, price exceeds marginal revenue, so price also exceeds marginal cost.

A monopoly charges a price that exceeds marginal cost, but does it always make an economic profit? In Fig. 13.4(b), Bobbie produces 3 haircuts an hour. Her average total cost is $10 (on the *ATC* curve) and her price is $14 (on the *D* curve), so her profit per haircut is $4 ($14 minus $10). Bobbie's economic profit is shown by the area of the blue rectangle, which equals the profit per haircut ($4) multiplied by the number of haircuts (3) for a total of $12.

If firms in a perfectly competitive industry make a positive economic profit, new firms enter. That does *not* happen in monopoly. Barriers to entry prevent new firms from entering the market, so a monopoly can make a positive economic profit and might continue to do so indefinitely. Sometimes that economic profit is large, as in the international diamond business.

Bobbie makes a positive economic profit. But suppose that Bobbie's landlord increases the rent on her salon. If Bobbie pays an additional $12 an hour for rent, her fixed cost increases by $12 an hour. Her marginal cost and marginal revenue don't change, so her profit-maximizing output remains at 3 haircuts an hour. Her profit decreases by $12 an hour to zero. If Bobbie's salon rent increases by more than $12 an hour, she incurs an economic loss. If this situation were permanent, Bobbie would go out of business.

Review Quiz

1 What is the relationship between marginal cost and marginal revenue when a single-price monopoly maximizes profit?

2 How does a single-price monopoly determine the price it will charge its customers?

3 What is the relationship between price, marginal revenue, and marginal cost when a single-price monopoly is maximizing profit?

4 Why can a monopoly make a positive economic profit even in the long run?

myeconlab   Work Study Plan 13.2 and get instant feedback.

Single-Price Monopoly and Competition Compared

Imagine an industry that is made up of many small firms operating in perfect competition. Then imagine that a single firm buys out all these small firms and creates a monopoly.

What will happen in this industry? Will the price rise or fall? Will the quantity produced increase or decrease? Will economic profit increase or decrease? Will either the original competitive situation or the new monopoly situation be efficient?

These are the questions we're now going to answer. First, we look at the effects of monopoly on the price and quantity produced. Then we turn to the questions about efficiency.

Comparing Price and Output

Figure 13.5 shows the market we'll study. The market demand curve is D. The demand curve is the same regardless of how the industry is organized. But the supply side and the equilibrium are different in monopoly and competition. First, let's look at the case of perfect competition.

Perfect Competition Initially, with many small perfectly competitive firms in the market, the market supply curve is S. This supply curve is obtained by summing the supply curves of all the individual firms in the market.

In perfect competition, equilibrium occurs where the supply curve and the demand curve intersect. The price is P_C, and the quantity produced by the industry is Q_C. Each firm takes the price P_C and maximizes its profit by producing the output at which its own marginal cost equals the price. Because each firm is a small part of the total industry, there is no incentive for any firm to try to manipulate the price by varying its output.

Monopoly Now suppose that this industry is taken over by a single firm. Consumers do not change, so the market demand curve remains the same as in the case of perfect competition. But now the monopoly recognizes this demand curve as a constraint on the price at which it can sell its output. The monopoly's marginal revenue curve is MR.

The monopoly maximizes profit by producing the quantity at which marginal revenue equals marginal

cost. To find the monopoly's marginal cost curve, first recall that in perfect competition, the industry supply curve is the sum of the supply curves of all the firms in the industry. Also recall that each firm's supply curve is its marginal cost curve (see Chapter 12, p. 279). So when the industry is taken over by a single firm, the competitive industry's supply curve becomes the monopoly's marginal cost curve. To remind you of this fact, the supply curve is also labelled MC.

The output at which marginal revenue equals marginal cost is Q_M. This output is less than the competitive output Q_C. The monopoly charges the price P_M, which is higher than P_C. We have established that

> Compared to a perfectly competitive industry, a single-price monopoly produces a smaller output and charges a higher price.

We've seen how the output and price of a monopoly compare with those in a competitive industry. Let's now compare the efficiency of the two types of market.

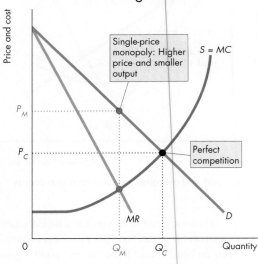

FIGURE 13.5 Monopoly's Smaller Output and Higher Price

A competitive industry produces the quantity Q_C at the price P_C. A single-price monopoly produces the quantity Q_M at which marginal revenue equals marginal cost and sells that quantity for the price P_M. Compared to perfect competition, a single-price monopoly produces a smaller output and charges a higher price.

myeconlab animation

Efficiency Comparison

Perfect competition (with no external costs and benefits) is efficient. Figure 13.6(a) illustrates the efficiency of perfect competition and serves as a benchmark against which to measure the inefficiency of monopoly. Along the demand curve and marginal social benefit curve ($D = MSB$), consumers are efficient. Along the supply curve and marginal social cost curve ($S = MSC$), producers are efficient. In competitive equilibrium, the price is P_C, the quantity is Q_C, and marginal social benefit equals marginal social cost.

Consumer surplus is the green triangle under the demand curve and above the equilibrium price (see Chapter 5, p. 111). *Producer surplus* is the blue area above the supply curve and below the equilibrium price (see Chapter 5, p. 113). The sum of the consumer surplus and producer surplus is maximized.

Also, in long-run competitive equilibrium, entry and exit ensure that each firm produces its output at the minimum possible long-run average cost.

To summarize: At the competitive equilibrium, marginal social benefit equals marginal social cost; the sum of consumer surplus and producer surplus is maximized; firms produce at the lowest possible long-run average cost; and resource use is efficient.

Figure 13.6(b) illustrates the inefficiency of monopoly and the sources of that inefficiency. A monopoly produces Q_M and sells its output for P_M. The smaller output and higher price drive a wedge between marginal social benefit and marginal social cost and create a *deadweight loss*. The grey triangle shows the deadweight loss and its magnitude is a measure of the inefficiency of monopoly.

Consumer surplus shrinks for two reasons. First, consumers lose by having to pay more for the good. This loss to consumers is a gain for monopoly and increases the producer surplus. Second, consumers lose by getting less of the good, and this loss is part of the deadweight loss.

Although the monopoly gains from a higher price, it loses some producer surplus because it produces a smaller output. That loss is another part of the deadweight loss.

A monopoly produces a smaller output than perfect competition and faces no competition, so it does not produce at the minimum possible long-run average cost. As a result, monopoly damages the consumer interest in three ways: A monopoly produces less, increases the cost of production, and raises the price by more than the increased cost of production.

FIGURE 13.6   Inefficiency of Monopoly

(a) Perfect competition

(b) Monopoly

In perfect competition in part (a), output is Q_C and the price is P_C. Marginal social benefit (*MSB*) equals marginal social cost (*MSC*); consumer surplus (the green triangle) plus producer surplus (the blue area) is maximized; and in the long run, firms produce at the lowest possible average cost. Monopoly in part (b) produces Q_M and raises the price to P_M. Consumer surplus shrinks, the monopoly gains, and a deadweight loss (the grey triangle) arises.

 myeconlab animation

Redistribution of Surpluses

You've seen that monopoly is inefficient because marginal social benefit exceeds marginal social cost and there is deadweight loss—a social loss. But monopoly also brings a *redistribution* of surpluses.

Some of the lost consumer surplus goes to the monopoly. In Fig. 13.6, the monopoly takes the difference between the higher price, P_M, and the competitive price, P_C, on the quantity sold, Q_M. So the monopoly takes the part of the consumer surplus. This portion of the loss of consumer surplus is not a loss to society. It is redistribution from consumers to the monopoly producer.

Rent Seeking

You've seen that monopoly creates a deadweight loss and is inefficient. But the social cost of monopoly can exceed the deadweight loss because of an activity called rent seeking. Any surplus—consumer surplus, producer surplus, or economic profit—is called **economic rent**. And **rent seeking** is the pursuit of wealth by capturing economic rent.

You've seen that a monopoly makes its economic profit by diverting part of consumer surplus to itself—by converting consumer surplus into economic profit. So the pursuit of economic profit by a monopoly is rent seeking. It is the attempt to capture consumer surplus.

Rent seekers pursue their goals in two main ways. They might

- Buy a monopoly
- Create a monopoly

Buy a Monopoly To rent seek by buying a monopoly, a person searches for a monopoly that is for sale at a lower price than the monopoly's economic profit. Trading of taxicab licences is an example of this type of rent seeking. In some cities, taxicabs are regulated. The city restricts both the fares and the number of taxis that can operate so that operating a taxi results in economic profit. A person who wants to operate a taxi must buy a licence from someone who already has one. People rationally devote time and effort to seeking out profitable monopoly businesses to buy. In the process, they use up scarce resources that could otherwise have been used to produce goods and services. The value of this lost production is part of the social cost of monopoly. The amount paid for a monopoly is not a social

cost because the payment is just a transfer of an existing producer surplus from the buyer to the seller.

Create a Monopoly Rent seeking by creating a monopoly is mainly a political activity. It takes the form of lobbying and trying to influence the political process. Such influence might be sought by making contributions to a political party in exchange for legislative support or by indirectly seeking to influence political outcomes through publicity in the media or more direct contacts with politicians and bureaucrats. An example of a monopoly created in this way is the cable television monopoly created and regulated by the Canadian Radio-television and Telecommunications Commission (CRTC). Another is a regulation that restricts "split-run" magazines. These regulations restrict output and increase price.

This type of rent seeking is a costly activity that uses up scarce resources. Taken together, firms spend billions of dollars lobbying MPs, MPPs, and bureaucrats in the pursuit of licences and laws that create barriers to entry and establish a monopoly.

Rent-Seeking Equilibrium

Barriers to entry create monopoly. But there is no barrier to entry into rent seeking. Rent seeking is like perfect competition. If an economic profit is available, a new rent seeker will try to get some of it. And competition among rent seekers pushes up the price that must be paid for a monopoly, to the point at which the rent seeker makes zero economic profit by operating the monopoly. For example, competition for the right to operate a taxicab in New York City leads to a price of more than $100,000 for a taxi licence, which is sufficiently high to eliminate the economic profit made by a taxicab operator.

Figure 13.7 shows a rent-seeking equilibrium. The cost of rent seeking is a fixed cost that must be added to a monopoly's other costs. Rent seeking and rent-seeking costs increase to the point at which no economic profit is made. The average total cost curve, which includes the fixed cost of rent seeking, shifts upward until it just touches the demand curve. Economic profit is zero. It has been lost in rent seeking.

Consumer surplus is unaffected, but the deadweight loss from monopoly is larger. The deadweight loss now includes the original deadweight loss triangle plus the lost producer surplus, shown by the enlarged grey area in Fig. 13.7.

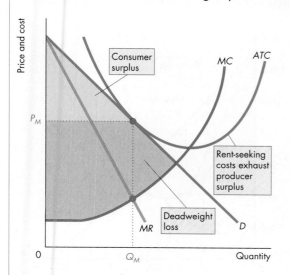

FIGURE 13.7 Rent-Seeking Equilibrium

With competitive rent seeking, a monopoly uses all its economic profit to maintain its monopoly. The firm's rent-seeking costs are fixed costs. They add to total fixed cost and to average total cost. The *ATC* curve shifts upward until, at the profit-maximizing price, the firm breaks even.

myeconlab animation

Review Quiz

1 Why does a single-price monopoly produce a smaller output and charge more than the price that would prevail if the industry were perfectly competitive?
2 How does a monopoly transfer consumer surplus to itself?
3 Why is a single-price monopoly inefficient?
4 What is rent seeking and how does it influence the inefficiency of monopoly?

myeconlab Work Study Plan 13.3 and get instant feedback.

So far, we've considered only a single-price monopoly. But many monopolies do not operate with a single price. Instead, they price discriminate. Let's now see how a price-discriminating monopoly works.

Price Discrimination

You encounter *price discrimination*—selling a good or service at a number of different prices—when you travel, go to the movies, get your hair cut, buy pizza, or visit an art museum or theme park. Many of the firms that price discriminate are not monopolies, but monopolies price discriminate when they can.

To be able to price discriminate, a firm must be able to identify and separate different buyer types and sell a product that cannot be resold.

Not all price *differences* are price *discrimination*. Some goods that are similar have different prices because they have different costs of production. For example, the price per kilogram of cereal is lower if you buy your cereal in a big box than if you buy individual serving size boxes. This price difference reflects a cost difference and is not price discrimination.

At first sight, price discrimination appears to be inconsistent with profit maximization. Why would a movie theatre allow children to see movies at a discount? Why would a hairdresser charge students and senior citizens less? Aren't these firms losing profit by being nice to their customers?

Capturing Consumer Surplus

Price discrimination captures consumer surplus and converts it into economic profit. It does so by getting buyers to pay a price as close as possible to the maximum willingness to pay.

Firms price discriminate in two broad ways. They discriminate

■ Among groups of buyers
■ Among units of a good

Discriminating Among Groups of Buyers People differ in the values they place on a good—their marginal benefit and willingness to pay. Some of these differences are correlated with features such as age, employment status, and other easily distinguished characteristics. When such a correlation is present, firms can profit by price discriminating among the different groups of buyers.

For example, a face-to-face sales meeting with a customer might bring a large and profitable order. So for salespeople and other business travellers, the marginal benefit from a trip is large and the price that such a traveller is willing to pay for a trip is high. In contrast, for a vacation traveller, any of several different trips and even no vacation trip are options. So for vacation travellers, the marginal benefit of a trip is small and the price that such a traveller is willing to pay for a trip is low. Because business travellers are willing to pay more than vacation travellers are, it is possible for an airline to profit by price discriminating between these two groups.

Discriminating Among Units of a Good Everyone experiences diminishing marginal benefit and has a downward-sloping demand curve. For this reason, if all the units of the good are sold for a single price, buyers end up with a consumer surplus equal to the value they get from each unit of the good minus the price paid for it.

A firm that price discriminates by charging buyers one price for a single item and a lower price for a second or third item can capture some of the consumer surplus. Buying one pizza and getting a second one free (or for a low price) is an example of this type of price discrimination.

(Note that some discounts for bulk arise from lower costs of production for greater bulk. In these cases, such discounts are not price discrimination.)

Let's see how price discriminating increases economic profit.

Profiting by Price Discriminating

Global Airlines has a monopoly on an exotic route. Figure 13.8 shows the market demand curve (*D*) for travel on this route. It also shows Global Airline's marginal revenue curve (*MR*), marginal cost curve (*MC*), and average total cost curve (*ATC*).

As a single-price monopoly, Global maximizes profit by producing the quantity at which *MR* equals *MC*, which is 8,000 trips a year, and charging $1,200 per trip. At this quantity, average total cost is $600 per trip, economic profit is $600 a trip, and Global's economic profit is $4.8 million a year, shown by the blue rectangle. Global's customers enjoy a consumer surplus shown by the green triangle.

Global is struck by the fact that many of its customers are business travellers, and it suspects they are willing to pay more than $1,200 a trip. Global does some market research, which reveals that some business travellers are willing to pay as much as $1,800 a trip. Also, these customers frequently change their travel plans at the last minute. Another group of

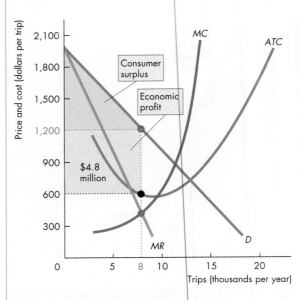

FIGURE 13.8   A Single Price of Air Travel

Global Airlines has a monopoly on an air route. The market demand curve is *D*. Global Airline's marginal revenue curve is *MR*, its marginal cost curve is *MC*, and its average total cost curve is *ATC*. As a single-price monopoly, Global maximizes profit by selling 8,000 trips a year at $1,200 a trip. Its profit is $4.8 million a year—the blue rectangle. Global's customers enjoy a consumer surplus—the green triangle.

myeconlab   animation

business travellers is willing to pay $1,600. These customers know a week ahead when they will travel, and they never want to stay over a weekend. Yet another group would pay up to $1,400. These travellers know two weeks ahead when they will travel and also don't want to stay away over a weekend.

Global announces a new fare schedule: no restrictions, $1,800; 7-day advance purchase, nonrefundable, $1,600; 14-day advance purchase, nonrefundable, $1,400; 14-day advance purchase, must stay over a weekend, $1,200.

Figure 13.9 shows the outcome with this new fare structure and also shows why Global is pleased with its new fares. It sells 2,000 seats at each of its four prices. Global's economic profit increases by the dark blue steps. Its economic profit is now its original $4.8 million a year plus an additional $2.4 million from its new higher fares. Consumer surplus shrinks to the sum of the smaller green areas.

FIGURE 13.9   Price Discrimination

Global revises its fare structure: no restrictions at $1,800, 7-day advance purchase at $1,600, 14-day advance purchase at $1,400, and must stay over a weekend at $1,200. Global sells 2,000 trips at each of its four new fares. Its economic profit increases by $2.4 million a year to $7.2 million a year, which is shown by the original blue rectangle plus the dark blue steps. Global's customers' consumer surplus shrinks.

 animation

Perfect Price Discrimination

Perfect price discrimination occurs if a firm is able to sell each unit of output for the highest price anyone is willing to pay for it. In such a case, the entire consumer surplus is eliminated and captured by the producer. To practise perfect price discrimination, a firm must be creative and come up with a host of prices and special conditions, each one of which appeals to a tiny segment of the market.

With perfect price discrimination, something special happens to marginal revenue—the market demand curve becomes the marginal revenue curve. The reason is that when the price is cut to sell a larger quantity, the firm sells only the marginal unit at the lower price. All the other units continue to be sold for the highest price that each buyer is willing to pay. So for the perfect price discriminator, marginal revenue *equals* price and the market demand curve becomes the marginal revenue curve.

With marginal revenue equal to price, Global can obtain even greater profit by increasing output up to the point at which price (and marginal revenue) is equal to marginal cost.

So Global seeks new travellers who will not pay as much as $1,200 a trip but who will pay more than marginal cost. Global offers a variety of vacation specials at different low fares that appeal only to new travellers. Existing customers continue to pay the higher fares. With all these fares and specials, Global increases sales, extracts the entire consumer surplus, and maximizes economic profit.

Figure 13.10 shows the outcome with perfect price discrimination. The fares paid by the original travellers extract the entire consumer surplus from this group. The new fares between $900 and $1,200 attract 3,000 additional travellers and take their entire consumer surplus also. Global now makes an economic profit of more than $9 million.

FIGURE 13.10   Perfect Price Discrimination

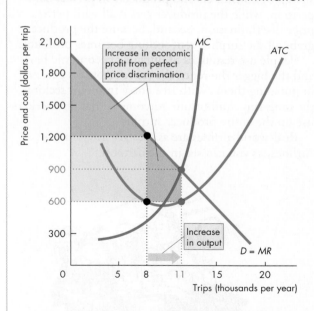

Dozens of fares discriminate among many different types of business traveller, and many new low fares with restrictions appeal to vacation travellers. With perfect price discrimination, the market demand curve becomes Global's marginal revenue curve. Economic profit is maximized when the lowest price equals marginal cost. Global sells 11,000 trips and makes an economic profit of $9.35 million a year.

 animation

Efficiency and Rent Seeking with Price Discrimination

With perfect price discrimination, output increases to the point at which price equals marginal cost—where the marginal cost curve intersects the demand curve (see Fig. 13.10). This output is identical to that of perfect competition. Perfect price discrimination pushes consumer surplus to zero but increases the monopoly's producer surplus to equal the sum of consumer surplus and producer surplus in perfect competition. With perfect price discrimination, deadweight loss is zero. So perfect price discrimination achieves efficiency.

The more perfectly the monopoly can price discriminate, the closer its output is to the competitive output and the more efficient is the outcome.

But there are two differences between perfect competition and perfect price discrimination. First, the distribution of the total surplus is different. It is shared by consumers and producers in perfect competition, while the producer gets it all with perfect price discrimination. Second, because the producer grabs all the surplus, rent seeking becomes profitable.

People use resources in pursuit of economic rent, and the bigger the rents, the more resources get used in pursuing them. With free entry into rent seeking, the long-run equilibrium outcome is that rent seekers use up the entire producer surplus.

Real-world airlines are as creative as Global Airlines, as you can see in the cartoon!

Would it bother you to hear how little I paid for this flight?

From William Hamilton, "Voodoo Economics," © 1992 by The Chronicle Publishing Company, p. 3. Reprinted with permission of Chronicle Books.

Attempting Perfect Price Discrimination
How Many Days at Disney World?

If you want to spend a day at Disney World in Orlando, it will cost you $75.62. You can spend a second (consecutive) day for an extra $72.42. A third day will cost you $68.17. But for a fourth day, you'll pay only $9.59, and for a fifth day, $3.20. For more, all the way up to 10, you'll pay only $2.12 a day.

Disney Corporation hopes that it has read your willingness to pay correctly and not left you with too much consumer surplus. Disney figures that after three days, your marginal benefit is crashing.

Disney's Ticket Prices

Review Quiz

1 What is price discrimination and how is it used to increase a monopoly's profit?
2 Explain how consumer surplus changes when a monopoly price discriminates.
3 Explain how consumer surplus, economic profit, and output change when a monopoly perfectly price discriminates.
4 What are some of the ways that real-world airlines price discriminate?

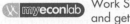 Work Study Plan 13.4 and get instant feedback.

You've seen that monopoly is profitable for the monopoly but costly for consumers. It results in inefficiency. Because of these features of monopoly, it is subject to policy debate and regulation. We'll now study the key monopoly policy issues.

Monopoly Regulation

Natural monopoly presents a dilemma. With economies of scale, it produces at the lowest possible cost. But with market power, it has an incentive to raise the price above the competitive price and produce too little—to operate in the self-interest of the monopolist and not in the social interest.

Regulation—rules administered by a government agency to influence prices, quantities, entry, and other aspects of economic activity in a firm or industry—is a possible solution to this dilemma.

To implement regulation, the government establishes agencies to oversee and enforce the rules. For example, the Canadian Transport Commission regulates transports under federal jurisdiction, including rail, air, water, and pipelines, and some interprovincial commercial motor transport. The Canadian Transport Commission became the focus of the federal Auditor's Report in 1979, and a process of deregulation began in 1980.

Deregulation is the process of removing regulation of prices, quantities, entry, and other aspects of economic activity in a firm or industry. During the past 25 years, deregulation has occurred in many Canadian markets, including domestic rail and air transportation, telephone service, natural gas, and grain transportation.

Regulation is a possible solution to the dilemma presented by natural monopoly but not a guaranteed solution. There are two theories about how regulation actually works: the *social interest theory* and the *capture theory*.

The **social interest theory** is that the political and regulatory process relentlessly seeks out inefficiency and introduces regulation that eliminates deadweight loss and allocates resources efficiently.

The **capture theory** is that regulation serves the self-interest of the producer, who captures the regulator and maximizes economic profit. Regulation that benefits the producer but creates a deadweight loss gets adopted because the producer's gain is large and visible while each individual consumer's is small and invisible. No individual consumer has an incentive to oppose the regulation, but the producer has a big incentive to lobby for it.

We're going to examine efficient regulation that serves the social interest and see why it is not a simple matter to design and implement such regulation.

Efficient Regulation of a Natural Monopoly

A cable TV company is a *natural monopoly*—it can supply the entire market at a lower price than two or more competing firms can. Shaw Cablesystems provides cable TV to households in Western Canada. The firm has invested heavily in satellite receiving dishes, cables, and control equipment and so has large fixed costs. These fixed costs are part of the firm's average total cost. Its average total cost decreases as the number of households served increases because the fixed cost is spread over a larger number of households.

Unregulated, Shaw Cablesystems produces the quantity that maximizes profit. Like all single-price monopolies, the profit-maximizing quantity is less than the efficient quantity, and underproduction results in a deadweight loss.

How can Shaw Cablesystems be regulated to produce the efficient quantity of cable TV service? The answer is by being regulated to set its price equal to marginal cost, known as the **marginal cost pricing rule**. The quantity demanded at a price equal to marginal cost is the efficient quantity—the quantity at which marginal benefit equals marginal cost.

Figure 13.11 illustrates the marginal cost pricing rule. The demand curve for cable TV is *D*. Shaw's marginal cost curve is *MC*. That marginal cost curve is (assumed to be) horizontal at $10 per household per month—that is, the cost of providing each additional household with a month of cable programming is $10. The efficient outcome occurs if the price is regulated at $10 per household per month with 10 million households served.

But there is a problem: At the efficient output, average total cost exceeds marginal cost, so a firm that uses marginal cost pricing incurs an economic loss. A cable TV company that is required to use a marginal cost pricing rule will not stay in business for long. How can the firm cover its costs and at the same time obey a marginal cost pricing rule?

There are two possible ways of enabling the firm to cover its costs: price discrimination and a two-part price (called a *two-part tariff*).

For example, local telephone companies charge consumers a monthly fee for being connected to the telephone system and then charge a price equal to marginal cost (zero) for each local call. A cable TV operator can charge a one-time connection fee that covers its fixed cost and then charge a monthly fee equal to marginal cost.

FIGURE 13.11   Regulating a Natural Monopoly

A natural monopoly cable TV supplier faces the demand curve *D*. The firm's marginal cost is constant at $10 per household per month, as shown by the curve labelled *MC*. The long-run average cost curve is *LRAC*.

Unregulated, as a profit-maximizer, the firm serves 5 million households at a price of $60 a month. An efficient marginal cost pricing rule sets the price at $10 a month. The monopoly serves 10 million households and incurs an economic loss. A second-best average cost pricing rule sets the price at $30 a month. The monopoly serves 8 million households and earns zero economic profit.

Second-Best Regulation of a Natural Monopoly

A natural monopoly cannot always be regulated to achieve an efficient outcome. Two possible ways of enabling a regulated monopoly to avoid an economic loss are

- Average cost pricing
- Government subsidy

Average Cost Pricing The **average cost pricing rule** sets price equal to average total cost. With this rule the firm produces the quantity at which the average total cost curve cuts the demand curve. This rule results in the firm making zero economic profit—breaking even. But because for a natural monopoly average total cost exceeds marginal cost, the quantity produced is less than the efficient quantity and a deadweight loss arises.

Figure 13.11 illustrates the average cost pricing rule. The price is $30 a month and 8 million households get cable TV.

Government Subsidy A government subsidy is a direct payment to a firm equal to its economic loss. To pay a subsidy, the government must raise the revenue by taxing some other activity. You saw in Chapter 6 that taxes themselves generate deadweight loss.

And the Second-Best Is ... Which is the better option, average cost pricing or marginal cost pricing with a government subsidy? The answer depends on the relative magnitudes of the two deadweight losses. Average cost pricing generates a deadweight loss in the market served by the natural monopoly. A subsidy generates deadweight losses in the markets for the items that are taxed to pay for the subsidy. The smaller deadweight loss is the second-best solution to regulating a natural monopoly. Making this calculation in practice is too difficult and average cost pricing is generally preferred to a subsidy.

Implementing average cost pricing presents the regulator with a challenge because it is not possible to be sure what a firm's costs are. So regulators use one of two practical rules:

- Rate of return regulation
- Price cap regulation

Rate of Return Regulation Under **rate of return regulation**, a firm must justify its price by showing that its return on capital doesn't exceed a specified target rate. This type of regulation can end up serving the self-interest of the firm rather than the social interest. The firm's managers have an incentive to inflate costs by spending on items such as private jets, free baseball tickets (disguised as public relations expenses), and lavish entertainment. Managers also have an incentive to use more capital than the efficient amount. The rate of return on capital is regulated but not the total return on capital, and the greater the amount of capital, the greater is the total return.

Price Cap Regulation For the reason that we've just examined, rate of return regulation is increasingly being replaced by price cap regulation. A **price cap regulation** is a price ceiling—a rule that specifies the highest price the firm is permitted to set. This type of regulation gives a firm an incentive to operate efficiently and keep costs under control. Price cap regulation has become common for the electricity and telecommunications industries and is replacing rate of return regulation.

To see how a price cap works, let's suppose that the cable TV operator is subject to this type of regulation. Figure 13.12 shows that without regulation, the firm maximizes profit by serving 5 million households and charging a price of $60 a month. If a price cap is set at $30 a month, the firm is permitted to sell any quantity it chooses at that price or at a lower price. At 5 million households, the firm now incurs an economic loss. It can decrease the loss by increasing output to 8 million households. To increase output above 8 million households, the firm would have to lower the price and again it would incur a loss. So the profit-maximizing quantity is 8 million households—the same as with average cost pricing.

Notice that a price cap lowers the price and increases output. This outcome is in sharp contrast to the effect of a price ceiling in a competitive market that you studied in Chapter 6 (pp. 130–132). The reason is that in a monopoly, the unregulated equilibrium output is less than the competitive equilibrium output, and the price cap regulation replicates the conditions of a competitive market.

In Fig. 13.12, the price cap delivers average cost pricing. In practice, the regulator might set the cap too high. For this reason, price cap regulation is often combined with *earnings sharing regulation*—a regulation that requires firms to make refunds to customers when profits rise above a target level.

FIGURE 13.12 Price Cap Regulation

A natural monopoly cable TV supplier faces the demand curve *D*. The firm's marginal cost is constant at $10 per household per month, as shown by the curve labelled *MC*. The long-run average cost curve is *LRAC*.

Unregulated, the firm serves 5 million households at a price of $60 a month. A price cap sets the maximum price at $30 a month. The firm has an incentive to minimize cost and serve the quantity of households that demand service at the price cap. The price cap regulation lowers the price and increases the quantity.

myeconlab animation

Review Quiz

1 What is the pricing rule that achieves an efficient outcome for a regulated monopoly? What is the problem with this rule?

2 What is the average cost pricing rule? Why is it not an efficient way of regulating monopoly?

3 What is a price cap? Why might it be a more effective way of regulating monopoly than rate of return regulation?

4 Compare the consumer surplus, producer surplus, and deadweight loss that arise from average cost pricing with those that arise from profit-maximization pricing and marginal cost pricing.

myeconlab Work Study Plan 13.5 and get instant feedback.

♦ You've now completed your study of monopoly. *Reading Between the Lines* on pp. 316–317 looks at Microsoft's near monopoly in PC operating systems and a court challenge the firm faced in Europe. In the next chapter, we study markets that lie between the extremes of perfect competition and monopoly and that blend elements of the two.

European View of Microsoft

European Court Faults Microsoft on Competition

September 18, 2007

Europe's second-highest court delivered a stinging rebuke to Microsoft Monday, ... [for] adding a digital media player to Windows, undercutting the early leader, RealNetworks.

It also ordered Microsoft to ... share confidential computer code with competitors. The court also upheld the record fine levied against the company, 497.2 million euros ($689.4 million).

But the court decision comes as the centre of gravity in computing is shifting away from the software for personal computers, Microsoft's stronghold. Increasingly, the e-mailing or word-processing functions of a computer can be performed with software delivered on a Web browser. Other devices like cell phones are now used as alternates to personal computers.

The real challenge to Microsoft, after more than a decade of dominating the technology industry, is coming not from the government, but from the marketplace. ...

[T]he Justice Department issued a statement expressing its concerns with the European decision, saying that tough restraints on powerful companies can be harmful. Thomas O. Barnett, assistant attorney general for the department's antitrust division, said that the effect "rather than helping consumers, may have the unfortunate consequence of harming consumers by chilling innovation and discouraging competition."

Consumer welfare, not protecting competitors, should be the guiding standard in antitrust, Mr. Barnett said. ...

In the United States, the Justice Department chose to settle the Microsoft antitrust case in 2001 without challenging the company's freedom to put whatever it wants in its operating system. ...

Essence of the Story

- A European court fined Microsoft $689 million for competing with RealNetworks by adding a digital media player to Windows, and the court ordered Microsoft to share its code with competitors.

- The market, not government, is Microsoft's main challenge because the emphasis is shifting from PC software to software delivered on a Web browser, and to cell phone software.

- The U.S. Justice Department did not challenge Microsoft's right to put whatever it wants in Windows and says that consumer welfare, not protecting competitors, should be the guide.

Economic Analysis

- Microsoft's operating system, Windows, enables the hardware of a PC to accept and execute instructions from word processors, spreadsheets, Web browsers, media players, and a host of other applications.

- In addition to creating the operating system for a PC, Microsoft develops and sells applications, the most famous of which are contained in its Office package (Word, Excel, Outlook, and PowerPoint).

- Other applications created by Microsoft are a Web browser, Internet Explorer, and a digital media player, Windows Media Player (the subject of the European court's decision).

- In the market for PC operating systems, Microsoft has a near monopoly.

- In the markets for applications, Microsoft faces stiff competition from other producers. The stiffest competition comes from the Internet.

- In 1994, a firm called Mosaic Communications launched the first easy-to-use Web browser, Netscape.

- A year later, RealNetworks Inc. launched its Real video and audio players.

- These two developments led to a rapid growth of Internet activity and left Microsoft behind the curve.

- PC users now needed Microsoft Windows, the Netscape browser, and the RealPlayer to enjoy the full scope of the Internet.

- Microsoft could have stood still and marketed Windows in its 1995 stripped-down form.

- If Microsoft had followed this strategy, it would have faced the market described in Fig. 1.

- As a profit-maximizing firm, Microsoft would have produced 20 million copies of Windows a year and sold them for $115 a copy.

- Instead, Microsoft improved Windows and added its own Web browser and media player.

- With a higher-value package, Microsoft faced the market shown in Fig. 2.

- Microsoft maximized profit by producing 20 million copies of Windows a year and selling them for $230 a copy.

- Microsoft's profit increased, but so did the consumer surplus of Windows users.

- As the U.S. Justice Department noted, limiting the actions of a monopoly doesn't always help the consumer.

Figure 1 Windows stripped down

Figure 2 Windows with bells and whistles

SUMMARY ◆

Key Points

Monopoly and How It Arises (pp. 300–301)

- A monopoly is an industry with a single supplier of a good or service that has no close substitutes and in which barriers to entry prevent competition.
- Barriers to entry may be legal (public franchise, licence, patent, copyright, firm owns control of a resource) or natural (created by economies of scale).
- A monopoly might be able to price discriminate when there is no resale possibility.
- Where resale is possible, a firm charges one price.

A Single-Price Monopoly's Output and Price Decision (pp. 302–305)

- A monopoly's demand curve is the market demand curve and a single-price monopoly's marginal revenue is less than price.
- A monopoly maximizes profit by producing the output at which marginal revenue equals marginal cost and by charging the maximum price that consumers are willing to pay for that output.

Single-Price Monopoly and Competition Compared (pp. 306–309)

- A single-price monopoly charges a higher price and produces a smaller quantity than a perfectly competitive industry.

- A single-price monopoly restricts output and creates a deadweight loss.
- The total loss that arises from monopoly equals the deadweight loss plus the cost of the resources devoted to rent seeking.

Price Discrimination (pp. 309–312)

- Price discrimination converts consumer surplus into economic profit.
- Perfect price discrimination extracts the entire consumer surplus; each unit is sold for the maximum price that each consumer is willing to pay; the quantity produced is the efficient quantity.
- Rent seeking with perfect price discrimination might eliminate the entire consumer surplus and producer surplus.

Monopoly Regulation (pp. 313–315)

- Regulation of natural monopoly might serve the social interest or the interest of the monopoly (the regulator being captured).
- Price equal to marginal cost achieves efficiency but results in economic loss.
- Price equal to average cost enables the firm to cover its cost but is inefficient.
- Rate of return regulation creates incentives for inefficient production and inflated cost.
- Price cap regulation with earnings share regulation can achieve a more efficient outcome than rate of return regulation.

Key Figures and Table

Figure 13.2   Demand and Marginal Revenue, 302
Figure 13.3   Marginal Revenue and Elasticity, 303
Figure 13.4   A Monopoly's Output and Price, 305
Figure 13.5   Monopoly's Smaller Output and Higher Price, 306
Figure 13.6   Inefficiency of Monopoly, 307

Figure 13.9   Price Discrimination, 311
Figure 13.10   Perfect Price Discrimination, 311
Figure 13.11   Regulating a Natural Monopoly, 314
Figure 13.12   Price Cap Regulation, 315
Table 13.1   A Monopoly's Output and Price Decision, 304

Key Terms

Average cost pricing rule, 314
Barriers to entry, 300
Capture theory, 313
Deregulation, 313
Economic rent, 308
Legal monopoly, 300

Marginal cost pricing rule, 313
Monopoly, 300
Natural monopoly, 300
Perfect price discrimination, 311
Price cap regulation, 315
Price discrimination, 301

Rate of return regulation, 314
Regulation, 313
Rent seeking, 308
Single-price monopoly, 301
Social interest theory, 313

PROBLEMS and APPLICATIONS

 Work problems 1–9 in Chapter 13 Study Plan and get instant feedback.
Work problems 10–16 as Homework, a Quiz, or a Test if assigned by your instructor.

1. Canada Post has a monopoly on residential mail delivery. Pfizer Inc. makes LIPITOR, a prescription drug that lowers cholesterol. Rogers Communications is the sole provider of cable television service in some parts of Ontario.

   a. What are the substitutes, if any, for the goods and services described above?
   b. What are the barriers to entry, if any, that protect these three firms from competition?
   c. Which of these three firms, if any, is a natural monopoly? Explain your answer and illustrate it by drawing an appropriate figure.
   d. Which of these three firms, if any, is a legal monopoly? Explain your answer.
   e. Which of these three firms is most likely to be able to profit from price discrimination and which is most likely to sell their good or service for a single price?

2. **Barbie's Revenge: Brawl over Doll is Heading to Trial**

   Four years ago, Mattel Inc. exhorted its executives to help save Barbie from a new doll clique called the Bratz. ... Market share was dropping at a "chilling rate," the presentation said. Barbie needed to be more "aggressive, revolutionary, and ruthless." That call to arms has led to a federal courthouse. ... Mattel accuses ... the maker of Bratz, of ... stealing the idea for the pouty-lipped dolls with the big heads. Mattel is trying to seize ownership of the Bratz line, ...

   Wall Street Journal, May 23, 2008

   a. Before Bratz entered the market, what type of monopoly did Mattel Inc. possess in the market for "the pouty-lipped dolls with the big heads"?
   b. What is the barrier to entry that Mattel might argue should protect it from competition in the market for Barbie dolls?
   c. Explain how the entry of Bratz dolls might be expected to change the demand for Barbie dolls.

3. **Inquiry Launched into Intel**

   The Federal Trade Commission in the United States has opened a formal probe into whether Intel, the world's largest chipmaker, has used its dominance to illegally stifle its few competitors. The move follows years of complaints from smaller chip rival Advanced Micro Devices. ... Intel is many times larger, holding 80 percent of the microprocessor market. ... In a sign that suggests the chip market remains competitive, Intel said, prices for microprocessors declined by 42.4 percent between 2000 and 2007 ... "evidence that this industry is fiercely competitive ..." Intel said.

   Washington Post, June 7, 2008

   a. Is Intel a monopoly in the chip market?
   b. Evaluate the argument made by Intel that the significant decline in prices is "evidence that this industry is fiercely competitive."

4. Minnie's Mineral Springs, a single-price monopoly, faces the market demand schedule:

Price (dollars per bottle)	Quantity demanded (bottles per hour)
10	0
8	1
6	2
4	3
2	4
0	5

   a. Calculate Minnie's total revenue schedule.
   b. Calculate its marginal revenue schedule.
   c. Draw a graph of the market demand curve and Minnie's marginal revenue curve.
   d. Why is Minnie's marginal revenue less than the price?
   e. At what price is Minnie's total revenue maximized?
   f. Over what range of prices is the demand for water from Minnie's Mineral Springs elastic?
   g. Why will Minnie not produce a quantity at which the market demand for water is inelastic?

5. Minnie's Mineral Springs faces the demand schedule in problem 4 and has the following total cost schedule:

Quantity produced (bottles per hour)	Total cost (dollars)
0	1
1	3
2	7
3	13
4	21
5	31

a. Calculate the marginal cost of producing each output listed in the table.

b. Calculate Minnie's profit-maximizing output and price.

c. Calculate the economic profit.

6. La Bella Pizza can produce a pizza for a marginal cost of $2. Its standard price is $15 a pizza. It offers a second pizza for $5. It also distributes coupons that give a $5 rebate on a standard-price pizza.

   a. How can La Bella Pizza make a larger economic profit with this range of prices than it could if it sold every pizza for $15?

   b. Draw a graph to illustrate your answer to a.

   c. Can you think of a way of increasing La Bella Pizza's economic profit even more?

   d. Is the outcome more efficient than it would be if La Bella Pizza charged just one price?

7. **Flying the "Open Skies"**

   The governments of Canada and the United States have negotiated an "Open Skies" air transport agreement, Transport Minister Jean–C. Lapierre and International Trade Minister Jim Peterson announced today. Potential benefits from the expansion of the 1995 agreement include greater access for Canadian passenger and cargo carriers to a much larger U.S. market as a platform from which to serve third countries; increased pricing flexibility for Canadian and U.S. carriers; more options for Canadian airports to attract U.S. carriers and lower prices for consumers.

   "This further liberalization of the Canada-U.S. air transport relationship will allow airlines of both countries to better meet the needs of travellers and shippers," said Mr. Lapierre. "It is my hope that this agreement will encourage the development of new markets, new services, lower prices and greater competition."

   "The flow of people, goods and services between Canada and the United States is crucial

to how we go about our daily business," said Mr. Peterson. This new flexibility which goes well beyond the 1995 agreement will improve how the NAFTA works and it will make North America more competitive."

   Transport Canada, November 11, 2005

   a. Before the "Open Skies" agreement came into effect, Air Canada was the only Canadian airline to fly to the United States. Did it operate in self-interest or in the social interest?

   b. Describe the change in price discrimination in the market for air travel when discount airlines entered the market under the "Open Skies" agreement.

   c. Explain the effect of the change in price discrimination when discount airlines entered the market under the "Open Skies" agreement on the price and the quantity of air travel.

8. The figure shows a situation similar to that of TransCanada, the firm that operates a natural gas distribution system in North America. The firm is a natural monopoly that cannot price discriminate.

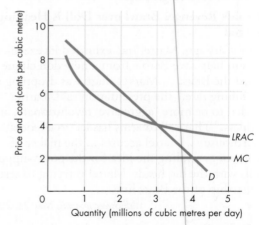

   What quantity will TransCanada produce and what is the price of natural gas if TransCanada is

   a. An unregulated profit-maximizing firm?

   b. Regulated to make zero economic profit?

   c. Regulated to be efficient?

9. What is the producer surplus, consumer surplus, and deadweight loss if TransCanada in problem 8 is

   a. An unregulated profit-maximizing firm?

   b. Regulated to make zero economic profit?

   c. Regulated to be efficient?

10. The following list gives some information about seven firms.

- Coca-Cola cuts its price below that of Pepsi-Cola in an attempt to increase its market share.
- A single firm, protected by a barrier to entry, produces a personal service that has no close substitutes.
- A barrier to entry exists, but the good has some close substitutes.
- A firm offers discounts to students and seniors.
- A firm can sell any quantity it chooses at the going price.
- The government issues Nike an exclusive licence to produce golf balls.
- A firm experiences economies of scale even when it produces the quantity that meets the entire market demand.

a. In which of the seven cases might monopoly arise?

b. Which of the seven cases are natural monopolies and which are legal monopolies?

c. Which can price discriminate, which cannot, and why?

11. Hot Air Balloon Rides, a single-price monopoly, has the demand schedule shown in columns 1 and 2 of the table and the total cost schedule shown in columns 2 and 3.

Price (dollars per ride)	Quantity demanded (rides per month)	Total cost (dollars per month)
220	0	80
200	1	160
180	2	260
160	3	380
140	4	520
120	5	680

a. Construct Hot Air's total revenue and marginal revenue schedules.

b. On a graph, show the market demand curve and Hot Air's marginal revenue curve.

c. Find Hot Air's profit-maximizing output and price and calculate the firm's economic profit.

d. If the government imposes a tax on Hot Air's profit, how does its output and price change?

e. If, instead of taxing Hot Air's profit, the government imposes a sales tax on balloon rides of $30 a ride, what are the new profit-maximizing quantity, price, and economic profit?

12. The figure illustrates the situation facing the publisher of the only newspaper containing local news in an isolated community.

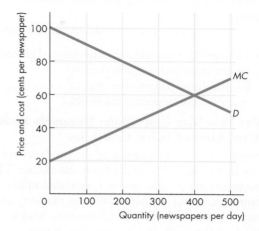

a. On the graph, mark the profit-maximizing quantity and price.

b. On the graph, show the publisher's total revenue per day.

c. At the price charged, is the demand for this newspaper elastic or inelastic? Why?

d. What are consumer surplus and deadweight loss? Mark each on your graph.

e. Explain why this market might encourage rent seeking.

f. If this market were perfectly competitive, what would be the quantity, price, consumer surplus, and producer surplus? Mark each on your graph.

13. **Telecoms Look to Grow by Acquisition**

A multibillion-dollar telecommunications merger announced Thursday ... shows how global cellular powerhouses are scouting for growth in emerging economies while consolidating in their own, crowded backyards.

France Télécom offered Thursday to buy TeliaSonera, a Swedish-Finnish telecommunications operator. ... Within hours, TeliaSonera rejected the offer as too low, but analysts said higher bids—either from France Télécom or others—could persuade [TeliaSonera] to accept a deal.

Meanwhile, in the United States, Verizon Wireless, ... agreed to buy Alltel for $28.1 billion, a deal that would make the company the biggest mobile phone operator in the country.

A combination of France Télécom and TeliaSonera would create the world's fourth-largest mobile operator ... smaller only than China Mobile, Vodafone and Telefónica of Spain.

International Herald Tribune, June 5, 2008

a. Explain the rent-seeking behaviour of global telecommunications companies.
b. Explain how mergers may affect the efficiency of the telecommunications market.

14. **Why Your Beer Costs More: Monopoly Boosts Prices, Limits Choice, Critics Say**

Imagine a store where most of the products are kept in the back. You order from the cashier. The products can't be sold below a legislated minimum price. And the overwhelming majority are made by one of three large companies, which also own the store. In Ontario, that is how $2.5 billion worth of beer is sold each year. ...

In reality, the retail chain responsible for just over 80 percent of beer sales in Ontario "is essentially a private monopoly" owned by the province's three largest brewers, Labatt, Molson, and Sleeman, the provincial study noted.

The brewers, in turn, belong to some of the highest-grossing beer makers in the world— Belgium's InBev SA, the United States' Molson Coors Brewing Co. and Japan's Sapporo. Analysts estimate that these foreign entities earn a combined $1 billion a year in profits in Canada, mostly in Ontario, making the province one of the most lucrative beer markets in the world.

And Ontario's beer consumers pay the freight, with higher prices, less choice and lack of convenience, the Beverage Alcohol System Review concluded three years ago. The review recommended opening beer sales to competition. But Ontario's government decided against sweeping changes. So little has changed.

A 24-pack of popular brands, such as Coors Light, is regularly priced at $36.95 in Ontario, at least 25 percent more than in such markets as Quebec and New York State, where beer is almost always on sale.

Toronto Star, July 05, 2008

a. Draw a graph to illustrate the market price, quantity of beer sold, and economic profit that the Beer Store in Ontario makes.

b. On your graph, identify consumer surplus, producer surplus, and deadweight loss.
c. How might the Beer Store's legal monopoly be justified?
d. Explain how the market price, quantity of beer sold, and the Beer Store's economic profit would change if the Ontario government decided to allow competition in the beer market.
e. Draw a graph to illustrate how an end to "essentially a private monopoly" would change the price and quantity in the beer market.
f. Explain how consumer surplus, producer surplus, and deadweight loss change with an end to "essentially a private monopoly" in the beer market.

15. **iShould!**

For gadget fans, ... today is a very big day indeed. A year after it launched in the U.S., Apple's iPhone finally arrives in Canada. ...

OK, but what's all the fuss? Aside from the innovative high-tech touchscreen, the iPhone ... [is] nice to look at, very easy to use, and backed by Apple's slick marketing. ...

Where can I buy it, and for how much? Rogers and its subsidiary Fido are the only cell-phone providers offering the iPhone, and it will only be sold through their stores, ... and the Rogers website. The version with 8 GB of storage will sell for $199. A three-year contract with Rogers or Fido is required ... [and] starts at $60 per month. They sell iPhones at Apple stores in the U.S., why not here?

Toronto Sun, September 7, 2008

a. How does Rogers being the exclusive provider of wireless service for the iPhone influence the wireless telecommunication market?
b. Would you expect the price of an iPhone to be higher or lower in Canada than in the United States? Explain your answer.

16. Study *Reading Between the Lines* on pp. 316–317 and then answer the following questions:

a. What does the news article mean when it says that Microsoft's main challenge comes from the marketplace rather than government?
b. How does Microsoft try to raise barriers to the entry of competitors?

14 Monopolistic Competition

After studying this chapter, you will be able to

- Define and identify monopolistic competition

- Explain how a firm in monopolistic competition determines its price and output in the short run and the long run

- Explain why advertising costs are high and why firms use brand names in a monopolistically competitive industry

Fifty years ago, Moncton, like most places in Canada, had no pizza restaurants. When Bernard Imbeault and two of his friends opened their first Pizza Delight in Sheldiac, New Brunswick, Pizza Delight was a local monopoly. The business grew, they moved to nearby Moncton, and now they operate 250 outlets across Canada as Pizza Delight, Mikes Restaurants, Scores Restaurants, and Bâton Rouge Restaurants. But the pizza market is highly competitive. Today in Moncton, about 50 pizza parlours compete for business: Pizza Delight, Pizza Shack, Domino's, Zio's Pizzeria, A1 Pizza, Norm's Pizza, Bravo Pizza, Wow Pizza, Vito's Pizza, Donairo's, Pizza Hut, Boston Pizza, and many others.

As you well know, a pizza is not just a pizza. People care about where they buy their pizza. They care about the crust, the sauce, the toppings, the style, and whether it's cooked in a wood-fired oven. The varieties are almost endless.

Because there are many different types of pizza, the market for pizza isn't perfectly competitive. Pizza producers compete, but each has a monopoly on its own special kind of pizza.

Most of the things that you buy are like pizza—they come in many different types. Running shoes and cell phones are two more striking examples.

The model of monopolistic competition that is explained in this chapter helps us to understand the competition we see every day in the markets for pizza, shoes, cell phones, and most other consumer goods and services.

In *Reading Between the Lines* at the end of the chapter, we apply the model of monopolistic competition to the market for 3G cell phones and the flurry of activity in that market following the launch of the new iPhone in 2008.

What Is Monopolistic Competition?

You have studied perfect competition, in which a large number of firms produce at the lowest possible cost, make zero economic profit, and are efficient. You've also studied monopoly, in which a single firm restricts output, produces at a higher cost and price than in perfect competition, and is inefficient.

Most real-world markets are competitive but not perfectly competitive, because firms in these markets have some power to set their prices, as monopolies do. We call this type of market *monopolistic competition*.

Monopolistic competition is a market structure in which

- A large number of firms compete.
- Each firm produces a differentiated product.
- Firms compete on product quality, price, and marketing.
- Firms are free to enter and exit the industry.

Large Number of Firms

In monopolistic competition, as in perfect competition, the industry consists of a large number of firms. The presence of a large number of firms has three implications for the firms in the industry.

Small Market Share   In monopolistic competition, each firm supplies a small part of the total industry output. Consequently, each firm has only limited power to influence the price of its product. Each firm's price can deviate from the average price of other firms by only a relatively small amount.

Ignore Other Firms   A firm in monopolistic competition must be sensitive to the average market price of the product, but the firm does not pay attention to any one individual competitor. Because all the firms are relatively small, no one firm can dictate market conditions and so no one firm's actions directly affect the actions of the other firms.

Collusion Impossible   Firms in monopolistic competition would like to be able to conspire to fix a higher price—called *collusion*. But because the number of firms in monopolistic competition is large, coordination is difficult and collusion is not possible.

Product Differentiation

A firm practices **product differentiation** if it makes a product that is slightly different from the products of competing firms. A differentiated product is one that is a close substitute but not a perfect substitute for the products of the other firms. Some people are willing to pay more for one variety of the product, so when its price rises, the quantity demanded of that variety decreases, but it does not (necessarily) decrease to zero. For example, Adidas, Asics, Diadora, Etonic, Fila, New Balance, Nike, Puma, and Reebok all make differentiated running shoes. If the price of Adidas running shoes rises and the prices of the other shoes remain constant, Adidas sells fewer shoes and the other producers sell more. But Adidas shoes don't disappear unless the price rises by a large enough amount.

Competing on Quality, Price, and Marketing

Product differentiation enables a firm to compete with other firms in three areas: product quality, price, and marketing.

Quality   The quality of a product is the physical attributes that make it different from the products of other firms. Quality includes design, reliability, the service provided to the buyer, and the buyer's ease of access to the product. Quality lies on a spectrum that runs from high to low. Some firms—such as Dell Computer Corp.—offer high-quality products. They are well designed and reliable, and the customer receives quick and efficient service. Other firms offer a lower-quality product that is less well designed, that might not work perfectly, and that the buyer must travel some distance to obtain.

Price   Because of product differentiation, a firm in monopolistic competition faces a downward-sloping demand curve. So, like a monopoly, the firm can set both its price and its output. But there is a tradeoff between the product's quality and price. A firm that makes a high-quality product can charge a higher price than a firm that makes a low-quality product.

Marketing   Because of product differentiation, a firm in monopolistic competition must market its product. Marketing takes two main forms: advertising and packaging. A firm that produces a high-quality product wants to sell it for a suitably high price. To be able to do so, it must advertise and package its product in a way that convinces buyers that they are getting the higher quality for which they are paying a higher price. For example, pharmaceutical companies advertise and package their brand-name drugs to persuade buyers that these items are superior to the lower-priced generic alternatives. Similarly, a low-quality producer uses advertising and packaging to persuade buyers that although the quality is low, the low price more than compensates for this fact.

Entry and Exit

Monopolistic competition has no barriers to prevent new firms from entering the industry in the long run. Consequently, a firm in monopolistic competition cannot make an economic profit in the long run. When existing firms make an economic profit, new firms enter the industry. This entry lowers prices and eventually eliminates economic profit. When firms incur economic losses, some firms leave the industry in the long run. This exit increases prices and eventually eliminates the economic loss.

In long-run equilibrium, firms neither enter nor leave the industry and the firms in the industry make zero economic profit.

Examples of Monopolistic Competition

The box below shows 10 industries that are good examples of monopolistic competition. These industries have a large number of firms (shown in parentheses after the name of the industry). In the most concentrated of these industries, upholstered household furniture, the largest 4 firms produce only 30 percent of the industry's total sales and the largest 20 firms produce 69 percent of total sales. The number on the right is the Herfindahl-Hirschman Index. Producers of clothing, bakery items, and plastic bags operate in monopolistic competition.

Review Quiz

1 What are the distinguishing characteristics of monopolistic competition?
2 How do firms in monopolistic competition compete?
3 Provide some examples of industries near your school that operate in monopolistic competition (excluding those in the figure below).

 Work Study Plan 14.1 and get instant feedback.

Monopolistic Competition Today

Almost Everything You Buy

These 10 industries operate in monopolistic competition. The number of firms in the industry is shown in parentheses after the name of the industry. The red bars show the percentage of industry sales by the largest 4 firms. The blue bars show the percentage of industry sales by the next 4 largest firms, and the orange bars show the percentage of industry sales by the next 12 largest firms. So the entire length of the combined red, blue, and orange bars shows the percentage of industry sales by the largest 20 firms. The Herfindahl-Hirschman Index is shown on the right.

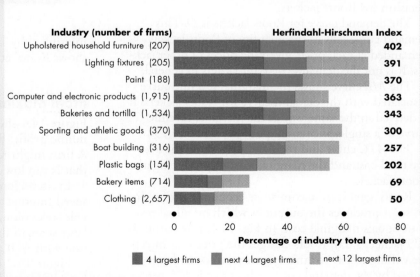

Measures of Concentration

Source of data: Adapted from Statistics Canada, Manufacturing, Construction, and Energy Division.

Price and Output in Monopolistic Competition

Suppose you've been hired by Michael Budman and Don Green, the co-founders of Roots Canada Ltd., to manage the production and marketing of Roots jackets. Think about the decisions that you must make at Roots. First, you must decide on the design and quality of jackets and on your marketing program. Second, you must decide on the quantity of jackets to produce and the price at which to sell them.

We'll suppose that Roots has already made its decisions about design, quality, and marketing and now we'll concentrate on the output and pricing decision. We'll study quality and marketing decisions in the next section.

For a given quality of jackets and marketing activity, Roots faces given costs and market conditions. Given its costs and the demand for its jackets, how does Roots decide the quantity of jackets to produce and the price at which to sell them?

The Firm's Short-Run Output and Price Decision

In the short run, a firm in monopolistic competition makes its output and price decision just like a monopoly firm does. Figure 14.1 illustrates this decision for Roots jackets.

The demand curve for Roots jackets is D. This demand curve tells us the quantity of Roots jackets demanded at each price, given the prices of other jackets. It is not the demand curve for jackets in general.

The MR curve shows the marginal revenue curve associated with the demand curve for Roots jackets. It is derived in the same way as the marginal revenue curve of a single-price monopoly (see Chapter 13).

The ATC curve and the MC curve show the average total cost and the marginal cost of producing a Roots jacket.

Roots' goal is to maximize its economic profit. To do so, it produces the output at which marginal revenue equals marginal cost. In Fig. 14.1, this output is 125 jackets a day. Roots charges the price that buyers are willing to pay for this quantity, which is determined by the demand curve. This price is $75 per jacket. When Roots produces 125 jackets a day, its average total cost is $25 per jacket and it makes an economic profit of $6,250 a day ($50 per jacket

FIGURE 14.1 Economic Profit in the Short Run

Roots maximizes profit by producing the quantity at which marginal revenue equals marginal cost, 125 jackets a day, and charging the price of $75 a jacket. This price exceeds the average total cost of $25 a jacket, so the firm makes an economic profit of $50 a jacket. The blue rectangle illustrates economic profit, which equals $6,250 a day ($50 a jacket multiplied by 125 jackets a day).

myeconlab animation

multiplied by 125 jackets a day). The blue rectangle shows Roots' economic profit.

Profit Maximizing Might Be Loss Minimizing

Figure 14.1 shows that Roots is earning a large economic profit. But such an outcome is not inevitable. A firm might face a level of demand for its product that is too low for it to make an economic profit.

Excite@Home was such a firm. Offering high-speed Internet service over the same cable that provides television, Excite@Home hoped to capture a large share of the Internet portal market in competition with AOL, MSN, and a host of other providers.

Figure 14.2 illustrates the situation facing Excite@Home in 2001. The demand curve for its portal service is D, the marginal revenue curve is MR, the average total cost curve is ATC, and the marginal cost curve is MC. Excite@Home maximized profit—

FIGURE 14.2 Economic Loss in the Short Run

Profit is maximized where marginal revenue equals marginal cost. The loss-minimizing quantity is 40,000 customers. The price of $40 a month is less than the average total cost of $50 a month, so the firm incurs an economic loss of $10 a customer. The red rectangle illustrates economic loss, which equals $400,000 a month ($10 a customer multiplied by 40,000 customers).

myeconlab animation

equivalently, it minimized its loss—by producing the output at which marginal revenue equals marginal cost. In Fig. 14.2, this output is 40,000 customers. Excite@Home charged the price that buyers were willing to pay for this quantity, which was $40 a month, as determined from the demand curve. With 40,000 customers, Excite@Home's average total cost was $50 per customer, so it incurred an economic loss of $400,000 a month ($10 a customer multiplied by 40,000 customers). The red rectangle shows Excite@Home's economic loss.

So far, the firm in monopolistic competition looks like a single-price monopoly. It produces the quantity at which marginal revenue equals marginal cost and then charges the price that buyers are willing to pay for that quantity, as determined by the demand curve. The key difference between monopoly and monopolistic competition lies in what happens next, when firms either make an economic profit or incur an economic loss.

Long Run: Zero Economic Profit

A firm like Excite@Home is not going to incur an economic loss for long. Eventually, it goes out of business. Also, there is no restriction on entry into monopolistic competition, so if firms in an industry are making economic profit, other firms have an incentive to enter that industry.

As the Gap, Eddie Bauer, and other firms start to make jackets similar to those made by Roots, the demand for Roots jackets decreases. The demand curve for Roots jackets and the marginal revenue curve shift leftward. As these curves shift leftward, the profit-maximizing quantity of Roots jackets decreases and the price falls.

Figure 14.3 shows the long-run equilibrium. The demand curve for Roots jackets and the marginal revenue curve have shifted leftward. The firm produces 75 jackets a day and sells them for $25 each. At this output level, average total cost is also $25 per jacket.

FIGURE 14.3 Output and Price in the Long Run

Economic profit encourages entry, which decreases the demand for each firm's product. When the demand curve touches the ATC curve at the quantity at which MR equals MC, the market is in long-run equilibrium. The output that maximizes profit is 75 jackets a day, and the price is $25 per jacket. Average total cost is also $25 per jacket, so economic profit is zero.

myeconlab animation

So Roots is making zero economic profit on its jackets. When all the firms in the market are making zero economic profit, there is no incentive for new firms to enter.

If demand is so low relative to costs that firms incur economic losses, exit will occur. As firms exit the market, the demand for the products of the remaining firms increases and their demand curves shift rightward. The exit process ends when all the firms in the market are making zero economic profit.

Monopolistic Competition and Perfect Competition

Figure 14.4 compares monopolistic competition and perfect competition and highlights two key differences between them:

- Excess capacity
- Markup

Excess Capacity A firm has **excess capacity** if it produces below its **efficient scale**, which is the quantity at which average total cost is a minimum—the quantity at the bottom of the U-shaped *ATC* curve. In Fig. 14.4, the efficient scale is 100 jackets a day. Roots in part (a) produces 75 jackets a day and has *excess capacity* of 25 jackets a day. But if all jackets are alike and are produced by firms in perfect competition in part (b), each firm produces 100 jackets a day, which is the efficient scale. Average total cost is the lowest possible only in *perfect* competition.

You can see the excess capacity in monopolistic competition all around you. Family restaurants (except for the truly outstanding ones) almost always have some empty tables. You can always get a pizza delivered in less than 30 minutes. It is rare that every pump at a gas station is in use with customers waiting in line. There are always many real estate agents ready to help find or sell a home. These industries are examples of monopolistic competition. The firms

FIGURE 14.4 Excess Capacity and Markup

(a) Monopolistic competition

(b) Perfect competition

The efficient scale is 100 jackets a day. In monopolistic competition in the long run, because the firm faces a downward-sloping demand curve for its product, the quantity produced is less than the efficient scale and the firm has excess capacity. Price exceeds marginal cost by the amount of the markup.

In contrast, because in perfect competition the demand for each firm's product is perfectly elastic, the quantity produced equals the efficient scale and price equals marginal cost. The firm produces at the least possible cost and there is no markup.

have excess capacity. They could sell more by cutting their prices, but they would then incur losses.

Markup A firm's **markup** is the amount by which price exceeds marginal cost. Figure 14.4(a) shows Roots' markup. In perfect competition, price always equals marginal cost and there is no markup. Figure 14.4(b) shows this case. In monopolistic competition, buyers pay a higher price than in perfect competition and also pay more than marginal cost.

Is Monopolistic Competition Efficient?

Resources are used efficiently when marginal social benefit equals marginal social cost. Price equals marginal social benefit and the firm's marginal cost equals marginal social cost (assuming there are no external benefits or costs). So if the price of a Roots jacket exceeds the marginal cost of producing it, the quantity of Roots jackets produced is less than the efficient quantity. And you've just seen that in long-run equilibrium in monopolistic competition, price *does* exceed marginal cost. So is the quantity produced in monopolistic competition less than the efficient quantity?

Making the Relevant Comparison Two economists meet in the street, and one asks the other "How is your husband?" The quick reply is "Compared to what?" This bit of economic wit illustrates a key point: Before we can conclude that something needs fixing, we must check out the available alternatives.

The markup that drives a gap between price and marginal cost in monopolistic competition arises from product differentiation. It is because Roots jackets are not quite the same as jackets from Eddie Bauer, Club Monaco, Banana Republic, Gap, Levi, Ralph Lauren, or any of the other dozens of producers of jackets that the demand for Roots jackets is not perfectly elastic. The only way that the demand for jackets from Roots might be perfectly elastic is if there is only one kind of jacket and all firms make it. In this situation, Roots jackets are indistinguishable from all other jackets. They don't even have identifying labels.

If there was only one kind of jacket, the total benefit of jackets would almost certainly be less than it is with variety. People value variety—not only because it enables each person to select what he or she likes best but also because it provides an external benefit. Most of us enjoy seeing variety in the choices of

others. Contrast a scene from China in the 1960s, when everyone wore a Mao tunic, with China today, where everyone wears the clothes of their own choosing. Or contrast a scene from Germany in the 1930s, when almost everyone who could afford a car owned a first-generation Volkswagen Beetle, with the world today with its enormous variety of styles and types of automobiles.

If people value variety, why don't we see infinite variety? The answer is that variety is costly. Each different variety of any product must be designed, and then customers must be informed about it. These initial costs of design and marketing—called setup costs—mean that some varieties that are too close to others already available are just not worth creating.

The Bottom Line Product variety is both valued and costly. The efficient degree of product variety is the one for which the marginal social benefit of product variety equals its marginal social cost. The loss that arises because the quantity produced is less than the efficient quantity is offset by the gain that arises from having a greater degree of product variety. So compared to the alternative—product uniformity—monopolistic competition might be efficient.

Review Quiz

1 How does a firm in monopolistic competition decide how much to produce and at what price to offer its product for sale?
2 Why can a firm in monopolistic competition make an economic profit only in the short run?
3 Why do firms in monopolistic competition operate with excess capacity?
4 Why is there a price markup over marginal cost in monopolistic competition?
5 Is monopolistic competition efficient?

 Work Study Plan 14.2 and get instant feedback.

You've seen how the firm in monopolistic competition determines its output and price in both the short run and the long run when it produces a given product and undertakes a *given* marketing effort. But how does the firm choose its product quality and marketing effort? We'll now study these decisions.

◆ Product Development and Marketing

When Roots made its price and output decision that we've just studied, it had already made its product quality and marketing decisions. We're now going to look at these decisions and see how they influence the firm's output, price, and economic profit.

Innovation and Product Development

The prospect of new firms entering the industry keeps firms in monopolistic competition on their toes! To enjoy economic profits, they must continually seek ways of keeping one step ahead of imitators—other firms who imitate the success of profitable firms.

One major way of trying to maintain economic profit is for a firm to seek out new products that will provide it with a competitive edge, even if only temporarily. A firm that introduces a new and differentiated product faces a demand that is less elastic and is able to increase its price and make an economic profit. Eventually, imitators will make close substitutes for the innovative product and compete away the economic profit arising from an initial advantage. So to restore economic profit, the firm must again innovate.

Profit-Maximizing Product Innovation   The decision to innovate and develop a new or improved product is based on the same type of profit-maximizing calculation that you've already studied.

Innovation and product development are costly activities, but they bring in additional revenues. The firm must balance the cost and revenue at the margin.

The marginal dollar spent on developing a new or improved product is the marginal cost of product development. The marginal dollar that the new or improved product earns for the firm is the marginal revenue of product development. At a low level of product development, the marginal revenue from a better product exceeds the marginal cost. At a high level of product development, the marginal cost of a better product exceeds the marginal revenue.

When the marginal cost and marginal revenue of product development are equal, the firm is undertaking the profit-maximizing amount of product development.

Efficiency and Product Innovation   Is the profit-maximizing amount of product innovation also the efficient amount? Efficiency is achieved if the marginal social benefit of a new and improved product equals its marginal social cost.

The marginal social benefit of an innovation is the increase in price that consumers are willing to pay for it. The marginal social cost is the amount that the firm must pay to make the innovation. Profit is maximized when marginal *revenue* equals marginal cost. But in monopolistic competition, marginal revenue is less than price, so product innovation is probably not pushed to its efficient level.

Monopolistic competition brings many product innovations that cost little to implement and are purely cosmetic, such as new and improved packaging or a new scent in laundry powder. And even when there is a genuine improved product, it is never as good as what some consumers are willing to pay. For example, "The Legend of Zelda: Twilight Princess" is regarded as an almost perfect and very cool game, but users complain that it isn't quite perfect. It is a game with features whose marginal revenue equal the marginal cost of creating them.

Advertising

A firm with a differentiated product needs to ensure that its customers know how its product is different from the competition. A firm also might attempt to create a consumer perception that its product is different from its competitors' even when that difference is small. Firms use advertising and packaging to achieve this goal.

Advertising Expenditures   Firms in monopolistic competition incur huge costs to ensure that buyers appreciate and value the differences between their own products and those of their competitors. So a large proportion of the price that we pay for a good covers the cost of selling it, and this proportion is increasing. Advertising in newspapers and magazines and on radio, television, and the Internet is the main selling cost. But it is not the only one. Selling costs include the cost of shopping malls that look like movie sets, glossy catalogues and brochures, and the salaries, airfares, and hotel bills of salespeople.

Advertising expenditures affect the profits of firms in two ways: They increase costs, and they change demand. Let's look at these effects.

Selling Costs in Canada

The Cost of Selling a Pair of Shoes

When you buy a pair of running shoes that cost you $110, you're paying $14.25 for the materials from which the shoes are made, $4.25 for the services of the Malaysian worker who made the shoes, $7.50 for the Asian manufacturing firm's capital cost and normal profit, and $0.75 for the cost of shipping the shoes to Canada. These numbers total $26.75. You pay $5.25 to the Canadian government in import duty. So we've now accounted for a total of $32. Where did the other $78 go? It is the cost of advertising, retailing, and other sales and distribution services.

The selling costs associated with running shoes are not unusual. Almost everything you buy includes a selling cost component that exceeds one-half of the total cost. Your clothing, food, electronic items, DVDs, magazines, and even your textbooks cost more to sell than they cost to manufacture.

Advertising costs are only a part and often a small part of total selling costs. For example, Nike spends about $6.25 on advertising per pair of running shoes sold.

For the North American economy as a whole, there are some 20,000 advertising agencies, which employ more than 200,000 people and have sales of $45 billion. These numbers are only part of the total cost of advertising because firms have their own internal advertising departments, the costs of which we can only guess.

But the biggest part of selling costs is not the cost of advertising. It is the cost of retailing services. The retailer's selling costs (and economic profit) are often as much as 50 percent of the price you pay.

| Raw materials $14.25 | Production costs $11.75 | Import duty $5.25 | Selling costs $78 |

Selling Costs and Total Cost Selling costs are fixed costs and they increase the firm's total cost. So like the fixed costs of producing a good, advertising costs per unit decrease as the quantity produced increases.

Figure 14.5 shows how selling costs change a firm's average total cost. The blue curve shows the average total cost of production. The red curve shows the firm's average total cost of production plus advertising. The height of the red area between the two curves shows the average fixed cost of advertising. The *total* cost of advertising is fixed. But the *average* cost of advertising decreases as output increases.

Figure 14.5 shows that if advertising increases the quantity sold by a large enough amount, it can lower average total cost. For example, if the quantity sold increases from 25 jackets a day with no advertising to 100 jackets a day with advertising, average total cost falls from $60 to $40 a jacket. The reason is that although the *total* fixed cost has increased, the greater fixed cost is spread over a greater output, so average total cost decreases.

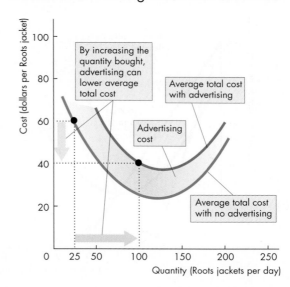

FIGURE 14.5   Selling Costs and Total Cost

Selling costs such as the cost of advertising are fixed costs. When added to the average total cost of production, selling costs increase average total cost by a greater amount at small outputs than at large outputs. If advertising enables sales to increase from 25 jackets a day to 100 jackets a day, average total cost *falls* from $60 to $40 a jacket.

Selling Costs and Demand Advertising and other selling efforts change the demand for a firm's product. But how? Does demand increase or does it decrease? The most natural answer is that advertising increases demand. By informing people about the quality of its products or by persuading people to switch from the products of other firms, a firm might expect to increase the demand for its own products.

But all firms in monopolistic competition advertise, and all seek to persuade customers that they have the best deal. If advertising enables a firm to survive, the number of firms in the market might increase. And to the extent that the number of firms does increase, advertising *decreases* the demand faced by any one firm. It also makes the demand for any one firm's product more elastic. So advertising can end up not only lowering average total cost but also lowering the markup and the price.

Figure 14.6 illustrates this possible effect of advertising. In part (a), with no advertising, the demand for Roots jackets is not very elastic. Profit is maximized at

75 jackets per day, and the markup is large. In part (b), advertising, which is a fixed cost, increases average total cost from ATC_0 to ATC_1 but leaves marginal cost unchanged at MC. Demand becomes much more elastic, the profit-maximizing quantity increases, and the markup shrinks.

Using Advertising to Signal Quality

Some advertising, like the Maria Sharapova Canon camera ads on television and in glossy magazines or the huge number of dollars that Coke and Pepsi spend, seems hard to understand. There doesn't seem to be any concrete information about a camera in the glistening smile of a tennis player. And surely everyone knows about Coke and Pepsi. What is the gain from pouring millions of dollars a month into advertising these well-known colas?

One answer is that advertising is a signal to the consumer of a high-quality product. A **signal** is an action taken by an informed person (or firm) to send

FIGURE 14.6   Advertising and Markup

(a) No firms advertise

(b) All firms advertise

If no firms advertise, in part (a), demand for each firm's product is low and not very elastic. The profit-maximizing output is small, the markup is large, and the price is high.

Part (b) shows that advertising increases average total

cost and shifts the ATC curve upward from ATC_0 to ATC_1. If all firms advertise, the demand for each firm's product becomes more elastic. Output increases, the price falls, and the markup shrinks.

a message to uninformed people. Think about two colas: Coke and Oke. Oke knows that its cola is not very good and that its taste varies a lot depending on which cheap batch of unsold cola it happens to buy each week. So Oke knows that while it could get a lot of people to try Oke by advertising, they would all quickly discover what a poor product it is and switch back to the cola they bought before. Coke, in contrast, knows that its product has a high-quality, consistent taste and that once consumers have tried it, there is a good chance they'll never drink anything else. On the basis of this reasoning, Oke doesn't advertise but Coke does. And Coke spends a lot of money to make a big splash.

Cola drinkers who see Coke's splashy ads know that the firm would not spend so much money advertising if its product were not truly good. So consumers reason that Coke is indeed a really good product. The flashy expensive ad has signalled that Coke is really good without saying anything about Coke.

Notice that if advertising is a signal, it doesn't need any specific product information. It just needs to be expensive and hard to miss. That's what a lot of advertising looks like. So the signalling theory of advertising predicts much of the advertising that we see.

Brand Names

Many firms create and spend a lot of money promoting a brand name. Why? What benefit does a brand name bring to justify the sometimes high cost of establishing it?

The basic answer is that a brand name provides information to consumers about the quality of a product, and is an incentive to the producer to achieve a high and consistent quality standard.

To see how a brand name helps the consumer, think about how you use brand names to get information about quality. You're on a road trip, and it is time to find a place to spend the night. You see roadside advertisements for Holiday Inn, Joe's Motel, and Annie's Driver's Stop. You know about Holiday Inn because you've stayed in it before. You've also seen their advertisements and know what to expect from them. You have no information at all about Joe's and Annie's. They might be better than the lodgings you do know about, but without that knowledge, you're not going to try them. You use the brand name as information and stay at Holiday Inn.

This same story explains why a brand name provides an incentive to achieve high and consistent quality. Because no one would know whether Joe's and Annie's were offering a high standard of service, they have no incentive to do so. But equally, because everyone expects a given standard of service from Holiday Inn, a failure to meet a customer's expectation would almost surely lose that customer to a competitor. So Holiday Inn has a strong incentive to deliver what it promises in the advertising that creates its brand name.

Efficiency of Advertising and Brand Names

To the extent that advertising and brand names provide consumers with information about the precise nature of product differences and about product quality, they benefit the consumer and enable a better product choice to be made. But the opportunity cost of the additional information must be weighed against the gain to the consumer.

The final verdict on the efficiency of monopolistic competition is ambiguous. In some cases, the gains from extra product variety unquestionably offset the selling costs and the extra cost arising from excess capacity. The tremendous varieties of books and magazines, clothing, food, and drinks are examples of such gains. It is less easy to see the gains from being able to buy a brand-name drug that has a chemical composition identical to that of a generic alternative, but many people willingly pay more for the brand-name alternative.

Review Quiz

1 How, other than by adjusting price, do firms in monopolistic competition compete?
2 Why might product innovation and development be efficient and why might it be inefficient?
3 How do selling costs influence a firm's cost curves and its average total cost?
4 How does advertising influence demand?
5 Are advertising and brand names efficient?

myeconlab Work Study Plan 14.3 and get instant feedback.

◆ Monopolistic competition is one of the most common market structures that you encounter in your daily life. *Reading Between the Lines* on pp. 334–335 applies the model of monopolistic competition to the market for 3G cell phones and shows you why you can expect continual innovation and the introduction of new phones from Apple and other producers.

Product Differentiation in the 3G Cell Phone Market

Watch Your Back Apple, These 10 iPhone Killers Are On The Prowl

July 17, 2008

It's been a week since the Apple iPhone 3G launched in earnest, to throngs of Mac-faithful Appleheads looking to get their hands on the second-generation of the device. It took just a weekend for Apple to sell one million 3G iPhones, so says Apple.

But as the lines at the Apple Store vanish, the dust starts to clear and iPhone-mania wanes, smart phone makers are lining up to try and take a bite out of Apple iPhone's success. Some take elements from the iPhone and put a new spin on them though they're not necessarily iPhone clones.

Others take mobile computing in a different direction. Regardless, there is a crop of device makers lurking around the corner, peeler in hand, hoping to skin the iPhone, or at least give Apple a flesh wound.

Here we take a look at 10 iPhone killers, devices that have the potential to cut the core right out of Apple. Anyone else smell apple pie?

[The ten iPhone killers are the BlackBerry Bold 9000, Palm Treo 800w, Palm Centro, Samsung Instinct, Samsung Omnia, Nokia E90 Communicator, Nokia E71, Nokia E66, HTC Touch Diamond, and OpenMoko Neo FreeRunner.]

Essence of the Story

- On July 11, 2008, Apple launched its new 3G iPhone.
- Worldwide interest in the new phone was high and Apple sold 1 million 3G iPhones in the first week.
- Anticipating Apple's success, other phone makers entered the market with 3G phones.
- Some of the new phones have features similar to those of the iPhone, but each phone is slightly different from the iPhone and from the other phones.

Economic Analysis

- On July 11, 2008, Apple launched its new 3G iPhone.

- By creating a substantially differentiated product, Apple was able to generate a great deal of interest in the new phone throughout the world.

- In the first weekend, Apple sold 1 million of the new phones.

- But within a month of the launch of the 3G iPhone, many competing but differentiated devices were on the market.

- The monopolistic competition model explains what is happening in the 3G cell phone market.

- Figure 1 shows the market for Apple's 3G iPhone in its first month. (The numbers are assumptions.)

- Because the Apple phone is different from its competitors and has features that users value, the demand curve, *D*, and marginal revenue curve, *MR*, provide a large short-run profit opportunity.

- The marginal cost curve is *MC* and the average total cost curve is *ATC*. Apple maximizes its economic profit by producing the quantity at which marginal revenue equals marginal cost, which in this example is 3 million iPhones a month.

- This quantity of phones can be sold for $200 each.

- The blue rectangle shows Apple's economic profit.

- Because this market is profitable, entry takes place.

- Within a month of the launch of the 3G iPhone, many competitors had entered the market.

- Figure 2 shows the the consequences of entry.

- The demand for the iPhone decreased as the market was shared with the other phones.

- Apple's profit-maximizing price decreased, and in the long run, economic profit is eliminated.

- With zero economic profit, Apple now has an incentive to develop an even better differentiated phone and start the cycle described here again, making an economic profit in a new phone in the short run.

Figure 1 Economic profit in the short run

Figure 2 Zero economic profit in the long run

SUMMARY

Key Points

What Is Monopolistic Competition? (pp. 324–325)

- Monopolistic competition occurs when a large number of firms compete with each other on product quality, price, and marketing.

Price and Output in Monopolistic Competition

(pp. 326–329)

- Each firm in monopolistic competition faces a downward-sloping demand curve and produces the profit-maximizing quantity.
- Entry and exit result in zero economic profit and excess capacity in long-run equilibrium.

Product Development and Marketing (pp. 330–333)

- Firms in monopolistic competition innovate and develop new products.
- Advertising expenditures increase total cost, but average total cost might fall if the quantity sold increases by enough.
- Advertising expenditures might increase demand, but demand might decrease if competition increases.
- Whether monopolistic competition is inefficient depends on the value we place on product variety.

Key Figures

Figure 14.1   Economic Profit in the Short Run, 326
Figure 14.2   Economic Loss in the Short Run, 327
Figure 14.3   Output and Price in the Long Run, 327
Figure 14.4   Excess Capacity and Markup, 328
Figure 14.5   Selling Costs and Total Cost, 331
Figure 14.6   Advertising and Markup, 332

Key Terms

Efficient scale, 328
Excess capacity, 328
Markup, 329
Monopolistic competition, 324
Product differentiation, 324
Signal, 332

PROBLEMS and APPLICATIONS

 Work problems 1–10 in Chapter 14 Study Plan and get instant feedback.
Work problems 11–20 as Homework, a Quiz, or a Test if assigned by your instructor.

1. Sara is a dot.com entrepreneur who has established a Web site at which people can design and buy a sweatshirt. Sara pays $1,000 a week for her Web server and Internet connection. The sweatshirts that her customers design are made to order by another firm, and Sara pays this firm $20 a sweatshirt. Sara has no other costs. The table sets out the demand schedule for Sara's sweatshirts.

Price (dollars per sweatshirt)	Quantity demanded (sweatshirts per week)
0	100
20	80
40	60
60	40
80	20
100	0

a. Calculate Sara's profit-maximizing output, price, and economic profit.

b. Do you expect other firms to enter the Web sweatshirt business and compete with Sara?

c. What happens to the demand for Sara's sweatshirts in the long run? What happens to Sara's economic profit in the long run?

2. The figure shows the situation facing Lite and Kool Inc., a producer of running shoes.

a. What quantity does Lite and Kool produce?

b. What is the price of a pair of Lite and Kool shoes?

c. What is Lite and Kool's economic profit or economic loss?

3. In the market for running shoes, all the firms face a similar demand curve and have similar cost curves to those of Lite and Kool in problem 2.

a. What happens to the number of firms producing running shoes in the long run?

b. What happens to the price of running shoes in the long run?

c. What happens to the quantity of running shoes produced by Lite and Kool in the long run?

d. What happens to the quantity of running shoes in the entire market in the long run?

e. Does Lite and Kool have excess capacity in the long run?

f. Why, if Lite and Kool has excess capacity in the long run, doesn't the firm decrease its capacity?

g. What is the relationship between Lite and Kool's price and marginal cost?

4. Is the market for running shoes described in problem 3 efficient or inefficient? Explain your answer.

5. Suppose that Tommy Hilfiger's marginal cost of a jacket is $100 (a constant marginal cost) and at one of the firm's shops, total fixed cost is $2,000 a day. The profit-maximizing number of jackets sold in this shop is 20 a day. Then the shops nearby start to advertise their jackets. The Tommy Hilfiger shop now spends $2,000 a day advertising its jackets, and its profit-maximizing number of jackets sold jumps to 50 a day.

a. What is this shop's average total cost of a jacket sold before the advertising begins?

b. What is this shop's average total cost of a jacket sold after the advertising begins?

c. Can you say what happens to the price of a Tommy Hilfiger jacket? Why or why not?

d. Can you say what happens to Tommy Hilfiger's markup? Why or why not?

e. Can you say what happens to Tommy Hilfiger's economic profit? Why or why not?

6. How might Tommy Hilfiger in problem 5 use advertising as a signal? How is a signal sent and how does it work?

7. How does having a brand name help Tommy Hilfiger in problem 5 to increase its economic profit?

8. **Wake Up and Sell the Coffee**

Traffic at [Starbucks] stores dropped for the first time in its history ... [amidst] ... mounting complaints ... that in its pursuit of growth, the company has strayed too far from its roots. ...

Starbucks will once again grind beans in its stores for drip coffee. It will give free drip refills ... and provide two hours of wi-fi. ...

Soon the company will roll out its new armor: a sleek, low-rise espresso machine that makes baristas more visible. ...

Of course, every change that Starbucks has made over the past few years—automated espresso machines, preground coffee, drive-throughs, fewer soft chairs and less carpeting—was made for a reason: to smooth operations or boost sales. ...Those may have been the right choices at the time ... but together they ultimately diluted the coffee-centric experience.

Time, April 7, 2008

a. Explain how Starbucks' past attempts to maximize profits ended up eroding product differentiation.

b. Explain how Starbucks' new plan intends to increase economic profit.

9 **The Shoe that Won't Quit**

I finally decided to take the plunge this past winter and buy a pair of Uggs. ... But when I got around to shopping for my Uggs in late January, the style that I wanted was sold out. ... The scarcity factor was not a glitch in the supply chain, but rather a carefully calibrated strategy by Ugg parent Deckers Outdoor that is one of the big reasons behind the brand's success.

Deckers tightly controls distribution to ensure that supply does not outstrip demand. ... If Deckers ever opened up the supply of Uggs to meet demand, sales would shoot up like a rocket, but they'd come back down just as fast.

Fortune, June 5, 2008

a. Explain why Deckers intentionally restricts the quantity of Uggs that the firm sells.

b. Draw a graph to illustrate how Deckers maximizes the economic profit from Uggs.

10. **Chocolate Market Goes High-End**

Last year, Gatineau chocolatier Gaetan Tessier turned 250 kilograms of raw, pure chocolate into delectable, high-end Easter treats. This year, he figures he'll be going through about three times that amount ... so strong is demand. ...

Earlier this month, ... chocolate giant Nestle announced it was investing $20 million in a research centre in Switzerland that will develop new products to meet anticipated growth in demand for luxury and premium confections.

Nestle said the $3.7-billion market for luxury chocolate expanded by eight percent annually between 2004 and 2006. The company added that it valued the potential premium chocolate market at about $14 billion and that it expects markets for luxury and premium chocolate to increase by more than 10 percent in the next new years.

"Premium chocolate continues to grow," said Joan Steuer, the U.S.-based founder of Chocolate Marketing, LLC. ... Steuer says there are two sides to the growth. On the one hand, there's the chocolate confections themselves—fancy artisan chocolates, such as those produced by Tessier's company, ChocoMotive. And then there's packaging. Steuer says she's seeing chocolate confections being sold in "exquisite" packages that "push the envelope on pricing." ...

Vancouver Sun, March 22, 2008

a. Explain how the "new products" that Nestle plans to create will change the demand for Nestle chocolates in the short run.

b. Explain how the strong demand for premium chocolate without exquisite packaging will affect the economic profit made by ChocoMotive.

c. Explain how the "exquisite" packages that "push the envelope on pricing" will affect the economic profit made by ChocoMotive in b.

d. Is long-run economic profit a possibility for ChocoMotive?

e. Does ChocoMotive have either excess capacity or a markup in long-run equilibrium?

11. Lorie teaches singing. Her fixed costs are $1,000 a month, and it costs her $50 of labour to give one class. The table shows the demand schedule for Lorie's singing lessons.

Price (dollars per lesson)	Quantity demanded (lessons per month)
0	250
50	200
100	150
150	100
200	50
250	0

a. Calculate Lorie's profit-maximizing output, price, and economic profit.

b. Do you expect other firms to enter the singing-lesson business and compete with Lorie?

c. What happens to the demand for Lorie's lessons in the long run? What happens to Lorie's economic profit in the long run?

12. The figure shows the situation facing Mike's Bikes Inc., a producer of mountain bikes.

a. What quantity does Mike's Bikes produce and what is its price?

b. Calculate the economic profit or economic loss that Mike's Bikes makes.

13. In the market for mountain bikes, the demand for each firm's bike and the firm's cost curves are similar to those of Mike's Bikes in problem 12.

a. What happens to the number of firms producing mountain bikes?

b. What happens to the price of mountain bikes in the long run?

c. What happens to the quantity of bikes produced by Mike's Bikes in the long run?

d. What happens to the quantity of mountain bikes in the entire market in the long run?

e. Is there any way for Mike's Bikes to avoid having excess capacity in the long run?

14. Do you expect that the market for mountain bikes described in problem 13 is efficient or inefficient? Explain your answer.

15. Bianca bakes delicious cookies. Her total fixed cost is $40 a day, and her average variable cost is $1 a bag. Few people know about Bianca's Cookies, and she is maximizing her profit by selling 10 bags a day for $5 a bag. Bianca thinks that if she spends $50 a day on advertising, she can increase her market share and sell 25 bags a day for $5 a bag.

a. If Bianca's belief about the effect of advertising is correct, can she increase her economic profit by advertising?

b. If Bianca advertises, will her average total cost increase or decrease at the quantity produced?

c. If Bianca advertises, will she continue to sell her cookies for $5 a bag or will she raise her price or lower her price?

16. **Pizza Hut Turns 50 in Tough Times**

Dan and Frank Carney borrowed $600 from their mother 50 years ago and opened a small pizzeria in Kansas ... in what was once a bar. The dream was to make enough pizzas to pay for college. ... That humble enterprise with a humble name—Pizza Hut—is now the world's largest pizza chain with $10 billion in annual sales. ...

The chain known for its red-roofed restaurants is now updating its look, with plasma TVs, sports bars and local sports memorabilia. It's also rolling out tubs of baked pasta and piles of fried chicken wings to go with its famous pizzas. It is a tough time for pizza makers, who are strapped by rising cheese and flour costs. ... Analysts say Pizza Hut was due for an overhaul—the new menu may help it through a rough time. ...

Restaurant analyst Larry Miller with RBC Capital Markets said "From a bigger picture, longer-term view, this is a brand that's starting to differentiate itself from the competition in some really unique ways." ... Pizza Hut began an aggressive advertising campaign this spring to publicize the new menu.

Associated Press, May 30, 2008

a. Explain how Pizza Hut is differentiating its brand to compete with other pizza outlets in terms of quality, price, and marketing.
b. Will Pizza Hut produce at, above, or below the efficient scale in the short run?
c. Do you think that aggressive advertising will change the efficiency of the fast-food market?

17. **Swinging for Female Golfers**
One of the hottest areas of innovation is in clubs for women, who now make up nearly a quarter of the 24 million golfers in the U.S. ... Callaway and Nike, two of the leading golf-equipment manufacturers, recently released new clubs designed specifically for women. ...
Time, April 21, 2008

a. How are Callaway and Nike attempting to maintain economic profit?
b. Draw a graph to illustrate the cost curves and revenue curves of Callaway or Nike in the market for golf clubs for women.
c. Show on your graph (in b) the short-run economic profit.
d. Explain why the economic profit that Callaway and Nike make on golf clubs for women is likely to be temporary.

18. **A Thirst for More Champagne**
Champagne exports have tripled in the past 20 years. That poses a problem for northern France, where the bubbly hails from—not enough grapes. So French authorities have unveiled a plan to extend the official Champagne grape-growing zone to cover 40 new villages. It's the first revision of the official appellation map since 1927, and—inevitably—it has provoked debate. Each plot must be tested for suitability, so the change will take several years to become effective. In the meantime the vineyard owners whose land values will jump markedly if the changes are finalized certainly have reason to raise a glass.
Fortune, May 12, 2008

a. Why is France so strict about designating the vineyards that can label their product Champagne?
b. Explain who would most likely oppose this plan.
c. Assuming that vineyards in these 40 villages are producing the same quality of grapes with or without this plan, why will their land values "jump markedly" if this plan is approved?

19. **Under Armour's Big Step Up**
Under Armour, the red-hot athletic-apparel brand, has joined Nike, Adidas, and New Balance as a major player on the market. ... [Under Armour CEO] Plank prepares to move the Under Armour brand out of its comfort zone into the cutthroat, $18.3 billion athletic-footwear market. ... Under Armour announced it would try to revive the long-dead cross-training category. ... Under Armour tested the footwear landscape about two years ago, when it started making American-football cleats. Selling soccer shoes against Adidas and Nike would have been suicidal. Football is a small, specialized market. ... "Our No. 1 goal was authenticating ourselves as a footwear brand," says Plank. "Does the consumer accept putting the Under Armour logo on a shoe?" ... But will young athletes really spend $100 for a [cross training] shoe to lift weights in? "They're spending $40 on a T shirt," quips Plank, nodding to the premium price that consumers are paying for Under Armour's sweat-sopping gear.
Time, May 26, 2008

a. Explain how brand names initially prevented Under Armour from competing in the athletic shoe market.
b. What factors influence Under Armour's ability to earn an economic profit?
c. Will Under Armour be able to make an economic profit in the cross-training shoe market?

20. Study *Reading Between the Lines* on pp. 334–335 and then answer the following questions.

a. How did the creation of the 3G iPhone influence the demand and marginal revenue curves faced by Apple in the market for 3G phones?
b. How do you think the creation of the 3G iPhone influenced the demand for older generation cell phones?
c. Explain the effect on Nokia of the introduction of the new iPhone in the market for 3G cell phones.
d. Draw a graph to illustrate the effect on Nokia in the market for 3G cell phones in c.
e. Explain the effect on Apple of the decisions by BlackBerry, Palm, Samsung, Nokia, HTC, and OpenMoko to bring "iPhone killers" to market.
f. Do you think the cell phone market is efficient? Explain your answer.

15 ◆ Oligopoly

After studying this chapter, you will be able to

- Define and identify oligopoly
- Explain two traditional oligopoly models
- Use game theory to explain how price and output are determined in oligopoly
- Use game theory to explain other strategic decisions
- Describe the antitrust laws that regulate oligopoly

An intense price war in the market for PCs has driven the price of a laptop below $1,000 and the price of a desktop below $500. A handful of firms—Dell, Hewlett-Packard, Lenovo, Acer, and Toshiba—account for more than half of the global market. Each of these firms must pay close attention to what the other firms are doing.

In some markets, there are only two firms. Computer chips are an example. The chips that drive most PCs are made by Intel and Advanced Micro Devices. How does competition between just two chip makers work?

When a small number of firms compete in a market, do they operate in the social interest, like firms in perfect competi-

tion? Or do they restrict output to increase profit, like a monopoly?

The theories of perfect competition and monopoly don't predict the behaviour of the firms we've just described. To understand how markets work when only a handful of firms compete, we need the richer models that are explained in this chapter. In *Reading Between the Lines* at the end of this chapter, we'll return to the market for personal computers and see how Dell and Hewlett-Packard slugged it out for dominance in that market.

What Is Oligopoly?

Oligopoly, like monopolistic competition, lies between perfect competition and monopoly. The firms in oligopoly might produce an identical product and compete only on price, or they might produce a differentiated product and compete on price, product quality, and marketing. **Oligopoly** is a market structure in which

- Natural or legal barriers prevent the entry of new firms.
- A small number of firms compete.

Barriers to Entry

Natural or legal barriers to entry can create oligopoly. You saw in Chapter 13 how economies of scale and demand form a natural barrier to entry that can create a *natural monopoly*. These same factors can create a *natural oligopoly*.

Figure 15.1 illustrates two natural oligopolies. The demand curve, *D* (in both parts of the figure), shows the demand for taxi rides in a town. If the average total cost curve of a taxi company is ATC_1 in part (a), the market is a natural **duopoly**—an oligopoly market with two firms. You can probably see some examples of duopoly where you live. Some cities have only two taxi companies, two car rental firms, two copy centres, or two college bookstores.

The lowest price at which the firm would remain in business is $10 a ride. At that price, the quantity of rides demanded is 60 a day, the quantity that can be provided by just two firms. There is no room in this market for three firms. But if there were only one firm, it would make an economic profit and a second firm would enter to take some of the business and economic profit.

If the average total cost curve of a taxi company is ATC_2 in part (b), the efficient scale of one firm is 20 rides a day. This market is large enough for three firms.

A legal oligopoly arises when a legal barrier to entry protects the small number of firms in a market. A city might license two taxi firms or two bus companies, for example, even though the combination of demand and economies of scale leaves room for more than two firms.

FIGURE 15.1 Natural Oligopoly

(a) Natural duopoly

(b) Natural oligopoly with three firms

The lowest possible price is $10 a ride, which is the minimum average total cost. When a firm produces 30 rides a day, the efficient scale, two firms can satisfy the market demand. This natural oligopoly has two firms—a natural duopoly.

When the efficient scale of one firm is 20 rides per day, three firms can satisfy the market demand at the lowest possible price. This natural oligopoly has three firms.

Small Number of Firms

Because barriers to entry exist, oligopoly consists of a small number of firms, each of which has a large share of the market. Such firms are interdependent, and they face a temptation to cooperate to increase their joint economic profit.

Interdependence With a small number of firms in a market, each firm's actions influence the profits of all the other firms. Zola Doré opened her coffee shop in downtown Whitehorse in 2005. In April 2008, Starbucks opened. The number of coffee shops increased to three. There was too much competition for coffee drinkers' dollars in the city of 20,500. Starbucks survived, but Zola went out of business in June 2008. Zola and Starbucks were interdependent.

Temptation to Cooperate When a small number of firms share a market, they can increase their profits by forming a cartel and acting like a monopoly. A **cartel** is a group of firms acting together—colluding—to limit output, raise price, and increase economic profit. Cartels are illegal, but they do operate in some markets. But for reasons that you'll discover in this chapter, cartels tend to break down.

Examples of Oligopoly

The box below shows some examples of oligopoly. The dividing line between oligopoly and monopolistic competition is hard to pin down. As a practical matter, we identify oligopoly by looking at concentration ratios, the Herfindahl-Hirschman Index, and information about the geographical scope of the market and barriers to entry. The HHI that divides oligopoly from monopolistic competition is generally taken to be 1,000. An HHI below 1,000 is usually an example of monopolistic competition, and a market in which the HHI exceeds 1,000 is usually an example of oligopoly.

Review Quiz

1 What are the two distinguishing characteristics of oligopoly?
2 Why are firms in oligopoly interdependent?
3 Why do firms in oligopoly face a temptation to collude?
4 Can you think of some examples of oligopolies that you buy from?

 Work Study Plan 15.1 and get instant feedback.

Oligopoly Today
Near Duopoly in Batteries

The figure shows some of the markets in Canada that are oligopolies. Although in some of these markets, the number of firms (in parentheses) is large, the share of the market held by the 4 largest firms (the red bars) is close to 100 percent.

The most concentrated markets—cigarettes, motor vehicles, breakfast cereals, chocolates, and batteries—are dominated by just one or two firms.

If you want to buy an AAA battery for your TV remote or toothbrush, you'll find it hard to avoid buying a Duracell or an Energizer.

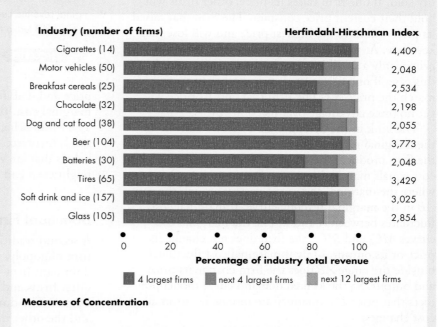

Source of data: Adapted from Statistics Canada, Manufacturing, Construction, and Energy Division.

Two Traditional Oligopoly Models

Suppose you run one of three gas stations in a small town. You're trying to decide whether to cut your price. To make your decision, you must predict how the other firms will react and calculate the effects of those reactions on your profit. If you cut your price and your competitors don't cut theirs, you sell more and the other two firms sell less. But won't the other firms cut their prices too and make your profits fall? What will you do?

Several models have been developed to explain the prices and quantities in oligopoly markets. The models fall into two broad groups: traditional models and game theory models. We'll look at examples of both types, starting with two traditional models.

The Kinked Demand Curve Model

The kinked demand curve model of oligopoly is based on the assumption that each firm believes that if it raises its price, others will not follow, but if it cuts its price, other firms will cut theirs.

Figure 15.2 shows the demand curve (D) that a firm believes it faces. The demand curve has a kink at the current price, P, and quantity, Q. At prices above P, a small price rise brings a big decrease in the quantity sold. If one firm raises its price, other firms will hold their current price constant. The firm that raised its price will have the highest price and will lose market share. At prices below P, even a large price cut brings only a small increase in the quantity sold. In this case, if one firm cuts its price, other firms will match the price cut. The firm that cuts its price will get no price advantage over its competitors.

The kink in the demand curve creates a break in the marginal revenue curve, MR. To maximize profit, the firm produces the quantity at which marginal cost equals marginal revenue. That quantity, Q, is where the marginal cost curve passes through the gap AB in the marginal revenue curve. If marginal cost fluctuates between A and B, like the marginal cost curves MC_0 and MC_1, the firm does not change its price or its output. Only if marginal cost fluctuates outside the range AB does the firm change its price and output. So the kinked demand curve model predicts that price and quantity are insensitive to small cost changes.

But this model has a problem. If marginal cost increases by enough to cause the firm to increase its

FIGURE 15.2 The Kinked Demand Curve Model

The price in an oligopoly market is P. Each firm believes it faces the demand curve D. At prices above P, a small price rise brings a big decrease in the quantity sold because other firms do not raise their prices. At prices below P, even a big price cut brings only a small increase in the quantity sold because other firms also cut their prices. Because the demand curve is kinked, the marginal revenue curve, MR, has a break AB. Profit is maximized by producing Q. The marginal cost curve passes through the break in the marginal revenue curve. Changes in marginal cost inside the range AB leave the price and quantity unchanged.

X myeconlab animation

price and if all firms experience the same increase in marginal cost, they all increase their prices together. The firm's belief that others will not join it in a price rise is incorrect. A firm that bases its actions on beliefs that are wrong does not maximize profit and might even end up incurring an economic loss.

Dominant Firm Oligopoly

A second traditional model explains a dominant firm oligopoly, which arises when one firm—the dominant firm—has a big cost advantage over the other firms and produces a large part of the industry output. The dominant firm sets the market price and the other firms are price takers. Examples of dominant firm oligopoly are a large gasoline retailer or a big box store that dominates its local market.

FIGURE 15.3   A Dominant Firm Oligopoly

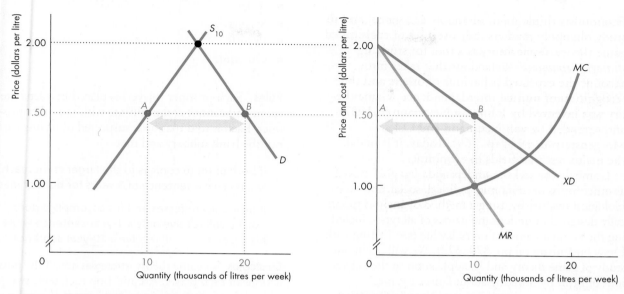

(a) Ten small firms and market demand

The demand curve for gas in a city is *D* in part (a). There are 10 small competitive firms that together have a supply curve of S_{10}. In addition, there is 1 large firm, Big-G, shown in part (b). Big-G faces the demand curve *XD*, determined as the market demand *D* minus the supply of the 10 small firms S_{10} —the demand that is not satisfied by the small firms.

(b) Big-G's price and output decision

Big-G's marginal revenue curve is *MR* and its marginal cost curve is *MC*. Big-G sets its output to maximize profit by equating marginal cost and marginal revenue. This output is 10,000 litres per week. The price at which Big-G can sell this quantity is $1.50 a litre. The 10 small firms take this price, and each firm sells 1,000 litres per week, point *A* in part (a).

To see how a dominant firm oligopoly works, suppose that 11 firms operate gas stations in a city. Big-G is the dominant firm. Figure 15.3 shows the market for gas in this city. In part (a), the demand curve *D* tells us the total quantity of gas demanded in the city at each price. The supply curve S_{10} is the supply curve of the 10 small firms. Part (b) shows the situation facing Big-G. Its marginal cost curve is *MC*. Big-G faces the demand curve *XD*, and its marginal revenue curve is *MR*. The demand curve *XD* shows the excess demand not met by the 10 small firms. For example, at a price of $1.50 a litre, the quantity demanded is 20,000 litres, the quantity supplied by the 10 small firms is 10,000 litres, and the excess quantity demanded is 10,000 litres, measured by the distance *AB* in both parts of the figure.

To maximize profit, Big-G operates like a monopoly. It sells 10,000 litres a week, where its marginal revenue equals its marginal cost, for a price of $1.50 a litre. The 10 small firms take the price of $1.50

a litre. They behave just like firms in perfect competition. The quantity of gas demanded in the entire city at $1.50 a litre is 20,000 litres, as shown in part (a). Of this amount, Big-G sells 10,000 litres and the 10 small firms each sell 1,000 litres.

Review Quiz

1   What does the kinked demand curve model predict and why must it sometimes make a prediction that contradicts its basic assumption?

2   Do you think a market with a dominant firm is in long-run equilibrium? Explain why or why not.

 Work Study Plan 15.2 and get instant feedback.

The traditional models don't enable us to understand all oligopoly markets and we're now going to study some newer models based on game theory.

Oligopoly Games

Economists think about oligopoly as a game, and to study oligopoly markets they use a set of tools called game theory. **Game theory** is a tool for studying *strategic behaviour*—behaviour that takes into account the expected behaviour of others and the recognition of mutual interdependence. Game theory was invented by John von Neumann in 1937 and extended by von Neumann and Oskar Morgenstern in 1944 (p. 369). Today, it is one of the major research fields in economics.

Game theory seeks to understand oligopoly as well as other forms of economic, political, social, and even biological rivalries by using a method of analysis specifically designed to understand games of all types, including the familiar games of everyday life (see Talking with Drew Fudenberg on pp. 370–372). We will begin our study of game theory and its application to the behaviour of firms by thinking about familiar games.

What Is a Game?

What is a game? At first thought, the question seems silly. After all, there are many different games. There are ball games and parlour games, games of chance and games of skill. But what is it about all these different activities that make them games? What do all these games have in common? We're going to answer these questions by looking at a game called "the prisoners' dilemma." This game captures the essential features of many games, including oligopoly, and it gives a good illustration of how game theory works and how it generates predictions.

The Prisoners' Dilemma

Art and Bob have been caught red-handed stealing a car. Facing airtight cases, they will receive a sentence of two years each for their crime. During his interviews with the two prisoners, the Crown attorney begins to suspect that he has stumbled on the two people who were responsible for a multimillion-dollar bank robbery some months earlier. But this is just a suspicion. The Crown attorney has no evidence on which he can convict Art and Bob of the greater crime unless he can get them to confess. But how can he extract a confession? The answer is by making the prisoners play a game. Let's look at the game they play.

All games share four common features:

- Rules
- Strategies
- Payoffs
- Outcome

Rules Each prisoner (player) is placed in a separate room and cannot communicate with the other prisoner. Each is told that he is suspected of having carried out the bank robbery and that

If both of them confess to the larger crime, each will receive a sentence of 3 years for both crimes.

If he alone confesses and his accomplice does not, he will receive only a 1-year sentence while his accomplice will receive a 10-year sentence.

Strategies In game theory, **strategies** are all the possible actions of each player. Art and Bob each have two possible actions:

1. Confess to the bank robbery.
2. Deny having committed the bank robbery.

Because there are two players, each with two strategies, there are four possible outcomes:

1. Both confess.
2. Both deny.
3. Art confesses and Bob denies.
4. Bob confesses and Art denies.

Payoffs Each prisoner can work out his *payoff* in each of these situations, and we can tabulate the four possible payoffs for each of the prisoners in what is called a payoff matrix for the game. A **payoff matrix** is a table that shows the payoffs for every possible action by each player for every possible action by each other player.

Table 15.1 shows a payoff matrix for Art and Bob. The squares show the payoffs for each prisoner—the red triangle in each square shows Art's and the blue triangle shows Bob's. If both prisoners confess (top left), each gets a prison term of 3 years. If Bob confesses but Art denies (top right), Art gets a 10-year sentence and Bob gets a 1-year sentence. If Art confesses and Bob denies (bottom left), Art gets a 1-year sentence and Bob gets a 10-year sentence. Finally, if both of them deny (bottom right), neither can be convicted of the bank robbery charge but both are sentenced for the car theft—a 2-year sentence.

Outcome The choices of both players determine the outcome of the game. To predict that outcome, we use an equilibrium idea proposed by John Nash of Princeton University (who received the Nobel Prize for Economic Science in 1994 and was the subject of the 2001 movie *A Beautiful Mind*). In **Nash equilibrium**, player *A* takes the best possible action given the action of player *B* and player *B* takes the best possible action given the action of player *A*.

In the case of the prisoners' dilemma, the Nash equilibrium occurs when Art makes his best choice given Bob's choice and when Bob makes his best choice given Art's choice.

To find the Nash equilibrium, we compare all the possible outcomes associated with each choice and eliminate those that are dominated—that are not as good as some other choice. Let's find the Nash equilibrium for the prisoners' dilemma game.

Finding the Nash Equilibrium Look at the situation from Art's point of view. If Bob confesses (top row), Art's best action is to confess because in that case, he is sentenced to 3 years rather than 10 years. If Bob denies (bottom row), Art's best action is still to confess because in that case he receives 1 year rather than 2 years. So Art's best action is to confess.

Now look at the situation from Bob's point of view. If Art confesses (left column), Bob's best action is to confess because in that case, he is sentenced to 3 years rather than 10 years. If Art denies (right column), Bob's best action is still to confess because in that case, he receives 1 year rather than 2 years. So Bob's best action is to confess.

Because each player's best action is to confess, each does confess, each goes to jail for 3 years, and the Crown attorney has solved the bank robbery. This is the Nash equilibrium of the game.

The Dilemma Now that you have found the outcome to the prisoners' dilemma, you can better see the dilemma. The dilemma arises as each prisoner contemplates the consequences of denying. Each prisoner knows that if both of them deny, they will receive only a 2-year sentence for stealing the car. But neither has any way of knowing that his accomplice will deny. Each poses the following questions: Should I deny and rely on my accomplice to deny so that we will both get only 2 years? Or should I confess in the hope of getting just 1 year (provided that my accomplice denies) knowing that if my accomplice does

TABLE 15.1   Prisoners' Dilemma Payoff Matrix

Each square shows the payoffs for the two players, Art and Bob, for each possible pair of actions. In each square, the red triangle shows Art's payoff and the blue triangle shows Bob's. For example, if both confess, the payoffs are in the top left square. The equilibrium of the game is for both players to confess and each gets a 3-year sentence.

confess, we will both get 3 years in prison? The dilemma leads to the equilibrium of the game.

A Bad Outcome For the prisoners, the equilibrium of the game, with each confessing, is not the best outcome. If neither of them confesses, each gets only 2 years for the lesser crime. Isn't there some way in which this better outcome can be achieved? It seems that there is not, because the players cannot communicate with each other. Each player can put himself in the other player's place, and so each player can figure out that there is a best strategy for each of them. The prisoners are indeed in a dilemma. Each knows that he can serve 2 years only if he can trust the other to deny. But each prisoner also knows that it is not in the best interest of the other to deny. So each prisoner knows that he must confess, thereby delivering a bad outcome for both.

The firms in an oligopoly are in a similar situation to Art and Bob in the prisoners' dilemma game. Let's see how we can use this game to understand oligopoly.

An Oligopoly Price-Fixing Game

We can use game theory and a game like the prisoners' dilemma to understand price fixing, price wars, and other aspects of the behaviour of firms in oligopoly. We'll begin with a price-fixing game.

To understand price fixing, we're going to study the special case of duopoly—an oligopoly with two firms. Duopoly is easier to study than oligopoly with three or more firms, and it captures the essence of all oligopoly situations. Somehow, the two firms must share the market. And how they share it depends on the actions of each. We're going to describe the costs of the two firms and the market demand for the item they produce. We're then going to see how game theory helps us to predict the prices charged and the quantities produced by the two firms in a duopoly.

Cost and Demand Conditions Two firms, Trick and Gear, produce switchgears. They have identical costs. Figure 15.4(a) shows their average total cost curve (*ATC*) and marginal cost curve (*MC*). Figure 15.4(b) shows the market demand curve for switchgears (*D*). The two firms produce identical switchgears, so one firm's switchgear is a perfect substitute for the other's, and the market price of each firm's product is identical. The quantity demanded depends on that price—the higher the price, the smaller is the quantity demanded.

This industry is a natural duopoly. Two firms can produce this good at a lower cost than either one firm or three firms can. For each firm, average total cost is at its minimum when production is 3,000 units a week. When price equals minimum average total cost, the total quantity demanded is 6,000 units a week, and two firms can just produce that quantity.

Collusion We'll suppose that Trick and Gear enter into a collusive agreement. A **collusive agreement** is an agreement between two (or more) producers to form a cartel to restrict output, raise the price, and increase profits. Such an agreement is illegal in Canada and is undertaken in secret. The strategies that firms in a cartel can pursue are to

- Comply
- Cheat

A firm that complies carries out the agreement. A firm that cheats breaks the agreement to its own benefit and to the cost of the other firm.

Because each firm has two strategies, there are four possible combinations of actions for the firms:

1. Both firms comply.
2. Both firms cheat.
3. Trick complies and Gear cheats.
4. Gear complies and Trick cheats.

FIGURE 15.4 Costs and Demand

(a) Individual firm

(b) Industry

The average total cost curve for each firm is *ATC*, and the marginal cost curve is *MC* (part a). Minimum average total cost is $6,000 a unit, and it occurs at a production of 3,000 units a week.

Part (b) shows the market demand curve. At a price of $6,000, the quantity demanded is 6,000 units per week. The two firms can produce this output at the lowest possible average cost. If the market had one firm, it would be profitable for another to enter. If the market had three firms, one would exit. There is room for only two firms in this industry. It is a natural duopoly.

Colluding to Maximize Profits Let's work out the pay-offs to the two firms if they collude to make the maximum profit for the cartel by acting like a monopoly. The calculations that the two firms perform are the same calculations that a monopoly performs. (You can refresh your memory of these calculations by looking at Chapter 13, pp. 304–305.) The only thing that the firms in duopoly must do beyond what a monopoly does is to agree on how much of the total output each of them will produce.

Figure 15.5 shows the price and quantity that maximize industry profit for the duopoly. Part (a) shows the situation for each firm, and part (b) shows the situation for the industry as a whole. The curve labelled MR is the industry marginal revenue curve. This marginal revenue curve is like that of a single-price monopoly (Chapter 13, p. 302). The curve labelled MC_I is the industry marginal cost curve if each firm produces the same quantity of output. This curve is constructed by adding together the outputs of the two firms at each level of marginal cost. Because the two firms are the same size, at each level of marginal cost, the industry output is twice the output of one firm. The curve MC_I in part (b) is twice as far to the right as the curve MC in part (a).

To maximize industry profit, the firms in the duopoly agree to restrict output to the rate that makes the industry marginal cost and marginal revenue equal. That output rate, as shown in part (b), is 4,000 units a week. The demand curve shows that the highest price for which the 4,000 switchgears can be sold is $9,000 each. Trick and Gear agree to charge this price.

To hold the price at $9,000 a unit, production must be 4,000 units a week. So Trick and Gear must agree on output rates for each of them that total 4,000 units a week. Let's suppose that they agree to split the market equally so that each firm produces 2,000 switchgears a week. Because the firms are identical, this division is the most likely.

The average total cost (ATC) of producing 2,000 switchgears a week is $8,000, so the profit per unit is $1,000 and economic profit is $2 million (2,000 units × $1,000 per unit). The economic profit of each firm is represented by the blue rectangle in Fig. 15.5(a).

We have just described one possible outcome for a duopoly game: The two firms collude to produce the monopoly profit-maximizing output and divide that output equally between themselves. From the industry point of view, this solution is identical to a monopoly. A duopoly that operates in this way is indistinguishable from a monopoly. The economic profit that is made by a monopoly is the maximum total profit that can be made by the duopoly when the firms collude.

But with price greater than marginal cost, either firm might think of trying to increase profit by cheating on the agreement and producing more than the agreed amount. Let's see what happens if one of the firms does cheat in this way.

FIGURE 15.5 Colluding to Make Monopoly Profits

(a) Individual firm

(b) Industry

The industry marginal cost curve, MC_I in part (b), is the horizontal sum of the two firms' marginal cost curves, MC in part (a). The industry marginal revenue curve is MR. To maximize profit, the firms produce 4,000 units a week (the quantity at which marginal revenue equals marginal cost). They sell that output for $9,000 a unit. Each firm produces 2,000 units a week. Average total cost is $8,000 a unit, so each firm makes an economic profit of $2 million (blue rectangle)—2,000 units multiplied by $1,000 profit a unit.

myeconlab animation

One Firm Cheats on a Collusive Agreement To set the stage for cheating on their agreement, Trick convinces Gear that demand has decreased and that it cannot sell 2,000 units a week. Trick tells Gear that it plans to cut its price so that it can sell the agreed 2,000 units each week. Because the two firms produce an identical product, Gear matches Trick's price cut but still produces only 2,000 units a week.

In fact, there has been no decrease in demand. Trick plans to increase output, which it knows will lower the price, and Trick wants to ensure that Gear's output remains at the agreed level.

Figure 15.6 illustrates the consequences of Trick's cheating. Part (a) shows Gear (the complier); part (b) shows Trick (the cheat); and part (c) shows the industry as a whole. Suppose that Trick increases output to 3,000 units a week. If Gear sticks to the agreement to produce only 2,000 units a week, total output is now 5,000 a week, and given demand in part (c), the price falls to $7,500 a unit.

Gear continues to produce 2,000 units a week at a cost of $8,000 a unit and incurs a loss of $500 a unit, or $1 million a week. This economic loss is shown by the red rectangle in part (a). Trick produces 3,000 units a week at an average total cost of $6,000 each. With a price of $7,500, Trick makes a profit of $1,500 a unit and therefore an economic profit of $4.5 million. This economic profit is the blue rectangle in part (b).

We've now described a second possible outcome for the duopoly game: One of the firms cheats on the collusive agreement. In this case, the industry output is larger than the monopoly output and the industry price is lower than the monopoly price. The total economic profit made by the industry is also smaller than the monopoly's economic profit. Trick (the cheat) makes an economic profit of $4.5 million, and Gear (the complier) incurs an economic loss of $1 million. The industry makes an economic profit of $3.5 million. This industry profit is $0.5 million less than the economic profit that a monopoly would make. But the profit is distributed unevenly. Trick makes a bigger economic profit than it would under the collusive agreement, while Gear incurs an economic loss.

A similar outcome would arise if Gear cheated and Trick complied with the agreement. The industry profit and price would be the same, but in this case, Gear (the cheat) would make an economic profit of $4.5 million and Trick (the complier) would incur an economic loss of $1 million.

Let's next see what happens if both firms cheat.

FIGURE 15.6   One Firm Cheats

(a) Complier   **(b) Cheat**   **(c) Industry**

One firm, shown in part (a), complies with the agreement and produces 2,000 units. The other firm, shown in part (b), cheats on the agreement and increases its output to 3,000 units a week. Given the market demand curve, shown in part (c), and with a total production of 5,000 units a week, the price falls to $7,500 a unit. At this price, the complier in part (a) incurs an economic loss of $1 million ($500 per unit × 2,000 units), shown by the red rectangle. In part (b), the cheat makes an economic profit of $4.5 million ($1,500 per unit × 3,000 units), shown by the blue rectangle.

Both Firms Cheat Suppose that both firms cheat and that each firm behaves like the cheating firm that we have just analyzed. Each tells the other that it is unable to sell its output at the going price and that it plans to cut its price. But because both firms cheat, each will propose a successively lower price. As long as price exceeds marginal cost, each firm has an incentive to increase its production—to cheat. Only when price equals marginal cost is there no further incentive to cheat. This situation arises when the price has reached $6,000. At this price, marginal cost equals price. Also, price equals minimum average total cost. At a price less than $6,000, each firm incurs an economic loss. At a price of $6,000, each firm covers all its costs and makes zero economic profit. Also, at a price of $6,000, each firm wants to produce 3,000 units a week, so the industry output is 6,000 units a week. Given the demand conditions, 6,000 units can be sold at a price of $6,000 each.

Figure 15.7 illustrates the situation just described. Each firm, in part (a), produces 3,000 units a week, and its average total cost is a minimum ($6,000 per unit). The market as a whole, in part (b), operates at the point at which the market demand curve (D) intersects the industry marginal cost curve (MC_I). Each firm has lowered its price and increased its output to try to gain an advantage over the other firm. Each has pushed this process as far as it can without incurring an economic loss.

We have now described a third possible outcome of this duopoly game: Both firms cheat. If both firms

cheat on the collusive agreement, the output of each firm is 3,000 units a week and the price is $6,000 a unit. Each firm makes zero economic profit.

The Payoff Matrix Now that we have described the strategies and payoffs in the duopoly game, we can summarize the strategies and the payoffs in the form of the game's payoff matrix. Then we can find the Nash equilibrium.

Table 15.2 sets out the payoff matrix for this game. It is constructed in the same way as the payoff matrix for the prisoners' dilemma in Table 15.1. The squares show the payoffs for the two firms—Gear and Trick. In this case, the payoffs are profits. (For the prisoners' dilemma, the payoffs were losses.)

The table shows that if both firms cheat (top left), they achieve the perfectly competitive outcome—each firm makes zero economic profit. If both firms comply (bottom right), the industry makes the monopoly profit and each firm makes an economic profit of $2 million. The top right and bottom left squares show the payoff if one firm cheats while the other complies. The firm that cheats makes an economic profit of $4.5 million, and the one that complies incurs a loss of $1 million.

Nash Equilibrium in the Duopolists' Dilemma The duopolists have a dilemma like the prisoners' dilemma. Do they comply or cheat? To answer this question, we must find the Nash equilibrium.

FIGURE 15.7 Both Firms Cheat

(a) Individual firm   **(b) Industry**

If both firms cheat by increasing production, the collusive agreement collapses. The limit to the collapse is the competitive equilibrium. Neither firm will cut its price below $6,000 (minimum average total cost) because to do so will result in losses. In part (a), each firm produces 3,000 units a week at an average total cost of $6,000. In part (b), with a total production of 6,000 units, the price falls to $6,000. Each firm now makes zero economic profit. This output and price are the ones that would prevail in a competitive industry.

TABLE 15.2   Duopoly Payoff Matrix

Gear's strategies

	Cheat	Comply
Cheat	$0 / $0	−$1.0m / +$4.5m
Comply	+$4.5m / −$1.0m	+$2m / +$2m

Trick's strategies

Each square shows the payoffs from a pair of actions. For example, if both firms comply with the collusive agreement, the payoffs are recorded in the bottom right square. The red triangle shows Gear's payoff, and the blue triangle shows Trick's. In Nash equilibrium, both firms cheat.

Look at things from Gear's point of view. Gear reasons as follows: Suppose that Trick cheats. If I comply, I will incur an economic loss of $1 million. If I also cheat, I will make zero economic profit. Zero is better than *minus* $1 million, so I'm better off if I cheat. Now suppose Trick complies. If I cheat, I will make an economic profit of $4.5 million, and if I comply, I will make an economic profit of $2 million. A $4.5 million profit is better than a $2 million profit, so I'm better off if I cheat. So regardless of whether Trick cheats or complies, it pays Gear to cheat. Cheating is Gear's best strategy.

Trick comes to the same conclusion as Gear because the two firms face an identical situation. So both firms cheat. The Nash equilibrium of the duopoly game is that both firms cheat. And although the industry has only two firms, they charge the same price and produce the same quantity as those in a competitive industry. Also, as in perfect competition, each firm makes zero economic profit.

This conclusion is not general and will not always arise. We'll see why not by looking first at some other games that are like the prisoners' dilemma. Then we'll broaden the types of games we consider.

Other Oligopoly Games

Firms in oligopoly must decide whether to mount expensive advertising campaigns; whether to modify their product; whether to make their product more reliable and more durable; whether to price discriminate and, if so, among which groups of customers and to what degree; whether to undertake a large research and development (R&D) effort aimed at lowering production costs; and whether to enter or leave an industry.

All of these choices can be analyzed as games that are similar to the one that we've just studied. Let's look at one example: an R&D game.

An R&D Game
Procter & Gamble Versus Kimberly-Clark

Disposable diapers have been around for a bit more than 40 years. Procter & Gamble (which has a 40 percent market share with Pampers) and Kimberly-Clark (which has a 33 percent market share with Huggies) have always been the market leaders.

When the disposable diaper was first introduced, it had to be cost effective in competition with reusable, laundered diapers. A costly R&D effort resulted in the development of machines that could make disposable diapers at a low enough cost to achieve that initial competitive edge. But new firms tried to get into the business and take market share away from the two industry leaders, and the industry leaders themselves battled each other to maintain or increase their own market shares.

During the early 1990s, Kimberly-Clark was the first to introduce Velcro closures. And in 1996, Procter & Gamble was the first to introduce "breathable" diapers.

The key to success in this industry (as in any other) is to design a product that people value highly relative to the cost of producing it. The firm that creates the most highly valued product and also develops the least-cost technology for producing it gains a competitive edge, undercutting the rest of the market, increasing its market share, and increasing its profit.

But the R&D that must be undertaken to improve product quality and cut cost is itself costly. So the cost of R&D must be deducted from the profit resulting from the increased market share that lower costs achieve. If no firm does R&D, every firm can be better off, but if one firm initiates the R&D activity, all must follow.

Table 15.3 illustrates the dilemma (with hypothetical numbers) for the R&D game that Kimberly-Clark and Procter & Gamble play. Each firm has two strategies: Spend $25 million a year on R&D or spend nothing on R&D. If neither firm spends on R&D, they make a joint profit of $100 million: $30 million for Kimberly-Clark and $70 million for Procter & Gamble (bottom right of the payoff matrix). If each firm conducts R&D, market shares are maintained but each firm's profit is lower by the amount spent on R&D (top left square of the payoff matrix). If Kimberly-Clark pays for R&D but Procter & Gamble does not, Kimberly-Clark gains a large part of Procter & Gamble's market. Kimberly-Clark profits, and Procter & Gamble loses (top right square of the payoff matrix). Finally, if Procter & Gamble conducts R&D and Kimberly-Clark does not, Procter & Gamble gains market share from Kimberly-Clark, increasing its profit, while Kimberly-Clark incurs a loss (bottom left square).

TABLE 15.3 Pampers Versus Huggies: An R&D Game

If both firms undertake R&D, their payoffs are those shown in the top left square. If neither firm undertakes R&D, their payoffs are in the bottom right square. When one firm undertakes R&D and the other one does not, their payoffs are in the top right and bottom left squares. The red triangle shows Procter & Gamble's payoff, and the blue triangle shows Kimberly-Clark's. The Nash equilibrium for this game is for both firms to undertake R&D. The structure of this game is the same as that of the prisoners' dilemma.

Confronted with the payoff matrix in Table 15.3, the two firms calculate their best strategies. Kimberly-Clark reasons as follows: If Procter & Gamble does not undertake R&D, we will make $85 million if we do and $30 million if we do not; so it pays us to conduct R&D. If Procter & Gamble conducts R&D, we will lose $10 million if we don't and make $5 million if we do. Again, R&D pays off. So conducting R&D is the best strategy for Kimberly-Clark. It pays, regardless of Procter & Gamble's decision.

Procter & Gamble reasons similarly: If Kimberly-Clark does not undertake R&D, we will make $70 million if we follow suit and $85 million if we conduct R&D. It therefore pays to conduct R&D. If Kimberly-Clark does undertake R&D, we will make $45 million by doing the same and lose $10 million by not doing R&D. Again, it pays us to conduct R&D. So for Procter & Gamble, R&D is also the best strategy.

Because R&D is the best strategy for both players, it is the Nash equilibrium. The outcome of this game is that both firms conduct R&D. They make less profit than they would if they could collude to achieve the cooperative outcome of no R&D.

The real-world situation has more players than Kimberly-Clark and Procter & Gamble. A large number of other firms share a small portion of the market, all of them ready to eat into the market share of Procter & Gamble and Kimberly-Clark. So the R&D efforts by these two firms not only serve the purpose of maintaining shares in their own battle but also help to keep barriers to entry high enough to preserve their joint market share.

The Disappearing Invisible Hand

All the games that we've studied are versions of the prisoners' dilemma. The essence of that game lies in the structure of its payoffs. The worst possible outcome for each player arises from cooperating when the other player cheats. The best possible outcome, for each player to cooperate, is not a Nash equilibrium because it is in neither player's *self-interest* to cooperate if the other one cooperates. It is this failure to achieve the best outcome for both players—the best social outcome if the two players are the entire economy—that led John Nash to claim (as he was portrayed as doing in the movie *A Beautiful Mind*) that he had challenged Adam Smith's idea that we are always guided, as if by an invisible hand, to promote the social interest when we are pursuing our self-interest.

A Game of Chicken

The Nash equilibrium for the prisoners' dilemma is called a **dominant strategy equilibrium**, which is an equilibrium in which the best strategy of each player is to cheat (confess) *regardless of the strategy of the other player*. Not all games have such an equilibrium, and one that doesn't is a game called "chicken."

In a graphic, if disturbing, version of this game, two cars race towards each other. The first driver to swerve and avoid a crash is "chicken." The payoffs are a big loss for both if no one "chickens," zero for the chicken, and a gain for the player who stays the course. If player 1 chickens, player 2's best strategy is to stay the course. And if player 1 stays the course, player 2's best strategy is to chicken.

For an economic form of this game, suppose the R&D that creates a new diaper technology results in information that cannot be kept secret or patented, so both firms benefit from the R&D of either firm. The chicken in this case is the firm that does the R&D.

Table 15.4 illustrates a payoff matrix for an R&D game of chicken between Kimberly-Clark and Procter & Gamble. Each firm has two strategies: Do the R&D (and "chicken") or do not do the R&D (and stand firm).

If neither "chickens," there is no R&D and each firm makes zero additional profit. If each firm conducts R&D—each "chickens"—each firm makes $5 million (the profit from the new technology minus the cost of the research). If one of the firms does the R&D, the payoffs are $1 million for the chicken and $10 million for the one who stands firm.

Confronted with the payoff matrix in Table 15.4, the two firms calculate their best strategies. Kimberly-Clark is better off doing R&D if Procter & Gamble does not undertake it. Procter & Gamble is better off doing R&D if Kimberly-Clark doesn't do it. There are two equilibrium outcomes: One firm does the R&D, but we can't predict which firm it will be.

You can see that it isn't a Nash equilibrium if no firm does the R&D because one firm would then be better off doing it. And you can see that it isn't a Nash equilibrium if both firms do the R&D because then one firm would be better off not doing it.

The firms could toss a coin or use some other random device to make a decision in this game. In some circumstances, such a strategy—called a mixed strategy—is actually better for both firms than choosing any of the strategies we've considered.

TABLE 15.4   An R&D Game of Chicken

If both firms undertake R&D, their payoffs are those shown in the top left square. If neither firm undertakes R&D, their payoffs are in the bottom right square. When one firm undertakes R&D and the other one does not, their payoffs are in the top right and bottom left squares. The red triangle shows Procter & Gamble's payoff, and the blue triangle shows Kimberly-Clark's. The equilibrium for this R&D game of chicken is for only one firm to undertake R&D. We cannot tell which firm will do the R&D and which will not.

Review Quiz

1   What are the common features of all games?
2   Describe the prisoners' dilemma game and explain why the Nash equilibrium delivers a bad outcome for both players.
3   Why does a collusive agreement to restrict output and raise price create a game like the prisoners' dilemma?
4   What creates an incentive for firms in a collusive agreement to cheat and increase production?
5   What is the equilibrium strategy for each firm in the duopolists' dilemma and why do the firms not succeed in colluding to raise the price and profits?
6   Describe two structures of payoffs for an R&D game and contrast the prisoners' dilemma and the chicken game.

 Work Study Plan 15.3 and get instant feedback.

Repeated Games and Sequential Games

The games that we've studied are played just once. In contrast, many real-world games are played repeatedly. This feature of games turns out to enable real-world duopolists to cooperate, collude, and make a monopoly profit.

Another feature of the games that we've studied is that the players move simultaneously. But in many real-world situations, one player moves first and then the other moves—the play is sequential rather than simultaneous. This feature of real-world games creates a large number of possible outcomes.

We're now going to examine these two aspects of strategic decision making.

A Repeated Duopoly Game

If two firms play a game repeatedly, one firm has the opportunity to penalize the other for previous "bad" behaviour. If Gear cheats this week, perhaps Trick will cheat next week. Before Gear cheats this week, won't it consider the possibility that Trick will cheat next week? What is the equilibrium of this game?

Actually, there is more than one possibility. One is the Nash equilibrium that we have just analyzed. Both players cheat, and each makes zero economic profit forever. In such a situation, it will never pay one of the players to start complying unilaterally because to do so would result in a loss for that player and a profit for the other. But a **cooperative equilibrium** in which the players make and share the monopoly profit is possible.

A cooperative equilibrium might occur if cheating is punished. There are two extremes of punishment. The smallest penalty is called "tit for tat." A *tit-for-tat strategy* is one in which a player cooperates in the current period if the other player cooperated in the previous period, but cheats in the current period if the other player cheated in the previous period. The most severe form of punishment is called a trigger strategy. A *trigger strategy* is one in which a player cooperates if the other player cooperates but plays the Nash equilibrium strategy forever thereafter if the other player cheats.

In the duopoly game between Gear and Trick, a tit-for-tat strategy keeps both players cooperating and making monopoly profits. Let's see why with an example.

Table 15.5 shows the economic profit that Trick and Gear will make over a number of periods under two alternative sequences of events: colluding and cheating with a tit-for-tat response by the other firm.

If both firms stick to the collusive agreement in period 1, each makes an economic profit of $2 million. Suppose that Trick contemplates cheating in period 1. The cheating produces a quick $4.5 million economic profit and inflicts a $1 million economic loss on Gear. But a cheat in period 1 produces a response from Gear in period 2. If Trick wants to get back into a profit-making situation, it must return to the agreement in period 2 even though it knows that Gear will punish it for cheating in period 1. So in period 2, Gear punishes Trick and Trick cooperates. Gear now makes an economic profit of $4.5 million, and Trick incurs an economic loss of $1 million. Adding up the profits over two periods of play, Trick would have made more profit by cooperating: $4 million compared with $3.5 million.

What is true for Trick is also true for Gear. Because each firm makes a larger profit by sticking with the collusive agreement, both firms do so and the monopoly price, quantity, and profit prevail.

In reality, whether a cartel works like a one-play game or a repeated game depends primarily on the number of players and the ease of detecting and punishing cheating. The larger the number of players, the harder it is to maintain a cartel.

TABLE 15.5 Cheating with Punishment

Period of play	Collude		Cheat with tit-for-tat	
	Trick's profit	Gear's profit	Trick's profit	Gear's profit
	(millions of dollars)		(millions of dollars)	
1	2	2	4.5	–1.0
2	2	2	–1.0	4.5
3	2	2	2.0	2.0
4	.	.	.	.

If duopolists repeatedly collude, each makes a profit of $2 million per period of play. If one player cheats in period 1, the other player plays a tit-for-tat strategy and cheats in period 2. The profit from cheating can be made for only one period and must be paid for in the next period by incurring a loss. Over two periods of play, the best that a duopolist can achieve by cheating is a profit of $3.5 million, compared to an economic profit of $4 million by colluding.

Games and Price Wars A repeated duopoly game can help us understand real-world behaviour and, in particular, price wars. Some price wars can be interpreted as the implementation of a tit-for-tat strategy. But the game is a bit more complicated than the one we've looked at because the players are uncertain about the demand for the product.

Playing a tit-for-tat strategy, firms have an incentive to stick to the monopoly price. But fluctuations in demand lead to fluctuations in the monopoly price, and sometimes, when the price changes, it might seem to one of the firms that the price has fallen because the other has cheated. In this case, a price war will break out. The price war will end only when each firm is satisfied that the other is ready to cooperate again. There will be cycles of price wars and the restoration of collusive agreements. Fluctuations in the world price of oil might be interpreted in this way.

Some price wars arise from the entry of a small number of firms into an industry that had previously been a monopoly. Although the industry has a small number of firms, the firms are in a prisoners' dilemma and they cannot impose effective penalties for price cutting. The behaviour of prices and outputs in the computer chip industry during 1995 and 1996 can be explained in this way. Until 1995, the market for Pentium chips for IBM-compatible computers was dominated by one firm, Intel Corporation, which was able to make maximum economic profit by producing the quantity of chips at which marginal cost equalled marginal revenue. The price of Intel's chips was set to ensure that the quantity demanded equalled the quantity produced. Then in 1995 and 1996, with the entry of a small number of new firms, the industry became an oligopoly. If the firms had maintained Intel's price and shared the market, together they could have made economic profits equal to Intel's profit. But the firms were in a prisoners' dilemma, so prices fell towards the competitive level.

Let's now study a sequential game. There are many such games, and the one we'll examine is among the simplest. It has an interesting implication and it will give you the flavour of this type of game. The sequential game that we'll study is an entry game in a contestable market.

A Sequential Entry Game in a Contestable Market

If two firms play a sequential game, one firm makes a decision at the first stage of the game and the other makes a decision at the second stage.

We're going to study a sequential game in a **contestable market**—a market in which firms can enter and leave so easily that firms in the market face competition from *potential* entrants. Examples of contestable markets are routes served by airlines and by barge companies that operate on the major waterways. These markets are contestable because firms could enter if an opportunity for economic profit arose and could exit with no penalty if the opportunity for economic profit disappeared.

If the Herfindahl-Hirschman Index (p. 238) is used to determine the degree of competition, a contestable market appears to be uncompetitive. But a contestable market can behave as if it were perfectly competitive. To see why, let's look at an entry game for a contestable air route.

A Contestable Air Route Agile Air is the only firm operating on a particular route. Demand and cost conditions are such that there is room for only one airline to operate. Wanabe Inc. is another airline that could offer services on the route.

We describe the structure of a sequential game by using a *game tree* like that in Fig. 15.8. At the first stage, Agile Air must set a price. Once the price is set and advertised, Agile can't change it. That is, once set, Agile's price is fixed and Agile can't react to Wanabe's entry decision. Agile can set its price at either the monopoly level or the competitive level.

At the second stage, Wanabe must decide whether to enter or to stay out. Customers have no loyalty (there are no frequent-flyer programs) and they buy from the lowest-price firm. So if Wanabe enters, it sets a price just below Agile's and takes all the business.

Figure 15.8 shows the payoffs from the various decisions (Agile's in the red triangles and Wanabe's in the blue triangles).

To decide on its price, Agile's CEO reasons as follows: Suppose that Agile sets the monopoly price. If Wanabe enters, it earns 90 (think of all payoff numbers as thousands of dollars). If Wanabe stays out, it earns nothing. So Wanabe will enter. In this case Agile will lose 50.

FIGURE 15.8   Agile Versus Wanabe: A Sequential Entry Game in a Contestable Market

If Agile sets the monopoly price, Wanabe makes 90 (thousand dollars) by entering and earns nothing by staying out. So if Agile sets the monopoly price, Wanabe enters.

If Agile sets the competitive price, Wanabe earns nothing if it stays out and incurs a loss if it enters. So if Agile sets the competitive price, Wanabe stays out.

myeconlab animation

Now suppose that Agile sets the competitive price. If Wanabe stays out, it earns nothing, and if it enters, it loses 10, so Wanabe will stay out. In this case, Agile will make zero economic profit.

Agile's best strategy is to set its price at the competitive level and make zero economic profit. The option of earning 100 by setting the monopoly price with Wanabe staying out is not available to Agile. If Agile sets the monopoly price, Wanabe enters, undercuts Agile, and takes all the business.

In this example, Agile sets its price at the competitive level and makes zero economic profit. A less costly strategy, called **limit pricing**, sets the price at the highest level that inflicts a loss on the entrant. Any loss is big enough to deter entry, so it is not always necessary to set the price as low as the competitive price. In the example of Agile and Wanabe, at the competitive price, Wanabe incurs a loss of 10 if it enters. A smaller loss would still keep Wanabe out.

This game is interesting because it points to the possibility of a monopoly behaving like a competitive industry and serving the social interest without regulation. But the result is not general and depends on one feature of the setup of the game: At the second stage, Agile is locked in to the price set at the first stage.

If Agile could change its price in the second stage, it would want to set the monopoly price if Wanabe stayed out—100 with the monopoly price beats zero with the competitive price. But Wanabe can figure out what Agile would do, so the price set at the first

stage has no effect on Wanabe. Agile sets the monopoly price and Wanabe might either stay out or enter.

We've looked at two of the many possible repeated and sequential games, and you've seen how these types of games can provide insights into the complex forces that determine prices and profits.

Review Quiz

1 If a prisoners' dilemma game is played repeatedly, what punishment strategies might the players employ and how does playing the game repeatedly change the equilibrium?

2 If a market is contestable, how does the equilibrium differ from that of a monopoly?

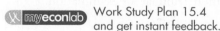 Work Study Plan 15.4 and get instant feedback.

So far, we've studied oligopoly with unregulated market power. Firms like Trick and Gear are free to collude to maximize their profit with no concern for the consumer or the law.

But when firms collude to achieve the monopoly outcome, they also have the same effects on efficiency and the social interest as monopoly. Profit is made at the expense of consumer surplus and a deadweight loss arises. Your next task is to see how Canadian anti-combine law limits market power.

◆ Anti-Combine Law

Anti-combine law is the law that regulates oligopolies and seeks to prevent them from becoming monopolies or behaving like monopolies. Anti-combine law can work in the public interest to maximize total surplus or in the self-interest of producers to maximize producer surpluses. We'll describe Canada's anti-combine law and examine some recent cases.

Canada's Anti-Combine Law

Canada's anti-combine law dates from 1889. At that time, monopoly was a major political issue and people were concerned about the absence of competition in industries as diverse as sugar and groceries, biscuits and confectionery, coal, binder twine, agricultural implements, stoves, coffins, eggs, and fire insurance. Canada's anti-combine law today is defined in the Competition Act of 1986, which is described in Table 15.6 on p. 360. The Act established a Competition Bureau and a Competition Tribunal. The Competition Act distinguishes between practices that are

1. Criminal
2. Noncriminal

Conspiracy to fix prices, bid-rigging, other anti-competitive price-fixing actions, and false advertising are criminal offences. The courts handle alleged offences, and the standard level of proof beyond a reasonable doubt must be established.

Mergers, abuse of a dominant market position, refusal to deal, and other actions designed to limit competition such as exclusive dealing are noncriminal offences. The Director of the Competition Bureau sends alleged violations of a noncriminal nature to the Competition Tribunal for examination.

Some Major Anti-Combine Cases

To see how the Competition Act has been working, we'll look at a few cases. The first case we'll examine is important because it confirms the Competition Tribunal's power to enforce its orders.

Chrysler In 1986, Chrysler stopped supplying auto parts to Richard Brunet, a Montreal auto dealer. Chrysler also discouraged other dealers from supplying Brunet. The Competition Tribunal claimed that Chrysler wanted Brunet's business for itself and ordered Chrysler to resume doing business with Brunet. Chrysler did not resume sending supplies and the Tribunal cited Chrysler for contempt. Appeals against this ruling eventually reached the Supreme Court of Canada, which confirmed the Tribunal's power over contempt for its ruling. But the Tribunal subsequently dropped its contempt charge.

The second case we'll look at concerns aspartame, the sweetener in many soft drinks.

NutraSweet NutraSweet, the maker of aspartame, tried to gain a monopoly in aspartame. It did so by licensing the use of its "swirl" only on products for which it had an exclusive deal. On October 4, 1990, the Competition Tribunal ruled that this action was an abuse of dominant position and unduly limited competition. The Competition Tribunal told NutraSweet that it may not enforce existing contracts, enter into new contracts in which it is the exclusive supplier, or give inducements to encourage the display of its "swirl." As a result of this case, competition increased and the price of aspartame fell in Canada.

The third case we'll examine concerns a publication you use almost every day: the Yellow Pages.

Bell Canada Enterprises Two subsidiaries of Bell Canada Enterprises have a 90 percent share of the market for the publication of telephone directories in their territories. These companies tie the sale of advertising services to the sale of advertising space in the Yellow Pages. If you want to advertise in the Yellow Pages, you must buy the advertising services of one of these two companies. As a result, other advertising agencies cannot effectively compete for business in Yellow Pages advertising.

The Director of the Competition Bureau applied for an order prohibiting the tied-sale practice of these two companies.

Other Recent Cases The Competition Bureau has investigated several high-profile cases in the past few years. These include a movie theatre merger when Cineplex Galaxy acquired Famous Players, a retail gasoline price-fixing cartel in Quebec, two proposed mergers between big Canadian banks, and the ownership transfer and relocation policies of the NHL when Jim Balsillie tried to buy the Predators.

Merger Allowed

Cineplex Galaxy Acquires Famous Players

In 2004, Cineplex Galaxy bought Famous Players. But before the deal could be confirmed, the Competition Bureau needed to vet and approve it.

The Firms

1. **Cineplex Galaxy** operated 86 theatres with 775 screens under the Cineplex Odeon and Galaxy brands in British Columbia, Alberta, Saskatchewan, Manitoba, Ontario, and Quebec.

2. **Famous Players** operated 77 theatres and 768 screens in the same six provinces as Cineplex Galaxy. The firm operated a number of brands other than its own name including Coliseum, Colossus, Paramount, and SilverCity.

By number of theatres and screens, Cineplex Galaxy was larger but Famous Players had larger box-office receipts.

The Markets

There isn't just one Canadian market for movie theatres. Each urban area is a separate market.

Barriers to Entry

The Competition Bureau identified three barriers to entry into the movie theatre industry:

1. Access to high box-office movies.
2. Access to suitable locations.
3. Sunk costs and risks.

Access to Movies The distribution policies of the major movie studios and distributors make entry risky. A new entrant cannot be sure before entering that the studios and distributors will provide it with movies capable of generating box-office revenue. So entry is highly risky.

Access to Locations During the late 1990s, a major building program created a large number of new stadium theatres, all of which occupied the best sites. As a consequence, it is difficult today to acquire a suitable site or location for a new movie theatre in many urban markets.

Sunk Costs and Risks Most new movie theatres are stadium-seating complexes that are single-purpose buildings. They are costly to build but have no resale

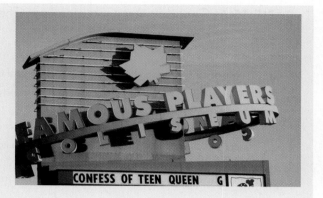

value so the cost of building them is a sunk cost, which makes entry very risky.

Concentration and Competition after the Merger

With Cineplex Galaxy and Famous Players operating as a single firm, many urban markets would become highly concentrated.

The Competition Bureau identified 17 local markets. In seven of them, the new merged firm would have had 100 percent market share and in five others, they would be near monopolies.

A few areas would have competition: in Montreal from Cinémas Guzzo; and in Montreal, Ottawa, and Toronto from AMC, a large U.S. operator. Outside of these major cities, the merged firm would have faced either no competition or very limited competition from small local firms.

The Competition Bureau's Decision

The Competition Bureau examined the competitive impact of the merger in each of the cities where Famous Players and Cineplex Galaxy competed and determined that the merger would likely reduce competition substantially in 17 of these areas. The Bureau was concerned about both price and non-price competition on such factors as theatre quality and film choice.

To resolve these concerns, in 17 cities the Bureau required the new firm to sell 35 of its theatres.

The general rule the Bureau employed was to reduce the new firm's market share in each city to a level similar to the pre-merger market share of the larger of Cineplex or Famous Players.

Source: The Competition Bureau, *Acquisition of Famous Players by Cineplex Galaxy.*

TABLE 15.6 Canada's Anti-Combine Law: The Competition Act, 1986

Abuse of Dominant Position

79 (1)   Where on application by the Director, the Tribunal finds that:

(a) one or more persons substantially or completely control, throughout Canada or any area thereof, a class or species of business,

(b) that person or those persons have engaged in or are engaging in a practice of anticompetitive acts, and

(c) the practice has had, is having or is likely to have the effect of preventing or lessening competition substantially in a market,

the Tribunal may make an order prohibiting all or any of those persons from engaging in that practice.

Mergers

92 (1)   Where on application by the Director, the Tribunal finds that a merger or proposed merger

prevents or lessens, or is likely to prevent or lessen, competition substantially ... the Tribunal

may ... [,]

in the case of a completed merger, order any party to the merger or any other person

(i) to dissolve the merger ...

(ii) to dispose of assets and shares ...

[or]

in the case of a proposed merger, make an order directed against any party to the proposed merger or any other person

(i) ordering the person ... not to proceed with the merger

(ii) ordering the person not to proceed with part of the merger.

Mergers Blocked

Canadian Banks

In January 1998, the Royal Bank of Canada and the Bank of Montreal announced that they wanted to merge and create a new bank. Soon after, in April 1998, CIBC and TD Bank announced their desire to combine.

After some months of deliberation, in December 1998, the Finance Minister, Paul Martin, told the banks that they could not proceed with their proposed mergers.

Why the Merger Was Blocked

The Finance Minister said that the bank mergers were not in the public interest because they would result in

- Too much concentration of economic power in the hands of too few financial institutions

- Reduced competition in the financial services markets

- Reduced government of Canada flexibility to address future concerns

A Competition Bureau report agreed.

Competition Bureau's View

The Competition Bureau investigated the impact of the proposed bank mergers on competition in the banking industry. The Bureau concluded that the mergers would substantially lessen competition and would result in bank branches being closed. Canadians would end up paying higher prices for reduced banking services.

Bank mergers in Canada are now so politically sensitive that any future attempts to merge will require the sanction of the federal government.

Price Fixing

Gasoline Cartel in Quebec

In June 2008, during a period of rapidly rising oil and gasoline prices, the Competition Bureau laid criminal charges against a number of individuals and companies in Victoriaville, Thetford Mines, Magog, and Sherbrooke (all in Quebec) for fixing the price of gasoline at the pump.

Price-fixing cartels are hard to detect. Evidence of identical prices does *not* prove the operation of a price-fixing agreement. Firms in perfect competition charge identical prices. Canadian law requires the Competition Bureau to provide evidence that proves, beyond a reasonable doubt, that the competitors *have an agreement to fix prices*.

In the Quebec gas prices case, the Competition Bureau used wiretaps and searches and took advantage of an immunity program that encourages people who are themselves breaking the law to provide evidence to investigators.

After extensive investigations, evidence emerged that gas retailers had made agreements by telephone on the prices they would charge. The evidence suggested that the overwhelming majority of gasoline retailers in these markets participated in the cartel.

The Court imposed fines totalling more than $2 million against the companies that pleaded guilty.

The Competition Bureau's investigation into potential price fixing in the retail gasoline market continues in other markets in Canada.

Source: Adapted from the Competition Bureau, *Competition Bureau Uncovers Gasoline Cartel in Quebec.*

Abuse of Dominant Position

NHL

In May 2007, Jim Balsillie did a tentative deal to buy the Nashville Predators with the intention, it was believed, of relocating the team to Hamilton, Ontario.

Locating the Predators in Hamilton would take some of the market from the Toronto Maple Leafs, who would demand compensation. The Buffalo Sabres might also be damaged and demand compensation, although NHL rules do permit relocation outside a radius of 80 kilometres of an existing team.

NHL policy requires that before a relocation can be accepted, a new owner must make a good-faith effort to keep the team in its city. Balsillie, it was claimed, had made no such attempt, and the NHL prevented him from completing the deal.

Following intense discussion in the media, the Competition Bureau investigated whether the NHL's transfer of ownership and relocation policies were anticompetitive or merely designed to protect the interests of the league.

After a major and highly detailed investigation, the Competition Bureau concluded that the NHL's policies were not anticompetitive and did not constitute an abuse of a dominant position. Rather, their aim was to maintain healthy rivalries among teams, to attract the largest possible audiences, and to encourage the investment in sports facilities by local governments.

Source: The Competition Bureau, *NHL Ownership Transfer and Relocation Policies.*

Review Quiz

1 What is the act of parliament that provides our anti-combine law?
2 What actions violate the anti-combine law?
3 Under what circumstances is a merger unlikely to be approved?

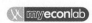 Work Study Plan 15.5 and get instant feedback.

Oligopoly is a market structure that you often encounter in your daily life. *Reading Between the Lines* on pp. 362–363 looks at a game played by Dell and HP in the market for personal computers.

Dell and HP in a Market Share Game

The Old Price-War Tactic May Not Faze Rivals Now

May 13, 2006

Dell is sharply reducing prices on its computers.

The tactic is classic, straight out of the playbook that made the company the world's largest computer maker. As overall demand for personal computers slows, lower your prices. Profit margins will take a temporary hit, but the move would hurt competitors worse as you take market share and enjoy revenue growth for years to come.

Dell did it in 2000 and it worked beautifully. But after Dell rolled out the plan last month, knocking as much as $700 off a $1,200 Inspiron and $500 off a $1,079 Dimension desktop, many of the securities analysts who follow the company, ... said that this time around it could be folly. ...

What changed? ... More than anything else, Dell's competitors have changed. In particular, Hewlett-Packard is no longer the bloated and slow-moving company it was six years ago. ...

The most telling evidence of the new landscape for PCs was seen in statistics on worldwide shipments. While the industry grew 12.9 percent in the first three months of the year, ... Dell's shipments grew 10.2 percent. It was the first time since analysts began tracking Dell that its shipments grew more slowly than the industry's. Hewlett's shipments, meanwhile, grew 22.2 percent. ...

Inside Hewlett, however, there is a feeling that it can beat Dell without resorting to price wars. ... The company has started an ambitious marketing campaign to make that point with ads that proclaim, "the computer is personal again." ...

The campaign ... will feature celebrities and how they individualize their computers ... [HP] has added technology like QuickPlay, which lets a user view a DVD or listen to a CD without waiting for the laptop's operating system to boot up. The ads will say, "Don't boot. Play." ...

Essence of the Story

- Dell cut its prices in 2000 and increased its market share and revenue in the years that followed.
- In April 2006, Dell slashed its prices.
- Experts say the price cut strategy will not work today.
- Hewlett-Packard (HP) is much stronger than it was six years ago.

- Total PC shipments increased by 12.9 percent in the first quarter of 2006: Dell's shipments increased by 10.2 percent, and HP's increased by 22.2 percent.
- HP says that it can beat Dell without a price cut. Instead it will launch a campaign to market PCs with new and improved features, such as one that plays DVDs and CDs without booting the operating system.

Economic Analysis

- The global PC market has many firms, but two firms dominate the market: Dell and Hewlett-Packard (HP).

- Figure 1 shows the shares in the global PC market. You can see that Dell and HP are the two biggest players but almost 50 percent of the market is served by small firms, each with less than 4 percent of the market.

- Table 1 shows the payoff matrix (millions of dollars of profit) for the game played by Dell and HP in 2000. (The numbers are hypothetical.)

- This game has a dominant strategy equilibrium similar to that for the duopoly game on p. 353.

- If HP cuts its price, Dell makes a larger profit by cutting its price (+$20m versus −$10m), and if HP holds its price constant, Dell again makes a larger profit by cutting its price (+$40m versus zero).

- So Dell's best strategy is to cut its price.

- If Dell cuts its price, HP makes a larger profit by cutting its price (+$5m versus −$20m), and if Dell holds its price constant, HP again makes a larger profit by cutting its price (+$10m versus zero).

- So HP's best strategy is to cut its price.

- Table 2 shows the payoffs from the game between Dell and HP in 2006.

- This game, too, has a dominant strategy equilibrium.

- If HP cuts its price, Dell makes a larger profit by cutting its price (+$10m versus −$10m), and if HP improves

its marketing and design, Dell again makes a larger profit by cutting its price (+$5m versus −$20m).

- So Dell's best strategy is to cut its price.

- If Dell cuts its price, HP makes a larger profit by improving its marketing and design (+$20m versus +$10m), and if Dell holds its price constant, HP again makes a larger profit by improving its marketing and design (+$40m versus +$20m).

- So HP's best strategy is to improve its marketing and design.

Table 1 The strategies and equilibrium in 2000

Table 2 The strategies and equilibrium in 2006

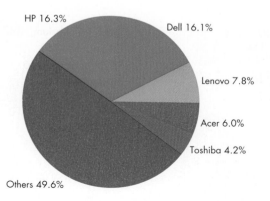

Figure 1 Market shares in the PC market in 2006

SUMMARY

Key Points

What Is Oligopoly? (pp. 342–343)

- Oligopoly is a market in which a small number of firms compete.

Two Traditional Oligopoly Models (pp. 344–345)

- If rivals match price cuts but do not match price hikes, each firm faces a kinked demand curve.
- If one firm dominates a market, it acts like a monopoly and the small firms act as price takers.

Oligopoly Games (pp. 346–354)

- Oligopoly is studied by using game theory, which is a method of analyzing strategic behaviour.
- In the prisoners' dilemma game, two prisoners acting in their own self-interest harm their joint interest.
- An oligopoly (duopoly) price-fixing game is the prisoners' dilemma in which the firms might collude or cheat.

- In Nash equilibrium, both firms cheat and output and price are the same as in perfect competition.
- Firms' decisions about advertising and R&D can be studied by using game theory.

Repeated Games and Sequential Games (pp. 355–357)

- In a repeated game, a punishment strategy can produce a cooperative equilibrium in which price and output are the same as in a monopoly.
- In a sequential contestable market game, a small number of firms can behave like firms in perfect competition.

Anti-Combine Law (pp. 358–361)

- Anti-combine law provides an alternative way for government to control monopoly and monopolistic practices.
- The Competition Act of 1986 sets out Canada's anti-combine law and places responsibility for enforcement with the Competition Tribunal.

Key Figures and Tables

Figure 15.1   Natural Oligopoly, 342
Figure 15.4   Costs and Demand, 348
Figure 15.5   Colluding to Make Monopoly Profits, 349

Figure 15.6   One Firm Cheats, 350
Figure 15.7   Both Firms Cheat, 351
Table 15.1   Prisoners' Dilemma Payoff Matrix, 347
Table 15.2   Duopoly Payoff Matrix, 352

Key Terms

Anti-combine law, 358
Cartel, 343
Collusive agreement, 348
Contestable market, 356
Cooperative equilibrium, 355
Dominant strategy equilibrium, 354
Duopoly, 342
Game theory, 346
Limit pricing, 357
Nash equilibrium, 347
Oligopoly, 342
Payoff matrix, 346
Strategies, 346

PROBLEMS and APPLICATIONS

 Work problems 1–11 in Chapter 15 Study Plan and get instant feedback.
Work problems 12–21 as Homework, a Quiz, or a Test if assigned by your instructor.

1. Two firms make most of the chips that power a PC: Intel and Advanced Micro Devices. What makes the market for PC chips a duopoly? Sketch the market demand curve and cost curves that describe the situation in this market and that prevent other firms from entering.

2. The price at which Wal-Mart can buy flat-panel TVs has fallen, and it is making a decision about whether to cut its selling price. Wal-Mart believes that if it cuts its price, all its competitors will cut their prices, but if it raises its price, none of its competitors will raise theirs.

   a. Draw a figure to illustrate the situation that Wal-Mart believes it faces in the market for flat-panel TVs.
   b. Do you predict that Wal-Mart will lower its price of a flat-panel TV? Explain and illustrate your answer.

3. Big Joe's Trucking has lower costs than the other 20 small truckers in the market. The market operates like a dominant firm oligopoly and is initially in equilibrium. Then the demand for trucking services increases. Explain the effects of the increase in demand on the price, output, and economic profit of

   a. Big Joe's.
   b. A typical small firm.

4. Consider a game with two players, who cannot communicate, and in which each player is asked a question. The players can answer the question honestly or lie. If both answer honestly, each receives $100. If one answers honestly and the other lies, the liar receives $500 and the honest player gets nothing. If both lie, then each receives $50.

   a. Describe the strategies and payoffs of this game.
   b. Construct the payoff matrix.
   c. What is the equilibrium of this game?
   d. Compare this game to the prisoners' dilemma. Are the two games similar or different? Explain.

5. Soapy Inc. and Suddies Inc. are the only producers of soap powder. They collude and agree to share the market equally. If neither firm cheats

on the agreement, each makes $1 million profit. If either firm cheats, the cheat makes a profit of $1.5 million, while the complier incurs a loss of $0.5 million. If both cheat, they break even. Neither firm can monitor the other's actions.

   a. What are the strategies in this game?
   b. Construct the payoff matrix for this game.
   c. What is the equilibrium of this game if it is played only once?
   d. Is the equilibrium a dominant strategy equilibrium? Explain.

6. If Soapy Inc. and Suddies Inc. repeatedly play the duopoly game that has the payoffs described in problem 5 on each round of play,

   a. What now are the strategies that each firm might adopt?
   b. Can the firms adopt a strategy that gives the game a cooperative equilibrium?
   c. Would one firm still be tempted to cheat in a cooperative equilibrium? Explain your answer.

7. **Oil City**

   In the late 1990s, Reliance spent $6 billion and employed 75,000 workers to build a world-class oil refinery at Jamnagar, India. ... Now Reliance is more than doubling the size of the facility, which ... will claim the title of the world's biggest ... with an output of 1.2 million litres of gasoline per day, or about 5% of global capacity. ... Reliance plans to aim Jamnagar's spigots westward, at the U.S. and Europe, where it's too expensive and politically difficult to build new refineries. ...The bulked-up Jamnagar will be able to move markets: Singapore traders expect a drop in fuel prices as soon as it's going full tilt.

   Fortune, April 28, 2008

   a. Explain this news article's claims that the global market for gasoline is not perfectly competitive.
   b. What barriers to entry might limit competition in this market and give a firm such as Reliance power to influence the market price?

8. Healthy and Energica are the only producers of a new energy drink. The firms collude and agree to

share the market equally. If neither firm cheats, each firm makes $4 million profit. If either firm cheats, the cheat makes $6 million profit, while the complier incurs a loss of $1.5 million. If both cheat, they break even. Neither firm can police the other's actions.

a. If the game is played once,
  (i) What is the payoff matrix?
  (ii) Describe the best strategy for each firm.
  (iii) What is the equilibrium of the game?
b. If this game can be played many times, what are two strategies that could be adopted?

9. **B.C. Cellphone Firm Eyes Competition in Yukon**

A Vancouver-based company wants to go head to head with Northwestel for cellular telephone service in the Yukon, offering its own service along much of the Alaska Highway corridor.

RuralCom Corp. has applied to Industry Canada seeking permission to set up a cellphone network that would extend nearly 1,700 kilometres from Wonowon in northern British Columbia to Beaver Creek, Yukon, near the Alaskan border.

Company president Robert Hillman [said] that the firm is ready to build more than 40 cellphone towers and transmitters along the corridor. ... "We would be a direct competitor to Northwestel when it comes to providing service," he said. "We would intend to ... do that very aggressively."

CBC News, June 27, 2007

Suppose that Industry Canada grants permission for RuralCom Corp. to set up the cell phone network.

a. Explain how the new entry into the market will influence the price of cell phone service.
b. Explain the game that RuralCom and Northwestel might play to gain or keep market share.
c. If a price war develops, how low might the price of cell phone service fall?
d. Explain why cell phone service in the Yukon might be a natural monopoly rather than a natural duopoly.

10. **Minister Reacts to Text Anger: Prentice Orders Meeting Over Telco's High Fees**

Two of Canada's biggest cell phone companies have some explaining to do. On Wednesday, Industry Minister Jim Prentice summoned the CEOs of both Telus and Bell Mobility to a meeting in his office before Aug. 8 to discuss their companies' decisions to begin charging clients 15 cents apiece for incoming text messages, including unsolicited spam. ...

Customers have been outraged. ... The companies both plan to introduce the new charge next month for customers who do not have a locked-in price plan that includes a text messaging fee. ... Canada's other major national cell provider, Rogers, says it has no plans to charge for incoming messages. ...

The companies themselves defended their position this week saying the use of text messaging has exploded in Canada—from an estimated 10 million texts per day in 2006 to over 45 million a day now—and they can't afford to continue to offer the service for free.

Winnipeg Free Press, July 10, 2008

a. Why does the Industry Minister want a meeting with CEOs of Telus and Bell Mobility?
b. Why do Telus and Bell Mobility want to charge for incoming text messages?
c. If Rogers does not charge for incoming text messages and Telus and Bell Mobility do, how might their market shares change?

11. **Coke and Pepsi Battle It Out**

For the first time since 1967, the red giant [Coca-Cola] swept into the Gulf. ... Today, Pepsi is fighting hard to hang onto its part of the cake in the Middle East, the only region where the company is number one. ... Coke and Pepsi have steered clear of a Middle East price war. Coca-Cola decided that display marketing, not cost, would clinch sales. ... Pepsi waffled, then stumbled along with copycat promotions. Coke pushed their point-of-sale plan further: ... Coca-Cola, the Middle East underdog with momentum, seems to relish the fight. ... [Coke and Pepsi] are at each other's throats, and that's good news for all of us.

AME Info, April 8, 2004

a. Describe the game that Coca-Cola and Pepsi-Co play in the Middle East. Why is it "good news for all" people in the Middle East?
b. Why would Coke and Pepsi steer clear of a price war even though they are "at each other's throats"?

12. Bud and Wise are the only two producers of aniseed beer, a New Age product designed to displace root beer. Bud and Wise are trying to figure out how much of this new beer to produce. They know that if they both limit production to 10,000 litres a day, they will make the maximum attainable joint profit of $200,000 a day—$100,000 a day each. They also know that if either of them produces 20,000 litres a day while the other produces 10,000 a day, the one that produces 20,000 litres will make an economic profit of $150,000 and the one that sticks with 10,000 litres will incur an economic loss of $50,000. Each also knows that if they both increase production to 20,000 litres a day, they will both make zero economic profit.

   a. Construct a payoff matrix for the game that Bud and Wise must play.
   b. Find the Nash equilibrium of the game that Bud and Wise play.
   c. What is the equilibrium of the game if Bud and Wise play it repeatedly?

13. Isolated Island has two taxi companies, one owned by Ann and the other owned by Zack. The figure shows the demand curve for taxi rides, *D*, and the average total cost curve of each of the firms, *ATC*. Suppose that Ann and Zack have two strategies: collude, fix the monopoly price, and limit the number of rides; or break the collusion, cut the price, and produce more rides.

   a. Create a payoff matrix for the game that Ann and Zack play, and find the Nash equilibrium for this game if it is played just once. Do the people of Isolated Island get the efficient quantity of taxi rides?

   b. If Ann and Zack play the game repeatedly, what additional strategies become available to them and how might the outcome change?

14. **Asian Rice Exporters to Discuss Cartel**
   Rice-exporting nations planned to discuss a proposed cartel to control the price of the staple food. ... Rice exporters Thailand, Cambodia, Laos and Myanmar planned to meet Tuesday to discuss a proposal by Thailand, the world's largest rice exporter, that they form a cartel. Ahead of the meeting ... the countries sought to assuage concerns that they might force up prices by limiting supplies.

   Unlike the Organization of Petroleum Exporting Countries, the purpose of the rice cartel would be "to contribute to ensuring food stability, not just in an individual country but also to address food shortages in the region and the world," Cambodian Prime Minister Hun Sen said Monday. "We shall not hoard (rice) and raise prices when there are shortages," Hun Sen said.

   The Philippines wasn't convinced. "It is a bad idea. ... It will create an oligopoly and it's against humanity," Edgardo Angara, chairman of the Philippine Senate's Committee on Agriculture, said Friday, adding that the cartel could price the grain out of reach for "millions and millions of people."
   CNN, May 6, 2008

   a. Assuming the rice-exporting nations become a profit-maximizing colluding oligopoly, explain how they would influence the global market for rice and the world price of rice.
   b. Assuming the rice-exporting nations become a profit-maximizing colluding oligopoly, draw a graph to illustrate their influence on the global market for rice.
   c. Even in the absence of international anti-combine law, why might it be difficult for this cartel to successfully collude? Use the ideas of game theory to explain.

15. **Rogers Woos iPhone Users with Discount Package; $30 a Month**
   Rogers Wireless Inc. caved to consumer pressure yesterday, temporarily slashing data fees on its smartphone plans just ahead of the carrier's launch of the vaunted iPhone 3G in Canada tomorrow. ... Customers who sign up for the new iPhone between July 11, when the device goes on sale, and the end of August will pay just $30 a

month for access to six gigabytes of data usage. ... The 6-GB plan would enable a customer to send and receive more than 157,000 e-mails a month, or visit more than 35,000 Web pages, according to figures provided by Rogers. ... Users can now use the iPhone the way it was intended, said Amit Kaminer, a consultant with Montreal-based Sea-Board Group, ... However, buyers will still be required to sign a three-year contract with Rogers, and the new offer would be in addition to any voice plan a wireless customer subscribes to. ...

National Post, July 10, 2008

a. Fido and its parent company Rogers Communications are the only carriers for the iPhone in Canada. How does this arrangement between Rogers and Apple (the producer of iPhone) affect competition in the market for cell phone service?

b. Does this arrangement between Rogers and Apple regarding the iPhone violate Canada's anti-combine law? Explain.

16. **An Energy Drink with a Monster of a Stock**

The $5.7 billion energy-drink category, in which Monster holds the No. 2 position behind industry leader Red Bull, has slowed down as copycat brands jostle for shelf space—and the attention of teen consumers. ... Over the past five years Red Bull's market share in dollar terms has gone from 91 percent to well under 50 percent ... and much of that loss has been Monster's gain.

Fortune, December 25, 2006

a. Describe the structure of the energy-drink market. How has that structure changed over the past few years?

b. Explain the various difficulties Monster and Red Bull would have if they attempted to collude and charge monopoly prices for energy drinks.

17. Microsoft with Xbox 360, Nintendo with Wii, and Sony with PlayStation 3 are slugging it out in the market for the latest generation of video-game consoles. Xbox 360 was the first to market; Wii has the lowest price; PS3 uses the most advanced technology and has the highest price.

a. Thinking of the competition among these firms in the market for consoles as a game, describe the firms' strategies concerning design, marketing, and price.

b. What, based on the information provided, turned out to be the equilibrium of the game?

c. Can you think of reasons why the three consoles are so different?

18. Suppose that Firefox and Microsoft each develop their own versions of an amazing new Web browser that allows advertisers to target consumers with great precision. Also, the new browser is easier and more fun to use than existing browsers. Each firm is trying to decide whether to sell the browser or to give it away. What are the likely benefits from each action? Which action is likely to occur?

19. Study *Reading Between the Lines* on pp. 362–363 and then answer the following questions.

a. What were the strategies of Dell and HP in 2000 and in 2006?

b. Why, according to the news article, was Dell having a harder time in 2006 than it had in 2000?

c. Why wouldn't HP launch its new product and marketing campaign *and* cut its price?

d. What do you think Dell must do to restore its place as market leader?

e. How would you describe the global market for PCs? Is it an example of oligopoly or monopolistic competition?

20. Describe the game known as the prisoners' dilemma. In describing the game,

a. Make up a story that motivates the game.

b. Work out a payoff matrix.

c. Describe how the equilibrium of the game is arrived at.

21. Why do Coca-Cola and PepsiCo spend huge amounts on advertising? Do they benefit? Does the consumer benefit? Explain your answer by constructing a game to illustrate the choices Coca-Cola and PepsiCo make.

UNDERSTANDING FIRMS AND MARKETS

Managing Change and Limiting Market Power

Our economy is constantly changing. Every year, new goods appear and old ones disappear. New firms are born, and old ones die. This process of change is initiated and managed by firms operating in markets.

When a new product appears, just one or two firms sell it: Apple and IBM were the only producers of personal computers; Microsoft was (and almost still is) the only producer of the PC operating system; Intel was the only producer of the PC chip. These firms had enormous power to determine the quantity to produce and the price of their products.

In many markets, entry eventually brings competition. Even with just two rivals, the industry changes its face in a dramatic way. *Strategic interdependence* is capable of leading to an outcome like perfect competition.

With the continued arrival of new firms in an industry, the market becomes competitive. But in most markets, the competition isn't perfect: it becomes *monopolistic competition* with each firm selling its own differentiated product.

Often, an industry that is competitive becomes less so as the bigger and more successful firms in the industry begin to swallow up the smaller firms, either by driving them out of business or by acquiring their assets. Through this process, an industry might return to oligopoly or even monopoly. You can see such a movement in the auto and banking industries today.

By studying firms and markets, we gain a deeper understanding of the forces that allocate resources and begin to see the invisible hand at work.

John von Neumann *was one of the great minds of the twentieth century. Born in Budapest, Hungary, in 1903, Johnny, as he was known, showed early mathematical brilliance. He was 25 when he published the article that changed the social sciences and began a flood of research on game theory—a flood that has not subsided. In that article, von Neumann proved that in a zero-sum game (such as sharing a pie), there exists a best strategy for each player.*

Von Neumann did more than invent game theory: He also invented and built the first practical computer, and he worked on the Manhattan Project, which developed the atomic bomb during World War II.

Von Neumann believed that the social sciences would progress only if they used their own mathematical tools, not those of the physical sciences.

"Real life consists of bluffing, of little tactics of deception, of asking yourself what is the other man going to think I mean to do."

JOHN VON NEUMANN, told to Jacob Bronowski (in a London taxi) and reported in *The Ascent of Man*

TALKING
WITH

Drew Fudenberg

Drew Fudenberg is the Frederic E. Abbe Professor of Economics at Harvard University. Born in New York City in 1957, he studied applied mathematics at Harvard and economics at M.I.T., where he was awarded a Ph.D. in 1981. He began his research and teaching career at the University of California, Berkeley, and moved to M.I.T. in 1987 and to Harvard in 1993.

Professor Fudenberg is a leading game theorist and has worked on an incredibly wide range of problems that arise in games when players don't have enough information to play in the way they play the games that we describe in Chapter 15. This work has resulted in more than 60 articles and two major books: with Jean Tirole, *Game Theory* (MIT Press, 1991) and with David K. Levine, *The Theory of Learning in Games* (MIT Press, 1998).

Michael Parkin and Robin Bade talked with Drew Fudenberg about his career, the promise held by game theory, and some of the results of his research.

Professor Fudenberg, was math a better undergraduate major than economics for a career in economics?

Math is a good preparation for graduate study in economics, particularly for economic theory, in part because some of the results are useful but mostly because it provides good training in abstract thinking and rigorous arguments.

That said, I didn't major in math but in "applied math," which at Harvard is a fairly flexible program that includes physics, computer science, and an area of application of the student's choice in addition to math and applied math classes. As an undergraduate, I actually took as many economics classes as math and applied math classes combined. Looking back, given how my research interests have developed, I probably should have taken more math and probability classes than I did. But I did leave college with what is probably the most important math skill for an economist: the willingness to pick up a textbook to learn new tools as they are needed.

Why did you become an economist?

I really enjoyed my economics classes in college, and by taking some graduate classes as an undergraduate, I found that I'd be able to hold my own in graduate school. I was lucky to have inspirational teachers such as Ken Arrow, Howard Raiffa, and Michael Spence, and to have an advisor (Steven Shavell) who encouraged me to think about graduate study and to start reading journals as an undergraduate. By senior year, I had narrowed things down to either economics or law, and I chose economics that spring.

Principles of economics texts (including this one) introduce game theory as a tool for understanding the strategic behaviour of oligopolies. Can you provide some examples of the wider use of game theory?

Game theory is used in many areas of economics. It helps us to study the credibility of a central bank in its pursuit of anti-inflationary monetary policy, the dilemma faced by a government about whether to tax capital or renege on its debt, the negotiations between labour unions and management, the decisions of developing economies to nationalize foreign-owned assets, pretrial negotiations by lawyers, and lobbying by interest groups.

Game theory is also used outside economics. Political scientists use it to gain insights into arms races and other strategic decisions, and biologists use it to study the dynamics of the evolution and survival of species.

Some economists think that game theory is the only game worth playing. Others think that it has no empirical content. How would you explain the achievements and the promise of game theory to a beginning student?

The current state of game theory is far from perfect, but it does help us understand and make predictions about a very large and important set of situations. Everything in economics can be viewed as a game. There is no real gain from doing so in the case of single-agent decisions (where there are no other agents) or in the case of a perfectly competitive economy (where each agent cares only about the market price and his own decisions). But in all other cases, the only alternative to a game theoretic analysis seems to be no analysis at all.

Game theory has proved to be a useful way to think about qualitative issues like "how does repeated interaction help support cooperation" and "how might a dominant firm in a market with network externalities exploit its position," and it has long been used to motivate and explain the outcomes of games played in economics laboratory experiments.

It is more difficult to use game theory in econometric studies of field data, but there has been a lot of progress in this area in recent years, in part due to my colleagues Ariel Pakes and Susan Athey. (You can read about Susan Athey on p. 178.)

The germs of truth behind the "no empirical content" criticism are that (a) seemingly small changes in the specification of a game can sometimes lead to large changes in its set of equilibria and (b) even when we are pretty sure we know the game being played, the predictions can be less accurate than we'd like. Of course, these same complaints can be made about many fields, but I have to admit that both academic and real-world life would be simpler if these complaints weren't true.

> ... the only alternative to a game theoretic analysis seems to be no analysis at all.

In the games that you study, players have limited knowledge. How is it possible for economists to study games in which the players don't know the payoffs and can't predict the actions of the other players?

The standard Nash equilibrium solution concept says that each player's strategy is a best response to the strategies being used by the others. The concept itself says nothing about the players' knowledge of the game being played nor about when and how a play might come to resemble an equilibrium. In some games, careful reasoning by sophisticated players will lead them to play the equilibrium the very first time they are in the game.

But in game theory experiments it is more typical for play to start away from the equilibrium and then move towards it as the players acquire more experience with the game. This adjustment can be the result of learning by human subjects who know they are in a game, but that's not necessary: Nash equilibrium can also arise when the players are genetically programmed agents who don't think at all, as in the games played by genes that evolutionary biologists study.

So the fact that the agents don't know the game doesn't make game theory irrelevant. However, these adaptive processes take time, and in many settings, it is not clear whether one should expect observed play to approximate an equilibrium.

It is fairly easy to distinguish equilibrium and non-equilibrium play in the lab, where the experimenter controls the payoff, and more difficult to do so in field data where the payoffs are part of what is being estimated.

The empirical application of game theory has advanced a lot in recent years but has mostly maintained equilibrium as an assumption. Devising empirical tests for equilibrium is one of the leading open problems in applied game theory.

How does someone get a reputation and how does that help to get a better outcome? Does reputation always improve the outcome?

To get a reputation for "doing x," you simply have to do x every chance you get! This may have some short-run costs, but if you will be playing this game very often and are patient, it can be worth incurring the costs to build the reputation you want.

Conversely, a short-run player or an impatient player isn't willing to invest in a reputation. The simplest case is of a single long-run player facing one short-run player after another in sequence, with the two sides choosing their actions simultaneously each round and the actions being observed by all subsequent players. Here, the opportunity to build a reputation can't hurt the long-run player, and it typically helps. Things get more complicated if there are two or more long-run players each trying to build their own reputation or if the actions played in a round are sequential instead of simultaneous.

For example, it's hard to build the reputation of "doing x after your opponent does y," if your opponent never plays y!

One of your earliest papers has the intriguing title "The Fat-Cat Effect, the Puppy-Dog Ploy, and the Lean and Hungry Look." What did you study in this paper and what did you discover?

Earlier papers by Michael Spence and Avinash Dixit had shown how an incumbent firm might want to "overinvest" in capital to induce a subsequent ("second period") entrant to enter on a smaller scale. The logic of those papers was that by investing more in capital, the firm would lower its second-period cost of production, which would lead it to have higher second-period output, and that in turn would lead the entrant to produce less, which is to the incumbent's advantage.

Jean Tirole and I provided a systematic analysis and taxonomy of the way that an incumbent can alter its investment decisions to influence the behaviour of a potential entrant. We identified four possible strategies and then spent several weeks looking for good names for each of them.

Here is the list: The "top dog" strategy is the one studied by Spence and Dixit, namely the incumbent does extra investment to make itself big and tough. With product competition, this strategy both induces

> To get a reputation for "doing x," you simply have to do x every chance you get!

the entrant to produce less and makes it more likely to stay out, so it is a good strategy for both entry accommodation and entry deterrence.

The "fat cat" strategy is to do extra investment to make oneself fat and nonaggressive. This strategy is a good way to accommodate if nonaggressive play induces a favourable response from the entrant, but it is never a good way to deter entry.

The "puppy dog ploy" is more or less the reverse: underinvestment to be small and nonthreatening.

Finally, the "lean and hungry look" is staying lean and mean to intimidate rivals. This strategy turns out to apply when the first-period investment is in advertising as opposed to physical capital.

What advice do you have for someone who is just beginning to study economics? What other subjects do you think work well alongside economics? Do you have some reading suggestions?

I read Heilbronner's *The Worldly Philosophers* as part of my first economics class, and I still like it for an overview of the field. I also recommend the economic history of Douglas North, notably his *Structure and Change in Economic History*, and David S. Landes' *The Unbound Prometheus: Technological Change and Industrial Development in Western Europe from 1750 to the Present.*

I advise my students to regularly skim periodicals such as the *Economist*, the *Financial Times*, and the *Wall Street Journal* for interesting articles. As the students become more advanced, they should make an effort to regularly look at economics journals to see what current research looks like and whether any of the topics interest them.

In terms of coursework in other subjects, I advise students who are interested in graduate study in economics to learn math through an introduction to real analysis and to take one class each in probability and statistics. Some familiarity with computer programming is useful and can be acquired in or out of class. Beyond that, it comes down to the student's interests.

16 Externalities

After studying this chapter, you will be able to

- Explain how externalities arise

- Explain why negative externalities lead to inefficient over-production and how property rights, emission charges, marketable permits, and taxes can be used to achieve a more efficient outcome

- Explain why positive externalities lead to inefficient under-production and how public provision, subsidies, vouchers, and patents can increase economic efficiency

We burn huge quantities of fossil fuels—coal, gas, natural gas, and oil—that cause acid rain and global warming. We dump toxic waste into rivers, lakes, and oceans. These environmental issues are simultaneously everybody's problem and nobody's problem. How can we take account of the damage that we cause others every time we turn on our heating or air-conditioning systems?

Almost every day, we hear about a new discovery—in medicine, engineering, chemistry, physics, or even economics. The advance of knowledge seems boundless. Ever more people are learning more and more of what is already known. The stock of knowledge is increasing, apparently without limit. We are getting smarter. But are we getting smarter fast enough? Are we spending enough on research and education? Do enough people remain in school for long enough?

And do we work hard enough at school? Would we be better off if we spent more on research and education?

In this chapter, we study the problems that arise because many of our actions create externalities. They affect other people, for good or ill, in ways that we do not usually take into account when we make our own economic choices. We will focus on two big areas—pollution and knowledge—in which externalities are especially important. In *Reading Between the Lines* at the end of the chapter, we look at the effects of a carbon tax designed to lower carbon emissions and address global warming.

Externalities in Our Lives

An **externality** is a *cost* or a *benefit* that arises from *production* and falls on someone other than the producer, or a *cost* or *benefit* that arises from *consumption* and falls on someone other than the consumer. We call an externality that imposes a cost a **negative externality**, and we call an externality that provides a benefit a **positive externality**.

We identify externalities as four types:

- Negative production externalities
- Negative consumption externalities
- Positive production externalities
- Positive consumption externalities

Negative Production Externalities

Congestion, pollution, and carbon emission are the sources of the most costly and widespread negative production externalities.

Congestion Every weekday morning and afternoon, Highway 401, which runs across the north of Toronto, slows to a crawl as trucks and commuters compete for position on what looks like an extensive parking lot.

The costs of congestion are time costs and fuel costs. Drivers and their passengers spend extra hours sitting in stalled traffic, burning additional fuel. Each rush-hour user of Highway 401 imposes a cost on the other users. This cost is a negative production externality.

The economic analysis of externalities looks at alternative ways of dealing with problems such as the cost of congestion on Highway 401.

Pollution and Carbon Emission When you run your air conditioning, use hot water, drive a car, take a trip by airplane, or even ride a bus or train, your action contributes to pollution and increases your carbon footprint.

Economic activity pollutes air, water, and land, and these individual areas of pollution interact through the *ecosystem*.

Air Pollution Sixty percent of our air pollution comes from road transportation and industrial processes. Only 20 percent arises from electric power generation. See the trends in air pollution in the United States since 1980 below.

A common belief is that air pollution is getting worse. In many developing countries, air pollution *is* getting worse. The rapid economic development of

Trends in Air Pollution

Cleaner and Safer

The figure shows the trends in the concentrations of six air pollutants in the United States. Lead has been almost eliminated from our air. Sulphur dioxide, carbon monoxide, and suspended particulates have been reduced to around half of their 1980 levels. And even the more stubborn ozone and nitrogen dioxide have been reduced to around 70 percent of their 1980 levels.

These reductions in air pollution levels are even more impressive when they are seen against the trends in economic activity. Between 1980 and 2007, total production increased by 123 percent. During this same period, vehicle kilometres travelled increased by 90 percent, energy consumption rose by 82 percent, and the population increased by 35 percent. While all this economic activity was on the increase, air pollution from all sources *decreased* by more than 30 percent.

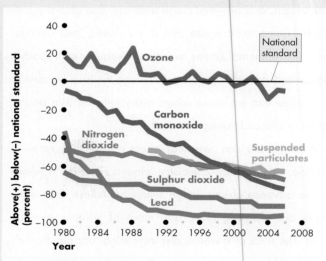

Six Sources of Air Pollution

Source of data: Latest Findings on National Air Quality: Status and Trends through 2006, United States Environmental Protection Agency, www.epa.gov/air/airtrends/2007/.

China has created a serious air quality problem for Beijing. During the 2008 Olympics, construction activity was halted and factories were closed in an attempt to provide temporary relief from air that would endanger the health of athletes.

But air pollution in the world's richest countries is getting less severe for most substances. Air pollution levels have been on a downward trend for more than 30 years.

In contrast to the trends in air pollution, carbon emissions and emissions of other global warming gases such as methane are on the increase, and consequently the carbon dioxide concentration in the Earth's atmosphere is increasing at an unprecedented pace.

The costs of air pollution and carbon emission are high and widespread. *Sulphur dioxide* and *nitrogen oxide* emissions from coal-fired and oil-fired generators of electric utilities cause *acid rain*, which damages trees and crops. Airborne substances such as lead from leaded gasoline are believed to cause cancer and other life-threatening conditions. Depletion of the *ozone layer* exposes us to higher doses of cancer-causing ultraviolet rays from the sun. And most costly of all, the increased carbon concentration is bringing global warming and potentially extremely costly climate change.

Some technological changes to cut costs, lessen air pollution, and slow the carbon buildup are possible either now or with further research and development.

Road vehicles can be made "greener" with new fuels including ethanol, alcohol, natural gas, propane and butane, and hydrogen. Vehicles can also be powered by electricity or batteries. But whether this change lessens air pollution and carbon emissions depends on how electricity is produced.

Global Temperature and CO_2 Trends
The Greatest Market Failure?

British economist Nicholas Stern prepared a major report on global warming and climate change for the United Kingdom government and his report, the Stern Review on the Economics of Climate Change, has attracted a great deal of attention. Stern calls climate change "the greatest market failure the world has ever seen." To avoid the risk of catastrophic damage from climate change, he says that greenhouse gas levels must be held at not more than 550 parts per million (ppm) of CO_2 (and its equivalent in other greenhouse gases). The level in 2007 was 430 ppm but it is rising at more than 2 ppm a year, so the world will reach the critical level by about 2070.

Global temperature and CO_2 trends are starkly opposite to those of air pollution, as the figure shows. Scientists debate the contribution of human economic activity to these trends but most say it is the major source. Although ice-core estimates show long swings in CO_2, there has never been a time when its concentration increased so rapidly.

To hold greenhouse gas levels at 550 ppm, emissions need to be cut to 75 percent or less of their current levels by 2050 and, eventually, cut to 20 percent of their current levels.

The cost of achieving these cuts is high. Stern's estimate is 1 percent of the value of global production. If this cost were to be met by the people who live in the rich countries, and realistically they are the only ones who could afford to pay, it would cost about $750 per person every year.

Global Warming Trends

Sources of data: Met Office Hadley Centre and Scripps Institution of Oceanography.

Some economists question Stern's assumptions and conclusions and argue that the cost of reducing emissions will be much lower if we go a bit more slowly and take advantage of future technological advances that will lower the cost of renewable energy sources—the sun, tide, and wind.

All economists agree that solving the global warming problem will require changes in the incentives that people face. The cost of carbon emitting activities must rise and the cost of the search for new energy technologies must fall.

Pollution-free electricity can be generated by harnessing wind power, solar power, tidal power, or geothermal power. Another alternative is nuclear power. This method is good for air pollution but creates a potential long-term problem for land and water pollution because there is no known entirely safe method of disposing of spent nuclear fuel.

Water Pollution The dumping of industrial waste and untreated sewage and the runoff from fertilizers pollute oceans, lakes, and rivers.

There are two main alternatives to polluting the waterways and oceans. One is the chemical processing of waste to render it inert or biodegradable. The other, in wide use for nuclear waste, is to use land sites for storage in secure containers.

Land Pollution Land pollution arises from dumping toxic waste products. Ordinary household garbage does not pose a pollution problem unless contaminants from dumped garbage seep into the water supply. Recycling is an apparently attractive alternative, but it requires an investment in new technologies to be effective. Incineration is a high-cost alternative to landfill, and it produces air pollution. Furthermore, these alternatives are not free, and they become efficient only when the cost of using landfill is high.

Negative Consumption Externalities

Negative consumption externalities are a source of irritation for most of us. Smoking tobacco in a confined space creates fumes that many people find unpleasant and that pose a health risk. Smoking creates a negative consumption externality. To deal with this externality, in many places and in almost all public places, smoking is banned. But banning smoking imposes a negative consumption externality on smokers! The majority imposes a cost on the minority—the smokers who would prefer to consume tobacco while dining or taking a plane trip.

Noisy parties and outdoor rock concerts are other examples of negative consumption externalities. They are also examples of the fact that a simple ban on an activity is not a solution. Banning noisy parties avoids the external cost on sleep-seeking neighbours, but it results in the sleepers imposing an external cost on the fun-seeking partygoers.

Permitting dandelions to grow in lawns, not picking up leaves in the fall, and allowing a dog to bark loudly or to foul a neighbour's lawn are other sources of negative consumption externalities.

Positive Production Externalities

If a honey farmer places beehives beside an orange grower's orchard, two positive production externalities arise. The honey farmer gets a positive production externality from the orange grower because the bees collect pollen and nectar from orange blossoms. And the orange grower gets a positive production externality because the bees pollinate the blossoms.

Positive Consumption Externalities

When you get a flu vaccination, you lower your risk of getting infected this winter. But if you avoid the flu, your neighbour who didn't get vaccinated has a better chance of avoiding it too. Flu vaccination generates positive consumption externalities.

When the owner of a historic building restores it, everyone who sees the building gets pleasure from it. Similarly, when someone erects a spectacular house—such as those built in Montreal's "Golden Square Mile" in the 1800s—or another exciting building—such as the CN Tower in Toronto—an external consumption benefit flows to everyone who has an opportunity to view it. Education, which we examine in this chapter, is another example of this type of externality.

Review Quiz

1 What are the four types of externality?
2 Give an example of each type of externality that is different from the ones described above.
3 How are the externalities that you've described addressed, either by the market or by public policy?

 Work Study Plan 16.1 and get instant feedback.

We've described the four types of externalities and provided some examples of each. Pollution is the most important of the negative externalities and it is this example that we use to study the economics of external costs.

Negative Externalities: Pollution

To study the economics of the negative externalities that arise from pollution, we distinguish between the private cost and the social cost of production.

Private Costs and Social Costs

A *private cost* of production is a cost that is borne by the producer of a good or service. *Marginal cost* is the cost of producing an *additional unit* of a good or service. So **marginal private cost** (*MC*) is the cost of producing an additional unit of a good or service that is borne by the producer of that good or service.

An *external cost* is a cost of producing a good or service that is *not* borne by the producer but borne by other people. A **marginal external cost** is the cost of producing an additional unit of a good or service that falls on people other than the producer.

Marginal social cost (*MSC*) is the marginal cost incurred by the producer and by everyone else on whom the cost falls—by society. It is the sum of marginal private cost and marginal external cost. That is,

$$MSC = MC + \text{Marginal external cost.}$$

We express costs in dollars, but we must always remember that a cost is an opportunity cost—something real, such as a clean river or clean air, is given up to get something.

Valuing an External Cost Economists use market prices to put a dollar value on the cost of pollution. For example, suppose that there are two similar rivers, one polluted and the other clean. Five hundred identical homes are built along the side of each river. The homes on the clean river rent for $2,500 a month, and those on the polluted river rent for $1,500 a month. If the pollution is the only detectable difference between the two rivers and the two locations, the rent decrease of $1,000 per month is the cost of the pollution. For the 500 homes on the polluted river, the external cost is $500,000 a month.

External Cost and Output Figure 16.1 shows an example of the relationship between output and cost in a chemical industry that pollutes. The marginal cost curve, *MC*, describes the marginal private cost borne by the firms that produce the chemical. Marginal cost increases as the quantity of chemical produced increases. If the firms dump waste into a river, they

impose an external cost that increases with the amount of the chemical produced. The marginal social cost curve, *MSC*, is the sum of marginal private cost and marginal external cost. For example, when output is 4,000 tonnes of chemical a month, marginal private cost is $100 a tonne, marginal external cost is $125 a tonne, and marginal social cost is $225 a tonne.

In Fig. 16.1, when the quantity of chemical produced increases, the amount of pollution increases and the marginal external cost of pollution increases.

Figure 16.1 shows the relationship between the quantity of chemical produced and the cost of the pollution it creates, but it doesn't tell us how much pollution gets created. That quantity depends on how the market for the chemical operates. First, we'll see what happens when the industry is free to pollute.

FIGURE 16.1 An External Cost

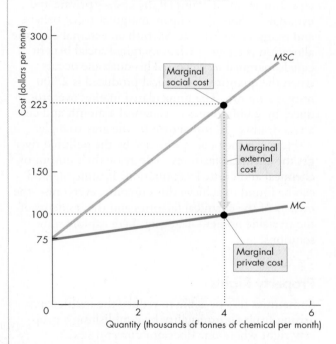

The *MC* curve shows the marginal private cost borne by the factories that produce a chemical. The *MSC* curve shows the sum of marginal private cost and marginal external cost. When output is 4,000 tonnes of chemical a month, marginal private cost is $100 a tonne, marginal external cost is $125 a tonne, and marginal social cost is $225 a tonne.

Production and Pollution: How Much?

When an industry is unregulated, the amount of pollution it creates depends on the market equilibrium price and quantity of the good produced. In Fig. 16.2, the demand curve for a pollution-creating chemical is *D*. This curve also measures the marginal social benefit, *MSB*, of the chemical. The supply curve is *S*. This curve also measures the producers' marginal private cost, *MC*. The supply curve is the marginal private cost curve because when firms make their production and supply decisions, they consider only the costs that they will bear. Market equilibrium occurs at a price of $100 a tonne and 4,000 tonnes of chemical a month.

This equilibrium is inefficient. You learned in Chapter 5 that the allocation of resources is efficient when marginal social benefit equals marginal social cost. But we must count all the costs—private and external—when we compare marginal social benefit and marginal social cost. So with an external cost, the allocation is efficient when marginal social benefit equals marginal *social* cost. This outcome occurs when the quantity of chemical produced is 2,000 tonnes a month. The unregulated market overproduces by 2,000 tonnes of chemical a month and creates a deadweight loss shown by the grey triangle.

How can the people who live by the polluted river get the chemical factories to decrease their output of chemical and create less pollution? If some method can be found to achieve this outcome, everyone—the owners of the chemical factories and the residents of the riverside homes—can gain. Let's explore some solutions.

Property Rights

Sometimes it is possible to reduce the inefficiency arising from an externality by establishing a property right where one does not currently exist. **Property rights** are legally established titles to the ownership, use, and disposal of factors of production and goods and services that are enforceable in the courts.

Suppose that the chemical factories own the river and the 500 homes alongside it. The rent that people are willing to pay depends on the amount of pollution. Using the earlier example, people are willing to pay $2,500 a month to live alongside a pollution-free river but only $1,500 a month to live with the pollution created by 4,000 tonnes of chemical a month. If

FIGURE 16.2   Inefficiency with an External Cost

The supply curve is the marginal private cost curve, *S* = *MC*. The demand curve is the marginal social benefit curve, *D* = *MSB*. Market equilibrium at a price of $100 a tonne and 4,000 tonnes a month is inefficient because marginal social cost exceeds marginal social benefit. The efficient quantity is 2,000 tonnes a month. The grey triangle shows the deadweight loss created by the pollution externality.

myeconlab   animation

the factories produce this quantity, they lose $1,000 a month for each home for a total of $500,000 a month. The chemical factories are now confronted with the cost of their pollution—forgone rent from the people who live by the river.

Figure 16.3 illustrates the outcome by using the same example as in Fig. 16.2. With property rights in place, the *MC* curve no longer measures all the costs that the factories face in producing the chemical. It excludes the pollution costs that they must now bear. The *MSC* curve now becomes the marginal private cost curve *MC*. All the costs fall on the factories, so the market supply curve is based on all the marginal costs and is the curve labelled *S* = *MC* = *MSC*.

Market equilibrium now occurs at a price of $150 a tonne and 2,000 tonnes of chemical a month. This outcome is efficient. The factories still produce some pollution, but it is the efficient quantity.

FIGURE 16.3 Property Rights Achieve an Efficient Outcome

With property rights, the marginal cost curve that excludes pollution costs shows only part of the producers' marginal cost. The marginal private cost curve includes the cost of pollution, so the supply curve is $S = MC = MSC$. Market equilibrium is at a price of $150 a tonne and 2,000 tonnes of chemical a month and is efficient because marginal social cost equals marginal social benefit. The efficient quantity of pollution is not zero.

The Coase Theorem

Does it matter how property rights are assigned? Does it matter whether the polluter or the victim of the pollution owns the resource that might be polluted? Until 1960, everyone thought that it did matter. But in 1960, Ronald Coase (see p. 413) had a remarkable insight, now called the Coase theorem.

The **Coase theorem** is the proposition that if property rights exist, if only a small number of parties are involved, and if transactions costs are low, then private transactions are efficient. There are no externalities because the transacting parties take all the costs and benefits into account. Furthermore, it doesn't matter who has the property rights.

Application of the Coase Theorem In the example that we've just studied, the factories own the river and the homes. Suppose that instead, the residents own their homes and the river. Now the factories must pay a fee to the homeowners for the right to dump their waste. The greater the quantity of waste dumped into the river, the more the factories must pay. So again, the factories face the opportunity cost of the pollution they create. The quantity of chemical produced and the amount of waste dumped are the same whoever owns the homes and the river. If the factories own them, they bear the cost of pollution because they receive a lower income from home rents. And if the residents own the homes and the river, the factories bear the cost of pollution because they must pay a fee to the homeowners. In both cases, the factories bear the cost of their pollution and dump the efficient amount of waste into the river.

The Coase solution works only when transactions costs are low. **Transactions costs** are the opportunity costs of conducting a transaction. For example, when you buy a house, you incur a series of transactions costs. You might pay a real estate agent to help you find the best place and a lawyer to run checks that assure you that the seller owns the property and that after you've paid for it, the ownership has been properly transferred to you.

In the example of the homes alongside a river, the transactions costs that are incurred by a small number of chemical factories and a few homeowners might be low enough to enable them to negotiate the deals that produce an efficient outcome. But in many situations, transactions costs are so high that it would be inefficient to incur them. In these situations, the Coase solution is not available.

Suppose, for example, that everyone owns the airspace above their homes up to, say, 10 miles. If someone pollutes your airspace, you can charge a fee. But to collect the fee, you must identify who is polluting your airspace and persuade them to pay you. Imagine the costs of negotiating and enforcing agreements with the 300 million people who live in Canada and the United States and the several thousand factories that emit sulphur dioxide and create acid rain that falls on your property! In this situation, we use public choices to cope with externalities. But the transactions costs that block a market solution are real costs, so attempts by the government to deal with externalities offer no easy solution. Let's look at some of these attempts.

Government Actions in the Face of External Costs

The three main methods that governments use to cope with externalities are

- Taxes
- Emission charges
- Marketable permits

Taxes The government can use taxes as an incentive for producers to cut back on pollution. Taxes used in this way are called **Pigovian taxes**, in honour of Arthur Cecil Pigou, the British economist who first worked out this method of dealing with externalities during the 1920s.

By setting the tax equal to the marginal external cost, firms can be made to behave in the same way as they would if they bore the cost of the externality directly. To see how government actions can change market outcomes in the face of externalities, let's return to the example of the chemical factories and the river.

Assume that the government has assessed the marginal external cost accurately and imposes a tax on the factories that exactly equals this cost. Figure 16.4 illustrates the effects of this tax.

The demand curve and marginal social benefit curve, $D = MSB$, and the firms' marginal cost curve, MC, are the same as in Fig. 16.2. The pollution tax equals the marginal external cost of the pollution. We add this tax to the marginal private cost to find the market supply curve. This curve is the one labelled $S = MC + tax = MSC$. This curve is the market supply curve because it tells us the quantity supplied at each price given the firms' marginal cost and the tax they must pay. This curve is also the marginal social cost curve because the pollution tax has been set equal to the marginal external cost.

Demand and supply now determine the market equilibrium price at $150 a tonne and a quantity of 2,000 tonnes of chemical a month. At this quantity of chemical, the marginal social cost is $150 a tonne and the marginal social benefit is $150 a tonne, so the outcome is efficient. Firms incur a marginal cost of $88 a tonne and pay a tax of $62 a tonne. The government's tax revenue is $124,000 a month.

Emission Charges Emission charges are an alternative to a tax for confronting a polluter with the external cost of pollution. The government sets a price per unit of pollution. The more pollution a firm creates,

FIGURE 16.4 A Pollution Tax to Achieve an Efficient Outcome

A pollution tax is imposed equal to the marginal external cost of pollution. The supply curve becomes the marginal private cost curve, MC, plus the tax—$S = MC + tax$. Market equilibrium is at a price of $150 a tonne and 2,000 tonnes of chemical a month and is efficient because marginal social cost equals marginal social benefit. The government collects a tax revenue shown by the purple rectangle.

the more it pays in emission charges. This method of dealing with pollution externalities has been used only modestly in North America but is common in Europe, where, for example, France, Germany, and the Netherlands make water polluters pay a waste disposal charge.

To work out the emission charge that achieves efficiency, the government needs a lot of information about the polluting industry that, in practice, is rarely available.

Marketable Permits Instead of taxing or imposing emission charges on polluters, each potential polluter might be assigned a permitted pollution limit. Each firm knows its own costs and benefits of pollution, and making pollution limits marketable is a clever way of using this private information that is unknown to the government. The government issues each firm a permit to emit a certain amount of pollution, and firms can buy and sell these permits. Firms that have a low marginal cost of reducing pollution sell their permits, and firms that have a high marginal cost of reducing pollution buy permits. The market in permits determines the price at which firms trade permits. Each firm buys or sells permits until its marginal cost of pollution equals the market price of a permit.

This method of dealing with pollution provides an even stronger incentive than emission charges to find lower-polluting technologies because the price of a permit to pollute rises as the demand for permits increases.

A Real-World Market for Emission Permits

Environment Canada has not used marketable permits, but the Environmental Protection Agency (EPA) in the United States has. The EPA first implemented air quality programs following the passage of the Clean Air Act in 1970.

Trading in lead pollution permits became common during the 1980s, and this marketable permit program has been rated a success. It enabled lead to be virtually eliminated from the atmosphere. But this success might not easily translate to other situations because lead pollution has some special features. First, most lead pollution came from a single source: leaded gasoline. Second, lead in gasoline is easily monitored. Third, the objective was clear: to eliminate lead in gasoline. The EPA is now considering using marketable permits to promote efficiency in the control of chlorofluorocarbons—the gases that are believed to damage the ozone layer.

Review Quiz

1 What is the distinction between private cost and social cost?

2 How does a negative externality prevent a competitive market from using resources efficiently?

3 How can a negative externality be eliminated by assigning property rights? How does this method of coping with an externality work?

4 How do taxes help us to cope with negative externalities? Can a pollution tax induce firms to produce the efficient quantity of pollution?

5 How do emission charges and marketable permits work?

 Work Study Plan 16.2 and get instant feedback.

Positive Externalities: Knowledge

Knowledge comes from education and research. To study the economics of knowledge, we distinguish between private benefits and social benefits.

Private Benefits and Social Benefits

A *private benefit* is a benefit that the consumer of a good or service receives. *Marginal benefit* is the benefit from an *additional unit* of a good or service. So a **marginal private benefit** (*MB*) is the benefit from an additional unit of a good or service that the consumer of that good or service receives.

The *external benefit* from a good or service is the benefit that someone other than the consumer receives. A **marginal external benefit** is the benefit from an additional unit of a good or service that people other than the consumer enjoy.

Marginal social benefit (*MSB*) is the marginal benefit enjoyed by society—by the consumer of a good or service (marginal private benefit) plus the marginal benefit enjoyed by others (the marginal external benefit). That is,

$$MSB = MB + \text{Marginal external benefit.}$$

Figure 16.5 shows an example of the relationship between marginal private benefit, marginal external benefit, and marginal social benefit. The marginal benefit curve, *MB*, describes the marginal private benefit—such as expanded job opportunities and higher incomes—enjoyed by college graduates. Marginal private benefit decreases as the quantity of education increases.

But college graduates generate external benefits. On the average, they tend to be better citizens. Their crime rates are lower, and they are more tolerant of the views of others. A society with a large number of college graduates can support activities such as high-quality newspapers and television channels, music, theatre, and other organized social activities.

In the example in Fig. 16.5, the marginal external benefit is $15,000 per student per year when 15 million students enroll in college. The marginal social benefit curve, *MSB*, is the sum of marginal private benefit and marginal external benefit. For example, when 15 million students a year enroll in college, the marginal private benefit is $10,000 per student and the marginal external benefit is $15,000 per student, so the marginal social benefit is $25,000 per student.

FIGURE 16.5   An External Benefit

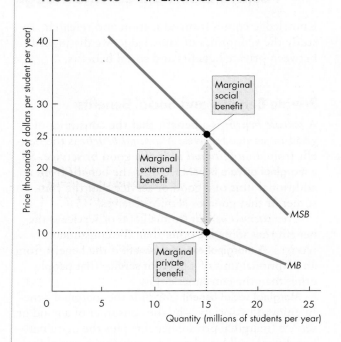

The *MB* curve shows the marginal private benefit enjoyed by the people who receive a college education. The *MSB* curve shows the sum of marginal private benefit and marginal external benefit. When 15 million students attend college, marginal private benefit is $10,000 per student, marginal external benefit is $15,000 per student, and marginal social benefit is $25,000 per student.

myeconlab animation

FIGURE 16.6 Inefficiency with an External Benefit

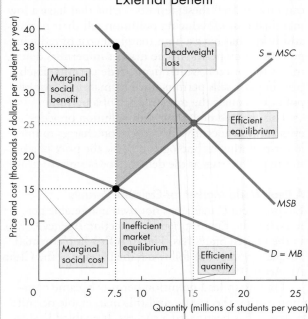

The market demand curve is the marginal private benefit curve, *D = MB*. The supply curve is the marginal social cost curve, *S = MSC*. Market equilibrium at a tuition of $15,000 a year and 7.5 million students is inefficient because marginal social benefit exceeds marginal social cost. The efficient quantity is 15 million students. A deadweight loss arises (grey triangle) because too few students enroll in college.

myeconlab animation

When people make schooling decisions, they ignore its external benefits and consider only its private benefits. So if education were provided by private schools that charged full-cost tuition, we would produce too few college graduates.

Figure 16.6 illustrates the underproduction that would exist if the government left education to the private market. The supply curve is the marginal social cost curve, *S = MSC*. The demand curve is the marginal private benefit curve, *D = MB*. Market equilibrium occurs at a tuition of $15,000 per student per year and 7.5 million students per year. At this equilibrium, marginal social benefit is $38,000 per student, which exceeds marginal social cost by $23,000. There are too few students in college. The efficient number is 15 million per year, where marginal

social benefit equals marginal social cost. The grey triangle shows the deadweight loss.

Underproduction similar to that in Fig. 16.6 would occur in grade school and high school if public education was left to an unregulated market. When children learn basic reading, writing, and number skills, they receive the private benefit of increased earning power. But even these basic skills bring the external benefit of developing better citizens.

External benefits also arise from the discovery of new knowledge. When Isaac Newton worked out the formulas for calculating the rate of response of one variable to another—calculus—everyone was free to use his method. When a spreadsheet program called VisiCalc was invented, Lotus Corporation and Microsoft were free to copy the basic idea and create

1-2-3 and Excel. When the first shopping mall was built and found to be a successful way of arranging retailing, everyone was free to copy the idea, and malls sprouted like mushrooms.

Once someone has discovered a basic idea, others can copy it. Because they do have to work to copy an idea, they face an opportunity cost, but they do not usually have to pay a fee for the idea. When people make decisions, they ignore the external benefits and consider only the private benefits.

When people make decisions about the amount of education or research to undertake, they balance the marginal private cost against the marginal private benefit. They ignore the external benefit. As a result, if we left education and research to unregulated market forces, we would get too little of these activities.

To get closer to producing the efficient quantity of a good or service that generates an external benefit, we make public choices, through governments, to modify the market outcome.

Government Actions in the Face of External Benefits

Four devices that governments can use to achieve a more efficient allocation of resources in the presence of external benefits are

- Public provision
- Private subsidies
- Vouchers
- Patents and copyrights

Public Provision Under **public provision**, a public authority that receives its revenue from the government produces the good or service. The education services produced by public universities, colleges, and schools are examples of public provision.

Figure 16.7(a) shows how public provision might overcome the underproduction that arises in Fig. 16.6.

FIGURE 16.7 Public Provision or Private Subsidy to Achieve an Efficient Outcome

(a) Public provision

(b) Private subsidy

In part (a), marginal social benefit equals marginal social cost with 15 million students per year, the efficient quantity. Tuition is set at $10,000 per student equal to marginal private benefit. Taxpayers cover the other $15,000 of cost per student.

In part (b), with a subsidy of $15,000 per student, the supply curve is $S_1 = MSC - subsidy$. The equilibrium price is $10,000, and the market equilibrium is efficient with 15 million students per year. Marginal social benefit equals marginal social cost.

myeconlab animation

Public provision cannot lower the cost of production, so marginal social cost is the same as before. Marginal private benefit and marginal external benefit are also the same as before.

The efficient quantity occurs where marginal social benefit equals marginal social cost. In Fig. 16.7(a), this quantity is 15 million students. Tuition is set to ensure that the efficient number of students enrolls. That is, tuition is set equal to the marginal private benefit at the efficient quantity. In Fig. 16.7(a), tuition is $10,000 a year. The rest of the cost of the public university is borne by the taxpayers and, in this example, is $15,000 per student per year.

Private Subsidies A **subsidy** is a payment that the government makes to private producers. By making the subsidy depend on the level of output, the government can induce private decision makers to consider external benefits when they make their choices.

Figure 16.7(b) shows how a subsidy to private colleges works. In the absence of a subsidy, the market supply curve is $S_0 = MSC$. The demand curve is the marginal private benefit curve, $D = MB$. If the government provides a subsidy to colleges of $15,000 per student per year, we must subtract the subsidy from the college's marginal cost to find the new market supply curve. That curve is $S_1 = MSC - subsidy$. The market equilibrium is tuition of $10,000 a year and 15 million students a year. The marginal social cost of educating 15 million students is $25,000 and the marginal social benefit is $25,000. So with marginal social cost equal to marginal social benefit, the subsidy has achieved an efficient outcome. The tuition and the subsidy just cover the colleges' marginal cost.

Vouchers A **voucher** is a token that the government provides to households, which they can use to buy specified goods or services. Milton Friedman, recipient of the 1976 Nobel Prize for Economic Science, long advocated vouchers as a means of providing parents with greater choice and control over the education of their children. Some people advocate them for college and university so that students can both receive financial help and exercise choice.

A school voucher allows parents to choose the school their children will attend and to use the voucher to pay part of the cost. The school cashes the vouchers to pay its bills. A voucher provided to a university student would work in a similar way. Because vouchers can be spent only on a specified item, they increase the willingness to pay for that item and so increase the demand for it.

FIGURE 16.8 Vouchers Achieve an Efficient Outcome

With vouchers, buyers are willing to pay MB plus the value of the voucher, so the demand curve becomes the marginal social benefit curve, D = MSB. Market equilibrium is efficient with 15 million students enrolled in college because price, marginal social benefit, and marginal social cost are equal. The tuition consists of the dollar price of $10,000 and a voucher valued at $15,000.

myeconlab animation

Figure 16.8 shows how a voucher system works. The government provides a voucher per student equal to the marginal external benefit. Parents (or students) use these vouchers to supplement the dollars they pay for education. The marginal social benefit curve becomes the demand for college education, $D = MSB$. The market equilibrium occurs at a price of $25,000 per student per year, and 15 million students attend college. Each student pays $10,000 tuition, and schools collect an additional $15,000 per student from the voucher.

If the government estimates the value of the external benefit correctly and makes the value of the voucher equal the marginal external benefit, the outcome from the voucher scheme is efficient. Marginal social cost equals marginal social benefit, and the deadweight loss is eliminated.

Vouchers are similar to subsidies, but their advocates say that they are more efficient than subsidies because the consumer can monitor school performance more effectively than the government can.

Patents and Copyrights   Knowledge might be an exception to the principle of diminishing marginal benefit. Additional knowledge (about the right things) makes people more productive. And there seems to be no tendency for the additional productivity from additional knowledge to diminish.

For example, in just 15 years, advances in knowledge about microprocessors have given us a sequence of processor chips that has made our personal computers increasingly powerful. Each advance in knowledge about how to design and manufacture a processor chip has brought ever larger increments in performance and productivity. Similarly, each advance in knowledge about how to design and build an airplane has brought apparently ever larger increments in performance: Orville and Wilbur Wright's 1903 Flyer was a one-seat plane that could hop a farmer's field. The Lockheed Constellation, designed in 1949, was an airplane that could fly 120 passengers from New York to London, but with two refueling stops in Newfoundland and Ireland. The latest Boeing 747 can carry 400 people nonstop from Singapore to New York (flights of 15,325 kilometres that take 20 hours). Similar examples can be found in agriculture, biogenetics, communications, engineering, entertainment, and medicine.

One reason why the stock of knowledge increases without diminishing returns is the sheer number of different techniques that can in principle be tried. Paul Romer, an economist at Stanford University, explains this fact. "Suppose that to make a finished good, 20 different parts have to be attached to a frame, one at a time. A worker could proceed in numerical order, attaching part one first, then part two. ... Or the worker could proceed in some other order, starting with part 10, then adding part seven. ... With 20 parts, ... there are [more] different sequences ... than the total number of seconds that have elapsed since the big bang created the universe, so we can be confident that in all activities, only a very small fraction of the possible sequences have ever been tried."[1]

Think about all the processes, all the products, and all the different bits and pieces that go into each, and you can see that we have only begun to scratch the surface of what is possible.

Because knowledge is productive and generates external benefits, it is necessary to use public policies to ensure that those who develop new ideas have incentives to encourage an efficient level of effort. The main way of providing the right incentives uses the central idea of the Coase theorem and assigns property rights—called **intellectual property rights**—to creators. The legal device for establishing intellectual property rights is the patent or copyright. A **patent** or **copyright** is a government-sanctioned exclusive right granted to the inventor of a good, service, or productive process to produce, use, and sell the invention for a given number of years. A patent enables the developer of a new idea to prevent others from benefiting freely from an invention for a limited number of years.

Although patents encourage invention and innovation, they do so at an economic cost. While a patent is in place, its holder has a monopoly. And monopoly is another source of inefficiency (which is explained in Chapter 13). But without a patent, the effort to develop new goods, services, or processes is diminished and the flow of new inventions is slowed. So the efficient outcome is a compromise that balances the benefits of more inventions against the cost of temporary monopoly in newly invented activities.

Review Quiz

1 What is special about knowledge that creates external benefits?

2 How might governments use public provision, private subsidies, and vouchers to achieve an efficient amount of education?

3 How might governments use public provision, private subsidies, vouchers, and patents and copyrights to achieve an efficient amount of research and development?

 Work Study Plan 16.3 and get instant feedback.

---

[1] Paul Romer, "Ideas and Things," in *The Future Surveyed*, supplement to the *Economist*, September 11, 1993, pp. 71–72.

◆ *Reading Between the Lines* on pp. 386–387 looks at the effects of a carbon tax and solar subsidy to reduce greenhouse gas emissions.

Fighting Carbon Emissions with a Carbon Tax and Solar Subsidy

On Carbon, Tax and Don't Spend

March 25, 2008

... a carbon tax isn't a new idea. Denmark, Finland, Norway and Sweden have had carbon taxes in place since the 1990s, but the tax has not led to large declines in emissions in most of these countries—in the case of Norway, emissions have actually increased by 43 percent per capita. ...

The one country in which carbon taxes have led to a large decrease in emissions is Denmark. ... What did Denmark do right? ...

Denmark avoids the temptation to maximize the tax revenue by giving the proceeds back to industry, earmarking much of it to subsidize environmental innovation. Danish firms are pushed away from carbon and pulled into environmental innovation, and the country's economy isn't put at a competitive disadvantage. So this is lesson No. 1 from Denmark.

The second lesson is that the carbon tax worked in Denmark because it was easy for Danish firms to switch to cleaner fuels. Danish policy makers made huge investments in renewable energy and subsidized environmental innovation. Denmark back then was more reliant on coal than the other three countries were (but not more so than the United States is today), so when the tax gave companies a reason to leave coal and the investments in renewable energy gave them an easy way to do so, they switched. The key was providing easy substitutes. ...

An increase in gasoline taxes ... would ... be the wrong policy. ... Higher gas taxes would raise revenue but do little to curb pollution.

Instead, if we want to reduce carbon emissions, then we should follow Denmark's example: tax the industrial emission of carbon and return the revenue to industry through subsidies for research and investment in alternative energy sources, cleaner-burning fuel, carbon-capture technologies and other environmental innovations.

Essence of the Story

- Denmark, Finland, Norway, and Sweden have had carbon taxes since the 1990s.

- Emissions increased in Norway, changed little in Finland and Sweden, and decreased in Denmark.

- Denmark used the carbon tax revenues to make it easy for power utilities to switch from coal.

- A gas tax increase would raise revenue but not curb pollution.

- North America should follow Denmark's example.

Economic Analysis

- Figure 1 illustrates why, as the article states, a carbon tax on gasoline would do little to curb pollution.

- The demand for gasoline in the short run, D_{SR}, is inelastic. If the Canadian gas price was raised (by a carbon tax) to the European level, gasoline consumption would decrease by very little.

- The demand for gasoline in the long run, D_{LR}, is elastic, so consumption might fall to the European level eventually, but it would take many years.

- Figure 2 illustrates why a carbon tax that is spent on subsidies to clean fuel cuts pollution.

- Figure 2(a) shows the costs of producing electricity using coal, which has an external cost: MSC exceeds MC. Figure 2(b) shows the cost using solar power, which has no external cost: $MC = MSC$.

- Assume that the marginal social cost of producing electricity equals the marginal benefit of electricity at 30 cents per kilowatt hour (kWh) and that the market price of electricity is also 30 cents per kWh.

- In Fig.2(a), a carbon tax equal to the marginal external cost raises the producer's marginal cost to equal the marginal social cost.

- With no subsidy for solar, a coal-fired power station continues to operate and produce 5 megawatt hours (MWh).

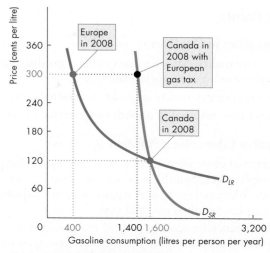

Figure 1 A carbon tax on gasoline

- But with a carbon tax and a solar subsidy, the marginal coal-fired power station shuts down and switches to solar power. As the article says, the subsidy makes fuel substitution easy for the producer.

- The combination of the tax and subsidy is *inefficient*. Electricity is now being produced by solar power at a marginal social cost of 50 cents per kWh instead of the efficient 30 cents per kWh using coal.

(a) Coal generation

(b) Solar generation

Figure 2 Using carbon tax to subsidize alternative fuels

387

SUMMARY

Key Points

Externalities in Our Lives (p. 374–376)

- An externality can arise from either a production activity or a consumption activity.
- A negative externality imposes an external cost.
- A positive externality provides an external benefit.

Negative Externalities: Pollution (pp. 377–381)

- External costs are costs of production that fall on people other than the producer of a good or service. Marginal social cost equals marginal private cost plus marginal external cost.
- Producers take account only of marginal private cost and produce more than the efficient quantity when there is a marginal external cost.
- Sometimes it is possible to overcome a negative externality by assigning a property right.
- When property rights cannot be assigned, governments might overcome externalities by using taxes, emission charges, or marketable permits.

Positive Externalities: Knowledge (pp. 381–385)

- External benefits are benefits that are received by people other than the consumer of a good or service. Marginal social benefit equals marginal private benefit plus marginal external benefit.
- External benefits from education arise because better-educated people tend to be better citizens, commit fewer crimes, and support social activities.
- External benefits from research arise because once someone has worked out a basic idea, others can copy it.
- Vouchers or subsidies to schools or the provision of public education below cost can achieve a more efficient provision of education.
- Patents and copyrights create intellectual property rights and an incentive to innovate. But they do so by creating a temporary monopoly, the cost of which must be balanced against the benefit of more inventive activity.

Key Figures

Figure 16.2   Inefficiency with an External Cost, 378
Figure 16.3   Property Rights Achieve an Efficient Outcome, 379
Figure 16.4   A Pollution Tax to Achieve an Efficient Outcome, 380

Figure 16.6   Inefficiency with an External Benefit, 382
Figure 16.7   Public Provision or Private Subsidy to Achieve an Efficient Outcome, 383
Figure 16.8   Vouchers Achieve an Efficient Outcome, 384

Key Terms

Coase theorem, 379
Copyright, 385
Externality, 374
Intellectual property rights, 385
Marginal external benefit, 381
Marginal external cost, 377
Marginal private benefit, 381

Marginal private cost, 377
Marginal social benefit, 381
Marginal social cost, 377
Negative externality, 374
Patent, 385
Pigovian taxes, 380
Positive externality, 374

Property rights, 378
Public provision, 383
Subsidy, 384
Transactions costs, 379
Voucher, 384

PROBLEMS and APPLICATIONS

 Work problems 1–8 in Chapter 16 Study Plan and get instant feedback.
Work problems 9–16 as Homework, a Quiz, or a Test if assigned by your instructor.

1. Consider each of the following activities or events and say for each one whether it is an externality. If so, say whether it is a positive or negative production or consumption externality.
   - Airplanes take off from Pearson International Airport during the Canadian Open tennis tournament, which is taking place nearby.
   - The sun sets over the Pacific Ocean.
   - The number of people who are studying for graduate degrees increases.
   - A person wears strong perfume while attending an orchestra concert.
   - A homeowner plants an attractive garden in front of his house.
   - A person drives while talking on a cell phone.
   - A bakery bakes bread.

2. The table provides information about costs and benefits that arise from the pesticide production that pollutes a lake used by a trout farmer.

Output of pesticide (tonnes per week)	Marginal cost	Marginal external cost	Marginal social benefit
		(dollars per tonne)	
0	0	0	250
1	5	33	205
2	15	67	165
3	30	100	130
4	50	133	100
5	75	167	75
6	105	200	55
7	140	233	40

   a. If no one owns the lake and if there is no regulation of pollution, what is the quantity of pesticide produced and what is the marginal cost of pollution borne by the trout farmer?
   b. If the trout farm owns the lake, how much pesticide is produced and what does the pesticide producer pay the farmer per tonne?
   c. If the pesticide producer owns the lake, and if a pollution-free lake rents for $1,000 a week, how much pesticide is produced and how much rent does the farmer pay the factory for the use of the lake?

   d. Compare the quantities of pesticide produced in b and c and explain the relationship between these quantities.

3. Back at the pesticide plant and trout farm described in problem 2, suppose that no one owns the lake and that the government introduces a pollution tax.

   a. What is the tax per tonne of pesticide produced that achieves an efficient outcome?
   b. Explain the connection between your answer to a and the answer to problem 2a.

4. Using the information provided in problem 2, suppose that no one owns the lake and that the government issues three marketable pollution permits, two to the farmer and one to the factory. Each permit allows the same amount of pollution of the lake, and the total amount of pollution is the efficient amount.

   a. What is the quantity of pesticide produced?
   b. What is the market price of a pollution permit? Who buys and who sells a permit?
   c. What is the connection between your answer and the answers to problems 2a and 3a?

5. The marginal cost of educating a student is $4,000 a year and is constant. The figure shows the marginal private benefit curve.

   a. With no government involvement and if the schools are competitive, how many students are enrolled and what is the tuition?

b. The external benefit from education is $2,000 per student per year and is constant. If the government provides the efficient amount of education, how many students will be accepted and what is the tuition?

6. **Waste Plan Pits City Against Industry**

A battle is brewing between the city of Toronto and the city's coffee shops. Not to mention the interest groups behind plastic water bottles, taxpayer rights and restaurants.

With this week's release of Toronto's report on in-store packaging—targeting disposable coffee cups, takeout food containers, water bottles and plastic bags. ...

"They (the industry) don't want to change," said Councillor Glenn De Baeremaeker, chair of the city works committee, who is pushing to make companies responsible for the packaging they create. ...

[The report recommended] banning non-recyclable coffee cups and bags as of Dec. 31, 2009. Giving customers who use their own coffee cups a 20-cent discount. Currently, Ontario's largest coffee chain, Tim Hortons, provides a 10-cent discount. ... Banning sales of bottled water ... at all city facilities by Dec. 31, 2011.

TheStar.com, November 6, 2008

a. Describe the externality that arises from plastic containers and bags.
b. Draw a graph to illustrate how plastic containers and bags create deadweight loss.
c. Explain the effects of a policy to ban the sale of plastic bottles and show in a graph the change in the deadweight loss that would arise.
d. Explain why a complete ban on plastic containers and bags might be inefficient.
e. Explain the effects on the use of plastic containers of Toronto's suggested policy of making manufacturers pay for recycling.

7. **US–Canada Propose Carbon Cutting Trade Plan**

Seven Western U.S. states and four Canadian provinces on Tuesday recommended a regional cap-and-trade program allowing offset credit trading in a plan designed to reduce global warming pollution by 15 percent from 2005 levels by 2020.

... The plan would allow up to 49 percent of emissions cuts through financing green efforts such as planting forests. ... The program seeks to set mandatory and "enforceable" limits on greenhouse gas emissions, the value for which will be determined by a market of trading them. ... The plan ...will help foster lower energy use through efficiency and using cleaner technologies. ... Each state could give allowances to entities that emit greenhouse gases or auction the allowances, or a combination of the two. The recommendations call for an auction level of at least 10 percent at the start and at least 25 percent by 2020. ...

Reuters, September 23, 2008

a. What will determine the cap and how will the auction of allowances bring about the planned decrease in pollution?
b. What incentives might be used to get companies that pollute to plant trees?
c. Explain how the plan might improve the efficiency of the use of cleaner technologies.

8. **The Case for School Choice**

School-choice policies in the United States, New Zealand, Denmark, and Sweden offer valuable lessons for the reform of education policy. They demonstrate the role competitive markets and parental choice play in the improvement both of student achievement and of parental satisfaction with the education system. Private vouchers could pave the way for education reform. ... The private voucher programs ... have demonstrated both the benefits of school choice for students and the demand for school choice from parents. ... Although the private sector is unlikely to commit enough resources to provide wide-spread school choice to Canadian children, a private voucher movement could prepare the way for broad-scale reform of public education.

Fraser Institute, September 20, 1999

a. Describe the private benefits and external benefits of parental school choice.
b. Explain why a market with private vouchers and parental choice would produce an efficient outcome.
c. Draw a graph to illustrate a market for education without school vouchers and no parental choice. Indicate the deadweight loss.
d. Explain how school vouchers and parental choice could achieve a better quality of education.

9. The figure illustrates the unregulated market for a pesticide. When factories produce pesticide, they also create waste, which they dump into a lake on the outskirts of the town. The marginal external cost of the dumped waste is equal to the marginal private cost of producing the pesticide (that is, the marginal social cost of producing the pesticide is double the marginal private cost).

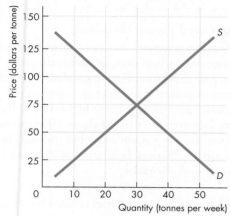

a. What is the quantity of pesticide produced if no one owns the lake and what is the efficient quantity of pesticide?
b. If the residents of the town own the lake, what is the quantity of pesticide produced and how much do residents of the town charge the factories to dump waste?
c. If the pesticide factories own the lake, how much pesticide is produced?
d. If no one owns the lake and the government levies a pollution tax, what is the tax that achieves the efficient outcome?

10. Betty and Anna work at the same office in Calgary. They both must attend a meeting in Edmonton, so they decide to drive to the meeting together. Betty is a cigarette smoker and her marginal benefit from smoking a package of cigarettes a day is $40. Cigarettes are $6 a pack. Anna dislikes cigarette smoke, and her marginal benefit from a smoke-free environment is $50 a day. What is the outcome if
a. Betty drives her car with Anna as a passenger?
b. Anna drives her car with Betty as a passenger?

11. The first two columns of the table show the demand schedule for electricity from a coal-burning utility; the second and third columns show the utility's cost of producing electricity.

Price (cents per kilowatt)	Quantity (kilowatts per day)	Marginal cost (cents per kilowatt)
4	500	10
8	400	8
12	300	6
16	200	4
20	100	2

Assume that the marginal external cost of the pollution created is equal to the marginal cost.

a. With no pollution control, what is the quantity of electricity produced, the price of electricity, and the marginal external cost of the pollution generated?
b. With no pollution control, what is the marginal social cost of the electricity generated and the deadweight loss?
c. Suppose that the government levies a pollution tax, such that the utility produces the efficient quantity. What are the price of electricity, the tax, and the tax revenue per day?

12. **China Vows to Clean Up Polluted Lake**
... Officials in Jiangsu Province [announced] plans to spend 108.5 billion yuan, or $14.4 billion, for a cleanup of Lake Tai, the country's third-largest freshwater lake. The campaign would focus initially on eradicating the toxic algal bloom that choked the lake this spring and left more than two million people without drinking water. ...

Lake Tai, known as China's ancient "land of rice and fish," is a legendary setting, once famous for its bounty of white shrimp, whitebait, and whitefish. But over time, an industrial buildup transformed the region. More than 2,800 chemical factories arose around the lake, and industrial dumping became a severe problem and, eventually, a crisis. ...

"The pollution of Lake Tai has sounded the alarm for us," Mr. Wen [Prime Minister] said, "The problem has never been tackled at its root."

New York Times, October 27, 2007

a. What are the externalities included in this news clip?
b. What are the external costs associated with the pollution of Lake Tai?
c. What was the "alarm" that the pollution of Lake Tai sounded and why has the problem "never been tackled at its root"?

13. **How Arts Funding Is Done Elsewhere**

When Rick van der Ploege became Holland's secretary of culture in 1998, he launched an arts-funding revolution that alarmed his quiet, multicultural country—but also became a potential model for smaller-population countries such as Canada. Dwarfed by cultural behemoths Germany and France, the Netherlands did not have the population or funding to compete with them. ... He felt that his country could become a destination—what he called a "cultural freeport."

Bursaries for about $100,000 a year were offered to foreign graduate students. Foreign filmmakers could also receive funding—as long as it met Dutch content requirement. More contentiously, artists would have to prove that there was a market for their creations if they wanted a subsidy. "My argument has always been to get the best people in the world." ... "Whether they be Canadian, Japanese, and maybe the Dutch, bring them together, and the locals would then have to compete on a global scale."

National Post, September 26, 2008

a. What external benefits are associated with the arts?

b. Draw a graph to illustrate and explain why the market for arts creates a deadweight loss.

c. Draw a graph to illustrate and explain how bursaries for foreign graduate students might improve efficiency.

14. **Light Bulbs: Shining a Light on Bulb Recycling**

We've received several questions about recycling light bulbs, ranging from regular incandescents to compact fluorescents (CFLs). First off, recycling incandescent bulbs is not ... on the priority list, because they don't contain toxic materials and don't offer much in the way of recoverable resources. ... It is important to recycle the far more energy-efficient CFLs. ...

Home Depot Canada is aiming to recycle 1.5 million bulbs by 2011 and says all components from the bulbs will be reused in creating a host of new products, including glass bottles and jars, baseball bats and products for the lighting industry. Lasting six to 10 times longer than the average incandescent bulb and using up to 75 per cent less electricity, CFLs save on power consumption and your electricity bill. When properly recycled, CFLs are definitely your best bet for the environment—and your pocketbook.

Calgary Herald, March 27, 2008

a. Relative to incandescents, what is the external benefit associated with CFLs?

b. Draw a graph to illustrate and explain why the market for CFLs is inefficient.

c. Draw a graph to illustrate and explain how government actions might achieve an efficient outcome in the market for bulbs.

15. **Clean Green Flying Machine?**

... Aviation generates 2–3 percent of man-made emissions of carbon dioxide, the main greenhouse gas. ... Most environmentalists think that the only solution is to make air travel more expensive, say through hefty fuel taxes. ... But the airline industry [says it] produces far more benefits than ills—8 percent of global [output] by transporting tourists, business travellers, and cargo around the globe.

Economist.com, August 14, 2007

a. What are the externalities created by the airline industry?

b. Why will hefty fuel taxes encourage airlines to operate in the social interest?

16. After you have studied *Reading Between the Lines* on pp. 386–387, answer the following questions:

a. How does a carbon tax change the costs faced by the operator of a coal-fired power plant?

b. How does a solar subsidy change the costs faced by a solar power station?

c. Why might the operator of a coal-fired power station be influenced by a solar subsidy?

d. Why might the combination of a carbon tax and social subsidy lead to producing electricity at too high a marginal social cost?

e. Would it ever make sense to impose a carbon tax *and* pay a solar subsidy?

17. Use the link on MyEconLab (Textbook Resources, Chapter 16, Web links) and read the article about wind farms.

a. What types of externalities arise in the production of electricity using wind technologies?

b. Comparing the externalities from wind technologies with those from burning coal and oil, which are more costly?

c. How do you think the external costs of using wind technologies should be dealt with? Compare the alternative range of solutions considered in this chapter.

17 Public Goods and Common Resources

After studying this chapter, you will be able to

- Distinguish among private goods, public goods, and common resources
- Explain how the free-rider problem arises and how the quantity of public goods is determined
- Explain the tragedy of the commons and its possible solutions

What's the difference between the Calgary Police Service and Brinks Security, between fish in the Atlantic Ocean and fish produced by a Newfoundland fish farm, and between a live U2 concert and a show on network television?

Why does government provide some goods and services such as the enforcement of law and order and national defence? Why don't we let private firms produce these items and let people buy the quantities that they demand in the marketplace? Is the scale of provision of these government-provided services correct? Or do governments produce either too much or too little of these items?

More and more people with ever-increasing incomes demand ever greater quantities of most goods and services. One of these items is fish grown wild in the ocean. The fish stocks of the world's oceans are not owned by anyone. They are common resources, and everyone is free to use them. Are our fish stocks being overused? Are we in danger of bringing

extinction to some species? Must the price of fish inevitably keep rising? What can be done to conserve the world's fish stocks?

These are the questions that we study in this chapter. We begin by classifying goods and resources. We then explain what determines the scale of government provision of public services. Finally, we study the tragedy of the commons.

In *Reading Between the Lines* at the end of the chapter, we look at a pressing tragedy of the commons in the world today: the problem of overuse of the tropical rainforests.

Classifying Goods and Resources

Goods, services, and resources differ in the extent to which people can be *excluded* from consuming them and in the extent to which one person's consumption *rivals* the consumption of others.

Excludable

A good is **excludable** if it is possible to prevent someone from enjoying its benefits. Brinks security services, Cooke Aquaculture's fish, and a U2 concert are examples. People must pay to consume them.

A good is **nonexcludable** if it is impossible (or extremely costly) to prevent anyone from benefiting from it. The services of the Calgary police, fish in the Atlantic Ocean, and a concert on network television are examples. When a police cruiser enforces the speed limit, everyone on the highway benefits; anyone with a boat can fish in the ocean; and anyone with a TV can watch a network broadcast.

Rival

A good is **rival** if one person's use of it decreases the quantity available for someone else. A Brinks truck can't deliver cash to two banks at the same time. A fish can be consumed only once.

A good is **nonrival** if one person's use of it does not decrease the quantity available for someone else. The services of the police and a concert on network television are nonrival. One person's benefit doesn't lower the benefit of others.

A Fourfold Classification

Figure 17.1 classifies goods, services, and resources into four types.

Private Goods A **private good** is both rival and excludable. A can of Coke and a fish on Cooke Aquaculture's farm are examples of private goods.

Public Goods A **public good** is both nonrival and nonexcludable. A public good can be consumed simultaneously by everyone, and no one can be excluded from enjoying its benefits. National defence is the best example of a public good.

Common Resources A **common resource** is rival and nonexcludable. A unit of a common resource can be

FIGURE 17.1   Fourfold Classification of Goods

	Excludable	Nonexcludable
Rival	**Private goods** Food and drink Car House	**Common resources** Fish in ocean Atmosphere City parks
Nonrival	**Natural monopolies** Internet Cable television Bridge or tunnel	**Public goods** National defence The law Air-traffic control

A private good is one for which consumption is rival and from which consumers can be excluded. A public good is one for which consumption is nonrival and from which it is impossible to exclude a consumer. A common resource is one that is rival but nonexcludable. A good that is nonrival but excludable is produced by a natural monopoly.

 animation

used only once, but no one can be prevented from using what is available. Ocean fish are a common resource. They are rival because a fish taken by one person isn't available for anyone else, and they are nonexcludable because it is difficult to prevent people from catching them.

Natural Monopolies In a natural monopoly, economies of scale exist over the entire range of output for which there is a demand (see p. 300). A special case of natural monopoly arises when the good or service can be produced at zero marginal cost. Such a good is nonrival. If it is also excludable, it is produced by a natural monopoly. The Internet and cable television are examples.

Review Quiz

1 Distinguish among public goods, private goods, common resources, and natural monopolies.

2 Provide examples of goods (or services or resources) in each of the four categories that differ from the examples in this section.

myeconlab Work Study Plan 17.1 and get instant feedback.

Public Goods

Why does the government provide our national defence? Why don't we buy our national defence from North Pole Protection, Inc., a private firm that competes for our dollars in the marketplace in the same way that McDonald's does? The answer is that national defence is a public good—nonexcludable and nonrival—and it has a free-rider problem.

The Free-Rider Problem

A *free rider* enjoys the benefits of a good or service without paying for it. Because a public good is provided for everyone to use and no one can be excluded from its benefits, no one has an incentive to pay his or her share of the cost. Everyone has an incentive to free ride. The **free-rider problem** is that the market would provide an inefficiently small quantity of a public good. Marginal social benefit from the public good would exceed its marginal social cost and a deadweight loss would arise.

Let's look at the marginal social benefit and marginal social cost of a public good.

Marginal Social Benefit of a Public Good

Lisa and Max (the only people in an imagined society) value national defence. Figures 17.2(a) and 17.2(b) graph their marginal benefits from a defence satellite system as MB_L for Lisa and MB_M for Max. A person's marginal benefit from a public good, like that from a private good, diminishes as the quantity of the good increases—the marginal benefit curves slope downward.

Figure 17.2(c) shows the marginal *social* benefit curve, *MSB*. Because everyone gets the same quantity of a public good, its marginal social benefit curve is the sum of the marginal benefits of all individuals at each *quantity*—it is the *vertical* sum of the individual marginal benefit curves. So the curve *MSB* in part (c) is the marginal social benefit curve for the economy made up of Lisa and Max. For each satellite, Lisa's marginal benefit is added to Max's marginal benefit.

Contrast the marginal social benefit curve for a public good with that of a private good. To obtain the marginal social benefit curve for a private good, we *sum the quantities demanded* by all individuals at each *price*—we sum the individual marginal benefit curves *horizontally* (see Chapter 5, p. 110).

FIGURE 17.2 Benefits of a Public Good

(a) Lisa's marginal benefit

(b) Max's marginal benefit

(c) Economy's marginal social benefit

The marginal social benefit at each quantity of the public good is the sum of the marginal benefits of all individuals. The marginal benefit curves are MB_L for Lisa and MB_M for Max. The economy's marginal social benefit curve is *MSB*.

Marginal Social Cost of a Public Good

The marginal social cost of a public good is determined in exactly the same way as that of a private good—see p. 112. The principle of increasing marginal cost applies to the marginal cost of a public good and the marginal social cost curve of a public good slopes upward.

Efficient Quantity of a Public Good

To determine the efficient quantity of a public good, we use the same principles that you learned in Chapter 5 and have used repeatedly: Find the quantity at which marginal social benefit equals marginal social cost.

Figure 17.3 shows the marginal social benefit curve, *MSB*, and the marginal social cost curve, *MSC*, for defence satellites. (We'll now think of society as consisting of Lisa and Max and 300 million others.)

If marginal social benefit exceeds marginal social cost, as it does when fewer than 2 satellites are provided, resources can be used more efficiently by increasing the quantity. The extra benefit exceeds the extra cost. If marginal social cost exceeds marginal social benefit, as it does when more than 2 satellites are provided, resources can be used more efficiently by decreasing the quantity. The saving in cost exceeds the loss of benefit.

If marginal social benefit equals marginal social cost, as it does when exactly 2 satellites are provided, resources cannot be used more efficiently. To provide more than 2 satellites would cost more than the additional coverage is worth, and to provide fewer satellites lowers the benefit by more than its cost saving. Resources are allocated efficiently.

Inefficient Private Provision

Could a private firm—North Pole Protection, Inc.—deliver the efficient quantity of satellites? Most likely, it couldn't because no one would have an incentive to buy his or her share of the satellite system. Everyone would reason as follows: "The number of satellites provided by North Pole Protection, Inc., is not affected by my decision to pay my share or not. But my own private consumption will be greater if I free ride and do not pay my share of the cost of the satellite system. If I don't pay, I enjoy the same level of security and I can buy more private goods. I will spend my money on private goods and free ride on the public good." Such

FIGURE 17.3 The Efficient Quantity of a Public Good

With fewer than 2 satellites, marginal social benefit, *MSB*, exceeds marginal social cost, *MSC*. With more than 2 satellites, *MSC* exceeds *MSB*. Only with 2 satellites is *MSC* equal to *MSB* and the quantity is efficient.

myeconlab animation

reasoning is the free-rider problem. If everyone reasons the same way, North Pole Protection, Inc., has no revenue and so provides no satellites. Because the efficient level is two satellites, private provision is inefficient.

Efficient Public Provision

The political process might be efficient or inefficient. We look first at an efficient outcome. There are two political parties: Hawks and Doves. They agree on all issues except for the number of satellites. The Hawks want 3 satellites, and the Doves want 1 satellite. But both parties want to get elected, so they run a voter survey and discover the marginal social benefit curve of Fig. 17.4. They also consult with satellite producers to establish the marginal cost schedule. The parties then do a "what-if" analysis. If the Hawks propose 3 satellites and the Doves propose 1 satellite, the voters will be equally unhappy with both parties. Compared to the efficient quantity, the Doves want an underprovision of 1 satellite and the Hawks want an overprovision of 1 satellite. The deadweight losses are equal. So the election would be too close to call.

FIGURE 17.4 An Efficient Political Outcome

The Doves would like to provide 1 satellite and the Hawks would like to provide 3 satellites. The political outcome is 2 satellites because unless each party proposes 2 satellites, the other party beats it in an election.

myeconlab animation

Contemplating this outcome, the Hawks realize that they are too hawkish to get elected. They figure that if they scale back to 2 satellites, they will win the election if the Doves propose 1 satellite. The Doves reason in a similar way and figure that if they increase the number of satellites to 2, they can win the election if the Hawks propose 3 satellites.

So they both propose 2 satellites. The voters are indifferent between the parties, and each party receives 50 percent of the vote.

Regardless of which party wins the election, 2 satellites are provided and this quantity is efficient. Competition in the political marketplace results in the efficient provision of a public good.

The Principle of Minimum Differentiation The tendency for competitors to make themselves similar to appeal to the maximum number of clients or voters is called the **principle of minimum differentiation**. This principle describes the behaviour of political parties. It also explains why fast-food restaurants cluster in the same block and even why new auto models have similar features. If McDonald's opens a new restaurant, it is likely that Wendy's will open near to McDonald's

rather than a mile down the road. If Chrysler designs a new van with a sliding door on the driver's side, most likely Ford will too.

For the political process to deliver the efficient outcome that you've just seen, voters must be well informed, evaluate the alternatives, and vote in the election. Political parties must be well informed about voter preferences. As the next section shows, we can't expect to achieve this outcome.

Inefficient Public Overprovision

If competition between two political parties is to deliver the efficient quantity of a public good, bureaucrats must cooperate and help to achieve this outcome. In the case of satellites, bureaucrats in the Department of National Defence (DND) must cooperate and accept this outcome.

Objective of Bureaucrats Bureaucrats want to maximize their department's budget because a bigger budget brings greater status and more power. So the DND's objective is to maximize the defence budget.

Figure 17.5 shows the outcome if the DND is successful in the pursuit of its goal. The DND might

FIGURE 17.5 Bureaucratic Overprovision

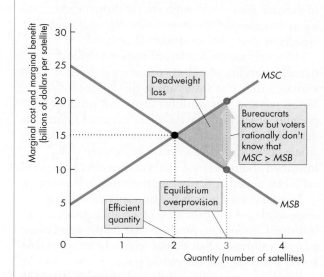

Well-informed bureaucrats want to maximize their budget and rationally ignorant voters enable the bureaucrats to go some way towards achieving their goal. A public good might be inefficiently overprovided with a deadweight loss.

myeconlab animation

try to persuade the politicians that 2 satellites cost more than the originally budgeted amount; or the DND might press its position more strongly and argue for more than 2 satellites. In Fig. 17.5, the DND persuades the politicians to go for 3 satellites.

Why don't the politicians block the DND? Won't overproducing satellites cost future votes? It will if voters are well informed and know what is best for them. But voters might not be well informed, and well-informed interest groups might enable the DND to achieve its objective and overcome the objections of the politicians.

Rational Ignorance A principle of the economic analysis of public choices is that it is rational for a voter to be ignorant about an issue unless that issue has a perceptible effect on the voter's economic welfare. **Rational ignorance** is the decision not to acquire information because the cost of doing so exceeds the expected benefit.

For example, each voter knows that he or she can make virtually no difference to the defence policy of the government of Canada. Each voter also knows that it would take an enormous amount of time and effort to become even moderately well informed about alternative defence technologies. So voters remain relatively uninformed about the technicalities of defence issues. Although we are using defence policy as an example, the same reasoning applies to all aspects of government economic activity.

All voters are consumers of national defence. But not all voters are producers of national defence. Only a small number of voters are in this latter category. Voters who own or work for firms that produce components of satellites have a direct personal interest in defence because it affects their incomes and careers. These voters have an incentive to become well informed about defence issues and to operate a political lobby aimed at furthering their own self-interests.

In collaboration with the bureaucrats who are responsible for the provision of a public good, informed voters who produce that public good exert a larger influence than do the relatively uninformed voters who only use the public good.

When the rationality of the uninformed voter and special interest groups are taken into account, the political equilibrium provides public goods in excess of the efficient quantity. So in the satellite example, 3 or more satellites might be installed rather than the efficient quantity of 2 satellites.

Health-Care and Security Spending
Canada Cares

In Canada, both health care and security are publically provided services. The federal government, the ten provinces, and the three territories have key roles to play. The figure shows how total expenditure on these two services has changed since 1989. The figure shows that spending on health care was about twice the spending on security at about $2,000 per person until 1997. Since then, health-care expenditure has increased by 45 percent.

Security spending includes national defence, the RCMP, provincial and local police services, and border services. The graph shows that expenditure per person on security has remained fairly constant at about $1,000 a person.

Health-care spending includes expenditure on hospitals, physicians, drugs, and public health. The largest component of this expenditure is spending on hospitals. The second largest, and fastest growing component, is expenditure on prescription and non-prescription drugs. Spending on physicians is the third largest component.

Health-care spending varies across the provinces and territories. Expenditure per person is higher in the Yukon and Northwest Territories and in Nunavut than in the provinces because of the higher costs of serving a large area with relatively few people scattered across it.

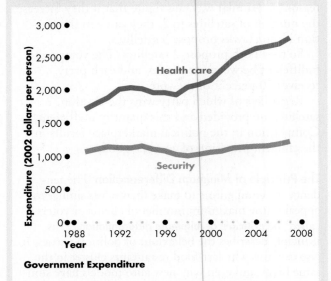

Government Expenditure

Source of data: Statistics Canada, CANSIM Table 385-0001.

Two Types of Political Equilibrium

We've seen that two types of political equilibrium are possible: efficient and inefficient. These two types of political equilibrium correspond to two theories of government:

- Social interest theory
- Public choice theory

Social Interest Theory   Social interest theory predicts that governments make choices that achieve an efficient provision of public goods. This outcome occurs in a perfect political system in which voters are fully informed about the effects of policies and refuse to vote for outcomes that can be improved upon.

Public Choice Theory   Public choice theory predicts that governments make choices that result in inefficient overprovision of public goods. This outcome occurs in political markets in which voters are rationally ignorant and base their votes only on issues that they know affect their own net benefit. Voters pay more attention to their self-interests as producers than their self-interests as consumers, and public officials also act in their own self-interest. The result is *government failure* that parallels market failure.

Why Government Is Large and Growing

Now that we know how the quantity of public goods is determined, we can explain part of the reason for the growth of government. Government grows in part because the demand for some public goods increases at a faster rate than the demand for private goods. There are two possible reasons for this growth:

- Voter preferences
- Inefficient overprovision

Voter Preferences   The growth of government can be explained by voter preferences in the following way. As voters' incomes increase (as they do in most years), the demand for many public goods increases more quickly than income. (Technically, the *income elasticity of demand* for many public goods is greater than one—see Chapter 4, pp. 94–95.) These goods include public health, education, national defence, highways, airports, and air-traffic control systems. If politicians did not support increases in expenditures on these items, they would not get elected.

Inefficient Overprovision   Inefficient overprovision might explain the *size* of government but not its *growth rate*. It (possibly) explains why government is *larger* than its efficient scale, but it does not explain why governments use an increasing proportion of total resources.

Voters Strike Back

If government grows too large relative to the value that voters place on public goods, there might be a voter backlash against government programs and a large bureaucracy. Electoral success during the 1990s at the provincial and federal levels required politicians of all parties to embrace smaller, leaner, and more efficient government. The September 11 attacks have led to a greater willingness to pay for security but have probably not lessened the desire for lean government.

Another way in which voters—and politicians—can try to counter the tendency of bureaucrats to expand their budgets is to privatize the production of public goods. Government *provision* of a public good does not automatically imply that a government-operated bureau must *produce* the good. Garbage collection (a public good) is often done by a private firm, and experiments are being conducted with even private prisons.

Review Quiz

1 What is the free-rider problem and why does it make the private provision of a public good inefficient?
2 Under what conditions will competition among politicians for votes result in an efficient quantity of a public good?
3 How do rationally ignorant voters and budget-maximizing bureaucrats prevent competition in the political marketplace from producing the efficient quantity of a public good? Do they result in too much or too little public provision of public goods?

myeconlab Work Study Plan 17.2 and get instant feedback.

You've seen how public goods create a free-rider problem that would result in the underprovision of such goods. We're now going to learn about common resources and see why they result in the opposite problem—the overuse of such resources.

Common Resources

Atlantic Ocean cod stocks have been declining since the 1950s, and some marine biologists fear that this species is in danger of becoming extinct in some regions. The whale population of the South Pacific has been declining also, and some groups are lobbying to establish a whale sanctuary in the waters around Australia and New Zealand to regenerate the population.

Logging, cattle ranching, mining, oil extraction, and damming rivers are destroying the tropical rainforests of Southeast Asia, Africa, and Central and South America at an alarming rate. At the present rate of destruction, most will be gone by 2030.

These situations involve common property, and the problem that we have identified is called the *tragedy of the commons*.

The Tragedy of the Commons

The **tragedy of the commons** is the absence of incentives to prevent the overuse and depletion of a commonly owned resource. If no one owns a resource, no one considers the effects of her or his use of the resource on others.

The Original Tragedy of the Commons The term "tragedy of the commons" comes from fourteenth-century England, where areas of rough grassland surrounded villages. The commons were open to all and used for grazing cows and sheep owned by the villagers.

Because the commons were open to all, no one had an incentive to ensure that the land was not overgrazed. The result was a severe overgrazing situation. Because the commons were overgrazed, the quantity of cows and sheep that they could feed kept falling.

During the sixteenth century, the price of wool increased and England became a wool exporter to the world. Sheep farming became profitable, and sheep owners wanted to gain more effective control of the land they used. So the commons were gradually privatized and enclosed. Overgrazing ended, and land use became more efficient.

A Tragedy of the Commons Today One of today's pressing tragedies of the commons is overfishing. To study the tragedy of the commons, let's look at what has been happening to Atlantic Cod—just one species of fish that has been seriously overfished.

Sustainable Production

Sustainable production is the rate of production that can be maintained indefinitely. In the case of ocean fish, the sustainable production is the quantity of fish (of a given species) that can be caught each year into the indefinite future without wiping out the species.

This production rate depends on the existing stock of fish and the number of boats that go fishing. For a given stock of fish, sending more boats to sea increases the quantity of fish caught. But sending too many boats to sea depletes the stock.

So as the number of boats increases, the quantity of fish caught increases as long as the stock is maintained. But above some crucial level, as more boats go fishing, the stock of fish decreases and the number of fish caught also decreases.

Table 17.1 provides some numbers that illustrate the relationship between the number of boats that go fishing and the quantity of fish caught. The numbers in this example are hypothetical.

TABLE 17.1 Sustainable Production: Total, Average, and Marginal Catch

	Boats (thousands)	Total catch (thousands of tonnes per month)	Average catch (tonnes per boat)	Marginal catch (tonnes per boat)
A	0	0		
				90
B	1	90	90	
				70
C	2	160	80	
				50
D	3	210	70	
				30
E	4	240	60	
				10
F	5	250	50	
				−10
G	6	240	40	
				−30
H	7	210	30	
				−50
I	8	160	20	
				−70
J	9	90	10	
				−90
K	10	0	0	

As the number of fishing boats increases, the quantity of fish caught increases up to the maximum sustainable catch and then decreases. The average catch and marginal catch decrease as the number of boats increases.

Total Catch The total catch is the sustainable rate of production. The numbers in the first two columns of Table 17.1 show the relationship between the number of fishing boats and the total catch, and Fig. 17.6 illustrates this relationship.

You can see that as the number of boats increases from zero to 5,000, the sustainable catch increases to a maximum of 250,000 tonnes a month. As the number of boats increases above 5,000, the sustainable catch begins to decrease. By the time 10,000 boats are fishing, the fish stock is depleted to the point at which no fish can be caught.

With more than 5,000 boats, there is overfishing. Overfishing arises if the number of boats increases to the point at which the fish stock begins to fall and the remaining fish are harder to find and catch.

Average Catch The average catch is the catch per boat and equals the total catch divided by the number of boats. The numbers in the third column of Table 17.1 show the average catch.

With 1,000 boats, the total catch is 90,000 tonnes and the catch per boat is 90 tonnes. With 2,000 boats,

the total catch is 160,000 tonnes, and the catch per boat is 80 tonnes. As more boats take to the ocean, the catch per boat decreases. By the time 8,000 boats are fishing, each boat is catching just 20 tonnes a month.

The decreasing average catch is an example of the principle of diminishing returns.

Marginal Catch The marginal catch is the change in the total catch that occurs when one more boat joins the existing number. It is calculated as the change in the total catch divided by the increase in the number of boats. The numbers in the fourth column of Table 17.1 show the marginal catch.

For example, in rows *C* and *D* of the table, when the number of boats increases by 1,000, the catch increases by 50,000 tonnes, so the increase in the catch per boat equals 50 tonnes. In the table, we place this amount midway between the two rows because it is the marginal catch at 2,500 boats, midway between the two levels that we used to calculate it.

Notice that the marginal catch, like the average catch, decreases as the number of boats increases. Also notice that the marginal catch is always less than the average catch.

When the number of boats reaches that at which the sustainable catch is a maximum, the marginal catch is zero. At a larger number of boats, the marginal catch becomes negative—more boats decrease the total catch.

An Overfishing Equilibrium

The tragedy of the commons is that common resources are overused. Why might the fish stock be overused? Why might overfishing occur? Why isn't the maximum number of boats that take to the sea the number that maximizes the sustainable catch— 5,000, in this example?

To answer this question, we need to look at the marginal cost and marginal private benefit to an individual fisher.

Suppose that the marginal cost of a fishing boat is the equivalent of 20 tonnes of fish a month. That is, to cover the opportunity cost of maintaining and operating a boat, the boat must catch 20 tonnes of fish a month. This quantity of fish also provides the boat owner with normal profit (part of the cost of operating the boat), so the boat owner is willing to go fishing.

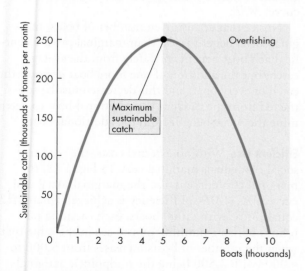

FIGURE 17.6 Sustainable Production of Fish

As the number of boats increases, the sustainable catch increases up to a maximum. Beyond that number, more boats will diminish the fish stock and the sustainable catch decreases. Overfishing occurs when the maximum sustainable catch decreases.

myeconlab animation

The marginal private benefit of operating a boat is the quantity of fish the boat can catch. This quantity is the average catch that we've just calculated. The average catch is the marginal private benefit because that is the quantity of fish that the boat owner gets by taking the boat to sea.

The boat owner will go fishing as long as the average catch (marginal private benefit) exceeds the marginal cost. The boat owner will maximize profit when marginal private benefit equals marginal cost.

Figure 17.7 shows the marginal cost curve, *MC*, and the marginal private benefit curve, *MB*. The *MB* curve is based on the average catch in Table 17.1.

You can see in Fig. 17.7 that with fewer than 8,000 boats, each boat catches more fish than it costs to catch them. Because boat owners can gain from fishing, the number of boats is 8,000 and there is an overfishing equilibrium.

If one boat owner stopped fishing, the overfishing would be less severe. But that boat owner would be giving up an opportunity to earn an economic profit.

The self-interest of the boat owner is to fish, but the social interest is to limit fishing. The quantity of

fish caught by each boat decreases as additional boats go fishing. But when individual boat owners are deciding whether to fish, they ignore this decrease. They consider only the marginal *private* benefit. The result is an *inefficient* overuse of the resource.

The Efficient Use of the Commons

What is the efficient use of a common resource? It is the use of the resource that makes the marginal cost of using the resource equal to the marginal *social* benefit from its use.

Marginal Social Benefit The marginal *social* benefit of a boat is the boat's marginal catch—the increase in the total catch that results from an additional boat. The reason is that when an additional boat puts to sea, it catches the average catch but it decreases the average catch for itself and for every other boat. The *marginal social benefit* is the *increase* in the quantity of fish caught per boat, not the average number of fish caught.

We calculated the marginal catch in Table 17.1 and we repeat part of that table for convenience in Fig. 17.8. The figure also shows the marginal private benefit curve, *MB*, and the marginal social benefit curve, *MSB*.

Notice that at any given number of boats, marginal social benefit is less than marginal private benefit. Each boat benefits privately from the average catch, but the addition of one more boat *decreases* the catch of every boat, and this decrease must be subtracted from the catch of the additional boat to determine the social benefit from the additional boat.

Efficient Use With no external costs, the marginal social cost equals marginal cost. In Fig. 17.8, the marginal cost curve is also the marginal social cost curve, *MC = MSC*. Efficiency is achieved when *MSB* equals *MSC* with 4,000 boats, each catching 60 tonnes of fish a month. You can see in the table that when the number of boats increases from 3,000 to 4,000 (with 3,500 being the midpoint), marginal social benefit is 30 tonnes, which exceeds marginal social cost. When the number of boats increases from 4,000 to 5,000 (with 4,500 being the midpoint), marginal social benefit is 10 tonnes, which is less than marginal social cost. At 4,000 boats, marginal social benefit is 20 tonnes, which equals marginal social cost.

FIGURE 17.7 Why Overfishing Occurs

The average catch decreases as the number of boats increases. The average catch per boat is the marginal private benefit, *MB*, of a boat. The marginal cost of a boat is equivalent to 20 tonnes of fish, shown by the curve *MC*. The equilibrium number of boats is 8,000—an overfishing equilibrium.

myeconlab animation

FIGURE 17.8   Efficient Use of a Common Resource

Boats (thousands)	Total catch (thousands of tonnes per month)	Marginal private benefit	Marginal social benefit
		(tonnes per boat)	
A 0	0		
			90
B 1	90	90	
			70
C 2	160	80	
			50
D 3	210	70	
			30
E 4	240	60	
			10
F 5	250	50	

The marginal social benefit of a fishing boat is the change in total benefit that results from an additional boat. The table shows that when the number of boats increases from 2,000 to 3,000 (from row C to row D), the total catch increases from 160,000 to 210,000 tonnes a month and marginal catch and marginal social benefit is 50 tonnes.

The figure graphs the marginal social benefit curve, MSB, and the marginal private benefit curve, MB. Marginal social benefit is less than marginal private benefit and decreases as the number of boats increases. The efficient number of boats is 4,000—the number at which marginal social benefit equals marginal social cost of $20 a boat. The common resource is used efficiently.

myeconlab   animation

Achieving an Efficient Outcome

Defining the conditions under which a common resource is used efficiently is easier than generating those conditions. To use a common resource efficiently, it is necessary to design an incentive mechanism that confronts the users of the resource with the marginal social consequences of their actions. The same principles apply to common resources as those that you met when you studied externalities in Chapter 16.

Three main methods might be used to achieve the efficient use of a common resource. They are

- Property rights
- Production quotas
- Individual transferable quotas (ITQs)

Property Rights   A common resource that no one owns and that anyone is free to use contrasts with *private property*, which is a resource that *someone* owns and has an incentive to use in the way that maximizes its value. One way of overcoming the tragedy of the commons is to remove the commons and make the resource private property. By assigning private property rights, each owner faces the same conditions as society faces. The *MSB* curve of Fig. 17.8 becomes the marginal *private* benefit curve, and the use of the resource is efficient.

The private property solution to the tragedy of the commons *is* available in some cases. It was the solution to the original tragedy of the commons in England's Middle Ages. It is also a solution that has been used to prevent overuse of the airwaves that carry our cell phone service. The right to use this space—called the frequency spectrum—has been auctioned by governments to the highest bidders, and the owner of a particular part of the spectrum is the only one permitted to use it (or to license someone else to use it).

But assigning private property rights is not always feasible. It would be difficult, for example, to assign private property rights to the oceans. It would not be impossible, but the cost of enforcing private property rights over thousands of hectares of ocean would be high. And it would be even more difficult to assign and protect private property rights to the atmosphere.

In some cases, there is an emotional objection to assigning private property rights. When private property rights are too costly to assign and enforce, some form of government intervention is used, and production quotas are the simplest.

Production Quotas You studied the effects of a production quota in Chapter 6 (pp. 141–142) and learned that a quota can drive a wedge between marginal social benefit and marginal social cost and create deadweight loss. In that earlier example, the market was efficient without a quota. But in the case of the use of a common resource, the market is inefficient. It is overproducing, so a quota that limits production can bring a move towards a more efficient outcome.

A quota might be placed either on the number of boats or on the catch. In our example, the catch is determined by the number of boats, so placing a quota on the number of boats is equivalent to placing a quota on the catch. We'll define the quota in terms of the number of boats permitted to fish.

Figure 17.9 shows a quota that achieves an efficient outcome. The quota limits the number of boats to 4,000, the number that catches the efficient quantity at which marginal social benefit, *MSB*, equals marginal social cost, *MSC*. If the boats allocated the

FIGURE 17.9 A Production Quota to Use a Common Resource Efficiently

A quota on the number of boats permitted to fish is set at 4,000, the number that catches the quantity of fish at which marginal social benefit, *MSB*, equals marginal social cost, *MSC*. If the quota is successfully enforced, the outcome is efficient.

right to fish are the only ones to do so, the outcome is efficient.

Implementing a production quota has two problems. First, it is in every boat owner's self-interest to cheat and send out more boats than the number permitted. The reason is that marginal private benefit exceeds marginal cost, so by using more boats, each boat owner gets a higher income. If enough boat owners break the quota, overfishing returns and the tragedy of the commons remains.

Second, marginal cost is not, in general, the same for all producers—as we're assuming here. Some producers have a comparative advantage in using a resource. Efficiency requires that the quota be allocated to the producers with the lowest marginal cost. But the government department that allocates quotas does not have information about the marginal cost of individual producers. Even if the government tried to get this information, producers would have an incentive to lie about their costs so as to get a bigger quota.

So a production quota can work, but only if the activities of every producer can be monitored and all producers have the same marginal cost. Where producers are difficult or very costly to monitor or where marginal costs vary across producers, a production quota cannot achieve an efficient outcome.

Individual Transferable Quotas Where producers are difficult to monitor or where marginal costs differ across producers, a more sophisticated quota system can be effective. It is an **individual transferable quota (ITQ)**, which is a production limit that is assigned to an individual who is then free to transfer (sell) the quota to someone else. A market in ITQs emerges and ITQs are traded at their market price.

The market price of an ITQ is the highest price that someone is willing to pay for one. That price is marginal benefit minus marginal cost. The price of an ITQ will rise to this level because the boat owners who don't have a quota would be willing to pay this amount to get one.

A boat owner with an ITQ could sell it for the market price, so by not selling the ITQ the boat owner incurs an opportunity cost. The marginal cost of fishing, which now includes the opportunity cost of the ITQ, equals the marginal social benefit of the efficient quantity.

Figure 17.10 illustrates how ITQs work. Each boat has a marginal cost equivalent to 20 tonnes per month. The efficient outcome is achieved with 4,000 boats, each catching 60 tonnes a month. The market

FIGURE 17.10   ITQs to Use a Common Resource Efficiently

ITQs are issued on a scale that keeps output at the efficient level. The market price of an ITQ equals the marginal private benefit minus marginal cost. Because each user of the common resource faces the opportunity cost of using the resource, self-interest achieves the social interest.

myeconlab   animation

price of an ITQ equals the equivalent of 40 tonnes of fish a month. The marginal cost of fishing rises from MC_0 to $MC_0 + price of ITQ$, 4,000 boats go fishing, and each catches 60 tonnes of fish. The outcome is efficient.

Individual differences in marginal cost do not prevent an ITQ system from delivering the efficient outcome. Boat owners with a low marginal cost are willing and able to pay more for a quota than are boat owners with a high marginal cost. The market price of an ITQ will equal 60 tonnes minus the marginal cost of the marginal producer. Boat owners with higher marginal costs will not go fishing.

Public Choice and the Political Equilibrium

When we studied the provision of public goods, we saw that a political equilibrium might be inefficient—government failure might arise. Such a political outcome might arise with the use of a common resource. Defining an efficient allocation of resources and designing an ITQ system to achieve that allocation is not sufficient to ensure that the political process will deliver the efficient outcome.

In the case of the ocean fish stock, some countries have achieved an efficient political equilibrium, but not all have done so.

Economists agree that ITQs offer an effective tool for achieving an efficient use of the stock of ocean fish. So a political commitment to ITQs is an efficient outcome, and an unwillingness to use ITQs is an inefficient political outcome.

Australia and New Zealand have introduced ITQs to conserve fish stocks in the South Pacific and Southern Oceans. The evidence from these countries suggests that ITQs work well. Fishing boat operators have an incentive to catch more than the assigned quota, but such cheating seems to be relatively rare. Also, boats with an ITQ have an incentive to monitor and report cheating by others without an ITQ.

ITQs help maintain fish stocks, but they also reduce the size of the fishing industry. This consequence of ITQs puts them against the self-interest of the fishing-boat owners. In all countries, the fishing industry opposes restrictions on its activities, but in Australia and New Zealand, the opposition is not strong enough to block ITQs.

In Canada, the opposition to ITQs has prevented this solution from being adopted. One parliamentary committee even went so far as to argue that evidence from Australia and New Zealand should not be used to justify ITQs in Canada. In the United States, Congress has outlawed ITQs in the Gulf of Mexico and the Northern Pacific.

Review Quiz

1 What is the tragedy of the commons? Give two examples, including one from your province.
2 Describe the conditions under which a common resource is used efficiently.
3 Review three methods that might achieve the efficient use of a common resource and explain the obstacles to efficiency.

myeconlab   Work Study Plan 17.3 and get instant feedback.

◆ *Reading Between the Lines* on pp. 406–407 looks at the overuse of tropical rainforests.

The next chapter begins a new part of your study of microeconomics and examines the third big question of economics: For whom are goods and services produced? We examine the markets for factors of production and discover how wage rates and other incomes are determined.

Rainforests: A Tragedy of the Commons

Puerto Rico Rainforest on Edge

April 23, 2006

The scent of flowering tropical plants fills the moist air amid a chorus of whistling birds and singing frogs. The only other sound for a mile in any direction is the roar of a 100-foot waterfall.

Despite 28,000 acres of such lovely scenes, the tropical rainforest that Puerto Rico's prehistoric Taino Indians called El Yunque, or "Land of the White Clouds," is in grave danger. Thousands of acres of forests and green lands … are being cleared at a torrid pace. …

There are consequences to clearing these lands, beyond harm to hundreds of rare plants and wildlife in El Yunque. The rainforest … provides one-third of the island's fresh drinking water. …

Tropical forests such as El Yunque constitute about 6% of Earth's surface and account for 50% to 80% of the world's plant species. Rainforests once covered 14% of the planet's land surface, but have shrunk due to development and deforestation. …

"I'd like to think we live in harmony with El Yunque," said Martha Herrera, 69, who bought a two-story house next to the rainforest a decade ago.

"Some people say I'm hurting El Yunque. But how am I hurting anything?" she asked as her three dogs and flock of chickens roamed in and out of the park one recent morning.

About a quarter-mile away, construction crews were pouring concrete as they rushed to finish a 20-acre condominium complex.

"People who buy these units want the views of the rainforest," said Hecter Ramirez, 35, a construction worker at the site. "I have a job. That's important to my family and me. People tell me this isn't going to damage anything."

El Yunque is home to 240 native tree species—more than any other national forest. Federally listed endangered plants grow in the forest too, such as the miniature orchid and palo de jazmin. …

Essence of the Story

- Puerto Rico's El Yunque tropical rainforest has 240 native tree species—more than any other national forest.
- Tropical forests, which have shrunk from 14 percent to 6 percent of Earth's surface, account for 50 to 80 percent of the world's plant species.
- The rainforest near San Juan provides one-third of the island's fresh drinking water.
- Puerto Rico's tropical rainforest is being cleared at a torrid pace.
- Condominium construction is taking place close to the rainforest.
- Construction workers and people who buy condominiums say they aren't doing any damage.

Economic Analysis

- The tropical rainforests of Puerto Rico grow on land that some people want to build on.

- These forests are home to many rare species of tree, a source of drinking water, and a carbon-dioxide sink that helps to maintain Earth's atmosphere.

- The forests are common property.

- The private incentive to exploit these forest resources is strong.

- Because no one owns the forests, there is no incentive to conserve the resources and use them on a sustainable basis.

- The result is overuse, just like the overuse of the commons of England in the Middle Ages.

- The figures illustrate the tragedy of the commons in a tropical rainforest.

- Figure 1 shows the relationship between the sustainable production of wood from a rainforest and the number of lumber producers working the forest.

- Figure 2 shows the marginal private benefit and marginal private cost of a producer and the marginal social benefit and marginal social cost of wood.

- The producer's marginal cost of felling a tree is assumed to be zero.

- For a common resource, the marginal private benefit received by a producer is MB and LD lumber producers acting in their self-interest deplete the resource. Sustainable production decreases to zero.

- For a privately owned resource, the marginal social benefit curve, MSB, becomes the marginal private benefit curve. Self-interest results in LP lumber producers who maximize the sustainable output of the rainforest.

- If the only benefit from the rainforest were its timber, maximum sustainable timber output would be efficient.

- But external benefits arise from the diversity of the wildlife supported by the forest, so marginal social cost exceeds the zero marginal private cost.

- Production in the social interest—the efficient level of production—is achieved with LS lumber producers and is less than the maximum sustainable production.

Figure 1 Rainforest timber production

Figure 2 Marginal benefits and marginal costs

SUMMARY

Key Points

Classifying Goods and Resources (p. 394)

- A private good is a good or service that is rival and excludable.
- A public good is a good or service that is nonrival and nonexcludable.
- A common resource is a resource that is rival but nonexcludable.

Public Goods (pp. 395–399)

- Because a public good is a good or service that is *nonrival* and *nonexcludable*, it creates a *free-rider* problem: No one has an incentive to pay their share of the cost of providing a public good.
- The efficient level of provision of a public good is that at which marginal social benefit equals marginal social cost.
- Competition between political parties, each of which tries to appeal to the maximum number of voters, can lead to the efficient scale of provision of a public good and to all parties proposing the same policies—the principle of minimum differentiation.
- Bureaucrats try to maximize their budgets, and if voters are rationally ignorant, public goods might be provided in quantities that exceed those that are efficient.

Common Resources (pp. 400–405)

- Common resources create a problem that is called the tragedy of the commons—no one has a private incentive to conserve the resources and use them at an efficient rate.
- A common resource is used to the point at which the marginal private benefit equals the marginal cost.
- A common resource might be used efficiently by creating a private property right, setting a quota, or issuing individual transferable quotas.

Key Figures

Figure 17.1   Fourfold Classification of Goods, 394
Figure 17.2   Benefits of a Public Good, 395
Figure 17.3   The Efficient Quantity of a Public Good, 396

Figure 17.4   An Efficient Political Outcome, 397
Figure 17.5   Bureaucratic Overprovision, 397
Figure 17.7   Why Overfishing Occurs, 402
Figure 17.8   Efficient Use of a Common Resource, 403

Key Terms

Common resource, 394
Excludable, 394
Free-rider problem, 395
Individual transferable quota (ITQ), 404
Nonexcludable, 394
Nonrival, 394
Principle of minimum different-iation, 397
Private good, 394
Public good, 394
Rational ignorance, 398
Rival, 394
Tragedy of the commons, 400

PROBLEMS and APPLICATIONS

myeconlab Work problems 1–7 in Chapter 17 Study Plan and get instant feedback.
Work problems 8–16 as Homework, a Quiz, or a Test if assigned by your instructor.

1. Classify each of the following items as excludable, nonexcludable, rival, nonrival, a public good, a private good, or a common resource.
   - Jasper National Park
   - A Big Mac
   - Peace Bridge
   - Air
   - Police protection
   - Sidewalks
   - Canada Post
   - FedEx courier service
   - The MyEconLab Web site

2. For each of the following goods, explain whether there is a free-rider problem. If there is no such problem, how is it avoided?
   - July 1st fireworks display
   - TransCanada Highway in rural Manitoba
   - Wireless Internet access in hotels
   - Sharing downloaded music
   - The public library in your city

3. The figure provides information about a sewage disposal system that a city of 1 million people is considering installing.

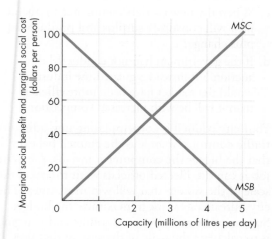

   a. What is the capacity that achieves an efficient outcome?
   b. How much will each person have to pay in taxes to pay for the efficient capacity level?
   c. What is the political equilibrium if voters are well informed?

   d. What is the political equilibrium if voters are rationally ignorant and bureaucrats achieve the highest attainable budget?

4. The table shows the value of cod caught in the North Atlantic Ocean by American, Canadian, and European fishing boats. The marginal cost of operating a boat is $80,000 a month.

Number of boats	Value of cod caught (thousands of dollars per month)
0	0
10	2,000
20	3,400
30	4,200
40	4,400
50	4,000
60	3,000
70	1,400

   a. What is the marginal private benefit of a fishing boat at each quantity of boats?
   b. What is the marginal social benefit of a fishing boat at each quantity of boats?
   c. With no regulation of cod fishing, what is the equilibrium number of boats and the value of cod caught?
   d. Is the equilibrium in c an overfishing equilibrium?
   e. What is the efficient number of boats?
   f. What is the efficient value of the cod catch?
   g. Do you think that the consumers of fish and the fishing industry will agree about how much cod should be caught?
   h. If Canada, the United States, and the European Union imposed a production quota to limit the catch to the efficient quantity, what would the total value of the catch be under the quota?
   i. If Canada, the United States, and the European Union issued ITQs to fishing boats to limit the catch to the efficient quantity, at what price would ITQs be traded?

5. The Wonder Fish

Our oceans are being drained of food. Doctors tell us to eat more fish. ... To meet this growing appetite, commercial fishermen are scooping up everything that's edible (and a lot of what's not). Couple that trend with the effects of global warming, and the situation has become so dire that some scientists think seafood stocks will totally collapse by 2048. ... A former fisheries researcher in the Cook Islands, [Kona Blue cofounder Neil] Sims was disgusted by how locals ravaged marine life there. But the scene also inspired his idea for a new (patents pending) style of deepwater fish farming. ... So just what is Kona Kampachi? Think of it as a more versatile cousin of hamachi. It's not genetically engineered in any way, just well bred. ... Sims fastidiously controls every variable in the life of a fish. Kona Blue houses 150 brood stock on shore a few miles north of Kona. These breeders are continually refreshed with deep-ocean water and left to do nothing but eat, swim, and procreate. Every few days a female lays as many as 300,000 eggs, which are harvested and transferred to a nursery ... When the fish reach an inch in length, they head to the ocean. In the wild the survival of two eggs would ensure sustainability for the species. Kona Blue does far better. "We get survival rates of 5% to 10%," says Sims.

Fortune, April 21, 2008

a. Why is the fish stock being overused?
b. How does Kona Blue help prevent overfishing, while at the same time allowing a greater amount of fish to be caught?
c. Use a model of the sustainable production of fish to illustrate your explanation.
d. Draw a graph to illustrate your answers to b and c.

6. Ottawa Opens Up Wireless Industry to More Competition

The Conservative government on Wednesday paved the way for new cellphone companies by announcing new rules for an auction of radio airwaves designed to spur competition in the wireless industry. About 40 per cent of the spectrum will be reserved for new entrants, with the remainder open to all bidders, including Canada's big three providers—Rogers, Bell and Telus. ... In handing down the rules, Industry Minister Jim Prentice gave potential newcomers, including Quebecor, MTS Allstream, Shaw and Eastlink, virtually everything they asked for. ... [H]e agreed with their assessment that prices are too high and the wireless industry needs more competition. "Our goal at the end of the day is lower prices, better services, and more choices," he said.

Those who had been arguing for more competition were delighted with the ruling. "This is a grand slam for consumers," telecom analyst Eamon Hoey told CBC News. "It really puts a heavy knife into the oligopolic style of structure we've had in the cellular business." Chris Peirce, chief regulatory officer of MTS Allstream, was pleased as well. "They have really gotten their policy right ..." he said.

But Liberal industry critic Scott Brison was not pleased. "There's no proof it will lead to lower prices," he argued, saying regulation would have been better. Brison said the auction decision will result in a $200-million windfall for the new entrants.

CBC News, November 28, 2007

a. Is the spectrum of the radio waves a private good, a common resource, or a public good? Explain why.
b. What in the news clip indicates that the auction is in the public interest?
c. When the new carriers commence to operate, how will consumer surplus and producer surplus change?
d. If the government had not conducted the auction but instead regulated the industry, would the market have been more efficient than it will be with increased competition?

7. Your city council is contemplating upgrading its traffic control system and the council believes that the bigger the computer it installs, the better job it can do. Elected officials want to install the scale of the system that will win most votes. The city bureaucrats want to maximize the budget. Suppose that you are an economist and your job is to calculate the scale of the system that uses resources efficiently.

a. What data would you need to reach your own conclusions?
b. What does the public choice theory predict will be the quantity chosen?
c. How could you, as an informed voter, attempt to influence the choice?

8. For each of the following goods, explain whether there is a free-rider problem. If there is no such problem, how is it avoided?

- Fire protection
- Niagara Falls
- Stanley Park
- Car licences
- Street lighting in urban areas
- Flood control in the Red River watershed
- Cavendish Beach on Prince Edward Island

9. The table provides information about a mosquito control program.

Quantity sprayed (hectares per day)	Marginal social cost	Marginal social benefit
	(dollars per day)	
0	0	0
1	1,000	5,000
2	2,000	4,000
3	3,000	3,000
4	4,000	2,000
5	5,000	1,000

a. What quantity of spraying would a private mosquito control program provide?

b. What is the efficient quantity of spraying?

c. Two political parties, the Conservers and the Eradicators, fight an election in which the only issue is the quantity of spraying to undertake. The Conservers want no spraying and the Eradicators want to spray 5 hectares per day. The voters are well-informed about the benefits and costs of mosquito control programs. What is the outcome of the election?

d. Draw a graph to illustrate the outcome of the election.

10. In problem 9, the government sets up a Mosquito Control Unit and appoints a bureaucrat to run the department.

a. Would the mosquito spraying most likely be underprovided, overprovided, or provided at the efficient quantity?

b. How do rational voters behave and why do they enable bureaucrats to behave in the way you described in a?

c. Draw a graph to illustrate the outcome when bureaucrats achieve their objective.

11. An oil reserve runs under plots of land owned by seven people. Each person has the right to sink a well on her or his land and take oil from the reserve. The amount of oil that is produced depends on the number of wells sunk and is shown in the table. The marginal private cost of a well is the equivalent of 4 litres a day.

Number of wells	Oil output (litres per day)
0	0
2	12
4	22
6	30
8	36
10	40
12	42
14	42

a. What is the marginal private benefit at each quantity of wells?

b. What are the equilibrium number of wells and quantity of oil produced?

c. What is the marginal social benefit at each quantity of wells?

d. What are the efficient number of wells and quantity of oil to produce?

e. If the common reserve were owned by only one person, how many wells would be sunk and how much oil would be produced?

f. How much would someone offer the seven owners to rent the rights to all the oil in the common reserve? (Use litres of oil as the units.)

12. If hikers were required to pay a fee to use the Overlander Trail in Jasper National Park,

a. Would the use of this common resource be more efficient?

b. Would it be even more efficient if the most popular spots had the highest prices?

c. Why do you think we don't see more market solutions to the tragedy of the commons?

13. **Who's Hiding under the [U.S.] Umbrella?**
Students of the Cold War learn that, to deter possible Soviet aggression, the United States placed a "strategic umbrella" over NATO Europe and Japan, declaring it would fight if their independence was threatened by the Soviet Union. ... European and Japanese allies have been taking

economic advantage of the fact that the United States was providing for most of their own national security.

Under President Ronald Reagan, approximately 6 percent of the GDP of the United States was spent on defence, whereas the Europeans tended to spend only 2 to 3 percent and the Japanese a miserly 1 percent, although all faced a common enemy. Thus the American taxpayer bore a disproportionate burden for the overall defence spending, whereas those sheltering under its umbrella spent more on social or consumer goods, or saved while the United States went further into debt. ... Today, the United States, like Rome and Britain in their time, is the provider of international public goods. ...

International Herald Tribune, January 30, 2008

a. Explain the free-rider problem described in this news clip.
b. Does the free-rider problem in international defence mean that the world has too little defence against aggression?
c. How do nations try to overcome the free-rider problem among nations?

14. **Commuting More than Pain at Pump**

... [T]he daily drive causes a large number of commuters everything from increased stress and anger to sleep deprivation and loss of productivity at work. ... Nearly half (45 percent) of the 4,091 respondents polled in 10 major metropolitan areas said that traffic congestion increased their stress levels. Another 28 percent said it heightened their feelings of anger. Almost one in five said commuting problems cut down on their productivity at work and in school and a full 12 percent said they were sleep deprived. ... The two biggest culprits: start-and-stop traffic and rude drivers.

Because traffic delays are typically random, commuters have to budget a larger amount of time to get from here to there. ... [IBM's Institute for Electronic Government] has been devising ways to help cities deal with increased traffic congestion, and has helped deploy automated tolling, congestion pricing plans and real-time traffic modeling in cities such as Brisbane, London, Singapore and Stockholm. ...

To help alleviate traffic problems, drivers said they wanted more options to work from home, improved public transportation, and better road condition information.

CNN, May 30, 2008

a. Are congested public roadways excludable or nonexcludable and rival or nonrival? Explain.
b. As a result of this classification, explain the problem associated with congested public roadways that results in an inefficient usage.
c. Draw a graph to illustrate the inefficient equilibrium.
d. How could government policies be used to achieve an efficient usage of roadways?

15. **Where the Tuna Roam**

... [T]o the first settlers, the Great Plains posed the same problem as the oceans today: It was a vast, open area where there seemed to be no way to protect animals against relentless human predators. ... But animals thrived [on the Prairies] once the settlers divvied up the land and ingeniously devised new ways to protect their livestock. ... Today the ocean is still pretty much an open range, and the fish are suffering the consequences. ... Fishermen have a personal incentive to make as much as they can this year, even if they're destroying their own profession in the process. They figure any fish they don't take for themselves will just be taken by someone else. ...

New York Times, November 4, 2006

a. What are the similarities between the problems faced by the earliest settlers on the Prairies and today's fishers?
b. Can the tragedy of the commons in the oceans be eliminated in the same manner used by the early settlers on the plains?
c. How can ITQs change the short-term outlook of fishers to a long-term outlook?

16. After you have studied *Reading Between the Lines* on pp. 406–407, answer the following questions:

a. What is happening in Puerto Rico that is causing the depletion of the country's tropical rainforests?
b. How would the creation of private property rights in Puerto Rico's rainforests change the way in which the forest resources are used?
c. Would private ownership solve all the problems of resource overuse? If not, why not?

UNDERSTANDING MARKET FAILURE AND GOVERNMENT

Making the Rules

Creating a a system of responsible democratic government is a huge enterprise and one that could easily go wrong. Creating a constitution that made despotic and tyrannical rule impossible was relatively easy. And we achieved such a constitution for Canada by using some sound economic ideas. We've designed a sophisticated system of incentives—of carrots and sticks—to make the government responsive to public opinion and to limit the ability of individual self-interests to gain at the expense of the social interest. But we have not been able to create a constitution that effectively blocks the ability of special interest groups to capture the consumer and producer surpluses that result from specialization and exchange.

We have created a system of government to deal with four market failures: (1) monopoly, (2) externalities, (3) public goods, and (4) common resources.

Government might help cope with these market failures. But as we know, government does not eliminate the pursuit of self-interest. Voters, politicians, and bureaucrats pursue their self-interest, sometimes at the expense of the social interest, and instead of market failure, we get government failure.

Many economists have thought long and hard about the problems discussed in this part. But no one has had as profound an effect on our ideas in this area as Ronald Coase.

Ronald Coase *(1910–), was born in England and educated at the London School of Economics, where he was deeply influenced by his teacher, Arnold Plant, and by the issues of his youth: communist central planning versus free markets.*

Professor Coase has lived in the United States since 1951. He first visited America as a 20-year-old on a travelling scholarship during the depths of the Great Depression. It was on this visit, and before he had completed his bachelor's degree, that he conceived the ideas that 60 years later were to earn him the 1991 Nobel Prize for Economic Science.

Ronald Coase discovered and clarified the significance of transactions costs and property rights for the functioning of the economy. He has revolutionized the way we think about property rights and externalities and has opened up the growing field of law and economics.

"The question to be decided is: is the value of fish lost greater or less than the value of the product which contamination of the stream makes possible?"

RONALD H. COASE
The Problem of Social Cost

TALKING
WITH

Caroline M. Hoxby

Caroline M. Hoxby is the Allie S. Freed Professor of Economics at Harvard University. Born in Cleveland, Ohio, she was an undergraduate at Harvard and a graduate student at Oxford and MIT.

Professor Hoxby is a leading student of the economics of education. She has written many articles on this topic and has published books entitled *The Economics of School Choice* and *College Choices* (both University of Chicago Press, 2003 and 2004, respectively). She is Program Director of the Economics of Education Program at the National Bureau of Economic Research, serves on several other national boards that study education issues, and has advised or provided testimony to several state legislatures and the United States Congress.

Michael Parkin and Robin Bade talked with Caroline Hoxby about her work and the progress that economists have made in understanding how the financing and provision of education influence the quality of education and the equality of access to it.

Why did you decide to become an economist?

I've wanted to be an economist from about the age of 13. That was when I took my first class in economics (an interesting story in itself) and discovered that all of the thoughts swimming around in my head belonged to a "science" and there was an entire body of people who understood this science—a lot better than I did, anyway. I can still recall reading *The Wealth of Nations* for the first time; it was a revelation.

What drew you to study the economics of education?

We all care about education, perhaps because it is the key means by which opportunity is (or should be) extended to all in the United States. Also, nearly everyone now acknowledges that highly developed countries like the United States rely increasingly on education as the engine of economic growth. Thus, one reason I was drawn to education is its importance. However, what primarily drew me was that education issues were so clearly begging for economic analysis and that there was so little of it. I try hard to understand educational institutions and problems, but I insist on bringing economic logic to bear on educational issues.

Why is education different from fast food? Why don't we just let people buy it from private firms that are regulated to maintain quality standards analogous to the safety standards that the FDA imposes on fast-food producers?

The thing that makes education different from fast food is not that we cannot buy it from private institutions that are regulated to maintain quality standards. We do this all the time—think of private schools and colleges. What makes education different is that it is (a) an investment, not consumption, and (b) the capital markets for financing the investments work poorly when left on their own. Essentially, our country has an interest in every person investing optimally in his or her education. To make investments, however, people need funds that allow them to attend good schools and take time away from work. Children don't have these funds and cannot arrange for loans that they may or may not pay off decades later. Therefore, children depend on their families for funds, and families do not necessarily have the funds to invest optimally or the right incentives to do so. Society has a role in filling the gaps in the capital market; it fills this role by public funding of elementary and secondary education, government guaranteed loans, college savings programs, and so on. There is no particular reason, however, why government needs to actually run schools; it can provide the funding without actually providing schooling.

In one of your papers, you posed the question: Does competition among public schools benefit students or taxpayers? What are the issues, what was your answer, and how did you arrive at it?

We are all familiar with the fact that families choose public schools when they choose where to live. This traditional form is by far the most pervasive form of school choice in the United States, and few parents who exercise it would be willing to give it up. Yet, until quite recently, we did not know whether having such traditional school choice was good for students (high achievement) or taxpayers (more efficient schools). It is important to know because some people in the United States, especially poor people who live in central cities, are unable to exercise this form of school choice. Economists hypothesized that this lack of choice might be a reason why many children from poor, central city families receive such a deficient education, especially considering the dollars spent in their schools (which spend significantly more than the median school).

To investigate this hypothesis, I examined all of the metropolitan areas in the United States. They vary a great deal in the degree of traditional choice available to parents. On one extreme, there is a group of metropolitan areas with hundreds of school districts. On the other extreme, there is a group of metropolitan areas with only one school district. Most are somewhere in between. A family in a metropolitan area with one district may have no easy way of "escaping" a badly run district administration. A family in a metropolitan area with hundreds of districts can choose among several districts that match well with its job location, housing preferences, and so on.

Looking across metropolitan areas with many districts (lots of potential competition from traditional school choice) and few districts (little potential competition), I found that areas with greater competition had substantially higher student achievement for any given level of school spending. This suggests that schools are more efficient producers of achievement when they face competition.

What do we know about the relative productivity of public and private schools?

It is somewhat difficult to say whether achievement is higher at public or private schools in the United States. The best studies use randomly assigned private school scholarships, follow the same children over time, or use "natural experiments" in which some areas accidentally end up with more private schools than others. These studies tend to find that, for the same student, private schools produce achievement that is up to 10 percent higher. However, for understanding which type of school is more productive, we actually do not need private schools to have higher achievement. For the sake of argument, let's "call it a draw" on the achievement question.

In recent studies comparing achievement in public and private schools, the public schools spent an average of $9,662 per student and the private schools spent an average of $2,427 per student. These spending numbers, combined with achievement that we will call equal, suggest that the private schools were 298 percent more productive. I would not claim that this number is precisely correct; we could think of some minor adjustments. But it is difficult not to conclude that the private schools are significantly more productive. They produce equal achievement for a fraction of the cost.

What can economists say about the alternative methods of financing education? Is there a voucher solution that could work?

There is definitely a voucher solution that could work because vouchers are inherently an extremely flexible policy. People often see the word "voucher" and think of, say, a $2,000 voucher being given to a small share of children. But this need not be so. Anything that we can do with public school financing we can do better with a voucher because vouchers can be specific to a student, whereas the government can never ensure that funds get to an individual student by giving those funds to his or her district.

Any well-designed voucher system will give schools an incentive to compete. However, when designing vouchers, we can also build in remedies for a variety of educational problems. Vouchers can be used to ensure that disabled children get the funding they need and the program choices they need. Compared to current school finance programs, vouchers can do a better job of ensuring that low-income families have sufficient funds to invest in the child's education. Well-designed vouchers can encourage schools to make their student bodies socio-economically diverse. Economists should say to policy makers: "Tell me your goals; I'll design you a voucher."

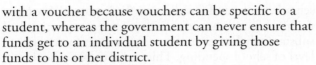

Economists should say to policy makers: "Tell me your goals; I'll design you a voucher."

Is there a conflict between efficiency and equity in the provision of quality education?

To raise the public funds that allow all families to invest optimally in their children's education, we have to have taxes. Taxes always create some deadweight loss, so we always create some inefficiency when we raise the funds we need to provide equitable educational opportunities. However, if the funds are used successfully and actually induce people to make optimal investments in their education, we have eliminated much more inefficiency than the taxes created. Thus, in an ideal world, there need not be a conflict between efficiency and equity.

In the real world, public funds are often raised with taxes (creating deadweight loss) and then are not successfully used. If we spend twice as much on public schools and do not have higher achievement to show for it, then there are no efficiency gains to overwhelm the efficiency losses from taxation. In other words, to avoid a conflict between equity and efficiency, we must learn how to use public funds productively in education. This is what the economics of education is all about.

What advice do you have for a student who is just starting to study economics? Is economics a good subject in which to major? What other subjects go well alongside it? And do you have anything special to say to women who are making a career choice? What must we do to get more women involved in our subject?

Students who are just starting to study economics should do two things. First, learn the tools even if they seem abstruse. Once you have mastered the tools, you will be able to "see the forest for the trees." As long as you don't master the tools, you will be in the trees and will find it hard to think about economic problems. Second, think about economic problems! The real world is a great moving textbook of economics, once you have the tools to analyze it.

Economics is a great subject in which to major because it trains you for life, for many careers, and for the thinking that you would need in a leadership position. I think that it is the best training for a future career in business, the law, or policy making. Don't forget nonprofits: every year, nonprofit organizations try to hire people with economics skills who are also interested in charitable schemes.

Math and statistics courses are complementary to economics because they make it easier for a student to master the tools quickly. Economics goes well with many studies in the arts and sciences, too. It all depends on what you want to use economics for. If you want to do health policy making, take economics along with premedical courses. If you want to be a policy maker in the performing arts, take economics along with music.

I wish that there were more women in economics. Our field loses far too many talented minds. Also, women who need to understand economics for their careers are sometimes without it. To aspiring women economists, I can only say to hang in there. Mastering economics is empowering. You will never have to worry about your opinion not being taken seriously if you are a good economist.

18 Markets for Factors of Production

After studying this chapter, you will be able to

- Describe the anatomy of factor markets

- Explain how the value of marginal product determines the demand for a factor of production

- Explain how wage rates and employment are determined and how labour unions influence the labour market

- Explain how capital and land rental rates and natural resource prices are determined

You know that wage rates vary a lot. A server at McDonald's earns $10 an hour. Ed Jones, who spends his days in a small container suspended from the top of Toronto's high-rise buildings cleaning windows, makes $12 an hour. Blue Jays pitcher A. J. Burnett collected a cool $13.2 million in 2008. Some differences in earnings might seem surprising. For example, some college football coaches earn much more than professors. What determines the wages that people earn?

The price of oil became a big issue in 2008 as new record highs were set. But then the price crashed. What determines the prices of the natural resources that we use to produce goods and services? Why do these prices fluctuate and sometimes seem to lose connection with the fundamentals of supply and value?

In this chapter, we study the markets for labour, capital, and natural resources and learn how their prices are determined. In *Reading Between the Lines* at the end of the chapter, we focus on the market for oil and look at the slowdown in the development of Alberta's huge oilsands resources.

417

◆ The Anatomy of Factor Markets

The four factors of production are

- Labour
- Capital
- Land (natural resources)
- Entrepreneurship

Let's take a brief look at the anatomy of the markets in which these factors of production are traded.

Markets for Labour Services

Labour services are the physical and mental work effort that people supply to produce goods and services. A labour market is a collection of people and firms who trade labour services. The price of labour services is the wage rate.

Some labour services are traded day by day. These services are called *casual labour*. People who pick fruit and vegetables often go to a farm and take whatever work is available that day. But most labour services are traded on a contract, called a **job**.

Most labour markets have many buyers and many sellers and are competitive. In these labour markets, the wage rate is determined by supply and demand, just like the price is determined in any other competitive market.

In some labour markets, a labour union organizes labour, which introduces an element of monopoly on the supply side of the labour market. In this type of labour market, a bargaining process between the union and the employer determines the wage rate.

We'll study both competitive labour markets and labour unions in this chapter.

Markets for Capital Services

Capital consists of the tools, instruments, machines, buildings, and other constructions that have been produced in the past and that businesses now use to produce goods and services. These physical objects are themselves goods—capital goods. Capital goods are traded in goods markets, just as bottled water and toothpaste are. The price of a dump truck, a capital good, is determined by supply and demand in the market for dump trucks. This market is not a market for capital services.

A market for *capital services* is a *rental market*—a market in which the services of capital are hired.

An example of a market for capital services is the vehicle rental market in which Avis, Budget, Hertz, U-Haul, and many other firms offer automobiles and trucks for hire. The price in a capital services market is a *rental rate*.

Most capital services are not traded in a market. Instead, a firm buys capital and uses it itself. The services of the capital that a firm owns and operates have an implicit price that arises from depreciation and interest costs (see Chapter 10, pp. 228–229). You can think of this price as the implicit rental rate of capital. Firms that buy capital and use it themselves are *implicitly* renting the capital to themselves.

Markets for Land Services and Natural Resources

Land consists of all the gifts of nature—natural resources. The market for land as a factor of production is the market for the *services of land*—the use of land. The price of the services of land is a rental rate.

Most natural resources, such as farm land, can be used repeatedly. But a few natural resources are nonrenewable. **Nonrenewable natural resources** are resources that can be used only once. Examples are oil, natural gas, and coal. The prices of nonrenewable natural resources are determined in global *commodity markets* and are called *commodity prices*.

Entrepreneurship

Entrepreneurial services are not traded in markets. Entrepreneurs receive the profit or bear the loss that results from their business decisions.

Review Quiz ◆

1 What are the factors of production and their prices?
2 What is the distinction between capital and the services of capital?
3 What is the distinction between the price of capital equipment and the rental rate of capital?

 Work Study Plan 18.1 and get instant feedback.

The rest of this chapter explores the influences on the demand and supply of factors of production. We begin by studying the demand for a factor of production.

The Demand for a Factor of Production

The demand for a factor of production is a **derived demand**—it is derived from the demand for the goods and services that it is used to produce. You've seen, in Chapters 10 through 15, how a firm determines its profit-maximizing output. The quantities of factors of production demanded are a consequence of firms' output decisions. A firm hires the quantities of factors of production that maximize its profit.

To decide the quantity of a factor of production to hire, a firm compares the cost of hiring an additional unit of the factor with its value to the firm. The cost of hiring an additional unit of a factor of production is the *factor price*. The value to the firm of hiring one more unit of a factor of production is called the factor's value of marginal product. The **value of marginal product** equals the price of a unit of output multiplied by the marginal product of the factor of production.

To study the demand for a factor of production, we'll use labour as the example. But what you learn here about the demand for labour applies to the demand for all factors of production.

Value of Marginal Product

Table 18.1 shows you how to calculate the value of the marginal product of labour at Angelo's Bakery. The first two columns show Angelo's total product

schedule—the number of loaves per hour that each quantity of labour can produce. The third column shows the marginal product of labour—the change in total product that results from a one-unit increase in the quantity of labour employed. (See Chapter 11, pp. 253–256 for a refresher on product schedules.)

Angelo can sell bread at the going market price of $2 a loaf. Given this information, we can calculate the value of marginal product (fourth column). It equals price multiplied by marginal product. For example, the marginal product of hiring the second worker is 6 loaves an hour. Each loaf sold brings in $2, so the value of the marginal product of the second worker is $12 (6 loaves at $2 each).

A Firm's Demand for Labour

The value of the marginal product of labour tells us what an additional worker is worth to a firm. It tells us the revenue that the firm earns by hiring one more worker. The wage rate tells us what an additional worker costs a firm.

The value of the marginal product of labour and the wage rate together determine the quantity of labour demanded by a firm. Because the value of marginal product decreases as the quantity of labour employed increases, there is a simple rule for maximizing profit: Hire the quantity of labour at which the value of marginal product equals the wage rate.

If the value of marginal product of labour exceeds the wage rate, a firm can increase its profit by hiring

TABLE 18.1   Value of Marginal Product at Angelo's Bakery

	Quantity of labour (L) (workers)	Total product (TP) (loaves per hour)	Marginal product (MP = ΔTP/ΔL) (loaves per worker)	Value of marginal product (VMP = MP × P) (dollars per worker)
A	0	0		
			7	14
B	1	7		
			6	**12**
C	2	13		
			5	10
D	3	18		
			4	8
E	4	22		
			3	6
F	5	25		

The value of the marginal product of labour equals the price of the product multiplied by marginal product of labour. If Angelo's hires 2 workers, the marginal product of the second worker is 6 loaves an hour (in the third column). The price of a loaf is $2, so the value of the marginal product of the second worker is $2 a loaf multiplied by 6 loaves an hour, which is $12 an hour (in the fourth column).

one more worker. If the wage rate exceeds the value of marginal product of labour, a firm can increase its profit by firing one worker. But if the wage rate equals the value of the marginal product of labour, the firm cannot increase its profit by changing the number of workers it employs. The firm is making the maximum possible profit.

So the quantity of labour demanded by a firm is the quantity at which the value of the marginal product of labour equals the wage rate.

A Firm's Demand for Labour Curve

A firm's demand for labour curve is derived from its value of marginal product curve. Figure 18.1 shows these two curves. Figure 18.1(a) shows the value of marginal product curve at Angelo's Bakery. The blue bars graph the numbers in Table 18.1. The curve labelled *VMP* is Angelo's value of marginal product curve.

If the wage rate falls and other things remain the same, a firm hires more workers. Figure 18.1(b) shows Angelo's demand for labour curve.

Suppose the wage rate is $10 an hour. You can see in Fig. 18.1(a) that if Angelo hires 2 workers, the value of the marginal product of labour is $12 an hour. At a wage rate of $10 an hour, Angelo makes a profit of $2 an hour on the second worker. If Angelo hires a third worker, the value of the marginal product of that worker is $10 an hour. So on this third worker, Angelo breaks even.

If Angelo hired 4 workers, his profit would fall. The fourth worker generates a value of marginal product of only $8 an hour but costs $10 an hour, so Angelo does not hire 4 workers. When the wage rate is $10 an hour, the quantity of labour demanded by Angelo is 3 workers, which is a point on Angelo's demand for labour curve, *D*, in Fig. 18.2(b).

If the wage rate increased to $12 an hour, Angelo would decrease the quantity of labour demanded to 2 workers. If the wage rate decreased to $8 an hour, Angelo would increase the quantity of labour demanded to 4 workers.

A change in the wage rate brings a change in the quantity of labour demanded and a movement along the demand for labour curve.

A change in any other influence on a firm's labour-hiring plans changes the demand for labour and shifts the demand for labour curve.

FIGURE 18.1   The Demand for Labour at Angelo's Bakery

(a) Value of marginal product

(b) Demand for labour

Angelo's Bakery can sell any quantity of bread at $2 a loaf. The blue bars in part (a) represent the firm's value of marginal product of labour (based on Table 18.1). The orange line is the firm's value of marginal product curve. Part (b) shows Angelo's demand for labour curve. Angelo hires the quantity of labour that makes the value of marginal product equal to the wage rate. The demand for labour curve slopes downward because the value of marginal product diminishes as the quantity of labour employed increases.

Changes in a Firm's Demand for Labour

A firm's demand for labour depends on

- The price of the firm's output
- The prices of other factors of production
- Technology

The Price of the Firm's Output The higher the price of a firm's output, the greater is the firm's demand for labour. The price of output affects the demand for labour through its influence on the value of marginal product of labour. A higher price for the firm's output increases the value of the marginal product of labour. A change in the price of a firm's output leads to a shift in the firm's demand for labour curve. If the price of the firm's output increases, the demand for labour increases and the demand for labour curve shifts rightward.

For example, if the price of bread increased to $3 a loaf, the value of the marginal product of Angelo's fourth worker would increase from $8 an hour to $12 an hour. At a wage rate of $10 an hour, Angelo would now hire 4 workers instead of 3.

The Prices of Other Factors of Production If the price of using capital decreases relative to the wage rate, a firm substitutes capital for labour and increases the quantity of capital it uses. Usually, the demand for labour will decrease when the price of using capital falls. For example, if the price of a bread-making machine falls, Angelo might decide to install one machine and lay off a worker. But the demand for labour could increase if the lower price of capital led to a sufficiently large increase in the scale of production. For example, with cheaper machines available, Angelo might install a machine and hire more labour to operate it. This type of factor substitution occurs in the long run when the firm can change the size of its plant.

Technology New technologies decrease the demand for some types of labour and increase the demand for other types. For example, if a new automated bread-making machine becomes available, Angelo might install one of these machines and fire most of his workforce—a decrease in the demand for bakery workers. But the firms that manufacture and service automated bread-making machines hire more labour, so there is an increase in the demand for this type of labour. An example occurred during the 1990s when electronic telephone exchanges decreased the demand for telephone operators and increased the demand for computer programmers and electronics engineers.

Table 18.2 summarizes the influences on a firm's demand for labour.

TABLE 18.2 A Firm's Demand for Labour

The Law of Demand

(Movements along the demand curve for labour)

The quantity of labour demanded by a firm

Decreases if:	Increases if:
■ The wage rate increases	■ The wage rate decreases

Changes in Demand

(Shifts in the demand curve for labour)

A firm's demand for labour

Decreases if:	Increases if:
■ The price of the firm's output decreases	■ The price of the firm's output increases
■ The price of a substitute for labour falls	■ The price of a substitute for labour rises
■ The price of a complement of labour rises	■ The price of a complement of labour falls
■ A new technology or new capital decreases the marginal product of labour	■ A new technology or new capital increases the marginal product of labour

Review Quiz

1 What is the value of marginal product of labour?
2 What is the relationship between the value of marginal product of labour and the marginal product of labour?
3 How is the demand for labour derived from the value of marginal product of labour?
4 What are the influences on the demand for labour?

 Work Study Plan 18.2 and get instant feedback.

Labour Markets

Labour services are traded in many different labour markets. Examples are markets for bakery workers, van drivers, crane operators, computer support specialists, air traffic controllers, dentists, and economists. Some of these markets, such as the market for bakery workers, are local. They operate in a given urban area. Some labour markets, such as the market for air traffic controllers, are national. Firms and workers search across the nation for the right match of worker and job. And some labour markets are global, such as the market for superstar hockey, basketball, and soccer players.

We'll look at a local market for bakery workers as an example. First, we'll look at a *competitive* labour market. Then, we'll see how monopoly elements can influence a labour market.

A Competitive Labour Market

A competitive labour market is one in which many firms demand labour and many households supply labour.

Market Demand for Labour Earlier in the chapter, you saw how an individual firm decides how much labour to hire. The market demand for labour is derived from the demand for labour by individual firms. We determine the market demand for labour by adding together the quantities of labour demanded by all the firms in the market at each wage rate. (The market demand for a good or service is derived in a similar way—see p. 110.)

Because each firm's demand for labour curve slopes downward, the market demand for labour curve also slopes downward.

The Market Supply of Labour The market supply of labour is derived from the supply of labour decisions made by individual households.

Individual's Labour Supply Decision People can allocate their time to two broad activities: labour supply and leisure. (Leisure is a catch-all term. It includes all activities other than supplying labour.) For most people, leisure is more fun than work so to induce them to work they must be offered a wage.

Think about the labour supply decision of Jill, one of the workers at Angelo's Bakery. Let's see how the wage rate influences the quantity of labour she is willing to supply.

Reservation Wage Rate Jill enjoys her leisure time, and she would be pleased if she didn't have to spend her time working at Angelo's Bakery. But Jill wants to earn an income, and as long as she can earn a wage rate of at least $5 an hour, she's willing to work. This wage is called her *reservation wage*. At any wage rate above her reservation wage, Jill supplies some labour.

The wage rate at Angelo's is $10 an hour, and at that wage rate, Jill chooses to work 30 hours a week. At a wage rate of $10 an hour, Jill regards this use of her time as the best available. Figure18.2 illustrates.

Backward-Bending Labour Supply Curve If Jill were offered a wage rate between $5 and $10 an hour, she would want to work fewer hours. If she were offered a wage rate above $10 an hour, she would want to work

FIGURE 18.2 Jill's Labour Supply Curve

Jill's labour supply curve is *S*. Jill supplies no labour at wage rates below her reservation wage of $5 an hour. As the wage rate rises above $5 an hour, the quantity of labour that Jill supplies increases to a maximum of 40 hours a week at a wage rate of $25 an hour. As the wage rate rises above $25 an hour, Jill supplies a decreasing quantity of labour; her labour supply curve bends backward. The income effect on the demand for leisure dominates the substitution effect.

more hours, but only up to a point. If Jill could earn $25 an hour, she would be willing to work 40 hours a week (and earn $1,000 a week). But at a wage rate above $25 an hour, with the goods and services that Jill can buy for $1,000, her priority would be a bit more leisure time. So if the wage rate increased above $25 an hour, Jill would cut back on her work hours and take more leisure. Jill's labour supply curve eventually bends backward.

Jill's labour supply decisions are influenced by a substitution effect and an income effect.

Substitution Effect At wage rates below $25 an hour, the higher the wage rate Jill is offered, the greater is the quantity of labour that she supplies. Jill's wage rate is her *opportunity cost of leisure*. If she quits work an hour early to catch a movie, the cost of that extra hour of leisure is the wage rate that Jill forgoes. The higher the wage rate, the less willing Jill is to forgo the income and take the extra leisure time. This tendency for a higher wage rate to induce Jill to work longer hours is a *substitution effect*.

Income Effect The higher Jill's wage rate, the higher is her income. A higher income, other things remaining the same, induces Jill to increase her demand for most goods and services. Leisure is one of those goods. Because an increase in income creates an increase in the demand for leisure, it also creates a decrease in the quantity of labour supplied.

Market Supply Curve Jill's supply curve shows the quantity of labour supplied by Jill as her wage rate changes. Most people behave like Jill and have a backward bending labour supply curve, but they have different reservation wage rates and wage rates at which their labour supply curves bend backward.

A market supply curve shows the quantity of labour supplied by all households in a particular job market. It is found by adding together the quantities of labour supplied by all households to a given job market at each wage rate. Also, along a supply curve in a particular job market, the wage rates available in other job markets remain the same. For example, along the supply curve of bakery workers, the wage rates of all other labour are constant.

Despite the fact that an individual's labour supply curve eventually bends backward, the market supply curve of labour slopes upward. The higher the wage rate for bakery workers, the greater is the quantity of labour supplied in that labour market.

Let's now look at labour market equilibrium.

Competitive Labour Market Equilibrium Labour market equilibrium determines the wage rate and employment. In Fig. 18.3, the market demand curve for bakery workers is D and the market supply curve of bakery workers is S. The equilibrium wage rate is $10 an hour, and the equilibrium quantity is 300 bakery workers. If the wage rate exceeded $10 an hour, there would be a surplus of bakery workers. More people would be looking for jobs in bakeries than firms were willing to hire. In such a situation, the wage rate would fall as firms found it easy to hire people at a lower wage rate. If the wage rate were less than $10 an hour, there would be a shortage of bakery workers. Firms would not be able to fill all the positions they had available. In this situation, the wage rate would rise as firms found it necessary to offer higher wages to attract labour. Only at a wage rate of $10 an hour are there no forces operating to change the wage rate.

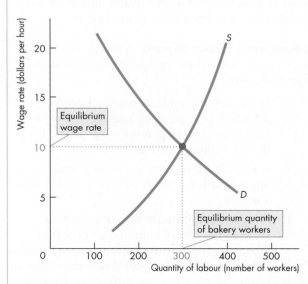

FIGURE 18.3 The Market for Bakery Workers

A competitive labour market coordinates firms' and households' plans. The market is in equilibrium—the quantity of labour demanded equals the quantity supplied at a wage rate of $10 an hour when 300 workers are employed. If the wage rate exceeds $10 an hour, the quantity supplied exceeds the quantity demanded and the wage rate will fall. If the wage rate is below $10 an hour, the quantity demanded exceeds the quantity supplied and the wage rate will rise.

myeconlab animation

A Labour Market with a Union

A **labour union** is an organized group of workers that aims to increase the wage rate and influence other job conditions. Let's see what happens when a union enters a competitive labour market.

Influences on Labour Supply One way of raising the wage rate is to decrease the supply of labour. In some labour markets, a union can restrict supply by controlling entry into apprenticeship programs or by influencing job qualification standards. Markets for skilled workers, doctors, dentists, and lawyers are the easiest ones to control in this way.

If there is an abundant supply of nonunion labour, a union can't decrease supply. For example, in the market for farm labour in southern Ontario, the flow of nonunion labour from Jamaica makes it difficult for a union to control the supply.

On the demand side of the labour market, the union faces a tradeoff: The demand for labour curve slopes downward, so restricting supply to raise the wage rate costs jobs. For this reason, unions also try to influence the demand for union labour.

Influences on Labour Demand A union tries to increase the demand for the labour of its members in four main ways:

1. Increasing the value of marginal product of its members by organizing and sponsoring training schemes and apprenticeship programs, and by professional certification

2. Lobbying for imports restrictions and encouraging people to buy goods made by unionized workers

3. Supporting minimum wage laws, which increase the cost of employing low-skilled labour and lead firms to substitute high-skilled union labour for low-skilled nonunion labour

4. Lobbying for restrictive immigration laws to decrease the supply of foreign workers

Labour Market Equilibrium with a Union Figure 18.4 illustrates what happens to the wage rate and employment when a union successfully enters a competitive labour market. With no union, the demand curve is D_C, the supply curve is S_C, the wage rate is $10 an hour, and 300 workers have jobs.

Now a union enters this labour market. First, look at what happens if the union has sufficient control

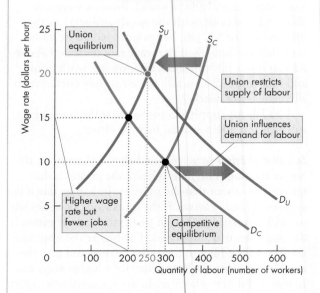

FIGURE 18.4   A Union Enters a Competitive Labour Market

In a competitive labour market, the demand curve is D_C and the supply curve is S_C. The wage rate is $10 an hour and 300 workers are employed. If a union decreases the supply of labour and the supply of labour shifts to S_U, the wage rate rises to $15 an hour and employment decreases to 200 workers. If the union can also increase the demand for labour and shift the demand curve to D_U, the wage rate rises to $20 an hour and 250 workers are employed.

[X] myeconlab animation

over the supply of labour to be able to restrict supply below its competitive level—to S_U. If that is all the union is able to do, employment falls to 200 workers and the wage rate rises to $15 an hour.

Suppose now that the union is also able to increase the demand for labour to D_U. The union can get an even bigger increase in the wage rate with a smaller fall in employment. By maintaining the restricted labour supply at S_U, the union increases the wage rate to $20 an hour and achieves an employment level of 250 workers.

Because a union restricts the supply of labour in the market in which it operates, the union's actions spill over into nonunion markets. Workers who can't get union jobs must look elsewhere for work. This action increases the supply of labour in nonunion markets and lowers the wage rate in those markets. This spillover effect further widens the gap between union and nonunion wages.

Monopsony in the Labour Market Not all labour markets in which unions operate are competitive. Rather, there are labour markets in which the employer possesses market power and the union enters to try to counteract that power.

A market in which there is a single buyer is called a **monopsony**. A monopsony labour market has one employer. Each of the provincial governments is the major employer of health-care professionals. In some isolated mining communities, the local mine is the main employer. These firms have monopsony power.

A monopsony acts on the buying side of a market in a similar way to a monopoly on the selling side. The firm maximizes profit by hiring the quantity of labour that makes the marginal cost of labour equal to the value of marginal product of labour and by paying the lowest wage rate at which it can attract this quantity of labour.

Figure 18.5 illustrates a monopsony labour market. Like all firms, a monopsony faces a downward-sloping value of marginal product curve, *VMP,* which is its demand for labour curve, *D*—the curve *VMP = D* in the figure.

What is special about monopsony is the marginal cost of labour. For a firm in a competitive labour market, the marginal cost of labour is the wage rate. For a monopsony, the marginal cost of labour exceeds the wage rate. The reason is that being the only buyer in the market, the firm faces an upward-sloping labour supply curve—the curve *S* in the figure.

To attract one more worker, the monopsony must offer a higher wage rate. But it must pay this higher wage rate to all its workers, so the marginal cost of a worker is the wage rate plus the increased wage bill that arises from paying all the workers the higher wage rate.

The supply curve is now the average cost of labour curve and the relationship between the supply curve and the marginal cost of labour curve, *MCL,* is similar to that between a monopoly's demand curve and marginal revenue curve (see p. 302). The relationship between the supply curve and the *MCL* curve is also similar to that between a firm's average cost curve and marginal cost curve (see pp. 258–259).

To find the profit-maximizing quantity of labour to hire, the monopsony sets the marginal cost of labour equal to the value of marginal product of labour. In Fig. 18.5, this outcome occurs when the firm employs 100 workers.

To hire 100 workers, the firm must pay $10 an hour (on the supply of labour curve). Each worker is

paid $10 an hour, but the value of marginal product of labour is $20 an hour, so the firm makes an economic profit of $10 an hour on the marginal worker.

If the labour market in Fig. 18.5 were competitive, equilibrium wage rate and employment would be determined by the demand and supply curves. The wage rate would be $15 an hour, and 150 workers would be employed. So compared with a competitive labour market, a monopsony pays a lower wage rate and employs fewer workers.

A Union and a Monopsony A union is like a monopoly. If the union (monopoly seller) faces a monopsony buyer, the situation is called **bilateral monopoly**. The National Hockey League (the owners) and the National Hockey League Players' Association (the union of players) is an example of bilateral monopoly. The NHL and the NHLPA negotiate a multi-year salary deal.

FIGURE 18.5 A Monopsony Labour Market

A monopsony is a market structure in which there is a single buyer. A monopsony in the labour market has a value of marginal product curve *VMP* and faces a labour supply curve *S*. The marginal cost of labour curve is *MCL*. Making the marginal cost of labour equal to value of marginal product maximizes profit. The monopsony hires 100 hours of labour and pays the lowest wage rate for which that quantity of labour will work, which is $10 an hour.

myeconlab animation

The outcome of bargaining depends on the costs that each party can inflict on the other. The firm can shut down the plant and lock out its workers, and the workers can shut down the plant by striking. Each party estimates the other's strength and what it will lose if it does not agree to the other's demands.

Usually, an agreement is reached without a strike or a lockout. The threat is usually enough to bring the bargaining parties to an agreement. When a strike or lockout does occur, it is because one party has misjudged the costs each party can inflict on the other. Such an event occurred on September 15, 2004, when negotiations failed and the owners locked out the players. The 88th NHL season was cancelled. Teams lost an estimated $2 billion in revenue from tickets, media, sponsorships, and concessions, while players gave up about $1 billion in lost salaries.

In the example in Fig. 18.5, if the union and employer are equally strong, and each party knows the strength of the other, they will agree to split the gap between $10 (the wage rate on the supply curve) and $20 (the wage rate on the demand curve) and agree to a wage rate of $15 an hour.

You've now seen that in a monopsony, a union can bargain for a higher wage rate without sacrificing jobs. A similar outcome can arise in a monopsony labour market when a minimum wage law is enforced. Let's look at the effect of a minimum wage.

Monopsony and the Minimum Wage

In a competitive labour market, a minimum wage that exceeds the equilibrium wage decreases employment (see pp. 133–134). In a monopsony labour market, a minimum wage can increase both the wage rate and employment. Let's see how.

Figure 18.6 shows a monopsony labour market without a union. The wage rate is $10 an hour and 100 workers are employed.

A minimum wage law is passed that requires employers to pay at least $15 an hour. The monopsony now faces a perfectly elastic supply of labour at $15 an hour up to 150 workers (along the minimum wage line). To hire more than 150 workers, a wage rate above $15 an hour must be paid (along the supply curve). Because the wage rate is $15 an hour up to 150 workers, so is the marginal cost of labour $15 an hour up to 150 workers. To maximize profit, the monopsony sets the marginal cost of labour equal to the value of marginal product of labour (on the demand curve). That is, the monopsony hires 150

FIGURE 18.6 Minimum Wage Law in Monopsony

In a monopsony labour market, the wage rate is $10 an hour and 100 workers are hired. If a minimum wage law increases the wage rate to $15 an hour, the wage rate rises to this level and employment increases to 150 workers.

myeconlab animation

workers and pays $15 an hour. The minimum wage law has succeeded in raising the wage rate and increasing the amount of labour employed.

Scale of the Union–Nonunion Wage Gap

You've seen how a union can influence the wage rate, but how much of a difference to wage rates do unions actually make? This question is difficult to answer. To measure the difference in wages attributable to unions, economists have looked at the wages of unionized and nonunionized workers who do similar work and have similar skills.

The evidence based on these comparisons is that the union–nonunion wage gap lies between 10 and 25 percent of the wage. For example, unionized airline pilots earn about 25 percent more than nonunion pilots with the same level of skill. In markets that have only a union wage rate, we might presume that the wage rate is 10 to 25 percent higher than it would be in the absence of a union.

Wage Rates in Canada
How School Pays

In 2008, the average wage rate in Canada was a bit less than $700 a week. The figure shows the *average weekly wage rates* for 15 jobs selected from those for which Statistics Canada reports wage-rate data.

You can see that a senior manager, on average, earns more than three times as much per week as a chef or cook and more than twice as much as the operator of a machine. Remember that these numbers are averages. Individual managers earn much more or much less than the average manager.

Many more occupations earn a wage rate below the national average than above it. And most of the occupations that earn more than the national average require a college degree and post-graduate training.

Earning differences are explained by differences in the value of the marginal product of the skills in the various occupations and in market power.

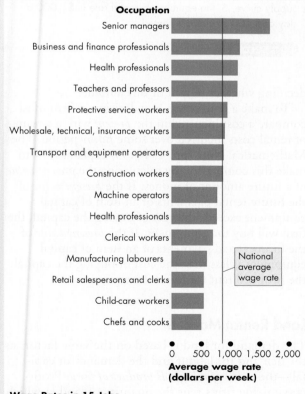

Wage Rates in 15 Jobs

Source of data: Statistics Canada.

Trends and Differences in Wage Rates

You can use what you've learned about labour markets to explain the trends and differences in wage rates.

Wage rates increase over time—trend upward. The reason is that the value of marginal product of labour trends upward. Technological change and the new types of capital that it brings make workers more productive. With greater labour productivity, the demand for labour increases and so does the average wage rate. Even jobs in which productivity doesn't increase experience an increase in the *value* of marginal product. Child care is an example. A child-care worker can't care for an increasing number of children, but an increasing number of parents who earn high wages are willing to hire child-care workers. The *value* of marginal product of these workers increases.

Wage rates are unequal, and in recent years, they have become increasingly unequal. High wage rates have increased rapidly while low wage rates have stagnated or even fallen. The reasons are complex and not fully understood.

One reason is that the new technologies of the 1990s and 2000s made skilled workers more productive and destroyed some low-skilled jobs. For example, the ATM took bank-teller jobs and lowered their wage rate but created jobs for computer programmers and electronic engineers and increased their wage rates. Another reason is that globalization has increased competition for low-skilled workers and opened global markets for high-skilled workers.

Review Quiz

1 What determines the amount of labour that households plan to supply?
2 How are the wage rate and employment determined in a competitive labour market?
3 How do labour unions influence wage rates?
4 What is a monopsony and why is a monopsony able to pay a lower wage rate than a firm in a competitive labour market?
5 How is the wage rate determined when a union faces a monopsony?
6 What is the effect of a minimum wage law in a monopsony labour market?

 Work Study Plan 18.3 and get instant feedback.

Capital and Natural Resource Markets

The markets for capital and land can be understood by using the same basic ideas that you've seen when studying a competitive labour market. But markets for nonrenewable natural resources are different. We'll now examine three groups of factor markets:

- Capital rental markets
- Land rental markets
- Nonrenewable natural resource markets

Capital Rental Markets

The demand for capital is derived from the *value of marginal product of capital*. Profit-maximizing firms hire the quantity of capital services that makes the value of marginal product of capital equal to the *rental rate of capital*. The *lower* the rental rate of capital, other things remaining the same, the *greater* is the quantity of capital demanded. The supply of capital responds in the opposite way to the rental rate. The *higher* the rental rate, other things remaining the same, the *greater* is the quantity of capital supplied. The equilibrium rental rate makes the quantity of capital demanded equal to the quantity supplied.

Figure 18.7 illustrates the rental market for tower cranes—capital used to construct high-rise buildings. The value of marginal product and the demand curve is $VMP = D$. The supply curve is S. The equilibrium rental rate is $1,000 per day and 100 tower cranes are rented.

Rent-Versus-Buy Decision Some capital services are obtained in a rental market, such as the market for tower cranes. And like tower cranes, many of the world's large airlines rent their airplanes. But not all capital services are obtained in a rental market. Instead, firms buy the capital equipment that they use. You saw in Chapter 10 (pp. 228–229) that the cost of the services of the capital that a firm owns and operates itself is an implicit rental rate that arises from depreciation and interest costs. Firms that buy capital *implicitly* rent the capital to themselves.

The decision to obtain capital services in a rental market rather than buying capital and renting it implicitly is made to minimize cost. The firm compares the cost of explicitly renting the capital and the cost of buying and implicitly renting it. This decision is the same as the one that a household makes in

FIGURE 18.7   A Rental Market for Capital

The value of marginal product of tower cranes, *VMP*, determines the demand, *D*, for tower crane rentals. With the supply curve, *S*, the equilibrium rental rate is $1,000 a day and 100 cranes are rented.

deciding whether to rent or buy a home.

To make a rent-versus-buy decision, a firm must compare a cost incurred in the *present* with a stream of rental costs incurred over some *future* period. The Mathematical Note (pp. 434–435) explains how to make this comparison by calculating the *present value* of a future amount of money. If the *present value* of the future rental payments of an item of capital equipment exceeds the cost of buying the capital, the firm will buy the equipment. If the *present value* of the future rental payments of an item of capital equipment is less than the cost of buying the capital, the firm will rent (or lease) the equipment.

Land Rental Markets

The demand for land is based on the same factors as the demand for labour and the demand for capital—the *value of marginal product of land*. Profit-maximizing firms rent the quantity of land at which the value of marginal product of land is equal to the *rental rate of land*. The *lower* the rental rate, other things remaining the same, the *greater* is the quantity of land demanded.

But the supply of land is special: Its quantity is fixed so the quantity supplied of each particular block of land cannot be changed by people's decisions and its supply is perfectly inelastic.

The equilibrium rental rate makes the quantity of land demanded equal to the quantity available. Figure 18.8 illustrates the market for a hectare of land in Toronto. The value of marginal product of this land and its demand curve is $VMP = D$. The quantity supplied is fixed and the supply curve is S. The equilibrium rental rate is $1,000 per hectare per day.

The rental rate of land is high on Bloor Street in downtown Toronto because the willingness to pay for the services produced by that land is high, which makes the VMP of land high. A Big Mac costs more at McDonald's on Bloor Street than at McDonald's on Mountain Road, Moncton, but not because the rental rate of land is higher in Toronto. The rental rate of land is higher in Toronto because of the greater willingness to pay for a Big Mac (and other goods and services) in Toronto.

FIGURE 18.8   A Rental Market for Land

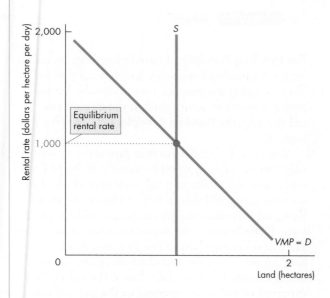

The value of marginal product of a 1 hectare block, *VMP*, determines the rental demand, *D*, for this land. With supply curve *S*, the land rents for $1,000 per day.

Nonrenewable Natural Resource Markets

The nonrenewable natural resources are oil, gas, and coal. Burning one of these fuels converts it to energy and other by-products, and the used resource cannot be re-used. The natural resources that we use to make metals are also nonrenewable, but they can be used again, at some cost, by recycling them.

Oil, gas, and coal are traded in global commodity markets. The price of a given grade of crude oil is the same in Calgary, London, and Singapore. Traders, linked by telephone and the Internet, operate these markets around the clock every day of the year.

Demand and supply determine the prices and the quantities traded in these commodity markets. We'll look at the influences on demand and supply by considering the global market for crude oil.

The Demand for Oil   The two key influences on the demand for oil are

1. The *value of marginal product* of oil
2. The expected future price of oil

The value of marginal product of oil is the *fundamental* influence on demand. It works in exactly the same way for a nonrenewable resource as it does for any other factor of production. The greater the quantity of oil used, the smaller is the value of marginal product of oil. Diminishing value of marginal product makes the demand curve slope downward. The lower the price, the greater is the quantity demanded.

The higher the expected future price of oil, the greater is the present demand for oil. The expected future price is a *speculative* influence on demand. Oil in the ground and oil in storage tanks are inventories that can be held or sold. A trader might plan to buy oil to hold now and sell later for a profit. Instead of buying oil to hold and sell later, the trader could buy a bond and earn interest. The forgone interest is the opportunity cost of holding the oil. If the price of oil is expected to rise by a bigger percentage than the interest rate, a trader will hold oil and incur the opportunity cost. In this case, the return from holding oil exceeds the return from holding bonds.

The Supply of Oil   The three key influences on the supply of oil are

1. The known oil reserves
2. The scale of current oil production facilities
3. The expected future price of oil

Known oil reserves are the oil that has been discovered and can be extracted with today's technology. This quantity increases over time because advances in technology enable ever less accessible sources to be discovered. The greater the size of known reserves, the greater is the supply of oil. But this influence on supply is small and indirect. It operates by changing the expected distant future price of oil. Even a major new discovery of oil would have a negligible effect on current supply.

The scale of current oil production facilities is the *fundamental* influence on supply. Producing oil is like any production activity: It is subject to increasing marginal cost. The increasing marginal cost of extracting oil means that the supply curve of oil slopes upward. The higher the price of oil, the greater is the quantity supplied. When new oil wells are sunk or when new faster pumps are installed, the supply of oil increases. When existing wells run dry, the supply of oil decreases. Over time, the factors that increase supply are more powerful than those that decrease supply, so changes in the fundamental influence increase the supply of oil.

Speculative forces based on expectations about the future price also influence the supply of oil. The *higher* the expected future price of oil, the *smaller* is the present supply of oil. A trader with an oil inventory might plan to sell now or to hold and sell later. You've seen that forgone interest is the opportunity cost of holding the oil. If the price of oil is expected to rise by a bigger percentage than the interest rate, it is profitable to incur the opportunity cost of holding oil rather than selling it immediately.

The Equilibrium Price of Oil The demand for oil and the supply of oil determine the equilibrium price and quantity traded. Figure 18.9 illustrates the market equilibrium.

The value of marginal product of oil, *VMP*, is the *fundamental determinant of demand*, and the marginal cost of extraction, *MC*, is the *fundamental determinant of supply*. Together, they determine the *market fundamentals price*.

If expectations about the future price are also based on fundamentals, the equilibrium price is the market fundamentals price. But if expectations about the future price of oil depart from what the market fundamentals imply, *speculation* can drive a wedge between the equilibrium price and the market fundamentals price.

FIGURE 18.9 A Nonrenewable Natural Resource Market

The value of marginal product of a natural resource, *VMP*, and the marginal cost of extraction, *MC*, determine the *market fundamentals price*. Demand, *D*, and supply, *S*, which determine the equilibrium price, are influenced by the expected future price. Speculation can bring a gap between the market fundamentals price and the equilibrium price.

The Hotelling Principle Harold Hotelling, an economist at Columbia University, had an incredible idea: Traders expect the price of a nonrenewable natural resource to rise at a rate equal to the interest rate. We call this idea the **Hotelling Principle**. Let's see why it is correct.

You've seen that the interest rate is the opportunity cost of holding an oil inventory. If the price of oil is expected to rise at a rate that exceeds the interest rate, it is profitable to hold a bigger inventory. Demand increases, supply decreases, and the price rises. If the interest rate exceeds the rate at which the price of oil is expected to rise, it is not profitable to hold an oil inventory. Demand decreases, supply increases, and the price falls. But if the price of oil is expected to rise at a rate equal to the interest rate, holding an inventory of oil is just as good as holding bonds. Demand and supply don't change and the price does not change. Only when the price of oil is expected to rise at a rate equal to the interest rate is the price at its equilibrium.

The World Market for Oil

Wild Prices Keep Returning to Hotelling Path

The world price shot up from $US93 a barrel in January 2008 to $137 a barrel in July, and then crashed to $US64 a barrel by October.

The Hotelling Principle tells us that we must expect the price of oil to rise at a rate equal to the interest rate. But expecting the price to rise at a rate equal to the interest rate doesn't mean that the price will rise at this rate.

As you can see in the figure below, over the past 50 or so years the price of oil has not followed the path predicted by the Hotelling Principle. But it has kept returning to that path.

The future is unpredictable and expectations about future prices keep changing. The forces that influence expectations are not well understood. The expected future price of oil depends on its expected future rate of use and the rate of discovery of new sources of supply. Guesses can change abruptly and become self-reinforcing. When the expected future price of oil changes for whatever reason, demand and supply change, and so does the price. Prices in speculative markets are always volatile.

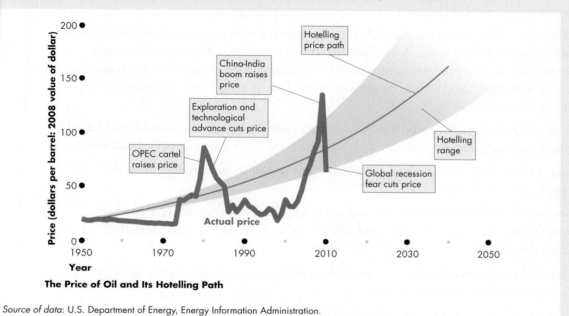

The Price of Oil and Its Hotelling Path

Source of data: U.S. Department of Energy, Energy Information Administration.

Review Quiz

1 What determines demand and supply in rental markets for capital and land?
2 What determines the demand for a nonrenewable natural resource?
3 What determines the supply of a nonrenewable natural resource?
4 What is the market fundamentals price and how might it differ from the equilibrium price?
5 Explain the Hotelling Principle.

myeconlab Work Study Plan 18.4 and get instant feedback.

You've now completed your study of markets for factors of production. You've seen that although the influences on supply are special to each factor of production, the core idea that value of marginal product determines the demand for a factor of production applies to all factors. *Reading Between the Lines* on pp. 432–433 looks at the development of Alberta's oilsands resources as the price of oil changes.

The next chapter looks at how the market economy distributes income and explains the trends in the distribution of income. The chapter also looks at the government's efforts to redistribute income and modify the market outcome.

Canada's Oilsands

Another Oilsands Project Pushed Aside for Now

October 30, 2008

Yet another multi-billion-dollar oilsands project has been put on hold as rising costs and uncertainty about financial markets and commodity prices grip a sector that had anticipated $126 billion in new investment over the next four years.

On Thursday, Royal Dutch Shell announced it would delay its decision on a second 100,000-barrel-per-day expansion of its Fort McMurray, Alta.-area oilsands-mining operations until costs come down. ...

Escalating costs for everything from labour to steel are noted in a new report by the Calgary-based Canadian Energy Research Institute that shows new large-scale integrated mining projects will cost $140,000 per flowing barrel of synthetic crude to construct and require oil prices of more than $80 US, at the current Canada–U.S. exchange rate, to ensure a 10 per-cent rate of return to investors.

"I don't think there will be a stop (in development)," said CERI oil economist David McColl. "Projects are just going to come on a little bit slower and that's not necessarily a bad thing. ...

In fact, I would suggest that slower growth will help us manage the production of the resource a little bit better." ...

"Given the combination of high costs and low crude prices we expect to see a number of project deferral announcements," said UBS Securities Canada Inc. research analyst Andrew Potter.

He has said rising costs, for labour in particular, could force a number of projects in the region to be delayed, reworked or sold.

Material reprinted with the express permission of "The National Post Company", a Canwest Partnership.

Essence of the Story

- Royal Dutch Shell has put a $126 billion Alberta oilsands project on hold.
- This is the second 100,000-barrel-per-day expansion to be delayed.
- A combination of high costs and low oil prices is the reason.
- The cost of labour, steel, and other resources has increased.
- The price of crude oil has fallen.
- A price of at least $US80 is needed to make oilsands profitable.

Economic Analysis

- The market for oil is a global market, and demand and supply in the global oil market determine the price.

- Both demand and supply depend on expectations of the future price of oil, which results in a highly volatile price.

- But in the long run and on average, the price of oil keeps returning to rise along the path implied by the Hotelling Principle.

- The sources of oil supply change in the long run as the price changes.

- Figure 1 shows how increases in the demand for oil bring higher prices that eventually make high-marginal cost sources of oil worth using.

- With demand at D_0, the price of oil is $20 a barrel and only easily tapped sources with a low marginal cost, such as those in the Middle East, are used.

- With demand at D_1, the price of oil is $40 a barrel and sources with a higher marginal cost, such as offshore sources like Hibernia, are used.

- With demand at D_0, the price of oil is $80 a barrel and sources with a high marginal cost, such as the Alberta oilsands, are used.

- When the price of oil was above $100 a barrel in mid-2008, plans were made to develop Alberta oilsands projects.

- When the price of oil fell to below $80 a barrel in October 2008, Alberta oilsands projects were put on hold.

- The market for oil and the Alberta labour market interact and Fig. 2 shows this interaction.

- With an expansion of oilsand development, the demand for labour in Alberta increased. The demand curve shifted rightward from D_0 to D_1. The wage rate and employment increased.

- When the world price of oil fell in the second half of 2008 and oilsands projects became unprofitable, the demand for labour (and other resources) decreased.

- The demand for labour curve shifted back to D_0 and the wage rate and employment decreased.

- But lower wage rates and lower costs of other resources used to develop oilsands projects didn't

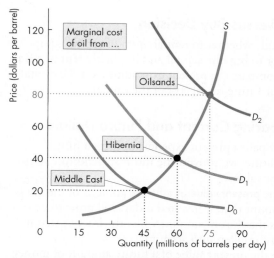

Figure 1 The crude oil market in the long run

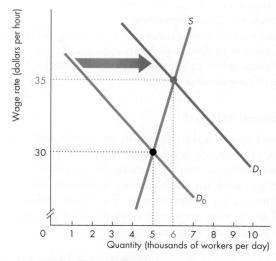

Figure 2 The Alberta labour market

overcome the low price of oil and reverse the decision to slow down the oilsands development.

- It was the low world price of oil, not high wage rates and other costs, that slowed the development of Alberta's oilsands projects.

433

MATHEMATICAL NOTE

Present Value and Discounting

Rent-Versus-Buy Decision

To decide whether to rent an item of capital equipment or to buy the capital and implicitly rent it, a firm must compare the present expenditure on the capital with the future rental cost of the capital.

Comparing Current and Future Dollars

To compare a present expenditure with a future expenditure, we convert the future expenditure to its "present value."

The **present value** of a future amount of money is the amount that, if invested today, will grow to be as large as that future amount when the interest that it will earn is taken into account.

So the present value of a future amount of money is smaller than the future amount. The calculation that we use to convert a future amount of money to its present value is called **discounting**.

The easiest way to understand discounting and present value is to first consider its opposite: how a present value grows to a future amount of money because of *compound interest*.

Compound Interest

Compound interest is the interest on an initial investment plus the interest on the interest that the investment has previously earned. Because of compound interest, a present amount of money (a present value) grows into a larger future amount. The future amount is equal to the present amount (present value) plus the interest it will earn. That is,

Future amount = Present value + Interest income.

The interest in the first year is equal to the present value multiplied by the interest rate, r, so

Amount after one year = Present value +
                      ($r \times$ Present value).

or

Amount after one year = Present value $\times (1 + r)$.

If you invest $100 today and the interest rate is 10 percent a year ($r = 0.1$), one year from today you will have $110—the original $100 plus $10 interest.

Check that the above formula delivers that answer: $100 \times 1.1 = \$110$.

If you leave this $110 invested to earn 10 percent during a second year, at the end of that year you will have

Amount after two years = Present value $\times (1 + r)^2$.

With the numbers of the previous example, you invest $100 today at an interest rate of 10 percent a year ($r = 0.1$). After one year you will have $110—the original $100 plus $10 interest. And after the second year, you will have $121. In the second year, you earned $10 on your initial $100 plus $1 on the $10 interest that you earned in the first year.

Check that the above formula delivers that answer: $100 \times (1.1)^2 = \$100 \times 1.21 = \$121$.

If you leave your $100 invested for n years, it will grow to

Amount after n years = Present value $\times (1 + r)^n$.

With an interest rate of 10 percent a year, your $100 will grow to $195 after 7 years ($n = 7$)—almost double the present value of $100.

Discounting a Future Amount

We have just calculated future amounts one year, two years, and n years in the future, knowing the present value and the interest rate. To calculate the present value of these future amounts, we just work backward.

To find the present value of an amount one year in the future, we divide the future amount by $(1 + r)$.

That is,

$$\text{Present value} = \frac{\text{Amount of money one year in future}}{(1 + r)}.$$

Let's check that we can use the present value formula by calculating the present value of $110 one year from now when the interest rate is 10 percent a year. You'll be able to guess that the answer is $100 because we just calculated that $100 invested today at 10 percent a year becomes $110 in one year. So the present value of $110 one year from today is $100. But let's use the formula. Putting the numbers into the above formula, we have

$$\text{Present value} = \frac{\$110}{(1 + 0.1)}$$

$$= \frac{\$110}{1.1} = \$100.$$

To calculate the present value of an amount of money two years in the future, we use the formula:

$$\text{Present value} = \frac{\text{Amount of money two years in future}}{(1 + r)^2}.$$

Use this formula to calculate the present value of $121 two years from now at an interest rate of 10 percent a year. With these numbers, the formula gives

$$\text{Present value} = \frac{\$121}{(1 + 0.1)^2}$$

$$= \frac{\$121}{(1.1)^2}$$

$$= \frac{\$121}{1.21}$$

$$= \$100.$$

We can calculate the present value of an amount of money n years in the future by using the general formula

$$\text{Present value} = \frac{\text{Amount of money } n \text{ years in future}}{(1 + r)^n}.$$

For example, if the interest rate is 10 percent a year, $100 to be received 10 years from now has a present value of $38.55. That is, if $38.55 is invested today at 10 percent a year it will accumulate to $100 in 10 years.

Present Value of a Sequence of Future Amounts

You've seen how to calculate the present value of an amount of money one year, two years, and n years in the future. Most practical applications of present value calculate the present value of a sequence of future amounts of money that are spread over several years. An airline's payment of rent for the lease of airplanes is an example.

To calculate the present value of a sequence of amounts over several years, we use the formula you have learned and apply it to each year. We then sum the present values for all the years to find the present value of the sequence of amounts.

For example, suppose that a firm expects to pay $100 a year for each of the next five years and the interest rate is 10 percent a year ($r = 0.1$). The present value (PV) of these five payments of $100 each is calculated by using the following formula:

$$PV = \frac{\$100}{1.1} + \frac{\$100}{1.1^2} + \frac{\$100}{1.1^3} + \frac{\$100}{1.1^4} + \frac{\$100}{1.1^5},$$

which equals

$$PV = \$90.91 + \$82.64 + \$75.13 + \$68.30 + \$62.09$$
$$= \$379.07.$$

You can see that the firm pays $500 over five years. But because the money is paid in the future, it is not worth $500 today. Its present value is only $379.07. And the farther in the future the money is paid, the smaller is its present value. The $100 paid one year in the future is worth $90.91 today, but the $100 paid five years in the future is worth only $62.09 today.

The Decision

If this firm could lease a machine for five years at $100 a year or buy the machine for $500, it would jump at leasing. Only if the firm could buy the machine for less than $379.07 would it want to buy.

Many personal and business decisions turn on calculations like the one you've just made. A decision to buy or rent an apartment, to lease or rent a car, to pay off a student loan or let the loan run another year can all be made using the above calculation.

SUMMARY ◆

Key Points

The Anatomy of Factor Markets (p. 418)

- The factor markets are: job markets for labour; rental markets (often implicit rental markets) for capital and land; and global commodity markets for nonrenewable natural resources.
- The services of entrepreneurs are not traded on a factor market.

The Demand for a Factor of Production (pp. 419–421)

- The value of marginal product determines the demand for a factor of production.
- The value of marginal product decreases as the quantity of the factor employed increases.
- The firm employs the quantity of each factor of production that makes the value of marginal product equal to the factor price.

Labour Markets (pp. 422–427)

- The value of marginal product of labour determines the demand for labour. A rise in the wage rate brings a decrease in the quantity demanded.
- The quantity of labour supplied depends on the wage rate. At low wage rates, a rise in the wage rate increases the quantity supplied. Beyond a high enough wage rate, a rise in the wage rate decreases the quantity supplied—the supply curve eventually bends backward.
- Demand and supply determine the wage rate in a competitive labour market.

- A labour union can raise the wage rate by restricting the supply or increasing the demand for labour.
- A monopsony can lower the wage rate below the competitive level.
- A union or a minimum wage in a monopsony labour market can raise the wage rate without a fall in employment.

Capital and Natural Resource Markets (pp. 428–431)

- The value of marginal product of capital (and land) determines the demand for capital (and land).
- Firms make a rent-versus-buy decision by choosing the option that minimizes cost.
- The supply of land is inelastic and the demand for land determines the rental rate.
- The demand for a nonrenewable natural resource depends on the value of marginal product and on the expected future price.
- The supply of a nonrenewable natural resource depends on the known reserves, the cost of extraction, and the expected future price.
- The price of nonrenewable natural resources can differ from the market fundamentals price because of speculation based on expectations about the future price.
- The price of a nonrenewable natural resource is expected to rise at a rate equal to the interest rate.

Key Figures and Tables

Figure 18.1   The Demand for Labour at Angelo's Bakery, 420
Figure 18.2   Jill's Labour Supply Curve, 422
Figure 18.3   The Market for Bakery Workers, 423
Figure 18.4   A Union Enters a Competitive Labour Market, 424

Figure 18.9   A Nonrenewable Natural Resource Market, 430
Table 18.1   Value of Marginal Product at Angelo's Bakery, 419
Table 18.2   A Firm's Demand for Labour, 421

Key Terms

Bilateral monopoly, 425
Compound interest, 434
Derived demand, 419
Discounting, 434

Hotelling Principle, 430
Job, 418
Labour union, 424
Monopsony, 425

Nonrenewable natural resources, 418
Present value, 434
Value of marginal product, 419

PROBLEMS and APPLICATIONS

myeconlab Work problems 1–9 in Chapter 18 Study Plan and get instant feedback.
Work problems 10–18 as Homework, a Quiz, or a Test if assigned by your instructor.

1. Wanda owns a fish shop. She employs students to sort and pack the fish. Students can pack the following amounts of fish in an hour:

Number of students	Quantity of fish (kilograms)
1	20
2	50
3	90
4	120
5	145
6	165
7	180
8	190

The fish market is competitive and Wanda can sell her fish for 50¢ a kilogram. The market for packers is competitive and their market wage rate is $7.50 an hour.

a. Calculate the marginal product of the students and draw the marginal product curve.
b. Calculate the value of marginal product of labour and draw the value of marginal product curve.
c. Find Wanda's demand for labour curve.
d. How many students does Wanda employ?

2. Back at Wanda's fish shop described in problem 1, the market price of fish falls to 33.33¢ a kilogram but the wage rate of fish packers remains at $7.50 an hour.

a. How does the students' marginal product change?
b. How does the value of marginal product of labour change?
c. How does Wanda's demand for labour change?
d. What happens to the number of students that Wanda employs?

3. Back at Wanda's fish shop described in problem 1, packers' wages increase to $10 an hour but the price of fish remains at 50¢ a pound.

a. What happens to the value of marginal product of labour?
b. What happens to Wanda's demand for labour curve?
c. How many students does Wanda employ?

4. **Wal-Mart Closes Quebec Lube Shop that Won Labour Contract**
Wal-Mart Stores Inc., … said it closed a unionized Quebec tire and lubrication shop because of costs tied to the first labour agreement imposed at any of its North American locations.

The closing is effective immediately because it would have raised operating costs by at least 30% and triggered "dramatic" price increases on products, …

Under the contract, wages would have increased by a third, or more than 10 times the average hourly rate of Quebec companies this year, the company said. Wal-Mart Tire and Lube Express's six employees in Gatineau won't be fired and will be offered jobs at other … shops. …

"A major cost increase like that can't be sustained" in a lube shop, Mr. Pelletier said. … Wal-Mart is telling employees "that if you join a union, they're going to close your shop," Wayne Hanley, Canadian president of the United Food and Commercial Workers said. …

National Post, October 16, 2008

a. Why do workers want to form a union?
b. If the market for lube services is competitive, explain why a major cost increase can't be sustained.
c. Draw a graph to illustrate the competitive labour market. Show on the graph the effect of the union wage rate that is 30 percent above the competitive wage rate.

5. Which of the following items are nonrenewable natural resources, which are renewable natural resources, and which are not natural resources? Explain your answers.
a. CN Tower
b. Lake Huron
c. Coal in an Alberta coal mine
d. The Internet
e. Algonquin Park
f. Power generated by wind turbines

6. **Metro Eyes Sky-Rise Farming**
… There are no known estimates of the cost of a vertical farm, … [I]t would likely be twice the price of keeping farmland intact.

[Surrey Councilor] Hunt agreed, "you certainly need a few dollars and a few sites to do [vertical farming]," but said Surrey is a growing community that could incorporate green walls or roofs into its buildings. "Why not have these green plants being broccoli or cabbage and everything else under the sun?" he said.

Although Surrey has about a third of its land in the [Agricultural Land Reserve] (ALR), Hunt said other communities have no farmland left. ... "Every decade, every council that comes along has taken 100 or 130 acres out [of the ALR]. When you keep doing that, pretty soon you won't have anything left," he said.

In 1973, when the ALR came into effect, about 86 percent of the vegetables needed to feed Metro Vancouver residents were grown locally. ... Today, that has dwindled to 43 percent. ... [T]o feed the region, Metro will need another 90,000 hectares of farmland. ...

Vancouver Sun, October 21, 2008

a. With farmland decreasing by 100 or 130 acres a year, what do you predict has happened to the price of farmland? Include in your answer a discussion of the demand for farmland and the supply of farmland.
b. Use a graph to show why the price of land in Surrey has risen over the past decade.
c. Will vertical farming raise or lower the price of land in Surrey and what effect will it have on the price of farmland? Is the supply of farmland in British Columbia perfectly inelastic?

7. Keshia operates a bookkeeping service. She is considering buying or leasing some new laptop computers. The purchase price of a laptop is $1,500 and after three years it is worthless. The annual lease rate is $550 per laptop. The value of marginal product of one laptop is $700 a year. The value of marginal product of a second laptop is $625 a year; of a third laptop is $575 a year; and of a fourth laptop is $500 a year.

a. How many laptops will Keshia lease or buy?
b. If the interest rate is 4 percent a year, will Keshia lease or buy her laptops?
c. If the interest rate is 6 percent a year, will Keshia lease or buy her laptops?

8. **British Construction Activity Falls**
Construction activity in Britain declined in June at the fastest rate in 11 years ... and a major home builder said it had been unable to raise more capital—both signs of worsening conditions in the battered housing industry. ... Construction employment declined in June after 23 months of growth. ... The housing market has been hit by falling prices. ... Average house prices in the United Kingdom fell 0.9 percent in June, the eighth consecutive month of declines, leaving the average 6.3 percent below June 2007.

Forbes, July 2, 2008

a. Explain how a fall in house prices influences the market for construction labour.
b. Draw a graph to illustrate the effect of a fall in house prices in the market for construction labour.
c. Explain how a fall in house prices influences the market for construction equipment leases.
d. Draw a graph to illustrate the effect of a fall in house prices in the market for construction equipment leases.

9. **Fixing Farming**
Backyard vegetable gardens are fine. So are organics, slow food and locavores—people who eat produce grown nearby. But solutions to the global food crisis will come from big business, genetically engineered crops and large-scale farms. ... The problem they face has made headlines lately. Demand for farm products—food, fiber and fuel—will keep growing, as the population grows and as hundreds of millions of people move into the middle class and consume more meat and dairy. Global per capita meat consumption has increased by 60 percent in the last 40 years—that's 60 percent per person. Meanwhile, the supply of farmland is limited. Agriculture already uses 55 percent of the habitable land on the planet. ... The answer is for farmers to become more productive—generating more output from fewer inputs.

Fortune, May 22, 2008

a. Is farmland a renewable or nonrenewable resource?
b. Explain how the growing demand for farm products will affect the market for land.
c. Draw a graph to illustrate how the growing demand for farm products will affect the market for land.
d. How might farmers meet the growing demand for farm products without having to use a greater quantity of farmland?

10. Kaiser's Ice Cream Parlor hires workers to produce smoothies. The market for smoothies is perfectly competitive, and the price of a smoothie is $4. The labour market is competitive, and the wage rate is $40 a day. The table shows the workers' total product schedule.

Number of students	Quantity of smoothies (number per day)
1	7
2	21
3	33
4	43
5	51
6	55

a. Calculate the marginal product and the value of the marginal product of the fourth worker.
b. How many workers will Kaiser's hire to maximize its profit and how many smoothies a day will Kaiser's produce?
c. If the price rises to $5 a smoothie, how many workers will Kaiser's hire?

11. Kaiser's in problem 10 installs a new soda fountain that increases the productivity of workers by 50 percent. If the price of a smoothie remains at $4 and the wage rises to $48 a day, how many workers does Kaiser's hire?

12. **Alberta Boosts Wages for Day-Care Staff**

The Alberta government is boosting funding for day-care centres, ... after complaints that such organizations are losing staff to higher-paying jobs in a bustling economy. The bulk of the money ... will go to improving salaries for 7,000 staff who work in licensed day-care centres. ...

"So with a shot in the arm like this, with a significant raise or bump in salary, that will keep those people we need to stay and it will also bring back some of those people who left to go work in other fields."

CBC News, March 5, 2007

a. Explain why the wage rate of day-care workers is below that in other competitive labour markets in Alberta.
b. Draw a graph to illustrate the effects of a wage rise on the market for day-care workers.
c. Explain why other jobs that a day-care worker could obtain might pay a higher wage rate. Would "people who left to go work in other fields" have an incentive to return to day care?

13. **You May be Paid More (or Less) than You Think**

It's so hard to put a price on happiness, isn't it? But if you've ever had to choose between a job you like and a better-paying one that you like less, you probably wished some economist would get on the stick and tell you how much job satisfaction is worth. ...

Economists John Helliwell and Haifang Huang at the University of British Columbia have done just that. Their estimates are based on an analysis of life satisfaction surveys that consider four key factors of job satisfaction. Trust in management is ... like getting a 36 percent pay raise. ... Having a job that offers a lot of variety in projects ... is the equivalent of a 21 percent hike in pay. Having a position that requires a high level of skill is the equivalent of a 19 percent raise. And having enough time to finish your work is the equivalent of an 11 percent boost in pay. ...

CNN, March 29, 2006

a. How might the job characteristics described here affect the supply of labour for different types of jobs?
b. How might this influence on supply result in different wage rates that reflect the attractiveness of a job's characteristics?

14. **The New War over Wal-Mart**

Today, Wal-Mart employs more people—1.7 million—than any other private employer, and by this measure is not just the largest company in the world but the largest company in the history of the world. With size comes power. ... The Wal-Mart effect drives down consumer prices ... and, some argue, it also drives down wages and benefits. ...

One of the major forces opposing Wal-Mart is organized labour. The United Food and Commercial Workers International Union has long wanted to organize Wal-Mart's stores. Last year, it succeeded at a Canadian Wal-Mart, which the company immediately shut down. ... What the war against Wal-Mart tends to gloss over is that it's not at all clear that the company behaves any worse than its competitors. When it comes to payroll and benefits, Wal-Mart's median hourly wage pretty much tracks the national median wage for general merchandise retail jobs. And its health-care benefits are a good deal more accessible ... than those of many of its competitors.

The Atlantic, June 2006

a. Assuming that Wal-Mart has market power in a labour market, explain how the firm could use that market power in setting wages.

b. Draw a graph to illustrate how Wal-Mart might use labour market power to set wages.

c. Explain how a union of Wal-Mart's employees would attempt to counteract Wal-Mart's wage offers (a bilateral monopoly).

d. Explain the response by the Canadian Wal-Mart to the unionization of employees.

e. Based on evidence presented in this article, does Wal-Mart function as a monopsony in labour markets, or is the market for retail labour more competitive? Explain.

f. If the market for retail labour is competitive, explain the potential effect of a union on the wage rates.

g. Draw a graph to illustrate the potential effect of a union on the wage rates in a competitive labour market.

15. **Demand Drives Up Costs for Industrial Land**

Lack of availability and rising demand has fuelled increasing costs for fully serviced industrial land in Calgary—now at nearly $600,000 per acre on average. ... The CB Richard Ellis report says there were 857,800 square feet of new developments in the second quarter and another 1.8 million square feet of new supply under construction. Iain Ferguson, senior sales associate for CB Richard Ellis Alberta Limited, said the rising industrial land prices per acre in Calgary are due to demand. "The demand continues to be high because vacancy continues to be a problem," said Ferguson. ... Demand has been fuelled by low interest rates and the booming energy sector. ...

Calgary Herald, June 28, 2007

a. Is industrial land a renewable or nonrenewable resource? Explain.

b. Explain why the demand for industrial land in Calgary has increased.

c. If companies are responding to the higher prices in the energy sector now, what does that imply about their assumptions about the future price of energy in relation to current interest rates?

d. What could cause the price of industrial land to fall in the future?

16. New technology has allowed oil to be pumped from much deeper offshore oil fields than before. For example, 28 deep ocean rigs operate in the deep waters of the Gulf of Mexico.

a. What effect do you think deep ocean sources have had on the world oil price?

b. Who will benefit from drilling for oil in the Gulf of Mexico? Explain your answer.

17. Water is a natural resource that is plentiful in Canada but not plentiful in Arizona and southern California.

a. If Canadians start to export bulk water to Arizona and southern California, what do you predict will be the effect on the price of bulk water?

b. Will Canada eventually run out of water?

c. Do you think the Hotelling Principle applies to Canada's water? Explain why or why not.

18. Study *Reading Between the Lines* on pp. 432–433 and answer the following questions:

a. Why were Alberta's oilsands such an attractive target for development in early 2008?

b. What changed during 2008 to put previously profitable projects on hold?

c. How did the *VMP* of oilsands change during 2008? Explain and illustrate your answer with an appropriate graphical analysis.

d. How does the Hotelling Principle tell us that the Alberta oilsands might eventually be used?

e. How does the development of oilsands influence the Alberta labour market?

f. Could the labour market become so tight that it prevents the profitable development of the oilsands?

g. When oilsands become profitable to use, what happens to producer surplus from Hibernia offshore oil production?

h. How might the development of efficient green energy sources to deal with climate change affect the world price of oil and the development of Alberta's oilsands?

i. If efficient green energy sources are developed, what will happen to the *VMP* of Alberta's oilsands? Explain and illustrate your answer with an appropriate graphical analysis.

19 ◆ Economic Inequality

After studying this chapter, you will be able to

- Describe the inequality in income and wealth in Canada in 2006 and the trends in inequality
- Explain the features of the labour market that contribute to economic inequality
- Describe the scale of income redistribution by governments

Every night, about 1,200 people sleep outside without shelter in Vancouver, a city with mansions that are home to some very wealthy Canadians. Vancouver is not unusual. More than 4,000 Calgarians are homeless. And in Toronto, where Isadore Sharp is building a luxury apartment tower with a penthouse priced at $30 million, more than 20,000 people, 9,000 of whom are children, seek a bed every night in a shelter for the homeless. Extreme poverty and extreme wealth exist side by side in every major city in Canada and in most parts of the world.

How many rich and poor people are there in Canada? How are income and wealth distributed? Are the rich getting richer and the poor getting poorer?

What causes inequality in the distribution of economic well-being? How much redistribution does the government do to limit extreme poverty?

In this chapter, we study economic inequality—its extent, its sources, and the things governments do to make it less extreme. We begin by looking at some facts about economic inequality in Canada. We end, in *Reading Between the Lines*, by looking at the changing gap between the highest and lowest incomes over the past twenty years.

◆ Measuring Economic Inequality

Statistics Canada provides measures of economic inequality based on three definitions of income: market income, total income, and after-tax income. **Market income** equals the wages, interest, rent, and profit earned in factor markets before paying income taxes. **Total income** equals market income plus cash payments to households by governments. **After-tax income** equals total income minus tax payments by households to governments.

The Distribution of Income

Figure 19.1 shows the distribution of annual after-tax income across the 13.7 million households in Canada in 2006. Note that the *x*-axis measures household after-tax income and the *y*-axis shows the percentage of households.

The most common household income, called the *mode* income, was received by the 7 percent of households whose after-tax incomes fell between $15,000 and $19,999.

The middle level of household after-tax income in 2006, called the *median* income, was $44,400. Fifty percent of households have an income that exceeds the median and 50 percent have an income below the median.

The average household after-tax income in 2006, called the *mean* income, was $54,300. This number equals total household after-tax income divided by the 13.6 million households.

You can see in Fig. 19.1 that the mode income is less than the median income and that the median income is less than the mean income. This feature of the distribution of income tells us that there are more households with low incomes than with high incomes. It also tells us that some of the high incomes are very high.

The income distribution in Fig. 19.1 is called a *positively skewed* distribution, which means that it has a long tail of high values. This distribution shape contrasts with the bell distribution of people's heights. In a bell-shaped distribution, the mean, median, and mode are all equal.

Another way of looking at the distribution of income is to measure the percentage of total income received by each given percentage of households. Data are reported for five groups—called *quintiles* or fifth shares—each consisting of 20 percent of households.

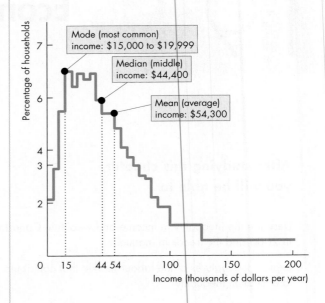

FIGURE 19.1 The Distribution of Income in Canada in 2006

The distribution of income is positively skewed. The mode (most common) income is less than the median (middle) income, which in turn is less than the mean (average) income. The shape of the distribution above $150,000 is an indication rather than a precise measure, and the distribution goes up to several million dollars a year.

Source of data: Statistics Canada, Table 202-0601.

myeconlab animation

Figure 19.2 shows the distribution based on these shares in 2006. The poorest 20 percent of households received 4.8 percent of total after-tax income; the second poorest 20 percent received 10.7 percent; the middle 20 percent received 16.4 percent; the next highest 20 percent received 24.0 percent; and the highest 20 percent received 44.0 percent of total after-tax income.

The distribution of income in Fig. 19.1 and the quintile shares in Fig. 19.2 tell us that income is distributed unequally. But we need a way of comparing the distribution of income in different periods and using different measures. A clever graphical tool called the *Lorenz curve* enables us to make such comparisons.

FIGURE 19.2 Quintile Shares in Canada in 2006

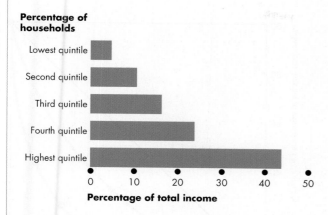

Percentage of households

Lowest quintile
Second quintile
Third quintile
Fourth quintile
Highest quintile

0 10 20 30 40 50
Percentage of total income

Households (percentage)	Income (percentage of total income)
Lowest 20	4.8
Second 20	10.7
Middle 20	16.4
Next highest 20	24.0
Highest 20	44.0

In 2006, the poorest 20 percent of households received 4.8 percent of total after-tax income; the second poorest 20 percent received 10.7 percent; the middle 20 percent received 16.4 percent; the next highest 20 percent received 24.0 percent; and the highest 20 percent received 44.0 percent.

Source of data: Statistics Canada, Table 202-0406.

myeconlab animation

The Income Lorenz Curve

The income **Lorenz curve** graphs the cumulative percentage of income against the cumulative percentage of households. Figure 19.3 shows the income Lorenz curve using the quintile shares from Fig. 19.2. The table shows the percentage of income of each quintile group. For example, row *A* tells us that the lowest quintile of households receives 4.8 percent of total after-tax income. The table also shows the *cumulative* percentages of households and income. For example, row *B* tells us that the lowest two quintiles (lowest 40 percent) of households receive 15.5 percent of

FIGURE 19.3 The Income Lorenz Curve in 2006

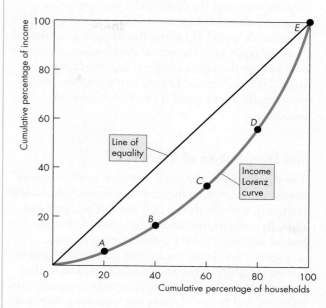

	Households		Income	
	Percentage	Cumulative percentage	Percentage	Cumulative percentage
A	Lowest 20	20	4.8	4.8
B	Second 20	40	10.7	15.5
C	Middle 20	60	16.4	31.9
D	Next highest 20	80	24.0	55.9
E	Highest 20	100	44.0	100.0

The cumulative percentage of income is graphed against the cumulative percentage of households. Points *A* through *E* on the Lorenz curve correspond to the rows of the table. If incomes were distributed equally, each 20 percent of households would receive 20 percent of total income and the Lorenz curve would fall along the line of equality. The Lorenz curve shows that income is unequally distributed.

Source of data: Statistics Canada, Table 202-0406.

myeconlab animation

total income (4.8 percent for the lowest quintile and 10.7 percent for the next lowest). The Lorenz curve graphs the cumulative income shares against the cumulative household percentages.

If income were distributed equally across all the households, each quintile would receive 20 percent of total income and the cumulative percentages of income received by the cumulative percentages of households would fall along the straight line labelled "Line of equality." The actual distribution of income is shown by the curve labelled "Income Lorenz curve." The closer the Lorenz curve is to the line of equality, the more equal is the distribution of income.

The Distribution of Wealth

The distribution of wealth provides another way of measuring economic inequality. A household's **wealth** is the value of the things that it owns at a *point in time*. In contrast, income is the amount that the household receives over a given *period of time*.

Figure 19.4 shows the Lorenz curve for wealth in Canada in 1999. Median household wealth in that year was $64,000. Wealth is extremely unequally distributed, and for this reason, the data are grouped by unequal groups of households. The poorest 40 percent of households owns only 1.1 percent of total wealth (row *A'* in the table). The next poorest 10 percent owns only 2.8 percent of total wealth (row *B'*) and the next poorest 10 percent owns only 4.7 percent of total wealth (row *C'*). So the poorest 60 percent of households owns only 8.6 percent of total wealth. At the other end of the wealth distribution, the wealthiest 10 percent of households owns 55.6 percent of total wealth (row *G'*).

Figure 19.4 shows the income Lorenz curve (from Fig. 19.3) alongside the wealth Lorenz curve. You can see that the Lorenz curve for wealth is much farther away from the line of equality than is the Lorenz curve for income, which means that the distribution of wealth is much more unequal than the distribution of income.

Wealth or Income?

We've seen that wealth is much more unequally distributed than is income. Which distribution provides the better description of the degree of inequality? To answer this question, we need to think about the connection between wealth and income.

Wealth is a stock of assets, and income is the flow of earnings that results from the stock of wealth. Suppose that a person owns assets worth $1 million—

FIGURE 19.4 Lorenz Curves for Income and Wealth in Canada

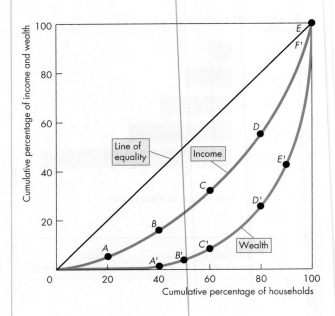

	Households		Income	
	Percentage	Cumulative percentage	Percentage	Cumulative percentage
A'	Lowest 40	40	1.1	1.1
B'	Next 10	50	2.8	3.9
C'	Next 10	60	4.7	8.6
D'	Next 10	70	7.4	16.0
E'	Next 10	80	11.0	27.0
F'	Next 10	90	17.4	44.4
G'	Next 10	100	55.6	100.0

The cumulative percentage of wealth is graphed against the cumulative percentage of households. Points *A'* through *G'* on the Lorenz curve for wealth correspond to the rows of the table. By comparing the Lorenz curves for income and wealth, we can see that wealth is distributed much more unequally than is income.

Sources of data: Statistics Canada, Table 202–0604 and Catalogue 75–202–XIE.

has a wealth of $1 million. If the rate of return on assets is 5 percent a year, then this person receives an income of $50,000 a year from those assets. We can describe this person's economic condition by using either the wealth of $1 million or the income of $50,000. When the rate of return is 5 percent a year, $1 million of wealth equals $50,000 of income in perpetuity. Wealth and income are just different ways of looking at the same thing.

But in Fig. 19.4, the distribution of wealth is more unequal than the distribution of income. Why? It is because the wealth data do not include the value of human capital, while the income data measure income from all wealth, including human capital.

Think about Lee and Peter, two people with equal income and equal wealth. Lee's wealth is human capital and his entire income is from employment. Peter's wealth is in the form of investments in stocks and bonds and his entire income is from these investments.

When an agent of Statistics Canada interviews Lee and Peter in a national income and wealth survey, their incomes are recorded as being equal, but Lee's wealth is recorded as zero, while Peter's wealth is recorded as the value of his investments. Peter looks vastly more wealthy than Lee in the survey data.

Because the national survey of wealth excludes human capital, the income distribution is a more accurate measure of economic inequality than the wealth distribution.

Annual or Lifetime Income and Wealth?

A typical household's income changes over its life cycle. Income starts out low, grows to a peak when the household's workers reach retirement age, and then falls after retirement. Also, a typical household's wealth changes over time. Like income, it starts out low, grows to a peak at the point of retirement, and falls after retirement.

Think about three households with identical lifetime incomes, one young, one middle-aged, and one retired. The middle-aged household has the highest income and wealth, the retired household has the lowest, and the young household falls in the middle. The distributions of annual income and wealth in a given year are unequal, but the distributions of lifetime income and wealth are equal.

The data on inequality share the bias that you've just seen. Inequality in annual income and wealth data arises because households are at different stages in their life cycles, which overstates lifetime inequality.

Trends in Inequality

To see trends in the income distribution, we need a measure that enables us to rank distributions on the scale of more equal and less equal. No perfect scale exists, but one that is much used is called the Gini coefficient. The **Gini coefficient** is based on the Lorenz curve and equals the coefficient of the area between the line of equality and the Lorenz curve to the entire area beneath the line of equality. If income is equally distributed, the Lorenz curve is the same as the line of equality, so the Gini coefficient is zero. If one person has all the income and everyone else has none, the Gini coefficient is 1.

The Trend in Income Distribution
The Rich Get Richer

The figure shows how the distribution of after-tax income changed between 1976 and 2006. The share of total income received by the richest 20 percent of households increased from 40 percent to 44 percent. The share received by the poorest 20 percent of households remained constant at 5 percent. The shares received by the other three groups decreased, and the share of the third (the middle) 20 percent of households decreased most from 17.9 percent to 16.4 percent.

No one knows for sure why these trends occurred, and a large amount of research has been done to try to explain them.

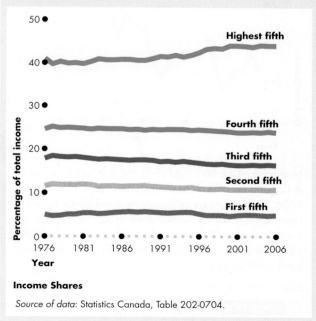

Income Shares

Source of data: Statistics Canada, Table 202-0704.

Figure 19.5 shows the Canadian Gini coefficient from 1976 to 2006. The figure shows a break in the data in 1996 because in that year, the Census Bureau changed its definition, so the numbers before and after the break can't be compared. Despite the break in the series, the Gini coefficient has clearly increased, which means that on this measure, the distribution of incomes in Canada has become more unequal.

The major change is that the share of income received by the richest households has increased. You saw on the previous page how the income of the richest 20 percent has increased. No one knows for sure *why* this trend has occurred, but a possibility that we'll explore in the next section is that technological change has increased the value of marginal product of high-skilled workers and decreased the value of marginal product of low-skilled workers.

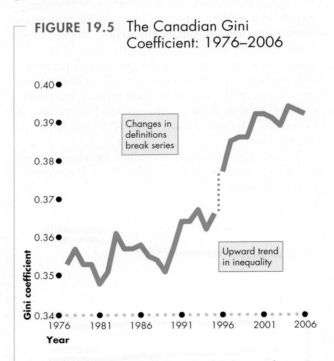

FIGURE 19.5 The Canadian Gini Coefficient: 1976–2006

Changes in definitions break series

Upward trend in inequality

Measured by the Gini coefficient, the distribution of income in Canada became more unequal between 1976 and 2006. The percentage of income received by the richest households increased through these years. The change in the definition in 1996 makes the numbers before and after 1996 not comparable. Despite the break in the data, the trend is still visible.

Source of data: Statistics Canada, Table 202-0705.

myeconlab animation

Who Are the Rich and the Poor?
More Evidence that Schooling Pays

The lowest incomes are earned by people who scratch out a living doing seasonal work on farms. But the poorest Canadians are people who earn nothing and rely on handouts to survive. The incidence of poverty varies systematically depending on household characteristics, and six characteristics stand out:

- Education
- Labour force status
- Source of income
- Household type
- Age of householder
- Number of children

Education Education makes a huge difference to a household's income and to the risk of being poor. A person who has not completed high school has the highest risk of being poor. University graduates and those with a post-graduate or professional degree have the lowest risk of being poor.

Labour Force Status Households in the labour force, even if unemployed, tend to have higher incomes than those not in the labour force—either they've retired or they have become discouraged by a persistent failure to find a suitable job.

Source of Income A household that earns its income either by working or from its wealth is unlikely to be poor and a household that receives its income in the form of a transfer payment from the government is more likely to be poor.

Household Type Households with two parents present are unlikely to be poor. The poorest household is most likely to be one with a single female parent—almost 50 percent of whom are poor.

Age of Householder The youngest and the oldest households have lower incomes and a greater incidence of poverty than middle-aged households.

Number of Children On average, the more children in a household, the smaller is the income per person and the more likely the household is to be poor.

Poverty

Poverty is a state in which a family's income is too low to be able to buy the quantities of food, shelter, and clothing that are deemed necessary.

Poverty is both an absolute and a relative concept. Millions of people in Africa and Asia live, barely, in *absolute* poverty with incomes of less than $400 a year.

In Canada, poverty is identified in *relative* terms using the concept of the **low-income cut-off**, defined as the income level below which a family normally spends 63.6 percent or more of its income on food, shelter, and clothing. (The low-income cut-off is determined separately for each family type.)

How much poverty (defined as the percentage of families with incomes below the low-income cut-off) is there in Canada, and is the problem getting worse or better? Figure 19.6 answers this question.

The incidence of poverty has fluctuated between a low of 14 percent in 1989 and a high of 20 percent in 1996 and 1997. But there has been no trend in poverty and on the average, 17 percent of Canadian families have incomes below the low-income cut-off.

FIGURE 19.6 The Incidence of Low Income

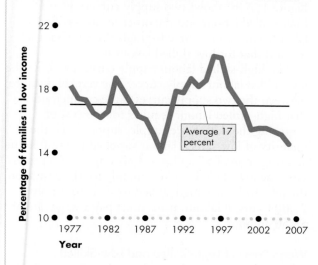

The incidence of low income in Canada has fluctuated between 14 and 20 percent of families. On the average, 17 percent of families have incomes below the low-income cut-off.

Source of data: Statistics Canada, Table 202-0804.

 animation

The Poverty Rate

How Long Does It Last?

Most poverty is temporary and short-lived. The figure shows the numbers: 75 percent of those in poverty remain in that state for less than a year and another 8 percent of those in poverty remain so for 1 year. Poverty rates for people who are in that state for 2 years or more are very low.

Given that the average poverty rate is 17 percent of families, you can see that around 2 percent of Canadian families experience poverty that persists for more than 2 years.

The duration of poverty, like its level, depends on household characteristics, and education is the key characteristic. The least educated tend to experience the most persistent poverty.

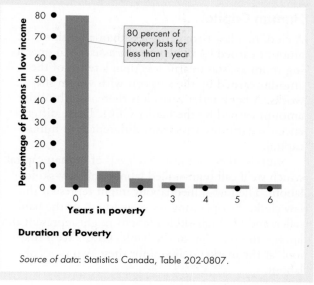

Source of data: Statistics Canada, Table 202-0807.

Review Quiz

1 Which is distributed more unequally, income or wealth? Why? Which is the better measure?

2 Has the distribution of income become more equal or more unequal?

3 What are the main characteristics of people who earn large incomes and those who earn small incomes?

4 What is poverty and how does its incidence vary across households?

myeconlab Work Study Plan 19.1 and get instant feedback.

◆ The Sources of Economic Inequality

We've described economic inequality in Canada. Our task now is to explain it. We began this task in Chapter 18 by learning about the forces that influence demand and supply in the markets for labour, capital, and land. We're now going to deepen our understanding of these forces.

Inequality arises from unequal labour market outcomes and from unequal ownership of capital. We'll begin by looking at labour markets and two of their features that contribute to income differences:

- Human capital
- Discrimination

Human Capital

A clerk in a law firm earns less than a tenth of the amount earned by the lawyer he assists. An operating room assistant earns less than a tenth of the amount earned by the surgeon with whom she works. A bank teller earns less than a tenth of the amount earned by the bank's CEO. These differences in earnings arise from differences in human capital.

Suppose there are just two levels of human capital, which we'll call high-skilled labour and low-skilled labour. The low-skilled labour might represent the law clerk, the operating room assistant, or the bank teller, and the high-skilled labour might represent the lawyer, the surgeon, or the bank's CEO. We'll first look at the market demand for these two types of labour.

The Demand for High-Skilled and Low-Skilled Labour

High-skilled workers can perform tasks that low-skilled labour would perform badly or perhaps could not perform at all. Imagine an untrained person doing open-heart surgery. High-skilled labour has a higher value of marginal product than does low-skilled labour. As we learned in Chapter 18, a firm's demand for labour curve is the same as the value of marginal product of labour curve.

Figure 19.7(a) shows the demand curves for high-skilled and low-skilled labour. The demand curve for high-skilled labour is D_H, and that for low-skilled labour is D_L. At any given level of employment, firms are willing to pay a higher wage rate to a high-skilled worker than to a low-skilled worker. The gap between the two wage rates measures the value of marginal product of skill; for example, at an employment level of 2,000 hours, firms are willing to pay $12.50 an hour for a high-skilled worker and only $5 an hour for a low-skilled worker, a difference of $7.50 an hour. So the value of marginal product of skill is $7.50 an hour.

The Supply of High-Skilled and Low-Skilled Labour

High-skilled labour contains more human capital than does low-skilled labour, and human capital is costly to acquire. The opportunity cost of acquiring human capital includes expenditures on tuition and textbooks and also forgone or reduced earnings while the skill is being acquired. When a person goes to school full time, that cost is the total earnings forgone. But some people acquire skills on the job—on-the-job training. Usually, a worker undergoing on-the-job training is paid a lower wage than one doing a comparable job but not undergoing training. In such a case, the cost of acquiring the skill is the difference between the wage paid to a person not being trained and that paid to a person being trained.

The position of the supply curve of high-skilled labour reflects the cost of acquiring human capital. Figure 19.7(b) shows two supply curves: one for high-skilled labour and the other for low-skilled labour. The supply curve for high-skilled labour is S_H, and that for low-skilled labour is S_L.

The high-skilled labour supply curve lies above the low-skilled labour supply curve. The vertical distance between the two supply curves is the compensation that high-skilled labour requires for the cost of acquiring the skill. For example, suppose that the quantity of low-skilled labour supplied is 2,000 hours at a wage rate of $5 an hour. This wage rate compensates the low-skilled workers mainly for their time on the job. To induce high-skilled workers to supply 2,000 hours of labour, firms must pay a wage rate of $8.50 an hour.

Wage Rates of High-Skilled and Low-Skilled Labour

The demand for and supply of high-skilled and low-skilled labour determine the two wage rates. Figure 19.7(c) brings together the demand curves and the supply curves for high-skilled and low-skilled labour. Equilibrium occurs in the market for low-skilled labour (on the blue curves) at a wage rate of $5 an hour, and a quantity of low-skilled labour of 2,000 hours. Equilibrium occurs in the market for

FIGURE 19.7 Skill Differentials

(a) Demand for high-skilled and low-skilled labour

(b) Supply of high-skilled and low-skilled labour

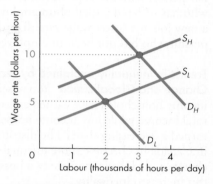

(c) Markets for high-skilled and low-skilled labour

Part (a) illustrates the value of marginal product of skill. Low-skilled labour has a value of marginal product that gives rise to the demand curve marked D_L. High-skilled labour has a higher value of marginal product than does low-skilled labour, so the demand curve for high-skilled labour, D_H, lies to the right of D_L. The vertical distance between these two curves is the value of marginal product of the skill.

Part (b) illustrates the cost of acquiring skill. The supply

curve for low-skilled labour is S_L. The supply curve for high-skilled labour is S_H. The vertical distance between these two curves is the required compensation for the cost of acquiring a skill.

Part (c) shows the equilibrium employment and the wage differential. Low-skilled workers provide 2,000 hours of labour at a wage rate of $5 an hour. High-skilled workers provide 3,000 hours of labour at a wage rate of $10 an hour.

myeconlab animation

high-skilled labour (on the green curves) at a wage rate of $10 an hour, and a quantity of high-skilled labour of 3,000 hours.

The equilibrium wage rate of high-skilled labour exceeds that of low-skilled labour for two reasons: First, high-skilled labour has a higher value of marginal product than low-skilled labour, so at a given wage rate, the quantity of high-skilled labour demanded exceeds that of low-skilled labour. Second, skills are costly to acquire, so at a given wage rate, the quantity of high-skilled labour supplied is less than that of low-skilled labour. The wage differential (here, $5 an hour) depends on both the value of marginal product of the skill and the cost of acquiring it. The higher the value of marginal product of a skill or the more costly it is to acquire, the larger is the wage differential between high-skilled and low-skilled labour.

Do Education and Training Pay? Rates of return on high school and college education have been estimated to be in the range of 5 percent to 10 percent a year after allowing for inflation, which suggests that a

college degree is a better investment than almost any other that a person can undertake.

Inequality Explained by Human Capital Differences
Human capital differences help to explain some of the inequality that we've described. They also help to explain some of the trends in the distribution of income that have occurred during the past 20 years.

Human capital differences are correlated with these household characteristics. Education contributes directly to human capital. Age contributes indirectly to human capital because older workers have more experience than younger workers. Human capital differences can also explain a small part of the inequality associated with sex. A larger proportion of men than women have completed a college or a university degree. These differences in education levels among the sexes are becoming smaller, but they have not been eliminated.

Career interruptions can decrease human capital. A person (most often a woman) who interrupts a career to raise young children usually returns to the labour force with a lower earning capacity than a similar person who has kept working. Likewise, a person who has suffered a spell of unemployment often finds a new job at a lower wage rate than that of a similar person who has not been unemployed.

Trends in Inequality Explained by Technological Change and Globalization You've seen that high-income households have earned an increasing share of total income while low-income households have earned a decreasing share: The distribution of income in Canada has become more unequal. Technological change and globalization are two possible sources of this increased inequality.

Technological Change Information technologies such as computers and laser scanners are *substitutes* for low-skilled labour: They perform tasks that previously were performed by low-skilled labour. The introduction of these technologies has lowered the marginal product and the demand for low-skilled labour. These same technologies require high-skilled labour to design, program, and run them. High-skilled labour and the information technologies are *complements*. So the introduction of these technologies has increased the marginal product and demand for high-skilled labour.

Figure 19.8 illustrates the effects on wages and employment. The supply of low-skilled labour in part (a) and that of high-skilled labour in part (b) are S, and initially, the demand in each market is D_0. The low-skill wage rate is $5 an hour, and the high-skill wage rate is $10 an hour. The demand for low-skilled labour decreases to D_1 in part (a) and the demand for high-skilled labour increases to D_1 in part (b). The low-skill wage rate falls to $4 an hour and the high-skill wage rate rises to $15 an hour.

Globalization The entry of China and other developing countries into the global economy has lowered the prices of many manufactured goods. Lower prices for the firm's output lowers the value of marginal product of the firm's workers and decreases the demand for their labour, such as Fig. 19.8(a) shows. The wage rate falls, and employment shrinks.

At the same time, the growing global economy increases the demand for services that employ high-skilled workers, and the value of marginal product and the demand for high-skilled labour increases, such as Fig. 19.8(b) shows. The wage rate rises, and employment opportunities for high-skilled workers expand.

FIGURE 19.8 Explaining the Trend in Income Distribution

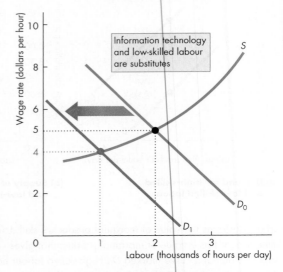

(a) A decrease in demand for low-skilled labour

(b) An increase in demand for high-skilled labour

Low-skilled labour in part (a) and information technologies are substitutes. Advances in information technology decrease the demand for low-skilled labour and lower its wage rate. High-skilled labour in part (b) and information technologies are complements. Advances in information technology increase the demand for high-skilled labour and raise its wage rate.

myeconlab animation

Discrimination

Human capital differences can explain some of the economic inequality that we observe. Discrimination is another possible source of inequality.

Suppose that females and males have identical abilities as investment advisors. Figure 19.9 shows the supply curves of females, S_F in part (a), and of males, S_M in part (b). The value of marginal product of investment advisors, shown by the two curves labelled *VMP* in parts (a) and (b), is the same for both groups.

If everyone is free of sex-based prejudice, the market determines a wage rate of $40,000 a year for investment advisors. But if the customers are prejudiced against women, this prejudice is reflected in the wage rate and employment.

Suppose that the perceived value of marginal product of the females, when discriminated against, is VMP_{DA}. Suppose that the perceived value of marginal product for males, the group discriminated in favour of, is VMP_{DF}. With these *VMP* curves, females earn $20,000 a year and only 1,000 females work as investment advisors whereas males earn $60,000 a year and 3,000 of them work as investment advisors.

Counteracting Forces Economists disagree about whether prejudice actually causes wage differentials, and one line of reasoning implies that it does not. In the above example, customers who buy from men pay a higher service charge for investment advice than do the customers who buy from women. This price difference acts as an incentive to encourage people who are prejudiced to buy from the people against whom they are prejudiced. This force could be strong enough to eliminate the effects of discrimination altogether.

Suppose, as is true in manufacturing, that a firm's customers never meet its workers. If such a firm discriminates against women (or against visible minorities), it can't compete with firms that hire these groups because the firm that discriminates has higher costs than those of the nonprejudiced firms. Only firms that do not discriminate survive in a competitive industry.

Whether because of discrimination or from some other source, women on average do earn lower incomes than men. Another possible source of lower wage rates of women arises from differences in the relative degree of specialization of women and men.

FIGURE 19.9 Discrimination

(a) Females

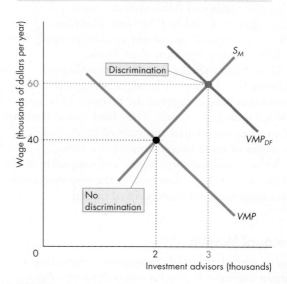

(b) Males

With no discrimination, the wage rate is $40,000 a year and 2,000 of each group are hired. With discrimination against women, the value of marginal product curve in part (a) is VMP_{DA} and that in part (b) is VMP_{DF}. The wage rate for women falls to $20,000 a year, and only 1,000 are employed. The wage rate for men rises to $60,000 a year, and 3,000 are employed.

Differences in the Degree of Specialization Couples must choose how to allocate their time between working for a wage and doing jobs in the home, such as cooking, cleaning, shopping, organizing vacations, and, most important, bearing and raising children. Let's look at the choices of Bob and Sue.

Bob might specialize in earning an income and Sue in taking care of the home. Or Sue might specialize in earning an income and Bob in taking care of the home. Or both of them might earn an income and share home production jobs.

The allocation they choose depends on their preferences and on their earning potential. The choice of an increasing number of households is for each person to diversify between earning an income and doing some household chores. But in most households, Bob will specialize in earning an income and Sue will both earn an income and bear a larger share of the task of running the home. With this allocation, Bob will probably earn more than Sue. If Sue devotes time and effort to ensuring Bob's mental and physical well-being, the quality of Bob's market labour will be higher than it would be if he were diversified. If the roles were reversed, Sue would be able to supply market labour that earns more than Bob's.

To test whether the degree of specialization accounts for earnings differences between the sexes, economists have compared the incomes of never-married men and women. They have found that, on the average, with equal amounts of human capital, the wages of these two groups are the same.

We've examined some sources of inequality in the labour market. Let's now look at the way inequality arises from unequal ownership of capital.

Unequal Wealth

You've seen that wealth inequality—excluding human capital—is much greater than income inequality. This greater wealth inequality arises from two sources: life-cycle saving patterns and transfers of wealth from one generation to the next.

Life-Cycle Saving Patterns Over a family's life cycle, wealth starts out at zero or perhaps less than zero. A student who has financed education all the way through graduate school might have a lot of human capital and an outstanding student loan of $30,000. This person has negative wealth. Gradually loans get paid off and a retirement fund is accumulated. At the point of retiring from full-time work, the family has maximum wealth. Then, during its retirement years, the family spends its wealth. This life-cycle pattern means that much of the wealth is owned by people in their sixties.

Intergenerational Transfers Households that inherit wealth from the previous generation or that save more than enough on which to live during retirement end up transferring wealth to the next generation. But intergenerational transfers are not always a source of increased inequality. If a generation that has a high income saves a large part of that income and leaves wealth to a succeeding generation that has a lower income, this transfer decreases the degree of inequality. But one feature of intergenerational transfers of wealth leads to increased inequality: wealth concentration through marriage.

Marriage and Wealth Concentration People tend to marry within their own socioeconomic class—a phenomenon called *assortative mating*. In everyday language, "like attracts like." Although there is a good deal of folklore that "opposites attract," perhaps such Cinderella tales appeal to us because they are so rare in reality. Wealthy people seek wealthy partners.

Because of assortative mating, wealth becomes more concentrated in a small number of families and the distribution of wealth becomes more unequal.

Review Quiz

1 What role does human capital play in accounting for income inequality?
2 What role might discrimination play in accounting for income inequality?
3 What are the possible reasons for income inequality by sex?
4 How might technological change and globalization influence the distribution of income?
5 Does inherited wealth make the distribution of income less equal or more equal?
6 Why does wealth inequality persist across generations?

 Work Study Plan 19.2 and get instant feedback.

Next, we're going to see how taxes and government programs redistribute income and decrease the degree of economic inequality.

Income Redistribution

The three main ways in which governments in Canada redistribute income are

- Income taxes
- Income maintenance programs
- Subsidized services

Income Taxes

Income taxes may be progressive, regressive, or proportional. A **progressive income tax** is one that taxes income at an average rate that increases with income. A **regressive income tax** is one that taxes income at an average rate that decreases with income. A **proportional income tax** (also called a *flat-rate income tax*) is one that taxes income at a constant average rate, regardless of the level of income.

The income tax rates that apply in Canada are composed of two parts: federal and provincial taxes. The highest income tax rates are in Quebec and the lowest are in Alberta. There is variety in the detailed tax arrangements in the individual provinces but the tax system, at both the federal and provincial levels, is progressive.

The poorest Canadians pay no income tax. Even those who earn $30,000 a year pay a very low rate of income tax. Those whose incomes are $50,000 a year pay about 21 percent of their income in income taxes; those whose incomes are $100,000 a year pay about 28 percent in income tax; and as incomes increase, the average tax rate increases to 45 percent or higher.

Income Maintenance Programs

Three main types of programs redistribute income by making direct payments (in cash, services, or vouchers) to people in the lower part of the income distribution. They are

- Social security programs
- Employment Insurance program
- Welfare programs

Social Security Programs Four programs—Old Age Security (OAS), Guaranteed Income Supplement (GIS), the Allowance, and the Allowance for the Survivor (AS)—ensure a minimum level of income for senior citizens. Cash payments to retired or disabled workers or their surviving spouses are paid for by compulsory payroll taxes on both employers and employees. In 2008, the maximum OAS was $516.96 a month, the maximum GIS for a single person was $562.51, the maximum Allowance was $947.86, and the maximum AS was $1,050.68.

Employment Insurance Program To provide an income to unemployed workers, the federal government has established an unemployment compensation program. The Employment Insurance program is funded by employee and employer contributions, and after a qualifying period the worker is entitled to receive a benefit if he or she becomes unemployed. In 2008, the maximum unemployment benefit was 55 percent of gross weekly earnings over the previous 26 weeks, adjusted for the unemployment rate in his or her region of Canada.

Welfare Programs Other welfare programs provide income maintenance for families and persons. They are

1. Canada Social Transfer (CST) in support of post-secondary education, social assistance, and social services, including early childhood development, are administered by the provinces and provide basic assistance to cover the cost of food, clothing, personal and household items, and in some provinces and territories, regularly recurring special needs.

2. Canada/Quebec Pension Plans, funded equally by employee and employer contributions, provide retirement benefits, survivor benefits, disability benefits, and death benefits.

3. Workers' Compensation, a provincial program funded by employers, is designed to provide financial assistance as well as medical care and rehabilitation of workers injured at work.

Subsidized Services

A great deal of redistribution takes place in Canada through the provision of subsidized services, which is the provision of goods and services by the government at prices below the cost of production. The taxpayers who consume these goods and services receive a transfer in kind from the taxpayers who do not consume them. The two most important areas in which this form of redistribution takes place are education—both kindergarten through Grade 12 and college and university—and health care.

The Scale of Income Redistribution

Only the Richest Pay

To determine the scale of income redistribution, we need to compare the distribution of *market income* with the distribution of *after-tax income*. The data available on benefits exclude the value of subsidized services (such as the value of university education and health-care services), so the resulting distribution might understate the total amount of redistribution from the rich to the poor.

The figures show the scale of redistribution based on the calculations just described. In Fig. 1, the blue Lorenz curve describes the market distribution of income and the green Lorenz curve shows the distribution of income after all taxes and benefits. (The Lorenz curve based on *total income*—market income plus transfer payments from governments—lies between these two curves.)

The distribution after taxes and benefits is much less unequal than the market distribution. In 2006, the lowest 20 percent of households received only 1.2 percent of market income but 4.8 percent of after-tax income. The second lowest 20 percent of households received 7.4 percent of market income but 10.7 percent of after-tax income. The highest 20 percent of households received 51.6 percent of market income but only 44.0 percent of after-tax income.

Figure 2 highlights the percentage of total income redistributed among the five groups. The share of total income received by the lowest three quintiles (60 percent) of households increased. The share received by the lowest increased by 3.6 percent and the share received by the second lowest increased by 3.3 percent. The share of total income received by the fourth quintile fell slightly. And the share of total income received by the highest quintile fell by almost 8 percent of total income.

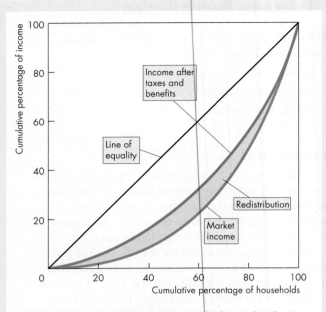

Figure 1 Income Distribution Before and After Redistribution

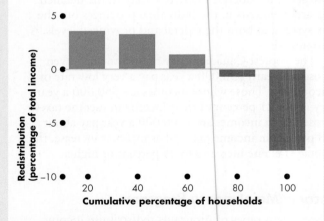

Figure 2 The Scale of Redistribution

Source of data: Statistics Canada, Table 202-0701.

Canadian students enrolled in the universities in Ontario pay annual tuition fees of around $5,000. The cost of a year's education at one of these universities is about $20,000. Thus families with a member enrolled in these institutions receive a benefit from the government of about $15,000 a year. Those with several college or university students receive proportionately higher benefits.

Government provision of health care to all residents has brought high-quality and high-cost health care to millions of people who earn too little to buy such services themselves. As a result, this program has contributed to reducing inequality.

The Big Tradeoff

The redistribution of income creates what has been called the **big tradeoff**, a tradeoff between equity and efficiency.

You learned in Chapter 5 that there are two views about equity (or fairness): the *fair rules* view and the *fair outcome* view. The fair rules view doesn't present a tradeoff between equity and efficiency because voluntary transactions are efficient and even if they result in inequality, they are considered fair.

The big tradeoff arises from the fair results view of equity. In this view, more equal is fairer: less equal is less fair. But there is a tradeoff—a big tradeoff—because redistributing income and wealth to achieve greater equality ends up creating inefficiencies.

There are two sources of inefficiency from redistributing income and wealth. They are

- Administrative cost
- Deadweight loss

Administrative Cost A dollar collected from a rich person does not translate into a dollar received by a poor person. Some of the dollar collected gets used up in the process of redistribution. Tax-collecting agencies such as the Canada Revenue Agency and welfare-administering agencies (as well as tax accountants and lawyers) use skilled labour, computers, and other scarce resources to do their work. The bigger the scale of redistribution, the greater is the opportunity cost of administering it.

But the cost of collecting taxes and making welfare payments is a small part of the total cost of redistribution.

Deadweight Loss The bigger cost of redistributing income and wealth arises from allocative inefficiency—from deadweight loss—of taxes and benefits.

Greater equality can be achieved only by taxing productive activities—from taxing work and saving. Taxing people's income from their work and saving lowers the after-tax income they receive. This lower after-tax income makes them work and save less, which in turn results in smaller output and less consumption not only for the rich who pay the taxes but also for the poor who receive the benefits.

It is not only taxpayers who face weaker incentives to work. Benefit recipients also face weaker incentives. In fact, under the welfare arrangements that prevail in Canada today, the weakest incentives to work are those faced by households that benefit most from welfare. When a welfare recipient gets a job, benefits are withdrawn and eligibility for support is withdrawn. In effect, these households face a marginal tax rate of more than 100 percent on their earnings. This arrangement locks poor households in a welfare trap.

So the scale and methods of income redistribution must pay close attention to the incentive effects of taxes and benefits.

A Major Welfare Challenge

The poorest people in Canada are women who have not completed high school, have a child (or children), and live without a partner. Single mothers present a major welfare challenge. Their numbers are large—approximately 1 million—and their economic plight and the economic prospects for their children are serious.

For physically fit single mothers, the long-term solution to their problem is education and on-the-job training—acquiring human capital. The short-term solution is welfare. But welfare must be designed to minimize the disincentive to pursue the long-term goal. This is the central challenge in designing an effective welfare program.

Review Quiz

1 How do governments in Canada redistribute income?
2 Describe the scale of redistribution in Canada.
3 What is one of the major welfare challenges today and how is it being tackled in Canada?

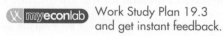 Work Study Plan 19.3 and get instant feedback.

We've examined economic inequality in Canada. We've seen how inequality arises and that inequality has been increasing. *Reading Between the Lines* on pp. 456–457 looks at the increasing inequality that began during the early 1980s and continues today.

You've now completed your study of microeconomics. You've seen how markets work and do a remarkable job of reconciling self-interest and social interest. You've seen situations in which market failure occurs and government action that might improve the market outcome. But you've also seen cases of government failure.

Trends in Poverty

What Can Be Done to Help?

September 18, 2008

The homeless are visible in big cities and small communities across Canada. Soup kitchens and shelters are busy, and some Canadians have more than one low-paying job and struggle to pay bills and buy the things they need for daily living.

There is poverty in Canada, but the numbers of people in the low-income bracket have fallen fairly dramatically in the last 10 years. ...

When Statistics Canada numbers regarding low income are considered, a clear downward trend in poverty numbers is apparent. ...

The agency has a low-income cut-off it uses to get its numbers. ...

Those numbers show that Canadians in the low income bracket dropped from 15.7 per cent, or 4.5 million people, in 1996 to 10.5 per cent, or 3.3 million people, in 2006. ...

However, one cannot consider those figures without looking at what has happened to income numbers and how these have affected Canadians hovering around the low-income line.

"Median earnings of Canadians employed on a full-time basis for a full year changed little during the past quarter century, edging up from $41,348 in 1980 to $41,401 in 2005," according to recent Statistics Canada findings (based on 2006 census figures and constant 2005 dollars adjusted for inflation).

"Earnings of full-time full year earners rose for those at the top of the earnings distribution, stagnated for those in the middle and declined for those at the bottom."

In fact, the median income for the low-income group dropped from $19,367 in 1980 to $15,375 in 2005 ...

Essence of the Story

- Using the low-income cut-off to get its numbers, Statistics Canada reports a decrease in the number of families living in poverty from 15.7 percent or 4.5 million in 1996 to 10.5 percent or 3.3 million in 2006.

- Median earnings of full-time, full-year workers remained at about $41,000 between 1980 and 2005.

- Median income rose for high-income earners while it fell from $19,367 to $15,375 for low-income earners.

Economic Analysis

- The news article reports the decrease in the incidence of low income (percentage of families with incomes below the low-income cut-off) between 1996 and 2006.

- That number fell from 15.7 percent in 1996 to 10.5 percent in 2006.

- The news article also reports that the median income has barely changed since 1985 and that the incomes of people below the low-income cut-off have decreased and the incomes of high-income groups have increased.

- These reported facts are consistent with what you have learned in this chapter. But taken on their own, they are misleading.

- Figure 19.6 on p. 447 shows the percentage of families below the low-income cut-off since 1997. The incidence of low income fluctuates around a constant average of 17 percent: 1996 was a peak year and 2006 a trough year. There is no clearly visible downward trend in the incidence of low income.

- The supply of low-skilled labour increased partly because of immigration. The demand for low-skilled labour increased, but by less than supply for the reason that we identify in the chapter: New technologies are a substitute for low-skilled labour.

- Figure 1 shows the distribution of after-tax family income in 1980 compared to that in 2006. The average increased, but the median decreased. This change tells us that inequality increased.

- The Lorenz curves for 1980 and 2006 in Fig. 2 confirm this increase in inequality. The Gini coefficient increased from 0.353 in 1980 to 0.392 in 2006.

- But one aspect of the data on family income distorts the impression of increased inequality: The average size of a family unit has been falling. In 1980 it was 2.6 persons and by 2006 it was 2.1 persons.

- Figure 3 shows what has happened to average family income holding family size constant at its 1980 level. Individuals have become much better off than family units because family units have shrunk. There were many more one-person family units in 2006 than in 1980.

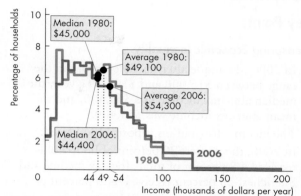

Figure 1 The income distribution in 1980 and 2006

Figure 2 The Lorenz curves in 1980 and 2006

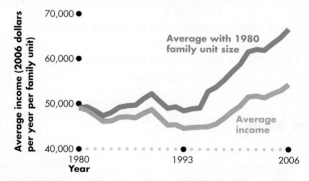

Figure 3 Two measures of average income: 1980 to 2006

SUMMARY

Key Points

Measuring Economic Inequality (pp. 442–447)

- In 2006, the mode after-tax income was in the range between $15,000 and $19,999 a year, the median after-tax income was $44,400, and the mean after-tax income was $53,400.
- The income distribution is positively skewed.
- In 2006, the poorest 20 percent of households received 4.8 percent of total after-tax income and the richest 20 percent received 44.0 percent of total after-tax income.
- Wealth is distributed more unequally than income because the wealth data exclude the value of human capital.
- Since 1976, the distribution of income has become more unequal.
- Education, type of household, age of householder, and source of income influence household income.

The Sources of Economic Inequality (pp. 448–452)

- Inequality arises from differences in human capital.
- Trends in the distribution of human capital that arise from technological change and globalization can explain some of the trend in increased inequality.
- Inequality might arise from discrimination.
- Inequality between men and women might arise from differences in the degree of specialization.
- Intergenerational transfers of wealth lead to increased inequality because people can't inherit debts and assortative mating tends to concentrate wealth.

Income Redistribution (pp. 453–455)

- Governments redistribute income through progressive income taxes, income maintenance programs, and subsidized services.
- Redistribution increases the share of total income received by the lowest 60 percent of households and decreases the share of total income received by the highest quintile. The share of the fourth quintile barely changes.
- Because the redistribution of income weakens incentives, it creates a tradeoff between equity and efficiency.
- Effective redistribution seeks to support the long-term solution to low income, which is education and job training—acquiring human capital.

Key Figures

Figure 19.1   The Distribution of Income in Canada in 2006, 442
Figure 19.4   Lorenz Curves for Income and Wealth in Canada, 444
Figure 19.5   The Canadian Gini Coefficient: 1976–2006, 446
Figure 19.7   Skill Differentials, 449
Figure 19.8   Explaining the Trend in Income Distribution, 450
Figure 19.9   Discrimination, 451

Key Terms

After-tax income, 442
Big tradeoff, 455
Gini coefficient, 445
Lorenz curve, 443
Low-income cut-off, 447
Market income, 442
Poverty, 447
Progressive income tax, 453
Proportional income tax, 453
Regressive income tax, 453
Total income, 442
Wealth, 444

PROBLEMS and APPLICATIONS

 Work problems 1–8 in Chapter 19 Study Plan and get instant feedback.
Work problems 9–15 as Homework, a Quiz, or a Test if assigned by your instructor.

1. The table shows after-tax income shares in Canada in 1986.

Households	After-tax income (percent of total)
Lowest 20%	5.5
Second 20%	11.4
Third 20%	17.6
Fourth 20%	24.7
Highest 20%	40.8

a. What is after-tax income?
b. Draw a Lorenz curve for Canada in 1986 and compare it with the Lorenz curve in 2006 shown in Fig. 19.3.
c. Was Canadian after-tax income distributed more equally or less equally in 2006 than it was in 1986?
d. What are some reasons for the differences in the distribution of after-tax income in Canada in 1986 and 2006?

2. The figure shows the demand for and supply of low-skilled labour.

The value of marginal product of high-skilled workers is $8 an hour greater than that of low-skilled workers. (The value of marginal product at each employment level is $8 greater than that of a low-skilled worker.) The cost of acquiring the skill adds $6 an hour to the wage that must be offered to attract high-skilled labour.

a. What is the wage rate of low-skilled labour?
b. What is the quantity of low-skilled labour employed?
c. What is the wage rate of high-skilled labour?
d. What is the quantity of high-skilled labour employed?
e. Why does the wage rate of a high-skilled worker exceed that of a low-skilled worker by exactly the cost of acquiring the skill?

3. The figure shows the demand for and supply of workers who are discriminated against. Suppose that there is a group of workers in the same industry who are not discriminated against, and their value of marginal product is perceived to be twice the value of marginal product of the workers who are discriminated against. Suppose also that the supply of workers who do not face discrimination is 2,000 hours per day less at each wage rate.

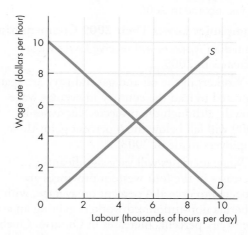

a. What is the wage rate of the workers who are discriminated against?
b. What is the quantity of workers employed who are discriminated against?
c. What is the wage rate of the workers who do not face discrimination?
d. What is the quantity of workers employed who do not face discrimination?

4. Incomes in China and India are a small fraction of incomes in Canada. But incomes in China and India are growing at more than twice the rate

of those in Canada. Given this information, what can you say about

a. Changes in inequality between people in China and India and people in Canada?
b. The world Lorenz curve and world Gini coefficient?

5. The tables show the average income received by the five quintiles in Canada in 2006.

Canadian households	Average income (dollars per household)
Lowest 20%	16,500
Second 20%	38,400
Third 20%	61,700
Fourth 20%	87,300
Highest 20%	161,000

a. Create a table that shows the income shares of the five quintiles.
b. Create a table that shows the cumulative distribution of income.
c. Draw the income Lorenz curve for income. Compare the distribution of income and after-tax income in 2006.

6. **Companies Lower Their 2009 Compensation**
Canadian workers will receive lower wage increases in 2009. ...

Workers in the oil and gas industry are again expected to lead the country in average wage growth, although the projected increases in 2009 will fall below the 6 percent gains these employees made in 2008. ...

Wage increases will vary significantly. ... Increases in the four western provinces are expected to exceed 4 percent on average, with Alberta's non-unionized workers gaining an average of 5.1 percent. Increases in Ontario, Quebec, and the Atlantic provinces are expected to fall below the national average [3 percent].

Conference Board of Canada, October 27, 2008

a. If wage rates rise, as expected, by more than the national average in Western Canada and less than the national average in Ontario, Quebec, and the Atlantic provinces, how will the economic well-being of households across the nation change?
b. Why are workers in Alberta's oil and gas industry expected to receive the largest average wage raises?

7. **Most Lucrative College Degrees for 2007 Grads**
... The class of 2007 is finding it easier than recent classes to get their foot in the work world. Employers have said they expect to hire 17.4 percent more ... than they did last year, and in many instances they plan to pay them more, too ... The average starting offer for seniors majoring in marketing is up 14 percent from last year to $41,323. Those majoring in business administration are seeing a 9.2 percent jump to $43,523. ... Finance: $47,905 ... Economics: $51,631. ... There have been slight decreases in the average starting salary offers for just a few majors, ... including psychology, political science, history, and English: Down 1.1 percent to $30,502.

CNN, February 8, 2007

a. Why do graduates with different majors have drastically different starting salaries?
b. Draw a graph of the labour markets for economics majors and political science majors to illustrate your explanation of the differences in the starting salaries of these two groups.

8. **Where Women's Pay Trumps Men's**
Men work more than women ... on the job anyway ... at least in terms of overall hours. That's just one reason why when you make a general comparison of men's and women's earnings in most fields, men usually come out ahead. ... [But Warren] Farrell ... found ... 39 ... occupations [in which] women's median earnings exceeded men's earnings by at least 5 percent and in some cases by as much as 43 percent. ... In fields like engineering, a company may get one woman and seven men applying for a job. ... If the company wants to hire the woman, they may have to pay a premium to get her. ... Also, where women can combine technical expertise with people skills—such as those required in sales and ... where customers may prefer dealing with a woman—that's likely to contribute to a premium in pay. ...

CNN, March 2, 2006

a. Draw a graph to illustrate why discrimination could result in female workers getting paid more than male workers for some jobs.
b. Explain how market competition could potentially eliminate this wage differential.
c. If customers "prefer dealing with a woman" in some markets, how might that lead to a persistent higher wage rate for women?

9. The tables show the money income shares in Canada and the United Kingdom. Money income equals market income plus cash payments.

Canadian households	Money income (percent of total)
Lowest 20%	7
Second 20%	13
Third 20%	18
Fourth 20%	25
Highest 20%	37

U.K. households	Money income (percent of total)
Lowest 20%	3
Second 20%	5
Third 20%	14
Fourth 20%	25
Highest 20%	53

a. Create a table that shows the cumulative distribution of income in Canada and the United Kingdom.
b. Draw Lorenz curves for Canada and the United Kingdom and compare them. In which country is income less equally distributed?
c. What are some reasons for the differences in the distribution of income in Canada and the United Kingdom?

10. The table shows three income-tax payment schemes.

Before-tax income (dollars)	Plan A tax (dollars)	Plan B tax (dollars)	Plan C tax (dollars)
10,000	1,000	1,000	2,000
20,000	2,000	4,000	2,000
30,000	3,000	9,000	2,000

Which income-tax payment plan

a. Is proportional?
b. Is regressive?
c. Is progressive?
d. Increases inequality?
e. Lessens inequality?
f. Has no effect on inequality?

11. The table shows the distribution of market income in Canada in 2006.

Households	Market income (percent of total)
Lowest 20%	1.1
Second 20%	7.3
Third 20%	14.8
Fourth 20%	24.8
Highest 20%	52.0

a. What is the definition of market income?
b. Draw the Lorenz curve for the distribution of market income.

12. The table shows the distribution of after-tax income in Canada in 2006.

Households	After-tax income (percent of total)
Lowest 20%	4.8
Second 20%	10.7
Third 20%	16.4
Fourth 20%	24.0
Highest 20%	44.1

Use the information provided in problem 11 about market income in 2006.

a. What is the percentage of total market income that is redistributed from the highest income group?
b. What are the percentages of total income that are redistributed to the lower income groups?
c. Describe the effects of increasing the amount of income redistribution in Canada to the point at which the lowest income group receives 15 percent of total income and the highest income group receives 30 percent of total income.

13. In an economy in 2000, 3 million people had full-time managerial and professional jobs that paid an average of $800 a week. At the same time, 1 million people had full-time sales positions that paid an average of $530 a week.

a. Explain why managers and professionals are paid more than salespeople.
b. Explain why, despite the higher weekly wage, more people are employed as managers and professionals than as salespeople.
c. If the online shopping trend continues, how do you think the market for salespeople will change in coming years?

14. The Cash Will Flow: A huge surplus and an upcoming election will likely mean a big-spending federal budget

... Budget surplus projections reach as high as $13 billion—and Conservative promises pile just as high. ... The Canadian Taxpayers Federation and National Citizens Coalition are already warning of a spending spree that will leave the ordinary Joe with less in his pocket. "The bottom line is, all of this spending puts meaningful tax relief in doubt," says John Williamson, federal director of the taxpayer group.

Flaherty has already signalled plans to announce a working income tax benefit. ... The benefit would provide tax relief aimed at eliminating the so-called welfare wall of people trying to get off the dole only to see taxes and other new expenses whittle down their employment income until taking a low-level job seems unaffordable.

Investors should watch for a break on the capital gains tax and other savings. Pensioners will be able to split their income with their spouse in order to lower the household tax bill. ...

NDP Leader Jack Layton says the budget will have to address the growing "prosperity gap" between Canada's rich and poor by investing in education, child care, seniors, and urban infrastructure. ... The entire exercise leaves the CTF's Williamson shaking his head.

CNEWS, Canoe, March 17, 2007

a. Explain how a "working income tax benefit" would work. Who would benefit most? Would it have any short-term or long-term effect on the incidence of poverty in Canada?

b. Why does the Canadian Taxpayers Federation and National Citizens Coalition say that "a spending spree will leave the ordinary Joe with less in his pocket"?

c. Explain why tax cuts in a progressive income tax system are consistently criticized for favouring the wealthy.

d. How might the benefits of tax cuts trickle down to others whose taxes are not cut?

e. Explain how Jack Layton's budget suggestion would change the "prosperity gap"? Would his suggestion have a short-term or long-term effect on the incidence of poverty in Canada?

15. After you have studied *Reading Between the Lines* on pp. 456–457, answer the following questions.

a. What are the facts reported in the news article about the change in the incidence of low income?

b. Explain why a comparison of low-income cut-off incidence in 1996 and 2006 tells us nothing about the trend in the incidence of low income.

c. Explain the link between the two distributions of income in Fig. 1 with the two Lorenz curves in Fig. 2.

d. Explain how the median income can fall while the average income rises. What does this feature of the income distribution tell us?

e. How does the size of the average family unit influence the impression created by the data reported in the news article?

16. Use the link on MyEconLab (Chapter Resources, Chapter 19, Web links) to download the Deininger and Squire Data Set on income distribution. Select two counties that interest you and obtain data on quintile shares of income for these two countries in two years, the most recent available and the earliest available.

a. In which of the countries you've selected is the distribution of income more unequal ?

b. What reasons might explain the differences in the distributions of income in the two countries you've selected?

c. How has the distribution of income changed in the two countries over the two years you've selected? Has the distribution of income become more equal or less equal? How do you know?

d. What reasons might explain the changes in the distributions of income in c?

e. Compare the distributions of income in your chosen countries with that in Canada and suggest explanations for the differences in the degree of inequality.

UNDERSTANDING FACTOR MARKETS AND INEQUALITY

For Whom?

During the past 35 years, the gap between the richest and the poorest in Canada has widened. But millions in Asia have been lifted from poverty and are now enjoying a high and rapidly rising standard of living. What are the forces that generate these trends? The answer to this question is the forces of demand and supply in factor markets. These forces determine wages, interest rates, rents, and the prices of natural resources. These forces also determine people's incomes.

In Canada, human capital and entrepreneurship are the most prized resources, and their incomes have grown most rapidly. In Asia, labour has seen its wage rates transformed. And in all regions rich in oil, incomes have risen on the back of high and fast-rising energy prices.

Many outstanding economists have advanced our understanding of factor markets and the role they play in helping to resolve the conflict between the demands of humans and the resources available. One of them is Thomas Robert Malthus.

Another is Harold Hotelling, whose prediction of an ever rising price of nonrenewable natural resources implies an ever falling rate of their use and an intensifying search for substitutes.

Yet another is Julian Simon, who challenged both the Malthusian gloom and the Hotelling Principle. He believed that people are the "ultimate resource" and predicted that a rising population lessens the pressure on natural resources. A bigger population provides a larger number of resourceful people who can discover more efficient ways of using scarce resources.

Thomas Robert Malthus *(1766–1834), an English clergyman and economist, was an extremely influential social scientist. In his best-selling* Essay on the Principle of Population, *published in 1798, he predicted that population growth would outstrip food production and said that wars, famine, and disease were inevitable unless population growth was held in check by marrying at a late age and living a celibate life. (He married at 38 a wife of 27, marriage ages that he recommended for others.)*

Malthus had a profound influence on Charles Darwin, who got the key idea that led him to the theory of natural selection from Essay on the Principle of Population. *But it was also Malthus' gloomy predictions that made economics the "dismal science."*

"The passion between the sexes has appeared in every age to be so nearly the same, that it may always be considered, in algebraic language, as a given quantity."

THOMAS ROBERT MALTHUS
An Essay on the Principle of Population

TALKING
WITH

David Card

David Card is Class of 1950 Professor of Economics and Director of the Center for Labor Economics at the University of California, Berkeley, and Faculty Research Associate at the National Bureau of Economic Research.

Born in Canada, Professor Card obtained his B.A. at Queen's University, Kingston, Ontario, in 1977 and his Ph.D. at Princeton University in 1983. He has received many honours, the most notable of which is the American Economic Association's John Bates Clark Prize, awarded to the best economist under 40.

Professor Card's research on labour markets and the effects of public policies on earnings, jobs, and the distribution of income has produced around 150 articles and several books. His most recent book (co-edited with Alan Auerbach and John Quigley) is *Poverty, the Distribution of Income, and Public Policy* (New York: Russell Sage Foundation, 2006). An earlier book (co-authored with Alan B. Krueger), *Myth and Measurement: The New Economics of the Minimum Wage* (Princeton, NJ: Princeton University Press, 1995), made a big splash and upset one of the most fundamental beliefs about the effects of minimum wages.

Michael Parkin and Robin Bade talked with David Card about his work and the progress that economists have made in understanding how public policies can influence the distribution of income and economic well-being.

Professor Card, what attracted you to economics?

When I went to university I had no intention of studying economics: I was planning to be a physics major. I was helping a friend with her problem set and started reading the supply and demand section of the textbook. I was impressed with how well the model seemed to describe the paradox that a bumper crop can be bad for farmers. I read most of the book over the next few days. The next year, I signed up as an economics major.

Almost all your work is grounded in data. You are an empirical economist. How do you go about your work, where do your data come from, and how do you use data?

The data I use come from many different sources. I have collected my own data from surveys; transcribed data from historical sources and government publications; and used computerized data files based on records from censuses and surveys in the United States, Canada, Britain, and other countries.

An economist can do three things with data. The first is to develop simple statistics on basic questions such as "What fraction of families live in poverty?" For this, one needs to understand how the data were collected and processed and how the questions were asked. For example, the poverty rate depends on how you define a "family." If a single mother and her child live with the mother's parents, the income of the mother and the grandparents is counted as "family income."

The second thing economists do with data is develop descriptive comparisons. For example, I have compared the wage differences between male and female workers. Again, the details are important. For example, the male–female wage differential is much bigger if you look at annual earnings than at earnings per hour, because women work fewer hours per year.

Once you've established some simple facts, you start to get ideas for possible explanations. You can also rule out a lot of other ideas.

The third and most difficult thing that empirical economists try to do is infer a causal relationship. In rare instances, we have a true experiment in which a random subgroup of volunteers is enrolled in a "treatment group" and the remainder become the "control group." The Self Sufficiency Program (SSP)—an experimental welfare reform demonstration in Canada—was conducted this way. Because of random assignment, we know that the treatment and control groups would have looked very similar in the absence of the treatment. Thus when we see a difference in behaviour, such as the higher level of work activity by single parents in the treatment group of SSP, we can infer that the financial incentives of SSP caused people to work more.

Most often, we don't have an experiment. We see a group of people who are subject to some "treatment" (such as a higher minimum wage) and we try to construct a comparison group by finding some other group similar to the treatment group who tell us what the treatment group would have looked like in the absence of treatment. If we can't find a compelling comparison group, we have to be cautious.

In your book on the minimum wage with Alan Krueger, you reported that an increase in the minimum wage increased employment—the opposite of the conventional wisdom. How did you reach that conclusion?

We studied several instances where minimum wages were raised in one place but not in another. For example, when we found out that the New Jersey legislature had recently voted to raise the minimum wage, we set up a survey of fast-food restaurants in New Jersey and in nearby parts of Pennsylvania. We surveyed the stores a few months before the New Jersey minimum went up and then again one year later, after the minimum had been raised. The first-round survey found that conditions were very similar in the two states. In the second round, we found that although wages were now higher in New Jersey, employment was also slightly higher. It was very important to have the first-round survey to

> The most difficult thing that empirical economists try to do is infer a causal relationship.

benchmark any differences that existed prior to the rise in the minimum. Thus, we argued that any differential changes in New Jersey relative to Pennsylvania from the first round to the second round were most plausibly due to the minimum wage.

How did you explain what you found?

We argued that many employers in New Jersey before the rise in the minimum were operating with vacancies and would have liked to hire more workers but could not do so without raising their wages. In this situation, an increase in the minimum wage can cause some employers to hire more and others to hire less. On average, the net effect on employment can be small. What we saw was a rise in wages and a reduction in vacancies in New Jersey, coupled with a small gain in employment.

You've examined just about every labour market policy. Let's talk about welfare payments to single mothers: How do they influence labour market decisions?

The Self Sufficiency Program welfare demonstration in Canada tested an earnings subsidy as an alternative to conventional welfare payments. The problem with conventional welfare is that recipients have no incentive to work: If they earn $1, their payments are reduced by $1. That led Milton Friedman in the early 1950s to advocate an alternative "negative income tax" program, such as SSP, in which recipients who earn more only lose a fraction of their benefits (in the case of SSP, 50 cents per dollar earned). The results showed that this alternative system encourages single parents to work more.

Immigration has been big news in recent years. Can you describe your work on this issue and your findings?

My research has tried to understand whether the arrival of low-skilled immigrants hurts the labour market opportunities for less-skilled natives. One of my papers studies the effect of the Mariel Boatlift, which occurred in 1980 following a political uprising that led Fidel Castro to declare that people who wanted to leave Cuba were free to exit from the port of Mariel. Within

465

days, a flotilla of small boats from the United States began transporting people to Miami, and 150,000 people eventually left. Over one-half stayed in Miami, creating a huge "shock" to the supply of low-skilled labour. I studied the effect by looking at wages and unemployment rates for various groups in Miami and in a set of comparison cities that had very similar wage and employment trends in the previous decade. I found that the influx of the boatlift had no discernible effect on wages or unemployment of other workers in Miami. My later work has confirmed that the Miami story seems to hold in most other cities. Cities can absorb big inflows of low-skilled immigrants with remarkably little negative impact on natives.

The distribution of income has become increasingly unequal. Do we know why?

There are many sources. Family incomes have become more unequal in part because of a rise in families with two very high-wage earners. These families have pulled away from the rest, creating a widening distribution. The very richest families, whose incomes are above the 95th or 99th percentile of the income distribution, earn an increasingly large share of national income. The trends in income for this group account for most of the rise in inequality we have seen in the last 10 years.

Unfortunately, it is very hard to study this group because they represent such a small fraction of families, and they are often under-reported on surveys. The best available data, from tax returns, don't tell us much about the sources of this group's success, though it seems to be due to labour market earnings rather than to previous investments or family wealth.

There is a large literature on wage inequality among the larger "middle" of the population: people who earn up to $150,000 per year, for example. Wage inequality for men in this group rose very sharply in the early 1980s in the United States, rose a little more between 1985 and 1990, and was fairly stable (or even

> ... find out what life is like for other people. ... The best economists are observant and thoughtful social scientists.

decreasing) in the 1990s. Some of the rise in the 1980s was due to decreases in unionization, and some was due to the changing effects of the minimum wage, which fell in real terms in the early 1980s, and then gained in the early to mid-1990s.

Some researchers ascribe the rest of the trend in wage inequality to the spread of computers and increasing demands for highly skilled workers. Others blame international trade and, most recently, immigration. Those explanations are hard to evaluate because we don't really see the forces of new technology or trade that affect any particular worker. One thing we do know is that wage inequality trends were quite different in many other countries. Canada, for instance, had relatively modest rises in inequality in the 1980s.

What advice do you have for someone who is just beginning to study economics? What other subjects do you think work well alongside economics? Do you have some reading suggestions?

The part of economics that most interests me is the behaviour of people in their everyday life. People constantly have to answer questions such as: Should I get more education? How much should I save? Should I send my children to the local public school? It's extremely important to see how these questions are answered by different people: people from poorer families or other countries or who had to make very different choices. Take any opportunity to find out what life is like for other people. You can learn a lot from reading novels, spending a year abroad, or taking classes in sociology or history. The best economists are observant and thoughtful social scientists. My other piece of advice is study mathematics. The more mathematics training you have, the more easily you can understand what economists are doing. Newton invented calculus to study the motion of planets, but economics benefits from the same tools.

20 Measuring GDP and Economic Growth

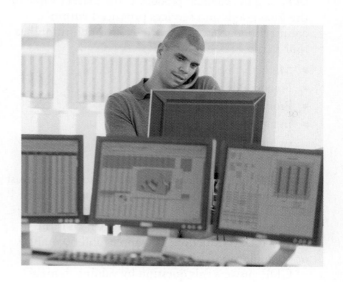

After studying this chapter, you will be able to

- Define GDP and use the circular flow model to explain why GDP equals aggregate expenditure and aggregate income

- Explain how Statistics Canada measures Canadian GDP and *real* GDP

- Describe how real GDP is used to measure economic growth and fluctuations and explain the limitations of real GDP as a measure of economic well-being

Will our economy remain weak through 2010 in a recession, or worse, a depression? Or will it begin to expand more rapidly? Many Canadian businesses wanted to know the answers to these questions in 2009. Nortel wanted to know whether to maintain its workforce or lay off some workers. Bombardier wanted to know whether to increase its capacity to build railroad engines. To assess the state of the economy and to make big decisions about business contraction or expansion, firms such as Nortel and Bombardier use forecasts of GDP. What exactly is GDP and what does it tell us about the state of the economy?

To reveal the rate of growth or shrinkage of production, we must remove the effects of inflation and assess how pro-

duction is *really* changing. How do we remove the effects of inflation to reveal *real* production?

Some countries are rich while others are poor. How do we compare economic well-being in one country with that in another? How can we make international comparisons of production?

In this chapter, you will find out how economic statisticians at Statistics Canada measure GDP and the economic growth rate. You will also learn about the uses and the limitations of these measures. In *Reading Between the Lines* at the end of the chapter, we'll look at the Canadian economy during the slowdown that began in 2008.

467

Gross Domestic Product

What exactly is GDP, how is it calculated, what does it mean, and why do we care about it? You are going to discover the answers to these questions in this chapter. First, what *is* GDP?

GDP Defined

GDP, or **gross domestic product**, is the market value of the final goods and services produced within a country in a given time period. This definition has four parts:

- Market value
- Final goods and services
- Produced within a country
- In a given time period

We'll examine each in turn.

Market Value   To measure total production, we must add together the production of apples and oranges, computers and popcorn. Just counting the items doesn't get us very far. For example, which is the greater total production: 100 apples and 50 oranges or 50 apples and 100 oranges?

GDP answers this question by valuing items at their *market values*—the prices at which items are traded in markets. If the price of an apple is 10 cents, then the market value of 50 apples is $5. If the price of an orange is 20 cents, then the market value of 100 oranges is $20. By using market prices to value production, we can add the apples and oranges together. The market value of 50 apples and 100 oranges is $5 plus $20, or $25.

Final Goods and Services   To calculate GDP, we value the *final goods and services* produced. A **final good** (or service) is an item that is bought by its final user during a specified time period. It contrasts with an **intermediate good** (or service), which is an item that is produced by one firm, bought by another firm, and used as a component of a final good or service.

For example, a Ford truck is a final good, but a Firestone tire on the truck is an intermediate good. A Dell computer is a final good, but an Intel Pentium chip inside it is an intermediate good.

If we were to add the value of intermediate goods and services produced to the value of final goods and services, we would count the same thing many times—a problem called *double counting*. The value of a truck already includes the value of the tires, and the value of a Dell PC already includes the value of the Pentium chip inside it.

Some goods can be an intermediate good in some situations and a final good in other situations. For example, the ice cream that you buy on a hot summer day is a final good, but the ice cream that a restaurant buys and uses to make sundaes is an intermediate good. The sundae is the final good. So whether a good is an intermediate good or a final good depends on what it is used for, not what it is.

Some items that people buy are neither final goods nor intermediate goods and they are not part of GDP. Examples of such items include financial assets—stocks and bonds—and secondhand goods—used cars or existing homes. A secondhand good was part of GDP in the year in which it was produced, but not part of GDP this year.

Produced Within a Country   Only goods and services that are produced *within a country* count as part of that country's GDP. Roots Canada Limited, a Canadian firm, produces T-shirts in Taiwan, and the market value of those shirts is part of Taiwan's GDP, not part of Canada's GDP. Toyota, a Japanese firm, produces automobiles in Cambridge, Ontario, and the value of this production is part of Canada's GDP, not part of Japan's GDP.

In a Given Time Period   GDP measures the value of production *in a given time period*—normally either a quarter of a year—called the quarterly GDP data—or a year—called the annual GDP data.

GDP measures not only the value of total production but also total income and total expenditure. The equality between the value of total production and total income is important because it shows the direct link between productivity and living standards. Our standard of living rises when our incomes rise and we can afford to buy more goods and services. But we must produce more goods and services if we are to be able to buy more goods and services.

Rising incomes and a rising value of production go together. They are two aspects of the same phenomenon: increasing productivity. To see why, we study the circular flow of expenditure and income.

GDP and the Circular Flow of Expenditure and Income

Figure 20.1 illustrates the circular flow of expenditure and income. The economy consists of households, firms, governments, and the rest of the world (the rectangles), which trade in factor markets and goods (and services) markets. We focus first on households and firms.

Households and Firms Households sell and firms buy the services of labour, capital, and land in factor markets. For these factor services, firms pay income to households: wages for labour services, interest for the use of capital, and rent for the use of land. A fourth factor of production, entrepreneurship, receives profit.

Firms' retained earnings—profits that are not distributed to households—are part of the household sector's income. You can think of retained earnings as being income that households save and lend back to firms. Figure 20.1 shows the total income—*aggregate income*—received by households, including retained earnings, by the blue flow labelled *Y*.

Firms sell and households buy consumer goods and services—such as inline skates and haircuts—in the goods market. The total payment for these goods and services is **consumption expenditure**, shown by the red flow labelled *C*.

Firms buy and sell new capital equipment—such as computer systems, airplanes, trucks, and assembly line equipment—in the goods market. Some of what firms produce is not sold but is added to inventory. For example, if GM produces 1,000 cars and sells 950 of them, the other 50 cars remain in GM's inventory of unsold cars, which increases by 50 cars. When a firm adds unsold output to inventory, we can think of the firm as buying goods from itself. The purchase of new

---

FIGURE 20.1   The Circular Flow of Expenditure and Income

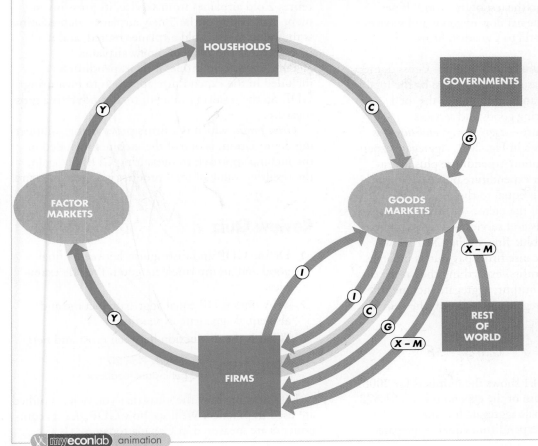

Households make consumption expenditures (*C*); firms make investments (*I*); governments buy goods and services (*G*); and the rest of the world buys net exports (*X – M*). Firms pay incomes (*Y*) to households. Aggregate income equals aggregate expenditure.

Billions of dollars in 2008

$$C = 885$$
$$I = 304$$
$$G = 357$$
$$X - M = 32$$
$$Y = 1{,}578$$

Source of data: Statistics Canada, CANSIM Table 380-0002. (The data are for the first quarter of 2008 annual rate.)

myeconlab animation

plant, equipment, and buildings and the additions to inventories are **investment**, shown by the red flow labelled *I*.

Governments   Governments buy goods and services from firms and their expenditure on goods and services is called **government expenditure**. In Fig. 20.1, government expenditure is shown as the red flow *G*.

Governments finance their expenditure with taxes. But taxes are not part of the circular flow of expenditure and income. Governments also make financial transfers to households, such as social security benefits and unemployment benefits, and pay subsidies to firms. These financial transfers, like taxes, are not part of the circular flow of expenditure and income.

Rest of the World   Firms in Canada sell goods and services to the rest of the world—**exports**—and buy goods and services from the rest of the world—**imports**. The value of exports (*X*) minus the value of imports (*M*) is called **net exports**, the red flow *X* − *M* in Fig 20.1. If net exports are positive, the net flow of goods and services is from Canadian firms to the rest of the world. If net exports are negative, the net flow of goods and services is from the rest of the world to Canadian firms.

GDP Equals Expenditure Equals Income   Gross domestic product can be measured in two ways: by the total expenditure on goods and services or by the total income earned producing goods and services.

The total expenditure—*aggregate expenditure*—is the sum of the red flows in Fig. 20.1. Aggregate expenditure equals consumption expenditure plus investment plus government expenditure plus net exports.

Aggregate income is equal to the total amount paid for the services of the factors of production used to produce final goods and services—wages, interest, rent, and profit. The blue flow in Fig. 20.1 shows aggregate income. Because firms pay out as incomes (including retained profits) everything they receive from the sale of their output, aggregate income (the blue flow) equals aggregate expenditure (the sum of the red flows). That is,

$$Y = C + I + G + X - M.$$

The table in Fig. 20.1 shows the numbers for 2008. You can see that the sum of the expenditures is $1,578 billion, which also equals aggregate income.

Because aggregate expenditure equals aggregate

income, the two methods of measuring GDP give the same answer. So

GDP equals aggregate expenditure and equals aggregate income.

The circular flow model is the foundation on which the national economic accounts are built.

Why Is Domestic Product "Gross"?

"Gross" means before subtracting the depreciation of capital. The opposite of "gross" is "net," which means after subtracting the depreciation of capital.

Depreciation is the decrease in the value of a firm's capital that results from wear and tear and obsolescence. The total amount spent both buying new capital and replacing depreciated capital is called **gross investment**. The amount by which the value of capital increases is called **net investment**. Net investment equals gross investment minus depreciation.

For example, if an airline buys 5 new airplanes and retires 2 old airplanes from service, its gross investment is the value of the 5 new airplanes, depreciation is the value of the 2 old airplanes retired, and net investment is the value of 3 new airplanes.

Gross investment is one of the expenditures included in the expenditure approach to measuring GDP. So the resulting value of total product is a gross measure.

Gross profit, which is a firm's profit before subtracting depreciation, is one of the incomes included in the income approach to measuring GDP. So again, the resulting value of total product is a gross measure.

Review Quiz

1   Define GDP and distinguish between a final good and an intermediate good. Provide examples.
2   Why does GDP equal aggregate income and also equal aggregate expenditure?
3   What is the distinction between gross and net?

myeconlab   Work Study Plan 20.1 and get instant feedback.

Let's now see how the ideas that you've just studied are used in practice. We'll see how GDP and its components are measured in Canada today.

Measuring Canada's GDP

Statistics Canada uses the concepts in the circular flow model to measure GDP and its components in the *National Income and Expenditure Accounts*. Because the value of aggregate production equals aggregate expenditure and aggregate income, there are two approaches available for measuring GDP, and both are used. They are

- The expenditure approach
- The income approach

The Expenditure Approach

The *expenditure approach* measures GDP as the sum of consumption expenditure (C), investment (I), government expenditure on goods and services (G), and net exports of goods and services ($X - M$), corresponding to the red flows in the circular flow model in Fig. 20.1. Table 20.1 shows the result of this approach for 2008. The table uses the terms in the *National Income and Expenditure Accounts*.

Personal expenditures on consumer goods and services are the expenditures by Canadian households on goods and services produced in Canada and in the rest of the world. They include goods such as pop and books and services such as banking and legal advice. They also include the purchase of consumer durable goods, such as TVs and microwave ovens. But they do *not* include the purchase of new homes, which Statistics Canada counts as part of investment.

Business investment is expenditure on capital equipment and buildings by firms and the additions to business inventories. It also includes expenditure on new homes by households.

Government expenditures on goods and services is the expenditure by all levels of government on goods and services, such as national defence and garbage collection. It does *not* include *transfer payments*, such as unemployment benefits, because they are not expenditures on goods and services.

Net exports of goods and services are the value of exports minus the value of imports. This item includes telephone equipment that Nortel sells to AT&T (a Canadian export), and Japanese DVD players that Sears buys from Sony (a Canadian import).

Table 20.1 shows the relative magnitudes of the four items of aggregate expenditure.

TABLE 20.1 GDP: The Expenditure Approach

Item	Symbol	Amount in 2008 (billions of dollars)	Percentage of GDP
Personal expenditures on consumer goods and services	C	885	56.1
Business investment	I	304	19.3
Government expenditures on goods and services	G	357	22.6
Net exports of goods and services	X – M	32	2.0
Gross domestic product	Y	1,578	100.0

The expenditure approach measures GDP as the sum of personal expenditures on consumer goods and services, (*C*), business investment (*I*), government expenditures on goods and services (*G*), and net exports (*X – M*).

In 2008, GDP measured by the expenditure approach was $1,578 billion. Personal expenditures on consumption goods and services is the largest expenditure item.

Source of data: Statistics Canada, CANSIM Table 380-0002.

The Income Approach

The *income approach* measures GDP by summing the incomes that firms pay households for the factors of production they hire—wages for labour, interest for capital, rent for land, and profit for entrepreneurship. The *National Income and Expenditure Accounts* divide incomes into five categories:

1. Wages, salaries, and supplementary labour income
2. Corporate profits
3. Interest and miscellaneous investment income
4. Farmers' income
5. Income from non-farm unincorporated businesses

Wages, salaries, and supplementary labour income is the payment for labour services. It includes net wages and salaries (called "take-home pay") plus taxes withheld on earnings plus benefits such as pension contributions.

Corporate profits are the profits of corporations, some of which are paid to households in the form of dividends and some of which are retained by corporations as undistributed profits. They are all income.

Interest and miscellaneous investment income is the interest households receive on loans they make minus the interest households pay on their own borrowing.

Farmers' income and *income from non-farm unincorporated businesses* are mixtures of the previous three items. They include compensation for the owner's labour, payment for the use of the owner's capital, and profit, lumped together in these two catch-all categories.

Table 20.2 shows these five incomes and their relative magnitudes. They sum to *net domestic income at factor cost*. The term "factor cost" is used because it is the cost of the factors of production used to produce final goods. When we sum the expenditures on final goods, we arrive at a total called *domestic product at market prices*. Market prices and factor cost diverge because of indirect taxes and subsidies.

An *indirect tax* is a tax paid by consumers when they buy goods and services. (In contrast, a *direct tax* is a tax on income.) Provincial sales taxes, GST, and taxes on alcohol, gasoline, and tobacco are indirect taxes. Because of indirect taxes, consumers pay more for some goods and services than producers receive. Market price exceeds factor cost. For example, if the sales tax is 7 percent, you pay $1.07 when you buy a $1 chocolate bar. The factor cost of the chocolate bar including profit is $1. The market price is $1.07.

A *subsidy* is a payment by the government to a producer. Payments made to grain growers and dairy farmers are subsidies. Because of subsidies, consumers pay less for some goods and services than producers receive. Factor cost exceeds market price.

To get from factor cost to market price, we add indirect taxes and subtract subsidies. Making this adjustment brings us to *net domestic income at market prices*. We still must get from a *net* to a *gross* measure.

Total expenditure is a *gross* number because it includes *gross* investment. Net domestic income at market prices is a net income measure because corporate profits are measured *after deducting depreciation*. They are a *net* income measure. To get from net income to gross income, we must *add depreciation*.

We've now arrived at GDP using the income approach. This number is not exactly the same as GDP using the expenditure approach. If a waiter doesn't report all his tips when he fills out his income

TABLE 20.2 GDP: The Income Approach

Item	Amount in 2008 (billions of dollars)	Percentage of GDP
Wages, salaries, and supplementary labour income	815	51.6
Corporate profits	226	14.3
Interest and miscellaneous investment income	75	4.7
Farmers' income	1	0.1
Income from non-farm unincorporated businesses	93	5.9
Net domestic income at factor cost	1,210	76.6
Indirect taxes *less* subsidies	165	10.5
Net domestic income at market prices	1,375	87.1
Depreciation	202	12.8
GDP (income approach)	**1,577**	**99.9**
Statistical discrepancy	1	0.1
GDP (expenditure approach)	**1,578**	**100.0**

The sum of all incomes equals *net domestic income at factor cost*. GDP equals net domestic income at factor cost plus indirect taxes less subsidies plus depreciation. In 2008, GDP measured by the income approach was $1,577 billion. This amount is $1 billion less than GDP measured by the expenditure approach—a statistical discrepancy of $1 billion or 0.1 percent of GDP.

Wages, salaries, and supplementary labour income is by far the largest part of aggregate income.

Source of data: Statistics Canada, CANSIM Table 380-0001.

tax return, they get missed in the income approach but they show up in the expenditure approach when he spends his income. Also because some expenditure items are estimated rather than directly measured, the sum of expenditures might exceed the sum of incomes.

The gap between the expenditure approach and the income approach is called the **statistical discrepancy** and it is calculated as the GDP expenditure total minus the GDP income total. The discrepancy is never large. In 2008, it was 0.1 percent of GDP.

Nominal GDP and Real GDP

Often, we want to *compare* GDP in two periods, say 2002 and 2008. In 2002, GDP was $1,153 billion and in 2008, it was $1,578 billion—37 percent higher than in 2002. This increase in GDP is a combination of an increase in production and a rise in prices. To isolate the increase in production from the rise in prices, we distinguish between *real* GDP and *nominal* GDP.

Real GDP is the value of final goods and services produced in a given year when *valued at the prices of a reference base year.* By comparing the value of production in the two years at the same prices, we reveal the change in production.

Currently, the reference base year is 2002 and we describe real GDP as measured in 2002 dollars—in terms of what the dollar would buy in 2002.

Nominal GDP is the value of final goods and services produced in a given year valued at the prices of that year. Nominal GDP is just a more precise name for GDP.

Economists at Statistics Canada calculate real GDP using the method described in the Mathematical Note on pp. 482–483. Here, we'll explain the basic idea but not the technical details.

Calculating Real GDP

We'll calculate real GDP for an economy that produces one consumption good, one capital good, and one government service. Net exports are zero.

Table 20.3 shows the quantities produced and the prices in 2002 (the base year) and in 2009. In part (a), we calculate nominal GDP in 2002. For each item, we multiply the quantity produced by its price to find the total expenditure on the item. We then sum the expenditures to find nominal GDP, which in 2002 is $100 million. Because 2002 is the base year, real GDP and nominal GDP both equal $100 million.

In Table 20.3(b), we calculate nominal GDP in 2009, which is $300 million. Nominal GDP in 2009 is three times its value in 2000. But by how much has production increased? Real GDP will tell us.

In Table 20.3(c), we calculate real GDP in 2009. The quantities of the goods and services produced are those of 2009, as in part (b). The prices are those in the reference base year—2002, as in part (a).

For each item, we multiply the quantity produced in 2009 by its price in 2002. We then sum these expenditures to find real GDP in 2009, which is

TABLE 20.3 Calculating Nominal GDP and Real GDP

	Item	Quantity (millions)	Price (dollars)	Expenditure (millions of dollars)
(a)	**In 2002**			
C	T-shirts	10	5	50
I	Computer chips	3	10	30
G	Security services	1	20	20
Y	Real and nominal GDP in 2002			100
(b)	**In 2009**			
C	T-shirts	4	5	20
I	Computer chips	2	20	40
G	Security services	6	40	240
Y	Nominal GDP in 2009			300
(c)	**Quantities of 2009 valued at prices of 2002**			
C	T-shirts	4	5	20
I	Computer chips	2	10	20
G	Security services	6	20	120
Y	Real GDP in 2009			160

In 2002, the reference base year, real GDP equals nominal GDP and was $100 million. In 2009, nominal GDP increased to $300 million. But real GDP in 2009 in part (c), which is calculated by using the quantities of 2009 in part (b) and the prices of 2002 in part (a), was only $160 million—a 60 percent increase from 2002.

$160 million. This number is what total expenditure would have been in 2009 if prices had remained the same as they were in 2000.

Nominal GDP in 2009 is three times its value in 2002, but real GDP in 2009 is only 1.6 times its 2002 value—a 60 percent increase in production.

Review Quiz

1 What is the expenditure approach to measuring GDP?
2 What is the income approach to measuring GDP?
3 What adjustments must be made to total income to make it equal GDP?
4 What is the distinction between nominal GDP and real GDP?
5 How is real GDP calculated?

myeconlab Work Study Plan 20.2 and get instant feedback.

The Uses and Limitations of Real GDP

Economists use estimates of real GDP for two main purposes:

- To compare the standard of living over time
- To compare the standard of living across countries

The Standard of Living Over Time

One method of comparing the standard of living over time is to calculate real GDP per person in different years. **Real GDP per person** is real GDP divided by the population. Real GDP per person tells us the value of goods and services that the average person can enjoy. By using *real* GDP, we remove any influence that rising prices and a rising cost of living might have had on our comparison.

We're interested in both the long-term trends and the shorter-term cycles in the standard of living.

Long-Term Trend   A handy way of comparing real GDP per person over time is to express it as a ratio of some reference year. For example, in 1971, real GDP per person was $20,127, and in 2007, it was $40,070. So real GDP per person in 2007 was (approximately) double its 1971 level. Measured by real GDP per person, people were twice as well off in 2007 as their parents had been in 1971.

Figure 20.2 shows the path of Canadian real GDP per person from 1961 to 2007 and highlights two features of our expanding living standard:

- The growth of potential GDP per person
- Fluctuations of real GDP around potential GDP

The Growth of Potential GDP   When all the economy's labour, capital, land, and entrepreneurial ability are fully employed, the value of real GDP is called **potential GDP**. Potential GDP per person, the smoother black line in Fig. 20.2, grows at a steady pace because the quantities of the factors of production and their productivity grow at a steady pace.

But potential GDP per person doesn't grow at a *constant* pace. During the 1960s, it grew at a rate of 3.4 percent per year. Its growth rate then slowed and the average after 1970 was only 2.4 percent per year. This slowdown in the growth of potential GDP per person might seem small, but it had big consequences, as you'll soon see.

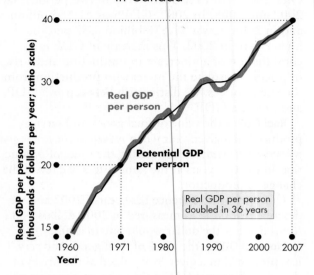

FIGURE 20.2   Rising Standard of Living in Canada

Real GDP per person in Canada doubled over the 36 years between 1971 and 2007. Real GDP per person, the red line, fluctuates around potential GDP, the black line.

Sources of data: Real GDP, Statistics Canada, CANSIM Tables 380-0017 and 051-0005. Potential GDP, based on Bank of Canada output gap estimate after 1985 and authors' assumptions before 1985.

myeconlab   animation

Fluctuations around Potential GDP   You can see that real GDP shown by the red line in Fig. 20.2 fluctuates around potential GDP. Sometimes, real GDP is above potential; sometimes, it is below potential; and sometimes, real GDP shrinks.

Let's take a closer look at the two features of our expanding living standard that we've just outlined.

Productivity Growth Slowdown   You've just seen that the growth rate of real GDP per person slowed after 1970. How costly was that slowdown? The answer is provided by a number that we'll call the **Lucas wedge**, which is the dollar value of the accumulated gap between what real GDP per person would have been if the 1960s growth rate had persisted and what real GDP per person turned out to be.

University of Chicago economist and Nobel Laureate Robert E. Lucas Jr., who drew attention to this measure, remarked that once he began to think about the benefits of faster economic growth, he found it hard to think about anything else.

Figure 20.3 illustrates the Lucas wedge. The red line is actual real GDP per person and the thin black line is the trend that real GDP per person would have followed if the 1960s growth rate of potential GDP had persisted through the years to 2007.

You can see in the figure that the gap—the wedge—had accumulated to an astonishing $316,000 per person by 2007. The gap started out small during the 1970s but in 2008, real GDP per person was $23,230 per year lower than it would have been with no growth slowdown.

Real GDP Fluctuations We call the fluctuations in the pace of expansion of real GDP the business cycle. A **business cycle** is a periodic but irregular up-and-down movement of total production and other measures of economic activity. The business cycle isn't a regular, predictable, and repeating cycle like the phases of the moon. The timing and the intensity of the business cycle vary a lot, but every cycle has two phases:

1. Expansion
2. Recession

and two turning points:

1. Peak
2. Trough

Figure 20.4 shows these features of the most recent Canadian business cycle.

An **expansion** is a period during which real GDP increases. In the early stage of an expansion real GDP returns to potential GDP and as the expansion progresses, potential GDP grows and real GDP eventually exceeds potential GDP. Canada experienced an expansion before the first quarter of 1990 and again after the first quarter of 1991.

A **recession** is a period during which real GDP decreases—its growth rate is negative—for at least two successive quarters. Canada's most recent recession occurred between the first quarter of 1990 and the first quarter of 1991.

FIGURE 20.3 The Cost of Slower Growth: The Lucas Wedge

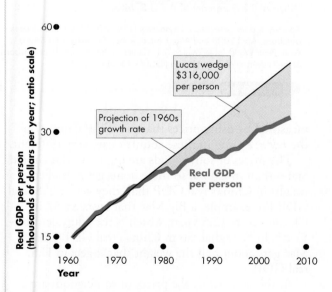

The black line projects the 1960s growth rate of real GDP per person to 2007. The Lucas wedge arises from the slowdown of productivity growth that began during the 1970s. The cost of the slowdown is $316,000 per person.

Sources of data: Statistics Canada, CANSIM Tables 380-0017 and 051-0005 and authors' calculations.

myeconlab animation

FIGURE 20.4 The Most Recent Canadian Business Cycle

The most recent business cycle peak occurred at the end of an expansion in the first quarter of 1990. A recession ran from that peak through the first quarter of 1991. A new expansion then began.

Sources of data: Statistics Canada, CANSIM Table 380-0002 and Bank of Canada estimate of the output gap.

myeconlab animation

A *peak* is the point in a business cycle at which real GDP reaches its highest level in an expansion and from which a recession begins. Canada's last business cycle peak occurred in the first quarter of 1990.

A *trough* is the point in a business cycle at the bottom of a recession when real GDP reaches a temporary low point from which the next expansion begins. Canada's last trough occurred in the first quarter of 1991.

You can see that recessions are infrequent and relatively short. Expansion is the normal state of the economy. The expansion that began in the first quarter of 1991 was still running in the second quarter of 2008, although a new recession was then predicted.

Let's now leave comparisons of the standard of living over time and look at those across countries.

The Standard of Living Across Countries

Two problems arise in using real GDP to compare living standards across countries. First, the real GDP of one country must be converted into the same currency units as the real GDP of the other country. Second, the goods and services in both countries must be valued at the same prices. We'll look at these two problems by using a striking example: a comparison of the United States and China.

China and the United States Compared In 2008, real GDP per person in the United States was $38,422. The official Chinese statistics published in the International Monetary Fund's *World Economic Outlook* says that real GDP per person in China in 2008 was 16,400 yuan. (The yuan is the currency of China.) On average, during 2008, $1 U.S. was worth 8.3 yuan. If we use this exchange rate to convert 16,400 yuan into U.S. dollars, we get $1,976. This comparison of real GDP per person in China and the United States makes China look extremely poor. In 2008, real GDP per person in the United States was 19 times that in China, or real GDP per person in China was 5 percent of that in the United States.

The red line in Fig. 20.5 shows real GDP per person in China from 1980 to 2008 when the market exchange rate is used to convert yuan to U.S. dollars.

Purchasing Power Parity Comparison Figure 20.5 shows another estimate of China's real GDP per person that is much larger than the one we've just calculated. Let's see how this alternative measurement is made.

U.S. real GDP is measured by using prices that prevail in the United States. China's real GDP is

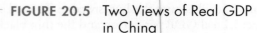

FIGURE 20.5 Two Views of Real GDP in China

Real GDP per person in China has grown rapidly. But how rapidly it has grown and to what level depends on how real GDP is valued. When GDP is valued at the market exchange rate, China is a poor developing country in which income per person in 2008 was 5 percent of the U.S. level. But when GDP is valued at purchasing power parity prices, China seems to be much less poor with real GDP per person in 2008 at 12.5 percent of the U.S. level.

Sources of data: International Monetary Fund, World Economic Outlook database, April 2008 and Alan Heston, Robert Summers, and Bettina Aten, Penn World Table Version 6.1, Center for International Comparisons at the University of Pennsylvania (CICUP), October 2002.

myeconlab animation

measured by using prices that prevail in China. But the *relative prices* in these countries are very different.

The prices of some goods are higher in the United States than in China, so these items get a smaller weight in China's real GDP than they get in U.S. real GDP. For example, a Big Mac that costs $3.57 in Chicago costs 12.5 yuan, which is the equivalent of $1.83, in Shanghai. So in China's real GDP, a Big Mac gets about half the weight that it gets in U.S. real GDP.

At the same time, the prices of some goods are higher in China than in the United States, so these items get a bigger weight in China's real GDP than they get in U.S. real GDP. For example, a Buick LaCrosse that costs $25,000 in Chicago costs 239,800 yuan, which is the equivalent of $35,000, in Shanghai. So a Buick LaCrosse made in China gets about 40 percent more weight than the same car made in Detroit gets in U.S. real GDP.

More prices are lower in China than in the United States, so Chinese prices put a lower value on China's production than do U.S. prices.

To avoid putting a lower value on China's production, we use **purchasing power parity** or **PPP** prices, which are the same prices for both countries when converted at the market exchange rate. By using PPP prices, we make a more valid comparison of real GDP in China and the United States.

Alan Heston, Robert Summers, and Bettina Aten, economists at the Center for International Comparisons at the University of Pennsylvania, have used PPP prices to construct real GDP data for more than 100 countries. The IMF now uses a method similar to that of Heston, Summers, and Aten to calculate PPP estimates of real GDP in all countries. The PPP comparisons tell a remarkable story.

Figure 20.5 shows the PPP view of China's real GDP, the green line. According to the PPP comparisons, real GDP per person in the United States in 2008 was 8 times that of China, or real GDP per person in China was 12.5 percent of that in the United States.

You've seen how real GDP is used to make standard of living comparisons over time and across countries. But real GDP isn't a perfect measure of the standard of living and we'll now examine its limitations.

Limitations of Real GDP

Real GDP measures the value of goods and services that are bought in markets. Some of the factors that influence the standard of living and that are not part of GDP are

- Household production
- Underground economic activity
- Health and life expectancy
- Leisure time
- Environmental quality
- Political freedom and social justice

Household Production An enormous amount of production takes place every day in our homes. Preparing meals, cleaning the kitchen, changing a light bulb, cutting the grass, washing the car, and caring for a child are all examples of household production. Because these productive activities are not traded in markets, they are not included in GDP.

The omission of household production from GDP means that GDP *underestimates* total production. But it also means that the growth rate of GDP *overestimates* the growth rate of total production. The reason is that some of the growth rate of market production (included in GDP) is a replacement for home production. So part of the increase in GDP arises from a decrease in home production.

Two trends point in this direction. One is the number of women who have jobs, which increased from 58 percent in 1970 to 62 percent in 2008. The other is the trend in the market purchase of traditionally home-produced goods and services. For example, more and more families now eat in fast-food restaurants—one of the fastest-growing industries in Canada—and use day-care services. This trend means that an increasing proportion of food preparation and child care that were part of household production are now measured as part of GDP. So real GDP grows more rapidly than does real GDP plus home production.

Underground Economic Activity The *underground economy* is the part of the economy that is purposely hidden from the view of the government to avoid taxes and regulations or because the goods and services being produced are illegal. Because underground economic activity is unreported, it is omitted from GDP.

The underground economy is easy to describe, even if it is hard to measure. It includes the production and distribution of illegal drugs, production that uses illegal labour that is paid less than the minimum wage, and jobs done for cash to avoid paying income taxes. This last category might be quite large and includes tips earned by cab drivers, hairdressers, and hotel and restaurant workers.

Estimates of the scale of the underground economy in Canada range between 5 and 15 percent of GDP ($66 billion to almost $200 billion). Provided that the underground economy is a reasonably stable proportion of the total economy, the growth rate of real GDP still gives a useful estimate of changes in economic well-being and the standard of living. But sometimes production shifts from the underground economy to the rest of the economy, and sometimes it shifts the other way. The underground economy expands relative to the rest of the economy if taxes become especially high or if regulations become especially restrictive. And the underground economy shrinks relative to the rest of the economy if the burdens of taxes and regulations are eased. During the 1980s, when tax rates were cut, there was an increase in the reporting of previously hidden income and tax revenues increased. So some part (but probably a very small part) of the expansion of real GDP during the 1980s represented a shift from the underground economy rather than an increase in production.

Health and Life Expectancy   Good health and a long life—the hopes of everyone—do not show up in real GDP, at least not directly. A higher real GDP enables us to spend more on medical research, health care, a good diet, and exercise equipment. And as real GDP has increased, our life expectancy has lengthened—from 70 years at the end of World War II to approaching 80 years today. Infant deaths and death in childbirth, two fearful scourges of the nineteenth century, have been greatly reduced.

But we face new health and life expectancy problems every year. AIDS and drug abuse are taking young lives at a rate that causes serious concern. When we take these negative influences into account, we see that real GDP growth overstates the improvements in the standard of living.

Leisure Time   Leisure time is an economic good that adds to our economic well-being and the standard of living. Other things remaining the same, the more leisure we have, the better off we are. Our working time is valued as part of GDP, but our leisure time is not. Yet that leisure time must be at least as valuable to us as the wage that we earn for the last hour worked. If it were not, we would work instead of taking leisure. Over the years, leisure time has steadily increased. The workweek has become shorter, more people take early retirement, and the number of vacation days has increased. These improvements in economic well-being are not reflected in real GDP.

Environmental Quality   Economic activity directly influences the quality of the environment. The burning of hydrocarbon fuels is the most visible activity that damages our environment, but it is not the only example. The depletion of nonrenewable natural resources, the mass clearing of forests, and the pollution of lakes and rivers are other major environmental consequences of industrial production.

Resources that are used to protect the environment are valued as part of GDP. For example, the value of catalytic converters that help to protect the atmosphere from automobile emissions is part of GDP. But if we did not use such pieces of equipment and instead polluted the atmosphere, we would not count the deteriorating air that we were breathing as a negative part of GDP.

An industrial society possibly produces more atmospheric pollution than an agricultural society does. But pollution does not always increase as we become wealthier. Wealthy people value a clean environment and are willing to pay for one. Compare the pollution in China today with pollution in Canada. China, a poor country, pollutes its rivers, lakes, and atmosphere in a way that is unimaginable in Canada.

Political Freedom and Social Justice   Most people in the Western world value political freedoms such as those provided by the Canadian Constitution. And they value social justice—equality of opportunity and of access to social security safety nets that protect people from the extremes of misfortune.

A country might have a very large real GDP per person but have limited political freedom and social justice. For example, a small elite might enjoy political liberty and extreme wealth while the vast majority are effectively enslaved and live in abject poverty. Such an economy would generally be regarded as having a lower standard of living than one that had the same amount of real GDP but in which political freedoms were enjoyed by everyone. Today, China has rapid real GDP growth but limited political freedoms, while Poland and Ukraine have moderate real GDP growth but democratic political systems. Economists have no easy way to determine which of these countries is better off.

The Bottom Line   Do we get the wrong message about the growth in economic well-being and the standard of living by looking at the growth of real GDP? The influences that are omitted from real GDP are probably important and could be large. Developing countries have a larger underground economy and a larger amount of household production than do developed countries. So as an economy develops and grows, part of the apparent growth of real GDP might reflect a switch from underground to regular production and from home to market production. This measurement error overstates the growth in economic well-being and the improvement in the standard of living.

A Broader Indicator of Economic Well-Being

The Human Development Index

The limitations of real GDP reviewed in this chapter affect the standard of living and general well-being of every country. So to make international comparisons of the general state of economic well-being, we must look at real GDP and other indicators.

The United Nations has constructed a broader measure called the Human Development Index (HDI), which combines real GDP, life expectancy and health, and education. Real GDP per person (measured on the PPP basis) is a major component of the HDI.

The dots in the figure show the relationship between real GDP per person and the HDI. Canada has the tenth highest real GDP per person but the fourth highest HDI. (The countries with higher HDIs and GDPs per person are named in the figure.)

The HDI of Canada is lower than that of 9 other countries because the people of those countries live longer and have better access to health care and education than do Canadians.

Five African nations have the lowest real GDP per person and Sierra Leone has the lowest HDI.

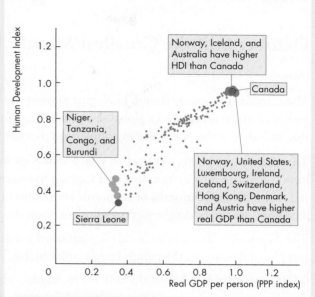

The Human Development Index

Source of data: United Nations hdr.undp.org/en/statistics/data/.

Other influences on the standard of living include the amount of leisure time available, the quality of the environment, the security of jobs and homes, and the safety of city streets.

It is possible to construct broader measures that combine the many influences that contribute to human happiness. Real GDP will be one element in those broader measures, but it will by no means be the whole of those measures.

The United Nations Human Development Index (HDI) is one example of attempts to provide broader measures of economic well-being and the standard of living. But this measure places a good deal of weight on real GDP.

Dozens of other measures have been proposed. One includes resource depletion and emissions in a "green" GDP measure. Another emphasizes the enjoyment of life rather than the production of goods in a "genuine progress index" or GPI.

Despite all the alternatives, real GDP per person remains the most widely used indicator of economic well-being.

Review Quiz

1 Distinguish between real GDP and potential GDP and describe how each grows over time.
2 How does the growth rate of real GDP contribute to an improved standard of living?
3 What is a business cycle and what are its phases and turning points?
4 What is PPP and how does it help us to make valid international comparisons of real GDP?
5 Explain why real GDP might be an unreliable indicator of the standard of living.

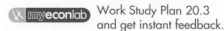 Work Study Plan 20.3 and get instant feedback.

You've now studied the methods used to measure GDP and real GDP. You've also learned about the uses of real GDP and some of its limitations. *Reading Between the Lines* on pp. 480–481 looks at Canadian real GDP in 2008.

Your next task is to learn how we measure employment and unemployment and the CPI.

Real GDP in the Slowing Economy of 2008

October Still the Cruellest Month: Recession Fears

November 1, 2008

The Canadian economy shrank in August as most sectors, including mines and petroleum, gave way to the pressure of a global slowdown. The contraction was by no means good, but that snapshot of the past paled in comparison to what followed.

The tumultuous events of October, which took root in the financial upheaval of September, have convinced most economists that Canada has entered recession. Even those not predicting the two consecutive months of economic contraction required to be classed as a "technical recession" are forecasting something close to borderline.

The diagnosis is that while Canada is positioned better than most to tackle the credit crisis and global downturn, the pain is largely unavoidable. ...

GDP contracted by an annualized 0.3% in August, with six of 10 sectors of the economy shrinking, Statistics Canada figures showed yesterday. The result followed a 0.7% rise in July and a flat reading in June. ...

David Wolf, an economist at Merrill Lynch, said the manufacturing and wholesale trades were the biggest drags on the Canadian economy in August. The energy sector, which was responsible for the jump in July, fell back to earth, while construction and transportation also contracted. ...

"We expect that the decline in August will cascade into the fourth quarter and likely into the first half of next year," said Douglas Porter, deputy chief economist at BMO Capital Markets. ...

Material reprinted with the express permission of "The National Post Company", a Canwest Partnership.

Essence of the Story

- The Canadian economy shrank in August 2008.
- Most economists say that Canada entered recession.
- Canada is positioned better than most nations to tackle global downturn but cannot avoid some pain.
- GDP contracted by an annualized rate of 0.3 percent in August 2008.
- Merrill Lynch economist David Wolf said the manufacturing and wholesale trades had the largest declines.
- BMO Capital Markets economist Douglas Porter expected the August decline to persist into the first half of 2009.

Economic Analysis

- This news article reports real GDP numbers for August 2008.

- The data for this month show a shrinking economy and had most economists predicting that Canada (with the entire world) was heading for recession.

- Figure 1 shows the real GDP growth rate (annualized) quarter to quarter from the first quarter of 2000 to the second quarter of 2008.

- The quarter-to-quarter growth rate fluctuated between a high of 5.5 percent in 2000 and a low of –0.6 percent in 2001.

- You can see slow growth in 2001 and then more rapid growth in 2004 through early 2007.

- The slow growth rate in 2007 turned slightly negative in 2008.

- Figure 2 shows the growth rates of the components of real GDP. The green bars are average growth rates from 2000 through 2007 and the orange bars are the growth rates for the first half of 2008.

- You can see that in the first half of 2008, consumption expenditure (C) grew a bit slower than average. You can also see that net exports grew rapidly—exports (X) increased by more than average and imports (M) decreased.

- Figure 2 shows that government expenditure decreased and so it contributed to the slowdown of real GDP growth.

- But Fig. 2 shows the major sign of future recession in the large decrease in investment (I).

- When investment collapses as it did in 2008, recession is usually not far away.

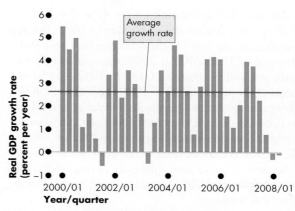

Figure 1 Real GDP growth rate: 2000–2008

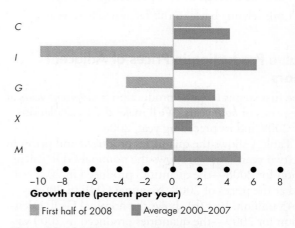

Figure 2 Real GDP components growth rate

MATHEMATICAL NOTE

Chained-Dollar Real GDP

In the real GDP calculation on pp. 473–474, real GDP in 2009 is three times its value in 2002. But suppose that we use 2009 as the reference base year and value real GDP in 2002 at 2009 prices. If you do the math, you will see that real GDP in 2002 is $150 million at 2009 prices. GDP in 2009 is $300 million (in 2009 prices), so now the numbers say that real GDP has doubled. Which is correct? Did real GDP double or triple? Should we use the prices of 2002 or 2009? The answer is that we need to use *both* sets of prices.

Statistics Canada uses a measure of real GDP called **chained-dollar real GDP**. Three steps are needed to calculate this measure:

- Value production in the prices of adjacent years.
- Find the average of two percentage changes.
- Link (chain) back to the reference base year.

Value Production in Prices of Adjacent Years

The first step is to value production in *adjacent* years at the prices of *both* years. We'll make these calculations for 2009 and its preceding year, 2008.

Table 1 shows the quantities produced and prices in the two years. Part (a) shows the nominal GDP calculation for 2008—the quantities produced in 2008 valued at the prices of 2008. Nominal GDP in 2008 is $145 million. Part (b) shows the nominal GDP calculation for 2009—the quantities produced in 2009 valued at the prices of 2009. Nominal GDP in 2009 is $172 million. Part (c) shows the value of the quantities produced in 2009 at the prices of 2008. This total is $160 million. Finally, part (d) shows the value of the quantities produced in 2008 at the prices of 2009. This total is $158 million.

Find the Average of Two Percentage Changes

The second step is to find the percentage change in the value of production based on the prices in the two adjacent years. Table 2 summarizes these calculations.

Part (a) shows that, valued at the prices of 2008, production increased from $145 million in 2008 to $160 million in 2009, an increase of 10.3 percent.

TABLE 1   GDP Calculation Step 1: Value Production in Adjacent Years at Prices of Both Years

Item		Quantity (millions)	Price (dollars)	Expenditure (millions of dollars)
(a)	**In 2008**			
C	T-shirts	3	5	15
I	Computer chips	3	10	30
G	Security services	5	20	100
Y	Real and nominal GDP in 2008			**145**
(b)	**In 2009**			
C	T-shirts	4	4	16
I	Computer chips	2	12	24
G	Security services	6	22	132
Y	Nominal GDP in 2009			**172**
(c)	**Quantities of 2009 valued at prices of 2008**			
C	T-shirts	4	5	20
I	Computer chips	2	10	20
G	Security services	6	20	120
Y	2009 production at 2008 prices			**160**
(d)	**Quantities of 2008 valued at prices of 2009**			
C	T-shirts	3	4	12
I	Computer chips	3	12	36
G	Security services	5	22	110
Y	2008 production at 2009 prices			**158**

Step 1 is to value the production of adjacent years at the prices of both years. Here, we value the production of 2008 and 2009 at the prices of both 2008 and 2009. The value of 2008 production at 2008 prices, in part (a), is nominal GDP in 2008. The value of 2009 production at 2009 prices, in part (b), is nominal GDP in 2009. Part (c) calculates the value of 2009 production at 2008 prices, and part (d) calculates the value of 2008 production at 2009 prices. We use these numbers in step 2.

Part (b) shows that, valued at the prices of 2009, production increased from $158 million in 2008 to $172 million in 2009, an increase of 8.9 percent. Part (c) shows that the average of these two percentage changes in the value of production is 9.6. That is, $(10.3 + 8.9) \div 2 = 9.6$.

By applying this average percentage change to real GDP, we can find the value of real GDP in 2009. Real GDP in 2008 is $145 million, so a 9.6 percent increase is $14 million, so real GDP in 2009 is

TABLE 2 Real GDP Calculation Step 2: Find Average of Two Percentage Changes

Value of Production	Millions of dollars
(a) At 2008 prices	
Nominal GDP in 2008	145
2009 production at 2008 prices	160
Percentage change in production at 2008 prices	10.3
(b) At 2009 prices	
2008 production at 2009 prices	158
Nominal GDP in 2009	172
Percentage change in production at 2009 prices	8.9
(c) Average of percentage change	**9.6**

Using the numbers calculated in step 1, the percentage change in production from 2008 to 2009 valued at 2008 prices is 10.3 percent, in part (a). The percentage change in production from 2008 to 2009 valued at 2009 prices is 8.9 percent, in part (b). The average of these two percentage changes is 9.6 percent, in part (c).

◆

$145 million plus $14 million, which equals $159 million. Because real GDP in 2008 is in 2008 dollars, real GDP in 2009 is also in 2008 dollars.

Although the real GDP of $159 million is expressed in 2008 dollars, the calculation uses the average of the prices of the final goods and services that make up GDP in 2008 and 2009.

Link (Chain) Back to the Base Year

Today, Statistics Canada uses 2002 as the reference base year. The third step in calculating real GDP is to express it in the prices of the reference base year. To do this, Statistics Canada performs calculations like the ones that you've just worked through to find the percentage change in real GDP in each pair of years going back to 2002.

We start with nominal GDP in 2002, which equals real GDP in 2002. We then use the calculated percentage change for 2003 to find real GDP in 2003 expressed in the prices of 2002. We repeat this calculation for each year. In this way, real GDP in 2009 is linked (chained) to the base-year real GDP.

Figure 1 shows an example. Starting with real GDP in 2002 (assumed to be $100 million), we apply the

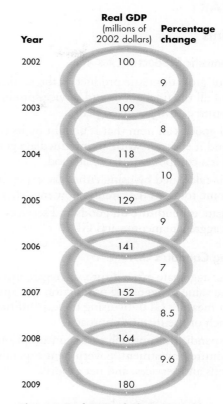

Year	Real GDP (millions of 2002 dollars)	Percentage change
2002	100	
		9
2003	109	
		8
2004	118	
		10
2005	129	
		9
2006	141	
		7
2007	152	
		8.5
2008	164	
		9.6
2009	180	

Figure 1 Real GDP calculation step 3: link (chain) back to base year

calculated percentage changes to obtain *chained-dollar real GDP* in 2002 dollars. By 2008, real GDP was $164 million (in 2002 dollars). In 2009, real GDP grew by 9.6 percent of $164 million, which is $16 million, so real GDP in 2009 was $180 million (in 2002 dollars).

Exercise

The table provides data on the economy of Tropical Republic that produces only bananas and coconuts.

Quantities	2008	2009
Bananas	1,000 bunches	1,100 bunches
Coconuts	500 bunches	525 bunches
Prices		
Bananas	$2 a bunch	$3 a bunch
Coconuts	$10 a bunch	$8 a bunch

Calculate Tropical Republic's nominal GDP in 2008 and 2009 and its chained-dollar real GDP in 2009 expressed in 2008 dollars.

SUMMARY

Key Points

Gross Domestic Product (pp. 468–470)

- GDP, or gross domestic product, is the market value of all the final goods and services produced in a country during a given period.
- A final good is an item that is bought by its final user, and it contrasts with an intermediate good, which is a component of a final good.
- GDP is calculated by using either the expenditure or income totals in the circular flow model.
- Aggregate expenditure on goods and services equals aggregate income and GDP.

Measuring Canada's GDP (pp. 471–473)

- Because aggregate expenditure, aggregate income, and the value of aggregate production are equal, we can measure GDP by using the expenditure approach or the income approach.
- The expenditure approach sums consumption expenditure, investment, government expenditure on goods and services, and net exports.

- The income approach sums wages, interest, rent, and profit (and indirect taxes less subsidies and depreciation).
- Real GDP is measured using a common set of prices to remove the effects of inflation from GDP.

The Uses and Limitations of Real GDP (pp. 474–479)

- Real GDP is used to compare the standard of living over time and across countries.
- Real GDP per person grows and fluctuates around the more smoothly growing potential GDP.
- Incomes would be much higher today if the growth rate of real GDP per person had not slowed during the 1970s.
- International real GDP comparisons use PPP prices.
- Real GDP is not a perfect measure of the standard of living because it excludes household production, the underground economy, health and life expectancy, leisure time, environmental quality, and political freedom and social justice.

Key Figures and Tables

Figure 20.1   The Circular Flow of Expenditure and Income, 469
Figure 20.2   Rising Standard of Living in Canada, 474
Figure 20.4   The Most Recent Canadian Business Cycle, 475
Table 20.1   GDP: The Expenditure Approach, 471
Table 20.2   GDP: The Income Approach, 472

Key Terms

Business cycle, 475
Chained-dollar real GDP, 482
Consumption expenditure, 469
Depreciation, 470
Expansion, 475
Exports, 470
Final good, 468
Government expenditure, 470
Gross domestic product (GDP), 468
Gross investment, 470
Imports, 470
Intermediate good, 468
Investment, 470
Lucas wedge, 474
Net exports, 470
Net investment, 470
Nominal GDP, 473
Potential GDP, 474
Purchasing power parity (PPP), 477
Real GDP, 473
Real GDP per person, 474
Recession, 475
Statistical discrepancy, 472

PROBLEMS and APPLICATIONS

 Work problems 1–11 in Chapter 20 Study Plan and get instant feedback.
Work problems 12–18 as Homework, a Quiz, or a Test if assigned by your instructor.

1. The figure below shows the flows of expenditure and income in Canada. During 2007, *B* was $852 billion, *C* was $342 billion, *D* was $311 billion, and *E* was $30 billion. Name the flows and then calculate

    a. Aggregate expenditure.
    b. Aggregate income.
    c. GDP.

2. The figure below shows the flows of expenditure and income in Canada during 2006. *B* was $803 billion, *C* was $320 billion, *D* was $291 billion, and *E* was $36 billion.

    Calculate the quantities in problem 1 during 2006.

3. The figure below shows the flows of expenditure and income in Canada during 2005. *A* was $1,373 billion, *B* was $759 billion, *D* was $264 billion, and *E* was $51 billion. Calculate

    a. Aggregate expenditure.
    b. Aggregate income.
    c. GDP.
    d. Government expenditure.

4. The firm that printed this textbook bought the paper from XYZ Paper Mills. Was this purchase of paper part of GDP? If not, how does the value of the paper get counted in GDP?

5. The table sets out some data for the United Kingdom in 2005.

Item	Billions of pounds
Wages paid to labour	685
Consumption expenditure	791
Taxes	394
Transfer payments	267
Profits	273
Investment	209
Government expenditure	267
Exports	322
Saving	38
Imports	366

    a. Calculate GDP in the United Kingdom.
    b. Explain the approach (expenditure or income) that you used to calculate GDP.

6. Tropical Republic produces only bananas and coconuts. The base year is 2008, and the tables give the quantities produced and the prices.

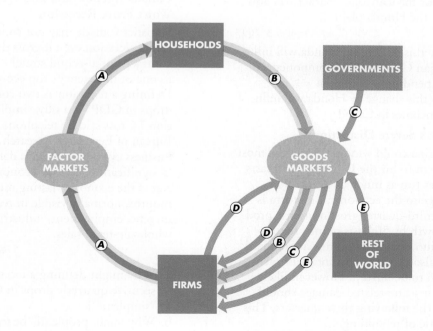

Quantities	2008	2009
Bananas	800 bunches	900 bunches
Coconuts	400 bunches	500 bunches

Prices		
Bananas	$2 a bunch	$4 a bunch
Coconuts	$10 a bunch	$5 a bunch

a. Calculate Tropical Republic's nominal GDP in 2008 and 2009.
b. Calculate real GDP in 2009 in terms of the base-year prices.

7. Use the Data Grapher in MyEconLab to answer the following questions. In 2007 in which country was
   a. The growth rate of real GDP highest: Canada, Japan, or the United States?
   b. The growth rate of real GDP lowest: France, China, or the United States?

8. **Honda Canada Begins Production of New 2006 Civic at its Canadian Plant**
   Honda Canada today celebrated the start of production of the new Honda Civic coupe at its Honda of Canada Manufacturing facility in Alliston, Ontario. The Civic [is] Canada's best-selling passenger car the past seven years. ... All global production for the new 2-door Civic coupes will come from the Honda of Canada Manufacturing facility in Alliston and all Civic sedan models for the Canadian market will also be produced at the Honda plant ...
   CNW Group, October 3, 2005
   a. Explain how this change by Honda will influence Canadian GDP and the components of aggregate expenditure.
   b. Explain how this change by Honda will influence factor incomes in Canada.

9. **Toting Katrina's Severe Distortions**
   Hurricane Katrina could wind up being the most devastating storm to hit the U.S. Early forecasts of insured losses run as much as $26 billion. ... As far as damage to the economy, the storm is likely to drop third-quarter gross domestic product (GDP) growth by 50 basis points, figures Beth Ann Bovino, senior economist at Standard & Poor's. She also expects consumer sentiment and production to be hurt. ... However, likely repairs from hurricane-related damage should boost GDP in the following three quarters. This is largely because of rebuilding. ...
   BusinessWeek, August 31, 2005

a. Explain how a devastating storm can initially decrease GDP.
b. How can a devastating storm then contribute to an increase in GDP?
c. Does the increase in GDP indicate a rise in the standard of living as a result of the storm?

10. **Poor India Makes Millionaires at Fastest Pace**
    India, with the world's largest population of poor people living on less than a dollar a day, also paradoxically created millionaires at the fastest pace in the world in 2007. ... Growing them at a blistering pace of 22.7 per cent, India added another 23,000 more millionaires in 2007 to its 2006 tally of 100,000 millionaires measured in dollars. ... In contrast, developmental agencies put the number of subsistence level Indians living on less than a dollar a day at 350 million and those living on less than $2 a day at 700 million. In other words, for every millionaire, India has about 7,000 impoverished people. ...
    Times of India, June 25, 2008
    a. Why might a measurement of real GDP per person misrepresent the standard of living of the average Indian?
    b. Why might $1 a day and $2 a day underestimate the standard of living of the poorest Indians?

11. **Canada Agency Says 2nd Quarter GDP Dip Won't Prove Recession**
    Statistics Canada may not conclude the economy is in a recession even if gross domestic product contracts for a second straight quarter, according to one of the agency's top economists. ... Defining a recession as two consecutive quarterly drops in GDP "is a silly, simplistic, simplification," Cross said by telephone. ... The National Bureau of Economic Research, which chronicles business cycles in the U.S., defines a recession as "a significant decline in economic activity spread across the economy, lasting more than a few months, normally visible in real GDP, real income, employment, industrial production, and wholesale-retail sales."
    Bloomberg, June 18, 2008
    a. Why might defining a recession as "two consecutive quarterly drops in GDP" be too "simplistic"?
    b. Why might people still be feeling the pain of recession after an expansion begins?

12. **GDP Expands 11.4 Percent, Fastest in 13 Years**

China's economy expanded at its fastest pace in 13 years in 2007. ... The country's Gross Domestic Product (GDP) grew 11.4 percent last year from 2006, to 24.66 trillion yuan ($3.42 trillion). ... That marked a fifth year of double-digit growth for the world's fourth largest economy after the U.S., Japan, and Germany. The increase was especially remarkable given the fact that the United States is experiencing a slowdown due to the sub-prime crisis and housing slump. ... According to Citigroup estimates, each one percent drop in the U.S. economy will shave 1.3 percent off China's growth, as Americans are heavy users of Chinese products. In spite of the uncertainties, the country's economy is widely expected to post its sixth year of double-digit growth in 2008 on investment and exports.

China Daily, January 24, 2008

a. Use the expenditure approach for calculating China's GDP to explain why "each one percent drop in the U.S. economy will shave 1.3 percent off China's growth."
b. Why might China's recent double-digit GDP growth rates overstate the actual increase in the level of production taking place in China?
c. Explain the complications involved with attempting to compare the economic welfare in China and the United States by using the GDP for each country.

13. **Study: Household Spending and Debt**

Canadian households have been spending more and saving less during the past two decades ... As a result almost one-half, or 47 percent of all households were spending more than their pre-tax income in 2001, up from 39 percent in 1982. ... Household deficit spending may be financed by drawing down savings or selling financial assets, but data indicate that borrowing is most closely tied to the increase in spending. Between 1982 and 2001, per capita debt doubled, stemming from dramatic increases in both mortgage and consumer debt. ...

The study suggests that a number of factors contributed to the increase in debt-financed spending. Interest rates fell dramatically over this period ... creating an "easy credit" environment.

At the same time, income taxes and Canada/Quebec Pension Plan and Employment Insurance premiums took a larger bite out of pre-tax income, squeezing the amount of income available for personal consumption and savings.

Other studies show that increasing financial wealth, particularly home equity, stimulates household spending. So the recent run-up in real estate values in many areas of the country may have helped to loosen the purse strings of homeowners.

Statistics Canada, March 22, 2005

a. How has consumer spending in relation to pre-tax income changed in Canada over the past two decades?
b. Explain the key influences on this change in consumer spending.
c. With home prices falling, as they were in 2008, how would you expect consumer spending and GDP to change in 2009?

14. **Consumer Spending a Big Factor: NBS**

When the [Chinese] National Bureau of Statistics (NBS) in October released its consumption figures for the first three quarters, people were surprised to discover that consumers are playing an ever-important role in the growth of the economy. ... Consumption contributed 37 percent of gross domestic product while foreign demand, or net exports, accounted for 21.4 percent. ... The remaining 41.6 percent was made by investment. ...

While exports are growing, imports are increasing at a faster pace, narrowing the gap and leading to shrinking net exports. ... But challenges lie ahead. Consumption will continue to grow, but only slowly, analysts said, because the public are still bothered by spending pressures like Social Security, health, education and housing. With those uncertainties, they prefer to save rather than spend.

China remains a developing country with a relatively low level of income, which cannot provide a strong back-up for consumption. ... The government has yet to provide adequate public services, such as education and health, and people prefer to save more in anticipation of rising future expenditure. ... In 2006, rural residents earned about one-third of the income earned by urban residents.

China Daily, December 11, 2007

a. Compare the relative magnitudes of consumption expenditure, net exports, and investment in China with those in Canada.

b. Why is consumption expenditure in China so low?

15. **Totally Gross**

Over the years, GNP and GDP have proved spectacularly useful in tracking economic change—both short-term fluctuations and long-run growth. Which isn't to say GDP doesn't miss some things. [Amartya] Sen, a development economist at Harvard, has long argued that health is a big part of living standards—and in 1990 he helped create the United Nations' Human Development Index, which combines health and education data with per capita GDP to give a more complete view of the wealth of nations (the United States currently comes in 12th, while on per capita GDP alone, it ranks second). [Joseph] Stiglitz, a Columbia professor and former World Bank chief economist, advocates a "green net national product" that takes into account the depletion of natural resources. Also sure to come up ... is the currently fashionable idea of trying to include happiness in the equation. The issue with these alternative benchmarks is not whether they have merit (most do) but whether they can be measured with anything like the frequency, reliability and impartiality of GDP.

Time, April 21, 2008

a. Explain the factors identified here that limit the usefulness of using GDP to measure economic welfare.

b. What are the challenges involved in trying to incorporate measurements of those factors in an effort to better measure economic welfare?

c. What does the ranking of Canada in the Human Development Index (10th) imply about the levels of health and education relative to other nations?

16. **Boeing Bets the House**

Boeing plans to produce some components of its new 787 Dreamliner in Japan. The aircraft will be assembled in the United States, and much of the first year's production will be sold to ANA (All Nippon Airways), a Japanese airline.

New York Times, May 7, 2006

a. Explain how Boeing's activities and its transactions affect U.S. and Japanese GDP.

b. Explain how ANA's activities and its transactions affect U.S. and Japanese GDP.

c. Use a circular flow diagram to illustrate your answers to a and b.

17. The United Nations Human Development Index (HDI) is based on real GDP per person, life expectancy at birth, and indicators of the quality and quantity of education.

a. Explain why the HDI might be better than real GDP as a measure of economic welfare.

b. Which items in the HDI are part of real GDP and which items are not in real GDP?

c. Do you think the HDI should be expanded to include items such as pollution, resource depletion, and political freedom? Explain.

d. What other influences on economic welfare should be included in a comprehensive measure?

18. Study *Reading Between the Lines* on pp. 480–481 and then answer the following questions:

a. Which components of aggregate expenditure increased at the fastest rate in the first half of 2008?

b. Which components of aggregate expenditure increased at the slowest rate (or decreased at the fastest rate) in the first half of 2008?

c. For how long has the Canadian economy been expanding since the last business cycle trough?

d. What is the main sign that the economy was heading for recession in 2009?

19. Use the link on MyEconLab (Chapter Resources, Chapter 20, Web links) to find the available data from Statistics Canada on GDP and the components of aggregate expenditure and aggregate income. The data are in current prices (nominal GDP) and constant prices (real GDP).

a. What are the levels of nominal GDP and real (chained-dollar) GDP in the current quarter?

b. What was the level of real GDP in the same quarter of the previous year?

c. By what percentage has real GDP changed over the past year?

21

Monitoring Jobs and Inflation

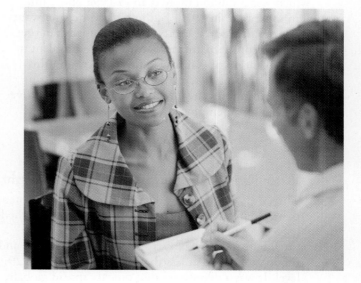

After studying this chapter, you will be able to

- Explain why unemployment is a problem, define the unemployment rate, the employment-to-population ratio, and the labour force participation rate, and describe the trends and cycles in these labour market indicators

- Explain why unemployment is an imperfect measure of underutilized labour, why it is present even at full employment, and how unemployment and real GDP fluctuate together over a business cycle

- Explain why inflation is a problem, how we measure the price level and the inflation rate, and why the CPI measure of inflation might be biased

Each month, we chart the course of employment and unemployment as measures of Canadian economic health. How do we count the number of people working and the number unemployed? What do the level of employment and the unemployment rate tell us? Are they reliable vital signs for the economy?

We always have some unemployment—we never get to a point at which no one is unemployed. So what is full employment? How many people are unemployed when there is full employment?

Having a good job that pays a decent wage is only half of the equation that translates into a good standard of living. The other half is the cost of living. We track the cost of the items that we buy with another number that is published every month: the Consumer Price Index, or CPI. What is the CPI? How is it calculated? And does it provide a reliable guide to the changes in our cost of living?

As the Canadian and global economies slowed in the wake of the financial crisis of 2007–2008, Canadian unemployment edged upward. *Reading Between the Lines* at the end of this chapter puts the spotlight on the labour market during the expansion of the years leading up to the 2008 slowdown.

We begin by looking at unemployment: What is it, why does it matter, and how do we measure it?

489

◆ Employment and Unemployment

What kind of job market will you enter when you graduate? Will there be plenty of good jobs to choose among, or will jobs be so hard to find that you end up taking one that doesn't use your education and pays a low wage? The answer depends, to a large degree, on the total number of jobs available and on the number of people competing for them.

The Canadian economy is an incredible job-creating machine. In 2008, 17 million people had jobs, which was 3 million more than in 1998 and 7 million more than in 1978. But not everyone who wants a job can find one. On a typical day, more than one million people are unemployed. That's equivalent to the population of Calgary. During a recession this number rises and during a boom year it falls. At its worst, during the Great Depression, one in every five workers was unemployed.

Why Unemployment Is a Problem

Unemployment is a serious personal and social economic problem for two main reasons. It results in

- Lost production and incomes
- Lost human capital

Lost Production and Incomes The loss of a job brings a loss of income for the unemployed worker and a loss of production. The loss of income is devastating for the people who bear it and makes unemployment a frightening prospect for everyone. Today, employment benefits create a safety net, but they don't fully replace lost earnings and not every person who becomes unemployed receives benefits.

Lost Human Capital Prolonged unemployment permanently damages a person's job prospects by destroying human capital. Think about a manager who loses his job when his employer downsizes. The only work

The Great Depression

What Keeps Ben Bernanke Awake at Night

The Great Depression began in October 1929, when the U.S. and global stock markets crashed. It reached its deepest point in 1933, when 25 percent of the Canadian and U.S. labour force was unemployed and production stood at less than 70 percent of its 1929 level. It was a depression that quickly spread globally to envelop most nations and lasted until 1941, when the United States entered World War II.

The 1930s were and remain the longest and worst period of high unemployment in history. Failed banks, shops, farms, and factories left millions of families all around the world without jobs, homes, and food. Without the support of governments and charities, millions would have starved.

The Great Depression was an enormous political event: It fostered the rise of the German and Japanese militarism that were to bring the most devastating war humans have ever fought. It also led to President Franklin D. Roosevelt's "New Deal," which enhanced the role of government in economic life and made government intervention in markets popular and the market economy unpopular.

The Great Depression also brought a revolution in economic ideas. In 1936, the English economist John Maynard Keynes published his *General Theory of Employment, Interest, and Money*, a book that created what we now call macroeconomics.

Many economists have studied the Great Depression and tried to determine why what started out as an ordinary recession became so devastating. Among them are Ben Bernanke, Chairman of the United States Federal Reserve (or U.S. Fed).

One of the reasons why the U.S. Fed has been so aggressive in cutting interest rates, saving Bear Stearns, and propping up Fannie Mae and Freddie Mac is because Ben Bernanke knows how financial collapse leads to broader economic collapse and is determined to avoid a repeat of the Great Depression.

he can find is driving a taxi. After a year in this work, he discovers that he can't compete with new MBA graduates. Eventually, he gets hired as a manager but in a small firm and at a lower wage than before. He has lost some of his human capital.

Governments make strenuous efforts to measure unemployment accurately and to adopt policies to moderate its level and ease its pain. Let's see how the Canadian government monitors unemployment.

Labour Force Survey

Every month, Statistics Canada conducts a *Labour Force Survey* in which it asks 54,000 households a series of questions about the age and job market status of the members of each household. Figure 21.1 shows the population categories used by Statistics Canada and the relationships among the categories.

The population divides into two broad groups: the working-age population and others who are too young to work or who live in institutions and are unable to work. The **working-age population** is the total number of people age 15 years and over. The working-age population is also divided into two groups: those in the labour force and those not in the labour force. Members of the labour force are either employed or unemployed. So the **labour force** is the sum of the employed and the unemployed. The employed are either full-time or part-time workers; and part-time workers are either want part-time work (voluntary part time) or full-time work (involuntary part time).

To be counted as employed in the Labour Force Survey, a person must have either a full-time job or a part-time job. To be counted as *un*employed, a person must be available for work and must be in one of three categories:

1. Without work but has made specific efforts to find a job within the previous four weeks
2. Laid off from a job and be waiting to be called back to work
3. Waiting to start a new job within four weeks

Anyone surveyed who satisfies one of these three criteria is counted as unemployed. People in the working-age population who are neither employed nor unemployed are classified as not in the labour force.

In 2007, the population of Canada was 32.9 million; the working-age population was 26.6 million. Of this number, 8.7 million were not in the labour

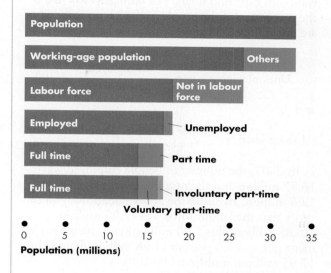

FIGURE 21.1 Population Labour Force Categories

The population is divided into the working-age population and others. The working-age population is divided into those in the labour force and those not in the labour force. The labour force is divided into the employed and the unemployed. The employed are divided into the full-time and part-time employed, and the part-time employed are divided into voluntary and involuntary part-time.

Source of data: Statistics Canada, CANSIM Tables 282-0002 and 051-0001.

force. Most of these people were in school full time or had retired from work. The remaining 17.9 million people made up the Canadian labour force. Of these, 16.9 million were employed and 1.0 million were unemployed. Of the 16.9 million employed, 3.1 million had part-time jobs, and of these, 0.7 million wanted a full-time job but couldn't find one.

Four Labour Market Indicators

Statistics Canada calculates four indicators of the state of the labour market. They are

- The unemployment rate
- The involuntary part-time rate
- The labour force participation rate
- The employment-to-population ratio

The Unemployment Rate The amount of unemployment is an indicator of the extent to which people who want jobs can't find them. The **unemployment rate** is the percentage of the people in the labour force who are unemployed. That is,

$$\text{Unemployment rate} = \frac{\text{Number of people unemployed}}{\text{Labour force}} \times 100.$$

and

$$\text{Labour force} = \frac{\text{Number of people employed}}{} + \frac{\text{Number of people unemployed}}{}$$

In 2007, the number of people employed was 16.87 million and the number unemployed was 1.08 million. By using the above equations, you can verify that the labour force was 17.95 million (16.87 million plus 1.08 million) and the unemployment rate was 6.0 percent (1.08 million divided by 17.95 million, multiplied by 100).

Figure 21.2 shows the unemployment rate from 1960 to 2007. The average unemployment rate during this period was 7.6 percent. The unemployment rate fluctuates over the business cycle: It increases as a recession deepens, reaches a peak after the recession ends, and decreases after a recovery gets going.

The Involuntary Part-Time Rate Part-time workers who want full-time work are underemployed and Statistics Canada counts their number. The *involuntary part-time rate* is the percentage of the people in the labour force who work part time but want full-time jobs.

$$\text{Involuntary part-time rate} = \frac{\text{Number of involuntary part-time workers}}{\text{Labour force}} \times 100.$$

In 2007, with 679,000 involuntary part-time workers and a labour force of 17.95 million, the involuntary part-time rate was 3.8 percent.

The Labour Force Participation Rate The number of people in the labour force is an indicator of the willingness of people of working age to take jobs. The **labour force participation rate** is the percentage of the working-age population who are members of the labour force. That is,

$$\text{Labour force participation rate} = \frac{\text{Labour force}}{\text{Working-age population}} \times 100.$$

In 2007, the labour force was 17.95 million and the working-age population was 26.55 million. By using the above equation, you can see that the labour

FIGURE 21.2 The Unemployment Rate: 1960–2007

The average unemployment rate from 1960 to 2007 was 7.6 percent. The unemployment rate increases in a recession, peaks after the recession ends, and decreases in an expansion. The unemployment rate was unusually high following the recessions of 1982 and 1991.

Source of data: Statistics Canada, CANSIM Table 282-0002.

myeconlab animation

FIGURE 21.3 Labour Force Participation and Employment: 1960–2007

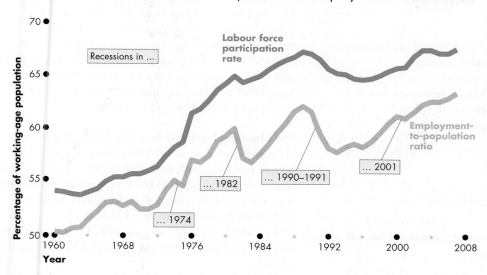

The labour force participation rate and the employment-to-population ratio have upward trends before 1990 and then flatten off after 1990. They fluctuate with the business cycle.

The employment-to-population ratio fluctuates more than the labour force participation rate and reflects cyclical fluctuations in the unemployment rate.

Source of data: Statistics Canada, CANSIM Table 282-0002.

myeconlab animation

force participation was 67.6 percent (17.95 million divided by 26.55 million, multiplied by 100).

The Employment-to-Population Ratio The number of people of working age who have jobs is an indicator of both the availability of jobs and the degree of match between people's skills and jobs. The **employment-to-population ratio** is the percentage of people of working age who have jobs. That is,

$$\text{Employment-to-population ratio} = \frac{\text{Number of people employed}}{\text{Working-age population}} \times 100.$$

In 2007, the number of people employed was 16.87 million and the working-age population was 26.55 million. By using the above equation, you can see that the employment-to-population ratio was 63.5 percent (16.87 million divided by 26.55 million, multiplied by 100).

Figure 21.3 shows the labour force participation rate and the employment-to-population ratio from 1960 to 2007. These indicators follows an upward trend before 1990 and then flatten off after 1990. The increase before 1990 means that the Canadian economy created jobs at a faster rate than the working-age population grew.

The employment-to-population ratio fluctuates with the business cycle: It falls in a recession and rises in an expansion. The labour force participation rate has milder business cycle swings that reflect movements into and out of the labour force.

Review Quiz

1   What determines whether a person is in the labour force?
2   What distinguishes an unemployed person from a person who is not in the labour force?
3   Describe the trends and fluctuations in the Canadian unemployment rate.
4   Describe the trends and fluctuations in the Canadian labour force participation rate and employment-to-population ratio.

myeconlab Work Study Plan 21.1 and get instant feedback.

You've seen how we measure employment and unemployment. Your next task is to see what the unemployment numbers tell us and what we mean by full employment.

Unemployment and Full Employment

What does the unemployment rate seek to measure and does it provide an accurate measure?

The purpose of the unemployment rate is to measure the underutilization of labour resources, but it is an imperfect measure for two sets of reasons.

- It excludes some underutilized labour.
- Some unemployment is unavoidable—is "natural."

Underutilized Labour Excluded

Two types of underutilized labour are excluded from the official unemployment measure. They are

- Marginally attached workers
- Part-time workers who want full-time jobs

Marginally Attached Workers A **marginally attached worker** is a person who currently is neither working nor looking for work but has indicated that he or she wants and is available for a job and has looked for work sometime in the recent past. A subset of marginally attached workers is a group called discouraged workers.

A **discouraged worker** is a marginally attached worker who has stopped looking for a job because of repeated failure to find one. The numbers of marginally attached and discouraged workers is small. In 2007, when the official unemployment rate was 6.0 percent, adding the discouraged workers raised the rate to 6.1 percent of the labour force.

Part-Time Workers Who Want Full-Time Jobs Many part-time workers want to work part time. This arrangement fits in with the other demands on their time. But some part-time workers would like full-time jobs and can't find them. In the official statistics, these workers are called *involuntary part-timers* and they are partly unemployed.

A large number of workers fall into this group, and the rate fluctuates with the overall unemployment rate. In 2007, when the official unemployment rate was 6.0 percent, the involuntary part-time unemployment rate was 1.7 percent, which means that the overall unemployment rate including marginally attached workers was 7.8 percent.

"Natural" Unemployment

Unemployment arises from job search activity. There is always someone without a job who is searching for one, so there is always some unemployment. The key reason why there is always someone who is searching for a job is that the economy is a complex mechanism that is always changing—it is a churning economy.

The Churning Economy Some of the change in the churning economy comes from the transitions that people make through the stages of life—from being in school to finding a job to working, perhaps to becoming unhappy with a job and looking for a new one, and finally to retiring from full-time work.

In Canada in 2007, almost 500,000 new workers entered the labour force and around 150,000 workers retired.

Other change comes from the transitions that businesses make. Every day, new firms are born, existing firms grow or shrink, and firms fail and go out of business. This process of business creation, expansion, contraction, and failure creates and destroys jobs.

Both of these transition processes—of people and businesses—create frictions and dislocations that make unemployment unavoidable.

The Sources of Unemployment In the churning economy that we've just described, people become unemployed if they

1. Lose their jobs and search for another job.
2. Leave their jobs and search for another job.
3. Enter or reenter the labour force to search for a job.

And people end a spell of unemployment if they

1. Are hired or recalled.
2. Withdraw from the labour force.

People who are laid off from their jobs, either permanently or temporarily, are called *job losers*. Some job losers become unemployed, but some immediately withdraw from the labour force. People who voluntarily quit their jobs are called *job leavers*. Like job losers, some job leavers become unemployed and search for a better job while others either withdraw from the labour force temporarily or permanently retire from work. People who enter or reenter the labour force are called *entrants* and *reentrants*.

Entrants are mainly people who have just left school. Some entrants get a job right away and are never unemployed, but many spend time searching for their first job, and during this period, they are unemployed. Reentrants are people who have previously withdrawn from the labour force. Most of these people are formerly discouraged workers.

Job losers are the biggest source of unemployment. On the average, they account for more than half of total unemployment. Also, their number fluctuates a great deal. At the troughs of the recessions of 1982 and 1991, on any given day, around 800,000 of the 1.4 million unemployed were job losers. In contrast, at the business cycle peaks of 1987 and 2001, around half a million of the 1 million unemployed were job losers.

Entrants and reentrants also make up a large component of the unemployed. Their number fluctuates but more mildly than the fluctuations in the number of job losers.

Job leavers are the smallest and most stable source of unemployment. On any given day, fewer than 1 million people are unemployed because they are job leavers. The number of job leavers is remarkably constant. To the extent that this number fluctuates, it does so in line with the business cycle: A slightly larger number of people leave their jobs in good times than in bad times.

Frictions, Structural Change, and Cycles The unemployment that arises from normal labour turnover—from people entering and leaving the labour force and from the ongoing creation and destruction of jobs—is **frictional unemployment**. Frictional unemployment is a permanent and healthy phenomenon in a dynamic, growing economy.

The flow of people into and out of the labour force and the processes of job creation and job destruction means that people must search for jobs and businesses must search for workers. There are always businesses with unfilled jobs and people seeking jobs. Businesses don't usually hire the first person who applies for a job, and unemployed people don't usually take the first job that comes their way. Both firms and workers spend time searching for what they believe will be the best available match. By this process of search, people match their skills and interests with the available jobs and find a satisfying job and a good income. While these unemployed people are searching, their unemployment is frictional.

The unemployment that arises when changes in technology or international competition change the skills needed to perform jobs or change the locations of jobs is called **structural unemployment**. Structural unemployment usually lasts longer than frictional unemployment because workers must usually retrain and possibly relocate to find a job. When a steel plant in Hamilton, Ontario, is automated, some jobs in that city disappear. Meanwhile, in the Ottawa valley and Vancouver, new jobs for security guards, retail clerks, and life-insurance salespeople are created. The unemployed former steelworkers remain unemployed for several months until they move, retrain, and get one of these jobs. Structural unemployment is painful, especially for older workers for whom the

Structural Unemployment in Canada
The Maritime Provinces
Unemployment rates across Canada's provinces range from almost 14 percent in Newfoundland and Labrador to less than 4 percent in Alberta. This range of unemployment rates arises from structural features of the Canadian economy. Alberta and the West in general are growing rapidly. The Maritimes and to a lesser extent Quebec are growing more slowly. People must leave the eastern provinces and move westward to find work. A reluctance to uproot keeps the unemployment rates widely dispersed.

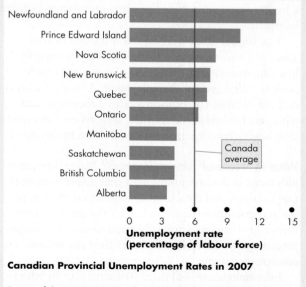

Canadian Provincial Unemployment Rates in 2007

Source of data: Statistics Canada CANSIM Table 282-0002.

best available option might be to retire early or take a lower-skilled, lower-paying job. At some times, the amount of structural unemployment is modest. At other times, it is large, and at such times, structural unemployment can become a serious long-term problem. It was especially large during the late 1970s and early 1980s. During those years, oil price hikes and an increasingly competitive international environment destroyed jobs in traditional Canadian industries, such as auto and steel, and created jobs in new industries, such as electronics and bioengineering, as well as in banking and insurance. Structural unemployment was also present during the early 1990s as many businesses and governments "downsized."

Two other structural sources of higher unemployment are a *minimum wage* and an *efficiency wage*. Chapter 6 (see pp. 133–135) explains how the minimum wage creates unemployment.

An **efficiency wage** is a wage set above the going market wage, and it creates unemployment just like the minimum wage does.

A firm might choose to pay an efficiency wage for four reasons. First, it enables the firm to face a steady stream of available new workers. Second, it attracts the most productive workers. Third, the fear of losing a well-paid job stimulates greater work effort. Fourth, workers are less likely to quit their jobs, so the firm faces a lower rate of labour turnover and lower recruiting and training costs.

The firm balances these benefits against the cost of a higher wage and offers the wage rate that maximizes its profit.

The higher-than-normal unemployment that arises at a business cycle trough and the unusually low unemployment that exists at a business cycle peak is called **cyclical unemployment**. A worker who is laid off because the economy is in a recession and who gets rehired some months later when the expansion begins has experienced cyclical unemployment.

What Is "Natural" Unemployment? Natural unemployment is the unemployment that arises from normal frictions and structural change when there is no cyclical unemployment—when all the unemployment is frictional and structural. Natural unemployment as a percentage of the labour force is called the **natural unemployment rate**.

Full employment is defined as a situation in which the unemployment rate equals the natural unemployment rate.

There can be a lot of unemployment at full employment, and the term "full employment" is an example of a technical economic term that does not correspond with everyday language. The term "natural unemployment rate" is another technical economic term whose meaning does not correspond with everyday language. For most people—especially for unemployed workers—there is nothing natural about unemployment. But if you think for a moment, you will come up with many other natural phenomena that are unpleasant. Floods, hurricanes, ice storms, and the feeding frenzy of sharks are just three examples.

So when economists call a situation with a lot of unemployment one of "full employment" and describe the unemployment rate at full employment as the "natural rate," they are talking about the unemployment that results from natural physical constraints on the ease with which the labour market can match workers with jobs.

There is not much controversy about the existence of a natural unemployment rate. Nor is there much disagreement that it changes. The natural unemployment rate arises from the existence of labour market frictions and structural change, and it fluctuates because the frictions and the amount of structural change fluctuate. But economists don't agree about the size of the natural unemployment rate and the extent to which it fluctuates. Some economists believe that the natural unemployment rate fluctuates frequently and that at times of rapid demographic and technological change, the natural unemployment rate can be high. Others think that the natural unemployment rate changes slowly.

Real GDP and Unemployment Over the Cycle

The quantity of real GDP at full employment is *potential GDP* (p. 474). Over the business cycle, real GDP fluctuates around potential GDP. The gap between real GDP and potential GDP is called the **output gap**. As the output gap fluctuates over the business cycle, the unemployment rate fluctuates around the natural unemployment rate.

Figure 21.4 illustrates these fluctuations in Canada between 1985 and 2007—the output gap in part (a) and the unemployment rate and natural unemployment rate in part (b).

FIGURE 21.4   The Output Gap and the Unemployment Rate

(a) Output gap

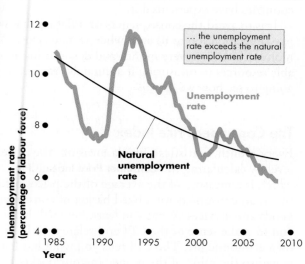

(b) Unemployment rate

As real GDP fluctuates around potential GDP in part (a), the unemployment rate fluctuates around the natural unemployment rate in part (b). At the end of the deep 1991 recession, the unemployment rate reached almost 12 percent. The natural unemployment rate decreased during the 1980s, 1990s, and 2000s. Fluctuations in unemployment and output do not exactly line up: The unemployment rate lags the output gap.

Sources of data: Bank of Canada output gap estimate and Statistics Canada, CANSIM Table 282-0002. Natural unemployment is the authors' assumption.

myeconlab animation

When the economy is at full employment, the unemployment rate equals the natural unemployment rate and real GDP equals potential GDP so the output gap is zero. When the unemployment rate is less than the natural unemployment rate, real GDP is greater than potential GDP and the output gap is positive. And when the unemployment rate is greater than the natural unemployment rate, real GDP is less than potential GDP and the output gap is negative.

Figure 21.4(b) shows one view of the natural unemployment rate. Keep in mind that economists do not know the magnitude of the natural unemployment rate and that shown in the figure is only one estimate. In Fig. 21.4(b), the natural unemployment rate was close to 11 percent in 1985 and it fell steadily through the 1980s, 1990s, and 2000s to about 6.5 percent by 2007. This estimate of the natural unemployment rate in Canada is one that many, but not all, economists would agree with.

The fluctuations in unemployment tend to lag behind the output gap fluctuations.

Review Quiz

1 What is the unemployment rate supposed to measure and why is it an imperfect measure?

2 Why might the official unemployment rate underestimate the underutilization of labour resources?

3 Why does unemployment arise and what makes some unemployment unavoidable?

4 Define frictional unemployment, structural unemployment, and cyclical unemployment. Give examples of each type of unemployment.

5 What is the natural unemployment rate?

6 How does the natural unemployment rate change and what factors might make it change?

7 How does the unemployment rate fluctuate over the business cycle?

myeconlab   Work Study Plan 21.2 and get instant feedback.

Your next task in this chapter is to see how we monitor the price level and the inflation rate. You will learn about the Consumer Price Index (CPI), a vital sign that gets monitored every month. You will also learn about other measures of the price level and inflation rate.

◆ The Price Level and Inflation

What will it *really* cost you to pay off your student loan? What will your parents' life savings buy when they retire? The answers depend on what happens to the **price level**, the average level of prices, and the value of money.

We are interested in the price level for two main reasons. First, we want to measure the **inflation rate**, which is the annual percentage change of the price level. Second, we want to distinguish between the money values and real values of economic variables such as your student loan and your parents' savings.

We will begin by explaining why we're interested in the inflation rate—why inflation is a problem. We'll then look at the ways in which we measure the price level and the inflation rate. Finally, we'll return to the task of separating real values from money values of economic variables.

Why Inflation Is a Problem

Inflation is a problem for several reasons, but the main one is that once it takes hold, its rate is unpredictable. Unpredictable inflation brings serious social and personal problems because it

- Redistributes income and wealth
- Diverts resources from production

Redistributes Income and Wealth   Inflation makes the economy behave like a casino in which some people gain some lose and no one can predict where the gains and losses will fall. Gains and losses occur because of unpredictable changes in the value of money. Money is used as a measuring rod of value in the transactions that we undertake. Borrowers and lenders, workers and employers all make contracts in terms of money. If the value of money varies unpredictably over time, then the amounts *really* paid and received—the quantities of goods that the money will buy—also fluctuate unpredictably. Measuring value with a measuring rod whose units vary is a bit like trying to measure a piece of cloth with an elastic tape measure. The size of the cloth depends on how tightly the elastic is stretched.

Diverts Resources from Production   In a period of rapid, unpredictable inflation, resources get diverted from productive activities to forecasting inflation. It

can even become more profitable to forecast the inflation rate correctly than to invent a new product. Doctors, lawyers, accountants, farmers—just about everyone—can make themselves better off, not by specializing in the profession for which they have been trained but by spending more of their time dabbling as amateur economists and inflation forecasters and managing their investments.

From a social perspective, this diversion of talent resulting from inflation is like throwing scarce resources onto the garbage heap. This waste of resources is a cost of inflation.

At its worst, inflation becomes **hyperinflation**, an inflation rate so rapid that workers are paid twice a day because money loses its value so quickly. As soon as workers are paid, they rush out to spend their wages before the money loses too much value. In this situation, the economy grinds to a halt and society collapses. Hyperinflation is rare, but Zimbabwe has it today and several European and Latin American countries have experienced it.

It is to avoid the consequences of inflation that we pay close attention to it, even when its rate is low. We monitor inflation every month and devote considerable resources to measuring it accurately. You're now going to see how we do this.

The Consumer Price Index

Every month, Statistics Canada measures the price level by calculating the **Consumer Price Index (CPI)**, which is a measure of the average of the prices paid by urban consumers for a fixed basket of consumer goods and services. What you learn here will help you to make sense of the CPI and relate it to your own economic life. The CPI tells you what has happened to the value of the money in your pocket.

Reading the CPI Numbers

The CPI is defined to equal 100 for a period called the **reference base period**. Currently, the reference base period is 2002. That is, for the average of the 12 months of 2002, the CPI equals 100.

In September 2008, the CPI was 115.7. This number tells us that the average of the prices paid by urban consumers for a fixed market basket of consumer goods and services was 15.7 percent higher in September 2008 than it was on the average during 2002.

Constructing the CPI

Constructing the CPI is a huge operation that involves three stages:

- Selecting the CPI basket
- Conducting the monthly price survey
- Calculating the CPI

The CPI Basket The first stage in constructing the CPI is to select what is called the *CPI basket*. This basket contains the goods and services represented in the index and the relative importance attached to each of them. The idea is to make the relative importance of the items in the CPI basket the same as that in the budget of an average urban household. For example, because people spend more on housing than on bus rides, the CPI places more weight on the price of housing than on the price of bus rides.

To determine the CPI basket, Statistics Canada conducts a survey of consumer expenditure. Today's basket is based on data gathered in a 2005 survey.

Figure 21.5 shows the CPI basket. It contains thousands of individual goods and services arranged in the eight large groups shown in the figure. The most important item in a household's budget is shelter, which accounts for 27 percent of total expenditure. Transportation comes next at 20 percent. Third in relative importance is food at 17 percent. These three groups account for almost two-thirds of the average household budget. Recreation, education, and reading take 12 percent. Another 11 percent is spent on household operations and furnishings, 5 percent on clothing and footwear, 5 percent on health and personal care, and 3 percent on alcoholic beverages and tobacco products.

Statistics Canada breaks down each of these categories into smaller ones. For example, the recreation, education, and reading category breaks down into textbooks and supplies, telephone services, and personal computer services.

As you look at the relative importance of the items in the CPI basket, remember that they apply to the *average* household. *Individual* households are spread around the average. Think about your own expenditure and compare the basket of goods and services you buy with the CPI basket.

The Monthly Price Survey Each month, Statistics Canada employees check the prices of the 80,000 goods and services in the CPI basket in 30 metropolitan areas. Because the CPI aims to measure price

FIGURE 21.5 The CPI Basket

The CPI basket consists of the items that an average urban household buys. It consists mainly of shelter (27 percent), transportation (20 percent), and food (17 percent). All other items add up to 36 percent of the total.

Source of data: Statistics Canada, CANSIM CPI Report, September 2008.

changes, it is important that the prices recorded each month refer to exactly the same item. For example, suppose the price of a box of jelly beans has increased but a box now contains more beans. Has the price of jelly beans increased? Statistics Canada employees must record the details of changes in quality or packaging so that price changes can be isolated from other changes.

Once the raw price data are in hand, the next task is to calculate the CPI.

Calculating the CPI To calculate the CPI, we

1. Find the cost of the CPI basket at base-period prices.
2. Find the cost of the CPI basket at current-period prices.
3. Calculate the CPI for the base period and the current period.

We'll work through these three steps for a simple example. Suppose the CPI basket contains only two goods and services: oranges and haircuts. We'll construct an annual CPI rather than a monthly CPI with the reference base period 2008 and the current period 2009.

Table 21.1 shows the quantities in the CPI basket and the prices in the base period and current period.

Part (a) contains the data for the base period. In that period, consumers bought 10 oranges at $1 each and 5 haircuts at $8 each. To find the cost of the CPI basket in the base-period prices, multiply the quantities in the CPI basket by the base-period prices. The cost of oranges is $10 (10 at $1 each), and the cost of haircuts is $40 (5 at $8 each). So total cost in the base period of the CPI basket is $50 ($10 + $40).

Part (b) contains the price data for the current period. The price of an orange increased from $1 to $2, which is a 100 percent increase—($1 ÷ $1) × 100 = 100. The price of a haircut increased from $8 to $10, which is a 25 percent increase—($2 ÷ $8) × 100 = 25.

The CPI provides a way of averaging these price increases by comparing the cost of the basket rather than the price of each item. To find the cost of the CPI basket in the current period, 2009, multiply the quantities in the basket by their 2009 prices. The cost of oranges is $20 (10 at $2 each), and the cost of haircuts is $50 (5 at $10 each). So total cost of the fixed CPI basket at current-period prices is $70 ($20 + $50).

TABLE 21.1   The CPI: A Simplified Calculation

(a) The cost of the CPI basket at base-period prices: 2008

CPI basket			Cost of
Item	Quantity	Price	CPI Basket
Oranges	10	$1.00	$10
Haircuts	5	$8.00	$40
Cost of CPI basket at base-period prices			$50

(b) The cost of the CPI basket at current-period prices: 2009

CPI basket			Cost of
Item	Quantity	Price	CPI Basket
Oranges	10	$2.00	$20
Haircuts	5	$10.00	$50
Cost of CPI basket at current-period prices			$70

You've now taken the first two steps towards calculating the CPI: calculating the cost of the CPI basket in the base period and the current period. The third step uses the numbers you've just calculated to find the CPI for 2008 and 2009.

The formula for the CPI is

$$\text{CPI} = \frac{\text{Cost of CPI basket at current-period prices}}{\text{Cost of CPI basket at base-period prices}} \times 100.$$

In Table 21.1, you established that in 2008 (the base period), the cost of the CPI basket was $50 and in 2009, it was $70. If we use these numbers in the CPI formula, we can find the CPI for 2008 and 2009. For 2008, the CPI is

$$\text{CPI in 2008} = \frac{\$50}{\$50} \times 100 = 100.$$

For 2009, the CPI is

$$\text{CPI in 2009} = \frac{\$70}{\$50} \times 100 = 140.$$

The principles that you've applied in this simplified CPI calculation apply to the more complex calculations performed every month by Statistics Canada.

Measuring the Inflation Rate

A major purpose of the CPI is to measure changes in the cost of living and in the value of money. To measure these changes, we calculate the *inflation rate* as the annual percentage change in the price level. To calculate the inflation rate, we use the formula:

$$\text{Inflation rate} = \frac{\text{CPI this year} - \text{CPI last year}}{\text{CPI last year}} \times 100.$$

We can use this formula to calculate the inflation rate in 2008. The CPI in September 2008 was 115.7, and the CPI in September 2007 was 111.9. So the inflation rate during the year to September 2008 was

$$\text{Inflation rate} = \frac{(115.7 - 111.9)}{111.9} \times 100 = 3.4\%.$$

Distinguishing High Inflation from a High Price Level

Figure 21.6 shows the CPI and the inflation rate in Canada during the 36 years between 1972 and 2008. The two parts of the figure are related and emphasize the distinction between high inflation and high prices.

Figure 21.6 shows that when the price level in part (a) *rises rapidly*, as it did during the 1970s and through 1982, the inflation rate in part (b) is *high*. When the price level in part (a) *rises slowly*, as it did after 1982, the inflation rate in part (b) is *low*.

A high inflation rate means that the price level is rising rapidly. A high price level means that there has been a sustained period of rising prices like that shown in Fig. 21.6(a).

The CPI is not a perfect measure of the price level and changes in the CPI probably overstate the inflation rate. Let's look at the sources of bias.

The Biased CPI

The main sources of bias in the CPI are

- New goods bias
- Quality change bias
- Commodity substitution bias
- Outlet substitution bias

New Goods Bias If you want to compare the price level in 2009 with that in 1969, you must somehow compare the price of a computer today with that of a typewriter in 1969. Because a PC is more expensive than a typewriter was, the arrival of the PC puts an upward bias into the CPI and its inflation rate.

Quality Change Bias Cars, CD players, and many other items get better every year. Part of the rise in the prices of these items is a payment for improved quality and is not inflation. But the CPI counts the entire price rise as inflation and so overstates inflation.

Commodity Substitution Bias Changes in relative prices lead consumers to change the items they buy. For example, if the price of beef rises and the price of chicken remains unchanged, people buy more chicken and less beef. This switch from beef to chicken might provide the same amount of protein and the same enjoyment as before and expenditure is the same as before. The price of protein has not changed. But because the CPI ignores the substitution of chicken for beef, it says the price of protein has increased.

FIGURE 21.6 The CPI and the Inflation Rate

(a) CPI

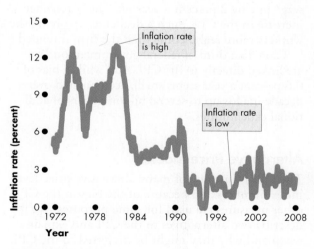

(b) Inflation rate

When the price level rises rapidly, the inflation rate is high, and when the price level rises slowly, the inflation rate is low.

During the 1970s and through 1982, the price level increased rapidly in part (a) and the inflation rate was high in part (b). The inflation rate averaged a bit more than 5 percent a year and sometimes exceeded 10 percent a year.

After 1982, the price level rose slowly in part (a) and the inflation rate was low in part (b). The inflation rate averaged 3 percent a year.

Source of data: Statistics Canada, CANSIM Table 326-0002.

myeconlab animation

Outlet Substitution Bias When confronted with higher prices, people use discount stores more frequently and convenience stores less frequently. This phenomenon is called *outlet substitution*. The CPI surveys do not monitor outlet substitutions.

The Magnitude of the Bias

You've reviewed the sources of bias in the CPI. But how big is the bias? This question is addressed periodically and the most recent estimate is provided in a study by Bank of Canada economist James Rossiter at about 0.6 percent per year.

Some Consequences of the Bias

The bias in the CPI distorts private contracts and increases government outlays. Many private agreements, such as wage contracts, are linked to the CPI. For example, a firm and its workers might agree to a three-year wage deal that increases the wage rate by 2 percent a year *plus* the percentage increase in the CPI. Such a deal ends up giving the workers more real income than the firm intended.

Close to a third of federal government outlays are linked directly to the CPI. And while a bias of 0.6 percent a year seems small, accumulated over a decade it adds up to several billion dollars of additional expenditures.

Alternative Price Indexes

The CPI is just one of many alternative price level index numbers and because of the bias in the CPI, other measures are used for some purposes. We'll describe two alternatives to the CPI and explain when and why they might be preferred to the CPI. The alternatives are

- GDP deflator
- Chained price index for consumption

GDP Deflator The **GDP deflator** is an index of the prices of all the items included in GDP and is the ratio of nominal GDP to real GDP. That is, to calculate the GDP deflator, we divide nominal GDP by real GDP and multiply by 100.

Because real GDP includes consumption expenditure, investment, government expenditure, and net exports, the GDP deflator is an index of the prices of all these items.

Real GDP is calculated using the *chained-dollar method* (see pp. 482–483), which means that the weights attached to each item in the GDP deflator are the components of GDP in both the current year and the preceding year.

Because it uses current period and previous period quantities rather than fixed quantities from an earlier period, a *chained-dollar* price index incorporates substitution effects and new goods and overcomes the sources of bias in the CPI.

Since 2000, the GDP deflator has increased at an average rate of 2.4 percent per year, which is 0.3 percentage points above the CPI inflation rate.

The GDP deflator is appropriate for macroeconomics because, like GDP, it is a comprehensive measure of the cost of the real GDP basket of goods and services. But as a measure of the cost of living, it is too broad—it includes items that people don't buy.

Chained Price Index for Consumption The **chained price index for consumption (CPIC)** is an index of the prices of all the items included in consumption expenditure in GDP and is the ratio of nominal consumption expenditure to real consumption expenditure. That is, to calculate the CPIC, we divide nominal consumption expenditure by real consumption expenditure and multiply by 100.

Like the GDP deflator, because the CPIC uses current period and previous period quantities rather than fixed quantities from an earlier period, it incorporates substitution effects and new goods and overcomes the sources of bias in the CPI.

Since 2000, the CPIC has increased at an average rate of 1.6 percent per year, which is 0.5 percentage points below the CPI inflation rate.

Core Inflation

No matter whether we calculate the inflation rate using the CPI, the GDP deflator, or the CPIC, the number bounces around a good deal from month to month or quarter to quarter. To determine whether the inflation rate is trending upward or downward, we need to strip the raw numbers of their volatility. The **core inflation rate**, which is the inflation rate excluding volatile elements, attempts to do just that and reveal the underlying inflation trend.

The most commonly used measure of core inflation is the *core CPI inflation rate* and as a practical matter, the core CPI inflation rate is calculated as the percentage change in the CPI *excluding food and fuel*.

The prices of these two items are among the most volatile.

While the core CPI inflation rate removes the volatile elements in inflation, it can give a misleading view of the true underlying inflation rate. If the relative prices of the excluded items are changing, the core inflation rate will give a biased measure of the true underlying inflation rate.

Such a misleading account was given during the years between 2000 and 2008 when the relative prices of food and fuel were rising. The result was a core CPI inflation rate that was systematically below the CPI rate by an average of 0.5 percentage points.

Figure 21.7 shows the two series since 1993. More refined measures of core inflation have been suggested that eliminate the bias but are not in common use.

The Real Variables in Macroeconomics

You saw in Chapter 3 the distinction between a *money price* and a *relative price* (see p. 58). Another name for a *money* price is a *nominal* price. In macroeconomics, we often want to distinguish between a real variable and its corresponding nominal variable. We want to distinguish a real price from its corresponding nominal price because a real price is an opportunity cost that influences choices. And we want to distinguish a real quantity (like real GDP) from a nominal quantity (like nominal GDP) because we want to see what is "really" happening to variables that influence the standard of living.

You've seen in this chapter how we view real GDP as nominal GDP deflated by the *GDP deflator*. Viewing real GDP in this way opens up the idea of using the same method to calculate other real variables. Using the GDP deflator, we can deflate any nominal variable and find its corresponding real value.

An important example is the wage rate, which is the price of labour. We measure the *real wage rate* as the nominal wage rate divided by the GDP deflator.

There is one variable that is a bit different—an interest rate. A real interest rate is *not* a nominal interest rate divided by the price level. You'll learn how to adjust interest rates for inflation to find a real interest rate in Chapter 23. But all the other real variables of macroeconomics are calculated by dividing a nominal variable by the price level.

FIGURE 21.7   CPI and Core CPI Inflation

The core CPI inflation rate excludes price changes of food and fuel. Since 2000, the core inflation rate has been 0.5 percentage points below the CPI inflation rate because the relative prices of food and fuel have been rising.

Sources of data: Statistics Canada, CANSIM Table 380-0002.

myeconlab animation

Review Quiz

1 What is the price level?
2 What is the CPI and how is it calculated?
3 How do we calculate the inflation rate and what is the relationship between the CPI and the inflation rate?
4 What are the four main ways in which the CPI is an upward-biased measure of the price level?
5 What problems arise from the CPI bias?
6 What are the alternative measures of the price level and how do they address the problem of bias in the CPI?

myeconlab Work Study Plan 21.3 and get instant feedback.

◆ You've now completed your study of the measurement of macroeconomic performance. Your task in the following chapters is to learn what determines that performance and how policy actions might improve it. But first, take a close-up look at the labour market in the slowdown of 2008 in *Reading Between the Lines* on pp. 504–505.

Jobs in the Slowdown of 2008

Canada adds 9,500 jobs, U.S. loses 240,000

November 7, 2008

The Canadian jobless rate held up remarkably well compared to the United States in October, as one country managed to add jobs while the other suffered yet another steep decline, new data showed on Friday.

Canadian employment rolls remained largely unchanged in October after September's surprising gains, however, a federal election that briefly added more than 40,000 jobs may have veiled mounting weakness elsewhere.

In stark contrast, the American economy shed more than 240,000 jobs last month, as the world's largest economy cooled further. The worse-than-expected results catapulted the jobless rate to 6.5 percent from 6.1 percent—a level last touched in 1994.

In Canada, the unemployment rate edged up to 6.2 percent in October, an increase of 0.1 percent from the previous month, Statistics Canada said. October witnessed an increase of 9,500 new jobs to add to September's surge of more than 107,000, even as the global credit crisis roiled on.

The figure was in line with what economists had expected. Employment increased in Alberta as that province added 15,000 more jobs and the unemployment rate remained the lowest in the country, at 3.7 percent. "There was little employment change in the other provinces," the federal agency said. ...

Essence of the Story

- Canadian employment increased by 107,000 in September 2008 and by 9,500 in October 2008.

- The unemployment rate increased from 6.1 percent in September to 6.2 percent in October.

- In the United States, employment decreased by 240,000 jobs in October 2008 and the unemployment rate increased from 6.1 percent in September to 6.5 percent in October, its highest level since 1994.

- Employment in Alberta increased by 15,000 and the unemployment rate remained at 3.7 percent, the lowest in Canada.

Economic Analysis

- This news article reports some labour market data for both Canada and the United States in 2008.

- The credit crisis that began in August 2007 and intensified through 2008 had a bigger effect on the U.S. economy than on the Canadian economy.

- The three figures compare the labour markets of United States and Canada during 2008.

- Figure 1 shows that the employment-to-population ratio in Canada is higher than in the United States.

- This figure also shows that although the employment-to-population ratio fell in both countries, the fall in the United States was large and Canadian employment held steady with only a very slight fall.

- Figure 2 shows the unemployment rates. Normally, Canada has a higher unemployment rate than the United States.

- At the beginning of 2008, the normal state of affairs prevailed, but during 2008, the U.S. unemployment rate climbed steeply and by July, it equalled the Canadian rate. In October, the U.S. rate pulled ahead of the Canadian rate.

- Figure 3 shows that most of the job growth during 2008 was in part-time work. In both Canada and the United States, the part-time employment rate increased by about half a percentage point.

- Figure 3 also shows that Canada has more part-time employment than the United States—about a full percentage point more.

- Canada's relatively strong performance through October 2008 is also reflected in estimates of the output gaps in the two countries. Canada's output gap was estimated at –0.6 percent of potential GDP while the U.S. gap was estimated to be –2.7 percent of potential GDP.

- The reasons for Canada's relatively strong performance through October 2008 are not well understood, but if the United States goes into a long and deep recession, it is unlikely that Canada will continue to perform as well as it did during the first 10 months of 2008.

Figure 1 Employment

Figure 2 Unemployment

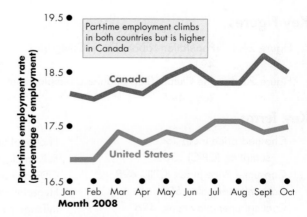

Figure 3 Part-time employment

SUMMARY

Key Points

Employment and Unemployment (pp. 490–493)

- Unemployment is a serious personal, social, and economic problem because it results in lost output and income and a loss of human capital.
- The unemployment rate averaged 7.6 percent between 1960 and 2007. It increases in recessions and decreases in expansions.
- The labour force participation rate and the employment-to-population ratio have an upward trend and fluctuate with the business cycle.

Unemployment and Full Employment (pp. 494–497)

- The unemployment rate is an imperfect measure of the underutilization of labour resources because it excludes some underutilized labour and some unemployment is unavoidable.
- The unemployment rate underestimates the underutilization of labour resources because it excludes marginally attached workers and part-time workers who want full-time jobs.
- Some unemployment is unavoidable because people are constantly entering and leaving the labour force and losing or quitting jobs; also firms that create jobs are constantly being born, expanding, contracting, and dying.
- Unemployment can be frictional, structural, or cyclical.

- When all unemployment is frictional and structural, the unemployment rate equals the natural unemployment rate, the economy is at full employment, and real GDP equals potential GDP.
- Over the business cycle, real GDP fluctuates around potential GDP and the unemployment rate fluctuates around the natural unemployment rate.

The Price Level and Inflation (pp. 498–503)

- Inflation is a problem because it redistributes income and wealth and diverts resources from production.
- The Consumer Price Index (CPI) is a measure of the average of the prices paid by urban consumers for a fixed basket of consumer goods and services.
- The CPI is defined to equal 100 for a reference base period—currently 2002.
- The inflation rate is the percentage change in the CPI from one period to the next.
- Changes in the CPI probably overstate the inflation rate because of the bias that arises from new goods, quality changes, commodity substitution, and outlet substitution.
- The bias in the CPI distorts private contracts and increases government outlays.
- Alternative price level measures avoid the bias of the CPI but do not make a large difference to the measured inflation rate.
- Real economic variables are calculated by dividing nominal variables by the price level.

Key Figures

Figure 21.1   Population Labour Force Categories, 491

Figure 21.4   The Output Gap and the Unemployment Rate, 497

Figure 21.5   The CPI Basket, 499

Key Terms

Chained price index for consumption (CPIC), 502
Consumer Price Index (CPI), 498
Core inflation rate, 502
Cyclical unemployment, 496
Discouraged worker, 494
Efficiency wage, 496
Employment-to-population ratio, 493

Frictional unemployment, 495
Full employment, 496
GDP deflator, 502
Hyperinflation, 498
Inflation rate, 498
Labour force, 491
Labour force participation rate, 492

Marginally attached worker, 494
Natural unemployment rate, 496
Output gap, 496
Price level, 498
Reference base period, 498
Structural unemployment, 495
Unemployment rate, 492
Working-age population, 491

PROBLEMS and APPLICATIONS

myeconlab Work problems 1–9 in Chapter 21 Study Plan and get instant feedback.
Work problems 10–18 as Homework, a Quiz, or a Test if assigned by your instructor.

1. Statistics Canada reported the following data for October 2008:
   Labour force: 18,345,500
   Employment: 17,215,800
   Working-age population: 27,044,100.
   Calculate for that month the

   a. Unemployment rate.
   b. Labour force participation rate.
   c. Employment-to-population ratio.

2. The Canadian unemployment rate was 6.4 percent in August 2006 and 6.1 percent in August 2008. Use this information to predict what happened between August 2006 and August 2008 to the numbers of

   a. Job losers and job leavers.
   b. Entrants and reentrants into the labour force.

3. In July 2009, on Sandy Island, 10,000 people were employed, 1,000 were unemployed, and 5,000 were not in the labour force. During August 2009, 80 people lost their jobs and didn't look for new ones, 20 people quit their jobs and retired, 150 people were hired or recalled, 50 people withdrew from the labour force, and 40 people entered or reentered the labour force to look for work. Calculate for July 2009

   a. The unemployment rate.
   b. The employment-to-population ratio.

   Calculate for the end of August 2009

   c. The number of people unemployed.
   d. The number of people employed.
   e. The unemployment rate.

4. Statistics Canada reported the following data:
   CPI in June 2006: 109.5
   CPI in June 2007: 111.9
   CPI in June 2008: 114.6

   a. What do these numbers tell you about the price level in these three years?
   b. Calculate the inflation rates for the years ending in June 2007 and June 2008.
   c. How did the inflation rate change in 2008?
   d. Why might these CPI numbers be biased?

   e. How do alternative price indexes help to avoid the bias in the CPI numbers?

5. The IMF *World Economic Outlook* reports the following price level data (2000 = 100):

Region	2006	2007	2008
United States	117.1	120.4	124.0
Euro area	113.6	117.1	119.6
Japan	98.1	98.1	98.8

   a. Which region had the highest inflation rate in 2007 and which had the highest inflation rate in 2008?
   b. Describe the path of the price level in Japan.

6. **September Job Gains Defy "Wisdom"**

   The Canadian economy produced a record number of new jobs in September, a perplexing development given the onset of a global recession in the midst of a horrendous financial crisis. A whopping 107,000 new jobs were created last month, a gain that not only defied "conventional wisdom but gravity as well," Douglas Porter, deputy chief economist at BMO Capital Markets said. ... But scrape below the surface and the details were not as impressive as the headline, Mr. Porter said. A large part of the gain—which predates the worst of the financial crisis—was in part-time youth employment, not necessarily the underpinnings of a sustainable economy. ...

   National Post, October 11, 2008

   a. Why did Douglas Porter say the September 2008 job numbers defied gravity and conventional wisdom?
   b. Why might the September job numbers overstate the rise in employment?
   c. Given the information in the news article, what do you predict happened to the gap between real GDP and potential GDP during September 2008?

7. **GM, Ford Cuts Show Difficult Times Far from Over**

   A pink slip is a nasty thing. In fact, next to death and divorce, it's the most devastating experience in one's lifetime. Sadly, workers at GM and Ford know it all too well. On top of the 2,600 layoffs coming next year in Oshawa when GM closes its truck plant, now 500 workers at the car plant face layoff early next year ... In total, another 3,600 in North America could be getting pink slips just before Christmas. And the number doesn't include the 1,400 workers who'll lose their jobs in 2010, when GM closes a Windsor transmission plant. ... Ford is also bleeding red ink, ... [and] announced a further 10-per-cent cut in white-collar, salaried positions, with 2,260 more layoffs. This is chilling news for Ontario, now a have-not province, where layoffs are piling high. ... Bottom line is that for every job in an assembly plant, there are 7.5 jobs with auto-parts suppliers and other companies, meaning the auto industry accounts for millions of jobs in North America. The Centre for Automotive Research estimates if the U.S. auto industry shrinks by 50 per cent, 2.5 million jobs will be lost. Now the question is will GM survive?

Timmins Daily Press, November 11, 2008

a. How will the events described in this news article change the employment rate, the labour force participation rate, and the unemployment rate in Ontario?
b. Will the change in Ontario's unemployment rate arise from a change in frictional, structural, or cyclical unemployment? Explain.
c. How will the events described in the news article change the natural unemployment rate? Explain.

8. **Canada Inflation Rate Rises More than Forecast on Gas**

Canada's annual inflation accelerated for the second straight month in May as gasoline prices surged, lending support to the Bank of Canada's prediction last week that prices may keep rising all year. Consumer prices rose 2.2 percent from a year earlier, the fastest pace since January, Statistics Canada said today. ... Gasoline prices spurred May's acceleration, soaring 15 percent from a year ago. Excluding gasoline, consumer prices would have gained 1.6 percent in April, the agency said. ... "It's no surprise that gasoline prices are leading the charge," said Pascal Gauthier, an economist with Toronto-Dominion Bank. ... Month-over-month inflation accelerated in May in part because of a 2.9 percent gain in transportation costs and a 1 percent gain in food prices, Statistics Canada said. The core inflation rate was unchanged from a year earlier

at 1.5 percent and the monthly core inflation rate stayed at 0.3 percent, in both cases matching economists' median forecast. The core rate, used by policy makers as a guide to future trends, excludes volatile items such as gasoline and fresh fruit and discounts tax changes such as a reduction in the federal sales tax earlier this year. An 8.1 percent drop in car prices kept the core index from rising in May, Statistics Canada said.

Bloomberg, June 13, 2008

a. How do the inflation rates described in this article compare to average inflation since 1993? How do they compare to average inflation during the 1970s and early 1980s?
b. Which components of the CPI basket are experiencing price increases faster than the average and which have price increases below the average?
c. What is the difference between the CPI and the core CPI? Why might the core CPI be a useful measurement and why might it be misleading?

9. **Dress for Less**

Since 1998, the price of a "Speedy" handbag—the entry-level style at Louis Vuitton—has more than doubled, to $685, indicative of a precipitous price increase throughout the luxury goods market. The price of Joe Boxer's "licky face" underwear, meanwhile, has dropped by nearly half, to $8.99, representing just as seismic a shift at the other end of the fashion continuum, where the majority of ... consumers do their shopping.

As luxury fashion has become more expensive, mainstream apparel has become markedly less so. ... Clothing is one of the few categories in the federal Consumer Price Index in which overall prices have declined—about 10 percent—since 1998 (the cost of communication is another). That news may be of solace to anyone whose budget has been stretched just to drive to work or to stop at the supermarket; in fashion, at least, there are still deals to be had. ...

New York Times, May 29, 2008

a. What percentage of the CPI basket does clothing and footware comprise?
b. If luxury clothing prices have increased dramatically since the late 1990s, why has the clothing category of the CPI actually declined by about 10 percent?

10. In the New Orleans metropolitan area in August 2005, the labour force was 634,512 and 35,222 people were unemployed. In September 2005 following Hurricane Katrina, the labour force fell by 156,498 and the number employed fell by 206,024. Calculate the unemployment rate in August 2005 and in September 2005.

11. The IMF *World Economic Outlook* reports the following unemployment rates:

Region	2007	2008
United States	4.6	5.4
Euro area	7.4	7.3
Japan	3.9	3.9

   a. What do these numbers tell you about the phase of the business cycle in the United States, the Euro area, and Japan in 2008?
   b. What do you think these numbers tell us about the relative size of the natural unemployment rates in the United States, the Euro area, and Japan?
   c. Do these numbers tell us anything about the relative size of the labour force participation rates and employment-to-population ratios in the three regions?
   d. Why might these unemployment numbers understate or overstate the true amount of unemployment?

12. A typical family on Sandy Island consumes only juice and cloth. Last year, which was the base year, the family spent $40 on juice and $25 on cloth. In the base year, juice was $4 a bottle and cloth was $5 a length. This year, juice is $4 a bottle and cloth is $6 a length. Calculate

   a. The CPI basket.
   b. The CPI in the current year.
   c. The inflation rate in the current year.

13. **A Half-Year of Job Losses**
   Employers trimmed jobs from their payrolls in June for the sixth straight month, as the government's closely watched report Thursday showed continued weakness in the labour market. ... The June number brought to 438,000 the number of jobs lost by the U.S. economy so far this year. ... The job losses in the monthly report were concentrated in manufacturing and construction, two sectors that have been badly battered in the current economic downturn. ...
   CNN, July 3, 2008

   a. How do the job losses for the first half of 2008 compare to the total number of people employed (as seen in this chapter)?
   b. Based on the news clip, what might be the main source of increased unemployment?
   c. Based on the news clip, what might be the main type of increased unemployment?

14. **Out of a Job and Out of Luck at 54**
   Too young to retire, too old to get a new job. That's how many older workers are feeling these days. ... Older job seekers are discovering the search is even rougher as many employers shy away from hiring those closer to retirement than to the start of their careers. ... After they get the pink slip, older workers spend more time on the unemployment line. Many lack the skills to search for jobs in today's online world and to craft resumes and cover letters, experts say. ... It took those age 55 and older an average of 21.1 weeks to land a new job in 2007, about five weeks longer than their younger counterparts, according to AARP. "Clearly older workers will be more adversely affected because of the time it takes to transition into another job," said Deborah Russell, AARP's director of workforce issues.
   CNN, May 21, 2008

   a. What type of unemployment might older workers be more prone to experience?
   b. Explain how the unemployment rate of older workers would be influenced by the business cycle.
   c. Why might older unemployed workers become marginally attached or discouraged workers during a recession?

15. **Unemployment Up, Even as Economy Sprouts New Jobs**
   Canada's unemployment rate edged up to 6.2 per cent in October from 6.1 per cent the previous month, Statistics Canada said Friday, even as the economy unexpectedly added thousands of new positions despite struggling to avoid a recession amid a global economic slowdown.
   There were 9,500 jobs created during the month, compared to a gain of 107,000 positions in September, the federal agency said. ... Alberta's unemployment rate remained the lowest in the country at 3.7 per cent, which added 15,000 jobs in October. "There was little employment change in the other provinces." Statistics Canada said.

Newfoundland and Labrador had the highest jobless rate at 13.7 per cent, followed by Prince Edward Island at 11.5 per cent. ...

Windsor Star, November 7, 2008

a. How can the unemployment rate increase when employment increases?
b. How would you explain the large difference in the unemployment rates in Alberta, Newfoundland and Labrador, and Prince Edward Island?
c. Explain why most of the difference in the unemployment rates in Alberta, Newfoundland and Labrador, and Prince Edward Island is a difference in the natural unemployment rate in each province.

16. **Economic "Misery" More Widespread**

Unemployment and inflation are typically added together to come up with a so-called "Misery Index." The "Misery Index" was often cited during periods of high unemployment and inflation, such as the mid 1970s and late 1970s to early 1980s.

And some fear the economy may be approaching those levels again. The official numbers produce a current Misery Index of only 8.9—inflation of 3.9% plus unemployment of 5%. That's not far from the Misery Index's low of 6.1 seen in 1998. ... Some worry it could even approach the post-World War II record of 20.6 in 1980. ...

CNN, May 13, 2008

a. Explain how the "Misery Index" might serve as a gauge of how the economy is performing.
b. How does the most current "Misery Index" compare to the high and low given in this article? (You may find it useful to use the link of MyEconLab—Chapter Resources, Chapter 21, Web links—to visit the Bureau of Labour Statistics Web site for the current unemployment rate and the most recent 12-month change in the CPI.)

17. **The Great Inflation Cover-Up**

The 1996 Boskin Commission ... was established to determine the accuracy of the [U.S.] CPI. The commission concluded that the CPI overstated inflation by 1.1%, and methodologies were adjusted to reflect that. Critics of the Boskin Commission suggest that the basis upon which the CPI was revised doesn't account for the way

people actually purchase and consume products. The commission pointed to four biases inherent in the way the CPI was determined that supposedly contribute to overstatement. ... But the Boskin critics note several reasonable exceptions to those biases. The Boskin Commission suggests that when customers substitute one good for another, the CPI should treat those goods equally. If [someone] orders a hanger steak instead of his beloved filet mignon because the hanger steak is cheaper, Boskin argues that the hanger steak prices should be compared with previous filet mignon prices. It's all beef, right? But critics of the Boskin report point to areas where substitution is so price-driven that consumers are pushed out of the category altogether. What happens when the consumer gives up steak entirely and switches to chicken? ... Boskin also says that whatever you're paying in price increases is offset by the additional pleasure you get from better goods. To put it another way, you adjust for improvement in quality over time. ... So, for example, energy price increases due to federally mandated environmental measures are offset by how much we all sit around enjoying the cleaner environment.

Fortune, April 3, 2008

a. What are the main sources of bias that are generally believed to make the CPI overstate the inflation rate?
b. Is the U.S. or Canadian CPI more biased?
c. Do the substitutions among different kinds of meat make the CPI biased up or down?
d. Why does it matter if the CPI overstates or understates the inflation rate?

18. Study *Reading Between the Lines* on pp. 504–505 and then answer the following questions:

a. What are the key differences in performance of the U.S. and Canadian job markets during 2008?
b. How do the part-time employment rates of the two countries compare?
c. Why might the United States job market have been so much weaker than the Canadian job market during 2008?
d. Are the differences between the U.S. and Canadian job markets in 2008 seasonal, frictional, structural, or cyclical unemployment?

UNDERSTANDING MACROECONOMIC TRENDS AND FLUCTUATIONS

The Big Picture

Macroeconomics is a large and controversial subject that is interlaced with political ideological disputes. And it is a field in which charlatans as well as serious thinkers have much to say.

You have just learned in Chapters 20 and 21 how we monitor and measure the main macroeconomic variables. We use real GDP to calculate the rate of economic growth and business cycle fluctuations. And we use the CPI and other measures of the price level to calculate the inflation rate and to "deflate" nominal values to find *real* values.

In the chapters that lie ahead, you will learn the theories that economists have developed to explain economic growth, fluctuations, and inflation.

First, in Chapters 22 through 25, you will study the long-term trends. This material is central to the oldest question in macroeconomics that Adam Smith tried to answer: What are the causes of the wealth of nations? You will also study three other old questions that Adam Smith's contemporary and friend David Hume first addressed: What causes inflation? What causes international deficits and surpluses? And why do exchange rates fluctuate?

In Chapters 26 through 28, you will study macroeconomic fluctuations.

Finally, in Chapters 29 and 30, you will study the policies that the federal government and the Bank of Canada might adopt to make the economy perform well.

David Hume, *a Scot who lived from 1711 to 1776, did not call himself an economist. "Philosophy and general learning" is how he described the subject of his life's work. Hume was an extraordinary thinker and writer. Published in 1742, his* Essays, Moral and Political, *range across economics, political science, moral philosophy, history, literature, ethics, and religion and explore such topics as love, marriage, divorce, suicide, death, and the immortality of the soul!*

His economic essays provide astonishing insights into the forces that cause inflation, business cycle fluctuations, balance of payments deficits, and interest rate fluctuations; and they explain the effects of taxes and government deficits and debts.

Data were scarce in Hume's day, so he was not able to draw on detailed evidence to support his analysis. But he was empirical. He repeatedly appealed to experience and evidence as the ultimate judge of the validity of an argument. Hume's fundamentally empirical approach dominates macroeconomics today.

"... in every kingdom into which money begins to flow in greater abundance than formerly, everything takes a new face: labour and industry gain life; the merchant becomes more enterprising, the manufacturer more diligent and skillful, and even the farmer follows his plow with greater alacrity and attention."

DAVID HUME
Essays, Moral and Political

TALKING
WITH

Peter Howitt

Peter Howitt is Lyn Crost Professor of Social Sciences in the Department of Economics at Brown University. Born in 1946 in Toronto, he was an undergraduate at McGill University and a graduate student at Northwestern University. He began his research and teaching career at the University of Western Ontario in 1972, where he spent many productive years before moving to the United States in 1996. Professor Howitt is a past president of the Canadian Economics Association and is one of the world's leading macroeconomists. He has done research on all aspect of macroeconomics, with a focus in recent years on economic growth.

Michael Parkin and Robin Bade talked with Peter Howitt about his work and the major macroeconomic problems facing Canada today.

Peter, what attracted you to economics?

When I was in high school I had a part-time job as office boy with a small company that imported wool from around the world and sold it to textile mills in Ontario and Quebec. I was fascinated by the way wool prices went up and down all the time, and this curiosity led me to enroll in an honours economics course. My interests soon switched to macroeconomics, but I was always driven by curiosity to find out more about the workings of the human anthill.

You have made outstanding contributions to our understanding of all the major problems of macroeconomics, notably unemployment, economic growth, and inflation. Which of these issues do you believe is the most serious one for Canada today? Can they be separated?

Right now [November 2008], we are in the midst of a global financial crisis. I hope that the attempts by governments and central banks around the world to stabilize financial markets will succeed, but I fear the worst. The financial situation has led to a contraction of new credit and a drop in global aggregate demand. If aggregate demand continues to fall, as many are predicting, our biggest economic problem will soon be unemployment.

I am also concerned that long-term economic growth will be set back by the crisis. Financial markets are likely to remain in their current state for several years, and as long as they do, many of the investments, in plant and equipment and in research and development, that are needed for long-term economic growth will be choked off for lack of credit. In this sense the problems of unemployment and growth are closely linked. As for inflation, I am confident that the Bank of Canada's inflation-targeting policy will probably keep it under control. I also think that inflation-targeting will help to dampen the downturn of aggregate demand and thus to mitigate the potential problems of unemployment and economic growth.

Of course, all of these problems are interrelated. Learning about all the interrelationships is one of the things that makes economics so interesting. Take the relationship between growth and unemployment, for example. If you take a short-run perspective, then these two variables would appear to be negatively related. If the economy grows faster, there will be more jobs, and better paying jobs, which will draw people out of unemployment. But in the long run it looks quite different. You can't maintain a high growth rate indefinitely by continuing to put idle people to work, because at some point you will have everyone in the economy working. Instead, to keep the economy growing at a high rate you have to keep finding ways to make people more productive. You get this from having technological progress, from innovations that improve the efficiency of production processes and that allow people to produce new goods that contribute to our material welfare in ways that previous generations never have imagined.

Now the industrial innovations that underlie economic growth in the long run usually come at a cost. This is what Schumpeter meant by the term "creative destruction." For example, if I invent a new good this will create new jobs for people to produce the good, but it will also destroy the jobs of people who produce the goods that mine will replace. So an economy that is going through a period of rapid technological change is likely to have good growth prospects, but it may also have a high rate of unemployment. The people whose jobs are destroyed may eventually find even better jobs but it will take time, so there will be a lot of people in a temporary situation of unemployment. To make a long story short, even though a short burst of growth from one quarter to the next is likely to reduce the rate of unemployment, a sustained rise in the rate of growth from one decade to the next will create a rise in the rate of unemployment.

> ... industrial innovations that underlie economic growth in the long run usually come at a cost. This is what Schumpeter meant by the term "creative destruction."

What does your research tell us about the main sources of Canada's persistently high unemployment rate during the 1980s and 1990s?

I think a lot of what has taken place in Canada is an example of the effects of creative destruction that I talked about. A lot of technological change destroys low-skill jobs, and also destroys the value of old skills. In particular, a lot of clerical and middle management jobs have been made redundant by computers. Computers open up new jobs for people able to master the technology, but a lot of people don't have the skills or the knowledge to profit from these opportunities.

This is a global phenomenon, not just limited to Canada. Computers are having a revolutionary effect on economic life all over the world. In the United States it hasn't appeared to produce much unemployment. Instead what you see is a growing gap between the wages of skilled and unskilled workers. In Canada that gap isn't as visible, largely because we have more generous minimum wages and unemployment insurance benefits, which means that a fall in the demand for low-skill workers shows up more in a rise in unemployment and less in a fall in their wages than in the United States.

Why did our economic growth rate slow during the 1980s?

The short answer is that no one knows. But I think the answer probably lies in the computer revolution that I have talked about. Ultimately I think this revolution is going to give us a higher growth rate. But we have to accumulate a lot of knowledge in order to profit from it. We have been going through a collective learning experience that has been enormously costly, and this has been a continual drag on productivity, even though in the end I expect it will greatly enhance productivity.

Also, I think we are underestimating growth rates nowadays. This is because we are investing a lot in knowledge—knowledge of how to harness the power of the computer and to exploit the opportunities that it presents. Investment in knowledge is like investment in machinery in that it entails the sacrifice of resources now in return for the promise of more income sometime in the future. But while the national income accountant measures investment in machines as part of the economy's output of final goods and services, investment in knowledge is just treated as wasted resources.

Was the pursuit of low inflation worthwhile? Have we now got too low an inflation rate?

I think the pursuit of low inflation was definitely worthwhile, although in retrospect we maybe should have been more patient. Inflation impairs one of the most useful devices in the economic system—the conventional measure of value. Now that we have almost eliminated inflation we have a much healthier economic system. I don't think we should go much further, however, because you may have to raise unemployment even higher in order to get inflation all the way down to zero, and once you have it down to 2 percent you have little more to gain by reducing it even further. Also, further reductions in inflation may impair the working of the labour market. That is, people whose real wages are falling for whatever reason may be more inclined to continue working if they can at least avoid having to submit to a nominal wage cut, but can instead take the real-wage cut through the back door of inflation. With 2 percent inflation there is still lots of room for this sort of real-wage flexibility, but with no inflation there is none at all.

Some economists say that the Bank of Canada can speed up the economic growth rate by forgetting about low inflation and keeping interest rates low. Others say the best hope for increasing the growth rate is low inflation. Who is right?

The first group is certainly now right, except perhaps in a very short-run sense. You can't sustain a high growth rate for long by printing more money. Before long you'll end up with a higher rate of inflation and even higher interest rates as lenders seek compensation for the fall in the value of money. A lot of recent econometric evidence has been produced by various writers studying the experience of different countries that

> ... one of the great things about economics is that you can be paid well for spending your time satisfying your curiosity.

shows over long periods of time that inflation and growth are negatively correlated. More inflation from one decade to the next is likely to produce a fall in the growth rate rather than a rise. The effect doesn't appear to be numerically very large, but even a small drop in the growth rate can have a significant depressing effect on the level of real income if sustained for a decade or two.

What advice would you give to a student who wants to become a professional economist today?

My first advice for anyone interested in doing economics is to give full reign to your curiosity. The greatest satisfaction that I have received as an economist has been from discovering things about how the world works, from seeing a little more clearly some of the complex interactions between the different parts of the economy. I can still remember the excitement I felt when I started to see how demand and supply work, and when I learned about the circular flow of economic activity and how it can be affected by saving and investment decisions. I am happy to say that this sense of excitement has never left me. Furthermore, one of the great things about economics is that you can be paid well for spending your time satisfying your curiosity. Satisfying your curiosity is enjoyable, but if you want to accomplish something you can't let yourself be satisfied easily. You have to keep asking questions, and trying to answer them. It's easy to think you have solved a problem when you haven't explored things deeply enough. The best way for a student to do this is to do lots of exercises, and to discuss what you are doing with others. The same applies throughout one's career.

22 ◆ Economic Growth

After studying this chapter, you will be able to

- Define and calculate the economic growth rate and explain the implications of sustained growth

- Describe the economic growth trends in Canada and other countries and regions

- Explain how population growth and labour productivity growth make potential GDP grow

- Explain and measure the sources of labour productivity growth

- Explain the theories of economic growth and policies designed to increase the growth rate

Real GDP *per person* in Canada tripled between 1958 and 2008. If you live in a dorm that was built during the 1960s, it is likely to have just two power outlets: one for a desk lamp and one for a bedside lamp. Today, with the help of a power bar (or two), your room bulges with a personal computer, television and DVD player, microwave, refrigerator, coffeemaker, and toaster—and the list goes on. What has brought about this growth in production, incomes, and living standards?

We see even greater economic growth in modern Asia. At the mouth of the Yangtze River in one of the world's great cities, Shanghai, people are creating businesses, investing in new technologies, developing local and global markets, and transforming their lives. Incomes have tripled in the short 13 years since 1995. Why are incomes in China growing so rapidly?

In this chapter, we study the forces that make real GDP grow, that make some countries grow faster than others, and that make growth rates sometimes slow down and sometimes speed up.

In *Reading Between the Lines* at the end of the chapter we return to the economic growth of China and see how it compares with that of the much richer United States.

The Basics of Economic Growth

Economic growth is a sustained expansion of production possibilities measured as the increase in real GDP over a given period. Rapid economic growth maintained over a number of years can transform a poor nation into a rich one. Such have been the stories of Hong Kong, South Korea, Taiwan, and some other Asian economies. Slow economic growth or the absence of growth can condemn a nation to devastating poverty. Such has been the fate of Sierra Leone, Somalia, Zambia, and much of the rest of Africa.

The goal of this chapter is to help you to understand why some economies expand rapidly and others stagnate. We'll begin by learning how to calculate the economic growth rate and by discovering the magic of sustained growth.

Calculating Growth Rates

We express the **economic growth rate** as the annual percentage change of real GDP. To calculate this growth rate, we use the formula:

$$\text{Real GDP growth rate} = \frac{\text{Real GDP in current year} - \text{Real GDP in previous year}}{\text{Real GDP in previous year}} \times 100.$$

For example, if real GDP in the current year is $11 trillion and if real GDP in the previous year was $10 trillion, then the economic growth rate is 10 percent.

The growth rate of real GDP tells us how rapidly the *total* economy is expanding. This measure is useful for telling us about potential changes in the balance of economic power among nations. But it does not tell us about changes in the standard of living.

The standard of living depends on **real GDP per person** (also called *per capita* real GDP), which is real GDP divided by the population. So the contribution of real GDP growth to the change in the standard of living depends on the growth rate of real GDP per person. We use the above formula to calculate this growth rate, replacing real GDP with real GDP per person.

Suppose, for example, that in the current year, when real GDP is $1,100 billion, the population is 20.2 million. Then real GDP per person is

$1,100 billion divided by 20.2 million, which equals $54,455. And suppose that in the previous year, when real GDP was $1 billion, the population was 20 million. Then real GDP per person in that year was $1,000 billion divided by 20 million, which equals $50,000.

Use these two values of real GDP per person with the growth formula above to calculate the growth rate of real GDP per person. That is,

$$\text{Real GDP per person growth rate} = \frac{\$54,455 - \$50,000}{\$50,000} \times 100 = 8.9 \text{ percent.}$$

The growth rate of real GDP per person can also be calculated (approximately) by subtracting the population growth rate from the real GDP growth rate. In the example you've just worked through, the growth rate of real GDP is 10 percent. The population changes from 20 million to 20.2 million, so the population growth rate is 1 percent. The growth rate of real GDP per person is approximately equal to 10 percent minus 1 percent, which equals 9 percent.

Real GDP per person grows only if real GDP grows faster than the population grows. If the growth rate of the population exceeds the growth of real GDP, then real GDP per person falls.

The Magic of Sustained Growth

Sustained growth of real GDP per person can transform a poor society into a wealthy one. The reason is that economic growth is like compound interest.

Compound Interest   Suppose that you put $100 in the bank and earn 5 percent a year interest on it. After one year, you have $105. If you leave that $105 in the bank for another year, you earn 5 percent interest on the original $100 *and on the $5 interest that you earned last year*. You are now earning interest on interest! The next year, things get even better. Then you earn 5 percent on the original $100 and on the interest earned in the first year and the second year. You are even earning interest on the interest that you earned on the interest of the first year.

Your money in the bank is growing at a rate of 5 percent a year. Before too many years have passed, your initial deposit of $100 will have grown to $200. But after how many years?

The answer is provided by a formula called the **Rule of 70**, which states that the number of years it

FIGURE 22.1   The Rule of 70

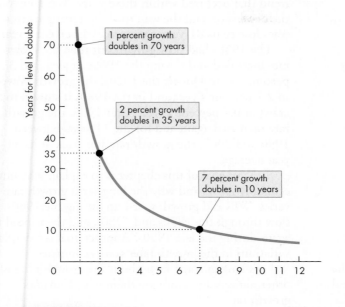

Growth rate (percent per year)	Years for level to double
1	70.0
2	35.0
3	23.3
4	17.5
5	14.0
6	11.7
7	10.0
8	8.8
9	7.8
10	7.0
11	6.4
12	5.8

The number of years it takes for the level of a variable to double is approximately 70 divided by the annual percentage growth rate of the variable.

In the graph: "1 percent growth doubles in 70 years"; "2 percent growth doubles in 35 years"; "7 percent growth doubles in 10 years"

myeconlab animation

takes for the level of any variable to double is approximately 70 divided by the annual percentage growth rate of the variable. Using the Rule of 70, you can now calculate how many years it takes your $100 to become $200. It is 70 divided by 5, which is 14 years.

Applying the Rule of 70

The Rule of 70 applies to any variable, so it applies to real GDP per person. Figure 22.1 shows the doubling time for growth rates of 1 percent per year to 12 percent per year.

You can see that real GDP per person doubles in 70 years (70 divided by 1)—an average human life span—if the growth rate is 1 percent a year. It doubles in 35 years if the growth rate is 2 percent a year and in just 10 years if the growth rate is 7 percent a year.

We can use the Rule of 70 to answer other questions about economic growth. For example, in 2000, real GDP per person in the United States was approximately 8 times that of China. China's recent growth rate of real GDP per person was 7 percent a year. If this growth rate were maintained, how long would it take China's real GDP per person to reach that of the

United States in 2000? The answer, provided by the Rule of 70, is 30 years. China's real GDP per person doubles in 10 years (70 divided by 7). It doubles again to 4 times its current level in another 10 years. And it doubles yet again to 8 times its current level in another 10 years. So after 30 years of growth at 7 percent a year, China's real GDP per person is 8 times its current level and equals that of the United States in 2000. Of course, after 30 years, real GDP per person in the United States would have increased, so China would still not have caught up to the United States.

Review Quiz

1   What is economic growth and how do we calculate its rate?
2   What is the relationship between the growth rate of real GDP and the growth rate of real GDP per person?
3   Use the Rule of 70 to calculate the growth rate that leads to a doubling of real GDP per person in 20 years.

myeconlab   Work Study Plan 22.1 and get instant feedback.

Economic Growth Trends

You have just seen the power of economic growth to increase incomes. At a 1 percent growth rate, it takes a human life span to double the standard of living. But at a 7 percent growth rate, the standard of living doubles every decade. How fast is our economy growing? How fast are other economies growing? Are poor countries catching up to rich ones, or do the gaps between the rich and poor persist or even widen? Let's answer these questions.

Growth in the Canadian Economy

Figure 22.2 shows real GDP *per person* in Canada for the 81 years from 1926 to 2007. The average growth rate over this period was 2.1 percent a year.

The earliest years in the graph are dominated by two extraordinary events: the Great Depression of the 1930s and World War II of the 1940s. The fall in real GDP during the depression and the bulge during the war obscure the changes in the long-term growth trend that occurred within these years. Averaging out the depression and the war, the long-term growth rate was close to its 81-year average of 2.1 percent a year.

The 1950s had slow growth but then the growth rate increased and during the 1960s, it averaged 3.3 percent a year. During the 1970s, the growth slowed to 2.1 percent a year and in the 1980s it slowed to a crawl of 0.7 percent a year. After 1996, the growth rate increased again and for the 11 years between 1996 and 2007, the growth rate was back at its 81-year average.

A major goal of this chapter is to explain why our economy grows and why the long-term growth rate varies. Why did growth speed up during the 1960s, slow through the 1970s and 1980s, and then speed up again during the late 1990s? Another goal is to explain variations in the growth rates across countries.

Let's look at some facts about the growth rates of other nations and compare them with Canada's growth rate.

FIGURE 22.2   Economic Growth in Canada: 1926–2007

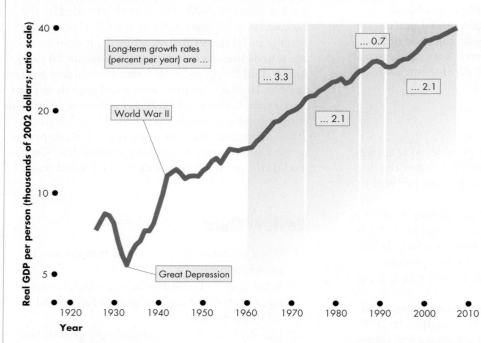

During the 81 years from 1926 to 2007, real GDP per person in Canada grew by 2.1 percent a year, on the average. Growth was the most rapid during the 1960s and slowest during the 1980s.

Sources of data: F.H. Leacy (ed.), *Historical Statistics of Canada*, 2nd ed., catalogue 11-516, series A1, F32, F55, Statistics Canada, Ottawa, 1983; and Statistics Canada, Tables 380-0002 and 051-0005.

myeconlab animation

Real GDP Growth in the World Economy

Figure 22.3 shows real GDP per person in Canada and in other countries between 1960 and 2008. Part (a) looks at the seven richest countries—known as the G7 nations. Among these nations, the United States has the highest real GDP per person. In 2008, Canada had the second-highest real GDP per person, ahead of Japan and France, Germany, Italy, and the United Kingdom (collectively the Europe Big 4).

During the 48 years shown here, the gaps between the United States, Canada, and the Europe Big 4 have been almost constant. But starting from a long way below, Japan grew fastest. It caught up to Europe in 1982 and to Canada in 1990. But during the 1990s, Japan's economy stagnated.

Many other countries are growing more slowly than, and falling farther behind, Canada. Figure 22.3(b) looks at some of these countries.

Real GDP per person in Central and South America was 34 percent of the Canadian level in 1960. It grew more quickly than Canada and reached 36 percent of the Canadian level by 1970. Growth slowed through 2004, then increased and by 2008, real GDP per person in these countries was 40 percent of the Canadian level.

In Central and Eastern Europe, real GDP per person has grown more slowly than anywhere except Africa, and has fallen from 32 percent of the Canadian level in 1980 to 26 percent in 2008.

Real GDP per person in Africa, the world's poorest continent, has fallen from 11 percent of the Canadian level in 1960 to 6 percent in 2008.

FIGURE 22.3 Economic Growth Around the World

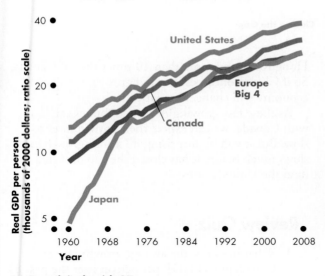

(a) Growth in the rich G7

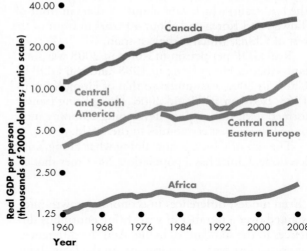

(b) Persistent gaps between rich and poor

Real GDP per person has grown throughout the world. Among the rich industrial countries in part (a), real GDP per person has grown slightly faster in the United States than in Canada and the four big countries of Europe (France, Germany, Italy, and the United Kingdom). Japan had the fastest growth rate before 1973 but then growth slowed and Japan's economy stagnated during the 1990s.

Part (b) shows real GDP per person in a wider range of countries. Central and South America was growing more quickly than Canada during the 1960s but slumped during the early 2000s before increasing again. Growth in Central and Eastern Europe and in Africa has been slower than in Canada, so the gaps between the real GDP per person in Canada and these countries have widened.

Sources of data: (1960–2004) Alan Heston, Robert Summers, and Bettina Aten, Penn World Table Version 6.2, Center for International Comparisons at the University of Pennsylvania (CICUP), September 2006; and (2005–2008) International Monetary Fund, *World Economic Outlook*, April 2008.

myeconlab animation

Catch-Up in Asia

Fast Trains on the Same Track

Five Asian economies, Hong Kong, Korea, Singapore, Taiwan, and China have experienced spectacular growth, which you can see in the figure. During the 1960s, real GDP per person in these economies ranged from 2.6 to 25 percent of that in Canada. But by 1993, real GDP per person in Singapore surpassed that of Canada. By 2005, real GDP per person in Hong Kong had overtaken that of Canada, and Taiwan and Korea were only a short distance behind.

The figure also shows that China is catching up but from a long way behind. China's real GDP per person increased from 2.6 percent of the Canadian level in 1960 to 15 percent in 2008.

The Asian economies shown here are like fast trains running on the same track at similar speeds and with a roughly constant gap between them. Singapore and Hong Kong are hooked together as the lead train, which runs about 15 years in front of Taiwan and Korea and about 40 years in front of the rest of China, which is the last train.

Real GDP per person in Korea in 2008 was similar to that in Hong Kong in 1988, and real GDP in China in 2008 was similar to that of Hong Kong in 1968. Between 1968 and 2008, Hong Kong transformed itself from a poor developing economy into one of the richest economies in the world.

The rest of China is now doing what Hong Kong has done. China has a population 200 times that of

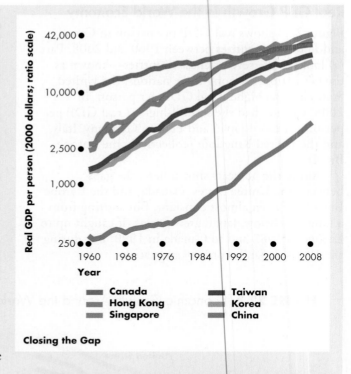

Closing the Gap

Hong Kong and more than 40 times that of Canada. So if China continues its rapid growth, the world economy will change dramatically.

As these fast-growing Asian economies catch up with Canada, we can expect their growth rates to slow. But it will be surprising if China's growth rate slows much before it has closed the gap on Canada (and the United States).

Even modest differences in economic growth rates sustained over a number of years bring enormous differences in the standard of living. And the differences that you've just seen are enormous. So the facts about economic growth in Canada and around the world raise some big questions.

What are the preconditions for economic growth? What sustains economic growth once it gets going? How can we identify the sources of economic growth and measure the contribution that each source makes? What can we do to increase the sustainable rate of economic growth?

We're now going to address these questions and discover the causes of economic growth. We start by seeing how potential GDP is determined and what makes it grow. We'll discover that labour productivity growth is the key to a rising living standard and go on to explore the sources of this growth.

Review Quiz

1 What has been the average growth rate of Canadian real GDP per person over the past 81 years? In which periods was growth the most rapid and in which periods was it the slowest?

2 Describe the gaps between real GDP per person across countries. For which countries is the gap narrowing? For which is it widening? And for which is it remaining the same?

3 Compare the growth rates and levels of real GDP per person in Hong Kong, Korea, Singapore, Taiwan, China, and Canada. How far is China's real GDP per person behind that of the other Asian economies?

 Work Study Plan 22.2 and get instant feedback.

How Potential GDP Grows

Economic growth occurs when real GDP increases. But a one-shot rise in real GDP or a recovery from recession isn't economic growth. Economic growth is a sustained, year-after-year increase in *potential GDP*.

We'll begin our study of the process of economic growth by looking at potential GDP. We'll see how it is determined and what forces make it grow.

How Potential GDP Is Determined

Labour, capital, land, and entrepreneurship produce real GDP, and the productivity of the factors of production determines the quantity of real GDP that can be produced.

The quantity of land is fixed and on any given day, the quantities of entrepreneurial ability and capital are also fixed and their productivities are given. The quantity of labour employed is the only *variable* factor of production. Potential GDP is the level of real GDP when the quantity of labour employed is the full-employment quantity.

To determine potential GDP, we use a model with two components:

- The aggregate production function
- The aggregate labour market

The Aggregate Production Function When you studied the limits to production in Chapter 2 (see p. 32), you learned that the *production possibilities frontier* is the boundary between the combinations of goods and services that can be produced and those that cannot. Let's think about the production possibilities frontier for two "goods": real GDP and the quantity of leisure time.

Think of real GDP as a number of big shopping carts. Each cart contains some of each kind of different goods and services produced, and one cartload of items costs $1 billion. To say that real GDP is $1,200 billion means that you can think of real GDP as 1,200 very big shopping carts of goods and services.

The quantity of leisure time is the number of hours spent not working. Each leisure hour could have been spent working. If we spent all our time taking leisure, we would do no work and produce nothing. Real GDP would be zero. The more leisure we forgo, the greater is the quantity of labour and the greater is the quantity of real GDP produced.

But labour hours are not all equally productive. We use our most productive hours first and as more hours are worked less and less productive hours are used. So for each additional hour of leisure forgone (each additional hour of labour), real GDP increases but by successively smaller amounts.

The **aggregate production function** is the relationship that tell us how real GDP changes as the quantity of labour changes when all other influences on production remain the same. Figure 22.4 shows this relationship—the curve labelled *PF*. An increase in the quantity of labour (and a corresponding decrease in leisure hours) brings a movement along the production function and an increase in real GDP.

The Aggregate Labour Market The aggregate labour market determines the quantity of labour hours employed and the quantity of real GDP supplied. To see how the labour market works, we need to study the demand for labour, the supply of labour, and labour market equilibrium.

The Demand for Labour The demand for labour is the relationship between the quantity of labour demanded and the real wage rate. The quantity of labour demanded is the number of labour hours hired by all the firms in the economy during a given period. This

FIGURE 22.4   The Aggregate Production Function

At point A on the aggregate production function PF, 20 billion hours of labour produce $1,200 billion of real GDP.

quantity depends on the price of labour, which is the real wage rate.

The **real wage rate** is the money (or nominal) wage rate divided by the price level. The *real wage rate* is the quantity of goods and services that an hour of labour earns. It contrasts with the money wage rate, which is the number of dollars that an hour of labour earns.

The *real* wage rate influences the quantity of labour demanded because what matters to firms is not the number of dollars they pay (money wage rate) but how much output they must sell to earn those dollars.

The quantity of labour demanded *increases* as the real wage rate *decreases*—the demand for labour curve slopes downward. Why? The answer lies in the shape of the production function.

You've seen that along the production function, each additional hour of labour increases real GDP by successively smaller amounts. This tendency has a name: the *law of diminishing returns.* Because of diminishing returns, firms will hire more labour only if the real wage rate falls to match the fall in the extra output produced by that labour.

The Supply of Labour The *supply of labour* is the relationship between the quantity of labour supplied and the real wage rate. The quantity of labour supplied is the number of labour hours that all the households in the economy plan to work during a given period. This quantity depends on the real wage rate.

The *real* wage rate influences the quantity of labour supplied because what matters to households is not the number of dollars they earn (money wage rate) but what they can buy with those dollars.

The quantity of labour supplied *increases* as the real wage rate *increases*—the supply of labour curve slopes upward. At a higher real wage rate, more people choose to work and more people choose to work longer hours if they can earn more per hour.

Labour Market Equilibrium The price of labour is the real wage rate. The forces of supply and demand operate in labour markets just as they do in the markets for goods and services to eliminate a shortage or a surplus. But a shortage or a surplus of labour brings only a gradual change in the real wage rate. If there is a shortage of labour, the real wage rate rises to eliminate it; and if there is a surplus of labour, the real wage rate eventually falls to eliminate it. When there is neither a shortage nor a surplus, the labour market is in equilibrium—a full-employment equilibrium.

FIGURE 22.5 Labour Market Equilibrium

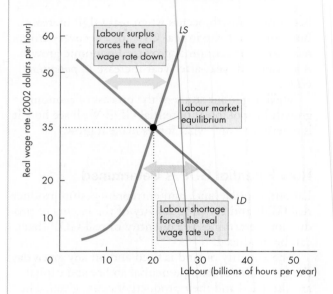

Labour market equilibrium occurs when the quantity of labour demanded equals the quantity of labour supplied. The equilibrium real wage rate is $35 an hour, and equilibrium employment is 20 billion hours per year.

At a wage rate above $35 an hour, there is a surplus of labour and the real wage rate falls to eliminate the surplus. At a wage rate below $35 an hour, there is a shortage of labour and the real wage rate rises to eliminate the shortage.

Figure 22.5 illustrates labour market equilibrium. The demand for labour curve is *LD* and the supply of labour curve *LS*. This labour market is in equilibrium at a real wage rate of $35 an hour and 20 billion hours a year are employed.

If the real wage rate exceeds $35 an hour, the quantity of labour supplied exceeds the quantity demanded and there is a surplus of labour. When there is a surplus of labour, the real wage rate falls towards the equilibrium real wage rate where the surplus is eliminated.

If the real wage rate is less than $35 an hour, the quantity of labour demanded exceeds the quantity supplied and there is a shortage of labour. When there is a shortage of labour, the real wage rate rises towards the equilibrium real wage rate where the shortage is eliminated.

If the real wage rate is $35 an hour, the quantity of labour demanded equals the quantity supplied and there is neither a shortage nor a surplus of labour. In this situation, there is no pressure in either direction on the real wage rate. So the real wage rate remains constant and the market is in equilibrium. At this equilibrium real wage rate and level of employment, the economy is at *full employment*.

Potential GDP You've seen that the production function tells us the quantity of real GDP that a given amount of labour can produce—see Fig. 22.4. The quantity of real GDP produced increases as the quantity of labour increases. At the equilibrium quantity of labour, the economy is at full employment, and the quantity of real GDP at full employment is potential GDP. So the full-employment quantity of labour produces potential GDP.

Figure 22.6 illustrates the determination of potential GDP. Part (a) shows labour market equilibrium. At the equilibrium real wage rate, equilibrium employment is 20 billion hours. Part(b) shows the production function. With 20 billion hours of labour, the economy can produce a real GDP of $1,200 billion. The amount is potential GDP.

What Makes Potential GDP Grow?

We can divide all the forces that make potential GDP grow into two categories:

- Growth of the supply of labour
- Growth of labour productivity

Growth of the Supply of Labour When the supply of labour grows, the supply of labour curve shifts rightward. The quantity of labour at a given real wage rate increases.

The quantity of labour is the number of workers employed multiplied by average hours per worker; and the number employed equals the employment-to-population ratio multiplied by the working-age population (see Chapter 21, p. 492). So the quantity of labour changes as a result of changes in

1. Average hours per worker
2. The employment-to-population ratio
3. The working-age population

Average hours per worker have decreased as the workweek has become shorter and the employment-to-population ratio has increased as more women have entered the labour force. The combined effects

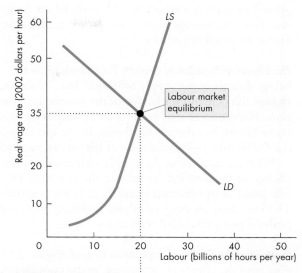

FIGURE 22.6 The Labour Market and Potential GDP

(a) The labour market

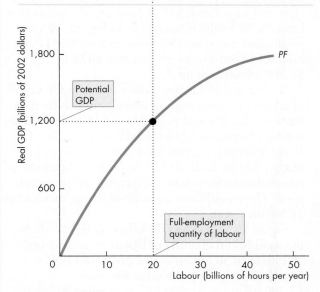

(b) Potential GDP

The economy is at full employment when the quantity of labour demanded equals the quantity of labour supplied, in part (a). The real wage rate is $35 an hour, and employment is 20 billion hours a year. Part (b) shows potential GDP. It is the quantity of real GDP determined by the production function at the full-employment quantity of labour.

myeconlab animation

of these two factors have kept average hours per working-age person (approximately) constant.

Growth in the supply of labour has come from growth in the working-age population. In the long run, the working-age population grows at the same rate as the total population.

The Effects of Population Growth Population growth brings growth in the supply of labour, but it does not change the demand for labour or the production function. The economy can produce more output by using more labour, but there is no change in the quantity of real GDP that a given quantity of labour can produce.

With an increase in the supply of labour and no change in the demand for labour, the real wage rate falls and the equilibrium quantity of labour increases. The increased quantity of labour produces more output and potential GDP increases.

Illustrating the Effects of Population Growth Figure 22.7 illustrates the effects of an increase in the population. In Fig. 22.7(a), the demand for labour curve is *LD* and initially the supply of labour curve is *LS*$_0$. The equilibrium real wage rate is $35 an hour and the quantity of labour is 20 billion hours a year. In Fig. 22.7(b), the production function (*PF*) shows that with 20 billion hours of labour employed, potential GDP is $1,200 billion at point *A*.

An increase in the population increases the supply of labour and the supply of labour curve shifts rightward to *LS*$_1$. At a real wage rate of $35 an hour, there is now a surplus of labour. So the real wage rate falls. In this example, the real wage rate will fall until it reaches $25 an hour. At $25 an hour, the quantity of labour demanded equals the quantity of labour supplied. The equilibrium quantity of labour increases to 30 billion a year.

Figure 22.7(b) shows the effect on real GDP. As the equilibrium quantity of labour increases from 20 billion to 30 billion hours, potential GDP increases along the production function from $1,200 billion to $1,500 billion at point *B*.

So an increase in the population increases the full-employment quantity of labour, increases potential GDP, and lowers the real wage rate. But the population increase *decreases* potential GDP per hour of labour. Initially, it was $60 ($1,200 billion divided by 20 billion). With the population increase, potential GDP per hour of labour is $50 ($1,500 billion divided by 30 billion). Diminishing returns are the source of the decrease in potential GDP per hour of labour.

FIGURE 22.7 The Effects of an Increase in Population

(a) The labour market

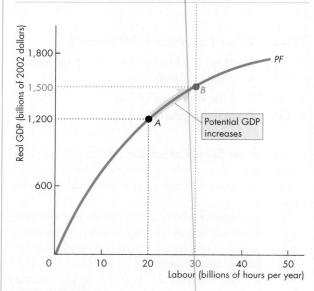

(b) Potential GDP

An increase in the population increases the supply of labour. In part (a), the supply of labour curve shifts rightward. The real wage rate falls and aggregate labour hours increase. In part (b), the increase in aggregate labour hours brings an increase in potential GDP. But diminishing returns bring a decrease in potential GDP per hour of labour.

 animation

Growth of Labour Productivity **Labour productivity** is the quantity of real GDP produced by an hour of labour. It is calculated by dividing real GDP by aggregate labour hours. For example, if real GDP is $1,200 billion and aggregate hours are 20 billion, labour productivity is $60 per hour.

When labour productivity grows, real GDP per person grows and brings a rising standard of living. Let's see how an increase in labour productivity changes potential GDP.

Effects of an Increase in Labour Productivity If labour productivity increases, production possibilities expand. The quantity of real GDP that any given quantity of labour can produce increases. If labour is more productive, firms are willing to pay more for a given number of hours of labour so the demand for labour also increases.

With an increase in the demand for labour and *no change in the supply of labour*, the real wage rate rises and the quantity of labour supplied increases. The equilibrium quantity of labour also increases.

So an increase in labour productivity increases potential GDP for two reasons: Labour is more productive and more labour is employed.

Illustrating the Effects of an Increase in Labour Productivity Figure 22.8 illustrates the effects of an increase in labour productivity.

In part (a), the production function initially is PF_0. With 20 billion hours of labour employed, potential GDP is $1,200 billion at point *A*.

In part (b), the demand for labour curve is LD_0 and the supply of labour curve is *LS*. The real wage rate is $35 an hour, and the equilibrium quantity of labour is 20 billion hours a year.

Now labour productivity increases. In Fig. 22.8(a), the increase in labour productivity shifts the production function upward to PF_1. At each quantity of labour, more real GDP can be produced. For example, at 20 billion hours, the economy can now produce $1,700 billion of real GDP at point *B*.

In Fig. 22.8(b), the increase in labour productivity increases the demand for labour and the demand for labour curve shifts rightward to LD_1. At the initial real wage rate of $35 an hour, there is now a shortage of labour. The real wage rate rises. In this example, the real wage rate will rise until it reaches $45 an hour. At $45 an hour, the quantity of labour demanded equals the quantity of labour supplied and the equilibrium quantity of labour is 22.5 billion a year.

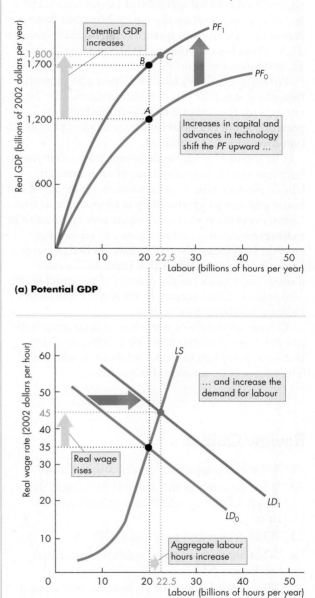

FIGURE 22.8 The Effects of an Increase in Labour Productivity

(a) Potential GDP

(b) The labour market

An increase in labour productivity shifts the production function upward from PF_0 to PF_1 in part (a) and shifts the demand for labour curve rightward from LD_0 to LD_1 in part (b). The real wage rate rises to $45 an hour, and aggregate labour hours increase to 22.5 billion. Potential GDP increases from $1,200 billion to $1,800 billion.

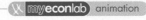

myeconlab animation

Figure 22.8(a) shows the effects of the increase in labour productivity on potential GDP. There are two effects. At the initial quantity of labour, real GDP increases to point *B* on the new production function. But as the equilibrium quantity of labour increases to 22.5 billion hours, potential GDP increases to $1,800 billion at point *C*.

Potential GDP per hour of labour also increases. Initially, it was $60 ($1,200 billion divided by 20 billion). With the increase in labour productivity, potential GDP per hour of labour is $80 ($1,800 billion divided by 22.5 billion).

The increase in aggregate labour hours that you have just seen is a consequence of an increase in labour productivity. This increase in aggregate labour hours and labour productivity is an example of the interaction effects that economists seek to identify in their search for the ultimate *causes* of economic growth. In the case that we've just studied, aggregate labour hours increase but that increase is a *consequence*, not a cause, of the growth of potential GDP. The source of the increase in potential GDP is an increase in labour productivity.

Labour productivity is the key to increasing output per hour of labour and rising living standards. But what brings an increase in labour productivity? The next section answers this question.

Review Quiz

1 What is the aggregate production function?
2 What determines the demand for labour, the supply of labour, and labour market equilibrium?
3 What determines potential GDP?
4 What are the two broad sources of potential GDP growth?
5 What are the effects of an increase in the population on potential GDP, the quantity of labour, the real wage rate, and potential GDP per hour of labour?
6 What are the effects of an increase in labour productivity on potential GDP, the quantity of labour, the real wage rate, and potential GDP per hour of labour?

 Work Study Plan 22.3 and get instant feedback.

Why Labour Productivity Grows

You've seen that labour productivity growth makes potential GDP grow; and you've seen that labour productivity growth is essential if real GDP per person and the standard of living are to grow. But *why* does labour productivity grow? What are the preconditions that make labour productivity growth possible and what are the forces that make it grow? Why does labour productivity grow faster at some times and in some places than others?

Preconditions for Labour Productivity Growth

The fundamental precondition for labour productivity growth is the *incentive* system created by firms, markets, property rights, and money. These four social institutions are the same as those described in Chapter 2 (see pp. 43–44) that enable people to gain by specializing and trading.

It was the presence of secure property rights in Britain in the middle 1700s that got the Industrial Revolution going, and it is their absence in some parts of Africa today that is keeping labour productivity stagnant.

With the preconditions for labour productivity growth in place, three things influence its pace:

- Physical capital growth
- Human capital growth
- Technological advances

Physical Capital Growth

As the amount of capital per worker increases, labour productivity also increases. Production processes that use hand tools can create beautiful objects, but production methods that use large amounts of capital per worker are much more productive. The accumulation of capital on farms, in textile factories, in iron foundries and steel mills, in coal mines, on building sites, in chemical plants, in auto plants, in banks and insurance companies, and in shopping malls has added incredibly to labour productivity of our economy. The next time you see a movie that is set in the Old West or colonial times, look carefully at the small amount of capital around. Try to imagine how productive you would be in such circumstances compared with your productivity today.

Human Capital Growth

Human capital—the accumulated skill and knowl-edge of human beings—is the most fundamental source of labour productivity growth. Human capi-tal grows when a new discovery is made and it grows when more and more people learn how to use past discoveries.

The development of one of the most basic human skills—writing—was the source of some of the earliest major gains in productivity. The ability to keep written records made it possible to reap ever-larger gains from specialization and trade. Imagine how hard it would be to do any kind of business if all the accounts, invoices, and agreements existed only in people's memories.

Later, the development of mathematics laid the foundation for the eventual extension of knowledge about physical forces and chemical and biological processes. This base of scientific knowledge was the foundation for the technological advances of the Industrial Revolution and of today's information revolution.

But a lot of human capital that is extremely pro-ductive is much more humble. It takes the form of millions of individuals learning and becoming remarkably more productive by repetitively doing simple production tasks. One much studied example of this type of human capital growth occurred in World War II. With no change in physical capital, thousands of workers and managers in U.S. shipyards learned from experience and accumulated human capital that more than doubled their productivity in less than two years.

Technological Advances

The accumulation of physical capital and human capital have made a large contribution to labour productivity growth. But technological change—the discovery and the application of new technologies—has made an even greater contribution.

Labour is many times more productive today than it was a hundred years ago but not because we have more steam engines and more horse-drawn carriages per person. Rather, it is because we have transporta-tion equipment that uses technologies that were unknown a hundred years ago and that are more pro-ductive than the old technologies were.

Technological advance arises from formal research and development programs and from informal trial and error, and it involves discovering new ways of getting more out of our resources.

To reap the benefits of technological change, capi-tal must increase. Some of the most powerful and far-reaching fundamental technologies are embodied in human capital—for example, language, writing, and mathematics. But most technologies are embodied in physical capital. For example, to reap the benefits of the internal combustion engine, millions of horse-drawn carriages had to be replaced with automobiles; and to reap the benefits of digital music, millions of Discmans had to be replaced by iPods.

Figure 22.9 summarizes the sources of labour pro-ductivity growth and more broadly of real GDP growth. The figure also emphasizes that for real GDP per person to grow, real GDP growth must exceed the population growth rate.

FIGURE 22.9 The Sources of Economic Growth

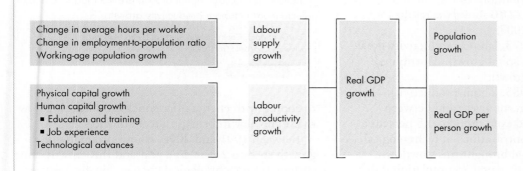

Change in average hours per worker
Change in employment-to-population ratio
Working-age population growth
— Labour supply growth

Physical capital growth
Human capital growth
■ Education and training
■ Job experience
Technological advances
— Labour productivity growth

Real GDP growth

Population growth

Real GDP per person growth

Labour supply growth and labour productivity growth combine to determine real GDP growth. Real GDP per person growth depends on real GDP growth and population growth.

myeconlab animation

Growth Accounting

The accumulation of physical capital and human capital and the discovery of new technologies bring increased labour productivity. But how much does each source of labour productivity growth contribute? Edward F. Denison, an economist at the Brookings Institution, provided the answer by developing **growth accounting**, a tool that calculates the quantitative contribution to labour productivity growth of each of its sources.

To make these calculations, we use information about the Canadian production function.

The Canadian Production Function   Using data on capital, labour hours, and real GDP in Canada, economists at the Centre for the Study of Living Standards (CSLS) in Ottawa has estimated the effect of capital on labour productivity. They have discovered that on average, with no change in technology, a 1 percent increase in capital per hour of labour brings a 0.49 percent increase in labour productivity. We can use this rule to calculate the contributions of capital growth and technological change to the growth of labour productivity.

Suppose that capital per hour of labour grows by 3 percent a year and labour productivity grows by 2.5 percent a year. The 0.49 percent rule tells us that capital growth contributed 0.49 of 3 percent, which is 1.47 percent, to the growth of labour productivity. The rest of the 2.5 percent growth of labour productivity comes from technological change. That is, technological change contributed 1.03 percent, which is the 2.5 percent growth of labour productivity minus the estimated 1.47 percent contribution of capital growth.

Accounting for the Productivity Growth Slowdown and Speedup   We can use Canada's production function to measure the contributions to Canadian productivity growth. Figure 22.10 shows the results for the years 1961 through 2007.

Between 1961 and 1973, labour productivity grew by 3 percent a year and capital growth contributed about one-third of this growth.

Between 1973 and 1985, labour productivity growth slowed to 1.5 percent a year and between 1985 and 1991, it slowed even more to 0.5 percent a year. A collapse of the contributions of technological change and human capital brought this slowdown. Technological change and capital accumulation didn't stop during the productivity growth slowdown, but its focus changed from increasing labour productivity

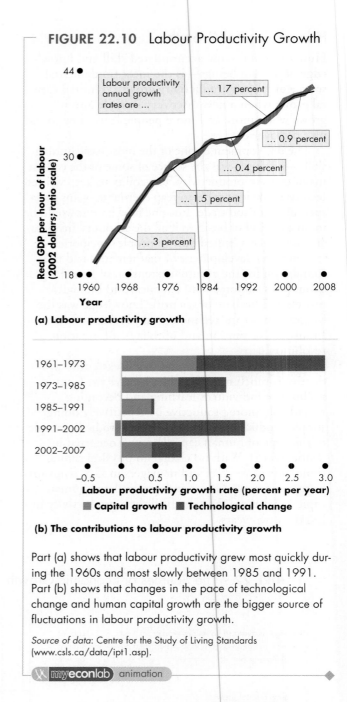

FIGURE 22.10 Labour Productivity Growth

(a) Labour productivity growth

(b) The contributions to labour productivity growth

Part (a) shows that labour productivity grew most quickly during the 1960s and most slowly between 1985 and 1991. Part (b) shows that changes in the pace of technological change and human capital growth are the bigger source of fluctuations in labour productivity growth.

Source of data: Centre for the Study of Living Standards (www.csls.ca/data/ipt1.asp).

myeconlab   animation

to coping with energy price shocks and learning how to use the new information technologies.

Between 1991 and 2002, labour productivity growth sped to 2 percent a year and this growth came entirely from technological change. Finally, between 2002 and 2007, labour productivity growth slowed again.

Accounting for Faster Growth in Asia You saw earlier in this chapter that some Asian economies are growing at much faster rates than Canada and other rich economies. Growth accounting can be used to quantify the sources of this more rapid growth. We don't have enough data to replicate the calculations that we have made for Canada, but we can use the general idea to see why these economies grow so fast.

The fast-growing Asian economies are starting from a long way behind Canada. In many industries in these economies, the technologies in use are not the latest and most productive. As a result, just by adopting more productive technologies that have already been developed elsewhere, these economies can grow faster than the rich economies.

In some cases, a developing economy can leapfrog over technologies still in use in developed economies. Telecommunication is a striking example. Developing economies are bypassing old technology land lines and installing cell phone networks.

To benefit from new technologies, developing economies must invest in new capital. The scale of investment influences how fast the new technologies spread. Table 22.1 shows some numbers. Most of the fast-growing Asian economies invest a larger percentage of their incomes in new capital than Canada invests. Because they invest such a large percentage of income, capital per hour of labour increases more rapidly, and so does labour productivity.

TABLE 22.1 Investment in Seven Economies

Economy	Investment (percentage of GDP)
China	28
Hong Kong	26
Korea	36
Singapore	44
Taiwan	19
Canada	25
United States	21

Source of data: (1960–2004) Alan Heston, Robert Summers, and Bettina Aten, Penn World Table Version 6.2, Center for International Comparisons at the University of Pennsylvania (CICUP), September 2006.

Microloans Boost Growth

Women Are the Better Borrowers

Microloans are very small loans made to poor and unemployed potential entrepreneurs, who are often women. These people have no credit history that enables them to borrow from a bank.

Microloans originated in Bangladesh but have now spread throughout the developing world. They have become so successful that some regular banks are beginning to get into the business. These loans enable poor people to start a small business, employ a few people, and start to earn an income. As their incomes grow, they can pay off their microloans, and begin to save and accumulate more capital.

Kiva.org and MicroPlace.com (owned by eBay) are Web sites that enable people to lend money that is used to make microloans in developing economies.

Throughout the developing world, microloans are helping women to feed and cloth their families and to grow their small businesses, often in agriculture.

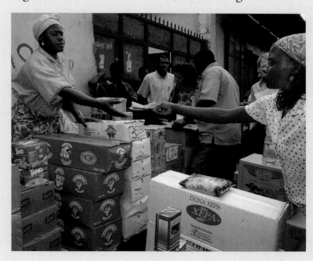

Review Quiz

1 What are the preconditions for and sources of labour productivity growth?
2 What is growth accounting and how is it used?
3 What brought about the slower labour productivity growth between 1973 and 1991?

 Work Study Plan 22.4 and get instant feedback

Canadian Economic Growth Since 1987

Productivity and Population Growth

We're going to look at the process that made Canadian real GDP grow between 1987 and 2007.

In 1987, employment was 29 billion labour hours, the real wage rate was $16.50 an hour, and real GDP and potential GDP were $933 billion. (We are measuring in 2002 dollars.)

By 2007, labour hours had increased to 32 billion, the real wage rate had risen to $21 an hour, and real GDP and potential GDP had increased to $1,320 billion (in 2002 dollars).

You can use the model that you've just studied to understand the process of growth that increased employment, the real wage rate, and potential GDP.

First, advances in technology and the investment in capital that brought us the Internet, the cell phone, MP3 audio, and MP4 video also brought us robots in factories and warehouses and more productive equipment in offices, shops, farms, and mines. As a result, labour productivity increased. The Centre for the Study of Living Standards estimates that the increase in labour productivity was 23 percent. These same advances in technology and growth of capital increased the demand for labour.

Second, the population grew. In 1987, the working-age population was 20.3 million. By 2007, that number was 26.6 million—a 31 percent increase. This increase in the working-age population increased the supply of labour.

Although the percentage increase in labour productivity was smaller than the percentage increase in population, labour demand is more responsive to the real wage rate than labour supply and the combined effects of these changes increased employment and potential GDP and raised the real wage rate.

The figures illustrate these outcomes. Figure 1 shows the Canadian production function in 1987 as PF_{1987}. Figure 2 shows the demand for labour in 1987 as LD_{1987} and the supply of labour as LS_{1987}. In 1987, the equilibrium real wage rate was $16.50 an hour, and 29 billion hours of labour were employed. On the production function PF_{1987}, this equilibrium quantity of labour produced a potential GDP of $933 billion.

By 2007, advances in technology and capital accumulation had increased labour productivity, which shifted the production function upward to PF_{2007} and shifted the demand for labour curve to LD_{2007}. The increase in the working-age population had increased

the supply of labour and shifted the supply of labour curve to LS_{2007}.

At the 2007 full-employment equilibrium, the real wage rate had increased to $21 an hour, employment had increased to 32 billion hours, and potential GDP had increased to $1,320 billion.

The process described here is the source of rising living standards in Canada.

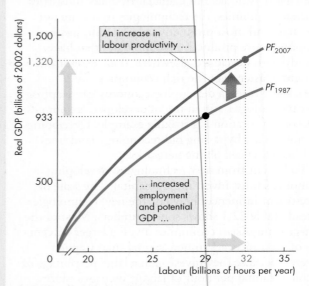

Figure 1 Canadian Production Function

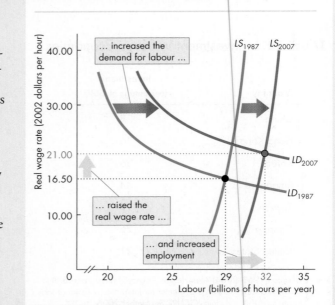

Figure 2 Canadian Labour Market

Growth Theories and Policies

You've seen how population growth and labour productivity growth make potential GDP grow. You've also seen that the growth of physical capital and human capital and technological advances make labour productivity grow. How do all these factors interact? Growth theory addresses this question.

You're going to study three theories of economic growth, each of which gives some insights into the process of economic growth. But none provides a complete and definite answer to the basic questions: What causes economic growth and why do growth rates vary? Economics has some way to go before it can provide a definite answer to these questions. We study the three theories of growth:

- Classical growth theory
- Neoclassical growth theory
- New growth theory

Classical Growth Theory

Classical growth theory is the view that the growth of real GDP per person is temporary and that when it rises above the subsistence level, a population explosion eventually brings it back to the subsistence level. Adam Smith, Thomas Robert Malthus, and David Ricardo—the leading economists of the late eighteenth century and early nineteenth century—proposed this theory, but the view is most closely associated with the name of Malthus and is sometimes called the *Malthusian theory*.

Modern-Day Malthusians Many people today are Malthusians. They say that if today's global population of 6.7 billion explodes to 11 billion by 2050 and perhaps to 35 billion by 2300, we will run out of resources, real GDP per person will decline, and we will return to a primitive standard of living. We must act, say the Malthusians, to contain the population growth.

Modern-day Malthusians also point to global warming and climate change as reasons to believe that eventually, real GDP per person will decrease. Doomsday conditions, they believe, will arise as a direct consequence of today's economic growth and the vast and growing amounts of activity that are increasing the amount of carbon dioxide in Earth's atmosphere.

Classical Theory of Population Growth When the classical economists were developing their ideas about population growth, an unprecedented population explosion was under way. In Britain and other Western European countries, improvements in diet and hygiene had lowered the death rate while the birth rate remained high. For several decades, population growth was extremely rapid. After being stable for several centuries, the population of Britain increased by 40 percent between 1750 and 1800 and by a further 50 percent between 1800 and 1830. Meanwhile, an estimated 1 million people (about 20 percent of the 1750 population) left Britain for America and Australia before 1800, and outward migration continued on a similar scale through the nineteenth century. These facts are the empirical basis for the classical theory of population growth.

To explain the high rate of population growth, the classical economists used the idea of a **subsistence real wage rate**, which is the minimum real wage rate needed to maintain life. If the actual real wage rate is less than the subsistence real wage rate, some people cannot survive and the population decreases. In classical theory, when the real wage rate exceeds the subsistence real wage rate, the population grows. But an increasing population brings diminishing returns to labour, so labour productivity eventually decreases. This dismal implication led to economics being called the *dismal science*. The dismal implication is that no matter how much technological change occurs, the real wage rate is always pushed back towards the subsistence level.

The dismal conclusion of classical growth theory is a direct consequence of the assumption that the population explodes if real GDP per hour of labour exceeds the subsistence real wage rate. To avoid this conclusion, we need a different view of population growth. Neoclassical growth theory provides a different view.

Neoclassical Growth Theory

Neoclassical growth theory is the proposition that real GDP per person grows because technological change induces an amount of saving and investment that makes capital per hour of labour grow. Growth ends only if technological change stops. Robert Solow of MIT suggested the most popular version of neoclassical growth theory in the 1950s.

Neoclassical growth theory's break with its classical predecessor is its view about population growth.

The Neoclassical Economics of Population Growth

The population explosion of eighteenth century Europe that created the classical theory of population eventually ended. The birth rate fell, and while the population continued to increase, its rate of increase became moderate. This slowdown in population growth seemed to make the classical theory less relevant. It also eventually led to the development of a modern economic theory of population growth.

The modern view is that although the population growth rate is influenced by economic factors, the influence is not a simple and mechanical one like that proposed by the classical economists. Key among the economic influences on population growth is the opportunity cost of a woman's time. As women's wage rates increase and their job opportunities expand, the opportunity cost of having children increases. Faced with a higher opportunity cost, families choose to have fewer children and the birth rate falls.

A second economic influence works on the death rate. The technological advance that brings increased labour productivity and increased incomes brings advances in health care that extend lives.

These two opposing economic forces influence the population growth rate. As incomes increase, both the birth rate and the death rate decrease. It turns out that these opposing forces almost offset each other, so the rate of population growth is independent of the economic growth rate.

This modern view of population growth and the historical trends that support it contradict the views of the classical economists. They also call into question the modern doomsday conclusion that the planet will one day be swamped with more people than it can support. Neoclassical growth theory adopts this modern view of population growth. Forces other than real GDP and its growth rate determine population growth.

Technological Change

In neoclassical growth theory, the pace of technological change influences the economic growth rate but economic growth does not influence the pace of technological change. It is assumed that technological change results from chance. When we're lucky, we have rapid technological change, and when bad luck strikes, the pace of technological advance slows.

The Basic Neoclassical Idea

To understand neoclassical growth theory, imagine the world of the mid-1950s, when Robert Solow is explaining his idea.

Americans are enjoying post–World War II prosperity. Income per person is around $12,000 a year in today's money. The population is growing at about 1 percent a year. Saving and investment are about 18 percent of GDP, enough to keep the quantity of capital per hour of labour constant. Income per person is growing but not by much.

Then technology begins to advance at a more rapid pace across a range of activities. The transistor revolutionizes an emerging electronics industry. New plastics revolutionize the manufacture of household appliances. The interstate highway system revolutionizes road transportation. Jet airliners start to replace piston-engine airplanes and speed air transportation.

These technological advances bring new profit opportunities. Businesses expand, and new businesses are created to exploit the newly available profitable technologies. Investment and saving increase. The economy enjoys new levels of prosperity and growth. But will the prosperity last? And will the growth last? Neoclassical growth theory says that the *prosperity* will last but the *growth* will not last unless technology keeps advancing.

According to neoclassical growth theory, the prosperity will persist because there is no classical population growth to induce the wage rate to fall.

But growth will eventually stop if technology stops advancing, for two related reasons. First, the high profit rates that result from technological change bring increased saving and capital accumulation. But second, as more capital is accumulated, more and more projects are undertaken that have lower rates of return. The return on capital falls and the incentive to keep investing weakens. With weaker incentives to save and invest, saving decreases and the rate of capital accumulation slows.

A Problem with Neoclassical Growth Theory

All economies have access to the same technologies, and capital is free to roam the globe, seeking the highest available real interest rate. Given these facts, neoclassical growth theory implies that growth rates and income levels per person around the world will converge. While there is some sign of convergence among the rich countries, as Fig. 22.3(a) shows, convergence is slow, and it does not appear to be imminent for all countries, as Fig. 22.3(b) shows.

New growth theory overcomes this shortcoming of neoclassical growth theory. It also explains what determines the pace of technological change.

New Growth Theory

New growth theory holds that real GDP per person grows because of the choices people make in the pursuit of profit and that growth will persist indefinitely. Paul Romer of Stanford University developed this theory during the 1980s based on the ideas of Joseph Schumpeter during the 1930s and 1940s.

The theory begins with two facts about market economies:

- Discoveries result from choices.
- Discoveries bring profit, and competition destroys profit.

Discoveries and Choices When people discover a new product or technique, they think of themselves as being lucky. They are right. But the pace at which new discoveries are made—and at which technology advances—is not determined by chance. It depends on how many people are looking for a new technology and how intensively they are looking.

Discoveries and Profits Profit is the spur to technological change. The forces of competition squeeze profits, so to increase profit, people constantly seek either lower-cost methods of production or new and better products for which people are willing to pay a higher price. Inventors can maintain a profit for several years by taking out a patent or a copyright, but eventually, a new discovery is copied, and profits disappear.

Two further facts play a key role in the new growth theory:

- Discoveries are a public capital good.
- Knowledge is capital that is not subject to the law of diminishing returns.

Discoveries Are a Public Capital Good Economists call a good a *public good* when no one can be excluded from using it and when one person's use does not prevent others from using it. National defence is one example of a public good. Knowledge is another.

In 1992, Marc Andreesen and his friend Eric Bina developed a browser they called Mosaic. This browser laid the foundation for today's Web browsers that have increased productivity by an unimaginably large amount.

While patents and copyrights protect the inventors or creators of new products and production processes and enable them to profit from their innovative ideas, once a new discovery has been made, everyone can benefit from its use. And one person's use of a new discovery does not prevent others from using it. Your use of a Web browser doesn't prevent someone else from using that same code simultaneously.

Because knowledge is a public good, as the benefits of a new discovery spread, free resources become available. These resources are free because nothing is given up when they are used. They have a zero opportunity cost. Knowledge is even more special because it is not subject to diminishing returns.

Knowledge Capital Is Not Subject to Diminishing Returns Production is subject to diminishing returns when one resource is fixed and the quantity of another resource changes. Adding labour to a fixed amount of capital or adding capital to a fixed amount of labour both bring diminishing marginal product—diminishing returns.

But increasing the stock of knowledge makes both labour and machines more productive. Knowledge capital does not bring diminishing returns.

The fact that knowledge capital does *not* experience diminishing returns is the central novel proposition of new growth theory. And the implication of this simple and appealing idea is astonishing. Unlike the other two theories, new growth theory has no growth-stopping mechanism. As physical capital accumulates, the return to capital—the real interest rate—falls. But the incentive to innovate and earn a higher profit becomes stronger. So innovation occurs, capital becomes more productive, the demand for capital increases, and the real interest rate rises again.

Labour productivity grows indefinitely as people discover new technologies that yield a higher real interest rate. This growth rate depends on people's ability to innovate.

Over the years, the ability to innovate has changed. The invention of language and writing (the two most basic human capital tools) and later the development of the scientific method and the establishment of universities and research institutions brought huge increases in the pace of innovation. Today, a deeper understanding of genes is bringing profit in a growing biotechnology industry. And advances in computer technology are creating an explosion of profit opportunities in a wide range of information-age industries.

A Perpetual Motion Economy New growth theory sees the economy as a perpetual motion machine, which Fig. 22.11 illustrates.

No matter how rich we become, our wants will always exceed our ability to satisfy them. We will always want a higher standard of living. In the pursuit of a higher standard of living, human societies have developed incentive systems—markets, property rights, and money—that enable people to profit from innovation. Innovation leads to the development of new and better techniques of production and new and better products. To take advantage of new techniques and to produce new products, new firms start up and old firms go out of business—firms are born and die. As old firms die and new firms are born, some jobs are destroyed and others are created. The new jobs created are better than the old ones and they pay higher real wage rates. Also, with higher wage rates and more productive techniques, leisure increases. New and better jobs and new and better products lead to more consumption goods and

services and, combined with increased leisure, bring a higher standard of living.

But our insatiable wants are still there, so the process continues, going round and round a circle of wants, incentives, innovation, and new and better products, and a yet higher standard of living.

New Growth Theory Versus Malthusian Theory

The contrast between the Malthusian theory and new growth theory couldn't be more sharp. Malthusians see the end of prosperity as we know it today and new growth theorists see unending plenty. The contrast becomes clearest by thinking about the differing views about population growth.

To a Malthusian, population growth is part of the problem. To a new growth theorist, population growth is part of the solution. People are the ultimate economic resource. A larger population brings forth

FIGURE 22.11 A Perpetual Motion Machine

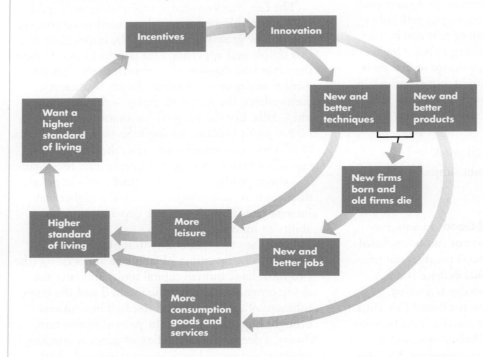

People want a higher standard of living and are spurred by profit incentives to make the innovations that lead to new and better techniques and new and better products. These new and better techniques and products, in turn, lead to the birth of new firms and the death of some old firms, new and better jobs, and more leisure and more consumption goods and services. The result is a higher standard of living. But people want a still higher standard of living, and the growth process continues.

Source: Based on a similar figure in *These Are the Good Old Days: A Report on U.S. Living Standards,* Federal Reserve Bank of Dallas 1993 Annual Report.

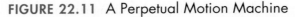 **myeconlab** animation

more wants, but it also brings a greater amount of scientific discovery and technological advance. So rather than being the source of falling real GDP per person, population growth generates faster labour productivity growth and rising real GDP per person. Resources are limited, but the human imagination and ability to increase productivity are unlimited.

Sorting Out the Theories

Which theory is correct? None of them tells us the whole story, but they all teach us something of value.

Classical growth theory reminds us that our physical resources are limited and that without advances in technology, we must eventually hit diminishing returns.

Neoclassical growth theory reaches the same conclusion but not because of a population explosion. Instead, it emphasizes diminishing returns to capital and reminds us that we cannot keep growth going just by accumulating physical capital. We must also advance technology and accumulate human capital. We must become more creative in our use of scarce resources.

New growth theory emphasizes the capacity of human resources to innovate at a pace that offsets diminishing returns. New growth theory fits the facts of today's world more closely than do either of the other two theories. But that doesn't make it correct.

Achieving Faster Growth

Growth theory tells us that to achieve faster economic growth, we must increase the growth rate of physical capital, the pace of technological advance, or the growth rate of human capital.

The main suggestions for achieving these objectives are

- Stimulate saving
- Stimulate research and development
- Encourage international trade
- Improve the quality of education

Stimulate Saving Saving finances investment, which brings capital accumulation. So stimulating saving can increase economic growth. The East Asian economies have the highest growth rates and the highest saving rates. Some African economies have the lowest growth rates and the lowest saving rates.

Tax incentives can increase saving. Registered Retirement Savings Plans (RRSPs) are a tax incentive to save. Economists claim that a tax on consumption rather than income provides the best saving incentive.

Stimulate Research and Development Everyone can use the fruits of *basic* research and development efforts. For example, all biotechnology firms can use advances in gene-splicing technology. Because basic inventions can be copied, the inventor's profit is limited and the market allocates too few resources to this activity.

Governments can direct public funds towards financing basic research, but this solution is not foolproof. It requires a mechanism for allocating the public funds to their highest-valued use. The National Science and Engineering Research Council is one possibly efficient channel for allocating public funds to universities to finance and stimulate basic research.

Encourage International Trade Free international trade stimulates growth by extracting all the available gains from specialization and trade. The fastest-growing nations today are those with the fastest-growing exports and imports.

Improve the Quality of Education The free market produces too little education because it brings benefits beyond those valued by the people who receive the education. By funding basic education and by ensuring high standards in basic skills such as language, mathematics, and science, governments can contribute to a nation's growth potential. Education can also be stimulated and improved by using tax incentives to encourage improved private provision.

Review Quiz

1 What is the key idea of classical growth theory that leads to the dismal outcome?
2 What, according to neoclassical growth theory, is the fundamental cause of economic growth?
3 What is the key proposition of new growth theory that makes economic growth persist?

myeconlab Work Study Plan 22.5 and get instant feedback.

◆ To complete your study of economic growth, take a look at *Reading Between the Lines* on pp. 536–537 to see how economic growth is transforming the economy of China.

Economic Growth in China

China Industrial-Output Growth Is Slowest in 6 Years

September 12, 2008

China's industrial production grew at the slowest pace in six years on weaker export demand and factory shutdowns for the Olympics, increasing the likelihood the government will stimulate the economy.

Output rose 12.8 percent in August from a year earlier, the statistics bureau said today, after gaining 14.7 percent in July. That was less than the 14.5 percent median estimate of 22 economists surveyed by Bloomberg News. ...

China's economic expansion slowed for a fourth quarter to 10.1 percent in the three months through June. Its growth remained the fastest of the world's 20 biggest economies. ...

Power shortages are also restraining output. Aluminum Corp. of China Ltd. and 19 of its peers signed an accord in July to reduce production by as much as 10 percent until the end of the year to ease the shortages. Electricity output growth slowed in August for the fifth straight month to 5.1 percent. ...

Still, the signs aren't all negative. Retail sales grew 23.2 percent last month, close to the fastest pace in nine years, the statistics bureau said today. While export growth slowed, the 21.1 percent increase was more than economists estimated.

Last month's industrial-output growth was the slowest since August 2002 after excluding the distortions in January and February each year caused by China's Lunar New Year holiday.

Essence of the Story

- China's industrial production grew by 12.8 percent in the year to August 2008, its slowest pace since 2002.

- China's real GDP growth slowed to 10.1 percent in the second quarter—the fourth successive quarter of slower growth.

- China's real GDP growth is the fastest of the world's 20 biggest economies.

- Power shortages limited production.

- Retail sales grew 23.2 percent in August 2008, close to the fastest pace in nine years.

- Export growth slowed to 21.1 percent.

Economic Analysis

- In 1978, under the leadership of Deng Xiaoping, China embarked on a program of economic reform.

- Gradually, state-owned monopolies were replaced by private competitive businesses, often financed with foreign capital and operated as joint ventures with foreign firms.

- By the early 1980s, China's real GDP was growing at one of the fastest rates in the world and the fastest ever known. We compare China's growth with that of the largest economy—the United States.

- In 2008, China's real GDP was more than $9 trillion (using U.S. dollars and PPP prices in 2000—see Chapter 20, p. 477).

- U.S. real GDP in 2008 was almost $12 trillion (2000 dollars).

- Although China's real GDP was not far behind U.S. real GDP in 2008, China used much more labour than the United States used.

- Aggregate labour hours in the United States in 2008 were about 250 billion.

- We don't know what China's aggregate labour hours were. But employment was 790 million and with an average workweek of 40 hours (an assumption), aggregate hours would be around 1,650 billion—more than 6 times the U.S. labour hours.

- So real GDP per hour of labour in China in 2008 was around $5 compared to about $48 in the United States.

- But China's real GDP is growing at about 10 percent a year. In contrast, U.S. real GDP is growing at about 2.5 percent a year.

- If these growth rates persist, China's real GDP will surpass that of the United States within the next decade.

- But China's real GDP per hour of labour will continue to lag well behind that of the United States.

- The figure shows the situation in China and the United States in 2008.

- The U.S. production function is PF_{US08}, and China's production function is PF_{C08}.

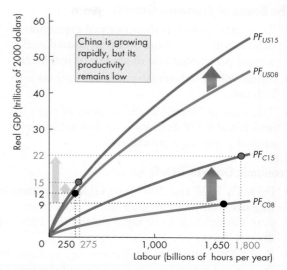

Figure 1 Growth in China and the United States

- With employment of 250 billion hours, the United States produces $12 trillion of real GDP, and with employment of 1,650 billion hours, China produces $9 trillion of real GDP.

- That is, an hour of labour in the United States produces around 10 times as much as an hour of labour in China produces.

- The figure also shows the situation in the United States and China in 2015 if current growth rates persist.

- The U.S. production function will be PF_{US15}, and China's production function will be PF_{C15}.

- With population growth at about 1 percent a year in both countries, labour hours will increase and so will real GDP.

- In 2015, China will be producing a larger real GDP than the United States but real GDP per hour of labour in China will still lag that in the United States.

SUMMARY ◆

Key Points

The Basics of Economic Growth (pp. 516–517)

- Economic growth is the sustained expansion of production possibilities and is measured as the annual percentage rate of change of real GDP.
- Sustained growth transforms poor nations into rich ones.
- The Rule of 70 tells us the number of years in which real GDP doubles—70 divided by the annual percentage growth rate.

Economic Growth Trends (pp. 518–520)

- Between 1926 and 2007, real GDP per person in Canada grew at an average rate of 2.1 percent a year. Growth was most rapid during the 1960s and slowest during the 1980s.
- Real GDP per person has grown slightly faster in the United States than in Canada and the four big countries of Europe.
- The gap in real GDP per person between Canada and Central and South America has narrowed. The gaps between Canada and Africa and Central Europe have widened.

How Potential GDP Grows (pp. 521–526)

- The aggregate production function and equilibrium in the aggregate labour market determine potential GDP.
- Potential GDP grows if the labour supply grows or if labour productivity grows.

- Only labour productivity growth makes real GDP per person and the standard of living grow.

Why Labour Productivity Grows (pp. 526–530)

- Labour productivity growth requires an incentive system created by firms, markets, property rights, and money.
- The sources of labour productivity growth are growth of physical capital and human capital and advances in technology.
- Growth accounting measures the contributions of capital accumulation and technological change to the growth of labour productivity.
- During the productivity growth slowdown of the 1970s, technological change did not stop growing but its focus changed to coping with energy price shocks and environmental protection.

Growth Theories and Policies (pp. 531–535)

- In classical theory, real GDP per person keeps returning to the subsistence level.
- In neoclassical growth theory, without further technological change, diminishing returns to capital bring economic growth to a halt.
- In new growth theory, economic growth persists indefinitely at a rate determined by decisions that lead to innovation and technological change.
- Policies for achieving faster growth include stimulating saving and research and development, encouraging international trade, and improving the quality of education.

Key Figures

Figure 22.1   The Rule of 70, 517
Figure 22.2   Economic Growth in Canada: 1926–2007, 518
Figure 22.3   Economic Growth Around the World, 519
Figure 22.6   The Labour Market and Potential GDP, 523

Figure 22.7   The Effects of an Increase in Population, 524
Figure 22.8   The Effects of an Increase in Labour Productivity, 525
Figure 22.11   A Perpetual Motion Machine, 534

Key Terms

Aggregate production function, 521
Classical growth theory, 531
Economic growth rate, 516
Growth accounting, 528

Labour productivity, 525
Neoclassical growth theory, 531
New growth theory, 533
Real GDP per person, 516

Real wage rate, 522
Rule of 70, 516
Subsistence real wage rate, 531

PROBLEMS and APPLICATIONS

myeconlab   Work problems 1–9 in Chapter 22 Study Plan and get instant feedback.
Work problems 10–18 as Homework, a Quiz, or a Test if assigned by your instructor.

1. Japan's real GDP was 561 trillion yen in 2007 and 569 trillion yen in 2008. Japan's population was 127.7 million in 2007 and 127.8 million in 2008. Calculate

   a. The economic growth rate.
   b. The growth rate of real GDP per person.
   c. The approximate number of years it takes for real GDP per person in Japan to double if the 2008 economic growth rate and population growth rate are maintained.

2. For three years, there was no technological change in Longland but capital per hour of labour increased from $10 to $20 to $30 and real GDP per hour of labour increased from $3.80 to $5.70 to $7.13. Then, in the fourth year, capital per hour of labour remained constant but real GDP per hour of labour increased to $10.

   a. Does Longland experience diminishing returns? Explain why or why not.
   b. In Longland, use growth accounting to calculate the effect on labour productivity of a 1 percent increase in capital.
   c. Explain how you would do the growth accounting for Longland and calculate the effect of technological change on growth in the fourth year described above.

3. If Canada cracks down on illegal immigrants and returns millions of workers to their home countries, explain what happens to

   a. Canadian potential GDP.
   b. Canadian employment.
   c. The real wage rate in Canada.

   In the countries to which the immigrants return, explain what happens to

   d. Potential GDP.
   e. Employment.
   f. The real wage rate.

4. In the economy of Cape Despair, the subsistence real wage rate is $15 an hour. Whenever real GDP per hour rises above $15, the population grows, and whenever real GDP per hour of labour falls below this level, the population falls. The table shows Cape Despair's production function:

Labour (billions of hours per year)	Real GDP (billions of 2002 dollars)
0.5	8
1.0	15
1.5	21
2.0	26
2.5	30
3.0	33
3.5	35

   Initially, the population of Cape Despair is constant and real GDP per hour of labour is at the subsistence level of $15. Then a technological advance shifts the production function upward by 50 percent at each level of labour.

   a. What are the initial levels of real GDP and labour productivity?
   b. What happens to labour productivity immediately following the technological advance?
   c. What happens to the population growth rate following the technological advance?
   d. What are the eventual levels of real GDP and real GDP per hour of labour?

5. Explain the processes that will bring the growth of real GDP per person to a stop according to

   a. Classical growth theory.
   b. Neoclassical growth theory.
   c. New growth theory.

6. **U.S. Workers World's Most Productive**
   American workers stay longer in the office, at the factory, or on the farm than their counterparts in Europe and most other rich nations, and they produce more per person over the year. ... Productivity ... is found by dividing the country's gross domestic product by the number of people employed. ... Only part of the U.S. productivity growth ... can be explained by the longer hours Americans are putting in. ... [The U.S.] also beats all 27 nations in the European Union, Japan, and Switzerland in the amount of wealth created per hour of work. ... The U.S. employee put in an average 1,804 hours of work in 2006 ... compared with 1,407.1 hours for the Norwegian worker and 1,564.4 for the French. It pales,

however, in comparison with the annual hours worked per person in Asia, where seven economies—South Korea, Bangladesh, Sri Lanka, Hong Kong, China, Malaysia and Thailand—surpassed 2,200 average hours per worker. But those countries had lower productivity rates. ...

CBS News, September 3, 2007

a. What is the difference between productivity in this article and per capita real GDP?
b. Identify and correct a confusion between levels and growth rates of productivity in the news article.
c. If workers in developing Asian economies work more hours than Americans, why are they not the world's most productive?

7. **You Have Seven Years to Learn Mandarin**

A recent study by the economist Angus Maddison projects that China will become the world's dominant economic superpower ... in 2015. ... If that happens, America will close out a 125-year run as the No. 1 economy. [The United States] assumed the title in 1890. ... China was the largest economy for centuries because everyone had the same type of economy —subsistence—and so the country with the most people would be economically biggest. Then the Industrial Revolution sent the West on a more prosperous path. Now the world is returning to a common economy, this time technology- and information-based, so once again population triumphs.

Fortune, May 12, 2008

a. Why was China the world's largest economy until 1890?
b. Why did the United States surpass China in 1890 to become the world's largest economy?
c. Explain why China is predicted to become the world's largest economy again.
d. When China becomes the world's largest economy, does that mean that the standard of living in China will be higher than that in the United States? Explain.

8. **Dodge's Successor Too Optimistic About Globalization**

Mark Carney, our new governor of the Bank of Canada, chose to use his first speech to extol the benefits of globalization, as well as to highlight some of the challenges ... "While it is true that

this [globalization] adjustment process can be, and has been, difficult for certain individuals and firms, the overall picture is quite positive," he said, suggesting that Canada, with flexible labour markets, has made it possible for workers to re-skill or retrain and, on balance, "find more productive employment" ... Carney's prescription focuses on promoting "flexibility," especially in labour markets, by helping workers to relocate, maintaining social safety nets that don't discourage employment, and investing in lifelong learning and retraining. But while investing in education and skills for lifelong learning is important, it will take more than this to prepare Canada for the next wave of globalization. Canada urgently needs ... increased public and private investment in research and development, more spending on infrastructure including high-speed broadband, more public-private risk-sharing to commercialize new knowledge and more incentives for entrepreneurial growth companies or gazelles.

Toronto Star, February 24, 2008

a. Explain which growth theory most closely describes the arguments made in this article.
b. Explain the suggestions in this article that can help Canada achieve faster economic growth.

9. **Aptera: Road Runner**

Steve Fambro was sick of people whizzing past him in the carpool lane, so he ... set out to design a three-wheeled vehicle—technically a motorcycle—that would make it legal for him to drive alone in that lane and be cozy enough for daily commuting. While researching designs, he realized something important about fuel efficiency: It's all about aerodynamics. By tearing up the rule book, he found a shape that would nearly eliminate wind resistance, thereby reducing by two thirds the energy needed to move a car. With ... $20 million from Idealab ... Fambro's company, Aptera, is scheduled to begin production later this year. The vehicle gets an average of 300 miles per gallon. ... Priced at around $30,000, Aptera's cars are already sold out.

Fortune, April 28, 2008

a. Explain which growth theory best describes the news article.
b. Use the model explained in this chapter to illustrate your answer in a.

10. If China's real GDP grows at 9 percent a year, its population grows at 1 percent a year, and these growth rates continue, in what year will China's real GDP per person be twice its 2008 level?

11. If a large increase in investment increases labour productivity, explain what will happen to

   a. Potential GDP.
   b. Employment.
   c. The real wage rate.

   If a severe drought decreases labour productivity, explain what will happen to

   d. Potential GDP.
   e. Employment.
   f. The real wage rate.

12. **The New New World Order**

   "If you're a consumer sitting in Paris and you're ... watching TV, it looks like the world is coming to an end," says [international grocery store chain] Carrefour executive David Shriver. "But consumers in places like China and Brazil simply don't see it that way." Welcome to the new, precariously bipolar world. While gross domestic product growth is cooling a bit in emerging markets, the results are still tremendous compared with the U.S. and much of Western Europe. The 54 developing markets surveyed by Global Insight will post a 6.7% jump in real GDP this year, down from 7.5% last year. The 31 developed countries will grow an estimated 1.6%. The difference in growth rates represents the largest spread between developed and developing markets in the 37-year history of the survey.

   Fortune, July 14, 2008

   a. Explain the "bipolar world" that is revealed by recent economic growth rates.
   b. Do growth rates over the past few decades indicate that gaps in per capita real GDP around the world are shrinking, growing, or staying the same? Explain.

13. **Underinvesting in the Future**

   South Korea, Hong Kong, Taiwan, and Singapore have over 40 years averaged roughly the highest consistent economic growth rates in the world. ... But change the national accounting principles behind these rosy numbers and a different picture emerges, one that the societies concerned have barely begun to grapple with. In one vital respect these countries (soon to be joined by China) collectively may have the worst record of

investment in the future since homo sapiens evolved: Investment in the next generation. They have the lowest fertility rates in the world. ... Economists forget that people as well as buildings depreciate at a roughly predictable rate. Child-rearing is at least as essential as building roads. Imagine if these four economies had invested less in infrastructure and ... more in people. ... They would not be facing a situation in which their workforces—unless replaced by immigrants—will decline dramatically within 20 years as the population over 65 continues to grow. The payback for years of what may well have been the misallocation of resources is not far in the future.

International Herald Tribune, July 7, 2008

   a. Explain why the rapid growth rates of these Asian economies might be masking a "misallocation of resources" that will result in lower income per person in the future.
   b. Explain the difficulties in balancing goals for immediate economic growth and future economic growth.

14. **India's Economy Hits the Wall**

   Just six months ago, India was looking good. Annual growth was 9%, corporate profits were surging 20%, the stock market had risen 50% in 2007, consumer demand was huge, local companies were making ambitious international acquisitions, and foreign investment was growing. Nothing, it seemed, could stop the forward march of this Asian nation. But stop it has. ... The country is reeling from 11.4% inflation, large government deficits, and rising interest rates. Foreign investment in India's stock market is fleeing, the rupee is falling, and the stock market is down over 40% from the year's highs. Most economic forecasts expect growth to slow to 7%—a big drop for a country that needs to accelerate growth, not reduce it. ... India needs urgently to spend $500 billion on new infrastructure and more on upgrading education and health-care facilities. ... A plan to build 30 Special Economic Zones is virtually suspended because New Delhi has not sorted out how to acquire the necessary land, a major issue in both urban and rural India, without a major social and political upheaval. Agriculture [is] ... technologically laggard ... [and] woefully unproductive. Simple and non-political reforms, like strengthening the legal system and adding more judges, have been ignored. ... A June 16 report by Goldman Sachs' Jim O'Neill and Tushar Poddar ... urges India to improve governance, raise educational achievement, and control inflation. It also advises reining in profligate expenditures, liberalizing its financial markets, increasing agricultural productivity, and improving infrastructure, the environment, and energy use.

Business Week, July 1, 2008

Explain five potential sources for faster economic growth in India suggested in this news clip.

15. **Makani Power: A Mighty Wind**

Makani Power aims to generate energy from what are known as high-altitude wind-extraction technologies. And that's about all its 34-year-old Aussie founder, Saul Griffith, wants to say about it. ... But Makani can't hide entirely, not when its marquee investor is Google.org, the tech company's philanthropic arm. Makani's plan is to capture that high-altitude wind ... with a very old tool: kites. Harnessing higher-altitude wind, at least in theory, has greater potential than the existing wind industry ... a thousand feet above ground, wind is stronger and more consistent.

Fortune, April 28, 2008

Explain which growth theory best describes the news article.

16. **Canadians Win Japan's Kyoto Prize**

Two Canadians have been honoured with Japan's equivalent of the Nobel Prize. Toronto-based biologist Anthony Pawson ... was picked in the basic sciences for research that deepened understanding of how cells communicate. [Pawson's] discoveries have spurred progress in a wide range of biomedical research and the development of anti-cancer drugs. ... American computer scientist Richard Karp ... was also honoured. He won the prize in advanced technology for his work in measuring how difficult certain computational problems are to solve—a fundamental step in designing computer algorithms. ... Each received a gold medal and 50 million yen, worth about US$500,000. ... Founded in 1985, the Kyoto Prize is given to people for their contribution in the scientific, cultural and spiritual betterment of humankind.

Toronto Star, November 10, 2008

a. Explain how the Kyoto Prize helps fuel the perpetual motion economic growth machine.
b. How does Japan benefit from awarding researchers in other countries?

17. **Make Way for India—The Next China**

... China ... [is] growing at around 9 percent a year. ... [China's] one-child policy will start to reduce the size of China's working population within the next 10 years. India, by contrast, will have an increasing working population for another generation at least.

The Independent, March 1, 2006

a. Given the expected population changes, do you think China or India will have the greater economic growth rate? Why?
b. Would China's growth rate remain at 9 percent a year without the restriction on its population growth rate?
c. India's population growth rate is 1.6 percent a year, and in 2005 its economic growth rate was 8 percent a year. China's population growth rate is 0.6 percent a year, and in 2005 its economic growth rate was 9 percent a year. In what year will real GDP per person double in each country?

18. After studying *Reading Between the Lines* on pp. 536–537, answer the following questions:

a. What was the growth rate of real GDP in China in the year ending in August 2008?
b. Is real GDP per hour of labour in China growing because labour productivity is increasing or only because the population is increasing? How would you determine the contribution of each factor?
c. With the population growth in both countries at about 1 percent a year, is China narrowing the gap in real GDP per person between China and the United States?
d. At the current rate of convergence in c, how long will it take for real GDP per person in China to equal that in the United States?

19. Use the link on MyEconLab (Chapter Resources, Chapter 22, Web links) to obtain data on real GDP per person for the United States, China, South Africa, and Mexico since 1960.

a. Draw a graph of the data.
b. Which country has the lowest real GDP per person and which has the highest?
c. Which country has experienced the fastest growth rate since 1960 and which the slowest?
d. Explain why the growth rates in these four countries are ranked in the order you have discovered.

23

Finance, Saving, and Investment

After studying this chapter, you will be able to

- Describe the financial markets and financial institutions and the flows of funds that finance investment
- Explain how investment and saving decisions and borrowing and lending decisions are made and how these decisions interact in the market for loanable funds
- Explain how a government deficit (or surplus) influences the real interest rate, saving, and investment in the market for loanable funds
- Explain how international borrowing or lending influences the real interest rate, saving, and investment in the global market for loanable funds

During normal times, financial markets play their quiet unseen role of funnelling funds from savers and lenders to investors and borrowers. But 2008 was not a normal time. Beginning in August 2007 and running through 2008, global financial markets were in crisis. The epicentre of the crisis was a collapse of house prices in the United States and a crash in the values of securities held by banks and other institutions that finance house purchases. Banks around the world took big losses and venerable Wall Street investment banks Bear Stearns and Lehman Brothers disappeared.

The strains spread to Canada and all the big Canadian banks sustained heavy losses. But the crisis was less severe here than in the United States and Europe.

This chapter explains how financial markets work and their place in the economy. We look mainly at the normal functioning of these markets. But at various points in the chapter and in *Reading Between the Lines* at the end of the chapter, we examine the unusual and fearful events of the 2008 financial crisis.

Financial Institutions and Financial Markets

The financial institutions and markets that we study in this chapter play a crucial role in the economy. They provide the channels through which saving flows to finance the investment in new capital that makes the economy grow.

In studying the economics of financial institutions and markets, we distinguish between

- Finance and money
- Physical capital and financial capital

Finance and Money

In economics, we use the term *finance* to describe the activity of providing the funds that finance expenditures on capital. The study of finance looks at how households and firms obtain and use financial resources and how they cope with the risks that arise in this activity.

Money is what we use to pay for goods and services and factors of production and to make financial transactions. The study of money looks at how households and firms use it, how much of it they hold, how banks create and manage it, and how its quantity influences the economy.

In the economic lives of individuals and businesses, finance and money are closely interrelated. And some of the main financial institutions, such as banks, provide both financial services and monetary services. Nevertheless, by distinguishing between *finance* and *money* and studying them separately, we will better understand our financial and monetary markets and institutions.

For the rest of this chapter, we study finance. Money is the topic of the next chapter.

Physical Capital and Financial Capital

Economists distinguish between physical capital and financial capital. *Physical capital* is the tools, instruments, machines, buildings, and other items that have been produced in the past and that are used today to produce goods and services. Inventories of raw materials, semifinished goods, and components are part of physical capital. When economists use the term capital, they mean *physical* capital. The

funds that firms use to buy physical capital are called **financial capital**.

Along the *aggregate production function* in Chapter 22, the quantity of capital is fixed. An increase in the quantity of capital increases production possibilities and shifts the aggregate production function upward. You're going to see, in this chapter, how investment, saving, borrowing, and lending decisions influence the quantity of capital and make it grow, and as a consequence, make real GDP grow.

We begin by describing the links between capital and investment and between wealth and saving.

Capital and Investment

The quantity of capital changes because of investment and depreciation. *Investment* (Chapter 20, p. 470) increases the quantity of capital and *depreciation* (Chapter 20, p. 470) decreases it. The total amount spent on new capital is called **gross investment**. The change in the value of capital is called **net investment**. Net investment equals gross investment minus depreciation.

Figure 23.1 illustrates these terms. On January 1, 2008, Ace Bottling Inc. had machines worth $30,000—Ace's initial capital. During 2008, the market value of Ace's machines fell by 67 percent—$20,000. After this depreciation, Ace's machines were valued at $10,000. During 2008, Ace spent $30,000 on new machines. This amount is Ace's gross investment. By December 31, 2008, Ace Bottling had capital valued at $40,000, so its capital had increased by $10,000. This amount is Ace's net investment. Ace's net investment equals its gross investment of $30,000 minus depreciation of its initial capital of $20,000.

Wealth and Saving

Wealth is the value of all the things that people own. What people own is related to what they earn, but it is not the same thing. People earn an *income*, which is the amount they receive during a given time period from supplying the services of the resources they own. **Saving** is the amount of income that is not paid in taxes or spent on consumption goods and services. Saving increases wealth. Wealth also increases when the market value of assets rises—called *capital gains*—and decreases when the market value of assets falls—called *capital losses*.

For example, at the end of the school year you have $250 in the bank and a coin collection worth

FIGURE 23.1 Capital and Investment

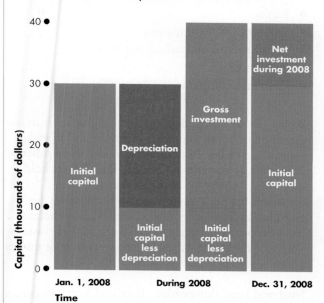

On January 1, 2008, Ace Bottling had capital worth $30,000. During the year, the value of Ace's capital fell by $20,000—depreciation—and Ace spent $30,000 on new capital—gross investment. Ace's net investment was $10,000 ($30,000 gross investment minus $20,000 depreciation) so at the end of 2008, Ace had capital worth $40,000.

myeconlab animation

$300, so your wealth is $550. During the summer, you earn $5,000 (net of taxes) and spend $1,000 on consumption goods and services, so your saving is $4,000. Your bank account increases to $4,250 and your wealth becomes $4,550. The $4,000 increase in wealth equals saving. If coins rise in value and your coin collection is now worth $500, you have a capital gain of $200, which is also added to your wealth.

National wealth and national saving work like this personal example. The wealth of a nation at the end of a year equals its wealth at the start of the year plus its saving during the year, which equals income minus consumption expenditure.

To make real GDP grow, saving and wealth must be transformed into investment and capital. This transformation takes place in the markets for financial capital and through the activities of financial institutions. We're now going to describe these markets and institutions.

Markets for Financial Capital

Saving is the source of the funds that are used to finance investment, and these funds are supplied and demanded in three types of financial markets:

- Loan markets
- Bond markets
- Stock markets

Loan Markets Businesses often want short-term finance to buy inventories or to extend credit to their customers. Sometimes they get this finance in the form of a loan from a bank. Households often want finance to purchase big-ticket items, such as automobiles or household furnishings and appliances. They get this finance as bank loans, often in the form of outstanding credit card balances.

Households also get finance to buy new homes. (Expenditure on new homes is counted as part of investment.) These funds are usually obtained as a loan that is secured by a **mortgage**—a legal contract that gives ownership of a home to the lender in the event that the borrower fails to meet the agreed loan payments (repayments and interest). Mortgage loans were at the centre of the 2007–2008 U.S. credit crisis that engulfed the global economy.

All of these types of financing take place in loan markets.

Bond Markets When Bombardier expands its airplane production plant, it gets the finance it needs by selling bonds. Governments—federal, provincial, and municipal—also raise finance by issuing bonds.

A **bond** is a promise to make specified payments on specified dates. For example, you can buy a Bombardier bond that promises to pay $7.35 every year and then to make a final payment of $100 in December 2026.

The buyer of a bond from Bombardier makes a loan to the company and is entitled to the payments promised by the bond. When a person buys a newly issued bond, he or she may hold the bond until the borrower has repaid the amount borrowed or sell it to someone else. Bonds issued by firms and governments are traded in the **bond market**.

The term of a bond might be long (decades) or short (just a month or two). Firms often issue very short-term bonds as a way of getting paid for their sales before the buyer is able to pay. For example, when Bombardier sells $100 million of airplanes to

Air Canada, Bombardier wants to be paid when the items are shipped. But Air Canada doesn't want to pay until the airplanes are earning an income. In this situation, Air Canada might promise to pay Bombardier $101 million three months in the future. TD Bank might be willing to buy this promise for (say) $100 million. Bombardier gets $100 million immediately and the bank gets $101 million in three months when Air Canada honours its promise. The government of Canada issues promises of this type, called Treasury bills.

Another type of bond is a **mortgage-backed security**, which entitles its holder to the income from a package of mortgages. Mortgage lenders create mortgage-backed securities. They make mortgage loans to home buyers and then create securities that they sell to obtain more funds to make more mortgage loans. The holder of a mortgage-backed security is entitled to receive payments that derive from the payments received by the mortgage lender from the home buyer–borrower.

Mortgage-backed securities were at the centre of the storm in the financial markets in 2007–2008.

Stock Markets When Petro-Canada wants finance to expand its oilsands operation in Alberta, it might issue stock. A **stock** is a certificate of ownership and claim to the firm's profits. Petro-Canada has issued 484 million shares of its stock. So if you owned 484 Petro-Canada shares, you would own one-millionth of the company and be entitled to receive one-millionth of its profits.

Unlike a stockholder, a bondholder does not own part of the firm that issued the bond.

A **stock market** is a financial market in which shares of stocks of corporations are traded. The Toronto Stock Exchange, the New York Stock Exchange, and the London Stock Exchange (in England) are all examples of stock markets.

Financial Institutions

Financial markets are highly competitive because of the role played by financial institutions in those markets. A **financial institution** is a firm that operates on both sides of the markets for financial capital. It is a borrower in one market and a lender in another.

Financial institutions also stand ready to trade so that households with funds to lend and firms or households seeking funds can always find someone on the other side of the market with whom to trade.

The key Canadian financial institutions are

- Banks
- Trust and loan companies
- Credit unions and caisses populaires
- Pension funds
- Insurance companies

Banks Banks accept deposits and use the funds to buy government bonds and other securities and to make loans. Canada has 14 domestic banks, and a further 33 foreign banks operate in Canada. These banks hold more than 70 percent of the total assets of the Canadian financial services sector. Economists distinguish banks from other financial institutions because bank deposits are money. We'll return to these institutions in Chapter 24, where we study the role of money in our economy.

Trust and Loan Companies Trust and loan companies provide similar services to banks and the largest of them are owned by banks. They accept deposits and make personal loans and mortgage loans. They also administer estates, trusts, and pension plans.

Credit Unions and Caisses Populaires Credit unions and caisses populaires are banks that are owned and controlled by their depositors and borrowers, are regulated by provincial rules, and operate only inside their own provincial boundaries. These institutions are large in number but small in size.

Pension Funds Pension funds are financial institutions that receive the pension contributions of firms and workers. They use these funds to buy a diversified portfolio of bonds and stocks that they expect to generate an income that balances risk and return. The income is used to pay pension benefits.

Some pension funds invest in mortgage-backed securities of the type that collapsed in value during the 2008 financial crisis.

Pension funds can be very large and play an active role in the firms whose stock they hold.

Insurance Companies Insurance companies provide risk-sharing services. They enter into agreements with households and firms to provide compensation in the event of accident, theft, fire, ill-health, and a host of other misfortunes. They receive premiums from their customers and make payments against claims.

Financial Failures

The Institutions at the Centre of the Storm

Bear Stearns: absorbed by JPMorgan Chase with help from the U.S. Federal Reserve. Lehman Brothers: gone. Fannie Mae and Freddie Mac: taken into government oversight with U.S. taxpayer guarantees. Merrill Lynch: absorbed by Bank of America. AIG: given an $85 billion lifeline by the Federal Reserve and sold off in parcels to financial institutions around the world. Wachovia: taken over by Citigroup. Washington Mutual: taken over by JPMorgan. Morgan Stanley: 20 percent bought by Mitsubishi, a large Japanese bank. These are some of the events in the financial crisis of 2008. What was going on?

Between 2002 and 2005, mortgage lending exploded and home prices rose. Mortgage lenders bundled their loans into *mortgage-backed securities* and sold them to eager buyers around the world.

In 2006, interest rates began to rise and the values of financial assets fell. With lower asset values, financial institutions took big losses. Some losses of some institutions were too big to bear and these institutions became insolvent.

Insurance companies use the funds they have received but not paid out as claims to buy bonds and stocks on which they earn an interest income.

Some insurance companies also insure corporate bonds and other risky financial assets. They provide insurance that pays out if a firm fails and cannot meet its bond obligations. Some insurance companies insure other insurers in a complex network of reinsurance.

In normal times, insurance companies have a steady flow of funds coming in from premiums and interest on the financial assets they hold and a steady, but smaller, flow of funds paying claims. Their profit is the gap between the two flows. But in unusual times, when large and widespread losses are being incurred, insurance companies can run into difficulty in meeting their obligations. Such a situation arose in 2008 for one of the world's biggest insurers, AIG, and the firm was taken into public ownership.

Canadian insurance companies have very large international operations and earn 70 percent of their income outside Canada.

All financial institutions face risk and this risk poses two problems: a solvency problem and a liquidity problem.

Solvency and Liquidity

A financial institution's **net worth** is the total market value of what it has lent minus the market value of what it has borrowed. If net worth is positive, the institution is *solvent* and can remain in business. But if net worth is negative, the institution is *insolvent* and goes out of business. The owners of an insolvent financial institution—usually its stockholders—bear the loss when the assets are sold and debts paid.

A financial institution both borrows and lends, so it is exposed to the risk that its net worth might become negative. To limit that risk, financial institutions are regulated and a minimum amount of their lending must be backed by their net worth.

Sometimes a financial institution is solvent but illiquid. A firm is *illiquid* if it has made long-term loans with borrowed funds and is faced with a sudden demand to repay more of what it has borrowed than its available cash. In normal times, a financial institution that is illiquid can borrow from another institution. But if all financial institutions are short of cash, the market for loans among financial institutions dries up.

Insolvency and illiquidity were at the core of the financial meltdown of 2007–2008.

Interest Rates and Asset Prices

Stocks, bonds, short-term securities, and loans are collectively called *financial assets*. The interest rate on a financial asset is the interest received expressed as a percentage of the price of the asset.

Because the interest rate is a percentage of the price of an asset, if the asset price rises, other things remaining the same, the interest rate falls. Conversely, if the asset price falls, other things remaining the same, the interest rate rises.

To see this inverse relationship between an asset price and the interest rate, look at the example of a Petro-Canada share. In November 2008, the price of a Petro-Canada share was $20 and each share entitled its owner to 80 cents of Petro-Canada profit. The interest rate on a Petro-Canada share was

Interest rate = ($0.80 ÷ $20) × 100 = 4 percent.

If the price of a Petro-Canada share increased to $40 and each share still entitled its owner to 80 cents of Petro-Canada profit, the interest rate on a Petro-Canada share would become

Interest rate = ($0.80 ÷ $40) × 100 = 2 percent.

This relationship means that the price of an asset and the interest rate on that asset are determined simultaneously—one implies the other.

This relationship also means that if the interest rate on the asset rises, the price of the asset falls, debts become harder to pay, and the net worth of the financial institution falls. Insolvency can arise from previously unexpected large rises in the interest rate.

In the next part of this chapter, we learn how interest rates and asset prices are determined in the financial markets.

Review Quiz

1 Distinguish between physical capital and financial capital and give two examples of each.

2 What is the distinction between gross investment and net investment?

3 What are the three main types of markets for financial capital?

4 Explain the connection between the price of a financial asset and its interest rate.

 Work Study Plan 23.1 and get instant feedback.

The Market for Loanable Funds

In macroeconomics, we group all the financial markets that we described in the previous section into a single market for loanable funds. The **market for loanable funds** is the aggregate of all the individual financial markets.

The circular flow model of Chapter 20 (see p. 469) can be extended to include flows in the market for loanable funds that finance investment.

Funds that Finance Investment

Figure 23.2 shows the flows of funds that finance investment. They come from three sources:

1. Household saving

2. Government budget surplus

3. Borrowing from the rest of the world

Households' income, Y, is spent on consumption goods and services, C, saved, S, or paid in net taxes, T. **Net taxes** are the taxes paid to governments minus the cash transfers received from governments (such as social insurance and unemployment benefits). So income is equal to the sum of consumption expenditure, saving, and net taxes:

$$Y = C + S + T.$$

You saw in Chapter 20 (p. 470) that Y also equals the sum of the items of aggregate expenditure: consumption expenditure, C, investment, I, government expenditure, G, and exports, X, minus imports, M. That is,

$$Y = C + I + G + X - M.$$

By using these two equations, you can see that

$$I + G + X = M + S + T.$$

Subtract G and X from both sides of the last equation to obtain

$$I = S + (T - G) + (M - X).$$

This equation tells us the investment, I, is financed by household saving, S, the government budget surplus, $(T - G)$, and borrowing from the rest of the world, $(M - X)$.

A government budget surplus $(T > G)$ contributes funds to finance investment, but a government budget deficit $(T < G)$, competes with investment for funds.

FIGURE 23.2 Financial Flows and the Circular Flow of Expenditure and Income

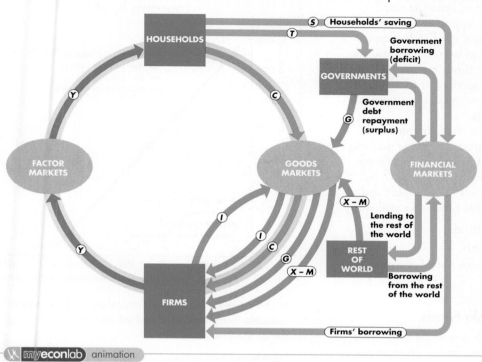

Households use their income for consumption expenditure (*C*), saving (*S*), and net taxes (*T*). Firms borrow to finance their investment expenditure. Governments borrow to finance a budget deficit or repay debt if they have a budget surplus. The rest of the world borrows to finance its deficit or lends its surplus.

myeconlab animation

If we export less than we import, we borrow (*M* – *X*) from the rest of the world to finance some of our investment. If we export more than we import, we lend (*X* – *M*) to the rest of the world and part of Canadian saving finances investment in other countries.

The sum of private saving, *S*, and government saving, (*T* – *G*), is called **national saving**. National saving and foreign borrowing finance investment.

In 2008, Canadian investment was $304 billion and lending to the rest of the world (positive net exports) was $32 billion. This total of $336 billion was financed by private saving of $296 billion and a government (federal, provincial, and local combined) budget surplus of $40 billion.

You're going to see how investment and saving and the flows of loanable funds—all measured in constant 2002 dollars—are determined. The price in the market for loanable funds that achieves equilibrium is an interest rate, which we also measure in real terms as the *real* interest rate. In the market for loanable funds, there is just one interest rate, which is an average of the interest rates on all the different types of financial securities that we described earlier. Let's see what we mean by the real interest rate.

The Real Interest Rate

The **nominal interest rate** is the number of dollars that a borrower pays and a lender receives in interest in a year expressed as a percentage of the number of dollars borrowed and lent. For example, if the annual interest paid on a $500 loan is $25, the nominal interest rate is 5 percent per year ($25 ÷ $500 × 100).

The **real interest rate** is the nominal interest rate adjusted to remove the effects of inflation on the buying power of money. The real interest rate is approximately equal to the nominal interest rate minus the inflation rate.

You can see why if you suppose that you have put $500 in a savings account that earns 5 percent a year. At the end of a year, you have $525 in your savings account. Suppose that the inflation rate is 2 percent per year—during the year, all prices increased by 2 percent. You need $510 to buy what a year earlier cost $500. So you can buy $15 more worth of goods and services than you could have bought a year earlier. You've earned goods and services worth $15, which is a real interest rate of 3 percent a year. And the bank has paid a real interest rate of 3 percent a year. So the real interest rate is the 5 percent nominal interest rate minus the 2 percent inflation rate.[1]

The real interest rate is the opportunity cost of loanable funds. The real interest *paid* on borrowed funds is the opportunity cost of borrowing. And the real interest rate *forgone* when funds are used either to buy consumption goods and services or to invest in new capital goods is the opportunity cost of not saving or not lending those funds.

We're now going to see how the loanable funds market determines the real interest rate, the quantity of funds loaned, saving, and investment. In the rest of this section, we will ignore the government and the rest of the world and focus on households and firms in the market for loanable funds. We will study

- The demand for loanable funds
- The supply of loanable funds
- Equilibrium in the market for loanable funds

The Demand for Loanable Funds

The *quantity of loanable funds demanded* is the total quantity of funds demanded to finance investment, the government budget deficit, and international investment or lending during a given period. Our focus here is on investment. We'll bring the other two items into the picture in later sections of this chapter.

What determines investment and the demand for loanable funds to finance it? Many details influence this decision, but we can summarize them in two factors:

1. The real interest rate
2. Expected profit

Firms invest in capital only if they expect to earn a profit, and fewer projects are profitable at a high real interest rate than at a low real interest rate, so

Other things remaining the same, the higher the real interest rate, the smaller is the quantity of loanable funds demanded; and the lower the real interest rate, the greater is the quantity of loanable funds demanded.

---

[1] The *exact* real interest rate formula, which allows for the change in the purchasing power of both the interest and the loan, is Real interest rate = (Nominal interest rate − Inflation rate) ÷ (1 + Inflation rate/100). If the nominal interest rate is 5 percent a year and the inflation rate is 2 percent a year, the real interest rate is (5 − 2) ÷ (1 + 0.02) = 2.94 percent a year.

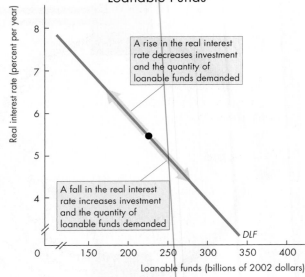

FIGURE 23.3 The Demand for Loanable Funds

A rise in the real interest rate decreases investment and the quantity of loanable funds demanded

A fall in the real interest rate increases investment and the quantity of loanable funds demanded

A change in the real interest rate changes the quantity of loanable funds demanded and brings a movement along the demand curve.

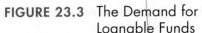

Demand for Loanable Funds Curve The **demand for loanable funds** is the relationship between the quantity of loanable funds demanded and the real interest rate, when all other influences on borrowing plans remain the same. The demand curve *DLF* in Fig. 23.3 is a demand for loanable funds curve.

To understand the demand for loanable funds, think about Bell Canada's decision to borrow $100 million to buy some new phone mail servers. If Bell expects to get a return of $5 million a year from this investment before paying interest costs and the interest rate is less than 5 percent a year, Bell would make a profit, so it buys the servers. But if the interest rate is more than 5 percent a year, Bell would incur a loss, so it doesn't buy the servers. The quantity of loanable funds demanded is greater, the lower is the real interest rate.

Changes in the Demand for Loanable Funds When the expected profit changes, the demand for loanable funds changes. Other things remaining the same, the greater the expected profit from new capital, the greater is the amount of investment and the greater is the demand for loanable funds.

Expected profit rises during a business cycle expansion and falls during a recession; rises when technological change creates profitable new products; rises as a growing population brings increased demand for goods and services; and fluctuates with contagious swings of optimism and pessimism, called "animal spirits" by Keynes and "irrational exuberance" by Alan Greenspan.

When expected profit changes, the demand for loanable funds curve shifts.

The Supply of Loanable Funds

The *quantity of loanable funds supplied* is the total funds available from private saving, a government budget surplus, and international borrowing during a given period. Our focus here is on saving. We'll bring the other two items into the picture later.

How do you decide how much of your income to save and supply in the market for loanable funds? Your decision is influenced by many factors, but chief among them are

1. The real interest rate
2. Disposable income
3. Expected future income
4. Wealth
5. Default risk

We begin by focusing on the real interest rate.

> Other things remaining the same, the higher the real interest rate, the greater is the quantity of loanable funds supplied; and the lower the real interest rate, the smaller is the quantity of loanable funds supplied.

The Supply of Loanable Funds Curve   The **supply of loanable funds** is the relationship between the quantity of loanable funds supplied and the real interest rate when all other influences on lending plans remain the same. The curve *SLF* in Fig. 23.4 is a supply of loanable funds curve.

Think about a student's decision to save some of what she earns from her summer job. With a real interest rate of 2 percent a year, she decides that it is not worth saving much—better to spend the income and take a student loan if funds run out during the semester. But if the real interest rate jumped to 10 percent a year, the payoff from saving would be high enough to encourage her to cut back on spending and increase the amount she saves.

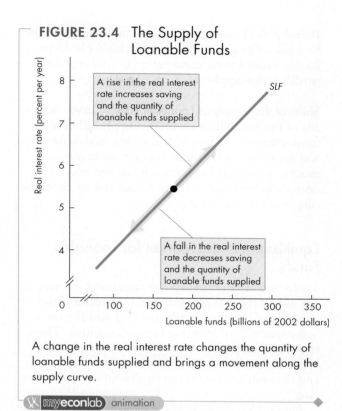

FIGURE 23.4   The Supply of Loanable Funds

A rise in the real interest rate increases saving and the quantity of loanable funds supplied

A fall in the real interest rate decreases saving and the quantity of loanable funds supplied

A change in the real interest rate changes the quantity of loanable funds supplied and brings a movement along the supply curve.

myeconlab   animation

Changes in the Supply of Loanable Funds   A change in disposable income, expected future income, wealth, or default risk changes the supply of loanable funds.

Disposable Income   A household's *disposable income* is the income earned minus net taxes. When disposable income increases, other things remaining the same, consumption expenditure increases but by less than the increase in income. Some of the increase in income is saved. So the greater a household's disposable income, other things remaining the same, the greater is its saving.

Expected Future Income   The higher a household's expected future income, other things remaining the same, the smaller is its saving today.

Wealth   The higher a household's wealth, other things remaining the same, the smaller is its saving. If a person's wealth increases because of a capital gain, the person sees less need to save. For example, from 2002 to 2006, when house prices were rising at more than 10 percent a year, wealth increased despite the fact that personal saving dropped to less than 34 percent.

Default Risk Default risk is the risk that a loan will not be repaid. The greater that risk, the higher is the interest rate needed to induce a person to lend and the smaller is the supply of loanable funds.

Shifts of the Supply of Loanable Funds Curve

When any of the four influences on the supply of loanable funds changes, the supply of loanable funds changes and the supply curve shifts. An increase in disposable income, a decrease in expected future income, a decrease in wealth, or a fall in default risk increases the supply of loanable funds.

Equilibrium in the Market for Loanable Funds

You've seen that, other things remaining the same, the higher the real interest rate, the greater is the quantity of loanable funds supplied and the smaller is the quantity of loanable funds demanded. There is one real interest rate at which the quantities of loanable funds demanded and supplied are equal, and that interest rate is the equilibrium real interest rate.

Figure 23.5 shows how the demand for and supply of loanable funds determine the real interest rate. The *DLF* curve is the demand curve and the *SLF* curve is the supply curve. If the real interest rate exceeds 6 percent a year, the quantity of loanable funds supplied exceeds the quantity demanded. Borrowers find it easy to get funds, but lenders are unable to lend all the funds they have available. The real interest rate falls until the quantity of funds supplied equals the quantity of funds demanded.

If the real interest rate is less than 6 percent a year, the quantity of loanable funds supplied is less than the quantity demanded. Borrowers can't get the funds they want, but lenders are able to lend all the funds they have available. So the real interest rate rises and continues to rise until the quantity of funds supplied equals the quantity demanded.

Regardless of whether there is a surplus or a shortage of loanable funds, the real interest rate changes and is pulled towards an equilibrium level. In Fig. 23.5, the equilibrium real interest rate is 6 percent a year. At this interest rate, there is neither a surplus nor a shortage of loanable funds. Borrowers can get the funds they want, and lenders can lend all the funds they have available. The investment plans of borrowers and the saving plans of lenders are consistent with each other.

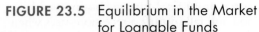

FIGURE 23.5   Equilibrium in the Market for Loanable Funds

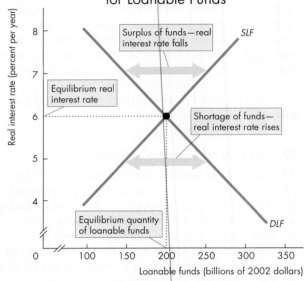

A surplus of funds lowers the real interest rate and a shortage of funds raises it. At a real interest rate of 6 percent a year, the quantity of funds demanded equals the quantity supplied and the market is in equilibrium.

myeconlab   animation

Changes in Demand and Supply

Financial markets are highly volatile in the short run but remarkably stable in the long run. Volatility in the market comes from fluctuations in either the demand for loanable funds or the supply of loanable funds. These fluctuations bring fluctuations in the real interest rate and in the equilibrium quantity of funds lent and borrowed. They also bring fluctuations in asset prices.

Here we'll illustrate the effects of *increases* in demand and supply in the market for loanable funds.

An Increase in Demand If the profits that firms expect to earn increase, firms increase their planned investment and increase their demand for loanable funds to finance that investment. With an increase in the demand for loanable funds, but no change in the supply of loanable funds, there is a shortage of funds. As borrowers compete for funds, the interest rate rises and lenders increase the quantity of funds supplied.

Figure 23.6(a) illustrates these changes. An increase in the demand for loanable funds shifts the demand curve rightward from DLF_0 to DLF_1. With

FIGURE 23.6 Changes in Demand and Supply

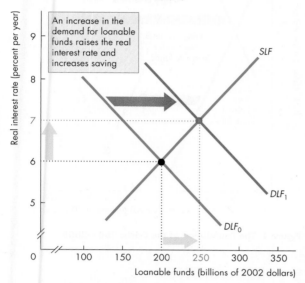

An increase in the demand for loanable funds raises the real interest rate and increases saving

(a) An increase in demand

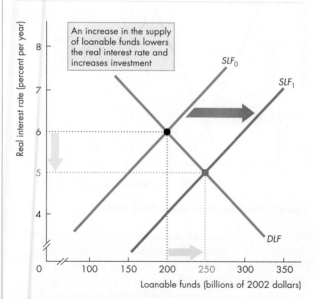

An increase in the supply of loanable funds lowers the real interest rate and increases investment

(b) An increase in supply

In part (a), the demand for loanable funds increases and supply doesn't change. The real interest rate rises (financial asset prices fall) and the quantity of funds increases.

In part (b), the supply of loanable funds increases and demand doesn't change. The real interest rate falls (financial asset prices rise) and the quantity of funds increases.

 myeconlab animation

no change in the supply of loanable funds, there is a shortage of funds at a real interest rate of 6 percent a year. The real interest rate rises until it is 7 percent a year. Equilibrium is restored and the equilibrium quantity of funds has increased.

An Increase in Supply If one of the influences on saving plans changes and increases saving, the supply of loanable funds increases. With no change in the demand for loanable funds, the market is flush with loanable funds. Borrowers find bargains and lenders find themselves accepting a lower interest rate. At the lower interest rate, borrowers find additional investment projects profitable and increase the quantity of loanable funds that they borrow.

Figure 23.6(b) illustrates these changes. An increase in supply shifts the supply curve rightward from SLF_0 to SLF_1. With no change in demand, there is a surplus of funds at a real interest rate of 6 percent a year. The real interest rate falls until it is 5 percent a year. Equilibrium is restored and the equilibrium quantity of funds has increased.

Long-Run Growth of Demand and Supply Over time, both demand and supply in the market for loanable funds fluctuate and the real interest rate rises and falls. Both the supply of loanable funds and the demand for loanable funds tend to increase over time. On average, they increase at a similar pace, so although demand and supply trend upward, the real interest rate has no trend. It fluctuates around a constant average level.

Review Quiz

1 What is the market for loanable funds?
2 Why is the real interest rate the opportunity cost of loanable funds?
3 How do firms make investment decisions?
4 What determines the demand for loanable funds and what makes it change?
5 How do households make saving decisions?
6 What determines the supply of loanable funds and what makes it change?
7 How do changes in the demand for and supply of loanable funds change the real interest rate and the quantity of loanable funds?

myeconlab Work Study Plan 23.2 and get instant feedback.

The Origins of the 2007–2008 Financial Crisis

Loanable Funds Fuel U.S. Home-Price Bubble

The financial crisis that gripped the U.S. and global economies in 2007 and cascaded through the financial markets in 2008 had its origins much earlier in events taking place in the market for loanable funds.

Between 2001 and 2005, a massive injection of loanable funds occurred in the United States. Some funds came from the rest of the world, but that source of supply has been stable. The U.S. Federal Reserve (the Fed) provided funds to keep interest rates low and that was a major source of the increase in the supply of funds. (The next chapter explains how a central bank does this.)

Figure 1 illustrates the U.S. loanable funds market starting in 2001. In that year, the demand for loanable funds was DLF_{01} and the supply of loanable funds was SLF_{01}. The equilibrium real interest rate was 4 percent a year and the equilibrium quantity of loanable funds was $29 trillion (in 2000 dollars).

During the ensuing four years, a massive increase in the supply of loanable funds shifted the supply curve rightward to SLF_{05}. A smaller increase in demand shifted the demand for loanable funds curve to DLF_{05}. The real interest rate fell to 1 percent a year and the quantity of loanable funds increased to $36 trillion—a 24 percent increase in just four years.

With this large increase in available funds, much of it in the form of mortgage loans to home buyers, the demand for homes increased by more than the increase in the supply of homes. Home prices rose and the expectation of further increases fuelled the demand for loanable funds.

By 2006, the expectation of continued rapidly rising home prices brought a very large increase in the demand for loanable funds. At the same time, the Fed began to tighten credit. (Again, you'll learn how this is done in the next chapter.) The result of the tighter credit policy was a slowdown in the pace of increase in the supply of loanable funds.

Figure 2 illustrates these events. In 2006, the demand for loanable funds increased from DLF_{05} to DLF_{06} and the supply of loanable funds increased by a smaller amount from SLF_{05} to SLF_{06}. The real interest rate increased to 3 percent a year.

The rise in the real interest rate (and a much higher rise in the nominal interest rate) put many homeowners in financial difficulty. Mortgage

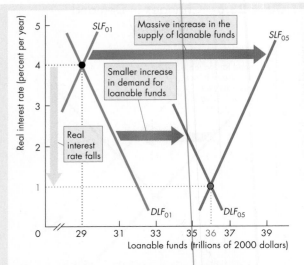

Figure 1   The Foundation of the Crisis: 2001–2005

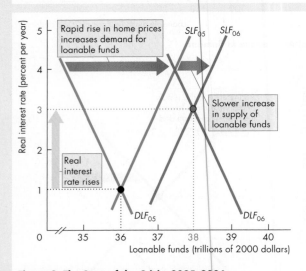

Figure 2   The Start of the Crisis: 2005–2006

repayments increased and some borrowers stopped repaying their loans. By August 2007, the damage from mortgage default and foreclosure was so large that the credit market began to dry up. A large decrease in both demand and supply kept interest rates roughly constant but decreased the quantity of new business.

The total quantity of loanable funds didn't decrease, but the rate of increase slowed to a snail's pace and the financial institutions most exposed to the bad mortgage debts and the securities that they backed (described on p. 546) began to fail.

These events illustrate the crucial role played by the loanable funds market in our economy.

Government in the Market for Loanable Funds

Government enters the market for loanable funds when it has a budget surplus or budget deficit. A government budget surplus increases the supply of loanable funds and contributes to financing investment; a government budget deficit increases the demand for loanable funds and competes with businesses for funds. Let's study the effects of government on the market for loanable funds.

A Government Budget Surplus

A government budget surplus increases the supply of loanable funds. The real interest rate falls, which decreases household saving and decreases the quantity of private funds supplied. The lower real interest rate increases the quantity of loanable funds demanded, and as a result investment increases.

FIGURE 23.7   A Government Budget Surplus

Government budget surplus increases the supply of loanable funds ...

PSLF

SLF

... lowers the real interest rate

... decreases saving

... increases investment

DLF

Loanable funds (billions of 2002 dollars)

A government budget surplus of $100 billion is added to private saving and the private supply of loanable funds (PSLF) to determine the supply of loanable funds, SLF. The real interest rate falls to 5 percent a year, private saving decreases, but investment increases to $250 billion.

myeconlab animation

Figure 23.7 shows these effects of a government budget surplus. The private supply of loanable funds curve is *PSLF*. The supply of loanable funds curve, *SLF*, shows the sum of private supply and the government budget surplus. Here, the government budget surplus is $100 billion, so at each real interest rate the *SLF* curve lies $100 billion to the right of the *PSLF* curve. That is, the horizontal distance between the *PSLF* curve and the *SLF* curve equals the government budget surplus.

With no government surplus, the real interest rate is 6 percent a year, the quantity of loanable funds is $200 billion a year, and investment is $200 billion a year. But with the government surplus of $100 billion a year, the equilibrium real interest rate falls to 5 percent a year and the quantity of loanable funds increases to $250 billion a year.

The fall in the interest rate decreases private saving to $150 billion, but investment increases to $250 billion, which is financed by private saving plus the government budget surplus (government saving).

A Government Budget Deficit

A government budget deficit increases the demand for loanable funds. The real interest rate rises, which increases household saving and increases the quantity of private funds supplied. But the higher real interest rate decreases investment and the quantity of loanable funds demanded by firms to finance investment.

Figure 23.8 shows these effects of a government budget deficit. The private demand for loanable funds curve is *PDLF*. The demand for loanable funds curve, *DLF*, shows the sum of private demand and the government budget deficit. Here, the government budget deficit is $100 billion, so at each real interest rate the *DLF* curve lies $100 billion to the right of the *PDLF* curve. That is, the horizontal distance between the *PDLF* curve and the *DLF* curve equals the government budget deficit.

With no government deficit, the real interest rate is 6 percent a year, the quantity of loanable funds is $200 billion a year, and investment is $200 billion a year. But with the government budget deficit of $100 billion a year, the equilibrium real interest rate rises to 7 percent a year and the quantity of loanable funds increases to $250 billion a year.

The rise in the real interest rate increases private saving to $250 billion, but investment decreases to $150 billion because $100 billion of private saving must finance the government budget deficit.

FIGURE 23.8 A Government Budget Deficit

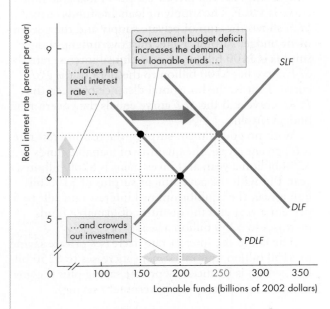

A government budget deficit adds to the private demand for loanable funds (*PDLF*) to determine the demand for loanable funds, *DLF*. The real interest rate rises, saving increases, but investment decreases—a crowding-out effect.

 animation

FIGURE 23.9 The Ricardo-Barro Effect

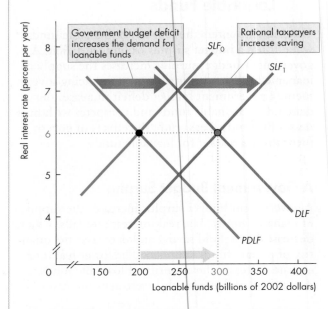

A budget deficit increases the demand for loanable funds to *DLF*. Rational taxpayers increase saving, which increases the supply of loanable funds from SLF_0 to SLF_1. Crowding out is avoided: Increased saving finances the budget deficit.

 animation

The Crowding-Out Effect The tendency for a government budget deficit to raise the real interest rate and decrease investment is called the **crowding-out effect**. The budget deficit crowds out investment by competing with businesses for scarce financial capital.

The crowding-out effect does not decrease investment by the full amount of the government budget deficit because the higher real interest rate induces an increase in private saving that partly contributes to financing the deficit.

The Ricardo-Barro Effect First suggested by the English economist David Ricardo in the nineteenth century and refined by Robert J. Barro of Harvard University, the Ricardo-Barro effect holds that both of the effects we've just shown are wrong and that the government budget, whether in surplus or deficit, has no effect on either the real interest rate or investment.

Barro says that taxpayers are rational. They can see that a budget deficit today means that future taxes will be higher and future disposable incomes will be smaller. With smaller expected future disposable

incomes, saving increases today. Private saving and the private supply of loanable funds increase to match the quantity of loanable funds demanded by the government. So the budget deficit has no effect on either the real interest rate or investment. Figure 23.9 shows this outcome.

Most economists regard the Ricardo-Barro view as extreme. But there might be some change in private saving that goes in the direction suggested by the Ricardo-Barro effect that lessens the crowding-out effect.

Review Quiz

1 How does a government budget surplus or deficit influence the market for loanable funds?
2 What is the crowding-out effect and how does it work?
3 What is the Ricardo-Barro effect and how does it modify the crowding-out effect?

 Work Study Plan 23.3 and get instant feedback.

The Global Loanable Funds Market

The loanable funds market is global, not national. Lenders on the supply side of the market want to earn the highest possible real interest rate and they will seek it by looking everywhere in the world. Borrowers on the demand side of the market want to pay the lowest possible real interest rate and they will seek it by looking everywhere in the world. Financial capital is mobile: It moves to the best advantage of lenders and borrowers.

International Capital Mobility

If a Canadian supplier of loanable funds can earn a higher interest rate in Tokyo than in Toronto, funds supplied in Japan will increase and funds supplied in Canada will decrease—funds will flow from Canada to Japan.

If a Canadian demander of loanable funds can pay a lower interest rate in Paris than in Toronto, the demand for funds in France will increase and the demand for funds in Canada will decrease—funds will flow from France to Canada.

Because lenders are free to seek the highest real interest rate and borrowers are free to seek the lowest real interest rate, the loanable funds market is a single, integrated, global market. Funds flow into the country in which the interest rate is highest and out of the country in which the interest rate is lowest.

When funds leave the country with the lowest interest rate, a shortage of funds raises the real interest rate in that country. When funds move into the country with the highest interest rate, a surplus of funds lowers the real interest rate in that country. The free international mobility of financial capital pulls real interest rates around the world towards equality.

Only when the real interest rates in Toronto, Tokyo, and Paris are equal does the incentive to move funds from one country to another stop.

Equality of real interest rates does not mean that if you calculate the average real interest rate in Toronto, Tokyo, and Paris, you'll get the same number. To compare real interest rates, we must compare financial assets of equal risk.

Lending is risky. A loan might not be repaid. Or the price of a stock or bond might fall. Interest rates include a risk premium—the riskier the loan, other things remaining the same, the higher is the interest rate. The interest rate on a risky loan minus that on a safe loan is called the *risk premium*.

International capital mobility brings *real* interest rates in all parts of the world to equality except for differences that reflect differences in risk—differences in the risk premium.

International Borrowing and Lending

A country's loanable funds market connects with the global market through net exports. If a country's net exports are negative ($X < M$), the rest of the world supplies funds to that country and the quantity of loanable funds in that country is greater than national saving. If a country's net exports are positive ($X > M$), the country is a net supplier of funds to the rest of the world and the quantity of loanable funds in that country is less than national saving.

Demand and Supply in the Global and National Markets

The demand for and supply of funds in the global loanable funds market determines the world equilibrium real interest rate. This interest rate makes the quantity of loanable funds demanded equal the quantity supplied in the world economy. But it does not make the quantity of funds demanded and supplied equal in each national economy. The demand for and supply of funds in a national economy determine whether the country is a lender to or a borrower from the rest of the world.

The Global Loanable Funds Market Figure 23.10(a) illustrates the global market. The demand for loanable funds, DLF_W, is the sum of the demands in all countries. Similarly, the supply of loanable funds, SLF_W, is the sum of the supplies in all countries. The world equilibrium real interest rate makes the quantity of funds supplied in the world as a whole equal to the quantity demanded. In this example, the equilibrium real interest rate is 5 percent a year and the quantity of funds is $10 trillion.

An International Borrower Figure 23.10(b) shows the market for loanable funds in a country that borrows from the rest of the world. The country's demand for loanable funds, DLF, is part of the world demand in Fig. 23.10(a). The country's supply of loanable funds, SLF_D, is part of the world supply.

FIGURE 23.10   Borrowing and Lending in the Global Loanable Funds Market

(a) The global market   **(b) An international borrower**   **(c) An international lender**

In part (a), the demand for loanable funds, *DLF*, and the supply of funds, *SLF*, determine the equilibrium real interest rate in the global loanable funds market.

The country in part (b) has a shortage of funds at the

world equilibrium real interest rate. The country borrows from the rest of the world and has negative net exports.

The country in part (c) has a surplus of funds at the world equilibrium real interest rate. The country lends to the rest of the world and has positive net exports.

If this country were isolated from the global market, the real interest rate would be 6 percent a year (where the *DLF* and *SLF_D* curves intersect). But if the country is integrated into the global economy, with a real interest rate of 6 percent a year, funds would flood into it. With a real interest rate of 5 percent a year in the rest of the world, suppliers of loanable funds would seek the higher return in this country. In effect, the country faces the supply of loanable funds curve *SLF*, which is horizontal at the world equilibrium real interest rate.

The country's demand for loanable funds and the world interest rate determine the equilibrium quantity of loanable funds—$2.5 billion in Fig. 23.10(b).

An International Lender Figure 23.10(c) shows the situation in a country that lends to the rest of the world. As before, the country's demand for loanable funds, *DLF*, is part of the world demand and the country's supply of loanable funds, *SLF_D*, is part of the world supply in Fig. 23.10(a).

If this country were isolated from the global economy, the real interest rate would be 4 percent a year (where the *DLF* and *SLF_D* curves intersect). But if this country is integrated into the global economy, with a real interest rate of 4 percent a year, funds

would quickly flow out of it. With a real interest rate of 5 percent a year in the rest of the world, suppliers of loanable funds would seek the higher return in other countries. Again, the country faces the supply of loanable funds curve *SLF*, which is horizontal at the world equilibrium real interest rate.

The country's demand for loanable funds and the world interest rate determine the equilibrium quantity of loanable funds—$1.5 billion in Fig. 23.10(c).

Changes in Demand and Supply A change in the demand or supply in the global market of loanable funds changes the real interest rate in the way shown in Fig. 23.6 (see p. 553). The effect of a change in demand or supply in a national market depends on the size of the country. A change in demand or supply in a small country has no significant effect on global demand or supply, so it leaves the world real interest rate unchanged and changes only the country's net exports and international borrowing or lending. A change in demand or supply in a large country has a significant effect on global demand or supply, so it changes the world real interest rate as well as the country's net exports and international borrowing or lending. Every country feels some of the effect of a large country's change in demand or supply.

Greenspan's Interest Rate Puzzle

The Role of the Global Market

The real interest rate paid by big U.S. corporations fell from 5.5 percent a year in 2001 to 2.5 percent a year in 2005. Alan Greenspan, then the chairman of the U.S. Federal Reserve, said he was puzzled that the real interest rate was falling at a time when the U.S. government budget deficit was increasing.

Why did the real interest rate fall?

The answer lies in the global loanable funds market. Rapid economic growth in Asia and Europe brought a large increase in global saving, which in turn increased the global supply of loanable funds. The supply of loanable funds increased because Asian and European saving increased strongly.

The U.S. government budget deficit increased the U.S. and global demand for loanable funds. But this increase was very small compared to the increase in supply.

The result of a large increase in supply and a small increase in demand was a fall in the world average real interest rate and an increase in the equilibrium quantity of loanable funds.

The figure illustrates these events. The supply of loanable funds increased from SLF_{01} in 2001 to SLF_{05} in 2005. (In the figure, we ignore the change in the global demand for loanable funds because it was very small relative to the increase in supply.)

With the increase in supply, the real interest rate fell from 5.5 percent to 2.5 percent a year and the quantity of loanable funds increased.

In the United States, borrowing from the rest of the world increased to finance the increased government budget deficit.

The interest rate puzzle illustrates the important fact that the loanable funds market is a global market, not a national market.

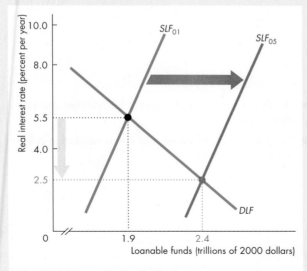

The Global Loanable Funds Market

Review Quiz

1 Why do loanable funds flow among countries?
2 What determines the demand for and supply of loanable funds in an individual economy?
3 What happens if a country has a shortage of loanable funds at the world real interest rate?
4 What happens if a country has a surplus of loanable funds at the world real interest rate?
5 How is a government budget deficit financed in an open economy?

 Work Study Plan 23.4 and get instant feedback.

To complete your study of financial markets, take a look at *Reading Between the Lines* on pp. 560–561 and see how you can use the model of the loanable funds market to understand the events in the financial market crisis of 2008.

Bailing Out Troubled U.S. Financial Markets

Bailout Plan Wins Approval

October 3, 2008

After the House reversed course and gave final approval to the $700 billion economic bailout package, President Bush quickly signed it into law on Friday, authorizing the Treasury to undertake what could become the most expensive government intervention in history.

But even as Mr. Bush declared that the measure would "help prevent the crisis on Wall Street from becoming a crisis in communities across our country," Congressional Democrats said that it was only a first step and pledged to carry out a sweeping overhaul of the nation's financial regulatory system. ...

Some measures of the credit markets improved after the bill was approved, but only modestly. Analysts said it was too soon to tell whether borrowing rates—the interest rates banks charge each other for loans, and a key indicator of the flow of credit—would fall. ...

Supporters said the bailout was needed to prevent economic collapse; opponents said it was hasty, ill conceived and risked too much taxpayer money to help Wall Street tycoons, while providing no guarantees of success. The rescue plan allows the Treasury to buy troubled securities from financial firms in an effort to ease a deepening credit crisis that is choking off business and consumer loans, the lifeblood of the economy, and contributing to a string of bank failures. ...

Essence of the Story

- In October 2008, the U.S. Congress passed a $700 billion economic bailout package for troubled financial institutions.

- The plan allows the U.S. Treasury to buy troubled securities from financial firms.

- The goal was to unfreeze credit and make loan markets work normally.

- Analysts said it was too soon to tell whether interest rates would fall.

- Supporters of the bailout said it was needed to prevent economic collapse.

Economic Analysis

- In the fall of 2008, the U.S. loanable funds market was in a distressed state.

- The spread in interest rates between safe U.S. government Treasury bills and risky commercial loans was unusually high and the quantity of loans was unusually low.

- Banks and other financial institutions were holding financial assets that they could sell only at a large loss—referred to as *toxic assets*.

- The financial markets were operating at an equilibrium that was hampering continued economic growth.

- The U.S. Congress hoped to inject life into the markets by creating a $700 billion fund to buy toxic assets and enable financial institutions to start lending again. (In the event, the Treasury used the funds to buy bank stocks.)

- It was feared that without the $700 billion of funds, financial institutions would not only fail to provide the funds required to make the economy grow but also slide into a deeper state of stress with the quantity of funds available decreasing further.

- The figures illustrate the hope and the fear.

- In 2008 (both figures), the demand for loanable funds was DLF_{08} and the supply was SLF_{08}. The real interest rate was 3 percent a year and quantity of funds was $40 trillion (2000 dollars).

- Figure 1 shows the hope. A rescue package increases the supply of loanable funds and increases optimism about the future. Increased optimism increases profit expectations and increases the demand for funds. The demand and supply curve shift rightward to DLF_{09} and SLF_{09}. The quantity of funds increases and the economy begins to expand again.

- Figure 2 shows the fear. With no rescue package, the supply of loanable funds decreases and pessimism about the future increases. The increased pessimism decreases profit expectations and decreases the demand for funds. The demand and supply curve shift leftward to DLF_{09} and SLF_{09}. The quantity of funds decreases and the economy goes into recession or worse.

Figure 1 The hope

Figure 2 The fear

- Whether a rescue would work as hoped or whether the dire consequences of no rescue would occur as feared is not known. We have no direct experience of events like the ones described here on which to base solid predictions.

561

SUMMARY ◆

Key Points

Financial Institutions and Financial Markets

(pp. 544–548)

- Capital (*physical capital*) is a real productive resource; financial capital is the funds used to buy capital.
- Gross investment increases the quantity of capital and depreciation decreases it. Saving increases wealth.
- The markets for financial capital are the markets for loans, bonds, and stocks.
- Financial institutions ensure that borrowers and lenders can always find someone with whom to trade.

The Market for Loanable Funds (pp. 548–554)

- Investment in capital is financed by household saving, a government budget surplus, and funds from the rest of the world.
- The quantity of loanable funds demanded depends negatively on the real interest rate and the demand for loanable funds changes when profit expectations change.
- The quantity of loanable funds supplied depends positively on the real interest rate and the supply of loanable funds changes when disposable income, expected future income, wealth, and default risk change.
- Equilibrium in the loanable funds market determines the real interest rate and quantity of funds.

Government in the Market for Loanable Funds

(pp. 555–556)

- A government budget surplus increases the supply of loanable funds, lowers the real interest rate, and increases investment and the equilibrium quantity of loanable funds.
- A government budget deficit increases the demand for loanable funds, raises the real interest rate, decreases investment in a crowding-out effect, and decreases the equilibrium quantity of loanable funds.
- The Ricardo-Barro effect is the response of rational taxpayers to a budget deficit: Private saving increases to finance the budget deficit. The real interest rate remains constant and the crowding-out effect is avoided.

The Global Loanable Funds Market (pp. 557–559)

- The loanable funds market is a global market.
- The equilibrium real interest rate is determined in the global loanable funds market and national demand and supply determine the quantity of international borrowing or lending.

Key Figures

Figure 23.2   Financial Flows and the Circular Flow of Expenditure and Income, 549
Figure 23.3   The Demand for Loanable Funds, 550
Figure 23.4   The Supply of Loanable Funds, 551
Figure 23.5   Equilibrium in the Market for Loanable Funds, 552

Figure 23.6   Changes in Demand and Supply, 553
Figure 23.7   A Government Budget Surplus, 555
Figure 23.8   A Government Budget Deficit, 556
Figure 23.10 Borrowing and Lending in the Global Loanable Funds Market, 558

Key Terms

Bond, 545
Bond market, 545
Crowding-out effect, 556
Demand for loanable funds, 550
Financial capital, 544
Financial institution, 546
Gross investment, 544

Market for loanable funds, 548
Mortgage, 545
Mortgage-backed security, 546
National saving, 549
Net investment, 544
Net taxes, 548
Net worth, 547
Nominal interest rate, 549

Real interest rate, 549
Saving, 544
Stock, 546
Stock market, 546
Supply of loanable funds, 551
Wealth,   544

PROBLEMS and APPLICATIONS

Work problems 1–10 in Chapter 23 Study Plan and get instant feedback.
Work problems 11–19 as Homework, a Quiz, or a Test if assigned by your instructor.

1. Michael is an Internet service provider. On December 31, 2007, he bought an existing business with servers and a building worth $400,000. During his first year of operation, his business grew and he bought new servers for $500,000. The market value of some of his older servers fell by $100,000.

   a. What was Michael's gross investment, depreciation, and net investment during 2008?
   b. What was the value of Michael's capital at the end of 2008?

2. Lori is a student who teaches golf on the weekend and in a year earns $20,000 after paying her taxes. At the beginning of 2007, Lori owned $1,000 worth of books, CDs, and golf clubs and she had $5,000 in a savings account at the bank. During 2007, the interest on her savings account was $300 and she spent a total of $15,300 on consumption goods and services. There was no change in the market values of her books, CDs, and golf clubs.

   a. How much did Lori save in 2007?
   b. What was her wealth at the end of 2007?

3. First Call is a cellular phone company. It plans to build an assembly plant that costs $10 million if the real interest rate is 6 percent a year. If the real interest rate is 5 percent a year, First Call will build a larger plant that costs $12 million. And if the real interest rate is 7 percent a year, First Call will build a smaller plant that costs $8 million.

   a. Draw a graph of First Call's demand for loanable funds curve.
   b. First Call expects its profit from the sale of cellular phones to double next year. If other things remain the same, explain how this increase in expected profit influences First Call's demand for loanable funds.

4. Draw a graph to illustrate how an increase in the supply of loanable funds and a decrease in the demand for loanable funds can lower the real interest rate and leave the equilibrium quantity of loanable funds unchanged.

5. The table shows an economy's demand for loanable funds and supply of loanable funds schedules when the government's budget is balanced.

Real interest rate (percent per year)	Loanable funds demanded	Loanable funds supplied
	(trillions of 2002 dollars)	
4	8.5	5.5
5	8.0	6.0
6	7.5	6.5
7	7.0	7.0
8	6.5	7.5
9	6.0	8.0
10	5.5	8.5

   a. If the government has a budget surplus of $1 trillion, what are the real interest rate, the quantity of investment, and the quantity of private saving? Is there any crowding out in this situation?
   b. If the government has a budget deficit of $1 trillion, what are the real interest rate, the quantity of investment, and the quantity of private saving? Is there any crowding out in this situation?
   c. If the government has a budget deficit of $1 trillion and the Ricardo-Barro effect occurs, what are the real interest rate and the quantity of investment?

6. In the loanable funds market in problem 5, the quantity of loanable funds demanded increases by $1 trillion at each real interest rate and the quantity of loanable funds supplied increases by $2 trillion at each real interest rate.

   a. If the government budget is balanced, what are the real interest rate, the quantity of loanable funds, investment, and private saving? Does any crowding out occur?
   b. If the government budget becomes a deficit of $1 trillion, what are the real interest rate, the quantity of loanable funds, investment, and private saving? Does any crowding out occur?
   c. If the government wants to stimulate the quantity of investment and increase it to $9 trillion, what must they do?

7. **Household Debt Now Rising Faster than Wealth**

   The debt of Canadian households is now rising faster than their wealth in the wake of the stock market correction and a housing market slow-down. ... The mortgage market is still expanding ... although it will likely slow by more than half ... due to the correction in the formerly overheated markets in western Canadian cities and the tightening up of federal mortgage lending restrictions. There are also early signs that the pace of growth in non-mortgage consumer credit is slowing. ... And that's a good thing, said CIBC economist and author of the report Benjamin Tal. "If household credit were to continue to rise by 13% a year at some point I would become concerned because you would have too much credit and not enough wealth to support it ... "During the first quarter of the year, overall household debt rose by almost 3%, while personal disposable income rose by 2%. ...

Financial Post Magazine, August 19, 2008

a. Explain why the growth of household wealth has slowed in Canada.
b. When a household buys stocks, does that represent consumption, saving, or investment? Explain.
c. When a household buys a new house, does that represent consumption, saving, or investment? Explain.
d. What factors may influence a household when deciding between buying stocks, bonds, or a house?

8. **The Global Saving Glut and the U.S. Current Account,** remarks by Ben Bernanke (then a governor of the U.S. Federal Reserve) on March 10, 2005:

On most dimensions the U.S. economy appears to be performing well. Output growth has returned to healthy levels, the labor market is firming, and inflation appears to be well controlled. However, one aspect of U.S. economic performance still evokes concern among economists and policy-makers: the nation's large and growing current account deficit [negative net exports]. ... Most forecasters expect the nation's current account imbalance to decline slowly at best, implying a continued need for foreign credit and a concomitant decline in the U.S. net foreign asset position. Bernanke went on to ask the following questions. What are *your* answers to his questions:

a. Why is the United States, with the world's largest economy, borrowing heavily on international capital markets—rather than lending, as would seem more natural?
b. What implications do the U.S. current account deficit (negative net exports) and the U.S. consequent reliance on foreign credit have for U.S. economic performance?
c. What policies, if any, should be used to address this situation?

9. **The New New World Order**

... While gross domestic product growth is cooling a bit in emerging markets, the results are still tremendous compared with the United States and much of Western Europe. The 54 developing markets surveyed by Global Insight will post a 6.7% jump in real GDP this year, down from 7.5% last year. The 31 developed countries will grow an estimated 1.6%. The difference in growth rates represents the largest spread between developed and developing markets in the 37-year history of the survey.

Fortune, July 14, 2008

a. Do growth rates of real GDP over the past few decades indicate that world saving is shrinking, growing, or staying the same? Explain.
b. If the world demand for loanable funds remains the same, will the world real interest rate rise, fall, or remain the same? Explain.

10. **IMF Warning Over Slowing Growth**

The global economy may face a marked slowdown next year as a result of the turmoil in financial markets, the International Monetary Fund has warned. The IMF said the global credit squeeze would test the ability of the economy to continue expanding at recent rates. While future economic stability could not be taken for granted, there was plenty of evidence that the global economy remained durable, it added.

BBC News, October 10, 2007

a. Explain how turmoil in global financial markets might affect the demand for loanable funds, investment, and global economic growth in the future.
b. What might be the evidence that the global economy will continue to grow?

11. Annie runs a fitness centre. On December 31, 2008, she bought an existing business with exercise equipment and a building worth $300,000. During 2009, business improved and she bought some new equipment for $50,000. At the end of 2009, her equipment and buildings were worth $325,000. Calculate Annie's gross investment, depreciation, and net investment during 2009.

12. Karrie is a golf pro, and after she paid taxes, her income from golf and interest from financial assets was $1,500,000 in 2008. At the beginning of 2008, she owned $900,000 worth of financial assets. At the end of 2008, Karrie's financial assets were worth $1,900,000.

    a. How much did Karrie save during 2008?
    b. How much did she spend on consumption goods and services?

13. In 2008, the Lee family had disposable income of $80,000, wealth of $140,000, and an expected future income of $80,000 a year. At a real interest rate of 4 percent a year, the Lee family saves $15,000 a year; at a real interest rate of 6 percent a year, they save $20,000 a year; and at a real interest rate of 8 percent, they save $25,000 a year.

    a. Draw a graph of the Lee family's supply of loanable funds curve.
    b. In 2009, suppose that the stock market crashes and the default risk increases. Explain how this increase in default risk influences the Lee family's supply of loanable funds curve.

14. Draw a graph that illustrates the effect of an increase in the demand for loanable funds and an even larger increase in the supply of loanable funds on the real interest rate and the equilibrium quantity of loanable funds.

15. **India's Economy Hits the Wall**

    Just six months ago, India was looking good. Annual growth was 9%, corporate profits were surging 20%, the stock market had risen 50% in 2007, consumer demand was huge, local companies were making ambitious international acquisitions, and foreign investment was growing. Nothing, it seemed, could stop the forward march of this Asian nation. But stop it has. ... The country is reeling from 11.4% inflation, large government deficits, and rising interest rates. ... Most economic forecasts expect growth to slow to 7%—a big drop for a country that needs to accelerate growth, not reduce it. ... A June 16 report by Goldman Sachs' Jim O'Neill and Tushar Poddar ... urges India to improve governance, raise educational achievement, and control inflation. It also advises ... liberalizing its financial markets. ...

    Business Week, July 1, 2008

    a. Suppose that the Indian government reduces its deficit and returns to a balanced budget. If other things remain the same, how will the demand or supply of loanable funds in India change?
    b. With economic growth forecasted to slow, future incomes are expected to fall. If other things remain the same, how will the demand or supply of loanable funds in India change?

16. **The Global Savings Glut and Its Consequences**

    The world is experiencing an unprecedented glut of savings, driving down real interest rates. It is a good time to borrow rather than lend. ... Several developing countries are running large current account surpluses (representing an excess of savings over investment). ... China has the biggest surplus of $1.2 trillion, but other developing countries put together have accumulated almost as much. ... Rapid growth leads to high saving rates: people save a large fraction of additional income. In India, GDP growth has accelerated from 6% to 9%, lifting the saving rate from 23% a decade ago to 33% today. China's saving rate is a dizzy 55%. Not even the investment boom in Asia can absorb these huge savings, which are therefore put into U.S. bonds. When a poor country buys U.S. bonds, it is in effect lending to the United States.

    Cato Institute, June 8, 2007

    a. Graphically illustrate and explain the impact of the "unprecedented glut of savings" on the real interest rate and the quantity of loanable funds.
    b. How do the high saving rates in China and India impact investment in the United States? How does this investment influence the production function and potential GDP in the United States?

17. **China's Integration Into the Global Financial System**

China's global economic significance is growing. Its gross domestic product (GDP) is the world's second largest when measured in terms of purchasing-power parities, and its share in world exports is exceeded only by Germany's and that of the United States. China is Canada's second-largest trading partner, and trade between the two countries is continuing to grow rapidly. ... Yet China has only a minor role in the global financial system. Its banks, some of which are the largest in the world by market capitalization and the size of their balance sheets, have only a modest international presence. ... China's currency ... is virtually not used outside the country and, with a few exceptions, Chinese capital markets are not a source of financing for foreign borrowers. China's lack of integration into the global financial system needs to be understood primarily in the context of China's own interests and domestic policy priorities. The central economic goal of the Chinese authorities has been to achieve growth with stability while radically restructuring the industrial sector and creating enough jobs each year to absorb layoffs and large numbers of new entrants into the labour force. ... As the Chinese economy matures, however, and as reforms strengthen the domestic financial system, China will become more important in global financial markets. Changes are already occurring as China's financial might is being channeled towards overseas investments. ...

Bank of Canada Review, Summer 2008

a. Explain the effects of increased integration of China into the global loanable funds market. Will the world equilibrium real interest rate rise or fall as China becomes more integrated? Draw a graph to illustrate your answer.

b. Explain the potential effect on Canada of an increased Chinese presence in global financial markets.

c. What are the advantages and disadvantages to China of isolating itself from the global loanable funds market?

18. **Greenspan's Conundrum Spells Confusion for Us All**

... At the beginning of the year, the consensus was that ... bond yields would rise. ... Gradually, over February, the consensus has started to reassert itself. ... Ten-year Treasury bond yields were hovering below 4 percent in the early part of the month but now they are around 4.3 percent.

Because the consensus was that bond yields should be 5 percent by the end of the year, most commentators have focused, not on why bond yields have suddenly risen, but on why they were so low before.

A number of explanations for this "conundrum" have been advanced. First, bond yields are being held artificially low by unusual buying. ... Another [is] ... bond yields reflect investors' expectations for an economic slowdown in 2005.

Financial Times, February 26, 2005

a. Explain how "unusual buying" might lead to a low real interest rate.

b. Explain how "investors' expectations for an economic slowdown" might lead to a lower real interest rate.

19. Study *Reading Between the Lines* on pp. 560–561 and then answer the following questions.

a. What was the financial rescue package passed by U.S. Congress and what was it supposed to do?

b. What did the U.S. Congress hope would occur after the rescue package was passed?

c. Based on what happened in the stock market, in the weeks after the package was passed, do you think we can conclude that suppliers of loanable funds believed that the rescue package was working? Explain your answer.

d. What did people fear would occur if the rescue package didn't work as intended?

e. Based on what happened in the stock market, do you think we can conclude that suppliers of loanable funds shared the fears? Explain your answer.

f. What other measures might the government take if it wants to boost supply and demand in the market for loanable funds?

g. How do you think the global nature of the loanable funds markets influences how the U.S. market would respond to no rescue?

24 ◆ Money, the Price Level, and Inflation

After studying this chapter, you will be able to

- Define money and describe its functions

- Describe the banking system and explain the economic functions of banks, the Bank of Canada, and the payments system

- Explain how the banking system creates money

- Explain what determines the demand for money, the supply of money, and the nominal interest rate

- Explain how the quantity of money influences the price level and the inflation rate in the long run

Money, like fire and the wheel, has been around for a long time, and it has taken many forms. Money was wampum (beads made from shells) for North American Indians, whale's teeth for Fijians, and tobacco for early American colonists. Cakes of salt served as money in Ethiopia and Tibet. Today, when we want to buy something, we use coins or dollar bills, write a cheque, or swipe a card. Soon, we'll be using a "smart card" that keeps track of spending and that our pocket computer can read. Are all these things money?

When we deposit some coins or notes into a bank, is that still money? And what happens when the bank lends the money we've deposited to someone else? How can we get our money back if it has been lent out?

The Bank of Canada regulates the quantity of money in our economy. How does the Bank of Canada influence the quantity of money and what happens if it creates too much money or too little money?

In this chapter, we study the functions of money; the banks that create it; the Bank of Canada, which influences the quantity of money; and the long-run consequences of changes in the quantity of money. In *Reading Between the Lines* at the end of the chapter, we look at a spectacular example of money, inflation, and economic collapse in the African nation, Zimbabwe.

What Is Money?

What do wampum, tobacco, and nickels and dimes have in common? They are all examples of **money**, which is defined as any commodity or token that is generally acceptable as a means of payment. A **means of payment** is a method of settling a debt. When a payment has been made, there is no remaining obligation between the parties to a trans-action. So what wampum, tobacco, and nickels and dimes have in common is that they have served (or still do serve) as the means of payment. Money serves three other functions:

- Medium of exchange
- Unit of account
- Store of value

Medium of Exchange

A *medium of exchange* is any object that is generally accepted in exchange for goods and services. Without a medium of exchange, goods and services must be exchanged directly for other goods and services—an exchange called **barter**. Barter requires a *double coincidence of wants*, a situation that rarely occurs. For example, if you want a hamburger, you might offer a CD in exchange for it. But you must find someone who is selling hamburgers and wants your CD.

A medium of exchange overcomes the need for a double coincidence of wants. Money acts as a medium of exchange because people with something to sell will always accept money in exchange for it. But money isn't the only medium of exchange. You can buy with a credit card, but a credit card isn't money. It doesn't make a final payment, and the debt it creates must eventually be settled by using money.

Unit of Account

A *unit of account* is an agreed measure for stating the prices of goods and services. To get the most out of your budget, you have to figure out whether seeing one more movie is worth its opportunity cost. But that cost is not dollars and cents. It is the number of ice cream cones, cases of pop, or cups of coffee that you must give up. It's easy to do such calculations when all these goods have prices in terms of dollars and cents (see Table 24.1). If the price of a movie is $8 and the price of a case of pop is $4, you know

---

TABLE 24.1 The Unit of Account Function of Money Simplifies Price Comparisons

Good	Price in money units	Price in units of another good
Movie	$8.00 each	2 cases of pop
Pop	$4.00 per case	2 ice cream cones
Ice cream	$2 per cone	4 packs of jelly beans
Jelly beans	$0.50 per pack	2 sticks of gum
Gum	$0.25 per stick	

Money as a unit of account: The price of a movie is $8 and the price of a stick of gum is 25¢, so the opportunity cost of a movie is 32 sticks of gum ($8.00 ÷ 25¢ = 32).

No unit of account: You go to a movie theatre and learn that the price of a movie is 2 cases of pop. You go to a candy store and learn that a pack of jelly beans costs 2 sticks of gum. But how many sticks of gum does seeing a movie cost you? To answer that question, you go to the convenience store and find that a case of pop costs 2 ice cream cones. Now you head for the ice cream shop, where an ice cream cone costs 4 packs of jelly beans. Now you get out your pocket calculator: 1 movie costs 2 cases of pop, or 4 ice cream cones, or 16 packs of jelly beans, or 32 sticks of gum!

---

right away that seeing one movie costs you 2 cases of pop. If jelly beans are $0.50 a pack, 1 movie costs 16 packs of jelly beans. You need only one calculation to figure out the opportunity cost of any pair of goods and services.

Imagine how troublesome it would be if your local movie theatre posted its price as 2 cases of pop, the convenience store posted the price of a case of pop as 2 ice cream cones, the ice cream shop posted the price of an ice cream cone as 4 packs of jelly beans, and the candy store priced a pack of jelly beans as 2 sticks of gum! Now how much running around and calculating will you have to do to find out how much that movie is going to cost you in terms of the pop, ice cream, jelly beans, or gum that you must give up to see it? You get the answer for pop right away from the sign posted at the movie theatre. But for all the other goods, you're going to have to visit many different stores to establish the price of each commodity in terms of another and then calculate the prices in units that are relevant for your own decision. The hassle of doing all this research might be enough to make a person swear off movies! You can see how much simpler it is if all the prices are expressed in dollars and cents.

Store of Value

Money is a *store of value* in the sense that it can be held and exchanged later for goods and services. If money were not a store of value, it could not serve as a means of payment.

Money is not alone in acting as a store of value. A house, a car, and a work of art are other examples.

The more stable the value of a commodity or token, the better it can act as a store of value and the more useful it is as money. No store of value has a completely stable value. The value of a house, a car, or a work of art fluctuates over time. The value of the commodities and tokens that are used as money also fluctuate over time.

Inflation lowers the value of money and the values of other commodities and tokens that are used as money. To make money as useful as possible as a store of value, a low inflation rate is needed.

Money in Canada Today

In Canada today, money consists of

- Currency
- Deposits at banks and other depository institutions

Currency The notes and coins held by individuals and businesses are known as **currency**. Notes are money because the government declares them so. Look at a Bank of Canada note and notice the words "Ce billet a cours légal–this note is legal tender." Currency is the most convenient type of money for settling small debts and buying low-priced items.

Deposits Deposits of individuals and businesses at banks and other depository institutions, such as trust and mortgage companies, credit unions, and caisses populaires, are also counted as money. Deposits are money because the owners of the deposits can use them to make payments.

Official Measures of Money in Canada
Currency a Small Part of the Total

The figure shows the relative magnitudes of the items that make up M1 and M2. Notice that M2 is a bit more than double M1 and that currency is a small part of our money.

	$ billions in November 2008
M2	838
Comprises all in M1, plus...	
Fixed term deposits	317
Non-chequable deposits, non-personal	11
Non-chequable deposits, personal	103
M1	407
Chequable deposits, non-personal	212
Chequable deposits, personal	145
Currency outside banks	50

Two Official Measures of Money

- M1
  - Currency outside banks
  - Personal chequable deposits
  - Non-personal chequable deposits
- M2
  - M1
  - Personal non-chequable deposits
  - Non-personal non-chequable deposits
  - Fixed term deposits

Source of data: Statistics Canada CANSIM Table 176-0020.

Official Measures of Money Two official measures of money[*] in Canada today are known as M1 and M2. **M1** consists of currency and chequable deposits of individuals and businesses. M1 does *not* include currency held by banks, or currency and chequable deposits of the government of Canada. **M2** consists of M1 plus all other deposits.

---

[*] In the Bank of Canada's official statistics, M1 is called M1+ (gross) and M2 is is called M2 (gross).

Are M1 and M2 Really Money? Money is the means of payment. So the test of whether an asset is money is whether it serves as a means of payment. Currency passes the test. But what about deposits? Chequable deposits are money because they can be transferred from one person to another by writing a cheque or using a debit card. Such a transfer of ownership is equivalent to handing over currency. Because M1 consists of currency plus chequable deposits and each of these is a means of payment, *M1 is money.*

But what about M2? Some of the savings deposits in M2 are just as much a means of payment as the chequable deposits in M1. You can use the ATM at the grocery store checkout or gas station and transfer funds directly from your savings account to pay for your purchase. But some savings deposits are not means of payment. These deposits are known as liquid assets. *Liquidity* is the property of being easily convertible into a means of payment without loss in value. Because the deposits in M2 that are not means of payment are quickly and easily converted into a means of payment—into currency or chequable deposits—they are counted as money.

Deposits Are Money but Cheques Are Not In defining money, we include, along with currency, deposits at banks and other depository institutions. But we do not count the cheques that people write as money. Why are deposits money and cheques not?

To see why deposits are money but cheques are not, think about what happens when Colleen buys some roller blades for $200 from Rocky's Rollers. When Colleen goes to Rocky's shop, she has $500 in her deposit account at the Laser Bank. Rocky has $1,000 in his deposit account—at the same bank, as it happens. The total deposits of these two people are $1,500. Colleen writes a cheque for $200. Rocky takes the cheque to the bank right away and deposits it. Rocky's bank balance rises from $1,000 to $1,200, and Colleen's balance falls from $500 to $300. The total deposits of Colleen and Rocky are still the same as before: $1,500. Rocky now has $200 more than before, and Colleen has $200 less.

This transaction has transferred money from Colleen to Rocky, but the cheque itself was never money. There wasn't an extra $200 of money while the cheque was in circulation. The cheque instructs the bank to transfer money from Colleen to Rocky.

If Colleen and Rocky use different banks, there is an extra step. Rocky's bank credits $200 to Rocky's

account and then takes the cheque to a cheque-clearing centre. The cheque is then sent to Colleen's bank, which pays Rocky's bank $200 and then debits Colleen's account $200. This process can take a few days, but the principles are the same as when two people use the same bank.

Credit Cards Are Not Money You've just seen that cheques are not money. What about credit cards? Isn't having a credit card in your wallet and presenting the card to pay for your roller blades the same thing as using money? Why aren't credit cards somehow valued and counted as part of the quantity of money?

When you pay by cheque, you are frequently asked to prove your identity by showing your driver's licence. It would never occur to you to think of your driver's licence as money. It's just an ID card. A credit card is also an ID card, but one that lets you take out a loan at the instant you buy something. When you sign a credit card sales slip, you are saying, "I agree to pay for these goods when the credit card company bills me." Once you get your statement from the credit card company, you must make at least the minimum payment due. To make that payment, you need money—you need to have currency or a chequable deposit to pay the credit card company. So although you use a credit card when you buy something, the credit card is not the *means of payment* and it is not money.

Review Quiz

1 What makes something money? What functions does money perform? Why do you think packs of chewing gum don't serve as money?
2 What are the problems that arise when a commodity is used as money?
3 What are the main components of money in Canada today?
4 What are the official measures of money? Are all the measures really money?
5 Why are cheques and credit cards not money?

  Work Study Plan 24.1 and get instant feedback.

We've seen that the main component of money in Canada is deposits at banks and other depository institutions. Let's take a closer look at these institutions.

The Banking System

The banking system consists of private and public institutions that create money and manage the nation's monetary and payments systems. These institutions play a crucial role in financial markets and have profound effects on overall economic performance. To describe these institutions and explain their functions, we'll divide them into three groups:

- Depository institutions
- The Bank of Canada
- The payments system

Depository Institutions

A **depository institution** is a private firm that takes deposits from households and firms and makes loans to other households and firms. The deposits of three types of depository institution make up the nations money. They are

- Chartered banks
- Credit unions and caisses populaires
- Trust and mortgage loan companies

Chartered Banks   A **chartered bank** is a private firm, chartered under the Bank Act of 1992 to receive deposits and make loans. The chartered banks are by far the largest institutions in the banking system and conduct all types of banking and financial business. In 2008, 14 Canadian-owned banks (including the Royal Bank of Canada, CIBC, Bank of Montreal, Bank of Nova Scotia, National Bank of Canada, and TD Canada Trust) and 33 foreign-owned banks had the bulk of the deposits in M1 and M2.

Credit Unions and Caisses Populaires   A **credit union** is a cooperative organization that operates under the Co-operative Credit Association Act of 1992 and that receives deposits from and makes loans to its members. A caisse populaire is a similar type of institution that operates in Quebec.

Trust and Mortgage Loan Companies   A **trust and mortgage loan company** is a privately owned depository institution that operates under the Trust and Loan Companies Act of 1992. These institutions receive deposits, make loans, and act as trustee for pension funds and for estates.

All Banks Now   Historically, Canada made a sharp legal distinction between banks and other depository institutions. But the economic functions of all depository institutions have grown increasingly similar. This fact is recognized in laws governing these institutions that became effective in 1992. Because they all perform the same essential economic functions, we'll call all these institutions banks unless we need to distinguish among them.

What Depository Institutions Do   Depository institutions provide services such as cheque clearing, account management, credit cards, and Internet banking, all of which provide an income from service fees. But depository institutions earn most of their income by using the funds they receive from depositors to make loans and buy securities that earn a higher interest rate than that paid to depositors. In this activity, a depository institution must perform a balancing act weighing return against risk. To see this balancing act, we'll focus on the chartered banks.

A chartered bank puts the funds it receives from depositors and other funds that it borrows into four types of assets:

1. Reserves   Reserves are notes and coins in a bank's vault or in a deposit account at the Bank of Canada. (We'll study the Bank of Canada later in this chapter.) These funds are used to meet depositors' currency withdrawals and to make payments to other banks. In normal times, a bank keeps about a half of one percent of deposits as reserves.

2. Liquid Assets   Liquid assets are government of Canada Treasury bills and commercial bills. These assets are the banks' first line of defence if they need reserves. Liquid assets can be sold and instantly converted into reserves with virtually no risk of loss. Because they have a low risk, they earn a low interest rate.

3. Securities   Securities are government of Canada bonds and other bonds such as mortgage-backed securities. These assets can be converted into reserves but at prices that fluctuate. Because their prices fluctuate, these assets are riskier than liquid assets, but they also have a higher interest rate.

4. Loans   Loans are commitments of funds for an agreed-upon period of time. Banks make loans to corporations to finance the purchase of capital. They also make mortgage loans to finance the purchase of homes, and personal loans to finance consumer durable goods, such as cars or boats. The outstanding balances on credit card accounts are also bank loans. Loans are the riskiest assets of a bank. They cannot be converted into reserves until they are due to be repaid. And some borrowers default and never repay. These assets earn the highest interest rate.

Table 24.2 provides a snapshot of the sources and uses of funds of all the chartered banks in 2008.

Economic Benefits Provided by Depository Institutions

You've seen that a depository institution earns part of its profit because it pays a lower interest rate on deposits than what it earns on loans. What benefits do these institutions provide that make depositors willing to put up with a low interest rate and borrowers willing to pay a higher one? They provide four benefits:

- Create liquidity
- Pool risk
- Lower the cost of borrowing
- Lower the cost of monitoring borrowers

Create Liquidity Depository institutions create liquidity by *borrowing short and lending long*—taking deposits and standing ready to repay them on short notice or on demand and making loan commitments that run for terms of many years.

TABLE 24.2 Chartered Banks: Sources and Uses of Funds

	$ billion September 2008	Percentage of deposits
Total funds	1,762.5	159.0
Sources		
Deposits	1,108.4	100.0
Borrowing and own capital	654.1	59.0
Uses		
Reserves	4.7	0.4
Liquid assets	216.0	19.5
Securities and other assets	194.7	17.6
Loans	1,347.1	121.5

Chartered banks get two-thirds of their funds from depositors and use the funds to make loans. Banks hold a very small amount of reserves—less than a half of one percent of deposits. They hold about 20 percent of deposits as liquid assets.

Source of data: Statistics Canada, CANSIM Table 176-0011.

◆

Pool Risk A loan might not be repaid—a default. If you lend to one person who defaults, you lose the entire amount loaned. If you lend to 1,000 people (through a bank) and one person defaults, you lose almost nothing. Depository institutions pool risk.

Lower the Cost of Borrowing Imagine there are no depository institutions and a firm is looking for $1 million to buy a new factory. It hunts around for several dozen people from whom to borrow the funds. Depository institutions lower the cost of this search. The firm gets its $1 million from a single institution that gets deposits from a large number of people but spreads the cost of this activity over many borrowers.

Lower the Cost of Monitoring Borrowers By monitoring borrowers, a lender can encourage good decisions that prevent defaults. But this activity is costly. Imagine how costly it would be if each household that lent money to a firm incurred the costs of monitoring that firm directly. Depository institutions can perform this task at a much lower cost.

You now know what money is and that the bulk of the nation's money is deposits in banks and other institutions. Your next task is to learn about the Bank of Canada and the ways in which it can influence the quantity of money.

The Bank of Canada

The Bank of Canada is Canada's **central bank**, a public authority that supervises other banks and financial institutions, financial markets, and the payments system, and conducts monetary policy.

The Bank of Canada is a bank. And like all banks, it accepts deposits, makes loans, and holds investment securities. But the Bank of Canada is special in three important ways. It is the

- Banker to banks and government
- Lender of last resort
- Sole issuer of bank notes

Banker to Banks and Government The Bank of Canada has a restricted list of customers. They are the chartered banks, credit unions and caisses populaires, and trust and mortgage loan companies that make up the banking system; the government of Canada; and the central banks of other countries. The Bank of Canada accepts deposits from these customers, and these deposits are part of the reserves of the banks.

Lender of Last Resort The Bank of Canada makes loans to banks. And it is the **lender of last resort**, which means that it stands ready to make loans when the banking system as a whole is short of reserves. If some banks are short of reserves while others have surplus reserves, the overnight loan market moves the funds from one bank to another.

Sole Issuer of Bank Notes The Bank of Canada is the only bank that is permitted to issue bank notes. You might think that such a monopoly is natural, but it isn't. In some banking systems—those of Ireland and Scotland are examples—private banks also issue bank notes. But in Canada and most other countries, the central bank has a monopoly on this activity.

The Bank of Canada's Balance Sheet The Bank of Canada influences the economy by changing interest rates. You'll learn the details of the Bank's monetary policy strategy in Chapter 30 when you've studied all the tools needed to understand monetary policy. But to influence interest rates, the Bank must change the quantity of money in the economy. And this quantity depends on the size and composition of its balance sheet—its assets and the liabilities. Lets look at the Bank of Canada's balance sheet starting with its assets.

The Bank of Canada's Assets The Bank of Canada has two main assets:

1. Government securities
2. Loans to depository institutions

The Bank of Canada holds government of Canada securities—Treasury bills—that it buys in the bills market. The Bank of Canada makes loans to depository institutions. When these institutions in aggregate are short of reserves, they can borrow from the Bank of Canada. In normal times this item is small, but during 2008, it grew as the Bank provided increasing amounts of relief from the sub-prime mortgage crisis. In September 2008, loans to depository institutions almost equalled government securities in the Bank of Canada's balance sheet (see Table 24.3).

The Bank of Canada's Liabilities The Bank of Canada has two liabilities:

1. Bank of Canada notes
2. Depository institution deposits

Bank of Canada notes are the dollar bills that we use in our daily transactions. Some of these notes are held by individuals and businesses; others are in the tills and vaults of banks and other depository institutions. Depository institution deposits at the Bank of Canada are part of the reserves of these institutions (see p. 571).

The Monetary Base The Bank of Canada's liabilities together with coins issued by the Royal Canadian Mint (coins are not liabilities of the Bank of Canada) make up the monetary base. That is, the **monetary base** is the sum of Bank of Canada notes, coins, and depository institution deposits at the Bank of Canada. The monetary base is so named because it acts like a base that supports the nation's money. Table 24.3 provides a snapshot of the sources and uses of the monetary base in September 2008.

To change the monetary base, the Bank of Canada conducts an **open market operation**, which is the purchase or sale of government of Canada securities—Treasury bills and bonds—by the Bank of Canada in the open market. When the Bank of Canada conducts an open market operation, it makes a transaction with a bank or some other business but it does not transact with the federal government.

We explain how open market operations work and their effects in Chapter 30 (pp. 736–737).

The Payments System

The **payments system** is the system through which banks make payments to each other to settle transactions by their customers. You saw why we need such a system when you thought about Colleen buying some new roller blades from Rocky. If Colleen banks at TD Canada Trust and Rocky's bank is CIBC, when

TABLE 24.3   The Sources and Uses of the Monetary Base

Sources (billions of dollars)		Uses (billions of dollars)	
Government of Canada securities	26.6	Currency	51.2
Loans to depository institutions	25.0	Reserves of depository institutions	0.4
Monetary base	51.6	Monetary base	51.6

Source of data: Statistics Canada, CANSIM Table 176-0011. The data are for September 2008.

Central Banks in a Credit Crisis

The Striking Contrast Between Canada and the United States

The balance sheets of central banks underwent some remarkable changes from mid-2007 to late 2008. The United States was at the epicentre of the financial tsunami, and its central bank, the Federal Reserve (the U.S. Fed), took steps to lower interest rates and boost the reserves of banks. The world's other major central banks, the Bank of Canada, the European Central Bank, and the Bank of Japan took steps to coordinate their actions with the U.S. Fed.

In normal times, a central bank's holding of its country's government securities are almost as large as the monetary base (currency and depository institution reserves). But during the 2007–2008 sub-prime crisis, central banks swapped a large volume of safe government securities for riskier loans to depository institutions.

The Bank of Canada, see Fig. 1(a), halved its holding of government securities and replaced them with loans to banks. The U.S. Fed, see Fig. 2(a), almost halved its holdings of government securities and increased its loans to depository institutions from zero to $1 trillion—an amount close to equalling the size of the entire Canadian economy.

Changes also occurred on the liabilities side of the central banks' balance sheets. But these changes were small in Canada and dramatic in the United States.

In Canada, see Fig. 1(b), currency increased somewhat but the reserves of depository institutions barely changed. In contrast, in the United States, see Fig. 2(b), the reserves of the banks increased a staggering *fifteenfold* from $44 billion to $650 billion.

The difference in the increase in reserves might, in part, arise from the fact that Canada has a small number of very large banks while the United States has a large number of very small banks. The Canadian banks are more willing to lend to each other, so small reserves are adequate. The U.S. banks are extremely reluctant to lend to each other, so much larger reserves are wanted.

When the credit crisis finally ends and banks' desired reserves decrease, the U.S. Fed will need to act swiftly to mop up the vast quantity of reserves to prevent the banks from creating an unprecedented quantity of money. The Bank of Canada doesn't face this problem.

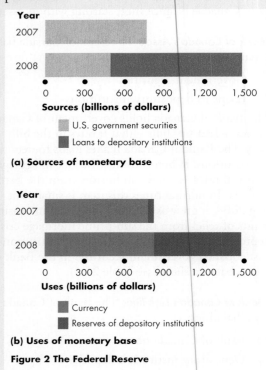

(a) Sources of monetary base

Sources (billions of dollars)
- Government securities
- Loans to depository institutions

(b) Uses of monetary base

Uses (billions of dollars)
- Currency
- Reserves of depository institutions

Figure 1 The Bank of Canada

(a) Sources of monetary base

Sources (billions of dollars)
- U.S. government securities
- Loans to depository institutions

(b) Uses of monetary base

Uses (billions of dollars)
- Currency
- Reserves of depository institutions

Figure 2 The Federal Reserve

Sources of data: Statistics Canada, CANSIM Table 176-0011 and Board of Governors of the Federal Reserve System.

Colleen writes her cheque to buy the roller blades, TD Canada Trust must take $200 from Colleen and pay that amount to CIBC, and CIBC must put the $200 into Rocky's account.

Most transactions between two parties involve two banks and so require one bank to pay another. Think about what happens when Jack, who banks at CIBC, gets $50 cash from an Interac ABM. Interac gives Jack the $50 in cash and his CIBC deposit balance goes down by $50. But now, CIBC owes Interac $50. The payments system enables banks to make payments to each other. This system in Canada is operated by the Canadian Payments Association (CPA). The CPA owns and operates the two national payments systems:

- Large Value Transfer System
- Automated Clearing Settlement System

Large Value Transfer System The **Large Value Transfer System (LVTS)** is an electronic payments system that enables financial institutions and their customers to make large payments instantly and with the sure knowledge that the payment has been made. On an average day, the LVTS handles more than 18,000 payments worth an astonishing $140 billion.

Automated Clearing Settlement System The **Automated Clearing Settlement System (ACSS)** is the system through which all payments not processed by the LVTS are handled. These payments include cheques and small-value electronic payments. On an average day, the ACSS handles more than 20 million payments worth around $17 billion.

Next, we're going to see how the banking system—the banks and the Bank of Canada—creates money.

Review Quiz

1 What are Canada's depository institutions?
2 What are the economic functions of banks?
3 How do banks balance risk and return?
4 How do banks create liquidity and pool risks?
5 How does the Bank of Canada differ from other banks?
6 What is the payments system?

 Work Study Plan 24.2 and get instant feedback.

How Banks Create Money

Banks create money. But this doesn't mean that they have smoke-filled back rooms in which counterfeiters are busily working. Remember, most money is bank deposits, not currency. What banks create is deposits, and they do so by making loans.

Creating Deposits by Making Loans

The easiest way to see that banks create deposits is to think about what happens when Andy, who has a Visa card issued by CIBC, uses his card to buy a tank of gas from Petro-Canada. When Andy signs the card sales slip, he takes a loan from CIBC and obligates himself to repay the loan at a later date. At the end of the business day, a Petro-Canada clerk takes a pile of signed credit card sales slips, including Andy's, to Petro-Canada's bank. For now, let's assume that Petro-Canada also banks at CIBC. The bank immediately credits Petro-Canada's account with the value of the slips (minus the bank's commission).

You can see that these transactions have created a bank deposit and a loan. Andy has increased the size of his loan (his credit card balance) and Petro-Canada has increased the size of its bank deposit. Because bank deposits are money, CIBC has created money.

If Andy and Petro-Canada use the same bank (as we just assumed), no further transactions take place. But the outcome is essentially the same when they use different banks. If Petro-Canada's bank is the Bank of Nova Scotia, then CIBC uses its reserves to pay the Bank of Nova Scotia. CIBC has an increase in loans and a decrease in reserves; the Bank of Nova Scotia has an increase in reserves and an increase in deposits. The banking system has an increase in loans and deposits but no change in reserves.

If Andy had swiped his card at an automatic payment pump, all these transactions would have occurred at the time he filled his tank, and the quantity of money would have increased by the amount of his purchase (minus the bank's commission for conducting the transactions).

The quantity of deposits that the banking system can create is limited by three factors:

- The monetary base
- Desired reserves
- Desired currency holdings

The Monetary Base You've seen that the *monetary base* is the sum of Bank of Canada notes, coins, and banks' deposits at the Bank of Canada. The size of the monetary base limits the total quantity of money that the banking system can create. The reason is that banks have a desired level of reserves, households and firms have a desired holding of currency, and both of these desired holdings of the monetary base depend on the quantity of money.

Desired Reserves A bank's *actual* **reserves** consist of the notes and coins in its vaults and its deposit at the Bank of Canada. A bank uses its reserves to meet depositors' demand for currency and to make payments to other banks.

You've also seen that banks don't have $100 of reserves for every $100 that people have deposited with them. If the banks did behave that way, they wouldn't make a profit.

In September 2008, banks had reserves of $1.20 for every $100 of M1 deposits and $0.60 for every $100 of M2 deposits. Most of these reserves are currency. You saw in the previous section that reserves in the form of deposits at the Bank of Canada are tiny. But there's no need for panic. Each bank holds the quantity of reserves that is adequate for its ordinary business needs.

The fraction of a bank's total deposits that are held in reserves is called the **reserve ratio**. So with reserves of $1.20 for every $100 of M1 deposits, the M1 reserve ratio is 0.012 or 1.2 percent, and with reserves of $0.60 for every $100 of M2 deposits, the M2 reserve ratio is 0.006 or 0.6 percent.

A bank's desired reserves are the reserves that it wishes to hold. Banks choose to hold reserves so that they can make payments—just as households and firms hold money to enable them to make payments. The quantity of reserves that a bank plans to hold is its *desired reserves*, and desired reserves expressed as a percentage of total deposits is called the **desired reserve ratio**. In Canada, with its highly efficient Large Value Transfer System that banks use to make payments, the desired reserve ratio is very small.

A bank's reserve ratio changes when its customers make a deposit or a withdrawal. If a bank's customer makes a deposit, reserves and deposits increase by the same amount, so the bank's reserve ratio increases. Similarly, if a bank's customer makes a withdrawal, reserves and deposits decrease by the same amount, so the bank's reserve ratio decreases.

A bank's **excess reserves** are its actual reserves minus its desired reserves. When a bank has excess reserves, it makes loans and creates money; when it is short of reserves—when desired reserves exceed actual reserves—its loans and deposits shrink.

When the entire banking system has excess reserves, banks make loans and deposits increase; when the banking system is short of reserves, banks decrease loans and deposits decrease.

The greater the desired reserve ratio, the smaller is the quantity of money that the banking system can create from a given monetary base.

Desired Currency Holding We hold our money in the form of currency and bank deposits. The proportion of money held as currency isn't constant but at any given time, people have a definite view as to how much they want to hold in each form of money.

In 2008, for every dollar of M1 deposits held, we held 12.3 cents of currency and for every dollar of M2 deposits, we held 6 cents of currency.

Because households and firms want to hold some proportion of their money in the form of currency, when the total quantity of bank deposits increases, so does the quantity of currency that they want to hold. Because desired currency holding increases when deposits increase, currency leaves the banks when loans are made and deposits increase. We call the leakage of currency from the banking system the *currency drain*, and we call the ratio of currency to deposits the **currency drain ratio**.

The greater the currency drain ratio, the smaller is the quantity of deposits and money that the banking system can create from a given amount of monetary base.

The Money Creation Process

The money creation process begins when the monetary base increases and the banking system has excess reserves. These excess reserves come from a purchase of securities by the Bank of Canada from a bank. (Chapter 30, pp. 736–737, explains exactly how the Bank of Canada conducts such a purchase—open market operation.)

When the Bank of Canada buys securities from a bank, the bank's reserves increase but its deposits do not change. So the bank has excess reserves. It lends those excess reserves and a sequence of events then plays out.

The sequence, which keeps repeating until all the reserves held are desired and banks have no excess reserves, has eight steps:

1. Banks have excess reserves.
2. Banks lend excess reserves.
3. The quantity of money increases.
4. New money is used to make payments.
5. Some of the new money remains on deposit.
6. Some of the new money is a *currency drain*.
7. Desired reserves increase because deposits have increased.
8. Excess reserves decrease but remain positive.

The sequence repeats in a series of rounds, but excess reserves shrink at each round. The process of money creation continues until excess reserves have been eliminated.

Figure 24.1 illustrates the first round in this process.

The Money Multiplier

The **money multiplier** is the ratio of the change in the quantity of money to the change in monetary base. For example, if an increase in the monetary base by $100,000 increases the quantity of money by $250,000, then the money multiplier is 2.5.

The Mathematical Note on pp. 586–587 explains how the size of the money multiplier depends on the reserve ratio and the currency drain ratio.

Review Quiz

1 How do banks create money?
2 What limits the quantity of money that the banking system can create?
3 A bank manager tells you that she doesn't create money: She just lends what people deposit. Explain why she is wrong.

myeconlab Work Study Plan 24.3 and get instant feedback.

FIGURE 24.1 How the Banking System Creates Money by Making Loans

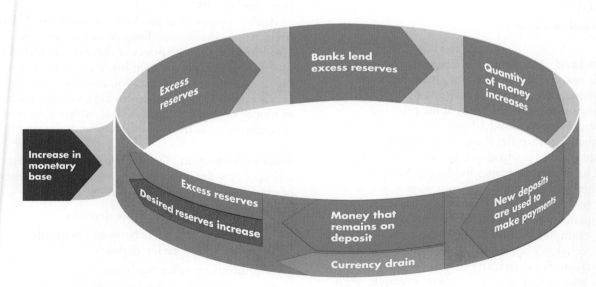

The Bank of Canada increases the monetary base, which increases bank reserves and creates excess reserves. Banks lend the excess reserves and create new deposits. The quantity of money increases. New deposits are used to make payments. Some of the new money remains on deposit at banks and some leaves the banks in a currency drain. The increase in bank deposits increases banks' desired reserves. But the banks still have excess reserves, though less than before. The process repeats until excess reserves have been eliminated.

myeconlab animation

The Market for Money

There is no limit to the amount of money we would like to *receive* in payment for our labour or as interest on our savings. But there *is* a limit to how big an inventory of money we would like to *hold* and neither spend nor use to buy assets that generate an income. The *quantity of money demanded* is the inventory of money that people plan to hold on any given day. It is the quantity of money in our wallets and in our deposit accounts at banks. The quantity of money held must equal the quantity supplied, and the forces that bring about this equality in the money market have powerful effects on the economy, as you will see in the rest of this chapter.

But first, we need to explain what determines the amount of money that people plan to hold.

The Influences on Money Holding

The quantity of money that people plan to hold depends on four main factors:

- The price level
- The *nominal* interest rate
- Real GDP
- Financial innovation

The Price Level The quantity of money measured in dollars is *nominal money*. The quantity of nominal money demanded is proportional to the price level, other things remaining the same. If the price level rises by 10 percent, people hold 10 percent more nominal money than before, other things remaining the same. If you hold $20 to buy your weekly movies and pop, you will increase your money holding to $22 if the prices of movies and pop—and your wage rate—increase by 10 percent.

The quantity of money measured in constant dollars (for example, in 2000 dollars) is real money. *Real money* is equal to nominal money divided by the price level and is the quantity of money measured in terms of what it will buy. In the above example, when the price level rises by 10 percent and you increase your money holding by 10 percent, your *real* money holding is constant. Your $22 at the new price level buys the same quantity of goods and is the same quantity of *real money* as your $20 at the original price level. The quantity of real money demanded is independent of the price level.

The Nominal Interest Rate A fundamental principle of economics is that as the opportunity cost of something increases, people try to find substitutes for it. Money is no exception. The higher the opportunity cost of holding money, other things remaining the same, the smaller is the quantity of real money demanded. The nominal interest rate on other assets minus the nominal interest rate on money is the opportunity cost of holding money.

The interest rate that you earn on currency and chequable deposits is zero. So the opportunity cost of holding these items is the nominal interest rate on other assets such as a savings bond or a Treasury bill. By holding money instead, you forgo the interest that you otherwise would have received.

Money loses value because of inflation, so why isn't the inflation rate part of the cost of holding money? It is. Other things remaining the same, the higher the expected inflation rate, the higher is the nominal interest rate.

Real GDP The quantity of money that households and firms plan to hold depends on the amount they are spending, and the quantity of money demanded in the economy as a whole depends on aggregate expenditure—real GDP.

Again, suppose that you hold an average of $20 to finance your weekly purchases of movies and pop. Now imagine that the prices of these goods and of all other goods remain constant but that your income increases. As a consequence, you now buy more goods and services and you also keep a larger amount of money on hand to finance your higher volume of expenditure.

Financial Innovation Technological change and the arrival of new financial products influence the quantity of money held. Financial innovations include

1. Daily interest chequable deposits
2. Automatic transfers between chequable deposits and saving deposits
3. Automatic teller machines
4. Credit cards and debit cards
5. Internet banking and bill paying

These innovations have occurred because of the development of computing power that has lowered the cost of calculations and record keeping.

We summarize the effects of the influences on money holding by using a demand for money curve.

The Demand for Money

The **demand for money** is the relationship between the quantity of real money demanded and the nominal interest rate when all other influences on the amount of money that people wish to hold remain the same.

Figure 24.2 shows a demand for money curve, *MD*. When the interest rate rises, other things remaining the same, the opportunity cost of holding money rises and the quantity of real money demanded decreases—there is a movement up along the demand for money curve. Similarly, when the interest rate falls, the opportunity cost of holding money falls, and the quantity of real money demanded increases—there is a movement down along the demand for money curve.

When any influence on money holding other than the interest rate changes, there is a change in the demand for money and the demand for money curve shifts. Let's study these shifts.

Shifts in the Demand for Money Curve

A change in real GDP or financial innovation changes the demand for money and shifts the demand for money curve.

Figure 24.3 illustrates the change in the demand for money. A decrease in real GDP decreases the demand for money and shifts the demand for money curve leftward from MD_0 to MD_1. An increase in real GDP has the opposite effect: It increases the demand for money and shifts the demand for money curve rightward from MD_0 to MD_2.

The influence of financial innovation on the demand for money curve is more complicated. It decreases the demand for currency and might increase the demand for some types of deposits and decrease the demand for others. But generally, financial innovation decreases the demand for money.

You can see the effects of changes in real GDP and financial innovation by looking at the demand for money in Canada on the next page.

FIGURE 24.2 The Demand for Money

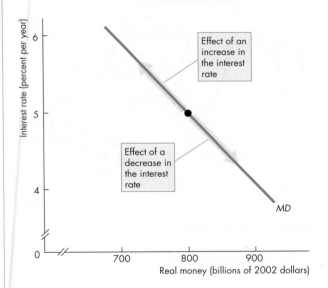

The demand for money curve, *MD*, shows the relationship between the quantity of real money that people plan to hold and the nominal interest rate, other things remaining the same. The interest rate is the opportunity cost of holding money. A change in the interest rate brings a movement along the demand for money curve.

FIGURE 24.3 Changes in the Demand for Money

A decrease in real GDP decreases the demand for money. The demand for money curve shifts leftward from MD_0 to MD_1. An increase in real GDP increases the demand for money. The demand for money curve shifts rightward from MD_0 to MD_2. Financial innovation generally decreases the demand for money.

Demand for Money in Canada

How Money Holding Bounces Around

The growth of real GDP brings sustained growth in the demand for money. If real GDP were the only influence on the demand for money, the demand for money curve would shift rightward whenever real GDP increased, which is most of the time.

But financial innovation also influences the demand for money. During the early 1970s, the spread of credit cards decreased the demand for currency and chequable deposits (M1).

A continued increase in the use of credit cards and the spread of ATMs further decreased the demand for M1 during the 1990s and 2000s. But debit cards and the payment of interest on chequable account balances increased the demand for M1 during the 1990s.

Similarly, financial innovation has changed the demand for the non-chequable deposits that make up M2. New interest-bearing deposits increased the demand for M2 during the 1970s. But during the 1990s, the interest-bearing chequable deposits that increased the demand for M1 had the opposite effect on M2. Also, innovations in financial products that compete with deposits of all kinds occurred and the demand for M2 decreased.

The figures illustrate the effects of financial innovation on the demand for M1 in part (a) and M2 in part (b). The effects of real GDP growth are removed by measuring money as a percentage of GDP.

Each dot represents the quantity of real money as a percentage of real GDP and the interest rate in each year between 1971 and 2007. In 1971, the demand for M1 curve was MD_0 in part (a). The demand for M1 decreased during the 1980s and the demand curve shifted leftward to MD_1. But the demand for M1 increased during the 1990s and the demand curve had shifted rightward to MD_2.

In 1971, the demand for M2 curve was MD_0 in part (b). During the 1970s, the demand for M2 increased and the demand curve shifted rightward to MD_1. During the 1990s, new substitutes for M2 decreased the demand for M2 and the demand curve shifted leftward to MD_2.

(a) Demand for M1+ gross

(b) Demand for M2+ gross

The Canadian Demand for Money

Sources of data: Statistics Canada, CANSIM Tables 176-0020, 176-0043, and 380-0002.

You now know what determines the demand for money, and you've seen how the banking system creates money.

Your next task is to bring the two sides of the money market together and see how the money market reaches an equilibrium. This matter is a bit complicated and we study it in two time frames, the short run and the long run.

Money Market Equilibrium

Money market equilibrium occurs when the quantity of money demanded equals the quantity of money supplied. The adjustments that bring about money market equilibrium are fundamentally different in the short run and the long run. Here, we explore the short run only briefly. We study the short run at length in Chapters 26–30, which explain the transmission of monetary policy through the economy.

Short-Run Equilibrium The quantity of money supplied is determined by the actions of the banks and the Bank of Canada. Each day, the Bank of Canada adjusts the quantity of money to hit its interest rate target. In Fig. 24.4, with the demand for money curve *MD*, if the Bank of Canada wants the interest rate to be 5 per-

cent a year, the Bank of Canada adjusts the quantity of money so that the quantity of real money supplied is $800 billion and the supply of money curve is *MS*.

The equilibrium interest rate is 5 percent a year. If the interest rate were 4 percent a year, people would want to hold more money than is available. They would sell bonds, bid down their price, and the interest rate would rise. If the interest rate were 6 percent a year, people would want to hold less money than is available. They would buy bonds, bid up their price, and the interest rate would fall.

Long-Run Equilibrium In the long run, supply and demand in the loanable funds market determines the real interest rate. The nominal interest rate equals the equilibrium real interest rate plus the expected inflation rate. Real GDP, which influences the demand for money, equals potential GDP. So the *only* variable that is left to adjust in the long run is the price level. The price level adjusts to make the quantity of real money supplied equal to the quantity demanded. If the Bank of Canada changes the nominal quantity of money, the price level changes (in the long run) by a percentage equal to the percentage change in the quantity of nominal money. In the long run, the change in the price level is proportional to the change in the quantity of money.

FIGURE 24.4 Money Market Equilibrium

Money market equilibrium occurs when the quantity of money demanded equals the quantity supplied.

Short run: In the short run, the quantity of real money and real GDP are given and the interest rate adjusts to achieve equilibrium, here 5 percent a year.

Long run: In the long run, supply and demand in the loanable funds market determines the interest rate, real GDP equals potential GDP, and the price level adjusts to make the quantity of real money supplied equal the quantity demanded, here $800 billion.

myeconlab animation

Review Quiz

1 What are the main influences on the quantity of real money that people and businesses plan to hold?
2 How does a change in the nominal interest rate change the quantity of money demanded? Illustrate the effect by using the demand for money curve.
3 How does a change in real GDP change the demand for money? Illustrate the effect by using the demand for money curve.
4 How has financial innovation changed the demand for M1 and the demand for M2?
5 How is money market equilibrium determined in the short run and in the long run?

myeconlab Work Study Plan 24.4 and get instant feedback.

Let's explore the long-run link between money and the price level more thoroughly.

The Quantity Theory of Money

In the long run, the price level adjusts to make the quantity of real money demanded equal the quantity supplied. A special theory of the price level and inflation—the quantity theory of money—explains this long-run adjustment of the price level.

The **quantity theory of money** is the proposition that in the long run, an increase in the quantity of money brings an equal percentage increase in the price level. To explain the quantity theory of money, we first need to define *the velocity of circulation*.

The **velocity of circulation** is the average number of times a dollar of money is used annually to buy the goods and services that make up GDP. But GDP equals the price level (P) multiplied by *real* GDP (Y). That is,

$$GDP = PY.$$

Call the quantity of money M. The velocity of circulation, V, is determined by the equation

$$V = PY/M.$$

For example, if GDP is $1,000 billion ($PY$ is $1,000 billion) and the quantity of money is $250 billion, then the velocity of circulation is 4.

From the definition of the velocity of circulation, the *equation of exchange* tells us how M, V, P, and Y are connected. This equation is

$$MV = PY.$$

Given the definition of the velocity of circulation, the equation of exchange is always true—it is true by definition. It becomes the quantity theory of money if the quantity of money does not influence the velocity of circulation or real GDP. In this case, the equation of exchange tells us that in the long run, the price level is determined by the quantity of money. That is,

$$P = M(V/Y),$$

where (V/Y) is independent of M. So a change in M brings a proportional change in P.

We can also express the equation of exchange in growth rates[1] in which form it states that

$$\text{Money growth rate} + \text{Rate of velocity change} = \text{Inflation rate} + \text{Real GDP growth rate}$$

Does the Quantity Theory Work?

Yes, on Average

On average, as predicted by the quantity theory of money, the inflation rate fluctuates in line with fluctuations in the money growth rate minus the real GDP growth rate. Figure 1 shows the relationship between money growth (M2 definition) and inflation in Canada. You can see a clear relationship between the two variables.

Figure 1 Canadian Money Growth and Inflation

Sources of data: Statistics Canada, CANSIM Tables 176-0020 and 380-0002.

Solving this equation for the inflation rate gives

$$\text{Inflation rate} = \text{Money growth rate} + \text{Rate of velocity change} - \text{Real GDP growth rate}$$

In the long run, the rate of velocity change is not influenced by the money growth rate. More strongly, in the long run, the rate of velocity change is approxi-

---

[1] To obtain this equation, begin with
$$MV = PY,$$
and then changes in these variables are related by the equation
$$\Delta MV + M\Delta V = \Delta PY + P\Delta Y.$$
Divide this equation by the equation of exchange to obtain
$$\Delta M/M + \Delta V/V = \Delta P/P + \Delta Y/Y.$$
The term $\Delta M/M$ is the money growth rate, $\Delta V/V$ is the rate of velocity change, $\Delta P/P$ is the inflation rate, and $\Delta Y/Y$ is the real GDP growth rate.

International data also support the quantity theory. Figure 2 shows a scatter diagram of the inflation rate and the money growth rate in 134 countries and Fig. 3 shows the inflation rate and money growth rate in countries with inflation rates below 20 percent a year. You can see a general tendency for money growth and inflation to be correlated but the quantity theory (the red line) does not predict inflation precisely.

The correlation between money growth and inflation isn't perfect, and the correlation does not tell us that money growth *causes* inflation. Money growth might cause inflation; inflation might cause money growth; or some third variable might cause both inflation and money growth. Other evidence does confirm, though, that causation runs from money growth to inflation.

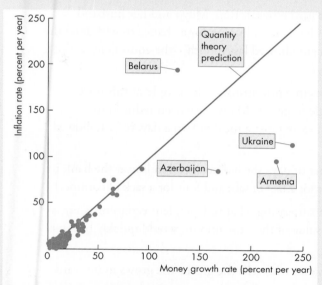

Figure 2 Money Growth and Inflation in the World

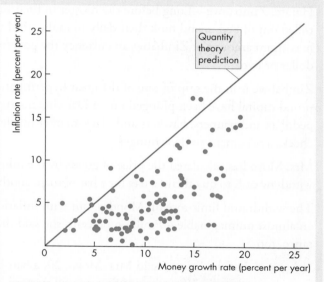

Figure 3 104 Lower-inflation countries: 1990–2005

Sources of data: International Financial Statistics Yearbook, 2008, and International Monetary Fund, *World Economic Outlook*, October 2008.

mately zero. With this assumption, the inflation rate in the long run is determined as

$$\text{Inflation rate} = \text{Money growth rate} - \text{Real GDP growth rate}$$

In the long run, fluctuations in the money growth rate minus the real GDP growth rate bring equal fluctuations in the inflation rate.

Also in the long run, with the economy at full employment, real GDP equals potential GDP, so the real GDP growth rate equals the potential GDP growth rate. This growth rate might be influenced by inflation, but the influence is most likely small and the quantity theory assumes that it is zero. So the real GDP growth rate is given and doesn't change when the money growth rate changes—inflation is correlated with money growth.

Review Quiz

1 What is the quantity theory of money?
2 How is the velocity of circulation calculated?
3 What is the equation of exchange? Can it be wrong?
4 Does the quantity theory correctly predict the effects of money growth on inflation?

myeconlab Work Study Plan 24.5 and get instant feedback.

You now know what money is, how the banks create it, and how the quantity of money influences the nominal interest rate in the short run and the price level in the long run. *Reading Between the Lines* rounds out the chapter by looking at the quantity theory of money in action in Zimbabwe today.

The Quantity Theory of Money in Zimbabwe

Life in Zimbabwe: Wait for Useless Money, Then Scour for Food

October 2, 2008

Harare, Zimbabwe—Long before the rooster in their dirt yard crowed, Rose Moyo and her husband rolled out of bed ... and took their daily moonlit stroll to the bank ... hoping for a chance to withdraw the maximum amount of Zimbabwean currency the government allowed last month—the equivalent of just a dollar or two.

Zimbabwe is in the grip of one of the great hyperinflations in world history. The people of this once proud capital have been plunged into a Darwinian struggle to get by. Many have been reduced to peddlers and paupers, hawkers and black-market hustlers, eating just a meal or two a day, their hollowed cheeks a testament to their hunger. ...

Mrs. Moyo has calculated the price of goods by the number of days she had to spend in line at the bank to withdraw cash to buy them: a day for a bar of soap; another for a bag of salt; and four for a sack of cornmeal.

The withdrawal limit rose on Monday, but with inflation surpassing what independent economists say is an almost unimaginable 40 million percent, she said the value of the new amount would quickly be a pittance, too.

"It's survival of the fittest," said Mrs. Moyo, 29, a hair braider who sells the greens she grows in her yard for a dime a bunch. "If you're not fit, you will starve."

Economists here and abroad say Zimbabwe's economic collapse is gaining velocity, radiating instability into the heart of southern Africa. As the bankrupt government prints ever more money, inflation has gone wild, rising from 1,000 percent in 2006 to 12,000 percent in 2007 to a figure so high the government had to lop 10 zeros off the currency in August to keep the nation's calculators from being overwhelmed. (Had it left the currency alone, $1 would now be worth about 10 trillion Zimbabwean dollars.) ...

Essence of the Story

- Hyperinflation in Zimbabwe is the worst in world history—40 million percent a year.

- $1 U.S. was heading towards $10 trillion Zimbabwean before 10 zeros were lopped off the currency unit.

- People get up in the middle of the night to stand in line for cash at the bank because the government limits cash withdrawals.

- Prices of goods are measured in the number of days spent in line to withdraw the cash to buy them: a day for a bar of soap or a bag of salt; four days for a sack of cornmeal.

- The people of Harare (the capital city) are on the edge of survival.

- The government fuels the inflation by printing ever more money.

Economic Analysis

- Zimbabwe has the highest inflation rate in world history, so it provides a good example of the quantity theory of money in action.

- The Zimbabwe economy is in a state of total collapse, so this case study also provides a graphic example of the devastating costs of high inflation.

- During 2008, the inflation rate in Zimbabwe was so high, it could not be measured accurately but it was reputed to be 231 million percent a year.

- To appreciate an inflation rate of 231 million percent a year, translate it into a monthly inflation rate. Every month, on average, prices rise by 239 percent. A cup of coffee that costs $3 in January costs $10 in February, $117 in April and $4,560 in July!

- Figure 1 shows Zimbabwe's reported inflation rate and money growth rate record from 2000 to 2007.

- The money growth rate increased from 52 percent a year in 2000 to 66,700 percent a year in 2007.

- The reported inflation rate increased slowly at first, from 56 percent a year in 2000 to 303 percent a year in 2005. In 2006, the inflation rate took off and climbed to a reported 1,100 percent in 2006 and 24,000 percent in 2007.

- The quantity theory predicts that inflation will outpace the money growth rate, not fall behind it as these reported inflation rates show.

- The reported inflation rate is almost certainly far lower than the true inflation rate.

- When people expect rapid inflation, they expect the money they hold to lose value rapidly, so they spend and hold goods rather than money.

- The velocity of circulation rises. The velocity of circulation is independent of the quantity of money but not independent of the money growth rate.

- We can measure the velocity of circulation in Zimbabwe by using the equation of exchange

$$MV = PY$$

along with data on M, P, and Y.

- Real GDP, Y, has fallen every year since 2000, and in 2007 it stood at 70 percent of its 2000 level.

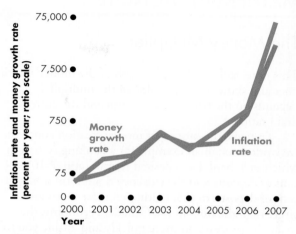

Figure 1 Money growth and inflation

- The velocity of circulation, based on the reported data, *fell* from 6.7 in 2000 to 0.6 in 2007.

- The true velocity of circulation could not have fallen. A lower velocity implies that people are hoarding more money.

- The explanation for the fall in the calculated velocity of circulation is that the true inflation rate is much higher than the reported rate.

- The unofficial reported inflation of 40 million percent a year in 2008 might be close to the truth. The inflation rate during the years 2003 through 2007 was almost certainly greater than the money growth rate.

- The reported change in the currency unit, lopping off 10 zeroes, has no effect on the inflation rate. It only changes the units in which prices are measured.

- To lower its inflation rate, the government of Zimbabwe must stop printing money to finance its expenditures.

MATHEMATICAL NOTE

The Money Multiplier

This note explains the basic math of the money multiplier and shows how the value of the multiplier depends on the banks' reserve ratio and the currency drain ratio.

To make the process of money creation concrete, we work through an example for a banking system in which each bank has a desired reserve ratio of 10 percent of deposits and the currency drain ratio is 50 percent of deposits or 0.5. (Although these ratios are larger than the ones in the Canadian economy, they make the process end more quickly and enable you to see more clearly the principles at work.)

The figure keeps track of the numbers. Before the process begins, the banks have no excess reserves. Then the monetary base increases by $100,000 and a bank has excess reserves of this amount.

The bank lends the $100,000 of excess reserves. When this loan is made, new money increases by $100,000.

With a currency drain ratio of 50 percent of deposits, $33,333 drains out of the banks as currency and $66,667 remains in the banks as deposits. The quantity of money has increased by $100,000—the increase in deposits plus the increase in currency holding.

The increased bank deposits of $66,667 generate an increase in desired reserves of 10 percent of that amount, which is $6,667. Actual reserves have increased by the same amount as the increase in deposits: $66,667. So the banks now have excess reserves of $60,000.

The process we've just described repeats but begins with excess reserves of $60,000. The figure shows the next two rounds. At the end of the process, the quantity of money has increased by a multiple of the increase in the monetary base. In this case, the increase is $250,000, which is 2.5 times the increase in the monetary base.

The sequence in the figure is the first stage of the process that finally reaches the total shown in the final row of the "money" column.

To calculate what happens at the later stages in the process and the final increase in the quantity of money,

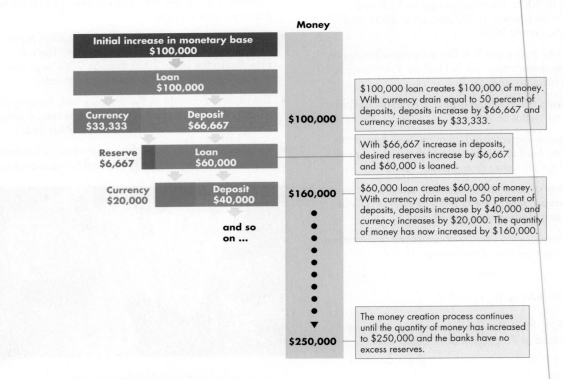

Figure 1 The money creation process

look closely at the numbers in the figure. The initial increase in reserves is $100,000 (call it A). At each stage, the loan is 60 percent (0.6) of the previous loan and the quantity of money increases by 0.6 of the previous increase. Call that proportion L ($L = 0.6$). We can write down the complete sequence for the increase in the quantity of money as

$$A + AL + AL^2 + AL^3 + AL^4 + AL^5 + \dots .$$

Remember, L is a fraction, so at each stage in this sequence, the amount of new loans and new money gets smaller. The total value of loans made and money created at the end of the process is the sum of the sequence, which is[2]

$$A/(1 - L).$$

If we use the numbers from the example, the total increase in the quantity of money is

$$\$100,000 + 60,000 + 36,000 + \dots$$

$$= \$100,000 (1 + 0.6 + 0.36 + \dots)$$

$$= \$100,000 (1 + 0.6 + 0.6^2 + \dots)$$

$$= \$100,000 \times 1/(1 - 0.6)$$

$$= \$100,000 \times 1/(0.4)$$

$$= \$100,000 \times 2.5$$

$$= \$250,000.$$

The magnitude of the money multiplier depends on the desired reserve ratio and the currency drain ratio. Call the monetary base MB and the quantity of money M. When there are no excess reserves,

------

[2] The sequence of values is called a convergent geometric series. To find the sum of a series such as this, begin by calling the sum S. Then write the sum as

$$S = A + AL + AL^2 + AL^3 + AL^4 + AL^5 + \dots .$$

Multiply by L to get

$$LS = AL + AL^2 + AL^3 + AL^4 + AL^5 + \dots .$$

Then subtract the second equation from the first to get

$$S(1 - L) = A$$

or

$$S = A/(1 - L).$$

$MB =$ Desired currency holding + Desired reserves.

$M =$ Deposits + Desired currency holding.

Call the currency drain ratio a and the desired reserve ratio b. Then

$$\text{Desired currency holding} = a \times \text{Deposits}$$

$$\text{Desired reserves} = b \times \text{Deposits}$$

$$MB = (a + b) \times \text{Deposits}$$

$$M = (1 + a) \times \text{Deposits}.$$

Call the change in monetary base ΔMB and the change in the quantity of money ΔM. Then

$$\Delta MB = (a + b) \times \text{Change in deposits}$$

$$\Delta M = (1 + a) \times \text{Change in deposits}.$$

The money multiplier is the ratio of ΔM to ΔMB, so divide the above equation for ΔM by the one for ΔMB. That is,

$$\text{Money multiplier} = (1 + a)/(a + b).$$

If we use the values of the example summarized in the figure, $a = 0.5$ and $b = 0.1$, the

$$\text{Money multiplier} = (1 + 0.5)/(0.5 + 0.1)$$

$$= 1.5/0.6 = 2.5.$$

The Canadian Money Multiplier

The money multiplier in Canada can be found by using the formula above along with the values of a and b in the Canadian economy.

Because we have two definitions of money, M1 and M2, we have two money multipliers. The numbers for M1 in 2008 are $a = 0.14$ and $b = 0.0004$. So

$$\text{M1 multiplier} = (1 + 0.14)/(0.14 + 0.0004)$$

$$= 1.14/0.1404 = 8.1.$$

For M2 in 2008, $a = 0.063$ and $b = 0.0002$, so

$$\text{M2 multiplier} = (1 + 0.063)/(0.063 + 0.0002)$$

$$= 1.063/0.0632 = 16.8.$$

SUMMARY

Key Points

What Is Money? (pp. 568–570)

- Money is the means of payment. It functions as a medium of exchange, a unit of account, and a store of value.
- Today, money consists of currency and deposits.

The Banking System (pp. 571–575)

- The banking system consists of the depository institutions (chartered banks, credit unions and caisses populaires, and trust and mortgage loan companies), the Bank of Canada, and the payments system.
- Depository institutions provide four main economic services: They create liquidity, minimize the cost of obtaining funds, minimize the cost of monitoring borrowers, and pool risks.
- The Bank of Canada is the central bank of Canada.

How Banks Create Money (pp. 575–577)

- Banks create money by making loans.
- The total quantity of money that can be created depends on the monetary base, the desired reserve ratio, and the currency drain ratio.

The Market for Money (pp. 578–581)

- The quantity of money demanded is the amount of money that people plan to hold.
- The quantity of real money equals the quantity of nominal money divided by the price level.
- The quantity of real money demanded depends on the nominal interest rate, real GDP, and financial innovation. A rise in the nominal interest rate brings a decrease in the quantity of real money demanded.
- In the short run, the Bank of Canada sets the quantity of money to hit a target nominal interest rate.
- In the long run, the loanable funds market determines the real interest rate and the quantity of money determines the price level.

The Quantity Theory of Money (pp. 582–583)

- The quantity theory of money is the proposition that money growth and inflation move up and down together in the long run.
- The Canadian and international evidence is consistent with the quantity theory, on average.

Key Figures

Figure 24.1   How the Banking System Creates Money by Making Loans, 577

Figure 24.2   The Demand for Money, 579
Figure 24.4   Money Market Equilibrium, 581

Key Terms

Automated Clearing Settlement System (ACSS), 575
Barter, 568
Central bank, 572
Chartered bank, 571
Credit union, 571
Currency, 569
Currency drain ratio, 576
Demand for money, 579
Depository institution, 571
Desired reserve ratio, 576
Excess reserves, 576
Large Value Transfer System (LVTS), 575
Lender of last resort, 573
M1, 569
M2, 569
Means of payment, 568
Monetary base, 573
Money, 568
Money multiplier, 577
Open market operation, 573
Payments system, 573
Quantity theory of money, 582
Reserve ratio, 576
Reserves, 576
Trust and mortgage loan company, 571
Velocity of circulation, 582

PROBLEMS and APPLICATIONS ◆

ⓧ myeconlab   Work problems 1–12 in Chapter 24 Study Plan and get instant feedback.
Work problems 13–22 as Homework, a Quiz, or a Test if assigned by your instructor.

1. In Canada today, money includes which of the following items?
   a. Bank of Canada bank notes in CIBC's ATMs
   b. Your Visa card
   c. Coins inside a vending machine
   d. Bank of Canada bank notes in your wallet
   e. The cheque you have just written to pay for your rent
   f. The student loan you took out last August

2. The chartered banks in Zap have

Reserves	$250 million
Loans	$1,000 million
Deposits	$2,000 million
Total assets	$2,500 million

   If banks have no excess reserves, calculate the banks' desired reserve ratio.

3. You are given the following information about the economy of Nocoin: The banks have deposits of $300 billion. Their reserves are $15 billion, two-thirds of which is in deposits with the central bank. Households and firms hold $30 billion in bank notes. There are no coins! Calculate

   a. The monetary base.
   b. The quantity of money.
   c. The banks' reserve ratio (as a percentage).
   d. The currency drain ratio (as a percentage).

4. [Study the Mathematical Note on pp. 586–587 to work this problem.] In problem 3, the banks have no excess reserves. Suppose that the Bank of Nocoin, the central bank, increases bank reserves by $0.5 billion.

   a. What happens to the quantity of money?
   b. Explain why the change in the quantity of money is not equal to the change in the monetary base.
   c. Calculate the money multiplier.

5. [Study the Mathematical Note on pp. 586–587 to work this problem.] In problem 3, the banks have no excess reserves. Suppose that the Bank of Nocoin, the central bank, decreases bank reserves by $0.5 billion.

   a. Calculate the money multiplier.
   b. What happens to the quantity of money?

   c. What happens to the quantity of deposits?
   d. What happens to the quantity of currency?

6. The spreadsheet provides information about the demand for money in Minland. Column A is the nominal interest rate, r. Columns B and C show the quantity of money demanded at two different levels of real GDP: Y_0 is $10 billion and Y_1 is $20 billion.

	A	B	C
1	r	Y_0	Y_1
2	7	1.0	1.5
3	6	1.5	2.0
4	5	2.0	2.5
5	4	2.5	3.0
6	3	3.0	3.5
7	2	3.5	4.0
8	1	4.0	4.5

   The quantity of money is $3 billion and, initially, real GDP is $20 billion. What happens in Minland if the interest rate

   a. Exceeds 4 percent a year?
   b. Is less than 4 percent a year?
   c. Equals 4 percent a year?

7. The Minland economy in problem 6 experiences a severe recession. Real GDP decreases to $10 billion. If the quantity of money supplied does not change,

   a. What happens in Minland if the interest rate is 4 percent a year?
   b. Do people buy bonds or sell bonds?
   c. Will the interest rate rise or fall? Why?

8. Quantecon is a country in which the quantity theory of money operates. The country has a constant population, capital stock, and technology. In year 1, real GDP was $400 million, the price level was 200, and the velocity of circulation was 20. In year 2, the quantity of money was 20 percent higher than in year 1. What was

   a. The quantity of money in year 1?
   b. The quantity of money in year 2?
   c. The price level in year 2?
   d. The level of real GDP in year 2?
   e. The velocity of circulation in year 2?

9. In Quantecon described in problem 8, in year 3, the quantity of money falls to one-fifth of its level in year 2.

   a. What is the quantity of money in year 3?
   b. What is the price level in year 3?
   c. What is the level of real GDP in year 3?
   d. What is the velocity of circulation in year 3?
   e. If it takes more than one year for the full quantity theory effect to occur, what do you predict happens to real GDP in Quantecon in year 3? Why?

10. **Financial System Review** The key risk to the [Canadian] financial system is that the downturn in the U.S. economy may be deeper than currently anticipated. ... The direct exposure of Canadian banks to the United States represents about 16 per cent of total bank assets, more than the combined exposure to any other group of foreign countries. ... In the mid-1990s, exposure to U.S. securities and loans represented roughly 3 per cent and 10 per cent of total Canadian bank assets, respectively. By 2007, these figures had converged, each representing just under 8 per cent of total Canadian bank assets. This shift towards increased holdings of U.S. securities, all else being equal, implies that the return on U.S. exposures has become more dependent on the performance of financial markets. ...

   Bank of Canada, June 2008

   a. Explain a bank's "balancing act."
   b. How and why have Canadian banks' holdings of U.S. assets changed?
   c. How might the over-pursuit of profit or underestimation of risk create problems for Canadian banks?

11. **"Boring" Canada's Financial Tips for the World**

   The financial crisis that began 14 months ago in the U.S. has intensified and spread around the world. ... Few countries are as dependent on trade or as integrated into the global financial system as Canada. Yet our financial sector continues to weather the turbulence better than many other countries. This did not happen by chance. Canadians by nature are prudent and our financial system has been characterized as unexciting. Canada's regulatory regime ensures that stability and efficiency are balanced. As a result, Canadian taxpayers have not had their money put at risk in response to this crisis. If Canada's financial system is boring, perhaps the world needs to be more like Canada ... capital and liquidity buffers need to be large enough to handle big shocks ... Some have criticized high Canadian capital requirements for banks as being too conservative. But the strong balance sheets of Canada's banks through this period speak for themselves ... The open market system did not fail in this crisis. However, some forgot Adam Smith's maxim that the invisible hand needs to be supported by an appropriate legal and regulatory framework.

   Financial Times, November 12, 2008

   a. Explain how Canada's financial system might be considered "boring."
   b. What are the advantages and disadvantages of a "boring" financial system?
   c. Explain how the last sentence of the news clip can be applied to organizing a country's financial system.

12. **Banks Drop on Higher Reserve Requirement**

   China's central bank will raise its reserve ratio requirement by a percentage point to a record 17.5 percent by June 25, stepping up a battle to contain lending growth. ... The increase will freeze up about 422 billion yuan of funds, equivalent to 91 percent of the value of new yuan-denominated loans extended in April. ... The latest move adds to the 614.7 billion yuan removed from the financial system through reserve ratio increases since January. China's banks had an average excess reserve deposit ratio of 2 percent as of March 31, down from 3.3 percent in December. The rate that banks charge each other for seven-day loans ... rose to 4.93 percent in Shanghai, the highest since Jan 24, according to China Bond Interbank Market. The gain suggests banks are hoarding cash in anticipation of further reserve ratio requirement increases. ... Every half-point increase in the reserve ratio requirement cuts banks' profits by as much as 1.5 percent, assuming they reduce lending to comply with it, said Li Qing, an analyst at CSC Securities HK Ltd.

   People's Daily Online, June 11, 2008

   a. Compare the reserve ratios in China and Canada.
   b. Explain how the reserve ratio influences China's money multiplier.
   c. Why would a higher reserve ratio decrease bank profits?

13. Sara withdraws $1,000 from her savings account at the Lucky Credit Union, keeps $50 in cash, and deposits the balance in her chequable account at the Royal Bank of Canada. What is the immediate change in M1 and M2?

14. Banks in New Transylvania have a desired reserve ratio of 10 percent and no excess reserves. The currency drain ratio is 50 percent. Then the central bank increases bank reserves by $1,200.

   a. What is the initial increase in the monetary base?
   b. How much do the banks lend in the first round of the money creation process?
   c. How much of the amount initially lent does not return to the banks but is held as currency?
   d. Set out the transactions that take place and calculate the amount of deposits created and the increase in the amount of currency held after the second round of the money creation process.

15. [Study the Mathematical Note on pp. 586–587 to work this problem.] In the United Kingdom, the currency drain ratio is 0.38 of deposits and the desired reserve ratio is 0.002. In Australia, the quantity of money is $150 billion, the currency drain ratio is 33 percent of deposits, and the desired reserve ratio is 8 percent.

   a. Calculate the U.K. money multiplier.
   b. Calculate the monetary base in Australia.

16. The table provides some data for the United States in the first decade following the Civil War.

	1869	1879
Quantity of money	$1.3 billion	$1.7 billion
Real GDP (1929 dollars)	$7.4 billion	Z
Price level (1929 = 100)	X	54
Velocity of circulation	4.50	4.61

Source: Milton Friedman and Anna J. Schwartz, *A Monetary History of the United States 1867–1960*.

   a. Calculate the value of X in 1869.
   b. Calculate the value of Z in 1879.
   c. Are the data consistent with the quantity theory of money? Explain your answer.

17. **Canada Backs Its Banks' Borrowing**
Canada guaranteed borrowing by its banks yesterday in a move that could find the government responsible for up to C$218bn in debt. ... The government this month [also] offered to buy as much as C$25bn in mortgages. ... The government offered to back any debt issued by Canadian banks with terms greater than three months and will charge a premium to those who opt into the guarantee. Laurence Booth, an economist at the University of Toronto, said: "I don't think [the guarantee] will be relied on heavily. It sounds like a fig leaf. It is not really needed but it shows concern for the banks."

Financial Times, October 24, 2008

   a. Explain how the government guaranteeing bank borrowing and buying up risky mortgages can change the risk-return balancing act by banks. How does charging a premium to banks who opt into the guarantee alter that balancing act?
   b. What is the government trying to accomplish by guaranteeing borrowing? How might this policy be successful even if few banks opt into the guarantee?

18. **U.S. Proposals to Increase Deposit Protection May Push Canada to Raise CDIC Limits**
Canada can bolster confidence in its financial institutions by insuring bank deposits beyond $100,000. ... Wilfrid Laurier finance professor Brian Smith said U.S. proposals to increase the federal deposit insurance on bank accounts will put pressure on Canada to also act. "It could be a useful measure to assure some Canadians that in fact that they're monies are protected and would instill some more confidence in the system," Smith said. ... Parliament increased coverage by the Canada Deposit Insurance Corp. for the first time in more than 20 years in 2005 by raising insurance for eligible deposits to $100,000 from $60,000. ... More than $512 billion of individual deposits in Canada are currently insured if financial institutions fail. ... [An increase in deposit insurance] would allow all members to increase their deposits at a time when the cost of interbanking borrowing is increasing. It could also help them to capture the growing liquidity that is available as Canadians extricate themselves from the stock market. ... Since the CDIC was created in 1967, 43 member financial institutions have failed.

Canoe Money, September 30, 2008

a. Explain how bank attempts to maximize profits can sometimes lead to bank failures.

b. How does CDIC insurance help minimize bank failures and bring more stability to the banking system?

c. How might CDIC insurance create a moral hazard situation for banks?

d. Explain how increasing CDIC deposit protection could improve liquidity for the banking system.

e. Even in the absence of a financial crisis, why might it be necessary to raise deposit protection limits over time?

19. **Fed at Odds with ECB over Value of Policy Tool**

Financial innovation and the spread of U.S. currency throughout the world has broken down relationships between money, inflation and growth, making monetary gauges a less useful tool for policy makers, the U.S. Federal Reserve chairman, Ben Bernanke, said. ... The European Central Bank, Bank of Japan and Bank of England all use growth in the supply of money in formulating policy. "Heavy reliance on monetary aggregates as a guide to policy would seem to be unwise in the U.S. context," Bernanke said. ... "The empirical relationship between money growth and variables such as inflation and nominal output growth has continued to be unstable." ... He said the Fed had "philosophical" and economic differences with European central bankers regarding the role of money and that debate between institutions was healthy. ... "Unfortunately, forecast errors for money growth are often significant," reducing their effectiveness as a tool for policy, Bernanke said. "There are differences between the U.S. and Europe in terms of the stability of money demand and financial innovation," Bernanke said. ... [Ultimately,] the risk of bad policy through a devoted following of money growth led the Fed to downgrade the importance of money measures.

International Herald Tribune, November 10, 2006

a. Explain how the debate surrounding the quantity theory of money could make "monetary gauges a less useful tool for policy makers."

b. What do Bernanke's statements reveal about his stance on the accuracy of the quantity theory of money?

20. Rapid inflation in Brazil in the early 1990s caused the cruzeiro to lose its ability to function as money. Which of the following commodities do you think would most likely have taken the place of the cruzeiro in the Brazilian economy? Explain why.

a. Tractor parts
b. Packs of cigarettes
c. Loaves of bread
d. Impressionist paintings
e. Baseball trading cards

21. **From Paper-Clip to House, in 14 Trades**

A 26-year-old Montreal man appears to have succeeded in his quest to barter a single, red paper-clip all the way up to a house. It took almost a year and 14 trades. ...

CBC News, 7 July 2006

a. Is barter a means of payment?
b. Is barter just as efficient as money when trading on eBay? Explain.

22. Study *Reading Between the Lines* on pp. 584–585 and then

a. Describe the money growth rate and the inflation rate in Zimbabwe since 2000.
b. How do we know that Zimbabwe's reported inflation between 2003 and 2007 is almost certainly below the true inflation rate?
c. What feature of Zimbabwe's economy provides a view of the cost of hyperinflation?
d. What must be done to stop Zimbabwe's inflation?
e. Why will knocking 10 zeroes off all prices not stop Zimbabwe's inflation?

23. Use the link on MyEconLab (Textbook Resources, Chapter 24, Web links) to visit "Money—Past, Present, and Future" and study the section on e-money.

a. What is e-money and what are the alternative forms that it takes?
b. Do you think that the widespread use of e-money will limit the ability of the Bank of Canada to control the quantity of money? Why or why not?
c. When you buy an item on the Internet and pay for it using PayPal, are you using money? Explain why or why not.
d. Why might e-money be superior to cash as a means of payment?

25

The Exchange Rate and the Balance of Payments

After studying this chapter, you will be able to

- Describe the foreign exchange market and distinguish between the nominal exchange rate and the real exchange rate

- Explain how the exchange rate is determined day by day

- Explain the long-run trends in the exchange rate and explain interest rate parity and purchasing power parity

- Describe the balance of payments accounts and explain what causes an international deficit

- Describe the alternative exchange rate policies and explain their long-run effects

The Canadian dollar—the loonie—is just one of more than a hundred different monies that circulate in the global economy. The loonie is an important money, but it isn't in the truly big league. The world's three big monies are the U.S. dollar ($), the euro (€), and the yen (¥). Most international payments are made using one of these monies.

In February 2007, one Canadian dollar bought 85 U.S. cents. By November 2007, the Canadian dollar had soared to $1.09 U.S. But for the next year, the Canadian dollar sank against the U.S. dollar to only 77 U.S cents. Why did our dollar rise and then fall against the U.S. dollar? Can or should Canada do anything to stabilize the value of the dollar?

From the early 1980s until 1999, the value of Canadian imports exceeded the value of Canadian exports and we borrowed a total of $223 billion from the rest of the world. During the 2000s, this situation reversed: The value of exports exceeded the value of imports and we repaid $178 billion of our earlier borrowing. Why do we sometimes have to borrow from foreigners and at other times repay our international debts?

In this chapter, you're going to discover why our dollar fluctuates against other currencies and what determines the amount of international borrowing and lending. In *Reading Between the Lines* at the end of the chapter, we'll look at China's foreign exchange rate policy and see why it troubles many people, especially Americans.

◆ Currencies and Exchange Rates

When Canadian Tire imports snow blowers from China, it pays for them using Chinese yuan. And when China Airlines buys an airplane from Bombardier, it pays using Canadian dollars. Whenever people buy things from another country, they use the currency of that country to make the transaction. It doesn't make any difference what the item is that is being traded internationally. It might be a snow blower, an airplane, insurance or banking services, real estate, the stocks and bonds of a government or corporation, or even an entire business.

Foreign money is just like Canadian money. It consists of notes and coins issued by a central bank and mint and deposits in banks and other depository institutions. When we described Canadian money in Chapter 24, we distinguished between currency (notes and coins) and deposits. But when we talk about foreign money, we refer to it as foreign currency. **Foreign currency** is the money of other countries regardless of whether that money is in the form of notes, coins, or bank deposits.

We buy these foreign currencies and foreigners buy Canadian dollars in the foreign exchange market.

The Foreign Exchange Market

The **foreign exchange market** is the market in which the currency of one country is exchanged for the currency of another. The foreign exchange market is not a place like a downtown flea market or a fruit and vegetable market. The foreign exchange market is made up of thousands of people—importers and exporters, banks, international travellers, and specialist traders called *foreign exchange brokers*.

The foreign exchange market opens on Monday morning in Sydney, Australia, and Hong Kong, which is still Sunday evening in Toronto. As the day advances, markets open in Singapore, Tokyo, Bahrain, Frankfurt, London, New York, Toronto, and San Francisco. As the West Coast markets close, Sydney is only an hour away from opening for the next day of business. The sun barely sets on the foreign exchange market. Dealers around the world are in continual contact by telephone and computer, and on a typical day in 2008, around $2 trillion (of all currencies) were traded in the foreign exchange market—or more than $400 trillion in a year.

Exchange Rates

An **exchange rate** is the price at which one currency exchanges for another currency in the foreign exchange market. For example, on December 1, 2008, one Canadian dollar would buy 80 U.S. cents—the exchange rate was $0.80 U.S per Canadian dollar.

The exchange rate fluctuates. A rise in the exchange rate is called an *appreciation* of the dollar, and a fall in the exchange rate is called a *depreciation* of the dollar. For example, when the exchange rate rises from 77 U.S. cents to 80 U.S. cents per dollar, the Canadian dollar appreciates, and when the exchange rate falls from 80 U.S. cents to 77 U.S. cents per dollar, the Canadian dollar depreciates.

The quantity of foreign money that we can buy with our dollar changes when the dollar appreciates or depreciates. But a change in the value of the dollar might not change what we *really* pay for our imports and earn from our exports. The reason is that prices of goods and services might change to offset the change in the value of the dollar and leave the terms on which we trade with other countries unchanged.

To determine whether a change in the exchange rate changes what we earn from exports and pay for imports, we need to distinguish between the *nominal* exchange rate and the *real* exchange rate.

Nominal and Real Exchange Rates

The **nominal exchange rate** is the value of the Canadian dollar expressed in units of foreign currency per Canadian dollar. It measures how much of one money exchanges for a unit of another money.

The **real exchange rate** is the relative price of Canadian-produced goods and services to foreign-produced goods and services. It is a measure of the quantity of the real GDP of other countries that a unit of Canadian real GDP buys.

The exchange rates that we've just discussed are *nominal* exchange rates. To understand the real exchange rate, suppose that China produces only snow blowers and Canada produces only airplanes. The price of a snow blower is 8,000 yuan, and the price of an airplane is $8 million. Also suppose that the exchange rate—the *nominal* exchange rate—is 10 yuan per dollar. With this information, we can calculate the *real* exchange rate, which is the number of snow blowers that one airplane buys. Let's do this calculation.

The Fluctuating Canadian Dollar

A Volatile Market

The figure shows the Canadian dollar exchange rate against the three big currencies that feature most prominently in global trade—the U.S. dollar, the Japanese yen, and the European euro—between 1988 and 2008.

The Canadian dollar has fluctuated most against the yen and least against the euro. The dollar depreciated sharply against the yen from 1990 to 1995 and appreciated from 2000 to 2007. The dollar depreciated against the U.S. dollar before 2002 and appreciated from 2002 to 2007. The dollar fluctuated around a constant 65 euro cents. In 2008, the dollar depreciated against these three currencies.

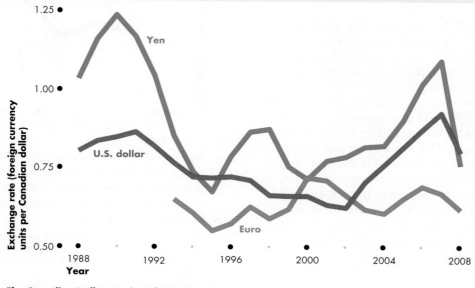

The Canadian Dollar Against Three Currencies

Source of data: PACIFIC Exchange Rate Service, http://fx.sauder.ubc.ca/.

At a price of 8,000 yuan and an exchange rate of 10 yuan per dollar, the price of a snow blower is $800. At a price of $8 million per airplane and $800 per snow blower, one airplane buys 10,000 snow blowers. The real exchange rate is 10,000 snow blowers per airplane.

Airplanes represent Canadian real GDP, and snow blowers represent Chinese real GDP. The price of a snow blower in China and the price of an airplane in Canada represent the price levels (GDP deflators) in the two countries. Call the Canadian price level P, the Chinese price level P^*, the nominal exchange rate E (yuan per dollar) and the real exchange rate RER (Chinese real GDP per unit of Canadian real GDP). Then the real exchange rate is

$$RER = E \times (P/P^*).$$

In words, the real exchange rate equals the nominal exchange rate multiplied by the ratio of the Canadian price level to the foreign price level.

The real exchange rate changes if the nominal exchange rate changes and prices remain constant. But if the dollar appreciates (E rises) and foreign prices rise (P^* rises) by the same percentage, the real exchange rate doesn't change. In the above example, if the exchange rate rises to 12 yuan per dollar and the price of a snow blower rises to 9,600 yuan, one airplane still buys 10,000 snow blowers.

How has the real exchange rate changed over time? Has it changed in the same way as the nominal exchange rate? We could answer these questions by calculating a real exchange rate in terms of each of the individual currencies of the countries with which we trade. But there is a more efficient way of measuring the real exchange rate. Instead of looking at the exchange rates between many different currencies, we look at an average of the exchange rates against all the currencies in which Canada trades.

Canadian-Dollar Effective Exchange Rate Index

The **Canadian-dollar effective exchange rate index (CERI)** is an average of the exchange rates of the Canadian dollar against the U.S. dollar, the European Union euro, the Japanese yen, the U.K. pound, the Chinese yuan, and the Mexican peso. In the CERI, each currency gets a weight that represents the importance of the currency in Canada's international trade.

The blue line in Fig. 25.1 shows the nominal CERI since 1997. We have defined the value of this index to be 100 in 1997. So the index tells us the value of the Canadian dollar against the other six currencies as a percentage of its value in 1997.

The index shows that the dollar depreciated on the average through 2002 and then appreciated through 2007 before depreciating again. The red line in Fig. 25.1 shows the real CERI. You can see that the nominal and real exchange rates moved in the same direction, but the nominal exchange rate appreciated by less and depreciated by more than the real exchange rate. The absence of a gap between the real exchange rate and the nominal exchange rate results from the fact that the inflation rates in Canada and the other countries were similar.

Questions About the Exchange Rate

The performance of the Canadian dollar in the foreign exchange market raises a number of questions that we address in the rest of this chapter.

First, how are the nominal exchange rate and real exchange rate determined? Why did the dollar appreciate from 2002 through 2007 and then depreciate?

Second, how do exchange rate fluctuations influence our international trade and international payments? In particular, could we use the exchange rate to maintain our international surplus?

Third, how do the Bank of Canada and other central banks operate in the foreign exchange market to change the value of the exchange rate? In some economies, the exchange rate is fixed, usually against the U.S. dollar. How did China fix the value of the yuan and keep it constant for many years? Could an appreciation of the yuan against the U.S. dollar change the balance of trade and payments between the United States (in deficit) and China (in surplus)?

We begin by learning how trading in the foreign exchange market determines the exchange rate.

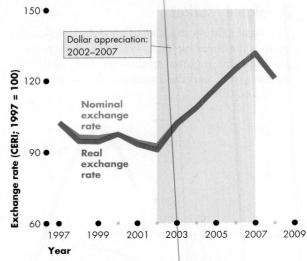

FIGURE 25.1 The Canadian-Dollar Effective Exchange Rate Index

The nominal CERI (blue line) and the real CERI (red line) depreciated slightly through 2002, appreciated through 2007, and then depreciated in 2008. The nominal CERI and real CERI are very similar because the inflation rates in the countries were similar.

Sources of data: PACIFIC Exchange Rate Service, http://fx.sauder.ubc.ca/, World Economic Outlook database, and Bank of Canada formula at www.bankofcanada.ca/en/rates/ceri.html. CERI calculated by authors with 1997 = 100.

myeconlab animation

Review Quiz

1 What is the foreign exchange market and what prices are determined in this market?

2 Distinguish between appreciation and depreciation of the dollar.

3 What are the world's major currencies?

4 Against which currencies and during which years has the Canadian dollar appreciated since 1998?

5 Against which currencies and during which years has the Canadian dollar depreciated since 1998?

6 What is the distinction between a nominal exchange rate and the real exchange rate?

7 What does the CERI measure?

myeconlab   Work Study Plan 25.1 and get instant feedback.

The Foreign Exchange Market

An exchange rate is a price—the price of one currency in terms of another. And like all prices, an exchange rate is determined in a market—the *foreign exchange market*.

The Canadian dollar trades in the foreign exchange market and is supplied and demanded by tens of thousands of traders every hour of every business day. Because the foreign exchange market has many traders and no restrictions on who may trade, it is a *competitive market*.

In a competitive market, demand and supply determine the price. So to understand the forces that determine the exchange rate, we need to study the factors that influence demand and supply in the foreign exchange market. But there is a feature of the foreign exchange market that makes it special.

The Demand for One Money Is the Supply of Another Money

When people want to exchange a foreign currency for Canadian dollars, they demand Canadian dollars and supply that other currency. And when people want to exchange Canadian dollars for a foreign currency, they supply Canadian dollars and demand that other currency.

Dealers in the foreign exchange market.

So the factors that influence the demand for Canadian dollars also influence the supply of European Union euros, U.S. dollars, or Japanese yen. And the factors that influence the demand for that other country's money also influence the supply of Canadian dollars.

We'll first look at the influences on the demand for Canadian dollars in the foreign exchange market.

Demand in the Foreign Exchange Market

People buy Canadian dollars in the foreign exchange market so that they can buy Canadian-produced goods and services—Canadian exports. They also buy Canadian dollars so that they can buy Canadian assets such as bonds, stocks, businesses, and real estate or so that they can keep part of their money in a Canadian dollar bank account.

The quantity of Canadian dollars demanded in the foreign exchange market is the amount that traders plan to buy during a given time period at a given exchange rate. This quantity depends on many factors, but the main ones are

1. The exchange rate
2. World demand for Canadian exports
3. Interest rates in Canada and other countries
4. The expected future exchange rate

To see how the exchange rate is determined, we'll look first at the relationship between the quantity of Canadian dollars demanded in the foreign exchange market and the exchange rate when the other three influences remain the same. This relationship is called the law of demand in the foreign exchange market. Then in the next section, we'll consider what happens when these other influences change.

The Law of Demand for Foreign Exchange

The law of demand applies to Canadian dollars just as it does to anything else that people value. Other things remaining the same, the higher the exchange rate, the smaller is the quantity of Canadian dollars demanded in the foreign exchange market. For example, if the price of the Canadian dollar rises from 70 U.S. cents to 80 U.S. cents but nothing else changes, the quantity of Canadian dollars that people plan to buy in the foreign exchange market decreases. The exchange rate influences the quantity of Canadian dollars demanded for two reasons:

- Exports effect
- Expected profit effect

Exports Effect The larger the value of Canadian exports, the larger is the quantity of Canadian dollars demanded in the foreign exchange market. But the value of Canadian exports depends on the prices of Canadian-produced goods and services *expressed in the currency of the foreign buyer*. And these prices depend on the exchange rate. The lower the exchange rate, other things remaining the same, the lower are the prices of Canadian-produced goods and services to foreigners and the greater is the volume of Canadian exports. So if the exchange rate falls (and other influences remain the same), the quantity of Canadian dollars demanded in the foreign exchange market increases.

To see the exports effect at work, think about orders for Bombardier regional jets. If the price of a plane is $8 million and the exchange rate is 75 euro cents per Canadian dollar, the price of this airplane to KLM, a European airline, is €6 million. KLM decides that this price is too high, so it doesn't buy a new Bombardier airplane. If the exchange rate falls to 60 euro cents per Canadian dollar and other things remain the same, the price of a Bombardier plan falls to €4.8 million. KLM now decides to buy the airplane and buys Canadian dollars in the foreign exchange market.

Expected Profit Effect The larger the expected profit from holding Canadian dollars, the greater is the quantity of Canadian dollars demanded in the foreign exchange market. But expected profit depends on the exchange rate. For a given expected future exchange rate, the lower the exchange rate today, the larger is the expected profit from buying Canadian dollars today and holding them, so the greater is the quantity of Canadian dollars demanded in the foreign exchange market today. Let's look at an example.

Suppose that Mizuho Bank, a Japanese bank, expects the exchange rate to be 110 yen per Canadian dollar at the end of the year. If today's exchange rate is also 110 yen per Canadian dollar, Mizuho Bank expects no profit from buying Canadian dollars and holding them until the end of the year. But if today's exchange rate is 100 yen per Canadian dollar and Mizuho Bank buys Canadian dollars, it expects to sell them at the end of the year for 110 yen per dollar and make a profit of 10 yen per Canadian dollar.

The lower the exchange rate today, other things remaining the same, the greater is the expected profit from holding Canadian dollars and the greater is the quantity of Canadian dollars demanded in the foreign exchange market today.

Demand Curve for Canadian Dollars

Figure 25.2 shows the demand curve for Canadian dollars in the foreign exchange market. A change in the exchange rate, other things remaining the same, brings a change in the quantity of Canadian dollars demanded and a movement along the demand curve. The arrows show such movements.

We will look at the factors that change demand in the next section of this chapter. But first, let's see what determines the supply of Canadian dollars.

FIGURE 25.2 The Demand for Canadian Dollars

The quantity of Canadian dollars demanded depends on the exchange rate. Other things remaining the same, if the exchange rate rises, the quantity of Canadian dollars demanded decreases and there is a movement up along the demand curve for Canadian dollars. If the exchange rate falls, the quantity of Canadian dollars demanded increases and there is a movement down along the demand curve for Canadian dollars.

Supply in the Foreign Exchange Market

People sell Canadian dollars and buy other currencies so that they can buy foreign-produced goods and services—Canadian imports. People also sell Canadian dollars and buy foreign currencies so that they can buy foreign assets such as bonds, stocks, businesses, and real estate or so that they can hold part of their money in bank deposits denominated in a foreign currency.

The quantity of Canadian dollars supplied in the foreign exchange market is the amount that traders plan to sell during a given time period at a given exchange rate. This quantity depends on many factors, but the main ones are

1. The exchange rate
2. Canadian demand for imports
3. Interest rates in Canada and other countries
4. The expected future exchange rate

Let's look at the law of supply in the foreign exchange market—the relationship between the quantity of Canadian dollars supplied in the foreign exchange market and the exchange rate when the other three influences remain the same.

The Law of Supply of Foreign Exchange

Other things remaining the same, the higher the exchange rate, the greater is the quantity of Canadian dollars supplied in the foreign exchange market. For example, if the exchange rate rises from 70 U.S. cents to 80 U.S. cents per Canadian dollar and other things remain the same, the quantity of Canadian dollars that people plan to sell in the foreign exchange market increases.

The exchange rate influences the quantity of dollars supplied for two reasons:

■ Imports effect
■ Expected profit effect

Imports Effect The larger the value of Canadian imports, the larger is the quantity of Canadian dollars supplied in the foreign exchange market. But the value of Canadian imports depends on the prices of foreign-produced goods and services *expressed in Canadian dollars*. These prices depend on the exchange rate. The higher the exchange rate, other things remaining the same, the lower are the prices of foreign-produced goods and services to Canadians and the greater are

Canadian imports. So if the exchange rate rises (and other influences remain the same), the quantity of Canadian dollars supplied in the foreign exchange market increases.

Expected Profit Effect This effect works just like that on the demand for the Canadian dollar but in the opposite direction. The higher the exchange rate today, other things remaining the same, the larger is the expected profit from selling Canadian dollars today and holding foreign currencies, so the greater is the quantity of Canadian dollars supplied.

Supply Curve for Canadian Dollars

Figure 25.3 shows the supply curve of Canadian dollars in the foreign exchange market. A change in the exchange rate, other things remaining the same, brings a change in the quantity of Canadian dollars supplied and a movement along the supply curve. The arrows show such movements.

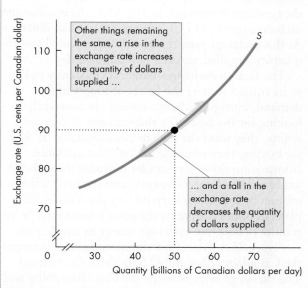

FIGURE 25.3 The Supply of Canadian Dollars

The quantity of Canadian dollars supplied depends on the exchange rate. Other things remaining the same, if the exchange rate rises, the quantity of Canadian dollars supplied increases and there is a movement up along the supply curve of Canadian dollars. If the exchange rate falls, the quantity of Canadian dollars supplied decreases and there is a movement down along the supply curve of Canadian dollars.

myeconlab animation

Market Equilibrium

Equilibrium in the foreign exchange market depends on how the Bank of Canada and other central banks operate. Here, we will study equilibrium when central banks keep out of this market. (We examine the effects of intervention in the foreign exchange market on pp. 611–613).

Figure 25.4 shows the demand curve for Canadian dollars, *D*, from Fig. 25.2, the supply curve of Canadian dollars, *S*, from Fig. 25.3, and the equilibrium exchange rate.

The exchange rate acts as a regulator of the quantities demanded and supplied. If the exchange rate is too high, there is a surplus—the quantity supplied exceeds the quantity demanded. For example, in Fig. 25.4, if the exchange rate is 100 U.S. cents per Canadian dollar, there is a surplus of Canadian dollars. If the exchange rate is too low, there is a shortage—the quantity supplied is less than the quantity demanded. For example, if the exchange rate is 80 U.S. cents per Canadian dollar, there is a shortage of Canadian dollars.

At the equilibrium exchange rate, there is neither a shortage nor a surplus—the quantity supplied equals the quantity demanded. In Fig. 25.4, the equilibrium exchange rate is 90 U.S. cents per Canadian dollar. At this exchange rate, the quantity demanded and the quantity supplied are each $50 billion a day.

The foreign exchange market is constantly pulled to its equilibrium by the forces of supply and demand. Foreign exchange traders are constantly looking for the best price they can get. If they are selling, they want the highest price available. If they are buying, they want the lowest price available. Information flows from trader to trader through the worldwide computer network, and the price adjusts minute by minute to keep buying plans and selling plans in balance. That is, the price adjusts minute by minute to keep the exchange rate at its equilibrium.

Figure 25.4 shows how the exchange rate between the Canadian dollar and U.S. dollar is determined. The exchange rates between the Canadian dollar and all other currencies are determined in a similar way. So are the exchange rates among the other currencies. Exchange rates are tied together so that no profit can be made by buying one currency, selling it for a second one, and then buying back the first one. If such a profit were available, traders would spot it, demand and supply would change, and the exchange rates would snap into alignment.

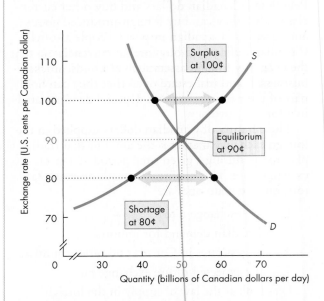

FIGURE 25.4 Equilibrium Exchange Rate

The demand curve for Canadian dollars is *D*, and the supply curve of Canadian dollars is *S*. If the exchange rate is 100 U.S cents per Canadian dollar, there is a surplus of Canadian dollars and the exchange rate falls. If the exchange rate is 80 U.S. cents per Canadian dollar, there is a shortage of Canadian dollars and the exchange rate rises. If the exchange rate is 90 U.S. cents per Canadian dollar, there is neither a shortage nor a surplus of Canadian dollars and the exchange rate remains constant. The foreign exchange market is in equilibrium.

 animation

Review Quiz

1 What are the influences on the demand for and supply of Canadian dollars in the foreign exchange market?
2 Provide an example of the exports effect on the demand for Canadian dollars and the imports effect on the supply of Canadian dollars.
3 How is the equilibrium exchange rate determined?
4 What happens if there is a shortage or a surplus of Canadian dollars in the foreign exchange market?

 Work Study Plan 25.2 and get instant feedback.

Changes in Demand and Supply: Exchange Rate Fluctuations

When the demand for Canadian dollars or the supply of Canadian dollars changes, the exchange rate changes. We'll now look at the factors that make demand and supply change, starting with the demand side of the market.

A Change in Demand for Canadian Dollars

The demand for Canadian dollars in the foreign exchange market changes when there is a change in

- World demand for Canadian exports
- Canadian and foreign interest rates
- The expected future exchange rate

World Demand for Canadian Exports An increase in world demand for Canadian exports increases the demand for Canadian dollars. For example, an increase in demand for air travel in Australia sends that country's airlines on a global shopping spree. They decide that the Bombardier regional jet is the ideal product, so they order 50 airplanes. The demand for Canadian dollars now increases.

Canadian and Foreign Interest Rates People buy financial assets to make a return. The higher the interest rate that people can earn on Canadian assets compared with foreign assets, the more Canadian assets they buy.

What matters is not the *level* of the Canadian interest rate, but the Canadian interest rate minus the foreign interest rate—a gap called the **Canadian interest rate differential**. If the Canadian interest rate rises and the foreign interest rate remains constant, the Canadian interest rate differential increases. The larger the Canadian interest rate differential, the greater is the demand for both Canadian assets and Canadian dollars.

The Expected Future Exchange Rate For a given current exchange rate, other things remaining the same, a rise in the expected future exchange rate increases the profit that people expect to make by holding Canadian dollars and the demand for Canadian dollars increases today.

Figure 25.5 summarizes the influences on the demand for Canadian dollars. An increase in the demand for Canadian exports, a rise in the Canadian interest rate differential, or a rise in the expected future exchange rate increases the demand for Canadian dollars and shifts the demand curve rightward from D_0 to D_1. A decrease in the demand for Canadian exports, a fall in the Canadian interest rate differential, or a fall in the expected future exchange rate decreases the demand for Canadian dollars and shifts the demand curve leftward from D_0 to D_2.

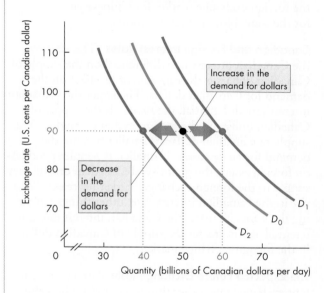

FIGURE 25.5 Changes in the Demand for Canadian Dollars

A change in any influence on the quantity of Canadian dollars that people plan to buy, other than the exchange rate, brings a change in the demand for Canadian dollars.

The demand for Canadian dollars

Increases if:
- World demand for Canadian exports increases
- The Canadian interest rate differential rises
- The expected future exchange rate rises

Decreases if:
- World demand for Canadian exports decreases
- The Canadian interest rate differential falls
- The expected future exchange rate falls

myeconlab animation

Changes in the Supply of Canadian Dollars

The supply of Canadian dollars in the foreign exchange market changes when there is a change in

- Canadian demand for imports
- Canadian and foreign interest rates
- The expected future exchange rate

Canadian Demand for Imports An increase in the Canadian demand for imports increases the supply of Canadian dollars in the foreign exchange market. For example, an increase in the demand for snow blowers sends Canadian Tire shopping in China. The supply of Canadian dollars increases as Canadian Tire goes to the foreign exchange market for Chinese yuan to pay for the snow blowers that it imports.

Canadian and Foreign Interest Rates The effect of the Canadian interest rate differential on the supply of Canadian dollars is the opposite of its effect on the demand for Canadian dollars. The larger the Canadian interest rate differential, the *smaller* is the supply of Canadian dollars in the foreign exchange market. The supply of Canadian dollars is smaller because the demand for *foreign* assets is smaller. If people spend less on foreign assets, the quantity of Canadian dollars they supply in the foreign exchange market decreases. So, a rise in the Canadian interest rate, other things remaining the same, increases the Canadian interest rate differential and decreases the supply of Canadian dollars in the foreign exchange market.

The Expected Future Exchange Rate For a given current exchange rate, other things remaining the same, a fall in the expected future exchange rate decreases the profit that can be made by holding Canadian dollars and decreases the quantity of Canadian dollars that people want to hold. To reduce their holdings of Canadian dollar assets, people must sell Canadian dollars. When they do so, the supply of Canadian dollars in the foreign exchange market increases.

Figure 25.6 summarizes the influences on the supply of Canadian dollars. If the supply of Canadian dollars decreases, the supply curve shifts leftward from S_0 to S_1. And if the supply of Canadian dollars increases, the supply curve shifts rightward from S_0 to S_2.

Changes in the Exchange Rate

If the demand for Canadian dollars increases and the supply does not change, the exchange rate rises.

FIGURE 25.6 Changes in the Supply of Canadian Dollars

A change in any influence on the quantity of Canadian dollars that people plan to sell, other than the exchange rate, brings a change in the supply of dollars.

The supply of Canadian dollars

Increases if:	*Decreases if:*
■ Canadian imports increase	■ Canadian imports decrease
■ The Canadian interest rate differential falls	■ The Canadian interest rate differential rises
■ The expected future exchange rate falls	■ The expected future exchange rate rises

myeconlab animation

If the demand for Canadian dollars decreases and the supply does not change, the exchange rate falls. Similarly, if the supply of Canadian dollars decreases and the demand does not change, the exchange rate rises. If the supply of Canadian dollars increases and the demand does not change, the exchange rate falls.

These predictions are the same as those for any other market and two episodes in the life of the Canadian dollar (next page) illustrate them.

Two Episodes in the Life of the Dollar

A Currency on a Roller Coaster

The foreign exchange market is a striking example of a competitive market. The expectations of thousands of traders around the world influence this market minute by minute throughout the 24-hour global trading day.

Demand and supply rarely stand still and their fluctuations bring a fluctuating exchange rate. Two episodes in the life of the dollar illustrate these fluctuations: 2005–2007, when the dollar appreciated, and 2007–2008, when the dollar depreciated.

An Appreciating Canadian Dollar: 2005–2007

Between 2005 and July 2007, the Canadian dollar appreciated against the U.S. dollar. It rose from 79 U.S. cents to 109 U.S. cents per Canadian dollar. Part (a) of the figure provides an explanation for this appreciation.

In 2005, the demand and supply curves were those labelled D_{05} and S_{05}. The exchange rate was 79 U.S. cents per Canadian dollar.

During 2005 and 2006, the global demand for resources increased the demand for Canadian exports. The increase in demand for Canadian exports increased the demand for the Canadian dollar. Also, currency traders, anticipating the increased demand, expected the dollar to appreciate against the U.S.

dollar. The demand for Canadian dollars increased, and the supply of Canadian dollars decreased.

In the figure, the demand curve shifted rightward from D_{05} to D_{07} and the supply curve shifted leftward from S_{05} to S_{07}. The exchange rate rose to 109 U.S. cents per Canadian dollar. In the figure, the equilibrium quantity remained unchanged—an assumption.

A Depreciating Canadian Dollar: 2007–2008

Between July 2007 and November 2008, the Canadian dollar depreciated against the U.S. dollar. It fell from 109 U.S. cents to 77 U.S. cents per Canadian dollar. Part (b) of the figure provides a possible explanation for this depreciation. The demand and supply curves labelled D_{07} and S_{07} are the same as in part (a).

During the last quarter of 2007 and the first three quarters of 2008, the U.S. economy entered a severe credit crisis and global demand for resources collapsed. A decrease in the demand for Canadian exports decreased the demand for Canadian dollars. Also, currency traders expected the Canadian dollar to depreciate against the U.S. dollar. The demand for Canadian dollars decreased and the supply of Canadian dollars increased.

In part (b) of the figure, the demand curve shifted leftward from D_{07} to D_{08}, the supply curve shifted rightward from S_{07} to S_{08}, and the exchange rate fell to 77 U.S. cents per Canadian dollar.

(a) 2005–2007

(b) 2007–2008

The Rising and Falling Canadian Dollar

Exchange Rate Expectations

The changes in the exchange rate that we've just examined occurred in part because the exchange rate was *expected to change*. This explanation sounds a bit like a self-fulfilling prophecy. So what makes expectations change? The answer is new information about the deeper forces that influence the value of one money relative to the value of another money. There are two such forces:

- Interest rate parity
- Purchasing power parity

Interest Rate Parity One definition of what money is worth is what it can earn. Two kinds of money—Canadian dollars and Japanese yen, for example—might earn different amounts. Suppose that the interest rate on a yen bank deposit in Tokyo is 1 percent a year and on a Canadian dollar bank deposit in Toronto is 3 percent a year. In this situation, why does anyone deposit money in Tokyo? Why doesn't all the money flow to Toronto? The answer is because of exchange rate expectations. Suppose that people expect the yen to appreciate by 2 percent a year. Canadian investors expect that if they buy and hold yen for a year, they will earn 1 percent interest and 2 percent from the higher yen (lower dollar) to give a total return of 3 percent. So the interest rate in terms of Canadian dollars is the same in Tokyo and Toronto. This situation is one of **interest rate parity**, which means equal rates of return.

Adjusted for risk, interest rate parity always prevails. Funds move to get the highest return available. If for a few seconds a higher return is available in Toronto than in Tokyo, the demand for Canadian dollars increases and the exchange rate rises until the expected rates of return are equal.

Purchasing Power Parity Another definition of what money is worth is what it will buy. But two kinds of money—Canadian dollars and Japanese yen, for example—might buy different amounts of goods and services. Suppose a memory stick costs 5,000 yen in Tokyo and $50 in Vancouver. If the exchange rate is 100 yen per dollar, the two monies have the same value. You can buy a memory stick in either Tokyo or Vancouver for the same price. You can express that price as either 5,000 yen or $50, but the price is the same in the two currencies.

The situation we've just described is called **purchasing power parity**, which means *equal value of money*. If purchasing power parity does not prevail, some powerful forces go to work. To understand these forces, let's suppose that the price of a memory stick in Vancouver rises to $60, but in Tokyo it remains at 5,000 yen. Further, suppose the exchange rate remains at 100 yen per dollar. In this case, a memory stick in Tokyo still costs 5,000 yen or $50, but in Vancouver, it costs $60 or 6,000 yen. Money buys more in Japan than in Canada. Money is not of equal value in the two countries.

If all (or most) prices have increased in Canada and not increased in Japan, then people will generally expect that the value of the Canadian dollar in the foreign exchange market must fall. In this situation, the exchange rate is expected to fall. The demand for Canadian dollars decreases, and the supply of Canadian dollars increases. The exchange rate falls, as expected. If the exchange rate falls to 83.33 yen per dollar and there are no further price changes, purchasing power parity is restored. A memory stick that costs $60 in Vancouver also costs the equivalent of $60 (60 × 83.33 = 5,000) in Tokyo.

If prices increase in Japan and other countries but remain constant in Canada, then people will generally expect that the value of the Canadian dollar in the foreign exchange market is too low and that it is going to rise. In this situation, the exchange rate is expected to rise. The demand for Canadian dollars increases, and the supply of Canadian dollars decreases. The exchange rate rises, as expected.

Instant Exchange Rate Response

The exchange rate responds instantly to news about changes in the variables that influence demand and supply in the foreign exchange market. You can see why the response is immediate by thinking about the expected profit opportunities that such news creates.

Suppose that the Bank of Japan is reported to be considering raising the interest rate next week. If this move is regarded as likely, then traders expect the demand for yen to increase and the demand for dollars to decrease. They also expect the yen to appreciate and the dollar to depreciate.

But to benefit from a yen appreciation and to avoid the loss from a dollar depreciation, yen must be bought and dollars must be sold *before* the exchange rate changes. Each trader knows that all the other traders share the same information and have similar expectations. And each trader knows that when people begin to sell dollars and buy yen, the exchange rate will change. To transact before the exchange rate changes means transacting right away, as soon as the information that changes expectations is received.

The Nominal and Real Exchange Rates in the Short Run and in the Long Run

Earlier in this chapter, we distinguished between the nominal exchange rate and the real exchange rate. So far we've explained only how the nominal exchange rate is determined and we've focused on the day-to-day fluctuations in the nominal exchange rate. We're going to turn now to the real exchange rate and explain how it is determined. We're also going to distinguish between the short run and the long run.

Continuing with the Canada–Japan example, the equation that links the nominal and real exchange rates is

$$RER = E \times (P^*/P).$$

where P is the Canadian price level, P^* is the Japanese price level, E is the nominal exchange rate (yen per Canadian dollar), and RER is the real exchange rate (the quantity of Japanese real GDP per unit of Canadian real GDP).

In the short run, this equation determines the real exchange rate. The price levels in Canada and Japan don't change every time the nominal exchange rate changes. So a change in E brings an equivalent change in RER.

But in the long run, demand and supply in the markets for goods and services determine the real exchange rate. If Japan and Canada produced identical goods (if GDP in both countries consisted only of memory sticks, for example), purchasing power parity would make the real exchange rate equal 1. One Japanese memory stick would exchange for one Canadian memory stick. In reality, although there is overlap in what each country produces, Canadian real GDP is a different bundle of goods and services from Japanese real GDP. So the relative price of Japanese and Canadian real GDP—the real exchange rate—is not 1 and it fluctuates. The forces of demand and supply in the markets for the millions of goods and services that make up real GDP determine the relative prices of Japanese and Canadian real GDP.

In the long run, with the real exchange rate determined by the real forces of demand and supply in

markets for goods and services, the above equation must be turned around to determine the nominal exchange rate. That is, the nominal exchange rate is

$$E = RER \times (P^*/P).$$

This equation tells us that in the long run, the nominal exchange rate is determined by the equilibrium real exchange rate and the price levels in the two countries. A rise in the Japanese price level, P^*, brings a rise in E and dollar appreciation; and a rise in the Canadian price level, P, brings a fall in E and dollar depreciation.

You learned in Chapter 24 (see pp. 582–583) that in the long run, the quantity of money determines the price level. But the quantity theory of money applies to all countries. So the quantity of money in Japan determines the price level in Japan, and the quantity of money in Canada determines the price level in Canada.

A nominal exchange rate, then, in the long run, is a monetary phenomenon. It is determined by the quantities of money in two countries.

The long-run forces that we've just described explain the broad trends in exchange rates. For example, the Canadian dollar has generally depreciated against the Japanese yen because Japan has created money at a slower pace than has Canada and the price level in Japan has risen more slowly than the Canadian price level. The Canadian dollar has been constant, on average, against the European euro because inflation rates have been similar in Canada and Europe.

Review Quiz

1 Why do the demand for and supply of Canadian dollars change?
2 What makes the Canadian dollar exchange rate fluctuate?
3 What is interest rate parity and what happens when this condition doesn't hold?
4 What is purchasing power parity and what happens when this condition doesn't hold?
5 What determines the real exchange rate and the nominal exchange rate in the short run?
6 What determines the real exchange rate and the nominal exchange rate in the long run?

 Work Study Plan 25.3 and get instant feedback.

Financing International Trade

You now know how the exchange rate is determined. What is the effect of the exchange rate? How does currency depreciation or currency appreciation influence our international trade and payments? We're going to lay the foundation for addressing these questions by looking at the scale of international trading, borrowing, and lending and at the way in which we keep our records of international transactions. These records are called the balance of payments accounts.

Balance of Payments Accounts

A country's **balance of payments accounts** records its international trading, borrowing, and lending in three accounts:

1. Current account
2. Capital account
3. Official settlements account

The **current account** records receipts from exports of goods and services sold abroad, payments for imports of goods and services from abroad, net interest income paid abroad, and net transfers abroad (such as foreign aid payments). The *current account balance* equals the sum of exports minus imports, net interest income, and net transfers.

The **capital account** records foreign investment in Canada minus Canadian investment abroad. (This account also has a statistical discrepancy that arises from errors and omissions in measuring international capital transactions.)

The **official settlements account** records the change in **official reserves**, which are the government's holdings of foreign currency. If official reserves *increase*, the official settlements account balance is *negative*. The reason is that holding foreign money is like investing abroad. Canadian investment abroad is a minus item in the capital account and in the official settlements account.

The sum of the balances on the three accounts *always* equals zero. If a country has a current account deficit, it either borrows more from abroad than it lends abroad or it uses its official reserves to cover the shortfall. A country with a current account surplus must lend more abroad than it borrows or increase its official reserves.

Table 25.1 shows the Canadian balance of payments accounts in 2007. Items in the current account and the capital account that provide foreign currency to Canada have a plus sign; items that cost Canada foreign currency have a minus sign. The table shows that in 2007, Canadian exports exceeded Canadian imports and the current account had a surplus of $14 billion. What do we do with our surplus of exports over imports? That is, how do we use our current account surplus?

We use our surplus by lending to the rest of the world. The capital account tells us how much we lend. We made loans of $167 billion (Canadian investment abroad) and borrowed $153 billion (foreign investment in Canada). Our *net* foreign lending was $167 billion minus $153 billion, which equals $14 billion. There is almost always a statistical discrepancy between our capital account and current account transactions, and in 2007, the discrepancy was $4 billion. Combining the discrepancy with the measured net foreign borrowing gives a capital account balance of –$10 billion.

TABLE 25.1 Canadian Balance of Payments Accounts in 2007

Current account	Billions of dollars
Exports of goods and services	+530
Imports of goods and services	–501
Net interest income	–14
Net transfers	–1
Current account balance	14

Capital account	
Foreign investment in Canada	+153
Canadian investment abroad	–167
Statistical discrepancy	4
Capital account balance	–10

Official settlements account	
Official settlements account balance	–4

Source of data: Statistics Canada, CANSIM Tables 376-0001 and 376-0002.

Our capital account balance plus our current account balance equals the change in Canadian official reserves. In 2007, our capital account balance of –$10 billion plus our current account balance of $14 billion equalled $4 billion. Our official reserves *increased* in 2007 by $4 billion. Holding more foreign reserves is like lending to the rest of the world, so this amount appears in the official settlements account in Table 25.1 as –$4 billion. The sum of the current account balance, the capital account balance. and the official settlements balance equals zero.

To see more clearly what the nation's balance of payments accounts mean, think about your own balance of payments accounts. They are similar to the nation's accounts.

An Individual's Balance of Payments Accounts An individual's current account records the individual's income from supplying the services of factors of production and expenditure on goods and services.

Consider Jackie, for example. She worked in 2005 and earned an income of $25,000. Jackie has $10,000 worth of investments that earned her an interest income of $1,000. Jackie's current account shows an income of $26,000. Jackie spent $18,000 buying consumption goods and services. She also bought a new house, which cost her $60,000. So Jackie's total expenditure was $78,000. Jackie's expenditure minus her income is $52,000 ($78,000 minus $26,000). This amount is Jackie's current account deficit.

The Canadian Balance of Payments Since 1984

From Deficit to Surplus

The numbers that you reviewed in Table 25.1 give a snapshot of the Canadian balance of payments accounts in 2007. The figure puts that snapshot into perspective by showing the balance of payments between 1984 and 2007.

Because the economy grows and the price level rises, changes in the dollar value of the balance of payments do not convey much information. To remove the influences of economic growth and inflation, the figure shows the balance of payments expressed as a percentage of nominal GDP.

As you can see, the current account was in deficit before 2000 (except for a brief and small surplus in 1996). After 2000, the current account was in surplus.

The capital account balance is almost a mirror image of the current account balance because the official settlements balance is very small in comparison with the balances of the other two accounts.

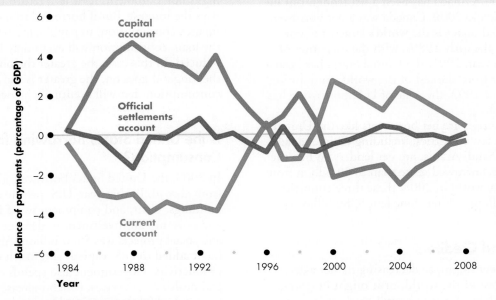

The Canadian Balance of Payments

Source of data: Statistics Canada, CANSIM Tables 376-0001 and 376-0002.

To pay for an expenditure of $52,000 in excess of her income, Jackie must either use the money that she has in the bank or take out a loan. Suppose that Jackie took out a loan of $50,000 to help buy her house and that this loan was the only borrowing that she did. Borrowing is an *inflow* in the capital account, so Jackie's capital account *surplus* was $50,000. With a current account deficit of $52,000 and a capital account surplus of $50,000, Jackie was still $2,000 short. She got that $2,000 from her own bank account. Her cash holdings fell by $2,000.

Jackie's income from her work is like a country's income from its exports. Her income from her investments is like a country's interest income from foreigners. Her purchases of goods and services, including her purchase of a house, are like a country's imports. Jackie's loan—borrowing from someone else—is like a country's borrowing from the rest of the world. The change in Jackie's bank account is like the change in the country's official reserves.

Borrowers and Lenders

A country that is borrowing more from the rest of the world than it is lending to the rest of the world is called a **net borrower**. Similarly, a **net lender** is a country that is lending more to the rest of the world than it is borrowing from the rest of the world.

Since 2000, Canada has been a net lender. But in most years before 2000, Canada was a net borrower.

The United States is the world's largest net borrower. Since the early 1980s, with the exception of only a single year, 1991, the United States has been a net borrower from the rest of the world. And during the years since 1992, the scale of U.S. borrowing has mushroomed.

Most countries are net borrowers like the United States. But a few countries, including China, Japan, and oil-rich Saudi Arabia, are net lenders. When the United States borrowed more than $700 billion from the rest of the world in 2008, these three countries lent $700 billion. China alone lent $380 billion.

Debtors and Creditors

A net borrower might be decreasing its net assets held in the rest of the world, or it might be going deeper into debt. A nation's total stock of foreign investment determines whether it is a debtor or a creditor. A **debtor nation** is a country that during its entire history has borrowed more from the rest of the world than it has lent to other countries. It has a stock of outstanding debt to the rest of the world that exceeds the stock of its own claims on the rest of the world. A **creditor nation** is a country that during its entire history has invested more in the rest of the world than other countries have invested in it.

Canada is a debtor nation. Throughout the nineteenth century we borrowed from Europe to finance our westward expansion, railroads, and industrialization. The capital-hungry developing countries (like Canada during the nineteenth century) are among the largest debtor nations. The international debt of these countries grew from less than a third to more than a half of their gross domestic product during the 1980s and created what was called the "Third World debt crisis."

But the United States is the world's largest debtor nation. Since 1984, the total stock of U.S. borrowing from the rest of the world has exceeded U.S. lending to the rest of the world by $7.4 trillion (almost as much as Canada's gross domestic product).

Should the world be concerned that the United States is the largest net borrower and debtor? The answer to this question depends mainly on what the net borrower is doing with the borrowed money. If borrowing is financing investment that in turn is generating economic growth and higher income, borrowing is not a problem. It earns a return that more than pays the interest. But if borrowed money is used to finance consumption, to pay the interest and repay the loan, consumption will eventually have to be reduced. In this case, the greater the borrowing and the longer it goes on, the greater is the reduction in consumption that will eventually be necessary.

Is the United States Borrowing for Consumption?

In 2008, the United States borrowed $700 billion from abroad. In that year, U.S. private investment in buildings, plant, and equipment was $1,980 billion and government investment in defence equipment and social projects was $480 billion. All this investment added to U.S. capital, and much of it increased productivity. Government also spends on education and health care services, which increase *human capital*. So U.S. international borrowing is financing private and public investment, not consumption. The same is true for most other international borrowers.

Current Account Balance

What determines a country's current account balance and net foreign borrowing? You've seen that net exports (*NX*) is the main item in the current account. We can define the current account balance (*CAB*) as

$$CAB = NX + \text{Net interest income} + \text{Net transfers.}$$

We can study the current account balance by looking at what determines net exports because the other two items are small and do not fluctuate much.

Net Exports

Net exports are determined by the government budget and private saving and investment. To see how net exports are determined, we need to recall some of the things that we learned in Chapter 23 about the flows of funds that finance investment. Table 25.2 refreshes your memory and summarizes some calculations.

Part (a) lists the national income variables that are needed, with their symbols. Part (b) defines three balances. **Net exports** are exports of goods and services minus imports of goods and services.

The **government sector balance** is equal to net taxes minus government expenditure on goods and services. If that number is positive, a government sector surplus is lent to other sectors; if that number is negative, a government deficit must be financed by borrowing from other sectors. The government sector deficit is the sum of the deficits of the federal, provincial, and local governments.

The **private sector balance** is saving minus investment. If saving exceeds investment, a private sector surplus is lent to other sectors. If investment exceeds saving, a private sector deficit is financed by borrowing from other sectors.

Part (b) also shows the values of these balances for Canada in 2007. As you can see, net exports were $31 billion, a surplus of $31 billion. The government sector's revenue from net taxes was $383 billion and its expenditure was $342 billion, so the government sector balance was $41 billion—a surplus of $41 billion. The private sector saved $301 billion and invested $311 billion, so the private sector balance was –$10 billion. The private sector had a deficit of $10 billion.

Part (c) shows the relationship among the three balances. From the national income accounts, we

know that real GDP, *Y*, is the sum of consumption expenditure (*C*), investment, government expenditure, and net exports. Real GDP also equals the sum of consumption expenditure, saving, and net taxes. Rearranging these equations tells us that net exports (*X* – *M*) equals the sum of the government sector balance (*T* – *G*) and the private sector balance (*S* – *I*). In Canada in 2007, the government sector balance was $41 billion and the private sector balance was –$10 billion. The government sector balance plus the private sector balance equalled net exports of $31 billion.

TABLE 25.2   Net Exports, the Government Budget, Saving, and Investment

	Symbols and equations	Canada in 2007 (billions of dollars)
(a) Variables		
Exports*	X	532
Imports*	M	501
Government expenditure	G	342
Net taxes	T	383
Investment	I	311
Saving	S	301
(b) Balances		
Net exports	X – M	532 – 501 = 31
Government sector	T – G	383 – 342 = 41
Private sector	S – I	301 – 311 = –10
(c) Relationship among balances		
National accounts	$Y = C + I + G + X - M$ $= C + S + T$	
Rearranging:	$(X - M) = (T - G) + (S - I)$	
Net exports	X – M	31
equals:		
Government sector	T – G	41
plus		
Private sector	S – I	–10

Source of data: Statistics Canada, CANSIM Tables 380-0002 and 380-0017.

*The national income accounts measures of exports and imports are slightly different from the balance of payments accounts measures in Table 25.1 on p. 606.

The Three Sector Balances

Deficits and Surpluses

You've seen that net exports equal the sum of the government sector balance and the private sector balance. How do these three sector balances fluctuate over time?

The figure answers this question. It shows the government sector balance (the red line), net exports (the blue line), and the private sector balance (the green line).

The private sector balance and the government sector balance move in opposite directions. When the government sector deficit was large during the 1980s and the first half of the 1990s, the private sector surplus was large. And when the government sector deficit was turned around to become a surplus during the second half of the 1990s and the 2000s, the private sector surplus decreased and eventually became a deficit.

Net exports are somewhat correlated with the government balance and are sometimes called twins. But the net exports balance does not follow the government sector balance closely. Rather, net exports respond to the *sum* of the government sector and private sector balances. When both the private sector and the government sector have a deficit, net exports are negative and the combined private and government deficit is financed by borrowing from the rest of the world.

The trend in Canada's net exports is slightly positive.

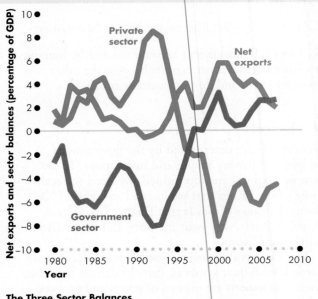

The Three Sector Balances

Source of data: Statistics Canada, CANSIM Tables 380-0017 and 380-0022.

Where Is the Exchange Rate?

In explaining the current account balance, we have not mentioned the exchange rate. Doesn't the exchange rate play a role?

In the short run, a fall in the nominal exchange rate lowers the real exchange rate, which makes our imports more costly and our exports more competitive. A higher price of imported consumption goods and services might induce a decrease in consumption expenditure and an increase in saving. A higher price of imported capital goods might induce a decrease in investment. Other things remaining the same, an increase in saving or a decrease in investment decreases the private sector deficit and decreases the current account deficit.

But in the long run, a change in the nominal exchange rate leaves the real exchange rate and all other real variables unchanged. So in the long run, the nominal exchange rate plays no role in influencing the current account balance.

Review Quiz

1 What are the transactions that the current account records?
2 What are the transactions that the capital account records?
3 What are the transactions that the official settlements account records?
4 What are the biggest net borrower and debtor nations and do they borrow to consume?
5 How are net exports and the government sector budget balance linked?

 Work Study Plan 25.4 and get instant feedback.

Exchange Rate Policy

Because the exchange rate is the price of a country's money in terms of another country's money, governments and central banks must have a policy towards the exchange rate. Three possible exchange rate policies are

- Flexible exchange rate
- Fixed exchange rate
- Crawling peg

Flexible Exchange Rate

A **flexible exchange rate** policy is one that permits the exchange rate to be determined by demand and supply with no direct intervention in the foreign exchange market by the central bank. Most countries —and Canada is prominent among them—operate a flexible exchange rate, and the foreign exchange market that we have studied so far in this chapter is an example of a flexible exchange rate regime.

But even a flexible exchange rate is influenced by central bank actions. If the Bank of Canada raises the Canadian interest rate and other countries keep their interest rates unchanged, the demand for Canadian dollars increases, the supply of Canadian dollars decreases, and the exchange rate rises. (Similarly, if the Bank of Canada lowers the Canadian interest rate, the demand for Canadian dollars decreases, the supply increases, and the exchange rate falls.)

In a flexible exchange rate regime, when the central bank changes the interest rate, its purpose is not to influence the exchange rate, but to achieve some other monetary policy objective. (We return to this topic at length in Chapter 30.)

Fixed Exchange Rate

A **fixed exchange rate** policy is one that pegs the exchange rate at a value decided by the government or central bank and that blocks the unregulated forces of demand and supply by direct intervention in the foreign exchange market. The world economy operated a fixed exchange rate regime from the end of World War II to the early 1970s. China had a fixed exchange rate against the U.S. dollar until recently. Hong Kong has had a fixed exchange rate for many years and continues with that policy today.

A fixed exchange rate requires active intervention in the foreign exchange market.

If the Bank of Canada wanted to fix the Canadian dollar exchange rate against the U.S. dollar, it would sell Canadian dollars to prevent the exchange rate from rising above the target value and buy Canadian dollars to prevent the exchange rate from falling below the target value.

There is no limit to the quantity of Canadian dollars that the Bank of Canada can *sell*. The Bank of Canada creates Canadian dollars and can create any quantity it chooses. But there is a limit to the quantity of Canadian dollars the Bank of Canada can *buy*. That limit is set by Canadian official foreign currency reserves because to buy Canadian dollars the Bank of Canada must sell foreign currency. Intervention to buy Canadian dollars stops when Canadian official foreign currency reserves run out.

Let's look at the foreign exchange interventions that the Bank of Canada can make.

Suppose the Bank of Canada wants the exchange rate to be steady at 90 U.S. cents per Canadian dollar. If the exchange rate rises above that level, the Bank of Canada sells dollars. If the exchange rate falls below 90 U.S. cents, the Bank of Canada buys dollars. By these actions, the Bank of Canada keeps the exchange rate close to its target rate.

Figure 25.7 shows the Bank of Canada's intervention in the foreign exchange market. The supply of dollars is S and initially the demand for dollars is D_0. The equilibrium exchange rate is 90 U.S. cents per dollar. This exchange rate is also the target exchange rate, shown by the horizontal red line.

When the demand for Canadian dollars increases and the demand curve shifts rightward to D_1, the Bank of Canada sells \$10 billion. This action prevents the exchange rate from rising. When the demand for Canadian dollars decreases and the demand curve shifts leftward to D_2, the Bank of Canada buys \$10 billion. This action prevents the exchange rate from falling.

If the demand for Canadian dollars fluctuates between D_1 and D_2 and on average is D_0, the Bank of Canada can repeatedly intervene in the way we've just seen. Sometimes it buys and sometimes it sells, but on average, it neither buys nor sells.

But suppose the demand for Canadian dollars *increases permanently* from D_0 to D_1. To maintain the exchange rate at 90 U.S. cents per Canadian dollar, the Bank of Canada must sell dollars and buy foreign currency, so Canadian official foreign currency reserves would be increasing. At some point, the

FIGURE 25.7 Foreign Exchange Market Intervention

Initially, the demand for Canadian dollars is D_0, the supply of Canadian dollars is S, and the exchange rate is 90 U.S. cents per Canadian dollar. The Bank of Canada can intervene in the foreign exchange market to keep the exchange rate close to its target rate. If demand increases from D_0 to D_1, the Bank of Canada sells dollars. If demand decreases from D_0 to D_2, the Bank of Canada buys dollars. Persistent intervention on one side of the market cannot be sustained.

 animation

Bank would abandon the exchange rate target to stop piling up foreign currency reserves.

Now suppose the demand for Canadian dollars *decreases permanently* from D_0 to D_2. In this situation, the Bank of Canada *cannot* maintain the exchange rate target indefinitely. To do so, it must *buy* Canadian dollars using the official foreign currency reserves. Eventually, the Bank would run out of foreign currency and have to abandon the target exchange rate.

Crawling Peg

A **crawling peg** exchange rate policy is one that selects a target for the exchange rate that changes periodically, with intervention in the foreign exchange market to achieve the target.

A crawling peg works like a fixed exchange rate except that the target value changes. Sometimes the

The People's Bank of China in the Foreign Exchange Market
Fixed Rate Followed by Crawling Peg

For several years, the exchange rate between the Chinese yuan and the U.S. dollar was constant. The reason for this near constant exchange rate is that China's central bank, the People's Bank of China, intervened to operate a fixed exchange rate policy. From 1997 until 2005, the yuan was pegged at 8.28 yuan per U.S. dollar. Since 2005, the yuan has appreciated slightly, but it has not been permitted to fluctuate freely. Since 2005, the yuan has been on a crawling peg.

The immediate consequence of the fixed yuan exchange rate (and crawling exchange rate) is that since 2000, China has piled up U.S dollar reserves on a huge scale. By mid-2006, China's official foreign currency reserves approached $1 trillion and by the end of 2007, they were fast approaching $2 trillion!

Part (a) of the figure shows the increase in China's official foreign currency reserves, some of which are euros and yen, but most of which are U.S. dollars. You can see that China's reserves increased by $200 billion in 2004 and 2005, by a bit more than $200 billion in 2006, and by $460 billion in 2007.

The demand and supply curves in part (b) of the figure illustrate what is happening in the market for U.S. dollars priced in terms of the yuan and explains why China's reserves have increased. The demand curve D and supply curve S intersect at 5 yuan per U.S. dollar. If the People's Bank of China takes no actions in the market, this exchange rate is the equilibrium rate (an assumed value).

By intervening in the foreign exchange market and buying U.S. dollars, the People's Bank pegs the yuan

target changes once a month, and sometimes it changes every day.

The Bank of Canada has never operated a crawling peg. But some prominent countries do use this system. When China abandoned its fixed exchange rate, it replaced it with a crawling peg. China and some other developing countries use a crawling peg as a method of trying to control inflation—a policy that we examine in Chapter 30, p. 748.

The ideal crawling peg sets a target for the exchange rate equal to the equilibrium exchange rate

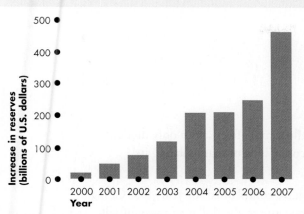

(a) Increase in U.S. Dollar Reserves

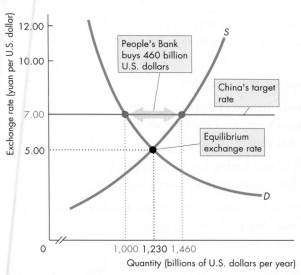

(b) Pegging the Yuan

China's Foreign Exchange Market Intervention

at 7 yuan per U.S. dollar. But to do so, it must pile up U.S. dollars. To hold the exchange rate at 7 yuan per dollar, the People's Bank bought $460 billion in 2007.

If the People's Bank stopped buying U.S. dollars, the U.S. dollar would depreciate, the yuan would appreciate, and China would stop piling up U.S. dollar reserves.

Why Does China Manage Its Exchange Rate? The popular story is that China manages its exchange rate to keep its export prices low and to make it easier to compete in world markets. You've seen that this story is correct in the short run. Given the prices in China and the rest of the world, a low yuan–U.S. dollar exchange rate brings lower U.S. dollar prices for China's exports. But the yuan–U.S. dollar exchange rate was fixed for almost 10 years and has been managed for 3 more years. This long period of a fixed exchange rate has long-run, not short-run, effects. In the long run, the exchange rate has no effect on competitiveness. The reason is that prices adjust to reflect the exchange rate and the real exchange rate is unaffected by the nominal exchange rate.

So why does China fix its exchange rate? The more convincing answer is that China sees a fixed exchange rate as a way of controlling its inflation rate. By making the yuan crawl against the U.S. dollar, China's inflation rate is anchored to the U.S. inflation rate and will not stray too far from that rate (see Chapter 30, p. 747).

The bottom line is that in the long run, exchange rate policy is monetary policy, not balance of payments policy. To change its balance of payments, a country must change its saving and investment.

on average. The peg seeks only to prevent large swings in the expected future exchange rate that change demand and supply and make the exchange rate fluctuate too wildly.

A crawling peg departs from the ideal if, as often happens with a fixed exchange rate, the target rate departs from the equilibrium exchange rate for too long. When this happens, the country either runs out of reserves or piles up reserves.

Reading Between the Lines on pp. 614–615 looks further at China's crawling peg exchange rate policy.

Review Quiz

1 What is a flexible exchange rate and how does it work?

2 What is a fixed exchange rate and how is its value fixed?

3 What is a crawling peg and how does it work?

4 How has China operated in the foreign exchange market, why, and with what effect?

 Work Study Plan 25.5 and get instant feedback.

The Rising Chinese Yuan

Bush Aides Struggling with Yuan

May 10, 2006

After nearly three years of pushing China to let its currency float more freely, with only modest results, the Bush administration still appears reluctant to accuse China of manipulating its exchange rate. ...

American manufacturers and many members of Congress have complained for years that China has kept its currency, the yuan, at an artificially low exchange rate to the dollar as a way of selling its exports at cheap prices.

Treasury Secretary John W. Snow has resisted demands to threaten Beijing, arguing that Chinese leaders are making "progress" towards a more flexible exchange rate and a more open financial system.

This week, a Treasury official again emphasized China's steps towards openness.

"If you look at what China is doing in exercising their commitment on putting in place a foreign-exchange regime that has greater flexibility," Mr. Snow's principal spokesman, Tony Fratto, told reporters on Monday, "you see some evidence that they're doing that."

But changes in the yuan's value have been relatively minor. Chinese leaders let the yuan climb about 2 percent against the dollar last July, and another similarly small amount more recently.

When President Hu Jintao visited President Bush in Washington last month, top Chinese officials re-emphasized a need for "stability" and offered no hint of when they might let the yuan move more freely. ...

The United States' trade deficit with China ballooned to $202 billion in 2005, an imbalance that might ordinarily have pushed up the value of the yuan in relation to the dollar. China has prevented the yuan from rising by buying hundreds of billions in dollar-denominated reserves. ...

Essence of the Story

- U.S. producers and members of Congress complain that China has kept the yuan artificially low to sell exports at low prices.
- Treasury Secretary John W. Snow says that China is moving towards a more flexible exchange rate.
- Changes in the yuan–dollar exchange rate have been small.

- The yuan appreciated in July 2005 and by small amounts more recently.
- The U.S. trade deficit with China was $202 billion in 2005.
- This imbalance should have pushed up the value of the yuan, but China prevented that from happening and increased its U.S. dollar reserves.

Economic Analysis

- China's exchange rate was pegged at 8.28 yuan per U.S. dollar until July 2005.

- In July 2005, the yuan appreciated against the U.S. dollar (the U.S. dollar depreciated) by 2.1 percent.

- Since July 2005, the yuan has slowly but persistently appreciated against the dollar (the dollar has depreciated against the yuan).

- Figure 1 shows the path of the depreciating dollar against the yuan.

- To peg the yuan before July 2005 and since then to keep the exchange rate from rising more than it wants, the People's Bank of China buys U.S. dollars in the foreign exchange market.

- The result of these foreign exchange market transactions has been a strong growth in China's foreign reserves.

- Figure 2 shows the buildup of China's reserves, which, by 2008, were approaching $2 trillion.

- Americans are concerned about the yuan–U.S. dollar exchange rate because China has a large trade surplus with the United States.

- But China's overall current account surplus is not large and is a fraction of the large U.S. current account deficit.

- Figure 3 shows the U.S. current account deficit and China's current account surplus.

- The analysis in this chapter explains that a current account deficit results from too little private and government saving relative to investment.

- China saves more than it invests, and the United States invests more than it saves.

- A change in the nominal exchange rate between the U.S. dollar and the Chinese yuan cannot make a large contribution to changing these imbalances.

- The main effect of the appreciation of the yuan against the U.S. dollar will be to slow China's inflation rate relative to the U.S. inflation rate.

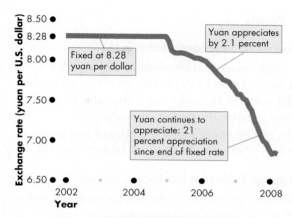

Figure 1 The yuan–U.S. dollar exchange rate

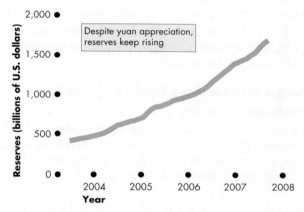

Figure 2 China's reserves pile up

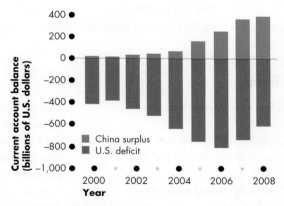

Figure 3 Current account balances

SUMMARY

Key Points

Currencies and Exchange Rates (pp. 594–596)

- Foreign currency is obtained in exchange for domestic currency in the foreign exchange market.
- The nominal exchange rate is the value of one currency in terms of another currency.
- The real exchange rate is the price of one country's real GDP in terms of another country's real GDP.

The Foreign Exchange Market (pp. 597–600)

- Demand and supply in the foreign exchange market determine the exchange rate.
- The higher the exchange rate, the smaller is the quantity of Canadian dollars demanded and the greater is the quantity of Canadian dollars supplied.
- The equilibrium exchange rate makes the quantity of Canadian dollars demanded equal the quantity of Canadian dollars supplied.

Changes in Demand and Supply: Exchange Rate Fluctuations (pp. 601–605)

- Changes in the world demand for Canadian exports, the Canadian interest rate differential, or the expected future exchange rate change the demand for Canadian dollars.

- Changes in the Canadian demand for imports, the Canadian interest rate differential, or the expected future exchange rate change the supply of Canadian dollars.
- Exchange rate expectations are influenced by purchasing power parity and interest rate parity.
- In the long run, the nominal exchange rate is a monetary phenomenon and the real exchange rate is independent of the nominal exchange rate.

Financing International Trade (pp. 606–610)

- International trade, borrowing, and lending are financed by using foreign currency.
- A country's international transactions are recorded in its current account, capital account, and official settlements account.
- The current account balance is similar to net exports and is determined by the government sector balance plus the private sector balance.

Exchange Rate Policy (pp. 611–613)

- An exchange rate can be flexible, fixed, or a crawling peg.
- To achieve a fixed or a crawling exchange rate, a central bank must intervene in the foreign exchange market and either buy or sell foreign currency.

Key Figures and Table

Figure 25.1   The Canadian-Dollar Effective Exchange Rate Index, 596

Figure 25.4   Equilibrium Exchange Rate, 600

Figure 25.7   Foreign Exchange Market Intervention, 612

Table 25.2   Net Exports, the Government Budget, Saving, and Investment, 609

Key Terms

Balance of payments accounts, 606

Canadian-dollar effective exchange rate index (CERI), 596

Canadian interest rate differential, 601

Capital account, 606

Crawling peg, 612

Creditor nation, 608

Current account, 606

Debtor nation, 608

Exchange rate, 594

Fixed exchange rate, 611

Flexible exchange rate, 611

Foreign currency, 594

Foreign exchange market, 594

Government sector balance, 609

Interest rate parity, 604

Net borrower, 608

Net exports, 609

Net lender, 608

Nominal exchange rate, 594

Official reserves, 606

Official settlements account, 606

Private sector balance, 609

Purchasing power parity, 604

Real exchange rate, 594

PROBLEMS and APPLICATIONS

myeconlab Work problems 1–14 in Chapter 25 Study Plan and get instant feedback.
Work problems 15–21 as Homework, a Quiz, or a Test if assigned by your instructor.

1. The U.S. dollar exchange rate increased from $0.97 Canadian in 2007 to $1.06 Canadian in 2008, and it decreased from 115 Japanese yen in 2007 to 107 Japanese yen in 2008.

   a. Did the U.S. dollar appreciate or depreciate against the Canadian dollar?
   b. Did the U.S. dollar appreciate or depreciate against the Japanese yen?
   c. What was the value of the Canadian dollar in terms of U.S. dollars in 2007 and 2008?
   d. What was the value of 100 Japanese yen in terms of U.S. dollars in 2007 and 2008?
   e. Did the Canadian dollar appreciate or depreciate against the U.S. dollar in 2008?
   f. Did the Japanese yen appreciate or depreciate against the U.S. dollar in 2008?

2. In 2004, the price level in the Eurozone was 112.4, the price level in the United States was 109.1, and the nominal exchange rate was 80 euro cents per U.S. dollar. What was the real exchange rate expressed as Eurozone real GDP per unit of U.S. real GDP?

3. In 2003, the price level in the United States was 106.3, the price level in Japan was 95.4, and the real exchange rate expressed as Japanese real GDP per unit of U.S. real GDP was 103.6. What was the nominal exchange rate?

4. There is a large increase in the global demand for roses and Colombia is the biggest producer of roses. At the same time, the central bank of Colombia increases the interest rate. What happens in the foreign exchange market for Colombian pesos to

   a. The demand for pesos?
   b. The supply of pesos?
   c. The quantity of pesos demanded?
   d. The quantity of pesos supplied?
   e. The exchange rate of the pesos against the U.S. dollar?

5. If a euro deposit in a bank in Paris, France, earns interest of 4 percent a year and a yen deposit in Tokyo, Japan, earns 0.5 percent a year, everything else remaining the same and adjusted for risk, what is the exchange rate expectation of the Japanese yen?

6. The U.K. pound is trading at 1.82 U.S. dollars per U.K. pound. There is purchasing power parity at this exchange rate. The interest rate in the United States is 2 percent a year and the interest rate in the United Kingdom is 4 percent a year.

   a. Calculate the U.S. interest rate differential.
   b. What is the U.K. pound expected to be worth in terms of U.S. dollars one year from now?
   c. Which country more likely has the lower inflation rate? How can you tell?

7. You can purchase a laptop in Mexico City for 12,960 Mexican pesos. If the exchange rate is 10.8 Mexican pesos per Canadian dollar and if purchasing power parity prevails, at what price can you buy an identical computer in Vancouver?

8. The table gives some information about a country's international transactions in 2008.

Item	Millions of dollars
Imports of goods and services	1,487
Foreign investment in the country	1,051
Exports of goods and services	990
Investment abroad	456
Net interest income	7
Net transfers	−68
Statistical discrepancy	−36

   a. Calculate the current account balance.
   b. Calculate the capital account balance.
   c. Did the country's official reserves increase or decrease?
   d. Was the country a net borrower or a net lender in 2008? Explain your answer.

9. A country has a lower inflation rate than all other countries. It has more rapid economic growth. The central bank does not intervene in the foreign exchange market. What can you say (and why) about

   a. The exchange rate?
   b. The current account balance?
   c. The expected exchange rate?
   d. The interest rate differential?
   e. Interest rate parity?
   f. Purchasing power parity?

10. **The Lesson: Buy Ruffles in Myanmar**

    ... A small bag of cheese-flavored Ruffles potato chips is $1.69 in Japan and only 8 cents in Myanmar. ... The price of spending 1 hour at an Internet cafe in Vietnam is $0.62 U.S., in China is $1.48 U.S., and in South Africa is $3.40 U.S.

    Los Angeles Times, April 23, 2006

    Do these prices indicate that purchasing power parity does not prevail? Why or why not?

11. **Peso's Party**

    It was bad enough when Canada's Loonie surpassed the U.S. dollar, but now the Mexican peso is gaining on the greenback, too. In April, the peso hit 10.44 to the U.S. dollar, its best rate in two years. Mexico's 4.2 percent GDP growth in January and February ... finally convinced currency investors that the peso shouldn't be tethered to the dollar, as it has been in recent years. ... At current levels, exports might soon become more expensive for gringos. In other words, time to stock up on Coronas.

    Fortune, May 12, 2008

    a. Is the news clip about the real exchange rate or the nominal exchange rate? Explain.

    b. Explain why "the Mexican peso is gaining on the greenback."

    c. Draw a graph to illustrate why "the Mexican peso is gaining on the greenback."

    d. Explain why Mexican goods might become more expensive for U.S. consumers.

12. **Canada's Experience with Flexible Exchange Rate in the 1950s: Valuable Lessons Learned**

    Canada's experience with a flexible exchange rate regime in the twentieth and twenty-first centuries is remarkable not only for sheer length, but also for its impact on macroeconomic theory and policy in open economies. ... Canada had a flexible exchange rate regime over the periods 1933–39 and 1950–62, and has maintained one since 1970 ... [There are] benefits of a flexible exchange rate regime: namely, its ability to insulate the domestic economy from external shocks by facilitating a smoother and thus less costly macroeconomic adjustment, and the fact that it permits the operation of an independent national monetary policy. ... Canada's experience led to a better understanding of the impact of monetary and fiscal policies in an open economy with a high degree of capital mobility ... Canada's floating-rate experience contributed to the postwar debate on exchange rate regimes by providing evidence to support the case for a flexible rate as a viable alternative to ... pegged exchange rates.

    Bank of Canada Review, Spring 2008

    a. Explain the difference between the flexible exchange rate policy that Canada pioneered and a fixed exchange rate policy.

    b. Explain the advantages of a flexible exchange rate policy over a fixed exchange rate policy.

    c. If a fixed exchange rate does not influence competitiveness in the long run, why might a country adopt this policy?

13. **The United States, Debtor Nation**

    The United States is a debtor nation, just like the poorest states in Africa, Latin America and Asia. ... For most of the past 30 years the United States has been piling up large trade deficits. The current account ... has now reached a deficit of 6 percent of GDP, and must be financed by capital inflows. Foreigners must purchase large amounts of US property, stocks, bonds, bank deposits and currency, or the current-account deficit cannot be financed. ...

    Asia Times, September 28, 2006

    a. Explain why a current account deficit "must be financed by capital inflows."

    b. Under what circumstances should the debtor nation status of the United States be a concern?

14. The *Economist* magazine uses the price of a Big Mac to determine whether a currency is undervalued or overvalued. In May 2006, the price of a Big Mac was $3.10 in New York, 10.5 yuan in Beijing, and 6.30 Swiss francs in Geneva. The exchange rates were 8.03 yuan per U.S. dollar and 1.21 Swiss francs per U.S. dollar.

    a. Was the yuan undervalued or overvalued relative to purchasing power parity?

    b. Was the Swiss franc undervalued or overvalued relative to purchasing power parity?

    c. Do you think the price of a Big Mac in different countries provides a valid test of purchasing power parity?

15. The table gives some information about the U.K. economy in 2003:

Item	Billions of U.K. pounds
Consumption expenditure	721
Exports of goods and services	277
Government expenditure	230
Net taxes	217
Investment	181
Saving	162

a. Calculate the private sector balance.
b. Calculate the government sector balance.
c. Calculate net exports.
d. What is the relationship between the government sector balance and net exports?

16. A country's currency appreciates, and its official holdings of foreign currency increase. What can you say about

a. The central bank's intervention in the foreign exchange market?
b. The country's current account balance?
c. The country's official settlements account?

17. **Top U.S. Real Estate Markets for Investment**

Rahul Reddy ... has been investing in commercial properties in Western Australia for the last two years. Now, with the Australian dollar growing in strength and the American housing market strained, he's got his eye on residential and commercial properties in Florida and California, areas he believes will recover over the long term. He's not alone. Encouraged by a weak dollar and a belief in the resiliency of the U.S. economy, individuals like Reddy, along with institutional investors such as pension funds and private equity groups, are seeking investment properties and development opportunities in the United States. ... "The U.S. is good for speculative higher-risk investments from our perspective because the strong Australian dollar will enable us to gain hold of properties at prices we will probably not see for a long time," says Reddy. "The U.S. is an economic powerhouse that I think will recover, and if the exchange rate goes back to figures from a few years ago, that will benefit us. ..."

Forbes, July 10, 2008

a. Explain why foreign individuals and institutions are "seeking investment properties and development opportunities in the United States."

b. Explain what would happen if the speculation made by Reddy became widespread. Would expectations become self-fulfilling?
c. Draw a graph of the foreign exchange market to illustrate your explanation in b.

18. **Canada's Dollar Depreciates as Stock Indexes in the U.S. Fall**

Canada's currency depreciated as U.S. stocks fell, signaling an increase in risk aversion.

The Canadian dollar has weakened 11 percent this quarter. ... The U.S. is Canada's largest trading partner. "The direction of the Canadian dollar is very much a function of how risk is seen in the global landscape," said Jack Spitz, managing director of foreign exchange at National Bank of Canada in Toronto. "Equities are off their highs, so the Canadian dollar gets swept up in this environment." ... Bank of Canada Governor Mark Carney signalled his country may slide into a recession like other industrialized nations, adding weight to economists' forecasts that he may pare interest rates to the lowest since 1960. ... Carney cut his key interest rate to 2.25 percent last month and said the world's eighth-largest economy would shrink this quarter and stall in the first three months of 2009. Three of the country's biggest banks predict a recession. ... The Canadian dollar will plunge 10 percent over the next three months ... as global growth slows, according to Barclays Capital.

Bloomberg, November 10, 2008

Explain and draw a graph to illustrate the individual effect of each of the following events on the exchange rate of the Canadian dollar against the U.S. dollar.

a. The Bank of Canada cuts the interest rate while foreign interest rates remain unchanged.
b. The Bank of Canada cuts the interest rate and foreign central banks cut their interest rates by the same amount and at the same time.
c. Expectations that the Bank of Canada will cut interest rates in the future increase.
d. A recession occurs in Canada but not in the United States.
e. A recession occurs in both the United States and Canada.

19. **U.S. Declines to Cite China as Currency Manipulator**

The Bush administration has declined to cite China for manipulating its currency to gain unfair trade advantages against the United States ... despite pressure in Congress for penalties. America's growing trade deficit with China, which last year hit an all-time high of $256.3 billion, [is] the largest deficit ever recorded with a single country. ... Chinese currency, the yuan, has risen in value by 18.4 percent against the dollar since the Chinese government loosened its currency system in July 2005. However, American manufacturers contend the yuan is still undervalued by as much as 40 percent, making Chinese products more competitive in this country and U.S. goods more expensive in China. ... China is a major holder of dollar-denominated investments such as U.S. Treasury securities, which it buys to keep the dollar from falling in value against the yuan.

MSN, May 15, 2008

a. Explain how China was able to maintain a fixed exchange rate with the dollar until July 2005.
b. Draw a graph to illustrate how China kept the exchange rate fixed.
c. Has China used a flexible exchange rate policy since July 2005?
d. Explain how fixed and crawling peg exchange rates can be used to manipulate trade balances in the short run, but not in the long run.
e. What is the long-run rationale behind a fixed or crawling peg exchange rate?

20. **Inside the Mind of a Debtor Nation**

Year after year, I am stunned by the decisions people make that get them into financial trouble. I've seen monthly car notes the size of mortgage payments. People take vacations or buy big-screen televisions and expensive jewelry while ignoring huge federal tax obligations. ... Why do they continue to use credit even though they are already weighed down by so much debt? ... What has made us into a nation of people who spend more than we earn? ... Part of the problem is our economy's reliance on personal consumption. On some level, we all know our buying is out of control, but we are constantly bombarded with messages encouraging us to shop. The steady stream blunts our reasoning power. ... Much of the difficulty stems from new retail technologies that make it easy to act without thinking. ... What's the long-term effect of our overspending?

Washington Post, March 2, 2008

a. Explain the effect on the dollar of "out of control" consumer spending and draw a graph of the foreign exchange market to illustrate your explanation.
b. How can "out of control" spending be used to explain the trends in balance of payments since the 1990s?
c. Explain whether or not Americans should be concerned that the United States is a net borrower and debtor nation.

21. Study *Reading Between the Lines* on pp. 614–615 and then answer the following questions.

a. Do you think the yuan–U.S. dollar exchange rate is a problem for Americans or the source of the U.S. current account deficit?
b. Do you think that appreciation of the yuan against the U.S. dollar can help the United States to eliminate its current account deficit?
c. What do you predict would be the main effects of an increase in the yuan–U.S. dollar exchange rate?
d. What, if anything, could U.S. policy do to reduce the U.S. current account deficit?

22. Use the link in MyEconLab (Textbook resources, Chapter 25, Weblinks) to visit PACIFIC, an exchange rate service, and read the page on purchasing power parity.

a. What is purchasing power parity?
b. Which currencies are the most overvalued relative to the U.S. dollar today?
c. Which currencies are the most undervalued relative to the U.S. dollar today?
d. Give some suggestions as to why some currencies are overvalued and some undervalued.
e. Do you think that the information on overvaluation and undervaluation is useful to currency speculators? Why or why not?

Expanding the Frontier

Economics is about how we cope with scarcity. We cope as individuals by making choices that balance marginal benefits and marginal costs so that we use our scarce resources efficiently. We cope as societies by creating incentive systems and social institutions that encourage specialization and exchange.

These choices and the incentive systems that guide them determine what we specialize in; how much work we do; how hard we work at school to learn the mental skills that form our human capital and that determine the kinds of jobs we get and the incomes we earn; how much we save for future big-ticket expenditures; how much businesses and governments spend on new capital—on auto assembly lines, computers and fibre cables for improved Internet services, shopping malls, highways, bridges, and tunnels; how intensively existing capital and natural resources are used and how quickly they wear out or are used up; and the problems that scientists, engineers, and other inventors work on to develop new technologies.

All the choices we've just described combine to determine the standard of living and the rate at which it improves—the economic growth rate.

Money that makes specialization and exchange in markets possible is a huge contributor to economic growth. But too much money brings a rising cost of living with no improvement in the standard of living.

Joseph Schumpeter, *the son of a textile factory owner, was born in Austria in 1883. He moved from Austria to Germany during the tumultuous 1920s when those two countries experienced hyperinflation. In 1932, in the depths of the Great Depression, he went to the United States and became a professor of economics at Harvard University.*

This creative economic thinker wrote about economic growth and development, business cycles, political systems, and economic biography. He was a person of strong opinions who expressed them forcefully and delighted in verbal battles.

Schumpeter saw the development and diffusion of new technologies by profit-seeking entrepreneurs as the source of economic progress. But he saw economic progress as a process of creative destruction—the creation of new profit opportunities and the destruction of currently profitable businesses. For Schumpeter, economic growth and the business cycle were a single phenomenon.

"Economic progress, in capitalist society, means turmoil."

JOSEPH SCHUMPETER
Capitalism, Socialism, and Democracy

621

Xavier Sala-i-Martin

Xavier Sala-i-Martin is Professor of Economics at Columbia University. He is also a Research Associate at the National Bureau of Economic Research, Senior Economic Advisor to the World Economic Forum, Associate Editor of the *Journal of Economic Growth*, founder and CEO of Umbele Foundation: A Future for Africa, and President of the Economic Commission of the Barcelona Football Club.

Professor Sala-i-Martin was an undergraduate at Universitat Autonoma de Barcelona and a graduate student at Harvard University, where he obtained his Ph.D. in 1990.

In 2004, he was awarded the Premio Juan Carlos I de Economía, a biannual prize given by the Bank of Spain to the best economist in Spain and Latin America.

With Robert Barro, he is the author of *Economic Growth Second Edition* (MIT Press, 2003), the definitive graduate level text on this topic.

Michael Parkin and Robin Bade talked with Xavier Sala-i-Martin about his work and the progress that economists have made in understanding economic growth.

What attracted you to economics?

It was a random event. I wanted to be rich, so I asked my mom, "In my family, who is the richest guy?" She said, "Your uncle John." And I asked, "What did he study?" And she said, "Economics." So I went into economics!

In Spain, there are no liberal arts colleges where you can study lots of things. At age 18, you must decide what career you will follow. If you choose economics, you go to economics school and take economics five years in a row. So you have to make a decision in a crazy way, like I did.

How did economic growth become your major field of research?

I studied economics. I liked it. I studied mathematical economics. I liked it too, and I went to graduate school. In my second year at Harvard, Jeffrey Sachs hired me to go to Bolivia. I saw poor people for the first time in my life. I was shocked. I decided I should try to answer the question "Why are these people so poor and why are we so rich, and what can we do to turn their state into our state?" We live in a bubble world in the United States and Europe, and we don't realize how poor people really are. When you see poverty at first hand, it is very hard to think about something else. So I decided to study economic growth. Coincidentally, when I returned from Bolivia, I was assigned to be Robert Barro's teaching assistant. He was teaching economic growth, so I studied with him and eventually wrote books and articles with him.

In your first research on economic growth, you tested the neoclassical growth model using data for a number of countries and for the states of the United States. What did you discover?

Neoclassical theory was criticized on two grounds. First, its source of growth, technological change, is exogenous—not explained. Second, its assumption of diminishing marginal returns to capital seems to imply that income per person should converge to the same level in every country. If you are poor, your marginal product should be high. Every cookie that you save should generate huge growth. If you are rich, your marginal product should be low. Every cookie you save should generate very little growth. Therefore poor countries should grow faster than rich countries, and convergence of income levels should occur. Convergence doesn't occur, so, said its critics, neoclassical theory must be wrong.

It turned out that it was this criticism that was wrong. Growth depends on the productivity of your cookies and on how many cookies you save. If you don't save any cookies, you don't grow, even if your marginal product is large.

Conditional convergence is the idea that income per person will converge only if countries have similar savings rates, similar technologies, and similar everything. That's what I tested. To hold every relevant factor equal, I tested the hypothesis using regions: states within the United States or countries that are similar. And once you're careful to hold other things equal, you see a perfect negative relationship between growth rates and income levels.

As predicted by neoclassical theory, poor countries grow faster than rich countries if they are similar. So my research shows that it is not so easy to reject neoclassical theory. The law of diminishing returns that comes from Adam Smith and Malthus and Ricardo is very powerful. Growth through capital accumulation is very, very hard. Growth has to come from other things, such as technological change.

What do we know today about the nature and causes of the wealth of nations that Adam Smith didn't know?

Actually, even though over the last two hundred years some of the best minds have looked at the question, we know surprisingly little. We have some general principles that are not very easy to apply in practice. We know, for example, that markets are good. We know that for the economy to work, we need property rights to be guaranteed. If there are thieves—government or private thieves—that can steal the proceeds of the

investment, there's no investment and there's no growth. We know that the incentives are very important.

These are general principles. Because we know these principles we should ask: How come Africa is still poor? The answer is, it is very hard to translate "Markets are good" and "Property rights work" into practical actions. We know that Zimbabwe has to guarantee property rights. With the government it has, that's not going to work. The U.S. Constitution works in the United States. If you try to copy the U.S. Constitution and impose the system in Zimbabwe, it's not going to work.

> Growth through capital accumulation is very, very hard. Growth has to come from other things, such as technological change.

You've done a lot of work on distribution of income, and you say we've made a lot of progress. What is the evidence to support this conclusion?

There are two issues: poverty and inequality. When in 2001 I said poverty is going down, everyone said I was crazy. The United Nations Development Report, which uses World Bank data, was saying the exact opposite. I said the World Bank methodology was flawed. After a big public argument that you can see in the *Economist*, the World Bank revised their poverty numbers and they now agree with me that poverty rates are falling.

Now why is poverty falling? In 1970, 80 percent of the world's poor were in Asia—in China, India, Bangladesh, and Indonesia. China's "Great Leap Forward" was a great leap backward. People were starving to death. Now, the growth of these countries has been spectacular and the global poverty rate has fallen. Yes, if you look at Africa, Africa is going backwards. But Africa has 700 million people. China has 1.3 billion. India has 1.1 billion. Indonesia has 300 million. Asia has 4 billion of the world's 6 billion people. These big guys are growing. It's impossible that global poverty is not going down.

But what we care about is poverty in different regions of the world. Asia has been doing very well, but Africa has not. Unfortunately, Africa is still going in the wrong direction.

You've made a big personal commitment to Africa. What is the Africa problem? Why does this continent lag behind Asia? Why, as you've just put it, is Africa going in the wrong direction?

Number one, Africa is a very violent continent. There are 22 wars in Africa as we speak. Two, nobody will invest in Africa. Three, we in the rich world—the United States, Europe, and Japan—won't let them trade. Because we have agricultural subsidies, trade barriers, and tariffs for their products, they can't sell to us.

Africans should globalize themselves. They should open, and we should let them open. They should introduce markets. But to get markets, you need legal systems, police, transparency, less red tape. You need a lot of the things we have now. They have corrupt economies, very bureaucratic, with no property rights, the judiciary is corrupt. All of that has to change.

They need female education. One of the biggest rates of return that we have is educating girls. To educate girls, they'll need to build schools, they need to pay teachers, they need to buy uniforms, they need to provide the incentives for girls to go to school, which usually is like a string. You pull it, you don't push it. Pushing education doesn't work. What you need is: Let the girls know that the rate of return on education is very high by providing jobs after they leave school. So you need to change the incentives of the girls to go to school and educate themselves. That's going to increase the national product, but it will also increase health, and it will also reduce fertility.

> Question!
> Question everything!

Returning to the problems of poverty and inequality, how can inequality be increasing within countries but decreasing globally—across countries?

Because most inequality comes from the fact that some people live in rich countries and some people live in poor countries. The big difference across people is not that there are rich Americans and poor Americans. Americans are very close to each other relative to the difference between Americans and people from Senegal.

What is closing today is the gap *across* countries—and for the first time in history. Before the Industrial Revolution, everybody was equal. Equal and poor. Equally poor. People were living at subsistence levels, which means you eat, you're clothed, you have a house, you die. No movies, no travel, no music, no toothbrush. Just subsist. And if the weather is not good, one-third of the population dies. That was the history of the world between 10,000 B.C. and today.

Yes, there was a king, there was Caesar, but the majority of the population were peasants.

All of a sudden, the Industrial Revolution means that one small country, England, takes off and there is 2 percent growth every year. The living standard of the workers of England goes up and up and up. Then the United States, then France, then the rest of Europe, then Canada all begin to grow.

In terms of today's population, 1 billion people become rich and 5 billion remain poor. Now for the first time in history, the majority of these 5 billion people are growing more rapidly than the rich guys. They're catching up quickly. The incomes of the majority of poor citizens of the world are growing faster than those of Americans.

What advice do you have for someone who is just beginning to study economics?

Question! Question everything! Take some courses in history and math. And read my latest favourite book, Bill Easterly's *White Man's Burden.* * It shows why we have not been doing the right thing in the aid business. I'm a little bit less dramatic than he is. He says that nothing has worked. I think some things have worked, and we have to take advantage of what has worked to build on it. But I agree with the general principle that being nice, being good, doesn't necessarily mean doing good. Lots of people with good intentions do harm. Economic science teaches us that incentives are the key.

---

*William Easterly, *The White Man's Burden: Why the West's Efforts to Aid the Rest Have Done So Much Ill and So Little Good.* New York, Penguin Books, 2006.

26

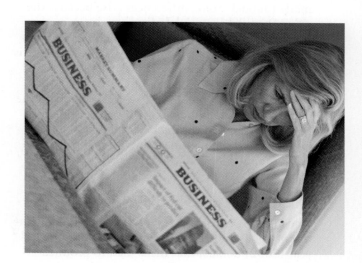

Aggregate Supply and Aggregate Demand

After studying this chapter, you will be able to

- Explain what determines aggregate supply in the long run and in the short run

- Explain what determines aggregate demand

- Explain how real GDP and the price level are determined and how changes in aggregate supply and aggregate demand bring economic growth, inflation, and the business cycle

- Describe the main schools of thought in macroeconomics today

Production grows and prices rise. But the pace at which production grows and prices rise is uneven. In 2006, real GDP grew by 3 percent, but in 2008, growth slowed to snail pace and was expected to shrink in in the last quarter of 2008 and the whole of 2009.

Similarly, during recent years, prices have increased at rates ranging from a barely perceptible 1 percent to a disturbing 4 percent a year.

The uneven pace of economic growth and inflation—the business cycle—is the subject of this chapter and the two that follow it. Here, you will discover the forces that bring fluctuations in the pace of real GDP growth and inflation and the associated fluctuations in employment and unemployment.

This chapter explains a *model* of real GDP and the price level—the *aggregate supply–aggregate demand model* or *AS–AD model*. This model represents the consensus view of macroeconomists on how real GDP and the price level are determined. The model provides a framework for understanding the forces that make our economy expand, that bring inflation, and that cause business cycle fluctuations. The *AS–AD* model also provides a framework within which we can see the range of views of macroeconomists in different schools of thought.

In *Reading Between the Lines* at the end of the chapter, we use the *AS–AD* model to interpret the course of Canadian real GDP and the price level in 2008.

Aggregate Supply

The purpose of the aggregate supply–aggregate demand model that you study in this chapter is to explain how real GDP and the price level are determined and how they interact. The model uses similar ideas to those that you encountered in Chapter 3 when you learned how the quantity and price in a competitive market are determined. But the *aggregate* supply–*aggregate* demand model (*AS–AD* model) isn't just an application of the competitive market model. Some differences arise because the *AS–AD* model is a model of an imaginary market for the total of all the final goods and services that make up real GDP. The quantity in this "market" is real GDP and the price is the price level measured by the GDP deflator.

One thing that the *AS–AD* model shares with the competitive market model is that both distinguish between *supply* and the *quantity supplied*. We begin by explaining what we mean by the quantity of real GDP supplied.

Quantity Supplied and Supply

The *quantity of real GDP supplied* is the total quantity of goods and services, valued in constant base-year (2002) dollars, that firms plan to produce during a given period. This quantity depends on the quantity of labour employed; the quantity of physical and human capital; and the state of technology.

At any given time, the quantity of capital and the state of technology are fixed. They depend on decisions that were made in the past. The population is also fixed. But the quantity of labour is not fixed. It depends on decisions made by households and firms about the supply of and demand for labour.

The labour market can be in any one of three states: at full employment, above full employment, or below full employment. At full employment, the quantity of real GDP supplied is *potential GDP*, which depends on the full-employment quantity of labour (see Chapter 22, pp. 521–523). Over the business cycle, employment fluctuates around full employment and the quantity of real GDP supplied fluctuates around potential GDP.

Aggregate supply is the relationship between the quantity of real GDP supplied and the price level. This relationship is different in the long run than in the short run and to study aggregate supply, we distinguish between two time frames:

- Long-run aggregate supply
- Short-run aggregate supply

Long-Run Aggregate Supply

Long-run aggregate supply is the relationship between the quantity of real GDP supplied and the price level when the money wage rate changes in step with the price level to achieve full employment. The quantity of real GDP supplied at full employment equals potential GDP and this quantity is the same regardless of the price level.

The long-run aggregate supply curve in Fig. 26.1 illustrates long-run aggregate supply as the vertical line at potential GDP labelled *LAS*. Along the long-run aggregate supply curve, as the price level changes, the money wage rate also changes so the real wage rate is constant and real GDP remains at potential GDP. The long-run aggregate supply curve is always vertical and is always located at potential GDP.

The long-run aggregate supply curve is vertical because potential GDP is independent of the price level. The reason for this independence is that a movement along the *LAS* curve is accompanied by a change in *two* sets of prices: the prices of goods and services—the price level—and the prices of the factors of production, most notably, the money wage rate. A 10 percent increase in the prices of goods and services is matched by a 10 percent increase in the money wage rate. Because the price level and the money wage rate change by the same percentage, the *real wage rate* remains constant at its full-employment equilibrium level. So when the price level changes and the real wage rate remains constant, employment remains constant and real GDP remains constant at potential GDP.

Production at a Pepsi Plant You can see more clearly why real GDP remains constant when all prices change by the same percentage by thinking about production decisions at a Pepsi bottling plant. How does the quantity of Pepsi supplied change if the price of Pepsi changes and the wage rate of the workers and prices of all the other resources used vary by the same percentage? The answer is that the quantity supplied doesn't change. The firm produces the quantity that maximizes profit. That quantity depends on the price of Pepsi relative to the cost of producing it. With no change in price *relative to cost*, production doesn't change.

Short-Run Aggregate Supply

Short-run aggregate supply is the relationship between the quantity of real GDP supplied and the price level *when the money wage rate, the prices of other resources, and potential GDP remain constant.* Figure 26.1 illustrates this relationship as the short-run aggregate supply curve *SAS* and the short-run aggregate supply schedule. Each point on the *SAS* curve corresponds to a row of the short-run aggregate supply schedule. For example, point *A* on the *SAS* curve and row *A* of the schedule tell us that if the price level is 100, the quantity of real GDP supplied is $1,100 billion. In the short run, a rise in the price level brings an increase in the quantity of real GDP supplied. The short-run aggregate supply curve slopes upward.

With a given money wage rate, there is one price level at which the real wage rate is at its full-employment equilibrium level. At this price level, the quantity of real GDP supplied equals potential GDP and the *SAS* curve intersects the *LAS* curve. In this example, that price level is 110. If the price level rises above 110, the quantity of real GDP supplied increases along the *SAS* curve and exceeds potential GDP; if the price level falls below 110, the quantity of real GDP supplied decreases along the *SAS* curve and is less than potential GDP.

Back at the Pepsi Plant You can see why the short-run aggregate supply curve slopes upward by returning to the Pepsi bottling plant. If production increases, marginal cost rises; if production decreases, marginal cost falls (see Chapter 2, p. 35).

If the price of Pepsi rises with no change in the money wage rate and other costs, Pepsi can increase profit by increasing production. Pepsi is in business to maximize its profit, so it increases production.

Similarly, if the price of Pepsi falls while the money wage rate and other costs remain constant, Pepsi can avoid a loss by decreasing production. The lower price weakens the incentive to produce, so Pepsi decreases production.

What's true for Pepsi bottlers is true for the producers of all goods and services. When all prices rise, the *price level rises.* If the price level rises and the money wage rate and other factor prices remain constant, all firms increase production and the quantity of real GDP supplied increases. A fall in the price level has the opposite effect and decreases the quantity of real GDP supplied.

FIGURE 26.1 Long-Run and Short-Run Aggregate Supply

	Price level (GDP deflator)	Real GDP supplied (billions of 2002 dollars)
A	100	1,100
B	105	1,150
C	**110**	**1,200**
D	115	1,250
E	120	1,300

In the long run, the quantity of real GDP supplied is potential GDP and the *LAS* curve is vertical at potential GDP. In the short run, the quantity of real GDP supplied increases if the price level rises, while all other influences on supply plans remain the same.

The short-run aggregate supply curve, *SAS,* slopes upward. The short-run aggregate supply curve is based on the aggregate supply schedule in the table. Each point *A* through *E* on the curve corresponds to the row in the table identified by the same letter.

When the price level is 110, the quantity of real GDP supplied is $1,200 billion, which is potential GDP. If the price level rises above 110, the quantity of real GDP supplied increases and exceeds potential GDP; if the price level falls below 110, the quantity of real GDP supplied decreases below potential GDP.

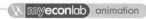 animation

Changes in Aggregate Supply

You've just seen that a change in the price level brings a movement along the aggregate supply curves, but it does not change aggregate supply. Aggregate supply changes when an influence on production plans other than the price level changes. These other influences include a change in potential GDP and the money wage rate and other factor prices. Let's begin by looking at factors that change potential GDP.

Changes in Potential GDP When potential GDP changes, aggregate supply changes. An increase in potential GDP increases both long-run aggregate supply and short-run aggregate supply.

Figure 26.2 shows the effects of an increase in potential GDP. Initially, the long-run aggregate supply curve is LAS_0 and the short-run aggregate supply curve is SAS_0. If potential GDP increases to $1,300 billion, long-run aggregate supply increases and the long-run aggregate supply curve shifts rightward to LAS_1. Short-run aggregate supply also increases, and the short-run aggregate supply curve shifts rightward to SAS_1. The two supply curves shift by the same amount only if the full-employment price level remains constant, which we will assume to be the case.

Potential GDP can increase for any of three reasons:

- An increase in the full-employment quantity of labour
- An increase in the quantity of capital
- An advance in technology

Let's look at these influences on potential GDP and the aggregate supply curves.

An Increase in the Full-Employment Quantity of Labour A Pepsi bottling plant that employs 100 workers bottles more Pepsi than does an otherwise identical plant that employs 10 workers. The same is true for the economy as a whole. The larger the quantity of labour employed, the greater is real GDP.

Over time, potential GDP increases because the labour force increases. But, with constant capital and technology, *potential* GDP increases only if the full-employment quantity of labour increases.

Fluctuations in employment over the business cycle bring fluctuations in real GDP. But these changes in real GDP are fluctuations *around* potential GDP. They are not changes in potential GDP and long-run aggregate supply.

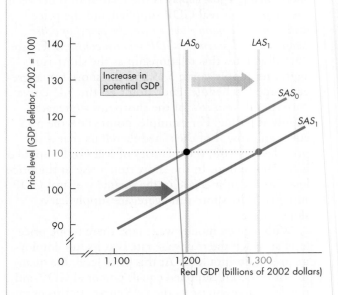

FIGURE 26.2   A Change in Potential GDP

An increase in potential GDP increases both long-run aggregate supply and short-run aggregate supply and shifts both aggregate supply curves rightward from LAS_0 to LAS_1 and from SAS_0 to SAS_1.

myeconlab animation

An Increase in the Quantity of Capital A Pepsi bottling plant with two production lines bottles more Pepsi than does an otherwise identical plant that has only one production line. For the economy, the larger the quantity of capital, the more productive is the labour force and the greater is its potential GDP. Potential GDP per person in capital-rich Canada is vastly greater than that in capital-poor China and Russia.

Capital includes *human capital*. One Pepsi plant is managed by an economics major with an MBA and has a labour force with an average of 10 years of experience. This plant produces a larger output than does an otherwise identical plant that is managed by someone with no business training or experience and that has a young labour force that is new to bottling. The first plant has a greater amount of human capital than the second. For the economy as a whole, the larger the quantity of *human capital*—the skills that people have acquired in school and through on-the-job training—the greater is potential GDP.

An Advance in Technology A Pepsi plant that has pre-computer age machines produces less than one that uses the latest robot technology. Technological change enables firms to produce more from any given amount of factors of production. So even with fixed quantities of labour and capital, improvements in technology increase potential GDP.

Technological advances are by far the most important source of increased production over the past two centuries. As a result of technological advances, one farmer in Canada today can feed 100 people and in a year one autoworker can produce almost 14 cars and trucks.

Let's now look at the effects of changes in the money wage rate.

Changes in the Money Wage Rate and Other Factor Prices

When the money wage rate (or the money price of any other factor of production such as oil) changes, short-run aggregate supply changes but long-run aggregate supply does not change.

Figure 26.3 shows the effect of an increase in the money wage rate. Initially, the short-run aggregate supply curve is SAS_0. A rise in the money wage rate *decreases* short-run aggregate supply and shifts the short-run aggregate supply curve leftward to SAS_2.

A rise in the money wage rate decreases short-run aggregate supply because it increases firms' costs. With increased costs, the quantity that firms are willing to supply at each price level decreases, which is shown by a leftward shift of the *SAS* curve.

A change in the money wage rate does not change long-run aggregate supply because on the *LAS* curve, the change in the money wage rate is accompanied by an equal percentage change in the price level. With no change in *relative* prices, firms have no incentive to change production and real GDP remains constant at potential GDP. With no change in potential GDP, the long-run aggregate supply curve *LAS* does not shift.

What Makes the Money Wage Rate Change?

The money wage rate can change for two reasons: departures from full employment and expectations about inflation. Unemployment above the natural rate puts downward pressure on the money wage rate, and unemployment below the natural rate puts upward pressure on it. An expected rise in the inflation rate makes the money wage rate rise faster, and an expected fall in the inflation rate slows the rate at which the money wage rate rises.

FIGURE 26.3 A Change in the Money Wage Rate

A rise in the money wage rate decreases short-run aggregate supply and shifts the short-run aggregate supply curve leftward from SAS_0 to SAS_2. A rise in the money wage rate does not change potential GDP, so the long-run aggregate supply curve does not shift.

myeconlab animation

Review Quiz

1 If the price level and the money wage rate rise by the same percentage, what happens to the quantity of real GDP supplied? Along which aggregate supply curve does the economy move?

2 If the price level rises and the money wage rate remains constant, what happens to the quantity of real GDP supplied? Along which aggregate supply curve does the economy move?

3 If potential GDP increases, what happens to aggregate supply? Does the *LAS* curve shift or is there a movement along the *LAS* curve? Does the *SAS* curve shift or is there a movement along the *SAS* curve?

4 If the money wage rate rises and potential GDP remains the same, does the *LAS* curve or the *SAS* curve shift or is there a movement along the *LAS* curve or the *SAS* curve?

myeconlab   Work Study Plan 26.1 and get instant feedback.

Aggregate Demand

The quantity of real GDP demanded (Y) is the sum of real consumption expenditure (C), investment (I), government expenditure (G), and exports (X) minus imports (M). That is,

$$Y = C + I + G + X - M.$$

The *quantity of real GDP demanded* is the total amount of final goods and services produced in Canada that people, businesses, governments, and foreigners plan to buy. These buying plans depend on many factors. Some of the main ones are

- The price level
- Expectations
- Fiscal policy and monetary policy
- The world economy

We first focus on the relationship between the quantity of real GDP demanded and the price level. To study this relationship, we keep all other influences on buying plans the same and ask: How does the quantity of real GDP demanded vary as the price level varies?

The Aggregate Demand Curve

Other things remaining the same, the higher the price level, the smaller is the quantity of real GDP demanded. This relationship between the quantity of real GDP demanded and the price level is called **aggregate demand**. Aggregate demand is described by an *aggregate demand schedule* and an *aggregate demand curve*.

Figure 26.4 shows an aggregate demand curve (AD) and an aggregate demand schedule. Each point on the AD curve corresponds to a row of the schedule. For example, point C' on the AD curve and row C' of the schedule tell us that if the price level is 110, the quantity of real GDP demanded is $1,200 billion.

The aggregate demand curve slopes downward for two reasons:

- Wealth effect
- Substitution effects

Wealth Effect When the price level rises but other things remain the same, *real* wealth decreases. Real

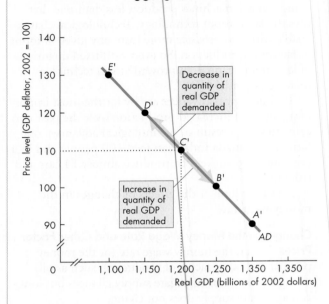

FIGURE 26.4   Aggregate Demand

	Price level (GDP deflator)	Real GDP demanded (billions of 2002 dollars)
A'	90	1,300
B'	100	1,250
C'	110	1,200
D'	120	1,150
E'	130	1,100

The aggregate demand curve (AD) shows the relationship between the quantity of real GDP demanded and the price level. The aggregate demand curve is based on the aggregate demand schedule in the table. Each point A' through E' on the curve corresponds to the row in the table identified by the same letter. When the price level is 110, the quantity of real GDP demanded is $1,200 billion, as shown by point C' in the figure. A change in the price level, when all other influences on aggregate buying plans remain the same, brings a change in the quantity of real GDP demanded and a movement along the AD curve.

myeconlab   animation

wealth is the amount of money in the bank, bonds, stocks, and other assets that people own, measured not in dollars but in terms of the goods and services that the money, bonds, and stock will buy.

People save and hold money, bonds, and stocks for many reasons. One reason is to build up funds for education expenses. Another reason is to build up enough funds to meet possible medical expenses or other big bills. But the biggest reason is to build up enough funds to provide a retirement income.

If the price level rises, real wealth decreases. People then try to restore their wealth. To do so, they must increase saving and, equivalently, decrease current consumption. Such a decrease in consumption is a decrease in aggregate demand.

Maria's Wealth Effect You can see how the wealth effect works by thinking about Maria's buying plans. Maria lives in Moscow, Russia. She has worked hard all summer and saved 20,000 rubles (the ruble is the currency of Russia), which she plans to spend attending graduate school when she has finished her economics degree. So Maria's wealth is 20,000 rubles. Maria has a part-time job, and her income from this job pays her current expenses. The price level in Russia rises by 100 percent, and now Maria needs 40,000 rubles to buy what 20,000 once bought. To try to make up some of the fall in value of her savings, Maria saves even more and cuts her current spending to the bare minimum.

Substitution Effects When the price level rises and other things remain the same, interest rates rise. The reason is related to the wealth effect that you've just studied. A rise in the price level decreases the real value of the money in people's pockets and bank accounts. With a smaller amount of real money around, banks and other lenders can get a higher interest rate on loans. But faced with a higher interest rate, people and businesses delay plans to buy new capital and consumer durable goods and cut back on spending.

This substitution effect involves substituting goods in the future for goods in the present and is called an *intertemporal* substitution effect—a substitution across time. Saving increases to increase future consumption.

To see this intertemporal substitution effect more clearly, think about your own plan to buy a new computer. At an interest rate of 5 percent a year, you might borrow $1,000 and buy the new computer. But at an interest rate of 10 percent a year, you might decide that the payments would be too high. You don't abandon your plan to buy the computer, but you decide to delay your purchase.

A second substitution effect works through international prices. When the Canadian price level rises and other things remain the same, Canadian-made goods and services become more expensive relative to foreign-made goods and services. This change in *relative prices* encourages people to spend less on Canadian-made items and more on foreign-made items. For example, if the Canadian price level rises relative to the Japanese price level, Japanese buy fewer Canadian-made cars (Canadian exports decrease) and Canadians buy more Japanese-made cars (Canadian imports increase). Canadian GDP decreases.

Maria's Substitution Effect In Moscow, Russia, Maria makes some substitutions. She was planning to trade in her old motor scooter and get a new one. But with a higher price level and a higher interest rate, she decides to make her old scooter last one more year. Also, with the prices of Russian goods sharply increasing, Maria substitutes a low-cost dress made in Malaysia for the Russian-made dress she had originally planned to buy.

Changes in the Quantity of Real GDP Demanded
When the price level rises and other things remain the same, the quantity of real GDP demanded decreases—a movement up along the *AD* curve as shown by the arrow in Fig. 26.4. When the price level falls and other things remain the same, the quantity of real GDP demanded increases—a movement down along the *AD* curve.

We've now seen how the quantity of real GDP demanded changes when the price level changes. How do other influences on buying plans affect aggregate demand?

Changes in Aggregate Demand

A change in any factor that influences buying plans other than the price level brings a change in aggregate demand. The main factors are

- Expectations
- Fiscal policy and monetary policy
- The world economy

Expectations An increase in expected future income increases the amount of consumption goods (especially big-ticket items such as cars) that people plan to buy today and increases aggregate demand.

An increase in the expected future inflation rate increases aggregate demand today because people decide to buy more goods and services at today's relatively lower prices.

An increase in expected future profits increases the investment that firms plan to undertake today and increases aggregate demand.

Fiscal Policy and Monetary Policy The government's attempt to influence the economy by setting and changing taxes, making transfer payments, and purchasing goods and services is called **fiscal policy**. A tax cut or an increase in transfer payments—for example, unemployment benefits or welfare payments—increases aggregate demand. Both of these influences operate by increasing households' *disposable* income. **Disposable income** is aggregate income minus taxes plus transfer payments. The greater the disposable income, the greater is the quantity of consumption goods and services that households plan to buy and the greater is aggregate demand.

Government expenditure on goods and services is one component of aggregate demand. So if the government spends more on hospitals, schools, and highways, aggregate demand increases.

Monetary policy consists of changes in the interest rate and in the quantity of money in the economy. The quantity of money is determined by the Bank of Canada and the banks (in a process described in Chapters 24 and 30). An increase in the quantity of money in the economy increases aggregate demand. To see why money affects aggregate demand, imagine that the Bank of Canada borrows the army's helicopters, loads them with millions of new $10 bills, and sprinkles them like confetti across the nation. People gather the newly available money and plan to spend some of it. So the quantity of goods and services demanded increases. But people don't plan to spend all the new money. They plan to save some of it and lend it to others through the banks. The interest rate falls, and with a lower interest rate, people plan to buy more consumer durables and firms plan to increase their investment.

The World Economy Two main influences that the world economy has on aggregate demand are the exchange rate and foreign income. The *exchange rate* is the amount of a foreign currency that you can buy with a Canadian dollar. Other things remaining the same, a rise in the exchange rate decreases aggregate

Fiscal Policy to Fight Recession

Relying on Automatic Stabilizers

In the slowing economy of 2008, the U.S. government used fiscal policy to stimulate business investment and consumption expenditure and increase aggregate demand.

In Canada, the government relied on the automatic tendency for tax revenues to fall and spending on unemployment benefits to rise as the economy slowed.

But by the end of 2008, a lively debate was underway between the government and the opposition parties on how much fiscal stimulus is needed.

Jim Flaherty versus John McCallum on fiscal stimulus

Monetary Policy to Fight Recession

Concerted Interest Rate Cuts

In the fall of 2008, the Bank of Canada, in concert with the U.S. Federal Reserve, the European Central Bank, and the Bank of England, cut the interest rate and took other measures to ease credit and encourage banks and others to increase their lending. The U.S. interest rate was the lowest (see below).

Like the earlier fiscal stimulus package, the idea of these interest rate cuts and easier credit was to stimulate business investment and consumption expenditure and increase aggregate demand.

 0.5%

Ben Bernanke
Federal Reserve

 2.5%

Jean-Claude Trichet
ECB

 2.0%

Mervyn King
Bank of England

 1.5%

Mark Carney
Bank of Canada

FIGURE 26.5 Changes in Aggregate Demand

Aggregate demand

Decreases if:

- Expected future income, inflation, or profits decrease

- Fiscal policy decreases government expenditure, increases taxes, or decreases transfer payments

- Monetary policy decreases the quantity of money and increases interest rates

- The exchange rate increases or foreign income decreases

Increases if:

- Expected future income, inflation, or profits increase

- Fiscal policy increases government expenditure, decreases taxes, or increases transfer payments

- Monetary policy increases the quantity of money and decreases interest rates

- The exchange rate decreases or foreign income increases

 animation

demand. To see how the exchange rate influences aggregate demand, suppose that the exchange rate is 80 euro cents per Canadian dollar. A Nokia cell phone from Finland costs 160 euros. An equivalent BlackBerry from Canada costs $220. In Canadian dollars, the Nokia phone costs $200, so people around the world buy the cheaper phone from

Finland. Now suppose the exchange rate falls to 70 euro cents per Canadian dollar. The Nokia phone now costs almost $230 and is more expensive than the BlackBerry. People will switch from the Nokia phone to the BlackBerry. Canadian exports increase and Canadian imports decrease, so Canadian aggregate demand increases.

An increase in foreign income increases Canadian exports and increases Canadian aggregate demand. For example, an increase in income in Japan and Germany increases Japanese and German consumers' and producers' planned expenditures on Canadian-produced goods and services.

Shifts of the Aggregate Demand Curve When aggregate demand changes, the aggregate demand curve shifts. Figure 26.5 shows two changes in aggregate demand and summarizes the factors that bring about such changes.

Aggregate demand increases and the *AD* curve shifts rightward from AD_0 to AD_1 when expected future income, inflation, or profit increases; government expenditure on goods and services increases; taxes are cut; transfer payments increase; the quantity of money increases and the interest rate falls; the exchange rate falls; or foreign income increases.

Aggregate demand decreases and the *AD* curve shifts leftward from AD_0 to AD_2 when expected future income, inflation, or profit decreases; government expenditure on goods and services decreases; taxes increase; transfer payments decrease; the quantity of money decreases and the interest rate rises; the exchange rate rises; or foreign income decreases.

Review Quiz

1 What does the aggregate demand curve show? What factors change and what factors remain the same when there is a movement along the aggregate demand curve?

2 Why does the aggregate demand curve slope downward?

3 How do changes in expectations, fiscal policy and monetary policy, and the world economy change aggregate demand and the aggregate demand curve?

myeconlab Work Study Plan 26.2 and get instant feedback.

Explaining Macroeconomic Fluctuations

The purpose of the *AS–AD* model is to explain changes in real GDP and the price level. The model's main purpose is to explain business cycle fluctuations in these variables. But the model also aids our understanding of economic growth and inflation trends. We begin by combining aggregate supply and aggregate demand to determine real GDP and the price level in equilibrium. Just as there are two time frames for aggregate supply, there are two time frames for macroeconomic equilibrium: a long-run equilibrium and a short-run equilibrium. We'll first look at short-run equilibrium.

Short-Run Macroeconomic Equilibrium

The aggregate demand curve tells us the quantity of real GDP demanded at each price level, and the short-run aggregate supply curve tells us the quantity of real GDP supplied at each price level. **Short-run macroeconomic equilibrium** occurs when the quantity of real GDP demanded equals the quantity of real GDP supplied. That is, short-run macroeconomic equilibrium occurs at the point of intersection of the *AD* curve and the *SAS* curve. Figure 26.6 shows such an equilibrium at a price level of 110 and real GDP of $1,200 billion (points *C* and *C'*).

To see why this position is the equilibrium, think about what happens if the price level is something other than 110. Suppose, for example, that the price level is 125 and that real GDP is $1,300 billion (at point *E* on the *SAS* curve). The quantity of real GDP demanded is less than $1,300 billion, so firms are unable to sell all their output. Unwanted inventories pile up, and firms cut both production and prices. Production and prices are cut until firms can sell all their output. This situation occurs only when real GDP is $1,200 billion and the price level is 110.

Now suppose the price level is 100 and real GDP is $1,100 billion (at point *A* on the *SAS* curve). The quantity of real GDP demanded exceeds $1,100 billion, so firms are unable to meet the demand for their output. Inventories decrease, and customers clamour for goods and services, so firms increase production and raise prices. Production and prices increase until firms can meet the demand for their output. This situation

FIGURE 26.6 Short-Run Equilibrium

Short-run macroeconomic equilibrium occurs when real GDP demanded equals real GDP supplied—at the intersection of the aggregate demand curve (*AD*) and the short-run aggregate supply curve (*SAS*). Here, such an equilibrium occurs at points *C* and *C'*, where the price level is 110 and real GDP is $1,200 billion.

If the price level is 120 and real GDP is $1,300 billion (point *E*), firms will not be able to sell all their output. They will decrease production and cut prices. If the price level is 100 and real GDP is $1,100 billion (point *A*), people will not be able to buy all the goods and services they demand. Firms will increase production and raise their prices.

Only when the price level is 110 and real GDP is $1,200 billion can firms sell all that they produce and can people buy all the goods and services they demand. This is the short-run macroeconomic equilibrium.

myeconlab animation

◆

occurs only when real GDP is $1,200 billion and the price level is 110.

In the short run, the money wage rate is fixed. It does not adjust to move the economy to full employment. So in the short run, real GDP can be greater than or less than potential GDP. But in the long run, the money wage rate does adjust and real GDP moves towards potential GDP. We are going to study this adjustment process. But first, let's look at the economy in long-run equilibrium.

Long-Run Macroeconomic Equilibrium

Long-run macroeconomic equilibrium occurs when real GDP equals potential GDP—equivalently, when the economy is on its *LAS* curve. Figure 26.7 shows the long-run macroeconomic equilibrium, which occurs at the intersection of the *AD* curve and the *LAS* curve (the blue curves). Long-run macroeconomic equilibrium comes about because the money wage rate adjusts. Potential GDP and aggregate demand determine the price level, and the price level influences the money wage rate. In long-run equilibrium, the money wage rate has adjusted to put the *SAS* curve through the long-run equilibrium point.

We'll look at this money wage adjustment process later in this chapter. But first, let's see how the *AS–AD* model helps us to understand economic growth and inflation.

Economic Growth in the *AS–AD* Model

Economic growth occurs because the quantity of labour and labour productivity grow. Population growth is the source of labour growth, and capital accumulation and technological change are the sources of labour productivity growth. Chapter 22 explains the effects of population growth and an increase in the supply of labour. That chapter also explains and illustrates the effects of labour productivity growth on the aggregate production function and on the demand for labour. These changes increase potential GDP.

The *AS–AD* model explains and illustrates potential GDP growth as a rightward shift of the *LAS* curve. For example, in Fig. 26.8, potential GDP grows from $1,200 billion to $1,300 billion and the *LAS* curve shifts rightward from LAS_0 to LAS_1.

FIGURE 26.7 Long-Run Equilibrium

FIGURE 26.8 Economic Growth and Inflation

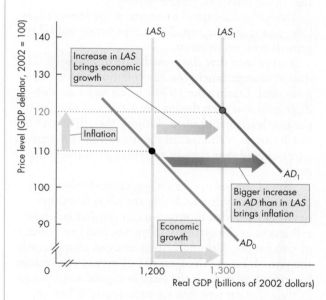

In long-run macroeconomic equilibrium, real GDP equals potential GDP. So long-run equilibrium occurs where the aggregate demand curve, *AD*, intersects the long-run aggregate supply curve, *LAS*. In the long run, aggregate demand determines the price level and has no effect on real GDP. The money wage rate adjusts in the long run, so that the *SAS* curve intersects the *LAS* curve at the long-run equilibrium price level.

Economic growth is the persistent increase in potential GDP. Economic growth is shown as an ongoing rightward shift of the *LAS* curve. The pace at which the *LAS* curve shifts rightward depends on the growth rate of the labour force and the growth rate of labour productivity.

Inflation is a persistently rising price level and it occurs when the quantity of money grows to make the *AD* curve shift rightward at a faster pace than that of the *LAS* curve.

myeconlab animation

Inflation in the *AS–AD* Model

Inflation occurs because the quantity of money grows more rapidly than potential GDP. In Chapter 24, the quantity theory of money, derived from the equation of exchange, explains inflation. With a constant velocity of circulation of money, the inflation rate equals the growth rate of the quantity of money minus the growth rate of real GDP. At full employment (in the macroeconomic long run), real GDP grows at the growth rate of potential GDP. So the inflation rate equals the growth rate of the quantity of money minus the growth rate of potential GDP.

We can explain and illustrate this inflation process using the *AS–AD* model. Inflation occurs when aggregate demand increases at a faster rate than the growth rate of potential GDP. That is, inflation occurs if the *AD* curve shifts rightward at a faster rate than the rate of rightward shift of the *LAS* curve. Figure 26.8 shows shifts of the *AD* and *LAS* curves that bring inflation.

If aggregate demand increases at the same rate as long-run aggregate supply, we experience real GDP growth with no inflation.

You've seen that the growth rate of potential GDP doesn't change much, but the inflation rate varies a great deal. During the 1970s, it reached a double-digit level and then during the 1980s, its rate fell to the low levels maintained through the 1990s and into the 2000s. It is changes in the growth rate of aggregate demand that explain the changes in the inflation rate.

Any of the influences on aggregate demand can change its growth rate. Using the ideas from the quantity theory of money, we can summarize those influences as the quantity of money and the velocity of circulation. Although either one can change, only the growth rate of the quantity of money can change by enough to explain the large and persistent changes in the inflation rate that we experience. When the quantity of money grows rapidly, aggregate demand grows rapidly and the inflation rate is high. When the growth rate of the quantity of money slows, the inflation rate eventually slows.

Our economy experiences periods of growth and inflation, like those shown in Fig. 26.8, but it does not experience *steady* growth and *steady* inflation. Real GDP fluctuates around potential GDP in a business cycle, and inflation fluctuates. When we study the business cycle, we ignore economic growth. By doing so, we see the business cycle more clearly.

The Business Cycle in the *AS–AD* Model

The business cycle occurs because aggregate demand and short-run aggregate supply fluctuate but the money wage rate does not adjust quickly enough to keep real GDP at potential GDP. Figure 26.9 shows three types of short-run equilibrium.

Figure 26.9(a) shows a below full-employment equilibrium. A **below full-employment equilibrium** is an equilibrium in which potential GDP exceeds real GDP. The gap between real GDP and potential GDP is the **output gap**. When potential GDP exceeds real GDP, the output gap is called a **recessionary gap**.

The below full-employment equilibrium in Fig. 26.9(a) occurs where the aggregate demand curve AD_0 intersects the short-run aggregate supply curve SAS_0 at a real GDP of $1,180 billion. Potential GDP is $1,200 billion. The recessionary gap is $20 billion.

The Canadian Business Cycle

The Fluctuating Output Gap

The Canadian economy had a recessionary gap in 2003 (at *A* in the figure), full employment in 2004 (at *B*), and an inflationary gap in 2007 (at *C*). The fluctuating output gap below is the real-world version of Fig. 26.9(d) and is generated by fluctuations in aggregate demand and short-run aggregate supply.

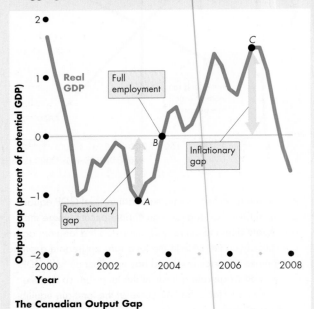

The Canadian Output Gap

Source of data: Bank of Canada output gap, www.bankofcanada.ca/en/rates/indinf/product_data_en.html.

Figure 26.9(b) is an example of **full-employment equilibrium**, in which real GDP equals potential GDP. In this example, the equilibrium occurs where the aggregate demand curve AD_1 intersects the short-run aggregate supply curve SAS_1 at an actual and potential GDP of $1,200 billion.

In part (c), there is an above full-employment equilibrium. An **above full-employment equilibrium** is an equilibrium in which real GDP exceeds potential GDP. When real GDP exceeds potential GDP, the output gap is called an **inflationary gap**.

The above full-employment equilibrium in Fig.

26.9(c) occurs where the aggregate demand curve AD_2 intersects the short-run aggregate supply curve SAS_2 at a real GDP of $1,220 billion. Potential GDP is $1,200 billion. The inflationary gap is $20 billion.

The economy moves from one type of macroeconomic equilibrium to another as a result of fluctuations in aggregate demand and in short-run aggregate supply. These fluctuations produce fluctuations in real GDP. Figure 26.9(d) shows how real GDP fluctuates around potential GDP.

Let's now look at some of the sources of these fluctuations around potential GDP.

FIGURE 26.9 The Business Cycle

(a) Below full-employment equilibrium

(b) Full-employment equilibrium

(c) Above full-employment equilibrium

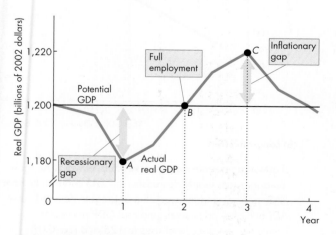

(d) Fluctuations in real GDP

Part (a) shows a below full-employment equilibrium in year 1; part (b) shows a full-employment equilibrium in year 2; and part (c) shows an above full-employment equilibrium in year 3. Part (d) shows how real GDP fluctuates around potential GDP in a business cycle.

In year 1, a recessionary gap exists and the economy is at point A in parts (a) and (d). In year 2, the economy is at full employment and the economy is at point B in parts (b) and (d). In year 3, an inflationary gap exists and the economy is at point C in parts (c) and (d).

Fluctuations in Aggregate Demand

One reason real GDP fluctuates around potential GDP is that aggregate demand fluctuates. Let's see what happens when aggregate demand increases.

Figure 26.10(a) shows an economy at full employment. The aggregate demand curve is AD_0, the short-run aggregate supply curve is SAS_0, and the long-run aggregate supply curve is LAS. Real GDP equals potential GDP at \$1,200 billion, and the price level is 110.

Now suppose that the world economy expands and that the demand for Canadian-produced goods increases in Japan and Europe. The increase in Canadian exports increases aggregate demand in Canada, and the aggregate demand curve shifts rightward from AD_0 to AD_1 in Fig. 26.10(a).

Faced with an increase in demand, firms increase production and raise prices. Real GDP increases to \$1,250 billion, and the price level rises to 115. The economy is now in an above full-employment equilibrium. Real GDP exceeds potential GDP, and there is an inflationary gap.

The increase in aggregate demand has increased the prices of all goods and services. Faced with higher prices, firms have increased their output rates. At this stage, prices of goods and services have increased but the money wage rate has not changed. (Recall that as we move along the SAS curve, the money wage rate is constant.)

The economy cannot produce in excess of potential GDP forever. Why not? What are the forces at work that bring real GDP back to potential GDP?

Because the price level has increased and the money wage rate is unchanged, workers have experienced a fall in the buying power of their wages and firms' profits have increased. Under these circumstances, workers demand higher wages, and firms, anxious to maintain their employment and output levels, meet those demands. If firms do not raise the money wage rate, they will either lose workers or have to hire less productive ones.

As the money wage rate rises, the short-run aggregate supply begins to decrease. In Fig. 26.10(b), the short-run aggregate supply curve begins to shift from

FIGURE 26.10 An Increase in Aggregate Demand

(a) Short-run effect

(b) Long-run effect

An increase in aggregate demand shifts the aggregate demand curve from AD_0 to AD_1. In short-run equilibrium, real GDP increases to \$1,250 billion and the price level rises to 115. In this situation, an inflationary gap exists. In the long run in part (b), the money wage rate rises and the

short-run aggregate supply curve shifts leftward. As short-run aggregate supply decreases, the SAS curve shifts from SAS_0 to SAS_1 and intersects the aggregate demand curve AD_1 at higher price levels and real GDP decreases. Eventually, the price level rises to 125 and real GDP decreases to \$1,200 billion—potential GDP.

SAS_0 towards SAS_1. The rise in the money wage rate and the shift in the SAS curve produce a sequence of new equilibrium positions. Along the adjustment path, real GDP decreases and the price level rises. The economy moves up along its aggregate demand curve as shown by the arrows in the figure.

Eventually, the money wage rate rises by the same percentage as the price level. At this time, the aggregate demand curve AD_1 intersects SAS_1 at a new full-employment equilibrium. The price level has risen to 125, and real GDP is back where it started, at potential GDP.

A decrease in aggregate demand has effects similar but opposite to those of an increase in aggregate demand. That is, a decrease in aggregate demand shifts the aggregate demand curve leftward. Real GDP decreases to less than potential GDP, and a recessionary gap emerges. Firms cut prices. The lower price level increases the purchasing power of wages and increases firms' costs relative to their output prices because the money wage rate is unchanged. Eventually, the money wage rate falls and the short-run aggregate supply increases.

Let's now work out how real GDP and the price level change when aggregate supply changes.

Fluctuations in Aggregate Supply

Fluctuations in short-run aggregate supply can bring fluctuations in real GDP around potential GDP. Suppose that initially real GDP equals potential GDP. Then there is a large but temporary rise in the price of oil. What happens to real GDP and the price level?

Figure 26.11 answers this question. The aggregate demand curve is AD_0, the short-run aggregate supply curve is SAS_0, and the long-run aggregate supply curve is LAS. Real GDP is $1,200 billion, which equals potential GDP, and the price level is 110. Then the price of oil rises. Faced with higher energy and transportation costs, firms decrease production. Short-run aggregate supply decreases, and the short-run aggregate supply curve shifts leftward to SAS_1. The price level rises to 120, and real GDP decreases to $1,150 billion. We call the combination of falling real GDP and a rising inflation rate **stagflation**. Canada has not experienced stagflation, but the United States and several other countries experienced it during the 1970s and early 1980s.

When the aggregate supply shock ends (in our example, when the price of oil returns to its original level), the economy returns to full employment.

FIGURE 26.11   A Decrease in Aggregate Supply

An increase in the price of oil decreases short-run aggregate supply and shifts the short-run aggregate supply curve from SAS_0 to SAS_1. Real GDP falls from $1,200 billion to $1,150 billion, and the price level rises from 110 to 120. The economy experiences stagflation.

 animation

Review Quiz

1   Does economic growth result from increases in aggregate demand, short-run aggregate supply, or long-run aggregate supply?

2   Does inflation result from increases in aggregate demand, short-run aggregate supply, or long-run aggregate supply?

3   Describe three types of short-run macroeconomic equilibrium.

4   How do fluctuations in aggregate demand and short-run aggregate supply bring fluctuations in real GDP around potential GDP?

myeconlab   Work Study Plan 26.3 and get instant feedback.

We can use the *AS–AD* model to explain and illustrate the views of the alternative schools of thought in macroeconomics. That is your next task.

Macroeconomic Schools of Thought

Macroeconomics is an active field of research, and much remains to be learned about the forces that make our economy grow and fluctuate. There is a greater degree of consensus and certainty about economic growth and inflation—the longer-term trends in real GDP and the price level—than there is about the business cycle—the short-term fluctuations in these variables. Here, we'll look only at differences of view about short-term fluctuations.

The *AS–AD* model that you've studied in this chapter provides a good foundation for understanding the range of views that macroeconomists hold about this topic. But what you will learn here is just a first glimpse at the scientific controversy and debate. We'll return to these issues at various points later in the text and deepen your appreciation of the alternative views.

Classification usually requires simplification, and classifying macroeconomists is no exception to this general rule. The classification that we'll use here is simple, but it is not misleading. We're going to divide macroeconomists into three broad schools of thought and examine the views of each group in turn. The groups are

- Classical
- Keynesian
- Monetarist

The Classical View

A **classical** macroeconomist believes that the economy is self-regulating and always at full employment. The term "classical" derives from the name of the founding school of economics that includes Adam Smith, David Ricardo, and John Stuart Mill.

A **new classical** view is that business cycle fluctuations are the efficient responses of a well-functioning market economy that is bombarded by shocks that arise from the uneven pace of technological change.

The classical view can be understood in terms of beliefs about aggregate demand and aggregate supply.

Aggregate Demand Fluctuations In the classical view, technological change is the most significant influence on both aggregate demand and aggregate supply. For this reason, classical macroeconomists don't use the

AS–AD framework. But their views can be interpreted in this framework. A technological change that increases the productivity of capital brings an increase in aggregate demand because firms increase their expenditure on new plant and equipment. A technological change that lengthens the useful life of existing capital decreases the demand for new capital, which decreases aggregate demand.

Aggregate Supply Response In the classical view, the money wage rate that lies behind the short-run aggregate supply curve is instantly and completely flexible. The money wage rate adjusts so quickly to maintain equilibrium in the labour market that real GDP always adjusts to equal potential GDP.

Potential GDP itself fluctuates for the same reasons that aggregate demand fluctuates: technological change. When the pace of technological change is rapid, potential GDP increases quickly and so does real GDP. And when the pace of technological change slows, so does the growth rate of potential GDP.

Classical Policy The classical view of policy emphasizes the potential for taxes to stunt incentives and create inefficiency. By minimizing the disincentive effects of taxes, employment, investment, and technological advance are at their efficient levels and the economy expands at an appropriate and rapid pace.

The Keynesian View

A **Keynesian** macroeconomist believes that left alone, the economy would rarely operate at full employment and that to achieve and maintain full employment, active help from fiscal policy and monetary policy is required.

The term "Keynesian" derives from the name of one of the twentieth century's most famous economists, John Maynard Keynes (see p. 703).

The Keynesian view is based on beliefs about the forces that determine aggregate demand and short-run aggregate supply.

Aggregate Demand Fluctuations In the Keynesian view, *expectations* are the most significant influence on aggregate demand. Those expectations are based on herd instinct, or what Keynes himself called "animal spirits." A wave of pessimism about future profit prospects can lead to a fall in aggregate demand and plunge the economy into recession.

Aggregate Supply Response In the Keynesian view, the money wage rate that lies behind the short-run aggregate supply curve is extremely sticky in the downward direction. Basically, the money wage rate doesn't fall. So if there is a recessionary gap, there is no automatic mechanism for getting rid of it. If it were to happen, a fall in the money wage rate would increase short-run aggregate supply and restore full employment. But the money wage rate doesn't fall, so the economy remains stuck in recession.

A modern version of the Keynesian view, known as the **new Keynesian** view, holds not only that the money wage rate is sticky but also that prices of goods and services are sticky. With a sticky price level, the short-run aggregate supply curve is horizontal at a fixed price level.

Policy Response Needed The Keynesian view calls for fiscal policy and monetary policy to actively offset changes in aggregate demand that bring recession.

By stimulating aggregate demand in a recession, full employment can be restored.

The Monetarist View

A **monetarist** is a macroeconomist who believes that the economy is self-regulating and that it will normally operate at full employment, provided that monetary policy is not erratic and that the pace of money growth is kept steady.

The term "monetarist" was coined by an outstanding twentieth-century economist, Karl Brunner, to describe his own views and those of Milton Friedman (see p. 757).

The monetarist view can be interpreted in terms of beliefs about the forces that determine aggregate demand and short-run aggregate supply.

Aggregate Demand Fluctuations In the monetarist view, *the quantity of money* is the most significant influence on aggregate demand. The quantity of money is determined by the Bank of Canada. If the Bank of Canada keeps money growing at a steady pace, aggregate demand fluctuations will be minimized and the economy will operate close to full employment. But if the Bank of Canada decreases the quantity of money or even just slows its growth rate too abruptly, the economy will go into recession. In the monetarist view, all recessions result from inappropriate monetary policy.

Aggregate Supply Response The monetarist view of short-run aggregate supply is the same as the Keynesian view: The money wage rate is sticky. If the economy is in recession, it will take an unnecessarily long time for it to return unaided to full employment.

Monetarist Policy The monetarist view of policy is the same as the classical view on fiscal policy. Taxes should be kept low to avoid disincentive effects that decrease potential GDP. Provided that the quantity of money is kept on a steady growth path, no active stabilization is needed to offset changes in aggregate demand.

The Way Ahead

In the chapters that follow, you're going to encounter Keynesian, classical, and monetarist views again. In the next chapter, we study the original Keynesian model of aggregate demand. This model remains useful today because it explains how expenditure fluctuations are magnified and bring changes in aggregate demand that are larger than the changes in expenditure. We then go on to apply the AS–AD model to a deeper look at Canadian inflation and business cycles. Our attention then turns to short-run macroeconomic policy—the fiscal policy of the government and the monetary policy of the Bank of Canada.

Review Quiz

1 What are the defining features of classical macroeconomics and what policies do classical macroeconomists recommend?
2 What are the defining features of Keynesian macroeconomics and what policies do Keynesian macroeconomists recommend?
3 What are the defining features of monetarist macroeconomics and what policies do monetarist macroeconomists recommend?

myeconlab   Work Study Plan 26.4 and get instant feedback.

To complete your study of the AS–AD model, take a look at the Canadian economy in 2008 through the eyes of this model in *Reading Between the Lines* on pp. 642–643.

Aggregate Supply and Aggregate Demand in Action

Canadians Shopped 'til Economy Dropped

November 25, 2008

Canadians shopped right up until the economy dropped, reports Tuesday suggest.

Consumers went on an unexpected shopping spree in September, just prior to the economy sliding into what a major international think-tank is projecting was the start of a prolonged recession that will linger right through to the middle of next year.

The Canadian economy is projected to contract 1.6 percent in the current quarter, reducing growth for the year to 0.5 percent, the Paris-based Organization for Economic Co-operation and Development said in a downwardly revised forecast for the Canadian and the global economy. Economic output will fall a further 1.4 percent in the first quarter of 2009 and by 0.3 percent in the second quarter and despite a slow recovery in the second half of the year output for the year as a whole will fall 0.5 percent. ...

Statistics Canada reported that retail sales jumped 1.1 percent in September, the largest gain since January, thanks to what was also the first increase in new car sales since January. ...

"Part of the explanation of the resilience in retailing activity is the fact that the Canadian job market has not cratered like in the U.S. and other domestic fundamentals, such as the housing market, have exhibited an orderly correction," said TD Securities analyst Charmain Buskas.

However, she and other analysts cautioned that it's in the fourth quarter where they expect sales and the overall economy to stumble, a view reinforced by the forecast by the OECD. ...

Essence of the Story

- Statistics Canada reported that retail sales increased by 1.1 percent in September 2008.

- A TD Securities analyst said that retail sales were strong because Canadian employment had not fallen and house price falls were moderate.

- The Organization for Economic Co-operation and Development (OECD) forecasted that the Canadian economy would contract at a 1.6 percent (annual) rate during the fourth quarter of 2008.

- The OECD forecasted that the economy would continue to contract through 2009.

- Analysts predicted that retail sales would fall in the fourth quarter of 2008 in line with the OECD forecast.

Economic Analysis

- Forecasters predicted that the Canadian economy would sink into recession at the end of 2008 and through 2009.

- The OECD predicted falling real GDP during the fourth quarter of 2008 and through 2009.

- The Bank of Canada estimate of potential GDP implied that an inflationary gap in 2007 and early 2008 became a widening recessionary gap in the second half of 2008.

- Figure 1 illustrates the path of real GDP and the estimate of potential GDP implied by the Bank of Canada's output gap estimates from the last quarter of 2006 through the last quarter of 2008.

- Real GDP grew faster than potential GDP from the last quarter of 2006 until the third quarter of 2007, so the inflationary gap widened.

- Real GDP stopped growing after the last quarter of 2007 and a recessionary gap opened up in the second quarter of 2008.

- In the third quarter of 2007, real GDP was $1,326 billion and the price level (GDP deflator) was 117. Potential GDP was $1,306 billion, so the inflationary gap was $20 billion (1.5 percent of potential GDP).

- Figure 2 illustrates the economy in the third quarter of 2007.

- Aggregate demand, AD_{07}, and short-run aggregate supply, SAS_{07}, intersect at a real GDP of $1,326 billion and a price level of 117.

- The Bank of Canada's implicit estimate of potential GDP of $1,306 billion provides the location of the LAS_{07} curve.

- Figure 3 illustrates the economy in the third quarter of 2008.

- Aggregate demand, AD_{08}, and short-run aggregate supply, SAS_{08}, intersect at a real GDP of $1,325 billion and a price level of 120.

- The Bank of Canada's implicit estimate of potential GDP of $1,346 billion provides the location of the LAS_{08} curve.

- Comparing Fig. 2 and Fig. 3, you can see that real GDP barely changed but potential GDP increased.

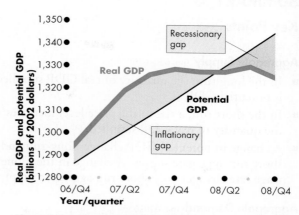

Figure 1 Actual and potential real GDP

Figure 2 Aggregate supply and aggregate demand in 2007

Figure 3 Aggregate supply and aggregate demand in 2008

SUMMARY ◆

Key Points

Aggregate Supply (pp. 626–629)

- In the long run, the quantity of real GDP supplied is potential GDP.
- In the short run, a rise in the price level increases the quantity of real GDP supplied.
- A change in potential GDP changes long-run and short-run aggregate supply. A change in the money wage rate changes only short-run aggregate supply.

Aggregate Demand (pp. 630–633)

- A rise in the price level decreases the quantity of real GDP demanded.
- Changes in expected future income, inflation, and profits; in fiscal policy and monetary policy; and in world real GDP and the exchange rate change aggregate demand.

Explaining Macroeconomic Fluctuations (pp. 634–639)

- Aggregate demand and short-run aggregate supply determine real GDP and the price level.
- In the long run, real GDP equals potential GDP and aggregate demand determines the price level.
- The business cycle occurs because aggregate demand and aggregate supply fluctuate.

Macroeconomic Schools of Thought (pp. 640–641)

- Classical economists believe that the economy is self-regulating and always at full employment.
- Keynesian economists believe that full employment can be achieved only with active policy.
- Monetarist economists believe that recessions result from inappropriate monetary policy.

Key Figures

Figure 26.1   Long-Run and Short-Run Aggregate Supply, 627
Figure 26.4   Aggregate Demand, 630
Figure 26.5   Changes in Aggregate Demand, 633
Figure 26.6   Short-Run Equilibrium, 634
Figure 26.7   Long-Run Equilibrium, 635
Figure 26.8   Economic Growth and Inflation, 635
Figure 26.9   The Business Cycle, 637
Figure 26.10   An Increase in Aggregate Demand, 638

Key Terms

Above full-employment equilibrium, 637
Aggregate demand, 630
Below full-employment equilibrium, 636
Classical, 640
Disposable income, 632
Fiscal policy, 632
Full-employment equilibrium, 637
Inflationary gap, 637
Keynesian, 640
Long-run aggregate supply, 626
Long-run macroeconomic equilibrium, 635
Monetarist, 641
Monetary policy, 632
New classical, 640
New Keynesian, 641
Output gap, 636
Recessionary gap, 636
Short-run aggregate supply, 627
Short-run macroeconomic equilibrium, 634
Stagflation, 639

PROBLEMS and APPLICATIONS

myeconlab   Work problems 1–7 in Chapter 26 Study Plan and get instant feedback.
Work problems 8–15 as Homework, a Quiz, or a Test if assigned by your instructor.

1. The following events occur at times in the history of Canada:

   - A deep recession hits the world economy.
   - The world oil price rises sharply.
   - Canadian firms expect future profits to fall.

   a. Explain for each event whether it changes short-run aggregate supply, long-run aggregate supply, aggregate demand, or some combination of them.
   b. Explain the separate effects of each event on real GDP and the price level, starting from a position of long-run equilibrium.
   c. Explain the combined effects of these events on real GDP and the price level, starting from a position of long-run equilibrium.
   d. Describe what a classical macroeconomist, a Keynesian, and a monetarist would want to do in response to each of the above events.

2. The table shows aggregate demand and short-run aggregate supply in Virtual Kingdom. Potential GDP is 1,100 billion (2007 pounds).

Price level	Real GDP demanded	Real GDP supplied in the short run
	(billions of 2007 pounds)	
100	1,250	1,050
110	1,200	1,100
120	1,150	1,150
130	1,100	1,200
140	1,050	1,250
150	1,000	1,300
160	950	1,350

   a. What is the short-run equilibrium real GDP and price level?
   b. What is the output gap and is it an inflationary gap or a recessionary gap?
   c. What is the long-run equilibrium price level?

3. U.S. real GDP during the second quarter of 2008 was $11,727 billion compared to $11,491 billion in the same quarter of 2007. The GDP deflator was 121.9, up from 119.5 in the second quarter of 2007. The Congressional Budget Office estimated potential GDP to be $11,888 billion in the second quarter of 2008 and $11,568 billion a year earlier.

   a. Draw a graph of the U.S. aggregate demand curve, the short-run aggregate supply curve, and the long-run aggregate supply curve in 2007 that is consistent with these numbers.
   b. On the graph, show how the aggregate demand curve, the short-run aggregate supply curve, and the long-run aggregate supply curve shifted during the year to the second quarter of 2008.

4. Initially, short-run aggregate supply is SAS_0 and aggregate demand is AD_0. Some events change aggregate demand, and later, some other events change aggregate supply.

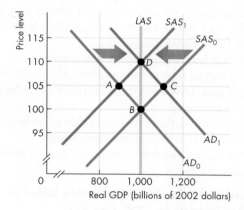

   a. What is the equilibrium after the change in aggregate demand?
   b. What is the equilibrium after the change in aggregate supply?
   c. Describe two events that could have changed aggregate demand from AD_0 to AD_1.
   d. Describe two events that could have changed aggregate supply from SAS_0 to SAS_1.

5. **Business Confidence Sinking**
   Business confidence in the economy has plunged to a near record low, suggesting that a fall in investment in new plants and equipment will follow, the Conference Board of Canada reported yesterday. ... The latest survey, conducted in the first three weeks of October, found that business leaders were much more concerned about the economy and their future financial situations than they had been in the summer survey. Expectations about future profitability also fell. "The ongoing financial and equity market

mayhem is having a significant impact on business leaders' views about near-term economic prospects," it said, noting the survey found that nearly 70 percent believed that the economy would be in worse shape in six months. Only 12 percent, and probably those that benefit from a weaker loonie, believed conditions would improve, it said, adding that ratio is the "worst" since the final quarter of 1990.

Gazette (Montreal), November 11, 2008

a. Explain and draw a graph to illustrate how declining business confidence can change the short-run equilibrium real GDP and price level.
b. If the economy was operating at full-employment equilibrium, describe the state of equilibrium after the fall in business confidence. In what way might business expectations have a self-fulfilling prophecy?
c. Explain how the economy can adjust in the long run to restore full-employment equilibrium and draw a graph to illustrate this adjustment process.
d. Explain the author's statement that those businesses who "believed conditions would improve" are "probably those that benefit from a weaker loonie."

6. **Canadian Dollar Provides Needed Relief to Quebec Exports in 2009, says EDC**

Quebec's international exports are expected to rise a modest 1 percent in 2009 after declining 4 percent in 2008, according to a provincial export outlook by Export Development Canada (EDC). "The slight rise in Quebec's exports in 2009 is possible thanks to an expected 10 percent depreciation of the Canadian dollar. Remove the exchange rate impact, and the province's export outlook is considerably weaker," said Peter Hall, Vice-President and Chief Economist. The industrial goods sector accounts for approximately 37 percent of Quebec's international exports. The outlook for this sector is defined by volatile ... commodity price movements. ... Lumber export volumes are unlikely to gain much of the ground lost since 2005, as existing home inven-

tories in the U.S. remain near all-time highs. ... In the aerospace sector, weak demand out of the United States, the destination for nearly half of total Canadian aerospace exports, will adversely impact the bottom line going forward. ...

Canadian Business, November 6, 2008

a. Explain the competing forces on exports for 2009 that are identified in this article.
b. Based upon the predictions made in this article for 2009, draw a graph to illustrate how these forces can change the short-run equilibrium real GDP and price level for Quebec.

7. **Harper to Canadian Consumers: "Keep Spending"**

Conservative Leader Stephen Harper reassured Canadian consumers amid economic turmoil in the United States that there will be no federal bailout of Canada's big banks. ...

He said the Canadian financial system is strong and its banks and insurance companies don't need any financial aid. ... While money is tighter these days, Harper said, consumers shouldn't panic and stop spending since they're the reason for the Canadian economy's strength. The Conservative Leader said this robust consumer spending is what has helped protect Canada from the same type of trouble currently affixing itself to the United States, and says his party's policies should be credited for encouraging this spending. "Some of the things we've done, in particular the tax changes we did ... the lowering of the GST, the lowering of the lowest personal income tax rate, the raising of the basic personal exemption," Harper said. "These have been important in sustaining strong consumer spending in this country. ... Canadian consumer spending has been a rock that has sustained the economy and we anticipate that that will continue," Harper said.

CTV News, September 19, 2008

a. Explain and draw a graph to illustrate the effects of the policy actions described by Stephen Harper.
b. Based upon his statements in this article, what macroeconomic school of thought does Stephen Harper most likely agree with?

8. The following events occur at times in the history of Canada:

  - The world economy goes into an expansion.
  - Canadian businesses expect future profits to rise.
  - The government increases its expenditure on goods and services in a time of war or increased international tension.

  a. Explain for each event whether it changes short-run aggregate supply, long-run aggregate supply, aggregate demand, or some combination of them.
  b. Explain the separate effects of each event on real GDP and the price level, starting from a position of long-run equilibrium.
  c. Explain the combined effects of these events on real GDP and the price level, starting from a position of long-run equilibrium.

9. In Japan, potential GDP is 600 trillion yen and the table shows the aggregate demand and short-run aggregate supply schedules.

Price level	Real GDP demanded	Real GDP supplied in the short run
	(trillions of 2000 yen)	
75	600	400
85	550	450
95	500	500
105	450	550
115	400	600
125	350	650
135	300	700

  a. Draw a graph of the aggregate demand curve and the short-run aggregate supply curve.
  b. What is the short-run equilibrium real GDP and price level?
  c. Does Japan have an inflationary gap or a recessionary gap and what is its magnitude?

10. **Fearful Consumers Reining in Spending**

Canadian consumer confidence took a nosedive ... amid continuing economic uncertainty, sparking fears that shoppers are already reining in their spending. Consumer confidence plunged to levels last seen in the 1982 recession. ... The findings suggest consumers are becoming especially leery about making big-ticket purchases such as appliances, cars and homes ahead of the all-important Christmas shopping season. ... "All we are hearing is doom and gloom and people seek-

ing advice on how they may be able to protect themselves and save money," said Bruce Cran, spokesperson for the Consumers' Association of Canada. ... Perhaps most striking is the parallels some Canadians are starting to draw between America's housing market meltdown and rapidly deflating home prices in this country. ... "The global credit crunch and major stock market declines clearly had an effect on consumer confidence in October," said Pedro Antunes, the [Conference] Board's director of national and provincial forecast. ... Respondents are increasingly worried about ... job prospects, the report found. ... The Conference Board says Canada will feel the knock-on effects of the global financial crisis but avoid a recession.

Toronto Star, October 18, 2008

  a. Explain the various factors that are weighing down consumer confidence.
  b. Explain and draw a graph to illustrate how declining consumer confidence can change real GDP and the price level in the short run.
  c. If the economy was operating at full-employment equilibrium, describe the state of equilibrium after the fall in consumer confidence. In what way might consumer expectations have a self-fulfilling prophecy? How does this complicate economic forecasting (such as the prediction offered by the Conference Board)?
  d. Why do changes in consumer spending play such a large role in the business cycle?
  e. Explain how the economy can adjust in the long run to restore full-employment equilibrium and draw a graph to illustrate this adjustment process.

11 **It's Pinching Everyone**

The rate of inflation [in India] has now touched a mind-boggling 11 percent. ... No one can predict when the process of spiraling prices will come to an end. ... [T]he current inflationary process is a global phenomenon and practically every country is suffering. ...

Emerging and developing countries have been growing significantly faster than the rest of the world, and there has been a steep surge in demand in these countries. ... Since there is no reason to believe that world production will rise miraculously at least in the immediate future, many people expect that prices will keep on rising. These expectations in turn exacerbate the inflationary process. Households buy more of non-perishable goods than they need for their immediate consumption because they expect prices to go up even further. What is worse is that traders withhold stocks from the market in the hope of being able to sell these at higher prices later on. In other words, expectations of higher prices become self-fulfilling.

Times of India, June 24, 2008

Explain and use a graph to show how inflation and inflation expectations "become self-fulfilling."

12. **Shoppers Stimulate Discount Stores**

Consumers sought the biggest bang for their economic stimulus bucks in June, sending the sales of discount merchants such as Wal-Mart and Costco surging. ... As the economy remains weak ... shoppers—rich and poor—are flocking to discounters for low-cost goods. ... Wal-Mart Stores Inc. trounced analyst expectations Thursday with a 5.8 percent jump in June sales ... attributing the increase to the government's economic stimulus payments. ... The retailer said sales jumped across the board. But the most dramatic increases were in entertainment, particularly for flat-screen televisions, and apparel, especially in swimwear and sportswear. ... Another major retailer, the warehouse club Costco Wholesale, beat analyst expectations with a 9 percent increase in same-store sales for June. ... Target, a top competitor to Wal-Mart, said that its same-store sales edged up 0.4 percent, well above the 0.5 percent decline projected by analyst consensus. ...

CNN, July 10, 2008

a. Explain and draw a graph to illustrate the effect of the fiscal stimulus payments on real GDP and the price level in the short run.
b. At which type of short-run equilibrium would the government want to use this policy?
c. Which macroeconomic school of thought would justify this policy?
d. If the government used this policy when the economy was at full employment, explain what would happen in the long run.
e. Draw a graph to illustrate your answer to d.

13. **Conditions Right for Stagflation**

Soaring energy prices are casting a long shadow over the economy, increasing the risk that Canadians face a period of low growth and high inflation, economists say. ... Monday saw a smattering of reports suggesting conditions are

right for stagflation. ... [T]he toxic brew of high oil prices and a deepening slump in the United States is increasing the risks to both growth and inflation this year, economists said. ... "Consumers are becoming increasingly wary about making major purchases," said the Conference Board.

Winnipeg Free Press, July 8, 2008

a. What is stagflation?
b. Explain how the rise in oil prices, the slump in the United States, and a decrease in purchases by consumers can cause stagflation. Draw a graph to illustrate this outcome.

14. The International Monetary Fund's World Economic Outlook database provides the following data for India.

	2004	2005	2006
	(percent per year)		
Real GDP growth rate	8.1	8.3	7.3
Inflation rate	4.2	4.7	4.6

a. What changes in aggregate demand and in long-run and short-run aggregate supply are consistent with these numbers?
b. Draw a graph to illustrate your answer to a.
c. List the main factors that might have produced the changes that you have described in your answer to a.
d. From the above data, do you think India has an inflationary gap, a recessionary gap, or is at full employment?

15. Study *Reading Between the Lines* on pp. 642–643 and then answer the following questions:

a. Did Canada have a recessionary gap or an inflationary gap in 2008? How do you know?
b. Use the *AS–AD* model to show the *changes* in aggregate demand and aggregate supply that brought the standstill in real GDP and rise in the price level between the third quarter of 2007 and the third quarter of 2008.
c. Use the *AS–AD* model to show the changes that would occur if monetary policy cut the interest rate and increased the quantity of money.
d. Use the *AS–AD* model to show the changes that would occur if the government increased its expenditure on goods and services or cut taxes.

27 Expenditure Multipliers: The Keynesian Model

After studying this chapter, you will be able to

- Explain how expenditure plans are determined when the price level is fixed

- Explain how real GDP is determined when the price level is fixed

- Explain the expenditure multiplier when the price level is fixed

- Explain the relationship between aggregate expenditure and aggregate demand and explain the multiplier when the price level changes

Céline Dion sings into a microphone in a barely audible whisper. Increasing in volume, through the magic of electronic amplification, her voice fills Toronto's Molson Amphitheatre.

Ed Stelmach, the premier of Alberta, and an assistant are being driven to a business meeting along one of Edmonton's less well-repaired streets. The car's wheels bounce and vibrate over the uneven road, but its passengers are undisturbed and the assistant's notes are written without a ripple, thanks to the car's efficient shock absorbers.

Investment and exports fluctuate like the volume of Céline Dion's voice and the uneven surface of an Edmonton street. How does the economy react to those fluctuations? Does it behave like an amplifier, blowing up the fluctuations and

spreading them out to affect the many millions of participants in an economic rock concert? Or does it react like a limousine, absorbing the shocks and providing a smooth ride for the economy's passengers?

You will explore these questions in this chapter. You will learn how a recession or an expansion begins when a change in investment or exports induces an amplified change in aggregate expenditure and real GDP. *Reading Between the Lines* at the end of the chapter looks at the role played by consumption expenditure during 2008 as the economy began to shrink.

Fixed Prices and Expenditure Plans

In the Keynesian model that we study in this chapter, all the firms are like your grocery store: They set their prices and sell the quantities their customers are willing to buy. If they persistently sell a greater quantity than they plan to and are constantly running out of inventory, they eventually raise their prices. And if they persistently sell a smaller quantity than they plan to and have inventories piling up, they eventually cut their prices. But on any given day, their prices are fixed and the quantities they sell depend on demand, not supply.

Because each firm's prices are fixed, for the economy as a whole

1. The *price level* is fixed, and
2. *Aggregate demand* determines real GDP.

The Keynesian model explains fluctuations in aggregate demand at a fixed price level by identifying the forces that determine expenditure plans.

Expenditure Plans

Aggregate expenditure has four components: consumption expenditure, investment, government expenditure on goods and services, and net exports (exports *minus* imports). These four components of aggregate expenditure sum to real GDP (see Chapter 20, pp. 469–470).

Aggregate planned expenditure is equal to the sum of the *planned* levels of consumption expenditure, investment, government expenditure on goods and services, and exports minus imports. Two of these components of planned expenditure, consumption expenditure and imports, change when income changes and so they depend on real GDP.

A Two-Way Link Between Aggregate Expenditure and Real GDP There is a two-way link between aggregate expenditure and real GDP. Other things remaining the same,

- An increase in real GDP increases aggregate expenditure, and
- An increase in aggregate expenditure increases real GDP.

You are now going to study this two-way link.

Consumption and Saving Plans

Several factors influence consumption expenditure and saving plans. The more important ones are

- Disposable income
- Real interest rate
- Wealth
- Expected future income

Disposable income is aggregate income minus taxes plus transfer payments. Aggregate income equals real GDP, so disposable income depends on real GDP. To explore the two-way link between real GDP and planned consumption expenditure, we focus on the relationship between consumption expenditure and disposable income when the other three factors listed above are constant.

Consumption Expenditure and Saving The table in Fig. 27.1 lists the consumption expenditure and the saving that people plan at each level of disposable income. Households can only spend their disposable income on consumption or save it, so planned consumption expenditure plus planned saving *always* equals disposable income.

The relationship between consumption expenditure and disposable income, other things remaining the same, is called the **consumption function**. The relationship between saving and disposable income, other things remaining the same, is called the **saving function**.

Consumption Function Figure 27.1(a) shows a consumption function. The *y*-axis measures consumption expenditure, and the *x*-axis measures disposable income. Along the consumption function, the points labelled *A* through *F* correspond to the rows of the table. For example, point *E* shows that when disposable income is $800 billion, consumption expenditure is $750 billion. As disposable income increases, consumption expenditure also increases.

At point *A* on the consumption function, consumption expenditure is $150 billion even though disposable income is zero. This consumption expenditure is called *autonomous consumption*, and it is the amount of consumption expenditure that would take place in the short run even if people had no current income. Consumption expenditure in excess of this amount is called *induced consumption*, which is the consumption expenditure that is induced by an increase in disposable income.

45° Line Figure 27.1(a) also contains a 45° line, the height of which measures disposable income. At each point on this line, consumption expenditure equals disposable income. Between A and D, consumption expenditure exceeds disposable income, between D and F, consumption expenditure is less than disposable income, and at point D, consumption expenditure equals disposable income.

Saving Function Figure 27.1(b) shows a saving function. Again, the points A through F correspond to the rows of the table. For example, point E shows that when disposable income is $800 billion, saving is $50 billion. As disposable income increases, saving increases. Notice that when consumption expenditure exceeds disposable income in part (a), saving is negative, called *dissaving*, in part (b).

FIGURE 27.1 Consumption Function and Saving Function

(a) Consumption function

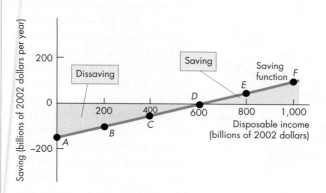

(b) Saving function

	Disposable income	Planned consumption expenditure	Planned saving
		(billions of 2002 dollars)	
A	0	150	−150
B	200	300	−100
C	400	450	−50
D	600	600	0
E	800	750	50
F	1,000	900	100

The table shows consumption expenditure and saving plans at various levels of disposable income. Part (a) of the figure shows the relationship between consumption expenditure and disposable income (the consumption function). The height of the consumption function measures consumption expenditure at each level of disposable income. Part (b) shows the relationship between saving and disposable income (the saving function). The height of the saving function measures saving at each level of disposable income. Points A through F on the consumption and saving functions correspond to the rows in the table.

The height of the 45° line in part (a) measures disposable income. So along the 45° line, consumption expenditure equals disposable income. Consumption expenditure plus saving equals disposable income. When the consumption function is above the 45° line, saving is negative (dissaving occurs). When the consumption function is below the 45° line, saving is positive. At the point where the consumption function intersects the 45° line, all disposable income is spent on consumption and saving is zero.

Marginal Propensities to Consume and Save

The **marginal propensity to consume** (*MPC*) is the fraction of a *change* in disposable income that is spent on consumption. It is calculated as the *change* in consumption expenditure (ΔC) divided by the *change* in disposable income (ΔYD). The formula is

$$MPC = \frac{\Delta C}{\Delta YD}.$$

In the table in Fig. 27.1, when disposable income increases by \$200 billion, consumption expenditure increases by \$150 billion. The *MPC* is \$150 billion divided by \$200 billion, which equals 0.75.

The **marginal propensity to save** (*MPS*) is the fraction of a *change* in disposable income that is saved. It is calculated as the *change* in saving (ΔS) divided by the *change* in disposable income (ΔYD). The formula is

$$MPS = \frac{\Delta S}{\Delta YD}.$$

In the table in Fig. 27.1, when disposable income increases by \$200 billion, saving increases by \$50 billion. The *MPS* is \$50 billion divided by \$200 billion, which equals 0.25.

Because an increase in disposable income is either spent on consumption or saved, the marginal propensity to consume plus the marginal propensity to save equals 1. You can see why by using the equation:

$$\Delta C + \Delta S = \Delta YD.$$

Divide both sides of the equation by the change in disposable income to obtain

$$\frac{\Delta C}{\Delta YD} + \frac{\Delta S}{\Delta YD} = 1.$$

$\Delta C/\Delta YD$ is the marginal propensity to consume (*MPC*), and $\Delta S/\Delta YD$ is the marginal propensity to save (*MPS*), so

$$MPC + MPS = 1.$$

Slopes and Marginal Propensities

The slope of the consumption function is the marginal propensity to consume, and the slope of the saving function is the marginal propensity to save.

Figure 27.2(a) shows the *MPC* as the slope of the consumption function. An increase in disposable income of \$200 billion is the base of the red triangle. The increase in consumption expenditure that results from this increase in disposable income is \$150 billion and is the height of the triangle. The slope of the consumption function is given by the formula "slope equals rise over run" and is \$150 billion divided by \$200 billion, which equals 0.75—the *MPC*.

Figure 27.2(b) shows the *MPS* as the slope of the saving function. An increase in disposable income of \$200 billion (the base of the red triangle) increases saving by \$50 billion (the height of the triangle). The slope of the saving function is \$50 billion divided by \$200 billion, which equals 0.25—the *MPS*.

FIGURE 27.2   The Marginal Propensities to Consume and Save

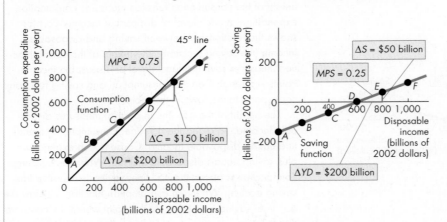

(a) Consumption function

(b) Saving function

The marginal propensity to consume, *MPC*, is equal to the change in consumption expenditure divided by the change in disposable income, other things remaining the same. It is measured by the slope of the consumption function. In part (a), the *MPC* is 0.75.

The marginal propensity to save, *MPS*, is equal to the change in saving divided by the change in disposable income, other things remaining the same. It is measured by the slope of the saving function. In part (b), the *MPS* is 0.25.

myeconlab animation

The Canadian Consumption Function

Other Things Not Always Equal

The figure shows the Canadian consumption function. Each point identified by a blue dot represents consumption expenditure and disposable income for a particular year. (The dots are for the years 1961 to 2007, and the dots of six of the years are identified in the figure.)

The Canadian consumption function is CF_0 in 1961 and CF_1 in 2007.

The slope of the consumption function in the figure is 0.85, which means that a $1 increase in disposable income brings an increase in consumption expenditure of 85 cents. This slope, which is an estimate of the marginal propensity to consume, is an assumption that is at the upper end of the range of values that economists have estimated for the marginal propensity to consume.

The consumption function shifts upward over time as other influences on consumption expenditure change. Of these other influences, the real interest rate and wealth fluctuate and bring upward and downward shifts in the consumption function.

But rising wealth and rising expected future income bring a steady upward shift in the consumption function. As the consumption function shifts upward, autonomous consumption increases.

The Canadian Consumption Function

Source of data: Statistics Canada, CANSIM Tables 380-0002 and 380-0004.

Consumption as a Function of Real GDP

Consumption expenditure changes when disposable income changes and disposable income changes when real GDP changes. So consumption expenditure depends not only on disposable income but also on real GDP. We use this link between consumption expenditure and real GDP to determine equilibrium expenditure. But before we do so, we need to look at one further component of aggregate expenditure: imports. Like consumption expenditure, imports are influenced by real GDP.

Import Function

Of the many influences on Canadian imports in the short run, Canadian real GDP is the main influence. Other things remaining the same, an increase in Canadian real GDP increases the quantity of Canadian imports.

The effect of real GDP on imports is determined by the **marginal propensity to import**, which is the fraction of an increase in real GDP that is spent on imports. It is calculated as the change in imports divided by the change in real GDP, other things remaining the same. For example, if a $100 billion increase in real GDP increases imports by $250 billion, the marginal propensity to import is 0.25.

Review Quiz

1 Which components of aggregate expenditure are influenced by real GDP?
2 Define and explain how we calculate the marginal propensity to consume and the marginal propensity to save.
3 How do we calculate the effects of real GDP on consumption expenditure and imports by using the marginal propensity to consume and the marginal propensity to import?

 Work Study Plan 27.1 and get instant feedback.

Real GDP influences consumption expenditure and imports, which in turn influence real GDP. Your next task is to study this second piece of the two-way link between aggregate expenditure and real GDP and see how all the components of aggregate planned expenditure interact to determine real GDP.

▶ Real GDP with a Fixed Price Level

You are now going to see how, at a given price level, aggregate expenditure plans determine real GDP. We start by looking at the relationship between aggregate planned expenditure and real GDP. This relationship can be described by an aggregate expenditure schedule or an aggregate expenditure curve. The *aggregate expenditure schedule* lists aggregate planned expenditure generated at each level of real GDP. The *aggregate expenditure curve* is a graph of the aggregate expenditure schedule.

Aggregate Planned Expenditure

The table in Fig. 27.3 sets out an aggregate expenditure schedule. To calculate aggregate planned expenditure at a given real GDP, we add the expenditure components together. The first column of the table shows real GDP, and the second column shows the planned consumption at each level of real GDP. A $100 billion increase in real GDP increases consumption expenditure by $70 billion—the *MPC* is 0.7.

The next two columns show investment and government expenditure on goods and services, both of which are independent of the level of real GDP. Investment depends on the real interest rate and the expected profit (see Chapter 23, p. 550). At a given point in time, these factors generate a given level of investment. Suppose this level of investment is $200 billion. Also, suppose that government expenditure is $220 billion.

The next two columns show exports and imports. Exports are influenced by events in the rest of the world, prices of foreign-produced goods and services relative to the prices of similar Canadian-produced goods and services, and exchange rates. But they are not directly affected by Canadian real GDP. Exports are a constant $180 billion. Imports increase as Canadian real GDP increases. A $100 billion increase in Canadian real GDP generates a $20 billion increase in imports—the marginal propensity to import is 0.2.

The final column shows aggregate planned expenditure—the sum of planned consumption expenditure, investment, government expenditure on goods and services, and exports minus imports.

Figure 27.3 plots an aggregate expenditure curve. Real GDP is shown on the *x*-axis, and aggregate planned expenditure is shown on the *y*-axis. The aggregate expenditure curve is the red line *AE*. Points *A* through *F* on that curve correspond to the rows of the table. The *AE* curve is a graph of aggregate planned expenditure (the last column) plotted against real GDP (the first column).

Figure 27.3 also shows the components of aggregate expenditure. The constant components—investment (*I*), government expenditure on goods and services (*G*), and exports (*X*)—are shown by the horizontal lines in the figure. Consumption expenditure (*C*) is the vertical gap between the lines labelled *I* + *G* + *X* and *I* + *G* + *X* + *C*.

To construct the *AE* curve, subtract imports (*M*) from the *I* + *G* + *X* + *C* line. Aggregate expenditure is expenditure on Canadian-produced goods and services. But the components of aggregate expenditure—*C*, *I*, and *G*—include expenditure on imported goods and services. For example, if you buy a new cell phone, your expenditure is part of consumption expenditure. But if the cell phone is an LG made in Korea, your expenditure on it must be subtracted from consumption expenditure to find out how much is spent on goods and services produced in Canada—on Canadian real GDP. Money paid to LG for cell phones imported from Korea does not add to aggregate expenditure in Canada.

Because imports are only a part of aggregate expenditure, when we subtract imports from the other components of aggregate expenditure, aggregate planned expenditure still increases as real GDP increases, as you can see in Fig. 27.3.

Consumption expenditure minus imports, which varies with real GDP, is called **induced expenditure**. The sum of investment, government expenditure, and exports, which does not vary with real GDP, is called **autonomous expenditure**. Consumption expenditure and imports can also have an autonomous component—a component that does not vary with real GDP. Another way to think about autonomous expenditure is that it would be the level of aggregate planned expenditure if real GDP were zero.

In Fig. 27.3, autonomous expenditure is $600 billion—aggregate planned expenditure when real GDP is zero. For each $100 billion increase in real GDP, induced expenditure increases by $50 billion.

The aggregate expenditure curve summarizes the relationship between aggregate *planned* expenditure and real GDP. But what determines the point on the aggregate expenditure curve at which the economy operates? What determines *actual* aggregate expenditure?

FIGURE 27.3   Aggregate Planned Expenditure: The *AE* Curve

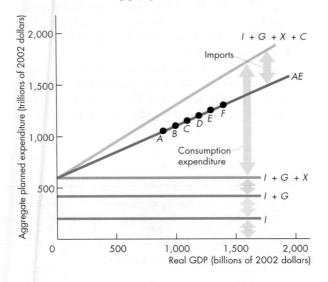

Aggregate planned expenditure is the sum of planned consumption expenditure, investment, government expenditure on goods and services, and exports minus imports. For example, in row *B* of the table, when real GDP is $1,000 billion, planned consumption expenditure is $700 billion, planned investment is $200 billion, planned government expenditure is $220 billion, planned exports are $180 billion, and planned imports are $200 billion. So when real GDP is $1,000 billion, aggregate planned expenditure is $1,100 billion ($700 + $200 + $220 + $180 − $200). The schedule shows that aggregate planned expenditure increases as real GDP increases. This relationship is graphed as the aggregate expenditure curve *AE*. The components of aggregate expenditure that increase with real GDP are consumption expenditure and imports. The other components—investment, government expenditure, and exports—do not vary with real GDP.

| | Real GDP (Y) | Planned expenditure | | | | | Aggregate planned expenditure (AE = C + I + G + X − M) |
		Consumption expenditure (C)	Investment (I)	Government expenditure (G)	Exports (X)	Imports (M)	
				(billions of 2002 dollars)			
	0	0	200	220	180	0	600
A	900	630	200	220	180	180	1,050
B	1,000	700	200	220	180	200	1,100
C	1,100	770	200	220	180	220	1,150
D	1,200	840	200	220	180	240	1,200
E	1,300	910	200	220	180	260	1,250
F	1,400	980	200	220	180	280	1,300

 myeconlab animation

Actual Expenditure, Planned Expenditure, and Real GDP

Actual aggregate expenditure is always equal to real GDP, as we saw in Chapter 20 (p. 470). But aggregate *planned* expenditure is not always equal to actual aggregate expenditure and therefore is not always equal to real GDP. How can actual expenditure and planned expenditure differ? The answer is that firms can end up with inventories that are greater or smaller than planned. People carry out their consumption expenditure plans, the govern-

ment implements its planned expenditure on goods and services, and net exports are as planned. Firms carry out their plans to purchase new buildings, plant, and equipment. But one component of investment is the change in firms' inventories. If aggregate planned expenditure is less than real GDP, firms sell less than they planned to sell and end up with unplanned inventories. If aggregate planned expenditure exceeds real GDP, firms sell more than they planned to sell and end up with inventories being too low.

Equilibrium Expenditure

Equilibrium expenditure is the level of aggregate expenditure that occurs when aggregate *planned* expenditure equals real GDP. Equilibrium expenditure is a level of aggregate expenditure and real GDP at which spending plans are fulfilled. At a given price level, equilibrium expenditure determines real GDP. When aggregate planned expenditure and actual

aggregate expenditure are unequal, a process of convergence towards equilibrium expenditure occurs. Throughout this process, real GDP adjusts. Let's examine equilibrium expenditure and the process that brings it about.

Figure 27.4(a) illustrates equilibrium expenditure. The table sets out aggregate planned expenditure at various levels of real GDP. These values are plotted as points *A* through *F* along the *AE* curve. The 45° line

FIGURE 27.4 Equilibrium Expenditure

(a) Equilibrium expenditure

(b) Unplanned inventory changes

Real GDP (Y)	Aggregate planned expenditure (AE)	Unplanned inventory change (Y – AE)
	(billions of 2002 dollars)	
A 900	1,050	–150
B 1,000	1,100	–100
C 1,100	1,150	–50
D 1,200	1,200	0
E 1,300	1,250	50
F 1,400	1,300	100

The table shows expenditure plans at different levels of real GDP. When real GDP is $1,200 billion, aggregate planned expenditure equals real GDP.

Part (a) of the figure illustrates equilibrium expenditure, which occurs when aggregate planned expenditure equals real GDP at the intersection of the 45° line and the *AE* curve. Part (b) of the figure shows the forces that bring about equilibrium expenditure. When aggregate planned expenditure exceeds real GDP, inventories decrease—for example, at point *B* in both parts of the figure. Firms increase production, and real GDP increases.

When aggregate planned expenditure is less than real GDP, inventories increase—for example, at point *F* in both parts of the figure. Firms decrease production, and real GDP decreases. When aggregate planned expenditure equals real GDP, there are no unplanned inventory changes and real GDP remains constant at equilibrium expenditure.

shows all the points at which aggregate planned expenditure equals real GDP. So where the *AE* curve lies above the 45° line, aggregate planned expenditure exceeds real GDP; where the *AE* curve lies below the 45° line, aggregate planned expenditure is less than real GDP; and where the *AE* curve intersects the 45° line, aggregate planned expenditure equals real GDP. Point *D* illustrates equilibrium expenditure. At this point, real GDP is $1,200 billion.

Convergence to Equilibrium

What are the forces that move aggregate expenditure towards its equilibrium level? To answer this question, we must look at a situation in which aggregate expenditure is away from its equilibrium level.

From Below Equilibrium Suppose that in Fig. 27.4, real GDP is $1,000 billion. Real GDP and actual aggregate expenditure are always equal, so actual aggregate expenditure is $1,000 billion. But aggregate *planned* expenditure is $1,100 billion, point *B* in Fig. 27.4(a). Aggregate planned expenditure exceeds *actual* expenditure. When people spend $1,100 billion and firms produce goods and services worth $1,000 billion, firms' inventories fall by $100 billion, point *B* in Fig. 27.4(b). Because the change in inventories is part of investment, *actual* investment is $100 billion less than *planned* investment.

Real GDP doesn't remain at $1,000 billion for very long. Firms have inventory targets based on their sales. When inventories fall below target, firms increase production to restore inventories to the target level. To increase inventories, firms hire additional labour and increase production.

Suppose that firms increase production in the next period by $100 billion. Real GDP increases by $100 billion to $1,100 billion. But again, aggregate planned expenditure exceeds real GDP. When real GDP is $1,100 billion, aggregate planned expenditure is $1,150 billion, point *C* in Fig. 27.4(a). Again, inventories decrease, but this time by less than before. With real GDP of $1,100 billion and aggregate planned expenditure of $1,150 billion, inventories decrease by $50 billion, point *C* in Fig. 27.4(b). Again, firms hire additional labour and production increases; real GDP increases yet further.

The process that we've just described—planned expenditure exceeds real GDP, inventories decrease, and production increases to restore inventories—ends

when real GDP has reached $1,200 billion. At this real GDP, there is equilibrium. Unplanned inventory changes are zero. Firms do not change their production.

From Above Equilibrium If, in Fig. 27.4, real GDP is $1,400 billion, the process that we've just described works in reverse. With real GDP at $1,400 billion, actual aggregate expenditure is also $1,400 billion. But aggregate planned expenditure is $1,300 billion, point *F* in Fig. 27.4(a). Actual expenditure exceeds planned expenditure. When people spend $1,300 billion and firms produce goods and services worth $1,400 billion, firms' inventories rise by $100 billion, point *F* in Fig. 27.4(b). Now, real GDP begins to fall. As long as actual expenditure exceeds planned expenditure, inventories rise and production decreases. Again, the process ends when real GDP has reached $1,200 billion, the equilibrium at which unplanned inventory changes are zero and firms do not change their production.

Review Quiz

1 What is the relationship between aggregate planned expenditure and real GDP at equilibrium expenditure?
2 How does equilibrium expenditure come about? What adjusts to achieve equilibrium?
3 If real GDP and aggregate expenditure are less than equilibrium expenditure, what happens to firms' inventories? How do firms change their production? And what happens to real GDP?
4 If real GDP and aggregate expenditure are greater than equilibrium expenditure, what happens to firms' inventories? How do firms change their production? And what happens to real GDP?

 Work Study Plan 27.2 and get instant feedback.

We've learned that when the price level is fixed, real GDP is determined by equilibrium expenditure. And we have seen how unplanned changes in inventories and the production response they generate bring a convergence towards equilibrium expenditure. We're now going to study *changes* in equilibrium expenditure and discover an economic amplifier called the *multiplier*.

The Multiplier

Investment and exports can change for many reasons. A fall in the real interest rate might induce firms to increase their planned investment. A wave of innovation, such as occurred with the spread of multimedia computers in the 1990s, might increase expected future profits and lead firms to increase their planned investment. An economic boom in Western Europe and Japan might lead to a large increase in their expenditure on Canadian-produced goods and services—on Canadian exports. These are all examples of increases in autonomous expenditure.

When autonomous expenditure increases, aggregate expenditure increases and so does equilibrium expenditure and real GDP. But the increase in real GDP is *larger* than the change in autonomous expenditure. The **multiplier** is the amount by which a change in autonomous expenditure is magnified or multiplied to determine the change in equilibrium expenditure and real GDP.

To get the basic idea of the multiplier, we'll work with an example economy in which there are no income taxes and no imports. So we'll first assume that these factors are absent. Then, when you understand the basic idea, we'll bring these factors back into play and see what difference they make to the multiplier.

The Basic Idea of the Multiplier

Suppose that investment increases. The additional expenditure by businesses means that aggregate expenditure and real GDP increase. The increase in real GDP increases disposable income, and with no income taxes, real GDP and disposable income increase by the same amount. The increase in disposable income brings an increase in consumption expenditure. And the increased consumption expenditure adds even more to aggregate expenditure. Real GDP and disposable income increase further, and so does consumption expenditure. The initial increase in investment brings an even bigger increase in aggregate expenditure because it induces an increase in consumption expenditure. The magnitude of the increase in aggregate expenditure that results from an increase in autonomous expenditure is determined by the *multiplier*.

The table in Fig. 27.5 sets out an aggregate planned expenditure schedule. Initially, when real GDP is $1,100 billion, aggregate planned expenditure is $1,125 billion. For each $100 billion increase in real GDP, aggregate planned expenditure increases by $75 billion. This aggregate expenditure schedule is shown in the figure as the aggregate expenditure curve AE_0. Initially, equilibrium expenditure is $1,200 billion. You can see this equilibrium in row B of the table and in the figure where the curve AE_0 intersects the 45° line at the point marked B.

Now suppose that autonomous expenditure increases by $50 billion. What happens to equilibrium expenditure? You can see the answer in Fig. 27.5. When this increase in autonomous expenditure is added to the original aggregate planned expenditure, aggregate planned expenditure increases by $50 billion at each level of real GDP. The new aggregate expenditure curve is AE_1. The new equilibrium expenditure, highlighted in the table (row D'), occurs where AE_1 intersects the 45° line and is $1,400 billion (point D'). At this real GDP, aggregate planned expenditure equals real GDP.

The Multiplier Effect

In Fig. 27.5, the increase in autonomous expenditure of $50 billion increases equilibrium expenditure by $200 billion. That is, the change in autonomous expenditure leads, like Céline Dion's electronic equipment, to an amplified change in equilibrium expenditure. This amplified change is the *multiplier effect*—equilibrium expenditure increases by *more than* the increase in autonomous expenditure. The multiplier is greater than 1.

Initially, when autonomous expenditure increases, aggregate planned expenditure exceeds real GDP. As a result, inventories decrease. Firms respond by increasing production so as to restore their inventories to the target level. As production increases, so does real GDP. With a higher level of real GDP, *induced expenditure* increases. Thus equilibrium expenditure increases by the sum of the initial increase in autonomous expenditure and the increase in induced expenditure. In this example, equilibrium expenditure increases by $200 billion and autonomous expenditure increases by $50 billion, so induced expenditure increases by $150 billion.

Although we have just analyzed the effects of an *increase* in autonomous expenditure, this analysis also applies to a decrease in autonomous expenditure. If initially the aggregate expenditure curve is AE_1, equilibrium expenditure and real GDP are $1,400 billion. A decrease in autonomous expenditure of $50 billion

FIGURE 27.5   The Multiplier

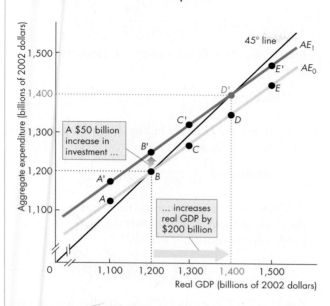

Real GDP (Y)	Aggregate planned expenditure			
	Original (AE₀)		New (AE₁)	
	(billions of 2002 dollars)			
1,100	A	1,125	A'	1,175
1,200	**B**	**1,200**	**B'**	**1,250**
1,300	C	1,275	C'	1,325
1,400	D	1,350	D'	1,400
1,500	E	1,425	E'	1,475

A $50 billion increase in autonomous expenditure shifts the AE curve upward by $50 billion from AE_0 to AE_1. Equilibrium expenditure increases by $200 billion from $1,200 billion to $1,400 billion. The increase in equilibrium expenditure is 4 times the increase in autonomous expenditure, so the multiplier is 4.

myeconlab animation

shifts the aggregate expenditure curve downward by $50 billion to AE_0. Equilibrium expenditure decreases from $1,400 billion to $1,200 billion. The decrease in equilibrium expenditure ($200 billion) is larger than the decrease in autonomous expenditure that brought it about ($50 billion).

Why Is the Multiplier Greater Than 1?

We've seen that equilibrium expenditure increases by more than the increase in autonomous expenditure. This makes the multiplier greater than 1. How come? Why does equilibrium expenditure increase by more than the increase in autonomous expenditure?

The multiplier is greater than 1 because induced expenditure increases—an increase in autonomous expenditure *induces* further increases in expenditure. If Rogers Cablesystems spends $10 million on a new pay-per-view system, real GDP increases by $10 million. But that is not the end of the story. Video systems designers now have more income, and they spend part of the extra income on goods and services. Real GDP now rises by the initial $10 million plus the extra consumption expenditure induced by the $10 million increase in income. The producers of automobiles, vacations, and other goods and services now have increased incomes, and they, in turn, spend part of the increase in their incomes on consumption goods and services. Additional income induces additional expenditure, which creates additional income.

How big is the multiplier effect?

The Size of the Multiplier

Suppose that the economy is in a recession. Now profit prospects start to look better, and firms are planning a large increase in investment. The world economy is heading towards expansion. The question on everyone's lips is: How strong will the expansion be? This is a hard question to answer, but an important ingredient in the answer is the size of the multiplier.

The *multiplier* is the amount by which a change in autonomous expenditure is multiplied to determine the change in equilibrium expenditure that it generates. To calculate the multiplier, we divide the change in equilibrium expenditure by the change in autonomous expenditure.

Let's calculate the multiplier for the example in Fig. 27.5. Initially, equilibrium expenditure is $1,200 billion. Then autonomous expenditure increases by $50 billion, and equilibrium expenditure increases by $200 billion, to $1,400 billion. Then

$$\text{Multiplier} = \frac{\text{Change in equilibrium expenditure}}{\text{Change in autonomous expenditure}}$$

$$\text{Multiplier} = \frac{\$200 \text{ billion}}{\$50 \text{ billion}} = 4.$$

The Multiplier and the Slope of the *AE* Curve

The magnitude of the multiplier depends on the slope of the *AE* curve. In Fig. 27.6, the *AE* curve in part (a) is steeper than the *AE* curve in part (b), and the multiplier is larger in part (a) than in part (b). To see why, let's do a calculation.

Aggregate expenditure and real GDP change because induced expenditure and autonomous expenditure change. The change in real GDP (ΔY) equals the change in induced expenditure (ΔN) plus the change in autonomous expenditure (ΔA). That is,

$$\Delta Y = \Delta N + \Delta A.$$

But the change in induced expenditure is determined by the change in real GDP and the slope of the *AE* curve. To see why, begin with the fact that the slope of the *AE* curve equals the "rise," ΔN, divided by the "run," ΔY. That is

$$\text{Slope of } AE \text{ curve} = \Delta N \div \Delta Y.$$

So

$$\Delta N = \text{Slope of } AE \text{ curve} \times \Delta Y.$$

Now, use this equation to replace ΔN in the first equation above to give

$$\Delta Y = \text{Slope of } AE \text{ curve} \times \Delta Y + \Delta A.$$

Now, solve for ΔY as

$$(1 - \text{Slope of } AE \text{ curve}) \times \Delta Y = \Delta A$$

and rearrange to give

$$\Delta Y = \frac{\Delta A}{1 - \text{Slope of } AE \text{ curve}}.$$

Finally, divide both sides of this equation by ΔA to give

$$\text{Multiplier} = \frac{\Delta Y}{\Delta A} = \frac{1}{1 - \text{Slope of } AE \text{ curve}}.$$

If we use the example in Fig. 27.5, the slope of the *AE* curve is 0.75, so

$$\text{Multiplier} = \frac{1}{1 - 0.75} = \frac{1}{0.25} = 4.$$

Where there are no income taxes and no imports, the slope of the *AE* curve equals the marginal propensity to consume (*MPC*). So

$$\text{Multiplier} = \frac{1}{1 - MPC}.$$

But $(1 - MPC)$ equals *MPS*. So another formula is

$$\text{Multiplier} = \frac{1}{MPS}.$$

Again using the numbers in Fig. 27.5, we have

$$\text{Multiplier} = \frac{1}{0.25} = 4.$$

Because the marginal propensity to save (*MPS*) is a fraction—a number between 0 and 1—the multiplier is greater than 1.

FIGURE 27.6 The Multiplier and the Slope of the *AE* Curve

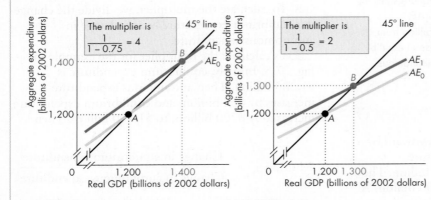

(a) Multiplier is 4

(b) Multiplier is 2

Imports and income taxes make the *AE* curve less steep and reduce the value of the multiplier. In part (a), with no imports and income taxes, the slope of the *AE* curve is 0.75 (the marginal propensity to consume) and the multiplier is 4. But with imports and income taxes, the slope of the *AE* curve is less than the marginal propensity to consume. In part (b), the slope of the *AE* curve is 0.5. In this case, the multiplier is 2.

myeconlab animation

Imports and Income Taxes

Imports and income taxes influence the size of the multiplier and make it smaller than it otherwise would be.

To see why imports make the multiplier smaller, think about what happens following an increase in investment. The increase in investment increases real GDP, which in turn increases consumption expenditure. But part of the increase in expenditure is on imported goods and services. Only expenditure on Canadian-produced goods and services increases Canadian real GDP. The larger the marginal propensity to import, the smaller is the change in Canadian real GDP.*

Income taxes also make the multiplier smaller than it otherwise would be. Again, think about what happens following an increase in investment. The increase in investment increases real GDP. Income tax payments increase so disposable income increases by less than the increase in real GDP and consumption expenditure increases by less than it would if taxes had not changed. The larger the income tax rate, the smaller is the change in real GDP.

The marginal propensity to import, the income tax rate, and the marginal propensity to consume determine the slope of the *AE* curve and the multiplier.

Over time, the value of the multiplier changes as tax rates change and as the marginal propensity to consume and the marginal propensity to import change. These ongoing changes make the multiplier hard to predict. But they do not change the fundamental fact that an initial change in autonomous expenditure leads to a magnified change in aggregate expenditure and real GDP.

The Multiplier Process

The multiplier effect isn't a one-shot event. It is a process that plays out over a few months. Figure 27.7 illustrates the multiplier process. Autonomous expenditure increases by $50 billion and real GDP increases by $50 billion (the green bar in round 1). This increase in real GDP increases induced expenditure in round 2. With the slope of the *AE* curve equal to 0.75, induced expenditure increases by 0.75 times the increase in real GDP, so the increase in real GDP of $50 billion induces a further increase in expenditure of $37.5 billion. This

change in induced expenditure (the green bar in round 2) when added to the previous increase in expenditure (the blue bar in round 2) increases real GDP by $87.5 billion. The round 2 increase in real GDP induces a round 3 increase in induced expenditure. The process repeats through successive rounds. Each increase in real GDP is 0.75 times the previous increase and eventually real GDP increases by $200 billion.

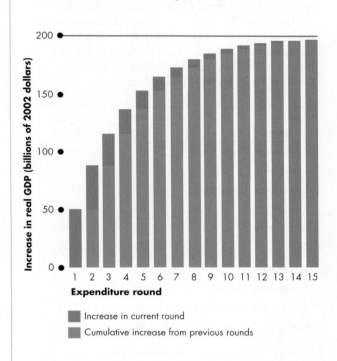

FIGURE 27.7 The Multiplier Process

Autonomous expenditure increases by $50 billion. In round 1, real GDP increases by the same amount. With the slope of the *AE* curve equal to 0.75, each additional dollar of real GDP induces an additional 0.75 of a dollar of induced expenditure. The round 1 increase in real GDP brings an increase in induced expenditure of $37.5 billion in round 2. At the end of round 2, real GDP has increased by $87.5 billion. The extra $37.5 billion of real GDP in round 2 brings a further increase in induced expenditure of $28.1 billion in round 3. Real GDP increases yet further to $115.6 billion. This process continues with real GDP increasing by ever-smaller amounts. When the process comes to an end, real GDP has increased by a total of $200 billion.

myeconlab animation

---

*The Mathematical Note on pp. 670–671 shows the effects of imports and income taxes on the multiplier.

The Multiplier in the Great Depression

Investment Collapse Kills the Economy

The aggregate expenditure model and its multiplier were developed during the 1930s by John Maynard Keynes to understand the most traumatic event in economic history, the *Great Depression*.

In 1929, the Canadian and global economies were booming. Canadian real GDP and real GDP per person had never been higher. By 1933, real GDP had fallen to 69 percent of its 1929 level and more than a quarter of the labour force was unemployed.

The table shows the GDP numbers and components of aggregate expenditure in 1929 and 1933. Investment collapsed with a decrease from $16 billion to $1 billion. Exports fell by $4 billion. Government expenditure held steady.

Item	1929	1933
	(billions of 2002 dollars)	
Consumption expenditure	50	40
Imvestment	16	1
Government expenditure	13	12
Exports	14	10
Less imports	−13	−8
GDP	**80**	**55**
Assumptions		
Induced expenditure	40	27.5
Autonomous expenditure	40	27.5
GDP	**80**	**55.0**

Source of data: Statistics Canada, *Historical Statistics of Canada*, Second Edition, F. H. Leacy (ed.), Ottawa, 1939, series F33, F34, F35, F51, F52, and F55 re-based to 2002 dollars.

If we assume that the marginal propensity to consume is 0.7 and the marginal propensity to import is 0.2, the slope of the *AE* curve is 0.5.

Autonomous expenditure and induced expenditure are each equal to a half of real GDP—$40 billion in 1929 and $27.5 billion in 1933.

The figure shows the *AE* curve in 1929 as AE_{29}. Equilibrium expenditure and real GDP were $80 billion. By 1933, autonomous expenditure had fallen by $12.5 billion to $27.5 billion and the *AE* curve had shifted downward to AE_{33}. Equilibrium expenditure and real GDP had fallen to $55 billion.

The decrease in autonomous expenditure of $12.5 billion brought a decrease in real GDP of $25 billion. The multiplier was $25/$12.5 = 2.

Aggregate Expenditure in the Great Depression

Business Cycle Turning Points

At business cycle turning points, the economy moves from expansion to recession or from recession to expansion. Economists understand these turning points as seismologists understand earthquakes. They know quite a lot about the forces and mechanisms that produce them, but they can't predict them. The forces that bring business cycle turning points are the swings in autonomous expenditure, such as investment and exports. The multiplier that you've just studied is the mechanism that gives momentum to the economy's new direction.

Review Quiz

1 What is the multiplier? What does it determine? Why does it matter?

2 How do the marginal propensity to consume, the marginal propensity to import, and the income tax rate influence the multiplier?

3 How do fluctuations in autonomous expenditure influence real GDP?

 Work Study Plan 27.3 and get instant feedback.

The Multiplier and the Price Level

We have just considered adjustments in spending that occur in the very short run when the price level is fixed. In this time frame, the economy's cobblestones, which are changes in investment and exports, are not smoothed by shock absorbers like those on Ed Stelmach's car. Instead, they are amplified like Céline Dion's voice. But these outcomes occur only when the price level is fixed. We now investigate what happens after a long enough time lapse for the price level to change.

Adjusting Quantities and Prices

When firms can't keep up with sales and their inventories fall below target, they increase production, but at some point, they raise their prices. Similarly, when firms find unwanted inventories piling up, they decrease production, but eventually they cut their prices. So far, we've studied the macroeconomic consequences of firms changing their production levels when their sales change, but we haven't looked at the effects of price changes. When individual firms change their prices, the economy's price level changes.

To study the simultaneous determination of real GDP and the price level, we use the *AS–AD model*, which is explained in Chapter 26. But to understand how aggregate demand adjusts, we need to work out the connection between the *AS–AD* model and the aggregate expenditure model that we've used in this chapter. The key to understanding the relationship between these two models is the distinction between the aggregate *expenditure* and aggregate *demand* and the related distinction between the aggregate *expenditure curve* and the aggregate *demand* curve.

Aggregate Expenditure and Aggregate Demand

The aggregate expenditure curve is the relationship between the aggregate planned expenditure and real GDP, all other influences on aggregate planned expenditure remaining the same. The aggregate demand curve is the relationship between the aggregate quantity of goods and services demanded and the price level, all other influences on aggregate

demand remaining the same. Let's explore the links between these two relationships.

Deriving the Aggregate Demand Curve

When the price level changes, aggregate planned expenditure changes and the quantity of real GDP demanded changes. The aggregate demand curve slopes downward. Why? There are two main reasons:

- Wealth effect
- Substitution effects

Wealth Effect Other things remaining the same, the higher the price level, the smaller is the purchasing power of wealth. For example, suppose you have $100 in the bank and the price level is 105. If the price level rises to 125, your $100 buys fewer goods and services. You are less wealthy. With less wealth, you will probably want to try to spend a bit less and save a bit more. The higher the price level, other things remaining the same, the lower is aggregate planned expenditure.

Substitution Effects For a given expected future price level, a rise in the price level today makes current goods and services more expensive relative to future goods and services and results in a delay in purchases—an *intertemporal substitution*. A rise in the Canadian price level, other things remaining the same, makes Canadian-produced goods and services more expensive relative to foreign-produced goods and services. As a result, Canadian imports increase and Canadian exports decrease—an *international substitution*.

When the price level rises, each of these effects reduces aggregate planned expenditure at each level of real GDP. As a result, when the price level *rises*, the aggregate expenditure curve shifts *downward*. A fall in the price level has the opposite effect. When the price level *falls*, the aggregate expenditure curve shifts *upward*.

Figure 27.8(a) shows the shifts of the *AE* curve. When the price level is 110, the aggregate expenditure curve is AE_0, which intersects the 45° line at point *B*. Equilibrium expenditure is $1,200 billion. If the price level increases to 130, the aggregate expenditure curve shifts downward to AE_1, which intersects the 45° line at point *A*. Equilibrium expenditure decreases to $1,100 billion. If the price level decreases to 90, the aggregate expenditure curve shifts upward to AE_2, which intersects the 45° line at point C. Equilibrium expenditure increases to $1,300 billion.

We've just seen that when the price level changes, other things remaining the same, the aggregate expenditure curve shifts and the equilibrium expenditure changes. But when the price level changes, other things remaining the same, there is a movement along the aggregate demand curve.

Figure 27.8(b) shows the movements along the aggregate demand curve. At a price level of 110, the aggregate quantity of goods and services demanded is $1,200 billion—point B on the AD curve. If the price level rises to 130, the aggregate quantity of goods and services demanded decreases to $1,100 billion. There is a movement up along the aggregate demand curve to point A. If the price level falls to 90, the aggregate quantity of goods and services demanded increases to $1,300 billion. There is a movement down along the aggregate demand curve to point C.

Each point on the aggregate demand curve corresponds to a point of equilibrium expenditure. The equilibrium expenditure points A, B, and C in Fig. 27.8(a) correspond to the points A, B, and C on the aggregate demand curve in Fig. 27.8(b).

Changes in Aggregate Expenditure and Aggregate Demand

When any influence on aggregate planned expenditure other than the price level changes, both the aggregate expenditure curve and the aggregate demand curve shift. For example, an increase in investment or exports increases both aggregate planned expenditure and aggregate demand and shifts both the AE curve and the AD curve. Figure 27.9 illustrates the effect of such an increase.

Initially, the aggregate expenditure curve is AE_0 in part (a) and the aggregate demand curve is AD_0 in part (b). The price level is 110, real GDP is $1,200 billion, and the economy is at point A in both parts of Fig. 27.9. Now suppose that investment increases by $100 billion. At a constant price level of 110, the aggregate expenditure curve shifts upward to AE_1. This curve intersects the 45° line at an equilibrium expenditure of $1,400 billion (point B). This equilibrium expenditure of $1,400 billion is the aggregate quantity of goods and services demanded at a price level of 110, as shown by point B in part (b). Point B lies on a new aggregate demand curve. The aggregate demand curve has shifted rightward to AD_1.

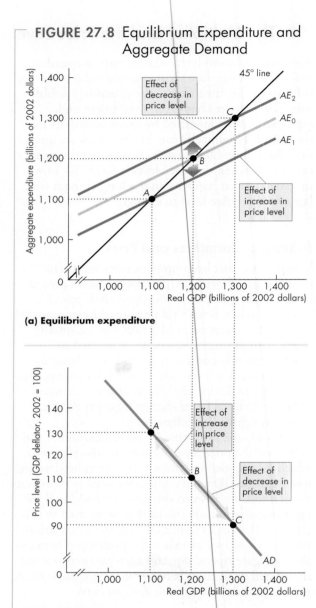

FIGURE 27.8 Equilibrium Expenditure and Aggregate Demand

(a) Equilibrium expenditure

(b) Aggregate demand

A change in the price level *shifts* the AE curve and results in a *movement along* the AD curve. When the price level is 110, the AE curve is AE_0 and equilibrium expenditure is $1,200 billion at point B. When the price level rises to 130, the AE curve is AE_1 and equilibrium expenditure is $1,100 billion at point A. When the price level falls to 90, the AE curve is AE_2 and equilibrium expenditure is $1,300 billion at point C. Points A, B, and C on the AD curve in part (b) correspond to the equilibrium expenditure points A, B, and C in part (a).

myeconlab animation

FIGURE 27.9   A Change in Aggregate Demand

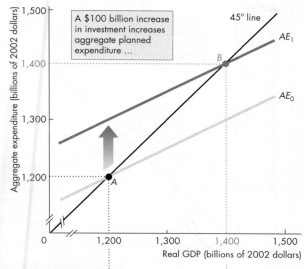

A $100 billion increase in investment increases aggregate planned expenditure ...

45° line

(a) **Aggregate expenditure**

... and increases aggregate demand. The multiplier in this example is 2

(b) **Aggregate demand**

The price level is 110. When the aggregate expenditure curve is AE_0 in part (a), the aggregate demand curve is AD_0 in part (b). An increase in autonomous expenditure shifts the AE curve upward to AE_1. In the new equilibrium, real GDP is $1,400 billion (at point B). Because the quantity of real GDP demanded at a price level of 110 increases to $1,400 billion, the AD curve shifts rightward to AD_1.

myeconlab animation

But how do we know by how much the AD curve shifts? The multiplier determines the answer. The larger the multiplier, the larger is the shift in the aggregate demand curve that results from a given change in autonomous expenditure. In this example, the multiplier is 2. A $100 billion increase in investment produces a $200 billion increase in the aggregate quantity of goods and services demanded at each price level. That is, a $100 billion increase in autonomous expenditure shifts the aggregate demand curve rightward by $200 billion.

A decrease in autonomous expenditure shifts the aggregate expenditure curve downward and shifts the aggregate demand curve leftward. You can see these effects by reversing the change that we've just described. If the economy is initially at point B on the aggregate expenditure curve AE_1 and on the aggregate demand curve AD_1, a decrease in autonomous expenditure shifts the aggregate expenditure curve downward to AE_0. The aggregate quantity of goods and services demanded decreases from $1,400 billion to $1,200 billion, and the aggregate demand curve shifts leftward to AD_0.

Let's summarize what we have just discovered:

> If some factor other than a change in the price level increases autonomous expenditure, the AE curve shifts upward and the AD curve shifts rightward. The size of the AD curve shift equals the change in autonomous expenditure multiplied by the multiplier.

Equilibrium Real GDP and the Price Level

In Chapter 26, we learned that aggregate demand and short-run aggregate supply determine equilibrium real GDP and the price level. We've now put aggregate demand under a more powerful microscope and have discovered that a change in investment (or in any component of autonomous expenditure) changes aggregate demand and shifts the aggregate demand curve. The magnitude of the shift depends on the multiplier. But whether a change in autonomous expenditure results ultimately in a change in real GDP, a change in the price level, or a combination of the two depends on aggregate supply. There are two time frames to consider: the short run and the long run. First we'll see what happens in the short run.

An Increase in Aggregate Demand in the Short Run
Figure 27.10 describes the economy. Initially, in part
(a), the aggregate expenditure curve is AE_0 and equilibrium expenditure is $1,200 billion—point A. In part
(b), aggregate demand is AD_0 and the short-run aggregate supply curve is SAS. (Chapter 26, pp. 627–629
explains the SAS curve.) Equilibrium is at point A in
part (b), where the aggregate demand and short-run
aggregate supply curves intersect. The price level is
110, and real GDP is $1,200 billion.

Now suppose that investment increases by
$100 billion. With the price level fixed at 110, the
aggregate expenditure curve shifts upward to AE_1.
Equilibrium expenditure increases to $1,400 bil-
lion—point B in part (a). In part (b), the aggregate
demand curve shifts rightward by $200 billion, from
AD_0 to AD_1. How far the aggregate demand curve
shifts is determined by the multiplier when the price
level is fixed.

But with this new aggregate demand curve, the
price level does not remain fixed. The price level rises,
and as it does, the aggregate expenditure curve shifts
downward. The short-run equilibrium occurs when
the aggregate expenditure curve has shifted downward to AE_2 and the new aggregate demand curve,
AD_1, intersects the short-run aggregate supply curve
at point C in both part (a) and part (b). Real GDP is
$1,330 billion, and the price level is 123.

When price level effects are taken into account,
the increase in investment still has a multiplier effect
on real GDP, but the multiplier is smaller than it
would be if the price level were fixed. The steeper the
slope of the short-run aggregate supply curve, the
larger is the increase in the price level and the smaller
is the multiplier effect on real GDP.

An Increase in Aggregate Demand in the Long Run
Figure 27.11 illustrates the long-run effect of an
increase in aggregate demand. In the long run, real
GDP equals potential GDP and there is full employment. Potential GDP is $1,200 billion, and the long-
run aggregate supply curve is LAS. Initially, the
economy is at point A in parts (a) and (b).

Investment increases by $100 billion. In Fig.
27.11, the aggregate expenditure curve shifts to AE_1
and the aggregate demand curve shifts to AD_1. With
no change in the price level, the economy would
move to point B and real GDP would increase to
$1,400 billion. But in the short run, the price level
rises to 123 and real GDP increases to only $1,330
billion. With the higher price level, the AE curve

FIGURE 27.10 The Multiplier in the
Short Run

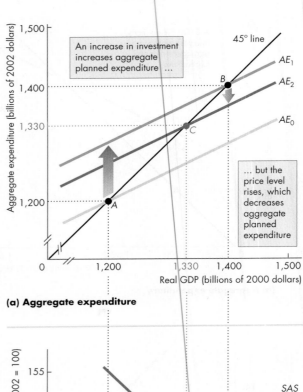

An increase in investment
increases aggregate planned
expenditure ...

... but the
price level
rises, which
decreases
aggregate
planned
expenditure

(a) Aggregate expenditure

(b) Aggregate demand

An increase in investment shifts the AE curve from AE_0 to
AE_1 and the AD curve from AD_0 to AD_1. The price level
rises, and the higher price level shifts the AE curve downward from AE_1 to AE_2. The economy moves to point C in
both parts. In the short run, when prices are flexible, the
multiplier effect is smaller than when the price level is fixed.

myeconlab   animation

FIGURE 27.11 The Multiplier in the Long Run

(a) Aggregate expenditure

(b) Aggregate demand

Starting from point A, an increase in investment shifts the AE curve to AE_1 and the AD curve to AD_1. In the short run, the economy moves to point C. In the long run, the money wage rate rises and the SAS curve shifts to SAS_1. As the price level rises, the AE curve shifts back to AE_0 and the economy moves to point A'. In the long run, the multiplier is zero.

myeconlab animation

shifts from AE_1 to AE_2. The economy is now in a short-run equilibrium at point C in both part (a) and part (b).

Real GDP now exceeds potential GDP. The labour force is more than fully employed, and in the long run, shortages of labour increase the money wage rate. The higher money wage rate increases firms' costs, which decreases short-run aggregate supply and shifts the SAS curve leftward towards SAS_1. The price level rises further, and real GDP decreases. There is a movement along AD_1, and the AE curve shifts downward from AE_2 towards AE_0. When the money wage rate and the price level have increased by the same percentage, real GDP is again equal to potential GDP and the economy is at point A'. In the long run, the multiplier is zero.

Review Quiz

1 How does a change in the price level influence the AE curve and the AD curve?

2 If autonomous expenditure increases with no change in the price level, what happens to the AE curve and the AD curve? Which shift is determined by the multiplier and why?

3 How does an increase in autonomous expenditure change real GDP in the short run? Does real GDP change by the same amount as the change in aggregate demand? Why or why not?

4 How does real GDP change in the long run when autonomous expenditure increases? Does real GDP change by the same amount as the change in aggregate demand? Why or why not?

myeconlab   Work Study Plan 27.4 and get instant feedback.

◆ You are now ready to build on what you've learned about aggregate expenditure fluctuations. We'll study the business cycle and the roles of fiscal policy and monetary policy in smoothing the cycle while achieving price stability and sustained economic growth. In Chapter 28, we study the Canadian business cycle and inflation, and in Chapters 29 and 30, we study fiscal policy and monetary policy respectively. But before you leave the current topic, look at *Reading Between the Lines* on pp. 668–669 to see the aggregate expenditure model in action in the Canadian economy during 2008.

Recession Coming

GDP Rise in Q3 Masks Layoffs, Recession to Come

December 1, 2008

Climbing inventories from producers and manufacturers helped spark an unexpected burst of economic growth in Canada last quarter. But excess product will drive unemployment higher as the country moves into recession, economists warned Monday.

"Inventories are building in the auto sector [and] much of the manufacturing sector, and that means factories will have to cut back production over the next while," said Sal Guatieri, a senior economist at BMO Capital Markets.

Warehouses brimming with unsold goods contributed to a stronger-than-expected 1.3 percent rise in real gross domestic product in the third quarter, as producers logged a robust level of output.

It does not mean they sold it.

Final domestic demand, which encompasses corporate and consumer spending, fell to its slowest pace in a dozen years in the three-month period, while exports declined for the fifth consecutive quarter.

Idle inventory combined with still-falling demand is a recipe for layoffs, Mr. Guatieri said. "We will likely see a wave of job losses because of that."...

"You could anticipate anywhere from 100 [thousand] to 200 thousand job losses over the next year," he said, adding BMO expects the unemployment rate to jump above 7 percent from 6.2 percent by this time next year. ...

Material reprinted with the express permission of "The National Post Company", a Canwest Partnership.

Essence of the Story

- Real GDP grew by 1.3 percent (annual rate) in the third quarter of 2008.

- Unwanted rising inventories were a large component of the increase in real GDP.

- Unwanted rising inventories will bring a cut in production.

- Final domestic demand in the three-month period fell to its slowest pace in a dozen years.

- Exports decreased for the fifth consecutive quarter.

- Economists say the economy is heading towards recession.

- BMO economists expect between 100,000 and 200,000 people to lose jobs and the unemployment rate to increase above 7 percent by the end of 2009.

Economic Analysis

- We can interpret this news article by using the analysis of convergence to equilibrium on p. 656 and in Fig. 27.4.

- The article reports that although real GDP increased during the third quarter of 2008, the main source of the increase was a rise in unplanned inventories.

- The table shows the real GDP and aggregate expenditure numbers for the second quarter and third quarter of 2008.

- Figure 1 illustrates the situation in the third quarter of 2008 and its implications for future quarters.

- Real GDP was $1,333 billion. Assuming that the $12 billion increase in inventories was unplanned, aggregate planned expenditure was $1,321 billion. These two numbers provide one point on the AE curve in part (a).

- The slope of the AE curve depends on the marginal propensity to consume, the marginal propensity to import, and the marginal tax rate (see the Mathematical Note on p. 670) and we'll assume that slope to be 0.2.

- Using this information and these assumptions, the aggregate expenditure curve in the third quarter of 2008 was AE and equilibrium real GDP was $1,318 billion.

- Part (b) shows the increase in unplanned inventories, which also equals the gap between the AE curve and the 45° line in part (a).

- With no further change in aggregate planned expenditure, real GDP can be expected to fall during the fourth quarter of 2008 (as predicted in the news article).

- With further cuts in aggregate planned expenditure, real GDP will fall by even more during the fourth quarter of 2008 and through 2009.

(a) Aggregate expenditure

(b) Unplanned inventory changes

Figure 1 Convergence to equilibrium expenditure in onset of recession

The Components of Aggregate Expenditure

	2008 Q2	2008 Q3	Change
	(billions of 2002 dollars)		
Consumption expenditure	815	816	1
Investment expenditure	329	332	3
Government expenditure	267	268	1
Exports	489	482	–7
Imports	583	575	–8
Residual*	12	10	–2
Real GDP	1,329	1,333	4
Change in inventories	10	12	2

*The residual arises because chain-linked real variables are calculated for each expenditure component independently of chain-linked real GDP and the components don't exactly sum to real GDP.

MATHEMATICAL NOTE

The Algebra of the Keynesian Model

This mathematical note derives formulas for equilibrium expenditure and the multipliers. We begin by defining the symbols we need:

- Aggregate planned expenditure, AE
- Real GDP, Y
- Consumption expenditure, C
- Disposable income, YD
- Investment, I
- Government expenditure, G
- Exports, X
- Imports, M
- Net taxes, T
- Autonomous consumption expenditure, a
- Autonomous taxes, T_a
- Marginal propensity to consume, b
- Marginal propensity to import, m
- Marginal tax rate, t
- Autonomous expenditure, A

Aggregate Expenditure

Aggregate planned expenditure (AE) is the sum of the planned amounts of consumption expenditure (C), investment (I), government expenditure (G), and exports (X) minus the planned amount of imports (M). That is,

$$AE = C + I + G + X - M.$$

Consumption Function Consumption expenditure (C) depends on disposable income (YD), and we write the consumption function as

$$C = a + bYD.$$

Disposable income (YD) equals real GDP minus net taxes ($Y - T$). So if we replace YD with ($Y - T$), the consumption function becomes

$$C = a + b(Y - T).$$

Net taxes, T, equal autonomous taxes (that are independent of income), T_a, plus induced taxes (that vary with income), tY.

So we can write net taxes as

$$T = T_a + tY.$$

Use this last equation to replace T in the consumption function. The consumption function becomes

$$C = a - bT_a + b(1 - t)Y.$$

This equation describes consumption expenditure as a function of real GDP.

Import Function Imports depend on real GDP, and the import function is

$$M = mY.$$

Aggregate Expenditure Curve Use the consumption function and the import function to replace C and M in the AE equation. That is,

$$AE = a - bT_a + b(1 - t)Y + I + G + X - mY.$$

Collect the terms that involve Y on the right side of the equation to obtain

$$AE = (a - bT_a + I + G + X) + [b(1 - t) - m]Y.$$

Autonomous expenditure (A) is ($a - bT_a + I + G + X$), and the slope of the AE curve is $[b(1 - t) - m]$. So the equation for the AE curve, which is shown in Fig. 1, is

$$AE = A + [b(1 - t) - m]Y.$$

Figure 1 The AE curve

Equilibrium Expenditure

Equilibrium expenditure occurs when aggregate planned expenditure (AE) equals real GDP (Y). That is,

$$AE = Y.$$

In Fig. 2, the scales of the x-axis (real GDP) and the y-axis (aggregate planned expenditure) are identical, so the 45° line shows the points at which aggregate planned expenditure equals real GDP.

Figure 2 shows the point of equilibrium expenditure at the intersection of the AE curve and the 45° line.

To calculate equilibrium expenditure, solve the equations for the AE curve and the 45° line for the two unknown quantities AE and Y. So starting with

$$AE = A + [b(1 - t) - m]Y$$

$$AE = Y,$$

replace AE with Y in the AE equation to obtain

$$Y = A + [b(1 - t) - m]Y.$$

The solution for Y is

$$Y = \frac{1}{1 - [b(1 - t) - m]}A.$$

The Multiplier

The multiplier equals the change in equilibrium expenditure and real GDP (Y) that results from a change in autonomous expenditure (A) divided by the change in autonomous expenditure.

A change in autonomous expenditure (ΔA) changes equilibrium expenditure and real GDP by

$$\Delta Y = \frac{1}{1 - [b(1 - t) - m]}\Delta A.$$

$$\text{Multiplier} = \frac{1}{1 - [b(1 - t) - m]}.$$

The size of the multiplier depends on the slope of the AE curve, $b(1 - t) - m$. The larger the slope, the larger is the multiplier. So the multiplier is larger,

- The greater the marginal propensity to consume (b)
- The smaller the marginal tax rate (t)
- The smaller the marginal propensity to import (m)

An economy with no imports and no income taxes has $m = 0$ and $t = 0$. In this special case, the multiplier equals $1/(1 - b)$. If b is 0.75, then the multiplier is 4, as shown in Fig. 3.

In an economy with imports and income taxes, if $b = 0.75$, $t = 0.2$, and $m = 0.1$, the multiplier equals 1 divided by $[1 - 0.75(1 - 0.2) + 0.1]$, which equals 2. Make up some more examples to show the effects of b, t, and m on the multiplier.

Figure 2 Equilibrium expenditure

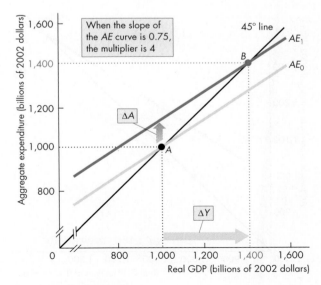

Figure 3 The multiplier

Government Expenditure Multiplier

The **government expenditure multiplier** equals the change in equilibrium expenditure (Y) that results from a change in government expenditure (G) divided by the change in government expenditure. Because autonomous expenditure is equal to

$$A = a - bT_a + I + G + X,$$

the change in autonomous expenditure equals the change in government expenditure. That is,

$$\Delta A = \Delta G.$$

You can see from the solution for equilibrium expenditure Y that

$$\Delta Y = \frac{1}{1 - [b(1 - t) - m]} \Delta G.$$

The government expenditure multiplier equals

$$\frac{1}{1 - [b(1 - t) - m]}.$$

In an economy in which $t = 0$ and $m = 0$, the government expenditure multiplier is $1/(1 - b)$. With $b = 0.75$, the government expenditure multiplier is 4, as Fig. 4 shows. Make up some examples and use the above formula to show how b, m, and t influence the government expenditure multiplier.

Autonomous Tax Multiplier

The **autonomous tax multiplier** equals the change in equilibrium expenditure (Y) that results from a change in autonomous taxes (T_a) divided by the change in autonomous taxes. Because autonomous expenditure is equal to

$$A - a - bT_a + I + G + X,$$

the change in autonomous expenditure equals minus b multiplied by the change in autonomous taxes. That is,

$$\Delta A = -b\Delta T_a.$$

You can see from the solution for equilibrium expenditure Y that

$$\Delta Y = \frac{-b}{1 - [b(1 - t) - m]} \Delta T_a.$$

The autonomous tax multiplier equals

$$\frac{-b}{1 - [b(1 - t) - m]}.$$

In an economy in which $t = 0$ and $m = 0$, the autonomous tax multiplier is $-b/(1 - b)$. In this special case, with $b = 0.75$, the autonomous tax multiplier equals -3, as Fig. 5 shows. Make up some examples and use the above formula to show how b, m, and t influence the autonomous tax multiplier.

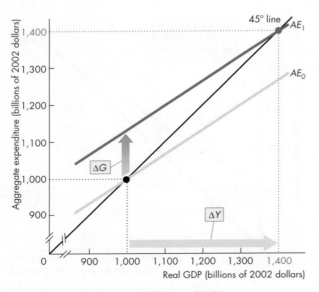

Figure 4 Government expenditure multiplier

Figure 5 Autonomous tax multiplier

Balanced Budget Multiplier

The **balanced budget multiplier** equals the change in equilibrium expenditure (Y) that results from equal changes in government expenditure and autonomous taxes divided by the change in government expenditure. Because government expenditure and autonomous taxes change by the same amount, the budget balance does not change.

The change in equilibrium expenditure that results from the change in government expenditure is

$$\Delta Y = \frac{1}{1 - [b(1 - t) - m]}\Delta G.$$

And the change in equilibrium expenditure that results from the change in autonomous taxes is

$$\Delta Y = \frac{-b}{1 - [b(1 - t) - m]}\Delta T_a.$$

So the change in equilibrium expenditure resulting from the changes in government expenditure and autonomous taxes is

$$\Delta Y = \frac{1}{1 - [b(1 - t) - m]}\Delta G +$$

$$\frac{-b}{1 - [b(1 - t) - m]}\Delta T_a.$$

Notice that

$$\frac{1}{1 - [b(1 - t) - m]}$$

is common to both terms on the right side. So we can rewrite the equation as

$$\Delta Y = \frac{1}{1 - [b(1 - t) - m]}(\Delta G - b\Delta T_a)$$

The AE curve shifts upward by $\Delta G - b\Delta T_a$, as shown in Fig. 6.

But the change in government expenditure equals the change in autonomous taxes. That is,

$$\Delta G = \Delta T_a.$$

And

$$\Delta Y = \frac{1 - b}{1 - [b(1 - t) - m]}\Delta G.$$

The balanced budget multiplier equals

$$\frac{1 - b}{1 - [b(1 - t) - m]}.$$

In an economy in which $t = 0$ and $m = 0$, the balanced budget multiplier is $(1 - b)/(1 - b)$, which equals 1, as Fig. 6 shows. Make up some examples and use the above formula to show how b, m, and t influence the balanced budget multiplier.

Figure 6 Balanced budget multiplier

SUMMARY

Key Points

Fixed Prices and Expenditure Plans (pp. 650–653)

- When the price level is fixed, expenditure plans determine real GDP.
- Consumption expenditure is determined by disposable income, and the marginal propensity to consume (*MPC*) determines the change in consumption expenditure brought about by a change in disposable income. Real GDP determines disposable income.
- Imports are determined by real GDP, and the marginal propensity to import determines the change in imports brought about by a change in real GDP.

Real GDP with a Fixed Price Level (pp. 654–657)

- Aggregate *planned* expenditure depends on real GDP.
- Equilibrium expenditure occurs when aggregate planned expenditure equals actual expenditure and real GDP.

The Multiplier (pp. 658–662)

- The multiplier is the magnified effect of a change in autonomous expenditure on equilibrium expenditure and real GDP.

- The multiplier is determined by the slope of the *AE* curve.
- The slope of the *AE* curve is influenced by the marginal propensity to consume, the marginal propensity to import, and the income tax rate.

The Multiplier and the Price Leve (pp. 663–667)

- The *AD* curve is the relationship between the quantity of real GDP demanded and the price level, other things remaining the same.
- The *AE* curve is the relationship between aggregate planned expenditure and real GDP, other things remaining the same.
- At a given price level, there is a given *AE* curve. A change in the price level changes aggregate planned expenditure and shifts the *AE* curve. A change in the price level also creates a movement along the *AD* curve.
- A change in autonomous expenditure that is not caused by a change in the price level shifts the *AE* curve and shifts the *AD* curve. The magnitude of the shift of the *AD* curve depends on the multiplier and on the change in autonomous expenditure.
- The multiplier decreases as the price level changes, and the multiplier in the long run is zero.

Key Figures

Figure 27.1   Consumption Function and Saving Function, 651

Figure 27.2   The Marginal Propensities to Consume and Save, 652

Figure 27.3   Aggregate Planned Expenditure: The *AE* Curve, 655

Figure 27.4   Equilibrium Expenditure, 656

Figure 27.5   The Multiplier, 659

Figure 27.6   The Multiplier and the Slope of the *AE* Curve, 660

Figure 27.7   The Multiplier Process, 661

Figure 27.8   Equilibrium Expenditure and Aggregate Demand, 664

Figure 27.9   A Change in Aggregate Demand, 665

Figure 27.10   The Multiplier in the Short Run, 666

Figure 27.11   The Multiplier in the Long Run, 667

Key Terms

Aggregate planned expenditure, 650

Autonomous expenditure, 654

Autonomous tax multiplier 672

Balanced budget multiplier, 673

Consumption function, 650

Disposable income, 650

Equilibrium expenditure, 656

Government expenditure multiplier, 672

Induced expenditure, 654

Marginal propensity to consume, 652

Marginal propensity to import, 653

Marginal propensity to save, 652

Multiplier, 658

Saving function, 650

PROBLEMS and APPLICATIONS

myeconlab Work problems 1–8 in Chapter 27 Study Plan and get instant feedback.
Work problems 9–14 as Homework, a Quiz, or a Test if assigned by your instructor.

1. You are given the following information about the economy of the United Kingdom.

Disposable income	Consumption expenditure
(billions of pounds per year)	
300	340
400	420
500	500
600	580
700	660

   a. Calculate the marginal propensity to consume.
   b. Calculate saving at each level of disposable income.
   c. Calculate the marginal propensity to save.

2. The figure illustrates the components of aggregate planned expenditure on Turtle Island. Turtle Island has no imports or exports, the people pay no incomes taxes, and the price level is fixed.

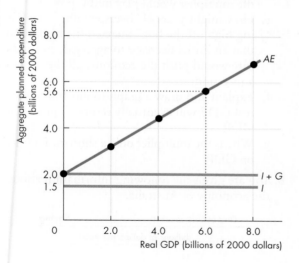

   a. Calculate autonomous expenditure and the marginal propensity to consume.
   b. What is aggregate planned expenditure when real GDP is $6 billion?
   c. If real GDP is $4 billion, what is happening to inventories?
   d. If real GDP is $6 billion, what is happening to inventories?
   e. Calculate the multiplier.

3. You are given the following information about the Canadian economy: Autonomous consumption expenditure is $50 billion, investment is $200 billion, and government expenditure is $250 billion. The marginal propensity to consume is 0.7 and net taxes are $250 billion—net taxes are assumed to be constant and not vary with income. Exports are $500 billion and imports are $450 billion.

   a. What is the consumption function?
   b. What is the equation of the *AE* curve?
   c. Calculate equilibrium expenditure.
   d. Calculate the multiplier.
   e. If investment decreases to $150 billion, what is the change in equilibrium expenditure?
   f. Describe the process in e that moves the economy to its new equilibrium expenditure.

4. Suppose that the economy is at full employment, the price level is 100, and the multiplier is 2. Investment increases by $100 billion.

   a. What is the change in equilibrium expenditure if the price level remains at 100?
   b. What is the immediate change in the quantity of real GDP demanded?
   c. Compare the increase in real GDP in the short run with the increase in the quantity of real GDP demanded in b.
   d. In the short run, does the price level remain at 100? Explain why or why not.
   e. Compare the increase in real GDP in the long run with the increase in the quantity of real GDP demanded in b.
   f. Explain how the price level changes in the long run.
   g. Are the values of the multipliers in the short run and the long run larger or smaller than 2?

5. **Canada's Harper Says Sales Tax Cut Likely the Last**

   Canadian Prime Minister Stephen Harper said on Monday that a New Year's Day cut to the country's sales tax will likely be the last. The one percentage point cut to the federal goods and services tax (GST) will ... [cut] the much-hated tax down to 5 percent ... Harper said the cut will bring $6 billion in tax relief for Canadians in 2008. The GST ... was at 7 percent before Harper's government took power in 2006... the move has proved popular with voters, and the Canadian Federation of Independent Business said on Monday the tax reduction will "provide a much-needed boost to the Canadian economy ... at a time when sales are traditionally sluggish in many sectors."

Reuters, December 31, 2007

a. Will the effect on aggregate expenditure of a cut in GST of $6 billion likely be larger or smaller than $6 billion? Explain.
b. Explain and draw graphs to illustrate how the GST cut will influence aggregate expenditure and aggregate demand in both the short run and the long run.

6. **The U.S. and China's Savings Problems**

Last year China saved about half of its gross domestic product. ... At the same time, the U.S. saved only 13 percent of its national income. ... And that's just looking at national averages that include saving by consumers, businesses, and governments. The contrast is even starker at the household level—a personal saving rate in China of about 30 percent of household income, compared with a U.S. rate that dipped into negative territory last year (–0.4% of after-tax household income). ... Similar extremes show up in the consumption shares of the two economies. ...

Fortune, March 8, 2006

Compare the *MPC* and *MPS* in China and the United States. Why might they differ?

7. **The Debt Demon**

... [T]he Conference Board predicts decent 2.2% growth for Canada—thanks to Canadians who love to spend and are undaunted about the misery their American cousins are suffering as families lose homes and life savings. "Canada's household sector seems oblivious to the concerns that the slowdown will spread north," said [economist Pedro] Antunes. ... Now, here's a warning: South of the border, our American cousins are learning a brutal lesson, after living high off the hog to let personal savings rates plunge to lows not seen since the Great Depression, while total household debt skyrocketed to trillions. ... Here in Canada, we're going down the same dark path

of overspending with household debt now at a record $1.1 trillion, which equates to more than 110% of personal disposable income. So far, rising real estate prices have kept many families afloat, especially for those who've borrowed against home equity to prop up their lifestyles. Now is the time to shed debt and set up an emergency fund. Not spend more.

Canoe Money, April 8, 2008

a. Explain and draw a graph to illustrate how the U.S. slowdown can "spread north" and influence aggregate planned expenditure.
b. Starting from equilibrium expenditure, why might aggregate planned expenditure and actual aggregate expenditure become unequal in this situation?
c. If actual aggregate expenditure and aggregate planned expenditure become unequal, how will they return to equilibrium expenditure?
d. Explain and draw a graph to illustrate the process by which Canada could be driven into a recession if consumers follow the advice offered at the end of this article. Explain the role that the multiplier would play in this process.
e. How might years of "overspending" and "living high off the hog" increase the likelihood that an initial decrease in aggregate expenditure would push the economy all the way into a recession?
f. Explain and draw a graph to illustrate how real GDP will eventually return to potential GDP.
g. Why is the multiplier only a short-run influence on GDP?

8. You are given the following information about the economy of Australia.

Disposable income	Saving
(billions of dollars per year)	
0	–5
100	20
200	45
300	70
400	95

a. Calculate the marginal propensity to save.
b. Calculate consumption at each level of disposable income.
c. Calculate the marginal propensity to consume.

9. The spreadsheet lists the components of aggregate planned expenditure in the United Kingdom. The numbers are in billions of pounds.

	A	B	C	D	E	F	G
1		Y	C	I	G	X	M
2	A	100	110	50	60	60	15
3	B	200	170	50	60	60	30
4	C	300	230	50	60	60	45
5	D	400	290	50	60	60	60
6	E	500	350	50	60	60	75
7	F	600	410	50	60	60	90

a. Calculate autonomous expenditure.
b. Calculate the marginal propensity to consume.
c. What is aggregate planned expenditure when real GDP is 200 billion pounds?
d. If real GDP is 200 billion pounds, what is happening to inventories?
e. If real GDP is 500 billion pounds, what is happening to inventories?
f. Calculate the multiplier.

10 **Does Canada Have a Household Debt Problem?**

Household spending has been rising at a significantly faster rate than household income ever since 1990. ... Canada's personal saving rate is now a negligible 1%, having steadily declined from 10% in 1990. ... Households have taken on a lot of debt, increasing their consumption through credit despite generally stagnant real incomes. Roughly the bottom 80% of households experienced little or no growth of real income from 1992 to 2002.

Progressive Economics Forum, February 14, 2008

a. What do the facts reported in this article imply about changes in the *MPC* and *MPS*?
b. Explain and use graphs to illustrate how the consumption function and saving function have changed in Canada since the early 1990s.
c. Is it possible for the personal saving rate to become negative?
d. Is a negative personal saving rate sustainable in the long run?

11. **Housing Prices and Consumer Spending**

The likely adverse effects on consumer spending and the aggregate economy of a significant downturn in house prices are an ongoing concern for policymakers.

Movements in house prices can affect consumer spending in two ways: through a direct wealth effect ... or through a collateral effect, by allowing greater access to credit. ... Households perceive their houses as wealth, and base their spending decisions in part on movements in net wealth positions. As well, if access to credit for some consumers is contingent on their housing wealth or equity, these credit-constrained households will be able to borrow and spend more, based on an increase in the collateral value of their homes. ... The effect of housing wealth on consumption may be larger than the effect from other forms of wealth. ... Households may view some forms of wealth as more uncertain and since house prices are typically less volatile than stock prices, households may view gains in housing wealth as more permanent. ...

Bank of Canada Review, Summer 2008

a. Explain and draw a graph to illustrate how increasing housing values can impact the consumption function and saving function.
b. Explain and draw aggregate expenditure and aggregate demand models to illustrate why a significant downturn in housing values would be a concern for an economy in the short run.
c. Explain and draw a graph to illustrate the long-run impact from b.
d. Why might the *MPC* depend upon the actual source of income and wealth changes, as opposed to being identical for all influences on income and wealth?

12. **We're Juggling Record Household Debt**

Canadians are juggling record debt loads averaging $80,000 per household including mortgage debt, says the author [Roger Sauvé] of a new report, and he warns job losses would push many families over a fiscal cliff. ... [Sauvé] describes a perfect storm of flat earnings, increased spending and plummeting savings. ... Total accumulated debt was 131 per cent of Canadian household income last year after income tax and transfers such as child benefits. That's up from 91 per cent in 1990, Sauvé says. Many consumers borrowed cash at lower interest rates to buy more expensive homes as real estate prices steadily rose. But many Canadians, especially those earning net middle incomes of about $60,000 a year, have racked up consumer debt that's almost doubled since 1990 to $22,500 from $12,000 on average, Sauvé says. "They've continued spending with more debt and less savings."

Toronto Star, February 12, 2008

a. Explain how lower interest rates and rising home values may have influenced the *MPC* and *MPS* in Canada and contributed to rising household debt.
b. Explain and use a graph to illustrate how combining job losses with the "perfect storm of flat earnings, increased spending and plummeting savings" has the potential to "push many families over a fiscal cliff" and ultimately cause a recession.
c. Why might consistently higher household saving rates make an economy less susceptible to being pushed into a recession by job losses?

13. **Survey Says Canadians Eager to Spend**

A new survey suggests Canadians could spend more money this holiday season than they did last year, despite recent widespread indications that consumer confidence has been rattled ... But Bruce Cran of the Consumers' Association of Canada said the bad economic news just keeps piling up and he has a hard time believing Canadians will be spending their way through the holiday season. ... A recent survey by the Conference Board of Canada found that consumer confidence fell in October to its lowest level in more than 25 years on dire global economic news. ... Deloitte said lower gas prices will mean a little more money in pockets. ... And the sagging loonie will mean more shopping at home, the survey suggested. ... "Compared to last year, when the Canadian dollar was at or above par leading up to the holiday season, we expect to see a significantly lower number of Canadians spending their holiday budget south of the border this year, which will help out our Canadian retailers," said [Deloitte's Bruce] Houlden. ...

According to the survey, shoppers in Toronto and Vancouver are the most likely to decrease their holiday spending this year.

CNEWS, November 11, 2008

a. What is induced consumption expenditure and what is autonomous consumption expenditure? Why isn't all consumption expenditure induced expenditure? What does the survey imply about how Canadian consumers view holiday expenditures?
b. Explain and draw a graph to illustrate Cran's predictions about how declining confidence will influence aggregate expenditure and aggregate demand in the short run.
c. Explain and draw a graph to illustrate the long-run effect on aggregate expenditure and aggregate demand of the decline in consumer confidence.
d. Explain and draw a graph to illustrate how the falling gas prices may impact aggregate expenditure and aggregate demand in the short run.
e. Explain how the depreciation of the Canadian dollar may impact the marginal propensity to import. How will this impact the multiplier effect from consumption expenditure?
f. Identify potential influences on consumption expenditure decisions that may be prompting the different spending patterns of Toronto and Vancouver consumers.

14. Study *Reading Between the Lines* on pp. 668–669 and then answer the following questions:

a. If the 2008 third quarter changes in inventories were mainly of planned changes, what role did they play in shifting the *AE* curve and changing equilibrium expenditure? Use a figure similar to that on p. 656 to answer this question.
b. If, as the news article reports, the world economy is slowing and Canadian exports stop growing, what will happen to the *AE* curve in future quarters and how will real GDP change?
c. What do you think will happen to real GDP, aggregate expenditure, and inventory investment in 2009? What clues do you get from the news article?

28 ◆ Canadian Inflation, Unemployment, and Business Cycle

After studying this chapter, you will be able to

- Explain how demand-pull and cost-push forces bring cycles in inflation and output

- Explain the short-run and long-run tradeoff between inflation and unemployment

- Explain how the mainstream business cycle theory and real businesses cycle theory account for fluctuations in output and employment

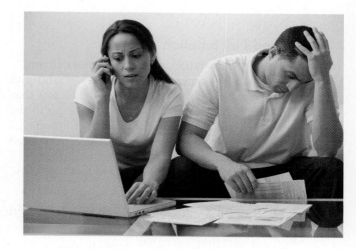

The 1920s were years of unprecedented prosperity for Canadians. After the horrors of the first World War (1914–1918), the economic machine was back at work producing such technological marvels as automobiles, airplanes, telephones, and vacuum cleaners. Houses were being built at a frantic pace. Then, in October 1929, the stock market crashed. Overnight, stock prices fell by 30 percent. The Great Depression had begun: By 1933, real GDP had fallen by 30 percent, the price level had fallen by 20 percent, and one person in five was unemployed.

The 1990s and 2000s were also years of unprecedented prosperity. Again, our lives were transformed by technological miracles: this time laptop computers, cell phones, large-format flat-panel video screens, and the Internet. Again,

homes, and especially city apartments, were built at a rapid pace. Then, in October 2008, stock prices tumbled, real GDP growth and inflation slowed, and the unemployment rate began to edge upward. People began to ask if we were on the verge of a new Great Depression.

We're going to use the *AS–AD* model that you studied in Chapter 26 and a related model, the Phillips curve, to explain the patterns in output, inflation, and unemployment. We then use the model of potential GDP that you studied in Chapter 22 to explain how business cycle fluctuations can arise without cost-push or aggregate demand forces.

In *Reading Between the Lines* at the end of the chapter, we examine the state of the Canadian economy in 2008 as the U.S economy slid into deeper recession.

Inflation Cycles

In the long run, inflation is a monetary phenomenon. It occurs if the quantity of money grows faster than potential GDP. But in the short run, many factors can start an inflation, and real GDP and the price level interact. To study these interactions, we distinguish between two sources of inflation:

- Demand-pull inflation
- Cost-push inflation

Demand-Pull Inflation

An inflation that starts because aggregate demand increases is called **demand-pull inflation**. Demand-pull inflation can be kicked off by *any* of the factors that change aggregate demand. Examples are a cut in the interest rate, an increase in the quantity of money, an increase in government expenditure, a tax cut, an increase in exports, or an increase in investment stimulated by an increase in expected future profits.

Initial Effect of an Increase in Aggregate Demand

Suppose that last year the price level was 110 and real GDP was $1,200 billion. Potential GDP was also $1,200 billion. Figure 28.1(a) illustrates this situation. The aggregate demand curve is AD_0, the short-run aggregate supply curve is SAS_0, and the long-run aggregate supply curve is LAS.

The Bank of Canada cuts the interest rate and increases the quantity of money and aggregate demand increases to AD_1. With no change in potential GDP and no change in the money wage rate, the long-run aggregate supply curve and the short-run aggregate supply curve remain at LAS and SAS_0, respectively.

The price level and real GDP are determined at the point where the aggregate demand curve AD_1 intersects the short-run aggregate supply curve. The price level rises to 113, and real GDP increases above potential GDP to $1,250 billion. Unemployment falls below its natural rate. The economy is at an above full-employment equilibrium and there is an inflationary gap. The next step in the unfolding story is a rise in the money wage rate.

FIGURE 28.1   A Demand-Pull Rise in the Price Level

(a) Initial effect

(b) The money wage adjusts

In part (a), the aggregate demand curve is AD_0, the short-run aggregate supply curve is SAS_0, and the long-run aggregate supply curve is LAS. The price level is 110, and real GDP is $1,200 billion, which equals potential GDP. Aggregate demand increases to AD_1. The price level rises to 113, and real GDP increases to $1,250 billion.

In part (b), starting from the above full-employment equilibrium, the money wage rate begins to rise and the short-run aggregate supply curve shifts leftward towards SAS_1. The price level rises further, and real GDP returns to potential GDP.

Money Wage Rate Response Real GDP cannot remain above potential GDP forever. With unemployment below its natural rate, there is a shortage of labour. In this situation, the money wage rate begins to rise. As it does so, short-run aggregate supply decreases and the *SAS* curve starts to shift leftward. The price level rises further, and real GDP begins to decrease.

With no further change in aggregate demand—that is, the aggregate demand curve remains at AD_1—this process ends when the short-run aggregate supply curve has shifted to SAS_1 in Fig. 28.1(b). At this time, the price level has increased to 121 and real GDP has returned to potential GDP of $1,200 billion, the level at which it started.

A Demand-Pull Inflation Process The events that we've just described bring a *one-time rise in the price level*, not an inflation. For inflation to proceed, aggregate demand must *persistently* increase.

The only way in which aggregate demand can persistently increase is if the quantity of money persistently increases. Suppose the government has a budget deficit that it finances by selling bonds. Also suppose that the Bank of Canada buys some of these bonds in the open market and creates more money. In this situation, aggregate demand increases year after year. The aggregate demand curve keeps shifting rightward. This persistent increase in aggregate demand puts continual upward pressure on the price level. The economy now experiences demand-pull inflation.

Figure 28.2 illustrates the process of demand-pull inflation. The starting point is the same as that shown in Fig. 28.1. The aggregate demand curve is AD_0, the short-run aggregate supply curve is SAS_0, and the long-run aggregate supply curve is *LAS*. Real GDP is $1,200 billion, and the price level is 110. Aggregate demand increases, shifting the aggregate demand curve to AD_1. Real GDP increases to $1,250 billion, and the price level rises to 113. The economy is at an above full-employment equilibrium. There is a shortage of labour, and the money wage rate rises. The short-run aggregate supply curve shifts to SAS_1. The price level rises to 121, and real GDP returns to potential GDP.

But the Bank of Canada increases the quantity of money again, and aggregate demand continues to increase. The aggregate demand curve shifts rightward to AD_2. The price level rises further to 125, and real GDP again exceeds potential GDP at

FIGURE 28.2   A Demand-Pull Inflation Spiral

Each time the quantity of money increases, aggregate demand increases and the aggregate demand curve shifts rightward from AD_0 to AD_1 to AD_2, and so on. Each time real GDP increases above potential GDP, the money wage rate rises and the short-run aggregate supply curve shifts leftward from SAS_0 to SAS_1 to SAS_2, and so on. The price level rises from 110 to 113, 121, 125, 133, and so on. There is a demand-pull inflation spiral. Real GDP fluctuates between $1,200 billion and $1,250 billion.

myeconlab   animation

$1,250 billion. Yet again, the money wage rate rises and decreases short-run aggregate supply. The *SAS* curve shifts to SAS_2, and the price level rises further, to 133. As the quantity of money continues to grow, aggregate demand increases and the price level rises in an ongoing demand-pull inflation process.

The process you have just studied generates inflation—an ongoing process of a rising price level.

Demand-Pull Inflation in Chatham You may better understand the inflation process that we've just described by considering what is going on in an individual part of the economy, such as a Chatham ketchup-bottling plant. Initially, when aggregate demand increases, the demand for ketchup increases and the price of ketchup rises. Faced with a higher price, the ketchup plant works overtime and increases production. Conditions are good for workers in Chatham, and the ketchup factory finds it hard to hang on to its best people. To do so, it offers a higher money wage rate. As the wage rate rises, so do the ketchup factory's costs.

What happens next depends on aggregate demand. If aggregate demand remains constant, the firm's costs increase but the price of ketchup does not increase as quickly as its costs. In this case, the firm cuts production. Eventually, the money wage rate and costs increase by the same percentage as the rise in the price of ketchup. In real terms, the ketchup factory is in the same situation as it was initially. It produces the same amount of ketchup and employs the same amount of labour as before the increase in demand.

But if aggregate demand continues to increase, so does the demand for ketchup, and the price of ketchup rises at the same rate as wages. The ketchup factory continues to operate at above full employment and there is a persistent shortage of labour. Prices and wages chase each other upward in a demand-pull inflation spiral.

Demand-Pull Inflation in Canada

A demand-pull inflation like the one you've just studied occurred in Canada during the late 1960s and early 1970s. In 1960, inflation was a moderate 2 percent a year, but its rate increased slowly through the mid-1960s. Then, between 1966 and 1969, the inflation rate surged upward. Inflation then decreased slightly during 1970 and 1971, but it took off again in 1972. By 1973, the inflation rate was almost 10 percent a year.

These increases in inflation resulted from increases in aggregate demand that had two main sources. The first was the large increase in U.S. government expenditures and in the quantity of money in the United States, which increased aggregate demand in the entire world economy. The second source was an increase in Canadian government expenditures and the quantity of money.

With the economy above full employment, the money wage rate started to rise more quickly and the *SAS* curve shifted leftward. The Bank of Canada responded with a further increase in the money growth rate, and a demand-pull inflation spiral unfolded. By 1974, the inflation rate had reached double digits.

Next, let's see how shocks to aggregate supply can create cost-push inflation.

Cost-Push Inflation

An inflation that is kicked off by an increase in costs is called **cost-push inflation**. The two main sources of cost increases are

1. An increase in the money wage rate
2. An increase in the money prices of raw materials

At a given price level, the higher the cost of production, the smaller is the amount that firms are willing to produce. So if the money wage rate rises or if the prices of raw materials (for example, oil) rise, firms decrease their supply of goods and services. Aggregate supply decreases, and the short-run aggregate supply curve shifts leftward.[1] Let's trace the effects of such a decrease in short-run aggregate supply on the price level and real GDP.

Initial Effect of a Decrease in Aggregate Supply

Suppose that last year the price level was 110 and real GDP was $1,200 billion. Potential real GDP was also $1,200 billion. Figure 28.3(a) illustrates this situation. The aggregate demand curve was AD_0, the short-run aggregate supply curve was SAS_0, and the long-run aggregate supply curve was *LAS*. In the current year, the world's oil producers form a price-fixing organization that strengthens their market power and increases the relative price of oil. They raise the price of oil, and this action decreases short-run aggregate supply. The short-run aggregate supply curve shifts leftward to SAS_1. The price level rises to 117, and real GDP decreases to $1,150 billion. The economy is at a below full-employment equilibrium and there is a recessionary gap.

This event is a *one-time rise in the price level*. It is not inflation. In fact, a supply shock on its own cannot cause inflation. Something more must happen to enable a one-time supply shock, which causes a one-time rise in the price level, to be converted into a process of ongoing inflation. The quantity of money must persistently increase. And it sometimes does increase, as you will now see.

---

[1] Some cost-push forces, such as an increase in the price of oil accompanied by a decrease in the availability of oil, can also decrease long-run aggregate supply. We'll ignore such effects here and examine cost-push factors that change only short-run aggregate supply. Later in the chapter, we study the effects of shocks to long-run aggregate supply.

FIGURE 28.3   A Cost-Push Rise in the Price Level

(a) Initial cost push

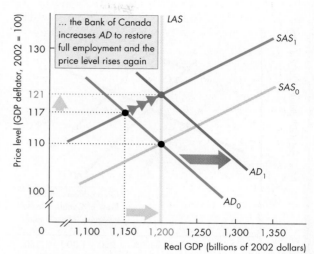

(b) The Bank of Canada responds

Initially, the aggregate demand curve is AD_0, the short-run aggregate supply curve is SAS_0, and the long-run aggregate supply curve is LAS. A decrease in aggregate supply (for example, resulting from a rise in the world price of oil) shifts the short-run aggregate supply curve to SAS_1. The economy moves to the point where the short-run aggregate supply curve SAS_1 intersects the aggregate demand curve

AD_0. The price level rises to 117, and real GDP decreases to $1,150 billion.

In part (b), if the Bank of Canada responds by increasing aggregate demand to restore full employment, the aggregate demand curve shifts rightward to AD_1. The economy returns to full employment, but the price level rises further to 121.

myeconlab animation

Aggregate Demand Response   When real GDP decreases, unemployment rises above its natural rate. In such a situation, there is often an outcry of concern and a call for action to restore full employment. Suppose that the Bank of Canada cuts the interest rate and increases the quantity of money. Aggregate demand increases. In Fig. 28.3(b), the aggregate demand curve shifts rightward to AD_1 and full employment is restored. But the price level rises further to 121.

A Cost-Push Inflation Process   The oil producers now see the prices of everything they buy increasing, so oil producers increase the price of oil again to restore its new high relative price. Figure 28.4 continues the story. The short-run aggregate supply curve now shifts to SAS_2. The price level rises and real GDP decreases.

The price level rises further, to 129, and real GDP decreases to $1,150 billion. Unemployment increases above its natural rate. If the Bank of Canada

responds yet again with an increase in the quantity of money, aggregate demand increases and the aggregate demand curve shifts to AD_2. The price level rises even higher—to 133—and full employment is again restored. A cost-push inflation spiral results. The combination of rising inflation and decreasing real GDP is **stagflation**.

You can see that the Bank of Canada has a dilemma. If it does not respond when producers raise the price of oil, the economy remains below full employment. If the Bank of Canada increases the quantity of money to restore full employment, it invites another oil price hike that will call forth yet a further increase in the quantity of money.

If the Bank of Canada responds to each oil price hike by increasing the quantity of money, inflation will rage along at a rate decided by oil producers. But if the Bank of Canada keeps the lid on money growth, the economy remains below full employment.

FIGURE 28.4   A Cost-Push Inflation Spiral

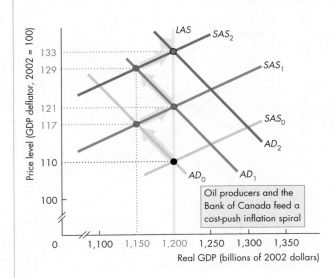

Each time a cost increase occurs, the short-run aggregate supply curve shifts leftward from SAS_0 to SAS_1 to SAS_2, and so on. Each time real GDP decreases below potential GDP, the Bank of Canada increases the quantity of money and the aggregate demand curve shifts rightward from AD_0 to AD_1 to AD_2, and so on. The price level rises from 110 to 117, 121, 129, 133, and so on. There is a cost-push inflation spiral. Real GDP fluctuates between $1,200 billion and $1,150 billion.

myeconlab animation

Cost-Push Inflation in Chatham
What is going on in the Chatham ketchup-bottling plant when the economy is experiencing cost-push inflation?

When the oil price increases, so do the costs of bottling ketchup. These higher costs decrease the supply of ketchup, increasing its price and decreasing the quantity produced. The ketchup plant lays off some workers.

This situation persists until either the Bank of Canada increases aggregate demand or the price of oil falls. If the Bank of Canada increases aggregate demand, the demand for ketchup increases and so does its price. The higher price of ketchup brings higher profits, and the bottling plant increases its production. The ketchup factory rehires the laid-off workers.

Cost-Push Inflation in Canada
A cost-push inflation like the one you've just studied occurred in Canada during the 1970s. It began in 1974 when the Organization of the Petroleum Exporting Countries (OPEC) pushed up the price of oil. The higher oil price decreased aggregate supply, which made the price level rise more quickly and made real GDP shrink. The Bank of Canada faced a dilemma: Would it accommodate the cost-push forces with money growth, or would it limit money growth to keep aggregate demand in check? From 1975 through 1977, the Bank of Canada allowed the quantity of money to grow quickly and inflation proceeded at a rapid rate. In 1979 and 1980, OPEC was again able to push oil prices higher. On that occasion, the Bank of Canada decided *not* to respond to the oil price hike with an increase in the quantity of money. The result was recession and, eventually, a fall in inflation.

Expected Inflation

If inflation is expected, the fluctuations in real GDP that accompany demand-pull and cost-push inflation that you've just studied don't occur. Instead, inflation proceeds with real GDP at potential GDP and unemployment at its natural rate. Figure 28.5 shows why.

Suppose that last year the aggregate demand curve was AD_0, the aggregate supply curve was SAS_0, and the long-run aggregate supply curve was LAS. The price level was 110, and real GDP was $1,200 billion, which is also potential GDP.

To keep things simple, suppose that potential GDP does not change, so the LAS curve doesn't shift. Also suppose that aggregate demand is *expected to increase* to AD_1.

In anticipation of this increase in aggregate demand, the money wage rate rises and the short-run aggregate supply curve shifts leftward. If the money wage rate rises by the same percentage as the price level is expected to rise, the short-run aggregate supply curve for next year is SAS_1.

If aggregate demand turns out to be the same as expected, the aggregate demand curve is AD_1. The short-run aggregate supply curve, SAS_1, and AD_1 determine the actual price level at 121. Between last year and this year, the price level increased from 110 to 121 and the economy experienced an inflation rate equal to that expected. If this inflation is ongoing, aggregate demand increases (as expected) in the

FIGURE 28.5 Expected Inflation

Potential real GDP is $1,200 billion. Last year, aggregate demand was AD_0 and the short-run aggregate supply curve was SAS_0. The actual price level was the same as the expected price level: 110. This year, aggregate demand is expected to increase to AD_1 and the price level is expected to rise from 110 to 121. As a result, the money wage rate rises and the short-run aggregate supply curve shifts to SAS_1.

If aggregate demand actually increases as expected, the actual aggregate demand curve AD_1 is the same as the expected aggregate demand curve. Real GDP is $1,200 billion, and the actual price level rises to 121. The inflation is expected.

Next year, the process continues with aggregate demand increasing as expected to AD_2 and the money wage rate rising to shift the short-run aggregate supply curve to SAS_2. Again, real GDP remains at $1,200 billion, and the price level rises, as expected, to 133.

 animation

following year and the aggregate demand curve shifts to AD_2. The money wage rate rises to reflect the expected inflation, and the short-run aggregate supply curve shifts to SAS_2. The price level rises, as expected, to 133.

What caused this inflation? The immediate answer is that because people expected inflation, the money wage rate increased and the price level increased. But the expectation was correct. Aggregate demand was expected to increase, and it did increase. The actual and expected increase in aggregate demand caused the inflation.

An expected inflation at full employment is exactly the process that the quantity theory of money

predicts. To review the quantity theory of money, see Chapter 24, pp. 582–583. This broader *AS–AD* model of inflation shows why the quantity theory of money doesn't explain the *fluctuations* in inflation. The economy follows the course described in Fig. 28.5, and as predicted by the quantity theory, only if aggregate demand growth is forecasted correctly.

Forecasting Inflation

To anticipate inflation, people must forecast it. Some economists who work for macroeconomic forecasting agencies, banks, insurance companies, labour unions, and large corporations specialize in inflation forecasting. The best forecast available is one that is based on all the relevant information and is called a **rational expectation**. A rational expectation is not necessarily a correct forecast. It is simply the best forecast with the information available. It will often turn out to be wrong, but no other forecast that could have been made with the information available could do better.

Inflation and the Business Cycle

When the inflation forecast is correct, the economy operates at full employment. If aggregate demand grows faster than expected, real GDP rises above potential GDP, the inflation rate exceeds its expected rate, and the economy behaves like it does in a demand-pull inflation. If aggregate demand grows more slowly than expected, real GDP falls below potential GDP and the inflation rate slows.

Review Quiz

1 How does demand-pull inflation begin?
2 What must happen to create a demand-pull inflation spiral?
3 How does cost-push inflation begin?
4 What must happen to create a cost-push inflation spiral?
5 What is stagflation and why does cost-push inflation cause stagflation?
6 How does expected inflation occur?
7 How do real GDP and the price level change if the forecast of inflation is incorrect?

 Work Study Plan 28.1 and get instant feedback.

Inflation and Unemployment: The Phillips Curve

Another way of studying inflation cycles focuses on the relationship and the short-run tradeoff between inflation and unemployment, a relationship called the **Phillips curve**—so named because it was first suggested by New Zealand economist A.W. Phillips.

Why do we need another way of studying inflation? What is wrong with the *AS–AD* explanation of the fluctuations in inflation and real GDP? The first answer to both questions is that we often want to study changes in both the expected and actual inflation rates, and for this purpose, the Phillips curve provides a simpler tool and clearer insights than the *AS–AD* model provides. The second answer to both questions is that we often want to study changes in the short-run tradeoff between inflation and real economic activity (real GDP and unemployment) and again, the Phillips curve serves this purpose well.

To begin our explanation of the Phillips curve, we distinguish between two time frames (similar to the two aggregate supply time frames). We study

- The short-run Phillips curve
- The long-run Phillips curve

The Short-Run Phillips Curve

The **short-run Phillips curve** shows the relationship between inflation and unemployment, holding constant

1. The expected inflation rate
2. The natural unemployment rate

You've just seen what determines the expected inflation rate. The natural unemployment rate and the factors that influence it are explained in Chapter 21, pp. 494–496.

Figure 28.6 shows a short-run Phillips curve, *SRPC*. Suppose that the expected inflation rate is 10 percent a year and the natural unemployment rate is 6 percent, point *A* in the figure. A short-run Phillips curve passes through this point. If inflation rises above its expected rate, unemployment falls below its natural rate. This joint movement in the inflation rate and the unemployment rate is illustrated as a movement up along the short-run Phillips curve from point *A* to point *B*. Similarly, if inflation falls below its expected rate, unemployment rises above its natural

FIGURE 28.6 A Short-Run Phillips Curve

The short-run Phillips curve (*SRPC*) shows the relationship between inflation and unemployment at a given expected inflation rate and a given natural unemployment rate. With an expected inflation rate of 10 percent a year and a natural unemployment rate of 6 percent, the short-run Phillips curve passes through point *A*.

With a given short-run aggregate supply curve, and starting at full employment, an increase in aggregate demand lowers unemployment and increases the inflation rate—a movement up along the short-run Phillips curve to point *B*; and a decrease in aggregate demand increases unemployment and lowers the inflation rate—a movement down along the short-run Phillips curve to point *C*.

myeconlab   animation

rate. In this case, there is movement down along the short-run Phillips curve from point *A* to point *C*.

The short-run Phillips curve is like the short-run aggregate supply curve. A movement along the *SAS* curve that brings a higher price level and an increase in real GDP is equivalent to a movement along the short-run Phillips curve from *A* to *B* that brings an increase in the inflation rate and a decrease in the unemployment rate.

Similarly, a movement along the *SAS* curve that brings a lower price level and a decrease in real GDP is equivalent to a movement along the short-run Phillips curve from *A* to *C* that brings a decrease in the inflation rate and an increase in the unemployment rate.

The Long-Run Phillips Curve

The **long-run Phillips curve** shows the relationship between inflation and unemployment when the actual inflation rate equals the expected inflation rate. The long-run Phillips curve is vertical at the natural unemployment rate. In Fig. 28.7, it is the vertical line *LRPC*.

The long-run Phillips curve tells us that any expected inflation rate is possible at the natural unemployment rate. This proposition is consistent with the *AS–AD* model, which predicts (and which Fig. 28.5 illustrates) that when inflation is expected, real GDP equals potential GDP and unemployment is at its natural rate.

The short-run Phillips curve intersects the long-run Phillips curve at the expected inflation rate. A change in the expected inflation rate shifts the short-run Phillips curve but it does not shift the long-run Phillips curve.

In Fig. 28.7, if the expected inflation rate is 10 percent a year, the short-run Phillips curve is $SRPC_0$.

If the expected inflation rate falls to 6 percent a year, the short-run Phillips curve shifts downward to $SRPC_1$. The vertical distance by which the short-run Phillips curve shifts from point *A* to point *D* is equal to the change in the expected inflation rate. If the actual inflation rate also falls from 10 percent to 6 percent, there is a movement down the long-run Phillips curve from *A* to *D*. An increase in the expected inflation rate has the opposite effect to that shown in Fig. 28.7.

The other source of a shift in the Phillips curve is a change in the natural unemployment rate.

Changes in the Natural Unemployment Rate

The natural unemployment rate changes for many reasons (see Chapter 21, pp. 494–496). A change in the natural unemployment rate shifts both the short-run and long-run Phillips curves. Figure 28.8 illustrates such shifts.

FIGURE 28.7 Short-Run and Long-Run Phillips Curve

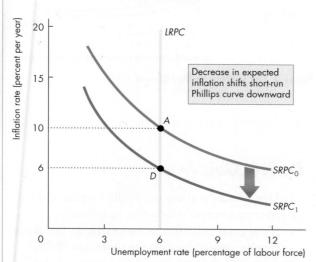

The long-run Phillips curve is *LRPC*. A fall in expected inflation from 10 percent a year to 6 percent a year shifts the short-run Phillips curve downward from $SRPC_0$ to $SRPC_1$. The long-run Phillips curve does not shift. The new short-run Phillips curve intersects the long-run Phillips curve at the new expected inflation rate—point *D*.

FIGURE 28.8 A Change in the Natural Unemployment Rate

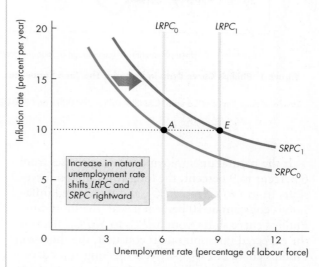

A change in the natural unemployment rate shifts both the short-run and long-run Phillips curves. An increase in the natural unemployment rate from 6 percent to 9 percent shifts the Phillips curves rightward to $SRPC_1$ and $LRPC_1$. The new long-run Phillips curve intersects the new short-run Phillips curve at the expected inflation rate—point *E*.

The Canadian Phillips Curve

The Shifting Short-Run Tradeoff

Figure 1 is a scatter diagram of the Canadian inflation rate (measured by the GDP deflator) and the unemployment rate since 1962. We can interpret the data in terms of the shifting short-run Phillips curve in Fig. 2.

During the 1960s, the short-run Phillips curve was $SRPC_0$, with a natural unemployment rate of 5 percent and an expected inflation rate of 2 percent a year (point A).

During the early 1970s, the short-run Phillips curve was $SRPC_1$, with a natural unemployment rate of 6 percent and an expected inflation rate of 10 percent a year (point B).

During the 1980s, the natural unemployment rate increased to 10 percent, the expected inflation rate fell to 8 percent (point C), and the short-run Phillips curve shifted to $SRPC_2$.

During the 1990s and 2000s, the expected inflation rate fell to 2 percent a year and and the natural unemployment rate decreased to 6 percent. The short-run Phillips curve shifted leftward to $SRPC_3$ and was almost back to $SRPC_0$, where it had been during the 1960s.

Figure 1 Phillips Curve Data in Canada: The Time Sequence

Figure 2 The Shifting Phillips Curves

Source of data: Statistics Canada, CANSIM Tables 380-0002 and 380-0056.

If the natural unemployment rate increases from 6 percent to 9 percent, the long-run Phillips curve shifts from $LRPC_0$ to $LRPC_1$, and if expected inflation is constant at 10 percent a year, the short-run Phillips curve shifts from $SRPC_0$ to $SRPC_1$. Because the expected inflation rate is constant, the short-run Phillips curve $SRPC_1$ intersects the long-run curve $LRPC_1$ (point E) at the same inflation rate at which the short-run Phillips curve $SRPC_0$ intersects the long-run curve $LRPC_0$ (point A).

Changes in both the expected inflation rate and the natural unemployment rate have shifted the Canadian Phillips curve but the expected inflation rate has had the greater effect.

Review Quiz

1 How would you use the Phillips curve to illustrate an unexpected change in inflation?

2 If the expected inflation rate increases by 10 percentage points, how do the short-run Phillips curve and the long-run Phillips curve change?

3 If the natural unemployment rate increases, what happens to the short-run Phillips curve and the long-run Phillips curve?

4 Does Canada have a stable short-run Phillips curve? Explain why or why not.

  Work Study Plan 28.2 and get instant feedback.

The Business Cycle

The business cycle is easy to describe but hard to explain and business cycle theory remains unsettled and a source of controversy. We'll look at two approaches to understanding the business cycle:

- Mainstream business cycle theory
- Real business cycle theory

Mainstream Business Cycle Theory

The mainstream business cycle theory is that potential GDP grows at a steady rate while aggregate demand grows at a fluctuating rate. Because the money wage rate is sticky, if aggregate demand grows faster than potential GDP, real GDP moves above potential GDP and an inflationary gap emerges. And if aggregate demand grows slower than potential GDP, real GDP moves below potential GDP and a recessionary gap emerges. If aggregate demand decreases, real GDP also decreases in a recession.

Figure 28.9 illustrates this business cycle theory. Initially, actual and potential GDP are $900 billion. The long-run aggregate supply curve is LAS_0, the aggregate demand curve is AD_0, and the price level is 110. The economy is at full employment at point A.

An expansion occurs when potential GDP increases and the LAS curve shifts rightward to LAS_1. During an expansion, aggregate demand also increases, and usually by more than potential GDP, so the price level rises. Assume that in the current expansion, the price level is expected to rise to 120 and that the money wage rate has been set on that expectation. The short-run aggregate supply curve is SAS_1.

If aggregate demand increases to AD_1, real GDP increases to $1,200 billion, the new level of potential GDP, and the price level rises, as expected, to 120. The economy remains at full employment but now at point B.

If aggregate demand increases more slowly to AD_2, real GDP grows by less than potential GDP and the economy moves to point C, with real GDP at $1,150 billion and the price level at 117. Real GDP growth is slower and inflation is lower than expected.

If aggregate demand increases more quickly to AD_3, real GDP grows by more than potential GDP and the economy moves to point D, with real GDP at $1,250 billion and the price level at 123. Real GDP growth is faster and inflation is higher than expected.

Growth, inflation, and the business cycle arise from the relentless increases in potential GDP, faster (on average) increases in aggregate demand, and fluctuations in the pace of aggregate demand growth.

FIGURE 28.9 The Mainstream Business Cycle Theory

In a business cycle expansion, potential GDP increases and the LAS curve shifts rightward from LAS_0 to LAS_1. A greater-than-expected increase in aggregate demand brings inflation.

If the aggregate demand curve shifts to AD_1, the economy remains at full employment. If the aggregate demand curve shifts to AD_2, a recessionary gap arises. If the aggregate demand curve shifts to AD_3, an inflationary gap arises.

This mainstream theory comes in a number of special forms that differ regarding the source of fluctuations in aggregate demand growth and the source of money wage stickiness.

Keynesian Cycle Theory In **Keynesian cycle theory**, fluctuations in investment driven by fluctuations in business confidence—summarized by the phrase "animal spirits"—are the main source of fluctuations in aggregate demand.

Monetarist Cycle Theory In **monetarist cycle theory**, fluctuations in both investment and consumption expenditure, driven by fluctuations in the growth rate of the quantity of money, are the main source of fluctuations in aggregate demand.

Both the Keynesian and monetarist cycle theories simply assume that the money wage rate is rigid and don't explain that rigidity.

Two newer theories seek to explain money wage rate rigidity and to be more careful about working out its consequences.

New Classical Cycle Theory In **new classical cycle theory**, the rational expectation of the price level, which is determined by potential GDP and *expected* aggregate demand, determines the money wage rate and the position of the *SAS* curve. In this theory, only *unexpected* fluctuations in aggregate demand bring fluctuations in real GDP around potential GDP.

New Keynesian Cycle Theory The **new Keynesian cycle theory** emphasizes the fact that today's money wage rates were negotiated at many past dates, which means that *past* rational expectations of the current price level influence the money wage rate and the position of the *SAS* curve. In this theory, both unexpected and currently expected fluctuations in aggregate demand bring fluctuations in real GDP around potential GDP.

The mainstream cycle theories don't rule out the possibility that occasionally an aggregate supply shock might occur. An oil price rise, a widespread drought, a major hurricane, or another natural disaster could, for example, bring a recession. But supply shocks are not the normal source of fluctuations in the mainstream theories. In contrast, real business cycle theory puts supply shocks at centre stage.

Real Business Cycle Theory

The newest theory of the business cycle, known as **real business cycle theory** (or RBC theory), regards random fluctuations in productivity as the main source of economic fluctuations. These productivity fluctuations are assumed to result mainly from fluctuations in the pace of technological change, but they might also have other sources, such as international disturbances, climate fluctuations, or natural disasters. The origins of RBC theory can be traced to the rational expectations revolution set off by Robert E. Lucas, Jr., but the first demonstrations of the power of this theory were given by Edward Prescott and Finn Kydland and by John Long and Charles Plosser. Today, RBC theory is part of a broad research agenda called dynamic general equilibrium analysis, and hundreds of young macroeconomists do research on this topic.

We'll explore RBC theory by looking first at its impulse and then at the mechanism that converts that impulse into a cycle in real GDP.

The RBC Impulse The impulse in RBC theory is the growth rate of productivity that results from technological change. RBC theorists believe this impulse to be generated mainly by the process of research and development that leads to the creation and use of new technologies.

To isolate the RBC theory impulse, economists use growth accounting, which is explained in Chapter 22, p. 528. Figure 28.10 shows the RBC impulse for Canada from 1962 through 2007. You can see that fluctuations in productivity growth are correlated with real GDP fluctuations.

Most of the time, technological change is steady and productivity grows at a moderate pace. But sometimes productivity growth speeds up, and occasionally productivity *decreases*—labour becomes less productive, on average. A period of rapid productivity growth brings a business cycle expansion, and a *decrease* in productivity triggers a recession.

It is easy to understand why technological change brings productivity growth. But how does it *decrease* productivity? All technological change eventually increases productivity. But if initially, technological change makes a sufficient amount of existing capital—especially human capital—obsolete, productivity temporarily decreases. At such a time, more jobs are destroyed than created and more businesses fail than start up.

FIGURE 28.10 The Real Business Cycle Impulse

The real business cycle is caused by changes in technology that bring fluctuations in the growth rate of productivity. The fluctuations in productivity growth shown here are calculated by using growth accounting to remove the contribution of capital accumulation to productivity growth. Productivity fluctuations are correlated with real GDP fluctuations. Economists are not sure what the productivity variable actually measures or what causes it to fluctuate.

Sources of data: Statistics Canada, CANSIM Table 380-0002 and Centre for the Study of Living Standards (www.csls.ca/data/ipt1.asp).

myeconlab animation

The RBC Mechanism Two effects follow from a change in productivity that gets an expansion or a contraction going:

1. Investment demand changes.
2. The demand for labour changes.

We'll study these effects and their consequences during a recession. In an expansion, they work in the direction opposite to what is described here.

Technological change makes some existing capital obsolete and temporarily decreases productivity. Firms expect their future profits to fall and see their labour productivity falling. With lower profit expectations, they cut back their purchases of new capital, and with lower labour productivity, they plan to lay off some workers. So the initial effect of a temporary fall in productivity is a decrease in investment demand and a decrease in the demand for labour.

Figure 28.11 illustrates these two initial effects of a decrease in productivity. Part (a) shows the effects of a decrease in investment demand in the loanable funds market. The demand for loanable funds is DLF and the supply of loanable funds is SLF (both of

which are explained in Chapter 23, pp. 548–554). Initially, the demand for loanable funds is DLF_0 and the equilibrium quantity of funds is $200 billion at a real interest rate of 6 percent a year. A decrease in productivity decreases investment demand, and the demand for loanable funds curve DLF shifts leftward to DLF_1. The real interest rate falls to 4 percent a year, and the equilibrium quantity of loanable funds decreases to $170 billion.

Figure 28.11(b) shows the demand for labour curve LD and the supply of labour curve LS (which are explained in Chapter 22, pp. 521–522). Initially, the demand for labour curve is LD_0, and equilibrium employment is 20 billion hours a year at a real wage rate of $35 an hour. The decrease in productivity decreases the demand for labour, and the LD curve shifts leftward to LD_1.

Before we can determine the new level of employment and real wage rate, we need to take a ripple effect into account—the key effect in RBC theory.

The Key Decision: When to Work? According to RBC theory, people decide *when* to work by doing a cost-benefit calculation. They compare the return from

FIGURE 28.11 Loanable Funds and Labour Markets in a Real Business Cycle

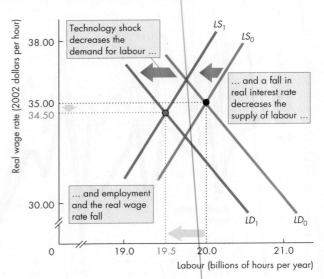

(a) **Loanable funds and interest rate**

(b) **Labour and wage rate**

In part (a), the supply of loanable funds *SLF* and initial demand for loanable funds *DLF*$_0$ determine the real interest rate at 6 percent a year. In part (b), the initial demand for labour, *LD*$_0$, and supply of labour, *LS*$_0$, determine the real wage rate at $35 an hour and employment at 20 billion hours. A technological change temporarily decreases productivity, and both the demand for loanable funds and the

demand for labour decrease. The two demand curves shift leftward to *DLF*$_1$ and *LD*$_1$. In part (a), the real interest rate falls to 4 percent a year. In part (b), the fall in the real interest rate decreases the supply of labour (the when-to-work decision) and the supply of labour curve shifts leftward to *LS*$_1$. Employment decreases to 19.5 billion hours, and the real wage rate falls to $34.50 an hour. A recession is underway.

 myeconlab animation

working in the current period with the *expected* return from working in a later period. You make such a comparison every day in school. Suppose your goal in this course is to get an A. To achieve this goal, you work hard most of the time. But during the few days before the midterm and final exams, you work especially hard. Why? Because you believe that the return from studying close to the exam is greater than the return from studying when the exam is a long time away. So during the term, you take time off for movies and other leisure pursuits, but at exam time, you study every evening and weekend.

RBC theory says that workers behave like you. They work fewer hours, sometimes zero hours, when the real wage rate is temporarily low, and they work more hours when the real wage rate is temporarily high. But to properly compare the current wage rate with the expected future wage rate, workers must use

the real interest rate. If the real interest rate is 6 percent a year, a real wage of $1 an hour earned this week will become $1.06 a year from now. If the real wage rate is expected to be $1.05 an hour next year, today's real wage of $1 looks good. By working longer hours now and shorter hours a year from now, a person can get a 1 percent higher real wage. But suppose the real interest rate is 4 percent a year. In this case, $1 earned now is worth $1.04 next year. Working fewer hours now and more next year is the way to get a 1 percent higher real wage.

So the when-to-work decision depends on the real interest rate. The lower the real interest rate, other things remaining the same, the smaller is the supply of labour today. Many economists believe this *intertemporal substitution* effect to be of negligible size. RBC theorists believe that the effect is large, and it is the key feature of the RBC mechanism.

You saw in Fig. 28.11(a) that the decrease in the demand for loanable funds lowers the real interest rate. This fall in the real interest rate lowers the return from current work and decreases the supply of labour.

In Fig. 28.11(b), the labour supply curve shifts leftward to LS_1. The effect of the decrease in productivity on the demand for labour is larger than the effect of the fall in the real interest rate on the supply of labour. That is, the LD curve shifts farther leftward than does the LS curve. As a result, the real wage rate falls to $34.50 an hour and employment decreases to 19.5 billion hours. A recession has begun and is intensifying.

What Happened to Money?

The name *real* business cycle theory is no accident. It reflects the central prediction of the theory. Real things, not nominal or monetary things, cause the business cycle. If the quantity of money changes, aggregate demand changes. But if there is no real change—with no change in the use of resources and no change in potential GDP—the change in the quantity of money changes only the price level. In RBC theory, this outcome occurs because the aggregate supply curve is the LAS curve, which pins real GDP down at potential GDP, so when aggregate demand changes, only the price level changes.

Cycles and Growth

The shock that drives the business cycle of RBC theory is the same as the force that generates economic growth: technological change. On average, as technology advances, productivity grows. But it grows at an uneven pace. You saw this fact when you studied growth accounting in Chapter 22, p. 528. There, we focused on slow-changing trends in productivity growth. RBC theory uses the same idea but says that there are frequent shocks to productivity that are mostly positive but that are occasionally negative.

Criticisms and Defences of RBC Theory

The three main criticisms of RBC theory are that (1) the money wage rate *is* sticky, and to assume otherwise is at odds with a clear fact; (2) intertemporal substitution is too weak a force to account for large fluctuations in labour supply and employment with small real wage rate changes; and (3) productivity shocks are as likely to be caused by *changes in aggregate demand* as by technological change.

If aggregate demand fluctuations cause the fluctuations in productivity, then the traditional aggregate demand theories are needed to explain them. Fluctuations in productivity do not cause the business cycle but are caused by it!

Building on this theme, the critics point out that the so-called productivity fluctuations that growth accounting measures are correlated with changes in the growth rate of money and other indicators of changes in aggregate demand.

The defenders of RBC theory claim that the theory explains the macroeconomic facts about the business cycle and is consistent with the facts about economic growth. In effect, a single theory explains *both growth and the business cycle*. The growth accounting exercise that explains the slowly changing trends also explains the more frequent business cycle swings. Its defenders also claim that RBC theory is consistent with a wide range of *micro*economic evidence about labour supply decisions, labour demand and investment demand decisions, and information on the distribution of income between labour and capital.

Review Quiz

1 Explain the mainstream theory of the business cycle.
2 What are the four versions of the mainstream theory and how do they differ?
3 What, according to RBC theory, is the source of the business cycle?
4 According to RBC theory, how does a fall in productivity growth influence investment demand, the market for loanable funds, the real interest rate, the demand for labour, the supply of labour, employment, and the real wage rate?
5 What are the main criticisms of RBC theory and how do its supporters defend it?

 Work Study Plan 28.3 and get instant feedback.

◆ To complete your study of economic fluctuations, take a look at the next two pages, where you will find an account of the Great Depression and an assessment of its possible return. Also, study *Reading Between the Lines* on pp. 696–697, which compares job losses in Canada and the United States during the 2007–2008 financial crisis and slowdown.

The Great Depression

From Recession to Deep Depression

The late 1920s were years of economic boom. New houses and apartments were built on an unprecedented scale, new firms were created, and the capital stock expanded. At the beginning of 1929, Canadian real GDP exceeded potential GDP and the unemployment rate was a low 2.9 percent. But the four years that followed saw a monstrous depression.

In a normal recession, the economy remains below full employment for a year or so and then starts to expand. But the recession of 1930 was not a normal one. In 1930 and the following two years, the economy was bombarded with huge negative aggregate demand shocks.

Why the Great Depression Happened

The late 1920s were years of economic boom, but they were also years of change and uncertainty. On the international scene, the patterns of world trade were changing, with Britain, the traditional economic powerhouse, in decline, and new powers, notably the United States and Japan, on the rise. Exchange rates fluctuated widely and some countries embarked on protectionist trade policies. On the domestic scene, uncertainty arose from the knowledge that the investment and housing boom couldn't last forever.

This environment of uncertainty led to a slow-down in consumer spending, especially on new homes and household appliances. By the fall of 1929, the uncertainty had reached a critical level and contributed to a major stock market crash. The stock market crash, in turn, heightened people's fears about economic prospects in the foreseeable future. Fear fed fear. Investment collapsed. The building industry almost disappeared. An industry that had been operating flat out just two years earlier was now building virtually no new houses and apartments. It was this drop in investment and the drop in consumer spending on durables that led to the initial decrease in aggregate demand.

At this stage, what became the Great Depression was no worse than many previous recessions had been. What distinguished the Great Depression from previous recessions were the events that occurred in the United States between 1930 and 1933. But economists, even to this day, have not come to agreement on how to interpret those events.

Nobel Laureate Milton Friedman and his co-researcher Anna J. Schwartz have argued that the contraction that turned recession into depression resulted from the worsening of financial and monetary conditions. Bank failures and a severe cut in the money supply lowered aggregate demand, prolonged the contraction, and deepened the depression.

Peter Temin has argued that spending continued to fall for a wide variety of reasons, including a continuation of increasing pessimism and uncertainty, but not from a collapse in the quantity of money.

It is a fact that the quantity of money fell: Between 1930 and 1933, it fell by 20 percent. This decrease in the quantity of money was not directly induced by the U.S. Fed's actions. The monetary base (currency in circulation and bank reserves) hardly fell at all, but the bank-deposits component of the money supply suffered an enormous collapse. It did so primarily because a large number of banks failed. Before the Great Depression, fuelled by increasing stock prices and booming business conditions, bank loans expanded. But after the stock market crash and the downturn, many borrowers found themselves in hard economic times. They could not pay the interest on their loans, and they could not meet their agreed repayment schedules. Bank deposits exceeded the value of the loans that the banks had made. When depositors withdrew funds from the banks, the banks lost reserves. Many of them simply couldn't meet their depositors' demands to be repaid.

Bank failures feed on themselves and create additional failures. Seeing banks fail, people become anxious to protect themselves and so take their money out of the bank. Such were the events of 1930. The quantity of notes and coins in circulation increased, and the volume of bank deposits declined. But the very action of taking money out of the bank to protect one's wealth accentuated the process of banking failure. Banks were increasingly short of cash and unable to meet their obligations.

What role did the stock market crash of 1929 play in producing the Great Depression? The crash certainly created an atmosphere of fear and panic and probably also contributed to the overall air of uncertainty that dampened investment spending. The crash also reduced the wealth of shareholders, encouraging them to cut back on their consumption spending. But the direct effect of the stock market crash on consumption, although a contributory factor to the Great Depression, was not the major source of the drop in aggregate demand. The collapse of investment arising from increased uncertainty brought the 1930 decline in aggregate demand.

The stock market crash was a predictor of severe recession. It reflected the expectations of shareholders concerning future profit prospects. As those expectations became pessimistic, people sold their shares. There were more sellers than buyers, and the share prices were bid lower and lower. That is, the behaviour of the stock market was a consequence of expectations about future profitability, and those expectations were lowered as a result of increased uncertainty.

Can It Happen Again?

Because we have an incomplete understanding of the causes of the Great Depression, we cannot be sure whether such an event will happen again. The economic turmoil of the 1920s that preceded the depression could certainly happen again. And the financial turmoil of 2007 and 2008 has an eerie similarity to the years leading into the Great Depression.

But there are significant differences between the economy of the 2000s and that of the 1930s that make a depression less likely today than it was 80 years ago. The most significant features of the economy that make severe depression less likely today are

- Bank deposit insurance
- Central banks as lenders of last resort
- Taxes and government spending
- Multi-income families

Bank Deposit Insurance As a direct result of the Great Depression, governments around the world, including in Canada, established institutions that insure bank deposits in the event of bank failure. If bank deposits had been insured before the Great Depression, the key event that turned an ordinary recession into the Great Depression is unlikely to have occurred. It was the fear of bank failure that caused people to withdraw their deposits from banks. The aggregate consequence of these individually rational acts was to cause the very bank failures that were feared. With deposit insurance, most depositors have nothing to lose if a bank fails and so have no incentive to take actions that are likely to give rise to that failure. But despite deposit insurance, the U.K. bank Northern Rock experienced a severe loss of deposits in the current financial crisis.

Lender of Last Resort Central banks today are making billions of dollars of both reserves and capital available to banks. It is generally agreed that the U.S. Federal Reserve made a serious mistake in its handling of monetary policy during the Great Depression by not being aggressive in keeping banks afloat. With an eye on the international situation, the Federal Reserve actually increased the overnight rate just when the banks needed to borrow more. Today, central banks are cutting interest rates.

Taxes and Government Spending The government sector was a much smaller part of the economy in 1929 than it is today. On the eve of that earlier recession, government purchases of goods and services were less than 11 percent of GDP. Today, they exceed 20 percent of GDP. Government transfer payments were less than 5 percent of GDP in 1929. Today, they too exceed 20 percent of GDP.

A larger level of government purchases of goods and services and transfer payments means that today we have a much more sensitive automatic stabilizer than the one available in 1929.

Multi-Income Families At the time of the Great Depression, families with more than one wage earner were much less common than they are today.

For the four reasons we have just reviewed, it appears that the economy has better shock-absorbing characteristics today than it had in the 1920s and 1930s. Even if there is a collapse of confidence, leading to a fall in investment, today's shock absorbers will not translate that initial shock into the large and prolonged fall in real GDP and rise in unemployment that occurred more than 70 years ago.

Because economies are now more immune to severe recession than they were in the 1930s, even a stock market crash of the magnitude that occurred in the United States in 2007 and 2008 had a small effect on spending. A crash of a similar magnitude in 1929 resulted in the near collapse of housing investment and consumer durable purchases. In the months following the current stock market crash, U.S. investment and spending on durable goods remained remarkably high.

None of this is to say that there might not be a deep recession or even a great depression in the 2010s (or beyond). But it would take a very severe shock to trigger one.

Onset of Recession in Canada and the United States

Massive Job Losses Hit Canada, U.S.

December 5, 2008

The Canadian economy lost a much greater than feared 71,000 jobs in November, the worst monthly loss in more than a quarter century, and a taste of what's to come, while the U.S. lost more than half a million more jobs, bringing the losses since the recession there began a year ago to nearly 1.9 million.

"With today's dismal employment reports, there is no doubt that the Canadian economy is in recession and the U.S. contraction is accelerating," said BMO Capital Markets chief economist Sherry Cooper. ...

... [T]he much worse than expected job losses were the most since the early-1980s recession, ending three straight months of gains and nudging the unemployment rate up a notch to a two-year high of 6.3 percent. ...

"Today's labour market report is further evidence that Canada's economy—particularly its manufacturing sector—is facing enormous challenges as a result of the global slowdown," said Finance Minister Jim Flaherty, adding that new measures needed to stimulate the economy will be included in his Jan. 27 budget. ...

The Canadian job market, however, is in a lot better shape than the U.S. labour market, having created 133,000 jobs during the first 11 months of the year, compared with the loss of nearly 2 million jobs there.

"For the 11th month in a row, U.S. employment shrank, and in November, shrank it did," BMO Capital Markets economist Jennifer Lee observed in the wake of news of the loss of a further 533,000 jobs, the worst in a third of a century. ...

Material reprinted with the express permission of "The National Post Company", a Canwest Partnership.

Essence of the Story

- Canadian employment decreased by 71,000 in November 2008, the worst monthly loss since the early 1980s recession.

- The unemployment rate reached a two-year high of 6.3 percent.

- Canadian employment increased by 133,000 during the first 11 months of 2008.

- U.S. employment decreased by 533,000 in November 2008.

- U.S. employment decreased every month in 2008 and the decrease totalled 1.9 million by November.

Economic Analysis

- The most recent phase of the Canadian business cycle is very different from that in the United States.

- The news article provides one indicator of the business cycle: employment numbers during 2008 for Canada and the United States.

- The data graphed in the figures put the 2008 employment numbers in a longer perspective.

- In 2001, the United States had a mild recession and Canada had a growth rate slowdown.

- Figure 1 shows that following the 2001 recession, the labour force participation rate in Canada surged upward from 66 percent to 68 percent. At the same time, the U.S. labour force participation rate sagged from 67 percent to 66 percent.

- Figure 2 shows that following the 2001 recession, the employment rate (the employment-to-population ratio) in the United States kept falling. It did not turn upward until late 2003 and it stopped rising at the end of 2006. Through 2007 and 2008, the U.S. employment rate plunged from 63 percent to 61 percent.

- Figure 2 also shows that Canadian employment surged upward from around 61 percent to 64 percent and kept on rising through 2007 when U.S. employment was falling. Canadian employment fell only slightly during 2008.

- Figure 3 shows that the Canadian unemployment rate has been higher than the U.S. rate. But the Canadian unemployment rate kept falling through 2007 while the U.S. rate was rising. The rapid rise in the U.S. unemployment rate during 2008 is not matched by the Canadian rate.

- Why did Canada escape the severe fall in employment and rise in unemployment that the United States experienced?

- The trigger that sent the U.S. economy crashing was a collapse in house prices and its effects on the credit markets. This problem was much less severe in Canada.

- Canada produces more resources (oil, natural gas, and minerals) than the United States and all of these items were still booming through 2007.

- The Canadian dollar depreciated, which helped to keep Canadian exports high and imports low and prevent aggregate demand from falling.

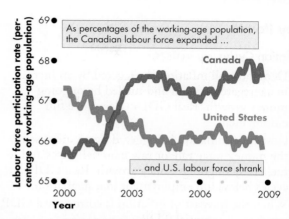

Figure 1 Labour force participation rates

Figure 2 Employment rates

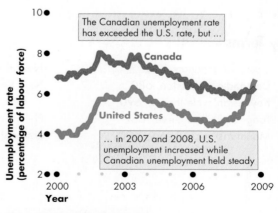

Figure 3 Unemployment rates

SUMMARY ▸

Key Points

Inflation Cycles (pp. 680–685)

- Demand-pull inflation is triggered by an increase in aggregate demand and fuelled by ongoing money growth. Real GDP cycles above full employment.
- Cost-push inflation is triggered by an increase in the money wage rate or raw material prices and is fuelled by ongoing money growth. Real GDP cycles below full employment in a stagflation.
- When the forecast of inflation is correct, real GDP remains at potential GDP.

Inflation and Unemployment: The Phillips Curve
(pp. 686–688)

- The short-run Phillips curve shows the tradeoff between inflation and unemployment when the expected inflation rate and the natural unemployment rate are constant.

- The long-run Phillips curve, which is vertical, shows that when the actual inflation rate equals the expected inflation rate, the unemployment rate equals the natural unemployment rate.

The Business Cycle (pp. 689–695)

- The mainstream business cycle theory explains the business cycle as fluctuations of real GDP around potential GDP and as arising from a steady expansion of potential GDP combined with an expansion of aggregate demand at a fluctuating rate.
- Real business cycle theory explains the business cycle as fluctuations of potential GDP, which arise from fluctuations in the influence of technological change on productivity growth.

Key Figures

Figure 28.2   A Demand-Pull Inflation Spiral, 681
Figure 28.4   A Cost-Push Inflation Spiral, 684
Figure 28.5   Expected Inflation, 685
Figure 28.7   Short-Run and Long-Run Phillips Curves, 687

Figure 28.9   The Mainstream Business Cycle Theory, 689
Figure 28.11   Loanable Funds and Labour Markets in a Real Business Cycle, 692

Key Terms

Cost-push inflation, 682
Demand-pull inflation, 680
Keynesian cycle theory, 690
Long-run Phillips curve, 687
Monetarist cycle theory, 690

New classical cycle theory, 690
New Keynesian cycle theory, 690
Phillips curve, 686
Rational expectation, 685

Real business cycle theory, 690
Short-run Phillips curve, 686
Stagflation,   683

PROBLEMS and APPLICATIONS

1. The spreadsheet provides information about the economy in Argentina. Column A is the year, Column B is real GDP in billions of 2000 pesos, and Column C is the price level.

	A	B	C
1	1997	277	105.6
2	1998	288	103.8
3	1999	278	101.9
4	2000	276	102.9
5	2001	264	101.8
6	2002	235	132.9
7	2003	256	146.8
8	2004	279	160.4
9	2005	305	174.5
10	2006	331	198.0
11	2007	359	226.1
12	2008	384	267.7

   a. In which years did Argentina experience inflation? In which years did it experience deflation (a falling price level)?
   b. In which years did recessions occur? In which years did expansions occur?
   c. In which years do you expect the unemployment rate was highest? Why?
   d. Do these data show a relationship between unemployment and inflation in Argentina?

   Use the following figure to answer problems 2, 3, 4, and 5. In each question the economy starts out on the curves AD_0 and SAS_0.

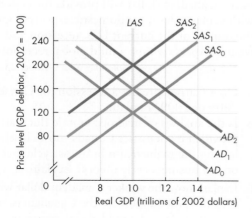

2. Some events occur and the economy experiences a demand-pull inflation.

   a. List the events that might cause a demand-pull inflation.
   b. Describe the initial effects of a demand-pull inflation.
   c. Describe what happens as a demand-pull inflation spiral proceeds.

3. Some events occur and the economy experiences a cost-push inflation.

   a. List the events that might cause a cost-push inflation.
   b. Describe the initial effects of a cost-push inflation.
   c. Describe what happens as a cost-push inflation spiral proceeds.

4. Some events occur and the economy is expected to experience inflation.

   a. List the events that might cause an expected inflation.
   b. Describe the initial effects of an expected inflation.
   c. Describe what happens as an expected inflation proceeds.

5. Suppose that people expect deflation (a falling price level), but aggregate demand remains at AD_0.

   a. What happens to the short-run and long-run aggregate supply curves? (Draw some new curves if you need to.)
   b. Describe the initial effects of an expected deflation.
   c. Describe what happens as it becomes obvious to everyone that the expected deflation is not going to occur.

6. **The Right Way to Beat Chinese Inflation**
   High inflation is threatening social stability in China, soaring from 3.3 percent in March 2007 to 8.3 percent in March 2008. ... China's accelerating inflation reflects a similar climb in its GDP growth rate, from the already high 11 percent in 2006 to 11.5 percent in 2007. The proximate cause of price growth since mid-2007 is the

appearance of production bottlenecks as domestic demand exceeds supply in an increasing number of sectors, such as power generation, transportation, and intermediate-goods industries. ... [T]he prolonged rapid increase in Chinese aggregate demand has been fueled by an investment boom, as well as a growing trade surplus. ...

Brookings Institution, July 2, 2008

a. Is China experiencing demand-pull or cost-push inflation? Explain.
b. Draw a graph to illustrate the initial rise in the price level and the money wage rate response to a one-time rise in the price level.
c. Draw a graph to illustrate and explain how China might experience an inflation spiral.

7. **Recession? Maybe. Depression? Get Real.**

The [U.S.] unemployment rate skyrocketed during the Depression, peaking at nearly 25 percent in 1933. The current [U.S.] unemployment rate is just 5 percent. And that's only up from 4.5 percent a year ago. Contrast that with the " far more explosive spike at the beginning of the Great Depression—from about 3 percent in 1929 to nearly 8.7 percent in 1930. ... Another hallmark of the Depression was deflation, which is obviously not happening today. ...

CNN, May 28, 2008

a. Can the inflation and unemployment trends during the Great Depression be explained by a movement along a short-run Phillips curve?
b. Can the inflation and unemployment trends during 2008 be explained by a movement along a short-run Phillips curve?

8. **Energy Power Inflation to 3.5%**

Canada's inflation rate last month was the highest in more than five years ... but economists say they're not overly concerned because the pace of increases appears to be slowing. Statistics Canada's consumer price index ... rose 3.5 percent between August 2007 and last month. ... "There are some grounds for optimism," said Dale Orr of the forecasting firm Global Insight Canada. "This inflation reading continues to support our forecast for a 2.7 percent increase in the over-all CPI this year, with the pace of inflation falling to the two percent level about mid-2009."... The Statistics Canada report Tuesday showed just how much inflation is tied to the price of oil. Overall, energy prices have risen 20.2

percent over the past 12 months, accounting for about half of the overall inflation run-up. ...

CNEWS, September 23, 2008

a. Explain the difference between demand-pull and cost-push inflation and use graphs to illustrate.
b. Which source more accurately describes the high inflation Canada was experiencing according to this article? Will this lead to an inflation spiral? Explain.
c. What factors may lead to a lower future inflation rate?

9. **Economy on Verge of Recession, Central Bank Warns**

The Canadian economy will be on the verge of recession until the spring, the Bank of Canada warned Thursday, slashing its forecast for growth to an anemic 0.6 percent this year and again next year, the weakest performance since the previous recession in the early 1990s. But the "sky is not falling," governor Mark Carney said. ... [H]e refused to label the downwardly revised forecast performance a recession, preferring instead to call it "sluggish." ... [Carney] projects strong growth of 3.4 percent in 2010. ... Statistics Canada in its report noted that in recent months growth and employment in Canada have been strong. ... Canadian employment last month and overall economic output earlier in the summer posted "large gains," Statistics Canada said, suggesting that the abrupt turnaround in both after months of weakness suggest that the earlier slack in output and employment growth was due to a shortfall in supply not in domestic demand. ... Meanwhile, the central bank said the sharp drop in the Canadian dollar will provide the economy with some cushion for domestic exporters against the impact of the current U.S. recession and what it expects will be a mild global recession.

Vancouver Sun, October 23, 2008

a. Does Carney predict a recession for Canada in 2008 or 2009? Explain.
b. Is the analysis of macroeconomic fluctuations provided by Statistics Canada most closely following the mainstream business cycle theory or real business cycle theory? Explain.
c. Explain how the weaker Canadian dollar will provide some support for the Canadian economy in the face of a mild global recession.

10. The Reserve Bank of New Zealand signed an agreement with the New Zealand government in which the Bank agreed to maintain inflation inside a low target range. Failure to achieve the target would result in the governor of the Bank of Canada losing his job.

   a. Explain how this arrangement might have influenced New Zealand's short-run Phillips curve.
   b. Explain how this arrangement might have influenced New Zealand's long-run Phillips curve.

11. An economy has an unemployment rate of 4 percent and an inflation rate of 5 percent a year at point A in the figure.

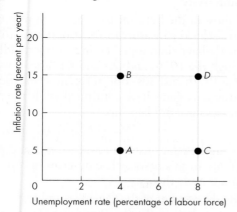

   Some events occur that move the economy in a clockwise loop from A to B to D to C and back to A.

   a. Describe the events that could create this sequence.
   b. Draw in the figure the sequence of the economy's short-run and long-run Phillips curves.
   c. Has the economy experienced demand-pull inflation, cost-push inflation, expected inflation, or none of these?

12. Suppose that the business cycle in Canada is best described by RBC theory. An advance in technology increases productivity.

   a. Draw a diagram to show the effect of the advance in technology in the market for loanable funds.
   b. Draw a diagram to show the effect of the advance in technology in the labour market.
   c. Explain the when-to-work decision when technology advances.

13. **Report Says Canadian Recession Is Here**

   Canadians are in store for a harsh winter of economic news with substantial job losses mounting in the next few months as recessionary times take hold, the Global Insight forecasting firm says. Managing director Dale Orr ... believes Canada has already entered the first recession in 17 years. ... Orr says the current October–December period will see the economy shrink 1.4 percent on an annualized basis, with a further 1.2 percent retreat occurring in the first quarter of 2009. For the next year as [a] whole, Orr says the economy will average zero growth. "That's quite a stretch of miserable growth," he said. Unlike the slowdown earlier this year, which was mainly been concentrated in the business community and the stock markets, this "will feel more like a recession" because of the significant job losses. ... Orr said Canada's jobless rate will rise from the current 6.2 percent to 7.2 percent at the end of next year.

   CNEWS, November 11, 2008

   a. What evidence does Orr present to support the view that Canada had entered a recession?
   b. Explain why Orr predicts that the end of 2008 and 2009 "will feel more like a recession" than the slowdown at the beginning of 2008.
   c. Use a short-run Phillips curve to explain why the inflation rate may decrease over the course of 2009.
   d. Under what circumstances might the inflation rate not decrease during 2009?

14. **Economy Facing Dual Threat—Slow Growth, High Inflation, says Bank of Canada**

   "I am not using the word stagflation," said Global Insight managing director Dale Orr. "But it's a very awkward trend when you have weak output and yet you have high inflation." He said traditionally the term stagflation—a word coined to reflect stagnant growth and price inflation—implies a prolonged condition in the economy, whereas the [central] bank's statement suggests the problem may only last a few months. Inflation had been a dead issue in Canada for months. ... But now that the central bank, and particularly record oil prices, has put inflation back on the table, future policy decisions have been made more problematic. ... Signs that Canada's economy continues to slow have been steadily building over the past month, from the recent report that gross domestic product shrank 0.3 percent in the first quarter, to last week's employment release showing job creation stalled in May, with full-time employment actually tumbling by 32,000. ... "Canada's job market has clearly weakened over the past two months because of the high Canadian dollar and its effect on the manufacturing and forestry sectors," [Canadian Labour Congress head Ken Georgetti] said. "Jobs are getting very hard to find for those entering the labour force and for those who are losing their current jobs."

CNEWS, June 10, 2008

a. Draw a graph to illustrate and explain how high oil prices might create cost-push inflation in Canada.
b. Explain why Orr refused to use the label "stagflation" to describe the situation.
c. Draw a graph to illustrate and explain how high oil prices could lead to a cost-push inflation spiral.
d. Explain why this situation makes the central bank's future monetary policy decisions "more problematic."
e. Explain and use a graph to illustrate Georgetti's claims about how the "high Canadian dollar" has weakened the job market. How might this also help to reduce inflationary pressure?

15. **Stagflation Is Back. Here's How to Beat It**

Three decades ago, in a bleak stretch of the 1970s, an economic phenomenon emerged that was as ugly as its name: stagflation. ... It created an existential crisis for the global economy, leading many to argue that the world had reached its limits of growth and prosperity. ... Fortunately, there is a better way forward than we took after 1974. We need to adopt coherent national and global technology policies to address critical needs in energy, food, water, and climate change. ... There is certainly no shortage of promising ideas, merely a lack of federal commitment to support their timely development, demonstration, and diffusion. Solar power ... high-mileage automobiles (like plug-in hybrids with advanced batteries), green buildings, carbon capture, cellulose-based ethanol, safe nuclear power, and countless other technologies on the horizon can reconcile a world of growing energy demands with increasingly scarce fossil fuels and rising

threats of human-made climate change. As for food supplies, new drought-resistant crop varieties have the potential to bolster global food security in the face of an already changing climate. New irrigation technologies can help impoverished farmers move from one subsistence crop to several high-value crops year round. Yet as promising as these alternatives are, we have not been investing enough to bring them to fruition. ...

Fortune, May 28, 2008

Does this analysis of macroeconomic performance reflect the mainstream business cycle theory or real business cycle theory? Explain.

16. **Real Wages Fail to Match a Rise in Productivity**

For most of the last century, wages and productivity—the key measure of the economy's efficiency—have risen together, increasing rapidly through the 1950s and 60s and far more slowly in the 1970s and 80s. But in recent years, the productivity gains have continued while the pay increases have not kept up.

New York Times, August 28, 2006

Explain the relationship between wages and productivity in this news article in terms of real business cycle theory.

17. Study the account of the Canadian and U.S. labour markets in *Reading Between the Lines* on pp. 696–697, then answer the following questions.

a. What are the main features of the labour force participation rate in Canada and the United States since 2000?
b. What are the main features of the employment rate (employment-to-population ratio) in Canada and the United States since 2000?
c. What are the main features of the unemployment rate in Canada and the United States since 2000?
d. Use the *AS–AD* model to show the changes in aggregate demand and aggregate supply that are consistent with the paths followed by employment in Canada and the United States from 2000 to 2006.
e. Use the *AS–AD* model to show the changes in aggregate demand and aggregate supply that are consistent with the paths followed by employment in Canada and the United States in 2007 and 2008.

UNDERSTANDING MACROECONOMIC FLUCTUATIONS

Boom and Bust

To cure a disease, doctors must first understand how the disease responds to different treatments. It helps to understand the mechanisms that operate to cause the disease, but sometimes a workable cure can be found even before the full story of the causes has been told.

Curing economic ills is similar to curing medical ills. We need to understand how the economy responds to the treatments we might prescribe for it. And sometimes we want to try a cure even though we don't fully understand the reasons for the problem we're trying to control.

You've seen how the pace of capital accumulation and technological change determine the long-term growth trend. You've learned how fluctuations around the long-term trend can be generated by changes in aggregate demand and aggregate supply. And you've learned about the key sources of fluctuations in aggregate demand and aggregate supply.

The *AS–AD* model explains the forces that determine real GDP and the price level in the short run. The model also enables us to see the big picture or grand vision of the different schools of macroeconomic thought concerning the sources of aggregate fluctuations. The Keynesian aggregate expenditure model provides an account of the factors that determine aggregate demand and make it fluctuate.

An alternative real business cycle theory puts all the emphasis on fluctuations in long-run aggregate supply. According to this theory, money changes aggregate demand and the price level but leaves the real economy untouched. The events of 2008 and 2009 will provide a powerful test of this theory.

John Maynard Keynes, *born in England in 1883, was one of the outstanding minds of the twentieth century. He represented Britain at the Versailles peace conference at the end of World War I, was a master speculator on international financial markets (an activity he conducted from bed every morning and which made and lost him several fortunes), and played a prominent role in creating the International Monetary Fund.*

He was a member of the Bloomsbury Group, a circle of outstanding artists and writers that included E. M. Forster, Bertrand Russell, and Virginia Woolf.

Keynes was a controversial and quick-witted figure. A critic once complained that Keynes had changed his opinion on some matter, to which Keynes retorted: "When I discover I am wrong, I change my mind. What do you do?"

Keynes' book, The General Theory of Employment, Interest, and Money, *written during the Great Depression and published in 1936, revolutionanized macroeconomics.*

"The ideas of economists and political philosophers, both when they are right and when they are wrong, are more powerful than is commonly understood. Indeed the world is ruled by little else."

JOHN MAYNARD KEYNES
The General Theory of Employment, Interest, and Money

703

TALKING
WITH

Ricardo J. Caballero

Ricardo J. Caballero is Ford Professor of International Economics at MIT. He has received many honours, the most notable of which are the Frisch Medal of the Econometric Society (2002) and being named Chile's Economist of the Year (2001). A highly regarded teacher, he is much sought as a special lecturer and in 2005 gave the prestigious Yrjo Jahnsson Lecture at the University of Helsinki.

Professor Caballero earned his B.S. degree in 1982 and M.A. in 1983 at Pontificia Universidad Católica de Chile. He then moved to the United States and obtained his Ph.D. at MIT in 1988.

Michael Parkin and Robin Bade talked with Ricardo Caballero about his work and the progress that economists have made in understanding economic fluctuations.

Professor Caballero, why did you decide to become an economist?

Did I decide? I'm convinced that one is either born an economist or not. I began studying business, but as soon as I took the first course in economics, I was captivated by the simple but elegant logic of (good) economic reasoning. Given the complexity of the real world, economic analysis is necessarily abstract. But at the same time, economics is mostly about concrete and important issues that affect the lives of millions of people. Abstraction and relevance—this is a wonderful but strange combination. Not everybody feels comfortable with it, but if you do, economics is for you.

Most of your work has been on business cycles and other high-frequency phenomena. Can we begin by reviewing the costs of recessions? Robert Lucas says that post-war U.S. recessions have cost very little. Do you agree?

No ... but I'm not sure Robert Lucas was really trying to say that. My sense is that he was trying to push the profession to focus a bit more on long-run growth issues. Putting down the costs of recessions was a useful debating device to make his important point.

I believe that the statement that recessions are not costly is incorrect. First, I think his calculation of this magnitude reflects some fundamental flaw in the way the workhorse models we use in economics fail to account for the costs of risk and volatility. This flaw shows up in many different puzzles in economics, including the well-known equity premium puzzle. Economic models underestimate, by an order of magnitude, how unhappy agents are about facing uncertainty. Second, it is highly unlikely that recessions and medium-term growth are completely separable. In particular, the ongoing process of restructuring, which is central to productivity growth, is severely hampered by deep recessions.

Recessions are costly because they waste enormous resources, affect physical and human investment decisions, have large negative distributional consequences, influence political outcomes, and so on.

What about the costs of recessions in other parts of the world, especially Latin America?

The cost of recessions grows exponentially with their size and the country's inability to soften the impact on the most affected. Less developed economies suffer much larger shocks because their economies are not well diversified, and they experience capital outflows that exacerbate the impact of recessionary shocks. Their domestic financial sectors are small and often become strained during recessions, making it difficult to reallocate scarce resources towards those who need them the most. To make matters worse, the government's ability to use fiscal policy becomes impaired by the capital outflows, and monetary policy is also out of the question when the currency is in free fall and liabilities are dollarized. There are many things that we take for granted in Canada and the United States that simply are not feasible for emerging markets in distress. One has to be careful with extrapolating too directly the countercyclical recipes used for developed economies to these countries.

Your first work, in your M.A. dissertation, was to build a macroeconomic model of the economy of Chile. What do we learn by comparing economies? Does the Chilean economy behave essentially like the U.S. economy or are there fundamental differences?

Chile is a special economy among emerging markets. It began pro-market reforms many years before the rest and has had very prudent macroeconomic management for several decades by now. For that reason, it is a bit more "like the U.S. economy" than most other emerging market economies. However, there are still important differences, of the sort described in my answer to the previous question.

Beyond the specifics of Chile, at some deep level, macroeconomic principles, and economic principles more generally, are the same everywhere. It is all about incentives, tradeoffs, effort, commitment, discipline, transparency, insurance, and so on. But different economies hurt in different places, and hence the practice of economics has plenty of diversity.

Recessions are costly because they waste enormous resources [and] affect physical and human investment decisions ...

During the most recent U.S. expansion, some asset prices—especially house prices—have looked as if they might be experiencing a speculative bubble, and you've done some recent work on bubbles. How can we tell whether we're seeing a bubble or just a rapid increase that is being driven by fundamental market forces?

First things first. I think we need to get used to the presence of speculative bubbles. The reason is that the world today has a massive shortage of financial assets that savers can use to store value. Because of this shortage, "artificial" assets are ready to emerge at all times. Specific bubbles come and go—from the NASDAQ, to real estate, to commodities—but the total is much more stable.

I do not think the distinction between bubbles and fundamentals is as clear-cut as people describe. Probably outside periods of liquidity crises, all assets have some bubble component in them. The question is how much.

You've studied situations in which capital suddenly stops flowing into an economy from abroad. What are the lessons you've learned from this research?

The most basic lesson for emerging markets is that capital flows are volatile. Sometimes they simply magnify domestic problems, but in many other cases, they are the direct source of volatility. However, the conclusion from this observation is not that capital flows should be limited, just as we do not close the banks in Canada and the United States to eliminate the possibility of bank runs. On the contrary, much of the volatility comes from insufficient integration with international capital markets, which makes emerging markets illiquid and the target of specialists and speculators. For the short and medium run, the main policy lesson is that sudden stops to the

The most basic lesson for emerging markets is that capital flows are volatile.

inflow of capital must be put at the centre of macroeconomic policy design in emerging markets. This has deep implications for the design of monetary and fiscal policy, as well as for international reserves management practices and domestic financial markets regulation.

Good growth potential in the United States over that of Europe and Japan and the much better quality of its financial assets over those of emerging Asian and oil-producing countries make the United States very attractive to international private and public investors.

The U.S. current account deficit has been large and increasing for many years, and dollar debt levels around the world have increased. Do you see any danger in this process for either the United States or the rest of the world?

I believe the persistent current account deficits in the United States are not the result of an anomaly that, as such, must go away in a sudden crash, as the conventional view has it. Instead, my view is that these deficits are just the counterpart of large capital inflows resulting from the global shortage of financial assets that I mentioned earlier. Good growth potential in the United States over that of Europe and Japan and the much better quality of its financial assets over those of emerging Asian and oil-producing countries make the United States very attractive to international private and public investors.

Absent major shocks, this process may still last for quite some time. But

Almost everything in life has an economic angle to it—look for it ...

of course shocks do happen, and in that sense, leverage is dangerous. However, there isn't much we can or should do, short of implementing structural reforms around the world aimed at improving growth potential in some cases and domestic financial development in others.

What advice do you have for someone who is just beginning to study economics but who wants to become an economist? If they are not in the United States, should they come here for graduate work as you did?

There is no other place in the world like the United States to pursue a Ph.D. and do research in economics. However, this is only the last stage in the process of becoming an economist. There are many superb economists, especially applied ones, all around the world.

I believe the most important step is to learn to think like an economist. I heard Milton Friedman say that he knows many economists who have never gone through a Ph.D. program, and equally many who have completed their Ph.D. but are not really economists. I agree with him on this one. A good undergraduate program and talking about economics is a great first step. Almost everything in life has an economic angle to it—look for it and discuss it with your friends. It will not improve your social life, but it will make you a better economist.

29

Fiscal Policy

After studying this chapter, you will be able to

- Describe how federal and provincial budgets are created and describe their recent history
- Explain the supply-side effects of fiscal policy
- Explain how fiscal policy is used to stabilize the business cycle

In 2007, the federal government spent 15 cents of every dollar that Canadians earned and collected 16 cents of every dollar earned in taxes. What are the effects of government spending and taxes on the economy? Does a dollar spent by the government have the same effect as a dollar spent by someone else? Does it create jobs, or does it destroy them? Do taxes harm employment and economic growth?

For many years during the 1980s and 1990s, the government had a large budget deficit and ran up a debt. During the late 1990s, spending cuts brought the deficit under control and created a surplus that is still in place today.

Despite recent budget surpluses, your share of government debt is $15,200. Does it matter if the government

doesn't balance its books? What are the effects of an ongoing government deficit and accumulating debt?

These are the fiscal policy issues that you will study in this chapter. At the end of the chapter, in *Reading Between the Lines*, we'll look at fiscal stimulus in the 2008–2009 global growth slowdown.

Government Budgets

The annual statement of the outlays and revenues of the government of Canada, together with the laws and regulations that approve and support those outlays and revenues, make up the **federal budget.** Similarly, a **provincial budget** is an annual statement of the revenues and outlays of a provincial government, together with the laws and regulations that approve or support those revenues and outlays.

Before World War II, the federal budget had no purpose other than to finance the business of government. But since the late 1940s, the federal budget has assumed a second purpose, which is to pursue the government's fiscal policy. **Fiscal policy** is the use of the federal budget to achieve macroeconomic objectives such as full employment, sustained long-term economic growth, and price level stability. Our focus is this second purpose.

Budget Making

The federal government and Parliament make fiscal policy. The process begins with long, drawn-out consultations between the Minister of Finance and Department of Finance officials and their counterparts in the provincial governments. These discussions deal with programs that are funded and operated jointly by the two levels of government. The Minister also consults with business and consumer groups on a wide range of issues.

After all these consultations, and using economic projections made by Department of Finance economists, the Minister develops a set of proposals, which are discussed in Cabinet and which become government policy. The Minister finally presents a budget plan to Parliament, which debates the plan and enacts the laws necessary to implement it.

Highlights of the 2008 Budget

Table 29.1 shows the main items in the federal budget. The numbers are projected amounts for the fiscal year beginning on April 1, 2008. The three main items shown are

- Revenues
- Outlays
- Budget balance

TABLE 29.1 The Federal Budget in 2008–09

Item	Projections (billions of dollars)	
Revenues	**242**	
Personal income taxes		119
Corporate income taxes		37
Indirect and other taxes		64
Investment income		22
Outlays	**240**	
Transfer payments		146
Expenditure on goods and services		62
Debt interest		32
Surplus	**2**	

Sources of data: Department of Finance, Budget Plan 2008 and Statistics Canada, CANSIM Table 183-0004.

Revenues Revenues are the federal government's receipts, which in the 2008–09 budget were projected at $242 billion. These revenues come from four sources:

1. Personal income taxes
2. Corporate income taxes
3. Indirect and other taxes
4. Investment income

The largest revenue source is *personal income taxes.* In 2008–09, personal income taxes were projected to be $119 billion. These are the taxes paid by individuals on their incomes. The second largest source of revenue is *indirect taxes*, which in 2008–09 were projected to be $64 billion. These taxes include the Goods and Services Tax (GST) and taxes on the sale of gasoline, alcoholic drinks, and a few other items. The smallest revenue sources are *corporate income taxes*, which are the taxes paid by companies on their profits, and *investment income*, which is the income from government enterprises and investments. In 2008–09, corporate income taxes were projected to raise $37 billion and investment income was projected at $22 billion.

Outlays Total federal government outlays in 2008–09 were projected at $240 billion. Outlays are classified in three categories:

1. Transfer payments
2. Expenditures on goods and services
3. Debt interest

The largest outlay, and by a big margin, is *transfer payments*. Transfer payments are payments to individuals, businesses, other levels of government, and the rest of the world. In 2008–09, this item was $146 billion. It includes unemployment cheques and welfare payments to individuals, farm subsidies, grants to provincial and local governments, aid to developing countries, and dues to international organizations such as the United Nations.

Expenditures on goods and services are expenditures on final goods and services, and in 2008–09 this item totalled $62 billion. These expenditures include those on national defence, computers for the Canada Revenue Agency, government cars, and highways. This component of the federal budget is the government expenditure on goods and services that appears in the circular flow of expenditure and income and in the national income and product accounts (see Chapter 20, pp. 469–470).

Debt interest is the interest on the government debt. In 2008–09, this item was $32 billion. At its peak percentage of GDP in 1990, it exceeded govern-ment expenditures on goods and services. This interest payment is large because the government has a large debt—$524 billion. This large debt has arisen because from 1971 to 1997 the federal government had a large and persistent budget deficit.

Budget Balance The government's budget balance is equal to its revenues minus its outlays. That is,

$$\text{Budget balance} = \text{Revenues} - \text{Outlays}.$$

If revenues exceed outlays, the government has a **budget surplus**. If outlays exceed revenues, the government has a **budget deficit**. If revenues equal outlays, the government has a **balanced budget**.

In 2008–09, with projected outlays of $240 billion and revenues of $242 billion, the government projected a budget surplus of $2 billion.

How typical is the federal budget of 2008–09? Let's look at its recent history.

The Budget in Historical Perspective

Figure 29.1 shows the government's revenues, outlays, and budget balance from 1961 to 2007. To get a better sense of the magnitudes of these items, they are shown as percentages of GDP. Expressing them in this way lets us see how large the government is relative to the size of the economy, and also helps us to study changes in the scale of government over

FIGURE 29.1 The Budget Surplus and Deficit

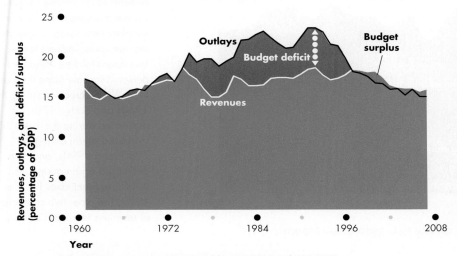

The figure records the federal government's revenues, outlays, and budget balance as percentages of GDP from 1961 to 2007. During the 1960s, outlays and revenues increased. During the late 1970s and through the 1980s, outlays continued to rise but revenues fell, so a budget deficit arose. During the 1990s, spending cuts eliminated the budget deficit, and after 1997, the federal government had a budget surplus.

Source of data: Statistics Canada, CANSIM Tables 380-0002 and 380-0007.

myeconlab   animation

time. You can think of the percentages of GDP as telling you how many cents of each dollar that Canadians earn get paid to and are spent by the government.

During the 1960s, government expanded but taxes and revenues kept pace with each other. But from 1971 through 1996, the federal budget was in deficit, and the average deficit over these years was 4.2 percent of GDP. The deficit climbed to a peak of 6.6 percent of GDP in 1985. It then decreased through the rest of the 1980s. During the recession of 1990–1991, the deficit increased again. The deficit remained above 4 percent of GDP for most of the 1980s and early 1990s.

Only in 1997 did the federal government finally eradicate its deficit. And it did so by cutting outlays, especially transfer payments to provincial governments.

Why did the government deficit grow during the early 1980s and remain high through the early 1990s? The immediate answer is that outlays increased while revenues remained relatively constant. But which components of outlays increased? And did all the sources of revenues remain constant?

To answer these questions, we need to examine each of the sources of revenues and outlays in detail. We'll begin by looking at the sources of revenues.

Revenues Figure 29.2 shows the components of government revenues since 1961. Total revenues have no strong trends. They increased through the 1960s and again through the 1980s. But they decreased during the 1970s and the first half of the 2000s. The main source of the fluctuations in revenues was personal income taxes. Indirect taxes also fluctuated but corporate income taxes and investment income were more stable than the other two revenue components.

The increase in personal income taxes during the 1980s resulted from increases in tax rates in successive budgets.

Indirect taxes decreased during the 1990s mainly because an old federal sales tax was replaced by the Goods and Services Tax or GST. Initially, this switch maintained revenues at a constant level, but gradually, the revenue from indirect taxes (as a percentage of GDP) fell.

Outlays Figure 29.3 shows the components of government outlays since 1961. Total outlays increased steadily from 1971 through 1985, were relatively flat through 1993, and then decreased sharply after 1993. The main source of the changing trends in outlays is transfer payments to provincial governments. These payments swelled during the 1980s and were cut drastically during the late 1990s.

FIGURE 29.2 Federal Government Revenues

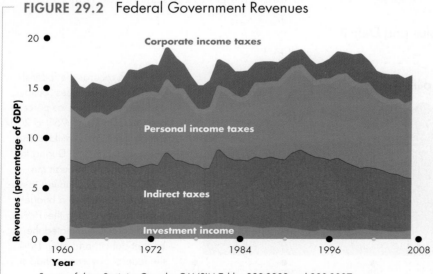

Source of data: Statistics Canada, CANSIM Tables 380-0002 and 380-0007.

The figure shows four main components of government revenues (as percentages of GDP): personal income taxes, corporate income taxes, indirect taxes, and investment income. Revenues from personal income taxes fluctuated most. They increased during the 1960s and early 1970s, decreased during the late 1970s, increased again during the 1980s and 1990s, and then decreased again during the 2000s. Indirect taxes fell after 1990. The other two components of revenues remained steady.

myeconlab animation

FIGURE 29.3 Federal Government Outlays

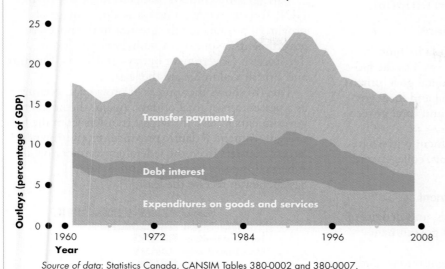

The figure shows three components of government outlays (as percentages of GDP): expenditures on goods and services, debt interest, and transfer payments. Expenditures on goods and services have had a downward trend. Transfer payments increased from 1965 to 1990 but decreased sharply during the 1990s. Debt interest increased steadily during the 1980s as the budget deficit fed on itself, but decreased during the late 1990s as surpluses began to lower the government's debt.

Source of data: Statistics Canada, CANSIM Tables 380-0002 and 380-0007.

myeconlab animation

To understand the changes in debt interest, we need to see the connection between the budget deficit and government debt.

Deficit and Debt The government borrows to finance its deficit. And **government debt** is the total amount of government borrowing. It is the sum of past deficits minus the sum of past surpluses.

When the government budget is in deficit, government debt increases, and when the government budget is in surplus, government debt decreases.

A persistent budget deficit emerged during the mid-1970s, and in such a situation, the deficit begins to feed on itself. A budget deficit increases borrowing; increased borrowing leads to larger debt; a larger debt leads to larger interest payments; and larger interest payments led to a larger deficit and yet larger debt. That is the story of the increasing budget deficit and rising debt of the 1980s.

Similarly, a persistent budget surplus creates a virtuous cycle of falling interest payments, larger surpluses, and falling debt.

Figure 29.4 shows the history of the government of Canada debt since 1940, at the start of World War II. Debt (as a percentage of GDP) was at an all-time high of 113 percent at the end of the war in 1945. Huge wartime deficits had increased Canada's debt to the point that it exceeded GDP. Post-war budget

FIGURE 29.4 The Federal Government Debt

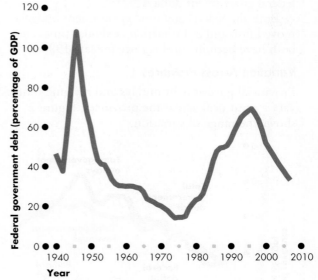

Federal government debt as a percentage of GDP increased during World War II, decreased from 1946 through 1974, increased through 1997, and then began to decrease again.

Source of data: Statistics Canada, CANSIM Tables 380-0002 and 380-0010.

myeconlab animation

Provincial and Local Governments

Bigger than Federal Government

The *total government* sector of Canada includes provincial and local governments as well as the federal government. In 2007, when federal government outlays were $230 billion, provincial and local government outlays were $390 billion and total government outlays were $620 billion.

Most provincial and local government outlays are on public hospitals and public schools, colleges, and universities.

Scale of Different Levels of Government

Figure 1 shows the revenues, outlays, and deficits of the federal government and of total government from 1961 to 2007.

You can see that federal government outlays and revenues and total government outlays and revenues fluctuate in similar ways, but the total government is much larger than the federal government. In other words, the provincial and local governments are a large component of total government. You can also see that total government outlays fluctuate more than federal government outlays.

Both the federal and total government budgets moved into and out of deficit at similar times and both have been in surplus since the late 1990s.

Variation Across Provinces

Provincial government outlays and revenue sources vary a great deal across the provinces. Figure 2 shows the range of variation.

Part (a) shows outlays as a percentage of provincial GDP. You can see that outlays as a percentage of provincial product are the greatest in the northern governments (Nunavut, Yukon, and Northwest Territories). Government outlays of Alberta, Ontario, and British Columbia are the least.

Part (b) shows the sources of provincial revenues as a percentage of total outlays. Again, the northern governments receive the largest transfers from the federal government. Atlantic provinces receive the next largest transfers from the federal government, while Alberta, Ontario, British Columbia, and Saskatchewan receive the least.

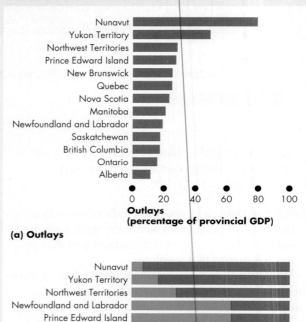

Outlays (percentage of provincial GDP)

(a) Outlays

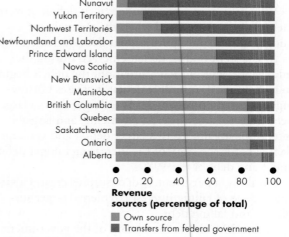

Revenue sources (percentage of total)

■ Own source
■ Transfers from federal government

(b) Revenues

Figure 2 Provincial Government Budgets

Source of data: Statistics Canada, CANSIM Tables 384-0002 and 385-0002.

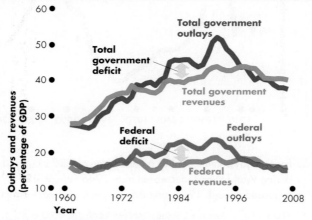

Figure 1 Total Government Budgets

Source of data: Statistics Canada, CANSIM Tables 380-0002 and 380-0007.

Canadian Government Surplus in Global Perspective

Deep Red in the United States and Japan

To compare government budgets across countries, we must take into account the differences in local and regional government arrangements. Some countries, and Canada is one of them, have large state/provincial and local governments. Other countries, and the United Kingdom is one, have larger central government and small local governments. These differences make the international comparison more valid at the level of *total government* rather than at the level of *central* (or *federal*) *government*. The figure shows the budget balances of total government in Canada and nine other countries.

The United States and Japan have the largest budget deficits, as a percentage of GDP. The United Kingdom, France, and Italy come next.

Norway, which has substantial oil wealth, has the largest government budget surplus. Other nations with budget surpluses include Finland, Korea, Sweden, and Australia.

Canada lies in the middle of the countries with budget surpluses and is the only major industrial economy with one.

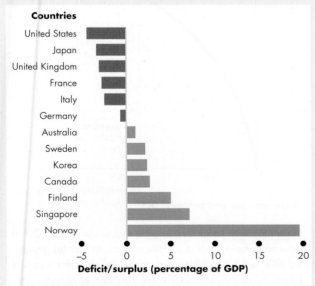

Government Budgets Around the World

Sources of data: International Monetary Fund, *World Economic Outlook*, April 2008, and Statistics Canada, CANSIM Tables 380-0002 and 380-0007.

surpluses lowered the debt-to-GDP ratio through 1974, by which time it stood at 18 percent, its lowest since World War II. Small budget deficits increased the debt-to-GDP ratio slightly through the 1970s, and large budget deficits increased it dramatically between 1981 and 1986. During the late 1980s, the ratio continued to increase but at a more moderate rate. It grew quickly again during the 1990–1991 recession, but its growth rate slowed after 1995 and debt interest as a percentage of GDP decreased.

Debt and Capital When individuals and businesses incur debts, they usually do so to buy capital—assets that yield a return. In fact, the main point of debt is to enable people to buy assets that will earn a return that exceeds the interest paid on the debt. The government is similar to individuals and businesses in this regard. Some government expenditure is investment—the purchase of public capital that yields a return. Highways, major irrigation schemes, public schools and universities, public libraries, and the stock of national defence capital all yield a social rate of return that probably far exceeds the interest rate the government pays on its debt.

But Canadian government debt, which is $500 billion, is much larger than the value of the public capital stock. This fact means that some government debt has been incurred to finance public consumption expenditure.

Review Quiz

1 What are the main items of government revenues and outlays?
2 Under what circumstances does the government have a budget surplus?
3 Explain the connection between a government budget deficit and a government debt.

 Work Study Plan 29.1 and get instant feedback.

Now that you know what the federal budget is and what the main components of revenues and outlays are, it is time to study the *effects* of fiscal policy. We'll begin by learning about the effects of taxes on employment, aggregate supply, and potential GDP. Then we'll look at the demand-side effects of fiscal policy and see how it provides a tool for stabilizing the business cycle.

Supply-Side Effects of Fiscal Policy

Fiscal policy has important effects on employment, potential GDP, and aggregate supply that we'll now examine. These effects are known as **supply-side effects**, and economists who believe these effects to be large ones are generally referred to as *supply-siders*. To study these effects, we'll begin with a refresher on how full employment and potential GDP are determined in the absence of taxes. Then we'll introduce an income tax and see how it changes the economic outcome.

Full Employment and Potential GDP

You learned in Chapter 22 (pp. 521–523) how the full-employment quantity of labour and potential GDP are determined. At full employment, the real wage rate adjusts to make the quantity of labour demanded equal the quantity of labour supplied. Potential GDP is the real GDP that the full-employment quantity of labour produces.

Figure 29.5 illustrates a full-employment situation. In part (a), the demand for labour curve is *LD*, and the supply of labour curve is *LS*. At a real wage rate of $30 an hour and 25 billion hours of labour a year employed, the economy is at full employment.

In Fig. 29.5(b), the production function is *PF*. When 25 billion hours of labour are employed, real GDP (which is also potential GDP) is $1,300 billion.

Let's now see how an income tax changes potential GDP.

The Effects of the Income Tax

The tax on labour income influences potential GDP and aggregate supply by changing the full-employment quantity of labour. The income tax weakens the incentive to work and drives a wedge between the take-home wage of workers and the cost of labour to firms. The result is a smaller quantity of labour and a lower potential GDP.

Figure 29.5 shows this outcome. In the labour market, the income tax has no effect on the demand for labour, which remains at *LD*. The reason is that the quantity of labour that firms plan to hire depends only on how productive labour is and what it costs—its real wage rate.

FIGURE 29.5   The Effects of the Income Tax on Aggregate Supply

(a) Income tax and the labour market

(b) Income tax and potential GDP

In part (a), with no income tax, the real wage rate is $30 an hour and employment is 25 billion hours. In part (b), potential GDP is $1,300 billion. An income tax shifts the supply of labour curve leftward to *LS + tax*. The before-tax wage rate rises to $35 an hour, the after-tax wage rate falls to $20 an hour, and the quantity of labour employed decreases to 20 billion hours. With less labour, potential GDP decreases.

myeconlab animation

But the supply of labour *does* change. With no income tax, the real wage rate is $30 an hour and 25 billion hours of labour a year are employed. An income tax weakens the incentive to work and decreases the supply of labour. The reason is that for each dollar of before-tax earnings, workers must pay the government an amount determined by the income tax code. So workers look at the after-tax wage rate when they decide how much labour to supply. An income tax shifts the supply curve leftward to *LS + tax*. The vertical distance between the *LS* curve and the *LS + tax* curve measures the amount of income tax. With the smaller supply of labour, the *before-tax* wage rate rises to $35 an hour but the *after-tax* wage rate falls to $20 an hour. The vertical gap between the before-tax and after-tax wage rates is the **tax wedge**.

The new equilibrium quantity of labour employed is 20 billion hours a year—less than in the no-tax case. Because the full-employment quantity of labour decreases, so does potential GDP. And a decrease in potential GDP decreases aggregate supply.

In this example, the tax rate is high—$15 tax on a $35 wage rate, about 43 percent. A lower tax rate would have a smaller effect on employment and potential GDP.

An increase in the tax rate to above 43 percent would decrease the supply of labour by more than the decrease shown in Fig. 29.5. Equilibrium employment and potential GDP would also decrease still further. A tax cut would increase the supply of labour, increase equilibrium employment, and increase potential GDP.

Taxes on Expenditure and the Tax Wedge

The tax wedge that we've just considered is only a part of the wedge that affects labour-supply decisions. Taxes on consumption expenditure add to the wedge. The reason is that a tax on consumption raises the prices paid for consumption goods and services and is equivalent to a cut in the real wage rate.

The incentive to supply labour depends on the goods and services that an hour of labour can buy. The higher the taxes on goods and services and the lower the after-tax wage rate, the less is the incentive to supply labour. If the income tax rate is 25 percent and the tax rate on consumption expenditure is 10 percent, a dollar earned buys only 65 cents worth of goods and services. The tax wedge is 35 percent.

Some Real-World Tax Wedges

Why Americans Work Longer Hours than Europeans

Edward C. Prescott of Arizona State University, who shared the 2004 Nobel Prize for Economic Science, has estimated the tax wedges for three countries: the United States, the United Kingdom, and France. We have estimated the tax wedge for Canada.

The wedges are a combination of taxes on labour income and taxes on consumption. They include *all* taxes on labour, including social insurance taxes. And the wedges are based on *marginal* tax rates—the tax rates paid on the marginal dollar earned.

The figure shows the tax wedges in these four countries. In the United States, the consumption tax wedge is 13 percent and the income tax wedge is 32 percent. Canada is very similar. In France, the consumption tax wedge is 33 percent and the income tax wedge is 49 percent. The tax wedges in United Kingdom fall between these two.

Does the Tax Wedge Matter?

Differences in potential GDP per person arise partly from productivity differences and partly from choices influenced by the tax wedge. Potential GDP (per person) in France is 14 percent below that of the United States and the entire difference is attributed to the difference in the tax wedge in the two countries. Potential GDP in Canada is 16 percent below that of the United States, but this difference is due to different productivities. Potential GDP in the United Kingdom is 41 percent below that of the United States, and about a third of the difference arises from the different tax wedges and two-thirds from productivity difference.

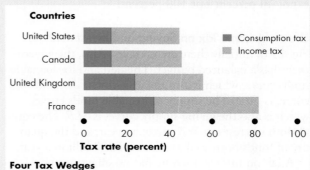

Four Tax Wedges

Source of data: Edward C. Prescott, *American Economic Review*, 2003, and authors' calculations.

Taxes and the Incentive to Save

A tax on interest income weakens the incentive to save and drives a wedge between the after-tax interest rate earned by savers and the interest rate paid by firms. These effects are analogous to those of a tax on labour income. But they are more serious for two reasons.

First, a tax on labour income lowers the quantity of labour employed and lowers potential GDP, while a tax on capital income lowers the quantity of saving and investment and *slows the growth rate of real GDP*.

Second, the true tax rate on interest income is much higher than that on labour income because of the way in which inflation and taxes on interest income interact. Let's examine this interaction.

Effect of Tax Rate on Real Interest Rate

The interest rate that influences investment and saving plans is the *real after-tax interest rate*. The real *after-tax* interest rate subtracts the income tax rate paid on interest income from the real interest rate. But the taxes depend on the nominal interest rate, not the real interest rate. So the higher the inflation rate, the higher is the true tax rate on interest income. Here is an example. Suppose the real interest rate is 4 percent a year and the tax rate is 40 percent.

If there is no inflation, the nominal interest rate equals the real interest rate. The tax on 4 percent interest is 1.6 percent (40 percent of 4 percent), so the real after-tax interest rate is 4 percent minus 1.6 percent, which equals 2.4 percent.

If the inflation rate is 6 percent a year, the nominal interest rate is 10 percent. The tax on 10 percent interest is 4 percent (40 percent of 10 percent), so the real after-tax interest rate is 4 percent minus 4 percent, which equals zero. The true tax rate in this case is not 40 percent but 100 percent!

Effect of Income Tax on Saving and Investment

In Fig. 29.6, initially there are no taxes. Also, the government has a balanced budget. The demand for loanable funds curve, which is also the investment demand curve, is *DLF*. The supply of loanable funds curve, which is also the saving supply curve, is *SLF*. The equilibrium interest rate is 3 percent a year, and the quantity of funds borrowed and lent is $200 billion a year.

A tax on interest income has no effect on the demand for loanable funds. The quantity of investment and borrowing that firms plan to undertake depends only on how productive capital is and what

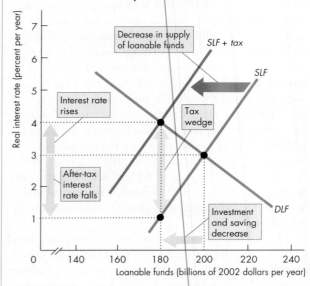

FIGURE 29.6 The Effects of a Tax on Capital Income

The demand for loanable funds and investment demand curve is *DLF*, and the supply of loanable funds and saving supply curve is *SLF*. With no income tax, the real interest rate is 3 percent a year and investment is $200 billion. An income tax shifts the supply curve leftward to *SLF + tax*. The interest rate rises to 4 percent a year, the after-tax interest rate falls to 1 percent a year, and investment decreases to $180 billion. With less investment, the real GDP growth rate decreases.

myeconlab animation

it costs—its real interest rate. But a tax on interest income weakens the incentive to save and lend and decreases the supply of loanable funds. For each dollar of before-tax interest, savers must pay the government an amount determined by the tax code. So savers look at the after-tax real interest rate when they decide how much to save.

When a tax is imposed, saving decreases and the supply of loanable funds curve shifts leftward to *SLF + tax*. The amount of tax payable is measured by the vertical distance between the *SLF* curve and the *SLF + tax* curve. With this smaller supply of loanable funds, the interest rate rises to 4 percent a year but the *after-tax* interest rate falls to 1 percent a year. A tax wedge is driven between the interest rate and the after-tax interest rate, and the equilibrium quantity of loanable funds decreases. Saving and investment also decrease.

Tax Revenues and the Laffer Curve

An interesting consequence of the effect of taxes on employment and saving is that a higher tax *rate* does not always bring greater tax *revenue*. A higher tax rate brings in more revenue per dollar earned. But because a higher tax rate decreases the number of dollars earned, two forces operate in opposite directions on the tax revenue collected.

The relationship between the tax rate and the amount of tax revenue collected is called the **Laffer curve**. The curve is so named because Arthur B. Laffer, a member of Ronald Reagan's Economic Policy Advisory Board, drew such a curve on a table napkin and launched the idea that tax cuts could *increase* tax revenue.

Figure 29.7 shows a Laffer curve. The tax *rate* is on the x-axis, and total tax *revenue* is on the y-axis. For tax rates below T^*, an increase in the tax rate increases tax revenue; at T^*, tax revenue is maximized; and a tax rate increase above T^* decreases tax revenue.

Most people think that Canada is on the upward-sloping part of the Laffer curve. But France might be close to the maximum point or perhaps even beyond it.

The Supply-Side Debate

Before 1980, few economists paid attention to the supply-side effects of taxes on employment and potential GDP. Then, when Ronald Reagan took office as president, a group of supply-siders began to argue the virtues of cutting taxes. Arthur Laffer was one of them. Laffer and his supporters were not held in high esteem among mainstream economists, but they were influential for a period. They correctly argued that tax cuts would increase employment and increase output. But they incorrectly argued that tax cuts would increase tax revenues and decrease the budget deficit. For this prediction to be correct, the United States would have had to be on the "wrong" side of the Laffer curve. Given that U.S. tax rates are among the lowest in the industrial world, it is unlikely that this condition was met. And when the Reagan administration did cut taxes, the budget deficit increased, a fact that reinforces this view.

Supply-side economics became tarnished because of its association with Laffer and came to be called "voodoo economics." But mainstream economists, including Martin Feldstein, a Harvard professor who was Reagan's chief economic advisor, recognized the

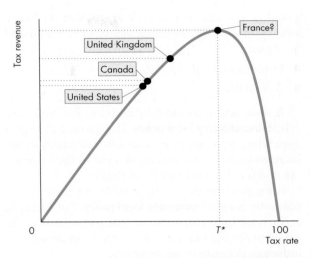

FIGURE 29.7   A Laffer Curve

A Laffer curve shows the relationship between the tax rate and tax revenues. For tax rates below T^*, an increase in the tax rate increases tax revenue. At the tax rate T^*, tax revenue is maximized. For tax rates above T^*, an increase in the tax rate decreases tax revenue.

myeconlab animation

power of tax cuts as incentives but took the standard view that tax cuts without spending cuts would swell the budget deficit and bring serious further problems. This view is now widely accepted by economists of all political persuasions.

Review Quiz

1 How does a tax on labour income influence the equilibrium quantity of employment?
2 How does the tax wedge influence potential GDP?
3 Why are income taxes on capital income more powerful than those on labour income?
4 What is the Laffer curve and why is it unlikely that Canada is on the "wrong" side of it?

myeconlab Work Study Plan 29.2 and get instant feedback.

You now know how taxes influence potential GDP and saving and investment. Next we look at the demand-side effects of fiscal policy and see how it is used as a tool for stabilizing the business cycle.

◆ Stabilizing the Business Cycle

Fiscal policy actions that seek to stabilize the business cycle work by changing aggregate demand and are either

- Discretionary or
- Automatic

A fiscal action initiated by an act of Parliament is called **discretionary fiscal policy**. It requires a change in a spending program or in a tax law. For example, an increase in defence spending or a cut in the income tax rate is a discretionary fiscal policy.

A fiscal action that is triggered by the state of the economy is called **automatic fiscal policy**. For example, an increase in unemployment induces an increase in payments to the unemployed. A fall in incomes induces a decrease in tax revenues.

Changes in government expenditure and changes in taxes have multiplier effects on aggregate demand. Chapter 27 explains the basic idea of the multiplier and the Mathematical Note on pp. 670–673 shows the algebra of the fiscal policy multipliers that we'll now study.

Government Expenditure Multiplier

The **government expenditure multiplier** is the magnification effect of a change in government expenditure on goods and services on aggregate demand. Government expenditure is a component of aggregate expenditure, so when government expenditure changes, aggregate demand changes. Real GDP changes and induces a change in consumption expenditure, which brings a further change in aggregate expenditure. A multiplier process ensues.

A Mackenzie Valley Pipeline Multiplier Canada's Arctic region is rich in natural gas. But to get that gas to market, a $16 billion pipeline must be built. If the project goes ahead (it is controversial because of its impact on the environment), it will have a large multiplier effect in northern Canada. Construction workers will spend much of their income in the Arctic region. Retail stores, schools, health-care centres, hotels and motels, and recreational facilities will open and hire yet more people who will spend yet more income. The initial increase in aggregate expenditure will induce a further increase in aggregate demand.

The Autonomous Tax Multiplier

The **autonomous tax multiplier** is the magnification effect of a change in autonomous taxes on aggregate demand. A *decrease* in taxes *increases* disposable income, which increases consumption expenditure. A decrease in taxes works like an increase in government expenditure. But the magnitude of the autonomous tax multiplier is smaller than the government expenditure multiplier. The reason is that a $1 tax cut generates *less than* $1 of additional expenditure. The marginal propensity to consume determines the increase in consumption expenditure induced by a tax cut. For example, if the marginal propensity to consume is 0.75, then a $1 tax cut increases consumption expenditure by only 75 cents. In this case, the tax multiplier is 0.75 times the magnitude of the government expenditure multiplier.

A GST Cut Multiplier The government has twice cut the GST. These tax cuts had a multiplier effect. With more disposable income, people increased consumption expenditure. This spending increased other people's incomes, which spurred yet more consumption expenditure. These tax cuts and their multiplier effects helped to keep the Canadian economy expanding through 2007 and 2008.

The Balanced Budget Multiplier

The **balanced budget multiplier** is the magnification effect on aggregate demand of a simultaneous change in government expenditure and taxes that leaves the budget balance unchanged. The balanced budget multiplier is positive because a $1 increase in government expenditure increases aggregate demand by more than a $1 increase in taxes decreases aggregate demand. So when both government expenditure and taxes increase by $1, aggregate demand increases.

Discretionary Fiscal Stabilization

If real GDP is below potential GDP, discretionary fiscal policy might be used in an attempt to restore full employment. The government might increase its expenditure on goods and services, cut taxes, or do some of both. These actions would increase aggregate demand. If they were timed correctly and were of the correct magnitude, they could restore full employment. Figure 29.8 shows how. Potential GDP is $1,200 billion, but real GDP is below potential at $1,100 billion and there is a $100 billion *recessionary gap* (see Chapter 26, p. 637). To restore full employment, the government takes a discretionary fiscal policy action. An increase in government expenditure or a tax cut increases aggregate expenditure by ΔE. If this were the only change in spending plans, the AD curve would become $AD_0 + \Delta E$ in Fig. 29.8. But the fiscal policy action sets off a multiplier process, which increases consumption expenditure. As the multiplier process plays out, aggregate demand increases further and the AD curve shifts rightward to AD_1.

With no change in the price level, the economy would move from point A to point B on AD_1. But the increase in aggregate demand combined with the upward-sloping SAS curve brings a rise in the price level. The economy moves to point C, and the economy returns to full employment.

Figure 29.9 illustrates the opposite case in which discretionary fiscal policy is used to eliminate inflationary pressure. The government decreases its expenditure

on goods and services or raises taxes to decrease aggregate demand. In the figure, the fiscal policy action decreases aggregate expenditure by ΔE and the AD curve shifts to $AD_0 - \Delta E$. The initial decrease in aggregate expenditure sets off a multiplier process, which decreases consumption expenditure. The multiplier process decreases aggregate demand further and the AD curve shifts leftward to AD_1.

With no change in the price level, the economy would move from point A to point B on AD_1 in Fig. 29.9. But the decrease in aggregate demand combined with the upward-sloping SAS curve brings a fall in the price level. So the economy moves to point C, where the inflationary gap has been eliminated, inflation has been avoided, and the economy is back at full employment.

Figures 29.8 and 29.9 make fiscal policy look easy: Calculate the recessionary gap or the inflationary gap and the multiplier, change government expenditure or taxes, and eliminate the gap. In reality, things are not that easy.

FIGURE 29.8 Expansionary Fiscal Policy

Potential GDP is $1,200 billion, real GDP is $1,100 billion, and there is a $100 billion recessionary gap. An increase in government expenditure or a tax cut increases expenditure by ΔE. A multiplier effect shifts the AD curve rightward to AD_1, the price level rises to 110, real GDP increases to $1,200 billion, and the recessionary gap is eliminated.

FIGURE 29.9 Contractionary Fiscal Policy

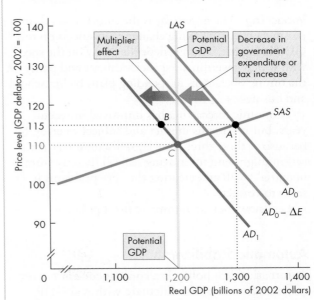

Potential GDP is $1,200 billion, real GDP is $1,300 billion, and there is a $100 billion inflationary gap. A decrease in government expenditure or a rise in taxes decreases expenditure by ΔE. A multiplier effect shifts the AD curve leftward to AD_1, the price level falls to 110, real GDP decreases to $1,200 billion, and the inflationary gap is eliminated.

Limitations of Discretionary Fiscal Policy

The use of discretionary fiscal policy is seriously hampered by three time lags:

- Recognition lag
- Law-making lag
- Impact lag

Recognition Lag The *recognition lag* is the time it takes to figure out that fiscal policy actions are needed. This process has two aspects: assessing the current state of the economy and forecasting its future state.

Law-Making Lag The *law-making lag* is the time it takes Parliament to pass the laws needed to change taxes or spending. This process takes time because each member of Parliament has a different idea about what is the best tax or spending program to change, so long debates and committee meetings are needed to reconcile conflicting views. The economy might benefit from fiscal stimulation today, but by the time Parliament acts, a different fiscal medicine is needed.

Impact Lag The *impact lag* is the time it takes from passing a tax or spending change to its effects on real GDP being felt. This lag depends partly on the speed with which government agencies can act and partly on the timing of changes in spending plans by households and businesses.

Economic forecasting has improved in recent years, but it remains inexact and subject to error. So because of these three time lags, discretionary fiscal action might end up moving real GDP away from potential GDP and creating the very problems it seeks to correct.

Let's now look at automatic fiscal policy.

Automatic Stabilizers

Automatic fiscal policy is a consequence of tax revenues and outlays that fluctuate with real GDP. These features of fiscal policy are called **automatic stabilizers** because they work to stabilize real GDP without explicit action by the government. Their name is borrowed from engineering and conjures up images of shock absorbers, thermostats, and sophisticated devices that keep airplanes and ships steady in turbulent air and seas.

The 2008 U.S. Fiscal Stimulus Package
Closing the Output Gap

As recession fears grew in the wake of the U.S. sub-prime mortgage crisis, U.S. Congress passed the *Economic Stimulus Act of 2008*. This act of *discretionary fiscal policy* was designed to increase aggregate demand and close a recessionary gap.

Tax rebates were the key component of the package and their effect on aggregate demand depends on the extent to which they are spent and saved.

The last time the U.S. federal government boosted aggregate demand with a tax rebate was in 2001 and a statistical investigation of the effects estimated that 70 percent of the rebates were spent within six months of being received.

The rebates in the 2008 fiscal package were targeted predominantly at low-income individuals and families, so the experience of 2001 would be likely to apply: Most of the rebates would be spent.

The cost of the package in 2008 was about $160 billion, so aggregate demand would be expected to increase by close to this amount and then by a multiplier as the initial spending became someone else's income and so boosted their spending.

The figure illustrates the effects of the package. Before the rebates, aggregate demand was AD_0 and real GDP was $11.7 trillion. The rebates increased aggregate demand to $AD_0 + \Delta E$, and a multiplier increased it to AD_1. Real GDP and the price level increased and the recessionary gap narrowed.

Effects of Fiscal Stimulus Act of 2008

Induced Taxes On the revenues side of the budget, tax laws define tax *rates*, not tax *dollars*. Tax dollars paid depend on tax rates and incomes. But incomes vary with real GDP, so tax revenues depend on real GDP. Taxes that vary with real GDP are called **induced taxes**. When real GDP increases in an expansion, wages and profits rise, so the taxes on these incomes—induced taxes—rise. When real GDP decreases in a recession, wages and profits fall, so the induced taxes on these incomes fall.

Transfer Payments On the outlays side of the budget, the government creates programs that pay benefits to suitably qualified people and businesses. The spending on such programs results in transfer payments that depend on the economic state of individual citizens and businesses. When the economy is in a recession, unemployment is high, the number of people experiencing economic hardship increases, and a larger number of firms and farms experience hard times. Transfer payments increase. When the economy expands, unemployment falls and the number of people, firms, and farms experiencing economic hardship decreases. Transfer payments decrease.

Induced taxes and transfer payments decrease the multiplier effects of changes in autonomous expenditure (such as investment and exports). So they moderate both expansions and recessions and make real GDP more stable. They achieve this outcome by weakening the link between real GDP and disposable income and so reduce the effect of a change in real GDP on consumption expenditure. When real GDP increases, induced taxes increase and transfer payments decrease, so disposable income does not increase by as much as the increase in real GDP. As a result, consumption expenditure does not increase by as much as it otherwise would and the multiplier effect is reduced.

We can see the effects of automatic stabilizers by looking at the way in which the government budget deficit fluctuates over the business cycle.

Budget Deficit Over the Business Cycle Figure 29.10 shows the business cycle in part (a) and fluctuations in the budget balance in part (b) between 1980 and 2008. Both parts highlight recessions by shading those periods. By comparing the two parts of the figure, you can see the relationship between the business cycle and the budget deficit. When the economy is in an expansion, the budget deficit declines. (In the figure, a declining deficit means a deficit that is getting closer to

FIGURE 29.10   The Business Cycle and the Budget Deficit

(a) Growth and recessions

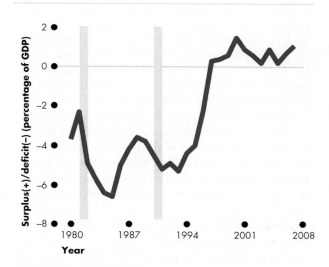

(b) Federal budget balance

As real GDP fluctuates around potential GDP in part (a), the budget deficit fluctuates in part (b). During a recession (shaded years), tax revenues decrease, transfer payments increase, and the budget deficit increases. The deficit also increases *before* a recession as real GDP growth slows and *after* a recession before real GDP growth speeds up.

Sources of data: Statistics Canada, CANSIM Tables 380-0002 and 380-0007, and the Bank of Canada's estimate of the output gap.

zero.) As the expansion slows before the recession begins, the budget deficit increases. It continues to increase during the recession and for a period after the recession is over. Then, when the expansion is well under way, the budget deficit declines again.

The budget deficit fluctuates with the business cycle because both revenues and outlays fluctuate with real GDP. As real GDP increases during an expansion, tax revenues increase and transfer payments decrease, so the budget deficit automatically decreases. As real GDP decreases during a recession, tax revenues decrease and transfer payments increase, so the budget deficit automatically increases. Fluctuations in investment and exports have a multiplier effect on real GDP. But fluctuations in the budget deficit decrease the swings in disposable income and make the multiplier effect smaller. They dampen both expansions and recessions.

Cyclical and Structural Balances Because the government budget balance fluctuates with the business cycle, we need a method of measuring the balance that tells us whether it is a temporary cyclical phenomenon or a persistent phenomenon. A government that wants to achieve a balanced budget can ignore a temporary cyclical surplus or deficit because it will vanish when full employment returns. But a surplus or deficit that persists even at full employment cannot be ignored and requires government action to remove it.

To determine whether the budget balance is persistent or temporary and cyclical, economists have developed the concepts of the structural budget balance and the cyclical budget balance. The **structural surplus or deficit** is the budget balance that would occur if the economy were at full employment and real GDP were equal to potential GDP. The **cyclical surplus or deficit** is the actual surplus or deficit minus the structural surplus or deficit. That is, the cyclical surplus or deficit is the part of the budget balance that arises purely because real GDP does not equal potential GDP. For example, suppose that the budget deficit is $100 billion, and that economists have determined that there is a structural deficit of $25 billion. In that case, there is a cyclical deficit of $75 billion.

Figure 29.11 illustrates the concepts of the cyclical surplus or deficit and the structural surplus or deficit. The blue curve shows government outlays. The outlays curve slopes downward because transfer payments, a component of government outlays, decrease

FIGURE 29.11   Cyclical and Structural Surpluses and Deficits

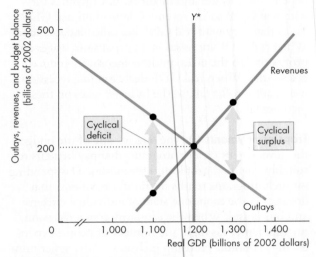

(a) Cyclical deficit and cyclical surplus

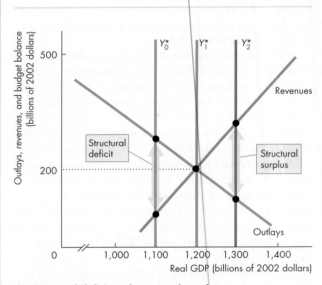

(b) Structural deficit and structural surplus

In part (a), potential GDP is $1,200 billion. When real GDP is less than potential GDP, the budget is in a *cyclical deficit*. When real GDP exceeds potential GDP, the budget is in a *cyclical surplus*. The government has a *balanced budget* when real GDP equals potential GDP. In part (b), if real GDP and potential GDP are $1,100 billion, there is a *structural deficit*. But if real GDP and potential GDP are $1,300 billion, there is a *structural surplus*.

myeconlab animation

Canada's 2009–10 Budget Deficit

Is It Structural or Cyclical?

Canada's Conservative government, first elected in January 2006 and re-elected in October 2008, has placed a high priority on maintaining a federal budget surplus.

The government wants to maintain a surplus for two reasons. First, it believes that the debt created by the long run of deficits during the 1980s and 1990s remains too large and it wants to see that debt lowered every year. Second, it believes that aiming for a surplus places a discipline on Parliament that can always find reasons to spend ever larger amounts on public projects and social programs.

Given this priority, when Canada began to feel the down draught of the U.S. and global growth slowdown of 2008 and the forecasted recession of 2009, the government faced a dilemma. Should it stick to its surplus priority or join the call for fiscal stimulus to lessen the recession's impact? The government's decision was to permit a cyclical deficit but to maintain a structural balanced budget.

The figure illustrates the situation in Canada in 2009. Potential GDP was (our estimate) $1,370 billion and if actual real GDP remained at that full-employment level, the budget would be in a small structural surplus.

The forecast for real GDP in 2009 was around $1,330 billion, a recessionary gap of about $40 billion. At that low level of real GDP, the budget moves into a cyclical deficit. A discretionary stimulus would lower the structural surplus and increase the cyclical deficit.

Canada's Structural Surplus and Cyclical Deficit

as real GDP increases. The green curve shows revenues. The revenues curve slopes upward because most components of revenues increase as real GDP increases.

In Fig. 29.11(a), potential GDP is $1,200 billion. If real GDP equals potential GDP, the government has a *balanced budget*. Outlays and revenues each equal $200 billion. If real GDP is less than potential GDP, outlays exceed revenues and there is a *cyclical deficit*. If real GDP is greater than potential GDP, outlays are less than revenues and there is a *cyclical surplus*.

In Fig. 29.11(b), if both real GDP and potential GDP are $1,100 billion ($Y^*_0$), the government has a budget deficit and it is a *structural deficit*. If both real GDP and potential GDP are $1,200 billion ($Y^*_1$), the budget is balanced—a *structural balance* of zero. If both real GDP and potential GDP are $1,300 billion ($Y^*_2$), the government has a budget surplus and it is a *structural surplus*.

Review Quiz

1 How can the federal government use fiscal policy to stabilize the business cycle?
2 Why is the government expenditure multiplier larger than the autonomous tax multiplier?
3 Why does a balanced budget increase in spending and taxes increase aggregate demand?
4 How do induced taxes and transfer payments work as automatic stabilizers to dampen the business cycle?
5 How do we tell whether a budget deficit needs government action to remove it?

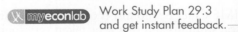 Work Study Plan 29.3 and get instant feedback.

You've seen how fiscal policy influences potential GDP and real GDP fluctuations. *Reading Between the Lines* on pp. 724–725 applies what you've learned and looks at the attempt by world leaders to coordinate fiscal stimulus and avoid global recession.

Global Coordinated Fiscal Policy

IMF Urges Stimulus as Global Growth Marked Down Sharply

November 6, 2008

IMF forecast cuts world growth by 3/4 percentage points to 2.2 percent for 2009. IMF says policies to stimulate growth can help cushion downturn. ...

The IMF is urging countries to stimulate their economies in the face of a bigger-than-expected slowdown in the global economy triggered by recent financial turmoil. ...

IMF Chief Economist Olivier Blanchard told a news conference: "We think that global fiscal expansion is very much needed at this point. If it comes, then the forecast we have will be on the pessimistic side." ...

Blanchard said the IMF would "advocate at the G-20 a global fiscal expansion as one of the measures that has to be taken fairly soon." Jorg Decressin, of the IMF's Research Department, told the news conference that the United States, Germany, and China were among the countries that have room for additional fiscal stimulus. ...

"There is a clear need for additional macroeconomic policy stimulus relative to what has been announced thus far. ... Room to ease monetary policy should be exploited, especially now that inflation concerns have moderated," [the IMF forecast] stated.

But the forecast said that monetary policy easing may not be enough. "Fiscal stimulus can be effective if it is well targeted, supported by accommodative monetary policy, and implemented in countries that have fiscal space. ...

At a meeting in Toronto on November 6, 2008, Prime Minister Stephen Harper is reported by Bloomberg to have said "governments and central banks face a balancing act deciding how much to stimulate the global economy. There is a very real concern that policy makers may overdo support for the economy, jeopardizing longer-term growth."

Essence of the Story

- The IMF forecasts that all the large industrialized economies will shrink in 2009.

- The IMF Chief Economist is calling for coordinated fiscal stimulus and that it be taken very soon.

- The IMF believes that there is also room to ease monetary policy.

- Prime Minister Stephen Harper said that Canada would take further steps but warned that deciding how much to stimulate the global economy is a balancing act and if policy makers overdo stimulation, longer-term growth might be jeopardized.

Economic Analysis

- The International Monetary Fund (IMF) reported the world real GDP growth rates shown in Fig. 1.

- The average world real GDP growth rate since 2000 is 3.7 percent per year.

- For 2009, the IMF forecasts a growth rate of 2.2 percent, which is similar to that for 2001.

- The outlook for 2009 is unusual in that all the major countries are expected to be in recession with positive world growth coming from the fast-growing developing economies, mainly in Asia.

- To help avoid a deep and long recession, the governments of the G-20 nations (the richest industrial countries and the biggest developing countries) held emergency meetings in Sao Paolo and Washington and discussed the possibility of coordinating fiscal stimulus.

- The United States and China were quick to announce and implement large increases in government expenditure and tax cuts in one of the largest fiscal stimulation measures ever taken.

- Other countries, including Canada, moved more cautiously and Stephen Harper cautioned that stimulus could be overdone.

- Figure 2 shows what Stephen Harper is concerned about.

- World aggregate demand in 2009 is forecasted to be AD_0. The world short-run aggregate supply curve is SAS. Equilibrium real GDP is forecasted to be $44 trillion, which is below potential GDP (here assumed to be $45 trillion).

- A well-judged coordinated fiscal stimulus would shift the AD curve rightward from AD_0 to AD_1. World real GDP would move to potential GDP and the price level would rise (inflation would temporarily rise).

- But the coordinated fiscal stimulus in combination with an expansionary monetary policy (see Chapter 30) might turn out to be more than enough to restore full employment.

- Greater fiscal stimulus (or monetary stimulus) might shift the AD curve further rightward to AD_2. In this case, an inflationary gap will open up and the inflation rate most likely will rise.

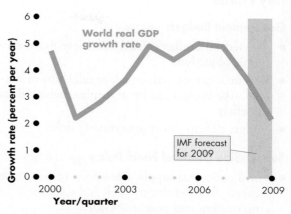

Figure 1 World real GDP growth rate: 2000–2009

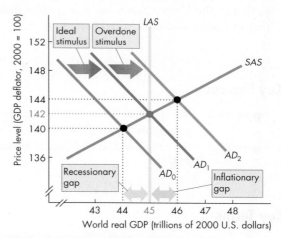

Figure 2 World aggregate supply and aggregate demand

- If the fiscal stimulus turns out to be too large, a further danger is that private investment will get crowded out (see Chapter 23, p. 555–556) and productivity growth will be damaged.

- If crowding out does occur, potential GDP growth will slow and the inflationary gap will become even wider. Rapid and unpredictable inflation will lower investment and slow real GDP growth even further.

- These longer-term consequences of overstimulation are what Stephen Harper is worried about in his remarks reported in the news article.

SUMMARY

Key Points

Government Budgets (pp. 708–713)

- The federal budget is used to achieve macroeconomic objectives.
- Revenues can exceed, equal, or fall short of outlays—the budget can be in surplus, balanced, or in deficit.
- Budget deficits create government debt.

Supply-Side Effects of Fiscal Policy (pp. 714–717)

- Fiscal policy has supply-side effects because taxes weaken the incentive to work and decrease employment and potential GDP.
- The Canadian labour market tax wedge is similar to that in the United States but it is smaller than that in France and the United Kingdom.

- Fiscal policy has supply-side effects because taxes weaken the incentive to save and invest, which lowers the growth rate of real GDP.
- The Laffer curve shows the relationship between the tax rate and the amount of tax revenue collected.

Stabilizing the Business Cycle (pp. 718–723)

- Fiscal stabilization can be discretionary or automatic.
- Discretionary changes in government expenditure or taxes can change aggregate demand but are hampered by law-making lags and the difficulty of correctly diagnosing and forecasting the state of the economy.
- Automatic changes in fiscal policy moderate the business cycle.

Key Figures

Figure 29.5   The Effects of the Income Tax on Aggregate Supply, 714
Figure 29.6   The Effects of a Tax on Capital Income, 716
Figure 29.8   Expansionary Fiscal Policy, 719
Figure 29.9   Contractionary Fiscal Policy, 719

Key Terms

Automatic fiscal policy, 718
Automatic stabilizers, 720
Autonomous tax multiplier, 718
Balanced budget, 709
Balanced budget multiplier, 718
Budget deficit, 709
Budget surplus, 709

Cyclical surplus or deficit, 722
Discretionary fiscal policy, 718
Federal budget, 708
Fiscal policy, 708
Government debt, 711
Government expenditure multiplier, 718

Induced taxes, 721
Laffer curve, 717
Provincial budget, 708
Structural surplus or deficit, 722
Supply-side effects, 714
Tax wedge, 715

PROBLEMS and APPLICATIONS

 Work problems 1–9 in Chapter 29 Study Plan and get instant feedback.
Work problems 10–18 as Homework, a Quiz, or a Test if assigned by your instructor.

1. The government is proposing to raise the tax rate on labour income. Use appropriate diagrams to show the directions of change, not exact magnitudes, of the supply-side effects of such a policy.

   a. What will happen to the supply of labour and the demand for labour and why?
   b. How will the equilibrium quantity of labour employed change and why?
   c. How will the equilibrium before-tax wage rate and after-tax wage rate change and why?
   d. What will happen to potential GDP?
   e. How would your answers to the above questions change if at the same time as raising the tax rate on labour income, the government cut the rate of sales tax to keep the amount of tax collected constant?
   f. What evidence would you present to the government to support the view that a lower tax on labour income will increase employment, potential GDP, and aggregate supply?

2. Suppose that in China, investment is $400 billion, saving is $400 billion, tax revenues are $500 billion, exports are $300 billion, and imports are $200 billion.

   a. Calculate government expenditure.
   b. What is the government budget balance?
   c. Is the government exerting a positive or negative impact on investment?
   d. What fiscal policy action might increase investment and speed economic growth? Explain how the policy action would work.

3. Suppose that instead of taxing nominal capital income, the government changed the tax code so that the inflation rate is subtracted from the interest rate before the taxable income from capital is calculated. Explain and illustrate the effect that this change would have on

   a. The tax rate on capital income.
   b. The supply of loanable funds.
   c. The demand for loanable funds.
   d. Investment and the real interest rate.

4. The economy is in a recession, and the recessionary gap is large.

   a. Describe the discretionary and automatic fiscal policy actions that might occur.
   b. Describe a discretionary fiscal stimulation package that could be used that would not bring a budget deficit.
   c. Explain the risks of discretionary fiscal policy in this situation.

5. The economy is in a recession, the recessionary gap is large, and there is a budget deficit.

   a. Do we know whether the budget deficit is structural or cyclical? Explain your answer.
   b. Do we know whether automatic stabilizers are increasing or decreasing aggregate demand? Explain your answer.
   c. If a discretionary increase in government expenditure occurs, what happens to the structural deficit or surplus? Explain.

6. **Strengthening Canada's Tax Advantage**

   The Government ... announc[ed] $60 billion in tax reductions for individuals, families, and businesses over this and the next five fiscal years. Combined with previous tax relief introduced by the Government, total tax relief over the same period approaches $200 billion. ... The actions in Budget 2008 are affordable, sustainable, and focused on key priorities ... reducing taxes on savings promotes investment, jobs and economic growth. ... The capital cost allowance (CCA) system determines how much of the cost of a capital asset a business may deduct each year for tax purposes. ... [An] accelerated CCA rate ... provides an incentive for ... businesses to accelerate or increase capital investments. ... Canada's scientific research and experimental development tax incentive program provid[ed] over $4 billion in tax assistance in 2007.

   Department of Finance Canada, February 26, 2008

   a. Explain the potential demand-side and supply-side effects of each of the tax policies.
   b. Explain the argument made that the tax cuts are "affordable" and "sustainable."

c. If the government provided $200 billion in tax cuts, does that mean that tax revenues will fall by $200 billion? Explain.

7. **Raise Corporate Taxes in Canada, Labour Group Argues**

Despite some reductions, corporate tax rates in Canada are still the 11th highest of about 80 developed and developing economies. ... "Canada's corporate income tax rate is on the wrong side of the Laffer curve," a C.D. Howe report said. ... [T]he CLC [Canadian Labour Congress] challenges the argument of business groups that cutting taxes will boost investment. Federal and provincial corporate tax revenues have fallen. ... A $15-billion-a-year loss in corporate tax revenues ... [and] past tax cuts have not been matched by increased business investment, the Canadian Labour Congress argues. ...

CanWest News, September 21, 2007

a. Explain the potential demand-side and supply-side effects of lower corporate tax rates and draw a graph to illustrate these effects.
b. Explain the argument that lower corporate tax rates can increase tax revenue in Canada.
c. Why might Canada's high corporate tax ranking support the C.D. Howe claim about being "on the wrong side of the Laffer curve?" What evidence does the CLC present to refute this claim?
d. If cutting corporate income tax rates resulted in a loss in corporate tax revenues, does that necessarily mean that the lower tax rates did not boost business investment? Explain.

8. **Canada May Offer New Economic Stimulus**

Finance Minister Jim Flaherty is suggesting the federal government may be willing to provide additional economic stimulus to inject life into Canada's dormant economy—and he's urging the provinces to consider following suit. ... "To the extent that provinces and territories can provide additional stimulus through their policies, that's a benefit to Canadians overall." One area that Canada can move on immediately, Flaherty said, is to speed up infrastructure projects already in the planning stages. ... Flaherty noted that previously introduced federal tax cuts are already adding $1.4 billion in stimulus to the Canadian economy this year and will provide a boost of almost $2 billion in 2009.

CTV News, November 9, 2008

a. Explain Jim Flaherty's statement that "To the extent that provinces and territories can provide additional stimulus through their policies, that's a benefit to Canadians overall."
b. How might Jim Flaherty's plan to "speed up infrastructure projects already in the planning stages" provide stimulus to stabilize the business cycle without imposing deficit pressure on the budget?
c. Explain and use a graph to show how income tax cuts can provide both supply-side and demand-side stimulus.
d. Why might the stimulus provided by the tax cuts be greater in 2009 than in 2008?
e. Explain which would have a larger impact on aggregate demand: a $1.4 billion tax cut or a $1.4 billion increase in government spending.

9. **Canada Will Try to Avoid Deficit: Harper**

Prime Minister Stephen Harper said ... "The Minister of Finance has been looking at a series of careful measures to try and preserve Canada's balanced budget position. ... But if there's a world-wide agreement we will engage in sufficient stimulus to do our part in carrying global economic demand." He said the government has not yet decided if it would go into deficit spending. ... "We are talking to our American counterparts. On the one hand we can't ignore what the Americans will do[;] on the other hand, we as the government of Canada have to ultimately undertake our own actions... in the best interests of the Canadian economy and the taxpayers. ... The world economy has difficult times ahead," he said. "Canada has so far been sheltered from most of those but will not be sheltered entirely from those problems. ... There is a view that monetary policy alone will not be sufficient to take the global economy through this crisis. ..."

Financial Post, November 15, 2008

a. Explain how Canada could experience a budget deficit even in the absence of discretionary stimulus.
b. Is it possible for Canada to use fiscal stimulus and still avoid a budget deficit? Explain.
c. Explain the potential advantages and disadvantages of coordinating discretionary fiscal policy decisions with other countries.
d. What does Stephen Harper imply about his view of the appropriate roles of monetary policy and fiscal policy?

10. Suppose that in Canada, investment is $160 billion, saving is $140 billion, government expenditure on goods and services is $150 billion, exports are $200 billion, and imports are $250 billion.

   a. What is the amount of tax revenue?
   b. What is the government budget balance?
   c. Is the government exerting a positive or negative impact on investment?
   d. What fiscal policy action might increase investment and speed economic growth? Explain how the policy action would work.

11. Suppose that capital income taxes are based (as they are in Canada and most countries) on nominal interest rates. And suppose that the inflation rate increases by 5 percent. Use appropriate diagrams to explain and illustrate the effect that this change would have on

   a. The tax rate on capital income.
   b. The supply of loanable funds.
   c. The demand for loanable funds.
   d. Equilibrium investment.
   e. The equilibrium real interest rate.

12. The economy is in a boom and the inflationary gap is large.

   a. Describe the discretionary and automatic fiscal policy actions that might occur.
   b. Describe a discretionary fiscal restraint package that could be used that would not produce serious negative supply-side effects.
   c. Explain the risks of discretionary fiscal policy in this situation.

13. The economy is in a boom, the inflationary gap is large, and there is a budget deficit.

   a. Do we know whether the budget deficit is structural or cyclical? Explain your answer.
   b. Do we know whether automatic stabilizers are increasing or decreasing aggregate demand? Explain your answer.
   c. If a discretionary decrease in government expenditure occurs, what happens to the structural balance? Explain your answer.

14. **Clueless Economists Find the Answer**
   "A month ago, when we would normally have released ... an updated Canadian outlook, the economic landscape was in major disarray, and we instead put out a memo titled We Don't Have a Clue and We're Not Going to Pretend That We

Do," economists at the University of Toronto's Institute for Policy Analysis noted. ... "Since that time, the situation has gradually settled down and important new information has been forthcoming such that we now feel that we have enough 'clues' to be able to present forecasts." ... For Canada, they predict the economy contracted at a 0.2-percent annual pace in the summer quarter, will shrink a further 0.2 percent this quarter, and then by a marginal 0.1 percent in the first quarter of 2009, before expanding by 0.4 percent in the spring, and picking up steam in the second half of next year ... an anemic 0.4-percent expansion for all of 2008, down from 2.7 percent in 2007, and then only marginal 0.6-per-cent growth in 2009, after which it projects a strong 3.6-per-cent expansion in 2010.

Ottawa Citizen, November 11, 2008

   a. Explain how economic forecasting can be used to improve discretionary fiscal policy.
   b. How does the uncertainty surrounding economic forecasting limit the effectiveness of discretionary fiscal policy?
   c. Given a forecast of an impending recession, explain how automatic stabilizers may help smooth out the business cycle.
   d. Assuming that automatic stabilizers are not enough to address an impending recession, explain and draw a graph to illustrate how discretionary fiscal policy could be used. What are the potential consequences if these discretionary policies suffer from significant law-making and impact lags?

15. **The Canadian Debt-Strategy Model**
   In its role as fiscal agent to the government, the Bank of Canada provides analysis and advice on decisions about the government's domestic debt portfolio. Debt-management decisions depend on assumptions about future interest rates, macroeconomic outcomes, and fiscal policy, yet when a debt-strategy decision is taken, none of these factors can be known with certainty. ... The debt managers who are responsible for the government's financing strategy have the complex task of choosing a strategy that minimizes the cost of the debt portfolio. ... In any given year, a government must borrow to finance any excess of government expenditures over revenues as well as any maturing debt issued in previous periods.

This borrowing requirement thus depends on past decisions regarding debt issuance and on the government's current surplus or deficit position. The government's position, in turn, depends on the general performance of the macroeconomy and on fiscal policy.

Bank of Canada Review, Summer 2008

a. Explain what is meant by "the cost of the debt portfolio."
b. Explain what factors determine whether or not Canada's government debt is worth the "cost."
c. Explain how annual imbalances impact the government's debt.
d. Explain how a persistent budget deficit can feed itself.
e. Why are managing and forecasting government debt so challenging?

16. **Bracing for Downturn**

Sixteen years of almost uninterrupted job growth has produced an embarrassment of riches in Canada's Employment Insurance account—a surplus, in fact, of $54 billion at current reckoning. But with economic storm clouds gathering south of the border, the Conservative government looks to be preparing for some turbulence ahead. It is creating a special cushion of $2 billion in a side account to help pay for any quick surge in payouts caused by an economic downturn. ...

CBC News, February 26, 2008

a. Explain how Employment Insurance (EI) serves as an automatic stabilizer. How does being prepared for a "quick surge" impact the effectiveness of EI?
b. Explain how EI impacts the budget balance over the business cycle.
c. What is the potential supply-side impact of EI?

17. **Conservative Canada Taking Fiscal Stimulus Slowly**

Canada says it will play its part in a global effort to stimulate the world economy, but Finance Minister Jim Flaherty said on Saturday he still did not foresee running a budget deficit in the current fiscal year. Flaherty said he would include fiscal measures when he presents his fall fiscal and economic update in the last week of November, but it would not likely contain new tax cuts and

it would also try to restrain public sector spending. ... [T]he country might move into a deficit as the result of future, undefined stimulus measures but that would likely only start in the fiscal year that begins April 1. ... Canada is the only one of the Group of Seven big industrial countries still to have a fiscal surplus, and Prime Minister Stephen Harper said this budget position gave it more latitude than many others, especially those with structural deficits. "What we've got to be sure is if we do short-term deficit spending as a deliberate policy—if we do that; we haven't settled on doing that—we will have to be able to demonstrate to Canadians that those deficits will genuinely be short-term and cyclical and we will come out of them quickly," he said.

Reuters, November 15, 2008

a. Explain how fiscal policy may still help stabilize the business cycle even if Canada fails to cut taxes and follows through with plans to "restrain public sector spending."
b. If the government did cut taxes and increase spending, which impact would have a larger multiplier effect? Explain.
c. What major limitation associated with the usage of discretionary fiscal policy is revealed in this article?
d. Explain why Prime Minister Harper believes Canada currently has more "latitude" when designing fiscal policy than other industrial nations.
e. Explain the difference between cyclical and structural deficits.
f. Explain why Prime Minister Harper places so much emphasis on pointing out that any deficit must be "short-term and cyclical."

18. Study *Reading Between the Lines* on pp. 724–725.

a. Describe the fiscal policy proposed by the G-20 finance ministers.
b. Explain the effects of the proposed fiscal policy if it is implemented well.
c. Explain Prime Minister Stephen Harper's concerns about overstimulating the global and Canadian economies.
d. Why are automatic stabilizers not sufficient to boost aggregate demand in the Canadian and global economies in 2009?

30 ◆ Monetary Policy

After studying this chapter, you will be able to

- Describe Canada's monetary policy objective and the framework for setting and achieving it

- Explain how the Bank of Canada makes its interest rate decision and achieves its interest rate target

- Explain the transmission channels through which the Bank of Canada influences the inflation rate

- Explain and compare alternative monetary policy strategies

At eight regularly scheduled meetings a year, the Bank of Canada announces whether the interest rate will rise, fall, or remain constant until the next decision date. And every business day, the Bank operates in financial markets to implement its decision and ensure that its target interest rate is achieved. Financial market traders, economic journalists, and pundits watch the economy for clues about what the Bank will decide at its next meeting.

How does the Bank of Canada make its interest rate decision? What exactly does it do every day to keep the interest rate where it wants it? And how does a change in the Bank's interest rate influence the economy? Can the Bank speed up economic growth and lower unemployment by lowering the interest rate and can the Bank keep inflation in check by raising the interest rate?

The Bank of Canada's monetary policy strategy gradually evolves, and the current strategy isn't the only one that might be used. Is the current monetary policy strategy the best one? What are the benefits and what are the risks associated with the alternative monetary policy strategies?

You learned about the functions of the Bank of Canada and its long-run effects on the price level and the inflation rate in Chapter 24. In this chapter, you will learn about the Bank's monetary policy in both the long run and the short run. You will learn how the Bank influences the interest rate and how a change in the interest rate influences the economy. You will also review the alternative ways in which monetary policy might be conducted. In *Reading Between the Lines* at the end of the chapter, you will see the Bank of Canada in an aggressive move to avoid a deep and prolonged recession in 2008 and 2009.

◆ Monetary Policy Objective and Framework

Canada's monetary policy objective and the framework for setting and achieving that objective stem from the relationship between the Bank of Canada and the government of Canada.

We'll first discuss the objective of monetary policy and then describe the framework and assignment of responsibility for achieving the objective.

Monetary Policy Objective

The objective of monetary policy is ultimately political, and it stems from the mandate of the Bank, which is set out in the Bank of Canada Act.

Bank of Canada Act The objective of monetary policy as set out in the preamble to the Bank of Canada Act of 1935 is to

> regulate credit and currency in the best interests of the economic life of the nation ... and to mitigate by its influence fluctuations in the general level of production, trade, prices and employment, so far as may be possible within the scope of monetary action ...

In simple language, these words have come to mean that the Bank's job is to control the quantity of money and interest rates in order to avoid inflation and, when possible, prevent excessive swings in real GDP growth and unemployment.

This emphasis on inflation has been made concrete by an agreement between the Bank and government.

Joint Statement of the Government of Canada and the Bank of Canada

In a joint statement (the most recent of which was made in 2006), the government of Canada and the Bank of Canada have agreed that

- The inflation-control target range will be 1 to 3 percent a year.
- Policy will aim at keeping the trend of inflation at the 2 percent target midpoint.
- The agreement will run for five years and be reviewed before the end of 2011.

A monetary policy strategy in which the central bank commits to an explicit inflation target and to explaining how its actions will achieve that target is called **inflation rate targeting**.

Interpretation of the Agreement The inflation-control target uses the Consumer Price Index (or CPI) as the measure of inflation. So the Bank has agreed to keep trend CPI inflation at a target of 2 percent a year.

But the Bank also pays close attention to *core inflation* (see pp. 502–503), which it calls its *operational guide*. The Bank believes that the core inflation rate provides a better measure of the underlying inflation trend and better predicts future CPI inflation.

Although the Bank watches the core inflation rate closely, it must take into account the possibility that the eight volatile elements that it excludes have a different trend inflation rate from the remaining items. As it turns out, between 1995 and 2000, the core and overall CPI trends were the same. But since 2000, the core rate has run at about 0.5 percent a year below the overall CPI inflation rate.

Actual Inflation The performance of Canada's inflation since the mid-1990s, when the current target was initially set, has been close to target. Figure 30.1 shows just how close.

In part (a), you can see the target range of 1 to 3 percent a year. And you can see that the actual inflation rate has only rarely gone outside the target range. You can also see that the inflation rate has been both above target and below target on occasion, so there is no bias or tendency for inflation to be persistently above or below target.

In part (b), you can see the trend of inflation at the 2 percent target midpoint. The actual path of the CPI was on trend from 1995 through 1998 and again from 2001 through 2007. Between 1999 and 2001, the CPI moved below the 2 percent trend line.

The general message of Fig. 30.1 is that the Bank of Canada has done a remarkable job of holding inflation to its 2 percent target with only small and temporary deviations from that goal.

Rationale for an Inflation-Control Target Two main benefits flow from adopting an inflation-control target. The first benefit is that the purpose of the Bank of Canada's policy actions are more clearly understood

FIGURE 30.1   Inflation-Control Target and Outcome

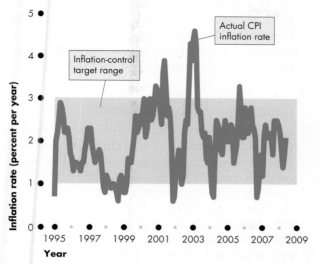

(a) Inflation target and outcome

(b) CPI trend at the 2 percent target midpoint

The Bank of Canada and the government of Canada agreed that the inflation-control target range will be 1 percent to 3 percent (part a) and that policy will aim at keeping the trend of inflation at the 2 percent target midpoint (part b).

Sources of data: Statistics Canada, CANSIM Table 326-0022, and Bank of Canada, Joint Statement of the Government of Canada and the Bank of Canada on the Renewal of the Inflation-Control Target, November 23, 2006.

myeconlab   animation

by financial market traders. A clearer understanding leads to fewer surprises and mistakes on the part of savers and investors.

The second benefit is that the target provides an anchor for expectations about future inflation. Firmly held expectations of low inflation make the short-run output-inflation (or unemployment-inflation) trade-off as favourable as possible. (see Chapter 28, pp. 686–688). Firmly held (and correct) inflation expectations also help to make better economic decisions, which in turn help to achieve a more efficient allocation of resources and more stable economic growth.

Controversy About the Inflation-Control Target Not everyone agrees that the adoption of an inflation-control target brings benefits. Critics argue that by focusing on inflation, the Bank of Canada sometimes permits the unemployment rate to rise or the real GDP growth rate to suffer.

The fear of these critics is that if the inflation rate begins to edge upward towards and perhaps beyond the upper limit of the target range, the Bank of Canada might reign in aggregate demand and push the economy into recession. Related, the Bank might end up permitting the value of the dollar on the foreign exchange market to rise and making exports suffer.

One response of supporters of inflation targeting is that by keeping inflation low and stable, monetary policy makes its maximum possible contribution towards achieving full employment and sustained economic growth.

Another response is, "Look at the record." The last time the Bank of Canada created a recession was at the beginning of the 1990s when it was faced with the threat of ongoing double-digit inflation. Since that time, monetary policy has been sensitive to the state of employment while maintaining its focus on achieving its inflation target.

Responsibility for Monetary Policy

The government of Canada and the Bank of Canada jointly agree on the monetary policy target, but the Bank of Canada Act places responsibility for the conduct of monetary policy on the Bank's Governing Council.

Governing Council of the Bank of Canada The members of the Bank's Governing Council are the Governor, Senior Deputy Governor, and four Deputy Governors.

All the members of the Governing Council are experts in monetary economics and monetary policymaking and, normally, they are people who have been promoted from within the ranks of economists working in the Bank's research and policy departments.

The current Governor (appointed in 2008) is Mark Carney, an economist who has had wide experience in private sector banking, government departments, and the Bank of Canada.

Bank of Canada Economists   The Bank of Canada employs research economists who write papers on monetary policy and the state of the Canadian and international economies. These economists provide the Governing Council with extensive briefings that guide monetary policy.

Consultations with the Government   The Bank of Canada Act requires regular consultations on monetary policy between the Governor and the Minister of Finance. The Act also lays out what must happen if the Governor and the Minister disagree in a profound way.

In such an event, the Minister would direct the Bank in writing to follow a specified course and the Bank would be obliged to accept the directive. The Governor would most likely resign in such a situation. While in the past there have been disagreements between the government and the Bank, no formal directive has ever been issued.

You now know the objective of monetary policy and can describe the framework and assignment of responsibility for achieving that objective. Your next task is to see how the Bank of Canada conducts its monetary policy.

Review Quiz

1 What is the Bank of Canada's objective of monetary policy?
2 What are the two parts of the inflation-control target?
3 How does the core inflation rate differ from the overall CPI inflation rate?
4 What is the Bank of Canada's record in achieving its inflation-control target?

 Work Study Plan 30.1 and get instant feedback.

The Conduct of Monetary Policy

In this section, we describe the way in which the Bank of Canada conducts its monetary policy. We follow this description in the final section with an account of alternative approaches to monetary policy and an evaluation of the Bank's approach.

Choosing a Policy Instrument

As the sole issuer of Canadian money, the Bank of Canada can decide to control the quantity of money (the monetary base), the price of Canadian money on the foreign exchange market (the exchange rate), or the opportunity cost of holding money (the short-term interest rate). If you need a quick refresher, check back to Chapter 24, p. 581 to see how the quantity of money affects the interest rate and to Chapter 25, pp. 611–613 to see how the interest rate or direct intervention in the foreign exchange market affects the exchange rate.

While the Bank of Canada can set any one of these three variables, it cannot set all three. The values of two of them are the consequence of the value at which the third one is set. If the Bank decided to decrease the quantity of money, both the interest rate and the exchange rate would rise. If the Bank decided to raise the interest rate, the quantity of money would decrease and the exchange rate would rise. And if the Bank decided to lower the exchange rate, the quantity of money would increase and the interest rate would fall.

So the Bank must decide which of these three instruments to use. It might decide to select one and stick with it. Or it might switch among them.

The Overnight Rate

The Bank of Canada's choice of policy instrument (which is the same choice as that made by most other major central banks) is a short-term interest rate. Given this choice, the Bank permits the exchange rate and the quantity of money to find their own equilibrium values and has no preset views about what those values should be.

The specific interest rate that the Bank of Canada targets is the **overnight loans rate**, which is the interest rate on overnight loans that members of the Large Value Transfer System or LVTS (the big banks) make to each other (see Chapter 24, p. 575.)

Figure 30.2 shows the overnight loans rate since 1995. You can see that the overnight loans rate was a bit more than 8 percent a year in 1995 and was increased to around 6 percent a year on two occasions. All of these periods with a high overnight rate are ones in which inflation was a concern.

In recent years, the overnight rate has been at historically low levels. The reason is that with inflation well anchored inside its target range, the Bank wanted to lean in the direction of avoiding recession.

Since late 2000, the Bank has established eight fixed dates on which it announces its overnight rate target for the coming period of approximately six weeks. Before 2000, the Bank announced changes in the overnight rate whenever it thought a change was required. And even now, the Bank sometimes acts in an emergency between normal announcement dates.

FIGURE 30.2 The Overnight Loans Rate

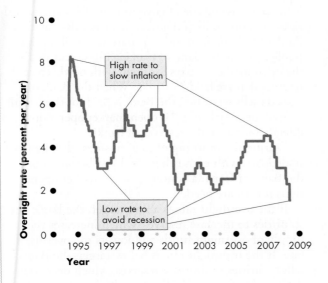

The Bank of Canada sets a target range for the overnight loans rate and then takes actions to keep the rate inside its target range. When the Bank wants to slow inflation, it takes actions that raise the overnight loans rate. When the Bank wants to avoid recession and inflation is low, it takes actions that lower the overnight loans rate.

Source of data: Statistics Canada, CANSIM Table 176-0048.

myeconlab animation

Although the Bank can change the overnight rate by any (reasonable) amount that it chooses, it normally changes the rate by only a quarter of a percentage point.[1]

How does the Bank decide the appropriate level for the overnight rate? And how, having made that decision, does the Bank get the overnight rate to move to the target level? We'll now answer these two questions.

The Bank's Decision-Making Process

Two alternative decision-making processes might be used. They are summarized by the terms:

- Instrument rule
- Targeting rule

Instrument Rule An **instrument rule** is a decision rule for monetary policy that sets the policy instrument at a level that is based on the current state of the economy. The best known instrument rule is the Taylor rule, which sets the interest rate at a level that depends on the deviation of the inflation rate from target and the size and direction of the output gap. For each percentage point by which inflation is above target, the interest rate is set one percentage point higher. And for each percentage point by which real GDP exceeds potential GDP (the percentage size of the output gap), the interest rate is set another percentage point higher. (We examine the Taylor rule later in this chapter—see p. 747.)

Targeting Rule A **targeting rule** is a decision rule for monetary policy that sets the policy instrument at a level that makes the forecast of the policy target equal to the target. Where the policy target is the inflation rate and the instrument is the overnight rate, the targeting rule sets the overnight rate at a level that makes the forecast of the inflation rate equal to the target for the inflation rate.

To implement such a targeting rule, a central bank must gather and process a large amount of information about the economy, the way it responds to shocks, and the way it responds to policy. It must then process all this data and come to a judgment about the best level for the policy instrument.

---

[1] A quarter of a percentage point is also called 25 basis points. A basis point is one-hundredth of one percentage point.

The Bank of Canada (along with most other central banks) follows a process that uses a targeting rule.

For the Bank of Canada, the process begins with an exercise that uses a model of the Canadian economy that you can think of as a sophisticated version of the aggregate supply–aggregate demand model (see Chapter 26). The Bank's economists provide the Governor and Governing Council with a baseline forecast that has the overnight loans rate set at a level that hits the inflation target two years in the future.

All the available regional, national, and international data on macroeconomic performance, financial markets, and inflation expectations are reviewed, discussed, and weighed in a careful deliberative process that ends with the Governing Council finding a consensus on the interest rate level to set.

After announcing an interest rate decision, the Bank engages in a public communication to explain the reasons for the Bank's decision.

Hitting the Overnight Rate Target

Once an interest rate decision is made, the Bank of Canada achieves its target by using two tools:

- Operating band
- Open market operations

Operating Band   The **operating band** is the target overnight rate plus or minus 0.25 percentage points. So the operating band is 0.5 percentage points wide. The Bank of Canada creates the operating band by setting two other interest rates: bank rate and the interest rate on reserves.

Bank rate is the interest rate that the Bank of Canada charges big (LVTS-participating) banks on loans. If a bank is short of reserves, it can always obtain reserves from the Bank of Canada but it must pay bank rate on the amount of borrowed reserves.

The Bank of Canada sets bank rate at the target overnight rate plus 0.25 percentage points. So, for example, when the target overnight rate is 4 percent, bank rate is 4.25 percent.

Because the Bank of Canada is willing to lend funds to banks at this interest rate, bank rate acts as a cap on the overnight loans rate. If a bank can borrow from the Bank of Canada at bank rate, it will not borrow from another bank unless the interest rate is lower than or equal to bank rate.

The Bank of Canada pays banks interest on their reserves at the Bank of Canada. The Bank calls these reserves "settlement balances" and the interest rate that they earn is the **settlement balances rate**. The Bank of Canada sets the settlement balances rate at the target overnight rate minus 0.25 percentage points, which also equals the low end of the Bank's target range for the overnight rate. If banks can earn the settlement balances rate from the Bank of Canada, they will not make overnight loans to other banks unless they earn a higher interest rate than what the Bank of Canada is paying.

You can see now that the Bank of Canada can always make the overnight rate remain within 0.25 percentage points of its target. But the Bank wants to do better than that and keep the overnight loans rate at its target, not at one end of the range or the other. The second policy tool is used to move the overnight rate to its target.

Open Market Operations   An **open market operation** is the purchase or sale of government of Canada securities—Treasury bills and government bonds—by the Bank of Canada from or to a chartered bank or the public. When the Bank of Canada buys securities on the open market, it pays for them with newly created reserves that are held by banks. When the Bank of Canada sells securities, the Bank is paid for them with reserves held by banks. So open market operations directly influence the reserves of banks.

During the morning of each business day, banks trade loans with each other. And just before noon, the Bank of Canada conducts open market operations if they are needed.

If the overnight rate is above target, the Bank buys securities to increase reserves, which increases the supply of overnight funds and lowers the overnight rate. If the overnight rate is below target, the Bank sells securities to decrease reserves, which decreases the supply of overnight funds and raises the overnight rate. If the overnight rate is at the target level, the Bank neither buys nor sells.

How an Open Market Operation Works

When the Bank of Canada conducts an open market operation, the reserves of the banking system change. To see why this outcome occurs, we'll trace the effects of an open market operation in which the Bank of Canada buys $100 million of government securities in the open market from CIBC.

After this transaction has been made,

1. CIBC has $100 million less securities, and the Bank of Canada has $100 million more securities.
2. The Bank of Canada pays for the securities by placing $100 million in CIBC's deposit account at the Bank of Canada.

Figure 30.3 shows the effects of these actions on the balance sheets of the Bank of Canada and CIBC. Ownership of the securities passes from CIBC to the Bank of Canada, so CIBC's assets decrease by $100 million and the Bank of Canada's assets increase by $100 million, as shown by the blue arrow running from CIBC to the Bank of Canada.

The Bank of Canada pays for the securities by placing $100 million in CIBC's reserve account at the Bank of Canada, as shown by the green arrow running from the Bank of Canada to CIBC.

The Bank of Canada's assets increase by $100 million, and its liabilities also increase by $100 million. CIBC's total assets are unchanged. It has sold securities in exchange for reserves.

If the Bank of Canada sells $100 million of government securities in the open market, the events that you've just seen occur in reverse.

When the Bank of Canada sells securities,

1. CIBC has $100 million more securities, and the Bank of Canada has $100 million less securities.
2. CIBC pays for the securities by using $100 million of its reserves deposit account at the Bank of Canada.

Figure 30.4 shows the effects of these actions on the balance sheets of the Bank of Canada and CIBC. Ownership of the securities passes from the Bank of Canada to CIBC, so CIBC's assets increase by $100 million and the Bank of Canada's assets decrease by $100 million, as shown by the blue arrow running from the Bank of Canada to CIBC.

CIBC uses $100 million of its reserve account at the Bank of Canada to pay for the securities, as the green arrow running from CIBC to the Bank of Canada shows.

The Bank of Canada's assets decrease by $100 million, and its liabilities also decrease by $100 million. CIBC's total assets are unchanged. It has used reserves to buy securities.

An increase or a decrease in reserves changes the overnight rate by changing the demand for and supply of overnight loans.

FIGURE 30.3 The Bank of Canada Buys Securities

When the Bank of Canada buys securities in the open market, it creates bank reserves. Bank of Canada assets and liabilities increase, and the selling bank exchanges securities for reserves.

FIGURE 30.4 The Bank of Canada Sells Securities

When the Bank of Canada sells securities in the open market, it reduces bank reserves. Bank of Canada assets and liabilities decrease, and the buying bank exchanges reserves for securities.

Equilibrium in the Market for Reserves

To see how an open market operation changes the overnight interest rate, we must see what happens in the market for the reserves of the banks.

Banks hold reserves so they can make payments. The amount that a bank will be called on to pay at any given moment fluctuates and cannot be forecasted accurately. If a bank runs out of reserves and is obliged to make a payment, reserves must be borrowed from the Bank of Canada. So bank rate is the opportunity cost of borrowed reserves.

The more reserves a bank holds, the less likely it is that the bank will need to borrow and pay bank rate. But reserves are costly to hold. The alternative to holding reserves is to lend them. The higher the interest rate at which reserves can be loaned, the higher is the opportunity cost of holding reserves. And the higher the opportunity cost, the greater is the incentive to economize on the quantity of reserves.

So the quantity of reserves demanded by banks depends on the overnight rate. The higher the overnight rate, other things remaining the same, the smaller is the quantity of reserves demanded.

Figure 30.5 shows the demand curve for reserves as the curve labelled *RD*. The *x*-axis measures the quantity of reserves held. If the entire banking system is borrowing from the Bank of Canada, reserves are negative. The *y*-axis measures the overnight rate. You can see that the overnight rate always lies inside the operating band. Why?

The overnight rate cannot exceed bank rate because if it did, a bank could earn a profit by borrowing from the Bank of Canada and lending to another bank. But all banks can borrow from the Bank of Canada at bank rate, so no bank is willing to pay more than bank rate to borrow reserves.

The overnight rate cannot fall below the settlement balances rate because if it did, a bank could earn a profit by borrowing from another bank and increasing its reserves at the Bank of Canada. But all banks can earn the settlement balances rate at the Bank of Canada, so no bank is willing to lend reserves at a rate below the settlement balances rate.

The Bank of Canada's open market operations determine the actual quantity of reserves in the banking system, and equilibrium in the market for reserves determines the actual overnight rate. So by using open market operations, the Bank of Canada can keep the overnight rate on target.

FIGURE 30.5 The Market for Bank Reserves

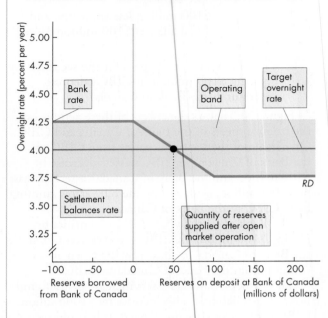

The demand curve for reserves is *RD*. If the overnight rate equals bank rate, banks are indifferent between borrowing reserves and lending reserves. The demand curve is horizontal at bank rate. If the overnight rate equals the settlement balances rate, banks are indifferent between holding reserves and lending reserves. The demand curve is horizontal at the settlement balances rate. Equilibrium, where the quantity of reserves demanded equals the quantity supplied, determines the overnight rate.

 animation

Review Quiz

1 What is the Bank of Canada's monetary policy instrument?

2 Summarize the Bank of Canada's monetary policy decision-making process.

3 What is the operating band? What does it do?

4 What happens when the Bank of Canada buys or sells securities in the open market?

5 How is the overnight rate determined in the market for reserves?

myeconlab Work Study Plan 30.2 and get instant feedback.

◆ Monetary Policy Transmission

You've seen that the Bank of Canada's goal is to keep the inflation rate as close as possible to 2 percent a year. And you've seen how the Bank can use its power to set the overnight rate at its desired level. We're now going to trace the events that follow a change in the overnight rate and see how those events lead to the ultimate policy goal. We'll begin with a quick overview of the transmission process and then look at each step a bit more closely.

Quick Overview

When the Bank of Canada lowers the overnight rate, other short-term interest rates and the exchange rate also fall. The quantity of money and the supply of loanable funds increase. The long-term real interest rate falls. The lower real interest rate increases consumption expenditure and investment. And the lower exchange rate makes Canadian exports cheaper and imports more costly, so net exports increase. Easier bank loans reinforce the effect of lower interest rates on aggregate expenditure. Aggregate demand increases, which increases real GDP and the price level relative to what they would have been. Real GDP growth and inflation speed up.

When the Bank raises the overnight rate, as the sequence of events that we've just reviewed plays out, the effects are in the opposite directions.

Figure 30.6 provides a schematic summary of these ripple effects for both a cut and a rise in the overnight rate. These effects stretch out over a period of between one and two years. The interest rate and exchange rate effects are immediate. The effects on money and bank loans follow in a few weeks and run for a few months. Real long-term interest rates change quickly. Spending plans change and real GDP growth slows after about one year. The inflation rate changes between one year and two years after the change in the overnight rate. But these time lags are not entirely predictable and can be longer or shorter.

We're going to look at each stage in the transmission process, starting with the interest rate effects.

Interest Rate Changes

The first effect of a monetary policy decision is a change in the overnight rate. Other interest rates

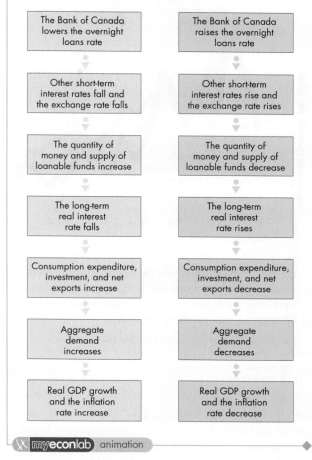

FIGURE 30.6 The Ripple Effects of a Change in the Overnight Loans Rate

myeconlab   animation

then change. These interest rate effects occur quickly and relatively predictably.

Figure 30.7 shows the fluctuations in four interest rates:

- The overnight rate
- The short-term bill rate
- The 10-year government bond rate
- The long-term corporate bond rate

Overnight rate As soon as the Bank announces a new setting for the overnight rate, it undertakes the necessary open market operations to hit the target.

Short-Term Bill Rate The short-term bill rate is the interest rate paid by the government of Canada on 3-month Treasury bills. Notice how closely the short-term

FIGURE 30.7 Four Interest Rates

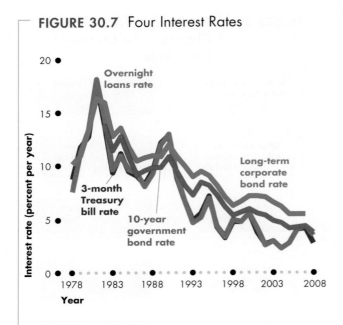

The short-term interest rates—the overnight rate and the short-term bill rate—move closely together. The long-term bond rates are higher than the short-term rates, and they fluctuate less than the short-term rates.

Source of data: Statistics Canada, CANSIM Table 176-0043.

myeconlab animation

bill rate follows the overnight rate. The two rates are almost identical. A powerful substitution effect keeps these two interest rates close. Chartered banks have a choice about how to hold their short-term liquid assets, and an overnight loan to another bank is a close substitute for short-term securities such as Treasury bills. If the interest rate on Treasury bills is higher than the overnight rate, the quantity of overnight loans supplied decreases and the demand for Treasury bills increases. The price of Treasury bills rises and the interest rate falls.

Similarly, if the interest rate on Treasury bills is lower than the overnight rate, the quantity of overnight loans supplied increases and the demand for Treasury bills decreases. The price of Treasury bills falls, and the interest rate rises.

When the interest rate on Treasury bills is close to the overnight rate, there is no incentive for a bank to switch between making an overnight loan and buying Treasury bills. Both the Treasury bill market and the overnight loans market are in equilibrium.

The 10-Year Government Bond Rate The 10-year government bond rate is the interest rate paid on bonds issued by the government of Canada. The government issues bonds of various maturities to manage its overall borrowing and finance the national debt.

The Long-Term Corporate Bond Rate The long-term corporate bond rate is the interest rate paid on bonds issued by large corporations. Businesses pay this interest rate on the loans that finance their purchases of new capital, so this interest rate influences investment decisions.

Two features of both of these longer-term bond rates stand out: They are higher than the short-term rates, and they fluctuate less than the short-term rates. The long-term interest rates are higher than the two short-term rates because longer-term loans are riskier than short-term loans. To provide the incentive that brings forth a supply of long-term loans, lenders must be compensated for the additional risk. Without compensation for the additional risk, only short-term loans would be supplied.

Long-term interest rates fluctuate less than short-term rates because expectations about future short-term interest rates as well as current short-term interest rates influence long-term interest rates. The alternative to borrowing or lending long term is to borrow or lend using a sequence of short-term securities. If the long-term interest rate exceeds the expected average of future short-term interest rates, people will lend long term and borrow short term. The long-term interest rate will fall. And if the long-term interest rate is below the expected average of future short-term interest rates, people will borrow long term and lend short term. The long-term interest rate will rise.

These market forces keep the long-term interest rate close to the expected average of future short-term interest rates (plus a premium for the extra risk associated with long-term loans). The expected average future short-term interest rate fluctuates less than the current short-term interest rate.

Exchange Rate Fluctuations

The exchange rate responds to changes in the interest rate in Canada relative to the interest rates in other countries—*the Canadian interest rate differential*. We explain this influence in Chapter 25 (see pp. 601–602).

When the Bank of Canada raises the overnight rate, the Canadian interest rate differential rises and, other things remaining the same, the Canadian dollar appreciates; when the Bank of Canada lowers the overnight rate, the Canadian interest rate differential falls and, other things remaining the same, the Canadian dollar depreciates.

Many factors other than the Canadian interest rate differential influence the exchange rate, so when the Bank of Canada changes the overnight rate, the exchange rate does not usually change in exactly the way it would with other things remaining the same. So while monetary policy influences the exchange rate, other factors also make the exchange rate change.

Money and Bank Loans

The quantity of money and bank loans change when the Bank of Canada changes the overnight rate target. A rise in the overnight rate decreases the quantity of money and bank loans, and a fall in the overnight rate increases the quantity of money and bank loans. These changes occur for two reasons: The quantity of deposits and loans created by the banking system changes and the quantity of money demanded changes.

You've seen that to change the overnight rate, the Bank of Canada must change the quantity of bank reserves. A change in the quantity of bank reserves changes the monetary base, which in turn changes the quantity of deposits and loans that the banking system can create. A rise in the overnight rate decreases bank reserves and decreases the quantity of deposits and bank loans created; a fall in the overnight rate increases bank reserves and increases the quantity of deposits and bank loans created.

The quantity of money created by the banking system must be held by households and firms. The change in the interest rate changes the quantity of money demanded. A fall in the interest rate increases the quantity of money demanded; a rise in the interest rate decreases the quantity of money demanded.

A change in the quantity of money and the supply of bank loans directly affects consumption and investment plans. With more money and easier access to loans, consumers and firms spend more. With less money and loans harder to get, they spend less.

The Long-Term Real Interest Rate

Demand and supply in the market for loanable funds determine the long-term *real interest rate*, which equals the long-term *nominal* interest rate minus the expected inflation rate. The long-term real interest rate influences expenditure decisions.

In the long run, demand and supply in the loanable funds market depend only on real forces—on saving and investment decisions. But in the short run, when the price level is not fully flexible, the supply of loanable funds is influenced by the supply of bank loans. Changes in the overnight rate change the supply of bank loans, which changes the supply of loanable funds and changes the real interest rate in the loanable funds market.

A fall in the overnight rate that increases the supply of bank loans increases the supply of loanable funds and lowers the equilibrium real interest rate. A rise in the overnight rate that decreases the supply of bank loans decreases the supply of loanable funds and raises the equilibrium real interest rate.

These changes in the real interest rate, along with the other factors we've just described, change expenditure plans.

Expenditure Plans

The ripple effects that follow a change in the overnight rate change three components of aggregate expenditure:

- Consumption expenditure
- Investment
- Net exports

Consumption Expenditure Other things remaining the same, the lower the real interest rate, the greater is the amount of consumption expenditure and the smaller is the amount of saving.

Investment Other things remaining the same, the lower the real interest rate, the greater is the amount of investment.

Net Exports Other things remaining the same, the lower the interest rate, the lower is the exchange rate and the greater are exports and the smaller are imports.

So eventually, a cut in the overnight rate increases aggregate expenditure and a rise in the overnight rate curtails aggregate expenditure. These changes in aggregate expenditure plans change aggregate demand, real GDP, and the price level.

The Change in Aggregate Demand, Real GDP, and the Price Level

The final link in the transmission chain is a change in aggregate demand and a resulting change in real GDP and the price level. By changing real GDP and the price level relative to what they would have been with no change in the overnight rate, the Bank of Canada influences its ultimate goal: the inflation rate. The Bank also influences the output gap.

The Bank of Canada Fights Recession

If inflation is low and real GDP is below potential GDP, the Bank acts to restore full employment and keep inflation steady. Figure 30.8 shows the effects of the Bank's actions, starting in the market for bank reserves and ending in the market for real GDP.

Market for Bank Reserves In Fig. 30.8(a), which shows the market for bank reserves, the Bank lowers the target overnight rate from 5 percent to 4 percent a year. To achieve the new target, the Bank buys

securities and increases the supply of reserves of the banking system from RS_0 to RS_1.

Money Market With increased reserves, the banks create deposits by making loans and the supply of money increases. The short-term interest rate falls and the quantity of money demanded increases. In Fig. 30.8(b), the supply of money increases from MS_0 to MS_1, the interest rate falls from 5 percent to 4 percent a year, and the quantity of money increases from $800 billion to $900 billion. The interest rate in the money market and the overnight rate are kept close to each other by the powerful substitution effect described on p. 740.

Loanable Funds Market Banks create money by making loans. In the long run, an increase in the supply of bank loans is matched by a rise in the price level and the quantity of *real* loans is unchanged. But in the short run, with a sticky price level, an increase in the supply of bank loans increases the supply of (real) loanable funds.

FIGURE 30.8   The Bank of Canada Fights Recession

(a) The market for bank reserves

In part (a), the Bank of Canada lowers the overnight rate target from 5 percent to 4 percent a year. The Bank buys securities in an open market operation and increases the supply of reserves from RS_0 to RS_1 to hit the new overnight rate target.

(b) Money market

In part (b), the supply of money increases from MS_0 to MS_1, the short-term interest rate falls, and the quantity of money demanded increases. The short-term interest rate and the overnight rate change by similar amounts.

In Fig. 30.8(c), the supply of loanable funds curve shifts rightward from SLF_0 to SLF_1. With the demand for loanable funds at DLF, the real interest rate falls from 6 percent to 5.5 percent a year. (We're assuming a zero inflation rate so that the real interest rate equals the nominal interest rate.) The long-term interest rate changes by a smaller amount than the change in the short-term interest rate for the reason explained on p. 740.

The Market for Real GDP Figure 30.8(d) shows aggregate demand and aggregate supply—the demand for and supply of real GDP. Potential GDP is $1,200 billion, where LAS is located. The short-run aggregate supply curve is SAS, and initially, the aggregate demand curve is AD_0. Real GDP is $1,180 billion, which is less than potential GDP, so there is a recessionary gap.

The increase in the supply of loans and the decrease in the real interest rate increase aggregate planned expenditure. (Not shown in the figure, a fall in the interest rate also lowers the exchange rate,

which increases net exports and aggregate planned expenditure.) The increase in aggregate expenditure, ΔE, increases aggregate demand and shifts the aggregate demand curve rightward to $AD_0 + \Delta E$. A multiplier process begins. The increase in expenditure increases income, which induces an increase in consumption expenditure. Aggregate demand increases further, and the aggregate demand curve eventually shifts rightward to AD_1.

The new equilibrium is at full employment. Real GDP is equal to potential GDP. The price level rises to 115 and then becomes stable at that level. So after a one-time adjustment, there is price stability.

In this example, we have given the Bank of Canada a perfect hit at achieving full employment and keeping the price level stable. It is unlikely that the Bank would be able to achieve the precision of this example. If the Bank stimulated aggregate demand by too little and too late, the economy would experience a recession. And if the Bank hit the gas pedal too hard, it would push the economy from recession to inflation and miss its inflation target.

(c) The market for loanable funds

In part (c), an increase in the supply of bank loans increases the supply of loanable funds from SLF_0 to SLF_1 and the real interest rate falls. Investment increases.

(d) Real GDP and the price level

In part (d), aggregate planned expenditure increases. The aggregate demand curve shifts rightward to $AD_0 + \Delta E$ and eventually to AD_1. Real GDP increases to potential GDP, and the price level rises.

The Bank of Canada Fights High Inflation

If the inflation rate is too high and real GDP is above potential GDP, the Bank takes actions that are designed to lower the inflation rate and restore price stability. Figure 30.9 shows the effects of the Bank's actions, starting in the market for bank reserves and ending in the market for real GDP.

Market for Bank Reserves In Fig. 30.9(a), which shows the market for bank reserves, the Bank raises the target overnight rate from 5 percent to 6 percent a year. To achieve the new target, the Bank sells securities in the open market and decreases the supply of reserves of the banking system from RS_0 to RS_1.

Money Market With decreased reserves, the banks shrink deposits by decreasing loans and the supply of money decreases. The short-term interest rate rises and the quantity of money demanded decreases. In Fig. 30.9(b), the supply of money decreases from MS_0 to MS_1, the interest rate rises from 5 percent to

6 percent a year, and the quantity of money decreases from $800 billion to $700 billion.

Loanable Funds Market With a decrease in reserves, banks must decrease the supply of loans. The supply of (real) loanable funds decreases, and the supply of loanable funds curve shifts leftward in Fig. 30.9(c) from SLF_0 to SLF_1. With the demand for loanable funds at DLF, the real interest rate rises from 6 percent to 6.5 percent a year. (Again, we're assuming a zero inflation rate so that the real interest rate equals the nominal interest rate.)

The Market for Real GDP Figure 30.9(d) shows aggregate demand and aggregate supply in the market for real GDP. Potential GDP is $1,200 billion where LAS is located. The short-run aggregate supply curve is SAS and initially the aggregate demand is AD_0. Real GDP is $1,220 billion, which is greater than potential GDP, so there is an inflationary gap. The Bank is reacting to this inflationary gap.

FIGURE 30.9 The Bank of Canada Fights Inflation

(a) The market for bank reserves

In part (a), the Bank of Canada raises the overnight rate from 5 percent to 6 percent a year. The Bank sells securities in an open market operation to decrease the supply of reserves from RS_0 to RS_1 and hit the new overnight rate target.

(b) Money market

In part (b), the supply of money decreases from MS_0 to MS_1, the short-term interest rate rises, and the quantity of money demanded decreases. The short-term interest rate and the overnight rate change by similar amounts.

myeconlab animation

The increase in the short-term interest rate, the decrease in the supply of bank loans, and the increase in the real interest rate decrease aggregate planned expenditure. (A rise in the interest rate also raises the exchange rate, which decreases net exports and aggregate planned expenditure.)

The decrease in aggregate expenditure, ΔE, decreases aggregate demand and shifts the aggregate demand curve to $AD_0 - \Delta E$. A multiplier process begins. The decrease in expenditure decreases income, which induces a decrease in consumption expenditure. Aggregate demand decreases further, and the aggregate demand curve eventually shifts leftward to AD_1.

The economy returns to full employment. Real GDP is equal to potential GDP. The price level falls to 115 and then becomes stable at that level. So after a one-time adjustment, there is price stability.

Again, in this example, we have given the Bank of Canada a perfect hit at achieving full employment and keeping the price level stable. If the Bank decreased aggregate demand by too little and too late,

the economy would have remained with an inflationary gap and the inflation rate would have risen above the rate that is consistent with price stability. And if the Bank hit the brakes too hard, it would push the economy from inflation to recession.

Loose Links and Long and Variable Lags

The ripple effects of monetary policy that we've just analyzed with the precision of an economic model are, in reality, very hard to predict and anticipate.

To achieve price stability and full employment, the Bank needs a combination of good judgment and good luck. Too large a cut in the overnight rate in an underemployed economy can bring inflation, as it did during the 1970s. And too large a rise in the overnight rate in an inflationary economy can create unemployment, as it did in 1981 and 1991. Loose links between the overnight rate and the policy goals make unwanted outcomes inevitable, and long and variable time lags add to the Bank's challenges.

(c) The market for loanable funds

In part (c), a decrease in the supply of bank loans decreases the supply of loanable funds from SLF_0 to SLF_1 and the real interest rate rises. Investment decreases.

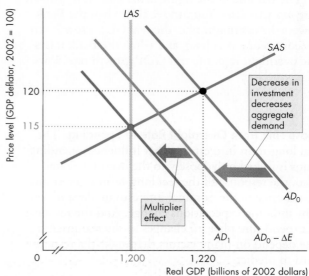

(d) Real GDP and the price level

In part (d), aggregate planned expenditure decreases. Aggregate demand decreases and the AD curve shifts leftward from AD_0 to AD_1. Real GDP decreases to potential GDP, and the price level falls.

A Reality Check

A View of the Long and Variable Lag

You've studied the theory of monetary policy. Does it really work in the way we've described? It does, and the figure provides some evidence to support this claim.

The blue line in the figure is the overnight rate that the Bank of Canada targets *minus* the long-term bond rate. (When the long-term bond rate exceeds the overnight rate, this gap is negative.)

We can view the gap between the overnight rate and the long-term bond rate as a measure of how hard the Bank is trying to steer a change in the economy's course.

When the Bank is more concerned about recession than inflation and is trying to stimulate real GDP growth, it cuts the overnight rate target and the overnight rate minus the long-term bond rate falls.

When the Bank is more concerned about inflation than recession and is trying to restrain real GDP growth, it raises the overnight rate target and the overnight rate minus the long-term bond rate rises.

The red line in the figure is the real GDP growth rate *one year later.* You can see that when the Bank lowers the overnight rate, the real GDP growth rate speeds up one year later, and when the Bank raises the overnight rate, the real GDP growth rate slows one year later.

Interest Rate and Real GDP Growth

Source of data: Statistics Canada, CANSIM Tables 176-0043 and 380-0002.

Not shown in the figure are the inflation rate increases and decreases that correspond to the fluctuations in the real GDP growth rate. But the effects on the inflation rate take even longer and are not as strong as the effects on the real GDP growth rate.

Loose Link from Overnight Rate to Spending The real long-term interest rate that influences spending plans is linked only loosely to the overnight rate. Also, the response of the *real* long-term interest rate to a change in the nominal interest rate depends on how inflation expectations change. And the response of expenditure plans to changes in the real interest rate depend on many factors that make the response hard to predict.

Time Lags in the Adjustment Process The Bank of Canada is especially handicapped by the fact that the monetary policy transmission process is long and drawn-out. Also, the economy does not always respond in exactly the same way to a policy change. Further, many factors other than policy are constantly changing and bringing new situations to which policy must respond.

Review Quiz

1   Describe the channels by which monetary policy ripples through the economy and explain why each channel operates.
2   Do interest rates fluctuate in response to the Bank of Canada's actions?
3   How do the Bank's actions change the exchange rate?
4   How do the Bank's actions influence real GDP and how long does it take for real GDP to respond to the Bank's policy changes?
5   How do the Bank's actions influence the inflation rate and how long does it take for inflation to respond to the Bank's policy changes?

 Work Study Plan 30.3 and get instant feedback.

Alternative Monetary Policy Strategies

The Bank of Canada must choose among alternative monetary policy strategies. What are the alternatives, and why has the Bank rejected them in favour of its interest rate strategy?

The Bank might have chosen any of four alternative monetary policy strategies: Two of them are instrument rules, and two are alternative targeting rules. The four alternatives are

- Overnight rate instrument rule
- Monetary base instrument rule
- Exchange rate targeting rule
- Money targeting rule

Overnight Rate Instrument Rule

The idea of setting the overnight rate based on a rule was suggested by Stanford University economist John B. Taylor, and the rule bears his name.

The **Taylor rule** sets the overnight rate in response to only the current inflation rate and the current estimate of the output gap. Calling the overnight rate R, the neutral real overnight rate R^*, the inflation rate π, the target inflation rate π^*, and the output gap (as a percentage of potential GDP) G, the Taylor rule says, set the overnight rate to equal

$$R = R^* + \pi + 0.5(\pi - \pi^*) + 0.5G.$$

Taylor suggests that the neutral real overnight rate is 2 percent a year, so if inflation was on target and the output gap was zero (full employment), with a 2 percent inflation target, the overnight rate would be 4 percent. It would be less than 4 percent if the economy were below full employment and above 4 percent if the economy were above full employment.

If the Bank of Canada had followed the Taylor rule, the overnight rate would have fluctuated by more than it did: On some occasions it would have been higher than the Bank wanted and on other occasions lower. For example, during 2005 when the overnight rate was 2.5 percent, the Taylor rule would have put it at 4.5 percent, and in 2008, when the overnight rate was 1.5 percent, the Taylor rule would have kept it close to 4 percent.

The Bank believes that because it uses much more information than just the current inflation rate and

the output gap, it is able to set the overnight rate more intelligently than Taylor rule would set it.

Monetary Base Instrument Rule

Instead of targeting the overnight rate, the Bank could target the monetary base. The idea of using a rule to set the monetary base was suggested by Carnegie-Mellon University economist Bennet T. McCallum, and a monetary base rule bears his name.

The **McCallum rule** makes the growth rate of the monetary base respond to the long-term average growth rate of real GDP and medium-term changes in the velocity of circulation of the monetary base.

The rule is based on the *quantity theory of money* (see Chapter 24, p 582). McCallum's idea is to make the monetary base grow at a rate equal to the target inflation rate plus the long-term real GDP growth rate minus the medium-term velocity growth rate, so that inflation will be kept close to target.

The Bank of Canada believes that shifts in the demand for money and the demand for monetary base would bring large fluctuations in the interest rate, which in turn would bring large fluctuations in aggregate demand.

Exchange Rate Targeting Rule

The Bank of Canada could intervene in the foreign exchange market to target the exchange rate. A fixed exchange rate is one possible exchange rate target. But with a fixed exchange rate, a country loses control over its inflation rate. The reason is that for internationally traded goods, *purchasing power parity* (see Chapter 25, p. 604) moves domestic prices in line with foreign prices.

The Bank of Canada could avoid a direct inflation link by using a *crawling peg exchange rate* (see Chapter 25, p. 612) as a means of achieving an inflation target. To do so, the Bank would make the exchange rate *change* at a rate equal to the world inflation rate minus the target inflation rate.

Some developing countries that have an inflation problem use this monetary policy strategy to lower the inflation rate.

The Bank of Canada rejects the crawling peg strategy because changes in the *real exchange rate* are unpredictable and even undetectable until after the event and these changes would bring instability to the inflation rate.

Extraordinary Policies for Extraordinary Times

Central Banks Get Creative

The financial crisis that began in the United States in August 2007 quickly spread though the global economy. You are now well equipped to understand the key elements in this crisis. The markets for loanable funds (Chapter 23), money (Chapter 24), and foreign exchange (Chapter 25) interacted in the financial crisis, which quickly became a broader economic crisis through its influence on aggregate demand and aggregate supply (Chapter 26).

The Key Elements of the Crisis

Figure 1 shows the stylized balance sheet of a bank: Deposits plus equity equals reserves plus loans and securities (see p. 572). A bank's equity is the market value of its stock—the value of the bank to its owners.

Three main events can put a bank under stress:

1. Widespread fall in asset prices
2. A significant currency drain
3. A run on the bank

Figure 1 summarizes the problems that each event presents to a bank. A widespread fall in asset prices means that the bank suffers a *capital loss*. It must write down the value of its assets, and the value of the

bank's equity decreases by the same amount as the fall in the value of its securities. If the fall in asset prices is large enough, the bank's equity might fall to zero, in which case the bank is *insolvent*. It fails.

A significant currency drain means that depositors withdraw funds and the bank loses reserves. This event puts the bank in a *liquidity* crisis. It is short of cash reserves, but isn't insolvent.

A run on the bank occurs when depositors lose confidence in the bank and massive withdrawals of deposits occur. The bank loses reserves and must call in loans and sell off securities at unfavourable prices. The banks' equity shrinks.

The red arrows in Fig. 1 summarize the effects of these events and the problems they brought in the 2007–2008 financial crisis.

A widespread fall in asset prices was triggered by the bursting of a house-price bubble that saw house prices in the United States switch from rapidly rising to falling. With falling house prices, sub-prime mortgage defaults occurred and the prices of mortgage-backed securities and derivatives, whose values are based on these securities, began to fall.

People began to withdraw deposits, which created a fear of a massive withdrawal of these funds analogous to a run on a bank. One U.K. bank, Northern Rock, did experience a bank run.

With low reserves and even lower equity, banks turned their attention to securing their balance sheets

Event	Deposits	+ Equity	= Reserves	+ Loans and securities	Problem
Widespread fall in asset prices		▼		▼	Solvency
Currency drain	▼		▼		Liquidity
Run on bank	▼	▼	▼	▼	Liquidity and solvency

Figure 1 The Ingredients of a Financial and Banking Crisis

Money Targeting Rule

As long ago as 1948, Nobel Laureate Milton Friedman proposed a targeting rule for the quantity of money. Friedman's **k-percent rule** makes the quantity of money grow at a rate of k percent a year, where k equals the growth rate of potential GDP.

Friedman's idea remained just that until the 1970s when inflation increased to double-digit rates and the central banks of most major countries—the Bank of Canada among them—adopted the k-percent rule.

The rule worked and inflation rates fell during the early 1980s. But financial innovation brought shifts in the demand for money and central banks began to search for an alternative approach.

Money targeting works when the demand for money is stable and predictable—when the velocity of circulation is stable. In the world of the 1980s, and possibly in the world of today, financial innovation leads to large and unpredictable fluctuations in the demand for money, which make the use of monetary targeting unreliable.

and called in loans. The loanable funds market and the money market dried up.

Because the loanable funds market is global, the same problems quickly spread to other economies, and foreign exchange markets became highly volatile.

Hard-to-get loans, market volatility, and increased uncertainty transmitted the financial and monetary crisis to real expenditure decisions.

The Policy Actions

Five types of policy action dribbled out over a period of more than a year. They were

1. Open market operations
2. Extension of deposit insurance
3. Central bank and government swapping government securities for toxic assets
4. Government buying bank shares
5. Fair value accounting

Figure 2 summarizes these actions, their effects on a bank's balance sheet (red and blue arrows), and the problem that each action sought to address.

An open market operation is the classic policy (described on pp. 736–737) for providing liquidity

and enabling a central bank to hit its overnight rate target. With substantial interest rate cuts, heavy open market operations were used to keep the banks well supplied with reserves. This action lowered bank holdings of securities and increased their reserves.

By extending deposit insurance (see p. 695), people with bank deposits had less incentive to withdraw them. Both deposits and bank reserves increased.

Some central banks bought troubled assets that no one could sell (so-called *toxic assets*) and sold good quality government securities in their place. These actions swapped bad loans and securities for good ones and addressed the liquidity problem.

Some governments bought shares in banks. This action boosted bank capital and addressed the insolvency problem.

The final action is not a monetary policy but a change in accounting standards. It relaxed the requirement for institutions to value their assets at current market value—called "mark-to-market"—and permitted them, in rare conditions, to use a model to assess "fair market value."

Taken as a whole, a huge amount of relief was thrown at the financial crisis and events through 2009 will show whether enough was done.

Action	Deposits	+ Equity	= Reserves	+ Loans and securities	Problem addressed
Open market operation			▲	▼	Liquidity
Extension of deposit insurance	▲		▲		Liquidity
Swap government securities for toxic assets			▲	▼	Liquidity
Buy bank shares		▲	▲		Solvency
Fair value accounting		▲		▲	Solvency

Figure 2 Policy Actions in a Financial and Banking Crisis

Why Rules?

You might be wondering why all monetary policy strategies involve rules. Why doesn't the Bank of Canada just do what seems best every day, month, and year, at its *discretion*? The answer is that monetary policy is about managing inflation expectations. In both financial markets and labour markets, people must make long-term commitments and these markets work best when plans are based on correctly anticipated inflation. A well-understood monetary policy rule makes it easier to forecast future inflation.

Review Quiz

1 What are the alternative strategies for conducting monetary policy?
2 Briefly, why does the Bank of Canada reject each of these alternatives?

myeconlab Work Study Plan 30.4 and get instant feedback.

You can complete your study of monetary policy in *Reading Between the Lines* on pages 750–751 and see the Bank of Canada's policy challenge in 2008.

Monetary Policy in Action

Bay Street Changes Rules of Rates Game

December 9, 2008

Bay Street's profit margins are starting to come under pressure as official interest rates creep closer to zero, prompting retail banks to change the rules of the game so customers pay more.

While the Bank of Canada on Tuesday cut interest rates to the lowest level since the 1950s, the country's five big banks indicated they would no longer march in lock step with the central bank. Instead, Bay Street is keeping the cost of borrowing for consumers more elevated in a bid to protect corporate earnings, passing on only part of the rate cut to customers.

While the decision of Bay Street to pocket part of the Bank of Canada rate cut is seen as good for shareholders and bad for customers, there is less certainty about how it will impact wider demand, partly because there are few historical precedents. ...

Nancy Hughes-Anthony, head of the Canadian Bankers Association ... said: "The banks are still borrowing in a very volatile marketplace. The Bank of Canada rate is only one component of their cost of funding, and while the cost of borrowing in international markets has come down a bit, it is still higher than before the crisis." ...

This willingness to pass on rate cuts is critical to determining the ability of the Bank of Canada to stimulate the economy in the midst of a downturn.

The central bank's own research shows "it is the real rate of interest that is most relevant" to the purchasing decisions of households, and that it can "influence demand only to the extent that adjustments to the [official] interest rate feed through to the real interest rate. ...

Essence of the Story

- The Bank of Canada cut the overnight rate target to its lowest level since the 1950s.

- The interest rates on loans from Canada's five big banks did not fall by as much as the Bank of Canada's rate cut.

- The banks borrow in volatile international markets where interest rates have not fallen much.

- The Bank of Canada's research shows that it is the real interest rate that influences the spending decisions of households.

- Changing the overnight rate influences aggregate demand only if it changes the real interest rate faced by borrowers.

Economic Analysis

- In December 2008, the Bank of Canada cut its overnight rate target to 1.5 percent a year, but other interest rates didn't fall by as much as the Bank's rate cut.

- By providing enough reserves to the banks (and by changing the other two interest rates that define the *operating band* (see p. 736), the Bank of Canada was able to achieve it target.

- Figure 1 shows how the Bank achieved the lower overnight rate in the market for reserves. With demand curve RD, the supply of reserves increased from RS_0 to RS_1 and the overnight rate fell to its 1.5 percent target.

- When the Bank of Canada cuts the overnight rate, the supply of loanable funds increases and the economy average real interest rate falls. But the fall in the real interest rate is much smaller than the cut in the overnight rate. Figure 2 shows why.

- Initially, the real interest rate is 3 percent at the intersection of the supply of loanable funds curve SLF_0 and the demand for loanable funds curve DLF. When the Bank lowers the overnight rate, the supply of loanable funds increases and the supply curve shifts rightward to SLF_1. The real interest rate falls, but by much less than the cut in the overnight rate.

- In Fig. 3, real GDP is $1,330 billion and the price level is 118 at the intersection of AD_0 and SAS. Potential GDP is $1,370 billion, so there is a recessionary gap.

- The lower overnight rate and lower real interest rate increase aggregate demand and the AD curve shifts rightward to AD_1. Real GDP increases and the price level rises.

- In 2008, credit markets were not working normally. The perception of risk was unusually high, and institutions normally willing to lend to each other were reluctant to do so.

- In the conditions of 2008, it was possible that a cut in the overnight rate would bring a very small increase in the supply of loanable funds, a small fall in the real interest rate cut, and only a small increase in aggregate demand.

- In this situation, monetary policy is a weak tool for influencing real GDP and the inflation rate.

Figure 1 The market for bank reserves

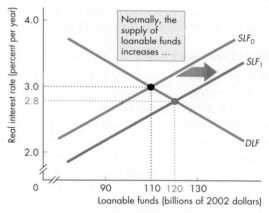

Figure 2 The market for loanable funds

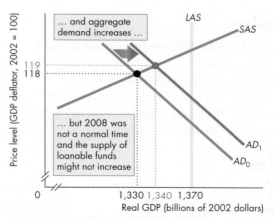

Figure 3 Real GDP and the price level

SUMMARY

Key Points

Monetary Policy Objective and Framework
(pp. 732–734)

- The Bank of Canada Act requires the Bank to use monetary policy to avoid inflation and moderate cycles in real GDP and employment.
- The government of Canada and the Bank of Canada have jointly agreed that the Bank will seek to keep CPI inflation between 1 percent and 3 percent a year and will aim for the 2 percent mid-point.
- The Bank has successfully achieved its inflation-control target.
- The Bank's Governing Council has the responsibility for the conduct of monetary policy, but the Bank and the government must consult regularly.

The Conduct of Monetary Policy (pp. 734–738)

- The Bank of Canada's instrument for monetary policy is the overnight loans rate.
- The Bank of Canada sets the overnight rate target and announces changes on eight dates each year.
- An *instrument rule* for monetary policy makes the instrument respond predictably to the state of the economy. The Bank of Canada does *not* use a mechanical instrument rule.

- A *targeting rule* for monetary policy sets the instrument to make the forecast of the inflation rate equal to the target inflation rate. The Bank of Canada *does* use such a rule.
- The Bank hits its overnight rate target by setting an operating band and using open market operations.
- By buying or selling government securities in the open market, the Bank of Canada is able to change bank reserves and change the overnight rate.

Monetary Policy Transmission (pp. 739–746)

- A change in the overnight rate changes other interest rates, the exchange rate, the quantity of money and loans, aggregate demand, and eventually real GDP and the price level.
- A change in the overnight rate changes real GDP about one year later and changes the inflation rate with an even longer time lag.

Alternative Monetary Policy Strategies (pp. 747–749)

- The main alternatives are the rule for setting the overnight rate, a monetary base rule, exchange rate targeting, or money targeting.
- Rules dominate discretion in monetary policy because they better enable the central bank to manage inflation expectations.

Key Figures

Figure 30.1 Inflation-Control Target and Outcome, 733
Figure 30.2 The Overnight Loans Rate, 735
Figure 30.5 The Market for Bank Reserves, 738
Figure 30.6 The Ripple Effects of a Change in the Overnight Loans Rate, 739
Figure 30.8 The Bank of Canada Fights Recession, 742–743
Figure 30.9 The Bank of Canada Fights Inflation, 744–745

Key Terms

Bank rate, 736
Inflation rate targeting, 732
Instrument rule, 735
k-percent rule, 748
McCallum rule, 747
Open market operation, 736
Operating band, 736
Overnight loans rate, 734
Settlement balances rate, 736
Targeting rule, 735
Taylor rule, 747

PROBLEMS and APPLICATIONS ◆

myeconlab   Work problems 1–10 in Chapter 30 Study Plan and get instant feedback.
Work problems 11–16 as Homework, a Quiz, or a Test if assigned by your instructor.

1. Suppose that the Bank of Canada is required to keep the inflation rate between 1 percent and 2 percent a year but with no requirement to keep trend inflation at the midpoint of this range. The Bank of Canada achieves its target.
   a. If initially the price level is 100,
      i. Calculate the highest price level that might occur after 10 years.
      ii. Calculate the lowest price level that might occur after 10 years.
      iii. What is the range of uncertainty about the price level after 10 years?
   b. Would this type of inflation goal serve the financial markets well and provide an anchor for inflation expectations?

2. Suppose that the Bank of England decides to follow the Taylor rule. In 2005, the United Kingdom has an inflation rate of 2.1 percent a year and its output gap is –0.3 percent. At what level does the Bank of England set the repo rate (the U.K. equivalent of the overnight rate)?

3. Suppose that the Bank of Canada is following the McCallum rule. The Bank of Canada has an inflation target range of between 1 percent a year and 3 percent a year. The long-term real GDP growth rate in Canada is 2.4 percent a year. If the velocity of circulation of the monetary base is 2, what is the

   a. Highest growth rate of monetary base that will occur?
   b. Lowest growth rate of monetary base that will occur?

4. In Freezone, shown in the figure, the aggregate demand curve is AD, potential GDP is $300 billion, and the short-run aggregate supply curve is SAS_B.

   a. What are the price level and real GDP?
   b. Does Freezone have an unemployment problem or an inflation problem? Why?
   c. What will happen in Freezone if the central bank takes no monetary policy actions?
   d. What monetary policy action would you advise the central bank to take and what do you predict will be the effect of that action?

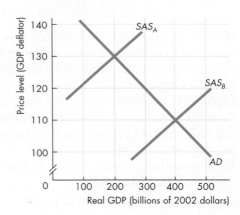

5. Suppose that in Freezone, shown in problem 4, the short-run aggregate supply curve is SAS_A and a drought decreases potential GDP to $250 billion.

   a. What happens in Freezone if the central bank lowers the overnight rate and buys securities on the open market?
   b. What happens in Freezone if the central bank raises the overnight rate and sells securities on the open market?
   c. Do you recommend that the central bank lower or raise the overnight rate? Why?

6. **Bank of Canada Lowers Overnight Rate Target**
   The Bank of Canada today announced that it is lowering its target for the overnight rate by one-quarter of a percentage point to 2 1/4 percent. The operating band for the overnight rate is correspondingly lowered. ... The outlook for growth and inflation in Canada is now more uncertain than usual. ... The weaker outlook for global demand will increase the drag on the Canadian economy coming from exports. ... The marked tightening in Canadian credit conditions in recent weeks will restrain business and housing investment. ... Core inflation is now projected to remain below 2 percent until the end of 2010. Total CPI inflation should peak during the third quarter of 2008, fall below 1 percent in the middle of 2009, and then return to the 2 percent target by the end of 2010. In the face of diminished inflationary pressures, the Bank of Canada lowered its policy interest rate by 50 basis points

on 8 October. ... This extraordinary move, combined with today's announcement, brings the cumulative reduction in our target for the overnight rate to 75 basis points. ...

Bank of Canada, October 31, 2008

a. What is the operating band? Explain how the operating band changed when the target for the overnight rate was lowered by one-quarter of a percentage point to 2.25 percent.
b. Explain the intended effect of the Bank of Canada's cumulative 0.75 percent rate cuts and illustrate your explanation with an appropriate graphical analysis.
c. What is core inflation and why might it be a useful measure of inflation?

7. **Global Bazookas, But No Silver Bullet**

Central bankers unleashed a broadside at the financial markets Wednesday. ... The [U.S.] Federal Reserve and five other central banks cut their interest rates, saying the crisis that has hammered stocks and locked up credit markets has also raised the risk of a serious recession. The Fed said the move ... is the latest in a series of "unprecedented joint actions" taken along with bankers in Canada, Europe, and the United Kingdom in a bid to restore confidence. ... "It is too late to avoid a slowdown, but strong and coordinated policies can avoid even worse scenarios," the IMF said in releasing its annual World Economic Outlook report. ... But no matter how good those plans are, making them work will take time—which is something policymakers seem to sense they don't have much of right now.

Fortune, October 8, 2008

a. How would the exchange rate respond if only the Bank of Canada cut the interest rate?
b. How would the exchange rate respond if the Bank of Canada cut the interest rate in a coordinated monetary policy action with other major central banks?
c. Evaluate the claim that "it is too late to avoid a slowdown." How does this fact complicate decisions on coordinated rate cuts?
d. How might these "unprecedented joint actions" that are meant to "restore confidence" actually end up diminishing confidence?

8. **Canada Moves to Restrict Bank Share Buybacks**

Canada has barred its domestic banks and insurers from buying back their own shares at a time when their priority is to strengthen their balance sheets. ... Governments worldwide have committed more than $1,000bn of state funds to support the financial system over the past month. But they have few tools available to ensure the funds are used to extend cheaper lending to other banks, businesses and individuals, as policymakers want ... local banks were criticized earlier this month for not immediately lowering their prime lending rates after the Bank of Canada reduced its key interest rate by 50 basis points. Finance minister Jim Flaherty said after the interest rate cut: "This isn't just about financial institutions; this is about making sure that credit is available for car loans, for mortgages, for businesses to finance their inventories."

Financial Times, October 28, 2008

a. Explain the intended effect of the Bank of Canada cutting the overnight lending rate by 50 basis points and illustrate your explanation with an appropriate graphical analysis.
b. Explain the factors that are limiting the effectiveness of this monetary stimulus.
c. In light of the limitations associated with both fiscal and monetary policy, explain and evaluate the rationale for using monetary policy as a first line of defence and reserving fiscal policy for deeper downturns when monetary policy has already been exhausted.

9 Suppose the Bank of Canada is required to keep the inflation rate between 0 and 3 percent a year and is also required to keep trend inflation at the midpoint of the range. The Bank of Canada achieves its target.

a. If initially the price level is 100, what is the likely price level after 10 years?
b. Compare this economy with the economy in problem 1. Which economy has the greater certainty about inflation over the longer term? Which has the greater short-term certainty?

10. Suppose that the Reserve Bank of New Zealand is following the Taylor rule. In 2009, it sets the official cash rate (the N.Z. equivalent of the overnight rate) at 4 percent a year. If the inflation rate in New Zealand is 2.0 percent a year, what is its output gap?

11. The figure shows the economy of Freezone. The aggregate demand curve is *AD* and the short-run aggregate supply curve is *SAS*$_A$. Potential GDP is $300 billion.

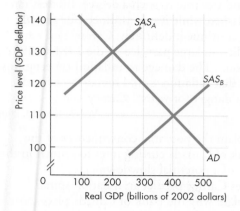

a. What are the price level and real GDP?
b. Does Freezone have an unemployment problem or an inflation problem? Why?
c. What do you predict will happen in Freezone if the central bank takes no monetary policy actions?
d. What monetary policy action would you advise the central bank to take and what do you predict will be the effect of that action?

12. Suppose that in Freezone, shown in problem 11, the short-run aggregate supply curve is *SAS*$_B$ and potential GDP increases to $350 billion.

a. What happens if the central bank lowers the overnight rate and buys securities on the open market?
b. What happens if the central bank raises the overnight rate and sells securities on the open market?
c. Do you recommend that the central bank lower or raise the overnight rate? Why?

13. **Policy and Infrastructure Developments**

Recent disruptions in financial markets have led central banks around the world to re-examine their roles in providing "liquidity" to the financial system. ... Central banks should provide liquidity to financial markets in extraordinary circumstances because markets require liquidity for efficient pricing, illiquidity can contribute to financial system instability with real economic

consequences, and a central bank's unique characteristics make it well suited to be the ultimate provider of liquidity to the financial system. A central bank should intervene to address financial market turbulence only when there is a significant market failure and significant financial instability with macroeconomic consequences could be avoided or mitigated. A central bank should price the provision of liquidity to financial markets competitively through auctions. A central bank should have a range of facilities with which to provide liquidity to the financial system, to better focus the provision of liquidity as needed.

Bank of Canada, June 2008

a. What are the primary functions of the Bank of Canada?
b. What does it mean for a central bank to provide "liquidity" to the financial system? How does this compare to the typical monetary policy tools used by the Bank of Canada?
c. Evaluate the claim that "Central banks should provide liquidity to financial markets in extraordinary circumstances."

14. **Canada Inflation Slows, Central Bank Expected to Cut Rates Again**

Inflation slowed dramatically. ... Canada's Consumer Price Index (CPI) increased by 1.8% in the 12-month period from February 2007 to February 2008, the slowest rate of growth in six months ... It's also a dramatic turn from the 12-month increase of 2.2% reported in January. ... Inflation is below the Bank of Canada's 2% target, meaning the Bank of Canada has room to lower interest rates at its next meeting. ... Canada's economy is facing a potential slowdown in the face of a possible U.S. recession. Already this month, the bank lowered its benchmark rate 50 points to 3.5%. "Inflation is under control and that's good news," Stefane Marion, an economist with National Bank Financial in Montreal, told Bloomberg. "Inflation is not an impediment to rate cuts in Canada, contrary to other countries where central bankers might be more hesitant." Unlike most rate cut scenarios, Canada's economy is operating above its production capacity and both core and total consumer price index (CPI) inflation are lower than projected. ... In this case, the rate cut was primarily a precautionary move—putting up its economic dukes to fend off threats of [and reactions to] a possible U.S. recession. ... Domestic demand remains strong because of rising incomes and commodity prices, the bank said. But effects of a weaker U.S. economy will stunt Canada's exports, and the bank projects that growth in 2008 will be weaker than it projected. ...

Money Morning, March 19, 2008

a. Explain the intended effect of the Bank of Canada's rate cuts and illustrate your explanation with an appropriate graphical analysis.
b. Why does the lower rate of inflation provide "room to lower interest rates?" Why are central bankers in other countries "more hesitant" to cut rates?
c. Evaluate the advantages and disadvantages of making "precautionary" monetary policy decisions.

15. **Carney: Bank of Canada's Focus on Inflation Key Amid Commodities Boom**

Keeping inflation in check is vital. ... Bank of Canada governor Mark Carney said Thursday, as he sought to explain the rationale behind last week's controversial decision to keep interest rates steady ... at three percent—a move that surprised many economists who were expecting a cut of a quarter of a percentage point. ... "This is not a question of what people think we say we're going to do. But it's a question of what we ought to do to fulfill our mandate. And that is proper transparency and communication." He said a 10 percent increase in commodity prices since April was enough of a reason for the Bank to change its view. "As a result the bank now judges that the current accommodative stance of monetary policy is appropriate to bring aggregate demand and supply into balance and to achieve the two percent inflation target," Carney said. "Going forward there remain important downside and upside risks to inflation, but these risks are now judged to be evenly balanced." Statistics Canada said Thursday Canada's inflation shot past the two percent level for the first time in four months in May. ... "The demand and supply fundamentals ... give reasons to expect firm commodity prices, but not necessarily persistent—let alone accelerating—commodity price increases," Carney said. The key is to avoid the pitfalls of monetary authorities in the 1970s—the last time commodities rose to such a degree. Interest rates were slashed while it was assumed our growth would continue indefinitely. Carney said that mentality, in large part, led to the 1981 to 1982 recession. "The damage to inflation expectations meant that inflation would remain a real and present danger for years," Carney said.

CNEWS, June 20, 2008

a. Explain the potential consequences of the Bank of Canada cutting rates too much in the face of a potential slowdown.
b. Does Carney predict an inflation spiral?
c. Explain why the Bank of Canada places so much emphasis on managing inflation expectations.
d. Why are public statements by the Bank of Canada actually an important component of successful monetary policy?
e. Evaluate the following statement made by Carney: "This is not a question of what people think we say we're going to do. But it's a question of what we ought to do to fulfill our mandate. And that is proper transparency and communication."

16. Study *Reading Between the Lines* on pp. 750–751 and then answer the following questions.

a. Given the policy action taken by the Bank of Canada, how do you think the Bank's expectation about future real GDP growth and future inflation differ from the most recent actual real GDP growth rate and inflation rate?
b. What would be the normal response to a large cut in the overnight rate in the market for loanable funds and to aggregate demand?
c. What made 2008 unusual and how would you analyze the special features of 2008 in the market for loanable funds?
d. If the Bank of Canada had not cut the overnight rate, what might the consequences have been?

UNDERSTANDING MACROECONOMIC POLICY

Tradeoffs and Free Lunches

A policy tradeoff arises if in taking an action to achieve one goal, some other goal must be forgone. The Bank of Canada wants to avoid a rise in the inflation rate and a rise in the unemployment rate. But if the Bank of Canada raises the interest rate to curb inflation, it might lower expenditure and increase unemployment. The Bank of Canada faces a short-run tradeoff between inflation and unemployment.

A policy free lunch arises if in taking actions to pursue one goal, some other (intended or unintended) goal is also achieved. The Bank of Canada wants to keep inflation in check and, at the same time, boost the economic growth rate. If lower inflation brings greater certainty about the future and stimulates saving and investment, the Bank of Canada gets both lower inflation and faster real GDP growth. It enjoys a free lunch.

The two chapters in this part have described the institutional framework in which fiscal policy (Chapter 29) and monetary policy (Chapter 30) are made, described the instruments of policy, and analyzed the effects of policy. This exploration of economic policy draws on almost everything you learned in previous chapters.

These policy chapters serve as a capstone on your knowledge of macroeconomics and draw together all the strands in your study of the previous chapters.

Milton Friedman, whom you meet below, has profoundly influenced our understanding of macroeconomic policy, especially monetary policy.

Milton Friedman *was born into a poor immigrant family in New York City in 1912. He was an undergraduate at Rutgers and a graduate student at Columbia University during the Great Depression. From 1977 until his death in 2006, Professor Friedman was a Senior Fellow at the Hoover Institution at Stanford University. But his reputation was built between 1946 and 1983, when he was a leading member of the "Chicago School," an approach to economics developed at the University of Chicago and based on the views that free markets allocate resources efficiently and that stable and low money supply growth delivers macroeconomic stability.*

Friedman has advanced our understanding of the forces that determine macroeconomic performance and clarified the effects of the quantity of money. For this work, he was awarded the 1977 Nobel Prize for Economic Science.

By reasoning from basic economic principles, Friedman (along with Edmund S. Phelps, the 2006 Economics Nobel Laureate) predicted that persistent

"Inflation is always and everywhere a monetary phenomenon."

MILTON FRIEDMAN

The Counter-Revolution in Monetary Theory

demand stimulation would not increase output but would cause inflation.

When output growth slowed and inflation broke out in the 1970s, Friedman seemed like a prophet, and for a time, his policy prescription, known as monetarism, was embraced around the world.

TALKING
WITH

Stephanie Schmitt-Grohé

Stephanie Schmitt-Grohé is Professor of Economics at Columbia University. Born in Germany, she received her first economics degree at Westfälische Wilhelms-Universität Münster in 1987, her M.B.A in Finance at Baruch College, City University of New York in 1989, and her Ph.D. in economics at the University of Chicago in 1994.

Professor Schmitt-Grohé's research covers a wide range of fiscal policy and monetary policy issues that are especially relevant in today's economy as the consequences of the 2007 U.S. mortgage crisis play out.

Working with her husband, Martin Uribe, also a Professor of Economics at Columbia University, she has published papers in leading economics journals on how best to conduct monetary policy and fiscal policy and how to avoid problems that might arise from the inappropriate use of a simple policy rule for setting the overnight rate. She has also contributed to the debate on inflation targeting.

In 2004, Professor Schmitt-Grohé was awarded the Bernácer Prize, awarded annually to a European economist under the age of 40 who has made outstanding contributions in the fields of macroeconomics and finance.

Michael Parkin and Robin Bade talked with Stephanie Schmitt-Grohé about her work and the challenges of conducting stabilization policy.

What attracted you to economics?

When I graduated from high school, I was interested in both chemistry and economics but I wasn't sure which I wanted to study, so I enrolled in both programs. Within the first year of study, I realized that I wanted to pursue a career in economics. I took a class in which we learned how fiat money can have value and how the central bank can control the inflation rate. This seemed very important to me at the time—and still does after so many years.

What led you to focus your research on monetary and fiscal stabilization policy?

I always was very interested in economic policy and both monetary and fiscal stabilization policy have large and clear effects on a society's well-being. The same is certainly true for other areas of economics, but the benefits of macroeconomic stabilization policy are particularly easy to see; and it isn't difficult to find historical examples where bad monetary and fiscal policies unnecessarily lowered the standard of living.

What was your first job as a professional economist? How did you get started?

My first job out of graduate school was at the Board of Governors of the Federal Reserve System in Washington. This was a fabulous experience. Watching the policy-making process, I became motivated to work on having a more consistent and compelling theoretical framework on which to base monetary policy advice, and in particular, learning to develop tools to perform evaluation of alternative monetary policy proposals.

Only a few years out of graduate school, you and your economist husband Martin Uribe accepted a challenge to contribute to an assessment of "dollarization" for Mexico. First, would you explain what dollarization is?

When a country dollarizes, the U.S. dollar becomes legal tender, replacing the domestic currency. Ecuador, for example, is dollarized. In the case of Mexico in 1999, there were proposals, mainly coming from the business community, to replace the peso with the U.S. dollar.

Why might dollarization be a good idea?

Such proposals are typically motivated by the desire to avoid excessive inflation and excessive exchange rate volatility. Dollarization also makes inflationary finance of the Treasury Department impossible.

And what are the costs of dollarization?

One cost is that the country loses the revenues it gains from issuing money. A second cost is that the country loses the ability to conduct monetary stabilization policy. In effect, the domestic central bank can no longer influence the business cycle through interest rate or exchange rate policy. The question that Martin and I wanted to answer was "How costly is it for a country to give up the ability to conduct monetary stabilization policy?" We quickly realized that we didn't have the tools to answer this question in a way that we regarded as satisfying.

Briefly, what did you have to do to enable you to say whether dollarization is a good or bad idea?

We wanted to be able to quantify the loss in economic welfare that comes from not being able to target monetary policy at stabilizing the domestic economy. To do this, we needed to compute two measures of economic welfare, one arising from Mexican monetary policy and another under dollarization. But we wanted our measures to be based on an empirically compelling and sufficiently detailed model of the Mexican business cycle. At that time there were no measurement techniques available that allowed us to perform this task. So over the course of the next five years we developed the tools that we needed. One tool is an algorithm that computes (approximately but with sufficient accuracy) economic welfare under any given monetary policy, including the two of interest to us: Mexican dollarization and actual Mexican monetary policy. A second tool that we developed is another algorithm to compute optimal monetary policy—the best available monetary policy.

Knowing the highest level of economic welfare that can be achieved allows us to judge how close practical policy proposals come to optimal policy.

And what was your biggest surprise?

I think our biggest surprise in this research program was how small the welfare costs of some very simple policy rules are vis-à-vis the optimal policy. Martin and I have shown in a number of papers that simple interest rate rules are very close to the best that can be achieved.

How would you describe the best stabilization policy for smoothing the business cycle and keeping inflation in check?

Good stabilization policy is not necessarily a policy that smoothes the business cycle, in the sense that it minimizes output fluctuations. On the contrary, it might be that trying to avoid cyclical fluctuations lowers economic welfare. Suppose, for example, that business-cycle fluctuations arise from fluctuations in the growth rate of productivity—as real business cycle theory suggests. Then economic welfare decreases if we limit the cyclical increase in output that comes from the increase in productivity.

The findings of my work with Martin suggest that a simple and highly effective monetary policy is one whereby the central bank raises the short-term interest rate by more than one-for-one when inflation exceeds the targeted level of inflation. Interest rate feedback rules of this type are similar to the Taylor rule, but contrary to Taylor's rule, our results suggest that the central bank should not respond to output variations in setting the short-term nominal interest rate. We find that if the central bank responds to the output gap, economic welfare suffers.

Regarding fiscal policies, the results of several of our papers strongly suggest smoothing out distortionary tax rates and using variations in the level of government debt to address cyclical budget shortfalls.

You've written about avoiding liquidity traps. What is the liquidity trap that we must avoid and how do we do so?

A liquidity trap is a situation in which the nominal interest rate is at zero. At this point, the central bank

> Good stabilization policy is not necessarily a policy that smoothes the business cycle ...

cannot lower the nominal interest rate any further to stimulate the economy.

In joint work with Jess Benhabib of New York University, Martin and I show that a liquidity trap can be avoided through the coordination of monetary and fiscal policy. In particular, liquidity traps—that is, zero nominal interest rates—can be avoided as equilibrium outcomes if the public becomes convinced that the government follows a fiscal policy that is inconsistent with zero nominal rates.

What is your assessment of the Taylor Rule?

Taylor-type interest rate feedback rules stipulate that the short-term nominal interest rate should be set as an increasing function of deviations of inflation from the target rate and of deviations of output from trend. In particular, the inflation coefficient of such a feedback rule should exceed unity, the so-called Taylor criterion. As mentioned above, in my work with Martin, I have found that simple interest rate rules that respond only to price inflation tend to bring outcomes with welfare levels very close to the optimal policy. In this sense Taylor-type interest rate feedback rules represent good monetary policy. An important caveat relative to Taylor's original specification of interest rate feedback rules is that our research (and that of several others) assigns very little, if any, value to including deviations of output from trend in the interest rate feedback rule. Moreover, such policies of leaning against the wind can under certain circumstances be harmful.

> ... interest rate rules that respond only to price inflation ... [are] very close to the optimal policy.

... and of inflation targeting?

Different people have different definitions of inflation targeting. This makes answering this question not straightforward. If inflation targeting is interpreted as a monetary policy specification, by which the short-term nominal interest rate responds only (or mainly) to inflation (as opposed to the output gap or other macroeconomic indicators), then the results of our work strongly support an inflation targeting policy.

What are the implications of your work for avoiding and living with the credit market conditions that emerged in August 2007 and dominated the global economy through 2008?

Over the past decade, financial institutions that act like banks have developed. They are not, however, required by law to be under the regulations and supervision of the government in the same way as regular banks are. Going forward, I believe that it is desirable to have an overhaul of the existing regulatory system in order to ensure equal regulation and supervision for all financial institutions.

What advice do you have for a student who is just starting to study economics? Is it a good choice of major? What subjects go well with it?

If you are just starting studying economics, be patient. Economics can be more formal than other social sciences, and because of this, it may take a little while before you can apply what you learn in your economics classes to enhance your understanding of the economy around you. Subjects that are nice complements with economics are statistics and applied math.

Do you have any special advice for young women who might be contemplating a career in economics?

About one-third of newly minted economics Ph.D.s are women, but only about 8 percent of full professors in a Ph.D.-granting economics department are women. Looking at statistics like this can be discouraging. However, from my 15 years of experience of working in this field, I don't see any reason why young women who are about to start a career in economics will not be able to change these statistics.

GLOSSARY

Above full-employment equilibrium A macroeconomic equilibrium in which real GDP exceeds potential GDP. (p. 637)

Absolute advantage A person has an absolute advantage if that person is more productive than another person. (p. 40)

After-tax income Total income minus tax payments by households to governments. (p. 442)

Aggregate demand The relationship between the quantity of real GDP demanded and the price level. (p. 630)

Aggregate planned expenditure The sum of planned consumption expenditure, planned investment, planned government expenditure on goods and services, and planned exports minus planned imports. (p. 650)

Aggregate production function The relationship between real GDP and the quantity of labour when all other influences on production remain the same. (p. 521)

Allocative efficiency A situation in which goods and services are produced at the lowest possible cost and in the quantities that provide the greatest possible benefit. We cannot produce more of any good without giving up some of another good that we *value more highly*. (p. 35)

Anti-combine law A law that regulates oligopolies and prevents them from becoming monopolies or behaving like monopolies. (p. 358)

Automated Clearing Settlement System (ACSS) The system through which all payments not processed by the LVTS are handled. (p. 575)

Automatic fiscal policy A fiscal policy action that is triggered by the state of the economy (p. 718)

Automatic stabilizers Mechanisms that stabilize real GDP without explicit action by the government. (p. 720)

Autonomous expenditure The sum of those components of aggregate planned expenditure that are not influenced by real GDP. Autonomous expenditure equals the sum of investment, government expenditure, exports, and the autonomous parts of consumption expenditure and imports. (p. 654)

Autonomous tax multiplier The magnification effect of a change in taxes on aggregate demand. (pp. 672, 718)

Average cost pricing rule A rule that sets price to cover cost including normal profit, which means setting the price equal to average total cost. (p. 314)

Average fixed cost Total fixed cost per unit of output. (p. 258)

Average product The average product of a factor of production. It equals total product divided by the quantity of the factor employed. (p. 253)

Average total cost Total cost per unit of output. (p. 258)

Average variable cost Total variable cost per unit of output. (p. 258)

Balanced budget A government budget in which tax revenues and outlays are equal. (p. 709)

Balanced budget multiplier The magnification effect on aggregate demand of a simultaneous change in government expenditure and taxes that leaves the budget balanced. (pp. 673, 718)

Balance of payments accounts A country's record of international trading, borrowing, and lending. (p. 606)

Bank rate The interest rate that the Bank of Canada charges big (LVTS-participating) banks on loans. (p. 736)

Barrier to entry A legal or natural constraint that protects a firm from potential competitors. (p. 300)

Barter The direct exchange of one good or service for other goods and services. (p. 568)

Behavioural economics A study of the ways in which limits on the human brain's ability to compute and implement decisions influence economic behaviour—both the decisions that people make and the consequences of those decisions for the way markets work. (p. 194)

Below full-employment equilibrium A macroeconomic equilibrium in which potential GDP exceeds real GDP. (p. 636)

Big tradeoff The tradeoff between equality and efficiency. (pp. 9, 119, 455)

Bilateral monopoly A situation in which a monopoly seller faces a monopsony buyer. (p. 425)

Black market An illegal market in which the price exceeds the legally imposed price ceiling. (p. 130)

Bond A promise to make specified payments on specified dates. (p. 545)

Bond market The market in which bonds issued by firms and governments are traded. (p. 545)

Budget deficit A government's budget balance that is negative—outlays exceed tax revenues. (p. 709)

Budget line The limits to a household's consumption choices. (p. 204)

Budget surplus A government's budget balance that is positive—tax revenues exceed outlays. (p. 709)

Business cycle The periodic but irregular up-and-down movement in production. (p. 475)

Canadian-dollar effective exchange rate index (CERI) An average of the exchange rates of the Canadian dollar against the U.S. dollar, the European Union euro, the Japanese yen, the U.K. pound, the Chinese yuan, and the Mexican peso. (p. 596)

Canadian interest rate differential The Canadian interest rate minus the foreign interest rate. (p. 601)

Capital The tools, equipment, buildings, and other constructions that businesses use to produce goods and services. (p. 4)

Capital account A record of foreign investment in Canada minus Canadian investment abroad. (p. 606)

Capital accumulation The growth of capital resources, including human capital. (p. 38)

Capture theory A theory that regulation serves the self-interest of the producer, who captures the regulator and maximizes economic profit. (p. 313)

Cartel A group of firms acting together—colluding—to limit output, raise the price, and increase economic profit. (p. 343)

Central bank A bank's bank and a public authority that regulates the nation's depository institutions and controls the quantity of money. (p. 572)

Ceteris paribus Other things being equal—all other relevant things remaining the same. (p. 24)

Chained-dollar real GDP A measure of real GDP derived by valuing production at the prices of both the current year and the previous year and linking (chaining) those prices back to the prices of the reference base year. (p. 482)

Chained price index for consumption (CPIC) An index of the prices of all the items included in consumption expenditure in GDP; the ratio of nominal consumption expenditure to real consumption expenditure. (p. 502)

Change in demand A change in buyers' plans that occurs when some influence on those plans other than the price of the good changes. It is illustrated by a shift of the demand curve. (p. 60)

Change in supply A change in sellers' plans that occurs when some influence on those plans other than the price of the good changes. It is illustrated by a shift of the supply curve. (p. 65)

Change in the quantity demanded A change in buyers' plans that occurs when the price of a good changes but all other influences on buyers' plans remain unchanged. It is illustrated by a movement along the demand curve. (p. 63)

Change in the quantity supplied A change in sellers' plans that occurs when the price of a good changes but all other influences on sellers' plans remain unchanged. It is illustrated by a movement along the supply curve. (p. 66)

Chartered bank A private firm, chartered under the Bank Act of 1992 to receive deposits and make loans. (p. 571)

Classical A macroeconomist who believes that the economy is self-regulating and that it is always at full employment. (p. 640)

Classical growth theory A theory of economic growth based on the view that the growth of real GDP per person is temporary and that when it rises above subsistence level, a population explosion eventually brings it back to subsistence level. (p. 531)

Coase theorem The proposition that if property rights exist, only a small number of parties are involved, and transactions costs are low, then private transactions are efficient. (p. 379)

Collusive agreement An agreement between two (or more) producers to form a cartel to restrict output, raise the price, and increase profits. (p. 348)

Command system A method of allocating resources by the order (command) of someone in authority. In a firm a managerial hierarchy organizes production. (pp. 108, 233)

Common resource A resource that is rival and nonexcludable. (p. 394)

Comparative advantage A person or country has a comparative advantage in an activity if that person or country can perform the activity at a lower opportunity cost than anyone else or any other country. (p. 40)

Competitive market A market that has many buyers and many sellers, so no single buyer or seller can influence the price. (p. 58)

Complement A good that is used in conjunction with another good. (p. 61)

Compound interest The interest on an initial investment plus the interest on the interest that the investment has previously earned. (p. 434)

Constant returns to scale Features of a firm's technology that lead to constant long-run average cost as output increases. When constant returns to scale are present, the *LRAC* curve is horizontal. (p. 264)

Consumer equilibrium A situation in which a consumer has allocated all his or her available income in the way that, given the prices of goods and services, maximizes his or her total utility (p. 184)

Consumer Price Index (CPI) An index that measures the average of the prices paid by urban consumers for a fixed "basket" of consumer goods and services. (p. 498)

Consumer surplus The value (or marginal benefit) of a good minus the price paid for it, summed over the quantity bought. (p. 111)

Consumption expenditure The total payment for consumer goods and services. (p. 469)

Consumption function The relationship between consumption expenditure and disposable income, other things remaining the same. (p. 650)

Contestable market A market in which firms can enter and leave so easily that firms in the market face competition from *potential* entrants. (p. 356)

Cooperative equilibrium The outcome of a game in which the players make and share the monopoly profit. (p. 355)

Copyright A government-sanctioned exclusive right granted to the inventor of a good, service, or productive process to produce, use, and sell the invention for a given number of years. (p. 385)

Core inflation rate The inflation rate excluding volatile elements—the underlying inflation trend. (p. 502)

Cost-push inflation An inflation that results from an initial increase in costs. (p. 682)

Crawling peg A policy regime that selects a target path for the exchange rate and uses intervention in the foreign exchange market to achieve that path. (p. 612)

Creditor nation A country that during its entire history has invested more in the rest of the world than other countries have invested in it. (p. 608)

Credit union A cooperative organization that operates under the Co-operative Credit Association Act of 1992 and receives deposits from and makes loans to its members. (p. 571)

Cross elasticity of demand The responsiveness of the demand for a good to a change in the price of a substitute or complement, other things remaining the same. It is calculated as the percentage change in the quantity demanded of the good divided by the percentage change in the price of the substitute or complement. (p. 93)

Cross-section graph A graph that shows the values of an economic variable for different groups or categories at a point in time. (p. 16)

Crowding-out effect The tendency for a government budget deficit to decrease investment. (p. 556)

Currency The notes and coins held by individuals and businesses. (p. 569)

Currency drain ratio The ratio of currency to deposits. (p. 576)

Current account A record of receipts from exports of goods and services sold abroad, payments for imports of goods and services from abroad, net interest income paid abroad, and net transfers abroad (such as foreign aid payments). (p. 606)

Cyclical surplus or deficit The actual surplus or deficit minus the structural surplus or deficit. (p. 722)

Cyclical unemployment The higher-than-normal unemployment that arises at a business cycle trough and the unusually low unemployment that exists at a business cycle peak. (p. 496)

Deadweight loss A measure of inefficiency. It is equal to the decrease in total surplus that results from an inefficient level of production. (p. 115)

Debtor nation A country that during its entire history has borrowed more from the rest of the world than it has lent to other countries. (p. 608)

Demand The entire relationship between the price of a good and the quantity demanded of it when all other influences on buyers' plans remain the same. It is illustrated by a demand curve and described by a demand schedule. (p. 59)

Demand curve A curve that shows the relationship between the quantity demanded of a good and its price when all other influences on consumers' planned purchases remain the same. (p. 60)

Demand for loanable funds The relationship between the quantity of loanable funds demanded and the real interest rate when all other influences on borrowing plans remain the same. (p. 550)

Demand for money The relationship between the quantity of money demanded and the interest rate when all other influences on the amount of money that people wish to hold remain the same. (p. 579)

Demand-pull inflation An inflation that starts because aggregate demand increases. (p. 680)

Depository institution A firm that takes deposits from households and firms and makes loans to other households and firms. (p. 571)

Depreciation The decrease in the value of a firm's capital that results from wear and tear and obsolescence. (p. 470)

Deregulation The process of removing regulation of prices, quantities, entry, and other aspects of economic activity in a firm or industry. (p. 313)

Derived demand Demand for a factor of production—it is derived from the demand for the goods and services produced by that factor. (p. 419)

Desired reserve ratio The ratio of reserves to deposits that banks want to hold. (p. 576)

Diminishing marginal rate of substitution The general tendency for a person to be willing to give up less of good y to get one more unit of good x, and at the same time remain indifferent, as the quantity of good x increases. (p. 208)

Diminishing marginal returns The tendency for the marginal product of an additional unit of a factor of production to be less than the marginal product of the previous unit of the factor. (p. 255)

Diminishing marginal utility The decrease in marginal utility as the quantity consumed increases. (p. 183)

Direct relationship A relationship between two variables that move in the same direction. (p. 18)

Discounting The calculation we use to convert a future amount of money to its present value. (p. 434)

Discouraged worker A marginally attached worker who has stopped looking for a job because of repeated failure to find one. (p. 494)

Discretionary fiscal policy A fiscal action that is initiated by an act of Parliament. (p. 718)

Diseconomies of scale Features of a firm's technology that lead to rising long-run average cost as output increases. (p. 264)

Disposable income Aggregate income minus taxes plus transfer payments. (pp. 632, 650)

Doha Development Agenda (Doha Round) Negotiations held in Doha, Qatar, to lower tariff barriers and quotas that restrict international trade in farm products and services. (p. 164)

Dominant strategy equilibrium An equilibrium in which the best strategy for each player is to cheat *regardless of the strategy of the other player*. (p. 354)

Dumping The sale by a foreign firm of exports at a lower price than the cost of production. (p. 165)

Duopoly A market structure in which two producers of a good or service compete. (p. 342)

Dynamic comparative advantage A comparative advantage that a person or country possesses as a result of having specialized in a particular activity and then, as a result of learning-by-doing, having become the producer with the lowest opportunity cost. (p. 43)

Economic depreciation The change in the market value of capital over a given period. (p. 229)

Economic efficiency A situation that occurs when the firm produces a given output at the least cost. (p. 231)

Economic growth The expansion of production possibilities that results from capital accumulation and technological change. (p. 38)

Economic growth rate The annual percentage change in real GDP. (p. 516)

Economic model A description of some aspect of the economic world that includes only those features of the world that are needed for the purpose at hand. (p. 11)

Economic profit A firm's total revenue minus its total cost. (p. 228)

Economic rent Any surplus—consumer surplus, producer surplus, or economic profit. (p. 308)

Economics The social science that studies the *choices* that individuals, businesses, governments, and entire societies make as they cope with *scarcity* and the *incentives* that influence and reconcile those choices. (p. 2)

Economies of scale Features of a firm's technology that lead to a falling long-run average cost as output increases. (pp. 243, 264)

Economies of scope Decreases in average total cost that occur when a firm uses specialized resources to produce a range of goods and services. (p. 243)

Efficiency wage A real wage rate that is set above the equilibrium wage rate. (p. 496)

Efficient scale The quantity at which average total cost is at a minimum—the quantity at the bottom of the U-shaped *ATC* curve. (p. 328)

Elastic demand Demand with a price elasticity greater than 1; other things remaining the same, the percentage change in the quantity demanded exceeds the percentage change in price. (p. 89)

Elasticity of supply The responsiveness of the quantity supplied of a good to a change in its price, other things remaining the same. (p. 96)

Employment-to-population ratio The percentage of people of working age who have jobs. (p. 493)

Entrepreneurship The human resource that organizes the other three factors of production: labour, land, and capital. (p. 4)

Equilibrium expenditure The level of aggregate expenditure that occurs when aggregate planned expenditure equals real GDP. (p. 656)

Equilibrium price The price at which the quantity demanded equals the quantity supplied. (p. 68)

Equilibrium quantity The quantity bought and sold at the equilibrium price. (p. 68)

Excess capacity A firm has excess capacity if it produces below its efficient scale. (p. 328)

Excess reserves A bank's actual reserves minus its desired reserves. (p. 576)

Exchange rate The price at which one currency exchanges for another in the foreign exchange market. (p. 594)

Excludable A good or service or a resource is excludable if it is possible to prevent someone from enjoying the benefit of it. (p. 394)

Expansion A business cycle phase between a trough and a peak—a period in which real GDP increases. (p. 475)

Exports The goods and services that we sell to people in other countries. (pp. 154, 470)

External diseconomies Factors outside the control of a firm that raise the firm's costs as the industry produces a larger output. (p. 287)

External economies Factors beyond the control of a firm that lower the firm's costs as the industry produces a larger output. (p. 287)

Externality A cost or a benefit that arises from production and falls on someone other than the producer, or a cost or a benefit that arises from consumption and falls on someone other than the consumer. (p. 374)

Factors of production The productive resources used to produce goods and services. (p. 3)

Federal budget The annual statement of the outlays and tax revenues of the government of Canada, together with the laws and regulations that approve and support those outlays and taxes. (p. 708)

Final good An item that is bought by its final user during a specified time period. (p. 468)

Financial capital The funds that firms use to buy physical capital. (p. 544)

Financial institution A firm that operates on both sides of the market for financial capital. It borrows in one market and lends in another. (p. 546)

Firm An economic unit that hires factors of production and organizes those factors to produce and sell goods and services. (pp. 43, 228)

Fiscal policy The government's attempt to achieve macroeconomic objectives such as full employment, sustained long-term economic growth, and price level stability by setting and changing tax rates, making transfer payments, and purchasing goods and services. (pp. 632, 708)

Fixed exchange rate An exchange rate pegged at a value decided by the government or central bank and that blocks the unregulated forces of demand and supply by direct intervention in the foreign exchange market. (p. 611)

Flexible exchange rate An exchange rate that is determined by demand and supply with no direct intervention in the foreign exchange market by the central bank. (p. 611)

Foreign currency The money of other countries, regardless of whether that money is in the form of notes, coins, or bank deposits. (p. 594)

Foreign exchange market The market in which the currency of one country is exchanged for the currency of another. (p. 594)

Four-firm concentration ratio A measure of market power that is calculated as the percentage of the value of sales accounted for by the four largest firms in an industry. (p. 238)

Free-rider problem The problem that the market would provide an inefficiently small quantity of a public good. (p. 395)

Frictional unemployment The unemployment that arises from normal labour turnover—from people entering and leaving the labour force and from the ongoing creation and destruction of jobs. (p. 495)

Full employment A situation in which the unemployment rate equals the natural unemployment rate. At full employment, there is no cyclical unemployment—all unemployment is frictional and structural. (p. 496)

Full-employment equilibrium A macroeconomic equilibrium in which real GDP equals potential GDP. (p. 637)

Game theory A tool for studying strategic behaviour—behaviour that takes into account the expected behaviour of others and the recognition of mutual interdependence. (p. 346)

GDP deflator An index of the prices of all the items included in GDP; the ratio of nominal GDP to real GDP. (p. 502)

General Agreement on Tariffs and Trade (GATT) An international agreement signed in 1947 to reduce tariffs on international trade. (p. 161)

Gini coefficient The ratio of the area between the line of equality and the Lorenz curve to the entire area beneath the line of equality. (p. 445)

Goods and services All the objects that people value and produce to satisfy human wants. (p. 3)

Government debt The total amount that the government has borrowed. It equals the sum of past budget deficits minus the sum of past budget surpluses. (p. 711)

Government expenditure Goods and services bought by government. (p. 470)

Government expenditure multiplier The magnification effect of a change in government expenditure on goods and services on equilibrium expenditure and real GDP. (pp. 672, 718)

Government sector balance An amount equal to net taxes minus government expenditure on goods and services. (p. 609)

Gross domestic product (GDP) The market value of all final goods and services produced within a country during a given time period. (p. 468)

Gross investment The total amount spent on purchases of new capital and on replacing depreciated capital. (pp. 470, 544)

Growth accounting A tool that calculates the contribution to labour productivity growth of each of its sources. (p. 528)

Herfindahl–Hirschman Index A measure of market power that is calculated as the square of the market share of each firm (as a percentage) summed over the largest 50 firms (or over all firms if there are fewer than 50) in a market. (p. 238)

Hotelling Principle The idea that traders expect the price of a nonrenewable resource to rise at a rate equal to the interest rate. (p. 430)

Human capital The knowledge and skill that people obtain from education, on-the-job training, and work experience. (p. 3)

Hyperinflation A rapid inflation that exceeds 50 percent a month. (p. 498)

Implicit rental rate The firm's opportunity cost of using its own capital. (p. 228)

Import quota A restriction that limits the maximum quantity of a good that may be imported in a given period. (p. 162)

Imports The goods and services that we buy from people in other countries. (pp. 154, 470)

Incentive A reward that encourages an action or a penalty that discourages one. (p. 2)

Incentive system A method of organizing production that uses a market-like mechanism inside the firm. (p. 233)

Income effect The effect of a change in income on consumption, other things remaining the same. (p. 212)

Income elasticity of demand The responsiveness of demand to a change in income, other things remaining the same. It is calculated as the percentage change in the quantity demanded divided by the percentage change in income. (p. 94)

Indifference curve A line that shows combinations of goods among which a consumer is indifferent. (p. 207)

Individual transferable quota (ITQ) A production limit that is assigned to an individual who is free to transfer (sell) the quota to someone else. (p. 404)

Induced expenditure The sum of the components of aggregate planned expenditure that vary with real GDP. Induced expenditure equals consumption expenditure minus imports. (p. 654)

Induced taxes Taxes that vary with real GDP. (p. 721)

Inelastic demand A demand with a price elasticity between 0 and 1; the percentage change in the quantity demanded is less than the percentage change in price. (p. 88)

Infant-industry argument The argument that it is necessary to protect a new industry to enable it to grow into a mature industry that can compete in world markets. (p. 165)

Inferior good A good for which demand decreases as income increases. (p. 62)

Inflationary gap The amount by which real GDP exceeds potential GDP. (p. 637)

Inflation rate The annual percentage change in the price level. (p. 498)

Inflation rate targeting A monetary policy strategy in which the central bank makes a public commitment to achieve an explicit inflation rate and to explain how its policy actions will achieve that target. (p. 732)

Instrument rule A decision rule for monetary policy that sets the policy instrument at a level that is based on the current state of the economy. (p. 735)

Intellectual property rights Property rights for discoveries owned by the creators of knowledge. (p. 385)

Interest The income that capital earns. (p. 4)

Interest rate parity A situation in which the rates of return on assets in different currencies are equal. (p. 604)

Intermediate good An item that is produced by one firm, bought by another firm, and used as a component of a final good or service. (p. 468)

Inverse relationship A relationship between variables that move in opposite directions. (p. 19)

Investment The purchase of new plant, equipment, and buildings, and additions to inventories. (p. 470)

Job A contract for the trade of labour services. (p. 418)

Keynesian A macroeconomist who believes that left alone, the economy would rarely operate at full employment and that to achieve full employment, active help from fiscal policy and monetary policy is required. (p. 640)

Keynesian cycle theory A theory that fluctuations in investment driven by fluctuations in business confidence—summarized in the phase "animal spirits"—are the main source of fluctuations in aggregate demand. (p. 690)

k-percent rule A rule that makes the quantity of money grow at a rate of k percent a year, where k equals the growth rate of potential GDP. (p. 748)

Labour The work time and work effort that people devote to producing goods and services. (p. 3)

Labour force The sum of the people who are employed and who are unemployed. (p. 491)

Labour force participation rate The percentage of the working-age population who are members of the labour force. (p. 492)

Labour productivity The quantity of real GDP produced by an hour of labour. (p. 525)

Labor union An organized group of workers that aims to increase the wage rate and influence other job conditions. (p. 424)

Laffer curve The relationship between the tax rate and the amount of tax revenue collected. (p. 717)

Land All the "gifts of nature" that we use to produce goods and services. (p. 3)

Large Value Transfer System (LVTS) An electronic payments system that enables financial institutions and their customers to make large payments instantly and with the sure knowledge that the payment has been made. (p. 575)

Law of demand Other things remaining the same, the higher the price of a good, the smaller is the quantity demanded of it; the lower the price of a good, the larger is the quantity demanded of it. (p. 59)

Law of diminishing returns As a firm uses more of a variable input, with a given quantity of other inputs (fixed inputs), the marginal product of the variable input eventually diminishes. (p. 255)

Law of supply Other things remaining the same, the higher the price of a good, the greater is the quantity supplied of it. (p. 64)

Learning-by-doing People become more productive in an activity (learning) just by repeatedly producing a particular good or service (doing). (p. 43)

Legal monopoly A market in which competition and entry are restricted by the granting of a public franchise, government licence, patent, or copyright. (p. 300)

Lender of last resort The Bank of Canada is the lender of last resort—depository institutions that are short of reserves can borrow from the Bank of Canada. (p. 573)

Limit pricing The practice of setting the price at the highest level that inflicts a loss on an entrant. (p. 357)

Linear relationship A relationship between two variables that is illustrated by a straight line. (p. 18)

Long run A period of time in which the quantities of all resources can be varied. (p. 252)

Long-run aggregate supply The relationship between the quantity of real GDP supplied and the price level when the money wage rate changes in step with the price level to achieve full employment. (p. 626)

Long-run average cost curve The relationship between the lowest attainable average total cost and output when both plant size and labour are varied. (p. 263)

Long-run macroeconomic equilibrium A situation that occurs when real GDP equals potential GDP—the economy is on its long-run aggregate supply curve. (p. 635)

Long-run market supply curve A curve that shows how the quantity supplied in a market varies as the market price varies after all the possible adjustments have been made, including changes in each firm's plant and the number of firms in the market. (p. 287)

Long-run Phillips curve A curve that shows the relationship between inflation and unemployment when the actual inflation rate equals the expected inflation rate. (p. 687)

Lorenz curve A curve that graphs the cumulative percentage of income or wealth against the cumulative percentage of households. (p. 443)

Low-income cut-off The income level below which a family spends 63.6 percent or more of its income on food, shelter, and clothing. (p. 447)

Lucas wedge The dollar value of the accumulated gap between what real GDP per person would have been if the 1960s growth rate had persisted and what real GDP per person turned out to be. (p. 474)

M1 A measure of money that consists of currency and chequable deposits of individuals and businesses. (p. 569)

M2 A measure of money that consists of M1 plus all other deposits. (p. 569)

Macroeconomics The study of the performance of the national economy and the global economy. (p. 2)

Margin When a choice is changed by a small amount or by a little at a time, the choice is made at the margin. (p. 10)

Marginal benefit The benefit that a person receives from consuming one more unit of a good or service. It is measured as the maximum amount that a person is willing to pay for one more unit of the good or service. (pp. 10, 36)

Marginal benefit curve A curve that shows the relationship between the marginal benefit of a good and the quantity of that good consumed. (p. 36)

Marginal cost The opportunity cost of producing one more unit of a good or service. It is the best alternative forgone. It is calculated as the increase in total cost divided by the increase in output. (pp. 10, 35, 258)

Marginal cost pricing rule A rule that sets the price of a good or service equal to the marginal cost of producing it. (p. 313)

Marginal external benefit The benefit from an additional unit of a good or service that people other than the consumer enjoy. (p. 381)

Marginal external cost The cost of producing an additional unit of a good or service that falls on people other than the producer. (p. 377)

Marginally attached worker A person who currently is neither working nor looking for work but has indicated that he or she wants and is available for a job and has looked for work sometime in the recent past. (p. 494)

Marginal private benefit The benefit from an additional unit of a good or service that the consumer of that good or service receives. (p. 381)

Marginal private cost The cost of producing an additional unit of a good or service that is borne by the producer of that good or service. (p. 377)

Marginal product The increase in total product that results from a one-unit increase in the variable input, with all other inputs remaining the same. It is calculated as the increase in total product divided by the increase in the variable input employed, when the quantities of all other inputs are constant. (p. 253)

Marginal propensity to consume The fraction of a change in disposable income that is consumed. It is calculated as the change in consumption expenditure divided by the change in disposable income. (p. 652)

Marginal propensity to import The fraction of an increase in real GDP that is spent on imports. (p. 653)

Marginal propensity to save The fraction of an increase in disposable income that is saved. It is calculated as the change in saving divided by the change in disposable income. (p. 652)

Marginal rate of substitution The rate at which a person will give up good y (the good measured on the y-axis) to get an additional unit of good x (the good measured on the x-axis) and at the same time remain indifferent (remain on the same indifference curve). (p. 208)

Marginal revenue The change in total revenue that results from a one-unit increase in the quantity sold. It is calculated as the change in total revenue divided by the change in quantity sold. (p. 274)

Marginal social benefit The marginal benefit enjoyed by society—by the consumer of a good or service (marginal private benefit) plus the marginal benefit enjoyed by others (marginal external benefit). (p. 381)

Marginal social cost The marginal cost incurred by the entire society—by the producer and by everyone else on whom the cost falls. It is the sum of marginal private cost and marginal external cost. (p. 377)

Marginal utility The change in total utility resulting from a one-unit increase in the quantity of a good consumed. (p. 182)

Marginal utility per dollar The marginal utility from a good divided by its price. (p. 184)

Market Any arrangement that enables buyers and sellers to get information from and to do business with each other. (p. 44)

Market for loanable funds The aggregate of all the individual markets in which households, firms, governments, banks, and other financial institutions borrow and lend. (p. 548)

Market income The wages, interest, rent, and profit earned in factor markets and before paying income taxes. (p. 442)

Markup The amount by which the firm's price exceeds its marginal cost. (p. 329)

McCallum rule A rule that makes the growth rate of the monetary base respond to the long-term average growth rate of real GDP and medium-term changes in the velocity of circulation of the monetary base. (p. 747)

Means of payment A method of settling a debt. (p. 568)

Microeconomics The study of the choices that individuals and businesses make, the way these choices interact in markets, and the influence of governments. (p. 2)

Minimum efficient scale The smallest quantity of output at which the long-run average cost curve reaches its lowest level. (p. 265)

Minimum wage A regulation that makes the hiring of labour below a specified wage rate illegal. The lowest wage at which a firm may legally hire labour. (p. 133)

Monetarist A macroeconomist who believes that the economy is self-regulating and that it will normally operate at full employment, provided that monetary policy is not erratic and that the pace of money growth is kept steady. (p. 641)

Monetarist cycle theory A theory that fluctuations in both investment and consumption expenditure, driven by fluctuations in the growth rate of the quantity of money, are the main source of fluctuations in aggregate demand. (p. 690)

Monetary base The sum of Bank of Canada notes, coins, and depository institution deposits at the Bank of Canada. (p. 573)

Monetary policy The Bank of Canada conducts the nation's monetary policy by changing interest rates and adjusting the quantity of money. (p. 632)

Money Any commodity or token that is generally acceptable as a means of payment. (pp. 44, 568)

Money multiplier The ratio of the change in the quantity of money to the change in the monetary base. (p. 577)

Money price The number of dollars that must be given up in exchange for a good or service. (p. 58)

Monopolistic competition A market structure in which a large number of firms make similar but slightly different products and compete on product quality, price, and marketing. (pp. 237, 324)

Monopoly A market structure in which there is one firm that produces a good or service that has no close substitutes and in which the firm is protected from competition by a barrier preventing the entry of new firms. (pp. 237, 300)

Monopsony A market in which there is a single buyer. (p. 425)

Mortgage A legal contract that gives ownership of a home to the lender in the event that the borrower fails to meet the agreed loan payments (repayments and interest). (p. 545)

Mortgage-backed security A type of bond that entitles its holder to the income from a package of mortgages. (p. 546)

Multiplier The amount by which a change in autonomous expenditure is magnified or multiplied to determine the change in equilibrium expenditure and real GDP. (p. 658)

Nash equilibrium The outcome of a game that occurs when player A takes the best possible action given the action of player B and player B takes the best

possible action given the action of player A. (p. 347)

National saving The sum of private saving (saving by households and businesses) and government saving. (p. 549)

Natural monopoly An industry in which economies of scale enable one firm to supply the entire market at the lowest possible price. (p. 300)

Natural unemployment rate The unemployment rate when the economy is at full employment—natural unemployment as a percentage of the labour force. (p. 496)

Negative externality An externality that arises from either production or consumption and that imposes an external cost. (p. 374)

Negative relationship A relationship between variables that move in opposite directions. (p. 19)

Neoclassical growth theory A theory of economic growth that proposes that real GDP per person grows because technological change induces an amount of saving and investment that makes capital per hour of labour grow. (p. 531)

Net borrower A country that is borrowing more from the rest of the world than it is lending to it. (p. 608)

Net exports The value of exports of goods and services minus the value of imports of goods and services. (pp. 470, 609)

Net investment The amount by which the value of capital increases—gross investment minus depreciation. (pp. 470, 544)

Net lender A country that is lending more to the rest of the world than it is borrowing from it. (p. 608)

Net taxes Taxes paid to governments minus cash transfers received from governments. (p. 548)

Net worth The total value of what a financial institution has lent minus the market value of what it has borrowed. (p. 547)

Neuroeconomics The study of the activity of the human brain when a

person makes an economic decision. (p. 195)

New classical A macroeconomist who holds the view that business cycle fluctuations are the efficient responses of a well-functioning market economy bombarded by shocks that arise from the uneven pace of technological change. (p. 640)

New classical cycle theory A rational expectations theory of the business cycle that regards unexpected fluctuations in aggregate demand as the main source of fluctuations of real GDP around potential GDP. (p. 690)

New growth theory A theory of economic growth based on the idea that real GDP per person grows because of the choices that people make in the pursuit of profit and holds that growth will persist indefinitely. (p. 533)

New Keynesian A macroeconomist who holds the view that not only is the money wage rate sticky but also that the prices of goods and services are sticky. (p. 641)

New Keynesian cycle theory A rational expectations theory of the business cycle that regards unexpected and currently expected fluctuations in aggregate demand as the main source of fluctuations of real GDP around potential GDP. (p. 690)

Nominal exchange rate The value of the Canadian dollar expressed in units of foreign currency per Canadian dollar. (p. 594)

Nominal GDP The value of the final goods and services produced in a given year valued at the prices that prevailed in that same year. It is a more precise name for GDP. (p. 473)

Nominal interest rate The number of dollars that a borrower pays and a lender receives in a year expressed as a percentage of the number of dollars borrowed and lent. (p. 549)

Nonexcludable A good or service or a resource is nonexcludable if it is impossible (or extremely costly) to prevent someone from benefiting from it. (p. 394)

Nonrenewable natural resources Natural resources that can be used only once. (p. 418)

Nonrival A good or service or a resource is nonrival if its use by one person does not decrease the quantity available for someone else. (p. 394)

Normal good A good for which demand increases as income increases. (p. 62)

Normal profit The return that an entrepreneur can expect to receive *on the average*. (p. 229)

Official reserves The government's holding of foreign currency. (p. 606)

Official settlements account A record of the change in official reserves—the government's holdings of foreign currency. (p. 606)

Offshore outsourcing A Canadian firm buys finished goods, components, or services from other firms in other countries. (p. 167)

Offshoring A Canadian firm hires foreign labour and produces in a foreign country or a Canadian firm buys finished goods, components, or services from firms in other countries. (p. 167)

Oligopoly A market structure in which a small number of firms compete. (pp. 237, 342)

Open market operation The purchase or sale of government of Canada securities—Treasury bills and bonds—by the Bank of Canada in the open market. (pp. 573, 736)

Operating band The target overnight loans rate plus or minus 0.25 percentage points.   (p. 736)

Opportunity cost The highest-valued alternative that we give up to get something.   (pp. 9, 33)

Output gap Real GDP minus potential GDP. (pp. 496, 636)

Outsourcing A Canadian firm buys finished goods, components, or services from other firms in Canada or from firms in other countries. (p. 167)

Overnight loans rate The interest rate that banks charge each other on overnight loans of reserves. (p. 734)

Patent A government-sanctioned exclusive right granted to the inventor of a good, service, or productive process to produce, use, and sell the invention for a given number of years. (p. 385)

Payments system The system through which banks make payments to each other to settle transactions by their customers. (p. 573)

Payoff matrix A table that shows the payoffs for every possible action by each player for every possible action by each other player. (p. 346)

Perfect competition A market in which there are many firms each selling an identical product; there are many buyers; there are no restrictions on entry into the industry; firms in the industry have no advantage over potential new entrants; and firms and buyers are well informed about the price of each firm's product. (pp. 237, 274)

Perfectly elastic demand Demand with an infinite price elasticity; the quantity demanded changes by an infinitely large percentage in response to a tiny price change. (p. 89)

Perfectly inelastic demand Demand with a price elasticity of zero; the quantity demanded remains constant when the price changes. (p. 88)

Perfect price discrimination Price discrimination that occurs when a firm sells each unit of output for the highest price that anyone is willing to pay for it. (p. 311)

Phillips curve A curve that shows a relationship between inflation and unemployment. (p. 686)

Pigovian taxes Taxes that are used as an incentive for producers to cut back on an activity that creates an external cost. (p. 380)

Positive externality An externality that arises from either production or consumption and that provides an external benefit. (p. 374)

Positive relationship A relationship between two variables that move in the same direction. (p. 18)

Potential GDP The value of production when all the economy's labour, capi-tal, land, and entrepreneurial ability are fully employed; the quantity of real GDP at full employment. (p. 474)

Poverty A state in which a household's income is too low to be able to buy the quantities of food, shelter, and clothing that are deemed necessary. (p. 447)

Preferences A description of a person's likes and dislikes. (p. 36)

Present value The amount of money that if invested today, will grow to be as large as a given future amount when the interest that it will earn is taken into account. (p. 434)

Price cap A regulation that makes it illegal to charge a price higher than a specified level. (p. 130)

Price cap regulation A rule that specifies the highest price that the firm is permitted to set—a price ceiling. (p. 315)

Price ceiling A regulation that makes it illegal to charge a price higher than a specified level. (p. 130)

Price discrimination The practice of selling different units of a good or service for different prices. (p. 301)

Price effect The effect of a change in the price on the quantity of a good consumed, other things remaining the same. (p. 211)

Price elasticity of demand A units-free measure of the responsiveness of the quantity demanded of a good to a change in its price, when all other influences on buyers' plans remain the same. (p. 86)

Price floor A regulation that makes it illegal to trade at a price lower than a specified level. (p. 133)

Price level The average level of prices as measured by a price index. (p. 498)

Price taker A firm that cannot influence the price of the good or service it produces. (p. 274)

Principal–agent problem The problem of devising compensation rules that induce an *agent* to act in the best interest of a *principal*. (p. 234)

Principle of minimum differentiation The tendency for competitors to make themselves similar to appeal to the maximum number of clients or voters. (p. 397)

Private good A good or service that is both rival and excludable. (p. 394)

Private sector balance An amount equal to saving minus investment. (p. 609)

Producer surplus The price of a good minus its minimum supply-price, summed over the quantity sold. (p. 113)

Product differentiation Making a product slightly different from the product of a competing firm. (pp. 237, 324)

Production efficiency A situation in which goods and services are produced at the lowest possible cost. (p. 33)

Production possibilities frontier The boundary between the combinations of goods and services that can be produced and the combinations that cannot. (p. 32)

Production quota An upper limit to the quantity of a good that may be produced in a specified period. (p. 141)

Profit The income earned by entrepreneurship. (p. 4)

Progressive income tax A tax on income at an average rate that increases with the level of income. (p. 453)

Property rights Social arrangements that govern the ownership, use, and disposal of anything that people value that are enforceable in the courts. (pp. 44, 378)

Proportional income tax A tax on income at a constant average rate, regardless of the level of income. (p. 453)

Provincial budget An annual statement of the revenues and outlays of a provincial government, together with the laws and regulations that approve or support those revenues and outlays. (p. 708)

Public good A good or service that is both nonrival and nonexcludable. It can be consumed simultaneously by everyone and no one can be excluded. (p. 394)

Public provision The production of a good or service by a public authority that receives its revenue from the government. (p. 383)

Purchasing power parity A situation in which the prices in two countries are equal when converted at the exchange rate. (pp. 477, 604)

Quantity demanded The amount of a good or service that consumers plan to buy during a given time period at a particular price. (p. 59)

Quantity supplied The amount of a good or service that producers plan to sell during a given time period at a particular price. (p. 64)

Quantity theory of money The proposition that in the long run, an increase in the quantity of money brings an equal percentage increase in the price level. (p. 582)

Rate of return regulation A regulation that requires the firm to justify its price by showing that its return on capital doesn't exceed a specified target rate. (p. 314)

Rational expectation The most accurate forecast possible; a forecast that uses all the available information, including knowledge of the relevant economic forces that influence the variable being forecasted. (p. 685)

Rational ignorance The decision not to acquire information because the cost of doing so exceeds the expected benefit. (p. 398)

Real business cycle theory A theory of the business cycle that regards random fluctuations in productivity as the main source of economic fluctuations. (p. 690)

Real exchange rate The relative price of Canadian-produced goods and services to foreign-produced goods and services. (p. 594)

Real GDP The value of final goods and services produced in a given year when valued at the prices of a reference base year. (p. 473)

Real GDP per person Real GDP divided by the population. (pp. 474, 516)

Real income A household's income expressed as a quantity of goods that the household can afford to buy. (p. 205)

Real interest rate The nominal interest rate adjusted for inflation, which is approximately equal to the nominal interest rate minus the inflation rate. (p. 549)

Real wage rate The money (or nominal) wage rate divided by the price level. The real wage rate is the quantity of goods and services that an hour of labour earns. (p. 522)

Recession A business cycle phase in which real GDP decreases for at least two successive quarters. (p. 475)

Recessionary gap The amount by which potential GDP exceeds real GDP. (p. 636)

Reference base period The period in which the CPI is defined to be 100. (p. 498)

Regressive income tax A tax on income at an average rate that decreases with the level of income. (p. 453)

Regulation Rules administered by a government agency to influence prices, quantities, entry, and other aspects of economic activity in a firm or industry. (p. 313)

Relative price The ratio of the price of one good or service to the price of another good or service. A relative price is an opportunity cost. (pp. 58, 205)

Rent The income that land earns. (p. 4)

Rent ceiling A regulation that makes it illegal to charge a rent higher than a specified level. (p. 130)

Rent seeking The lobbying for special treatment by the government to create economic profit or to divert consumer surplus or producer surplus away from others. The pursuit of wealth by capturing economic rent. (pp. 169, 308)

Reserve ratio The fraction of a bank's total deposits that are held in reserves. (p. 576)

Reserves A bank's reserves consist of notes and coins in its vaults plus its deposit at the Bank of Canada. (p. 576)

Rival A good or service or a resource is rival if its use by one person decreases the quantity available for someone else. (p. 394)

Rule of 70 A rule that states that the number of years it takes for the level of a variable to double is approximately 70 divided by the annual percentage growth rate of the variable. (p. 516)

Saving The amount of income that households have left after they have paid their taxes and bought their consumption goods and services. (p. 544)

Saving function The relationship between saving and disposable income, other things remaining the same. (p. 650)

Scarcity Our inability to satisfy all our wants. (p. 2)

Scatter diagram A diagram that plots the value of one variable against the value of another. (p. 17)

Search activity The time spent looking for someone with whom to do business. (p. 130)

Self-interest The choices that you think are the best ones available for you are choices made in your self-interest. (p. 5)

Settlement balances rate The interest rate that the Bank of Canada pays on reserves (settlement balances) at the Bank of Canada. (p. 736)

Short run The period of time in which the quantity of at least one factor of production is fixed and the quantities of the other factors can be varied. The fixed factor is usually capital—that is, the firm has a given plant size. (p. 252)

Short-run aggregate supply The relationship between the quantity of real GDP supplied and the price level when the money wage rate, the prices of other resources, and potential GDP remain constant. (p. 627)

Short-run macroeconomic equilibrium A situation that occurs when the quantity of real GDP demanded equals the quantity of real GDP supplied—at the point of intersection of the *AD* curve and the *SAS* curve. (p. 634)

Short-run market supply curve A curve that shows the quantity supplied in a market at each price when each firm's plant and the number of firms remain the same. (p. 280)

Short-run Phillips curve A curve that shows the tradeoff between inflation and unemployment, when the expected inflation rate and the natural unemployment rate remain the same. (p. 686)

Shutdown point The output and price at which the firm just covers its total variable cost. In the short run, the firm is indifferent between producing the profit-maximizing output and shutting down temporarily. (p. 278)

Signal An action taken by an informed person (or firm) to send a message to uninformed people. (p. 332)

Single-price monopoly A monopoly that must sell each unit of its output for the same price to all its customers. (p. 301)

Slope The change in the value of the variable measured on the *y*-axis divided by the change in the value of the variable measured on the *x*-axis. (p. 22)

Social interest Choices that are the best ones for society as a whole. (p. 5)

Social interest theory A theory that the political and regulatory process relentlessly seeks out inefficiency and introduces regulation that eliminates deadweight loss and allocates resources efficiently. (p. 313)

Speculative bubble A process in which the price is rising because expectations that it will rise bring a rising actual price. (p. 72)

Stagflation The combination of inflation and recession. (pp. 639, 683)

Statistical discrepancy The gap between GDP measured by total expenditure and GDP measured by total income. (p. 472)

Stock A certificate of ownership and claim to the firm's profits. (p. 546)

Stock market A financial market in which shares of stocks of corporations are traded. (p. 546)

Strategies All the possible actions of each player in a game. (p. 346)

Structural surplus or deficit The budget balance that would occur if the economy were at full employment and real GDP were equal to potential GDP. (p. 722)

Structural unemployment The unemployment that arises when changes in technology or international competition change the skills needed to perform jobs or change the locations of jobs. (p. 495)

Subsidy A payment made by the government to a producer. (pp. 142, 384)

Subsistence real wage rate The minimum real wage rate needed to maintain life. (p. 531)

Substitute A good that can be used in place of another good. (p. 61)

Substitution effect The effect of a change in price of a good or service on the quantity bought when the consumer (hypothetically) remains indifferent between the original and the new consumption situations—that is, the consumer remains on the same indifference curve. (p. 213)

Sunk cost The past cost of buying a plant that has no resale value. (p. 252)

Supply The entire relationship between the price of a good and the quantity supplied of it when all other influences on producers' planned sales remain the same. It is described by a supply schedule and illustrated by a supply curve. (p. 64)

Supply curve A curve that shows the relationship between the quantity supplied of a good and its price when all other influences on producers' planned sales remain the same. (p. 64)

Supply of loanable funds The relationship between the quantity of loanable funds supplied and the real interest rate when all other influences on lending plans remain the same. (p. 551)

Supply-side effects The effects of fiscal policy on employment, potential GDP, and aggregate supply. (p. 714)

Symmetry principle A requirement that people in similar situations be treated similarly. (p. 120)

Targeting rule A decision rule for monetary policy that sets the policy instrument at a level that makes the forecast of the ultimate policy target equal to the target. (p. 735)

Tariff A tax that is imposed by the importing country when an imported good crosses its international boundary. (p. 159)

Tax incidence The division of the burden of the tax between the buyer and the seller. (p. 135)

Tax wedge The gap between the before-tax and after-tax wage rates. (p. 715)

Taylor rule A rule that sets the federal funds rate at the equilibrium real interest rate (which Taylor says is 2 percent a year) plus amounts based on the inflation rate and the output gap. (p. 747)

Technological change The development of new goods and of better ways of producing goods and services. (p. 38)

Technological efficiency A situation that occurs when the firm produces a given output by using the least amount of inputs. (p. 231)

Technology Any method of producing a good or service. (p. 230)

Time-series graph A graph that measures time (for example, months or years) on the x-axis and the variable or variables in which we are interested on the y-axis. (p. 16)

Total cost The cost of all the productive resources that a firm uses. (p. 257)

Total fixed cost The cost of the firm's fixed inputs. (p. 257)

Total income Market income plus cash payments to households by the government. (p. 442)

Total product The total output produced by a firm in a given period of time. (p. 253)

Total revenue The value of a firm's sales. It is calculated as the price of the good multiplied by the quantity sold. (pp. 90, 274)

Total revenue test A method of estimating the price elasticity of demand by observing the change in total revenue that results from a change in the price, when all other influences on the quantity sold remain the same. (p. 90)

Total utility The total benefit that a person gets from the consumption of goods and services. (p. 182)

Total variable cost The cost of all the firm's variable inputs. (p. 257)

Tradeoff A constraint that involves giving up one thing to get something else. (p. 8)

Tragedy of the commons The absence of incentives to prevent the overuse and depletion of a commonly owned resource. (p. 400)

Transactions costs The opportunity costs of making trades in a market. The costs that arise from finding someone with whom to do business, of reaching an agreement about the price and other aspects of the exchange, and of ensuring that the terms of the agreement are fulfilled. (pp. 117, 242, 379)

Trend The general tendency for a variable to move in one direction. (p. 16)

Trust and mortgage loan company A privately owned depository institution that operates under the Trust and Loan Companies Act of 1992. (p. 571)

Unemployment rate The percentage of the people in the labour force who are unemployed. (p. 492)

Unit elastic demand Demand with a price elasticity of 1; the percentage change in the quantity demanded equals the percentage change in price. (p. 88)

Utilitarianism A principle that states that we should strive to achieve "the greatest happiness for the greatest number of people." (p. 118)

Utility The benefit or satisfaction that a person gets from the consumption of a good or service. (p. 182)

Value of marginal product The price of a unit of output multiplied by the marginal product of the factor of production. (p. 419)

Velocity of circulation The average number of times a dollar of money is used annually to buy the goods and services that make up GDP. (p. 582)

Voucher A token that the government provides to households, which they can use to buy specified goods and services. (p. 384)

Wages The income that labour earns. (p. 4)

Wealth The value of all the things that people own—the market value of their assets—at a point in time. (pp. 444, 544)

Working-age population The total number of people age 16 years and over who are not in jail, hospital, or some other form of institutional care. (p. 491)

World Trade Organization (WTO) An international organization that places greater obligations on its member countries to observe the GATT rules. (p. 164)

INDEX

Note: Key terms and the pages on which they are defined are **bolded**. References to *"f"* denote a figure and *"t"* denote a table.

A

ability to pay, 60
ability-to-pay principle, 140
above full-employment equilibrium, 636
absolute advantage, 40–41
abuse of dominant position, 358, 361
accounting profit, 228
actual aggregate expenditure, 655
administrative cost, 455
advertising
  costs, 331
  efficiency, 333
  expenditures, 330
  and markup, 332*f*
  monopolistic competition, 330–333
  to signal quality, 332–333
affordable quantities, 204
after-tax income, 442
after-tax wage rate, 715
age of householder, and poverty, 446
agent, 234
aggregate demand, 630
  in action, 642
  change in quantity of real GDP demanded, 631
  changes in, 631, 633*f*, 664–665, 665*f*
  classical view, 640
  cost-push inflation, 683
  and demand-pull inflation, 680
  equilibrium expenditure, 664*f*
  exchange rate, 632–633
  expectations, 631–632, 640
  fiscal policy, 632
  fluctuations in, 638–639, 638*f*, 640, 641
  foreign income, 633
  government expenditure, 632
  graph, 630*f*
  Keynesian view, 640–641
  long-run increase, 666–667
  monetarist view, 641
  monetary policy, 632
  and monetary policy, 742
  short-run increase, 666
  substitution effects, 631
  wealth effect, 630–631
  world economy, 632–633
aggregate demand curve, 630, 630*f*, 633
aggregate expenditure
  algebra of, 670
  and *AS-AD* model, 663–667
  changes in, 664–665
  and gross domestic product, 470
  monetary policy, 741

aggregate expenditure curve, 655*f*, 660, 660*f*, 663–664, 670, 670*f*
aggregate income, 469, 470
aggregate labour market, 521–522
aggregate planned expenditure, 650, 654–655, 655*f*
aggregate production function, 521, 521*f*, 544
aggregate supply
  in action, 642
  changes in, 628–629, 628*f*, 629*f*
  classical view, 640
  cost-push inflation, 682
  fluctuations in, 639, 639*f*
  income tax, effects of, 714*f*
  Keynesian view, 640–641
  long-run aggregate supply, 626, 627*f*
  meaning of, 626
  monetarist view, 641
  money wage rate, 629, 629*f*
  response, 640, 641
  short-run aggregate supply, 627, 627*f*
aggregate supply-aggregate demand model (*AS-AD* model). *See AS-AD* model
Agricultural Revolution, 53
AIG, 547
air pollution, 374–375
Alchian, Armen, 243
allocative efficiency, 35, 37
the Allowance, 453
the Allowance for the Survivor, 453
Amazon.com, 216
Anarchy, State, and Utopia, 120
Andreesen, Marc, 533
annual income and wealth, 445
anti-combine law, 358–361, 360*t*
antidumping duties, 165
AS-AD model
  aggregate demand, 630–633, 638–639, 638*f*
  and aggregate expenditure model, 663–667
  aggregate supply, 626–629, 639, 639*f*
  business cycle, 636–637
  economic growth, 635, 635*f*
  fluctuations in aggregate demand, 638–639, 638*f*
  fluctuations in aggregate supply, 639, 639*f*
  inflation, 635*f*, 636
  macroeconomic fluctuations, 634–639
  macroeconomic schools of thought, 640–641
  purpose of, 626
Asian economies, 520, 529
aspartame, 358
asset prices, 548
assortative mating, 452
Athey, Susan, 178–180
auto production, 265

Automated Clearing Settlement System (ACSS), 575
automatic fiscal policy, 718
automatic stabilizers, 632, 720–723
autonomous consumption, 650
autonomous expenditure, 654
autonomous tax multiplier, 672, 672*f*, 718
average cost pricing rule, 314
average fixed cost, 258
average grades, 256
average price, 87–88
average product, 253, 253*t*, 256*f*
average product curve, 256
average quantity, 87–88
average total cost, 258, 262–263
average total cost curve, 258–259, 259*f*
average variable cost, 258
average variable cost curve, 258, 259*f*

B

balance of payments, 606
balance of payments accounts, 606–608, 606*f*
balanced budget, 709, 723
balanced budget multiplier, 673, 673*f*, 718
Balsillie, Jim, 358, 361
bank deposit insurance, 695
bank failures, 694
bank loans. *See* loans
bank mergers, 360
bank notes, 573
Bank of America, 547
Bank of Canada
  see also monetary policy
  assets, 573
  balance sheet, 573
  bank notes, issuer of, 573
  bank rate, 736
  banker to banks and government, 572–573
  as central bank, 572
  consultations with government, 734
  decision-making process, 735–736
  economists, 734
  equilibrium in market for reserves, 738, 738*f*
  and Federal Reserve, 574
  Governing Council, 733–734
  high inflation, 744–745, 744*f*
  inflation-control target, 732–733
  and interest rates, 611, 731
  joint statement of Government of Canada and Bank of Canada, 732
  lender of last resort, 573
  liabilities, 573
  monetary base, 573, 576
  open market operation, 573, 736–737
  operating band, 736

overnight loans rate, 734–735, 735*f*, 739–740, 739*f*
overnight rate target, 736
policy instrument, choice of, 734
recession, 742–743, 742*f*
settlement balances rate, 736
targeting rule, 736
Bank of Canada Act, 732, 734
Bank of Canada balance sheet, 573
Bank of Japan, 574
Bank of Montreal, 360
bank rate, 736
bank reserves. *See* reserves
banking system
    Automated Clearing Settlement System (ACSS), 575
    Bank of Canada, 572–573
    depository institutions, 571–572
    deposits, 575–576
    desired currency holding, 576
    desired reserves, 576
    Large Value Transfer System (LVTS), 575
    money creation, 575–577, 577*f*
    payments system, 573
    reserves, 738, 738*f*
banks, 546, 571
bar chart, 16, 17*f*
barrier to entry, 300
    concentration measures, 240
    legal barrier to entry, 300–301
    natural barrier to entry, 300
    oligopoly, 342
    ownership barrier to entry, 300
    and rent seeking, 308
Barro, Robert J., 556
barter, 568
base year, 483
batteries, 343
Bay Street, 750
Bear Stearns, 547
behavioural economics, 194
    bounded rationality, 194
    bounded self-interest, 194–195
    bounded will-power, 194
    endowment effect, 195
Bell Canada Enterprises, 358
below full-employment equilibrium, 637
benefit
    external benefit, 117, 382*f*
    marginal benefit. *See* marginal benefit
    marginal external benefit, 381
    marginal private benefit, 381
    marginal social benefit. *See* marginal social benefit
    of offshoring, 167–168
    private benefits, 381–383
    of public good, 395*f*
    social benefits, 381–383
benefits principle, 140
Bentham, Jeremy, 118, 223
Bernanke, Ben, 490
Berners-Lee, Tim, 227
best affordable choice, 210–211, 210*f*
Bhagwati, Jagdish, 54–56
bias in CPI, 501–502
big tradeoff, 9, 119, 455
bilateral monopoly, 425

Bina, Eric, 533
black market, 130–131
bond, 545
bond market, 545–546
    borrowers, 608
    borrowing costs, 572
    borrowing for consumption, 608–609
    bounded rationality, 194
    bounded self-interest, 194–195
    bounded will-power, 194
    brand names, 333
Brunet, Richard, 358
BSE (mad cow disease), 164
budget. *See* government budget
budget balance, 709
budget deficit, 555–556, 556*f*, **709**, 709*f*, 711–713, 721–723, 721*f*
budget equation, 205–206
budget line, 204
    best affordable point, 211
    graph, 204*f*
    income-time budget line, 214
budget surplus, 555, 555*f*, **709**, 709*f*, 713
bureaucratic overprovision, 397–398, 397*f*
business cycle, 475
    above full-employment equilibrium, 636, 637*f*
    AS-AD model, 636–637
    below full-employment equilibrium, 637, 637*f*
    budget deficit, 721–722, 721*f*
    Canadian business cycle, 636
    cyclical surplus or deficit, 722–723, 722*f*
    employment-to-population ratio, 493
    expansion, 475
    full-employment equilibrium, 637, 637*f*
    and inflation, 685
    Keynesian cycle theory, 690
    mainstream business cycle theory, 689–690, 689*f*
    monetarist cycle theory, 690
    most recent Canadian business cycle, 475*f*
    new classical cycle theory, 690
    new Keynesian cycle theory, 690
    peak, 676
    phases, 475
    real business cycle theory, 690–693
    real GDP, fluctuations in, 637*f*
    recession, 475
    stabilization of, 718–723
    structural surplus or deficit, 722–723, 722*f*
    trough, 676
    turning points, 662
business economic policy, 12
business investment, 471
business organization, 234–235
buyers
    discrimination among groups of buyers, 309–310
    equivalence of tax on buyers and sellers, 136–137
    illegal goods markets, 144–145
    taxes on, 136, 137*f*

C

Caballero, Ricardo J., 704–706
caisses populaires, 546, 571
Canada
    anti-combine law, 358, 360*t*
    balance of payments accounts, 606*f*, 607
    budget deficit in 2009-10, 723
    business cycle, 636
    central bank, 574–575. *See also* Bank of Canada
    concentration measures in, 239
    consumption function, 653
    cost-push inflation, 684
    demand for imports, 602
    demand for money, 580–581
    demand-pull inflation, 682
    economic growth, 39*f*, 518, 518*f*, 530, 530*f*
    financial institutions, 546–547
    firms, size distribution of, 236
    four-firm concentration ratio, 239
    Gini coefficient, 446, 446*f*
    government sector, 712
    health care spending, 398
    job losses, 696
    jobs in slowdown of 2008, 504
    labour productivity, 530
    money, 569–570
    money growth and inflation, 582*f*
    money multiplier, 587
    most traded items, 154
    oilsands, 432
    output gap, 636
    Phillips curve, 688
    population growth, 530
    production possibilities per person, 39
    real GDP in slowing economy of 2008, 480
    real GDP per person, 515
    recession, 668, 696
    retail sales, 642
    security spending, 398
    selling costs, 331
    softwood lumber dispute, 170–171
    standard of living over time, 474, 474*f*
    structural unemployment, 495
    tariffs, 161
    underground economy, 477–478
    wage rates in, 427
    working-age population, 491
Canada/Quebec Pension Plan, 453
Canada Revenue Agency, 119
Canada Social Transfer (CST), 453
Canadian Constitution, 478
Canadian dollar
    change in demand, 601, 601*f*
    change in supply, 602, 602*f*
    demand curve, 598, 598*f*
    fluctuations, 595, 603
    supply curve, 599, 599*f*
    value of, 593
Canadian-dollar effective exchange rate index (CERI), 596, 596*f*
Canadian Food Inspection Agency, 164
Canadian interest rate differential, 601, 740
Canadian production function, 528

Canadian Radio-television and Telecommunications Commission (CRTC), 308
capital, 4
  described, 418
  diminishing marginal product of capital, 262
  financial capital, 544, 545–546
  and government budgets, 713
  implicit rental rate, 228–229
  income, 716f
  increase in quantity of, 628
  international capital mobility, 557
  and investment, 544, 545f
  physical capital, 544
  physical capital growth, 526
  services, 418
capital account, 606
capital accumulation, 38
capital gains, 544
Capital Good Economists, 533
capital goods, 418
capital losses, 544
capital markets
  described, 418
  land rental markets, 428–429, 429f
  rent-vs-buy decision, 428
  rental market, 418, 428, 428f
capture theory, 313
carbon emissions, 6, 374, 386
carbon tax, 386
Card, David, 134–135, 464–466
career interruptions, 449–450
cars, elasticities of demand for, 100
cartel, 343, 361
casual labour, 418
causation, 18
cause and effect, 11
central banks, 572, 574–575, 748–749
central economic planning, 43
Centre for the Study of Living Standards (CSLS), 528, 530
ceteris paribus, **24–25**
chained-dollar real GDP, 482–483, 482t, 483f, 483t, 502
chained price index for consumption (CPIC), 502
change
  and choices, 9
  in demand. *See* change in demand
  management, 369
  in supply. *See* change in supply
change in demand, 60
  aggregate demand, 631, 633f
  all possible changes, 75
  Canadian dollar, 601, 601f
  vs. change in the quantity demanded, 62–63, 63f
  decrease in both demand and supply, 75
  decrease in demand, 70–71
  and decrease in supply, 75
  demand for labour, 421
  effects of, 70f
  expected future income and credit, 62
  expected future prices, 61–62
  income, 62
  and income effect, 212f

increase in both demand and supply, 75
increase in demand, 61f, 70
and increase in supply, 75
loanable funds, 550–551, 552–553, 553f
with no change in supply, 75
permanent change in demand, 286–287, 287f
population, 62
preferences, 62
price, effect on, 96f
prices of related goods, 61
quantity, effect on, 96f
real GDP, 631
short-run equilibrium, 281
change in supply, 65
  aggregate supply, 628–629, 628f, 629f
  Canadian dollar, 602, 602f
  vs. change in the quantity supplied, 66–67, 67f
  decrease in both demand and supply, 75
  and decrease in demand, 75
  decrease in supply, 71
  effects of, 71f
  expected future prices, 66
  increase in both demand and supply, 75
  and increase in demand, 75
  increase in supply, 66, 66f, 71
  loanable funds, 551, 552–553, 553f
  with no change in demand, 75
  price, effect on, 86f
  prices of factors of production, 65
  prices of related goods produced, 65
  and production quotas, 141
  quantity, effect on, 86f
  state of nature, 66
  subsidy, 142
  suppliers, number of, 66
change in the quantity demanded, 62–63, 63, 63f
change in the quantity supplied, 66–67, 67f
chartered banks, 571, 572t
cheating, 142
cheques, 570
chicken, game of, 354, 354f
chief executive officer (CEO), 233
children, number of, 446
China
  central economic planning, 43
  economic growth in, 520, 536
  exchange rate, 613
  in foreign exchange market, 612–613
  political freedom, 478
  purchasing power parity, 476–477
  real GDP, 476, 476f, 517
  relative prices, 476
  the yuan, 614
choice
  consumer choices. *See* consumer choices
  public choice and the political equilibrium, 405
  work-leisure choices, 214–215
Chrysler, 358
churning economy, 494
CIBC, 360
Cineplex Galaxy, 359
circular flows

expenditure and income, 469–470, 469f, 549f
  through markets, 44, 45f
Citigroup, 547
classical growth theory, 531
classical theory of population growth, 531
classical view, 640
classification of goods and resources, 394
climate change, 6, 375
close substitutes, 209
CO_2 trends, 375
Coase, Ronald, 413
Coase theorem, 379
cod stocks, 400
collusion, 324, 343, 348–350, 349f
collusive agreement, 348
command system, 108, 233
commodity markets, 418
commodity prices, 418
commodity substitution, 501
common resource, 394
  and efficiency, 117
  efficient outcome, achievement of, 403–405
  efficient use of the commons, 402, 403f
  individual transferable quota (ITQ), 404–405, 405f
  overfishing equilibrium, 401–402
  production quotas, 404, 404f
  property rights, 403–404
  public choice and the political equilibrium, 405
  sustainable production, 400–401, 400t, 401f
  tragedy of the commons, 400, 406
comparative advantage, 40
  described, 40–41
  as driver of international trade, 154
  dynamic comparative advantage, 43, 165
  of offshoring, 167–168
Competition Act, 358–361, 360t
Competition Bureau, 359, 360, 361
Competition Tribunal, 358
competitive environment
  concentration measures, 238–241
  market types, 237–238
  in North America, 241
competitive equilibrium, 114, 290
competitive labour market
  backward-bending labour supply curve, 422–423, 422f
  described, 422
  equilibrium, 423, 423f
  income effect, 423
  individual's labour supply decision, 422
  labour union, entry of, 424f
  market demand for labour, 422
  market supply curve, 423
  market supply of labour, 422
  reservation wage rate, 422
  substitution effect, 423
competitive market, 58
  efficiency of, 114–117, 114f
  fairness of, 118–121
complement, 61
  cross elasticity of demand, 94
  perfect complements, 209–210

in production, 65
compound interest, 434, 516–517
computer chip, 6
concentration measures
    barriers to entry, 240
    in Canada, 239
    firm turnover, 240
    four-firm concentration ratio, 238, 238*t*
    geographical scope of market, 240
    Herfindahl-Hirschman Index (HHI), 238–239
    limitations of, 240–241
    market and industry correspondence, 240–241
congestion, 374
constant returns to scale, 264
constraints of the firm, 230–231
consumer choices
    best affordable choice, 210–211, 210*f*
    and change, 9
    consumption possibilities, 204–206
    discoveries and choices, 533
    explanations for, 194–195
    incentives, 2
    income effect, 212, 212*f*, 213, 213*f*
    at the margin, 10
    opportunity cost, 9
    perfect competition, 290
    predicting consumer choices, 210–214
    price changes and, 211–212
    self-interest, and social interest, 5–7
    substitution effect, 213, 213*f*
    and tradeoffs, 8
    understanding households' choices, 223
    utility-maximizing choice, 184, 184*t*
    what, how, and for whom?, 3–4
consumer equilibrium, 184
Consumer Price Index (CPI), 498
    bias, 501–502
    calculation of, 499–500, 500*t*
    commodity substitution bias, 501
    construction of, 499–500
    core CPI inflation rate, 502–503, 503*f*
    CPI basket, 499, 499*f*
    high inflation *vs.* high price level, 501
    and inflation rate, 500, 501*f*
    monthly price survey, 499
    new goods bias, 501
    outlet substitution bias, 502
    quality change bias, 501
    reading the CPI numbers, 498
    reference base period, 498
    target, 732
consumer surplus, 111
    demand and, 111*f*
    gains from trade, 290
    import quota, 163
    monopoly, 307, 307*f*
    perfect competition, 307, 307*f*
    price discrimination, 309–310
    tariffs, 160
    value and, 191
consumption
    affordable and unaffordable quantities, 204
    autonomous consumption, 650
    borrowing for consumption, 608–609
    budget equation, 205–206

chained price index for consumption (CPIC), 502
    disposable income, 650
    divisible and indivisible goods, 204
    induced consumption, 650
    influencing factors, 650–651
    marginal propensity to consume, 652, 652*f*
    negative consumption externalities, 376
    positive consumption externalities, 376
    possibilities, 204–206
    and real GDP, 653
consumption expenditure, 469, 650, 653, 741
consumption function, 650, 651*f*, 653, 670
contest, 108
contestable market, 356–357
contractionary fiscal policy, 719*f*
convergence to equilibrium, 657
cooperation, 343
cooperative equilibrium, 355
copyright, 301, 385
core inflation, 732
core inflation rate, 502–503, 503*f*
corn, 73, 73*f*
corporate bond rate, 740
corporate income tax, 708
corporate profits, 472
corporation, 235
correlation, 18
cost curves
    average total cost curve, 258
    average variable cost curve, 258–259, 259*f*
    long-run average cost curve, 263, 264
    marginal cost curve, 258, 259*f*
    and product curves, 260, 260*f*
    shifts in, 260–261
    total cost curves, 257*f*
cost-push inflation, 682–684, 683*f*, 684*f*
costs
    administrative cost, 455
    advertising, 331
    average cost, 258–259
    average fixed cost, 258
    average total cost, 258
    average variable cost, 258
    of borrowing, 572
    clean electricity, 266
    of economic growth, 38
    external cost, 116, 377*f*, 378*f*
    factor cost, 472
    glossary of, 261*t*
    long-run cost, 262–265
    marginal cost. *See* marginal cost
    marginal external cost, 377
    marginal private cost, 377
    marginal social cost. *See* marginal social cost
    opportunity cost. *See* opportunity cost
    and output, 257
    private costs, 377
    selling costs, 331, 331*f*, 332
    short-run cost, 257–261
    social costs, 377
    sunk cost, 252
    tax-collecting agencies, 119
    total cost, 257, 276*f*, 331, 331*f*

total fixed cost, 257
    total variable cost, 257
    transactions costs, 117, 242–243, 379
    transition costs, 169
    welfare-administering agencies, 119
CPI. *See* Consumer Price Index (CPI)
CPI basket, 499, 499*f*
crawling peg, 612–613, 747
credit, expected future, 62
Credit Association Act, 571
credit cards, 570
credit crisis, 574–575
credit crunch, 7
credit unions, 546, **571**
creditor nation, 608
cross elasticity of demand, 93–94, 93*f*
cross-section graph, 16, 17*f*
crowding-out effect, 556
crude oil, 34, 72, 72*f*, 429–430, 431
currency, 569
currency drain, 576
currency drain ratio, 576
current account, 606
current account balance, 606, 609
curve, 18
    see also specific curves
cyclical surplus or deficit, 722–723, 722*f*
cyclical unemployment, 496

D

data, graphing, 15–18
De Beers, 301
deadweight loss, 115
    import quotas, 163
    income redistribution, 455
    monopoly, 307
    tariffs, 160
debtor nation, 608
decentralized coordination. *See* economic coordination
decentralized markets, 43
decision time frames
    long run, 252
    short run, 252
default risk, 552
degree of substitutability, 209–210, 209*f*
Dell Computer, 362
demand, 59
    see also demand and supply model
    all possible changes, 75
    Canadian demand for imports, 602
    change in demand, 60–62, 70*f*, 75
    change in the quantity demanded, 62–63, 63*f*
    and consumer surplus, 111, 111*f*
    decrease in both demand and supply, 75
    decrease in demand, 70–71
    decrease in demand and increase in supply, 75
    demand equation, 78
    derived demand, 419
    effects of all possible changes, 74*f*
    elastic demand, 88–89, 88*f*, 275, 303
    elasticities of demand. *See* elasticities of demand
    foreign exchange market, 597
    illustration of, 59–60

income elastic demand, 94
income inelastic demand, 94
increase in both demand and supply, 75
increase in demand, 61*f*, 70
increase in demand and decrease in sup-
    ply, 75
individual demand, 110–111, 110*f*
inelastic demand, 88–89, 88*f*, 303
for labour, 419–420, 420*f*, 421*t*
law of demand, 59
loanable funds, 550–551, 550*f*
and marginal benefit, 110–111
and marginal revenue, 302*f*
market demand, 110–111, 110*f*
for money, 579, 579*f*
for oil, 429
in perfect competition, 274–275, 275*f*
perfectly elastic demand, 88*f*, 89, 138,
    138*f*
perfectly inelastic demand, 88, 88*f*, 137*f*
quantity demanded, 59
and selling costs, 332
unit elastic demand, 88, 88*f*, 303
willingness to pay, and value, 110
world demand for Canadian exports, 601
demand and supply model
    see also demand; supply
    all possible changes, 75
    changes in demand, 70–71
    changes in supply, 71
    effects of all possible changes, 74*f*
    gasoline prices, 76–77
    global market, 557–558
    price, prediction of changes in, 70–75
    quantity, prediction of changes in, 70–75
demand curve, 60
    for Canadian dollars, 598, 598*f*
    demand equation, 78
    demand for labour curve, 420
    demand for loanable funds curve, 550
    demand for money curve, 579, 579*f*
    described, 59–60
    graph, 60*f*, 78*f*
    and income effect, 212
    marginal benefit curve, 110
    movement along demand curve, 63
    and price effect, 211*f*, 212
    shift of demand curve, 63
    straight-line demand curve, and elasticity,
        89, 89*f*
    willingness and ability to pay, 60
demand equation, 78
demand for loanable funds, 550–551, 550*f*
demand for loanable funds curve, 550
demand for money, 579, 579*f*, 580–581
demand for money curve, 579, 579*f*
demand-pull inflation, 680–682, 680*f*,
    681*f*
demand schedule, 60
Demsetz, Harold, 243
deposit insurance, 695
depository institutions, 571
    economic benefits, 572
    function of, 571–572
    types of, 571
deposits, 569, 570, 575–576
depreciation, 228, 229, **470,** 544
deregulation, 313

derived demand, 419
desired reserve ratio, 576
developing economies
    exploitation, prevention of, 167
    investment in, 529*t*
    microloans, 529
    rapid expansion of production, 72
    telecommunication, 529
diamonds, 191
diminishing marginal product of capital, 262
diminishing marginal returns, 255
diminishing marginal utility, 183
diminishing returns, 262, 533
direct relationship, 18
direct tax, 472
disappearing invisible hand, 353
discounting, 434–435, **434**–435
discouraged worker, 494
discoveries
    and choices, 533
    and profits, 533
    public good, 533
discretionary fiscal policy, 718, 720
discretionary fiscal stabilization, 718–719
discrimination, 451, 451*f*
diseconomies of scale, 264
dismal science, 531
Disney World, 312
disposable income, 551, 632, 650
dissaving, 651
distribution of income. *see* income distribu-
    tion
divisible goods, 204
Doha Development Agenda, 164
Doha Round, 164
domestic product at market prices, 472
dominant firm oligopoly, 344–345, 345*f*
dominant strategy equilibrium, 354
double coincidence of wants, 568
double counting, 468
drugs
    illegal drugs, 144–145, 144*f*
    legalization of, 145
    prohibition, 145
    taxing drugs, 145
dumping, 165–166
duopoly, 342, 352*f*
dynamic comparative advantage, 43, 165

E

e-books, 216
eBay, 299, 301, 529
economic accounting, 228–229, 229*t*
economic coordination
    central economic planning, 43
    circular flows through markets, 44, 45*f*
    coordinating decisions, 44
    decentralized markets, 43
    firms, 43–44
    markets, 44
    money, 44
    property rights, 44
economic depreciation, 229
economic efficiency, 231
economic experiment, 11
economic growth, 38
    in *AS-AD* model, 635, 635*f*

basics of, 516–517
in Canada, 518, 518*f*
in China, 536
compound interest, 516–517
cost of economic growth, 38
economic growth rate, 516
graph, 38*f*
growth theories and policies, 531–535
Hong Kong, 39
and inflation, 635*f*
labour productivity, growth of, 526–530
Lucas wedge, 474–475, 475*f*
magic of sustained growth, 516–517
nation's economic growth, 39
real business cycle theory, 693
real GDP growth in world economy, 519,
    519*f*
sources of, 527*f*
and standard of living, 38
trends, 518–520
economic growth rate, 516
economic inequality
    annual *vs.* lifetime income and wealth,
        445
    big tradeoff, 455
    discrimination, 451, 451*f*
    Gini coefficient, 445–446, 446*f*
    globalization, 450
    human capital and, 448–450
    income distribution, 442, 442*f*
    income maintenance programs, 453
    income redistribution, 453–455
    income taxes, 453
    Lorenz curve, 443–444, 443*f*
    measurement of, 442–447
    poverty, 447
    sources of, 448–452
    specialization, differences in degree of,
        452
    subsidized services, 453–454
    technological change, 450
    trends in inequality, 445–446
    understanding, 463
    wealth, distribution of, 444, 452
    wealth *vs.* income, 444–445
economic instability, 7
economic loss, 278, 327
economic model, 11
    described, 18
    graphs in, 18–21
economic problem
    economic coordination, 43–44
    economic growth, 38–39
    efficient use of resources, 35–37
    the firm, 228–230
    gains from trade, 40–43
    production possibilities and opportunity
        cost, 32–34
economic profit, 228, 274, 276*f*, 304, 326*f*,
    327–328
economic rent, 308
economic revenue, 274
economic revolution, 53, 621
Economic Stimulus Act of 2008 (U.S.), 720
economic way of thinking
    change, and choices, 9
    choosing at the margin, 10

human nature, incentives, and institu-
    tions, 10
incentives, response to, 10
opportunity cost, 9
tradeoffs, and choices, 8
economics, 2
behavioural economics, 194–195
cause and effect, 11
dismal science, 531
economic experiment, 11
economic way of thinking, 8–10
macroeconomics, 2
microeconomics, 2
natural experiment, 11
neuroeconomics, 195
normative statements, 11
as policy tool, 12
positive statements, 11
scope of, 3–7, 53
self-interest *vs.* social interest, 5–7
as social science, 11
statistical investigation, 11
two big economic questions, 3–7
economies of scale, 243, 264–265
economies of scope, 243
economies of team production, 243
the economy. *See* Canada
education
    effect of, 449
    and poverty, 446
    quality, improvement of, 535
    and wage rates, 427
efficiency
    see also inefficiency
    advertising, 333
    allocative efficiency, 35
    brand names, 333
    and common resource, 117
    competitive equilibrium, 114
    and competitive equilibrium, 290
    competitive market, 114–117, 114*f*
    economic efficiency, 231–232
    efficient use of the commons, 402, 403*f*
    and fairness, 120
    and monopolistic competition, 329
    monopoly, 307
    obstacles to efficiency, 116–117
    perfect competition, 290–291, 291*f*, 307
    price discrimination, 312
    and product innovation, 330
    production efficiency, 33
    and public good, 117, 396
    public provision, 397–398, 397*f*
    regulation of natural monopoly, 313
    taxes, 139–140, 139*f*
    technological efficiency, 231
    of water use, 122
efficiency wage, 496
efficient scale, 328
elastic demand, 88–89, 88*f*, 275, 303
elastic supply, 97*f*
elasticities of demand
    cross elasticity of demand, 93–94, 93*f*
    gasoline, trucks and cars, 100
    income elasticity of demand, 94, 95
    and marginal revenue, 303, 303*f*
    minus sign and, 88

price elasticity of demand, 86–92
summary of, 99*t*
and tax incidence, 137–138
units-free measure, 88
elasticity of supply, 96
calculation of, 96–97
elastic supply, 97*f*
inelastic supply, 97*f*
influencing factors, 97–98
resource substitution possibilities, 97–98
summary of, 99*t*
tax incidence, 138
time frame for supply decision, 98
emission charges, 380
emission permits, 380–381
employment
    see also unemployment
    in Canada, 490
    employment-to-population ratio, 493, 493*f*
    full employment, 496, 523
    imports, effects of, 166
    international trade restrictions, effect of, 166
    involuntary part-time rate, 492
    jobs in slowdown of 2008, 504
    potential GDP, and full employment, 714
Employment Insurance program, 453
Employment Insurance tax, 137
employment-to-population ratio, 493, 493*f*
endowment effect, 195
entrants, 494–495
entrepreneurship, 4
and markets, 418
supply of, 229
entry, 283–284, 285, 325
entry barriers. *See* barrier to entry
the environment
    air pollution, 374–375
    carbon emissions, 374
    climate change, 6, 375
    congestion, 374
    global warming, 6, 373, 375
    land pollution, 376
    lax environmental standards, 166–167
    pollution, 374–376
    and real GDP, 478
    tropical rainforests, 7
    water pollution, 376
Environment Canada, 381
Environmental Protection Agency (EPA), 381
equality of opportunity, 120
equilibrium
    above full-employment equilibrium, 636
    below full-employment equilibrium, 637
    competitive equilibrium, 114, 290
    consumer equilibrium, 184
    convergence to, 657
    cooperative equilibrium, 355
    defined, 68
    dominant strategy equilibrium, 354
    equilibrium price, 68
    equilibrium quantity, 68
    with exports, 156*f*
    foreign exchange market, 600, 600*f*

full-employment equilibrium, 637
graph, 68, 79*f*
with imports, 155*f*
labour market equilibrium, 423, 423*f*, 424, 522–523, 522*f*
long-run equilibrium, 284*f*
long-run macroeconomic equilibrium, 635, 635*f*
market equilibrium, 68
market for loanable funds, 552, 552*f*
in market for reserves, 738, 738*f*
mathematical determination, 79
money market equilibrium, 581, 581*f*
Nash equilibrium, 347, 351–352
no international trade, 155*f*, 156*f*
overfishing equilibrium, 401–402
political equilibrium, 399, 405
price adjustments, 69
price as regulator, 68–69
real GDP and the price level, 665–667
rent-seeking equilibrium, 308, 309*f*
short-run equilibrium, 281, 281*f*
short-run macroeconomic equilibrium, 634, 634*f*
equilibrium expenditure, 656–657, 656*f*, 664*f*, 671, 671*f*
equilibrium price, 68, 430
equilibrium quantity, 68
equity
    ability-to-pay principle, 140
    benefits principle, 140
    big tradeoff, 119
    case study, 120–121
    competitive market, 118–121
    and efficiency, 120
    fair results view, 118–119
    fair rules view, 120
    minimum wage, 134
    poorest as well off as possible, 119
    rent ceiling, 132
    taxes, 140
    utilitarianism, 118–119, 119*f*
European Central Bank, 574
European Union, 164
excess capacity, 328–329, 328*f*
excess reserves, 576
exchange rate, 594
    aggregate demand, 632–633
    changes in, 602
    China, 613
    crawling peg, 612–613, 747
    expectations, 604
    expected future exchange rate, 601, 602
    fixed exchange rate, 611–612
    flexible exchange rate, 611
    fluctuations, 601–605, 740–741
    instant exchange rate response, 604–605
    nominal exchange rate, 594–595, 605
    policy, 611–613
    questions about, 596
    real exchange rate, 594, 605, 747
    role of, 610
exchange targeting rule, 747
excludable, 394
exit, 283, 284, 285, 325
expansion, 475
expansionary fiscal policy, 719*f*

expectations
    aggregate demand, 631–632, 640
    exchange rate, 604
    Keynesian view, 640–641
    rational expectation, 685
expected future exchange rate, 601, 602
expected future income, 551
expected future prices, 61–62
expected inflation, 684–685, 685f
expected profit effect, 598, 599
expenditure
    actual aggregate expenditure, 655
    aggregate expenditure, 470
    aggregate planned expenditure, 650,
        654–655, 655f
    autonomous expenditure, 654
    circular flows, 469–470, 469f
    consumption expenditure, 469
    equilibrium expenditure, 656–657, 656f,
        671, 671f
    government expenditure, 470, 471
    induced expenditure, 654
    personal expenditures, 471
    planned expenditure, 655
    plans, 650
    and price elasticity of demand, 91
expenditure approach, 471, 471f
export subsidies, 164
exports, 154, 470
    export subsidies, 164
    gains and losses, 158, 158f
    market with exports, 156f
    net exports, 470, 471, 609–610, 609t,
        741
    reasons for, 156
    world demand for Canadian exports, 601
exports effect, 598
external benefit, 117, 381–384, 382f
external cost, 116, 377, 377f, 378f
external diseconomies, 287–289
external economies, 287–289
externality, 374
    negative consumption externalities, 376
    negative externality, 374, 377–381
    negative production externalities,
        374–376
    as obstacle to efficiency, 116–117
    positive consumption externalities, 376
    positive externality, 374, 381–385
    positive production externalities, 376
extinction, 400

F
factor cost, 472
factor markets
    anatomy of, 418
    capital markets, 418, 428–431
    capital services, 418
    circular flow, 44
    commodity markets, 418
    and entrepreneurship, 418
    labour market. See labour market
    labour services, 418
    land services, 418
    natural resource markets, 418, 428–431
    rental market, 418

    understanding, 463
factor price, 419
factors of production, 3
    capital, 4
    demand, 419–421
    derived demand, 419
    entrepreneurship, 4
    labour, 3
    land, 3
    price, and change in demand, 421
    price, and change in supply, 65
    price, change in, 261
    value of marginal product, 419, 419f
fairness. See equity
Famous Players, 359
Fannie Mae, 547
farm machines, 285
farm subsidies, 143, 164
farmers, 142–143
farmers' income, 472
federal budget, 708
federal government, 712
Federal Reserve (U.S.), 7, 547, 554, 559,
    574
fertilizers, 73
final good, 468
finance
    funds that finance investment, 548–549
    vs. money, 544
    study of, 544
financial assets, 548
financial capital, 4, 544, 545–546
financial failures, 547
financial implications of marketing practice,
    2
financial innovation, 578
financial institutions, 546
    net worth, 547
    solvency and liquidity, 547
    types of, 546–547
financial markets
    bond market, 545–546
    capital, 544, 545f
    changes in demand and supply, 552–553,
        553f
    finance vs. money, 544
    financial capital, 544, 545–546
    financial flows and circular flows of
        expenditure and income, 549f
    investment, 544, 545f
    loan markets, 545
    market for loanable funds. See market for
        loanable funds
    physical capital, 544
    saving, 544–545
    stock market, 546
    United States, 560
    wealth, 544–545
financial property, meaning of, 44
financial stress, 7
firm, 43, 228
    accounting profit, 228
    business organization, types of, 234–235
    constraints, 230–231
    consumption expenditure, 469
    as coordinators of economic activity,
        242–243

    and decentralized coordination, 43–44
    decisions of, 229, 275
    described, 469
    economic accounting, 228–229, 229t
    economic profit, 228
    goal, 228
    information constraints, 230
    and its economic problem, 228–230
    market constraints, 230
    and markets, 242–243
    opportunity cost of production, 228–229
    output decision in perfect competition,
        276–279
    price takers, 274
    principal-agent problem, 234
    profit maximization, 228, 275
    pros and cons of different types of, 235,
        235t
    retained earnings, 469
    size distribution, in Canada, 236
    technology constraints, 230
    temporary shutdown decision, 278, 278f
    turnover, 240
first-come, first-served, 108–109
fiscal policy, 632, 708
    automatic fiscal policy, 718
    automatic stabilizers, 720–723
    autonomous tax multiplier, 718
    balanced budget multiplier, 718
    contractionary fiscal policy, 719f
    discretionary fiscal policy, 718, 720
    discretionary fiscal stabilization, 718–719
    expansionary fiscal policy, 719f
    global coordinated, 724
    government budgets, 708–713
    government expenditure multiplier, 718
    GST cut multiplier, 718
    impact lag, 720
    Laffer curve, 717, 717f
    law-making lag, 720
    recognition lag, 720
    stabilization of business cycle, 718–723
    supply-side effects, 714–717
fixed exchange rate, 611–612
flexible exchange rate, 611
food
    crisis, 46
    genetically modified foods, 164
    marginal utility, 196–197
    price elasticities of demand for food, 92
for whom (economic question), 4
for whom tradeoffs, 8–9
force, and resource allocation, 109
forecasting inflation, 685
foreign currency, 594
foreign exchange market, 594
    China, 612–613
    competitive market, 597
    demand, 597
    demand curve for Canadian dollars, 598,
        598f
    expected profit effect, 598, 599
    exports effect, 598
    imports effect, 599
    intervention, 612f
    law of demand, 597–598
    law of supply, 599

market equilibrium, 600, 600f
supply, 599
supply curve for Canadian dollars, 599, 599f
foreign income, 633
foreign interest rates, 601, 602
forgone interest, 229
fossil fuels, 373
four-firm concentration ratio, 238, 238t, 239
four-fold classification of goods, 394, 394f
Freakonomics (Levitt), 11
Freddie Mac, 547
free-rider problem, 395
frictional unemployment, 495
Friedman, Milton, 384, 748, 757
Fudenberg, Drew, 370–372
full employment, 496, 523, 714
full-employment equilibrium, 637
full-employment quantity of labour, 628
future value, 434–435

G

G-20, 724
3G cell phone market, 334
gains from trade
  achievement of, 41–43
  comparative advantage, 40–41
  consumer surplus, 290
  dynamic comparative advantage, 43
  graphs, 42f
  net gains from trade, 157–158
  producer surplus, 290
  specialization, 40
game theory, 346
  see also oligopoly
  Nash equilibrium, 347, 351–352
  oligopoly price-fixing game, 348–352
  payoff matrix, 346, 347t, 351, 352f
  prisoners' dilemma, 346–347, 347t
  strategies, 346
gasoline
  see also oil
  elasticities of demand for, 100
  prices, 76–77
gasoline cartel, 361
Gates, Bill, 6
GDP. *See* gross domestic product (GDP)
GDP deflator, 502
General Agreement on Tariffs and Trade (GATT), 161
General Motors of Canada, 100
genetically modified foods, 164
Gini coefficient, 445–446, 446f
global coordinated, 724
global market
  demand and supply, 557–558
  global market for loanable funds, 557–558, 559
  international borrowing and lending, 557, 558f
  money growth and inflation, 583f
global monopoly, 165, 237
global warming, 6, 373, 375
globalization
  and economic inequality, 450

self-interest and the social interest, 5
goods, 3
  capital goods, 418
  classification of, 394, 394f
  discrimination among units of a good, 310
  divisible goods, 204
  excludable, 394
  final good, 468
  four-fold classification, 394, 394f
  indivisible goods, 204
  inferior good, 62, 94, 214
  intermediate good, 468
  new goods bias, 501
  nonexcludable, 394
  nonrival, 394
  normal good, 62
  private good, 394
  public good, 117, 394, 395–399
  related goods, 61, 65
  rival, 394
goods markets
  circular flow, 44
  described, 58
Google, 244, 299, 301
Governing Council of Bank of Canada, 733–734
government
  crowding-out effect, 556
  economic policy, 12
  expenditures. *See* government expenditure
  external benefits and, 383–385
  external costs and, 380–381
  federal government, 712
  growth of, 399
  inefficient overprovision, 399
  joint statement of Government of Canada and Bank of Canada, 732
  levels of, 712
  and market failure, 413
  in market for loanable funds, 555–556
  minimum wage, 133–135
  outlays, 709, 710–711
  payments to farmers, 142–143
  production quotas, 141–142, 141f
  provincial government, 712
  rent ceilings, 130–132
  revenue, 708
  subsidies, 142–143
  taxes, 135–140
  transfer payments, 709, 721
  voter preferences, 399
government budget
  balanced budget, 709, 723
  budget balance, 709
  budget deficit, 555–556, 556f, 709, 709f, 713, 721–722, 723
  budget equation, 205–206
  budget making, 708
  budget surplus, 555, 555f, 709, 709f, 713
  capital, 713
  federal budget, 708
  government debt, 711–713, 711f
  highlights of 2008 budget, 708–709
  historical perspective, 709–711
  outlays, 709, 710–711
  provincial budget, 708

revenues, 708, 710
government debt, 711–713, 711f
government expenditure, 470, 471, 632, 695, 709, 710–711
government expenditure multiplier, 672, 672f, **718**
government licence, 300
government sector balance, 609
graphs
  breaks in axes, 18
  causation, 18
  ceteris paribus, 24–25
  correlation, 18
  cross-section graph, 16, 17f
  curve, 18
  data, 15–18
  in economic models, 18–21
  making a graph, 15f
  misleading graphs, 18
  relationships among more than two variables, 24–25, 25f
  scatter diagrams, 17–18, 17f
  slope of a relationship, 22–24
  time-series graph, 16, 16f
  unrelated variables, 21, 21f
  variables moving in opposite directions, 19–20
  variables moving in same direction, 18–19
  variables with maximum or minimum, 20, 21f
Great Depression, 7, 168, 490, 662, 679, 694–695
Greenspan, Alan, 559
gross domestic product (GDP), 468
  aggregate expenditure, 470
  aggregate income, 470
  base year, 483
  and circular flow of expenditure and income, 469–470
  defined, 468
  expenditure approach, 471, 471f
  final goods and services, 468
  GDP deflator, 502
  "gross," meaning of, 470
  income approach, 471–472, 472t
  limitations of, 477–478
  market value, 468
  measurement of, 471–473
  nominal GDP, 473, 473t
  potential GDP, growth of, 474, 521–526
  produced within a country, 468
  real GDP, 473, 473t, 474–479
  statistical discrepancy, 472
  uses of, 474–477
gross investment, 470, 544
gross profit, 470
Group of 20, 724
growth accounting, 528–529
growth theories and policies
  classical growth theory, 531
  faster growth, achievement of, 533
  Malthusian theory, 534–535
  neoclassical growth theory, 531–532
  new growth theory, 533–535
GST cut multiplier, 718
Guaranteed Income Supplement (GIS), 453

guns *vs.* butter tradeoff, 8

H
Hamermesh, Daniel, 135
health and safety barriers, 164, 478
health care spending, 398
**Herfindahl-Hirschman Index (HHI),
    238**–239
Hewlett-Packard, 362
high-skilled labour, 448
homelessness, 441
Hong Kong
    economic growth, 39*f,* 520
    production possibilities per person, 39
Hotelling, Harold, 430, 463
Hotelling principle, 430
households
    aggregate income, 469
    consumption expenditure, 469
    and CPI basket, 499
    described, 469
    disposable income, 551, 632
    production, and real GDP, 477
    type, 446
housing market with rent ceiling, 130–132
housing shortage, 130
how (economic question), 3
how tradeoffs, 8
Howitt, Peter, 512–514
Hoxby, Caroline M., 414–416
human capital, 3
    career interruptions, 449–450
    differences in, 449–450
    and economic inequality, 448–450
    growth of, 38, 527
    high- and low-skilled labour, demand and
        supply, 448–449
    measure of, 4*f*
    quantity of, 629
    skill differentials, 449*f*
    unemployment and, 490–491
Human Development Index (HDI), 479
human nature, 10
Human Resources and Social Development
    Canada, 119
Hume, David, 511
hyperinflation, 498, 584

I
IBM, 285
illegal goods markets, 144–145, 144*f*
illiquid firm, 547
Imbeault, Bernard, 323
impact lag, 720
implicit rental rate, 228–229
import function, 653, 670
import quota, 162
    effects of, 162, 162*f*
    social loss, 162–163
    winners and losers, 162–163, 163*f*
imports, 154, 470
    gains and losses, 157–158, 157*f*
    health, safety and regulation barriers, 164
    import quota, 162–163
    jobs, effects on, 166
    market with imports, 155*f*

multiplier, 661
    reasons for, 155
    tariffs, 159–160, 161*f*
    voluntary export restraint, 164
imports effect, 599
incentive, 2, 10
incentive pay, 234
incentive system, 233
income
    after-tax income, 442
    aggregate income, 469, 470
    annual, 445
    capital income, 716*f*
    change in, and budget equation, 206,
        206*f*
    change in, and consumer choices, 212
    and change in demand, 62
    circular flows, 469–470, 469*f*
    definitions of, 442
    disposable income, 551, 632, 650
    distribution of income. *See* income distri-
        bution
    expected future income, 62, 551
    factors, 446
    farmers' income, 472
    foreign income, 633
    income-time budget line, 214
    investment, 708
    lifetime, 445
    Lorenz curve, 443–444, 443*f,* 444*f*
    market income, 442
    mean income, 442
    median income, 442
    miscellaneous investment income, 472
    mode income, 442
    net domestic income at factor cost, 472
    net domestic income at market prices,
        472
    from non-farm unincorporated business-
        es, 472
    real income, 205
    redistribution of, 453–455, 454*f,* 498
    rise in, and marginal utility, 190, 190*f*
    total income, 442
    unemployment and, 490
    vs. wealth, 444–445
income approach, 471–472, 472*t*
income distribution
    big tradeoff, 455
    in Canada, 442, 442*f*
    income redistribution, 453–455, 454*f,*
        498
    positively skewed distribution, 442, 442*f*
    quintiles, 442, 443*f*
    trend in, 445, 450*f*
    unequal distribution of income, 4
income effect, 59, 212, 212*f,* 213, 213*f,*
    423
income elastic demand, 94
income elasticity of demand, 94, 95
income inelastic demand, 94
income maintenance programs, 453
income taxes, 453, 661, 708, 714–715, 714*f,*
    716
    see also taxes
income-time budget line, 214
increasing marginal returns, 254–255
India, 122

indifference curve, 207
    degree of substitutability, 209–210, 209*f*
    highest attainable indifference curve, 211
    marginal rate of substitution, 208, 208*f*
indirect tax, 472, 708
individual demand, 110–111, 110*f*
individual supply, 112–113, 112*f*
**individual transferable quota (ITQ),
    404**–405, 405*f*
indivisible goods, 204
induced consumption, 650
induced expenditure, 654
induced taxes, 721
Industrial Revolution, 53
Industry Canada, 236
inefficiency
    see also efficiency
    administrative cost, 455
    big tradeoff, 119
    deadweight loss. *See* deadweight loss
    external benefit, 382*f*
    external cost, 378*f*
    and government growth, 399
    income redistribution, 455
    inefficient production, 33
    minimum wage, 133–134, 134*f*
    monopoly, 307, 307*f*
    overproduction, 116
    production quotas, 142
    public overprovision, 397–398
    rent ceiling, 131, 131*f*
    underproduction, 115–116
inefficient production, 33
inelastic demand, 88–89, 88*f,* 303
inelastic supply, 97*f*
inequality. *See* economic inequality
infant-industry argument, 165
inferior good, 62, 94, 214
inflation
    actual inflation, 732
    AS-AD model, 635*f,* 636
    Bank of Canada and high inflation,
        744–745, 744*f*
    and business cycle, 685
    core inflation, 502–503, 732
    cost-push inflation, 682–684, 683*f,* 684*f*
    cycles, 680
    demand-pull inflation, 680–682, 680*f,*
        681*f*
    diversion of resources, 498
    economic growth, 635*f*
    expected inflation, 684–685, 685*f*
    forecasting inflation, 685
    high inflation *vs.* high price level, 501
    hyperinflation, 498, 584
    income redistribution, 498
    money, value of, 569
    money growth and inflation, 582*f,* 583*f*
    Phillips curve, 686–688, 686*f,* 687*f*
    problem of, 498
    sources of, 680
    stagflation, 639, 683
    and unemployment, 686–688, 686*f,* 687*f*
    wealth redistribution, 498
inflation-control target, 732–733, 733*f*
inflation rate, 498
    core CPI inflation rate, 502–503, 503*f*
    core inflation rate, 502–503, 503*f*

measurement of, 500
inflation rate targeting, 732
inflationary gap, 636
information-age economy
   self-interest and the social interest, 6
   source of the information age, 6
information-age monopolies, 301
information constraints, 230
Information Revolution, 6, 53
innovation, 301, 330, 578
insolvency, 547, 548
institutions, role of, 10
instrument rule, 735
   McCallum rule, 747
   Taylor rule, 747
insurance companies, 546–547
Intel, 6
intellectual property, 44
intellectual property rights, 385
interdependence, 343
interest, 4
   compound interest, 434, 516–517
   foregone interest, 229
   and income approach, 472
interest rate parity, 604
interest rates
   and asset prices, 548
   bank rate, 736
   Canadian interest rate, 602
   Canadian interest rate differential, 601, 740
   cuts, 632
   cuts in, 750
   foreign interest rates, 601, 602
   long-term corporate bond rate, 740
   long-term real interest rate, 741
   nominal interest rate, 549, 578
   overnight loans rate, 734–735, 735f, 739–740, 739f
   real interest rate, 549–550, 550n, 557, 716, 741
   settlement balances rate, 736
   short-term bill rate, 739–740
   10-year government bond rate, 740
intergenerational transfers, 452
intermediate good, 468
international borrowing and lending, 557
international capital mobility, 557
International Harvester, 285
international substitution, 663
international trade
   balance of payments accounts, 606–608
   borrowers, 608
   comparative advantage, 154
   current account balance, 609
   debtor and creditor nations, 608
   drivers of, 154
   encouragement of, 535
   exchange rate. *See* exchange rate
   exports, 156, 156f
   financing international trade, 606–610
   how global markets work, 154–156
   imports, 155, 155f
   lenders, 608
   losers, 157–158
   net exports, 609–610, 609t
   net gains from trade, 157–158

restrictions. *See* international trade restrictions
   statistics, 154
   winners, 157–158
International Trade Commission (ITC), 166
international trade restrictions
   case against protection, 165–169
   compensation of losers, 169
   competition with cheap foreign labour, 166
   dumping, 165–166
   exploitation of developing countries, 167
   export subsidies, 164
   health, safety and regulation barriers, 164
   import quota, 162–163
   infant-industry argument, 165
   jobs, effect on, 166
   lax environmental standards, 166–167
   offshore outsourcing, 167–168
   reasons for, 168–169
   rent seeking, 169
   tariff revenue, 168–169
   tariffs, 159–160, 161f
   trade wars, avoidance of, 168
   voluntary export restraint, 164
Internet search leaders, 244
intertemporal substitution, 663, 692
invention, 301
inventories
   additions to, as investment, 469–470
   change in, as business investment, 471
   inventory targets, 657
   as physical capital, 544
   and short-run equilibrium, 634
   unplanned inventory changes, 656f
   unwanted inventories, 634, 663
inverse relationship, 19, 20f
investment, 470
   business investment, 471
   and capital, 544, 545f
   funds that finance investment, 548–549
   Great Depression, 662
   gross investment, 470, 544
   income, 708
   miscellaneous investment income, 472
   national saving, 549
   net investment, 470, 544
   real interest rate, 741
   in seven economies, 529t
   taxes, effect of, 716
invisible hand, 115
involuntary part-time rate, 492
involuntary part-time workers, 494
iPhone, 334

J
Japan, budget deficit in, 713
Jevons, William Stanley, 194
job, 418
job leavers, 494
job losers, 494
job losses, 696
joint unlimited liability, 235
JPMorgan Chase, 547

K
k-percent rule, 748
key money, 130
Keynes, John Maynard, 490, 703
Keynesian cycle theory, 690
Keynesian model
   algebra of, 670–673
   described, 640–641
   fixed prices and expenditure plans, 650–653
   multiplier, 658–662
   multiplier and the price level, 663–667
   new Keynesian view, 641
   real GDP with fixed price level, 654–657
Kimberly-Clark, 352–353, 354, 354f
Kindle, 216
kinked demand curve model, 344, 344f
Kiva.org, 529
knowledge
   copyright, 385
   and diminishing returns, 533
   external benefit, 382f
   government actions, 383–385
   inefficiency with an external benefit, 382f
   patents, 385
   private benefits, 381–383
   private subsidy, 383f, 384
   public provision, 383–384, 383f
   social benefits, 381–383
   vouchers, 384–385, 384f
known oil reserves, 430
Korea, economic growth in, 520
Krueger, Alan, 134–135

L
labour, 3
   casual labour, 418
   demand. *See* labour demand
   full-employment quantity of labour, 628
   owner's supply of, 229
   quality of labour, 3
   quantity of, and output, 253
   services, 418, 422
   skill differentials, 449f
   supply. *See* labour supply
   underutilized labour, 494
   value of marginal product, 419
   work-leisure choices, 214
labour demand
   aggregate labour market, 521–522
   change in demand, 421
   in competitive labour market, 422
   demand for labour, 419–420, 420f, 421t
   high-skilled labour, 448
   labour union, influences of, 424
   low-skilled labour, 448
labour demand curve, 420
labour force, 491
   entrants, 494–495
   graph, 491f
   reentrants, 494–495
   status, 446
labour force participation rate, 492–493, 493f
labour force status, 446
Labour Force Survey, 491

labour market
  aggregate labour market, 521–522
  competitive labour market, 422–423
  described, 418
  equilibrium, 522–523, 522*f*
  indicators, 491–493
  minimum wage, 133–135, 133*f*
  monopsony, 425–426, 425*f*
  and potential GDP, 523, 523*f*
  real business cycle theory, 692*f*
  trends and differences in wage rates, 427
  with a union, 424–427
labour market equilibrium
  in competitive labour market, 423, 423*f*
  with a union, 424
labour productivity, 525
  Asia, faster growth in, 529
  in Canada, 530
  growth accounting, 528–529
  growth of, 525–526, 525*f*, 528*f*
  human capital growth, 527
  increase, 525–526, 525*f*
  physical capital growth, 526
  and potential GDP, 525–526, 525*f*
  preconditions for growth, 526
  productivity growth slowdown, 474–475
  reasons for growth, 526–530
  slowdown and speedup, 528
  technological advances, 527, 533
labour supply
  aggregate labour market, 522
  in competitive labour market, 422–423
  graph, 215*f*
  high-skilled labour, 448
  labour union, influence of, 424
  low-skilled labour, 448
  and potential GDP, 523–524
  work-leisure choices, 214, 214*f*
labour supply curve, 215, 215*f*, 422–423, 422*f*
labour union, 424
  in competitive labour market, 424*f*
  labour demand, influences on, 424
  labour market equilibrium, 424
  labour market with a union, 424–427
  labour supply, influences on, 424
  monopsony, 425–426, 425*f*
  union-nonunion wage gap, 426
Laffer, Arthur B., 717
Laffer curve, 717, 717*f*
land, 3
  described, 418
  land pollution, 376
  markets for land services, 418
  nonrenewable natural resources, 418
  rental markets, 428–429, 429*f*
  services of land, 418
land pollution, 376
Large Value Transfer System (LVTS), 575
law-making lag, 720
law of demand, 59, 597–598
law of diminishing returns, 255, 522
law of supply, 64, 599
Lazaridis, Mike, 227
learning-by-doing, 43, 165
legal barrier to entry, 300–301
legal monopoly, 300–301
legalization of drugs, 145

Lehman Brothers, 547
leisure time, 478
lender of last resort, 573, 695
lenders, 608
Levitt, Steven, 11, 223, 224–226
life-cycle saving patterns, 452
life expectancy, 478
lifestyle income and wealth, 445
limit pricing, 357
limited liability, 235
line. *See* straight line
linear equation, 26
linear relationship, 18–19, 26, 26*f*
liquid assets, 571
liquidity, 547, 570, 572
loan markets, 545
loanable funds, 692*f*
  see also market for loanable funds
loans, 571–572, 575–576, 577*f*, 741
Loblaw Companies Limited, 236
long and variable lags, 745–746
long run, 252
  aggregate demand, increase in, 666–667
  demand and supply, growth of, 553
  monopolistic competition, 327–328
  multiplier, 667*f*
  nominal exchange rates, 605
  output, price and profit in perfect competition, 283–285
  real exchange rates, 605
long-run aggregate supply, 626, 627*f*
long-run average cost curve, 263, 264
long-run cost production function, 262, 262*t*
long-run equilibrium, 284*f*
long-run macroeconomic equilibrium, 635, 635*f*
long-run market supply curve, 287
long-run Phillips curve, 687, 687*f*
long-run supply curve, 98
long-term contracts, 234
long-term corporate bond rate, 740
long-term real interest rate, 741
Lorenz curve, 443–444, 443*f*, 444*f*
loss comparisons, 278
losses
  economic loss, 278, 327
  in short run, 281–282
lottery, 109
low-income cut-off, 447
low-skilled labour, 448
Lucas, Robert E. Jr., 474
Lucas wedge, 474–475, 475*f*
luxuries, 91, 95

M

M1, 569–570
M1+, 569*n*
M2, 569–570
M2 (gross), 569*n*
Mackenzie Valley Pipeline, 718
macroeconomic policy
  fiscal policy. *See* fiscal policy
  monetary policy. *See* monetary policy
  understanding, 757
macroeconomics, 2
  classical view, 640
  fluctuations, 634–639, 703

Keynesian view, 640–641
long-run macroeconomic equilibrium, 635, 635*f*
monetarist, 641
new Keynesian view, 641
real variables in, 503
schools of thought, 640–641
short-run macroeconomic equilibrium, 634, 634*f*
themes of macroeconomics, 511
trends, 621
mainstream business cycle theory, 689–690, 689*f*
majority rule, 108
Malthus, Thomas Robert, 463, 531
Malthusian theory, 531, 534–535
margin, 10
  choosing at the margin, 10, 184–186
  total utility, 184–186
marginal analysis, 186, 277
marginal benefit, 10, 36
  and demand, 110–111
  marginal social benefit, 110*f*
  and preferences, 36, 36*f*
  principle of decreasing marginal benefit, 36
  willingness and ability to pay, 60
marginal benefit curve, 36, 110
marginal cost, 10, 35, 258
  equals marginal revenue, in single-price monopoly, 304
  increase in, and quantity supplied, 64
  marginal external cost, 377
  marginal private cost, 377
  marginal social cost, 377
  minimum supply price as, 65
  and output, 258
  and production possibilities frontier (PPF), 35, 35*f*
  and production quotas, 142
  and subsidies, 142
  and supply, 112–113
marginal cost curve, 112, 258, 259*f*
marginal cost pricing rule, 313
marginal external benefit, 381
marginal external cost, 377
marginal grades, 256
marginal private benefit, 381
marginal private cost, 377
marginal product, 253, 253*t*, 255*f*, 419
marginal product curve, 254–255
marginal propensity to consume, 652, 652*f*
marginal propensity to import, 653
marginal propensity to save, 652, 652*f*
marginal rate of substitution, 208, 208*f*, 211
marginal revenue, 274
  and demand, 302*f*
  and elasticity, 303, 303*f*
  equals marginal cost, in single-price monopoly, 304
  and price, in single-price monopoly, 302
marginal social benefit, 381
  efficient use of the commons, 402
  of public good, 395
  rent ceilings and, 131
  taxes, 139

marginal social benefit (MSB) curve, 111
marginal social cost, 377
    of public good, 396
    rent ceilings and, 131
    taxes, 139
marginal social cost (MSC) curve, 113
marginal utility, 182
    see also utility
    diminishing marginal utility, 183
    fall in price, 187–188, 188*f*
    food, 196–197
    graph, 183*f*
    paradox of value, 191, 191*f*
    positive marginal utility, 182–183
    predictions of, 187–192
    rise in income, 190, 190*f*
    rise in price, 189, 189*f*
    vs. total utility, 191
marginal utility per dollar, 184
marginally attached worker, 494
Maritime provinces, 495
market, 44
    alternatives to the market, 117
    buyers and sellers, 58
    circular flows through markets, 44, 45*f*
    commodity markets, 418
    and competitive environment, 237–241
    competitive market, 58
    constraints, 230
    corn, 73*f*
    crude oil, 72*f*
    and decentralized coordination, 44
    with exports, 156*f*
    factor markets. *See* factor markets
    fertilizers, 73*f*
    financial markets. *See* financial markets
    and firms, 242–243
    geographical scope, 240
    global markets. *See* international trade
    goods markets, 44, 58
    how markets work, 177
    illegal goods, 144–145, 144*f*
    with imports, 155*f*
    for money, 578–579
    oil, world markets for, 431
    and prices, 58
    reallocation of resources, 72–73
    rental market, 418
market coordination, 242
market demand, 110–111, 110*f*
market demand curve, 111
market equilibrium, 68
    see also equilibrium
market failure, understanding, 413
market for loanable funds, 548
    changes in demand and supply, 552–553, 553*f*
    demand for loanable funds, 550–551
    equilibrium, 552, 552*f*
    financial crisis in United States, 554
    funds that finance investment, 548–549
    global market for loanable funds, 557–558, 559
    government and, 555–556
    high inflation and, 744
    international borrowing and lending, 557, 558*f*
    international capital mobility, 557

real interest rate, 549–550
    recession and, 742–743
    supply of loanable funds, 551–552, 551*f*
market income, 442
market power, limit on, 369
market price
    domestic product at market price, 472
    net domestic income at market prices, 472
    as resource allocation method, 108
market structures
    monopolistic competition, 237. *See also* monopolistic competition
    monopoly, 237. *See also* monopoly
    in North America, 241
    oligopoly, 237. *See also* oligopoly
    perfect competition, 237. *See also* perfect competition
    summary of, 240*t*
    types of, 237–238
market supply, 112–113, 112*f*
market supply curve, 113
market value, 229, 468
marketable permits, 380–381
marketing, in monopolistic competition, 324–325
markup, 328*f*, 329, 332*f*
marriage and wealth concentration, 452
Marshall, Alfred, 177
Martin, Paul, 360
maximum point, 20, 21*f*
McCallum rule, 747
mean income, 442
means of payment, 568
median income, 442
medium of exchange, 568
men, and wage gap, 4
Merrill Lynch, 547
microeconomics, 2
microloans, 529
MicroPlace.com, 529
microprocessor, 6
Microsoft, 299, 301, 316–317
Mill, John Stuart, 118
minimum efficient scale, 265, 274
minimum point, 20, 21*f*
minimum-supply price, 112
minimum wage, 133
    effects of, 146
    fairness, 134
    inefficiency of, 133–134, 134*f*
    and monopsony, 426, 426*f*
    in practice, 134–135
    and unemployment, 133, 133*f*
minus sign, 88
misallocation of resources, 33
miscellaneous investment income, 472
misleading graphs, 18
Mitsubishi, 547
mode income, 442
monetarist, 641
monetarist cycle theory, 690
monetary base, 573, 576
monetary policy, 632
    see also Bank of Canada
    in action, 750
    alternative monetary policy strategies, 747–749

    conduct of, 734–738
    exchange rate fluctuations, 740–741
    exchange targeting rule, 747
    expenditure plans, 741
    framework, 732–734
    inflation-control target, 732–733, 733*f*
    instrument rule, 735
    interest rate changes, 739–740
    k-percent rule, 748
    long and variable lags, 745–746
    McCallum rule, 747
    money and bank loans, 741
    money targeting rule, 748
    objective, 732–733
    responsibility for, 733–734
    ripple effects, 745
    targeting rule, 735–736
    Taylor rule, 747
    time lags, 745–746
    transmission, 739–746
money, 44, 568
    in Canada today, 569
    vs. cheques, 570
    creation of, 575–577
    creation process, 576–577
    vs. credit cards, 570
    currency, 569
    and decentralized coordination, 44
    demand for money, 579, 579*f*
    demand for money in Canada, 580–581
    deposits, 569, 570
    described, 544
    vs. finance, 544
    financial innovation, 578
    growth and inflation, 582*f*, 583*f*
    influences on money holding, 578
    liquidity, 570
    M1, 569–570
    M1+, 569*n*
    M2, 569–570
    M2 (gross), 569*n*
    market for money, 578–579
    as medium of exchange, 568
    money market equilibrium, 581, 581*f*
    nominal interest rate, 578
    nominal money, 578
    official measures of money in Canada, 569–570
    overnight rate target, changes in, 741
    quantity theory of money, 582–583, 584, 747
    real business cycle theory, 693
    and real GDP, 578
    real money, 578
    shifts in demand for money curve, 579, 579*f*
    as store of value, 569
    as unit of account, 568–569, 568*t*
    velocity of circulation, 582
money market, 742
money market equilibrium, 581, 581*f*
money multiplier, 577, 586–587
money price, 58
money targeting rule, 748
money wage rate, 629, 629*f*, 681
monopolistic competition, 237, 324
    advertising, 330–333
    brand names, 333

collusion, impossibility of, 324
economic loss in short run, 327
economic profit in short run, 326*f*
efficiency and, 329
entry and exit, 325
examples of, 325
excess capacity, 328–329, 328*f*
individual competitors and, 324
large number of firms, 324
long-run output and price, 327–328,
    327*f*
marketing, 324–325
markup, 328*f*, 329
output, 326–329
vs. perfect competition, 328–329
price, 324, 326–329
product development, 330–333
product differentiation, 324
profit maximization, 326–327
quality of product, 324
selling costs, 331, 331*f*, 332
short-run output and price decision, 326
signal of quality, 332–333
small market share, 324
total cost, 331, 331*f*
zero economic profit in long run,
    327–328, 327*f*
monopoly, 237, 300
    average cost pricing rule, 314
    barrier to entry, 300–301
    bilateral monopoly, 425
    buying a monopoly, 308
    creating a monopoly, 308
    efficiency, 307, 307*f*
    elastic demand, 303
    global monopoly, 165, 237
    government subsidy, 314
    how monopoly arises, 300–301
    inefficiency, 307, 307*f*
    information-age monopolies, 301
    legal barrier to entry, 300–301
    legal monopoly, 300–301
    natural barrier to entry, 300
    natural monopoly, 300, 300*f*, 301,
        313–315, 314*f*, 394
    no close substitute, 300
    as obstacle to efficiency, 117
    output and price decision, 302–305
    ownership barrier to entry, 300
    vs. perfect competition, 301, 306–309
    price, 306, 306*f*
    price cap regulation, 315, 315*f*
    price discrimination, 301, 309–312
    price-setting strategies, 301
    rate of return regulation, 314
    redistribution of surpluses, 308
    regulation, 313–315
    regulation of natural monopoly, 313–315,
        314*f*
    rent seeking, 308
    rent-seeking equilibrium, 308, 309*f*
    single-price monopoly, 301, 302–309
monopsony, 425
    in labour market, 425–426, 425*f*
    and labour union, 425–426
    and minimum wage, 426, 426*f*
Moore, Gordon, 6
Moore's law, 6

Morgan Stanley, 547
Morgenstern, Oskar, 346
mortgage, 545
mortgage-backed security, 546, 547
Mosaic, 533
Motor Coach Industries (MCI), 283
multi-income families, 695
Multifiber Arrangement, 166
multiplier, 658
    algebra of, 671, 671*f*
    autonomous tax multiplier, 672, 672*f*,
        718
    balanced budget multiplier, 673, 673*f*,
        718
    basic idea of, 658
    business cycle turning points, 662
    government expenditure multiplier, 672,
        672*f*, 718
    graph, 659*f*
    Great Depression, 662
    greater than 1, 659
    GST cut multiplier, 718
    imports, 661
    long run, 667*f*
    multiplier effect, 658–659
    and price level, 663–667
    process, 661, 661*f*
    in short run, 666*f*
    size of, 659
    and slope of aggregate expenditure curve,
        660, 660*f*
multiplier effect, 658–659
Murphy, Kevin, 135
music downloads, 192–193

N

Nash, John, 353
Nash equilibrium, 347, 351–352
National Hockey League (NHL), 361, 437
National Hockey League Players Association
    (NHLPA), 437
National Income and Expenditure Accounts,
    471
national saving, 549
natural barrier to entry, 300
natural disaster case study, 120–121
natural experiment, 11
natural monopoly, 300, 300*f*, 301,
    313–315, 314*f*, 394
natural oligopoly, 342, 342*f*
natural resources. *See* resources
natural unemployment, 494–496
natural unemployment rate, 496,
    687–688, 687*f*
necessities, 91, 95
negative consumption externalities, 376
negative externality, 374, 377–381
negative production externalities, 374–376
negative relationship, 19, 20*f*, 27, 27*f*
negative slope, 22*f*
neoclassical economics of population growth,
    532
neoclassical growth theory, 531–532
net borrower, 608
net domestic income at factor cost, 472
net domestic income at market prices, 472
net exports, 470, 471, 609–610, 609*t*, 741
net investment, 470, 544

net lender, 608
net taxes, 548
net worth, 547
neuroeconomics, 195
new classical cycle theory, 690
new classical view, 640
new goods bias, 501
new growth theory, 533–535
new Keynesian cycle theory, 690
new Keynesian view, 641
no free lunch, 9
nominal exchange rate, 594–595, 605
nominal GDP, 473, 473*t*
nominal interest rate, 549, 578
nominal money, 578
non-farm unincorporated businesses, 472
nonexcludable, 394
nonrenewable natural resources, 418,
    429–431, 430*f*
nonrival, 394
normal good, 62
normal profit, 229, 274
normative statements, 11
Nozick, Robert, 120
NutraSweet, 358

O

obstacles to efficiency, 116–117
official reserves, 606
official settlements account, 606
offshore outsourcing, 167–168
offshoring, 167
oil, 34, 72, 72*F*, 429–430, 431, 682*f*
oilsands project, 432
Old Age Security (OAS), 453
oligopoly, 237, 342
    anti-combine law, 358–361
    barriers to entry, 342
    both firms cheat, 351, 351*f*
    cheating with punishment, 355*t*
    collusion, 348–350, 349*f*
    collusive agreement, 348
    cooperative equilibrium, 355
    disappearing invisible hand, 353
    dominant firm oligopoly, 344–345, 345*f*
    duopoly, 342
    duopoly payoff matrix, 352*f*
    examples of, 343
    game of chicken, 354, 354*f*
    game theory, 346–354
    interdependence, 343
    kinked demand curve model, 344, 344*f*
    limit pricing, 357
    Nash equilibrium, 351–352
    natural oligopoly, 342, 342*f*
    one firm cheats, 350, 350*f*
    other games, 352–354
    payoff matrix, 351
    price-fixing game, 348–352
    price wars, 356
    repeated duopoly games, 355–356
    research and development game, 352
    sequential entry game in contestable mar-
        ket, 356–357
    small number of firms, 343
    temptation to cooperate, 343
    tit-for-tat strategy, 355, 356
    traditional oligopoly models, 344–345

trigger strategy, 355
open market operation, 573, 736–737
operating band, 736
operational guide, 732
opportunity cost, 9, 33
  calculation of, 58
  crude oil, 34
  of food, 46
  forgone interest, 229
  of housing, 130
  implicit rental rate, 228–229
  increasing opportunity cost, 34
  of production, 228–229
  production possibilities frontier *(PPF)*,
    33–34
  as ratio, 33–34
  relative price, 58
  total cost, 274
  tradeoffs, 33
organization
  business organization, types of, 234–235
  command systems, 233
  incentive system, 233
  mixture of systems, 233
outlays, 709, 710–711
outlet substitution, 502
output
  average cost, 257, 258–259
  average product, 253
  and change for demand for labour, 421
  and external cost, 377
  firm's output decision in perfect competi-
    tion, 276–279
  long-run cost, 262–265
  marginal analysis, 277
  marginal cost, 257, 258
  marginal product, 253
  minimum efficient scale, 274
  monopolistic competition, 326–329
  profit-maximizing output, 276–279, 277*f*
  and quantity of labour, 253
  short run, in perfect competition,
    280–282
  short-run costs, 257–261
  single-price monopoly, 304–305, 305*f*
  total cost, 257
  total product, 253
output gap, 496, 497*f,* **636,** 720
outsourcing, 167
overfishing equilibrium, 401–402
overnight loans rate, 734–735, 735*f,*
  739–740, 739*f*
overnight rate instrument rule, 747
overnight rate target, 736
overproduction, 116, 116*f,* 142, 143
overprovision, 397–398, 397*f*
ownership, 234
ownership barrier to entry, 300

P

paradox of value, 191, 191*f*
partnership, 235
patent, 301, 385
payments system, 573
payoff matrix, 346, 347*t,* 351, 352*f*
peak, 476
pension funds, 546
People's Bank of China. *See* China

per capita real GDP. *See* real GDP per person
perfect competition, 237, 274
  changing tastes, 286–289
  choices, 290
  consumer surplus, 307, 307*f*
  demand for firm's product, 274–275,
    275*f*
  economic profit, 274
  efficiency, 290–291, 291*f,* 307
  firm's decisions, 275
  how perfect competition arises, 274
  long-run output, price and profit,
    283–285
  minimum efficient scale, 274
  vs. monopolistic competition, 328–329
  vs. monopoly, 301, 306–309
  output decision, 276–279
  price, 275*f,* 306
  price takers, 274
  producer surplus, 307, 307*f*
  resources, efficient use of, 290
  revenue, 274, 275*f*
  short-run outcomes, 282, 282*f*
  short-run output, price and profit,
    280–282
  vs. single-price monopoly, 306–309
  supply curve, 279, 279*f*
  technological change, 289
perfect price discrimination, 311, 311*f,*
  312
perfectly elastic demand, 88*f,* **89,** 138, 138*f*
perfectly elastic supply, 97*f,* 138
perfectly inelastic demand, 88, 88*f,* 137,
  137*f*
perfectly inelastic supply, 97*f,* 138
permanent change in demand, 286–287,
  287*f*
perpetual motion economy, 534, 534*f*
personal characteristics, and resource allocation, 109
personal computers, 285, 341
personal economic policy, 12
personal expenditures, 471
personal income taxes, 708
Phillips curve, 686
  Canada, 688
  long-run Phillips curve, 687, 687*f*
  short-run Phillips curve, 686, 686*f,* 687*f*
physical capital, 544
physical capital growth, 526
Pigou, Arthur Cecil, 380
Pigovian taxes, 380
Pizza Delight, 323
planned expenditure, 655
plant size, and average total cost, 262–263
policy
  business economic policy, 12
  economics as policy tool, 12
  exchange rate policy, 611–613
  fiscal policy. *See* fiscal policy
  government economic policy, 12
  Keynsian view, 641
  monetarist policy, 641
  monetary policy. *See* monetary policy
  personal economic policy, 12
political equilibrium, 399, 405
political freedom, 478
pollution
  air pollution, 374–376

  Coase theorem, 379
  emission charges, 380
  emission permits, 380–381
  external cost and output, 377
  government actions, 380–381
  inefficiency with external cost, 378*f*
  land pollution, 376
  marketable permits, 380–381
  Pigovian taxes, 380
  private costs, 377
  and production, 378
  property rights, 378
  social costs, 377
  taxes, 380, 380*f*
  valuation of external cost, 377
  water pollution, 376
pooling risk, 572
population, and change in demand, 62
population growth
  in Canada, 530
  classical theory of population growth, 531
  neoclassical economics of population
    growth, 532
  and potential GDP, 524, 524*f*
positive consumption externalities, 376
positive externality, 374, 381–385
positive marginal utility, 182–183
positive production externalities, 376
positive relationship, 18, 19*f,* 27
positive slope, 22*f*
positive statements, 11
positively skewed distribution, 442, 442*f*
potential GDP, 474
  aggregate labour market, 521–522
  aggregate production function, 521, 521*f*
  changes in, 628, 628*f*
  determination of, 521–523
  at full employment, 626, 714
  growth of, 474
  and labour market, 523, 523*f*
  labour productivity, growth of, 525–526,
    525*f*
  labour supply, growth of, 523–524
  population growth, effects of, 524, 524*f*
  sources of growth, 523–526
  and technological change, 629
poverty, 447
  duration of, 447
  factors, 446
  incidence of low income, 447*f*
  low-income cut-off, 447
  rate, 447
  trends in poverty, 456–457
  welfare challenge, 455
PPP. *See* purchasing power parity
preference map, 207, 207*f*
preferences, 36
  and change in demand, 62
  changes in, 286–289
  and indifferences curves, 207–210
  and marginal benefit, 36, 36*f*
  preference map, 207, 207*f*
prejudice, 451
Prescott, Edward C., 715
present value, 434–435
price
  adjustment of, 663
  adjustments, 69
  asset prices, 548

average price, and price elasticity of demand, 87–88
change in demand, effect of, 96*f*
change in supply, effect of, 86*f*
changes in. *See* price change
commodity prices, 418
equilibrium price. *See* equilibrium price
expected future prices, 61–62, 66
factor price, 419
of factors of production, 65
long-run changes in, 288*f*
and marginal revenue, in monopoly, 302
marginal utility, and fall in price, 187–188, 188*f*
marginal utility, and rise in price, 189, 189*f*
market price, 108, 472
and markets, 58
minimum supply price, 65
minimum-supply price, 112
money price, 58
monopolistic competition, 324, 326–329
monopoly, 301, 306, 306*f*
in perfect competition, 275*f*, 306
and production quotas, 142
as regulator, 68–69
related goods, 61, 65
relative price, 58, 59, 205, 211, 476
as resource allocation method, 108
short run, in perfect competition, 280–282
and shortages, 69
single-price monopoly, 304–305, 305*f*
and subsidies, 142
and surplus, 69
vs. value, 110
price cap, 130
price cap regulation, 315, 315*f*
price ceiling, 130
above equilibrium price, 130
below equilibrium price, 130
housing market with rent ceiling, 130–132
price change
change in, and budget equation, 205–206
and consumer choices, 211–212
factors of production, 261
prediction of changes in, 70–75
price effect, 211–212, 211*f*
time elapsed since, and price elasticity of demand, 92
price discrimination, 301
consumer surplus, 309–310
efficiency, 312
graph, 311*f*
in monopoly, 309–312
perfect price discrimination, 311, 311*f*, 312
profiting by, 310
rent seeking, 312
price effect, 211–212, 211*f*
price elasticity of demand, 86
average price and quantity, 87–88
calculation of, 87–88, 87*f*
closeness of substitutes, 91
elastic demand, 88–89
and expenditure, 91
food, 92
inelastic demand, 88–89, 88*f*

influencing factors, 91–92
minus sign and, 88
percentage changes, 88
proportion of income spent on good, 92
proportionate change, 88
real-world elasticities of demand, 91
straight-line demand curve, 89, 89*f*
time elapsed since price change, 92
and total revenue, 90, 90*f*
units-free measure, 88
price fixing, 361
price-fixing game, 348–352
price floor, 133
above equilibrium price, 133
below equilibrium price, 133
labour market with minimum wage, 133–135
price indexes
chained price index for consumption (CPIC), 502
Consumer Price Index (CPI), 498–502
GDP deflator, 502
price level, 498
and equilibrium real GDP, 665–667
high inflation *vs.* high price level, 501
and monetary policy, 742
money holding and, 578
and multiplier, 663–667
one-time rise in, 682
price regulations, 116
price takers, 274
price wars, 356, 362
principal-agent problem, 234
principle of decreasing marginal benefit, 36
principle of minimum differentiation, 397
prisoners' dilemma, 346–347, 347*t*
private costs, 377
private good, 394
private provision, 396
private sector balance, 609
private subsidy, 383*f*, 384
Procter & Gamble, 352–353, 354, 354*f*
produced within a country, 468
producer surplus, 113
gains from trade, 290
import quotas, 163
monopoly, 307, 307*f*
perfect competition, 307, 307*f*
supply and, 113*f*
tariffs, 160
product curves
average product curve, 256
and cost curves, 260, 260*f*
described, 253
marginal product curve, 254–255
total product curve, 254, 254*f*
product development, and monopolistic competition, 330–333
product differentiation, 237, 324, 334
product innovation, 330
product quality, 324
product schedules, 253
production
aggregate production function, 521*f*
auto production, 265
command system, 233
economic efficiency, 231–232
economies of team production, 243
efficiency, 33

the firm and its economic problem, 228–230
household production, 477
incentive system, 233
inefficient production, 33
mixture of systems, 233
natural forces and, 66
opportunity cost of, 228–229
organization, 233–235
overproduction, 116
and pollution, 378
positive production externalities, 376
technological efficiency, 231
trends, 3*f*
underproduction, 115–116
unemployment and, 490
production efficiency, 33
production function
aggregate production function, 521, 544
Canadian production function, 528
long-run cost, 262, 262*t*
production possibilities frontier (PPF), 32
allocative efficiency, 37
described, 32–33
economic growth, 38*f*
graph, 32*f*
and marginal cost, 35, 35*f*
opportunity cost, 33–34
production efficiency, 33
real GDP and the quantity of leisure time, 521
scarcity, illustration of, 32
tradeoff along, 33
production quotas, 141
common resource, 404, 404*f*
effects of, 141*f*
incentive to cheat and overproduce, 142
inefficiency, 142
marginal cost, decrease of, 142
price, rise in, 142
supply, decrease in, 141
productivity growth. *See* labour productivity
profit, 4
accounting profit, 228
corporate profits, 472
and discoveries, 533
economic profit, 228, 274, 276*f*, 304, 326*f*, 327–328
expected profit effect, 598
gross profit, 470
normal profit, 229, 274
short run, in perfect competition, 280–282
profit maximization
as firm's goal, 228, 275
in monopolistic competition, 326–327
product innovation, 330
profit-maximizing output, 276–279, 277*f*
progressive income tax, 453
prohibition, 145
property rights, 44, 378
Coase theorem, 379
common resource, 403–404
and decentralized coordination, 44
and pollution, 378, 379*f*
proportional income tax, 453
protectionism. *See* international trade restrictions
provincial budget, 708

provincial government, 712
public choice theory, 399
public franchise, 300
public good, 394
  benefits of, 395f
  discoveries, 533
  efficiency and, 117
  efficient political outcome, 397f
  efficient public provision, 396–397
  efficient quantity of, 396, 396f
  free-rider problem, 395
  government, growth of, 399
  inefficient private provision, 396
  inefficient public overprovision, 397–398
  marginal social benefit, 395
  marginal social cost, 396
  political equilibrium, 399
  principle of minimum differentiation, 397
  privatization of, 399
  public choice theory, 399
  rational ignorance, 398
  social interest theory, 399
public overprovision, 397–398, 397f
public provision, 383–384, 383f, 396–397
Puerto Rico, 406
purchasing power parity, 476–477, 604, 747

Q
quality
  advertising to signal quality, 332–333
  of education, 535
  of product, and monopolistic competition, 324
  quality change bias, 501
quantity
  adjustment of, 663
  affordable quantities, 204
  average quantity, and price elasticity of demand, 87–88
  change in demand, effect of, 96f
  change in supply, effect of, 86f
  divisible goods, 204
  equilibrium quantity, 68
  long-run changes in, 288f
  prediction of changes in, 70–75
  public good, efficient quantity of, 396, 396f
  of real GDP supplied, 626
  and subsidies, 142
  unaffordable quantities, 204
quantity demanded, 59, 550
quantity regulations, 116
quantity supplied, 64, 551
quantity theory of money, 582–583, 584, 747
Quebec gas prices case, 361
quintiles, 442, 443f

R
rainforests, 7, 406
rate of return regulation, 314
rational expectation, 685
rational ignorance, 398
ratios, and opportunity cost, 33–34
Rawls, John, 119
Reading Between the Lines

  The Rising Opportunity Cost of Food, 46
  Demand and Supply: The Price of Gasoline, 76
  The Elasticities of Demand for Gasoline, Trucks, and Cars, 100
  Is Water Use Efficient? 122
  The Minimum Wage in Action, 146
  The United States Protects its Lumber Producers, 170
  The Marginal Utility of Food, 196
  Paper Books Versus e-Books, 216
  Battling for Markets in Internet Search, 244
  Cutting the Cost of Clean Electricity, 266
  Temporary Shutdown or Exit, 292
  European View of Microsoft, 316
  Product Differentiation in the 3G Cell Phone Market, 334
  Dell and HP in a Market Share Game, 362
  Fighting Carbon Emissions with a Carbon Tax and Solar Subsidy, 386
  Rainforests: A Tragedy of the Commons, 406
  Canada's Oilsands, 432
  Trends in Poverty, 456
  Real GDP in the Slowing Economy of 2008, 480
  Jobs in the Slowdown of 2008, 504
  Economic Growth in China, 536
  Bailing Out Troubled U.S. Financial Markets, 560
  The Quantity Theory of Money in Zimbabwe, 584
  The Rising Chinese Yuan, 614
  Aggregate Supply and Aggregate Demand in Action, 642
  Recession Coming, 668
  Onset of Recession in Canada and the United States, 696
  Global Coordinated Fiscal Policy, 724
  Monetary Policy in Action, 750
Reagan, Ronald, 717
real business cycle theory, 690
  criticisms of, 693
  defenses, 693
  economic growth, 693
  impulse, 690, 691f
  labour markets, 692f
  loanable funds, 692f
  mechanism, 691
  money, 693
  when-to-work decision, 691–693
real exchange rate, 594, 605, 747
real GDP, 473
  and actual expenditure, 655
  and aggregate planned expenditure, 650
  business cycle, 475–476, 475f
  calculation of, 473, 473t
  chained-dollar real GDP, 482–483, 482t, 483f, 483t, 502
  changes in quantity demanded, 631
  China, 476, 476f, 517
  consumption, 653
  environmental quality, 478
  equilibrium real GDP and the price level, 665–667
  fluctuations, 475–476, 637f
  growth in world economy, 519, 519f

  health and life expectancy, 478
  Human Development Index (HDI), 479
  leisure time, 478
  limitations, 477–479
  long-term trend, 474
  Lucas wedge, 474–475, 475f
  market for, 743, 744–745
  and monetary policy, 742
  and money, 578
  and planned expenditure, 655
  political freedom, 478
  potential GDP, growth of, 474
  productivity growth slowdown, 474–475
  purchasing power parity, 476–477
  quantity of real GDP demanded, 630
  quantity of real GDP supplied, 626
  real GDP per person, 474, 516
  real GDP per person in Canada, 515
  in slowing economy of 2008, 480
  social justice, 478
  standard of living across countries, 476–477
  standard of living over time, 474, 474f
  underground economy, 477–478
  and unemployment, 496–497
  United States, 476, 517
  uses of, 474–479
real GDP per person, 474, 516
real income, 205
real interest rate, 549–550, 550n, 557, 716, 741
real money, 578
real property, meaning of, 44
real wage rate, 503, 522
recession, 475, 632, 668, 694–695, 696, 742–743, 742f
recessionary gap, 637
recognition lag, 720
redistribution of income, 453–455, 454f
redistribution of surpluses, 308
reentrants, 494–495
reference base period, 498
regressive income tax, 453
regulation, 313
  capture theory, 313
  deregulation, 313
  monopoly, 313–315
  natural monopoly, 313–315, 314f
  rate of return regulation, 314
  social interest theory, 313
regulation barriers, 164
related goods, 61, 65
relative price, 58, 59, **205,** 211, 476
rent, 4
rent ceiling, 130
  black market, 130–131
  fairness of, 132
  graph, 131f
  housing market with rent ceiling, 130–132
  housing shortage, 130
  inefficiency, 131, 131f
  in practice, 132
  search activity, 130
rent seeking, 169, 308, 312
rent-seeking equilibrium, 308, 309f
rent-vs-buy decision, 428, 434
rental market, 418, 428–429, 428f, 429f
rental rate, 418

repeated duopoly games, 355–356
research and development
    game, 352
    stimulation of, 535
Research in Motion (RIM), 227
reservation wage, 422
reserve ratio, 576
reserves, 571, **576,** 738, 738*f,* 742, 744
resource allocation methods
    command, 108
    contest, 108
    first-come, first-served, 108–109
    force, 109
    lottery, 109
    majority rule, 108
    market price, 108
    personal characteristics, 109
resources
    allocative efficiency, 35, 37
    brought to market, 228
    classification of, 394, 394*f*
    commodity markets, 418
    common resource, 117, 394, 400–405
    depletion, 7
    described, 3
    diversion of, in inflation, 498
    efficient use of, 35–37, 37*f*
    extinction, 400
    four-fold classification, 394, 394*f*
    Hotelling principle, 430
    misallocation of, 33
    nonrenewable natural resources, 418,
        429–431, 430*f*
    oil. *See* oil
    owned by the firm, 228
    reallocation of resources, 72–73
    resource allocation methods, 108–109
    tropical rainforests, 7
    unused resources, 33
    use of, in perfect competition, 290
results, fairness of, 118–119
retained earnings, 469
revenue
    economic revenue, 274
    government, 708, 710
    marginal revenue, 274
    in perfect competition, 274, 275*f*
    tariff revenue, 168–169
    total revenue, 90, 90*f,* 274, 276*f*
Ricardo, David, 531, 556
Ricardo-Barro effect, 556, 556*f*
risk
    default risk, 552
    pooling risk, 572
risk premium, 557
rival, 394
Romer, Paul, 385, 533
Royal Bank of Canada, 360
Rule of 70, 516–517, 517*f*
rules, fairness of, 120
Russia, 43

S

Sala-i-Martin, Xavier, 622–624
saving, 544
    disposable income, 650
    dissaving, 651
    influencing factors, 650–651
    marginal propensity to save, 652, 652*f*

national saving, 549
    stimulation of, 535
    and taxes, 716
    taxes, effect of, 716
    and wealth, 551
saving function, 650, 651, 651*f*
scarcity, 2, 32
scatter diagrams, 17–18, 17*f*
Schmitt-Grohé, Stephanie, 758–760
school vouchers, 384
Schumpeter, Joseph, 533, 621
search activity, 130
securities, 571
security spending, 398
self-interest, 5
    bounded self-interest, 194–195
    institutions, role of, 10
    pursuit of, and social interest, 5–7
sellers
    equivalence of tax on buyers and sellers,
        136–137
    illegal goods markets, 144, 145
    tax on sellers, 135–136, 136*f*
selling costs, 331, 331*f,* 332
sequential entry game, 356–357
services, 3
    labour services, 418, 422
    offshoring, 167
    subsidized services, 453–454
settlement balances rate, 736
short run, 252
    aggregate demand, increase in, 666
    losses, 281–282
    market supply, 280
    monopolistic competition, 326
    multiplier, 666*f*
    nominal exchange rates, 605
    output, price and profit in perfect compe-
        tition, 280–282
    real exchange rates, 605
short-run aggregate supply, 627, 627*f*
short-run cost
    average cost, 258–259
    different quantities of capital, 263*f*
    total cost, 257
short-run equilibrium, 281, 281*f*
**short-run macroeconomic equilibrium,
    634,** 634*f*
short-run market supply curve, 280, 280*f*
short-run Phillips curve, 686, 686*f,* 687*f*
short-run supply curve, 98
short-run technology constraint
    product curves, 253–256
    product schedules, 253
short-term bill rate, 739–740
shortages
    housing shortage, 130
    and price, 69
shutdown decision, 278, 278*f*
shutdown point, 278
signal, 332–333
Simon, Julian, 463
Singapore, economic growth in, 520
single mothers, 455
single-price monopoly, 301
    economic profit, 304
    marginal revenue and elasticity, 303, 303*f*
    marginal revenue equals marginal cost,
        304

maximum price market will bear,
    304–305
    output and price decision, 302–305, 305*f*
    vs. perfect competition, 306–309
    price and marginal revenue, 302
    price and output decision, 304–305
    redistribution of surpluses, 308
    rent seeking, 308
skill differentials, 449*f*
slope, 22
    across an arc, 23–24, 24*f*
    calculation of, 26*f*
    curved line, 23–24
    and marginal propensities, 652
    negative slope, 22*f*
    at a point, 23, 23*f*
    positive slope, 22*f*
    straight line, 22–23, 22*f,* 26–27, 26*f*
Smith, Adam, 53, 115, 353, 531
Smoot-Hawley tariff, 168
social benefits, 381–383
social costs, 377
social interest, 5–7
social interest theory, 313, 399
social justice, 478
social science, economics as, 11
social security programs, 453
softwood lumber dispute, 170–171
solar power, 266
solar subsidy, 386
sole proprietorship, 234
Solow, Robert, 531, 532
solvency, 547
Sony Reader, 216
specialization, 40, 452
speculative bubble, 72
speculative forces, 429, 430
stagflation, 639, 683
standard of living
    across countries, 476–477
    and economic growth, 38
    influences on, 478–479
    over time, 474, 474*f*
state of nature, 66
statistical discrepancy, 472
statistical investigation, 11
Statistics Canada, 239, 240, 442, 499
Stern, Nicholas, 375
Stern Review on the Economics of Climate
    Change, 375
stock, 546
stock market, 546
stock market crash, 694–695
store of value, 569
straight line
    equations of, 26–27
    linear equation, 26
    negative relationships, 27, 27*f*
    position of line, 27
    positive relationships, 27
    slope of, 22–23, 22*f,* 26–27
    y-axis intercept, 27, 27*f*
straight-line demand curve, 89, 89*f*
strategic behaviour, 346
    see also game theory
strategies, 346
structural surplus or deficit, 722–723,
    722*f*
structural unemployment, 495–496

subsidy, 142, 384
  described, 472
  effects of, 142–143, 143f
  export subsidies, 164
  fall in price and increase in quantity produced, 142
  farm subsidies, 143
  government payments to farmers, 142–143
  inefficient overproduction, 143
  marginal cost, increase in, 142
  monopoly, 314
  as obstacle to efficiency, 116
  private subsidy, 383f, 384
  solar subsidy, 386
  subsidized services, 453–454
  supply, increase in, 142
subsistence real wage rate, 531
substitute, 61
  close substitutes, 209
  closeness of, and price elasticity of demand, 91
  cross elasticity of demand, 93
  degree of substitutability, 209–210, 209f
  monopoly, and no close substitute, 300
  in production, 65
substitution
  commodity substitution, 501
  international substitution, 663
  intertemporal substitution, 663, 692
  marginal rate of substitution, 208, 208f, 211
  outlet substitution, 502
  resource substitution possibilities, and elasticity of supply, 97–98
substitution effect, 59, 213, 213f, 423, 631, 663–664
sunk cost, 252
suppliers, number of, 66
supply, 64
  see also demand and supply model
  all possible changes, 75
  change in supply, 65–66, 75
  change in the quantity supplied, 66–67, 67f
  decision, and marginal analysis, 277
  decrease in both demand and supply, 75
  decrease in supply, 71
  decrease in supply and increase in demand, 75
  effects of all possible changes, 74f
  elastic supply, 97f
  elasticity of supply, 96–99
  foreign exchange market, 599
  increase in both demand and supply, 75
  increase in supply, 66, 66f, 71
  increase in supply and decrease in demand, 75
  individual supply, 112–113, 112f
  inelastic supply, 97f
  law of supply, 64
  loanable funds, 551–552, 551f
  and marginal cost, 112–113
  market supply, 112–113, 112f
  and minimum supply-price, 112
  of oil, 429–430
  perfectly elastic supply, 97f, 138
  perfectly inelastic supply, 97f, 138

and producer surplus, 113, 113f
quantity supplied, 64
supply equation, 78
unit elastic supply, 97f
supply curve, 64
  for Canadian dollars, 599, 599f
  graph, 65f, 78f
  long-run market supply curve, 287
  long-run supply curve, 98
  marginal cost curve, 112
  minimum supply price, 65
  in perfect competition, 279, 279f
  short-run market supply curve, 280, 280f
  short-run supply curve, 98
  supply equation, 78
  supply of loanable funds curve, 552
supply equation, 78
supply of loanable funds, 551–552, 551f
supply of loanable funds curve, 552
supply schedule, 64
supply-side effects, 714
surplus
  budget surplus. *See* budget surplus
  consumer surplus. *See* consumer surplus
  cyclical surplus, 722–723, 722f
  government budget surplus, 555, 555f
  net exports, 610
  and price, 69
  producer surplus. *See* producer surplus
  redistribution, in monopoly, 308
  structural surplus, 722–723, 722f
sustainable production, 400–401, 400t, 401f
symmetry principle, 120

T

Taiwan, economic growth in, 520
targeting rule, 735
  described, 735–737
  exchange targeting rule, 747
  k-percent rule, 748
  money targeting rule, 748
tariff, 159
  antidumping duties, 165
  in Canada, 161
  effects of, 159–160, 159f
  revenues from, 168–169
  social loss, 160
  two-part tariff, 313
  winners and losers, 160, 161f
tax-collecting agencies, 119
tax incidence, 135
  and elasticity of demand, 137–138
  and elasticity of supply, 138
  perfectly elastic demand, 138
  perfectly elastic supply, 138
  perfectly inelastic demand, 137
  perfectly inelastic supply, 138
tax wedge, 715
taxes
  ability-to-pay principle, 140
  autonomous tax multiplier, 672, 672f
  benefits principle, 140
  big tradeoff, 119
  on buyers, 136, 137f
  and capital income, 716f
  carbon tax, 386
  corporate income tax, 708
  direct tax, 472

on drugs, 145
and efficiency, 139–140, 139f
and elasticity of demand, 137–138
and elasticity of supply, 138, 139f
Employment Insurance tax, 137
equivalence of tax on buyers and sellers, 136–137
on expenditure, 715
fairness, 140
incentive to save, 716
income taxes, 453, 716
indirect tax, 472, 708
induced taxes, 721
and investment, 716
Laffer curve, 717, 717f
level of, 695
multiplier, 661
net taxes, 548
as obstacle to efficiency, 116
with perfectly elastic demand, 138
with perfectly inelastic demand, 137f
personal income taxes, 708
Pigovian taxes, 380
pollution, 380, 380f
in practice, 140
progressive income tax, 453
vs. prohibition, 145
proportional income tax, 453
real interest rate and, 716
regressive income tax, 453
saving, effect on, 716
on sellers, 135–136, 136f
tax incidence, 135, 137–138
Taylor, John B., 747
Taylor rule, 747
TD Bank, 360
team production, 243
technological change, 38
  and economic inequality, 450
  effects of, 691
  and labour productivity, 527, 533
  neoclassical growth theory, 532
  and perfect competition, 289
  and potential GDP, 629
technological efficiency, 231
technology, 230
  and change in demand for labour, 421
  and change in supply, 66
  cost curves, shifts in, 260–261
technology constraint
  the firm and, 230
  short-run technology constraint, 253–256
telecommunications, 6
temperature analogy, 192
temporary shutdown decision, 278, 278f
10-year government bond rate, 740
theft, 109
themes of macroeconomics, 511
A Theory of Justice (Rawls), 119
time lags, 745–746
time-series graph, 16, 16f
tit-for-tat strategy, 355, 356
total cost, 257, 274, 276f, 331, 331f
total cost curves, 257f
total fixed cost, 257
total income, 442
total product, 253, 253t, 255f
total product curve, 254, 254f

total revenue, 90, 90*f,* **274,** 276*f*
total revenue test, 90
total utility, 182
   see also utility
   choosing at the margin, 184–186
   graph, 183*f*
   vs. marginal utility, 191
total variable cost, 257
trade restrictions. *See* international trade
   restrictions
trade wars, 168
tradeoffs, 8
   along production possibilities frontier
     (PPF), 33
   big tradeoff, 9
   and choices, 8
   guns *vs.* butter, 8
   how tradeoffs, 8
   opportunity cost, 33
   what tradeoffs, 8
   for whom tradeoffs, 8–9
tragedy of the commons, 400, 406
training. *See* education
transactions costs, 117, 242–243, **379**
transfer payments, 709, 721
transition costs, 169
trend, 16
trigger strategy, 355
tropical rainforests, 7
trough, 476
trucks, elasticities of demand for, 100
trust and loan companies, 546
trust and mortgage loan company, 571
two big economic questions, 3–7
two-part tariff, 313

U

unaffordable quantities, 204
underground economy, 477–478
underproduction, 115–116, 116*f*
underutilized labour, 494
unemployment
   see also employment
   cyclical unemployment, 496
   efficiency wage, 496
   frictional unemployment, 495
   and inflation, 686–688, 686*f,* 687*f*
   job leavers, 494
   job losers, 494
   natural unemployment, 494–496
   natural unemployment rate, 496
   Phillips curve, 686–688, 686*f,* 687*f*
   problem of, 490–491
   and real GDP, 496–497
   sources of unemployment, 494–495
   structural unemployment, 495–496
   underutilized labour, exclusion of, 494
   unemployment rate, 492, 492*f,* 494
unemployment rate, 492
   full employment and, 497
   graph, 492*f*
   natural unemployment rate, 687–688,
     687*f*
   and output gap, 497*f*
   purpose of, 494
union. *See* labour union
union-nonunion wage gap, 426
unit elastic demand, 88, 88*f,* 303
unit elastic supply, 97*f*
unit of account, 568–569, 568*t*

United Nations, 479
United States
   borrowing for consumption, 608–609
   budget deficit, 713
   central bank, 574–575
   credit crunch, 7
   Federal Reserve. *See* Federal Reserve
     (U.S.)
   financial crisis, 554, 748–749
   financial markets, 560
   fiscal stimulus package, 720
   job losses, 696
   money multiplier, 587
   Multifiber Arrangement, 166
   purchasing power parity, 476–477
   real GDP, 476, 517
   recession, 696
   relative prices, 476
   Smoot-Hawley tariff, 168
   softwood lumber dispute, 170–171
   tax wedges, 715
unlimited liability, 234
unplanned inventory changes, 656*f*
unrelated variables, 21, 21*f*
unused resources, 33
utilitarianism, 118–119, 119*f*
utility, 182
   choosing at the margin, 184–186
   graph, 183*f*
   marginal analysis, 186
   marginal utility, 182–183, 187–192
   marginal utility per dollar, 184
   temperature analogy, 192
   total utility, 182
   units of utility, 186
   utility maximization, 184–186, 192–193
   utility-maximizing choice, 184, 184*t*

V

value
   and consumer surplus, 191
   demand, and willingness to pay, 110
   market value, 229
   paradox of value, 191, 191*f*
   vs. price, 110
value of marginal product, 419, 419*f*
variables
   direct relationship, 18
   graphing relationships among more than
     two variables, 24–25, 25*f*
   inverse relationship, 19, 20*f*
   linear relationship, 18–19
   with maximum or minimum, 20, 21*f*
   moving in opposite directions, 19–20
   moving in same direction, 18–19
   negative relationship, 19, 20*f*
   positive relationship, 18, 19*f*
   real variables in macroeconomics, 503
   unrelated variables, 21, 21*f*
velocity of circulation, 582
voluntary export restraint, 164
von Neumann, John, 346, 369
voter preferences, 399
vouchers, 384–385, 384*f*

W

Wachovia, 547
wage gap
   gender-based, 4
   union-nonunion wage gap, 426

wages, 4
   after-tax wage rate, 715
   in Canada, 427
   education, effect of, 427
   efficiency wage, 496
   high-skilled labour, 448–449
   low-skilled labour, 448–449
   minimum wage. *See* minimum wage
   real wage rate, 503, 522
   reservation wage, 422
   subsistence real wage rate, 531
   trends and differences in wage rates, 427
wages, salaries, and supplementary labour,
   471
wants, 59, 568
Washington Mutual, 547
water, 191
water pollution, 376
water shortage case study, 120–121
water use, 122
wealth, 444, 544
   and aggregate demand, 630–631
   annual, 445
   distribution of, 444
   vs. income, 444–445
   intergenerational transfers, 452
   life-cycle saving patterns, 452
   lifetime, 445
   Lorenz curve, 444*f*
   marriage and wealth concentration, 452
   redistribution, and inflation, 498
   and saving, 551
   sources of wealth inequality, 452
wealth effect, 630–631, 663
Wealth of Nations (Smith), 53, 115
Welch, Finis, 135
welfare-administering agencies, 119
welfare programs, 453
what (economic question), 3
what tradeoffs, 8
willingness to pay, 60, 110
women
   discrimination, 451
   microloans, 529
   single mothers, 455
   wage gap, 4
work-leisure choices, 214–215
Workers' Compensation, 453
working-age population, 491
world demand for Canadian exports, 601
world economy
   see also international trade
   aggregate demand, 632–633
   economic growth in, 519, 519*f*
World Trade Organization (WTO), 164,
   165

Y

y-axis intercept, 27, 27*f*
Yahoo, 244
Yellow Pages, 358
the yuan, 614

Z

Zimbabwe, 584
Zoom Airlines, 292

PHOTO CREDITS

READING BETWEEN THE LINES

2   The Rising Opportunity Cost of Food   46

3   Demand and Supply: The Price of Gasoline   76

4   The Elasticities of Demand for Gasoline, Trucks, and Cars   100

5   Is Water Use Efficient?   122

6   The Minimum Wage in Action   146

7   The United States Protects its Lumber Producers   170

8   The Marginal Utility of Food   196

9   Paper Books Versus e-Books   216

10   Battling for Markets in Internet Search   244

11   Cutting the Cost of Clean Electricity   266

12   Temporary Shutdown or Exit   292

13   European View of Microsoft   316

14   Product Differentiation in the 3G Cell Phone Market   334

15   Dell and HP in a Market Share Game   362

16   Fighting Carbon Emissions with a Carbon Tax and Solar Subsidy   386

17   Rainforests: A Tragedy of the Commons   406

18   Canada's Oilsands   432

19   Trends in Poverty   456

20   Real GDP in the Slowing Economy of 2008   480

21   Jobs in the Slowdown of 2008   504

22   Economic Growth in China   536

23   Bailing Out Troubled U.S. Financial Markets   560

24   The Quantity Theory of Money in Zimbabwe   584

25   The Rising Chinese Yuan   614

26   Aggregate Supply and Aggregate Demand in Action   642

27   Recession Coming   668

28   Onset of Recession in Canada and the United States   696

29   Global Coordinated Fiscal Policy   724

30   Monetary Policy in Action   750